Introduction to

Computers and Information Systems with BASIC

The Scott, Foresman Series in Computers and Information Systems

Thomas H. Athey, Consulting Editor

Athey and Zmud
INTRODUCTION TO COMPUTERS AND INFORMATION SYSTEMS

Day
MICROCOMPUTERS IN BUSINESS

Pierson and Horn
STRUCTURED COBOL PROGRAMMING

Tom
MANAGING INFORMATION RESOURCES

Zmud
INFORMATION SYSTEMS IN ORGANIZATIONS

Zmud and Eagle Software, Inc.
BASIC PROGRAMMING

Introduction to

Computers and Information Systems with BASIC

Thomas H. Athey

California State Polytechnic University at Pomona

Robert W. Zmud

The University of North Carolina at Chapel Hill

Scott, Foresman and Company

Glenview, Illinois

London, England

A Study Guide to Accompany Introduction to Computers and Information Systems has been prepared to help you master the concepts discussed in your text. The *Guide* contains chapter summaries, detailed annotated chapter outlines, drill sections made up of multiple-choice, true/false, fill-in-the-blank, matching, and essay questions, as well as practice tests made up of true/false and multiple-choice questions. Page-referenced answers are provided for all questions. If the *Guide* (ISBN 0-673-18168-5) is not available in your bookstore, your bookstore manager will be able to order it for you.

Acknowledgments

Acknowledgments for literary selections, charts and graphs, illustrations, and photographs appear in a section at the back of the book beginning on page R-1, an extension of the copyright page.

Copyright © 1986 Scott, Foresman and Company.
All Rights Reserved.
Printed in the United States of America.

Library of Congress Cataloging-in-Publication Data

Athey, Thomas H.
Introduction to computers and information systems with BASIC.

Bibliography: p. R-5
Includes index.
1. Computers. 2. Information storage and retrieval systems. 3. BASIC (Computer program language)
I. Zmud, Robert W., 1946- . II. Title.
QA76.A84235 1986 004 85-22070
ISBN 0-673-18185-5

12345-VHJ-9089888786

PREFACE

In this, the Information Age, educators are finding it increasingly easy to convince students they should learn about computers. Indeed, the demand for this knowledge is growing almost as fast as the number of computer products and applications. It is not so easy to decide what—or how—to teach these students. Many textbooks focus on the "what"—computers and information systems in and of themselves. We call this the "computer literacy" approach and feel that it neglects the "why"—the reasons we use computers.

We wanted to write a book that was different. Both of us feel a strong conviction that today's students need *computing literacy,* the ability to use the computer as a tool to enrich their personal and professional lives. As computers become more common, the likelihood increases that students will need to understand and use computers in their careers, even if they do not become computer professionals. Like many employees, they may someday find themselves on a steering committee charged with developing or evaluating a computer application.

Our goal in this book is to help students become good consumers of computer technology and information systems. This goal is expressed in three major ways.

1. *Understandable depth.* First, we made a commitment to present each topic in understandable depth. This means that we are careful to focus on the information that students need to be able to understand how and why computers and information systems can be used to simplify and improve our lives. This does not mean that we avoid technical detail or ignore recent advances, however. As required by today's computing environment, we explain the workings of the most recent technological advances, including pointing devices, flat-panel displays, local area networks, and the Fifth Generation Computing Project. We are careful, though, to highlight trends and show students what these technologies mean to the users of computers and information systems.

2. *Integration of technology and its applications.* We also made a commitment to focus on applications and to explain how technology affects our use of computers. Thus, every major discussion of technology is illustrated by an application. This deliberate integration can also be seen in the section entitled "Special Feature: A Systems Approach to Selecting a Microcomputer," which shows students how to apply systems development techniques to their own computer-selection decisions.

3. *Focus on the microcomputer.* Microcomputer systems are used in almost every chapter to illustrate and explain concepts that are relevant to our discussion of larger systems. In addition, "Special Feature: A Systems Approach to Selecting a Microcomputer" offers practical advice for students contemplating the purchase of a microcomputer. We chose this strategy for two reasons. First, the importance of the microcomputer in today's business world is undeniable. Second, the microcomputer is probably the first computer students will use, either at home or in the micro lab at school. For many students, the micro is a convenient way to get hands-on experience—something we feel is important in helping students understand computers and information systems.

We also developed some recurring features to help us meet our goal.

"Professional Issue" sections within chapters address concerns that will affect students as business professionals and provide further insight into a variety of issues. Computing literacy, computer classification, the human-computer interface, printer selection, local area networks, fitting microcomputers into an MIS plan, cultivating the human touch in systems development, promoting and managing end-user computing, and telecommuting are some of the topics discussed.

"Computers at Work" features in each chapter excerpt articles from business and computer magazines that show the varied, real-world uses computers in product inventory, motel reservations, talent agency bookings, film, telecommunications, medicine, product design, and the music industry.

Full-color illustrations explain and clarify both technical processes and business procedures. We also feel that color photographs of computer applications are most useful when integrated within the text, rather than grouped in isolated collages. Thus, the text features a functional, as well as attractive, illustration program that is interwoven with the text.

In addition, we have provided a number of study aids to reinforce important text concepts, such as chapter outlines, bold-faced key terms, detailed chapter summaries with key terms reviewed in context, end-of-chapter review questions, and a bibliography of sources for further reading. Our text is also offered in two versions: one with extensive appendices on BASIC programming and one without these appendices.

THE SUPPLEMENT PROGRAM

We were also aware that a good book alone is not enough, given the demands of today's teaching environment. Understanding computers and information systems can be challenging for both instructor and student. Instructors must keep abreast of developments and trends, as well as offer students opportunities for hands-on experience through computer exercises that reflect real-world applications. Thus, our text provides a full range of supplements, designed to meet the needs of both instructors and students. These supplements include innovative software teaching aids, outstanding paper-based supplements, and the *CIS Profiles in Excellence* newsletter that showcases outstanding CIS programs around the nation.

Innovative Software Teaching Aids

1. The Scott, Foresman Electronic Bulletin Board is an online resource designed to meet the dynamic and diverse needs of data processing and information systems instructors nationwide. The Bulletin Board offers the following features to users of this text:

regularly updated information on computer technology and its application to business information systems;

an electronic mail and message system to allow instructors to leave messages for and interact with other instructors as well as Scott, Foresman marketing and editorial personnel; and

file transfer capabilities. Files available for transfer from the Bulletin Board to your computer include the following:

—fully functioning and documented spreadsheet, word processing, and data base management software for the IBM PC, as well as a variety of utilities and games

—class-tested assignments, exercises, problems, and applications for major software packages such as Lotus 1–2–3, VisiCalc/SuperCalc, DBase II and III, etc.

—BASIC programming assignments and exercises for the IBM PC, along with solutions

—additional teaching material for both the classroom and the microcomputer lab

The Scott, Foresman Electronic Bulletin Board is a resource designed to grow and become more useful with time. We encourage instructors to use the Electronic Bulletin Board to exchange ideas and to share successful teaching strategies and materials by uploading their own teaching materials into the Bulletin Board. The Bulletin Board will support baud rates up to 2400 and can be accessed by any computer. For instructors' convenience, microlab exercises and assignments, as well as spreadsheet, word processing, data base management, and telecommunications software, will also be made available on diskettes upon request.

2. A complete, interactive BASIC programming tutorial for the IBM PC, *BASIC Programming* by Robert W. Zmud, with the PC-Professor software tutorial by Eagle Software, Inc., features the most sophisticated and useful BASIC programming educational software available, along with a 128-page text on BASIC programming reprinted from the text and referenced to corresponding lessons in the software tutorial.

3. For the Apple IIe and IIc, an integrated spreadsheet, word processing, and data base management software package, available Spring 1986.

4. A revolutionary new electronic classroom management system, DIPLOMA, consists of four programs that assist instructors in testing, grading, and course management. DIPLOMA operates on IBM, Apple IIe and IIc, and compatible microcomputers.

EXAM provides almost 2000 true/false and multiple-choice questions keyed to our text. In addition, EXAM lets you create and edit questions, allowing you to develop personalized test files. EXAM accommodates an unlimited number of multiple-choice, true/false, matching, and short-answer/essay questions. Fourteen test-printing options can be used to leave space for figures or graphs, set margins, minimize page count, insert page headings, number pages, scramble questions and/or answers, generate answer keys, and provide student answer sheets.

GRADEBOOK, an electronic grade book, provides a work area that looks like the familiar grid of traditional paper grade books. In addition, GRADEBOOK offers these four advantages: (1) Student records can be located by name or ID number and can be sorted using combinations of four sorting options. In addition, comments about students, tests, or classes can be entered. (2) GRADEBOOK automatically calculates running averages for both students and tests and can be tailored to display letter grades, percentage averages, GPA, or points earned. (3) Tests can be given independent weights and curved using a variety of options. The program automatically generates and displays a test's bell curve during curving operations. (4) Graphic report screens monitor the effectiveness of a test or a student's progress.

STUDY GUIDE allows students to take tests generated by EXAM at a computer. As with tests given on paper, students can browse, skip difficult questions, and review or alter their answers. Upon completion, STUDY GUIDE will grade each test and present results in the form of graphs that depict overall performance, as well as performance by subtopic.

CALENDAR is a free-form scheduling tool that allows instructors to enter up to nine events or messages for any particular date. Messages can be easily entered, edited, saved, and displayed, while a transfer feature allows recurring events to be entered for several dates without retyping. The program can be set up to automatically load and save information.

Paper-Based Supplements

5. An Exercise/Case Book, *Microcomputers in Business: Spreadsheet, Word Processing, and Data Base Management Systems,* by John Day, Ohio University, was designed for use as a microcomputer lab manual. Through business-oriented problems and assignments, students learn how to use the microcomputer as a business tool. Unlike other lab manuals, *Microcomputers in Business* contains general problem descriptions and can be used with any available hardware and software.

6. Instructor's Manual provides an overview and summary of each text chapter, as well as lecture outlines, ideas for lecture and discussion, answers to in-text review questions, class projects and activities, additional essay and review questions, and abstracts from popular and academic literature.

7. Test File contains approximately 2000 questions, 30 true/false and 70 multiple-choice items for each chapter. These same questions are available through the DIPLOMA class management software.

8. One hundred full-color **Transparency Acetates** plus an additional fifty **Transparency Masters** have been prepared to enhance classroom lectures.

9. Study Guide includes chapter summaries, detailed annotated chapter outlines, drill sections made up of multiple-choice, true/false, fill-in-the-blank, matching, and essay questions, as well as practice tests made up of true/false and multiple-choice questions. Page-referenced answers are provided for all questions.

A Newsletter to Keep You Informed

10. The Scott, Foresman CIS Profiles in Excellence Newsletter, published three times annually, showcases outstanding CIS programs in two-year, undergraduate, and graduate schools around the nation, allowing readers to see how their colleagues have coped with the challenges of establishing curricula, developing courses, choosing hardware and software, and obtaining the funding for such programs.

ACKNOWLEDGMENTS

To Our Publisher and Family

It is a rare experience for authors to work with a team of professionals who are committed to excellence in everything that they do. We were privileged to become part of the Scott Foresman team.

Our appreciation goes to the top management of Scott, Foresman—to Jim Levy, Senior Vice-President and General Manager, College Division, Dick Welna, Vice-President and Editor-in-Chief, and Jim Sitlington, Editorial Vice-President, Business and Economics. From the beginning, they shared our commitment to create a new type of introductory text and provided the people and money to support our effort.

We must also thank: Jim Boyd, Acquisitions Editor in Computer Information Systems, whose innovativeness and charm enabled him to orchestrate the overall project; Linda Muterspaugh, Developmental Editor, who worked beyond the call of duty to make certain text explanations were integrated and clear; Elizabeth Fresen, Project Editor, who did the copy editing and kept smiling while keeping track of a million details; Barbara Schneider, Art Director, who created a stunning design and clear and attractive illustrations; and Cheryl Kucharzak, Picture Researcher, who found the perfect photos to clarify our concepts.

But, most important, Tom Athey had the understanding and support of his wife, Nancy, and children, Tim, Jay, and Carol, and Bob Zmud had the understanding and support of his wife, Jo Anne, and children, Danny and Jana. Their contributions were invaluable.

To Our Colleagues

We owe a special debt to the many colleagues who reviewed our manuscript and gave us valuable feedback. Special thanks must go to Kate Kaiser, University of Wisconsin at Milwaukee, for her contribution to the "Special Feature: A Systems Approach to Selecting a Microcomputer," to Robert F. Zant for his excellent technical comments, and to James Wynne and Fred Scott for their insightful comments on content. To all our reviewers, we extend our gratitude.

James Adair	*Bentley College*
Virginia Bender	*William Rainey Harper College*
Kathy Blicharz	*Pima Community College*
James Buxton	*Tidewater Community College*
Frank E. Cable	*Pennsylvania State University*
Mary J. Culnan	*University of California, Berkeley*
M. H. Goldberg	*Pace University*
Jean Margaret Hynes	*University of Illinois, Chicago*
Durward P. Jackson	*California State University, Los Angeles*
Richard Kapperman	*El Camino College*
James Kasum	*University of Wisconsin, Milwaukee*
James Kho	*California State University, Sacramento*

Lyle Langlois	*Glendale Community College*
Jeffrey I. Mock	*Diablo Valley College*
Christopher W. Pidgeon	*California State Polytechnic University*
Janet Pipkin	*University of South Florida*
Leonard Presby	*William Patterson College*
Herbert F. Rebhun	*University of Houston*
Leonard C. Schwab	*California State University, Hayward*
Fred Scott	*Broward Community College*
Sumit Sircar	*University of Texas, Arlington*
Vince Skudrna	*Baruch College (CUNY)*
Glenn Smith	*James Madison University*
Bob Tesch	*Northeast Louisiana University*
James Wynne	*Virginia Commonwealth University*
Robert F. Zant	*North Texas State University*

Thomas H. Athey

Robert W. Zmud

OVERVIEW

CONTENTS

PART I THE INFORMATION SOCIETY

PART II COMPUTER SYSTEM HARDWARE

PART III SYSTEM SUPPORT SOFTWARE

PART IV COMPUTER-BASED INFORMATION SYSTEMS

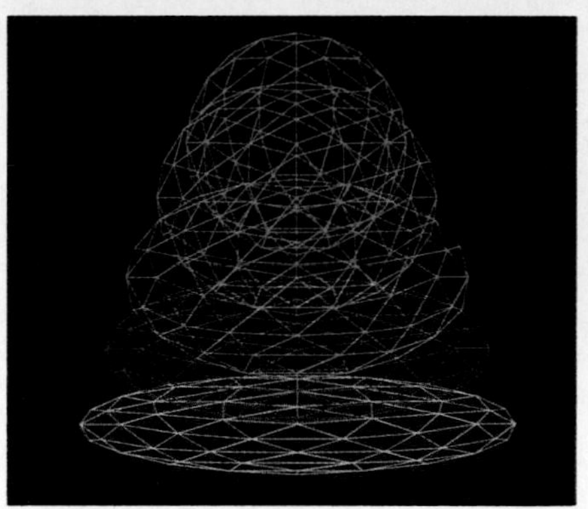

PART V APPLICATIONS SOFTWARE

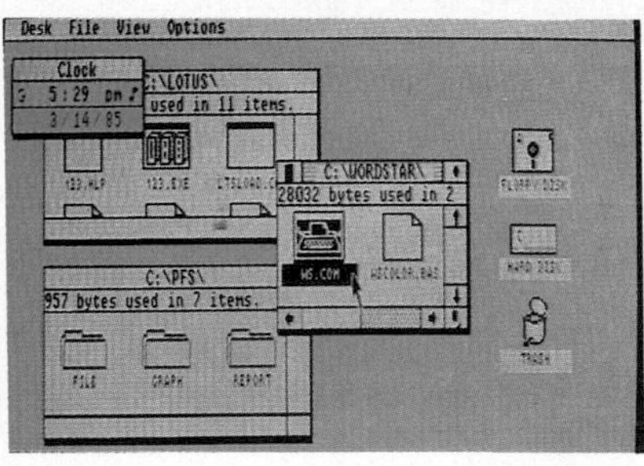

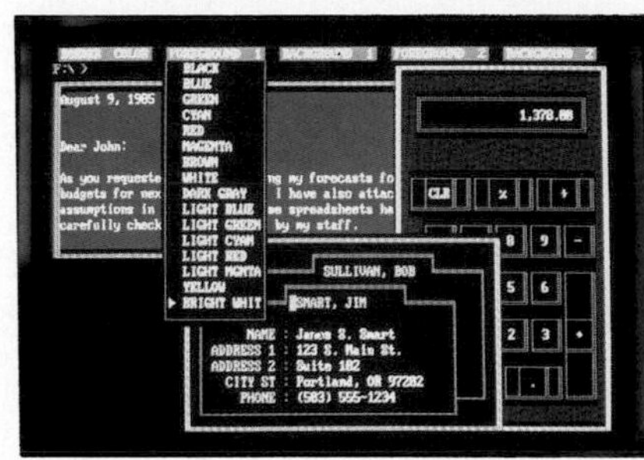

PART VI COMPUTERS AND SOCIETY

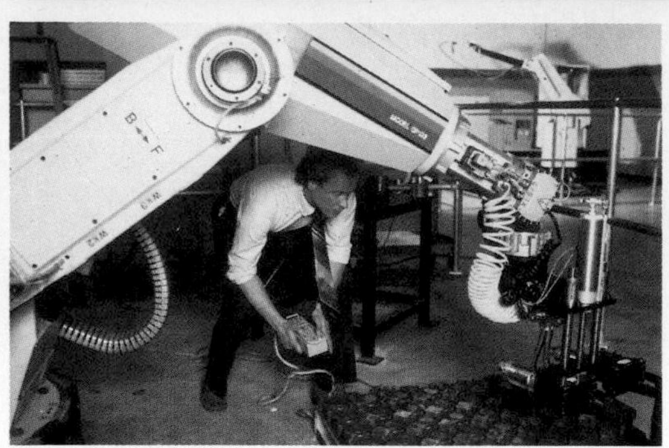

CHAPTER 16
The Information Age Society 463

PART VII APPENDICES

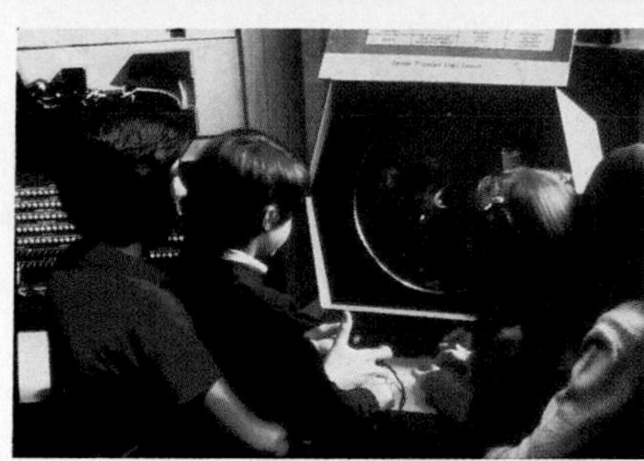

APPENDIX C

The BASIC Programming Language C-1

PART I THE INFORMATION SOCIETY

CHAPTER 1

Welcome to the Information Society

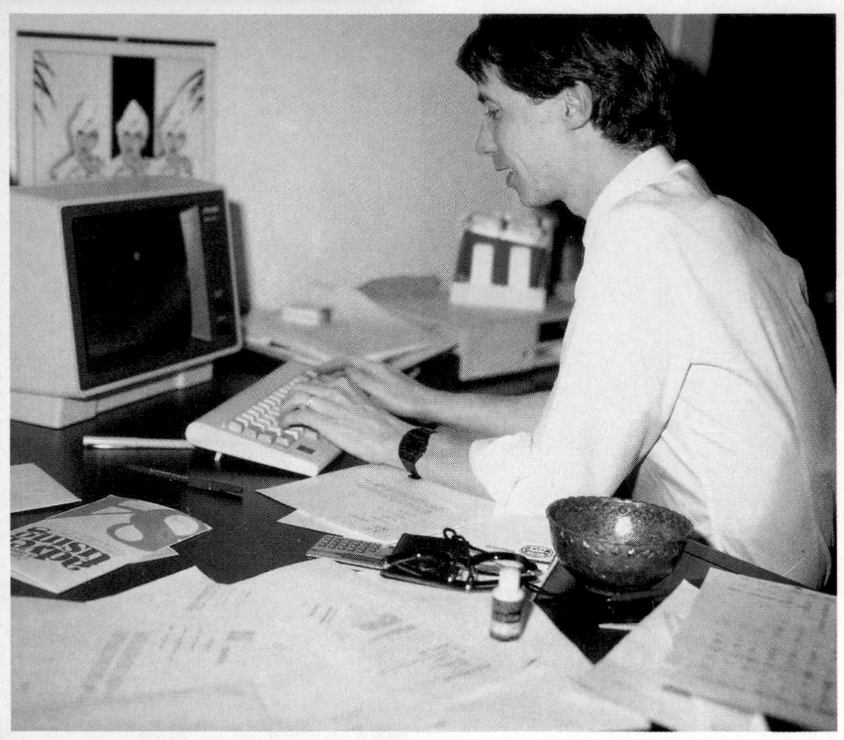

COMPUTERS AT WORK

PCs Polish a PR Firm's Image

Everyone is using PCs.

When you walk into the main reception area of the New York headquarters of Ruder, Finn & Rotman (RF&R), you might think you have mistakenly entered the lobby of the Museum of Modern Art. Life-sized mannequin sculptures and handsome black and white photographs impart an atmosphere of cultural sophistication. As you pass through the lobby's rich wooden doors and enter the offices, however, the decor changes. The clean lines of IBM PCs replace the lobby's free-form sculptures. The mood here is one of technical innovation. And so it should be: RF&R is one of the most computerized public relations firms in the industry.

If RF&R produces a tangible product, it is the vast quantity of written material that it creates. These materials—news releases, speeches, articles, brochures, annual reports, and radio and TV commercial scripts—are approved by clients and then released to the masses via print or broadcast media.

"If you want to oversimplify the role of an organization such as this," says Felix Kaufman, executive vice-president and director of RF&R's PC implementation strategy, "it strives to help its clients express themselves effectively in public—explain their policies, their values, their goals. This may involve interfacing with the media, with government officials, with the public. It can be part of a marketing function or investor relations, or it can relate to some public-spirited activity."

The emphasis on written material is one reason that, unlike many other companies, there is an IBM typewriter on virtually every executive's desk, from senior management on down. And now, PCs are beginning to join those typewriters.

Source: S. Kariya, "PCs Polish a PR Firm's Image," *PC Magazine,* 6 March, 1984, p. 166.

Are you surprised to find computers being used in a public relations firm? Actually, it might be more unusual to read about a business that does not use computers. We live in an age in which computers now outnumber the people living on Earth. This fact may scare people who do not understand what computers are, what they do, or how they do it. The sheer number of computers now in use is a bit surprising, even for those of us who have been working with and around computers for more than twenty years. The overpowering fact is that we are seeing just the beginning of a surge in the use of computers. How will they all be used? How will their use affect people, businesses, and society? And, perhaps most importantly, how might computers affect you and your career?

While no text can fully answer all of these questions, this text can give you the information you need to understand and deal effectively with the growing number of computers in your personal and professional life. In this chapter, you will begin by learning to do the following:

1. Define the term *information society* and explain its meaning within the world of work.
2. Define the term *microelectronics* and describe three major impacts of microelectronic technology.
3. Define the term *computing literacy* and describe its five levels.
4. Define the term *information system* and describe the three basic elements that make up an information system.
5. List and describe the four stages of the *information processing cycle.*

Professional Issue:
Computing Literacy in an Information Society

Throughout this text we will be highlighting issues that will affect you as a business professional, even if you do not go on to become a computer professional. We'll begin by focusing on the information society. Are you aware that our society has been transformed from an industrial society into an information society? In fact, in this **information society,** collection, processing, and distribution of information have actually replaced the manufacture of goods as the primary source of wealth and work.

For most of the twentieth century, economic growth has been fueled by "heavy" manufacturing industries, such as the steel and auto industries. These industries transformed basic raw materials such as iron, coal, and oil into a wide range of products for markets across the world. Beginning in the 1970s, however, intense worldwide competition in these markets led many experts to believe that some of the leading industrialized nations, such as the United States, were losing their world economic leadership.

But these experts overlooked two things. First, the demand for one "product"—the knowledge being accumulated by workers, technicians, scientists, and managers—increased more than ever. Information had become and continues to be America's primary business. Second, the 1960s witnessed the birth and growth of a major new American industry, the microelectronics industry.

Microelectronics refers to the miniaturization of electronic circuits and components. These devices process information. The most obvious use of microelectronics is, of course, the computer. A key aspect of today's computers is that they can process information in all of its forms—words, numbers, voice, and pictures. As we can see in Appendix A, many years of effort went into the development of this fast, reliable, and relatively inexpensive way to process information using electricity instead of human labor.

Much of this technology has been developed in Silicon Valley, around Palo Alto, California. This area, home of Stanford University and Hewlett-Packard Corporation, became a haven for innovative engineers during the late 1950s and the 1960s. The engineers' major accomplishment has been the development of the **integrated circuit,** also called a **microchip** or simply a **chip.** Over the years, engineers have perfected the means by which thousands of complete electronic circuits are contained on a single sliver of silicon. And, while the chip's size and cost have dropped, its power has increased. For example, consider the following:

> The prices of electronic devices have been cut in half every two to three years.
>
> The speed of electronic devices has doubled every two to three years.
>
> The **microprocessor,** a "computer on a chip," did not exist in 1974, cost about $400 to manufacture in 1975, about $30 by 1976, $3 by 1977, and less than $1 today. Some of today's microprocessors are more powerful than some of the large computers of the early 1960s.
>
> The most powerful electronic devices in 1980 performed around 5 million operations a second and occupied a cubic yard of space. By the late 1980s, the most powerful devices will likely perform 100 million operations a second, but will occupy less than a six-inch cube of space.

This technological progress is illustrated by the increasing complexity of the integrated circuits (see Exhibit 1.1).

These advances in microelectronics have had three major effects. First, microelectronic technology has "liberated" the computer, that almost mystical machine of the 1950s and 1960s. The electronic circuitry of these early computers was awkward, delicate, and expensive. For this reason, the computer was used primarily in large organizations, was usually locked away in rooms with carefully controlled environments, and was operated only by specialists. With microelectronics, computers became much smaller, more powerful, more durable, less expensive, and much easier to use. A variety of businesses and employees at many levels are using computers today. Throughout the text, we'll explore the broad range of uses for computers.

Today, the fastest growing segment of the computer industry involves **personal computers,** or computers meant to be used by an individual. Other terms for these computers are **microcomputers,** a reference to the microchips that

Exhibit 1.1

Integrated circuit technology began the process of combining multiple components within a single piece of silicon material (left). Modern microelectronic technology allows hundreds of thousands of electrical components and wiring to be imprinted on a single "chip" (right).

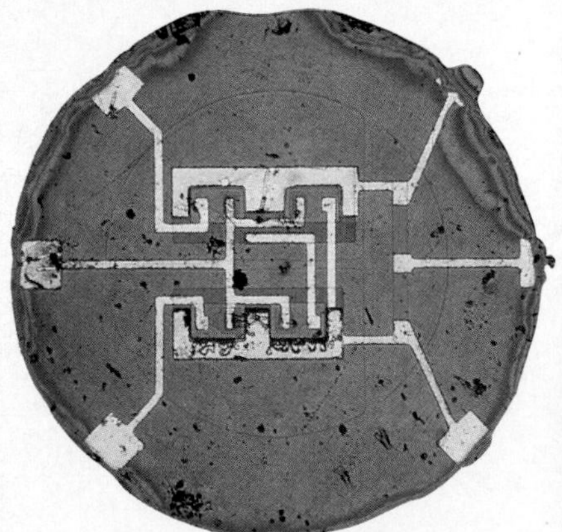

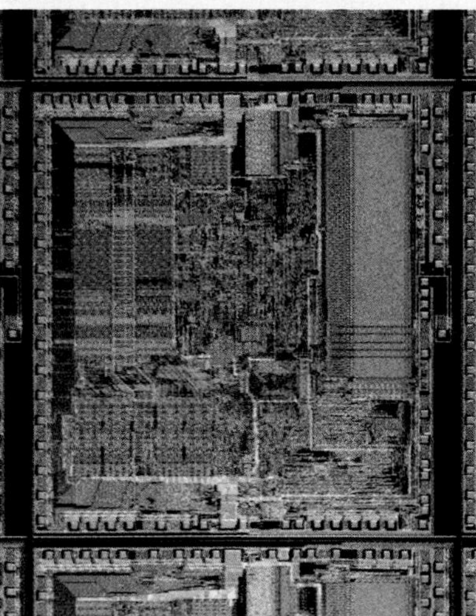

enable these computers to function, and **desktop computers,** a reference to their usual location. Exhibit 1.2 is a chart showing recent sales trends in North America for personal computers. Descriptions of this and other segments of the computer industry are given in Chapter 18.

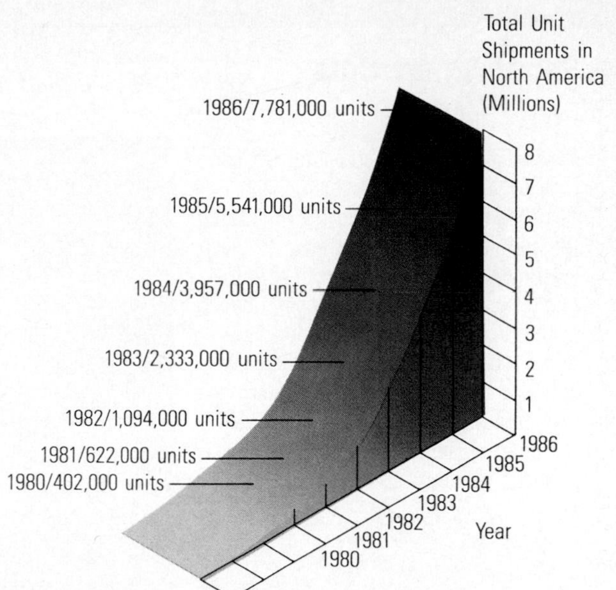

Exhibit 1.2
Recent and Expected Sales of Personal Computers in North America

By bringing the computer down in scale, personal computer manufacturers allowed people to hold it and prod it and play with it. As a result, it is common to find people without formal training in computers improving their professional and personal lives by using personal computers. Some of these people might even say the computer has "liberated" them from much of their work's monotony and tedium.

The second major impact of microelectronics involves its role in creating the information society. The economies of many nations are becoming increasingly dependent on the processing of information. The need to create, collect, store, and dispense this information has launched many new industries. Consulting firms, public and private information services, and research organizations represent just a few examples, along with the public relations firm described in the introduction to this chapter. Older industries have been affected as well. For example, insurance and banking are, first and foremost, information processing businesses. Insurance companies process vast amounts of customer and claim information, while banks process vast amounts of data describing the financial transactions of their customers. Even in government and the more traditional manufacturing, retail, and service industries, the movement of information is fast becoming the lifeblood of business and management. As a consequence, industries directly supporting information processing, such as communications, transportation, and office equipment, are growing. None of this would have been possible without microelectronics.

The third major impact of microelectronics finds these tiny and inexpensive devices being used to control a variety of other products. When connected to a sensing device, a microprocessor can capture and then process information to "control" the product within which it has been inserted. Microprocessors, in particular, seem to be able to improve the performance of almost anything, anywhere:

A microwave oven can vary cooking time and temperature depending on what is being cooked.

A videocassette recorder can be scheduled to tape a series of television shows in the middle of the night.

A cardiac pacemaker, perhaps the ultimate *personal* computer, maintains the functions of a sick or aging heart.

A sewing machine automatically handles a number of complex stitching operations.

A camera automated by a microprocessor allows an amateur photographer to easily take excellent pictures.

Adding **intelligence,** the apparent capability to act in an informed manner, to consumer products not only makes them more sophisticated, it also makes them easier to use. Computers at Work: "Super-Smart Cars" describes

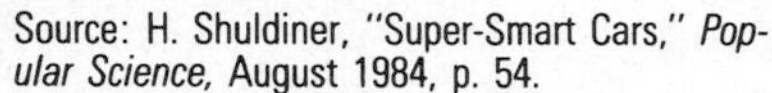

COMPUTERS AT WORK

Super-Smart Cars

A new generation of computerized controls is taking over our automobiles. Computers not only make cars run better, cleaner, and safer—they also give the driver an amazing amount of information on his car's metabolism. Coming in the next few years are other electronic wonders such as computerized anti-skid braking systems, touch-screen CRT controls for computers, and new anti-theft systems that eliminate the need for keys.

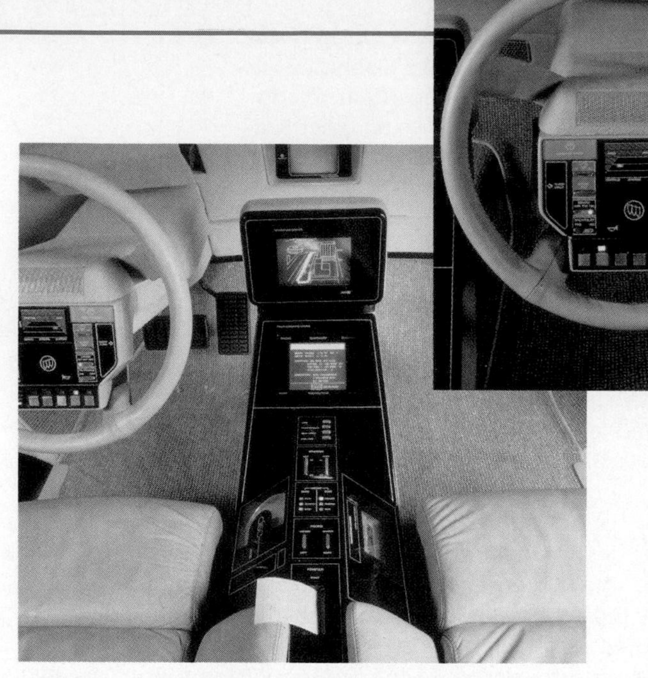

Source: H. Shuldiner, "Super-Smart Cars," *Popular Science,* August 1984, p. 54.

some of the exciting ways in which microprocessors are being incorporated within automobiles to make driving safer and more enjoyable.

The consumer products within the average American household contain over forty microprocessors. Think of your own house, apartment, or dormitory room. How many microprocessors do you own? All of us use computers on a daily basis—they make life more convenient and more enjoyable. More importantly, this use of microprocessors means that you may be more familiar and comfortable with computers than you realize.

Computing, Not Computer, Literacy

What impact does the information society have on you? It primarily affects the career options open to you. In 1976, white-collar workers outnumbered blue-collar workers for the first time. Today, "information occupations" represent over 60 percent of the U.S. work force. Some examples include programmers, teachers, clerks, secretaries, accountants, stockbrokers, managers, salespeople, lawyers, bankers, and engineers. Not only are you likely to find yourself in an "information occupation," but the odds favor your working with computers in that occupation. Because computers will probably play an important part in your career, Part VI will discuss in more detail the information society and its impact on people and work.

You are probably already aware of the key role computers play in today's world of work. The news media are constantly running stories about computers and about the need to educate people so that they can fill meaningful and productive roles in an information society. Computers in education, computer camps, computer magazines, computers on Sesame Street—the list goes on and on (see Exhibit 1.3). In the business world, computer training has become

Exhibit 1.3

Computer education and training, in all its forms, has become a growth industry. People of all ages are using computers at home, at school, and in the work place.

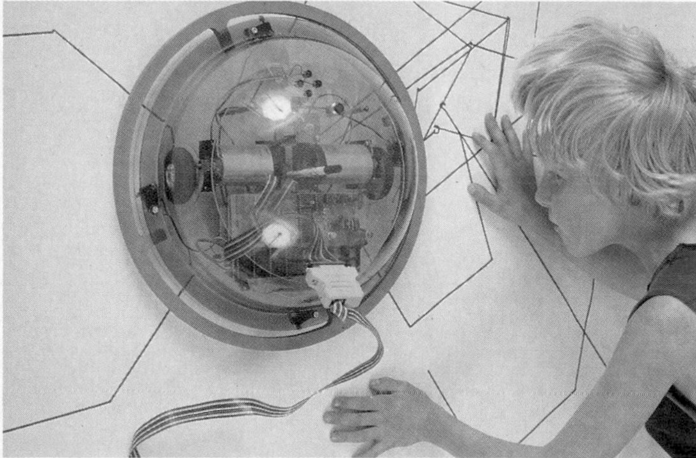

a major new industry. It is estimated, for example, that in 1986 $3 billion of the $14 billion to be spent on personal computers in the United States will go toward computer training seminars and workshops.

Some debate exists today regarding the type of computer education, or **computer literacy,** people need in order to function in an information society. Must everyone become a computer expert? More directly, what should you learn in order to be able to benefit from computers? The answer, as you might suspect, depends on how you intend to use computers.

Computer professionals certainly need to understand how computers work. Few computer users, however, really need to understand all the technology that makes up today's computers. Fortunately, you can take advantage of most of the computer's capabilities without knowing how electrical circuits function or even how to program. Programming is the process of developing the instructions or **programs** that direct a computer in its information processing. On the other hand, you may find computer technology interesting and computer programming fun. And learning these skills may even be useful in your career.

What most computer users need is an understanding of what computers can do and an ability to feel comfortable when using a computer. You need to develop the same sense of command and confidence toward computers that you have toward automobiles. While you do not need to be an engineer to drive a car, you do need to know the "rules of the road" and to feel at ease while driving. **Computing literacy** is the ability to use the computer as a tool to enrich your personal and professional life. Computing literacy—not computer literacy—should be the educational goal for most students.

Yet even with that understanding, there are levels of computing literacy (see Exhibit 1.4). These levels reflect the fact that people differ in their involvement with computers. As this involvement grows, a deeper and broader understanding of computers is needed. These five levels of computing literacy also

Exhibit 1.4
The Staircase of Computing Literacy

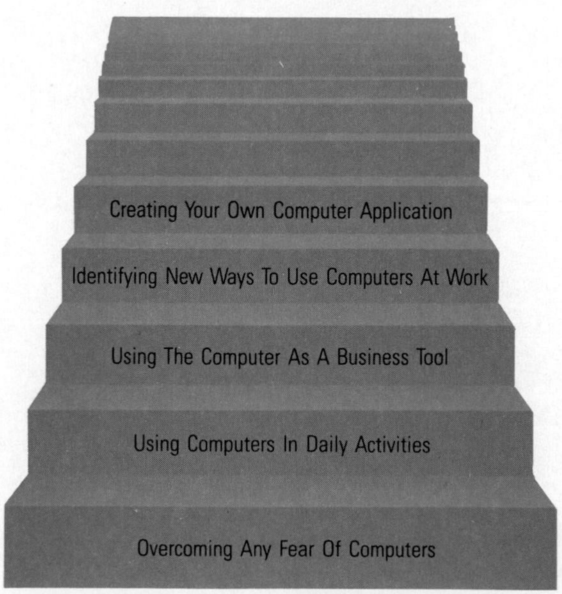

indicate the variety of ways you are likely to become involved with computers:

1. *You develop an understanding of the basic roles that computers serve in an information society well enough to overcome any fear of computer use.* The computer will touch even those people who never come into physical contact with it. It is unlikely that a person with a true fear of computers would be able to cope in such a world. This first level of computing literacy must be acquired by all members of an information society.
2. *You become comfortable with the use of computers as machines.* This involves the use of computers in handling everyday tasks that have been automated. Examples include banking, shopping, health care, and education tasks, as well as information search tasks in libraries and government agencies. People not acquiring this second level of computing literacy will find they are not taking advantage of many of the services and conveniences of an information society.
3. *You develop a willingness and an ability to use computers as tools to support routine business activities.* This includes using the computer for typing tasks, clerical tasks, and other tasks involved in the collection, storage, and retrieval of information. An inability to reach this third level of computing literacy will exclude an applicant from many kinds of jobs.
4. *You understand the strengths and weaknesses of computers, as well as the tasks being performed with computer support, in order to identify new ways of improving work performance.* Business and professional success is increasingly being tied to the innovative use of computers. Employees not acquiring this fourth level of computing literacy may be bypassed for promotions and other professional rewards.
5. *You design a computer application by specifying what the computer is to do, how it will do it, and perhaps do some of the programming.* While these activities are usually performed by computer specialists, computer technology is so advanced that most employees can be trained to develop some computer applications. People reaching this fifth level of computing literacy do not have to depend on others to meet their computing needs.

What is fascinating about this list is that none of these literacy levels requires a detailed knowledge of the inner workings of computers. Only the people who will go on to become full-time computer professionals will need to attain higher levels of computing literacy.

The Purpose of This Text

The topics covered in this text will help you achieve each of these five levels of computing literacy. Part I, "The Information Society," introduces you to the computer's capabilities, its uses in business, and its history. Part II, "Computer System Hardware," explains the information processing devices that make up modern computers. Part III, "System Support Software," describes the programs that direct these devices in handling information processing tasks. Part IV, "Computer-Based Information Systems," goes into more detail on the ways in which modern businesses are using computers and describes how these computer applications are developed. Part V, "Applications Software," describes the complete process of writing a new computer program to handle a specific business task or application. Part VI, "Computers and Society," discusses current and future effects of computers on the work environment and on society in general. Part VII, "Appendices," introduces you to the history of computers and computer arithmetic.

It takes very little time to get started in developing your computing literacy, particularly with today's personal computers. Personal computer hardware and software are fairly easy to understand, are simple to use, and can provide immediate practical benefits to anyone willing to learn about them. But before beginning, you need to recognize that simply reading about computer use and computer technology will not move you up many of the levels of computing literacy. Just as in playing tennis or any other sport, you must personally be using computers if you wish to gain any kind of familiarity with them. Computing literacy can only be achieved through practice. Computers at Work: "Thumbs Up for Hands-On," emphasizes that computing literacy is a participation sport! Acquiring computing literacy requires both an investment of your time and a willingness to make mistakes and learn from them. As you'll see, though, this learning need not be all hard work.

This text will start you on your progress up the ladder of computing literacy. How far you go and what you do with this knowledge, however, depends on your willingness to experience computer technology on a firsthand basis. The remaining sections of this chapter help you begin by taking a closer look at both computers and computing.

WHAT A COMPUTER IS

We have been using the term **computer** as if it refers to a single electronic device, but computers are actually composed of many electronic and electromechanical devices. **Electromechanical devices** contain both electronic and mechanical parts; all of these devices taken together are referred to as computer **hardware.** Hardware is the focus of Part II of this text.

But hardware, by itself, is useless. Hardware must be directed in its information processing by programs, and all of these programs are collectively referred to as computer **software.** Software is the focus of Parts III, IV, and V of this text.

When people refer to "a computer," they are usually referring to a set of hardware and software used as a single unit. In fact, it is more correct to use the phrase **computer system.** A wide variety of computer systems exist. The common link of all of these computer systems, however, is that they are composed of the same basic set of hardware and software components.

The primary purpose of this text is not to study the computer as an end in itself, but rather as a means to an end—the productive use of computers in business. When a computer system serves a practical use in a business, the application is termed an **information system.** An information system processes data to produce information. The term **data** refers to symbols used to represent a fact, event, or thing. Information is the meaning given a set of data.

Information systems are actually made up of three components: hardware, software, and people. People both build and use information systems. Parts IV and V of the text focus on these "people" roles. In the rest of this section we will discuss the ways in which hardware, software, and people interact.

Hardware

Hardware refers to the devices that physically enter, process, store and retrieve, and deliver data and information. All computer systems contain four types of hardware components: a computer processor, input devices, output

COMPUTERS AT WORK

Thumbs Up For Hands-On

American philosopher John Dewey thought humans learn best by doing. "You don't learn to play tennis by first reading about it in a book. Find a congenial companion, go to a tennis court, and get your hands on a racket. Flail around and make mistakes, and then, ask questions. Most of all, have fun. You're a learner and learning is fun," he might have said to someone who asked how to learn to play tennis. There is something elemental, existential, and very pure about Dewey's theory. And it works for me.

There is still much I don't know about computers. But I am learning at my own pace, in my own ornery, and very, very efficient way. And, as I said, I don't think I am all that unusual.

I think John Dewey would have loved computers. I think, too, that he would have had something to say about learning to use them; that something might be like this:

Go to a computer store;

find a congenial companion who knows more than you do;

get your hands on a keyboard;

flail around and make mistakes;

ask questions;

most of all, have fun.

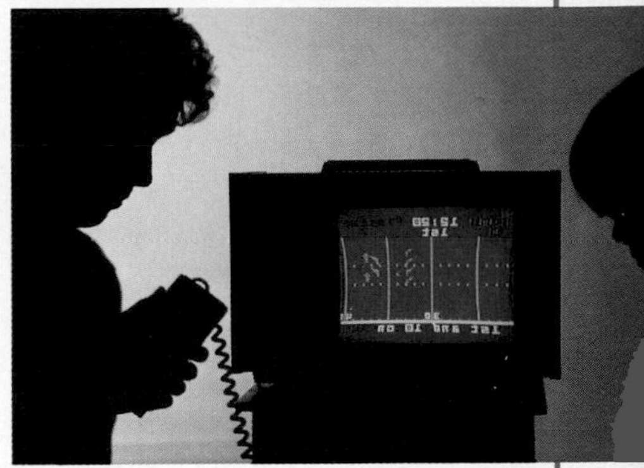

Source: I. Garvey, "Thumbs Up for Hands-On," *PC Magazine,* August 1983, pp. 137 and 142.

devices, and secondary storage devices. These components are diagrammed in Exhibit 1.5 on page 12. Occasionally, input, output, and secondary storage devices are called **peripheral devices** to reflect the fact that they are added onto the computer processor.

Computer Processor. The **computer processor** is made up of two parts: primary memory and the central processing unit. **Primary memory** provides temporary storage for all the data and information being processed, as well as the software directing this processing. The most crucial hardware component, however, is the **central processing unit (CPU).** It is there that all processing operations take place.

The CPU is made up of an arithmetic-logic unit and a control unit. The **arithmetic-logic unit (ALU)** contains the electronic circuits that actually perform the data processing operations. Data items flow between primary memory and the ALU as this processing occurs. A **control unit (CU)** contains electronic circuits that direct and coordinate these processing activities. A complete description of how these computer processor components function together is given in Chapter 3, "The Central Processing Unit." Generally, the more primary memory available in the computer processor and the more numerous and complex the ALU and CU circuits, the more powerful the computer system.

While the computer processor is usually referred to as a single hardware device, its three parts may be contained in different boxes, which are connected through electrical wires. This is most evident with supercomputers, today's largest and fastest computer systems. Even in modern microcomputers, the ALU and the CU may be on a different chip than primary memory, which may by itself occupy several specialized chips.

Exhibit 1.5

The four basic hardware components are the computer processor, input devices, output devices, and secondary storage devices. As data and information are processed, they flow between these components.

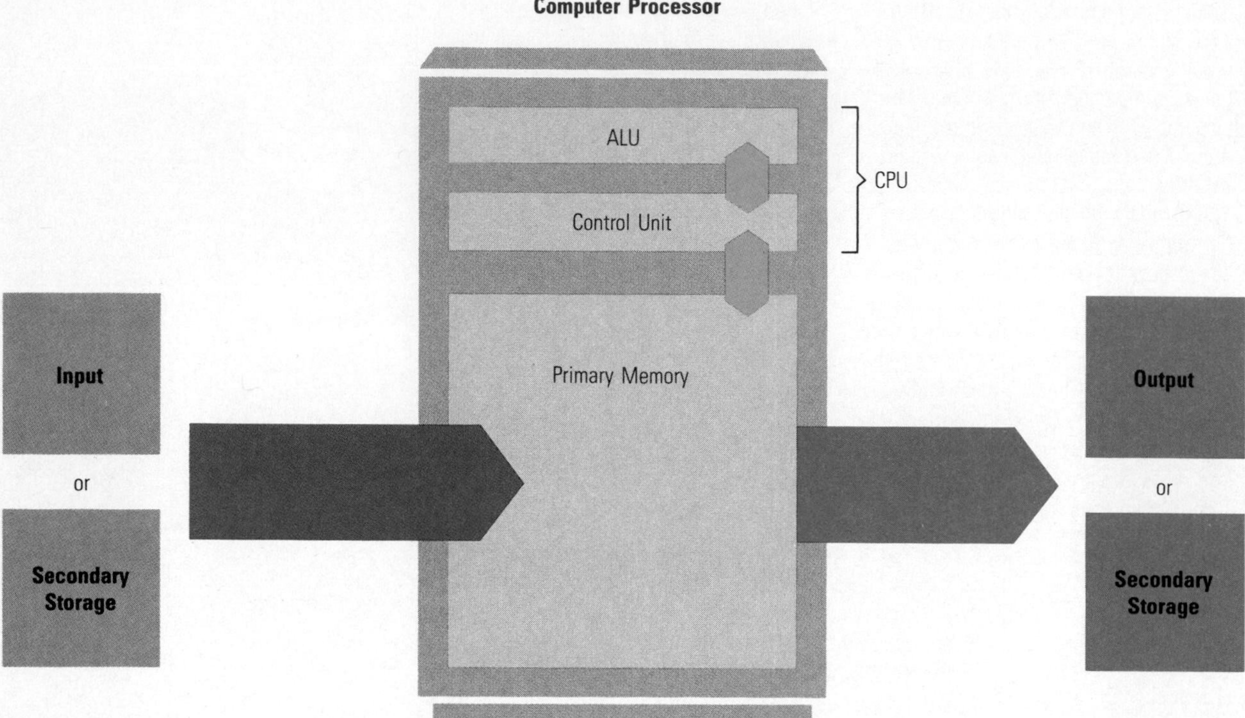

Input and Output Devices. **Input** and **output devices** are used to move data and information, respectively, into and out of the primary memory.

The most common type of input device is the computer **terminal.** Terminals have keyboards similar to those used with electric typewriters. With a **cathode ray tube (CRT)** terminal, the data being entered appear on a television-like screen, making it easy to spot and correct typing errors. CRT terminals are also called **video display terminals,** or simply **VDTs.**

Other input devices use **media,** or special kinds of material. When you take notes in class, you are placing your thoughts on paper, perhaps the most common medium. Some of these input devices include the following:

A **disk drive** uses a diskette as its input medium. A "floppy," or flexible, diskette looks like a small 45 rpm record. Just as a record "stores" sound on its surface, a diskette stores data on its surface. A diskette reader, then, picks up these data from the diskette's surface, translates them into electrical signals, and transmits them to the primary memory.

A **magnetic tape drive** uses **magnetic tape** as its input medium. Just as with recorded music, two forms of tape media are used: reels and cassettes. The magnetic tape drive senses the data items stored on a tape, translates them into electrical signals, and transmits them to the primary memory.

A variety of devices are capable of producing computer output:

A VDT displays data and information on the terminal screen. Output can be displayed on a VDT very quickly. However, once information leaves the screen, it is gone. To produce **hard copy,** a permanent form of the information being displayed, a printer or plotter can be used along with the VDT.

A **printer** uses paper as its output medium. A printer is very similar to a typewriter except that electrical signals from the computer processor direct the printing rather than a typist.

A **plotter** also uses paper as its output medium. By following electrical signals sent from the computer processor, a plotter can produce detailed graphics.

Did you notice that VDTs can be used both as input devices and output devices? A worker using a VDT can thus interact with a computer system in both directions. A clerk at a utility company, for example, can quickly answer questions about your bill by typing your account number into the CRT keyboard (input) and viewing a display of your recent billing history on the VDT screen (output).

Secondary Storage Devices. It is relatively costly to store data, information, and programs in primary memory. Furthermore, if a computer system's power source is turned off, anything stored in primary memory will probably be lost. As a result, most of the data, information, and programs used within a computer system are kept in **secondary storage** until they are needed. It takes longer to store data on or retrieve data from secondary storage devices because these devices use mechanical as well as electronic parts. But, secondary storage is less expensive than primary memory storage. More importantly, data placed in secondary storage are not lost when a computer system's power is cut.

The two most common secondary storage media are **magnetic tape** and **magnetic disk.** Tapes can take the form of reels or cassettes. Disks can be flexible (a floppy disk) or rigid (a **hard disk**). **Secondary storage devices** are the hardware that places data onto and reads data from these media. Once data and information are stored on tape or disk, secondary storage devices can also serve as input devices.

Exhibit 1.6 shows some of these hardware components in the type of microcomputer system with which you may already be familiar.

Exhibit 1.6

Input and output devices are used to move data and information, respectively, into and out of primary memory. The CRT terminal has a keyboard for entering data and a television-like screen on which the data appear. To the left of the CRT terminal is a printer, an output device that uses paper as its medium. The businessman pictured here is holding a secondary storage medium called a diskette, or floppy disk.

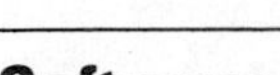

Software

Software refers to the programs, or sets of instructions, that direct the information processing operations performed by hardware. There are two types of software: applications software and systems software.

Applications Software. The general term for programs that perform specific user-oriented tasks is **applications software.** These tasks can range from playing chess to solving business problems. Some of the first business applications software was written to handle such basic but important business tasks as payroll, accounting, and customer billing.

Applications software is normally acquired in one of two ways. First, it can be "customized," or created especially for a specific business. Second, it can be bought in a ready-made, or "packaged," form. Exhibit 1.7, on page 14, shows a number of business **software packages** available for microcomputers.

Exhibit 1.7

One of the driving forces behind the surge in the business use of microcomputers is the ready availability of applications software.

Systems Software. Coordinating the flow of data, information, and programs within a computer system is a complex task. Today, most of these functions are performed by **systems software**—the general term for programs that direct hardware-related tasks. Exhibit 1.8 illustrates the relationship between computer hardware, systems software, and applications software.

The most important systems software is the **operating system.** This set of programs supervises all the activity that takes place within a computer system. For now, think of the operating system as an office manager who assigns work to a computer system's different components and who also helps out with the more important and difficult tasks. Chapter 7 discusses the role of the operating system in more depth. Most computer systems also use other types of systems software. Chapters 8 and 9, respectively, discuss the systems software involved in managing data in secondary storage and in communicating between computer systems.

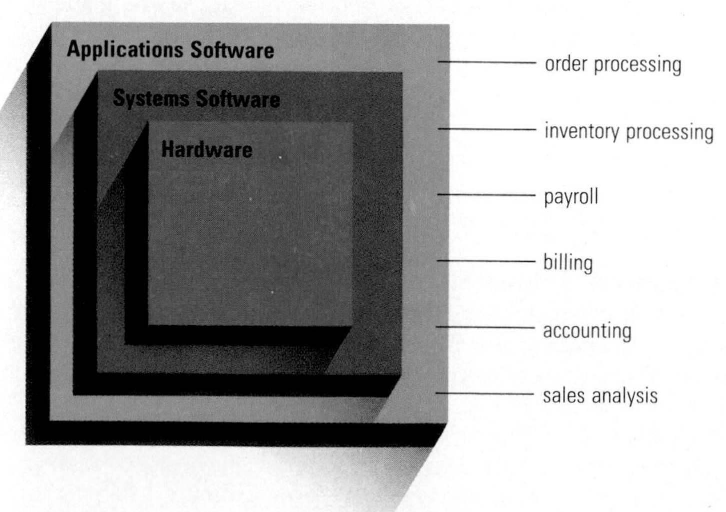

Exhibit 1.8

Systems software allows applications software to handle user-oriented problems rather than the details of directing the hardware.

People

People, most simply, breathe "life" into an information system. People play two major roles in information systems: that of information system user and that of information system creator.

User Role. Almost all the data used by information systems must be either directly input into the computer by a person or placed on a computer-readable medium by a person. Most information system outputs are sent to a person, who then makes use of the information. Without these users, there would be no data to process and no reason to create or use information systems.

Exhibit 1.9

A programmer works closely with an information system user to create a customized program.

Creator Role. Before an information system can be used effectively, it must be brought into a business. For this to occur, systems analysis, systems design, and programming activities must take place. Systems analysts do the following:

Determine whether an information system is needed.

Describe the business activities to be computerized.

Specify the exact nature of the needed information system.

Systems designers perform specific tasks:

Design the information system.

Decide whether applications software needs to be customized.

Decide whether additional hardware is needed.

Programmers have a single goal:

Create a customized program.

Often, computer specialists perform all or most of these creation activities. Three of the most common occupations found in an Information Systems Department are **systems analyst, systems designer,** and **programmer.** These computer specialists must work closely with an information system's eventual users to create a truly useful information system (see Exhibit 1.9). This cooperative process of developing information systems will be discussed in Part IV.

WHAT A COMPUTER DOES

On the surface, computers may seem to have mysterious and limitless powers. The computer applications pictured in Exhibit 1.10 on page 16 include some of the sophisticated uses of computers. With these or any other computer applications, however, the computer is merely processing information. But what exactly do we mean by "processing information"? And why are computers increasingly being used to process information? To understand this, it may help to look first at how people process information.

Exhibit 1.10

Many of today's computer applications seem to go far beyond our human capabilities to meet diverse needs. Examples include (clockwise from top) auto design, air-traffic control, sculpture, computerization of artificial limbs, control of factory equipment, and athletic performance analysis.

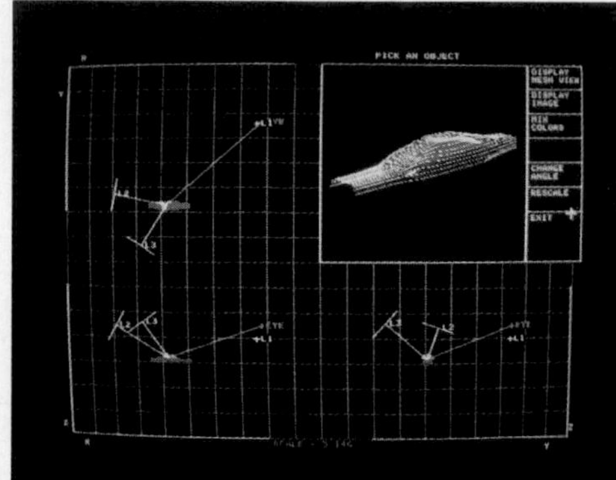

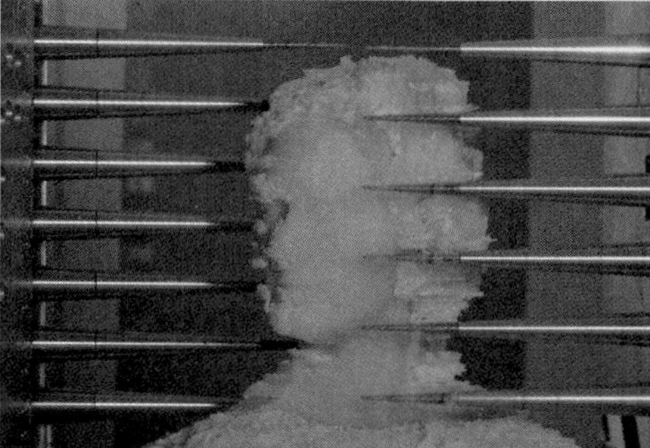

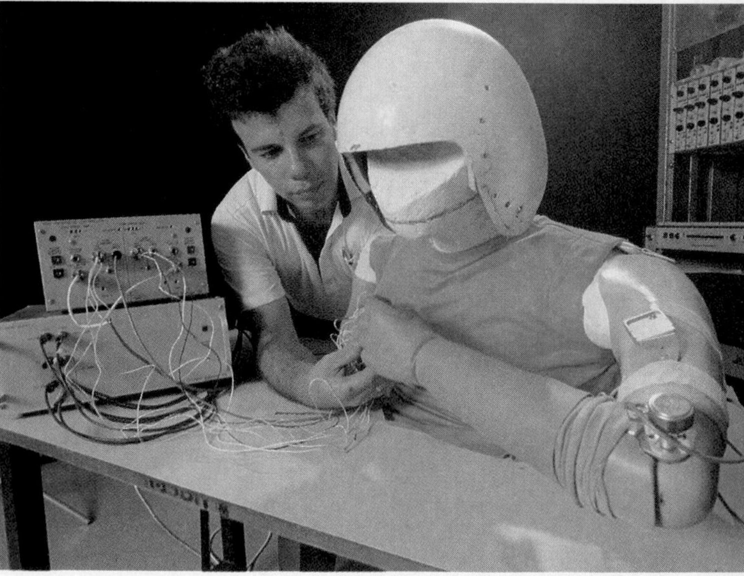

Exhibit 1.11

Solving a crossword puzzle provides a good illustration of what is meant by the term *information processing.*

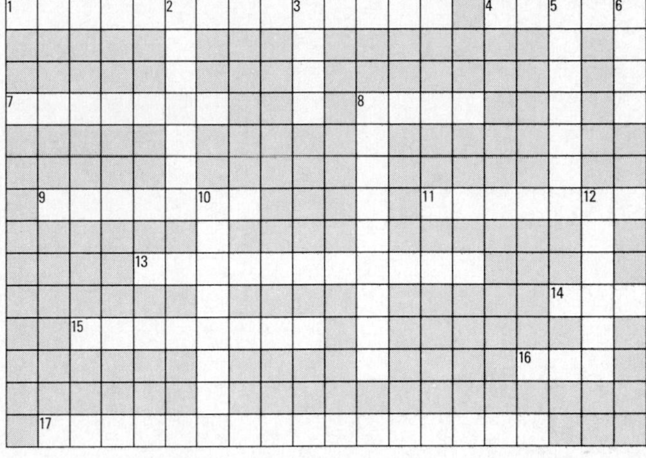

Across
1. A computer on a chip.
4. Devices that move data into the computer processor.
7. Software that coordinates the flow of data, information, and programs between hardware devices.
8. An integrated circuit is also called (a/an) ________ .
9. A systems ________ recognizes an information system is needed, describes the business activities to be computerized, and specifies the exact nature of the needed information system.
11. The ________ unit directs and coordinates all computer processing.
13. Hardware, software, and people working together to serve a practical business purpose are called (a/an) ________ system.
14. Abbreviation for computer system component made up of ALU and CU.
15. Electronic and electromechanical devices used to process data.
16. Abbreviation for video display terminal.
17. Refers to the miniaturization of electronic circuits and components used to process information.

Down
2. Temporary storage for data and information being processed is provided by ________ memory.
3. Getting started with personal computers is ________ .
5. An output device that is similar to a typewriter.
6. A common media for secondary storage is magnetic ________ .
8. The ability to use computers as tools to enrich our personal and professional lives is called ________ literacy.
10. Another term for computer programs.
12. A computer terminal can be used for both input and ________ .

(Answers appear on page 20.)

At one time or another, you have probably worked a crossword puzzle. Solving a crossword puzzle is purely an information processing activity. Using the puzzle shown in Exhibit 1.11, consider the steps you would go through in solving it:

1. Read the clue given in "1 across." This involves identifying each of the letters or numbers making up the clue.
2. Combine these symbols to interpret and understand the clue.
3. Try to relate the clue to a fact or concept you may have in your memory.
4. Produce an answer.
5. Try to match the letters in your "correct" answer to the spaces provided.
6. If the number of letters match, write this answer in the spaces provided. If the number of letters do not match, go back to step 1.

Step 1 required you to enter some data into your mind. Step 2 required you to process these data in order to interpret the clue. Step 3 required you to retrieve some data or information previously stored in your memory. Step 4 required you to process all the data and information now active in your mind in order to produce a new set of symbols representing your answer to the puzzle clue. In Step 5, you tested your answer by seeing if it fit into the puzzle spaces. Step 6 required you either to transfer your answer to the clue onto the puzzle or to go back to Step 1. In this information processing task, you engaged in a number of input, processing, storage and retrieval, and output activities.

Exhibit 1.12

A mail-order book firm processing a customer order with an information system follows each of the stages of the information processing cycle. The order is entered into the computer processor. Product information is retrieved from secondary storage. Processing operations calculate the total cost of the order. An invoice, a packing list, a shipping label, and possibly a back-order note are printed by the computer.

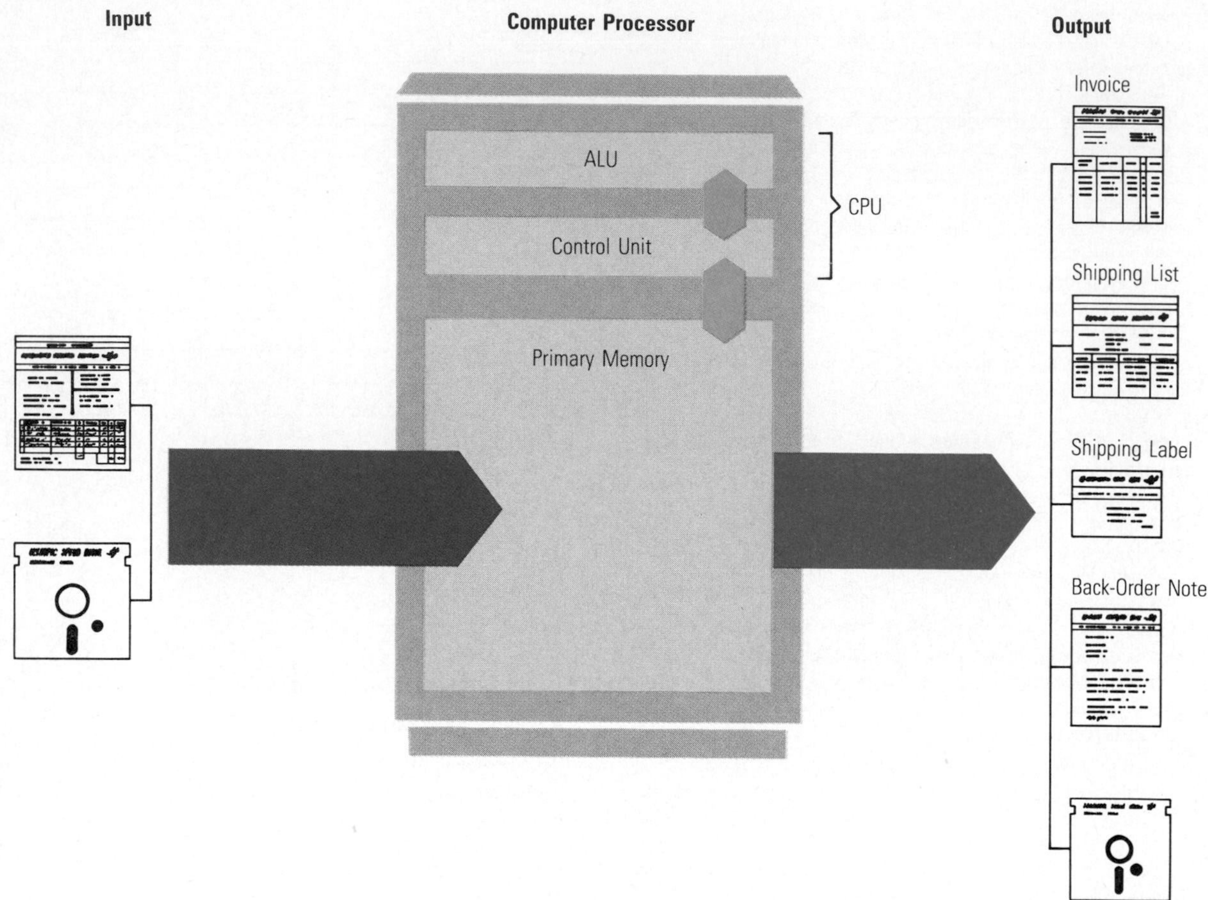

These stages of input, processing, storage and retrieval, and output activities are exactly what a computer does when it processes information and are referred to as the **information processing cycle.** Exhibit 1.12 portrays these stages for a relatively simple business information processing task, the processing of a customer order by a mail-order book firm. We will be looking at this example throughout the rest of this chapter.

Inputs Data

Both people and computers "take in" data. We, for example, capture data through our senses of sight, hearing, touch, smell, and taste. Most people, however, do not realize that our sensory organs are much more sophisticated than are a computer system's input devices. Much of the data we capture is in its original form. The computer is not so flexible. It must have data prepared in special ways and must be instructed, through a program, to look for and collect these data. The computer then "translates" the data into a pattern of electrical signals it can process. We will discuss this series of activities in greater detail in Part II of the text.

The book order form has been enlarged in Exhibit 1.13. To process the order, the computer will need to do the following:

1. Read the customer name and address.
2. Read the identification number, title, author, quantity, and price of each book being ordered.
3. Read the total cost of the order.

Notice in Exhibit 1.13 that this set of input data includes both letters and numbers. Both are easily captured by computers. However, it is unlikely that the computer will be able to enter this data directly from the handwritten order form. Instead, a clerk will prepare the data for entry, perhaps using a computer terminal.

Given these limitations, you may wonder why computers are used as much as they are. The answer lies in the computer's speed and reliability. Once the order data are organized and entered in a form that the computer can handle, termed a **computer-readable form,** the data can be captured and processed in a fraction of the time it would take a person to read the data items.

While this speed may be of little benefit when processing a single book order, the benefit is significant when thousands of orders are processed each day. Not only can all these orders be processed in a short period of time, but the cost of processing the orders is far less than if they were processed by hand. Furthermore, it is unlikely that the computer will make any errors in processing the data. People, in contrast, are prone to typing mistakes and mathematical errors. Finally, once the order data have been entered into the computer, they become available for further computer-based information processing. The advantages of this will become clearer as the remaining stages of the information processing cycle are discussed.

Exhibit 1.13
Handwritten Book Order Form

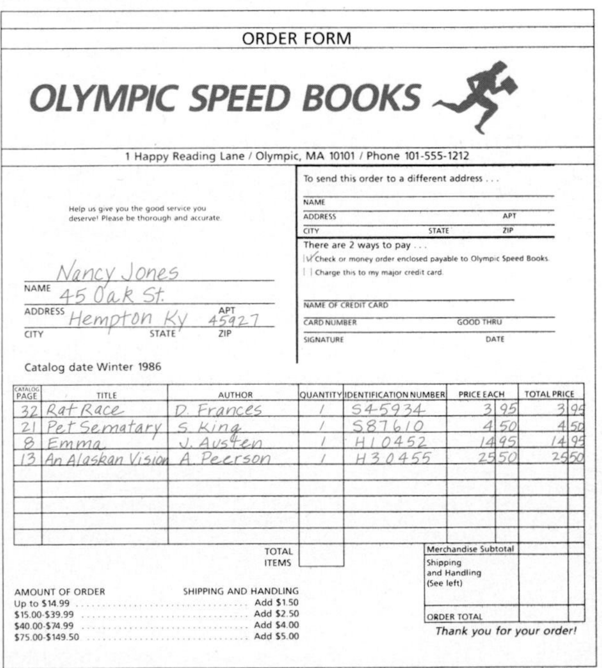

ORDER FORM

OLYMPIC SPEED BOOKS

1 Happy Reading Lane / Olympic, MA 10101 / Phone 101-555-1212

Help us give you the good service you deserve! Please be thorough and accurate.

NAME Nancy Jones
ADDRESS 45 Oak St. APT
CITY Hempton STATE Ky ZIP 45927

To send this order to a different address . . .
NAME
ADDRESS APT
CITY STATE ZIP

There are 2 ways to pay . . .
[✓] Check or money order enclosed payable to Olympic Speed Books.
[ ] Charge this to my major credit card.

NAME OF CREDIT CARD
CARD NUMBER GOOD THRU
SIGNATURE DATE

Catalog date Winter 1986

CATALOG PAGE	TITLE	AUTHOR	QUANTITY	IDENTIFICATION NUMBER	PRICE EACH	TOTAL PRICE
32	Rat Race	D. Frances	1	S45934	3 95	3 95
21	Pet Sematary	S. King	1	S87610	4 50	4 50
8	Emma	J. Austen	1	H10452	14 95	14 95
13	An Alaskan Vision	A. Peerson	1	H30455	25 50	25 50

TOTAL ITEMS

AMOUNT OF ORDER	SHIPPING AND HANDLING
Up to $14.99	Add $1.50
$15.00-$39.99	Add $2.50
$40.00-$74.99	Add $4.00
$75.00-$149.50	Add $5.00

Merchandise Subtotal
Shipping and Handling (See left)
ORDER TOTAL

Thank you for your order!

Processes Data

Both people and computers process data. People, in fact, possess some very sophisticated information processing capabilities. Our ability to work with incomplete sets of data and to generalize meanings across sets of data is very powerful. Most important, however, is our ability to create. When we are faced with a new problem, we are often able to arrive at a solution by piecing together prior experiences, sketchy facts, and "human intuition."

Computers, on the other hand, have extremely limited data processing capabilities. They are limited to a few rather basic processing operations:

Computers perform simple **arithmetic operations,** such as addition, subtraction, multiplication, and division.

Computers perform simple **text manipulation operations,** such as inserting or deleting characters and moving characters, words, and longer pieces of text.

Computers perform simple **logic operations,** such as comparing the values of two numbers or determining whether or not two words contain the same letters.

Furthermore, computers must be directed in a step-by-step fashion to perform these operations.

Given these limitations, why should we use computers? Again, the computer's speed and reliability prove to be key factors. Today's computers can perform thousands of error-free processing operations in the time it takes a person to perform one operation. Most computers perform their operations in **milliseconds,** one-thousandth of a second, **microseconds,** one-millionth of a second, and **nanoseconds,** one-billionth of a second. These speeds are so great they are difficult to comprehend. How long does it take you to add two numbers together in your head? One second? A computer might take one nanosecond to perform the same addition. The computer, then, is about 1,000,000,000 (one billion) times faster than you. Just how much faster is this? You may have a better idea if you consider that a commercial jet liner is about 100 times faster than your walking speed, a jet fighter about 400 times faster, the space shuttle about 4000 times faster, and the speed of light about 150,000,000 times faster.

The speed of today's computer systems enables them to process vast amounts of data very quickly. As a result, the overall cost of processing large sets of data is far less than it would be if people did the data processing. Some tasks, such as processing today's U.S. Census, would be virtually impossible to complete without the processing power of computer systems.

The fact that computer systems can perform only very simple arithmetic, text manipulation, and logic data processing operations turns out to be a fairly minor limitation. Computer programs can be developed to handle just about any information processing task. The limit to what can be done with computer systems lies not in the computer, but rather in our skill in using the computer's capabilities.

The data processing operations required in processing the book order described in Exhibit 1.12 are fairly simple. In fact, most of the resulting information is the same data that were entered into the computer: customer name and address; book identification numbers, titles, and authors; quantities and prices; and total cost of an order. As a double check, the computer will probably calculate the total price charged the customer.

The process becomes a bit more complex when a book is out of stock. In these cases, the applications program will direct the information system to perform two additional tasks. First, the computer system will recalculate the amount due. Second, the computer system will print a back-order notice to be sent to the customer. Producing this back-order notice is easy, since much of the message remains the same whenever it is written. What changes from note to note are data items that come directly from the order form: the customer's name and address and the identification numbers, titles, authors, and prices of the out-of-stock books.

Stores and Retrieves Data and Information

Both people and computers store and then retrieve data and information. Your mind, in fact, can hold more data than the largest of today's computers. Just think about it. The "data" stored in your memory include all your past experiences, all the facts and concepts that you ever learned, and all the ideas that ever occurred to you. Our ability to retrieve data from our memories also turns out to be far more sophisticated than that available with computer systems.

Why, then, are computers used so extensively in storing data and information? Again, we come back to the computer's speed and reliability. If information is stored in an organized manner within a computer, it can be retrieved quickly and accurately when it is needed. "Organizing" a set of data means storing it in a way that fits the data retrieval operations to be performed. Also, the cost of storing a large quantity of data within a computer system has become much less than the cost of storing these same data in file cabinets.

In the book order-processing example, data are retrieved from a data file. A **data file** refers to an organized set of related data items. In this case, data describing all of the books offered by the mail-order firm are kept in a book file (see Exhibit 1.14). All the data for a particular book are stored in a **data record** within this book file. Each of the data items that describes a feature of a book is termed a **data field.**

When the data file is organized in this way, retrieving the record for a particular book becomes easy—just search through the book file until a match is found between the identification number of a book being ordered and the "identification number" field of a particular record. When a match occurs, the correct data record, or book in this case, has been found.

FIELD	FIELD	FIELD	FIELD	FIELD	FIELD	
I.D. Number	Title	Author	Price	On-Hand	Publisher	RECORD
H30450	Roman Holidays	Elem	$15.95	14	Watkins	RECORD
H30451	The Greek Islands	Hays	$14.99	0	Wilson	RECORD
H30452	Peru and You	Thomas	$12.99	11	Sims	RECORD
H30454	Japanese Inns	Suola	$15.99	2	Wilson	RECORD
H30455	An Alaskan Vision	Peerson	$25.50	3	Sims	RECORD

Exhibit 1.14

Organizing the book file in a systematic manner makes it fairly easy for the information system to locate the record for a particular book. Once located, the data stored in this data record can be retrieved for use in processing a book order.

Exhibit 1.15

By capturing data from an order form, an information system can produce much of the paperwork necessary for handling a customer's book order.

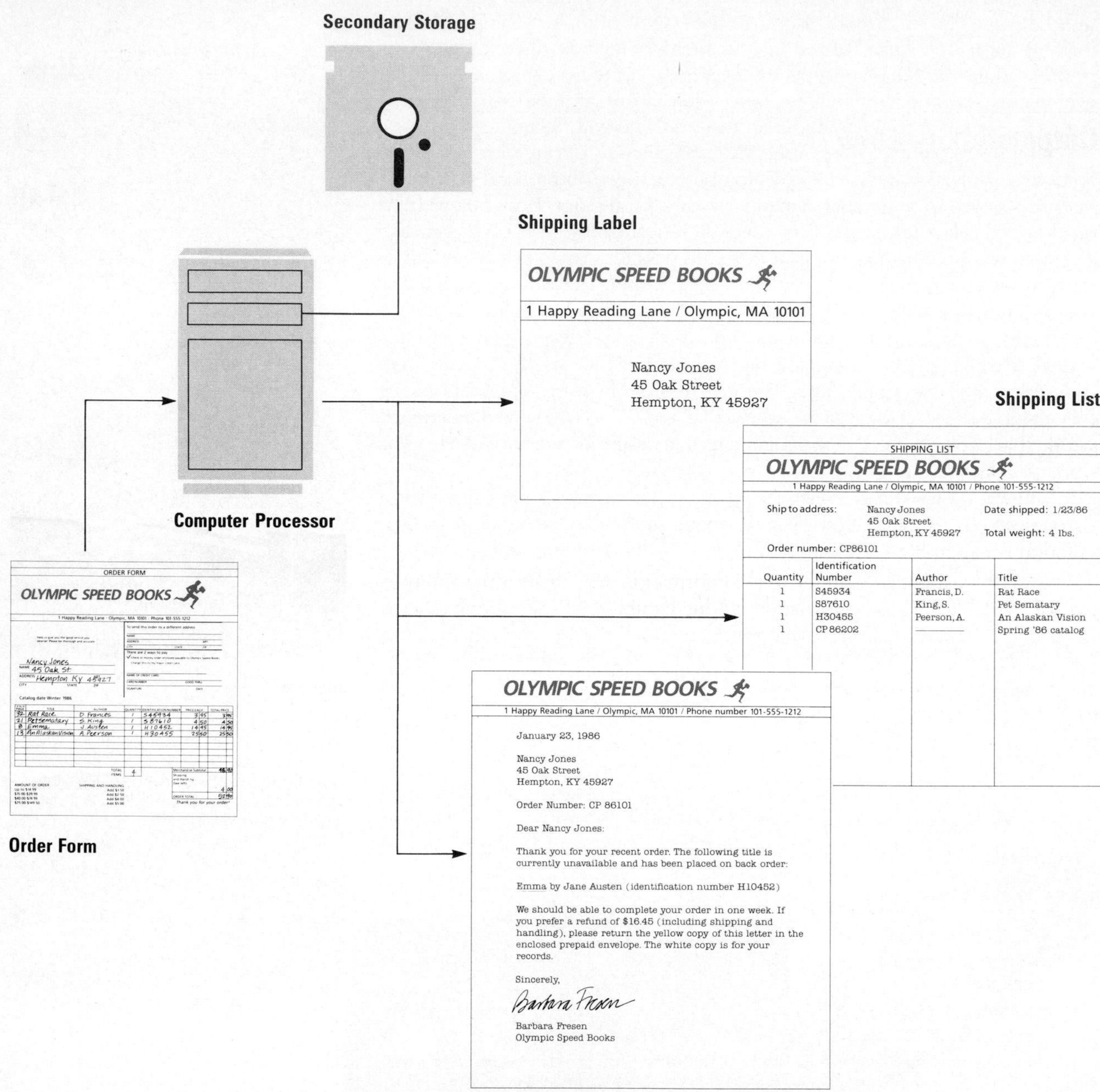

Notice that the operations to be performed in processing a book order may be affected by this retrieved information. What if no match was found in the book file for an ordered book? Or, what if a match is found, but the book's title, author, or price do not agree with what is on the book order? In such cases, it may be best to return the order form to the customer with a polite form letter—generated by the information system.

Outputs Information

Both people and computers communicate information. People, however, are much more versatile than computers in expressing their information. People, for example, have developed sophisticated abilities to transmit quite different messages with only slight changes in the information being communicated. Have you ever said one thing while indicating just the opposite through your tone or facial expression? Computers simply do not have the versatility or the sophistication that people have when communicating.

What computers provide, not surprisingly, is the ability to produce information quickly, accurately, and inexpensively. An obvious benefit is the ability to process the large number of outputs, such as the shipping lists, shipping labels, and back-order notices needed by the mail-order book company in processing thousands of book orders each month. A more detailed view of these outputs is illustrated in Exhibit 1.15 on page 22. It is common, as shown here, to find that a few input data items "trigger" a number of information system outputs.

Another benefit of computer-based information processing is the ability to easily vary the form of an information output. Exhibit 1.16, for example, shows the same information in three different forms—table, graph, and chart. Each form might be useful for different situations. In producing these "user-oriented" outputs, each information item is translated from the electrical signals used to represent it within the computer to the symbols used to print it on paper.

Exhibit 1.16

The same information can appear in different forms on a computer system. Information outputs can thus be tailored to meet the information user's needs.

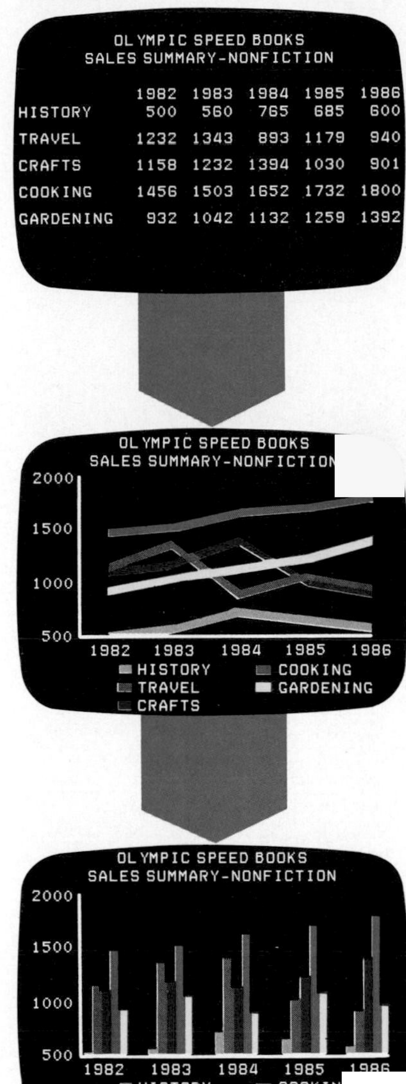

OLYMPIC SPEED BOOKS
SALES SUMMARY-NONFICTION

	1982	1983	1984	1985	1986
HISTORY	500	560	765	685	600
TRAVEL	1232	1343	893	1179	940
CRAFTS	1158	1232	1394	1030	901
COOKING	1456	1503	1652	1732	1800
GARDENING	932	1042	1132	1259	1392

Summarizing the Computer's Basic Capabilities

What, then, does a computer do?

1. Both numbers and letters can be entered into a computer. These data items can then be stored within a data file and output from the computer in this original form.
2. New data items can be created by performing arithmetic operations on numbers and by changing or rearranging text. These newly created data can also be stored within a data file or communicated from the computer. Also, any of the data items currently being processed can also be used to determine the information processing operations to be performed.
3. Data or information previously stored within the computer can be retrieved for processing (numerical operations or text manipulations) or for output. Often, these retrieved data are combined with data that have just been entered in order to create still other data items.
4. Information produced by earlier input, processing, and storage and retrieval operations can be output in a number of forms.

The real advantage of computer-based information processing, however, is that these operations can be performed more quickly, more reliably, and less expensively when done by a computer rather than by people. You will begin to learn in Chapter 2 how to spot situations where these advantages are likely to arise.

Finally, it is important to recognize exactly how computer-based information processing supports people in doing work. The computer does not do any of the physical labor involved in sending shipments of books to customers. However, it does perform the following activities:

The computer processes the "paper" that goes along with shipping a book order.

The computer provides the people performing specific tasks associated with shipping a book order with information that helps them perform their tasks.

The Automated Agent Helps Performers Get Gigs

What's your picture of a talent agent? Is it a sweaty man chomping a cigar while he sweet-talks a deal on the telephone? Is it a small-town arts administrator, searching through index cards, trying to promote her favorite folksinger into a big-city music festival? Or is it the manager of a band, trying to remember who it was that came backstage last night offering them another job?

The common thread in talent management is information-processing: knowing who's playing where, when, and for how much. Personal attention and endless hours on the phone give successful managers an edge, because they can parlay that information into signed contracts. Since so much of the business depends on managing knowledge, not just performers, automation via computers was inevitable. Now, one agent has teamed up with a programmer to create a vertical software package that is an "integrated booking information system"—*Ibis.* (Vertical software packages are specific to one industry or business.) It was designed for music talent agencies, but is also suitable for fashion model agencies and speakers' bureaus.

John Ullman runs the nationwide Traditional Arts Services from Portland, Oregon. He finds audiences for folk musicians such as Bill Monroe (the "father" of bluegrass), Mike Seeger, Elizabeth "Libba" Cotten (who wrote "Freight Train") and a variety of black, Irish, Cajun and Celtic performers. He said that an agent's biggest problem is knowing who to call or write to line up gigs, or performances.

"Here's a typical problem," he explained. "Let's say someone calls me and wants Libba Cotten in Carlsbad, New Mexico, in July. That's just one gig, and it pays well, but it's months in advance; we don't want to pass it up, but we couldn't just send her there from her home in Syracuse, New York, without some connecting dates along the way. My problem is to put together a tour—to find every potential sponsor who could put her on in the Southwest in July.

The PC breaks into show biz.

"Now, before we got the computer, I would scratch my head and say, 'Where are the sponsors around Carlsbad?' or go through my Rolodex file looking up names and start making phone calls. But what happens? I call somebody and they say, 'No, I can't use her, but how about so-and-so?' and right away I have to take some time away from what I was doing to put together a contract for another performer and another gig."

The software Ullman helped to write is a [data] management program that lets him find those potential sponsors with just one pass through the data. By keying in the categories he wants, Ullman makes the PC sort out those sponsors whose zip code or area code is in the Southwestern states. It will look for those among them who have expressed interest in folk artists like Ms. Cotten, and it may also include anyone whose season covers the month of July, and who can be expected to meet her fee. What Ullman gets is a printout of mailing labels that he can stick on a promotional flyer for Ms. Cotten. He knows, when he sends those flyers out, that the sponsors will be predisposed to considering her.

"In the time it would take to make just a few phone calls," said Ullman, "I can send out a hundred direct-mail pieces, and be certain that I am reaching the right people. I can use my time for other things, and my phone bill will be smaller. Then, when Libba Cotten makes her tour, it will be so efficiently scheduled that her travel expenses will be lower, meaning more money for her."

ENTER THE PROGRAMMER

Since Ullman knew the music business, but not the ins and outs of programming, he turned for help to an old friend, Robert Harper, of Seattle, Washington. As Harper Business Systems, he wrote software for mainframes, minis and micros.

Ibis, as they developed it, became a software package, with one part dedicated to sponsor information and mailing list management, and a second part for contract-writing and artist information.

Each page of sponsor data holds up to 28 categories (what data management system programmers call "fields"), including not only the sponsor's name, address, and phone number, but the size of the performance hall, availability of housing nearby, the kinds of music the sponsor sponsors, and room for the agent's remarks. A sample sponsor record is reproduced in Figure 1. There is also a process for creating new categories.

```
            ENTER NEW SPONSOR DATA     DELETE N                    FILEDATE 12-13-82
SPONSOR#  160                                 SEASON
   INDEX CONCERTHALL PRODUCTIONS       BEGINS  1                    MAILINGS 000
 ORGNAME Concerthall Productions         ENDS 12                    LIST ACUCAA
DIVISION Classical Artists Series        HALL Madison Sq.           SPECIAL INTERESTS
 ADDRESS 5500 Broadway Ave.             SEATS 20000                 1INT ALL
    CITY New York                       HIGH$ 150000                2INT
   STATE NY ZIP 10101                 HOUSING N                     CONTRACT RECAP
    ATTN Mr. Connoisseur                 AREA 201                  NUMBER 000
 1REMARK Mr. C. likes only                TEL 999-9999 X9999 TOTVAL 0000000
 2REMARK World-Class artists. 3REMARK                                LAST
                                                                     PERF 00-00-00
FIELD?                        (JUST HIT RETURN IF NO FIELDS ARE TO BE UPDATED.)
```

Users select fields, and change their "values," by entering new data on a line at the bottom of each page. Harper simplified the process, for novices. "Remember, these people are talent agents, or performers setting up their own gigs—not computer professionals."

The contract and artist information module uses the same procedure. Harper said, "The agent can create or update a performer's schedule, create or make changes in a contract, and keep track of important arrangements, such as who to call on arrival."

THE VALUE OF TEAMWORK

Harper and Ullman teamed up because each had a skill to share. "Ours is a partnership between a person who is a working part of the real market and a person who understands how to program what that market needs," said Ullman. "It's a paradigm for how small-business software should be designed."

The software finds potential sponsors with just one pass through the data. The system they unveiled to 125 agencies at the Western Alliance of Arts Administrators, in Seattle last September, costs about $8000. Included in the package were [an IBM] PC with two disk drives and a printer for about $5000; and the *Ibis* software at a price of $3000. Ullman said, "*Ibis* can help generate $10,000–15,000 a year, in income or savings, from an investment of under $10,000, and should pay for itself in a year."

To people in the business, he said, "The things *Ibis* does are the core of what an arts agency does. It reduces paperwork and cuts way down on office overhead. It enforces sound business practices, which are not always done, because they require a large staff to do them by hand. And it makes possible a lot of extras that, until now, could only be done by larger agencies, such as making multiple copies of itineraries, so everybody who needs one can get one.

"A neat trick is, when you're printing copies of the itinerary, you can put in or leave out certain information. The performers need everything, all on one page," says Ullman, "but the sponsor should not see what fees other sponsors on that tour are paying; the local publicity person needs only the days and dates for that particular city.

"It's basically a virgin market," he said. "Agencies and artists—either as individuals or in cooperatives—can make use of them right away. Only a few of the people I talked to are 'technophobic.' Maybe about ten percent will not put a computer in their office. The rest say they're interested. [An IBM] PC with *Ibis* will cost about as much as a modest-priced car, but the agency gains it back in savings by not hiring part-timers to type mailing labels or contracts. That cost me $4000–5000 last year alone. The artists gain, too, because the agent gets more time to give them more personal attention.

"Speed is crucial. When I finish talking with a sponsor and I ask, 'Is that date firm?' and he says 'Yes,' then as soon as I get off the phone, I want to hit the PRINT button and get the contract in the mail right away. There's no agent in the world who doesn't recognize *that* need!"

Source: H. Glatzer, "The Automated Agent Helps Performers Get Gigs," *PC Magazine,* March 1983, pp. 286–91.

SUMMARY

In an *information society,* the collection, processing, and distribution of information have become the primary source of wealth and work.

The 1960s witnessed the birth and growth of the microelectronics industry. *Microelectronics* refers to the miniaturization of electronic circuits and components used to process information.

The major microelectronic device is the *integrated circuit,* also called a *microchip* or *chip.* The *microprocessor* is a computer on a chip. Technological improvements will continue, perhaps at an even greater rate, in the foreseeable future.

Microelectronic advances have "liberated" the computer, as evidenced by the growing use of *personal computers,* also called *microcomputers* or *desktop* computers. Microelectronic advances have also transformed the U.S. into an information society. In addition, microprocessors are being used to add *intelligence,* the apparent ability to act in an informed manner, to a variety of familiar products.

In the future, most workers will probably work in "information careers" using computers. Some debate exists about the type of computer education, or *computer literacy,* people need to function in an information society. Computer professionals need to understand computer technology and how to write *programs,* or computer instructions. Most people, however, need *computing literacy,* the ability to use the computer as a tool to enrich their personal and professional lives. Exhibit 1.4 shows five levels of computing literacy.

The purpose of this text is to help you achieve the five levels of computing literacy. To do so, however, requires participation, whether it be working with a personal computer or even playing a computer game.

Computers are made up of electronic and electromechanical devices. *Electromechanical* devices contain both electronic and mechanical parts. Another term for computer devices is *hardware.*

Hardware is useless without *software,* the programs that direct information processing. Hardware and software used as a single unit make up a *computer system.* An *information system,* a computer system that serves a practical business purpose, is made up of hardware, software, and people.

Information systems process data to produce information. The term *data* refers to symbols used to represent a fact, event, or thing. *Information* is the meaning given to a set of data.

The four types of hardware components are computer processors, input devices, output devices, and secondary storage devices. The computer processor is made up of primary memory and the central processing unit. *Primary memory* provides temporary storage for data and programs. The *central processing unit (CPU)* performs all processing. The CPU is made up of the *arithmetic-logic unit (ALU),* which performs arithmetic, data manipulation, and logical processing operations, and the *control unit (CU),* which directs and coordinates all processing.

Input and *output devices* move data into and out of the computer processor. The most common input device is the *computer terminal,* also called a *video display terminal (VDT).* Most VDTs use a *cathode ray tube (CRT).* Diskette readers use diskettes as input media. Magnetic tape readers use *magnetic tapes* as input media.

Common output devices include the *CRT screen, printers,* and *plotters. Hard copy,* a permanent copy of computer output, is produced by printers and plotters. Computer terminals can function as both input and output devices.

Because primary memory is relatively expensive, it is used only for temporary storage of data. Most data and programs are stored on *secondary storage.* The most common secondary storage media are magnetic tape and magnetic disk. The hardware devices that place data onto and read data from these media are called *secondary storage devices.*

Applications software, the general term for practical computer applications, can be customized or bought ready-made in the form of a *software package. Systems software* are programs that coordinate the flow of data, information, and programs within a computer system. The most important systems software is the *operating system,* which functions as an office manager for the computer system.

In an information system, people act as both users and creators. Without users, there would be no data to process and no reason to use computers. Information system creators perform systems analysis, systems design, and programming. A *systems analyst* recognizes an information system is needed, describes the business activities to be computerized, and specifies the exact nature of the needed information system. A *systems designer* designs the information system, decides whether applications software needs to be customized, and decides whether additional hardware is needed. A *programmer* creates customized software (programs).

Computers transform data into information through an *information processing cycle* made up of input, processing, storage and retrieval, and output stages.

A computer can only accept data in *computer-readable form.* Data in this form can be captured quickly and accurately and are available for further *computer-based information processing.*

In *processing* data, computers need detailed instructions to perform simple *arithmetic, text manipulation,* and *logic operations.* Computers are used to process data because they are reliable and fast. Computer speeds are given in *milliseconds, microseconds,* and *nanoseconds.*

For *storage and retrieval,* data must be organized in a way that suits the application. *Data files* are made up of *data records,* and data records are made up of *data fields.* In many cases, processing can be affected by retrieved information.

Computers can be used to quickly and accurately produce the paperwork associated with routine business tasks. Computers can also be used to produce information that can help a person perform his or her job better. This information can be produced in many forms, including tables, graphs, and charts.

In the next chapter, we will look more closely at how business uses computers.

REVIEW QUESTIONS

1. What is the difference between information and knowledge?
2. Discuss the importance and impact of integrated circuitry.
3. Identify and discuss four ways in which the computer has impacted upon your life.
4. What is the difference between computer literacy and computing literacy?
5. List and briefly describe the five levels of computer literacy.
6. Differentiate between hardware and software. Which is more important to computer users? Explain your answer.
7. Identify the four basic types of hardware and briefly describe their functions.
8. Differentiate between the two basic types of software.
9. Briefly describe the steps contained in the information processing cycle.
10. What two advantages does the computer offer over human information processing? Under what conditions do these advantages become most important?
11. Compare the computer's ability to process data with that of the human being.
12. Evaluate the following statement: "The computer is overrated—it is not as creative as a human being, cannot accept as wide a range of inputs, cannot store as much data, and is not as flexible in presenting the results of its efforts."

CHAPTER 2
Computers in Business

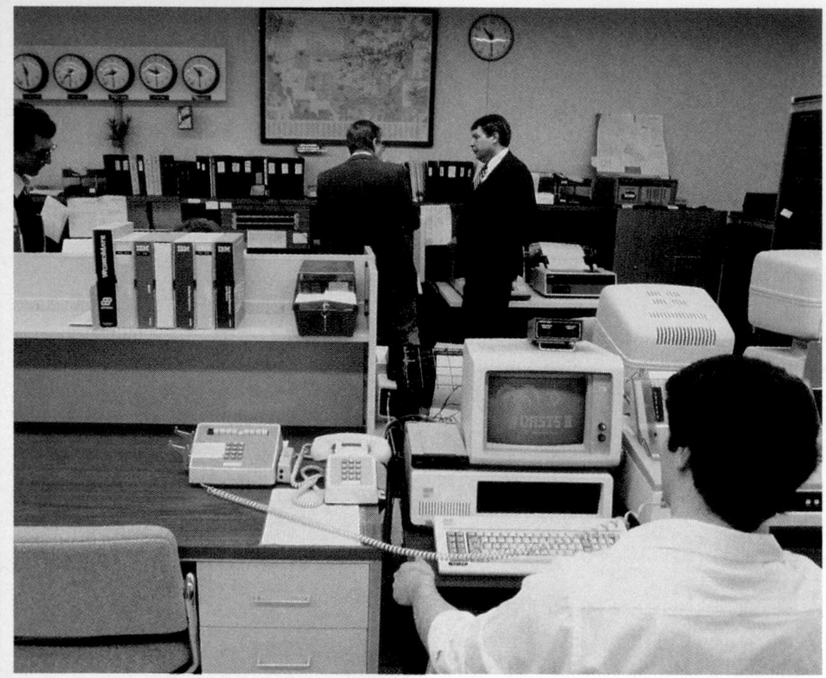

COMPUTERS AT WORK

Computers Keep Details Clean and Colorful

People don't always smile when John Whittemore comes into the room.

He's an insurance agent for Connecticut Mutual Life Insurance, a man who talks about sickness and death. Nobody wants to talk about that.

Then there are the numbers. When Whittemore sells a policy he has to show clients boring lists full of numbers—annual premiums and dividends and accrued benefits—all detailing the policy they'll buy.

"They don't want to see the numbers. They want to see how much they put in and how much money they are going to get back," Whittemore said.

Now they can. When Whittemore goes to visit a client these days, the numbers don't travel with him. Now clients can see policy details illustrated in a more understandable fashion through clean, colorful bar and line charts produced with Lotus Development Corp.'s 1-2-3[1] on Whittemore's IBM PC and printed on his Hewlett Packard color plotter.

For Whittemore, who sells Connecticut Mutual products through his own agency, the PC has been a blessing. Recently, he was selling a disability plan to a group of managers at a large Southern utility, competing against several large national agencies. Whittemore admits his proposal wasn't much better than his competitors'. But he used the PC to produce it.

"The client was worried about the effects of the plan on their earnings per share," Whittemore recalled. He prepared a bar chart with one bar showing the cost of the plan and another detailing the effect on earnings. The color graphics "blew them away" and Whittemore got the account.

"My competitors called me and invited me to come down to their headquarters at their expense to tell how I did it," Whittemore said.

[1]An integrated software package that combines electronic spreadsheet, computer graphics, and file management capabilities.

Source: M. Kramer, "Connecticut Mutual: Where PCs Sell Insurance," *PC Week*, 24 April, 1984, p. 54.

John Whittemore's success in selling the disability plan can obviously be traced to his experience in sales. But just as important was his skill in spotting an opportunity in which he could gain an advantage by using a computer. The ability to identify situations where computers can be used in business is an extremely valuable one, and this chapter will help you begin to develop that skill. You will learn to do the following:

1. List and explain the two major forces behind the increasing use of computers in business.
2. Describe what a business does and the three types of computer-based information systems used in business.
3. List and describe the six most popular "personal computing" applications in business.
4. List and discuss the two major factors to be considered in deciding whether to use a computer-based information system.

WHY BUSINESS COMPUTER USE IS GROWING

As Exhibit 2.1 shows, the use of computers in business of all sizes has grown rapidly over the last ten years. There are two reasons for this growth. First, advances in microelectronics have increased the power and reduced the cost of business computing. Second, many employees have achieved the levels of computing literacy needed to allow their firms to benefit from computer use.

Advances in Computer Systems

Stated simply, today's hardware provides more capability for less money. For example, the IBM PC, a common fixture on many managers' desks, can be purchased today for less than $3000. In terms of processor speed and primary memory, this personal computer is equivalent to the System/360 series computer system offered by IBM in the 1960s. Yet, the price of a comparable System/360 computer at that time was over $1 million. In addition, System/360 computer systems also required large, costly computer staffs. Computers at Work: "From Bigger to Better" may give you an idea of some of the obstacles that faced early computer users (see page 35). Given the expense and inconvenience, it isn't surprising that only large and wealthly corporations could justify frequent computer use. As hardware prices have dropped, however, more and more businesses are able to afford a computer system.

While hardware advances prompted this surge in business computing, software is now the driving force. Hardware provides a tool for solving business problems, but software puts this tool to use. Why has software become such a key factor in today's world of business computing?

First, the growing number of businesses owning computer systems have created a thriving market for software packages that perform standard business applications. And, as more specialized software packages become available, even more businesses become convinced that they can benefit from computer use.

Exhibit 2.1
The Growth of Business Computing

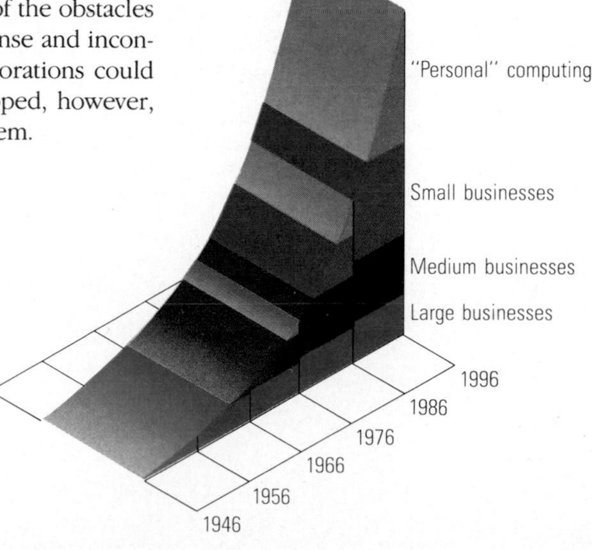

Exhibit 2.2

The Lotus 1–2–3 microcomputer software package offers users a variety of features, including display graphics and spreadsheet.

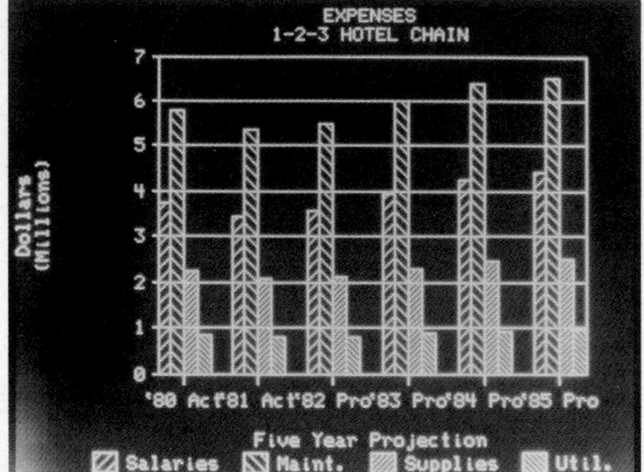

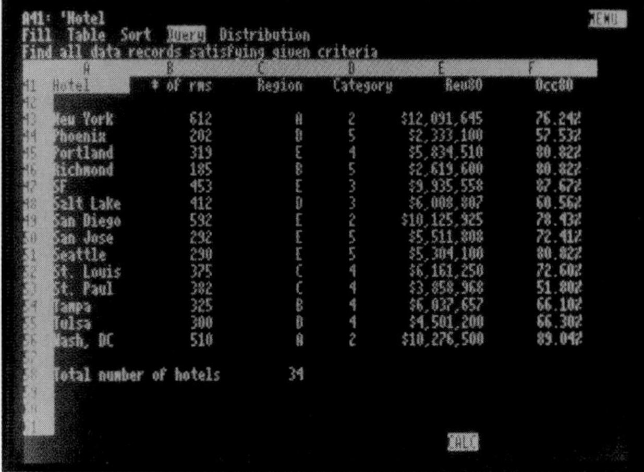

The attraction of "ready-made" software packages is not hard to understand. When you take a trip, you don't draw your own map because you can buy very good maps at low prices. The same reasoning applies to standard business software. Why should a firm develop its own programs when it can buy them from a software company, which spreads the development cost over a large sales volume?

Second, improvements in today's hardware allow programmers to develop software that is far more powerful and far simpler to use than software developed only a decade ago. Sophisticated and easy-to-use business software requires large amounts of primary memory and secondary storage as well as fast processing and data retrieval speeds. Much of the success of today's popular microcomputer software packages, such as LOTUS 1-2-3, is traced to the fact that the software packages are very capable and convenient to use (see Exhibit 2.2).

As we will see in Chapter 4, "Input," today's computer users are gaining the ability to interact with software in very "natural" ways. Managers at Filene's department store in Boston, for example, are using the Intellect software package to retrieve information from their computer system's data files in the following way:

> *Show me all the salespeople in Region 5 who have exceeded their sales quotas by 20 percent or more.*

Software that works in this manner requires a very powerful central processor unit.

The result of these advances in information systems is a spiral of computer use. As hardware becomes more advanced and less expensive, more businesses use computers. With more computer systems in place, the cost of sophisticated, easy-to-use software decreases, prompting even more business computing.

Progress in Achieving Computing Literacy

Successful business computing requires the efforts of many employees in user and in creator roles. Users must minimally attain literacy level 3, using computers as business tools, and creators need to attain literacy level 4, identifying new computer applications, or level 5, designing information systems, depending on the role being performed.

Many employees today have already attained these levels of computing literacy. Exhibit 2.3 shows the results of a recent study of employee attitudes toward computing. Two groups of people were surveyed. First, middle managers were questioned about their attitudes toward computers. Second, the firms' computer trainers were asked to predict the middle managers' responses. The computer trainers were surprised—these middle managers had more positive attitudes about using computers than was expected.

An increasingly important aspect of computing literacy occurs when a person becomes aware of the opportunities for human-computer synergy. **Synergy** occurs whenever a "team" produces greater results than the members of that team can produce when working separately. As it turns out, the information processing strengths of people and computer systems blend well. Exhibit 2.4 lists some of the human and computer characteristics that can lead

Exhibit 2.3

The computing literacy level within many firms is often higher than computer professionals realize. In this study, computer trainers, labeled "corporate policy," underestimated the computing literacy of the middle managers, labeled "end users."

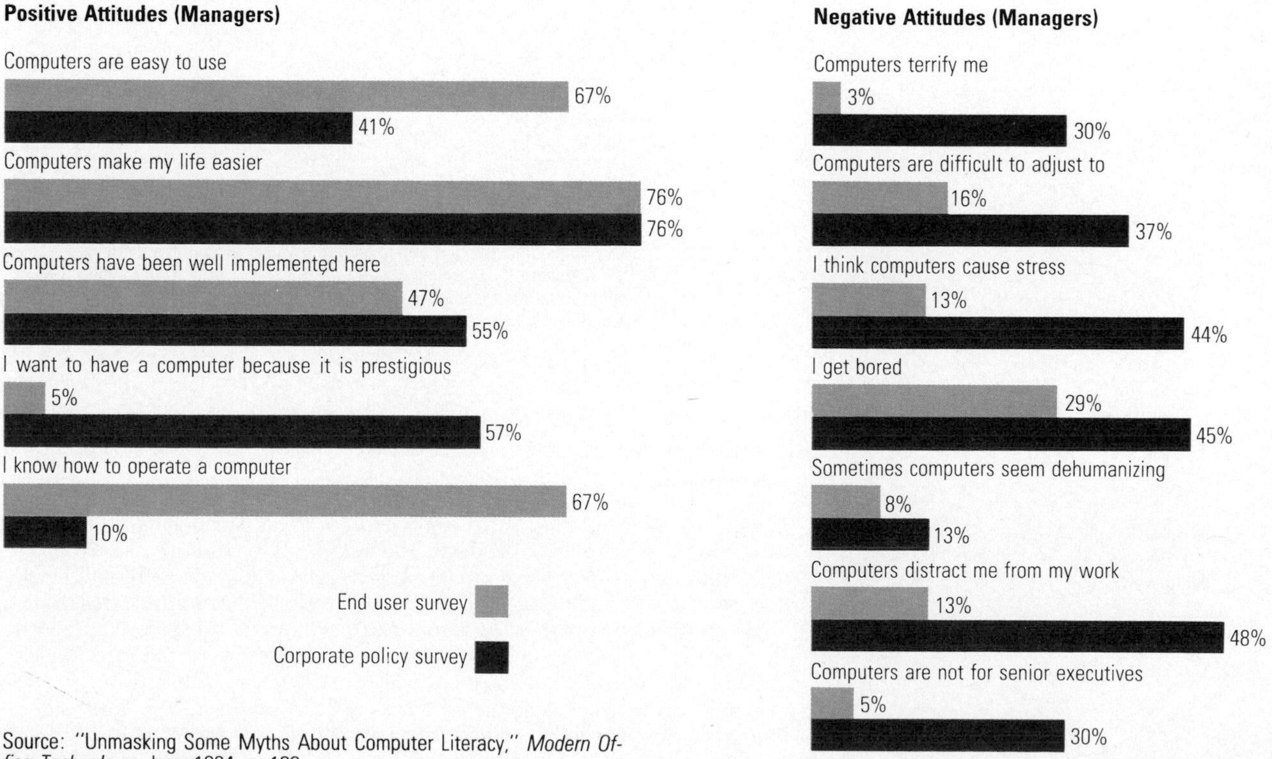

Positive Attitudes (Managers)

Computers are easy to use
67%
41%

Computers make my life easier
76%
76%

Computers have been well implemented here
47%
55%

I want to have a computer because it is prestigious
5%
57%

I know how to operate a computer
67%
10%

End user survey

Corporate policy survey

Negative Attitudes (Managers)

Computers terrify me
3%
30%

Computers are difficult to adjust to
16%
37%

I think computers cause stress
13%
44%

I get bored
29%
45%

Sometimes computers seem dehumanizing
8%
13%

Computers distract me from my work
13%
48%

Computers are not for senior executives
5%
30%

Source: "Unmasking Some Myths About Computer Literacy," *Modern Office Technology,* June 1984, p. 122.

Exhibit 2.4

Human-computer synergy occurs when the information processing strengths of humans and computers are combined.

	Human Weaknesses +	Computer Strengths →	Synergy	← Human Strengths +	Computer Weaknesses
INPUT	slow limited attention inaccurate biased	fast unlimited attention accurate unbiased	computer allows human to quickly accumulate masses of data		
			human enters data not prespecified or not computer-readable	able to capture data in original form	unable to capture data not computer-readable
				able to shift attention as need arises	all actions must be prespecified
PROCESSING	slow inaccurate small capacity	fast accurate large capacity	computer performs many calculations accurately, letting human assess a vast number of options		
			human creates new alternative for computer to compare against prior solutions	able to create	all actions must be prespecified
STORAGE AND RETRIEVAL	retrieval inaccurate retrieval cues lost easily	retrieval accurate retrieval cues stored and quickly retrieved	computer reduces human memory task to a few retrieval cues		
			human identifies an absent memory link	able to create sophisticated retrieval cues	all actions must be prespecified limited to fairly simple and inflexible retrieval cues
OUTPUT	slow limited capacity inaccurate inconsistent	fast high capacity accurate consistent	computer enables human to quickly produce many high quality information outputs		
			human communicates subtle aspects of computational results	many communication modes	limited variety of output channels

to human-computer synergy at each stage of the information processing cycle. Some illustrations may help you think of other opportunities for human-computer synergy:

> A sales manager is given one day to prepare for a staff meeting to discuss sales trends for a new family of products. From each of two hundred sales offices, daily sales figures over a five-month period are available for each of the eight new products. In addition, the manager has been asked to compile this data in a way that will compare sales across twelve different consumer categories. How much of this data could the manager "digest" by reading through it? Probably not very much. But, if the data is in computer-readable form, the sales manager can use the computer to "massage" the raw data. The computer is limited to capturing prespecified data available in a computer-readable form though, so important data may be missing. However, the sales manager can phone a key sales office and pose a few pertinent questions to some of the

sales force. This "soft" data combined with the "hard" sales figures produced by the computer should provide an accurate picture of the sales trends.

An engineer designing the wing structure for a new jet needs to evaluate several design options. Hundreds of stress calculations for each design variation must be performed. Working manually, or even working with a calculator, the engineer might need a week or more to assess each design option. Fortunately, in a process known as **computer-aided design (CAD)** a computer can perform these calculations in a couple of seconds. But, because the computer, in performing these stress calculations, can't gain any insights from the results, it's left to the engineer to detect any design flaws. Working with the computer through a CRT, he or she may note a slight but critical design problem. The engineer can consider possible solutions to this problem and quickly analyze them with the help of the computer. A design flaw that otherwise might have gone undetected has thus been prevented by the human-computer team.

A personal manager in a large corporation has been asked to locate an employee with experience in a particular task. She can picture a suitable employee's face, but can't recall the employee's name. Here, the face is a **retrieval cue**—a "tag" that is associated with a given fact, or data item. Unfortunately this retrieval cue is of little help to the personnel manager, who estimates it will take a week to go through the personnel records of the 850 employees who might have the needed skill. A "skills location" information system with a retrieval cue for the needed skill could instantly retrieve the names of all appropriate employees. Of course, the "skills location" system might not have a retrieval cue for the particular skill that's needed, but in this case, the personnel manager can substitute similar cues that are available. Now, when the personnel manager glances over the files of the employees listed by the information system, her memory is "jogged" and she can associate the employee's face with the information she has been given. A task that might otherwise take a week to complete has been handled in a few minutes by this human-computer team.

The financial manager of an East Coast chain of men's clothing stores has been asked to present the financial implications of moving to the West Coast. The financial manager has prepared a lengthy set of fifteen tables to be distributed at the meeting, but he has a few concerns: Were all the figures typed correctly? Can the executives really understand what all these numbers mean? Even more important, will all the information, presented in this fashion, put the executives to sleep? Using a computer system to produce color charts that summarize major points might capture more attention. On the other hand, it is often difficult to transmit complex or ambiguous messages with computer outputs. (One of the universal rules of business computing is **KISS,** or Keep It Simple, Stupid!) Though you can make a few small points very clear with high-quality computer graphics, it is unlikely that a complete picture of any situation can be presented. To get around this, the financial manager can improve communication by preparing simple, computer-generated charts and then personally explaining the complete picture. In addition, this human-computer team can be made even better by using a color graphics CRT display during the presentation. When the executives have questions about a particular aspect of the presentation, the financial manager can quickly retrieve and display more detailed information.

COMPUTERS AT WORK

From Bigger to Better

I've told this story before, but it's worth repeating.[1] In 1954 I was invited to the University of Illinois to see the ILIAC, which at that time was the world's most powerful computer. Housed in a gymnasium, it was supported by the world's largest air-conditioning system.

ILIAC was a vacuum-tube machine. Two undergraduates had the singular job of rushing about inside ILIAC with shopping carts full of tubes; when one burned out, they'd replace it. It did all its calculations three times and took a majority vote on the answer, because a tube might burn out while it was making a calculation.

For all that, time was scheduled on ILIAC months in advance; it really was the world's most powerful machine.

The TI-59 programmable scientific calculator is considerably more powerful than ILIAC was.

[1]Jerry Pournelle is a former aerospace engineer and current science-fiction writer who loves to play with computers.

Source: J. Pournelle, "The Next Five Years in Microcomputers," *BYTE*, September 1983, p. 233.

COMPUTERS IN BUSINESS

By now, you may have an idea of how computers can help people in business. In this section, we want to discuss in general terms some facets of business operations, the types of information systems used in business, and how these information systems interact.

What Doing Business Involves

Businesses produce goods and services and they buy and sell them, and all of this necessitates a great deal of clerical work in handling and controlling these functions.

Manufacturing. If you have ever assembled anything, you probably have a basic understanding of the work activities involved in manufacturing. People who work in manufacturing must consider the following:

Determine whether the products can be built. (Are there enough materials in stock? Are there enough workers and machinery available?)

Schedule the steps involved in making the products. (How can we best use the available workers and machinery? Will all the parts needed be available at the proper time?)

Perform each of the tasks required to make the product.

Deliver the completed products to a finished goods storage area.

Manufacturing, the general term for these activities, requires careful coordination. Similar needs for planning and monitoring also exist in businesses such as law firms and advertising agencies, where services, rather than manufactured goods, are provided.

Buying and Selling. Other important aspects of business operations include, of course, buying and selling. You might be surprised to learn that business buying behaviors are very similar to your own behaviors as a consumer. For example, a business must do the following:

Assess needs. (What stock levels are low? How many units do we need to purchase?)

Set purchase rules. (Is quick delivery more important than low price? Is a 3 percent rejection rate for "bad" supplies too high?)

Evaluate the goods offered by suppliers. (Is the higher quality of product "A" worth its higher price?)

Make the purchase.

Receive the purchased goods.

Examine the quality of the received goods.

Pay for the purchase.

A general term for this business function is **purchasing.** The business activity of paying suppliers is termed **accounts payable.**

The other side of the coin is business selling. Here, the considerations are somewhat different. A business must make specific decisions and implement them:

Decide what goods it will offer to others.

Create a demand for its products.

Maintain a sufficient inventory of its products to meet customer demand. (How many do we expect to sell this week?)

Accept a customer order.

Process the customer order.

Deliver the goods the customer ordered.

Bill the customer.

Receive and process customer payments.

Deciding what products to offer and creating a demand for those products is the general responsibility of **marketing,** while selling and delivering goods is the responsibility of **sales.** The business activity of receiving and processing customer payments is termed **accounts receivable.**

The activities of buying, manufacturing, and selling are the obvious aspects of doing business that occur to most of us. What might not be so obvious, however, is the crucial link between buying and manufacturing and between manufacturing and selling. This link is provided by **inventory,** a supply of goods held in reserve. As seen in Exhibit 2.5, inventory acts as a buffer between a business's manufacturing, buying, and selling activities. Without this buffer, manufacturing, buying, and selling would have to be perfectly coordinated. Imagine how difficult that would be! Monitoring inventory is important, particularly because inventory is a major business expense. Too little inventory means the company runs the risk of being unable to fill important customer orders. Too much inventory means that company money is tied up in unneeded products stored in a warehouse. Computers at Work: "Keeping 'Fun' in Stock" describes how one company has turned to computers to manage its inventory (see pp. 38-39).

Office Work. Do you want an "office" job? **Office** is a term people use every day. It's no wonder—a majority of the labor force works in offices. Even people who do not have "office" jobs spend a great deal of their time in offices. What types of work do "office" jobs entail? There is surprising variety in answers to this question.

A common view of the office sees it as those parts of a business that handle the paperwork that keeps a business going. Most of this paperwork falls into one of four categories:

1. accounting—the financial transactions involved with business activities
2. various sets of administrative records, such as payroll, personnel, and equipment records
3. general management activities, such as planning, budgeting, evaluating employee and department performances, and evaluating major investment decisions
4. general "office work" that occurs throughout all businesses, such as typing, document copying, and company mail

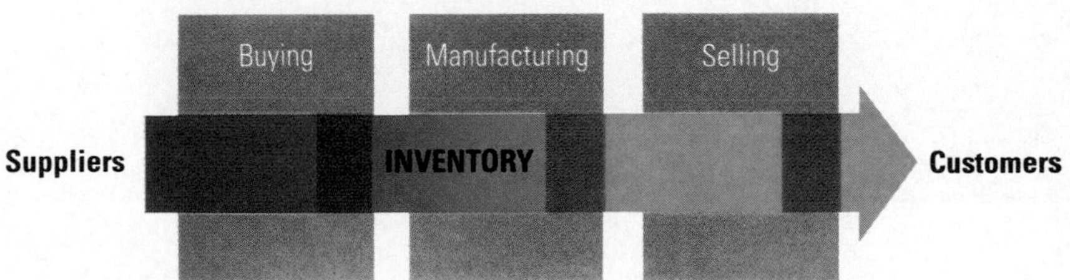

Exhibit 2.5

Product inventories serve as a buffer between a business's buying and selling activities.

Keeping "Fun" in Stock

Even though its products are called "Falling Star," "Zipper" and "Yo-Yo," business isn't necessarily fun and games. And speed of information retrieval can be as critical in inventory control as speed and excitement are on the carnival grounds.

This was the problem faced by Chance Manufacturing Co., a 250-employee, Wichita, KS-based firm that bills itself as the world's largest innovator, manufacturer and marketer of amusement rides. When Chance purchased its largest domestic competitor in 1972, it found itself with a parts inventory that soared from 8000 to nearly 30,000 items almost overnight—and was still growing. The manual "one-part-on-a-card" inventory control system that had worked until then was totally inadequate for the company's expanding needs.

"It is vital for us to maintain tight controls on our parts inventories for two reasons," explains Richard Chance, son of the founder and now second-generation president of the company. "First, the cost of each ride can easily run into six figures (Chance's newest, "Falling Star," lists at $550,000). If a $5 part is not available when we need it, the whole production line shuts down while the ride sits and waits for what should have been in our inventory to begin with. And labor costs obviously increase while workers stand idle." There is no way to "make do" with a compromise part, he adds, because the ride must be assembled with critical safety factors in mind.

"Secondly, a customer may need a replacement part overnight. If he doesn't get it, he's in real trouble. Carnival contracts impose a stiff penalty for every day a ride is inoperable," Chance points out. "We simply must have all parts available at all times."

Enter Roger Douthett, President of R. L. Douthett & Associates, a Wichita DP consulting firm. His recommendation: Wang Laboratories, Inc.'s Wang 2200, an advanced system capable of handling the sophisticated software program he would develop. Working closely with Douthett was Steve Jacobson, Chance's manager of data processing, who joined the company to effect the transition to in-house, on-line computing.

Douthett's program is used to access some 65,000 items of on-line inventory, about 4000 work orders, records of more than 1200 customers and 1500 vendors, plus all payroll records.

There is no way to "make do" with a compromise part.

Serving the needs of all departments is a single, integrated software package originally customized for Chance by Douthett, but now marketed commercially as "General On-Line Database Management." In addition to a program dealing with parts inventory control, production needs, and materials costs, an accounting program was built into Douthett's original package. As Chance's needs have changed and grown, the program has been extensively modified and enhanced.

To see how it's used, let's follow a typical sales order through the Chance computer operation:

A "bill of materials" is generated in the engineering department, where the parts list for a specific structure is defined. Once entered in the computer, the bill of materials goes to Steve Tandy, production/inventory control manager. Tandy takes the sales order and, using the bill of materials program, summarizes the requirements for each job. Parts are divided into those manufactured in-house (about 50 percent) and those purchased outside. A work order is then prepared for those that need fabricating and a production run planned; a request for purchase orders is sent to purchasing agent Jim Ramsey for other parts.

Purchasing uses the program to place items on order, reference purchasing history records, and retain information on vendors. Because all forms are generated and maintained on the system, there is tight control on all stock. That, in turn, makes it easy to locate parts, quickly check quantities on hand, plus obtain the latest inventory information on in-house manufactured parts as well as those received from vendors.

"In practice," says Jacobson, "an operator can key-in a number on his terminal for a particular ride; the system then runs through the program and identifies every single component that goes into that assembly. A powerful advantage is that the same program can be used to order parts, check on inventory status, and even track work-in-progress at any point along the production cycle."

The sales department uses the system heavily, too. An in-house staff maintains extensive information on prospective customers—names of individual contacts, what products they already own, records of contacts made (what was discussed, dates, level of interest, etc.). All of this information is entered directly into the computer. Moreover, using a modified commercially-available package, Jacobson merged data and word processing. That allows, for example, highly personalized follow-ups to leads, and annual letters of appreciation and greetings. Mass mailings also are dispatched about new products.

Chance has another vital application: Readily available on the computer is the summertime schedule of traveling carnival customers, permitting immediate delivery of parts and service.

Proud of its reputation for quality and safety, the firm whose slogan is "Fun Is Our Business" is solidly committed to a key role for computers in its expanding markets. At Chance, nothing is left to chance . . . except the name.

Source: "Riding High on Interactive Computing," *Modern Office Technology,* February 1984, pp. 132–36.

How Business Uses Computers

Our simplified description of what a business does may give you some idea of the vast amount of data processing that is involved in everyday business activities. Computer information systems provide a fast and accurate way of handling and controlling these data. They can also be a powerful tool for the managers responsible for setting and meeting the goals of a business. Information systems that are used for managerial support are called **management information systems,** or **MIS.**

There are three categories of management information systems: transaction processing systems; information reporting systems; and decision support systems. Each type of information system serves a distinct information processing role. Brief discussions of these three types of information systems will be given here. Chapter 10, "Management Information Systems," will cover these systems in more depth.

Transaction Processing Systems.

A **transaction** is a single business event, such as taking an item out of or adding it to inventory, making a sale, making a purchase, or paying a bill. **Transaction processing systems** are used to record, process, and manage data about these everyday business activities. Often, many of these basic business tasks, such as entering orders, paying bills, maintaining accounting ledgers, and keeping track of the flow of supplies and materials into and out of inventories, are the responsibility of the business' accounting department. Historically, the earliest, and still one of the heaviest, users of business information systems is the accountant.

Exhibit 2.6 illustrates the standard inputs and outputs normally associated with a transaction processing system. The input data describe a business transaction, such as ordering supplies. The transaction is then recorded in secondary storage. In this example, the data are placed in an "open purchase" file. The firm now has a permanent record that it ordered these supplies on this date. A business document, in this case a "purchase order," may be printed. Usually in processing transactions, data also need to be retrieved from other data files. In printing a purchase order, for example, the computer may be instructed to read the supplier's name and address from a "supplier" file.

A key point to note is that transaction processing systems build and maintain data files. The data contained in these files provide a detailed description of a firm's business activities. The term **data base** is often used when referring to such a computerized pool of business data.

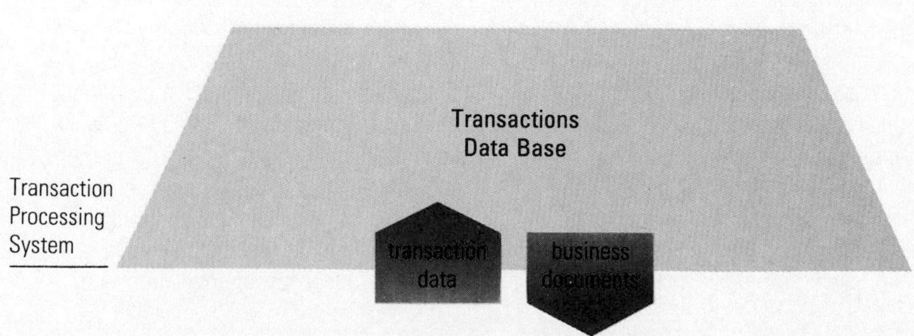

Exhibit 2.6
A Transaction Processing System
Transaction processing systems support the day-to-day activities of a business. Here, business purchases are processed and recorded.

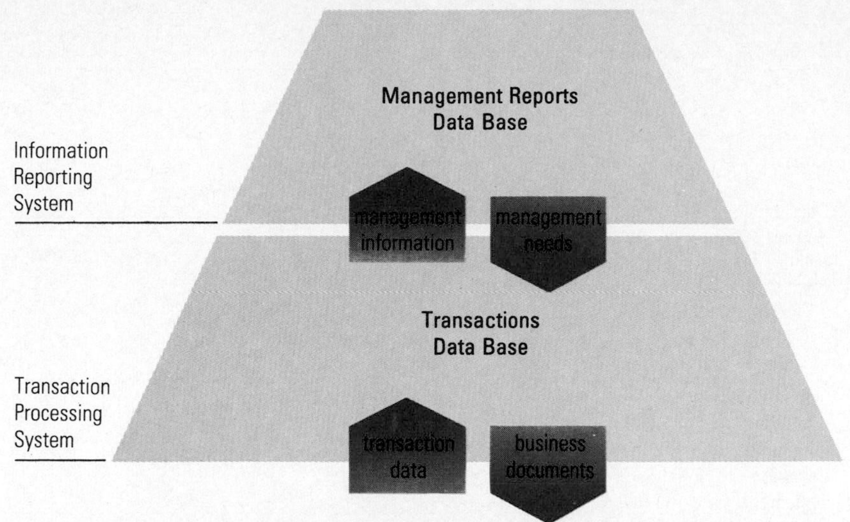

Exhibit 2.7
An Information Reporting System
Information reporting systems provide managers with the information they need to keep a business performing at a productive level.

Information Reporting Systems. While transaction processing systems help a business to carry out its day-to-day activities, they do not provide much support to mid- and upper-level managers. To do their jobs well, these managers need more general types of information—what should be done, what was done, and how well it was done. The data available in transaction processing systems are just too detailed, and thus not very useful, for most managers. **Information reporting systems** "massage" these raw data to produce summary reports that are useful to managers.

For example, a sales manager is not interested in knowing how many wrenches Joe Smith sold to the Acme Company on April 15 or how much Joe spent on a business lunch that day. What the sales manager needs to know, however, are answers to questions such as:

Has Joe Smith met his sales quota yet?
Is the overall sales goal for wrenches on schedule?
Are the department's travel expenses within budget?

To answer questions such as these, previously stored data about sales and travel transactions need to be analyzed and presented in a summary report to the sales manager at regular intervals. Information reports such as this help managers keep abreast of important issues.

Exhibit 2.7 illustrates the inputs and outputs that are found in an information reporting system. Raw data are retrieved from data files, transformed into meaningful information, and distributed in the form of **management reports.** The information produced for one report may also be stored in the data base. Then, this "information" can become the "data" for yet another management report.

Decision Support Systems. While information reporting systems inform managers about the general well-being of their departments, this type of information system is often not particularly helpful when a manager must make a specific decision. This is the role of the **decision support system,** which allows managers to produce management reports in an ad hoc fashion. The phrase *ad hoc* means that the need for a specific set of information could not have been anticipated.

Exhibit 2.8
A Decision Support System
Decision support systems allow managers to interact with an information system and define ad hoc information reports.

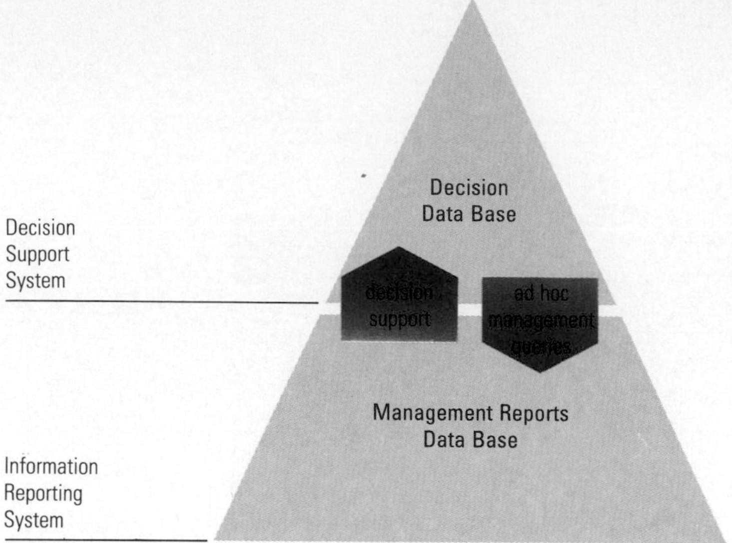

Consider, for example, a plant manager who receives the following urgent request from a senior executive:

> *How long would it take to manufacture and deliver a rush order to a new customer? If we can meet the customer's request, we will get more of their business in the future.*

How useful are the following reports: a weekly status report on inventory levels (three days old), a monthly sales forecast (two weeks old), and a daily status report on all customer orders (twelve hours old)? While each of these reports provides the plant manager with some picture of how well the plant is operating, they are not much help in answering the executive's question.

What the plant manager needs is some way to pull together current data on inventory levels, manufacturing operations, and order priorities so that he or she can determine whether it would be possible to rearrange manufacturing schedules for this rush order. Decision support systems provide this type of *ad hoc* information reporting.

Exhibit 2.8 illustrates the inputs and outputs normally found within a decision support system. A manager can directly interact with this information system to indicate which data are needed and what processing operations are to be performed. The decision support system then retrieves the requested data from the data base, sets up the needed processing operation, processes the data, and produces the results. The phrase "decision support" is used because these information systems support managers in making decisions.

How Information Systems Interact

Transaction processing systems, information reporting systems, and decision support systems fill three levels of business computing needs (see Exhibit 2.9). These "levels" reflect two ideas:

1. Information systems at higher levels make use of data stored by information systems at lower levels. Information reporting systems "feed" off transaction processing systems, and decision support systems "feed" off both transaction processing systems and information reporting systems.

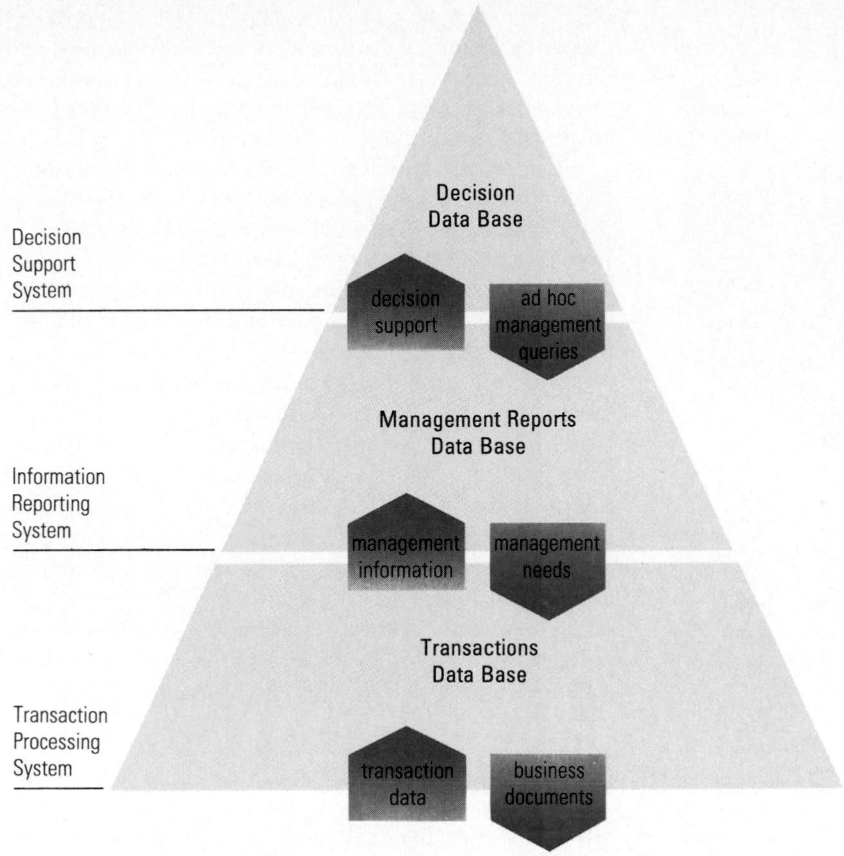

Exhibit 2.9
The Triangle of Management Information Systems
Transaction processing systems, information reporting systems, and decision support systems tend to serve three distinct levels of business computing.

2. Information systems at higher levels tend to serve "higher" business needs. Recall that transaction processing systems primarily support a firm's day-to-day activities. Information reporting systems are chiefly used by the managers responsible for making sure these day-to-day activities can be performed and are being performed well. Managers responsible for a firm's major business decisions depend upon decision support systems for vital information to give them a broad picture backed up by and based upon specific details.

Did you notice that we moved from talking about information systems that support business activities to information systems that support individual managers in a business? This dual nature of many business information systems emphasizes the key role that people play in an effective information system.

PERSONAL COMPUTING IN BUSINESS

The most recent addition to the world of business computing is the microcomputer. **Personal computing,** or the use of personal computers to directly support business professionals in their work, is the main force behind the explosive business demand for microcomputers (see Exhibit 2.10 on page 44). A **business professional** is an employee who holds an information occupation that requires judgment, such as a manager, a planning analyst, a legal specialist, or an engineer.

Professional employees spend a great deal of their time processing data. The typical professional seems to constantly be sifting through mail, memos,

Exhibit 2.10
Predicted Total Personal Computer Units Installed in the U.S., 1981–91

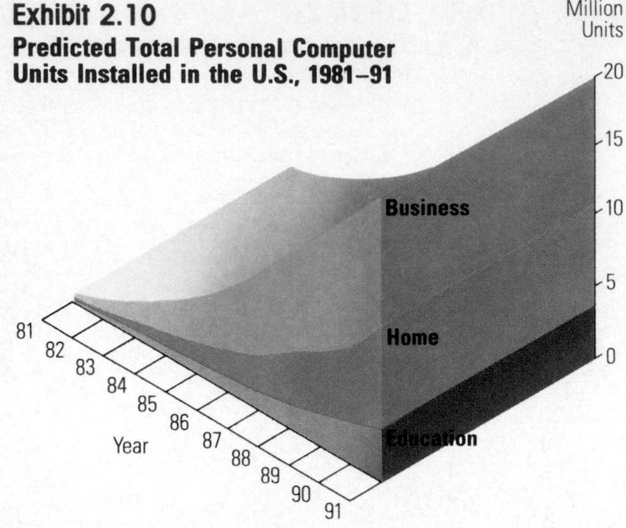

Source: G. S. Blundell, "Personal Computers in the Eighties," *BYTE*, January 1983, p. 171.

magazines, technical documents, reports, and books, or preparing memos, letters, reports, and presentations. And through these work activities, business professionals use their experience, knowledge, judgment, and creativity to create and communicate information.

The microcomputer can relieve much of the time-consuming frustrations of the business professional's job (see Computers at Work: "PC Support for Transportation-Technology Managers" on page 47). It's the low cost of microcomputers that makes them affordable—a $3000 expense item can be squeezed into most office budgets without too much trouble.

Personal computing software has been successful for two major reasons. First, it is aimed at a set of tasks performed by all business professionals. Second, it handles these tasks in much the same manner that business professionals perform them. As a result, most business professionals realize almost immediate benefits once they begin using a software package. The personal computing tools introduced here represent the most popular personal computing software applications. These applications will be covered in more depth in Chapter 15, "Applications Development Without Programmers."

Electronic Spreadsheets

What if you had studied engineering rather than business, or history, or psychology? What if you had gone to Europe instead of buying a car? Questions like these tantalize us largely because we can't answer them. In the business world, however, "what if" questions often determine a firm's profit—or even its survival.

Electronic spreadsheets, software that divides a terminal screen into a table of rows and columns, provide business professionals with a quick and accurate means of performing the mathematical calculations involved in answering "what if" questions. These packages provide the following capabilities:

Text can easily be inserted into the spreadsheet to form report titles and row and column headings.

Data can quickly be entered into a spreadsheet's **cells,** the points of intersection between rows and columns.

The spreadsheet's cells can then be related to one another, through arithmetic and logical formulas representing "business rules," to create business information; whenever data are changed, the software instantly calculates the effects of the change on all cells and displays the results.

These spreadsheets can easily be printed onto paper.

Once a spreadsheet has been built, it is simple to store on a floppy disk or diskette so that it can be retrieved later to be used again, and again . . .

A recent survey found that a remarkable 90 percent of the businesses questioned used their microcomputers for spreadsheet software applications. Exhibit 2.11 pictures a display screen for a typical electronic spreadsheet package.

Exhibit 2.11

This spreadsheet allows a user to make monthly mortgage payment comparisons.

Word Processing

Have you ever handed in a report late because you realized at the last moment it could be improved? Have you ever had to retype a full page or more of text simply because you made a typing error or left out a word or a whole sentence? These are the kinds of annoying delays business professionals encounter frequently.

Word processors, software that transforms a terminal screen into "sheets of paper" to be electronically written on, provide a quick and accurate way to create and revise business documents. These packages have the following capabilities:

Text can easily be written onto an "electronic document."

Any part of the document, whether a letter, word, sentence, paragraph, page, or group of pages, can be instantly changed or moved elsewhere in the document.

A document's **format,** such as margins, spacing, page numbers, and headings can be set automatically and easily adjusted.

A partially completed document can be stored on a floppy disk or diskette to be retrieved later for completion.

Once completed, a document can be stored on a floppy disk or diskette and then retrieved later for printing or revisions.

The complete document, or perhaps just a portion of it, can be retrieved from secondary storage and inserted anywhere within another document.

Exhibit 2.12 pictures the display screen for a typical word processing package.

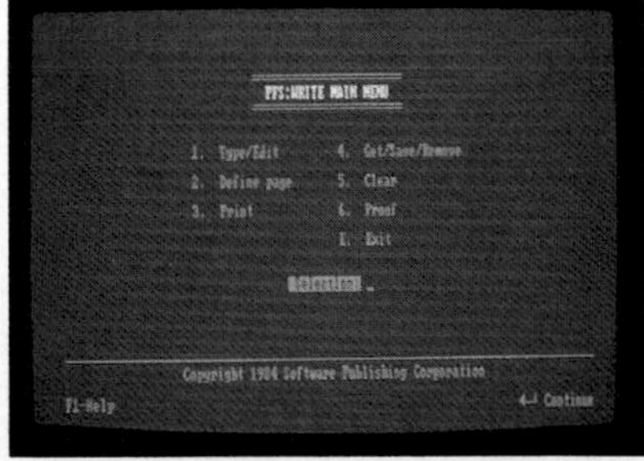

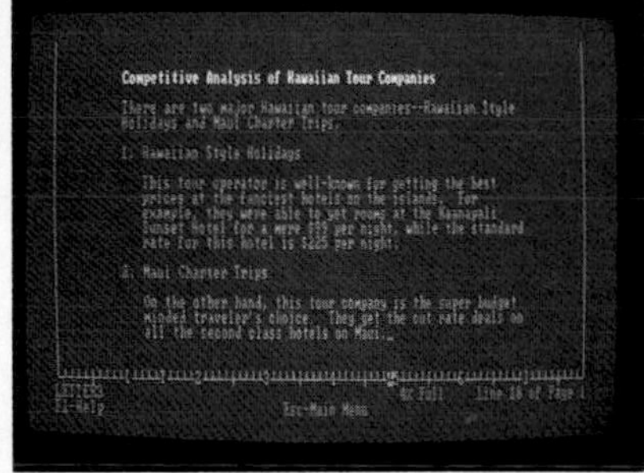

Exhibit 2.12

A word processing package makes preparing business reports a simple and convenient process. As the menu shows, this package can perform a number of useful tasks, including editing and proofreading.

Business Graphics

In writing a report or preparing an oral presentation, have you ever wished you were a good enough artist to express yourself visually as well as with words? Even people with the talent to produce quality art or graphics often don't have the time needed to prepare such presentation materials.

Business graphics, software that transforms primary memory into an electronic drawing board, provide business professionals with a quick and accurate means of creating quality presentation graphics. These packages have impressive capabilities:

Tables of raw data can easily be represented in bar chart, pie chart, and line graph forms.

When data values change, the graphic displays can instantly reflect the changes.

Text, including headings, titles, and legends, can easily be inserted into charts and graphs.

Color can be used to improve the meaning and visual appeal of a chart or graph.

A graph or chart can easily be printed on paper, or even on a 35mm slide.

Once a graph or chart has been created, it can be stored on a floppy disk or diskette to be retrieved later for printing, for revision, or to become part of an automated "slide show."

Exhibit 2.13 shows examples of the presentation materials that can be produced with business graphics software.

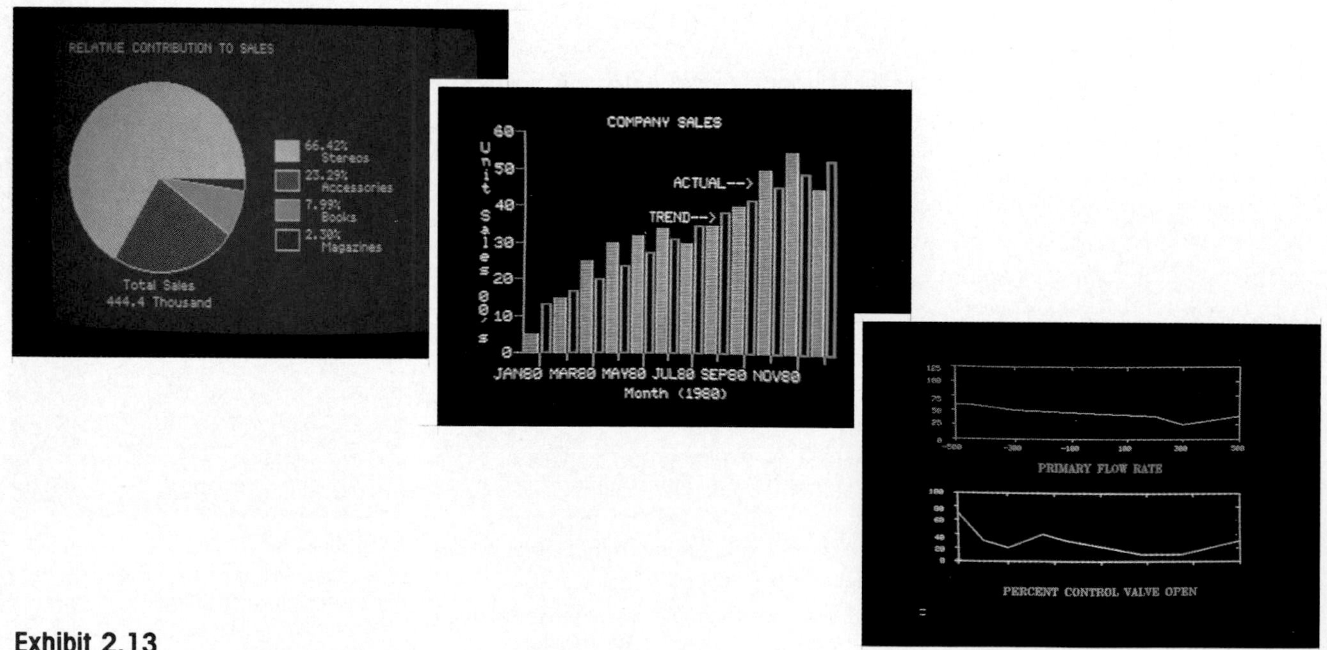

Exhibit 2.13

Charts and graphs illustrate trends and quantities in a clear and interesting fashion. Pie charts, bar charts, and line graphs are often used in business reports.

COMPUTERS AT WORK

PC Support for Transportation-Technology Managers

Todd Burger's metamorphosis from computer agnostic to his section's personal computer guru may be a pattern that's repeating itself all around Arthur D. Little Inc.

Currently the safety and engineering technology section's expert in transportation-technology management, Burger had little formal exposure to computers before he came to the company. Then, while working on a broad study of the United States rail network for the Electric Power Research Institute, he discovered what the *VisiCalc* and the Apple II in a downstairs office could do for his consulting practice.

"I had my share of late nights trying to understand some little glitch in the model I was building," Burger recalled. "But soon I was fluent to the point where I was coaching others."

Burger next applied his growing computer interest to a study for the New York Metropolitan Transit Authority. The MTA hired ADL to perform a comprehensive analysis of the implications of installing different types of automatic fare-collection equipment on its buses, subways and commuter trains. Burger was to perform the financial analysis for the project.

He spent almost two months developing a Lotus 1-2-3* model to calculate the effect of changes in circumstances on the MTA's discounted cash flow. Using data stored on 30 different floppy disks, the model answered millions of possible "what if" questions:

What if capital costs change?

What if a fine is imposed for non-payment of fares?

What if vandalism increases?
What if the cost of armored trucks changes?

What if the equipment is installed for entire stations instead of at selected gates?

"Every single operating, maintenance and capital input is accounted for," Burger said. "The other night, I did about a quarter-million calculations and printed out the results in 30 minutes. That type of analysis just would not have been possible without Lotus and the PC."

*An integrated software package that combines electronic spreadsheet, computer graphics, and file management capabilities.

Source: "Rides PC Wave," *PC Week,* 8 May, 1984, p. 41.

File Management

Where do you keep important names and addresses? Can you find them when you need them? Is your personal filing system organized? Can you find notes, memos, tables of figures, important dates, or reports when you want them? Most business professionals spend a lot of time organizing, storing, and then locating the information their work requires.

File management software transforms secondary storage into an electronic filing cabinet, allowing business professionals a quick and accurate way to organize, store, and retrieve the information that they depend on in doing their jobs. These packages have the following capabilities:

Numbers and text can easily be organized as a data file and then stored on a floppy disk or diskette.

Automatic retrieval cues for retrieving these numbers and text are simple to establish.

Data stored previously can quickly be located, retrieved, and changed.

Reports making use of stored data can be designed and then displayed on a terminal screen or printed onto paper.

On the following page, Exhibit 2.14 shows a data record that a typical file manager package has retrieved from secondary storage and displayed.

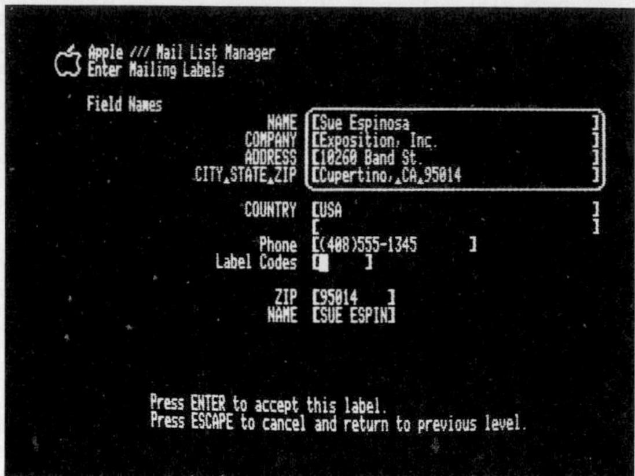

Exhibit 2.14

This is a data record from a typical file management package.

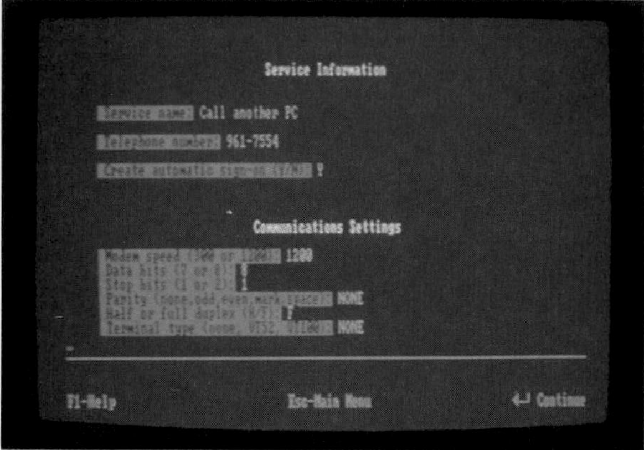

Exhibit 2.15

Communications software links one personal computer to another computer system.

Communications Software

Have you ever been working on a report and suddenly realized that a piece of information you need is missing? Worse, you know where to find it, say at a library or at a friend's home or office, but don't have the time to go get it. This is another of the frustrating problems that tend to plague business professionals.

Communications software, software that electronically links a personal computer to another computer system, provides a way to quickly and accurately communicate with distant sources of information. These packages have the following capabilities:

- A personal computer can easily be linked to a friend's or co-worker's personal computer so that messages, programs, or data can be exchanged.
- A personal computer is easily linked to a larger computer system so that data or programs stored on the larger computer can be transferred, or **downloaded,** to the personal computer.

Exhibit 2.15 illustrates some options offered by a typical communications package.

Integrated Software Packages

Once business professionals began to use these personal computing wonders, they soon wanted the convenience of combining the capabilities of several software packages. In preparing a report, for example, a manager might want to insert a graph without having to create the text with a word processing program, create the graph with a graphics program, and then manually cut and paste the two pieces together. Instead, business professionals wanted to be able to use—at any point in time—combinations of electronic spreadsheets, word processing, graphics, file management, or communications.

Integrated software combines a number of these personal computing tools in one software package. An integrated package provides the following capabilities:

- A user can easily switch back and forth among the software tools made available in the package.
- Data entered via one tool, such as a spreadsheet, are automatically available to the other tools, such as graphics.
- Documents displaying data and text in multiple forms are easily created with electronic "cut and paste" commands.

One of the most popular integrated software packages is Lotus 1-2-3, which combines software for an electronic spreadsheet with graphics and file management. Exhibit 2.16 pictures an example of the type of business documents that can be created with integrated packages.

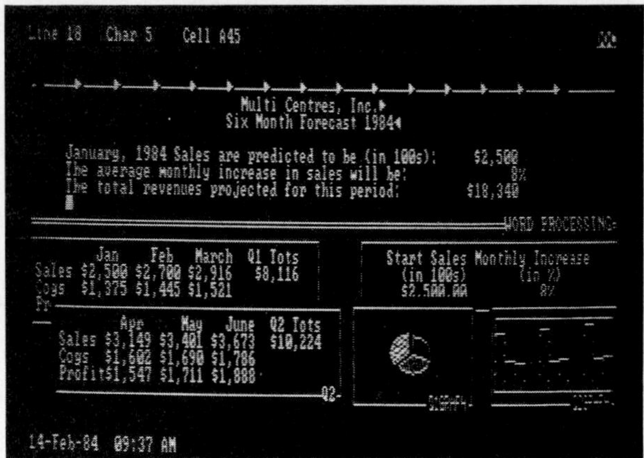

Exhibit 2.16
This is a sales forecast prepared with integrated software.

Professional Issue

Deciding When Computers Should Be Used

Two major questions need to be answered in deciding to computerize a business task. One, do the information processing characteristics of the task match the information processing strengths of a computer system? Second, do the benefits of computer use outweigh the costs? Answering the first question provides a quick means of identifying likely computer applications. A "yes" answer here, however, is not a guarantee that a firm should computerize the task. Business investments need to produce economic benefits. If this rule isn't followed, a business won't be around for very long! Decisions to computerize should only follow "yes" answers to *both* questions.

Analyzing the Task

We looked at some of the advantages of computer-based information processing in Chapter 1 and examined the strengths and weaknesses of computers earlier in this chapter when describing the opportunities for human-computer synergy. Exhibit 2.17, which summarizes these discussions, can serve as a checklist of task characteristics favorable to computer use (see page 50). Let's examine this checklist in detail.

Input. A task in which a large amount of data needs to be entered is usually a good candidate for computerization. Entering large amounts of data by computer will probably cost less per data item, and data entry will certainly be completed a lot sooner. Computerized data input, however, requires that special equipment be used and that the data be in computer-readable form. If only a small amount of data needs to be entered, it might be best to do so manually. A factory having to enter the number of hours worked for each of 3,500 workers is sure to benefit from putting its payroll on a computer. A factory with 15 employees would not.

Processing. The computer is well suited for tasks that involve many complex calculations. In planning each day's work, for example, a factory supervisor might have to determine the best way to process 80 orders for 6 different products through 3 or 4 manufacturing steps. Figuring out the best of all possible schedules by hand would be a very time-consuming task. Performing this task with a computer would seem a far better solution.

A "scheduling" program, however, must exist to perform this task on a computer. Can the factory supervisor list all the decisions he or she makes in putting together a daily work schedule? Are all these steps clearly defined, are they somewhat ambiguous, or do they vary? Without a clear set of processing rules, it will be difficult for a programmer to develop the needed program. Even if a clear set of rules can be defined for the scheduling task, it might take a long time and cost a lot of money to develop the program.

Storage and Retrieval. If a large amount of data needs to be stored, such as the parts inventory for a Boeing 747, it will probably be less expensive to store the data in a computer system than in filing cabinets. If only a small amount of data needs to be stored, however, such as warranty information on 3 company cars, it makes little sense to computerize. What about storing a medium amount of information? The answer may depend on how often the data items need to be retrieved.

Consider the following two situations:

> A purchasing clerk must refer to a list of 1,500 supplier names and addresses one day each month in order to mail out about 15 purchase orders.

Exhibit 2.17
Checklist: Task Characteristics Favorable to Computerization

	YES	NO
Input: Does a *large volume* of data need to be entered? Is the data *already stored* in a computer system? Can the data be easily converted to *computer-readable form*?		
Processing: Do a *large number* of calculations need to be performed? Do *complex* calculations need to be performed? Can a *clear set of rules* be stated that define the processing operations to be performed? Will these rules *remain fixed* for the forseeable future? Are these processing operations performed on a *frequent basis*?		
Storage and Retrieval: Does a *large volume* of data need to be stored? Does stored data need to be retrieved *frequently*?		
Output: Does a *large volume* of data need to be printed?		
Overall Task Needs: Is *accuracy* important? Is *speed* important? Are *current* data needed?		

Another purchasing clerk must constantly refer to another list of 1,500 supplier names and addresses in mailing out about 60 purchase orders per day.

In the first case, computer use is probably not needed. In the second case, it would be extremely helpful.

Output. As with data input, a task that requires a large amount of data output is a good candidate for automation. Preparing 3,500 paychecks by hand would take a great deal of time, but could be done quickly and inexpensively by a computer. But typing 15 paychecks would probably cost less than printing the paychecks on a computer.

Overall Task Needs. This final set of issues can be critical for task success—the accuracy, speed, and currentness of information processing. Accuracy and speed are a computer's primary advantages. Whenever task accuracy or speed are important, computer use should be considered. The need for high levels of accuracy in a firm's financial records is one reason accounting applications are usually one of the first information systems used in most businesses. And the speed with which travel agents need to access airline schedules make this an extremely important computer application for travel agencies.

The speed of computers can also result in very current data files. If it is crucial that information outputs are "up-to-date," then computer use might be very appropriate. When an important customer demands to know when an order is to be delivered, a salesperson would naturally want access to the most current data possible from the manufacturer.

Exhibit 2.18
The Decision to Computerize: Benefits and Costs

Benefit Categories	Cost Categories
Reducing Costs labor equipment materials	**Hardware** purchase installation maintenance
Avoiding Future Costs labor equipment materials	**Software** development purchase maintenance
Products or Services improvements new	**People** training use
Management Information improvements new	**Operations** data preparation overhead

Weighing the Benefits and Costs

As you might imagine, assigning dollar values to information system benefits and costs can be very difficult. Performing these calculations also requires more information about computer hardware and software than this text has presented so far. For now, Exhibit 2.18 introduces you to the major categories of benefits and costs. You will learn more about calculating information system benefits and costs in Chapter 11, "Systems Development I."

Benefits. There are four categories of information system benefits. With some proposed computer applications, only one of the categories may apply. With other applications, all may be pertinent.

The most common information system benefit occurs when *costs are reduced* with computer use. The costs normally affected are labor costs, equipment costs, and materials costs. An inventory control application, for example, may have the following impacts:

Inventory clerks no longer need to work overtime.

Two rather than three warehouses are needed.

The amount of inventory kept in stock is reduced by 40 percent.

Another common information system benefit is that computer use *avoids some future costs.* Again, labor, equipment, and supplies costs are typically involved. By replacing an old accounts receivable information system with one using newer technology, the following benefits might arise:

Clerks in the accounting department can handle increased work loads without working overtime.

The cost of the computer equipment needed to process these customer payments is cut in half.

The cost of office supplies is reduced by 20 percent.

A less common, but very important, benefit is realized when the information system allows a firm to offer its customers *new products and services* or *improved products and services.* Examples of these benefits include:

new product	A savings and loan institution offers its customers a combination savings/checking account, in which savings are automatically transferred into the checking account when the checking account balance is low.
new service	A bank offers its business customers the service of managing the excess cash in these customer's checking accounts.
improved product	An information system helps an automobile manufacturer turn out engines with fewer defects.
improved service	A mail-order firm reduces the time it takes to process a customer's order.

The final category of information system benefits, *management information,* is common, but often very difficult to state in dollar terms. A new marketing information system, for example, may provide the marketing staff with customer surveys that previously were not available, as well as more current sales information on competitors' products.

Costs. There are four categories of information system costs: hardware, software, people, and operating expenses. All four cost categories usually apply to all information systems.

The most obvious cost category involves *hardware* costs. The cost of new hardware, such as terminals or microcomputers, is a major factor in estimating the cost of a proposed information system. Hardware costs also include installation and maintenance costs. **Hardware maintenance** refers to the technical work involved in repairing or servicing equipment.

Another cost category that is usually considered is *software* costs. New information systems always require investment in computer programs. Software costs include the price of a software package, the labor costs involved with any software development, and software maintenance costs. **Software maintenance** involves fixing software errors and keeping the information system up-to-date.

A third cost category, and one often overlooked, is *people* costs. Computer use may take employees away from other tasks they need to perform, particularly when an information system is first introduced. Also, all computer users require training if they are to make good use of an information system.

The final set of information system costs are those directly associated with the *day-to-day operation of an information system.* Data input often requires that data first be placed in computer-readable form and then entered into a computer system. Also, the overhead costs and any supplies involved with input, processing, storage and retrieval, and output activities must also be considered as part of an information system's costs.

For McKesson, Computers Are the Magic in Profit Margins

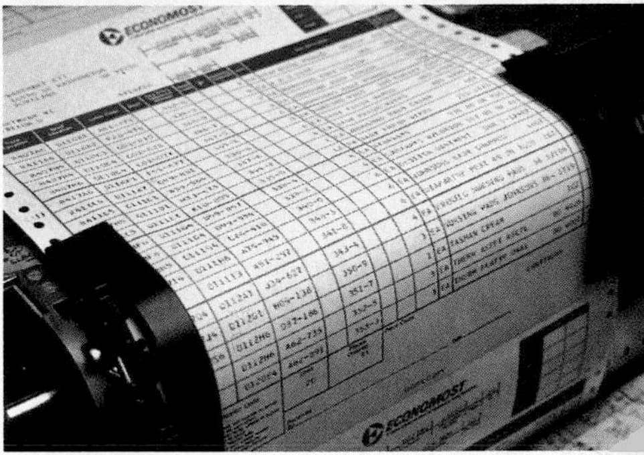

As the country's leading wholesale distributor of drugs, chemicals, and liquor, McKesson Corp. would like to banish the phrases "out of stock" and "hasn't come in yet." Unfortunately, strikes, shipping delays, and clerical mistakes make that impossible. But to minimize stock problems, the company over the last few years has developed a sophisticated computer system that does everything from placing orders with manufacturers to packing boxes with goods for delivery to retail drugstores.

Now McKesson is pushing computerization even further. It recently acquired two computer software companies, and is using its expertise to launch a new line of business—providing computer services to retail stores. Indeed, McKesson's commitment to high technology is so complete that Neil A. Harlan, its chairman, president, and chief executive, remarks that he isn't sure "whether we are a distribution business offering computer-based services or a computer-services business that distributes products."

Distribution is a cost- and labor-intensive business with notoriously thin profit margins. As Harlan explains it, "It was clear we needed to set ourselves apart from the large number of wholesale distributors serving the health care and other industries. We also felt that too much manual work was being done. Procurement, stocking, picking products to distribute—all needed to be made more efficient."

A PRIMITIVE SYSTEM AT FIRST

Computers were the obvious answer. Until 1970, customers ordered products by checking off a form preprinted with 2000 items and then mailed the form to the distribution center. On January 1, 1970, McKesson introduced Economost, a computerized order-entry system for the Drug Group, on an experimental basis. Five of McKesson's customers signed up for this primitive system, which consisted of modified Victor adding machines hooked up to an order-entry device that was mounted on a motorized cart. The orders were verbally transmitted via telephone to an IBM 360-20 computer.

The system was modified and improved over the next few years, and, in 1973, it was implemented nationwide. McKesson's competitors in the distribution business did not follow the leader into computers until the mid-1970s. Impressed by the success of Economost in the Drug Group, they set out to automate the other operating divisions as well—a process that is still going on.

Computers play a role in every stage of McKesson's distribution operation—from the manufacturer to the distributor and from the distributor to the marketplace. On the corporate side, 60 percent of the products McKesson distributes are ordered directly from the manufacturers' computers. McKesson's computers keep track of the inventory in some 260 warehouses on a day-to-day basis. When a certain item reaches a specific supply level, the computer automatically calls the manufacturer's computer and places a refill order. This one aspect of computerization has reduced the number of buyers at McKesson from 140 to 12.

But most of the computer links are made between McKesson and the stores that rely on it for their merchandise. The Drug & Health Care Group has the most sophisticated computer system and it is also the largest division. It distributes everything from pharmaceuticals to Kleenex to more than 16,000 drugstores and hospital pharmacies. To keep the operation running smoothly, it uses an automated order-entry system.

In addition to the ease of ordering, McKesson provides value-added services such as inventory control, accounting recordkeeping, and profit and loss statements. There are 52 distribution centers—down from the 92 that were needed before computers—serving McKesson's drugstore customers and 99 percent of those customers use the automated system.

To enhance these value-added services, McKesson acquired a computer-services company in 1983 called 3 P.M. that supplies on-line and standalone computer services to drugstores. The software package for pharmacies includes inventory control, price updates, patients' prescription records, side effects of drugs, accounts receivable, and third-party payment of bills. 3 P.M. customers receive a Digital Equipment Corp. personal computer for use in the pharmacy.

At McKesson Chemical, an on-line distribution system, which was devel-

How Econoscan Speeds Up Orders

McKesson supplies goods to 16,000 retail drugstores nationwide—a mindboggling undertaking made easier and more efficient by a computerized order-entry system. Since this was the first computer application developed to enhance McKesson's distribution business, it has been streamlined to peak operating performance. A typical transaction goes like this:

1. Using a scanning device called Econoscan, the retail store clerk reads the computer-printed shelf labels for each product. The device, which is leased to the retail drugstore through McKesson, has been manufactured exclusively for McKesson by Azur Data of Richland (Wash.), and will soon be made by Telxon of Kansas City.
2. The clerk then dials an 800-number that hooks the store up with McKesson's IBM System 36 computer data center in either Oakland or Kalamazoo. The Econoscan transmits the order to the computer at 600 items per minute.
3. The data center transmits the order to the drug distribution warehouse nearest to the retailer's location.
4. At the warehouse, the order is received by the computer and printed out.
5. The printout contains the name of the product, the quantity ordered, and a description of the product. The computer also automatically prints price labels for each item.

The hand of man finally enters the system at the warehouse where the items are taken off the shelves and packed in boxes according to the layout of the particular store that is placing the order. Warehouse employees also put the price labels on each of the items before they are boxed.

The boxes are loaded onto the trucks in "first on, last off" order to speed up the delivery process. At the drugstore, the items are simply unpacked and put on the shelves.

oped and designed over a three-year period at a cost exceeding $5 million, is moving ahead smartly. Once it is fully installed in 63 distribution branches, the system will provide data on safety, shipping, customer product needs, inventory, and prices for some 1000 chemicals.

To bring St. Pauli Girl beer, Folonari wines, or Ballantine's Scotch to American tables, McKesson is automating its third major operating unit, the Beverage Group. The process of automating some 36 wholesale houses that distribute alcoholic beverages is no simple matter, in view of the regulatory tangle in the retail liquor industry. "There are some complicating factors in this area," Harlan explains. "First, we have a network of state laws and regulations we have to work around. Second, wine and spirits is a franchise business. By that I mean that the stores have a lot of distributors. The liquor store guy would have to have a computer system for every distributor. It just won't work. But we think we can bring some order to the chaos." McKesson's system will help liquor store owners manage their inventories better, showing them, for example, how quickly items are selling.

A recent addition to the Beverage Group is Alhambra Water, which has been testing a computer system that centralizes customer service functions. Customers in northern California can call a toll-free number for service. Operators enter customer information into a terminal, and messages are printed out moments later at the appropriate service location.

The water division has also experimented with an "on-truck" computerized order-entry system at its Sparkletts operation in Los Angeles. The system permits route drivers to enter customer information into a portable computer terminal that is carried in the delivery truck.

Another electronic brainchild from McKesson is teleshopping. The company's new "Teletouch" system, developed in cooperation with Nolan Bushnell's ByVideo organization, will introduce electronic shopping at home to the McKesson distribution system. The system consists of a standalone terminal with a touch-screen. Customers touch the screen to select goods and pay by inserting a credit card into a slot in the terminal. McKesson polls its terminals daily, fills the orders, and updates prices electronically. The system is currently being tested in a variety of California locations.

This type of technology will probably be commonplace in the 21st century and it may be brought to the consumer by McKesson. The company has proved that it can weather the storms and now seems to be sailing in smooth waters into the Information Age.

Source: J. Cortino and E. C. Peck, "For McKesson, Computers Are the Magic in Profit Margins," *Management Technology,* July 1984, pp. 50–53.

SUMMARY

The use of computer systems by business is increasing at a rapid rate. Two major forces behind this growth are the remarkable advances in computer technology and the progress made in increasing the computing literacy levels of business employees.

Today's computer hardware continually provides greater information processing capabilities for less money. While hardware prompted the surge in business computing, advances in computer software are now the driving force. This is due to the ready availability of powerful and easy-to-use business software packages.

Successful business computing requires the efforts of many employees in user and creator roles. An important aspect of this computing literacy is an ability to recognize opportunities for *human-computer synergy,* such as that obtained through *computer-aided design.* Today, many business employees have achieved high levels of computing literacy.

Businesses create goods and services and buy and sell them. Coordinating and controlling these functions requires a great deal of office work.

Regardless of whether a firm is in the business of *manufacturing* products for customers or dealing with manufacturers in offering services to clients, the activities involved require careful coordination.

Business buying includes *purchasing* supplies and materials from suppliers. *Accounts payable* are accounts to be paid to these suppliers. Business selling includes *marketing,* or creating a demand for a business's goods, *selling,* and processing customer payments, which is termed *accounts receivable.* Manufacturing, buying, and selling are linked through *inventory.*

A majority of business employees work in *offices,* where they handle the paperwork that keeps their businesses going. Most of this paperwork falls into four categories: accounting, storing and keeping current administrative records, general management activities, and general office work, such as typing.

These business activities require that a vast amount of data be processed. Computer information systems provide a fast, accurate way of handling and controlling these data and can also serve as a powerful tool for business managers. Information systems serving managers are called *management information systems,* or *MIS.*

There are three categories of management information systems. *Transaction processing systems* record, process, and manage data about everyday business activities. Much of the data processed by transaction processing systems is placed in a *data base,* which refers to all the data files stored on a business's computer systems. *Information reporting systems* process the raw data kept in this data base to produce summary *management reports. Decision support systems* allow managers to access this data base in an ad hoc fashion to obtain information needed to make specific decisions. Transaction processing systems, information reporting systems, and decision support systems thus fill three distinct levels of business computing needs.

Personal computing, using microcomputers to directly support business professionals in their work, is the main force behind the growing use of microcomputers in business. A *business professional* is an employee who holds an information occupation requiring the use of judgment. Personal computing can relieve much of the time-consuming and frustrating aspects of business professionals' jobs.

Personal computing software owes its great success to two factors: it is aimed at a set of tasks performed by all business professionals, and it handles these tasks in much the same manner that business professionals perform them.

The five most popular personal computing software applications are *electronic spreadsheets, word processors, business graphics, file managers,* and *communications.*

Two major questions need to be asked in deciding whether or not to computerize a business task: "Do the information processing characteristics of the task match the information processing strengths of computers?" and "Do the benefits of computer use outweigh the costs?"

Tasks that are good candidates for computerization have the following characteristics: large amounts of data are entered; many complex calculations are required; the rules to follow in operating on data can be stated in a clear and precise manner; a large amount of data needs to be stored; stored data are frequently retrieved for use; large amounts of data are output, and accuracy, speed, and currentness are important for task success.

There are four categories of information system benefits. First, labor, equipment, and materials costs can be reduced. Second, future labor, equipment, and materials costs can be avoided. Third, better or improved products and services can be provided to a business's customers. And fourth, better or improved information can be provided to business managers.

There are four categories of information system costs: the cost of acquiring, installing, and maintaining hardware; the cost of developing and maintaining software; the training and related "people" costs that occur when introducing an information system; and, the costs associated with the day-to-day operation of an information system.

In the next chapters, you will be introduced to the different hardware devices used in business computing.

REVIEW QUESTIONS

1. Explain why software has become the driving force in computing today.
2. Explain the concept of human-computer synergy. Why is such a concept important?
3. Identify and discuss two examples of synergy in addition to those mentioned in the text.
4. Briefly list and discuss the activities performed in a typical manufacturing process. How can the computer be applied?
5. Briefly list the major activities involved in a typical purchasing process. How can the computer be applied?
6. What activities are required in the sales function? How can the computer be applied?
7. Explain how the computer can be used in each of the four basic types of office work.
8. Briefly describe the three categories of management information systems.
9. Briefly explain how information systems interact.
10. What is a business professional? How has the computer revolution aided these employees?
11. What is integrated software? What advantages does it offer?
12. Assume that the corporation for which you work knows that computerization of its operations is feasible. How can the firm decide whether or not it *should* computerize?

PART II COMPUTER SYSTEM HARDWARE

CHAPTER 3
The Central Processing Unit

COMPUTERS AT WORK

Computerizing the Olympic Games

In the 1984 Olympics, the computer was a visible presence, acting as coach, timekeeper, and interpreter, to name just a few roles. Indeed, the computer juggled a variety of tasks, from biomechanical training and security of Olympic athletes to ticketing and information flow for the spectators. Anyone who bought a ticket, watched an event, kept score, looked up a performer's past records, or even explored Olympic Stadium was at some point exposed to a computer.

Very large mainframe computers were used to process the results of the sport events. Computers handled much of the scoring and judging, flashing the results instantaneously to control centers along elaborate fiber-optic highways that knit together the huge Olympic complexes. A special device linked the starter's gun with photo finish cameras that were capable of pinpointing separations of as little as two millimeters. For example, long-jump events were measured by a slide carriage trained on an optical detector that measured down to the millimeter. All competition results were instantly processed by large mainframe computers some 30 miles away. Those results were flashed back to the event locations, on to the press centers, and finally to the Olympic committee headquarters, where they were available on display screens and as computer printouts.

Minicomputers also played a part, easing communication among the athletes and the thousands of people behind the scenes and on camera. These medium-sized computers were programmed to accommodate 10 languages, which were spoken by 95 percent of the athletes competing in Los Angeles. An athlete or official who wanted to send a message simply signed on to the computer in his or her language and specified the language of the receiver. The individual's message was then delivered electronically in a language understood by the recipient.

In addition, small microcomputers were helpful for coordinating inventory and housing and for matching equipment and facilities with teams, monitoring and updating as necessary. Other microcomputers were used to directly analyze an athlete's performance, which was filmed at 300 to 400 frames a second. To do so, film of the performance was projected onto a grid dotted with thousands of coordinates which the computer scanned, digitized, and displayed on a graphics terminal as three-dimensional stick figures. Athletes' performances were markedly improved by refocusing training and altering technique in ways suggested by the all-seeing eye of the computer.

Source: B. Ward and T. Maremaa, "Computerizing the Olympic Games," *Popular Computing,* August 1984, pp. 97–109.

Computers, from very large maxicomputers down to small microcomputers, played a vital role in virtually all aspects of the Olympic Games. Every day, computers perform valuable functions in the workplace and the home. They are a popular source of entertainment for both children and adults. Clearly, computers are becoming an important part of this modern society. Yet many people interact with computers without learning how they actually work, and thus they are missing an exciting and valuable part of the computing experience.

In this chapter, we introduce you to the workings of the central processing unit, the computer's "brain." This knowledge can be useful in many ways. First, it can take the mystery out of the way a computer works. Too often, people think computers are capable of magic. In this chapter, you'll learn how and where the so-called magic happens. Second, understanding how a computer works can help you evaluate the relative merits of various computer models. This knowledge will be critical if you are faced with the responsibility of either choosing a computer for a specific business application or responding to the proposal of a systems analyst. This chapter concludes with a section on evaluating the relative power of computers, and Part IV will discuss the process of systems analysis and design. In this chapter, you will learn to do the following:

1. Describe the problem-solving process used in creating instructions for the computer and explain why it is needed.
2. Describe and explain the basic steps in the two phases of the machine cycle.
3. Explain the ways data and program instructions are made computer-readable.
4. Describe the architecture of the central processing unit and explain the function of each part.
5. Define the technology used for the major functions in microcomputers.
6. Explain three primary means for classifying computers.
7. Define and explain the two criteria used to determine computer power.
8. Describe the effect of computer evolution on price and performance.

THE PROBLEM-SOLVING PROCESS

The reason computers are becoming so widely used in business, in government, at school, and even at home is that they help users solve problems. To understand how computers do this, we need to first understand the general problem-solving process. Then, we will look at some of the requirements for using computers to solve problems.

To solve many problems we must first specify a step-by-step procedure that will lead to a solution or a desired result. This type of process is quite common in everyday life. Assume, for example, you are having friends over to your home, and you want to bake a pecan pie to serve them. The general procedure for solving this problem is listed in a recipe, which is made up of a list of ingredients and a list of instructions.

First, you need to get the ingredients: pecans, corn syrup, eggs, a pastry shell, etc. Second, you need to follow the step-by-step procedure for preparing

Exhibit 3.1

A computer's problem-solving process is analogous to the procedures involved in baking a pie. Data or ingredients are input and processed according to a computer program or recipe. The outcome with computers is information, which satisfies a need as a baked pie does.

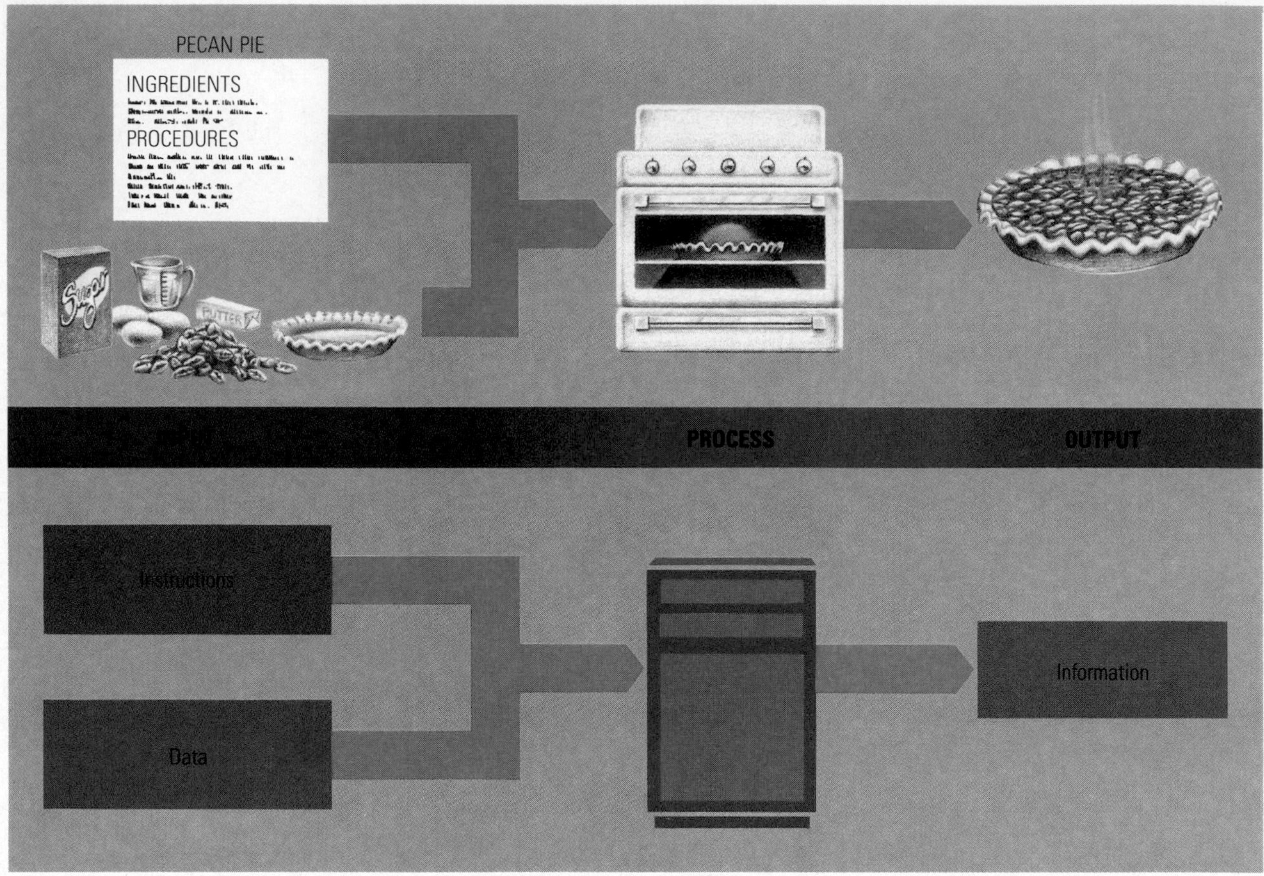

these ingredients and baking the pie. Step 1 is to cream the butter and sugar until light. Step 2 is to mix the eggs with a fork, and so on. In later steps, the pie is placed in the oven and baked for 35 to 40 minutes at 425 degrees. The result of this procedure is a baked pecan pie.

The major aspects of this problem-solving method are the input, process, and output functions. The input is a recipe and ingredients. The oven performs the process of transforming the raw ingredients into a baked pie. The baked pecan pie itself is the output and the desired solution to our problem (see Exhibit 3.1).

We can use this baking example to see how problem solving works when using a computer. Computer instructions, or programs, function as the recipe, and the data are the ingredients. The computer is used to process the data according to the program instructions, and produces the desired output. The computer's output could be a management report of sales activities, payroll checks, or a patient's medical record.

There are several key differences between the baking analogy and actual computer processing. One is that the oven is a rather simple single-purpose machine. Computers are general-purpose machines that can be instructed to do a variety of tasks, such as generating musical output, controlling traffic lights, or even playing chess. The second difference is that, while recipes contain step-by-step procedures, this type of instruction would not be specific enough to direct a computer.

For example, the recipe assumes you had or would get the ingredients and utensils needed to perform each instruction. Furthermore, some of the instructions are unclear and need interpretation. You are advised to "cream butter and sugar until light," but how light is "light"? When, for example, is the pie really baked to perfection? The suggested period of 35 to 40 minutes is just a general guideline. The instructions in recipes leave gaps that must be filled by experience and interpretation. Computers have neither of these skills.

To process information, the computer needs very specific instructions that explicitly state what is to be done. There is no room for vagueness. Like a mathematical formula, the step-by-step instructions given a computer must make no assumptions and must lead to the same result every time. Precise instructions such as these are called **algorithms.** Algorithms are used as the basis of computer programs or software.

To see how this concept is applied, consider the simple payroll example in Exhibit 3.2. John Avery worked 40 hours last week, and he gets paid $7 per hour. What is his gross pay? Even without your calculator, you know that the answer is $280. But how did you figure this out? More importantly, what list of instructions would a computer need to execute in order to calculate the gross pay for all employees of this company? Keep in mind that the computer cannot do anything beyond your instructions. The step-by-step instructions might be the following:

For each employee:

1. Get employee pay record.
2. Locate number of hours worked.
3. Locate hourly pay rate.
4. Calculate gross pay by multiplying number of hours worked by hourly pay rate.

Exhibit 3.2
The Payroll Problem-Solving Process

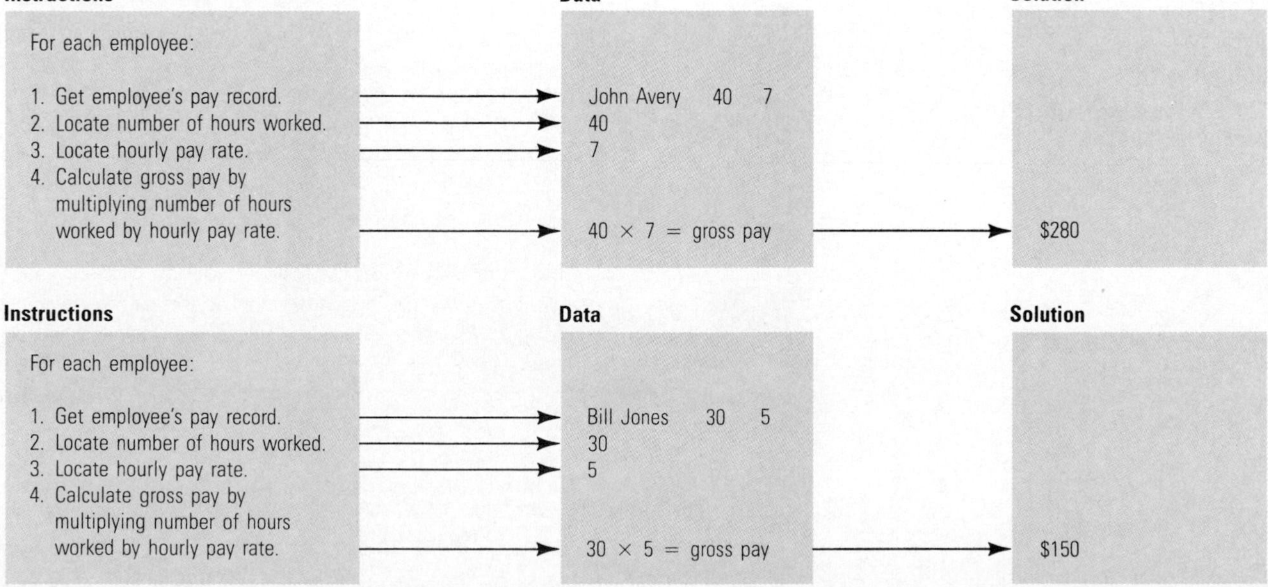

This set of instructions would be an algorithm for calculating gross pay. The problem-solving process would be to apply the instructions to a set of data. In John Avery's case, the resulting solution would be $280.

This procedure would work equally well for determining the gross pay of any employee. One would simply change the data (employee name, hours worked, and pay rate) and reapply the algorithm. For example, Bill Jones worked 30 hours and gets paid $5 per hour. Thus, his gross pay is calculated to be $150.

THE COMPUTER AT WORK

Let's take the payroll problem-solving steps and see how a computer could be used to determine the solution. A simplified version of the computer system will be used, so that we may highlight the main concepts and not be overloaded with complex details at this point.

Computer Processing Overview

The major components of a computer system are the input and output devices, primary memory, and the central processing unit (CPU). The CPU contains the control unit and the arithmetic-logic unit (ALU). Generally, the CPU and primary memory are housed in the computer processor (see Exhibit 3.3).

The first step in using a computer system to solve a problem is to enter or **load** the appropriate instructions into primary memory. In Exhibit 3.4, the control unit will show which events are being processed. The dotted lines indicate the sequence of steps being carried out. After the instructions are loaded (see Exhibit 3.4a), the data records are loaded into primary memory (see Exhibit 3.4b).

This process instructs a part of the control unit to go to primary memory and select the first instruction, which in this case is "Get employee pay record." To carry out this instruction, the control unit sends a signal to primary memory and retrieves the pay record for John Avery (see page 64). The completion of

Exhibit 3.3
The Major Components of a Computer System

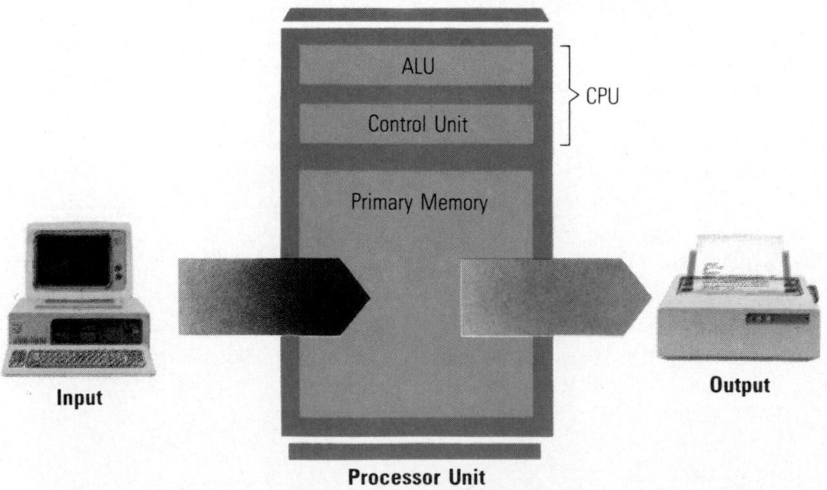

Exhibit 3.4a

In using a computer system to solve a problem, the first step is to enter, or load, instructions into primary memory.

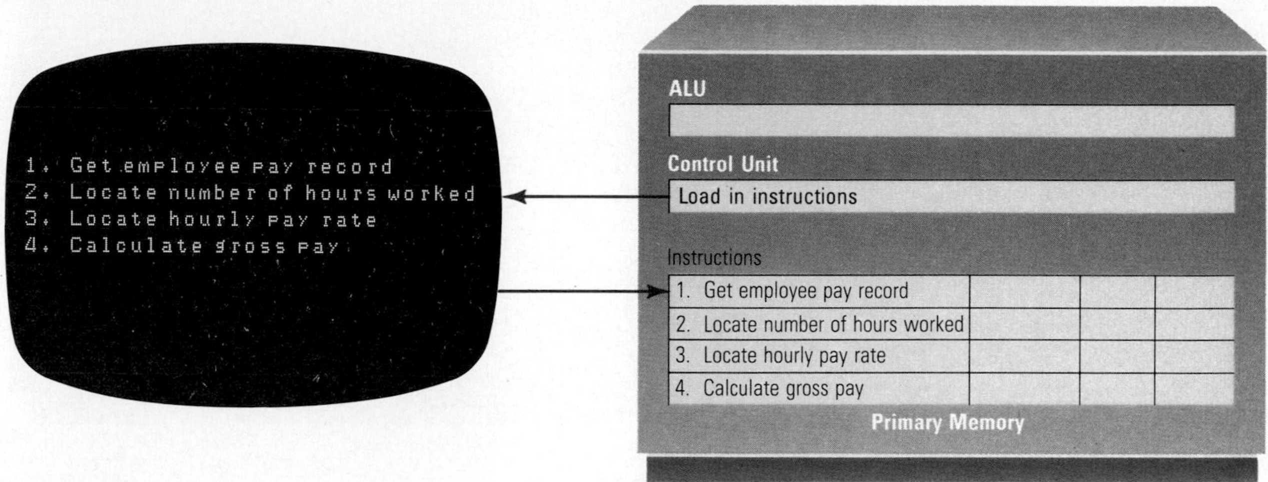

Exhibit 3.4b

Once the appropriate instructions have been loaded, the data records are loaded into primary memory.

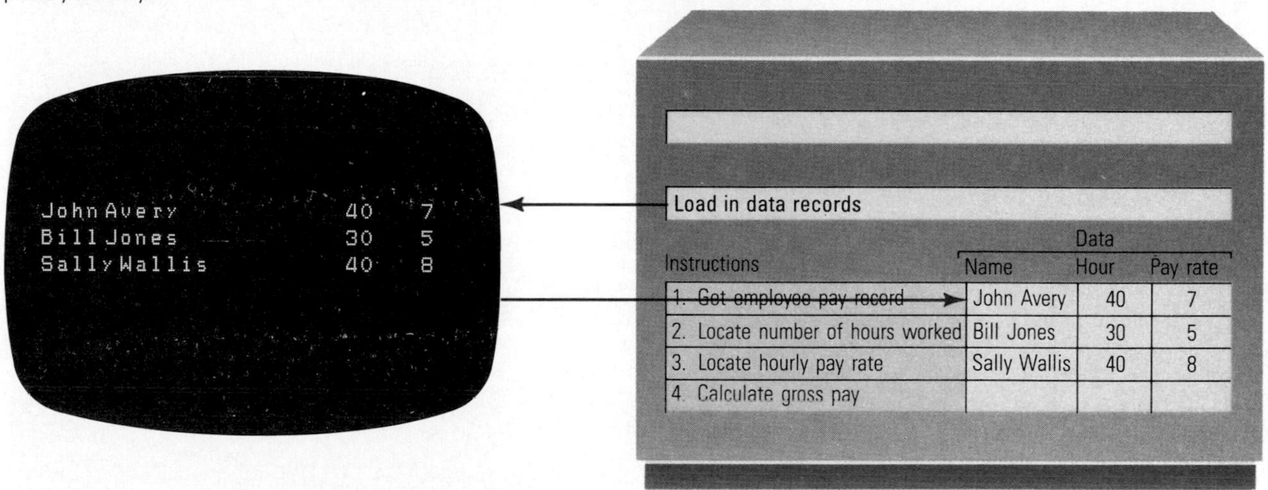

this task signals the control unit to start processing the second instruction (see Exhibit 3.5a).

The second instruction in memory is "Locate number of hours worked." The control unit copies the value of "hours" from the record for John Avery and places that value (40) in the arithmetic-logic unit for later use in the calculation of gross pay (see Exhibit 3.5b). The control unit then continues to execute the next instruction in sequence. Instruction 3 is "Locate hourly pay rate." John Avery is paid $7 per hour. A copy of this value is put into the arithmetic-logic unit by the control unit (see Exhibit 3.5c).

The fourth instruction is "Calculate gross pay." To carry out this instruction, recall that the formula to be used was the following: "multiply the number of hours worked by the hourly pay rate." The control unit sends a signal of

Exhibit 3.5
Process First Instruction: "Get Employee Pay Record"

(a)

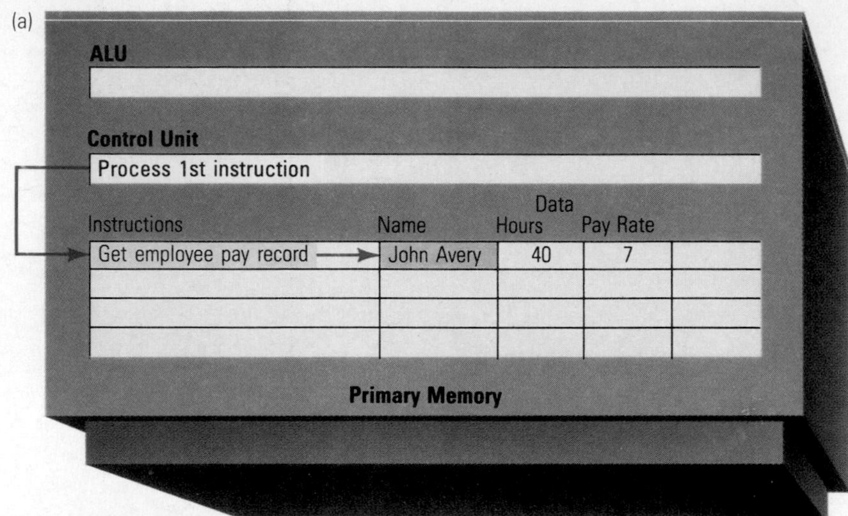

Process Second Instruction: "Locate Number of Hours Worked"

(b)

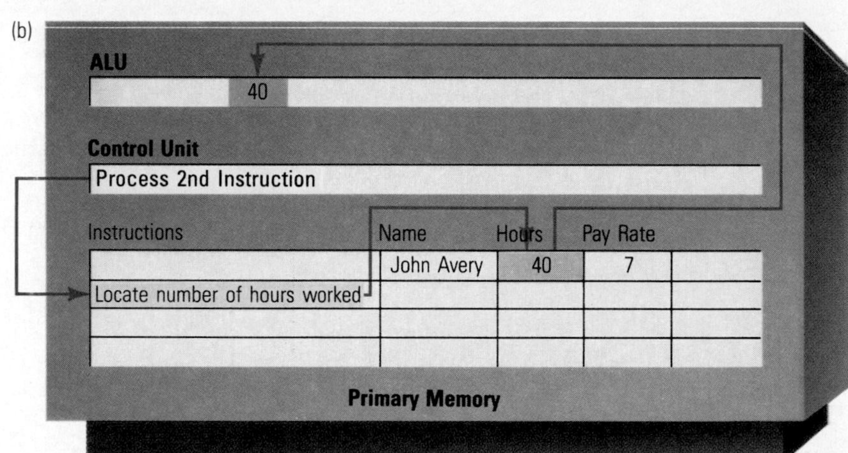

Process Third Instruction: "Locate Hourly Pay Rate"

(c)

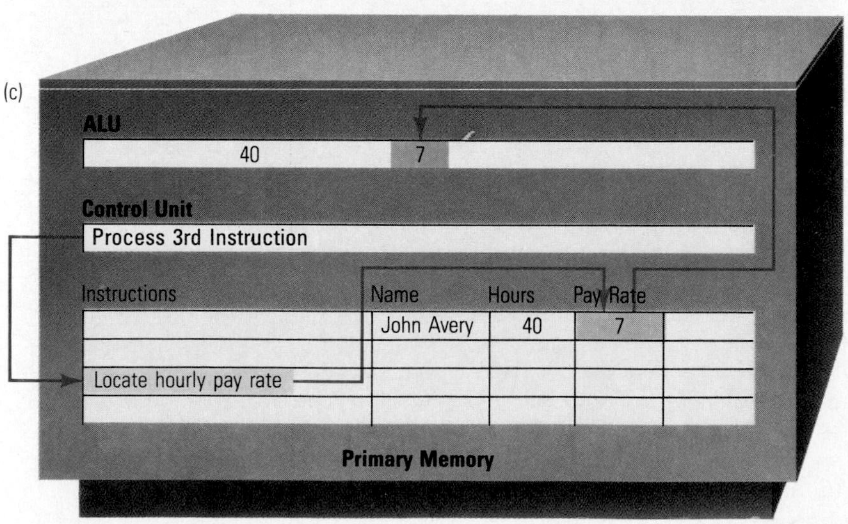

(d)

Process Fourth Instruction: "Calculate Gross Pay"

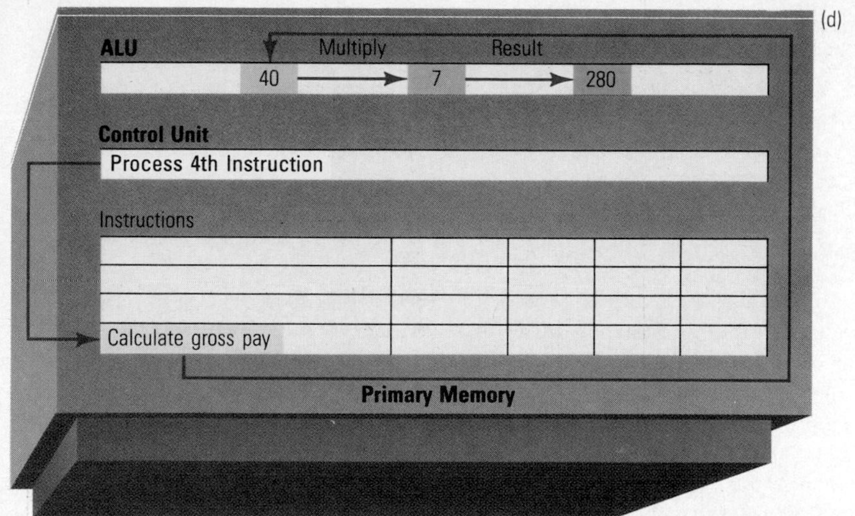

(e)

Start Sequence Over

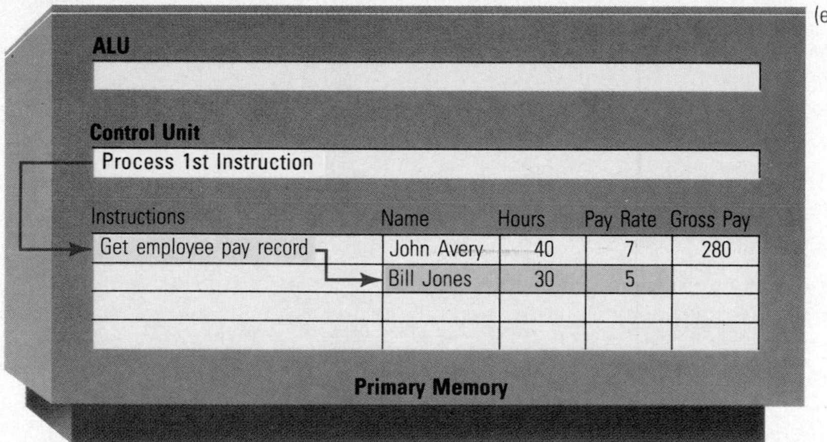

Process Print Instruction

(f)

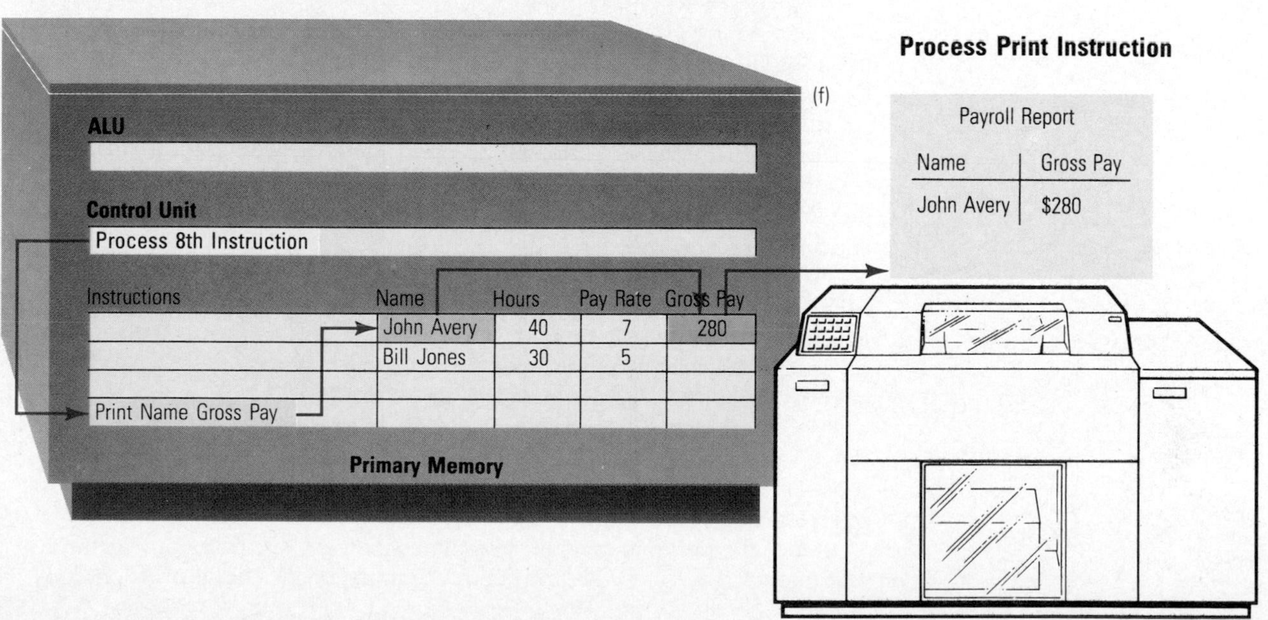

"multiply" to the arithmetic-logic unit. The ALU multiplies the two values it contains (40 times 7). The result of the calculation equals 280. At this point all instructions of the Gross Pay Algorithm have been carried out (see Exhibit 3.5d).

One additional major point that needs to be covered is the statement, "for each employee," in the Gross Pay Algorithm. After the instructions have been carried out for one employee, this statement would reset the control unit to cycle through the algorithm for the next employee, Bill Jones. This cycling would continue until all employee records had been processed (see Exhibit 3.5e).

But the algorithm didn't state a way to get the information, gross pay, out of the computer and display it for use. To do this, we would have to add several instructions to the algorithm. These would involve storing the result of the ALU calculation in primary memory as Gross Pay and associating it with the employee name, John Avery. For convenience we will skip showing these steps and proceed to a final instruction, which would order the printing of the employee name and gross pay amount (see Exhibit 3.5f).

While this payroll problem is very straightforward and the complex workings of the computer have been greatly simplified, it is helpful for understanding the following key points about computer processing:

Instructions, in the form of an algorithm, must provide a step-by-step procedure leading to the desired result.

Instructions and data must be loaded into the computer's primary memory to be processed.

The control unit sequences the events within the computer system according to the instructions of the program.

All calculations and logic comparisons take place in the ALU of the CPU.

The set of instructions within the algorithm are applied to one case and then recycled as necessary.

In order to see the results of computer processing, the solution must be displayed by means of an output device (printer or video display terminal).

The CPU and the Machine Cycle

Now that we have a conceptual overview of how instructions and data are processed in the computer to produce programming results, let's take a closer look at the CPU and how it functions.

In our gross pay example, we saw that the control unit was used to load program instructions and data into primary memory. It was also used to process instructions and sequence events. To accomplish these tasks, the control unit contains a program counter, an instruction register, an address register, and an instruction decoder.

The **program counter** is used to keep track of where the next instruction is in primary memory. Instructions are usually stored in consecutive memory locations and executed in order. Once the program counter is set to the memory location containing the first instruction, it can simply proceed to the next memory location. As you will learn later, there may be times when the program will specify the need to branch or jump to instructions outside the normal sequence. In either case, the program counter will retrieve instructions in the proper sequence. The process of retrieving an instruction is sometimes referred to as a **fetch.**

Once the program counter determines the next instruction, the control unit interprets it. To do this, the control unit first divides the instruction into two parts: an operation and an address. An **operation** is the action to be taken, such as multiply, store, or print. The **address** portion of the instruction refers to the location of the data in primary memory. After dividing the instruction into two parts, the control unit then puts the operation portion of the instruction in the instruction register. The address portion is entered in the address register. **Registers** are storage locations within the CPU that are used as temporary staging areas. The **instruction decoder** then sets the internal computer circuits to perform the operation.

The fetching of an instruction and its decoding are referred to as the **I–cycle,** for instruction cycle. Once the CPU has completed the I–cycle, it is then ready to execute the program instruction.

The control unit uses the ALU to perform arithmetic calculations or logic comparisons. Data are retrieved from the primary memory location stored in the address register and transferred to a storage register within the ALU. There can be several registers within the ALU that function as general-purpose staging areas.

Once the needed data are in place, the control unit signals the ALU to perform the operation specified in the instruction register. In our case, the operation is to multiply the contents of register X (40) and register Y (7). The result is stored in register Z, which is called the **accumulator.** To reduce the number of registers, the accumulator sometimes functions as the source for one of the values to be used in the arithmetic or logical operations.

The execution of the instruction and the storing of the result is the **E–cycle** or execution cycle. Together the I–cycle and the E–cycle are referred to as the **machine cycle** (see Exhibit 3.6). Although it may seem that the machine cycle is made up of many time-consuming steps, it is important to realize that the CPU is very fast. Machine cycles for different size computers are measured in milliseconds (thousandths of seconds), microseconds (millionths of seconds), and even nanoseconds (billionths of seconds).

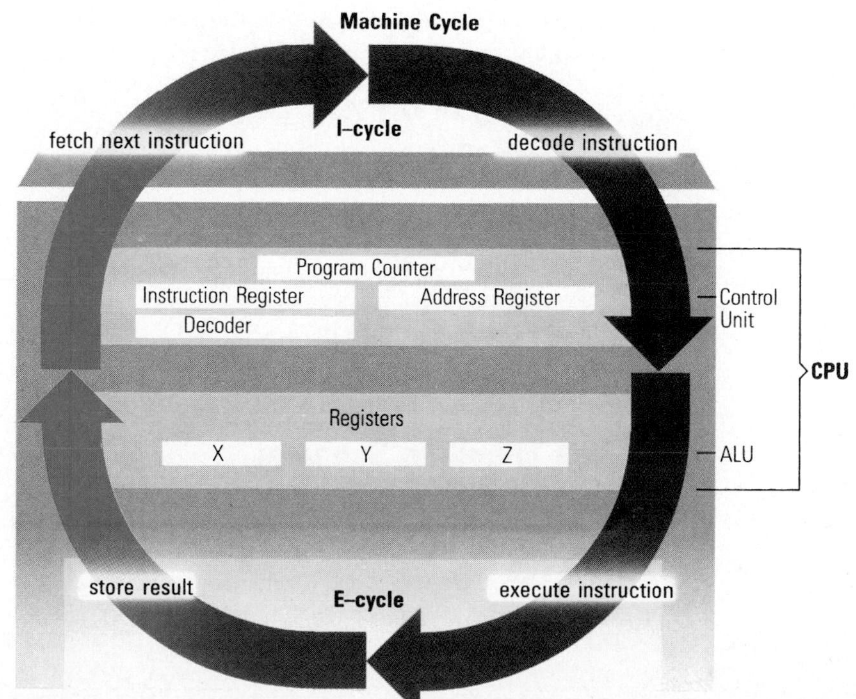

Exhibit 3.6

The fetching of an instruction and its decoding are referred to as the I–cycle, or instruction cycle. The execution of the instruction and the storing of the result are referred to as the E–cycle, or execution cycle. Together, the I–cycle and the E–cycle are referred to as the machine cycle.

CODING DATA AND INSTRUCTIONS FOR COMPUTER USE

Although computers are very complex electronic devices, they work on a very simple principle. Data can be represented by two states. For example, an electrical current is either flowing or not flowing; a particle is either magnetized or it isn't; or a voltage is either high or low. These two "on/off" or "high/low" states are the basis for everything the computer does. Thus all computer problems such as payroll calculations, word processing, or graphics must be broken down to this fundamental level. That is, all data, program instructions, and arithmetic-logic operations must be represented in the binary systems of 1s and 0s. To see how this works, let's start by discussing what a binary number system is, and how data and instructions are coded for computer use.

The Binary Number System

A **number system** is simply a way of representing numbers. The number system we commonly use is the base 10 or decimal system. In base 10, there are 10 symbols, 0 through 9. Numbers higher than 9 are represented through the use of place values. Each place value is represented by a digit. For example, the number 5812 is made up of four digits and could also be represented as shown in Exhibit 3.7. In the notation 10^n, 10 represents base 10 and the exponent n indicates the place value. Any number with an exponent of zero equals 1. Because it is familiar to us, we usually don't bother to break each number down to its place values. This knowledge is useful, however, when dealing with number systems with bases other than 10.

Exhibit 3.7

In the binary, or base 2, system, the symbols used are limited to one and zero, which correspond to the two-state nature of computer systems.

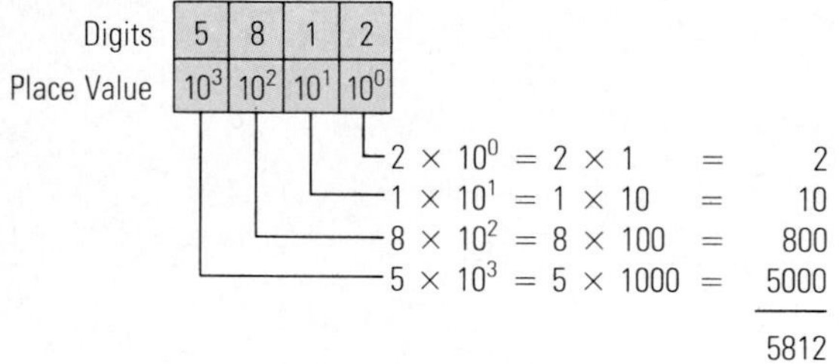

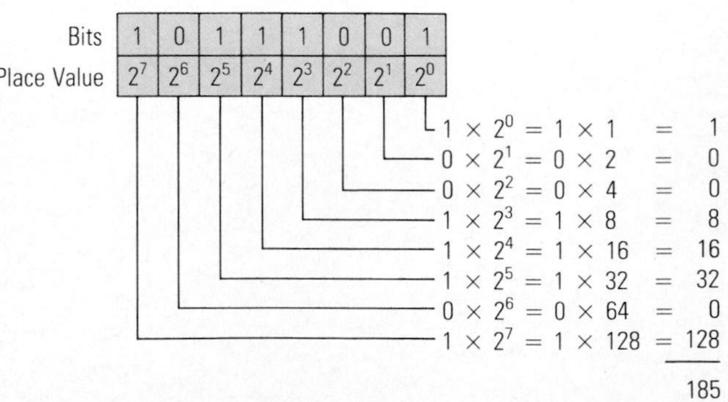

In the binary or base 2 system, the symbols used are limited to 1 and 0, which correspond to the two-state nature of computer systems. Higher numbers are shown by using place values. Each place value is called a binary digit or **bit.** A bit is the smallest piece of data. The binary number 10111001 would be equivalent to 185 in the decimal system.

Any decimal number can be converted to its binary equivalent and vice versa. It is also true that other number systems such as base 8 (octal) and base 16 (hexidecimal) have value when working with computer systems. We will discuss the numbering systems and the various conversion methods in Appendix B, "Arithmetic Operations and Number Systems."

Data Encoding Schemes

How are alphabetic letters, such as *A* or *j,* or special characters, such as $ or !, represented in computer systems? What about numbers used as characters in ZIP codes, phone numbers, or mechanical part numbers? A modification to the pure binary number system has been developed for encoding alphabetic letters, special characters, and numbers.

Exhibit 3.8
EBCDIC and ASCII-8 Binary Codes

EBCDIC

Uppercase Alpha		Lowercase Alpha		Special Characters		Numeric	
A	11000001	a	10000001	!	01011010	0	11110000
B	11000010	b	10000010	"	01111111	1	11110001
C	11000011	c	10000011	#	01111011	2	11110010
D	11000100	d	10000100	$	01011011	3	11110011
E	11000101	e	10000101	%	01101100	4	11110100
F	11000110	f	10000110	&	01010000	5	11110101
G	11000111	g	10000111	(	01001101	6	11110110
H	11001000	h	10001000	)	01011101	7	11110111
I	11001001	i	10001001	*	01011100	8	11111000
J	11010001	j	10010001	+	01001110	9	11111001

ASCII-8

Uppercase Alpha		Lowercase Alpha		Special Characters		Numeric	
A	10100001	a	11100001	!	01000001	0	01010000
B	10100010	b	11100010	"	01000010	1	01010001
C	10100011	c	11100011	#	01000011	2	01010010
D	10100100	d	11100100	$	01000100	3	01010011
E	10100101	e	11100101	%	01000101	4	01010100
F	10100110	f	11100110	&	01000110	5	01010101
G	10100111	g	11100111	(	01001000	6	01010110
H	10101000	h	11101000	)	01001001	7	01010111
I	10101001	i	11101001	*	01001010	8	01011000
J	10101010	j	11101010	+	01001011	9	01011001

Two popular coding schemes are the Extended Binary Coded Decimal Interchange Code (EBCDIC) and the American Standard Code for Information Interchange (ASCII). IBM developed EBCDIC, and uses it, as do several other computer manufacturers, on its large mainframe computers. ASCII was developed by the American Standards Institute, and it is used on almost all microcomputers, including IBM's, and on many minicomputers and large computers as well. Software is available to translate from one code to the other.

For our purposes, the importance of these codes is that each letter, special character, and number is given a unique code that is made up of a fixed number of bits. For example, in the EBCDIC system, the digit 1 would be coded as 1111 0001, the uppercase letter J would be 1101 0001, and special character $ is 0101 1011 (see Exhibit 3.8). Notice that the ASCII codes are different.

The combination of bits that may be used to represent a character is called a **byte.** An eight-bit coding scheme allows up to 256 unique symbols to be defined. This is more than enough for representing all digits, lower- and uppercase letters, and a variety of special characters, graphic symbols, and data communication codes.

An important aspect of these coding schemes is the change they make in the way numbers are represented. Under normal circumstances, base 2 would require four bits—1111—to represent the decimal number 15. In a similar way, base 2 would require eight bits—10111001—to represent the decimal number 185. The problem is that base 2 requires a different number of bits to represent different decimal numbers. Both EBCDIC and ASCII avoid this problem by converting each digit individually. Thus, the decimal number 15 would be encoded in EBCDIC as two bytes of eight bits each, 1111 0001 (the 1) and 1111 0101 (the 5).

Instruction Encoding

We have shown how data (numbers and characters) can be coded for computer use. But what about program instructions? If the computer is to "understand" and follow program instructions, they have to be translated from word phrases, such as "Get employee record," to the 1s and 0s language of the computer. Thus, a typical machine language instruction would look like this:

Instruction = Operation + Address

00010110   0110011111100110

The first part of the instruction would be the binary code of a computer operation such as load data into a primary memory location, or multiply numbers in the ALU, or print out the result. The second part of the instruction is used to represent the address of data located in computer memory.

Fortunately, we do not have to use the binary codes directly. Computer scientists have developed high-level languages such as BASIC, FORTRAN, and COBOL that are much closer to the spoken languages of English, French, or Spanish, making it easier to write programs. Programs written in high-level languages are translated by special computer programs into the binary codes of machine language. We will see how this is done in Chapter 14, "Programming Languages."

Binary Arithmetic-Logic Operations

The ALU uses binary mathematics in performing arithmetic and logic comparisons. The mathematics of adding, subtracting, multiplying, and dividing binary numbers are similar to the operations performed in the decimal number system.

Logic comparisons can be made using a form of subtraction. Assume, for example, the computer was instructed to determine if 40 is greater than 30. To do this, the first number (40) could be subtracted from the second number (30). If the result were a negative number, 40 would indeed be greater than 30.

Similar techniques are used when comparing text, as in a word processing application. Assume we want the computer to search a lengthy report and find all instances of the word *microcomputer*. The computer would compare the binary string of bits that represent the word *microcomputer* with the binary string of bits for the first word in the report. One bit pattern would be subtracted from the other. If the result were 0, then the words were identical, and a match would have been found. A positive or negative remainder would signify no match. The computer would proceed through the whole document in this fashion.

Fortunately, you do not need to learn binary coding to use a computer. It is enough to realize that the computer is a binary-based machine, and this quality is reflected in both the hardware and the fundamental operations. If you would like to learn more about different number systems and some elementary forms of binary arithmetic, however, see Appendix B.

MICROCOMPUTER ARCHITECTURE

If we took the "lid" off a computer, we might think we were looking at a science fiction city, with clusters of low buildings connected by superhighways. In fact, the engineers who design modern computers often play the role of architects in planning the layout and design of these computer "cities." The microcomputer system in Exhibit 3.9 is typical of what you might see the next time you go to a computer store or visit a computer lab. And what you have learned thus far has given you a good foundation for understanding what it all means.

Exhibit 3.9

Many components, chips, boards, and peripherals are necessary to build a microcomputer.

Semiconductor Chip Technology

The basic building block of this computer system is the semiconductor chip. These chips are composed of anywhere from several thousand to hundreds of thousands of transistors.

Transistors are electronic components that function as semiconductors. Solid materials, such as copper or silver, can serve as conductors meaning they will always transmit electricity. Other solid materials, such as plastic or rubber, will never transmit electricity, and are classified as insulators. A transistor is made up of silicon (a product of sand, which acts as an insulator or nonconducting material) that has been injected with small amounts of conducting materials. The result is a **semiconductor,** a device that can be made to serve as a conductor or as an insulator, depending upon conditions. Thus, a transistor can be made to represent a 1 (conductor) or a 0 (insulator). The transistor is highly reliable, requires little power, and can be manufactured very inexpensively. In addition, unlike vacuum tubes, which had to have air-conditioned environments in order to function, transistors give off very little heat.

Individual transistors can be combined to encode and store information, or they can be used to carry out arithmetic or logic operations. Semiconductor chips are used for the CPU, for primary memory, and for the interface devices between various hardware components. **Interface devices** are used to coordinate the flow of electrical signals between two hardware units.

As shown in Exhibit 3.9, a collection of chips are mounted on printed circuit boards to perform particular functions, such as connecting a printer or disk drive to the microcomputer. The largest circuit board, called the **motherboard,** generally contains the central processing unit. Other boards are used to adapt the microcomputer to a particular user's needs. Add-on boards for increasing primary memory or connecting a graphics monitor can be plugged into **expansion slots,** built-in brackets for holding additional circuit boards. With this overview, let's study the major parts in more detail.

Primary Memory Chips

In explaining how the computer could be used to process employee gross pay, we saw the importance of using primary memory as a storage area. The two main types of memory chips used in primary memory are called RAM and ROM.

RAM stands for **Random Access Memory,** which means that instructions or data can be written into this form of primary memory as needed. These instructions or data can also be read out of memory as needed, and transferred to the CPU for processing. Thus, RAM is sometimes referred to as **read/write memory.**

On the other hand, **Read Only Memory,** or **ROM,** can only be used to read data or instructions that have been permanently loaded onto the chip. Nothing can be written into this memory by the computer user. It is common, for example, to put a software language such as BASIC in ROM. This makes the language readily available to translate programming instructions and still protects it from users who might accidentally order the computer to write over this valuable information. Software that is stored in ROM hardware is called **firmware.**

RAM primary memory is used for temporarily storing user's program instructions and data. A programmer using a high-level language such as BASIC or COBOL can refer to data as "hours" or "pay rate" and not be concerned with knowing exactly where data are physically stored within primary memory. Instead, the control unit will handle the task of finding that information.

To do this, the control unit maintains a map of primary memory in much the way that streets are mapped. As shown in Exhibit 3.10, both maps and memory chips are made of grids formed by the intersection of horizontal and vertical lines. Each intersection is assigned a set of coordinates. If you look up the entry South Street in the map index, for example, its coordinates would be

Exhibit 3.10

Primary memory is mapped in a way analogous to street maps. Horizontal and vertical coordinates are used to directly find a specific location. For RAM chips, these would be memory addresses, which contain data, or instructions.

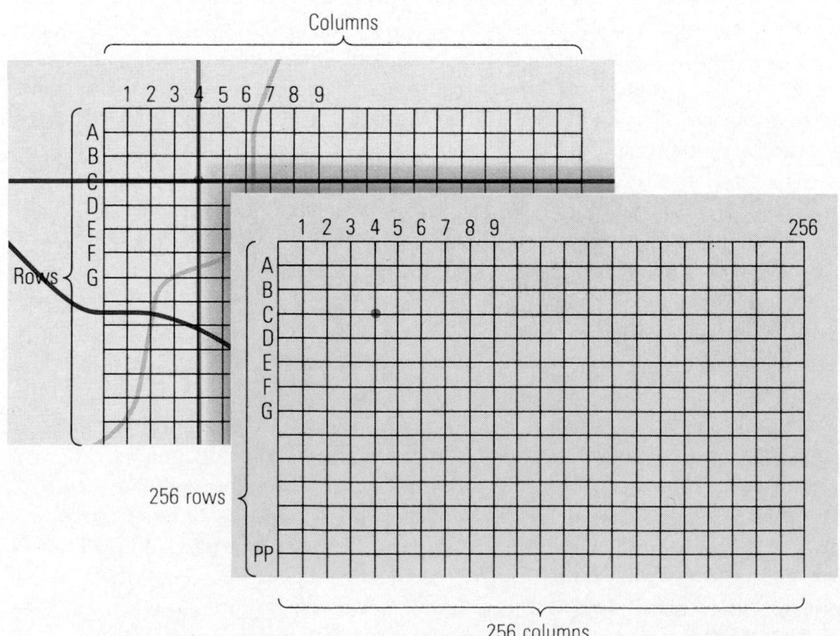

C4. To find this location, you would look down the left side of the map until you located sector C. Then you would proceed horizontally until you reached sector 4. Primary memory addressing works in a similar fashion. Assume, for example, that our computer has 64K of primary memory. **K,** or **kilo,** is an abbreviation for kilobyte, or 2^{10}, or 1024 bytes. A 64K memory would be arranged in a grid of 256 rows by 256 columns. Each address, or intersection on this grid, could be found by using two coordinates, one for the particular row and one for the particular column.

In computers that have larger amounts of primary memory, the RAM chips are arranged in banks, and the bank number is added to the address. This is similar to using a set of maps to represent a large area. For example the city map for a large city might give the address of South Street as page 17, coordinates 4C.

The type of RAM memory chips most commonly used today have the major disadvantage that whenever electric power is turned off, the contents of RAM are lost. This is known as **volatile** RAM. To keep this from happening accidentally during temporary power outages, a backup power supply must be used. ROM uses a different storage technology which is nonvolatile, and thus is not affected by power problems.

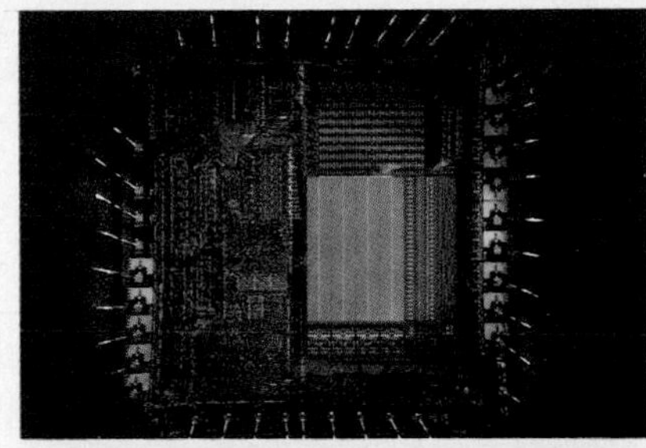

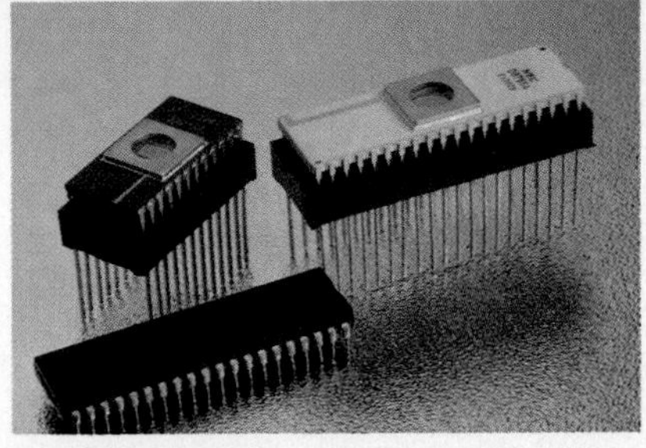

Exhibit 3.11

Typical microelectronic chips used in computer systems

ROM's major advantage—its ability to protect valuable information by storing it permanently—is also a disadvantage when that information needs to be changed. However, ROM chips have been developed that can be modified. Ultraviolet light is used to erase the information stored on the chip. These types of chips are called **Erasable Programmable ROM** or **EPROM.** They can be recognized by the clear glass window built into the chip package to absorb the ultraviolet light. To change the EPROM, it must be removed from the computer. After the chip is cleared, it can be reprogrammed.

The latest advancement has been the **EEPROM,** the **Electrically Erasable Programmable ROM.** This chip can be used for applications that require an occasional updating of the program or data being stored. The big advantage of EEPROM chips is that their contents can be changed without removing them from the computer. Rather, electrical signals can be sent to the chip, and changes can be made on a byte-by-byte basis. EEPROMs are being used to hold price lists in **point-of-sale terminals,** the electronic cash registers used in many stores. EEPROMS can be updated on a selective basis by sending signals over telephone lines. Their disadvantage is that they cost three to four times more than regular ROM chips. Exhibit 3.11 shows some of the chips currently used in primary memory.

Microprocessor Chips

We have seen that the key element of the computer is the central processor unit. A CPU that has been implemented on a single silicon chip is called a **microprocessor.** This chip would contain at least the control unit and the arithmetic-logic unit. In more advanced designs, the chip could also include RAM, ROM, and other support devices.

Microprocessor chips use many different internal designs, and the chips vary in appearance and capability. For example, microprocessors differ in the type of transistor technology used, the range of instructions they are capable of executing, the speed of their machine cycles, and their physical packaging. The most popular microprocessors are the MOS Technology 6502, Zilog Z–80A, Intel 8088, and Motorola 68000. As shown in Exhibit 3.12, the Apple IIe uses the

Exhibit 3.12
Popular Microprocessor Chips
The 68000 computer chip shown below contains 70,000 transistors.

Microprocessor Chip	Manufacturer	Dataword Length	Microcomputers Using This Chip
6502	MOS Technology	8	Apple IIe Atari 800 Commodore 64
Z–80A	Zilog	8	Radio Shack Personal Desktop Sanyo Business Systems MBC/250 Epson QX–10
8088	Intel	16	IBM PC and XT COMPAQ Portable HP 150 (touch screen)
68000	Motorola	32	Radio Shack TRS–80 Model 16B Corvus Concept Apple Macintosh
80286	Intel	24	IBM–AT

6502; the Epson QX–10 uses the Z–80A; the IBM PC uses the 8088; and Apple Macintosh uses the 68000. An example of the newest generation of microprocessor chips from INTEL is the 80286, which is used in the IBM-AT microcomputer.

When you visit the computer store or read ads in your local newspaper, you will often see microcomputers referred to as using 8-, 16-, or 32-bit processors. "Eight-bit" is a measure of a computer's dataword length. **Dataword length** refers to the number of bits of data that can be retrieved from memory each machine cycle. In a computer with an 8-bit microprocessor chip, 8 bits or 1 byte would be retrieved or processed each machine cycle. Each byte would contain one character such as a $ or 4 or c. An 8-bit machine would therefore require four machine cycles to fetch four characters. A 32-bit machine could perform this same task in a single cycle. Thus, dataword length is an important indicator of a computer's power, somewhat akin to the way horsepower is an overall indication of the power of a car's engine.

In this simple comparison, it is important to stress first that the 8-bit processor can do any job the 32-bit processor can, but at a much slower rate. This slower rate may be unacceptable for certain time-dependent applications, however. Second, computers with 32-bit processors are faster than computers with 16-bit processors, but not twice as fast. Many other variables affect overall computer speed. Third, 32-bit processors are much more complex to design and build than 8- or 16-bit chips, and thus cost more.

Support Units

To perform its tasks, the control unit needs the support of a variety of devices. One support device is a **clock,** which plays an important part in the computer's performance. Each event in a computer needs to be sequenced, and many things need to be going on simultaneously. To orchestrate this, the control unit needs to set a certain beat. This beat is established by the timing signal of the clock, and is measured in MegaHertz, or millions of cycles per second. Typical microcomputer clocks are 2, 5, or 10 MHz. Therefore, with a 5 MHz clock, events could be sequenced 5 million times per second!

If you looked inside a microcomputer, you could see sets of tiny lines connecting the various chips. These electronic highways, called **buses,** are used to send electrical signals between functional units. Some microcomputers contain one main bus for all internal communication, while other systems use separate buses for control, for address, and for data communication.

The control unit also needs the support of interface devices to enter data by means of a keyboard or joystick, or to output data from the computer to a peripheral device such as a printer, disk drive, or video monitor. Frequently, a separate interface device is required for each input and output device. Interface devices are needed for two reasons. First, there are often tremendous differences in the rates at which the processor, primary memory, and peripherals can transfer data. The interface device adjusts these rates so that various devices can communicate. Second, not every equipment vendor uses the same standards for electronic voltage levels, and the physical connections may even differ. In addition, vendors may use different methods for encoding data. This is especially true when a computer system is made up of equipment from different vendors, as is so common with microcomputers. Interface units overcome these obstacles. The technical details of how interfaces work will be discussed in Chapter 9, "Data Communications."

We have used the microcomputer to understand the technology used in the CPU, primary memory, and support devices. As you will learn later in this chapter, large computers and small computers work in the same fundamental way. But while a microprocessor is very complex, it is not yet sophisticated or powerful enough to use as the CPU in a large computer system. The large systems generally require the use of several chips and take advantage of faster, more advanced (and more expensive) circuit technology.

Professional Issue

Understanding Computer Classification

In this chapter you have gained a conceptual understanding of how computer systems work and some of the technology that they use. But it is also important for you to learn about the power, capability, and prices of different classes of computer systems. In Chapters 11 and 12, on systems development, and the Special Feature, "A Systems Approach to Selecting a Microcomputer," you will learn how to use this knowledge and become familiar with some other important factors in selecting computer systems to match users' needs.

The primary areas in which computers differ are in terms of their flexibility, purpose, and power. **General-purpose computer systems** are extremely flexible in that they can be programmed at different times to perform significantly different tasks. These computers can be used to do accounting, then word processing or graphics, and later even music composition. In contrast are the special-purpose or **dedicated computer systems,** which have been designed to do one task very efficiently. Video games and digital watches are examples of dedicated, nonprogrammable computer systems.

A second classification scheme is based on whether or not the computer has been designed for use in scientific work such as weather forecasting, medical imaging, and nuclear research, which are all highly mathematical. These applications require a computer system that can perform arithmetic operations in a rapid, accurate way. Such computers are sometimes called **number crunchers.** In contrast, **business computing** involves calculating and producing payroll checks, retrieving medical records, word processing, and mailing brochures to a selected clientele. These activities use relatively simple mathematics for any calculations. But a heavy demand is placed on the quick retrieval of records from secondary storage, or, in other words, on efficient input and output operations.

Computer Power

A third classification—and one more meaningful to us—is based on computing power. This text discusses four of the major classes: the micro-, the mini-, the maxi-, and the supercomputer. One measure of **computing power** is the number of instructions that can be processed in a given time period. More powerful maxi- and supercomputers can process millions of instructions per second, whereas less powerful microcomputers handle thousands in that amount of time. Exhibit 3.13 shows an example from each of the four classes of computing power.

Exhibit 3.13

The four major classes of computing power discussed in this text are, from left to right, the micro-, the mini-, the maxi-, and the supercomputer.

In practice, this means that more powerful computers can be programmed to handle more complex applications and/or service more users at the same time. Thus, there is a direct relationship between power and performance. For example, microcomputers often are used as personal computers in the home or in the office for word processing, spreadsheet analysis, or business graphics applications. Generally, they can be used by only one person at a time. Microcomputer systems generally cost less than $5000.

Minicomputers can be used to do accounting applications such as payroll, accounts receivable, and income statements for small-and medium-sized businesses. They can also be used for processing orders and for inventory control. Minicomputers generally can support ten to thirty users at one time, and cost between $10,000 and $100,000.

Mainframe or maxicomputers have been the mainstay of business, government, and education for most of the history of computers. These large computer systems can usually be found in special air-conditioned rooms at the data processing center of large corporations. Maxicomputers are used by airlines to support their reservation systems. Government agencies use maxicomputer systems for processing the records of millions of people. Imagine the data processing demands of the Social Security Administration, the Department of Motor Vehicles, or the Internal Revenue Service. Colleges often use a maxicomputer to provide hundreds of terminals for use by students for programming projects, while handling the administrative tasks of servicing 20,000 students. Maxicomputers vary in cost from $500,000 to $10 million dollars.

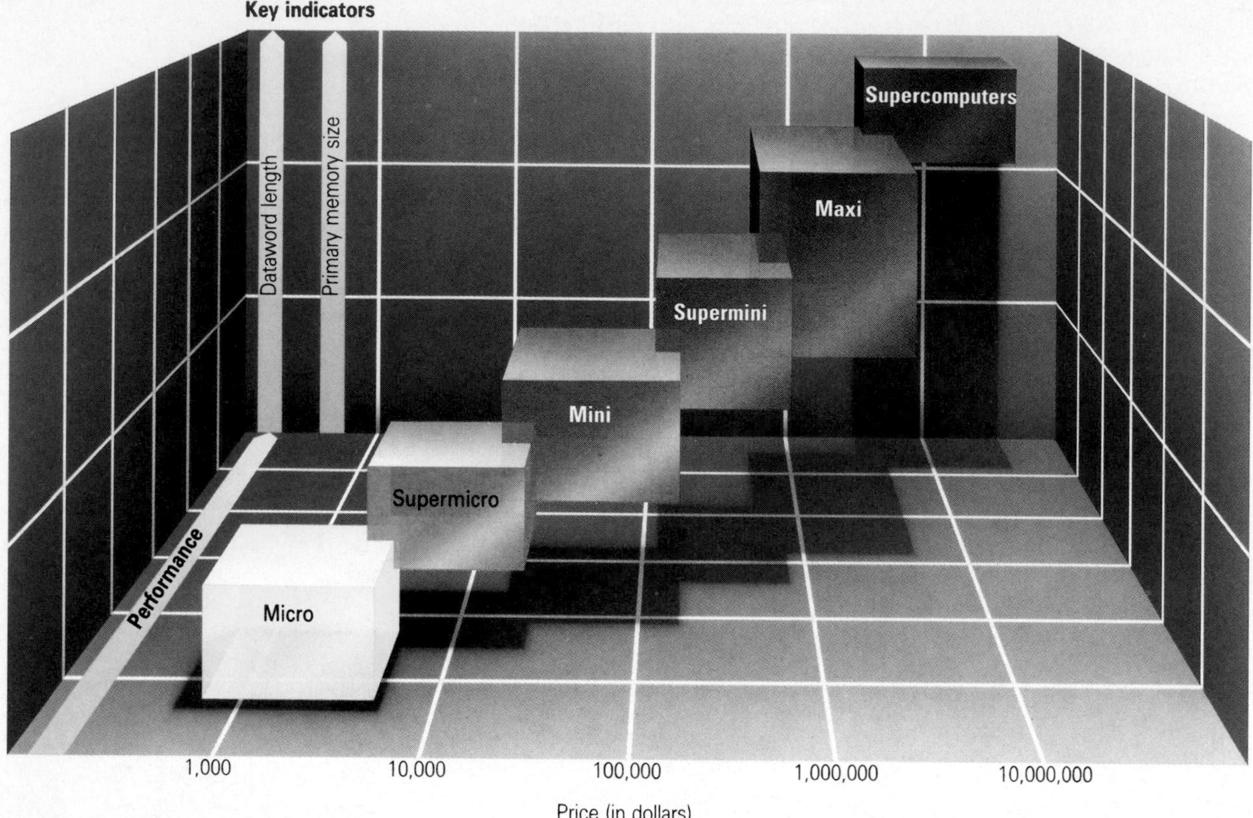

Exhibit 3.14

Two main indicators of a computer system's power are dataword length and size of primary memory. Selling price is a reasonably good indicator of computing power, with the purchase price for each computer category showing an upward trend as performance increases.

The supercomputers are the most powerful computers available today. These computers are the true number crunchers and have been designed for use in scientific work. They are also used to produce the graphic designs for special effects movies, such as *Tron* and the *Star Wars* series. Computer-generated images are based on manipulating mathematical formulas that describe geometric shapes very quickly to give the illusion of movement. Supercomputers cost over $10 million.

Actually, classifying computers into performance categories is not this straightforward. Tremendous advances in technology have meant that computer users can buy more computing power for less money. This, in turn, has blurred the boundaries between traditional classifications. Furthermore, superminicomputers such as DEC VAX and the supermicro have been introduced within the last five to ten years. A supermicro is a microcomputer, such as the IBM–AT, that uses an advanced microprocessor chip and is capable of supporting several users—at a price under $15,000.

Exhibit 3.14 reflects these new classifications and shows the overall relationship between increased performance and increased price of the computer systems. While a multitude of factors determine how powerful a computer system is, two of the main indicators are dataword length and the size of primary memory. Longer dataword lengths indicate more power, since fewer machine cycles are needed to respond to an instruction. Response time is shorter, and less time will be needed to do a particular job. The greater the capacity of primary memory, the more sophisticated the programs that can be used with that computer system.

Dataword length varies from 8 bits to 64 bits. Microcomputers generally have either 8- or 16-bit microprocessors; maxicomputers use either 32- or 64-bit processors; and supercomputers generally use 64-bit datawords. Primary memory varies from around 64K bytes to over 50 megabytes. *Mega* is a prefix meaning million. Microcomputers used as personal computers generally have between 64K bytes and 512K bytes of primary memory. Maxicomputer primary memory ranges from around 12 megabytes to 64 megabytes.

In the highly competitive world of computing, marketing forces tend to equate value with price. Therefore, selling price is a reasonably good indicator of computing power, particularly if one looks at prices by order of magnitude (that is, powers of 10 such as $100, $1,000, $10,000, etc.). While the purchase price for each computer category shows a general upward trend as performance increases, there is some overlap between classifications. This overlap reflects the fact that the overall worth of a computer system is affected by computing power and such factors as the availability of applications software and maintenance, as well as the marketing strategy of the manufacturer.

Evolutionary Path

Because computer performance increases every year and prices drop even faster, an indirect indication of computing price/performance is the date the computer was designed. The computer evolution traced in Exhibit 3.15 shows the effect of this interesting progression (see page 80). The red line shows vertical comparison, and the green line shows horizontal comparison.

For any given year, the larger computer systems have greater computer performance than smaller computer systems. Thus for the year 1975, performance for supermini (6) is greater than that of the minicomputer (5), which in turn is greater than the microcomputer (4). For any level of performance, the smaller computer system will equal a larger computer system some time in the near future. Thus the performance of the small mainframe in 1970 (3) was equaled by the supermini around 1975 (6), which was equaled by the mini around 1980 (8), and will be equaled by the micro around 1985 (10).

Another dimension is shown by the purple diagonal lines. They show that each classification of computer system increases in relative power over time. Therefore, a computer's classification is relative to both other computer system classifications and a particular time frame. One of the conclusions that can be drawn is that the inexpensive microcomputer of tomorrow will have the power of the expensive superminicomputer of today.

Future Performance Increases

The concept of the evolutionary path shows us that the computer classifications in Exhibit 3.15 are really valid for a very narrow time period. The advances in technology and competition among computer vendors constantly increase performance and decrease the costs associated with any category.

How far can manufacturers go toward increasing computer performance? Many experts believe that there will continue to be progress for the foreseeable future, but there will be no spectacular breakthroughs in performance.

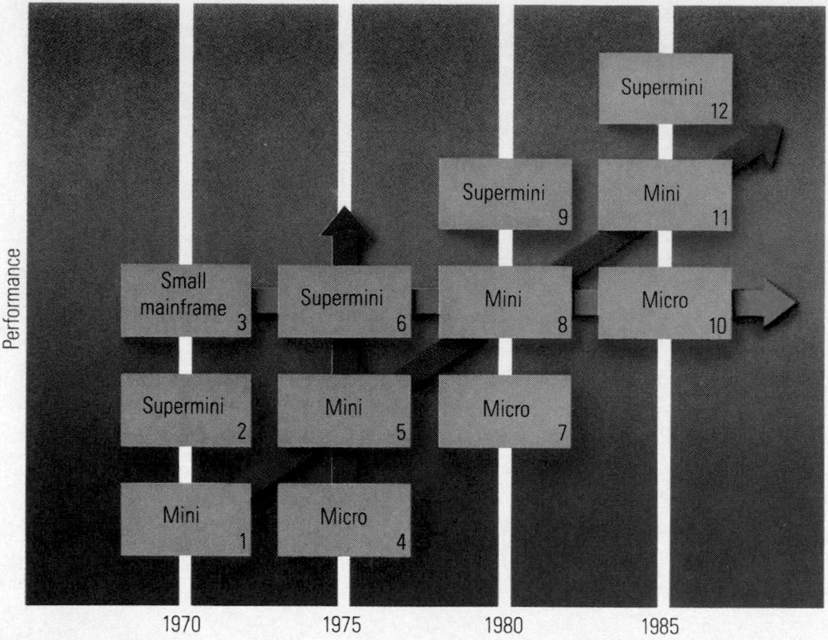

Exhibit 3.15

For any given year, the larger computer systems have greater performance than the smaller systems. For any level of performance, the smaller computer systems will equal larger systems sometime in the near future. Each classification of computer systems increases in relative power over time.

To understand the experts' thinking, we need to know a somewhat surprising fact. For the most part, the smallest microcomputer and the largest supercomputers work in the same fundamental way described in the early part of this chapter. These computer systems are based on the principles of John von Neumann, the mathematician credited with designing the von Neumann architecture, in which digital computers use program instructions stored in primary memory to sequence computer actions. Large computers are significantly faster than smaller computers, primarily because they use much faster—not different—circuitry for the CPU, main memory, and disk storage.

In addition to increasing the speed of each component in the computer system, larger computers use more concurrent, or simultaneous, processing. Because the CPU is so much faster than any of the other computer components, an input/output bottleneck occurs when the CPU works in a strictly sequential manner. One solution is to instruct the control unit to retrieve data from storage, while the CPU is performing another task. This is called **overlap processing.**

Another approach is to program the CPU to perform multiprogramming. In **multiprogramming,** the computer is processing more than one person's job on a time-share basis. Speed can also be increased by using multiple specialized processors. For example, an auxiliary processor can be designed to handle all the input/output communication. This would allow the CPU to concentrate solely on internal processing functions. We will learn more about these techniques in Part III, "Systems Support Software." For now, however, you can turn to the end of this chapter to Computers at Work: "Supercomputers Make Way for Teams of Micros" for an interesting discussion about how microcomputers may eventually replace supercomputers.

Each technique for increasing the speed of processing means increased complexity and, in turn, significant increases in cost. Instead of continuing to try to find ways to speed up the Von Neumann architecture, a fundamentally different kind of computer system is being designed for the future. It is called the Fifth Generation Computer. The Japanese are making a major commitment to developing a computer system that would work more like the human brain. These computers are expected to have a great impact on our society, since they will be significantly faster than the supercomputers of today, and more importantly, they will have "intelligence." Chapter 18 will discuss this very exciting project.

Supercomputers Make Way for Teams of Micros

Commodore Grace Hopper, at 78, is as sharp as ever in calling for the computer industry to recognize the effects of technological advancements on the direction in which the industry moves. The unbridled spread of single-user machines will cause the same kinds of problems that the wash of autos has created, Hopper said. Just as our nation's railways and mass transit systems have crumbled under the pounding of radial tires, so we are proceeding into the information age without a plan or a goal. That worries Grace Hopper very much.

The industry is hamstrung by a misguided belief that bigger processors are necessarily better processors, she asserted. If you can't move a big, heavy boulder with one ox, you don't grow a bigger ox, she said; you just add another ox. Similarly, large volumes of data are not better handled by a bigger machine; they are better managed with multiple machines, each doing a specialized task. Networked computers are the wave of the future, Hopper believes.

Hopper travels extensively, speaking to every flavor of audience from high school students to high-powered industry executives. Her wide-ranging, spirited talk contains kernels of insight for everyone. Hopper calls herself "the third programmer on the world's first electromechanical computer" (Harvard University's Mark I), but her message is light on nostalgia and heavy on current issues.

Anyone who relies on computers for a living should listen closely to what Grace Hopper has to say. Clearly, the field is poised for incredible growth, the kind which Hopper believes will make it the largest industry in the country by the end of the century. But she believes lack of standards and reluctance to adopt new ideas could send it careening into chaos just as quickly.

Hopper draws a parallel between the current state of the computer industry and the auto industry of the early part of the century. Microcomputers are the Model Ts of computing, she said. Like the early automobile, they are inexpensive and easily available. Just as Henry Ford offered the Model T in any color as long as it was black, the industry leader offers any color micro, as long as it is blue, she said.

Researchers at one of the leading universities are proving that linking sufficient quantities of microprocessors together can result in computer power that can rival the performance of the fastest processors in the world. California Institute of Technology (CalTech) has built a scientific processor dubbed the Cosmic Cube. It is made up of Intel 8086 and 8087 microprocessors—the same microprocessor chips that are used in the IBM PC.

Currently, CalTech has developed three computer systems employing microprocessors linked together. The largest system has 64 microprocessors, reportedly offering approximately one-tenth the power of a supercomputer such as the Cray–1 developed by Cray Research, Inc. According to one of the CalTech project's lead researchers, Charles L. Seitz, an associate professor of computer science, the unit costs about $80,000, compared with the Cray–1's $7 million-plus price tag.

The advantage of the Cosmic Cube design, Seitz said, is that a virtually unlimited number of microprocessors can be linked to tackle a large program.

Supercomputers operate by identifying similar operations (such as additions, subtractions and divisions) and performing them concurrently. However, current supercomputer architectures suffer from limits on how many concurrent operations can be performed at one time.

The Cosmic Cube architecture, Seitz explained, can be expanded with a virtually unlimited number of microprocessors that would, in effect, solve the concurrency limitations.

But one problem is that the Cosmic Cube's architecture does not lend itself to processing the same algorithms used on conventional supercomputers such as the Cray–1 or Control Data Corp.'s Cyber 205. While the Cosmic Cube is capable of executing the Fortran-based applications developed for supercomputers, many of those applications may have to be rewritten to take advantage of the concurrency offered by the Cosmic Cube.

Both Seitz and Fox estimated it could take ten to twenty years before processors like the Cosmic Cube take the place of currently used supercomputers.

But Seitz believes a commercial product using the Cosmic Cube architecture may be available in about five years.

Source: Adapted from P. Gillin, "Grace Hopper: Conscience of the Industry," *Computerworld,* 10 September, 1984, pp. 51–53, and T. Henkel, "Caltech Microprocessors May Rival Supercomputers," *Computerworld,* 30 January, 1984, p. 68.

To process information, a computer needs very specific instructions that explicitly state what is to be done. Special step-by-step instructions that lead to the same result every time are called *algorithms.* They are used as the basis for computer programs.

The computer processor unit is made up of a CPU and primary memory. The *CPU* contains the arithmetic-logic unit (ALU) and a control unit. The *ALU* is where all arithmetic and logic operations are performed. The *control unit* is used to sequence computer events according to program instructions, such as moving data between primary memory and the CPU or between input/output devices and primary memory. *Primary memory* is used to hold data and program instructions.

The control unit is composed of a program counter, instruction register, instruction decoder, and address register. *Registers* are storage locations within the CPU that are used as temporary staging areas. The ALU is composed of several registers, one of which functions as an *accumulator* to store ongoing results.

The *program counter* is used to keep track of where the next instruction is in primary memory. The process of retrieving an instruction is referred to as a *fetch.* Each program instruction is made up of an operation and address portion. The *operation* code refers to the action that needs to be taken, such as multiply, store, or print. The *address* portion refers to where the data can be found or should be placed. The operation portion of the instruction is put into the *instruction register.* It is then interpreted by the *instruction decoder,* and the internal computer circuits are set to perform the action specified.

The processing of a program instruction is called a *machine cycle.* It is composed of two parts. The first part is the *instruction cycle (I–Cycle),* in which the next program instruction is fetched from primary memory and then is decoded. The second part is the *execution cycle (E–Cycle),* in which the operation specified in the program instruction is carried out, and then the results of this action are stored.

A *number system* is simply a way of representing numbers. The number system we commonly use is the base 10 or decimal system. In the binary or base 2, the symbols used are limited to 1 and 0, which correspond to the binary nature of computer systems. Higher numbers are shown by using place values. Each place value is called a binary bit or *bit.*

A modification to the pure binary number system has been developed for encoding alphabetic letters, special characters, and numbers. Two of the more popular coding schemes are the *EBCDIC* and *ASCII.* The combination of bits referring to a complete character is called a *byte.*

A basic building block of modern computer circuitry is the semiconductor chip. These chips are composed of thousands of *transistors,* which are electronic components that function as semiconductors. A *semiconductor* is a solid-state device that can be made to conduct electricity under certain conditions and act as an insulator inhibiting electrical flow at other times.

Individual transistors can be combined to encode and store information, or they can be used to carry out arithmetic or logic operations. Semiconductor chips are used for the CPU, for primary memory, and for interface devices. *Interface devices* are used to coordinate the flow of electrical signals between two hardware units.

Primary memory chips are designed as RAM or ROM. *RAM* stands for *Random Access Memory,* which means that instructions or data can be read from this memory or written into it. Thus, RAM is sometimes referred to as *read/write memory.* The type of RAM chips most commonly used today are *volatile,* meaning that the memory contents will be lost when the electrical power is turned off.

ROM, or *Read Only Memory,* can only be used to read permanently loaded instructions or data. It is common, for example, to put a software language such as BASIC in ROM. Software that is stored in ROM hardware is called *firmware.* ROM uses storage technology that is nonvolatile, and thus is not affected by loss of power.

Erasable Programmable ROM or *EPROM* chips have been developed in which ultraviolet light can be used to erase the information stored on the chip. *EEPROM* or *Electrically Erasable Programmable ROM* chips can be used in situations where selected bytes of information need to be changed electronically.

A CPU that has been implemented on a single silicon chip is called a *microprocessor.* Microprocessor chips use many different internal designs, and the chips vary in appearance and capability. One of the specific ways in which they vary is in *dataword length.* This refers to the number of bits of data that can be retrieved from memory each machine cycle.

Several devices are used to support the microprocessor. One is the *clock* used by the control unit to establish the precise timing for when computer events are sequenced. *Buses* are electronic highways that are used to send electrical signals between functional units.

General-purpose computers are systems that can be programmed at different times to perform significantly different tasks. In contrast are special-purpose or *dedicated computers.* These systems are designed and configured to do one task very efficiently.

Computers differ in their *computer power.* This can be measured in a number of ways, such as the number of instructions that can be processed in a given time period. Other indicators of computer power are the dataword length and the size of primary memory.

For the most part, the smallest microcomputers and the largest supercomputers work in the same fundamental way. They use the von Neumann architecture, in which program instructions are stored in primary memory and used to sequence computer actions. But because the CPU is so much faster than any other computer components, an input/output bottleneck occurs when the

CPU works in a strictly sequential manner. More advanced computer systems use *overlap processing,* where data are being retrieved from storage while the CPU is performing another task. This allows *multiprogramming*, where the computer is processing more than one person's job on a time-share basis.

In the next chapter we will look at how input devices are used to collect data and enter them into the computer system for processing.

REVIEW QUESTIONS

1. How do computer algorithms differ from general instructions we use in everyday life?
2. What is the CPU? What are its major components? Where is the CPU housed?
3. Briefly describe the components and functions of the control unit.
4. Describe the machine cycle. Briefly discuss each of its components.
5. Briefly explain the binary system and describe its role in the operation of the computer. Convert 01000110 (binary) to its decimal equivalent.
6. How can letters, special characters, and numbers be encoded into binary code?
7. What is a semiconductor? Why is it important to the operation of a computer?
8. Compare RAM/ROM memory.
9. What is meant by the term *volatile?* How can volatility be overcome in RAM?
10. What is a microprocessor? How is the computer's microprocessor related to its power?
11. What are interface devices? Why are they needed?
12. The Alto Corporation is considering the purchase of a computer to carry out its quality control operations. Evaluate the firm's alternatives in terms of the three classification criteria mentioned in the text.

PART II COMPUTER SYSTEM HARDWARE

CHAPTER 4
INPUT

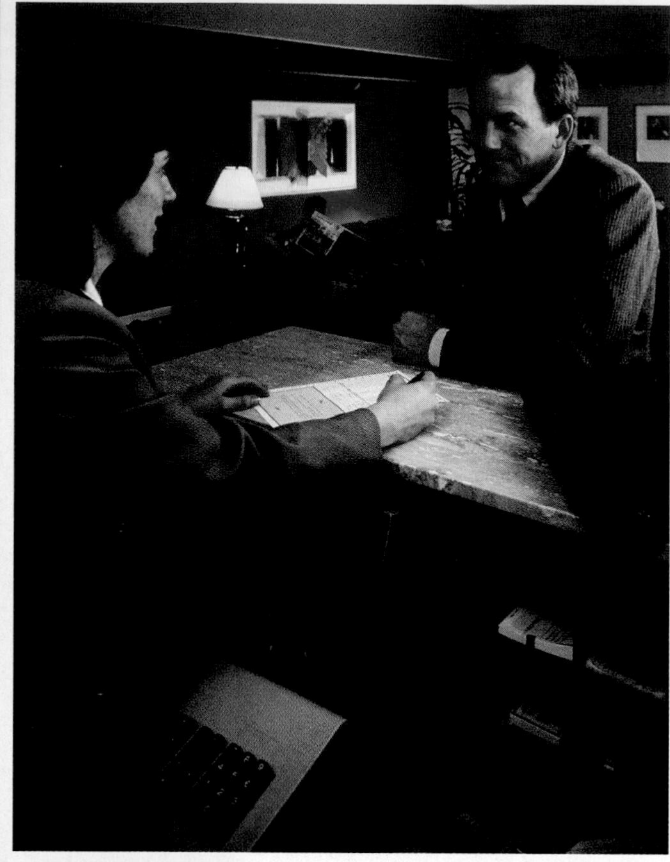

COMPUTERS AT WORK

Ramada Inn Uses Personal Computers to Take Reservations

PCs Are Permanent Guests

Personal computers are becoming permanent guests at hotels belonging to the world's third largest hotel firm.

With the installation of 635 IBM Personal Computers in hotels throughout the U.S. and Canada, Ramada Inns, Inc. has become the first hotel chain to use the micros as reservations terminals.

The Personal Computers have been linked to the company's main reservations computers in Phoenix and to other hotels in the chain which has 97,000 rooms in more than 600 inns and hotels.

Reservations can be sent via the Personal Computer to individual Ramada Inns or to one of four reservations centers in Omaha, Neb., Toronto, London and Frankfurt, West Germany. Presently, the Personal Computers have been installed only in the company's North American hotels.

Ramada personnel are able to make, change, and confirm reservations as well as supply guests with detailed information about any Ramada Inn worldwide.

When a travel agent or Pacesetter card holder calls for a reservation, all a clerk needs is the agent's code or the card holder's number.

The computer then prints all of the pertinent reservation information, including home address and credit card number.

A tutorial system was included right in the software because it was designed for people who have no prior experience with computers, and it actually shows them what every key on the keyboard does.

Besides saving time and adding to guest convenience, the Personal Computers are expected to reduce Ramada's communications costs, which will supposedly allow the hotel chain to keep its prices down.

Source: "Hotel Chain Using Micros in Reservations Net," *Computerworld,* 7 November, 1983, p. 36.

The foundation of computer processing is data. Data are so important to the basic operations of organizations that many managers now regard data as a corporate asset in the same way that money, buildings, and people are considered to be assets. Accessing, organizing, updating, and checking data are, therefore, essential and frequently performed tasks. We will focus on them in Chapter 8, "File and Data Base Systems."

For the present, we will concentrate on the fundamental devices and techniques used to collect data and enter it into a computer system for further processing. The preceding discussion of Ramada Inn's practice of using personal computers to make, change, and confirm hotel reservations illustrates a specific and very efficient means for data entry for that particular industry. Of course, organizations will have differing data entry needs, and this chapter will discuss various approaches, methods, and devices for data entry as well as how the way in which people interact with computers is changing.

You will learn to do the following:

1. Describe the two major approaches that are used in the data entry process.
2. Explain the methods that have been used to automate the collection of data at its source.
3. Describe some of the special computer devices that have been developed for use in specific industries such as supermarkets, banks, and distribution centers.
4. Explain how computer terminals used as data entry devices are becoming increasingly more like computers themselves.
5. Describe the present way that people must use to communicate with computers, and how this is progressing to a more natural human approach.

THE DATA ENTRY PROCESS

Every year the Internal Revenue Service processes the federal income tax returns of around 100 million Americans. How should the data from those returns be entered into a computer system? A supermarket serves hundreds of customers each day. How should the buying transaction be recorded and the thousands of items sold be accounted for? A small business pays its employees twice a month. When and how should the data from their time sheets be entered into the computer for processing? Each semester colleges need to update student records to reflect the classes taken and the grades received. In what form should the course grades be collected, and how should they be processed?

These are examples of the kinds of data processing tasks faced in organizations every day. In each case, data input is a major factor. For certain government agencies, retail operations, and industries such as insurance and medicine, the cost of entering data into a computer system has been estimated as one-third or more of the total data processing budget.

Organizations can enter data into a computer system in one of two ways or **modes.** First, an event can be recorded and processed as it happens. This is called a **transaction processing mode,** where the word **transaction** refers to a specific event. Or, a batch of similar transactions can be grouped for input and processing at a later time. This is called a **batch processing mode.** Each is appropriate in certain situations.

For example, in the reservation systems of airlines and hotels, the inventory of available flight seats or hotel rooms must reflect the current situation in an accurate and timely fashion. Therefore, each flight or room request, a transaction, needs to be processed immediately. In this case, transaction processing is the appropriate mode.

In contrast, a business that pays its employees twice a month doesn't need to update its payroll files daily. Rather, the time cards used for recording transactions can be collected every two weeks. This batch of data will then be entered and processed at a single time. This allows each employee's pay record, in turn, to be updated and a paycheck to be written. For this task, batch processing is most appropriate.

In the rest of this section, we will look at the ways Local College could use both the batch and transaction processing modes to input the data needed to register students for classes. As we will see, the devices and procedures associated with each mode vary in number of machines and amount of labor required, number of steps necessary, and flexibility, speed, and cost.

Batch Processing Examples

To register for classes, Local College requires each student to complete a Class Schedule Form. Bob Barker has elected to take Psychology 101, Math 105, and English 103. Along with 15,000 other students, Bob submits this form to the college administration during the one-week registration period. At the end of each day, all the forms are collected and sent to the Data Processing Center for processing. The DP Center must: (1) transform the human-readable data on the Class Schedule Forms into computer-readable data; (2) enter these data into the main college computer for processing; and (3) produce as output a class schedule for each student.

The DP Center could do this by using key-to-media equipment. For much of tne history of data processing, this approach has been the primary means for data entry. **Key-to-media equipment** is a general term for a number of keyboard devices that perform the single function of encoding data in a computer-readable form and placing it on material, or **media.** These media are then used to input data into the computer. In this example we will assume the DP Center is using keypunch equipment to produce punched cards, one of the oldest forms of computer media. In this technology, an operator types the data on the device's keyboard. Each keystroke causes a pattern of holes to be punched in a specially shaped card. A hole represents a "one", while no hole represents a "zero". Exhibit 4.1 shows a three-stage procedure for entering registration data using keypunch equipment.

In Stage I, a batch of completed class schedule forms is given to an operator at a keypunch machine. These forms, the source of data, are called **source documents.** In other applications, the source documents might be payroll time sheets, sales invoices, or credit card sales slips. The operator selects certain data from each source document for keying. The result is a set of punched cards representing the encoded student class schedule data.

In Stage II, each punched card and source document are given to a second operator. The goal here is to minimize the chance that data were keyed incorrectly. To do this, the operator rekeys the original data on a **verifier machine,** which compares the holes punched in the card with the rekeyed data. Any mismatches between the data, as first keyed, and the rekeyed data are shown by notches cut in the appropriate column of the card. If there were errors, a new card would then be repunched and verified. Cards without mismatches are notched on the right edge of the card.

Exhibit 4.1
Data Entry Using Punched Card Media for Batch Processing

In Stage I, data are keyed from each class schedule form, or source document. The resulting punched card is given to an operator, along with the source document, and the original data are rekeyed and verified in Stage II. In Stage III, a card reader reads the verified punched cards and sends computer memory a series of electrical signals. The result is a class schedule.

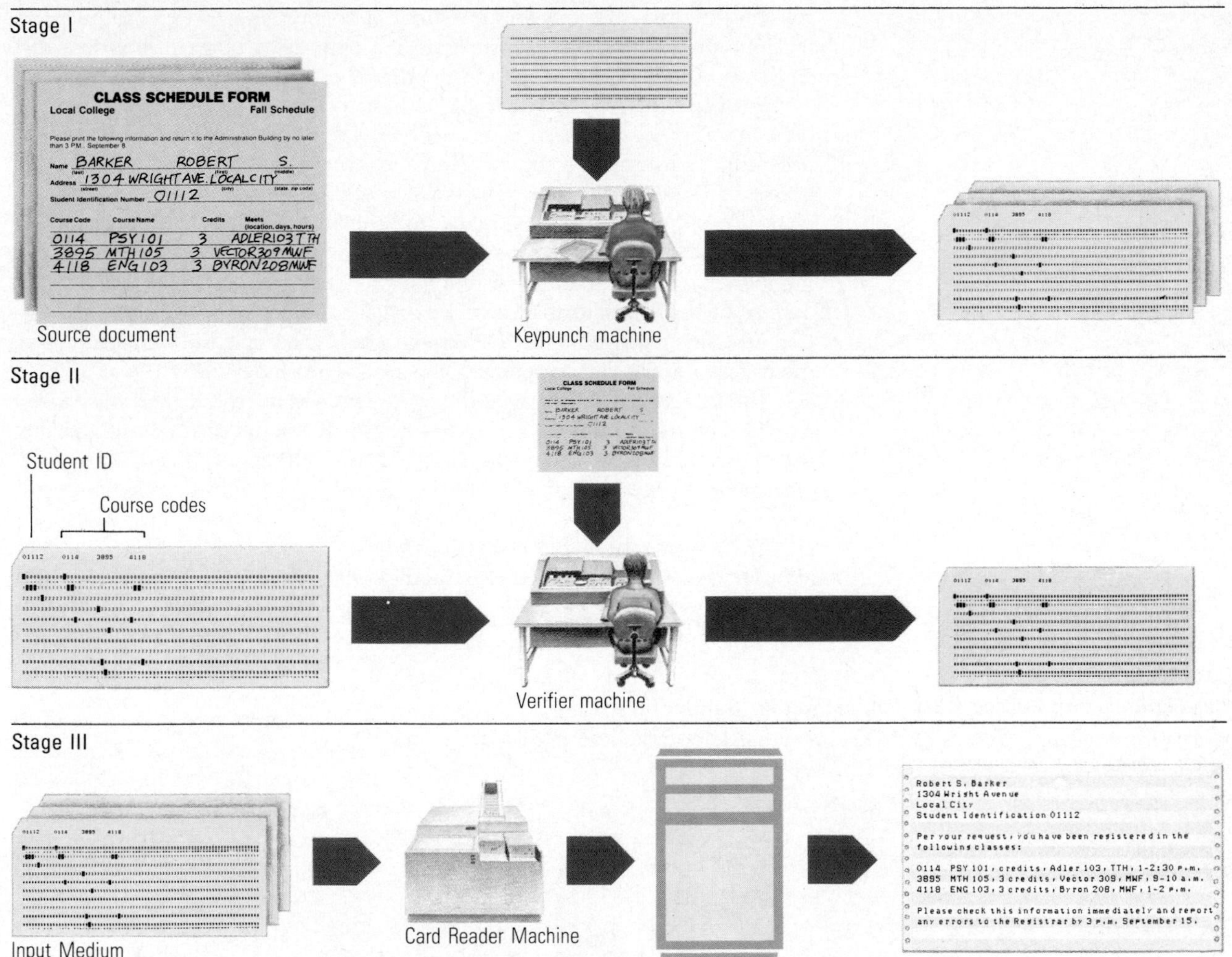

Stage III would begin later, when the DP Center schedules the computer to **run** or process the student's class schedule program. An operator would load a batch of verified punched cards in the input tray of the **card reader.** Upon appropriate signals from the computer program, the card reader would read each punched card and send computer memory a series of electrical signals representing the holes that were or were not punched in the card. These signals represent data encoded in some standard code such as ASCII. The result of this processing would be a class schedule for Bob Barker and each of the other students represented in the batch of punched cards.

This three-stage process has both advantages and disadvantages. One advantage is the verification process, which minimizes the chance that data were incorrectly keyed. GIGO ("garbage in, garbage out") is a familiar acronym that describes what happens when inaccurate data are entered into a computer system. If, for example, the first operator keyed 01111 instead of 01112 for Bob Barker's student identification number, the resulting class schedule would be completely useless. Thus, much effort and expense are involved in ensuring data are accurate when entered.

The main disadvantages of this three-stage process are the amount of labor and the special machinery required to ensure data accuracy. For example, rekeying the data is a costly duplication of labor and requires a special-purpose machine. In addition, there is a significant time delay between the time the source document is filled out and the time the processing actually occurs.

Source Data Automation (SDA) is a process that avoids the rekeying of data. In this process, special machines read data directly from the source document and convert it to computer-readable form. Assume, for example, that the Class Schedule Form was presented as a **mark-sense form,** in which rows of circles or bubbles replace the blank lines reserved for handwritten data (see page 95). A student would indicate his or her name, address, identification number, and course requests by filling in the appropriate bubbles (see Exhibit 4.2). As before, these forms would be collected in batches and sent to the DP Center. One employee in the DP Center would then take the forms and feed them into a **mark-sense reader,** a special-purpose device.

The mark-sense reader would be programmed to read data from specific locations on the document. To verify the accuracy of the reading process, the machine could be set to read a character several times and do a comparison. Mismatches between readings would be flagged for handling by a human operator.

The mark-sense reader could copy this data onto magnetic tape or a disk for later use as an input medium. Another approach would be to electrically

Exhibit 4.2
Data Entry Using Source Data Automation for Batch Processing

Source Data Automation (SDA) is a process in which special machines read data directly from a source document and convert the data to computer-readable form.

LOCAL COLLEGE — COURSE REQUEST
NAME BARKER ROBERT S. QUARTER 1 YEAR 86

Source document

Mark-sense reader

Offline
Magnetic tape
Magnetic disk

Online

Robert S. Barker
1304 Wright Avenue
Local City
Student Identification 01112

Per your request, you have been registered in the following classes:

0114 PSY 101, 3 credits, Adler 103, TTH, 1-2:30 p.m.
3895 MTH 105, 3 credits, Vector 309, MWF, 9-10 a.m.
4118 ENG 103, 3 credits, Byron 208, MWF, 1-2 p.m.

Please check this information immediately and report any errors to the Registrar by 3 p.m. September 15.

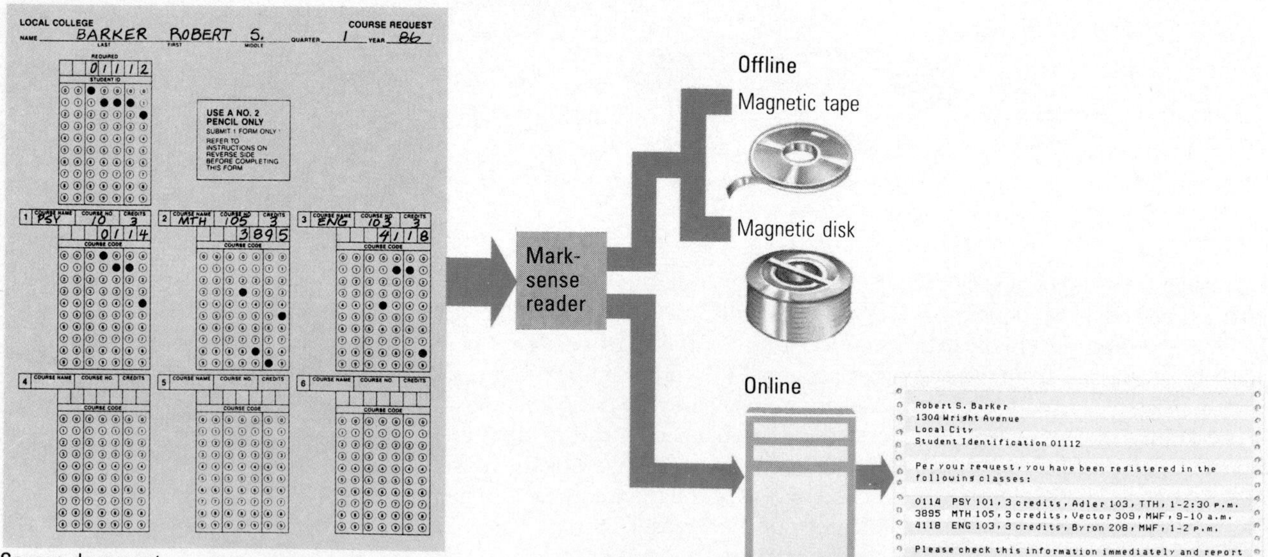

connect the SDA machine directly to the computer system. Then, under control of the computer program, a source document would be read by the SDA machine and the data entered into the computer's primary memory.

This latter case is an example of online processing. When devices are directly controlled by the computer's CPU, they are considered **online.** If the mark-sense machine was transferring data to a magnetic tape, however, it would be **offline** because the SDA machine would not be directly connected to the computer CPU or under its control.

The advantages of data entry via source data automation are significant. The process requires the labor of fewer people because the data do not have to be keyed. Reading and verification are done by the same machine. Another labor-saving feature is that an operator gets involved only on an exception basis. In contrast, the punched card method requires one operator to verify (retype) 100 percent of the data and another operator to handle the mismatches. With SDA, an operator has to resolve only the mismatches, which occur in approximately 1 in 1000 characters. And the speed of an SDA reader is generally measured in thousands of characters per second, compared to the tens of characters per second keyed by a keypunch operator.

The major disadvantage is that SDA machines are expensive and thus are generally limited to high-volume applications. Also, some SDA machines can read only a limited number of **fonts** or type styles. Later in the chapter we will discuss the advantages and disadvantages of several devices. Generally SDA devices have been used primarily with batch processing applications, but they can also be used in certain transaction processing situations.

Transaction Processing Examples

The two data entry examples just discussed both used the batch processing approach. Though the media are different (punched cards and mark-sense forms), data were collected and processed in batches. The two examples differed only in the way in which the source data were transcribed and verified.

A different approach to processing is shown in Exhibit 4.3a. Here, Local College Student Bob Barker completes the regular class scheduling form. He takes the form to the scheduling desk, where an operator keys student ID and

Exhibit 4.3a
Data Entry Using Computer Terminals for Transaction Processing

A terminal connected online to the computer allows an operator to make visual verification of data by comparing the screen display with the source document.

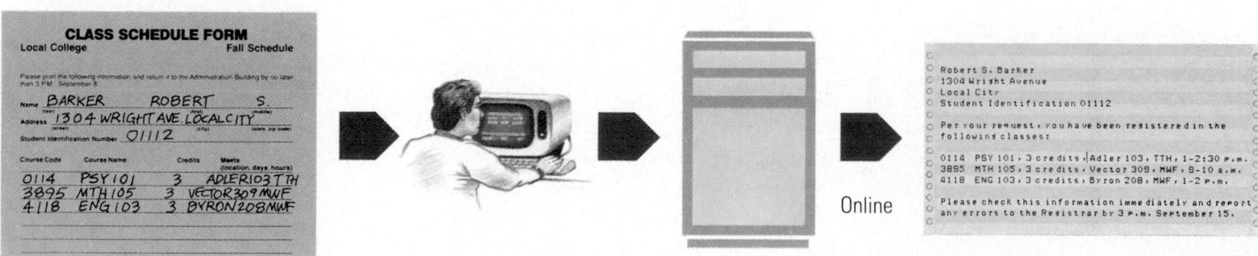

Source Document — Scheduling Desk — Student Class Schedule

course codes into a terminal connected online to the computer. Both the operator and Bob can make a visual verification of the data on the screen by comparing the screen display with the source document. The computer can also be used to test the accuracy of the data being entered—a process referred to as an **editing check.** For example, the computer could be programmed to reject any student ID or course numbers that contained characters other than digits. Or, the computer might perform a **range check,** ascertaining that certain data values fall within a specified range. If no students had been issued ID numbers above 55555, for example, the range check would immediately signal an error if the operator entered an ID number of 63281.

After these accuracy checks have been made, the computer would immediately process the request, check class openings, and display on the screen the results of this processing. The operator could then ask Bob if the information is correct and make necessary corrections at once. If the information was correct, but Bob got only two of the three classes requested, he could immediately request an alternate class. The final output would be a printed class schedule, which could be handed to the student instantly. In this case, both Bob and the operator are interacting with the computer. This interactive approach is an example of transaction processing.

There are several advantages to transaction processing. One is that business is taken care of at once, instead of hours or days later. Since the processing is done immediately, the information is more timely. If Bob didn't get all the classes he requested, this interactive approach would allow him to promptly make new choices based on what he has learned. Another advantage is that special-purpose machines, such as card readers or SDA machines, aren't eeded. Instead of having to rekey the data for accuracy, the computer is used to perform editing and range checks. In addition, the operator can visually verify the accuracy of both input and output.

The major disadvantage is that transaction processing requires sophisticated computer systems. The computer terminals are generally located at a distance from the computer, which requires additional hardware and software for remote data communication. To be cost-effective, these types of computer systems must have from ten to one hundred users sharing the computer. This will be discussed further in Part III, "System Support Software."

To carry this interactive approach one step further, why not let Bob interact directly with the computer? The computer terminal operator's main contribution is knowing how to interact with the computer system to handle the student's request. The need for a special operator could be eliminated if the computer program was revised. First, the computer could be programmed to display a **menu** or list of options, as well as **prompts,** or simple instructions that would tell Bob what to do (see Exhibit 4.3b). In addition, the DP Center would need to prepare a simple set of instructions that explained how to correct typing mistakes and move the **cursor,** a blinking symbol that shows where the next typed character will appear. Then Bob could easily select choices from a menu and type the required information. This conversational approach is one example of the significant move toward having users with no computer backgrounds interact directly with the computer, without having to go through intermediaries, such as keypunch, SDA, or computer terminal operators.

In this chapter we will be discussing the characteristics of key-to-media, source data automation, and computer terminal devices. Chapter 12, "Systems Development II," will show you how to apply this knowledge in choosing input devices appropriate for any given situation.

Exhibit 4.3b
Direct Interaction with the Computer

This conversational approach allows users without computer backgrounds to interact directly with the computer.

Menu

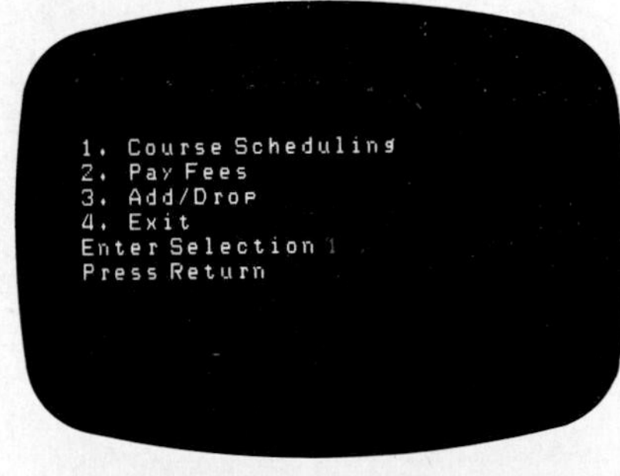

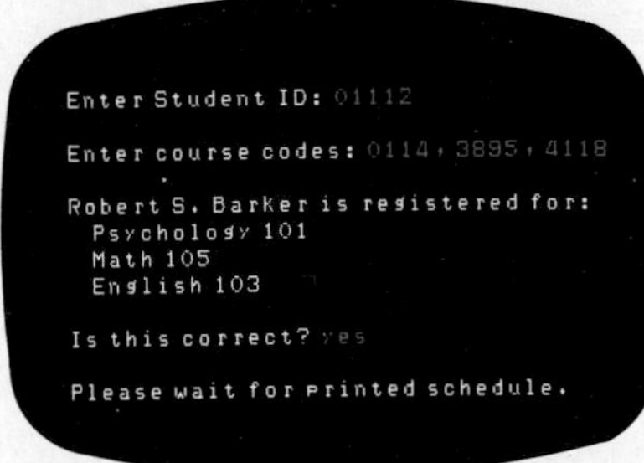

Enter Student ID: 01112
Enter course codes: 0114, 3895, 4118
Robert S. Barker is registered for:
Psychology 101
Math 105
English 103
Is this correct? yes
Please wait for printed schedule.

KEY-TO-MEDIA DEVICES

Key-to-media devices are used primarily for batch data entry. These devices include keypunch or key-to-punched card, key-to-tape, and key-to-disk devices. In each case, they are used to key data from source documents onto an input medium, which can be used later to input data under control of the main computer system.

In our example of the class scheduling, we explained the procedure of using **key-to-punched card devices.** Historically, this has been the most prevalent means of data entry, and was, in fact, the only method used for many years. The **punched card,** sometimes called the IBM card, has 80 columns in which particular combinations of holes represent numbers, alphabetic letters, or special characters (see Exhibit 4.4). The holes are patterned according to the Hollerith Code. This binary approach (hole or no hole) forms the basis for producing computer-readable data.

In the mid-1960s, **key-to-tape devices** were developed (see Exhibit 4.5). Because these devices allowed an operator to key data directly onto magnetic tape, this method of data entry offered significant advantages over key-to-punched card devices. First, one key-to-tape unit can be used for both keying and verifying. An input record keyed in and recorded on magnetic tape is read into a temporary storage unit. The original data are then rekeyed from the source document and the two results are compared to detect errors.

Second, since these devices operate electronically, they are quieter and allow quicker data entry than the mechanical punched-card equipment. Third, magnetic tape is a reusable medium and one tape can store the data equivalent of several thousand punched cards. Lastly, once keyed, data can be transferred to the computer hundreds of times faster from magnetic tape than from punched cards.

Exhibit 4.5

Key-to-tape devices allow an operator to key data directly onto magnetic tape. This method of data entry offers several significant advantages over mechanical punched-card equipment.

Exhibit 4.4

The punched card has 80 columns in which specific combinations of holes represent numbers, letters, or special characters. The absence or presence of a hole is the basis for producing computer-readable data.

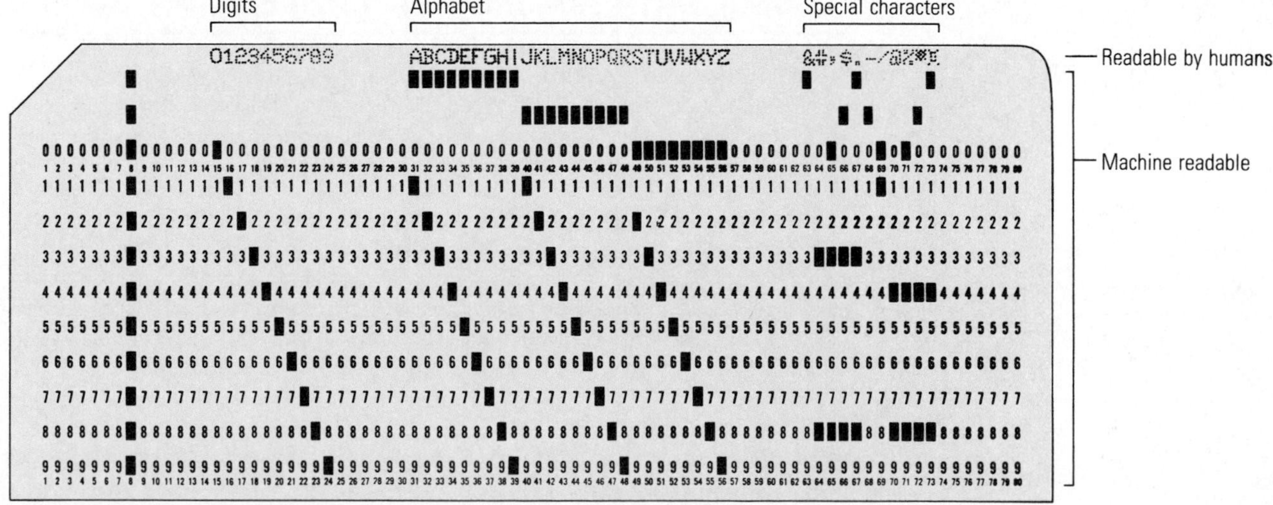

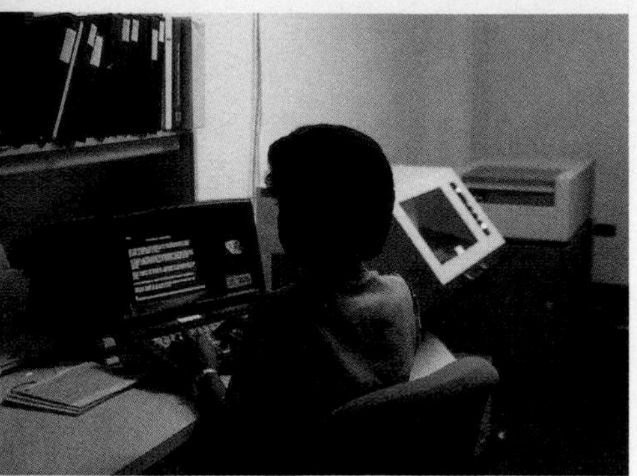

Exhibit 4.6

This operator keys data into the disk drive at her right. Developed in the late 1960s, key-to-disk devices replaced the key-to-tape unit by offering most of the same advantages along with several important new options to make data entry easier and more accurate.

In the late 1960s, **key-to-disk devices** were developed. These devices replaced key-to-tape units because they offered most all of the same advantages, as well as several significant new options. Key-to-disk data entry is generally done in a clustered or shared processor environment. Multiple data entry terminals or workstations are connected to and share one minicomputer. One of the major advantages is that the minicomputer can run editing checks on the data as they are being entered, and the operator can make corrections immediately. Second, stored programs can be used to display an image of the source document on the screen, with prompts being used to show what data items to enter next (see Exhibit 4.6).

The key-to-disk approach not only makes data entry easier, it is also less prone to error. The "clean" data can be combined with data previously stored on disk, such as customer name and address or part number and description. This significantly reduces the time necessary for entering data and prevents many errors because much keying is eliminated. When the data entry is complete, the appropriate data records are transferred to magnetic tape, where they can later be used for batch processing on the main computer system.

There are also **key-to-diskette data entry systems.** Often, these are microcomputers that are operated as single, or stand-alone, units, but more powerful computer systems can also function in a clustered environment. The data stored on the diskettes can be transferred to magnetic tape or, in some units, read directly from the diskettes into primary memory.

One important advantage of the key-to-media devices is that **data capture,** or conversion to computer-readable form, can occur at a different time than data processing. For batch processing applications, this allows a more efficient scheduling and utilization of the computer. A second advantage is that transferring encoded data to primary memory from input media (punched cards, magnetic tape, or disk) is thousands of times faster than entering the same data via a keyboard. Thus, the expensive, high-speed computer is used more efficiently.

The major disadvantage of key-to-media devices is that they are best used with batch processing. Further, at some point in the process, data must be keyed. This disadvantage can be avoided with source data automation devices.

SOURCE DATA AUTOMATION DEVICES

As we have seen, keying data is a slow and time-consuming process. Source data automation (SDA) speeds this tedious process by having a machine capture the data. Three common types of SDA are optical character recognition, magnetic character recognition, and voice recognition.

Optical Character Recognition

Source data automation devices that use light images to read data are classified as **optical character recognition (OCR)** machines. The many types of OCR machines differ significantly in the complexity of data that they can interpret.

Mark-Sense. One of the simplest optical readers used in SDA is the **mark-sense reader.** As described earlier in this chapter, the source document, the mark-sense form, is a form with rows of bubbles or circles on it

(Exhibit 4.7). A machine has been programmed to scan for marks in specific locations on these sheets. The mark-sense reader can distinguish only between dark, a space that's been filled in, and light, a space left blank. We saw in the class scheduling example how these forms are used. You may recall using a similar form when you took tests for admission to college or graduate school. The Educational Testing Service is one of the biggest users of these forms to score tests such as the Scholastic Aptitude Test (SAT).

Bar Codes. The use of **bar codes** represents the next level of optical complexity. You have probably seen bar codes on many things, from grocery items to paperback books. While about a dozen bar coding standards are in use, they all work on a similar coding principle. Numbers and letters are encoded by different combinations of bar widths and different widths of space between bars. For example, in the Universal Product Code (UPC) used in retail operations, bar widths are thin, medium, and thick, and the spacings between the bars are narrow, medium, or wide (see Exhibit 4.8).

Supermarket applications account for about two-thirds of the market for **bar-code readers.** Before the use of bar-code labels, supermarket checkers had to identify the item, read the price sticker, and then key in the item description and its price. This complete process can now be handled in one step, as a clerk passes the item

Exhibit 4.7

A portion of a mark-sense form

Copyright © 1983 by Educational Testing Service. All rights reserved. Princeton, NJ 08541 Reprinted by permission of Educational Testing Service.

SECONDARY SCHOOL ADMISSION TEST SIDE 1

1. YOUR NAME

Use a No. 2 pencil only. Make sure each mark is dark and completely fills the intended oval. Completely erase any errors or stray marks.

2. SEX: MALE / FEMALE

3. SCHOOL TYPE: PUBLIC / PRIVATE

4. GRADE: 5 6 7 8 9 10 11 12

5. REGISTRATION NUMBER

DO NOT MARK IN THIS AREA.

6. DATE OF BIRTH: MONTH DAY YEAR — JAN. FEB. MAR. APR. MAY JUNE JULY AUG. SEPT. OCT. NOV. DEC.

7. YOUR NAME: / HOME ADDRESS: / CENTER: / SIGNATURE: / TODAY'S DATE:

8. Indicate below the name and code number of each school you wish to receive your score report (maximum of six schools). Indicate only the schools that appear on the school list.

SCHOOL NAME (Print.) — NUMBER

Exhibit 4.8

Typical Bar Codes

Bar codes are frequently used today in retail stores to identify merchandise. Data are represented by varying bar widths and spacing between bars.

Courtesy Uniform Code Council, Inc.

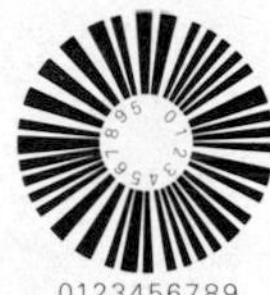

Number system character
0 = grocery products
3 = drugs and health-related products etc.

Manufacturer's identification number

Product/part code number

across a bar-code reader. In addition to speeding up the checkout process, the scanner is 10,000 times less prone to error than is a clerk keying in the data. Furthermore, the cost of adding bar codes to packages or canned goods is minimal, since it can be done as part of the manufacturing process.

Manufacturing and distribution account for the remaining third of the bar-code market. Railroads use trackside scanners to read the bar codes on the sides of passing cars. Traffic management applications such as train-yard scheduling and track switching are performed based on this information. Raw materials and parts in factories are laser-etched or labeled with bar codes. Scanner devices can then track these items as they move on conveyor belts. United Parcel Service uses gate-controlled conveyor belts to automatically sort bar-coded packages by destination.

OCR Fonts. While bar codes are adequate for product identification, they would require too much space in many of the paper-based transactions in industries such as banking and the utilities. Special fonts such as OCR-A and OCR-B (Exhibit 4.9) have been successfully used for printing machine-readable data on credit card slips, utility bills, insurance forms, and airline tickets.

Retailers such as Sears, Roebuck and J. C. Penney use **OCR wands** (Exhibit 4.10) to read merchandise tags coded in OCR-A font. This information is passed directly to a point-of-sale (POS) cash register, which processes the data to complete the sales transaction. The information on the sale amount and the merchandise sold can later be transferred to a central computer system for updating inventory and sales records and developing management reports.

Exhibit 4.9
A variety of OCR fonts are in use today.

TYPE	*INDUSTRY*	*EXAMPLE*	
OCR-A	Retail Manufacturing Remittance processing File tracking Distribution Libraries	ACDMNPRUXY0123456789>$/+#"⑀⑂⑁	
OCR-A Alphanumeric	Retail Manufacturing Remittance processing	ABCDEFGHIJKLMNOPQRSTUVWXYZ 0123456789>$/-+-#"	
OCR-B/Miti	(Europe/Japan) Retail	ACENPSTVX00123456789<+>-¥	
Multifont	Manufacturing Remittance processing European Giro market Airline	OCR-B 12L/12F 1403—OCR 407/1403	¥00123456789><++# ¥0123456789+# 00123456789><+# 0123456789

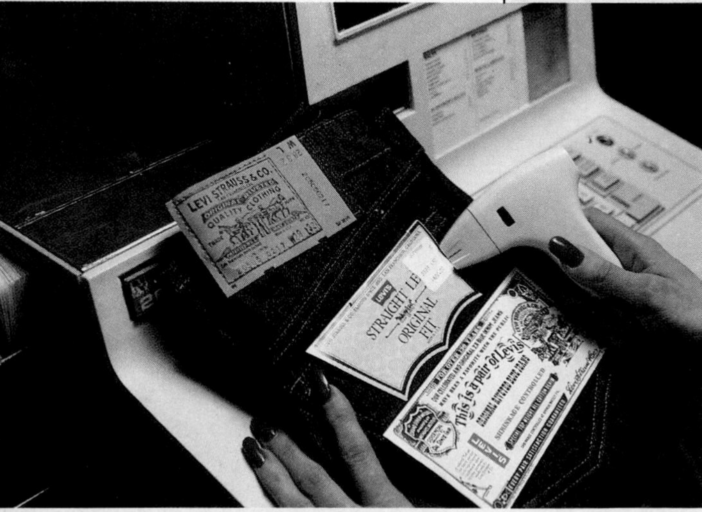

Exhibit 4.10
An OCR Wand
At J. C. Penney stores, OCR wands are used to read product and price information into the electronic cash register for processing.

OCR machines work by scanning a line of data and determining the shape of individual characters. Each character shape is digitized by shining a light beam on it and capturing the reflected pattern on a matrix grid. Because ink absorbs light and white space reflects it, the matrix grid can be digitized as a series of ones (dark spots) and zeroes (light spots). Each digitized matrix is then compared to a **template,** or predetermined pattern, representing each of the characters in a specified font style. The template with the fewest number of discrepancies is assumed to be a match for the character (see Exhibit 4.11).

Over the last twenty years OCR machines have been limited to reading primarily OCR-A and OCR-B fonts. Presently, inexpensive microprocessors are being used in OCR machines to give the capability of reading a wide variety of fonts, including those used in regular correspondence typing and by word processing systems. In addition, OCR machines made by Compuscan and Hendrix have multifont recognition capability within the same document, and perform this function without being told by an operator which styles are present.

In 1982, the United States Post Office began using OCR to automatically sort all first-class mail. All first-class envelopes are scanned by an OCR machine to read the bottom line of the address. The city, state, and ZIP code data are fed into an electronic directory to determine that the proper ZIP code has been used for the city. If it has, the machine then encodes the envelope with a bar-code label representing the ZIP code. This bar-code label is used for all sorting by the mail distribution centers. Those letters with handwritten addresses, which account for less than 20 percent of first-class mail, are processed without OCR support.

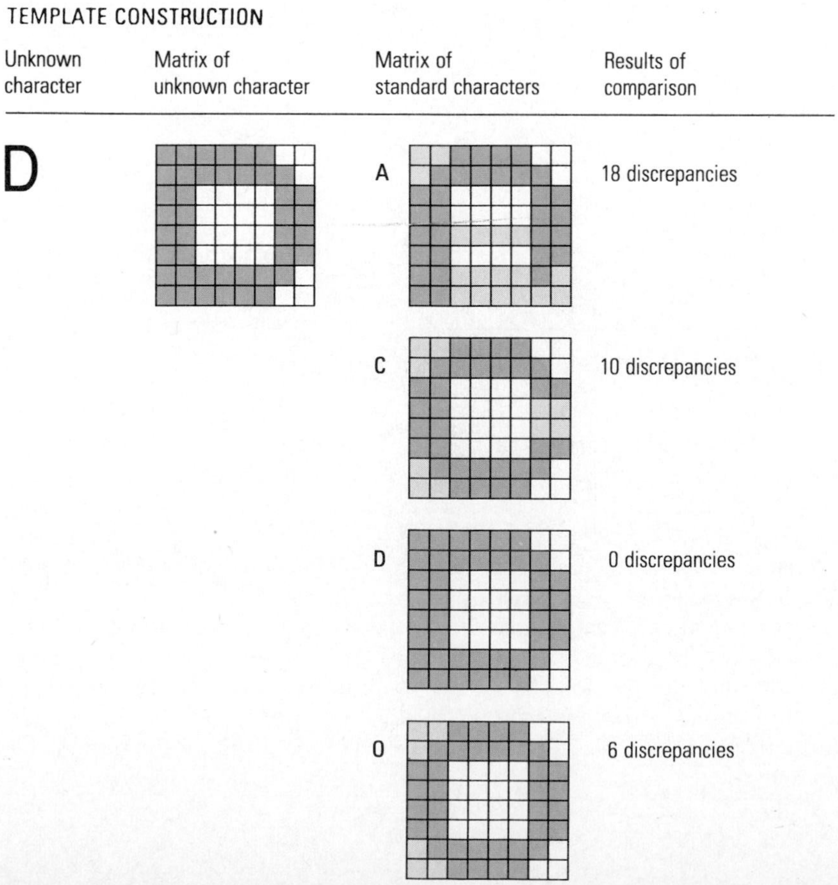

TEMPLATE CONSTRUCTION

Unknown character	Matrix of unknown character	Matrix of standard characters	Results of comparison
D		A	18 discrepancies
		C	10 discrepancies
		D	0 discrepancies
		O	6 discrepancies

Exhibit 4.11
Character Recognition Technique

For each unknown character, its digitized matrix is compared to a set of templates. The template with the fewest discrepancies is assumed to be a match for the character.

Handwritten Characters. The capability of OCR machines to accurately read handwritten characters has been quite limited so far. The greatest success has come in restricting handwriting to printing a particular style of number in designated boxes. Handwritten ZIP codes are being used by Federal Express as a means of sorting and rerouting packages in their overnight distribution centers. The Internal Revenue Service is using OCR machines to capture data from handwritten entries on tax form 1040EZ, the so-called short form. Note the directions given for writing numbers in Exhibit 4.12.

The tremendous variations in handwriting styles makes it very difficult to develop a general algorithm that will lead to an acceptable level of accuracy. Shape analysis, the most promising approach, counts the features of a character's geometry, such as the number of vertical lines, loops, and line endings. Thus an *o* would be characterized as a simple loop, and a *t* would be described as being comprised of a short horizontal line, a vertical line, a small loop, and four line endings.

Exhibit 4.12
Handwriting Instructions on an IRS Form

Department of the Treasury - Internal Revenue Service
1984 **Form 1040EZ Income Tax Return for Single filers with no dependents** (0) OMB No. 1545-0675

Name & address Use the IRS mailing label. If you don't have one, please print:

Please print your numbers like this.
1 2 3 4 5 6 7 8 9 0

Print your name above (first, initial, last)

Social security number

Present home address (number and street)

City, town, or post office, State, and ZIP code

Presidential Election Campaign Fund
Check box if you want $1 of your tax to go to this fund. ▶

Dollars Cents

Figure your tax

1 Total wages, salaries, and tips. This should be shown in Box 10 of your W-2 form(s). (Attach your W-2 form(s).) 1

2 Interest income of $400 or less. If the total is more than $400, you cannot use Form 1040EZ. 2

Optical scanner reading 1040EZ tax forms

Magnetic Ink Character Recognition

One of the earliest uses of character recognition machines was **Magnetic Ink Character Recognition (MICR).** MICR has been used since the 1950s in the banking industry as the standard method for processing checks. Checks are preprinted with the bank identification code and customer account number encoded in MICR characters (see Exhibit 4.13). After a check is presented for payment, the first bank to receive the check will encode the amount of money specified using a **MICR enscriber.**

Batches of checks are processed by the **MICR reader-sorter unit.** Data from the checks are read, and can be transferred to magnetic tape or directly entered into the CPU for processing. Daily updating of customer checking account balances would be done in this manner. Checks are then sorted for further routing to other banks, the Federal Reserve Bank, or the customer's account file.

Exhibit 4.13
Magnetic Ink Characters Shown on a Sample Check

Since the 1950s, the banking industry has used Magnetic Ink Character Recognition (MICR) as the standard method for processing checks.

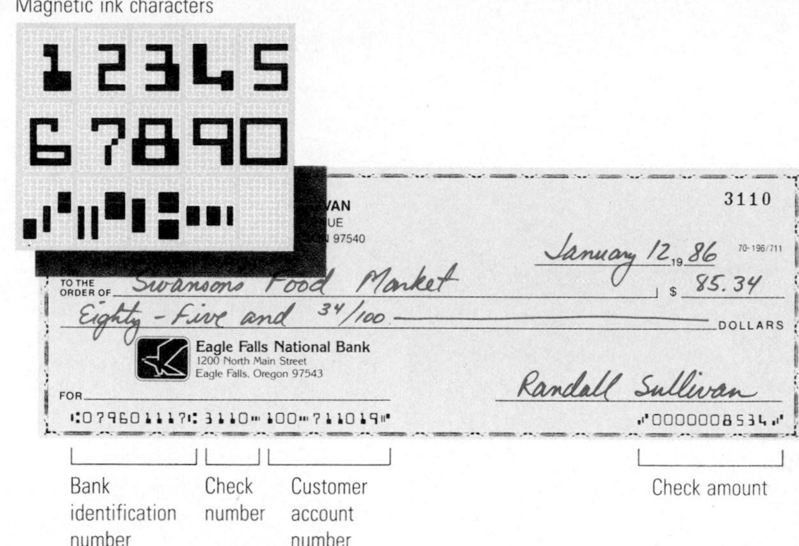

Recognition Equipment, Inc., has developed a system that optically and magnetically reads checks. The account numbers are still used for sorting checks, but the new aspect is that a digitized image of the check is created. The customer's monthly bank statement contains images of the cancelled checks rather than the checks themselves.

For MICR to be a true form of source data automation, checks would have to be read directly by a machine. Unfortunately, the handwritten check amount can't be consistently and accurately read by an OCR machine. Therefore, the amount has to be keyed in. This, of course, is a costly and time-consuming process, given the tremendous number of checks written each year (over 100 billion checks in the United States alone). Once the check amount has been keyed, however, machines can be used to automatically read and process the check data in the remaining stages (see Exhibit 4.14).

Exhibit 4.14
MICR Encoding Process and Sorter/Reader

A handwritten check amount can't be accurately read by an OCR machine and must therefore be encoded as MICR characters (left). The check data can then be read and processed automatically (right).

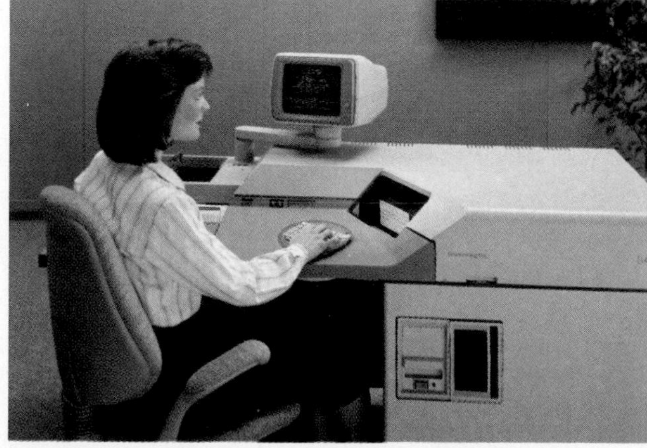

Voice Recognition

One of the newer technologies for automating source data entry is voice recognition. Quality control inspectors are able to speak into a microphone and specify which defects need to be corrected on specific parts on the assembly line (see Exhibit 4.15). This frees the inspector from the task of writing information on a form or typing it into a keyboard terminal. Voice recognition is a more natural, direct, and expedient source of data input.

Exhibit 4.15

Voice recognition in a quality control inspection application

In **voice recognition** systems, a microphone converts the spoken word into electrical signals. The signal patterns are processed to extract a set of identifying features, which are then compared to a set of voice templates stored in machine memory. The templates form the vocabulary of words the machine can recognize.

One technological obstacle to voice recognition devices is the consistency of the spoken word and its relationship to the stored template. An individual will say the same word differently at different times, depending on his or her energy level, mood, and health. Both colds and allergies, for example, can change voice quality. Even more variability occurs when different speakers say the same word. Physiology, age, sex, and geographic origin all contribute to this variation.

To reduce variability, speaker-dependent voice recognition systems have been developed. In this case, a specific individual "trains" the voice recognition machine by speaking a word a number of times. The resulting signal patterns are averaged, and a template is developed for the word. This process is repeated for each word that is to be recognized.

The other major technological obstacle in voice recognition is in developing instructions that allow the machine to recognize when one word has ended and another has begun. On the following page Exhibit 4.16 shows the demarcation between words as a silence. In reality, most people run their words together when speaking, rather than enunciating slowly and distinctly. This in turn greatly limits the accuracy of what is called continuous speech. To make a voice recognition system a viable option with today's technology, a number of restrictions have been required to increase the accuracy to an acceptable level. Most voice recognition machines are speaker-dependent, require a pause between words, and are limited to a vocabulary of about one hundred words.

The applications that can function within these constraints are generally warehouse and inventory operations, where codes often consist of single letters and numbers, and control is frequently handled by a few operators. The advantages of voice input in these cases are that users can communicate more naturally with a computer, continue doing other tasks with their hands, and move about as they input data.

COMPUTER TERMINALS

According to the International Data Corporation (IDC), a computer industry research firm, computer terminals are the predominant data entry device. The ubiquitous computer terminal can be designed for specialized industry applications or can be used for data entry and a multitude of other general-purpose functions.

Exhibit 4.16
The Voice Recognition Process

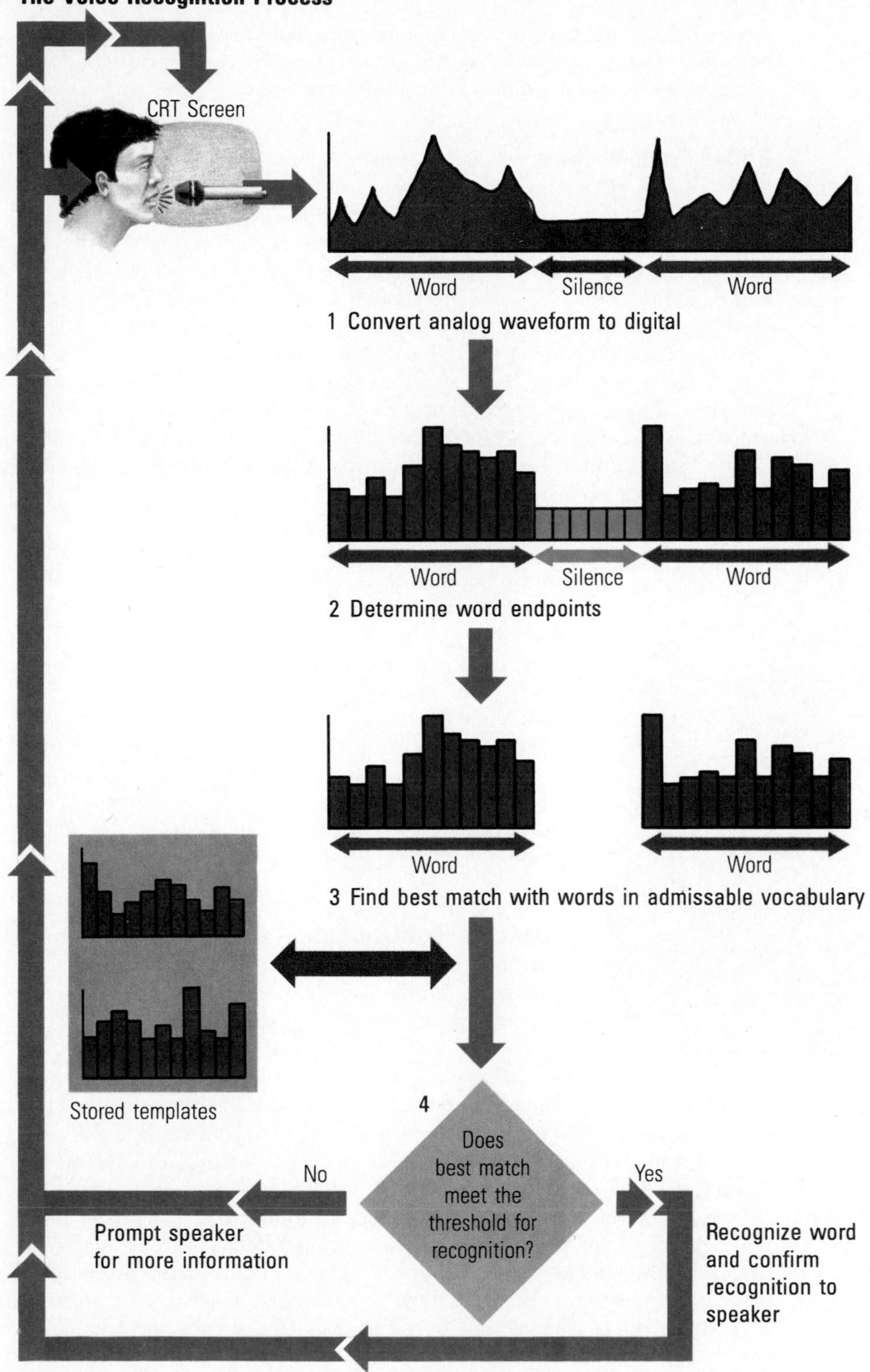

Special Function Terminals

There is an extensive market for computer terminals designed for special data entry functions. Specialized terminals are being used in retail, financial, source data collection, and word processing applications.

Retail Point-of-Sale. You are probably already somewhat familiar with **point-of-sale (POS) terminals,** as they are frequently found in supermarkets, department stores, and other retail operations. POS systems in supermarkets generally include an optical scanner, a cash register terminal, a printer, and often a voice-output unit, all of which are connected to a minicomputer located in the store, or to a larger computer located elsewhere. We have seen how optical scanners are used to read the bar codes on merchandise; the bar code identification number is used to check computer storage for a file containing the current price (see Exhibit 4.17). For systems with a voice-output unit, the computer file also contains the "voice print" for each item. The CPU processes these data and sends the results to the printer, which prints out a receipt listing product and price information. At the same time, a computer-generated voice may speak the item price.

Department store POS systems usually include an optical wand, a cash register terminal, and, often, a credit/authorization unit. The optical wand is used to read merchandise tags coded in special OCR fonts. For payments made with a credit card, the wand can be used to read the magnetic strip on the back of the card. The identification number can be transmitted over phone lines to a computer at the appropriate authorization center. A message approving or denying credit would be transmitted back and displayed on the POS terminal. These transaction data could then be used to update the customer's credit record and also to provide sales analysis and inventory control information for store managers.

Exhibit 4.17
Optical scanning in a supermarket

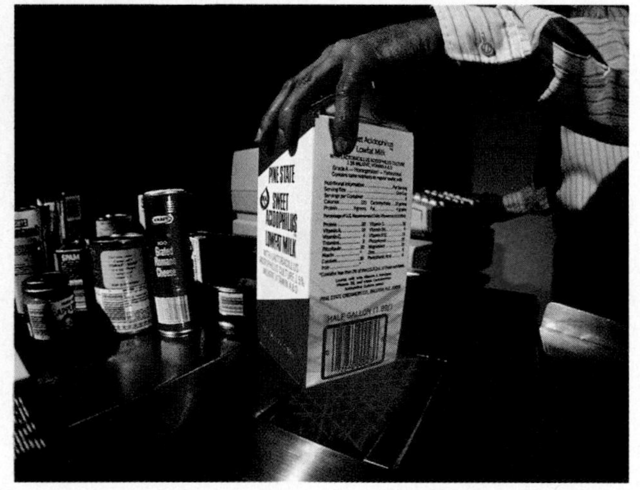

Financial Transaction. Savings and loan institutions and banks use special terminals to conduct financial transactions online from regional offices to computers located at some central site. When the savings account book is inserted into a specified slot in the terminal, the customer account number is read by the terminal. Amounts to be deposited or withdrawn are then entered into the terminal. The central computer updates the customer financial record and sends the information to the local printer, to be recorded in the savings account book.

Today, banks, supermarkets, gas stations, airlines, and many other businesses are providing services to consumers through automated teller machines (ATM). Customers have readily accepted and even demanded self-service in many retail operations. The ATM allows consumers to make routine financial transactions directly, at any time of the day or night, at convenient locations where they bank, work, shop, and travel. In addition, using ATMs to comput-

Exhibit 4.18

Today many businesses are providing services to consumers through automated teller machines and consumer transaction terminals. Diebold, Inc., is the leading supplier of these.

erize transactions, such as cash withdrawals and account queries, has reduced the number of employees needed by financial institutions.

Diebold, Inc., the leading supplier of ATMs, has also introduced a consumer transaction terminal used for displaying catalog listings and merchandise presently in stock. When a customer selects an item for purchase, the system can authorize the sale based on customer account information. The customer's account is automatically debited. This approach should be attractive to catalog merchants, because they can provide better customer service and reduce the personnel needed for check cashing, as well as minimize losses due to bad checks (see Exhibit 4.18).

Source Data Collection. In some instances, it's preferable to collect data at their source. For example, employees of utility companies need to record current readings of water, gas, or electric meters at residential and business sites. At the time of the reading, the customer ID number and meter information can be keyed into the terminal. Later, these data can be used by a utility's computer system to determine customer usage (see Exhibit 4.19).

Another task for which source data collection is suited is to record inventory status in retail stores and warehouses. A bar code reader is used to identify the product, and the operator keys in the number of units that are in stock. These lightweight, hand-held units are battery powered and have semiconductor memory chips to store the data for several hours. After the inventory is finished, the terminal can be connected to a telephone line and the data transmitted to a computer system for updating inventory stock records. Generally, these portable units cannot receive data from the computer system, however.

Exhibit 4.19

A utility meter reader using a portable terminal

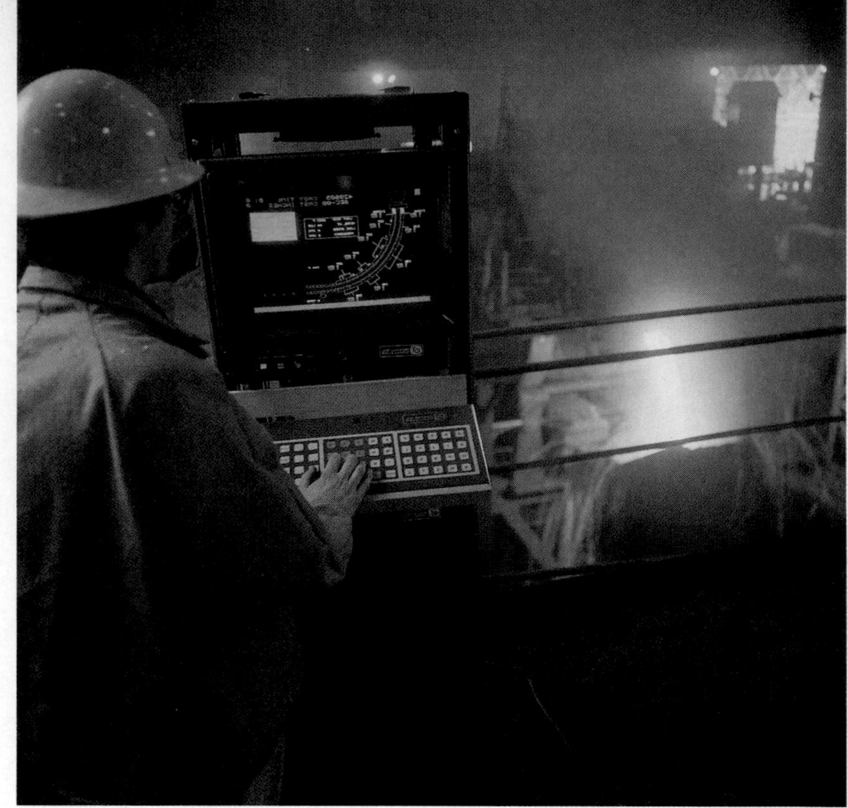

Exhibit 4.20

Terminals used in factories must be able to withstand extreme temperatures, dust, and other environmental conditions. At a U.S. Steel plant in Lorain, Ohio, this terminal is monitoring a continuous casting operation.

Many specialized terminals are used to collect data in factories. These terminals must be able to withstand extremes of heat or cold, high and low humidity, dusty conditions, and somewhat rugged handling. Rarely is entering data the primary job of the machinist, the assembler, the dockworker, or the forklift driver. Thus, terminals used in factory environments need to be both durable and easy to operate (see Exhibit 4.20).

Word Processing. The first step in the automation of the office has been the word processing system. These terminal-based systems enable a secretary or executive to create, edit, and print letters, memos, manuscripts, and reports faster and more accurately than with a typewriter. These computer systems have special software that makes the processing of text more effective and efficient. For letters and reports prepared in multiple drafts, the ability to electronically "cut and paste" eliminates the need for retyping the complete document. In addition, documents can be stored in electronic memory files and retrieved as needed. For mass mailings, form letters can be merged with names from mailing lists to personalize correspondence.

With some word processing systems, the screen will show a complete 8½-by-11-inch page of text. Many of these systems have special function keys to facilitate word processing. For example, there is a key for delete character, delete word, bold type, underline, and switching to next page.

However, general-purpose microcomputer systems have become quite powerful, and now have the large internal memory required for text processing. Many software packages now available for microcomputers provide extensive word processing capability and cost only a few hundred dollars. Because of this, the future for dedicated word processors—computers designed solely for this function—seems limited.

These two types of word processing systems are useful for someone who can come into the office to use them. But what about those people whose jobs require them to be at many different locations during the day, yet have the need to do word processing and the ability to send or receive data from a host computer?

For users in such circumstances, there are teleprinter terminals with keyboards and built-in printers to give hard copy output. The more advanced terminal also includes a small display screen. The terminal is portable and has a communication adapter to connect it to a standard telephone. Sportswriters, for example, need to be able to type articles in the press box as a game is being played (see Exhibit 4.21). At the conclusion of the game, the writer can quickly file the story by sending the text and statistics over the telephone lines to the newspaper's computer. At that point, the text can be checked by an editor and electronically typeset, ready for immediate use.

Exhibit 4.21

This sportswriter uses a portable terminal to cover a game between the Celtics and the Kings.

Portable Units. In recent years, complete microcomputer systems have become available as portable units, which can be used as data entry devices or as stand-alone processing systems. Osborne–1, the initial entry into this market, had a five-inch screen, two diskette drives, a full keyboard, and software packages for word processing, BASIC programming language, and file retrieval. All of this was packaged in a carrying case that could fit under an airplane seat. Although the Osborne–1 itself is no longer offered, it is easy to see why portable computers are a fast-growing segment of the personal computer market. Their portability adds to their usefulness, allowing a business professional to make constructive use of time that would ordinarily be wasted, such as time between appointments or during travel (see Exhibit 4.22).

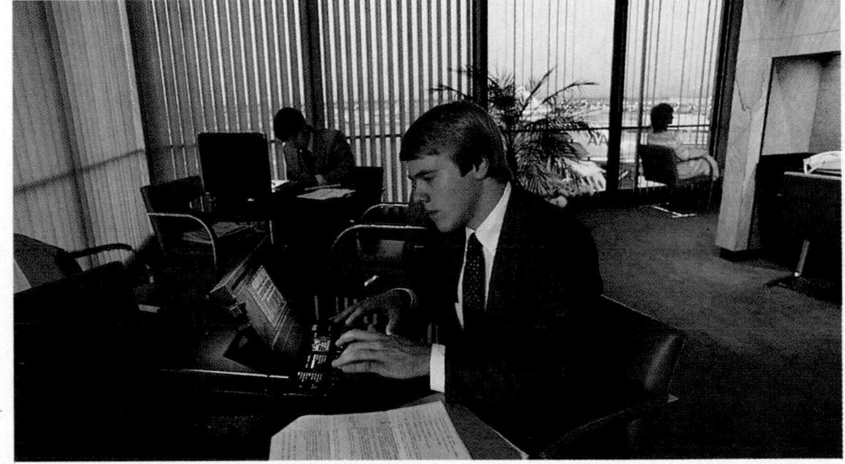

Exhibit 4.22

Portable computers are a fast-growing segment of the personal computer market, allowing business professionals to make use of time spent in travel or between appointments.

General-Purpose Terminals

Computer terminals that can be used for online data entry and many other functions such as word processing, electronic mail, time-sharing, and program development have become widely used. Five years ago CRTs were classified as dumb, smart, and intelligent, but these distinctions are blurring as more and more capability is being added to all terminals.

Dumb Terminals. Very basic devices used to enter data and display results were called **dumb terminals.** These terminals were connected to a computer system that did all editing of data and whatever processing that was required. Since the dumb terminals always had to be in a conversational mode with the host computer, much of the CPU time was taken up with data communication and processing of relatively simple tasks.

Smart Terminals. To avoid tying up so much CPU time, the **smart terminal** was designed with its own memory and editing capability. It enabled users to store several pages of text or data locally and edit them for correctness. Simple editing includes functions such as moving the cursor easily around the screen and adding or deleting characters or a line of text. The editing capabilities of a terminal are permanently programmed by the vendor and put into ROM. The clean data can then be sent as a block of data for more extensive processing. Thus, the CPU could be used primarily for processing programs, rather than being tied up by editing and data communications tasks.

As it became cheaper to increase memory capacity and the terminal market became very competitive, vendors added more capability to terminals and lowered their prices. Terminal memory capacities grew, and more sophisticated editing functions were provided. Since the resulting price for a smart terminal with increased performance capability was about equal to that for the dumb terminal, the demand for dumb terminals all but disappeared.

Intelligent Terminals. As inexpensive microprocessor chips became available, **intelligent terminals** were developed in the late 1970s. These terminals each had their own small CPU, which provided significantly more processing capability than smart terminals had. An intelligent terminal can run certain kinds of programs without being connected to the host computer, allowing it to process as a stand-alone computer would. This advance provided increased computing power to local users. However, if more sophisticated programming tasks were required, the intelligent terminal could make use of the capabilities of a large host computer.

Unfortunately, not every terminal can be connected to every computer, because encoding schemes, transmission standards, and other features vary among different vendors. Increased data communication capability has been built into the intelligent terminal to facilitate connection to a variety of host computers. These concepts and concerns will be discussed in detail in Chapter 9, "Data Communications."

Microcomputers. A major use of the microcomputer has been as a personal computer. That is, a person at home or at work does his or her computing tasks on a stand-alone machine. As users become more sophisticated in their use of personal computers, they sometimes want to connect their computers to larger computers for special applications. To facilitate this, data communication equipment was added, allowing the microcomputer to do all the data entry functions of an intelligent terminal, in addition to doing stand-alone computing. TeleVideo Systems, Inc., has shown how an intelligent terminal can be made into a microcomputer system.

Workstations. The latest development in general-purpose terminals is called the **workstation.** This is an enhanced microcomputer that can perform data or word processing functions, work as a dumb terminal connected to a host computer, and do data communication tasks such as electronic mail. These exciting advances are just the beginning of a trend bringing more flexible capability to the user.

Professional Issue

Human-Computer Interface

The **human-computer** interface, often called the man-machine interface, refers to the basic problem that arises when people have to communicate with machines. What is best and most comfortable for an individual is not always the most efficient use of the machine.

When any technology is new, it is costly and awkward to use. However, because they perform a necessary task of some kind, people are forced to adapt to the machine. As the technology reaches a certain level of maturity, it can then be designed in a cost-effective manner to meet its users' needs more efficiently and conveniently.

For much of the history of computing, people have been limited to using some form of keyboard as the primary way to enter data or give commands to the computer. At first, this was through keypunch machines and, more recently, through key-to-disk systems. Computer terminals, both special function and general-purpose, are now the primary data entry device, and they use different types of keyboards. But alternative ways of interacting, including touchscreens, "mice," and voice, have emerged as methods for more natural human interaction with the computer.

Keyboard

Keyboard designs reflect the nature of users and their purposes. Note that, in the collection of keyboards shown in Exhibit 4.23 on page 108, there are significant differences in the number, placement, and function of the keys.

For example, the point-of-sale cash register used at McDonald's has keys bearing the names of McDonald's products. "Big Mac" appears on one key and "Reg Fries" on another. The clerk presses the key once for each time the particular item was requested. In other words, for an order of two cheeseburgers, the cheeseburger key would be pressed twice. The microprocessor inside the cash register is programmed to retrieve from memory the current price of that item. The appropriate price is used to automatically calculate the cost of the order. This keyboard simplifies the data entry process because the employee doesn't have to know either product codes or prices. Results are totaled quickly and accurately.

Also shown is a keyboard typically used with general-purpose terminals. The main body of this keyboard is very similar to the keyboard arrangement of a standard typewriter. The history of the **QWERTY** keyboard goes back to the early days of the typewriter, in the late 1800s. To keep the closely spaced mechanical arms from tangling, the keyboard was designed so that the arms for frequently typed characters would be far apart.

Exhibit 4.23

Keyboard designs reflect the nature of users and their purposes. Shown (clockwise from top left) are keyboards used in food service, automated teller services, bookkeeping, and graphics design.

Since computer systems use electronic keyboards, it would seem that the keyboard should be rearranged to increase productivity rather than continue the tradition of the early mechanical typewriters. An alternate keyboard arrangement has been proposed by **Dvorak** (see Exhibit 4.24). His philosophy is that people could increase their typing speeds if the most frequently used keys were put in the home row and arranged to make better use of both hands. The home row includes the vowels under the fingertips of the left hand and the most common consonants under the fingertips of the right hand.

Studies have shown increased productivity in typing speeds of between 10 to 50 percent over standard keyboards. Many computer manufacturers now offer Dvorak keyboards. The chances that this approach would displace the QWERTY keyboard seem limited, however. First, it would require retraining millions of people. Second, alphabetic letters are really only a small part of computer input. Third, other than for batch data entry, keystroke speed is less important than having a keyboard that is familiar and easy to use.

Until ten years ago, the standard keyboard was sufficient for keying in data or entering programming instructions in various computer languages. However, as computer systems became more interactive, users, many now not computer experts, needed to be able to select functions from a menu. What was needed was an enhanced keyboard, to simplify word processing, spreadsheet analysis, and data queries.

A **numeric keypad,** a set of numeric keys similar to those on a calculator keyboard, was added to the regular typewriter keyboard. These keys allow faster entry of numeric data. (Recall that, on a standard typewriter keyboard, numbers are in the top row.) **Arrow keys** were added to facilitate the movement of the cursor. **Function keys** were added to provide a way to command certain common tasks in one step, rather than making several keystrokes to accomplish the same thing. For example, a function key could be defined for activities such as HELP, PRINT, GRAPH, and END. Even though the enhanced keyboard can provide more efficiency, it has several important drawbacks for people using the computer interactively. Many people who don't know how to type feel uncomfortable with a keyboard system. And there are those who don't want to use a keyboard—regardless of its convenient design. Some executives consider keyboarding to be clerical work, and thus are concerned about loss of status. Using a keyboard is also slow, and often requires you to split your attention between the screen and the keyboard to find special keys.

Exhibit 4.24
The Dvorak Keyboard Layout

Alternatives to the Keyboard

There are several alternatives to the keyboard that allow a user to point to options or functions on the screen. One is the light pen, shown in use below. Instead of actual function keys to press, the screen will display boxes that contain the names of functions or a menu of options. Selections are made by touching the light pen to a specific area on the screen. Touching the screen at a particular location with the light pen causes a change in electrical potential, which signals the computer to perform specific actions.

Exhibit 4.25
Touching a light pen to a specific area of a screen causes a change in electric potential and signals the computer to perform specific actions.

Exhibit 4.26

With the Hewlett-Packard Touchscreen, a user can interact with the computer simply by touching a fingertip to the screen.

Instead of a light pen, the Touchscreen by Hewlett-Packard allows the user to interact with the computer through the touch of a finger. Shown above is a spreadsheet program using the HP Touchscreen. Functions such as LOAD and STORE, EDIT, and EXIT are shown on the bottom of the screen. These can be touched with a finger to select the function desired. Showing where data should be located or where they should be moved can be done by pointing to a specific location on the screen.

In these different methods for selecting functions or moving data to different locations on the screen, the functions have been specified in words such as LOAD, DISPLAY, and EXIT. The next advancement for making the human-computer interface more natural is the use of **icons.** These are graphic symbols for functions. Icons used with Apple's Lisa computer are shown below. There are symbols for new document creation, application tools, and documents in computer storage.

Exhibit 4.27

Icons are graphic symbols for functions that make the human-computer interface more natural. Shown here are icons first made popular by Apple's Lisa computer.

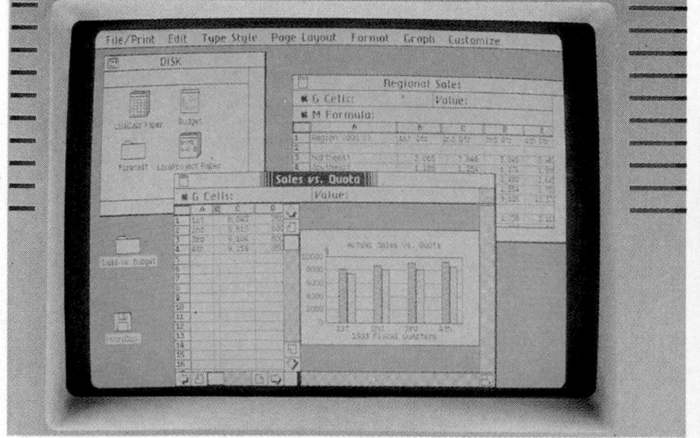

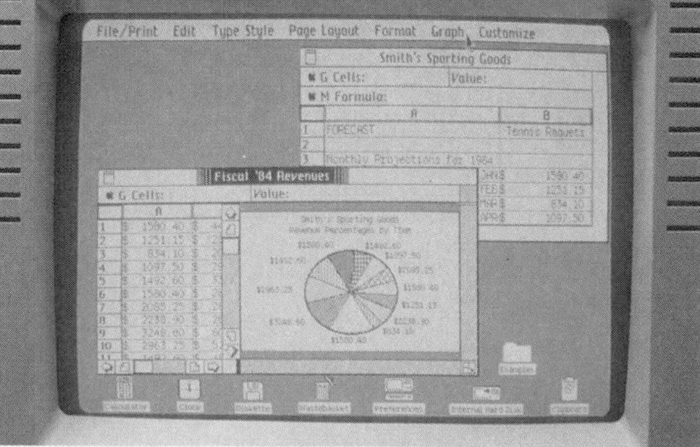

The Lisa computer was introduced in 1983. Though the concept was exciting, the computer had limited success primarily because it was very expensive for a personal computer (around $10,000). In 1984, Apple introduced several microcomputers that were derived from the Lisa concept. The one having the greatest impact is the Macintosh. It uses the icon approach and is priced around $2000. In its first year, Macintosh sales were $500 million! The Macintosh is being used in small, medium, and large organizations. One of the largest single purchases was by the University of Texas at Austin, which bought 13,000 Macintosh microcomputers for educational and administrative uses.

Apple's concept with the Lisa and the Macintosh is to make the screen layout resemble a desk top and allow you to function as you normally would at your desk. That is, you select documents from the file folders, use a calculator to do arithmetic, write letters and file them, and throw away waste in the trash can (see Exhibit 4.28).

With the Lisa and the Macintosh, you select functions by moving the cursor over the icon. The movement of the cursor is controlled with a hand-sized box called a **mouse.** As you move the mouse around your desk top, the cursor moves accordingly on the screen. For example, if you move the mouse to the left, the cursor moves to the left on the screen. To select an item, you simply position the cursor on it and push the button on the top of the mouse. Note, in Exhibit 4.29 on page 112, the rather dramatic picture contrasting the usual way of selecting functions by using function keys or keystrokes with the pointer-icon approach of MacIntosh.

Exhibit 4.28

Apple's Macintosh screen layout resembles a desk top, complete with calculator and file folders. Moving the mouse around a desk top causes the cursor to move accordingly on the screen.

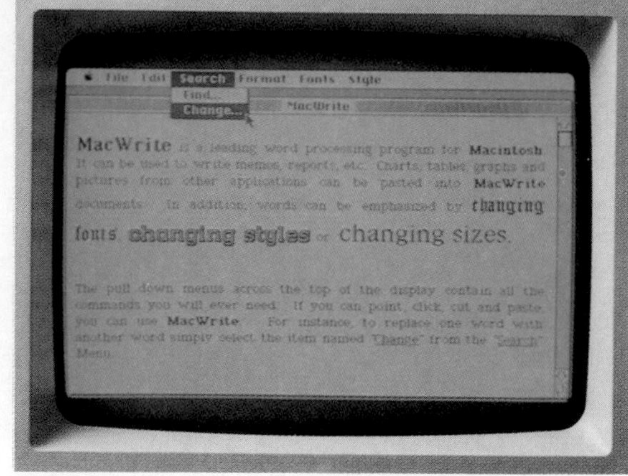

Exhibit 4.29

The pointer-icon approach of Macintosh greatly simplifies the usual way of selecting functions with keystrokes or function keys.

Earlier in this chapter, we discussed voice recognition systems and their use for source data entry. The same technology could be used to select functions or enter data.

Texas Instruments has a voice recognition unit that has been used successfully with, for example, spreadsheet applications on microcomputers. This type of application is not constrained by speaker-dependent voice systems, which can recognize only a limited number of word sounds. A spreadsheet program would generally be used by one executive on his or her personal computer. The individual functions are specified by speaking one or two words such as *Worksheet, Column Width, Move, Copy,* and *Add.* Numbers would be communicated in the same manner.

We have discussed the keyboard, pointing devices that are used with text or icons, and voice input as ways of interacting with the computer. The dominant technology is the keyboard, and most experts believe it will continue to be so for the forseeable future. A major reason is that the pointing devices don't do away with the keyboard. Any applications requiring substantial data or text input can be done faster with the keyboard. Pointing devices are a complementary input means, primarily useful for selecting functions.

The study of the best way for people to interact with the computer is part of what is called ergonomics. **Ergonomics** is the science of designing machines for use by people. In this section we have concentrated on the input interface. In the next chapter we will discuss various forms of obtaining information output. In Chapter 19, "Issues and Concerns," we will examine the broader issues of ergonomics to determine how computers, the work itself, and the worker's environment can be better designed to accommodate the needs and concerns of users, while enabling them to attain a high level of productivity.

Hand-Held Computers Speed Service Reports

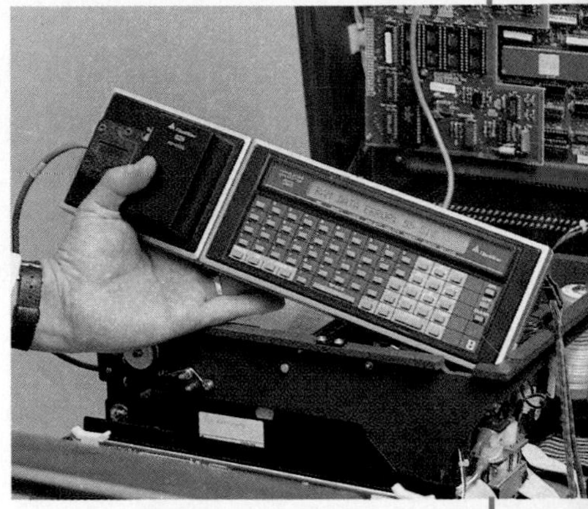

After several hours of intricate electronic repair, the job is finally done. The equipment is back in perfect working order. The service technician, rather than reflecting on a job well done, now has to concern himself with completing those cursed service call reports and submitting them to the home office.

Sound familiar? Not anymore at Marquette Electronics, Inc., a manufacturer of high-tech computerized electrocardiogram equipment. The reason is that Marquette's service technicians use the very things that they are most comfortable with to compile and transmit their service call reports: computers.

With the use of hand-held computers manufactured by Quasar Co., Marquette technicians save time in writing out each report and mailing it to Marquette's headquarters.

"We figure the hand-held computers will pay for themselves in just two years—even less depending on how much we can utilize them for diagnostic purposes," commented David L. Ivers, Marquette's vice-president of technical services.

He indicated that the use of the hand-held computers has resulted in more timely and accurate service call reporting and, therefore, more timely and accurate invoicing for service. After choosing the Quasar systems, Marquette began to develop software in January and had the service call reporting system on-line by May.

SPEEDS SUBMISSIONS

Marquette has approximately 80 service technicians who prepare a total of 50 to 60 work orders per day. When the technicians were preparing them manually, they would tend to wait two or three weeks and then submit several at a time.

This resulted in service invoices being mailed as long as six weeks after the service was performed in some cases. Today, 80% of the service call reports are prepared and transmitted in the same week the service was performed, Ivers said.

Each technician's hand-held computer incorporates, among other programs, a program to provide "prompts" for the technician to enter the information that Marquette will need to record and invoice properly the service call he has made.

The computer "asks" the technician for such information as his identification number; the customer's account number, P.O. box number and address; repair start and stop dates and times; model number(s) of equipment serviced; parts numbers and quantities used; and other expenses incurred by the technicians in performing the work.

All of this is transmitted via a modem, also supplied by Quasar, over a WATS line to Marquette's internal computer system. From that point, each service report is edited for errors, used to prepare an invoice if necessary, and then permanently filed, Ivers said.

Source: "Hand-Held Computers Speed Service Reports," *Computerworld,* 28 November, 1983, p. 57.

SUMMARY

The foundation of computer processing is data. A major effort is expended in entering data into the computer and ensuring their accuracy. Organizations can enter data into a computer system in one of two modes. An event or *transaction* can be recorded and processed as it happens, in the *transaction processing mode.* Or, a batch of similar transactions can be grouped for input and processed at a later time, in the *batch processing mode.* Transaction processing is used when time and currentness are important, as in reservation systems for airlines and hotels. Batch processing is used when immediacy of results is not as important as processing efficiency.

Key-to-media equipment is a general term for a number of keyboard devices that perform the single function of encoding data into a computer-readable form and placing them on material or *media.* Key-to-media devices are used primarily for batch data entry. These include key-to-punched cards, key-to-tape, and key-to-disk devices. Historically, the punched card was the primary input medium, but the key-to-disk units are now the predominant form of this approach to data entry.

Source documents, such as payroll time sheets, sales invoices, and credit card sales slips, are the source of data used as input for computer processing. *Source data automation (SDA)* is a process that avoids the keying and rekeying of data. These special machines read data directly from the source document and convert it to computer-readable form. Three major types of SDA are optical character recognition, magnetic character recognition, and voice recognition.

SDA devices that use light images to read data are classified as *optical character recognition (OCR)* machines. These include *mark-sense readers,* where data are encoded as dark (a filled-in space) or light (a space left blank) marks on a sheet, and *bar codes,* where numbers and letters are encoded by different combinations of bar widths and different widths of space between bars. For more complex applications, special character type styles called *fonts* are used. OCR-A and OCR-B are fonts used for printing machine-readable data. The capability of OCR machines to accurately read handwritten characters has been quite limited. *Magnetic ink character recognition* (MICR) has been the standard method used since the 1950s in the banking industry for processing checks using MICR characters. In *voice recognition systems,* the electrical signal pattern of spoken words is compared to that of the stored voice templates vocabulary. Most voice recognition machines are speaker-dependent, require a pause between words, and are limited to a vocabulary of around one hundred words.

When devices such as SDA or key-to-media machines are used to copy data onto magnetic tape or disk for later use as an input medium to the main computer system, they are considered *offline.* When the devices are directly connected to the computer and controlled by the computer's CPU, they are considered *online.*

Much time and effort are expended to ensure that data encoded are accurate. With key-to-media devices, the input is keyed two separate times, and the results are compared or *verified.* Differences are shown as errors and rekeyed. SDA machines are programmed to reread a character several times for verification. The computer can also be used to test the accuracy of the data entered. This process is called an *editing check.* It could involve *range checks* to ensure that data are within certain reasonable value limits.

Computer terminals are the predominant data entry device. They can be designed for specialized industry applications, or can be used for data entry and a multitude of other general-purpose functions. Specialized terminals are used in retail, financial, source data collection, and word processing applications.

General-purpose computer terminals can be used for online data entry and many other functions such as word processing, electronic mail, time-sharing, and program development. Very basic computer terminal devices used to enter data and display results are called *dumb terminals.* These terminals are connected to a computer system, which does all the editing of data and whatever processing that is required. *Smart terminals* have their own memory and editing capability. This enables users to store several pages of text or data locally and edit them for correctness. *Intelligent terminals* have their own small CPU, so users can prepare programs and data and do processing as a stand-alone computer would. A *workstation* is an enhanced microcomputer that can perform data or word processing functions, work as a dumb terminal connected to a host computer, and do data communication tasks such as electronic mail.

The *human-computer interface* refers to the means of interaction between a human being and the machine. The basic problem that arises when people have to communicate with machines is that what is best and most comfortable for people is not always the most efficient use of a machine.

Keyboards are the primary means through which humans interact with a computer. Keyboard designs differ significantly in terms of the number, placement, and function of the keys. A typical keyboard used with general-purpose terminals is very similar to the QWERTY keyboard arrangement of a standard typewriter. An alternate keyboard arrangement has been proposed by *Dvorak,* in which the home row includes the vowels under the fingertips of the left hand and the most common consonants under the fingertips of the right hand.

To make it easier for users to interact with computer systems, the computer can be programmed to display a *menu,* or list of options, as well as *prompts.* These are simple instructions that guide the user in what entries are needed. A *cursor* is a blinking symbol that shows where the next typed character will appear. To simplify word processing, spreadsheet analysis, or data queries, users needed an enhanced keyboard. To the typewriter keyboard has been added a *numeric keypad,* which functions as a quicker way to enter numeric data than using the top row of the keyboard. *Arrow keys* were added to facilitate the movement of the cursor. *Function keys* were added to provide a way to command certain common tasks in one step, rather than making several keystrokes to accomplish the same thing.

The dominant technology has been the keyboard. Most experts believe it will continue to be so for the forseeable future. A major reason is that the pointing devices don't do away with the keyboard. Any applications requiring substantial data or text input can be done faster with the keyboard.

Pointing devices are a complementary input means, primarily useful for selecting functions.

The study of the best way for people to interact with the computer is part of what is called ergonomics. *Ergonomics* is the science of designing machines for use by people. A recent advancement that makes the human-computer interface more natural is the use of *icons.* These are graphic symbols for functions such as selecting documents from the file folders, using a calculator to do arithmetic, writing and filing letters, even removing unwanted data or documents by selecting the "trash can." These functions are selected by the movement of the cursor, which is controlled with a hand-sized box called a *mouse.*

In the next chapter we will look at the wide variety of devices that can be used for information output.

REVIEW QUESTIONS

1. Briefly evaluate batch processing. How can SDA enhance the use of this approach to data processing?
2. What advantages and disadvantages are offered by transaction processing?
3. Briefly describe the major key-to-media devices discussed in the text. What advantages and disadvantages are offered by such devices?
4. The Good Life supermarket chain is considering the introduction of an OCR system. Which type is it most likely to utilize? Why?
5. How can OCR systems benefit retailers?
6. What problems must be overcome in order to allow OCR readers to handle handwritten characters?
7. Explain why the MICR system currently used by the banking industry is not a true SDA system.
8. Briefly explain the advantages offered by a voice recognition system. What technological problems must still be overcome in order to fully utilize such a system?
9. Compare the POS terminals used by supermarkets and department stores.
10. The Ajax Company is considering the installation of word processing equipment. What benefits might the firm expect?
11. Briefly compare so-called dumb, smart, and intelligent terminals.
12. What is *ergonomics?* How is communication with computers becoming more natural for people?

CHAPTER 5
Output

COMPUTERS AT WORK

Stevie Wonder: Computers Are Changing His Life

Having to depend on others is a little frustrating for Stevie Wonder. But thanks to new computer developments, he will have more freedom and flexibility to do what he likes. Best of all, he can function independently.

Two of the many new computer products designed specifically to aid the blind will help Stevie do this. One is the Kurzweil Reading Machine (KRM). The other is the Versabraille.

The KRM is really two machines in one: a computer that can scan the words on a printed page and interpret them, and a speech synthesizer that can speak those words out loud, at speeds of up to 250 words a minute.

The KRM helps Stevie work with his computers. It can read what's on another computer's screen. This allows Stevie to teach himself. When, for example, he got a portable Osborne computer to use on the road, Stevie was able to learn all about it himself by hooking the KRM up to the Osborne. The Osborne company had put their instruction manual on a floppy disk for Stevie, so all he had to do was put the disk in the Osborne and turn it, and the KRM, on. Then he listened as the KRM read everything to him straight off the disk!

Stevie's other system, the Versabraille, is a lap-sized computer designed specifically to use braille. Until computers came along, braille information wasn't very portable. A braille book could weigh as much as ten pounds. But the Versabraille can store tens of thousands of braille characters on a lightweight data cassette. It can then use this information in a variety of ways. The Versabraille can be connected to a KRM, so that the braille characters will be instantly translated into speech. The information can even be read back to the user by the Versabraille itself, one line at a time, using a special plastic readout strip on the machine's top. This strip has many tiny holes, with small plastic pinpoints that extend and retract to create different braille characters.

Right now, Stevie uses his Versabraille on and off the road as a kind of portable electronic notebook. It helps him do business, take notes, write letters and song lyrics, and keep track of addresses. But Stevie is building a complete integrated system, and soon the Versabraille will do a lot more.

When the Versabraille, KRM, and his instruments are all hooked up together, Stevie's musical tools will literally be able to talk to him—either in braille with the Versabraille's readout strip, or with the KRM's synthetic voice. He will be able to talk back to them and control what they do by writing in braille.

Source: Freff, "Stevie Wonder: Computers Make the Music in His Life," *Enter,* April 1984, pp. 25–28.

Useless. That's what even the most sophisticated computer would be if it couldn't process data and present them in a form that people could understand. For some users, printed output is adequate. However, for others, such as those with Stevie Wonder's handicap, voice output or a Braille printout is much more practical. For the most part, these alternatives to printed output have become available relatively recently. Historically, printed output—often referred to as hard copy—was the only means for showing results of computer processing. Though paper remains the primary medium for computer output, a variety of alternative means to communicate information has emerged, and we will discuss some of them. In this chapter, you will learn to do the following:

1. Describe three different ways to classify computer output.
2. Explain the two major technologies used in visual display devices and their advantages and disadvantages.
3. Use three primary factors to differentiate the dozen or so technologies used with printers.
4. Describe the two different ways computer voice output is formed.
5. List and explain the major criteria that can be used for printer selection.

CLASSIFYING COMPUTER OUTPUT

The routine at a supermarket checkout is one with which you are probably familiar. After making your merchandise selections, you approach the checkout stand. There, a clerk passes each item you chose over an optical scanner, which reads a bar-coded label to determine the product identification number. This number is used to check the electronic files for the appropriate product description and current price of the item. The computer then records this individual transaction and generates three forms of output, each of which can be understood by you, the customer (see Exhibit 5.1 on page 120).

What are these three forms of output? First, the product description and price of the item you selected are shown on a small video display terminal. Second, this same data is printed on a paper receipt, which gives an itemized listing of the entire sales transaction. Third, a computer-generated voice speaks the price of the item, and, with some systems, also the item description. After all goods have been recorded, the point-of-sale terminal calculates the total cost of taxable items, determines the appropriate sales tax on this amount, and then figures the total due. You pay the amount specified with cash, check, or credit card. The amount you hand over or sign for is entered by the clerk into the POS terminal, and any change due is indicated by all three displays.

For you, the customer, the primary information that results from this transaction processing is: (1) a terminal display and voice output of the total amount due; and (2) a paper receipt listing what was bought. For the business you chose to shop in, a very important by-product of this transaction processing is electronically stored data that can be used to update inventory files and determine the total daily sales for each store.

Why the need for three forms of output that people can understand? The customer needs a physical receipt of the total transaction for personal records and to simplify returning merchandise if necessary. The most convenient form for that receipt is paper. The visual display gives both the checkout clerk and the customer a way of checking that the optical scanner is reporting the correct price for each item. The computer-generated voice is another way of verifying the identity and price of an item.

Exhibit 5.1
Forms of Computer Output Used in a Supermarket

INPUT

OUTPUT

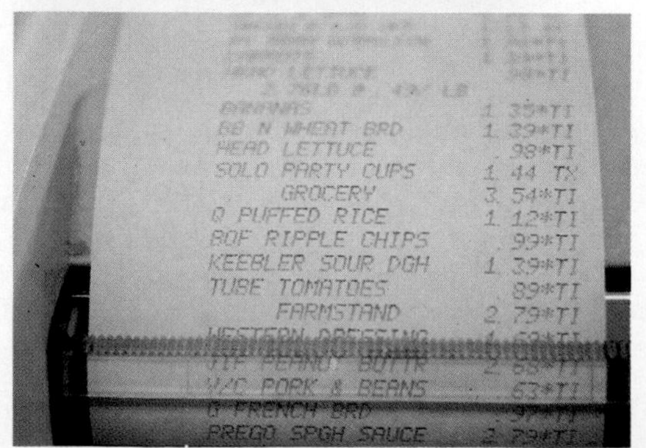

In a way, the visual display and voice generation are duplication. But because some people prefer visual information, others prefer audible information, and some like both, the process just described was developed to accommodate differing needs of people. The voice output is also of great help to those shoppers who are visually impaired.

Computer output can be classified in several different ways. **Hard copy** output, such as paper printouts, provides the user with a permanent record. **Soft copy** output, such as the visual display on a terminal or computer voice output, provides a temporary record. Both hard and soft copy output can be understood by human users, whereas the electronic data stored on magnetic tape or disk are computer-readable only. Information presented in the form of letters, numbers, and special characters is termed **alphanumeric.** In contrast, **graphics** are pictures or graphs depicting information.

The daily collection of all sales transactions would be stored on magnetic tape and used to generate monthly reports for management. An example would be a detailed report of daily sales of each item for the month. Because many managers and staff would need to read this report, which could be several hundred pages long, it would generally be prepared on a high-speed printer that could supply multiple copies at one time.

Collection and storage of daily transactions is an effective method for preparing periodic reports when most of the items in a file need to be reviewed and the timeliness of the information isn't critical. But looking through computer printouts—even those generated for one day of business activity—to determine inventory status of selected items would be time-consuming and potentially very inaccurate. Such inquiries are best handled with an on-line terminal. Not only is the information current, the process goes more quickly because the computer is used to search through electronic files stored on disk, and displays only those items requested by the user.

The various displays of information discussed so far use devices (printers, display terminals) that can output alphanumeric data. But often it is more effective to show information output in graphical form. For example, if a manager was trying to compare the monthly sales for a particular store, it would be awkward and tedious to try to visualize the breakdown by looking through a lengthy computer printout. On the other hand, a graphical display could effectively highlight those months in which sales were highest and those times when sales fell below the quota. Also, it would be quite easy to manipulate these data to see different graphical views (see Exhibit 5.2).

Exhibit 5.2

Implications from graphical displays of data are often easier to grasp than those from alphanumeric printouts.

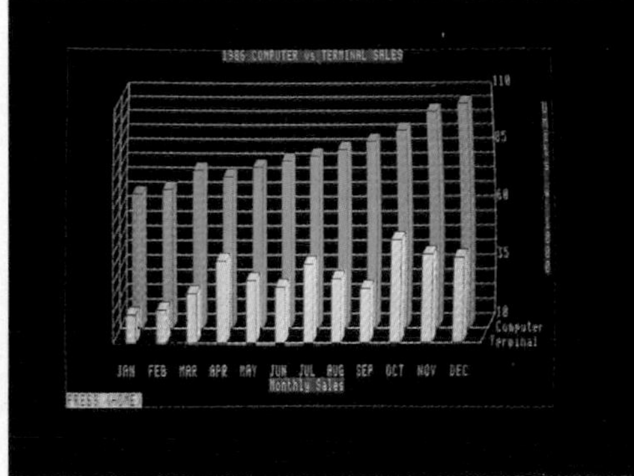

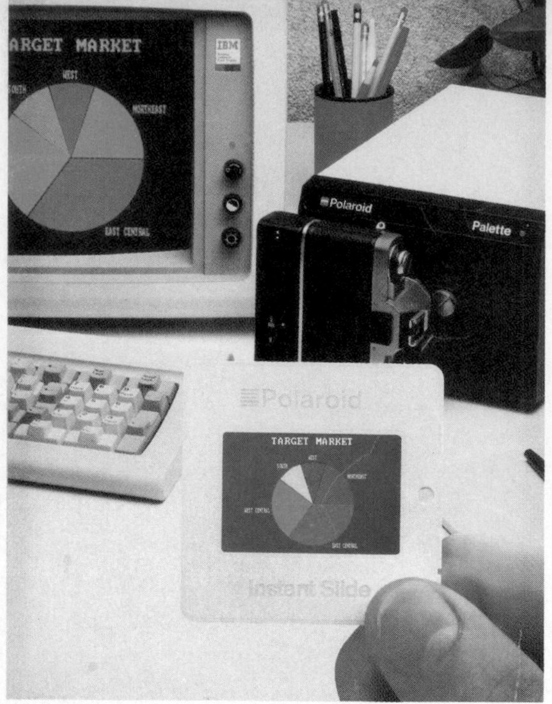

Exhibit 5.3

Slides can be made of video displays and used for illustration in presentations.

In addition to the video display of the graphics data, certain types of printers or plotters can be used to make hard copy printouts of the graphics. Often, staff members need to make a presentation to management regarding organizational performance. Special cameras are available to make slide film output of any image on the computer screen. These slides can then be used to add interest and emphasis to a discussion (see Exhibit 5.3).

These examples of practical uses give you a glimpse into the different ways computers meet the information needs of users in different business situations. And just as situations and needs differ, so do the computer devices used to meet these needs. Output devices vary in several respects: Is the output form a medium? Can the device display alphanumeric and/or graphic information? Is the output in a form understood by people and/or is it computer-readable?

In this chapter we will discuss the technology and capabilities of visual display, print and film, and synthesized speech devices. Chapters 11 and 12, on systems development, will show you how to use this knowledge to select the most appropriate output devices for any given situation.

VISUAL DISPLAY DEVICES

Visual display of information is one of the most effective means for communicating the results of computer processing. The primary technologies for producing and displaying the images on the terminal screen are the cathode-ray tube and the flat-panel.

Cathode-Ray Tube Displays

For many years, the primary technology used to create a visual image on the terminal screen has been the **cathode-ray tube (CRT).** In fact, this technology has become so dominant that computer terminals are often called CRTs. CRTs, like television picture tubes, electronically paint characters on a screen. Inside the tube, an electronic "gun" shoots a beam of electrons upon the back of the phosphor-coated glass face of the screen. The movement of the beam creates images on the face of the screen. We'll discuss two processes by which images are created on CRT screens: raster scan and vector technology.

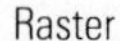

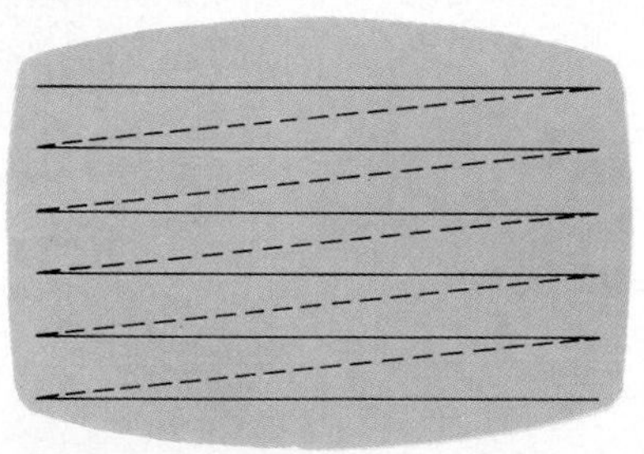

Exhibit 5.4
The Raster Scan Process

A beam of electrons sweeps across a CRT screen and the electrical current is increased or decreased to create brighter (on) or darker (off) points.

Raster Scan. In a CRT using raster scan, a beam of electrons sweeps back and forth horizontally across the screen. As the beam moves across the screen, the electrical current is increased or decreased to create brighter (on) or darker (off) points. These points are **pixels,** or picture elements. This sequence is continued for each line of the screen. The process is called **raster scan** (see Exhibit 5.4).

The color of the phosphor coating on the glass face of the screen determines whether the characters displayed are green, amber, or some other color. As the beam of electrons passes across the screen, the phosphors emit light instantaneously and then decay (go dark) quickly. This means that an image must be constantly refreshed. Typically, the whole screen is repainted at least thirty times per second. The advantage of the fast decay rate is that screen displays can be changed rapidly. The disadvantage is that, to the viewer's eye, the display may seem to flicker slightly. The intensity of the electron beam determines the brightness of the image on the screen. This is regulated by varying the voltage applied to the electron gun.

CRTs are used in monochrome and color monitors. **Monochrome monitors** display one color, such as green or amber, on a black background. Each pixel is represented by a green or amber phosphor dot. A single electron gun directs the beam to each dot (see Exhibit 5.5).

Exhibit 5.5
Monochrome Monitors

Color monitors use a triad, or trio, of dots to form a pixel. The three phosphor dots are red, green, and blue in color. In a **composite video monitor,** one electron gun is used to turn on the appropriate colors within each triad. In contrast, **RGB** (red, green, and blue) **monitors** use three electronic guns—one for each color. This results in sharper graphical images than are possible with composite video monitors, because of the finer control allowed by using three electron beams.

Since only red, green, and blue phosphor dots are used, you may wonder how the other colors you also see can be displayed. The answer is that these three primary colors can be "electronically" mixed to produce other colors. For example, when the red and green phosphors within a triad are turned on, a yellow pixel will be viewed on the screen. When all three dots are turned on, the pixel will be viewed as white (see Exhibit 5.6 on page 124). The more intense the beam is, as it strikes a phosphor, the brighter or deeper the color. This same concept is used by artists mixing the primary colors red, yellow, and blue. For computer purposes, it is the difference between color pigments and electronic waves that requires the use of green, rather than yellow, for the third primary color.

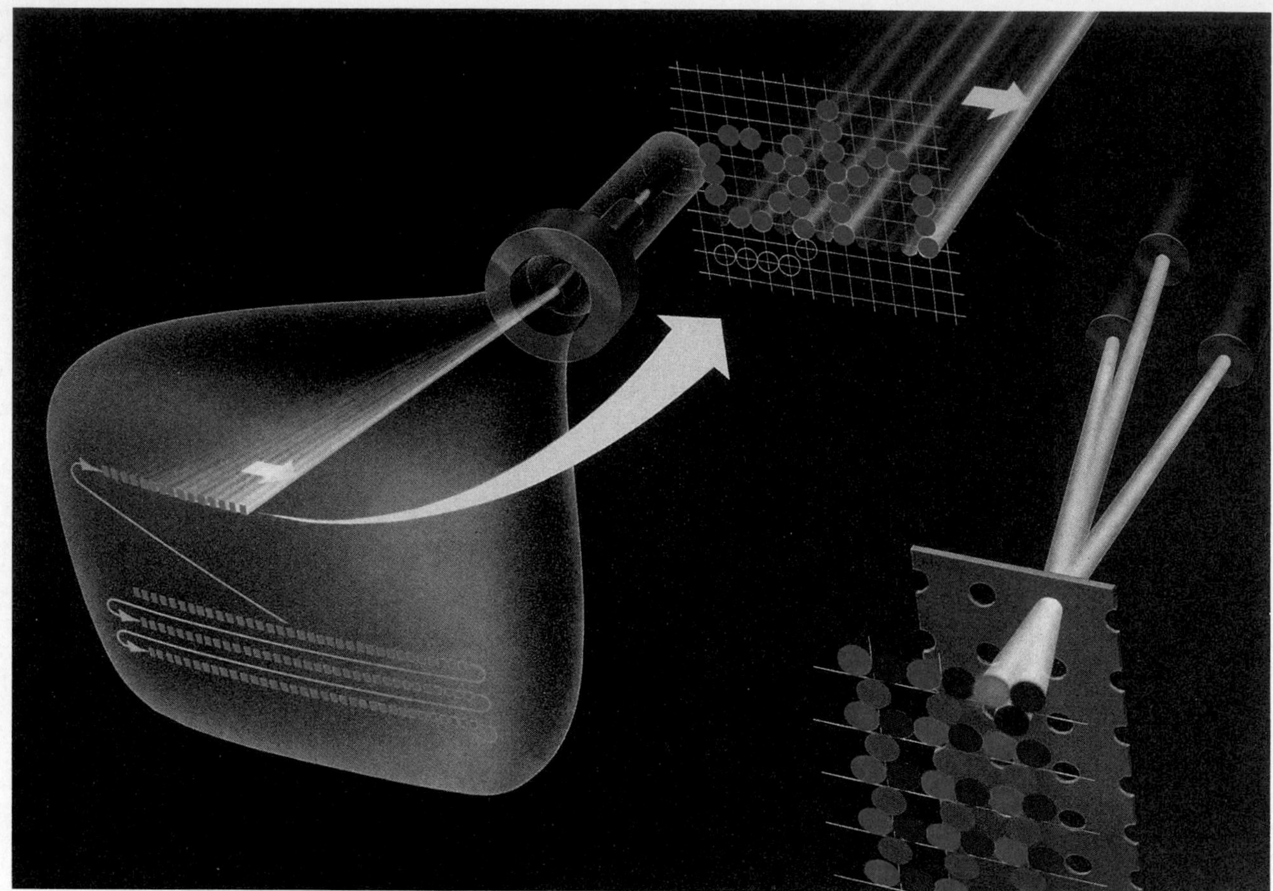

Exhibit 5.6

Red, green, and blue are the three primary colors that are "electronically" mixed to produce other colors. A spectrum of color is generated by turning on different combinations of the RGB electron guns on a triad of phosphor dots.

Reprinted with permission, *High Technology* Magazine, February 1985. Copyright © 1985 by High Technology Publishing Corporation, 38 Commercial Wharf, Boston, MA 02110.

One other major factor affects display screens, and that is whether a character- or dot-addressable scheme is being used. These terms refer to the number of addressable locations on a screen. In a **bit-map** or **dot-addressable display,** each individual pixel is addressable. Only blocks of pixels can be addressed or manipulated in **character-addressable displays.** The major advantage of the character-addressable approach is that it requires much less memory capacity. The number of locations is specified by the number of characters that can be displayed on a row and the number of rows on the screen. Typically, CRT screens can display 80 characters per row, and have 24 or 25 rows. **Resolution** is a measure of the number of pixels that can be addressed on the screen.

Monochrome screens are generally character-addressable, and primarily used for displaying alphanumeric data. When character-addressable screens are used to display graphics, the resolution quality of the resulting pictures is rather crude, and usually shows a stair-step effect because it is necessary to address the pixels in blocks, rather than individually (see Exhibit 5.7).

Dot-addressable displays, frequently used for graphical displays, can also be used to display alphanumeric data or text. The quality of the picture is a

Exhibit 5.7

Crude resolution quality usually shows a stair-step effect. These display graphics range in quality from crude to high resolution.

function of many variables, including the number of pixels on the screen itself and the computer's memory size. In a bit-map display, each pixel on the screen is represented by several bits in memory. A bit is used to indicate whether the pixel should be turned on or off. Several bits are used with color monitors to specify which of the triad dots should be turned on to form the desired color. You could even have the pixel blink on and off, though this would require another bit in memory. As you will discover in the next section, there are other display characteristics possible. The point is that, in dot-addressable displays, there is a direct correlation between the amount of primary memory required and the resolution and display capabilities of the display screen.

With some monitors you can select one of several levels of resolution. For example with the IBM color monitor, the highest resolution (with the most addressable pixels) allows only a black and white display. In the medium resolution mode (half the pixels are addressable), four colors can be displayed at one time. In the lowest resolution mode (only "character" blocks of pixels are addressable), a full palette of colors can be displayed.

In addition to color/monochrome and alphanumeric/graphical characteristics of a display device, there are a number of features that make using a CRT terminal an effective means for communicating information. When displaying data, text, or program listings that have more lines or rows than can be shown on the screen at any one time, scrolling or paging can be used to move through the document. **Scrolling,** usually controlled through the keyboard, allows the user to move up or down on the document, one line at a time. As a new line is added to the screen, one is removed. **Paging** allows a user to, in one move, move up or down the document by the depth of an entire screen. These options are necessary in applications such as word processing and spreadsheet analysis, and helpful in many other programming situations.

Some programs allow a computer's display screen to be divided into separate areas or boxes called **windows.** Special software that uses the characteristics of the display screen allows you to view various portions of your data processing work side-by-side on a single screen. For example, one window could display a business letter, another window could be a graphic display, and a third window could show a spreadsheet program. The Macintosh computer uses a bit-map display and special software to provide pull-down windows, text and graphical displays, and icons for selecting functions (see Exhibit 5.8).

Exhibit 5.8

A Macintosh Bit-Map Screen

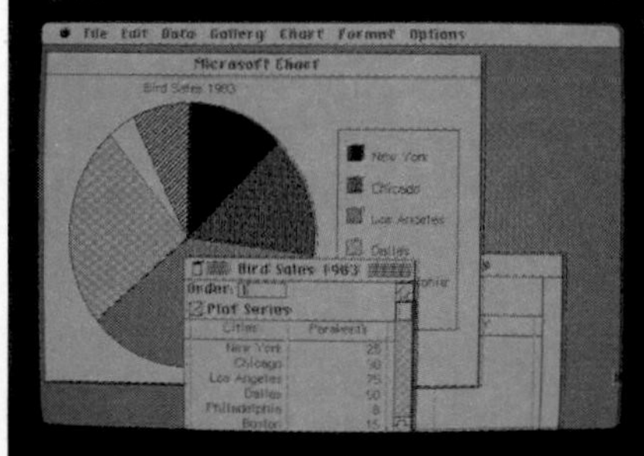

Exhibit 5.9
Reverse Video
On this screen, reverse video characters will appear in black on the amber background areas.

To highlight specific data within a screen display, features such as double size, bold, underline, and blink can be used. Characters or words that are displayed at twice their normal size, that appear in boldface type, that are underlined, or that blink will be effectively emphasized. These features also add interest to a presentation.

As the terminology suggests, in reverse video the displayed characters and background are reversed. The reverse video feature is useful for highlighting a character, word, line, or even a complete screen. For example, if a screen normally displayed amber characters on a black background, reverse video characters would be black on an amber background. This feature is frequently used in formatting a screen for data entry. Reverse video allows the programmer to design a CRT screen to look like a familiar printed form, such as an invoice or a medical history record (see Exhibit 5.9). This generally results in fewer data entry errors and, often, increased performance.

Vector. Producing high-quality graphics using the raster scan approach requires a significant amount of memory. This, in turn, limits the resolution of terminals used for graphics to around 300,000 pixels, although there are some terminals with the capability to display over 1 million pixels. However, for many years engineers and scientists working in the computer aided design and manufacturing (CAD/CAM) field, in particular, have needed displays with much higher resolution. They work with special graphics terminals, which use a vector display rather than raster scan.

Vector technology is based on the use of lines or vectors drawn on the screen. To see the difference between the vector and raster methods, see Exhibit 5.10. With a raster display, the letter *Z* is produced by a beam, sweeping line by line. At each pixel that is to be displayed, the beam intensity is increased. The turned-on pixels form a Z. With a vector display, the electron beam starts at the point labeled 1. The beam intensity is increased (turned on), and a line or vector is drawn until point 2 is reached, where the intensity is turned off. The electron gun is redirected at point 2 and the intensity is turned on until it reaches point 3, and so on. The result is a Z that has been traced out with the vectors.

As shown by these examples, the main difference between the vector and the raster methods is in how the electron beam is moved. With the raster

Exhibit 5.10
The two major processes used in cathode ray tube displays are raster scan and vector.

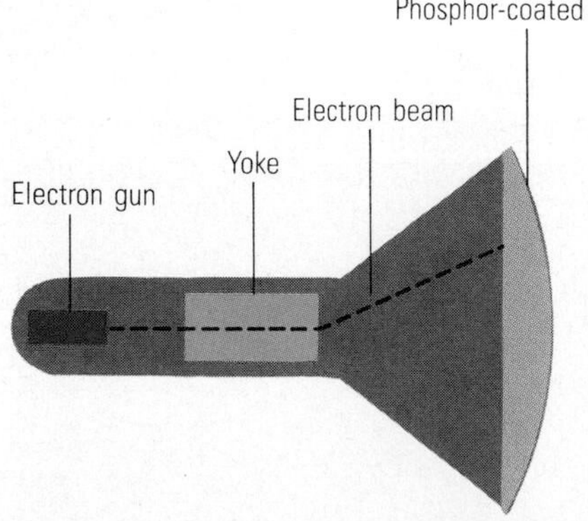

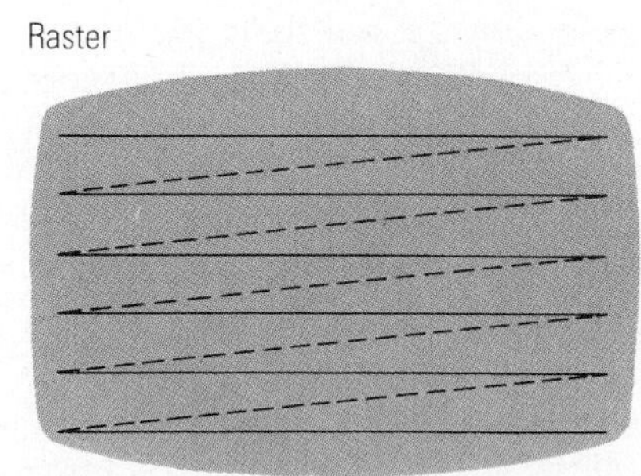

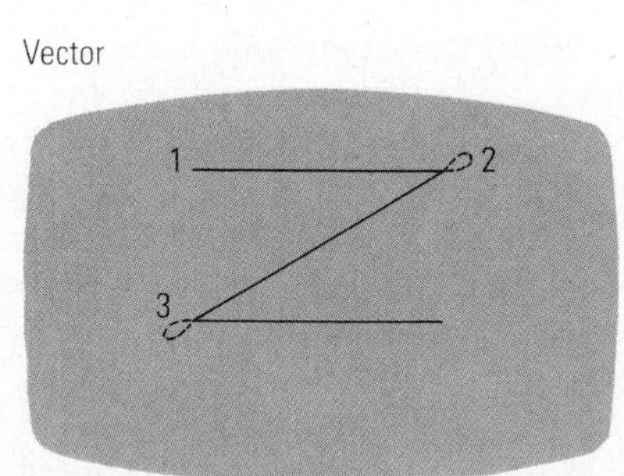

approach, the whole screen is always scanned in a fixed pattern, regardless of how much "action" is on the screen. In contrast, the vector approach scans only where necessary. As you might expect, this difference has a major effect on the amount of primary memory required to show a graphic image.

The vector approach functions with much less memory. Unlike the bit-map method, which requires characteristics of each pixel to be stored, the vector approach stores only the coordinates of the start and end points of each line. Mathematical equations can be used to derive the vector connecting these coordinates. Vector screens can thus achieve very high resolution with quite modest memory requirements. Screens with 4000 horizontal × 4000 vertical pixel resolution (16 million pixels) are common with vector graphics and require only a 64K–128K range of memory. A comparable resolution for screens using raster scan would require many megabytes of primary memory.

Thus, vector graphics can produce very high resolution pictures of line drawings with limited memory capacity terminals. Since the structure is determined by mathematical equations, these pictures can easily be manipulated and rotated to see different views. This makes vector graphics ideal for CAD/CAM applications (see Exhibit 5.11). The major disadvantage with the vector method is that it can't show solid objects. Further, it tends to be limited to monochrome displays.

Most experts, however, believe that raster graphics will be the technology of the future. Its primary disadvantage is that high resolution displays require significant memory capacity. However, as prices for memory capability continue to fall and increasingly capable microprocessors become available, this disadvantage will be overcome. The major advantages of the raster graphics approach are that it provides solid modeling capability and access to a wide spectrum of colors (see Exhibit 5.12). These factors are critical to the success of color graphics.

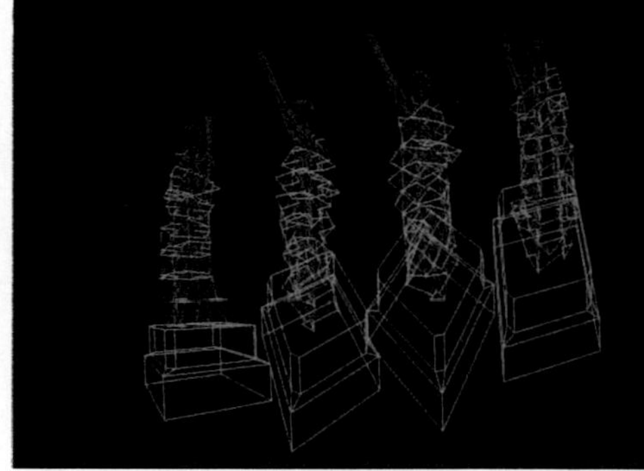

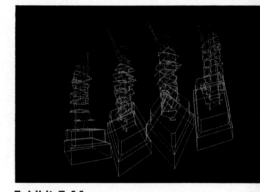

Exhibit 5.11

Vector graphics produce high-resolution line drawings that can be manipulated and rotated to show different views.

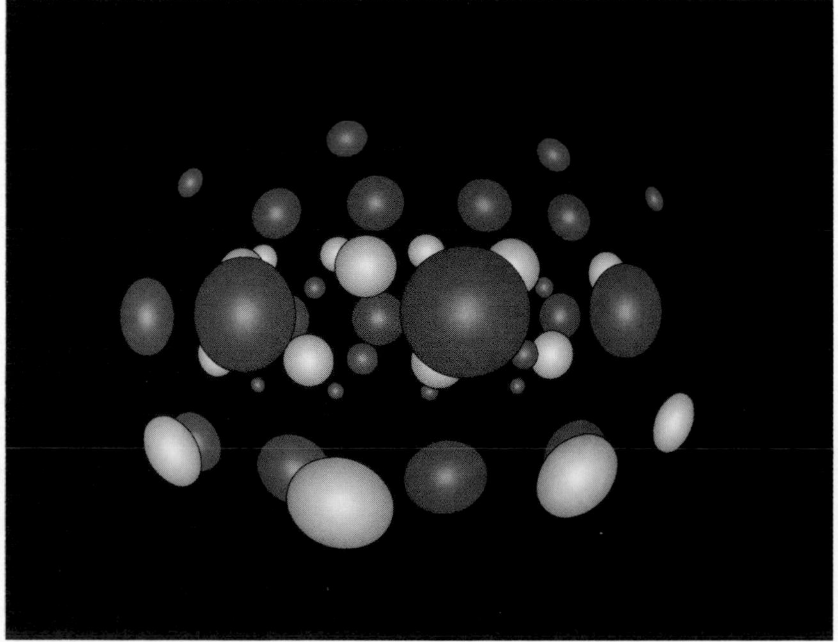

Exhibit 5.12

Raster graphics can show solid objects in a wide spectrum of colors. Here raster graphics were used to depict an antimony sulfur iodine crystal.

Flat-Panel Displays

A new technology is emerging to challenge the CRT as the primary means of displaying alphanumeric and graphical images. It is the flat-panel display. Plasma and liquid crystal are two of the primary technologies used with it.

The CRT has several disadvantages. One is that the screen-painting approach has a strobe light effect. The flicker causes eye fatigue in many people who interact with a computer for hours at a time. Second, the shooting of electrons against the phosphors causes radiation, as well as light, to be given off. Studies seem to indicate that the levels of radiation are too low to be dangerous, but many people are still concerned. Third, displays using CRTs have a large footprint, a reference to the amount of the desk space occupied by the terminal. The culprit is the electronic gun. For a typical CRT with a 12-inch display screen, the gun measures approximately six inches long from front to back. To accommodate the gun, most CRTs are about one foot deep, one foot wide, and weigh as much as a 12-inch TV. The flat-panel display, a possible successor to the CRT, does not have these disadvantages.

The flat-panel display shown in Exhibit 5.13 is a computer terminal using plasma technology. The display is only 3 inches thick, is lightweight, and has a resolution rivaling that of a photograph. Here is how the plasma display works. An ionized gas (plasma) is held between two glass plates. A set of horizontal wires is embedded in one of the glass plates, and a set of vertical wires is embedded in the other glass plate. These wires form a grid or matrix in which each intersection is a pixel. A particular pixel can be turned on by sending current through the appropriate horizontal and vertical wires. The current at the intersection excites the plasma—a neon-argon gas mixture—between the plates, and this produces orange light at that pixel. Flat-panel displays create a screen image by illuminating a pattern of discrete dots to display alphanumeric data, graphics, and video images.

Exhibit 5.13
A Flat-Panel Plasma Display
Glowing neon-argon gas produces a high-resolution, flicker-free image.

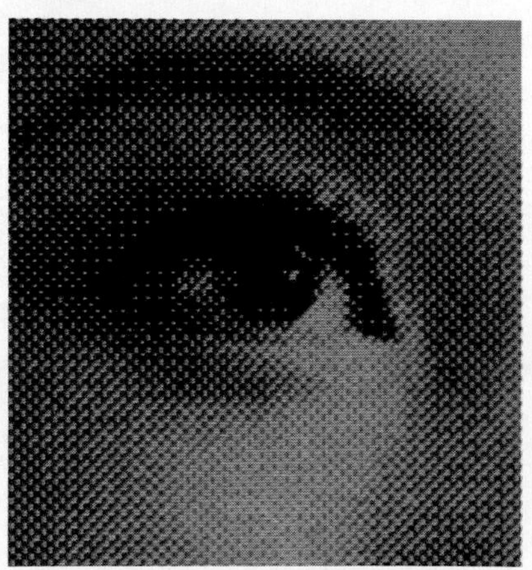

High resolution and steadiness of flat-panel displays yield high-quality results. CRTs using raster-scan to refresh the screen sometimes produce images with a wavy quality. In contrast, plasma display images are stable, with each pixel emitting a steady glow until it is turned off. Though the plasma flat-panel display technology has many exciting advantages, the terminals cost significantly more than CRTs. This high price tag will slow market penetration. Further disadvantages are that this type of display requires a great deal of power and gives off a large amount of heat.

To meet the needs of people who want to use their computers in the office, at home, and on business trips, the portable computer was developed. The initial entry was the Osborne 1, which used CRT technology to drive a 5-inch display screen. The complete computer was designed to fold up small enough to fit under an airplane seat. Companies such as COMPAQ took this concept one step further by developing a portable computer system with a larger, more workable 9-inch display screen. However, because these portables use the CRT technology, they are quite heavy, weighing around 20 to 30 pounds. Thus, they are more accurately described as "luggable" (see Exhibit 5.14).

Truly portable, lightweight computers with full-size screens became available in 1984 with the introduction of Data General's DG/One. This briefcase-size computer weighs 10 pounds and has a flat-panel display using the liquid crystal display (LCD) technology (see Exhibit 5.15).

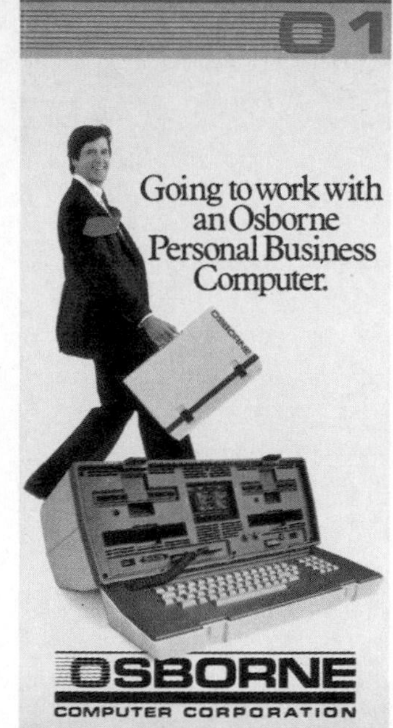

01
Going to work with an Osborne Personal Business Computer.
OSBORNE
OSBORNE
COMPUTER CORPORATION

Exhibit 5.14
The "Luggable" Computer
Osborne 1 had a five-inch display screen and could be folded for storage under an airplane seat.

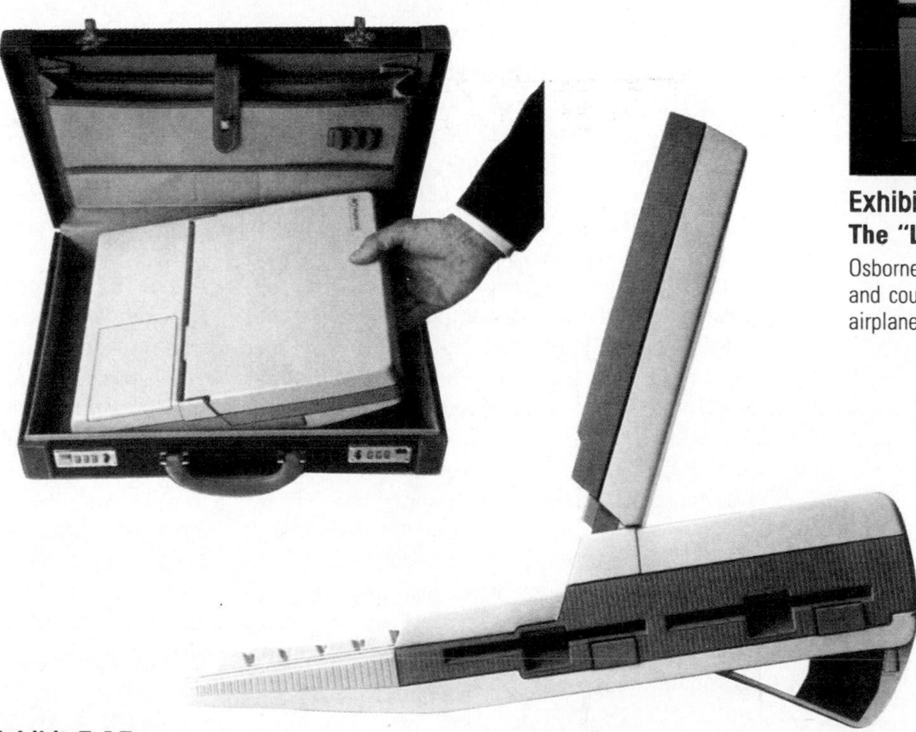

Exhibit 5.15
The Portable Computer
The Data General/One, introduced in 1984, had a full-size, flat-panel display using liquid crystal display (LCD) technology.

You may be familiar with LCD technology, as it is used in a variety of products, including pocket calculators and digital watches. A thin layer of liquid crystal molecules are put between two sheets of glass and separated into little squares. When a voltage is applied to the liquid crystal in an individual cell or square, the normally clear material will turn opaque and block light reflected from behind it. The result is a black square. The display screen is thus a pixel grid, which can be controlled so that characters can be shown by patterns of dots.

The major advantages of an LCD computer screen are that it doesn't give off radiation and it has no flicker. It also has a very low power requirement, so it can run off a small battery pack for many hours before recharging is necessary.

One disadvantage of the LCD, however, has been the small screen display. Typically, this was a 40-character by 8-line display. The breakthrough with the DG/One allows a standard 12-inch screen with display dimensions of 80-characters by 24-rows. But the resolution and brightness of the LCD display for a standard-size screen are less than those of a CRT of comparable size. Another disadvantage is that the quality of the LCD picture is dependent on the ambient (surrounding) light. Under low light conditions, the screen is very hard to read. With proper lighting, the display is sharpest when viewed directly, and loses resolution or crispness when viewed on an angle.

PRINT AND FILM DEVICES

Our supermarket example showed the need for some form of output that could be read by a person and would serve as a permanent record. The number and type of output forms used to communicate results will vary from situation to situation, of course, but paper has traditionally been the dominant form of output. In spite of all the talk about the concept of the "paperless office," it appears that paper will continue to be the major medium for communication documentation.

Historically, it is also true that alphanumeric data has been the primary information output. Thus, the computer printer, with its capability to print alphanumeric data on paper, has been the predominant means of generating hard copy output. More recently, the need for graphical displays has changed the type of printers that are in demand and also encouraged the development of plotters. Filmed output, such as microfilm and microfiche, is attractive as a computer output medium because of its lower storage cost and reduced space requirements, relative to those for paper.

In this first section, we will discuss the technology for computer printers that have been used primarily to print alphanumeric data. In the next section, printers and plotters used mainly for printing graphics will be described. Keep in mind that, generally, output devices that can print graphics can also print alphanumeric data. However, not all devices that print alphanumeric data can print high-quality graphics.

Alphanumeric Printers

The computer printer industry has not yet settled on a limited number of ways to print alphanumeric information. Rather, a dozen or so technologies are being used today. These technologies differ in three basic ways: the way in

Exhibit 5.16
Golf Ball, Daisy-Wheel, and Thimble Print Mechanisms

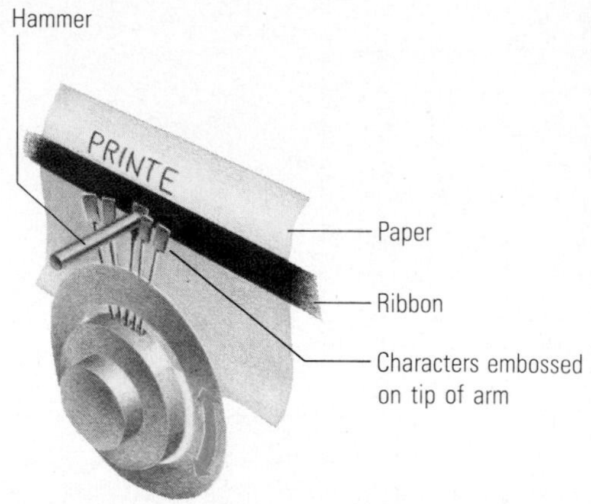

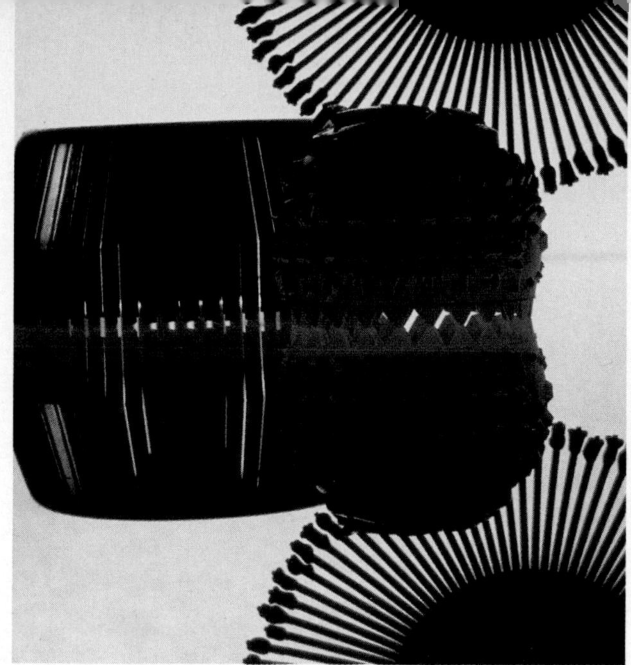

which characters are formed; the way in which characters are transferred to paper or another medium; and the number of characters that are printed at any one time.

Character Formation. There are three methods for forming a character: fully formed, dot-matrix, and image. The old manual typewriters and the new electric ones both use the fully formed character approach. Both the striker arms on the manual style and the "golf ball" typing element on the electric model have permanently shaped, or fully formed, characters. The electric typewriter is more versatile in that different type fonts can be used by changing the typing element.

In computer printers, the fully formed character approach has been implemented by using either a **golf ball, daisy-wheel, thimble, band, belt,** or **chain** as the print mechanism (see Exhibit 5.16). In a daisy-wheel printer, each "petal" contains an embossed character. The wheel is rotated until the appropriate character is in place, and then a hammer presses the character against a ribbon, which transfers an impression onto the paper. A variation in which the petals appear to be folded back is called a thimble.

The dot-matrix approach has become the most widely used character formation method of computer printers. In dot-matrix printers, characters are formed by a pattern of dots. In a 5 × 7 dot-matrix, the *5* refers to the number of horizontal dots and the *7* refers to the number of vertical dots. Selective pins are activated to form characters, as shown with the letter *T* (see Exhibit 5.17 on page 132).

The third way to form a character is by image. The dot-matrix approach uses a fixed block pattern of dots, such as 9 × 18 or 18 × 36, for each character. Image processing differs in that it generates characters through a raster scan type of approach, in which selected dots are "turned on" on a line-by-line basis. When all lines have been scanned, the resulting image will show the characters in their appropriate positions. This method is used by laser printers, and we will discuss that particular technology later.

Character Transfer. Characters can be transferred by either an impact or nonimpact method. The impact method of character transfer is widely used with computer printers. It works much like a typewriter in that an impression-

Exhibit 5.17
Dot-Matrix Computer Printing

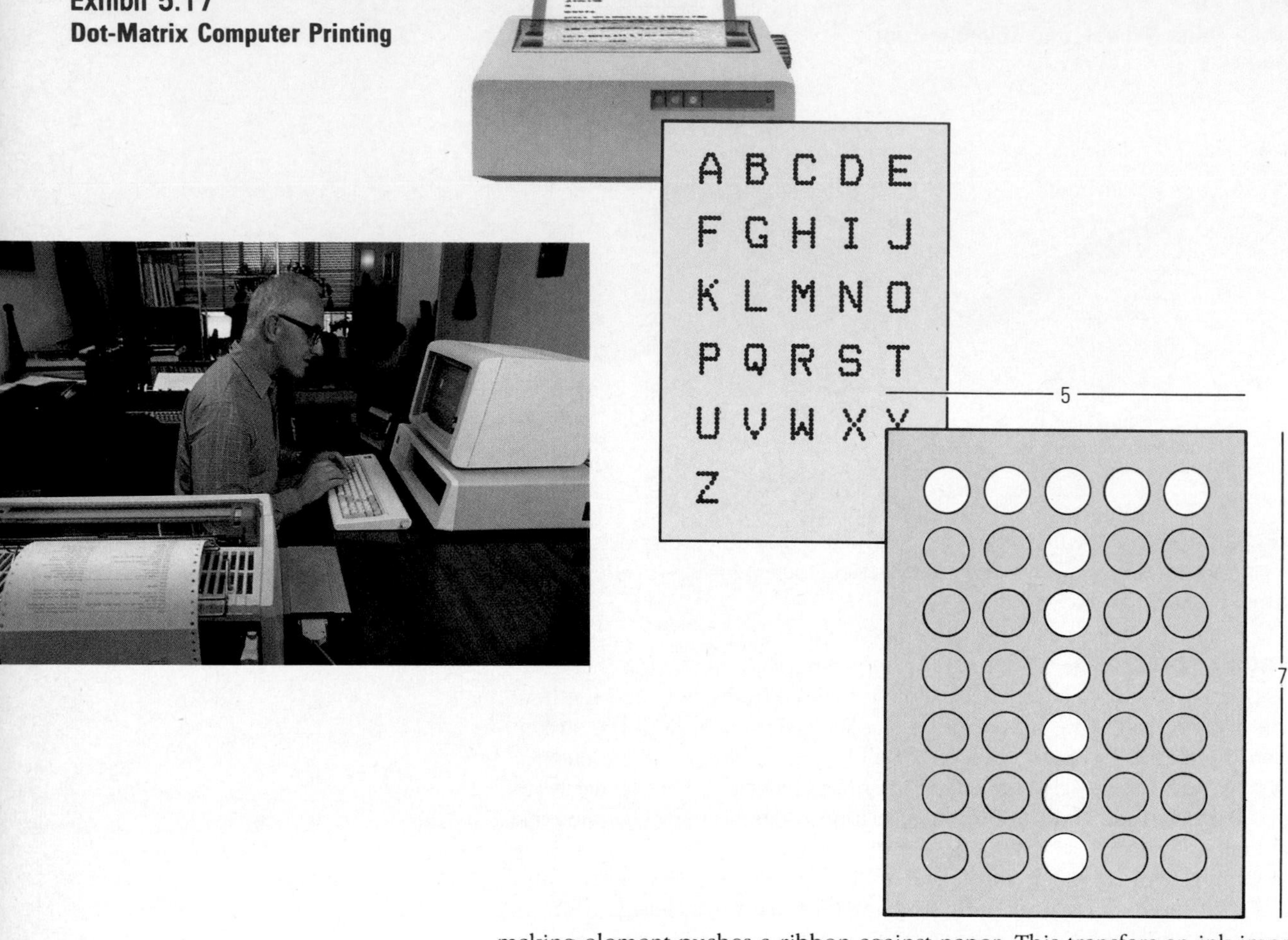

making element pushes a ribbon against paper. This transfers an ink impression onto the paper in the color of the ribbon. Daisy-wheel and thimble printers use this approach, as do belt, band, and chain printers. There is variation in whether the ribbon, paper, or fully formed character is struck first.

At one time, the impact method was limited to fully formed characters. But dot-matrix impact printers now make wide use of the impact method. Dot-matrix printers that form characters using columns of "dot hammers" are classified as impact printers.

The other major approach to character transfer is nonimpact. No physical hammering is used with this method. The character is transferred to the paper by means of heat, electrostatic charge, magnetism, or ink shot against selected parts of the paper. The nonimpact technique can be used with either the dot-matrix or image method of character formation. An application of this concept is shown with thermal and electrostatic dot-matrix printers. Each method forms characters on specially treated paper. Thermal printers use heated printheads to burn dots onto heat-sensitive paper. Electrostatic printers use electrically charged printheads to melt away dots in thin aluminum-coated paper.

Characters Printed at a Time. Most of the inexpensive printers print one character at a time. Thus, a line of text is generated as with a typewriter. Serial printers move the printhead from left to right, line by line. This is a relatively slow process, however. A modification used in many printers is **bi-directional printing,** or printing right to left and then left to right (see Exhib-

Unidirectional printing

Bidirectional printing

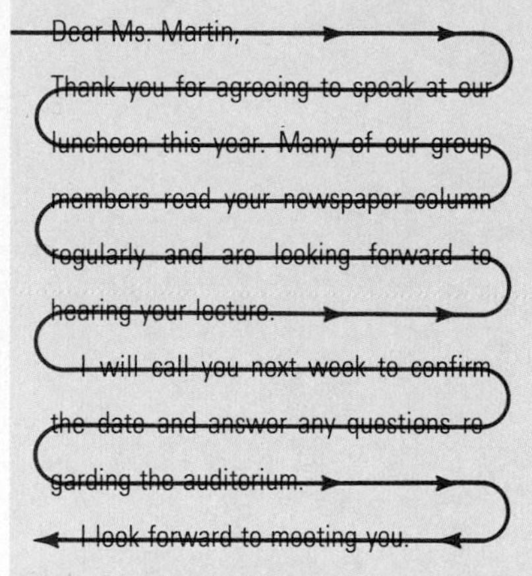

Bidirectional printing with logic seeking

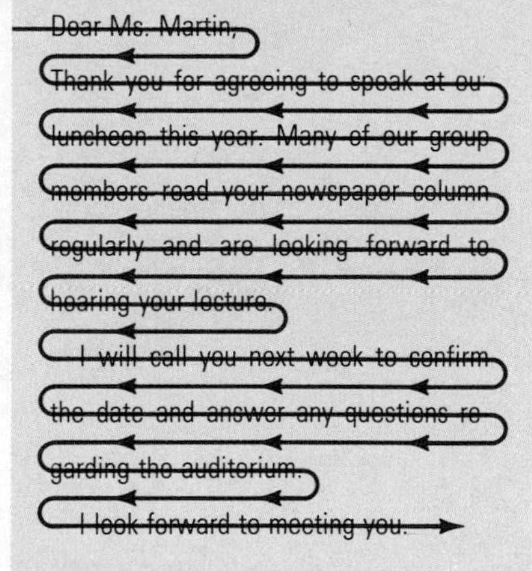

Exhibit 5.18

Bidirectional Printing

Printing in a bidirectional pattern saves the time it takes for the printhead to move from the end of one line to the beginning of the next line.

it 5.18). This saves the time it takes the printhead to return from the end of one line to the beginning of the next one.

A faster method is parallel, or line-at-a-time, printing. Instead of having the printhead move back and forth as in serial printing, multiple print hammers are used by line printers. For example, one type of chain printer has 132 print hammers. A chain of characters rotates past the print hammers at a very high speed. When the proper character is in front of a hammer, it releases and strikes the paper against the ribbon, and then against the chain. Since the chain contains several 48-character sections, multiple characters can be printed at the same time. On one pass of the chain, the complete line will have been printed (see Exhibit 5.19).

Exhibit 5.19

Band printers use a hammer to impact the paper against the ribbon and the fully formed character. The embossed characters are on a band that rotates horizontally. Chain printers use multiple hammers that are each released when the correct character slugs contained on the rotating chain are in the proper print position.

Band Printer

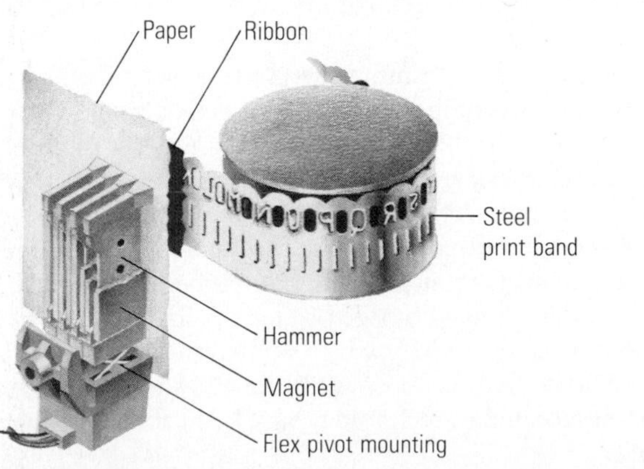

Chain Printer

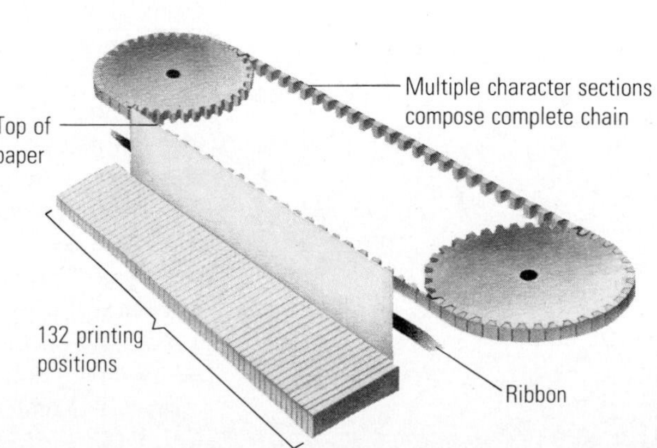

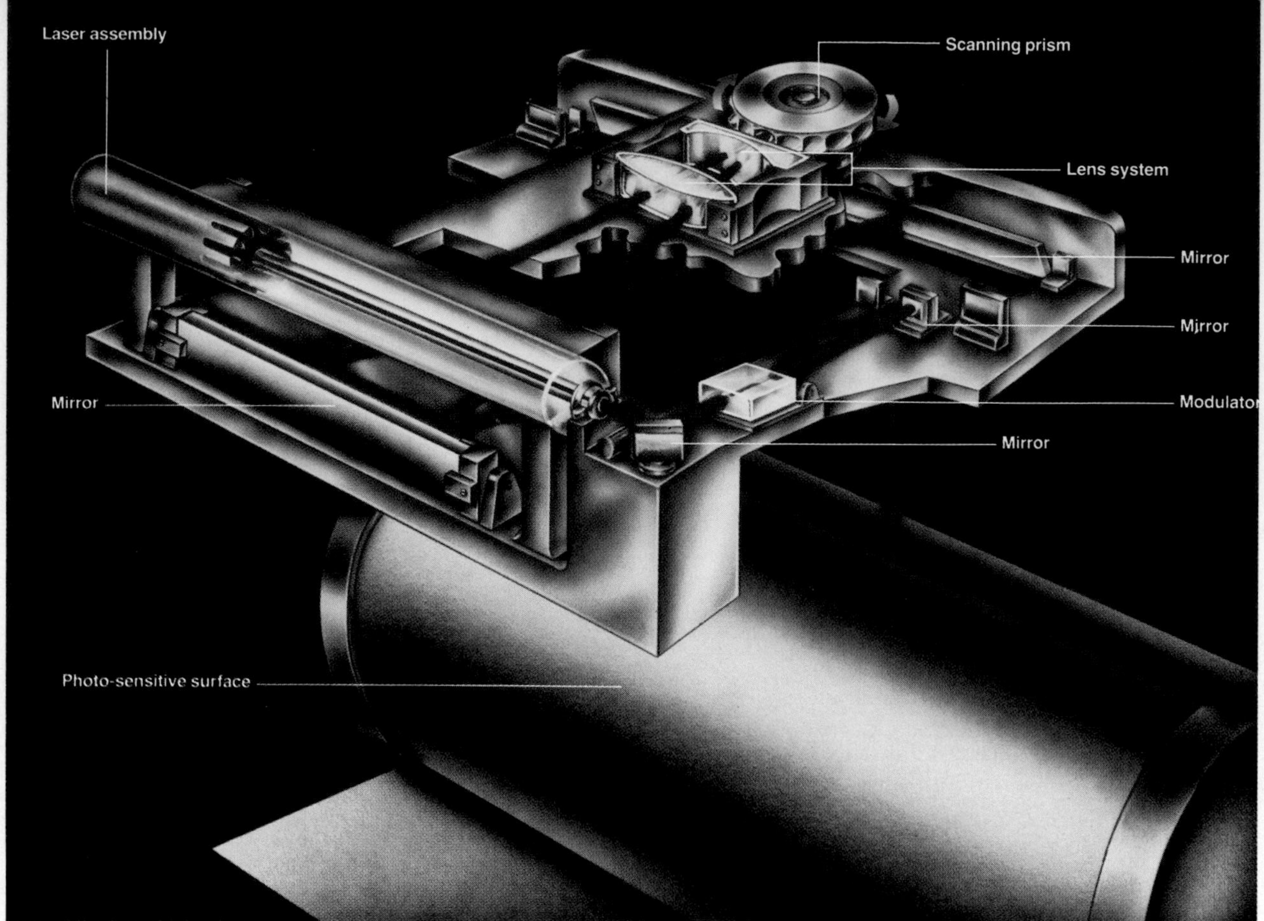

Exhibit 5.20

Laser printers use a series of mirrors and a scanning prism to trace the image of an entire page onto the photo-sensitive surface. The modulator is used to vary the intensity of the laser beam. The drum is rotated and the image, a pattern of charges, is transferred to paper by attracting toner. The image is then fused to the paper with heat.

The very high-speed printers are page printers. Typical of this process is the electrophotographic approach used with laser printers. They use a combination of raster scan and xerographic copy machine technologies. The raster scan approach is used to trace an image of an entire page onto a photosensitive drum. The drum is rotated and the image, a pattern of charges, is transferred to a plain sheet of paper by attracting toner that is fused on by heat (see Exhibit 5.20).

A summary of the key approaches to printing characters is given in Exhibit 5.21. Character formation options are: fully formed, dot-matrix, or image. Characters, once formed, can be transferred by an impact or nonimpact method. The number of characters to be transferred at a time can range from a single character to an entire line or a complete page.

Printer technology has evolved from the possible combinations within the three key aspects of printing characters. At present, state-of-the-art image formation is always nonimpact and is used with page printers. Fully formed characters are always used with impact technology, which is characteristic of either a character or line printer. The dot-matrix approach is the most flexible. It can be used with either impact or nonimpact technology, and is suitable for either character or line printing.

Exhibit 5.21
Key Approaches to Printing Characters

Character formation	Fully formed	Dot-matrix	Image
Character transfer	Impact	Nonimpact	
Number of characters	Character	Line	Page

Graphics Printers and Plotters

The growing popularity of graphics terminals has been accompanied by an increasing need for hard copy of the graphics developed on the computer terminal. For a long time, the only option available was to use the printer to make a graphical representation.

Thus, business graphics were first printed by plotting points using fully-formed characters. For example, to show a trend line, a character was printed at specific points. The letter *P* could be used to represent profits and the letter *S* to represent sales. Some clever programmers developed quite impressive computer drawings of holiday greetings, calendars, and even centerfolds with patterns of characters such as *X*s and *O*s.

Dot-matrix printing improved on the quality of graphics possible with fully formed characters. The dot-matrix approach is used in multifunction dot-matrix impact printers, as well as in printers using nonimpact thermal and ink-jet technology. For example, low-cost text and graphics printers used with personal computers can print business graphics such as bar graphs and pie charts.

Ink-jet technology is being used to generate higher-quality images. Fine-nozzle jets spray individual ink drops at the paper. By using multiple nozzles, several different colors of ink can be printed. This form of dot-matrix projection is useful for printing text and graphics. The nonimpact process is also used for printing on packages or odd-shaped objects. Exhibit 5.22 shows the excellent resolution possible with ink-jet technology. Flexibility in printing, color, and high resolution make this technology useful in a variety of areas, including engineering and business.

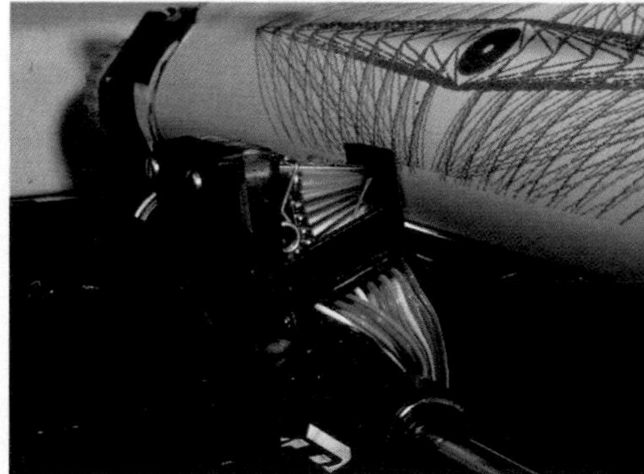

Exhibit 5.22
Ink-Jet Technology
Ink-jet printers using the drop-on-demand technology eject individual ink drops through a nozzle onto paper. Primary colors and black inks are used to produce high-resolution graphics.

Very expensive laser printers offer the best quality in hard copy graphics. Because they make use of the raster scan method, higher resolution is possible. This form of image processing is so good that it is being used as the base technology for electronic publishing (see Exhibit 5.23 on page 136). For example, banking and insurance industries and governmental agencies conduct many of their business activities using a multitude of preprinted forms. Previously, in-house printing departments had to run off thousands of copies of each form and store them for later use. Now, the computer is being used to operate laser printers, which produce each form as it is needed, and fill in the appropriate data as part of the output process.

Plotters are output devices that are specialized to produce graphics. Plotters use the vector concept to produce a picture made up of a series of straight lines. A pen plotter can only be programmed to move right, left, up, down, or diagonally. Curves are drawn as a series of very short lines. The quality of the

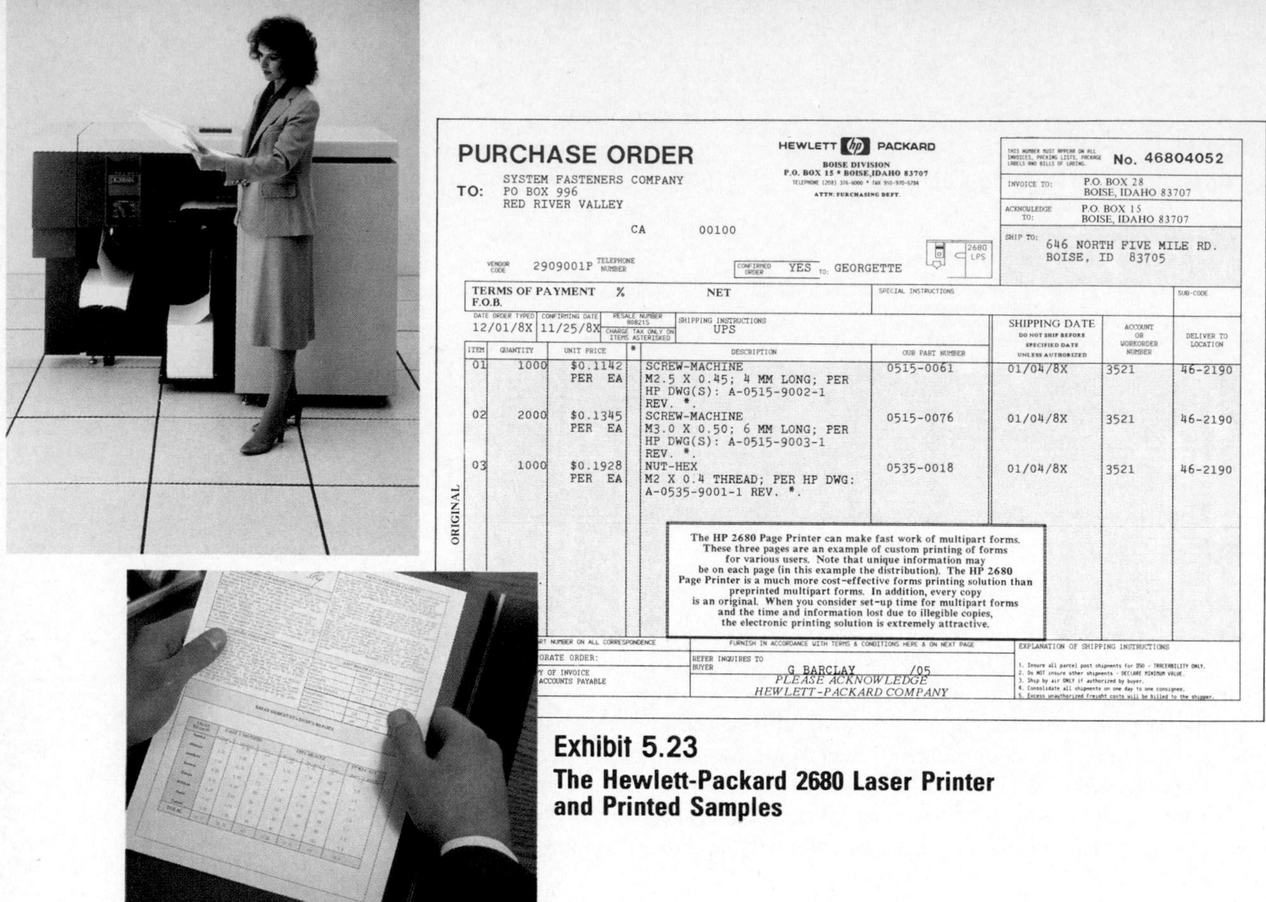

PURCHASE ORDER

HEWLETT PACKARD
BOISE DIVISION
P.O. BOX 15 * BOISE, IDAHO 83707
TELEPHONE (208) 376-6000 * TWX 910-970-5784
ATTN: PURCHASING DEPT.

TO: SYSTEM FASTENERS COMPANY
PO BOX 996
RED RIVER VALLEY
CA 00100

THIS NUMBER MUST APPEAR ON ALL INVOICES, PACKING LISTS, PACKAGE LABELS AND BILLS OF LADING. No. 46804052

INVOICE TO: P.O. BOX 28, BOISE, IDAHO 83707

ACKNOWLEDGE TO: P.O. BOX 15, BOISE, IDAHO 83707

SHIP TO: 646 NORTH FIVE MILE RD. BOISE, ID 83705

VENDOR CODE 2909001P TELEPHONE NUMBER

CONFIRMED ORDER YES TO: GEORGETTE

2680 LPS

TERMS OF PAYMENT % NET
F.O.B.

SPECIAL INSTRUCTIONS

SUB-CODE

DATE ORDER TYPED 12/01/8X
CONFIRMING DATE 11/25/8X
RESALE NUMBER 80821S
CHARGE TAX ONLY ON ITEMS ASTERISKED
SHIPPING INSTRUCTIONS UPS

ITEM	QUANTITY	UNIT PRICE	*	DESCRIPTION	OUR PART NUMBER	SHIPPING DATE DO NOT SHIP BEFORE SPECIFIED DATE UNLESS AUTHORIZED	ACCOUNT OR WORKORDER NUMBER	DELIVER TO LOCATION
01	1000	$0.1142 PER EA		SCREW-MACHINE M2.5 X 0.45; 4 MM LONG; PER HP DWG(S): A-0515-9002-1 REV. *.	0515-0061	01/04/8X	3521	46-2190
02	2000	$0.1345 PER EA		SCREW-MACHINE M3.0 X 0.50; 6 MM LONG; PER HP DWG(S): A-0515-9003-1 REV. *.	0515-0076	01/04/8X	3521	46-2190
03	1000	$0.1928 PER EA		NUT-HEX M2 X 0.4 THREAD; PER HP DWG: A-0535-9001-1 REV. *.	0535-0018	01/04/8X	3521	46-2190

ORIGINAL

The HP 2680 Page Printer can make fast work of multipart forms. These three pages are an example of custom printing of forms for various users. Note that unique information may be on each page (in this example the distribution). The HP 2680 Page Printer is a much more cost-effective forms printing solution than preprinted multipart forms. In addition, every copy is an original. When you consider set-up time for multipart forms and the time and information lost due to illegible copies, the electronic printing solution is extremely attractive.

RT NUMBER ON ALL CORRESPONDENCE
ORATE ORDER:
Y OF INVOICE
ACCOUNTS PAYABLE

FURNISH IN ACCORDANCE WITH TERMS & CONDITIONS HERE & ON NEXT PAGE
REFER INQUIRES TO BUYER G BARCLAY /05
PLEASE ACKNOWLEDGE
HEWLETT-PACKARD COMPANY

EXPLANATION OF SHIPPING INSTRUCTIONS
1. Insure all parcel post shipments for $50 - TRACEABILITY ONLY.
2. Do NOT insure other shipments - DECLARE MINIMUM VALUE.
3. Ship by air ONLY if authorized by buyer.
4. Consolidate all shipments on one day to one consignee.
5. Excess unauthorized freight costs will be billed to the shipper.

Exhibit 5.23
The Hewlett-Packard 2680 Laser Printer and Printed Samples

outcome is a direct function of the fineness of the lines, the type of pen tips used, and the number of color pens available. This low-cost approach can give surprisingly high-resolution graphics. Note in Exhibit 5.24 the complex surface drawing produced by the plotter on the far left.

Plotters come in a wide variety of sizes ranging from small desktop models to enormous devices that can be used to draw full-scale airplane designs. The two basic types of plotters are flat-bed and drum (see Exhibit 5.24). Flat-bed plotters move the pens along the X and Y axes according to software instructions. The material being printed on is flat and stationary. With drum plotters, the pen moves perpendicularly to the direction of the rotating drum, which can move the paper backward and forward. The major advantage of the drum plotter is that the length of the paper roll allows very long printouts, which are useful for scientific work such as seismic tracings, and for other applications as well.

Computer Output Microform

One of the options for producing hard copy output of data or graphical images is **Computer Output Microform (COM).** This is a technique in which a microphotographic copy of information is recorded on a microform such as a microfilm reel or a microfiche card. With some systems, the computer data are first recorded on magnetic tape. The tape is later used as input to a COM

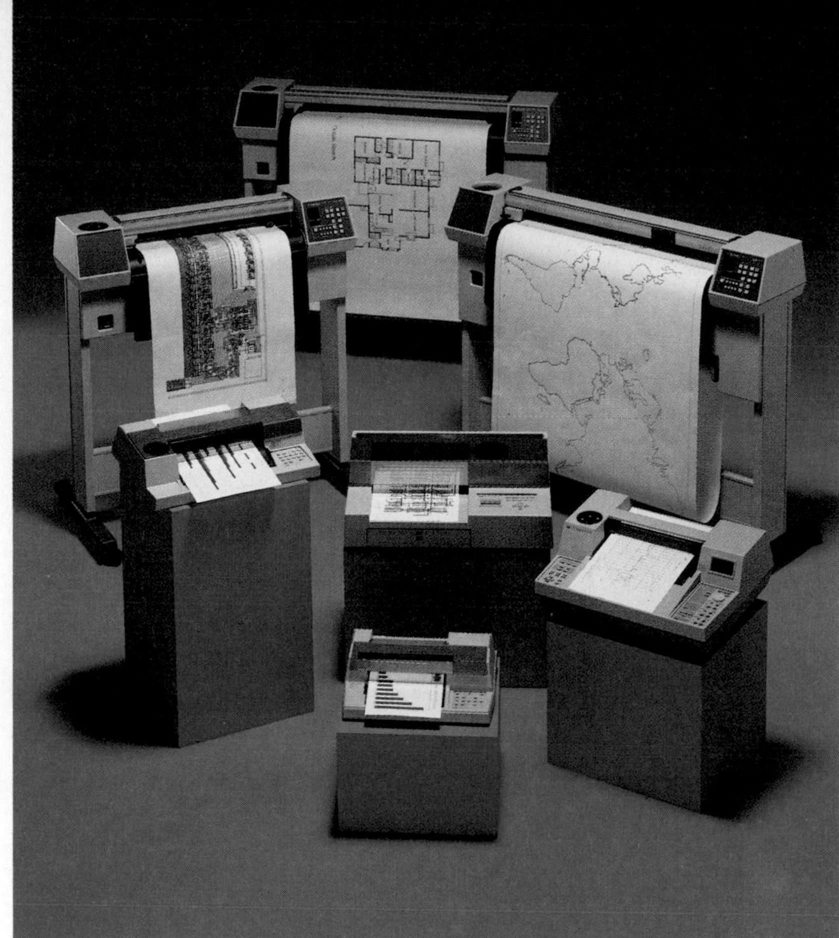

Exhibit 5.24
Plotters
Using the vector concept, plotters can produce high-resolution graphics at low cost. Computer plotters are used in a variety of applications.

machine, which reads the data and produces a microform copy of the information. In other systems, the computer can directly transfer data to the COM machine.

COM is especially useful in those situations where certain computer records stored on magnetic tape or disk are no longer active, but need to be referenced occasionally or kept to meet a legal requirement. Examples include the medical and financial records of patients after they have left a hospital, the transcript records of students after they have graduated from college, and old insurance claims. To store this type of data on computer disk or tape would cost approximately 20 times more than storing it on microfilm. The other option has been to store computer printouts of inactive data. But printouts cost 10 times as much to produce, and take up 50 times more physical space than microfilm. These cost relationships are also affecting how active data is being stored and retrieved.

To access data stored on a microform, one can use microfilm or microfiche readers. But **computer-assisted retrieval (CAR)** is also available. These systems are generally minicomputer-based and use an index to locate the specific cartridge of film that contains the desired data. This cartridge is then manually mounted for viewing by the operator, or, in more advanced systems, the cartridge is loaded automatically (see Exhibit 5.25 on page 138).

The cost advantage of microforms and the availability of CAR is affecting the extent of storage and retrieval of active data. Some 50 percent of CAR applications today relate to active order entry, accounts payable/receivable files, invoicing, and mortgage and installment loans.

Exhibit 5.25

The Kodak IMT-250 Microimage Terminal

The operator is seated at the microimage terminal, which can be linked with a minicomputer to find an image automatically. The CRT terminal in the background is then used to retrieve the microimage address from the minicomputer.

Thus, COM is an attractive medium for inactive, archival, and even, in certain cases, active data. Its major disadvantages are that COM equipment is expensive and slow at retrieving data. But the emerging optical disk technology, which will be discussed in Chapter 6, "Secondary Storage," overcomes many of the disadvantages of COM. In fact, it is expected to replace microfilm in many computer applications.

SPEECH SYNTHESIS DEVICES

HAL was the name of the computer in *2001: A Space Odyssey,* a movie about the future. HAL could listen, understand, speak, and almost outwit its masters. As you are learning, computers are very far from this level of sophistication in reality. Though perhaps not as dramatic as Hollywood special effects make them appear, there have been some exciting developments in the areas of voice recognition, artificial intelligence, and voice output. No longer limited to toys and arcade games, computer-generated voice output has been incorporated into medical systems, talking terminals, and voice message systems.

You are already familiar, no doubt, with one of the earliest uses of computer-activated voice output systems: a telephone company's phone message, "The number you have dialed has been changed." Dialing the old number activated a prerecorded taped message. Because an actual human voice was reproduced, the speech quality was very good.

In more recent years, telephone companies have used digital sound recording techniques to record the messages in bubble memory. (This form of storage will be discussed in Chapter 6). While the resulting speech quality is excellent, the inherent flexibility of systems using message reproduction is quite limited. All possible responses must be thought out in advance.

For a limited number of conditions, this isn't a drawback. But imagine using this method to announce, for example, every phone number change. It would require that a voice recording be made for each and every changed phone number—literally thousands! Clearly, this would be an unworkable solution. A more advanced concept called **speech synthesis** is needed for these situations.

Speech synthesizers work in one of two ways. They use either the analysis technique or the constructive method. With the **analysis technique,** digitized versions of individual words are stored in memory. The computer analyzes the message needed for a specific situation. It then selects the appropriate words from the vocabulary in memory. A computer-generated voice message is made by stringing these words together. The output is quite understandable, since the individual words are a reproduction of natural speech. However, the resulting phrases sound robotic, since there are none of the inflections or emphases that make speech sound natural. Telephone companies use the analysis approach to produce the voice output of the computer that announces, "That number has been changed. The new number is nine (pause), six (pause), three (pause), ..."

The breakthrough for low-cost speech output using the analysis approach occurred when Texas Instruments developed the first single-chip speech synthesizer. In 1978, this chip was used to generate the voice of Speak 'n' Spell, a computer educational toy. The same technique is also used in many vehicle warning systems, talking elevators, emergency medical systems, and grocery store checkout systems. A major disadvantage with the analysis method is its memory requirement. The larger the vocabulary, the more memory is needed. Applications using word analysis are therefore restricted to those that can function with a small vocabulary.

In general, the larger the vocabulary available, the greater the range of situations to which the computer can be programmed to respond. To develop computer voice-generated systems with large vocabularies, yet small memory requirements, is the goal of the **constructive technique** of speech synthesis. Instead of using stored words as the basic units of voice generation, this method uses **phonemes,** the basic elements of speech, to construct a vocabulary. For example, to say the word *peach* one would use three phonemes: *pea, ee,* and *ch.* In the English language, all words can be constructed from about 40 phonemes, made up of 16 vowel phonemes and 24 consonant phonemes. Thus, the constructive synthesis method requires the storage of only 40 phonemes, plus the rules for combining phonemes into words. This approach requires a relatively small memory to generate a large, if not unlimited, vocabulary.

The disadvantage of the constructive method is that the resulting computer speech is practically unrecognizable if the phonemes are simply strung together. Thus, more complex rules and synthesis techniques are needed to control the timing, pitch, and inflection of the sounds.

Exhibit 5.26
The DECtalk Voice Synthesizer

DECtalk, by Digital Equipment Corporation, is an example of a voice synthesis machine that can generate natural-sounding voice output using phonemes. DECtalk is a self-contained unit that receives text output from a computer system. Instead of printing the text, DECtalk speaks it through a speaker, or over a telephone line. Voices of male or female adults or children can be used, and the speaking rate can be varied (see Exhibit 5.26).

Voice synthesis systems such as DECtalk have many applications. One example is computer-aided instruction systems that allow a student to both see and hear the information that is displayed on the video screen. This reinforcement can make the instruction clearer and the system more pleasant to use. An example of another use for this system is to allow people to use their telephones to consult computer files. For example, a sales representative could get immediate inventory information needed during a customer meeting. A lawyer

Exhibit 5.27
Voice Output Applications
Constructive and analysis techniques of speech synthesis have many applications. Those listed here vary in terms of their complexity and their required vocabulary.

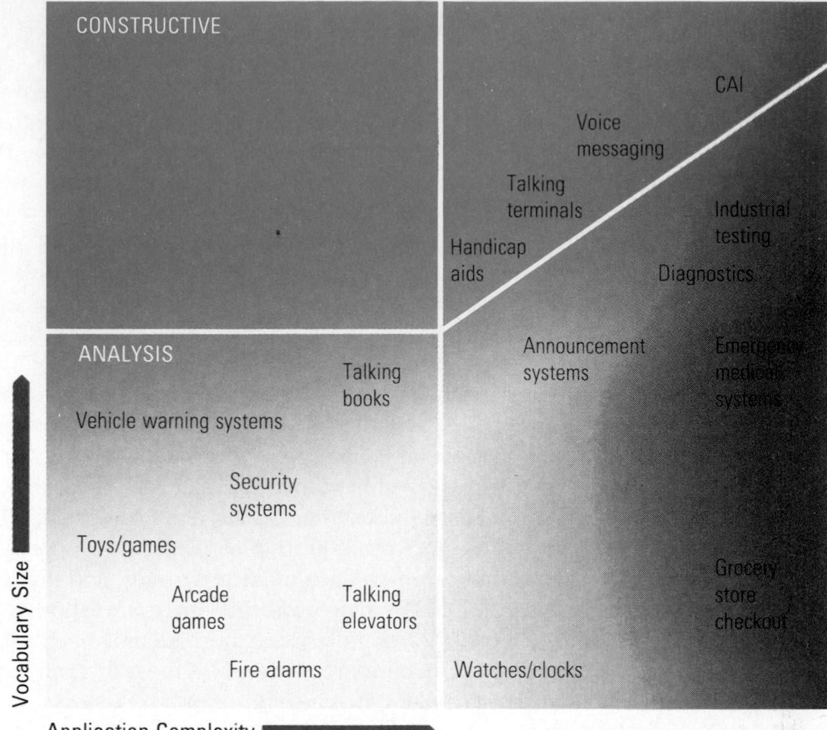

could check records in an office file during a break in court proceedings. An investor could get up-to-the-minute quotes from stock brokerage firms. Clearly, a voice synthesis system can be a useful tool for professionals in a variety of work situations.

Voice synthesis systems are also being used to aid the handicapped. To accomplish this, OCR systems have been combined with voice systems for use by visually impaired people. The OCR scans the text in a book or report and transmits it to a computer system, where it is processed. The output is synthesized speech. Exhibit 5.27 shows the relationship between these sorts of applications and their complexity and vocabulary requirements.

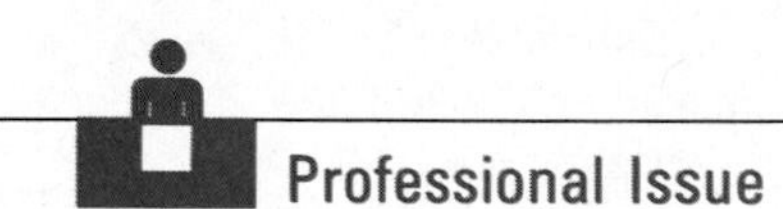

Printer Selection Criteria

Historically, the typewriter has been the major apparatus for producing printed material used in business communication, but increasingly, the computer printer is taking over this role. According to a Yankee Group report, major computer centers in the United States printed out 240 billion pages of information in 1980. This is equal to approximately 1000 pages for every person in the country. In 1985, the total was estimated at 20 trillion pages, or 10,000 pages of computer printout for each person. This trend is forecasted to continue for the near future. It stands to reason that the topic of computer printers deserves more discussion, because printers are the primary way to produce hard copy printouts, and the demand for hard copy printouts is increasing significantly. In addition, printers are a major cost item with any computer system. They are expensive because of their mechanical nature.

In this section we'll examine the major criteria used to select printers. These include performance, price, print quality, flexibility, and operational costs. A printer's **performance** is measured by its speed. Serial printer speeds are given in characters per second (cps), line printers in lines per minute (lpm), and page printers in pages per minute (ppm).

Several generalizations can be drawn from Exhibit 5.28. First, impact serial printers are generally slower than nonimpact serial printers. Second, impact line printers are significantly faster than serial printers. The top speed of fully formed impact serial printers is around 200 cps. Although this rate is relatively slow, it is considerably faster than a good typist's speed of 10 cps. Third, impact line printers are much slower than nonimpact page printers. The top speed for impact line printers is around 3000 lpm. In contrast, a medium-speed laser page printer rated at 40 ppm can print the equivalent of about 5000 lpm, and the pace of high-speed page printers with capability to print 120 ppm is about equal to a speed of 14,000 lpm.

However, the **price** for printers with increased print speed capability is generally significantly higher. For example, dot-matrix serial printers rated at 80 cps are available for around $500. An impact dot-matrix line printer at 150 lpm would cost around $5000. Impact printers rated at 2000 lpm would cost $60,000–$70,000. To get printers with top speeds in the 10,000 lpm range would cost hundreds of thousands of dollars.

The speed needed in a printer is very much related to the amount of printing that a company does. John Harker of Dataproducts Corporation believes that organizations that print more than a million pages per month are candidates for the very high-speed printers (10,000–20,000 lpm). This would be true of paper-intensive organizations such as banks, insurance companies, and governmental agencies.

Organizations generating 200,000–600,000 pages per month often use the high-speed printers (1000 to 3000 lpm). Small businesses generating 20,000–150,000 pages per month can use printers with speed capabilities of 300–1000 lpm. Serial printers are economical for the small printing jobs usually associated with personal computers.

Exhibit 5.28
Printer Performance Versus Price Factors

	Character Transfer	Technology	Speed	Price
Serial Printers	Impact	Dot-Matrix	20–200 cps	$400–3000
	Nonimpact	Dot-Matrix	80–500 cps	$300–4000
Line Printers	Impact	Dot-Matrix	150–600 lpm	$5000–15,000
	Impact	Drum	300–2000 lpm	$10,000–60,000
	Impact	Chain or Train	300–2000 lpm	$15,000–70,000
	Impact	Band or Belt	150–3000 lpm	$7,000–100,000
Page Printers	Nonimpact	Electrostatic	5–100 ppm	$3000–165,000
	Nonimpact	Xerographic	12–120 ppm	$18,000–400,000

Print quality is a major consideration in printer selection. The degree of quality needed is dependent on the type of organizational application. Invoices, statements, and other correspondence going outside a company usually require clean, legible copy. In general, fully formed characters used in drum, chain or train, band or belt, and some dot-matrix printers give good quality output. Page printers that use image processing give exceptionally high-quality output, rivaling offset printing used by publishers.

The lower print quality of nonimpact dot-matrix printers is acceptable for most organizations' internal uses. The quality of dot-matrix methods is a function of the density of the character matrix. Characters formed by a 5 × 7 dot-matrix are very low quality, whereas 5 × 9 are better, and 18 × 36 are quite good.

A printer's **flexibility** in handling a range of tasks is a fourth selection criterion. How easy is it to use different fonts? Many impact printers can work with only one type font at a time. To use a different font set, the type element must be changed, whether it is a golf ball or daisy-wheel style, or sections of a chain. In contrast, the characters produced by dot-matrix printers are defined electronically. Thus, it is relatively easy to change fonts by simply defining different matrix patterns. Mixed fonts can be used within a document.

The printer's ability to handle forms is another dimension of its flexibility. Many printers are designed to be used strictly for data processing and, therefore, use the common fanfold, single-sheet paper. But often, companies use multicopy forms for invoices and purchase orders. This sort of form requires an impact printer. Exhibit 5.29 shows an example of the versatility that some printers offer in printing alphanumerics, graphics, bar codes, and form designs in monochrome or color on paper of varying sizes and other such media.

The last major criterion for selecting a printer concerns **operational cost.** This covers both maintenance and supply considerations. Because print-

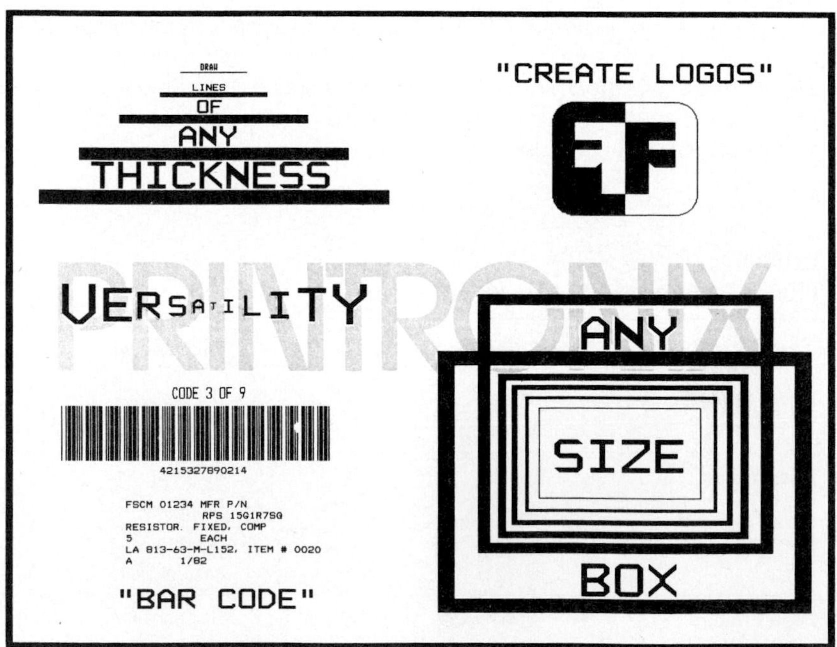

Exhibit 5.29

Samples printed on the Intelligent Graphics Processor by Printronix demonstrate its versatility.

ers have many moving parts, there is a significant chance for malfunction. In general, nonimpact printers require less maintenance than impact printers, but there are several exceptions to this rule. A good indicator of a printer's reliability is its **mean time between failures (MTBF) rating,** a measure of the expected average time between breakdowns. Service companies will quote their prices per hour for maintenance, or an annual charge for a service contract. In addition to comparing repair costs, it also will be important to check the reputation and reliability of the companies offering these repair services.

Supply costs are a function of the amount of printing that will be done and the rate at which paper, ribbons, and other consumable items are used up. The need for special paper or ink cartridges can add significantly to these costs.

We have discussed five major criteria that should be considered when selecting a computer printer. Other considerations for printer selection include operating noise level and any special environmental restrictions such as temperature or power requirements. In addition, there is a need to consider interfaces between the printer and the computer hardware and software. These will be discussed in Section III, "Systems Support Software." Chapter 12, "Systems Development II," will discuss ways to use the knowledge you gained here for specific applications.

Filming by Computer

Before long, synthetic images will be common in movies and television, and not for reasons of mere novelty. The lure is cost, speed, and quality.

Most computer-generated imagery, whether of a jumbo jet in a wind tunnel or a giant electric shaver flying through a TV commercial, is produced by computer graphic systems.

Cray Research in Minneapolis makes what many people consider the world's most powerful computers. When the first of Cray's new $12.6 million X–MP/22 machines rolls off the line later this year, it will be installed at Digital Productions, a Hollywood film studio. "The Cray was a natural choice," says John Whitney, Jr., the studio's president. But why does his company need something even the Pentagon doesn't have yet?

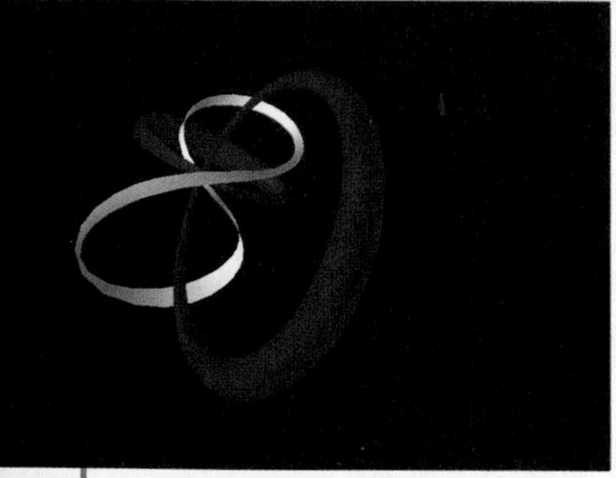

Well, for one thing, Whitney's studio is interested in creating full-screen computer simulations. These would be many times higher in resolution than a standard TV picture, possibly 4000 pixels high by 6000 pixels wide, for a total of 24 million pixels per frame. To create one frame, suppose the computer needs to make only 10 calculations to determine the value of each pixel. Commercial motion pictures run at 24 frames per second. Repeating the entire procedure for every frame, it would take 24 × 10 × 24,000,000, or 5,760,000,000, calculations to produce one second's worth of film. The entire image doesn't change in every frame, of course, and computer-graphics specialists know some shortcuts for reducing the number of calculations. But it's a task that is, as mathematicians say, "computer-intensive."

To deliver realistic images, computer graphics must be able to shade objects and represent motion. The most basic shading programs present the object in space as a solid form, its surface shown in any of millions of colors. The memory for each of the pixels in a high-resolution picture is at least 32 bits deep; that is, each pixel is stored in the computer's memory as a 32-digit binary number. Of this, 24 bits specify the exact color value of the particular pixel. Some pixels, those depicting parts of an object exposed to the brightest light, will show the full values of the assigned color; pixels in shadowy areas will be dimmer. As the object is rotated or moved, some or all of the pixel values change.

The next step is movement. This, of course, is created by recomputing the pixel values from frame to frame. The computer animator decides on the starting and ending points of the particular move, along with a time span. For example, to create a 24-frame (one-second) "zoom out" from a 13-degree to an 85-degree viewing angle, the computations are made to bring more and more of the image into view until all parts of the scene are visible by the 24th frame.

A program that moves objects around on a screen can be as simple to write as programs that draw the objects themselves. The "camera/eye" can fly around, under, and through objects with none of the physical limitations of real life. The movement is as smooth, effortless, and gravity-defying as the programmer wishes. (Not that it's always a snap for the computer.

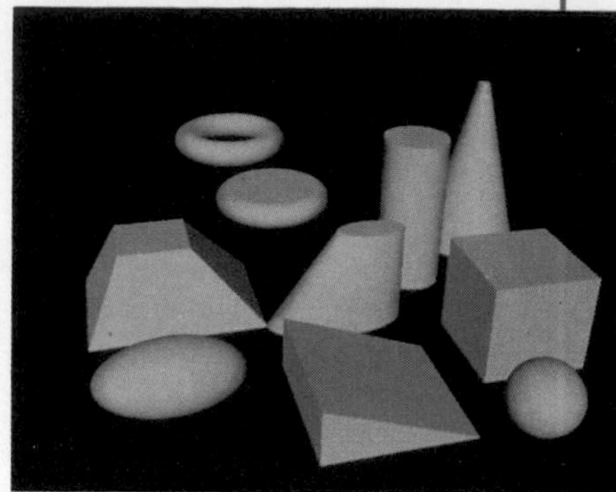

One second of film—24 frames per second, from 30 seconds to 30 minutes of computer time per frame—can take 12 hours to shoot.)

With all these advances in computer-created imagery, many insiders are convinced that we are on the brink of a major revolution in filmmaking technology, with computer graphics leading the way. What is probably the most ambitious image-synthesis project at the moment is underway at NYIT. There, Lance Williams, yet another graduate of the Utah computer-graphics program, is heading up a team that hopes to produce a feature-length computer-generated film called *The Works.* Several characters are already stored away in the computer's memory, including a digitally created robot composed of highly reflective metal that trundles down a hall on tanklike treads. Unfortunately, due to the monumental amount of computer time required, the team has only completed a few minutes of test footage.

Perhaps the ultimate in computer imaging is still years away: synthetic people, acting out scenes with one another, completely defined by numbers in a computer's data base. The usefulness of such an experiment is not as strikingly apparent as that of a wind-tunnel simulation—but for many researchers, the challenge may be too intriguing to pass up.

Source: From "Filming by Computer" by Robert Rivlin. Reprinted with permission, *Technology Illustrated,* (February 1983). Copyright © 1983 by High Technology Publishing Corporation, 38 Commercial Wharf, Boston, MA 02110.

SUMMARY

For computer-processed data to be of any value, it must be in a form that users can understand. Historically, printed output was the primary way of showing computer processing results. While paper is still the dominant output medium, there are now many other alternative ways to communicate information.

Computer output can be classified in several different ways. *Hard copy* output, such as paper printouts, provides the user with a permanent record. *Soft copy* output, such as the visual display on a terminal, or computer voice output provide a temporary record. These three forms of output can also be understood by human users, whereas the electronic data stored on magnetic tape or disk are *computer-readable.* Information that is presented in the form of letters, numbers, and special characters is *alphanumeric.* In contrast, *graphics* are pictures or graphs depicting information.

Visual display of information is one of the most effective means for showing users the results of computer processing. The primary technology for producing and displaying the images on the terminal screen are the cathode-ray tube and the flat-panel.

Cathode-ray tubes (CRTs), like television picture tubes, electronically paint characters on a screen. CRT screens can create images using raster scan or vector technology. In a CRT using the *raster scan* process, a beam of electrons sweeps back and forth horizontally across the screen. As the beam moves across the screen, the current is increased or decreased to create brighter (on) or darker (off) points. These points are called *pixels,* or picture elements. *Resolution* is a measure of the number of pixels that can be addressed on the screen.

CRTs are used in monochrome and color monitors. *Monochrome monitors* display one color such as green or amber on a black background. *Color monitors* use a triad or trio of dots to form a pixel. The three dots are red, green, and blue phosphor. In a *composite video monitor* one electron gun is used to turn on the appropriate colors within each triad. RGB *monitors* have much sharper graphical images than composite video monitors because of the finer control possible when using three electron beams.

If each individual pixel is addressable, this is known as a *bit-map* or *dot-addressable* display. When only blocks of pixels can be addressed or manipulated in displays, this is known as *character-addressable* display.

Vector technology is based on the use of lines or vectors drawn on the screen. In contrast to the raster scan approach, in which the whole screen is always scanned in a fixed pattern, regardless of how much is on the screen, the vector approach scans only where necessary. This difference has a major effect on the amount of primary memory required to show a graphic image.

A new technology is emerging to challenge the CRT as the primary means of displaying alphanumeric and graphical images. It is the *flat-panel* display. Plasma and liquid crystal are two of the primary technologies used with it. Flat-panel displays create a screen image by illuminating a pattern of discrete dots to display alphanumeric data, graphics, and video images. The high resolution and steady image of flat-panel displays yield high-quality results.

Historically, alphanumeric data has been the primary information output. The *computer printer,* with its capability to print alphanumeric data on paper, has been the predominant means of generating hard copy output. More recently, the need for graphical displays has changed the type of printers that are in demand and also encouraged the development of plotters.

The computer printer field has not settled on a limited number of ways of printing alphanumeric information. Rather, a dozen or so technologies are being used. These technologies differ in three basic ways: *character formation, character transfer* (to paper or another *medium*), and *number of characters printed at a time.* Character formation options are: fully formed, dot-matrix, and image. Characters, once formed, can be transferred by an impact or nonimpact method. The number of characters to be transferred at a time can range from one character to an entire line or a complete page.

The growing popularity of graphics terminals has been accompanied by an increasing need for hard copy of the graphics developed on the computer terminal. Business graphics were first printed by plotting points using fully formed characters. This approach is used in multifunction dot-matrix impact printers, as well as in printers using nonimpact thermal and ink-jet technology.

Plotters are output devices that are specialized to produce graphics. Plotters use the vector concept to produce a picture made up of a series of straight lines. Plotters come in a wide variety of sizes ranging from small desktop models to enormous devices used to draw full-scale airplane designs. The two basic types of plotters are flat-bed and drum.

One of the options for producing hard copy output of data or graphical images is *computer output microform (COM).* This is a technique in which a microphotographic copy of information is recorded on a microform such as a microfilm reel or a microfiche card. Filmed output, such as microfilm and microfiche, is attractive as a computer output medium because of its lower storage cost and reduced space requirements.

Computer-generated voice output using *speech synthesis* techniques is used in talking terminals and voice message systems. Speech synthesizers work in one of two ways. With the *analysis* technique, digitized versions of individual words are stored in memory, appropriate words are selected from the vocabulary in memory, and a computer-generated voice message is made by stringing the words together. The *constructive* technique differs in that *phonemes,* the basic elements of speech, are used to construct a word vocabulary.

The typewriter has been the major apparatus for producing printed material used in business communication, but increasingly, the computer printer is taking over this role. The major criteria used to select printers are: performance, price, print quality, flexibility, and operational costs.

A printer's *performance* is measured by its speed. The *price* for printers with increased print speed capability is generally significantly higher than for a low-speed model.

Print quality is a major consideration in printer selection. The degree of quality needed is dependent on the type of organizational application. Invoices, statements, and correspondence going outside a company usually require clean, legible copy. The lower print quality of nonimpact dot matrix printers is acceptable for most organizations' internal uses.

A printer's *flexibility* in handling a range of tasks is a fourth selection criterion. How easy is it to use different fonts? The printer's ability to handle forms is another dimension of its flexibility. Many printers are designed to be used strictly for traditional data processing output, such as alphanumeric data printed on paper. The last major criterion for selecting a printer concerns *operational cost.* This covers both maintenance and supply considerations.

In the next chapter we will discuss the various forms of secondary storage.

REVIEW QUESTIONS

1. Briefly describe the basic classifications of computer output. Why do some systems provide "redundant" outputs?
2. How does a CRT display work? What is meant by the term *raster scan?*
3. Distinguish between dot-addressable and character-addressable displays. What is *resolution,* and why is it important?
4. Briefly describe the advantages offered by each of the following special CRT features: scrolling, paging, windows, double size, blinking, underlining, and reverse video.
5. Build-Rite, an engineering firm, is considering the purchase of computer terminals for CAD/CAM applications. Should the firm purchase a graphics terminal featuring a vector display or raster scan display? Defend your position.
6. In spite of the resolution/memory advantages offered by vector displays, many experts believe that raster graphics will be the technology of the future. Why?
7. Compare flat-panel displays and CRT displays. What advantages does the flat-panel display offer?
8. Briefly summarize the text's conclusions regarding current printer technology. Which of the current printer technologies is the most flexible?
9. What is a plotter? How can a device that is capable of drawing only straight lines produce curves?
10. The CPM Corporation is considering the use of a COM system for the storage of its accounts receivable/accounts payable records. What are the advantages of this approach?
11. Briefly explain the two approaches currently employed by speech synthesizers.
12. Briefly describe the major criteria for selecting printers. Is it possible for one alternative to excel on all criteria? If not, how must a firm proceed with regard to the selection of a printer?

CHAPTER 6

Secondary Storage

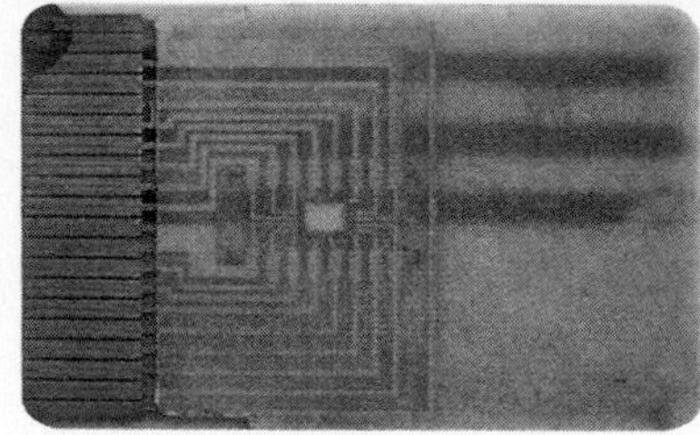

COMPUTERS AT WORK

Putting Intelligence In Your Wallet

Tomorrow's bank card may replace your checkbook with a digital storage system. It will be compact enough to fit in a wallet, yet powerful enough to hold records of all personal financial transactions. Its security will be so high, it will be accepted in place of cash in banks and stores worldwide. It may even balance your checkbook automatically. Two approaches are vying for dominance: a mass-memory card, and a computer-chip card.

The memory card could serve as an all-purpose ID, perhaps replacing driver's licenses, passports, etc. The card could store digital data signifying the bearer's fingerprint, voiceprint, or the pattern made by capillaries in the retina. A stand-alone card-reading machine, equipped with a microprocessor, would check whether this biological data on the card matched that of the card-holder. In addition, the card could carry such important information as a person's medical history, which can be vital in an emergency and which is often hard to obtain quickly today.

Just such a mass-storage card is being developed by Drexler Technology (Mountain View, Calif.). The company's Drexon card stores 2 megabits, or roughly 50,000 words—nearly 1000 times more than a magnetic strip card.

The Drexler cards are coated with a two-layer plastic film. The top layer is embedded with microscopic pieces of silver, giving the material a highly reflective, metallic look. To write data, a low power laser pits in the top layer to expose the unsilvered—and unreflective—bottom layer. To read the card, a laser scans the surface and a photodetector senses the presence and absence of pits as highs and lows in the intensity of the reflected light.

The computer-chip cards, often dubbed smart cards, draw their power from an embedded microprocessor. There's also a nonvolatile memory that holds its contents even when disconnected from an electrical power source. Present chip cards have memories of about 16 kilobits.

Although it has other potential uses, the smart card was originally developed for French banks as a replacement for the checkbook. The French tend to write lots of small checks, which are expensive for the banks to process. The banks hope the smart card will automate checking and drastically reduce the cost of check processing. Because the card shows the holder's account balance at the moment of the sale, it is as "bounce-proof" as cash. The card carries its owner's copy of the transaction; the terminal records the store's copy on a magnetic tape or disk which can be taken to the store's bank for deposit whenever convenient.

Source: From "Putting Intelligence In Your Wallet" by G. Berton Latamore. Reprinted with permission, *High Technology* magazine, (June 1983). Copyright © 1983 by High Technology Publishing Corporation, 38 Commercial Wharf, Boston, MA 02110.

As you read in the chapter opener, different storage media are emerging to handle increasingly diverse computer applications. A major function of all these secondary or auxiliary storage media is the storage of information in a computer-readable form that allows rapid retrieval for computer processing.

In Chapter 3, we studied a simple payroll application in which both program instructions and data were entered via the keyboard of a CRT. This approach is fine for programs that are going to be run once, or very infrequently. But in real payroll applications, the instructions for calculating and deducting taxes and insurance premiums make the program longer and more complicated, and an employer may have hundreds of employees to pay weekly, twice a month, or monthly. Entering the necessary program and data via a keyboard for each pay period would be a waste of time and money, as well as increase the chance of error.

In applications such as these, it makes more sense to store both the payroll program and employee pay records in secondary storage, such as on magnetic tape or disk. When it was time to run the payroll program, the computer instructions and master data for each employee would be read into primary memory from secondary storage. A payroll clerk would have to key in only those changes to the payroll records that had occurred since the last run. For example, an operator might have to key in the number of hours an employee worked in the latest pay period.

The move from batch processing of transactions to the more interactive requirements of information reporting, decision support systems, and computer aided design has had significant implications for the type of storage medium that is best for each application. In addition, different forms of data are being processed. Historically, data have been primarily alphanumeric. The 1970s saw the additional need for text processing, and the 1980s appear to be the decade for adding graphics. Different storage devices and media are emerging to handle these diverse needs. In this chapter you will learn to do the following:

1. Explain the major ways secondary storage devices are classified.
2. Describe available magnetic disk technologies and compare their capabilities and limitations.
3. Identify the unique characteristics of optical disks and bubble memory.
4. Identify the types of magnetic tape units that are used with large computers and personal computers.
5. Define the role of mass storage devices.
6. Explain what the memory hierarchy is and how it is used in computer systems.

CLASSIFYING COMPUTER STORAGE

In this chapter we will be discussing the characteristics of direct-access storage devices such as magnetic disk, optical disk, and bubble memory. Since computers are being used more and more for interactive applications, direct-access storage devices are becoming the dominant storage medium. But sequential-access media have an important role to play also. They are now being used primarily for batch processing applications and for inexpensive offline storage. Our discussion of sequential-access media will center on magnetic tape. We will also discuss mass storage, which allows relatively slow, but economical, computer access to vast numbers of inactive records. Lastly, we will put the uses of the traditional and emerging secondary and primary storage media into perspective by discussing the reasons each is used. First, however, we need to examine the ways computer storage is classified and explain some of the terms that apply. Computer storage can be divided into three basic categories: volatile vs. nonvolatile, sequential vs. direct access, and fixed vs. removable.

Volatile Versus Nonvolatile Storage

To be processed, computer programs and data have to be loaded into primary memory. But the present primary memory technology has several major problems. One is that read/write primary memory such as RAM can only be used for temporary storage of information, since it is *volatile.* That is, when power to the computer is cut off, the information in RAM is lost. In contrast, secondary storage is *nonvolatile.* Tapes and disks use magnetic recording techniques that retain the data when the power is off.

A second problem is that primary memory has limited storage capacity. Often, the complete program and all data records needed cannot fit into primary memory at one time. This limitation can be overcome, in part, by special support software called an operating system, which can be used to bring in only the active portions of instructions and data records from secondary storage. This allows large programs and extensive data records to be run on smaller computer systems. This type of support software will be discussed in detail in Chapter 7, "Operating Systems."

Sequential-Access Versus Direct-Access Storage

The limitations of primary memory—that it is volatile and has limited capacity—are two of the reasons secondary or auxiliary storage is needed. The particular type of secondary storage medium that is most appropriate depends on the kinds of programs being run. As we saw in Chapter 4, "Input," there are batch processing and transaction processing applications. These two approaches differ significantly in the way they access specific data in secondary storage. Batch processing usually uses sequential access, while transaction processing requires direct access.

To understand the terms **sequential-** and **direct-access,** imagine that you are playing recorded music on an audio cassette player and on a jukebox. Songs are recorded on audio cassette tapes sequentially. In other words, if you want to play song number four, you must first pass or play songs numbered one, two, and three. This method is called **sequential access.** In contrast, a jukebox lets you select any particular song from all that are available. By pushing button E4, you have direct access to your song without having to pass or play any other songs. This method is called **direct,** or **random,** access.

Magnetic tape, which works like an audio cassette, is the foremost sequential-access storage medium. To access a specific data record on magnetic tape, you must check each record key, in sequence, prior to the desired one. Thus, to find Sally Wallis's record, the magnetic tape unit would have to first check the record keys for John Avery and Bill Jones. Imagine the search time that would be required if Sally's record were the thousandth one on the tape. Without sequential access, the *entire* record would have to be read for each of the 999 records preceding Sally's. Clearly, sequential access holds a distinct disadvantage for a user interested only in specific records. However, if it is

Exhibit 6.1

Sequential-access media require that each record prior to the desired one be checked. Direct-access media allow the desired record to be located directly.

Sequential-Access Media | Direct-Access Media

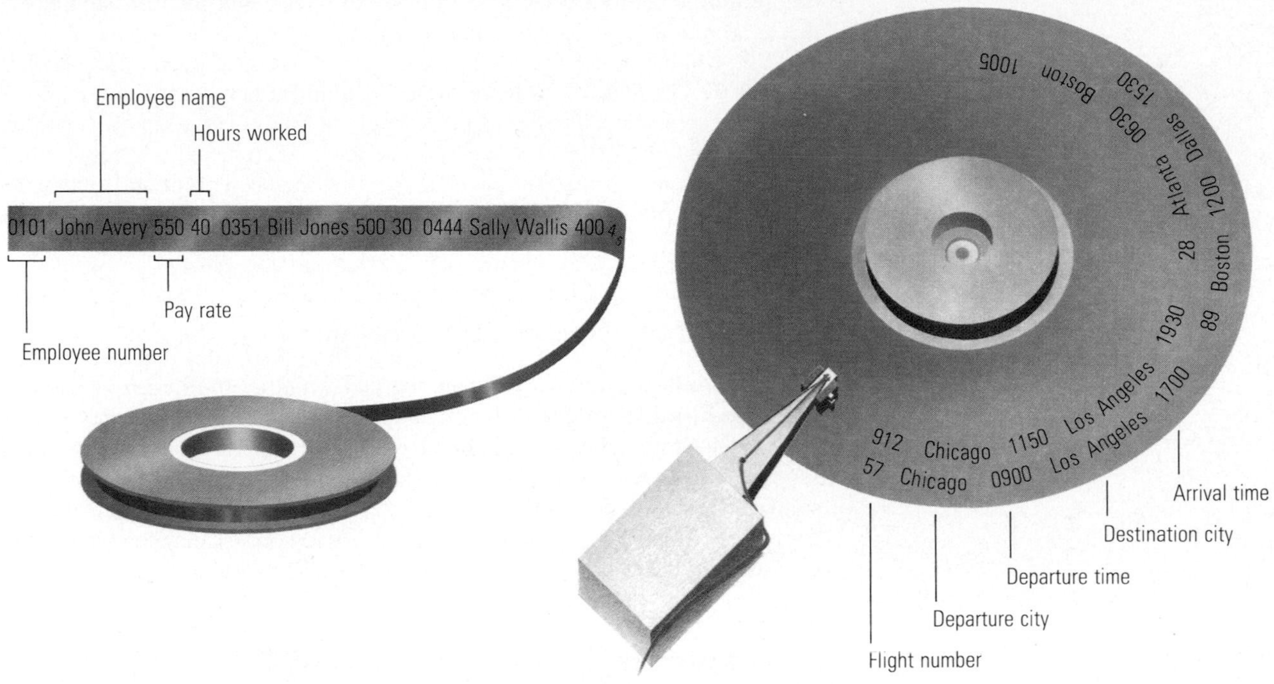

necessary to process almost all the records on the tape anyway, the lack of sequential-access capability would not be a limitation (see Exhibit 6.1).

Magnetic tape is ideal for batch processing applications such as a weekly payroll, monthly inventory status report, monthly accounts receivable billing, or for quarterly income statements. All of these programs are run rather infrequently, and when they are run almost all data records are processed to produce the required checks or reports. Thus, individual records do not have to be located directly. Since almost all records in the file will be affected, they can be processed in their existing sequence, or they can be sorted beforehand to produce the desired output.

Magnetic disk is the foremost direct-access secondary storage medium. Data are recorded on the disk in concentric circles. A **read/write head** is used to directly locate the place where the data record is to be read or written, in much the same way you can move the tone arm of a phonograph player to a particular song on a record album.

One instance in which direct access is essential is for transaction processing applications such as airline reservations. Assume you call the XYZ Airline to find out which flights are available between Chicago and Los Angeles on a specific date. The computer needs to be able to directly locate the records for only those particular flights from among thousands of records about flight schedules for the XYZ Airline.

With disk storage, direct access to specific records is readily available. Since there is no way to anticipate exactly which records will be needed when, or in what order, this capability is crucial. In most interactive applications, the ability to quickly respond to inquiries and to update records immediately as change occurs is also essential. For example, in an airline reservation system it is important not only to confirm flight information, but also to change the record for the number of open seats left on the Los Angeles-to-Chicago flight so that it accurately reflects availability.

You will learn more about how data access and data organization work in Chapter 8, "File and Data Base Systems." The important point to note here is that the access characteristics of the storage medium need to effectively meet the needs of the specific application. In general, batch processing applications are most efficient using a sequential-access storage medium and interactive processing applications are most efficient using a direct-access storage medium.

Fixed Versus Removable Storage

A third important variable of storage media is whether they are removable or fixed. **Removable media** such as magnetic tape and many disk systems allow the user to swap one set of data for another. This gives almost unlimited secondary storage capacity. In addition, this characteristic allows the storage media to be used as a backup. A **backup** is a duplicate set of computer-readable data or equipment that is used only when the original data or equipment are damaged, lost, or destroyed. When needed, the backup of

Exhibit 6.2

Removable media allow almost unlimited storage capacity, as one set of data can be swapped for another. Fixed secondary storage media offer higher reliability and extensive storage capacity without operator intervention.

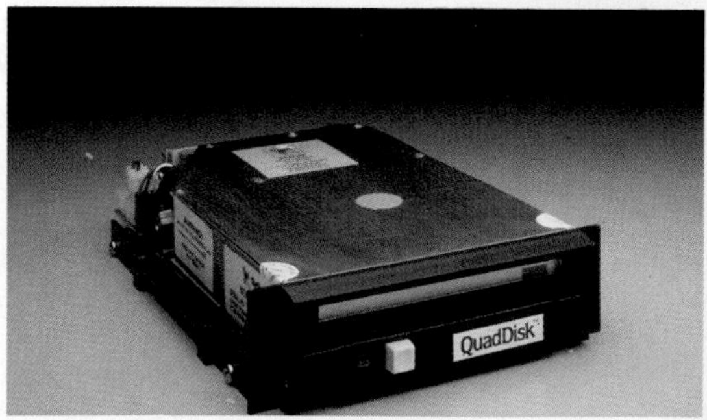

computer-readable data can be connected online and used either directly, or to reconstruct the destroyed information.

One of the major disadvantages of removable media is that they can be damaged by fingerprints, dust, or being dropped. Thus, they are less reliable than fixed media. In contrast, **fixed media** cannot be touched or removed by the user. For example, fixed hard disk systems are often used in secondary storage systems requiring high reliability and extensive storage capacity. Generally these high-precision systems have their read/write heads and disk platters sealed in contaminant-free environments (see Exhibit 6.2).

DIRECT-ACCESS STORAGE DEVICES

The medium that has come to clearly dominate the secondary storage market is the magnetic disk. This is primarily a reflection of an overall move from batch to transaction processing. With batch processing, the sequential access of records on magnetic tape was fine. However, transaction processing requires that a user have direct access to a specific record, and this is exactly what disks allow. Disks even offer the additional flexibility of doing traditional sequential processing, if desired.

One direct-access secondary storage device, the optical disk, is emerging as an important secondary storage medium. It is attractive because of its very large storage capacity and its ability to store high-quality video images. Bubble memory, on the other hand, is useful when the application requires compact, nonvolatile storage in harsh environments. Both the optical disk and bubble memory will be discussed further later in this chapter.

Magnetic Disks

There are two basic forms of magnetic disks—hard and floppy. **Hard disks** are rigid aluminum platters coated with a magnetic oxide. They come in a variety of physical sizes and have significantly different storage capacities. They can be further categorized in terms of being fixed or removable. **Diskettes** (also called floppy disks) are made of a flexible Mylar plastic coated with magnetic oxide. These diskettes also come in several physical sizes, but all are designed to be removable.

Before we consider the variety of disks available, let's see how they are designed to store and gain access to data. The disk itself is sometimes compared to a phonograph record, but there is a major difference. The disk has a series of invisible concentric circles called **tracks.** Note that this differs from a phonograph record, which has a single, visible groove that spirals toward the center of the record. Disk tracks are invisible, since they are simply composed of magnetically encoded data.

Along each track, data are encoded in the form of magnetic bit patterns. A read/write head is used to sense the magnetic direction of each bit, or to change magnetic patterns in the appropriate place on a specific track. The magnetic bit pattern for the letter *K,* using an 8-bit ASCII code, is shown in Exhibit 6.3. To read or write data, one or more disk platters are mounted on a spindle, which

Exhibit 6.3

Along each invisible concentric track, data are encoded in the form of magnetic bit patterns.

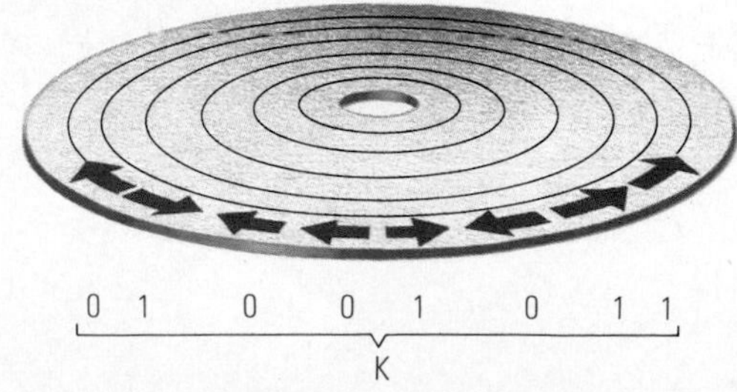

Exhibit 6.4

The storage capacity of disks is a function of the number of tracks per surface, the bit density, and the number of recording surfaces.

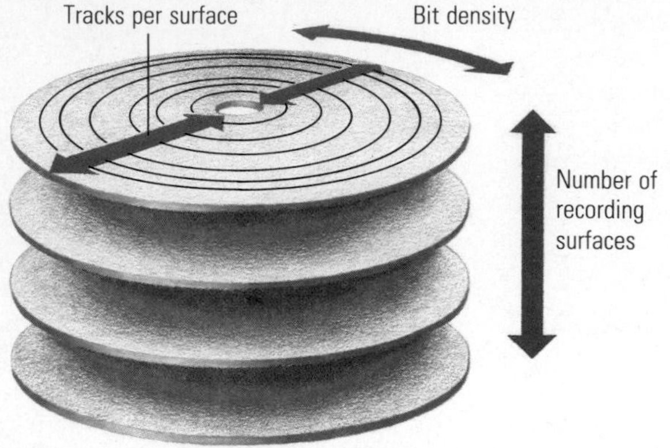

rotates at a fixed speed. For hard disk systems, this is commonly 3600 revolutions per minute (rpm), whereas the floppy disk systems spin at around 400 rpm.

The storage capacity of a disk is a function of the number of tracks per surface, the bit density, and the number of recording surfaces (see Exhibit 6.4). The number of tracks per surface is influenced by the physical size of the disk and the technology used to record the data. Platter sizes are commonly either 14-inches, 8-inches, or 5-1/4-inches in diameter for the large-capacity hard disk systems, and are primarily 5-1/4-inches and less than 4-inches in diameter for the diskette systems (see Exhibit 6.5). The number of tracks on a surface can range from 40–80 on the smaller diskettes to 200–800 on the larger disks. The trend is to pack more and more data onto a physically smaller and smaller disk.

Bit density is measured in terms of the number of bits per inch (bpi). The bpi measure ranges from 2000 in diskette systems to, commonly, 12,000 bpi in hard disks. The latest technology uses a thin-film layer of magnetic metal, as opposed to iron-oxide particles, to record bit densities of 24,000 bpi. The metal layer allows a greater, more uniform concentration of magnetic particles.

To increase the bpi for magnetic disks even more, a means of vertically recording magnetic patterns has emerged. Instead of trying to squeeze magnets lengthwise, magnets will be placed vertically instead. This allows much tighter compaction. The forecasts are for an increase of ten times the storage capacity for a vertically recorded disk, when compared to a conventional horizontally recorded disk of the same physical size (see Exhibit 6.6).

Overall, disk storage capacity ranges from less than 1 megabyte on the smaller diskette systems used with microcomputers up to several gigabytes on maxicomputers. A **gigabyte** is 1 billion bytes, or 1 thousand megabytes. About

Exhibit 6.5

Disk platters come in a variety of sizes. The smallest is 3–½ inches in diameter (left) and the largest is 14 inches in diameter (right).

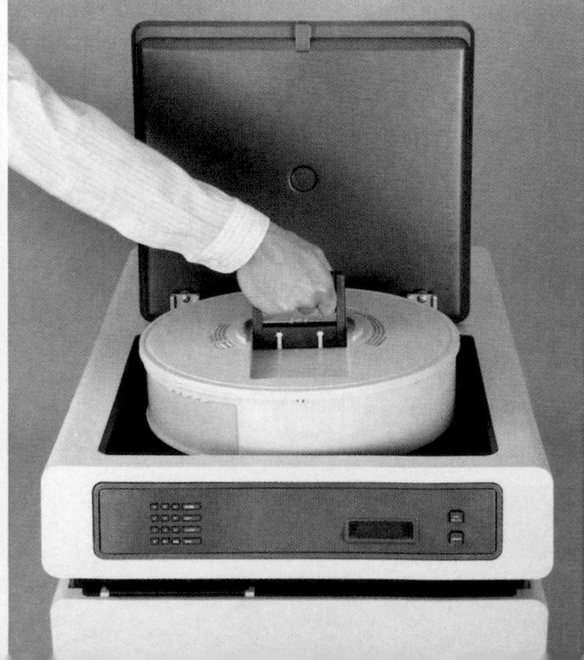

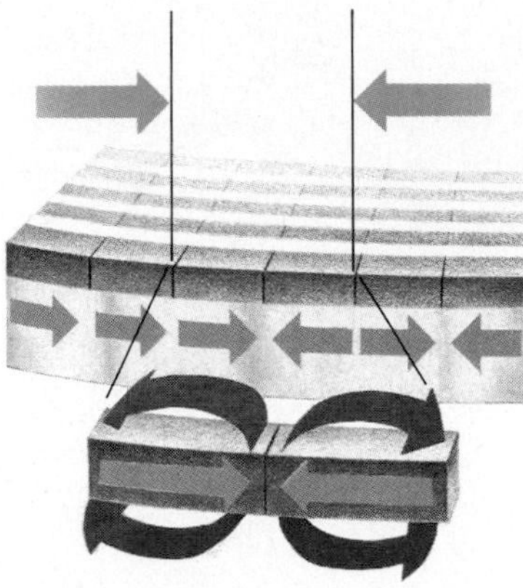

Horizontal recording
Conventional technology attempts to squeeze magnets lengthwise

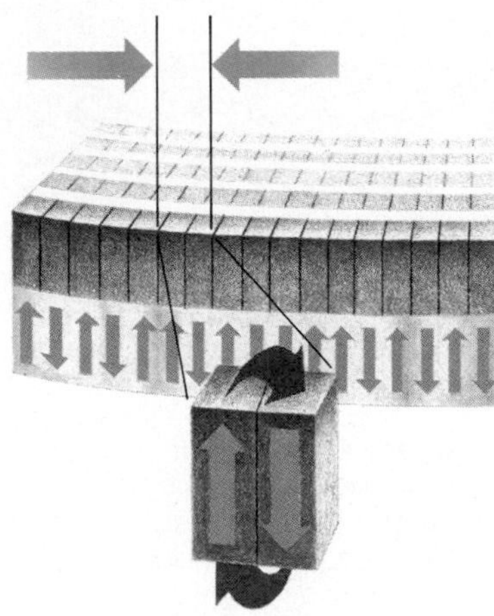

Vertical recording squeezes magnets' thickness

Exhibit 6.6

Vertically recording magnetic patterns by increasing bit density promises to increase disk storage capacity ten times over conventional horizontal recording techniques.

Reprinted with permission, *High Technology* magazine, (January 1983). Copyright © 1983 by High Technology Publishing Corporation, 38 Commercial Wharf, Boston, MA 02110.

500 typewritten pages can be recorded in a megabyte of storage. While at first glance it may be hard to imagine what people would do with a gigabyte of storage, the reality is that disk storage demand is growing at a rate of 20–30 percent per year, and there seems to be no end in sight. Even now, only a small percentage of the data used daily in commerical, educational, and government organizations is stored on computer disks. Most is still on paper, stored in crowded file cabinets (see Exhibit 6.7).

The number of platters used with disk systems ranges from one on microcomputer diskettes to nineteen on large-capacity hard disks on maxicomputers. Sometimes only one side of a single platter is used to record data. More frequently both sides of a platter are used, however. In any case, the storage capacity of a disk is directly related to the number of recording surfaces.

To read or write data, a read/write (r/w) head must be positioned over the appropriate track. For single platter systems, an **actuator,** which contains the read/write head, swings in and out over the disk surface to locate the correct track. Once the r/w head is positioned, the needed data record is found by letting the disk rotate beneath the r/w head. For multiple platter disk systems, a set of **access arms** is used. The access arms move in and out to position the r/w heads over the appropriate tracks. Generally, each access arm has two r/w heads—one for the surface above, and one for the surface below.

The two basic ways of organizing data on the disk are the sector and cylinder methods (see Exhibit 6.8 on page 156). With the **sector method,** the disk surface is logically divided into sectors (like slices of pie). Often, there are eight or more sectors on a surface. Data are then located by specifying the surface number, the sector, and the track number.

The **cylinder** method is based on a vertical plane. In a multiple platter disk system, each recording surface would contain a Track 30. The collection of all Track 30s would be considered Cylinder 30. When data are recorded with the cylinder method, the data in a file are recorded on Track 30 of Surface 1 and continued on Track 30 of Surface 2, 3, 4, etc., until all data are recorded or

Exhibit 6.7

Only a small percentage of data used daily by organizations is stored on computer disks. But this is changing as we recognize the convenience of computer retrieval of information.

Sector Method

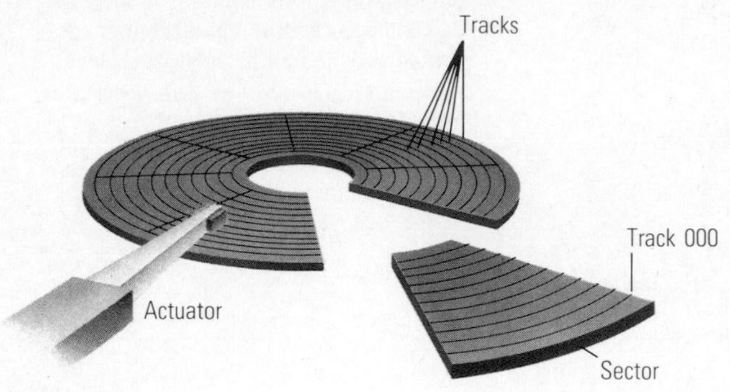

Cylinder Method

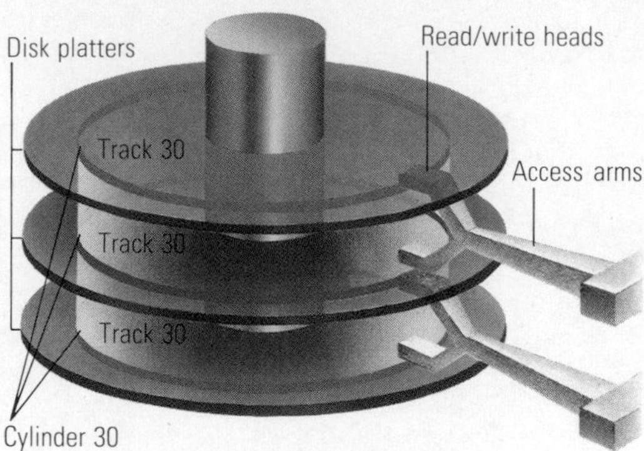

Exhibit 6.8

Two ways of organizing data on disk are the sector and cylinder methods. With the sector method, the disk surface is logically divided into sectors or horizontal sections. Data are located by specifying surface number, sector, and track number. The cylinder method is based on a vertical plane. The collection of all Track 30s, for example, would comprise Cylinder 30. Data are located by specifying cylinder and surface numbers.

the cylinder is filled. In the latter case, an additional cylinder would be used. The advantage of this approach is that once the first record is located, the access arm does not have to be repositioned to read sequential records. This reduces the time needed to retrieve data.

The speed at which data can be found and retrieved is a function of access time. **Access time** is the amount of time it takes from the point of requesting data until the data are retrieved. With disks, access time is composed of seek, search, and data transfer time. **Seek time** is the time it takes to position the r/w head over the desired track. Generally, the greater the track density and the more r/w heads, the shorter the seek time. **Search time** is the time it takes for the requested data to rotate under the r/w head. This is directly related to the rpm of the disk drive. Floppy disk drives rotate at about 400 rpm, whereas hard disks are close to ten times faster. The faster the rpm, the shorter the search time.

Once located, how quickly can the data be transferred into primary memory? It depends upon the **data transfer rate.** There is a significant difference in transfer rates between floppy and hard disk systems. Diskettes can transfer 50,000 characters per second (cps), while the large hard disk systems can transfer data at the rate of several million characters per second. Overall, the access time for floppy disk systems is around 250 milliseconds, whereas hard disk systems can access much larger amounts of data in 25 milliseconds.

Hard Disks. The largest capacity magnetic disks have been the hard disk systems. They come in three standard sizes: 14-inch, 8-inch, and 5-1/4-inch. Maxicomputers tend to use 14-inch disks with a storage capacity of several gigabytes. These disk systems cost under one hundred thousand dollars. Superminicomputer applications generally do not need that much online capacity. More typical of this group are 8-inch fixed disks with several hundred megabytes of storage, for around ten thousand dollars.

To attain high storage capacities and quick access rates, very close tolerances are required between the r/w head and the surface of the disk. When the

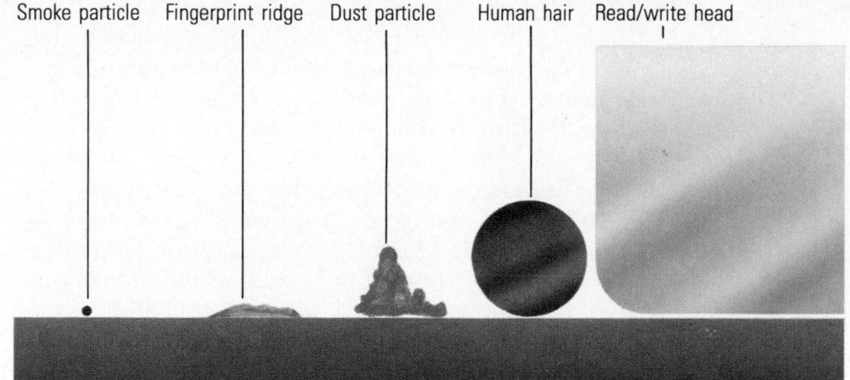

Exhibit 6.9

To attain high storage capacities and quick access rates, very close tolerances between the read/write head and the surface of the disk are necessary. Dust or a hair can cause the disk head to scratch the disk surface, resulting in the loss of data stored in those areas. Winchester technology helps to prevent this by hermetically sealing the disks.

disk is at rest, the r/w head rests on the disk surface. As the disk starts to spin, the r/w head takes off like an airplane, because of centrifugal force. The r/w head flies a fraction of an inch above the disk surface. Because the strength of the magnetic field diminishes quickly as vertical distance above the surface increases, the greatest storage capacities are gained when the head is as close as possible to the surface, without touching it.

The tolerances are so close, any kind of dust or human hair can make the disk head crash (see Exhibit 6.9). A head crash causes the disk head to scratch the disk surface, resulting in loss of the data stored in those areas. To cope with the need for dust-free environments, the **Winchester technology** is used. Basically, this technology seals the disk inside a hermetic (airtight) container. This approach has greatly increased the reliability of hard disk systems. The major disadvantage has been that Winchester disks were not removable. However, removable Winchester disks have recently been developed (see p. 160, Computers at Work: "Whence the Name Winchester").

A **disk pack** is a multiplatter hard disk that can be loaded onto, and later removed from, a disk drive. These packs are very useful for data that don't have to be online at all times. A single-platter removable disk is called a **disk cartridge.** These are often used with minicomputers for loading programs and for use as backup storage. The major disadvantage with removable disks that do not use the Winchester technology is that they are very susceptible to damage from fingerprints, dust particles, and from being dropped.

For business applications, mini- and microcomputers primarily use 5-1/4-inch Winchester disks. Typically a 50 Mbyte hard disk would sell for several thousand dollars. For professional microcomputers, a 10 Mbyte hard disk has become quite common as part of the standard configuration.

Diskettes. Diskettes, or floppy disks, are used primarily with microcomputers in the business, professional, and home markets. The diskette market is rapidly approaching annual sales of a billion dollars.

A diskette resembles a 45 rpm record with a square jacket on it (see Exhibit 6.10 on page 158). The most popular size diskette is 5-1/4 inches in diameter. It is made of Mylar plastic and is coated with a thin layer of metallic oxide particles. Diskettes vary in capacity from 100K to 2 Mbytes. Capacity depends on whether the diskette is **single, double,** or **quad density,** and whether it is **single-** or **double-sided.** Advances in recording technology have allowed more bits per inch and more tracks per surface.

Exhibit 6.10
The Diskette in Its Protective Cover

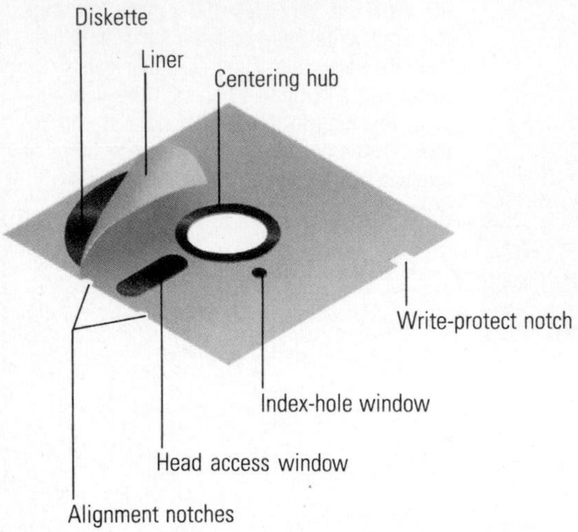

The actual amount of data that can be stored on a diskette is a function of how the data are formatted by the computer operating system. Often single-density disk systems have 40 tracks, each of which has 10 sectors that store 256 bytes of data. This results in a capacity of 100K bytes for a single surface.

Double-density disk systems can pack more than 500K bytes on a surface by using 80 tracks instead of 40, 16 sectors per track, and 512 bytes per sector. To increase the capacity even more, both sides of the disk can be used. Thus, a double-sided, double-density disk system would hold over 1 Mbyte. To obtain even larger capacities, several disk drives can be hooked together.

The standard for diskettes is now the 5-1/4-inch size. The previous standard of 8-inch diskettes is slowly disappearing. The latest trend is toward smaller diameter diskettes called microfloppies or **microdiskettes.** Four major groups of disk manufacturers are vying to set the standard for the market segment of microdiskettes under 4 inches. But 3-1/2-inch disks designed by Sony seem to have the lead, since they are being used in leading microcomputer systems, such as the Macintosh and the Hewlett-Packard portable.

A disk drive for a typical 5-1/4-inch diskette has a 2 Mbyte storage capacity and a transfer speed of 50,000 cps. It costs several hundred dollars, making it useful for personal and home computers where direct access is desired. Microfloppy disk systems provide around 1 Mbyte of storage for approximately two hundred dollars in a physically smaller package.

By their very nature, diskettes are a removable form of storage. The read/write head rides on the surface of the disk. This causes wear and tear, which eventually results in low reliability. To counter the limited online storage capacity and low reliability of diskette systems, removable hard disk cartridges are emerging. The rigid cartridge allows greater storage capacity, yet is more reliable and durable than the diskette because the removable disk is housed in an airtight plastic cartridge (see Exhibit 6.11).

Exhibit 6.11
A Removable Hard-Disk Cartridge

The door on the airtight plastic hard-disk cartridge slides open when the cartridge is inserted into the disk drive. This allows read/write heads access to the disk, while maintaining an airtight environment.

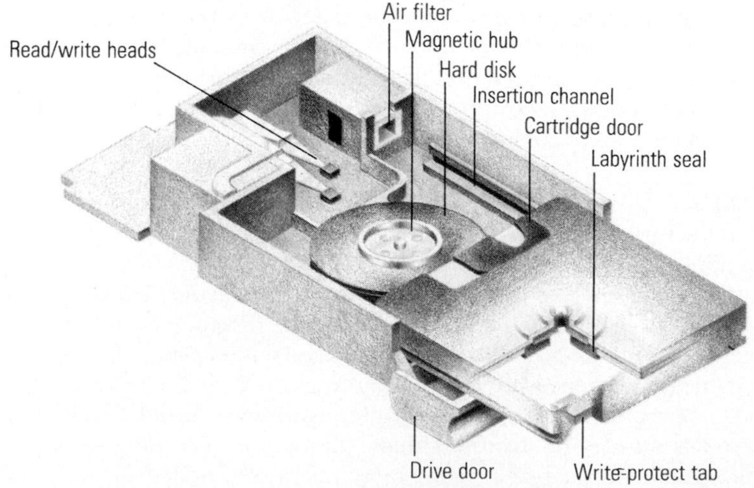

Optical Disks

Optical technology used with laser disk systems is providing a very high capacity storage medium with the **optical disk,** also called a **videodisc** (see Exhibit 6.12). Videodiscs will open new applications, since they can be used to store data, text, audio, and video images.

Optical disk systems look like magnetic disk systems. Each has a rotating platter and a head mechanism to record information. However, optical systems differ in that they use light energy rather than magnetic fields to store data. A high-powered laser beam records data by one of two methods. With the **ablative method,** a hole is burned in the disk surface (see Exhibit 6.13). With the **bubble method,** the disk surface is heated until a bubble forms.

The laser beam, in a lower power mode, reads the data by sensing the presence or absence of holes or bumps. The light beam will be reflected at different angles from a flat or disfigured surface. A series of mirrors is used to reflect the light beam to a photodiode, which transforms the light energy into an electric signal. The photodiode process works like the automatic doors at your local supermarket. As you walk toward the door, you deflect a light beam, which signals the door to open.

The optical properties of this device allow very high-density recording, so that an optical disk can store 100 times more than a magnetic disk of the same size. At present, optical disks have storage capacities in the gigabyte range. This implies that a single 12-inch optical disk can store over 400,000 pages—more than the complete contents of the Encyclopedia Britannica.

As discussed previously, to achieve high storage capacity, the magnetic r/w heads have to be very, very close to the surface of the magnetic disk. This necessitates the dust-free environment of Winchester technology. The usual result is a hard disk that is not removable. With optical disks, however, high density can be achieved without these restrictions. Due to the levels of light energy used, the recording mechanism doesn't have to be as close to the disk surface as for a magnetic disk. Further, optical disks can be coated in plastic so that people can handle them freely, without lessening the disk's readability.

Exhibit 6.12

Optical disk systems use light energy rather than magnetic fields to store data. This allows storage densities 100 times greater than the magnetic disk's and the ability to store high-quality video images and sounds.

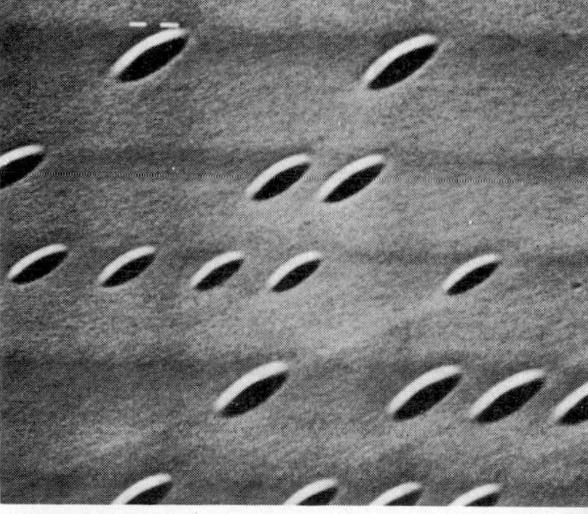

Exhibit 6.13

The ablative method of recording data uses a high-power laser to burn holes in the disk surface. In a lower power mode, the laser beam reads the data by sensing the presence or absence of holes in the disk surface.

COMPUTERS AT WORK

Whence the Name Winchester

Mystery shrouds the origins of the term "Winchester."

The original drive was introduced in 1976 by IBM. Winchester was the code name for the IBM project during development. That is all that's known for sure.

One story has it that the project code number was 30–30, a number that also happens to be a popular Winchester rifle caliber.

Another story says that the 30–30 designation arose because the original device's access time was 30 milliseconds and the read/write head flew 30 microns above the disk.

According to a third tale, the number came about because the original drive had two 30-megabyte disks.

Whatever the reason, the name stuck, and Winchester is on its way (wrongly) to becoming a generic term for hard disks. A subtle irony in all this is that IBM no longer uses the Winchester name for its hard disk drives.

Source: "Whence the Name Winchester," *Business Computer Systems,* October 1982, p. 119.

Also, the optical disk doesn't wear out like a diskette does. To summarize, the optical disk is removable, has high storage capacity, and is very reliable.

The cost of a typical optical disk system storing 1 gigabyte of data on a 12-inch removable platter is around ten thousand dollars. It has a data transfer rate of 500,000 cps, with an average access time of 150 milliseconds. The recording density is 14,500 bits per inch. Cost per Mbyte would be around $12. Since the technology is in its infancy, it is reasonable to expect dramatic improvement in both price and performance over the next several years.

In addition to having a large storage capacity, optical disks have another very important attribute. They can be used to store not only data and text, but also high-quality video images and sounds. Digitized patterns of images and sounds are stored in **frames.** A typical optical disk has 54,000 frames, which can be used to store screen images or a 30-minute audio and video presentation.

As described at the end of this chapter, in Computers at Work: "Resuscitation on Videodisc," each frame can be directly addressed, so that various applications such as CPR training or interactive video games can be learned in nonsequential patterns. In addition, extremely high-quality video pictures are possible that are superior to the more limited graphical images possible with magnetic media.

Unfortunately, at present, optical disk systems do not have the capability to erase or rewrite data onto the disk. The ablative and bubble methods of recording data by deforming the disk surface provide only the capability to read data. However, Matsushita, a Japanese company, has produced a prototype erasable optical disk, which uses a combination of optical and magnetic properties to provide read/write capabilities.

But even as a read-only device, optical disks have great potential as a medium for archiving important records and documents for long-term storage. Organizations are often required by law to store documents from ten to twenty years, and sometimes even longer. To date, much of the archiving has been done on microfilm or microfiche, but overall, this micrographics approach has never really taken off. It is too expensive, people intensive, and awkward a method to use. Edward Rothchild, publisher of *Optical Memory Newsletter,* predicts that optical disk systems will make film-based document storage obsolete. Lower costs and greatly improved access times will be its important advantages.

Exhibit 6.14

Bubble memory is nonvolatile, durable, and lightweight storage with low power requirements.

Bubble Memory

An alternative to semiconductor memory and traditional secondary storage is bubble memory. **Bubble memory** is a solid-state chip in which magnetic bubbles are formed and moved within a thin film of garnet (see Exhibit 6.14). It is somewhat a cross between RAM and disk technologies.

Like RAM, bubble memory uses a high-density, solid-state chip. However, instead of silicon, bubble memory uses a thin film of garnet, a transparent mineral. As in disk storage media, bubble memory uses magnetic properties to record 1s and 0s. The presence of a bubble indicates a 1, its absence indicates a 0. A bubble is not a physical bulge raised in the garnet wafer. Instead, it is a cylinder of magnetism that has been polarized in a specific direction.

Unlike disk storage, where read/write heads are moved over the disk to locate the data, bubble memory technology writes data by generating bubbles and moving them to the proper storage location. To perform the reading function, bubbles are duplicated from the storage location and moved to a reading mechanism.

Because bubble memory is on a chip, it is compact, and its magnetic properties make it nonvolatile. Since it has no mechanical parts, it is extremely reliable. Intel Corporation, the leading producer of bubble memory, has produced a 512K byte chip for which it quotes the mean time between failures to be forty years! Unfortunately, bubble memory is expensive, and has much slower access time than does RAM, though it is faster than disk.

When Bell Labs announced in 1971 that it had the first working bubble memory, the computer industry predicted that this approach would become a predominant storage medium. Since then, however, great performance breakthroughs and price decreases have taken place with semiconductor chips and disk storage. Bubble memory now appears to be a complementary storage medium, which will find its niche in special applications.

Bubble memory is often used in factories where extreme environmental conditions—dust, heat, and vibrations—require durability. Such factory conditions would render most disk drives inoperable. Bubble memory is also being used in portable terminals and computers. These systems can take advantage of bubble memory's ability to provide nonvolatile, yet durable, compact and lightweight storage with low power requirements (see Exhibit 6.15).

Exhibit 6.15

The Grid compact computer uses bubble memory.

SEQUENTIAL-ACCESS STORAGE DEVICES

Magnetic tape, a sequential-access storage device, comes in three forms—reel-to-reel, cartridge, and cassette. All magnetic tapes work in a similar fashion, very much like the audio cassettes with which you are probably familiar. A thin plastic tape is coated with magnetic material. The tape is passed over a read/write head, which either creates or senses a magnetic pattern of bits. Data tapes can be written over, and the tape itself can be reused many times. Tapes are portable, compact, and relatively inexpensive. However, they are vulnerable to dust, breakage, and stretching.

In this section, we will discuss the technology and most common applications of magnetic tape storage. We will start first with tape units that have been used with large computers, and then cover the cartridge and cassette tape units used with small computer systems.

Magnetic Tape

To understand how data are stored on magnetic tape, imagine that a piece of tape has been divided into parallel lanes or tracks that run its length. Within each track, a magnetic spot represents a 1, while no magnetic spot represents a 0. A column of tracks, each containing a byte, represents a single character. Most magnetic tapes are recorded using an 8-bit coding scheme like EBCDIC. A ninth track is reserved for a parity bit. A **parity bit** is used to check for errors that might have occurred during transmission (see Exhibit 6.16). This bit will either be a 0 or 1, depending on the method used. In an even parity system, the sum of the bits should be an even number. With odd parity, the sum of the bits should be an odd number. The wrong sum will cause an error message to be generated. Although the parity bit scheme cannot catch all errors, its ability to catch most transmission errors has made it a standard feature of magnetic tape.

Exhibit 6.16

Characters on magnetic tape are recorded by bit patterns on a column of tracks. The most common coding scheme is the 8-bit EBCDIC. A ninth track is reserved for a parity bit, used in checking for errors.

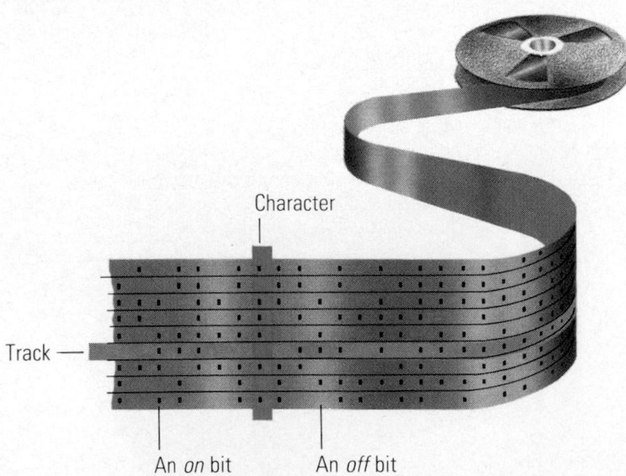

The storage capacity of a tape is determined by the number of bits per inch that can be recorded, the length of the tape, and the blocking factor. The majority of tape drives record at either 800 or 1600 bpi. For tape, a character or byte is represented by a vertical column of bits, so the terms *bit per inch* or *byte per inch* are interchangeable in measuring density. The standard reel-to-reel width is ½-inch wide. A 2400 foot reel recorded at 1600 bpi gives a potential storage capacity of 35 Mbytes. The very high performance tapes can be recorded at 6250 bpi, yielding a capacity of one hundred megabytes. Exhibit 6.17 shows a typical magnetic tape unit.

The actual storage capacity of a magnetic tape is dependent on the blocking factor used. Tape units can read or write on a tape only when it is moving at full speed. To allow the tape to accelerate to the needed speed, records stored on tape are separated by gaps. The size of the gap can be a half inch or so. To minimize the amount of wasted space, a set of records is blocked together. The blocks of records are separated by **inter-block gaps (IBG)** (see Exhibit 6.18). This approach also

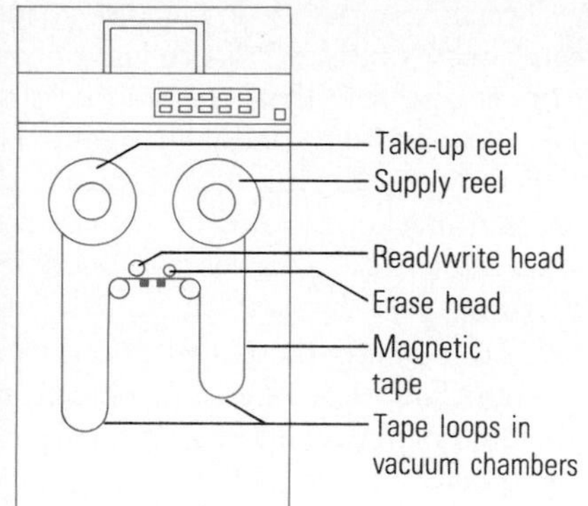

Exhibit 6.17
Magnetic Tape Units

reduces the time it takes to retrieve records from tape, because a block of records is read into computer memory in one operation, rather than having a separate reading operation for each record.

Because it is a sequential-access device, magnetic tape is subject to limitations that direct-access devices do not share. Tapes have another major disadvantage, however. The contents of a record on tape cannot be changed, nor can records be added or deleted. Rather, a new set of records has to be written onto a different tape in the sequence desired. We will discuss this process in Chapter 8, "File and Database Systems." For now, it is important to recognize that the direct access read and write capability of the disk has made it much more attractive than magnetic tape for most roles in the era of interactive processing.

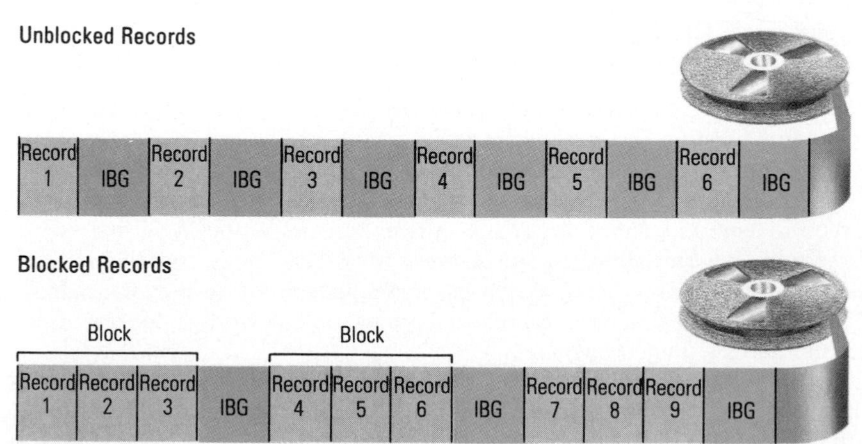

Exhibit 6.18

Because tape units can read or write on a tape only when it is moving at full speed, records stored on tape are separated by gaps. The result is wasted tape space. This can be minimized by blocking a set of records. Blocking also reduces the time it takes to retrieve records from tape.

Since computers do fail, disk systems do crash, and programs do inadvertently wipe out files, it is prudent to have a backup copy of data and programs. This is one role that magnetic tape does perform well, and at a low cost. Programs and data on disk are often backed up by dumping them onto magnetic tape. **Dumping** means moving all the files, intact, from one location to another. Backup is a function that makes good use of the sequential nature of tape. If the backup copy is later needed to reconstruct data lost from a disk, the programs and data are loaded from tape onto disk for processing.

To increase the speed of producing tape backups and to reduce the cost, vendors have developed tape units that can do streaming. **Streaming** refers to the elimination of interblock gaps. Since a backup copy will not be searched for specific records, there is no need for gaps within. Therefore, expensive, precision start/stop mechanisms can be eliminated. A streaming tape unit reads or writes a backup tape as a continuous set of records. With more sophisticated and costly magnetic tape units, the start/stop or streaming mode of operation can be selected as needed.

Cartridge and Cassette Tapes

Expensive magnetic tape units aren't a practical backup alternative for many minicomputers or most microcomputer systems. Smaller computer systems such as these are generally strictly disk-based and use a diskette as a means of backup. However, since a diskette can hold only a megabyte or so, 30 diskettes would be needed to back up a 30 Mbyte Winchester hard disk. This approach is expensive, awkward, and slow.

Magnetic tape vendors have developed the ¼-inch wide data cartridge as a backup alternative to the diskette. Very small, inexpensive, and convenient, these units use the streaming concept. They can store up to 60 megabytes, and can transfer this amount of data in 10 minutes (see Exhibit 6.19).

Exhibit 6.19

Data cartridge tapes can be used as a high-speed backup alternative to the diskette. These streaming tape units can store 60 megabytes of data and transfer it in 10 minutes.

Cassette tapes have been used primarily for home computers as a means of entering programs and data. While this is a very inexpensive form of secondary storage, the overall results have been quite poor. Cassette tapes were designed for audio—not for data—recording. They tend to be slow, and have fairly high error rates. This market will probably be taken over by microfloppy systems, which can provide accurate results at a price in line with inexpensive microcomputers.

MASS STORAGE DEVICES

Governmental organizations, such as the Census Bureau and the Social Security Administration, insurance companies, and banks have massive secondary storage requirements that cannot be met by the disk and tape devices we have discussed. There are several reasons for this. Disk systems that provide online access to large amounts of data are expensive. Tape units provide much cheaper storage, but only allow sequential access to the data. Both types of systems require a great deal of physical space in a computer room. Further, mounting magnetic tapes or disk packs causes a substantial time delay, is prone to error, and requires a trained operator.

One solution to these dilemmas is a **mass storage system (MSS).** The IBM 3850 Mass Storage System uses honeycomblike cells to store cylindrical data cartridges. Each cartridge contains a spool of magnetic tape that can hold 50 megabytes of data. Close to 10,000 total cartridges can be stored, providing online access to almost 500 gigabytes or ½ terabytes of storage. A *terabyte* is one trillion bytes.

When particular data are needed by the computer system, it sends a signal to an electromechanical device to retrieve the proper data cartridge. The data cartridge is automatically mounted on a read/write station, where the data contents are transferred to a magnetic disk for processing. When the processing of the data has been completed, any new or changed data are written back to the data cartridge, and the cartridge is returned to its storage cell (see Exhibit 6.20).

Exhibit 6.20

The IBM 3850 Mass Storage System uses honeycomblike cells to store cylindrical data cartridges. Data cartridges are retrieved by an electromechanical device and the contents are transferred to a magnetic disk for processing. Online access is provided for up to 500 gigabytes of data.

Access time for retrieving data in this way is around ten seconds. While that is considerably slower than the retrieval in milliseconds available with online disk storage, it is much faster than having an operator locate and mount a disk pack or tape.

The most appropriate users of mass storage units, which can cost almost a million dollars, are those organizations needing occasional online access to massive amounts of data, where quick access time is not critical and the cost per megabyte for storage must be low. MSS can provide online storage at an average cost of about a dollar per megabyte. As you will learn in the discussion that follows, this rate is relatively inexpensive when compared to that for other media.

Professional Issue

The Memory Hierarchy

Throughout our discussion of primary and secondary storage technologies, you may have noticed a significant difference in storage capacity, access time, and cost. In this section, these tradeoffs, as they are reflected in the traditional memory hierarchy, will be examined. Then we will consider storage trends that are changing the traditional memory hierarchy. In Chapter 11, "Systems Development I," this information will help you understand how storage methods are selected for various applications.

The Traditional Memory Hierarchy

Throughout the history of computer processing, it has been critical to take advantage of the fact that the CPU is much faster than other parts of the computer system. Thus, the major goal of computer storage is to make data available to the CPU as quickly as practical, considering the dollar cost of the storage medium. This goal is reflected in the traditional memory hierarchy, which ranks storage methods on their storage capacity, access time, and storage cost.

The total **storage capacity** of these memory units is usually measured in terms of kilobytes. As you may remember, a kilobyte is 1024 bytes. Hard disks hold around 100,000 Kbytes or 100 Mbytes, whereas primary memory capacity is more often in the range of 1000 Kbytes. Registers generally hold less than 100 bytes and sometimes as few as 2 bytes on small microcomputers.

Access time is measured in minutes, seconds, and even microseconds. Registers provide the fastest access, in the neighborhood of .01 microseconds. Semiconductor memory is fifty times slower than registers, though it works in millionths of a second. There is a tremendous drop in access speed as storage is moved to disk or tape. Hard disk, which is one of the fastest secondary storage media, is 50,000 times slower than primary memory! Disks work in terms of milliseconds, as compared to micro- or nanoseconds of registers and semiconductor memory.

Storage cost is measured in the number of bytes per dollar. At the cost of 2 bytes per dollar, registers are the most expensive devices for storing data. Primary memory using solid-state devices averages 200 bytes per dollar. The least expensive magnetic disk storage is the large-capacity hard disk system, which averages 40,000 bytes per dollar. Magnetic tape is relatively inexpensive storage, as is optical disk, at 100,000 bytes per dollar. Exhibit 6.21 shows how different forms of storage compare on these dimensions. This exhibit also includes information on three comparatively new and important forms of storage—cache memory, RAM disk, and optical disk—which we will be discussing in more detail.

To understand how these forms of storage are ranked in a memory hierarchy, we have to look at the computer in a slightly different way. In essence, a computer system is a set of **staging areas.** The only real work goes on in the registers within the CPU. Everything else is for support.

Exhibit 6.21
Memory Comparisons

Type of Memory	Total Storage Capacity (Kbytes)	Access Time	Relative Rate (operations per second)	Storage Cost (bytes per dollar)
Register	.1	.01 microsec	100,000,000	2
Cache	1	.1 microsec	10,000,000	20
RAM	1000	.5 microsec	2,000,000	200
RAM Disk	1000	.5 millisec	2000	400
Hard Disk	100,000	.25 millisec	40	40,000
Floppy Disk	2000	250 millisec	4	4,000
Optical Disk	1,000,000	150 millisec	7	100,000
Magnetic Tape	100,000	10 sec	1/10	100,000

The CPU performs millions of operations per second, but can only store a few bytes of data in the fast-working registers. Technically, there is no reason computer memory couldn't consist only of registers. The only problem is that 1 Mbyte of this quick-access storage would cost $2 million!

To make the cost of computer storage more reasonable, primary memory is used as a temporary storage area. The CPU draws program instructions and then data from primary memory into the registers as needed. RAM is 100 times less costly than register memory. The trade-off is that it is also fifty times slower.

Because primary memory is still expensive, ways to reduce the cost were developed. Since only a few data records are active within any short period of time, primary memory space can be further conserved by bringing data into memory only as they are needed. So secondary storage, such as disk or tape, is used to initially store all the data records. This form of storage is 200 times less costly than primary memory. However, the access rate is tens of thousands of times slower. A limited solution to the slow access speed of secondary storage media is to read in not just the record that is immediately needed, but ten to fifty records at one time. This keeps the primary memory requirements low, while reducing the number of slow accesses required from secondary storage.

Thus, the standard processing cycle uses these different levels of memory as staging areas. A typical sequence might be the following: Programs and data would be stored on the hard disk. To run a particular program, that complete set of instructions would be found on the disk and then read into primary memory. The program instructions would then be used by the CPU to sequence events. A small set of data records from the file would be retrieved from the hard disk (secondary storage) and loaded into primary memory. Particular data elements would be moved into working registers, and arithmetic or logical operations would be performed. The results would be transferred back into a section of primary memory.

As new data records were needed by the program, they would be read from the disk into primary memory in the same locations as were used for the previous records processed. When the program was completely run, results of computations could be written from primary memory onto disk. The computer could then be used to run another program, or turned off.

Because hard disk storage is nonvolatile, programs and data can be stored there permanently. However, this can be an expensive way to operate, especially if certain programs and data are used infrequently. More commonly, programs and data are transferred to a less expensive medium such as a diskette or magnetic tape, and stored offline.

When data are not directly connected to the computer system, they are considered offline. When magnetic tapes are loaded in the tape unit or diskettes are inserted in the disk unit, the data they contain are accessible by the computer. Under these conditions, the data are online. A significant advantage of fixed hard disk storage is that the data are always online. In most applications, however, it is more economical to use a variety of less expensive offline storage media. For example, a biweekly payroll program and payroll records can be stored offline on magnetic tape. When it is time to run the program, it, and the payroll records, can be transferred to a disk. Then the program and records can be loaded into primary memory and processed.

Exhibit 6.22 shows the traditional memory hierarchy, which represents these staging areas as four different levels. The need to move from, for example, Level IV, magnetic tape, to Level III, hard disk, to Level II, primary memory, to Level I, registers, is determined by differences in storage capacity, access

Exhibit 6.22
Memory Hierarchy

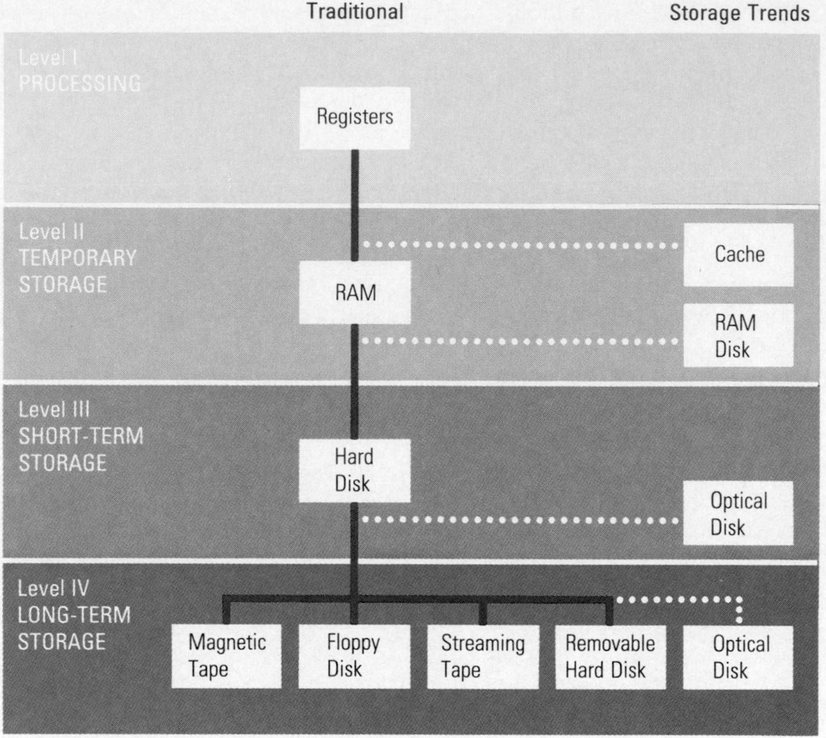

time, and cost. As we move from Level IV, the lowest level, up the hierarchy, storage capacity and access time decrease as cost increases. An important function of the memory hierarchy is to show how to reduce the cost of storage for different applications. And, as we will see in Chapter 7, "Operating Systems," this same knowledge is useful for developing computer systems that can be used by many people at the same time. Exhibit 6.22 also indicates three new forms of technology, which represent important trends in storage.

Storage Trends

Recent advances in memory technologies have made the memory hierarchy even more pronounced. To increase the effective speed of the CPU, **cache memory** is often used. Cache memory is a set of memory locations that are 5 to 10 times faster than primary memory, but cost 1/10 as much as registers.

Since most program instructions are taken in sequence, instruction 8 can be loaded in cache memory while the CPU is executing instruction 7. As soon as the CPU completes instruction 7, it can retrieve instruction 8 from the quick-access cache memory. This retrieval from cache memory would take 1/5 of the time needed to retrieve the same instruction directly from primary memory. The trade-off for this increase in access speed is that cache memory is 10 times more expensive than regular primary memory.

The biggest bottleneck to cost-effective computer operations, however, often occurs between primary memory and secondary storage. This can result from the constant need to swap data back and forth between disk and primary memory at speeds 50,000 times slower than the CPU. The disk, because of its electromechanical nature, will always slow down access time.

Semiconductor vendors are proposing a solid-state solution called a RAM disk. **RAM disks** are external add-on memory devices that can add up to 1 megabyte of storage for under ten thousand dollars. RAM "disks" are actually semiconductor chips that emulate, or imitate, disks. These chips provide a high-speed, nonrotating memory that is 50 times faster than magnetic disks. RAM disks are used primarily to provide a faster staging area than regular magnetic disks. They can transfer data 100 times faster than a Winchester disk and 200 times faster than a floppy disk. Because they are all solid-state, RAM disks are also much more reliable than hard disks. The major disadvantage of RAM disks is that they are volatile, and therefore cannot be used for permanent storage.

The *optical disk* is the latest addition to the memory hierarchy. Its access time is similar to the diskette, but it provides massive storage at a relatively low cost per byte. In other ways, it is a unique storage medium because of its ability to store more forms of information. For interactive video applications, it would be used in place of a hard disk. But optical disks can also be used for low-cost, long-term storage needs (see Exhibit 6.23).

Exhibit 6.23

Hitachi's optical disk filing system stores the equivalent of 40 thousand letter-size documents on a single optical disk.

In summary, it is critical to take advantage of the fact that the CPU is much faster than other parts of the computer system. To do so, data are moved through a series of temporary staging areas, each offering progressively faster access, as data move closer for use by the CPU. Unfortunately, the trade-off is that the faster the access of memory, the more costly it is and, generally, the less storage capacity it has.

The current flow of data in computers configured for high efficiency is from tape or diskette to (1) hard disk to (2) RAM disk to (3) primary memory RAM to (4) cache memory to (5) registers. For less demanding situations, personal computers have a data path from hard disk to primary memory RAM to registers (see Exhibit 6.24).

Exhibit 6.24

Temporary staging areas are used to take advantage of the high speed of the CPU, while balancing the trade-offs of access speed and capacity and cost of storage devices.

SECONDARY STORAGE
PRIMARY MEMORY
Online
Offline
Magnetic tape
5
Cache
Hard disk
RAM disk
2
Registers
3
4
1
Diskette
RAM

COMPUTERS AT WORK

Resuscitation on Videodisc

A paramedic leans over the figure of a woman, his hands pumping her chest to revive her heartbeat. At his side, a calm, silver-haired physician coaches, "A little more gently this time."

The scene is not an accident, but a classroom. The prone victim is an electronic manikin, and the doctor's reassurance emanates from a television screen. His comments on the trainee's progress in learning cardiopulmonary resuscitation (CPR) are prerecorded on an optical videodisc.

The American Heart Association's CPR Learning System uses interactive videodisc technology. The tactile-response doll communicates through a console with two television monitors and a high-speed audiotape system. Pictures, sound, and text are summoned by an Apple IIe microcomputer to answer students' questions or to react to their jostling, pressing, or mouth resuscitation of the figure.

"A human instructor can't get inside the manikin the way technology has," says David Hon, the CPR project's director and chief inventor.

The familiar Resusci-Annie CPR training figures were implanted with 14 sensors that monitor more than 6000 variables in psychomotor response. From the sensors, the computer can infer whether trainees are performing correctly. The system can discern subtle differences in rhythm and pressure, which are vital to learning CPR.

The courseware can judge the learner's comprehension and branch off to appropriate instructions at 700 points in the course, so a student receives immediate feedback. Reaction time ranges from microseconds for an audio response to about two seconds for a switch to new video. The doctor may appear on the color monitor to demonstrate a procedure, a voice may suggest moving the hands, or a graph may pop up on a screen to register the depth of each chest compression as the student presses down and the on-screen doctor warns, "Too deep."

At any time, students can call up a menu on a black-and-white screen and, using a light pen, choose one of nine options such as "Quiz me," "I know this," or "Call a live person for assistance." The computer instantly evaluates performance and instructs students according to their level of understanding.

One design challenge, says Hon, was to make possible a precise heart-pumping rhythm that alternates between the student and corescuer during the segment teaching the two-rescuer CPR. The computer can adjust the speed of the on-screen medic's push so that it occurs exactly in counterpoint to the student's movements on the manikin.

The goal of the project, begun in 1980, was to teach and maintain CPR skills among health and emergency professionals and laypersons. As many as 200,000 of the half-million Americans who die each year in emergencies die because no one at hand can rekindle a heartbeat. Though CPR classes abound in hospitals and adult-education centers, the number of people who learn and maintain their knowledge has plateaued for the past 10 years at less than 5 percent of the U.S. population. Committing instruction to disc, Hon says, will help cut the 18-to-1 odds against today's cardiac victims.

Not only is performance significantly better than with human instruction, according to tests, but the system cuts 50 percent to 75 percent of instruction time for such costly personnel as doctor, nurse, and paramedic instructors. With the system, first-timers can learn CPR in less than four hours. Recertification takes an average of 45 minutes.

Kaiser Medical of Northern California purchased two of the first units released in July. Jack Chapman, Kaiser visual-aids director, calls it "highly cost-effective" at $20,000 per system, plus $2500 for the optional infant model. Actronics, the Pittsburgh-based manufacturer, is also marketing the system to industry, the military, and several government agencies. Seven other videodiscs will follow to instruct medical staffs in advanced cardiac life support.

Ahead for medical applications of interactive technology, Hon believes, may be a manikin to train medical students to insert catheters. He speculates, though, that "a liver transplant simulation would probably never make it," because such surgery demands high tactility and intense monitoring of internal temperature. But, he muses, "The delivery of a baby? Perhaps."

Source: From "Resuscitation on Videodisc" by Paul Kleyman. Reprinted with permission, *Technology Illustrated,* (November 1983). Copyright © 1983 by High Technology Publishing Corporation, 38 Commercial Wharf, Boston, MA 02110.

SUMMARY

We have learned that, for computer programs and data to be processed, they have to be put into primary memory. Read/write primary memory such as RAM can only be used for temporary storage of information, since it is *volatile.* That is, when the computer is turned off, the information in RAM is lost. In contrast, secondary storage is *nonvolatile.* Tapes or disks use magnetic recording techniques that retain the data when the power to the computer is turned off.

Which type of secondary storage medium is most appropriate? It depends on the types of programs that are being run, and whether they require sequential or direct access to the data records. With *sequential-access* media, you must check each record key, in sequence, for all prior records in order to gain access to the desired one. With *direct,* or *random, access,* you can directly access the data record desired.

The medium that has come to clearly dominate the secondary storage market is the magnetic disk. This is primarily a reflection of the move from batch to transaction processing. With *batch processing,* the sequential access of records on magnetic tape was efficient. However, *transaction processing* requires direct access to a specific record, and this is what disks allow. Disks offer the additional flexibility of doing sequential processing if desired.

A third important variable of storage media is whether they are *removable* or *fixed.* Removable media, such as magnetic tape and many disk systems, allow the user to swap one set of data for another. However, removable media are generally susceptible to fingerprints, dust, and being dropped, and thus have lower reliability than fixed media. For secondary storage systems where there is a need for high reliability and extensive storage capacity, fixed hard disk systems are used. Generally, these high-precision systems use the *Winchester technology,* in which the read/write heads and disk platters are sealed in an environment free from contaminants.

There are two basic forms of magnetic disks: hard disks and floppy disks, or diskettes. *Hard disks* are rigid aluminum platters coated with a magnetic oxide. They come in a variety of physical sizes and have significantly different storage capacities. They can be further categorized in terms of being fixed or removable. A major disadvantage of Winchester hard disks has been that they could not be removed. However, removable Winchester disks have recently been developed to overcome this limitation.

Disk packs are a multiplatter hard disk which can be loaded onto, and later removed from, a disk drive. These packs are very useful for data that don't have to be online at all times. A single-platter removable disk is called a *disk cartridge.*

The *storage capacity* of a disk is a function of the number of tracks per surface, the bit density, and the number of recording surfaces. The speed with which data can be found and retrieved is a function of access time. *Access time* is the amount of time it takes from the point of requesting data until the data are retrieved.

Diskettes, or floppy disks, are made of a flexible Mylar plastic coated with a thin layer of metallic oxide particles. These diskettes also come in several physical sizes, and all are designed to be removable. Diskettes vary in storage capacity, depending on whether the diskette is single, double, or quad density, and whether it is single- or double-sided.

Optical disk systems use light energy rather than magnetic fields to store data. A high-powered laser beam is used to record data by either burning a hole in the disk surface or heating the disk surface until a bubble forms. The optical disk is emerging as an important direct-access secondary storage medium. It is attractive because of its large storage capacity and its ability to store high-quality video images.

An alternative to semiconductor memory and traditional secondary storage is bubble memory. *Bubble memory* is a solid-state chip where magnetic bubbles are formed and moved within a thin film of garnet. This cross between RAM and disk technologies makes bubble memory useful when compact, nonvolatile storage in harsh environments is needed.

Magnetic tapes are thin plastic tapes coated with magnetic material. They come in three forms: *reel-to-reel, cartridge,* and *cassette.* All magnetic tapes work in a similar fashion, very much like audio cassettes. The *storage capacity* of a tape is determined by the number of bits per inch that can be recorded, the length of the tape, and the blocking factor.

Mass storage devices use cylindrical data cartridges to provide online access to a massive amount of data, where short access time is not critical and the cost per megabyte for storage must be low.

There are significant differences in *storage capacity, access time,* and *cost* among storage media. These performance and cost differences have been classified into a *memory hierarchy* of temporary, short-term, and long-term storage.

Traditionally, the CPU uses registers for processing and RAM primary memory for temporary storage. Hard disk systems are the dominant means of providing online secondary storage. For long-term offline storage, magnetic tape, diskettes, streaming tape, and removable hard disk systems are used for archival and backup purposes. Recent advancements in memory technologies have made the memory hierarchy even more pronounced with the addition of *cache memory, RAM disks,* and *optical disks.*

In summary it is critical to take advantage of the fact that the CPU is much faster than other parts of the computer system. To do so, data are moved through a series of temporary *staging areas.* Each area offers progressively faster access, as data move closer for use by the CPU. Unfortunately, the trade-off is that the faster the access of memory, the more costly it is and, generally, the less storage capacity it has.

REVIEW QUESTIONS

1. What are the two major disadvantages of primary memory? How are these limitations most frequently overcome?
2. Compare sequential and direct access. Under what conditions would direct access be most needed?
3. What are the major advantages/disadvantages of removable media?
4. What factors influence the storage capacity of a disk?
5. Compare the two basic methods of organizing data on a disk.
6. Briefly describe the components of access time as applied to disks. Assuming that a firm requires the fastest possible access times, would diskettes or hard disks be more likely to be used?
7. What are *videodiscs?* What advantages do such storage systems have? How are data recorded on videodiscs?
8. The Ruff n' Tuff Corporation is considering several types of direct-access storage devices for use in its factories. Which type of storage would you suggest? Defend your choice.
9. What determines the actual storage capacity of magnetic tape? Why must tape records be separated? What is an interblock gap?
10. Explain how a mass storage system (MSS) works.
11. Briefly describe the traditional memory hierarchy. What types of trade-offs occur in progressing up the hierarchy?
12. Explain how data flows in computers configured for high efficiency. What is cache memory?

CHAPTER 7
Operating Systems

COMPUTERS AT WORK

Microsoft's Drive to Dominate Software

At the relatively ripe old age of nine years, privately held Microsoft Corp. of Bellevue, Washington, has emerged as the most powerful company in the fast-growing microcomputer software industry. With fiscal 1983 revenues of $50 million, Microsoft dominates the markets for the software that runs the current generation of business microcomputers. Now its fiercely ambitious 28-year-old co-founder and chairman, William H. Gates III, wants to make Microsoft the General Motors of the industry by taking command of a much bigger and more promising market segment, the so-called applications software that consumers buy.

The move will be Microsoft's most challenging undertaking yet. Although it is now a standard setter in both microcomputer languages and the operating systems that allow the machines to function, its success is largely due to its role as the supplier of these programs to IBM. To make their machines compatible with the vast numbers of applications written for IBM personal computers, other manufacturers have been compelled to license Microsoft's software. In turn, software companies that want to sell to owners of all those machines have had to design programs that work with Microsoft's products.

Gates' biggest problem may be Microsoft itself. In the course of its frantic growth the company has churned out a bewildering variety of products. Besides seven languages and three different operating systems, Microsoft has four applications products as well as several games, a forthcoming line of computer books, and miscellaneous pieces of hardware. None of Microsoft's competitors offers such a diverse group of products.

That makes for management headaches, since each additional product can add exponentially to the complex task of maintaining compatibility across product lines. To distinguish their machines from the competition, computer makers build in proprietary components to which Microsoft's operating systems must be adapted. In the same way, each of Microsoft's applications must be compatible with several operating systems, including some made by other companies such as Apple. Moreover, technology is moving so fast that the typical program must be updated, sometimes radically, every eighteen months or so. That creates a ripple effect throughout the whole product line.

Source: S. P. Sherman, "Microsoft's Drive to Dominate Software," *Fortune,* 23 January, 1984, pp. 82–90.

For William H. Gates III, business couldn't be better. At 28 years of age, Gates is chairman of Microsoft, the corporation that is a leader in the microcomputer software industry—a market that is growing fast. It is Microsoft's operating system and other support software that have earned the firm its powerful position. Now the strategy is to enhance its position by developing compatible application software packages.

As explained in Parts I and II of this textbook, a computer is directed by a series of program instructions. The types of programs that we have already discussed—payroll, inventory control, and spreadsheets—are called application software. Their purpose is to produce payroll checks, invoices, or management reports. These outputs are directly usable by an employee, customer, or manager. Thus, application programs have as their focus the needs of the end-user.

There is another series of programs that has been written to act as an interface between the application program and the computer itself. These programs are called **system software.** The system software first interprets and then carries out the commands necessary to run an application program. This intermediary role allows users to be less concerned with the inner details of computer operations, and provides for more efficient use of computer resources.

In this chapter we will concentrate on the operating system, which is the foundation of system software. In Chapters 8 and 9 we will discuss data management and data communications, two other important facets of support software. In this chapter you will learn to do the following:

1. Explain the different roles that operating software and support software play.
2. Describe the primary ways operating systems differ.
3. Specify the three major functions of an operating system.
4. Describe the types of operating systems that are being used.
5. Identify which brands of operating system are becoming predominant for use with microcomputers.

THE ROLE OF SYSTEM SOFTWARE

Application software is programs such as billing, order entry, and word processing that are written to meet the needs of users. System software is a series of programs that have been written to simplify the interface between the programmer and the computer hardware.

System Software Functions

System software is generally composed of an operating system, language translators and utilities, data management, and data communication systems.

The overall function of the **operating system (OS)** is to control the activities of the computer system. It serves as the traffic cop, directing and managing computer events. To do this, the OS has a set of programs called a **supervisor,** an executive, or a monitor. The supervisor handles the overall management of the many jobs and tasks that are being conducted by the computer system. First, the supervisor selects the application program to be run next, based on predefined rules. Then the resource management function is concerned with making the computer resources such as the CPU, primary memory, input/output devices, and support software available in an efficient way.

To enable efficient use of the computer system, the operating system must perform a variety of tasks. In large computer systems, the OS measures performance in terms of the number of jobs that have been processed and the resources that are being underutilized or are creating bottlenecks. In order to account for computer use, the OS also provides information on who is using the system, for how long, and what resources and data are used. This type of information can also be valuable for security purposes, to prevent accidental or purposeful abuse of computer systems and data resources.

Supplementing the OS are **language translators.** These are programs that translate the English-like program instructions of a high-level language such as BASIC or COBOL into the binary code of ones and zeros of machine language. A survey of computer languages and the system software techniques used to translate them into machine language will be covered in Chapter 14, "Programming Languages." **Utilities** are programs that have been written to accomplish common tasks such as sorting records or copying disk files to magnetic tape for backup. Operating systems enable programmers to increase their productivity by using utilities directly, or by incorporating them into their applications programs, rather than writing their own code for these tasks.

Data management routines can be used to: create new files; make additions, deletions, and alterations; reorganize or merge existing files; and extract data selected by user inquiries. The procedures for doing this and the variety of data management options available will be discussed in Chapter 8, "File and Data Base Systems."

In executing computer programs, data must be transferred between primary memory and peripherals. This involves providing data paths, interfacing with many different types of input and output devices, and often moving data over long distances through telephone networks and other telecommunication links. These types of data communication functions will be discussed in more detail in Chapter 9, "Data Communication." Exhibit 7.1 shows the varied roles of system software.

Exhibit 7.1
Varying Roles of System Software

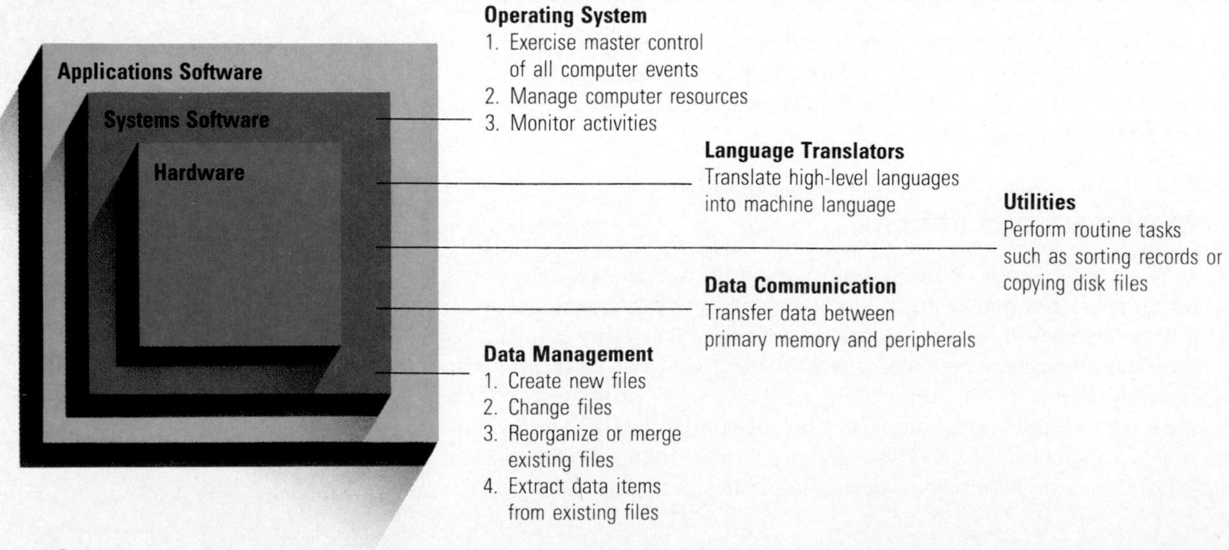
Applications Software
Systems Software
Hardware
Operating System
1. Exercise master control of all computer events
2. Manage computer resources
3. Monitor activities
Language Translators
Translate high-level languages into machine language
Utilities
Perform routine tasks such as sorting records or copying disk files
Data Communication
Transfer data between primary memory and peripherals
Data Management
1. Create new files
2. Change files
3. Reorganize or merge existing files
4. Extract data items from existing files

How Operating Systems Differ

In this chapter we will concentrate on the operating system. As potential users of computer systems, it is important to recognize the vital role the OS plays in effective computer systems. Many people consider it the factor that gives the computer hardware its "personality." That is, different operating systems will make the same computer appear different to users. For example, ease in interaction with the computer system and the degree of efficiency with which various applications programs run are two aspects of use that can vary.

In order to be able to distinguish among operating systems, a user must ask several questions. First, was the OS designed to be used primarily with batch or interactive processing jobs? The initial function of operating systems was to facilitate the running of a series of programs, one after another. An OS that performs this type of sequential processing of jobs is called a **batch-oriented operating system.** In contrast, some operating systems have been designed to handle conversational responses with a programmer or end-user doing BASIC programming or word processing from a CRT. These types of operating systems are **interactive-oriented.** Most operating systems today can accommodate both batch and interactive processing. However, it does make a difference in efficiency if the OS was designed primarily for one approach and adapted to accommodate the other type of processing.

Second, is the OS designed to be a single or multiuser system? Most microcomputer systems today are used as personal computers. That is, they serve only a *single user* at any one time. However, certain other operating systems can be used with some microcomputers to allow them to serve *multiple users* at any one time. Multiuser operating systems designed for microcomputer and small minicomputer systems generally accommodate from two to sixteen users, depending on the system. The larger, more powerful computer systems, when combined with more sophisticated multiuser operating systems, allow the computer to be shared by hundreds of users at the same time (see Exhibit 7.2).

Exhibit 7.2

Operating systems can be designed to accommodate a single user or hundreds of users.

Another important question is whether the OS has been designed for use on a specific computer model or on a variety of computer systems. The history of computer systems has been that computer manufacturers have also developed their own operating systems. This allowed the vendor to tailor the OS to the specific hardware characteristics of a particular computer in order to optimize its performance. This type of OS is **computer-specific.** The major disadvantage of these proprietary operating systems, is that application software written to run on a specific computer using a particular OS cannot, in general, be used on another computer model. When software written for one computer will not run on a different computer, the two machines are said to be **incompatible.** This has greatly limited the user's flexibility in changing computer models or upgrading to a more powerful computer system, since existing application software was not transferrable without extensive rewriting or purchase of new software.

The introduction of the IBM 360 computers in the mid-1960s developed the concept of a **family of computers,** a series of computer models based on the same computer architecture. A single OS was designed to accommodate users of the least powerful 360 models up through those owning the most powerful versions. The standard interface meant that users could acquire more powerful computer models in the series and still have their original application software be compatible (see Exhibit 7.3).

Exhibit 7.3

The IBM 360 computers were based on a single operating system to allow application software to be compatible on a series of computer models based on the same computer architecture. The computers by Zenith and Panasonic also shown are IBM PC-compatible.

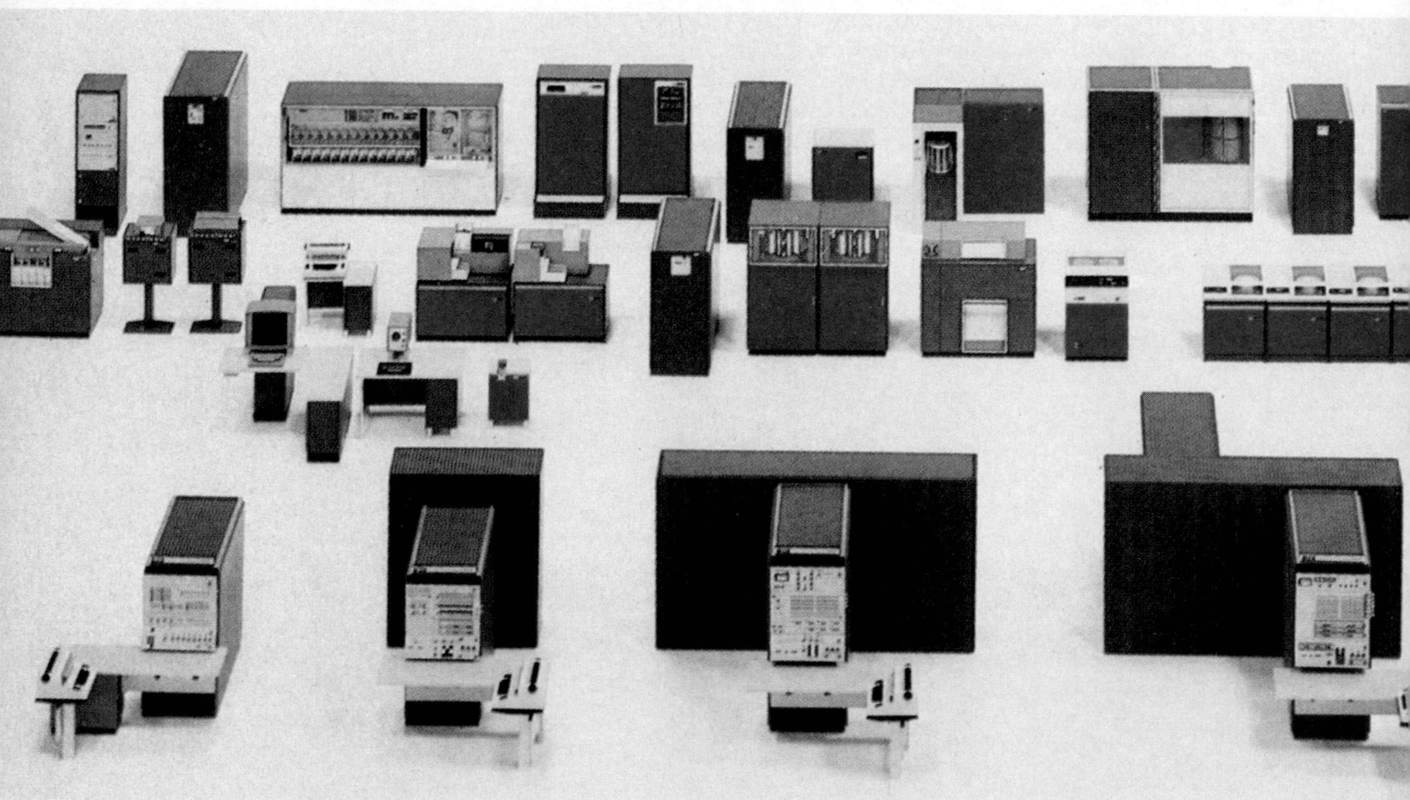

In the case of the IBM 360, the OS was usable across a family of computers, all based on the same computer architecture and made by the same computer manufacturer. A variation of this is seen with the microcomputer. Here, operating systems have been written by third-party vendors, not computer manufacturers, for use on *clones*—computers with very similar architecture. For example, the IBM PC microcomputer is based on the Intel 8088 microprocessor, as are COMPAQ, TANDY 1000, and many other personal computers. Microsoft has written the MSDOS operating system, which will run on each of these computers. It provides a relatively standard interface for application software programs. This trend is making it much easier for third-party software houses to develop application software packages that will run on several different computers, and thus users are not so limited to a particular computer model. However, one must be cautious. At the end of this chapter, Computers at Work: "Why Software Won't Run on All PC Clones" will explain why this is so.

The latest advancement is to have an OS that can accommodate application software written for a series of computer models spanning different generations. For example, IBM has developed an OS called Virtual Machine. It has been written for use on the latest IBM maxicomputers. With this higher order operating system, a user can run other operating systems designed for previous generation IBM computers on the new computer system. The virtual machine operating system makes the new computer look like any of several

previous computer models with their appropriate operating systems. This enables users to move to more powerful computer systems and take advantage of their capabilities for new applications while still being able to use their previously written application software as is.

OPERATING SYSTEM FUNCTIONS

In writing application programs, we usually make two simplifying assumptions: (1) the computer will be available exclusively for use by our program, and (2) we can specify logically what we want done.

In a multiuser environment, the computer is being shared. Thus, for the first assumption to be valid, the OS must take responsibility for managing the flow of computer jobs and the assignment of computer resources. This is necessary not only to relieve the users of any concern beyond their own individual program, but also to make effective use of expensive computer resources.

For the second assumption to be correct, the OS must provide an interface that allows us to concentrate more on what we want to accomplish rather than the details of how it is done. For example, we explained in Chapter 6 how data was stored on a magnetic disk. Further, we discussed how the read/write heads need to be positioned over the correct track to read data from a particular sector. Without an OS, we would have to know exactly where that data was stored on the disk and how to tell the read/write head to find the specific sector and track. This information is described as the physical details. An OS allows us to simply specify logically to get the next employee pay record without concern for where that record is or how to retrieve it.

Thus, one major function of an OS is to provide a useful interface that allows users to concentrate on what they want to accomplish—not the details of how the computer internally carries out their instructions. Another important service of the OS is to make effective use of expensive computer resources in supporting a number of users. How does the OS accomplish these objectives? It does so through overall master control, resource management, and monitoring activities.

Master Control

A program called a supervisor, executive, or monitor exercises overall master control of computer operations and coordinates work within the computer system. The way an OS exercises master control is, in many ways, similar to what you may have experienced when you visited a doctor with a large practice. You wait with the other patients in the outer waiting room. When one of the examining rooms is free, the nurse asks the next patient to enter it.

There are a number of examining rooms in which patients wait to be examined by the doctor. When the doctor completes the examination of one patient, he or she then goes into the examining room occupied by the next patient. The doctor starts that examination and (1) either completes it, upon which the patient leaves the examining room, or (2) the doctor determines that more data are needed in order to complete the examination. The doctor then calls in the technician to take the patient to X ray. When the X rays are ready, the doctor will begin the exam at the point at which he or she left off. In the meantime, while waiting for X-ray results, the doctor goes into the examination room of the next patient and begins the examination.

The reason for this process is that, by sharing valuable resources in a controlled way, more patients can be diagnosed and treated each day. As one of the most vital resources, it is important to keep the doctor busy examining patients and diagnosing illnesses.

In computer systems, the CPU is analogous to the doctor. In other words, the CPU is where the real work gets done. The CPU can process only one program at a time, just as a doctor can see only one patient at a time. The CPU works on one program until it is either completed or there is a need for input/output (I/O) data (such as an X ray or blood tests). Then it is directed by the OS to go on to the next scheduled program in primary memory.

The head nurse functions as the overall supervisor of what gets done, when, and by whom. For computers, the operating system performs this overall control function.

The outer office waiting room is analogous to application programs waiting on disk to be read into primary memory and executed. The OS decides which of these programs should be loaded into primary memory next using predefined rules. Primary memory, like the inner examining rooms at the doctor's office, is divided into areas that can hold different programs.

As we have seen, the supervisor plays a major role in deciding which programs get run, and when. But the OS is not an autonomous unit. Rather, it is carrying out policies set by the data processing center management or programmers.

For example, the computer operator working at the console in Exhibit 7.4 is directing the OS via a command language. At the beginning of the day, the computer operator will start the computer and use the command language to set policy parameters such as priority rules, I/O device assignments, and prespecified or **default** memory allocations. Later, while the computer is processing jobs, the computer operator can check the status of jobs, change priorities for jobs that are awaiting processing, terminate jobs, and so on. At the end of the day, the operator gives commands to shut down the computer system.

While the computer operator is in charge of monitoring the overall flow of work and makes changes as needed, the programmer is responsible for instructing how his or her particular job should be processed. The concept of a **job control language (JCL)** was introduced to allow the user to communicate to the operating system the special tasks associated with a particular program. Through a JCL, the programmer can specify that the program instructions are written in COBOL and that the data are found on a certain magnetic tape. In addition, the programmer can direct the output to a high-speed printer, which might be located in another building altogether.

A command language is also used by programmers using personal computers. Exhibit 7.5 shows the *DIR*ectory command, used to check the status of files on disk. There are many other common commands: *TYPE* is used to see what a particular file contains; *COPY* can be used to copy a file from one diskette to another; and *ERASE* is used to erase a single file or a collection of files.

Exhibit 7.4

The computer operator working at the console is directing the operating system via a command language. The operator can check the status of jobs, change priorities for jobs awaiting processing, and terminate jobs.

Exhibit 7.5

*DIR*ectory is used to check the status of files on disk.

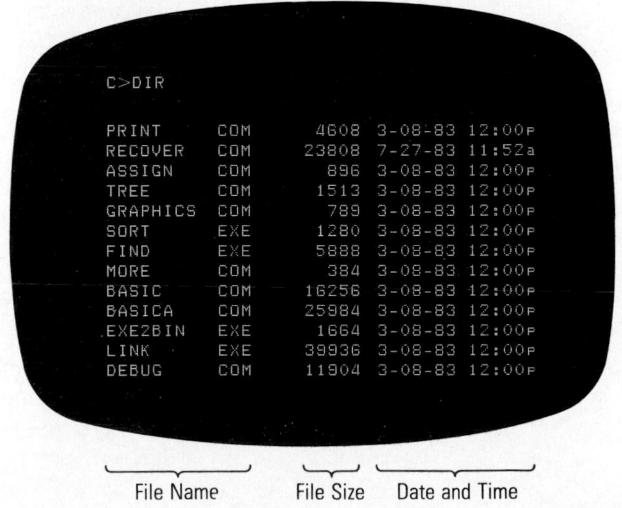

C>DIR
PRINT COM 4608 3-08-83 12:00p
RECOVER COM 23808 7-27-83 11:52a
ASSIGN COM 896 3-08-83 12:00p
TREE COM 1513 3-08-83 12:00p
GRAPHICS COM 789 3-08-83 12:00p
SORT EXE 1280 3-08-83 12:00p
FIND EXE 5888 3-08-83 12:00p
MORE COM 384 3-08-83 12:00p
BASIC COM 16256 3-08-83 12:00p
BASICA COM 25984 3-08-83 12:00p
EXE2BIN EXE 1664 3-08-83 12:00p
LINK EXE 39936 3-08-83 12:00p
DEBUG COM 11904 3-08-83 12:00p
File Name
File Size
Date and Time

Resource Management

The supervisor initiates and controls the execution of jobs. To accomplish this, it must allocate and schedule computer resources. This function is known as **resource management.** Computer resources include the CPU, primary memory, input/output devices, and support software.

CPU. One of the primary computer resources that needs to be shared is the CPU itself. The CPU can work only on one program at a time. But it can be shared by taking advantage of the fact that it is thousands of times faster than I/O devices or users working interactively with the system. Two factors to be determined are the length of time a program should be able to use the CPU uninterrupted and which of the many programs in primary memory awaiting the use of the CPU should be chosen next.

Once a program is being run, the CPU continues to process the program's instructions until either some interrupting event occurs or a predetermined period of time elapses. For example, a convenient place to have the CPU switch to the next program is when there is a need to get data from or send data to an I/O device. This form of interrupt processing is based on **events.** Another means of redirecting the CPU is to allow it to process program instructions for a certain time period, typically several milliseconds. At the end of this time, the CPU is switched to the next program. This form of interrupt processing is based on **time slicing.**

Once it is determined that the CPU should be switched to another program, there are several scheduling schemes that are used. The simplest is the **first-come-first-serve scheme.** A list is kept of the order in which jobs arrive to be processed. When the CPU is available, the job at the head of the list is then scheduled. Conceptually, this method is similar to the "take-a-number" approach at the local ice-cream store.

A second CPU scheduling method is the use of a **priority scheme.** External to the computer system, some programs are more important than others. An administration running semester grade reports may need to have priority over students running instructional programs. Some computer systems allow a user to set priority levels from 1 to 5. To keep everyone from designating his or her program as having top-priority level 5, many computer departments use a charge system. Top-priority programs cost much more to run than low-priority programs. This is analogous to a phone company charging more for a long-distance call placed during weekday business hours as compared to charges for calls made on weekends.

Memory. In the early computer systems, there was no management of memory. Only one application program at a time was loaded into memory. All primary memory was available for use by the program being run, regardless of whether that program needed only 10 percent of the space available, or 80 percent. If the program required 150 percent of the memory space, it would have to be rewritten to accommodate the limited memory available.

As operating systems were developed, there was a need to divide primary memory into a number of sections. One section contains the operating system itself, and the remaining section of memory was made available for several different user programs. With the move to multiuser computer systems, there was a need to share user memory in more efficient ways. The allocation of memory is called **memory management.** To accommodate multiple pro-

Single User Systems

Operating System

Single Program

Primary Memory

Multiuser Systems

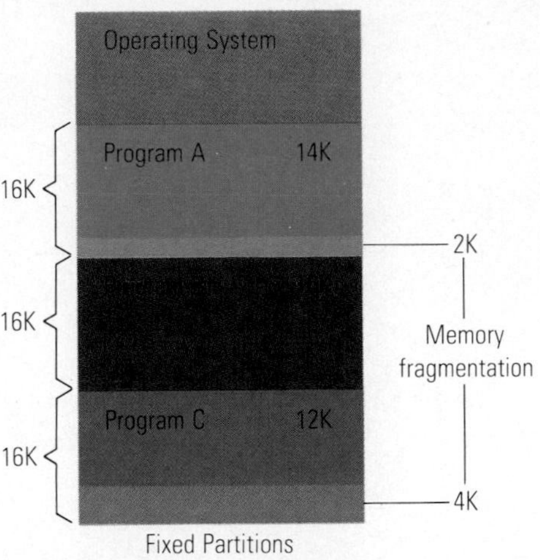

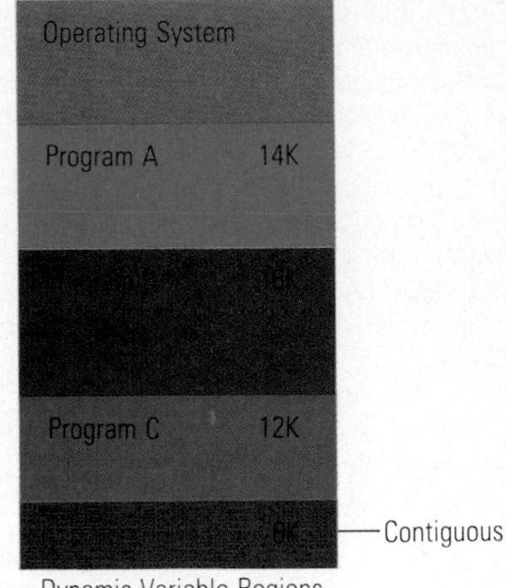

Exhibit 7.6
Memory Management

Multiuser operating systems require more sophisticated management of primary memory than single user systems. After space has been reserved for the operating system itself, the remaining memory locations can be allocated as fixed or variable size partitions. Fixed size partitions are sections of predefined, fixed memory size. Variable size partitions—partitions defined dynamically based upon the needs of the program—result in reduced memory fragmentation.

grams in memory at one time required a way of allocating that space, as well as a means for moving programs in and out of memory.

One allocation method was that of **fixed partitions.** Primary memory for use by user programs was divided into sections of a defined, fixed memory size. For example, with small minicomputers it is quite common to allocate a fixed partition of 16K to each CRT. This assures that, if the terminal is available, the user can process his or her program (see Exhibit 7.6).

One of the problems with fixed partitions is **memory fragmentation.** That is, not every program will use all of the memory available to it, thus leaving memory locations unused. Further, there is the problem of programs needing more than the fixed amount of memory available. One solution for accommodating programs of different sizes is to have fixed partitions of different sizes. However, this reduces but doesn't eliminate the fragmentation problem.

For larger computer systems that need to both accommodate a greater variety of programs and efficiently use a large, expensive primary memory, the concept of **variable size partitions or regions** was introduced. Partition size is defined dynamically, depending on the needs of the program. Thus, if a program were to need just 20K, that is what would be assigned. Similarly, a very large program could be given 512K. The only restriction is that the memory locations must be **contiguous,** or assigned as a block. In other words, a program using 16K of memory must have all the locations next to each other. It wouldn't work to have 4K in one part of memory, another 8K in a second part of memory, and the remaining 4K located in a different area.

While variable size partitions give flexibility and yield better memory utilization, there can still be memory fragmentation. Also, the number of programs that can be handled is limited to the number of complete programs that can be loaded into the primary memory partitions at any one time.

Exhibit 7.7

With *swapping,* a program waiting on disk to be processed is exchanged with a program in primary memory. Since the number of programs that can be handled is limited to the number of complete programs that can be loaded into the primary memory partitions at any one time, swapping allows the running of more programs than there are partitions. The exchange would take place at the end of a time slice. The intermediate processing results of Program B in memory are copied and written back to disk. The next waiting program, Program E, is placed in those primary memory locations. At the end of the time slice, Programs C and F are swapped.

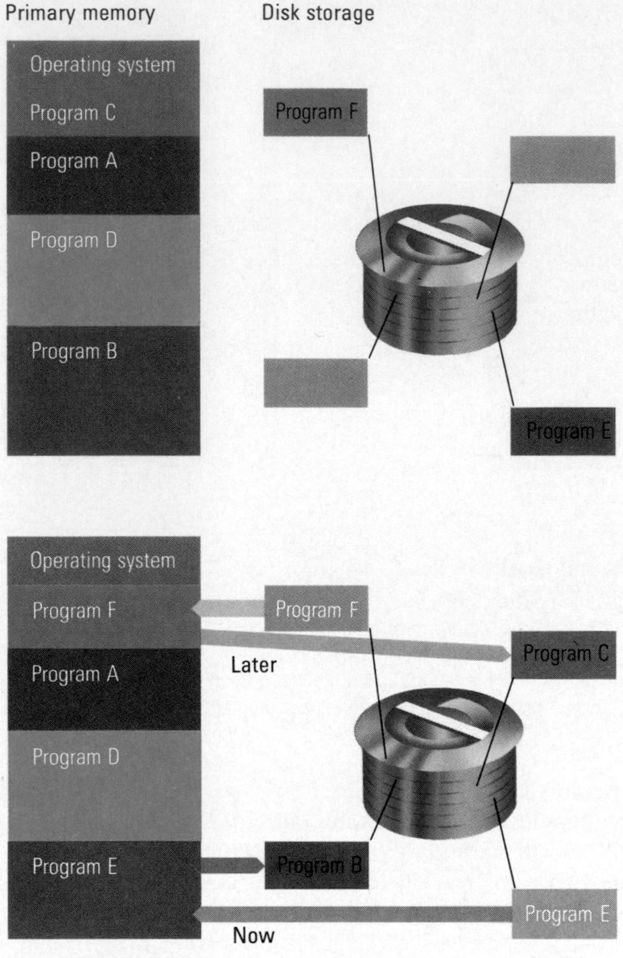

One way to accommodate more programs is for the OS to perform **swapping,** in which a program that is waiting on disk to be processed is exchanged with a program in primary memory. Exhibit 7.7 shows a memory divided into four partitions, which could be fixed or variable, with the OS occupying its own memory space. Programs A, B, C, and D are being processed. Waiting to be processed are programs E and F, which are held on the disk. At the end of a time slice, the intermediate processing results of program B in memory are copied and written back to the disk. The next waiting program, E, is read from the disk to the primary memory location now available. At the next time slice, program C and program F are swapped.

The next major advance in memory management is based on the concept that, even with large and complex programs, very few of the instructions need to be in primary memory at any one time. Therefore, it is a waste of resources to be swapping the complete program in and out of memory, or to have the total program in primary memory at one time. Why not bring in only those instructions that are relevant to the present state of processing for a particular program? This is the scheme implemented in *virtual memory using demand paging.*

To understand how demand paging works, consider the following analogy. When studying this textbook, you use, at any one time, only several pages out of the total number available. You could be actively reading one page, on which a certain paragraph could refer you to a diagram on the next page. Later, you may need to turn to the glossary to look up the definition of a term introduced in a previous chapter. When you have finished studying, or completed processing, the page, you then turn to the next page.

In a similar way, programs can be subdivided into sections containing instructions. These sections are of a fixed length and are called **pages.** With previous memory management schemes, the complete program had to reside in primary memory for processing to be accomplished. The concept of **virtual memory** means that only relevant pages need to be in primary memory at any one time, while the remainder of the program is stored on disk, available on demand (see Exhibit 7.8).

With the use of virtual memory, very large programs that either couldn't fit in small fixed partitions or dominated dynamic partitions, can now be run efficiently. In general, more users can be accommodated in an interactive environment, since each user's program takes up much less primary memory space. The major disadvantage is that virtual memory is a very complex undertaking for an OS. Because the OS is more complex, it takes more memory for the OS itself and requires more CPU resources to run the OS.

Input/Output Devices. Another key resource for any computer system is input and output devices such as magnetic tapes, magnetic disks, and printers. Contention for the use of a limited number of these devices is inevitable, and some type of management is needed.

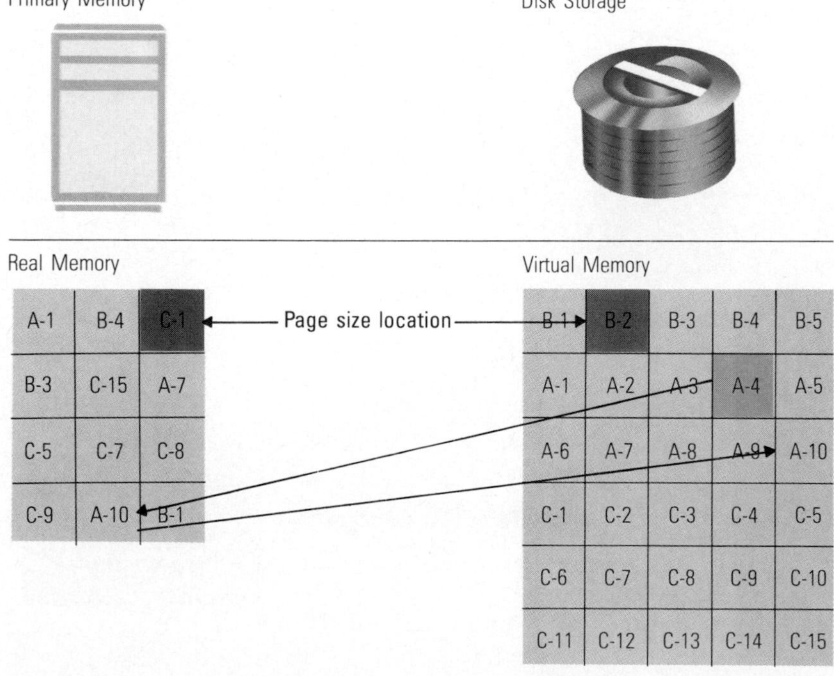

Exhibit 7.8
Virtual Memory

An advanced memory management technique, *virtual memory,* makes it appear that primary memory is of unlimited size and can therefore readily accommodate very large programs. Primary memory and disk memory are both divided into locations of a fixed page size. Program A has been divided into 10 pages, which are stored on disk. Pages A–1, A–7, and A–10 are actively being processed in primary memory. When, in processing the instructions of Program A, it becomes necessary to get a new Page A–4, for example, it could be swapped for Page A–10. But a problem comes about if Page A–10 is later needed along with Pages A–1, A–7, and A–4. Since all other memory locations are occupied by other programs, one of the A pages, which will be needed very soon, is swapped. When A–4 replaces A–10, and moments later Page A–10 must be referred to for information, another swap will have to take place. When a large portion of CPU time is used shuffling pages back and forth from disk to primary memory, the system is said to be *thrashing.*

The way in which I/O devices are allocated or assigned varies with the type of device. Secondary storage devices such as magnetic tape and disk are assigned by the OS in response to the requirements of the application program being run. For a program that will require access to magnetic tape units, the OS assigns the required number of devices to *that* program only for the duration of its processing. This practice is somewhat wasteful of storage resources, since the tape units won't be continuously active for a program, but it does eliminate the problem of two different programs trying to write on the same tape unit.

Disk units, however, are not assigned to a particular program for the duration of its processing. Because they are direct-access devices, they are shareable, and thus can be assigned and released as needed for an I/O operation. There are special precautions that need to be taken for controlling concurrent use, though, and these will be discussed in Chapter 8, "File and Data Base Systems."

In a multiuser environment, several programs could be backed up, waiting for the use of a printer. This could cause the CPU to become idle when all programs in memory are waiting on I/O operations. A concept called **spooling** allows the output to be printed to be put onto disk, freeing the CPU to process other programs. When the job is over and the printer is ready, the print will be read from disk and printed on the high-speed printer (see Exhibit 7.9). Spooling can also be used to read programs and data from input devices. Here, the information is stored on disk, forming a job pool. From the pool, the OS selects the next program to be sent to the CPU.

Exhibit 7.9

Spooling allows programs and data to be read from input devices and placed in a job pool on disk to await processing. Computer output to be printed can be placed in a print queue on disk, where it will remain until the printer becomes available. The spooling concept allows the CPU to be kept continuously active processing jobs.

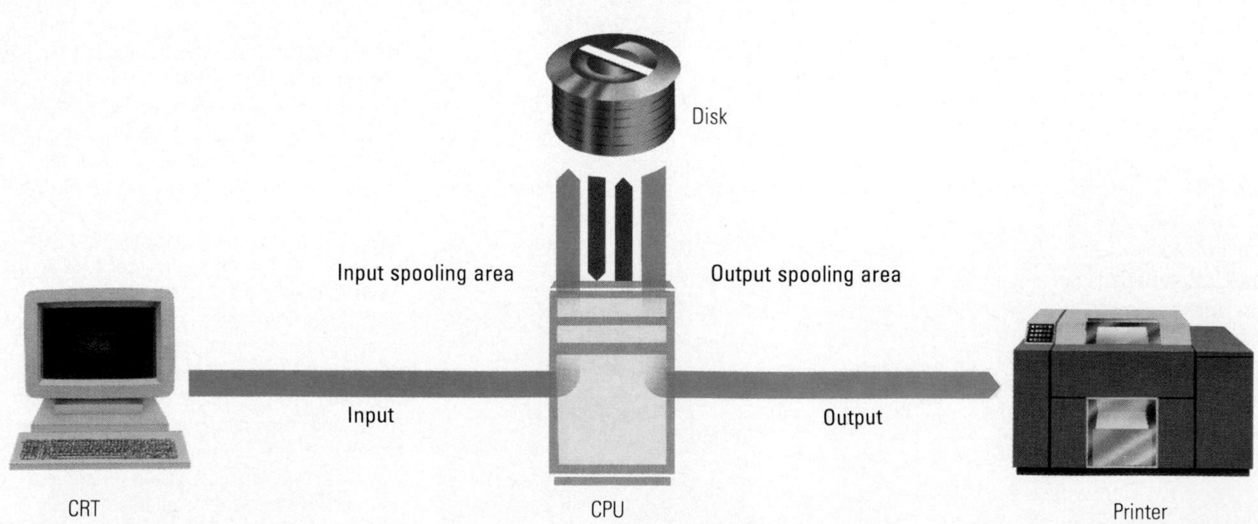

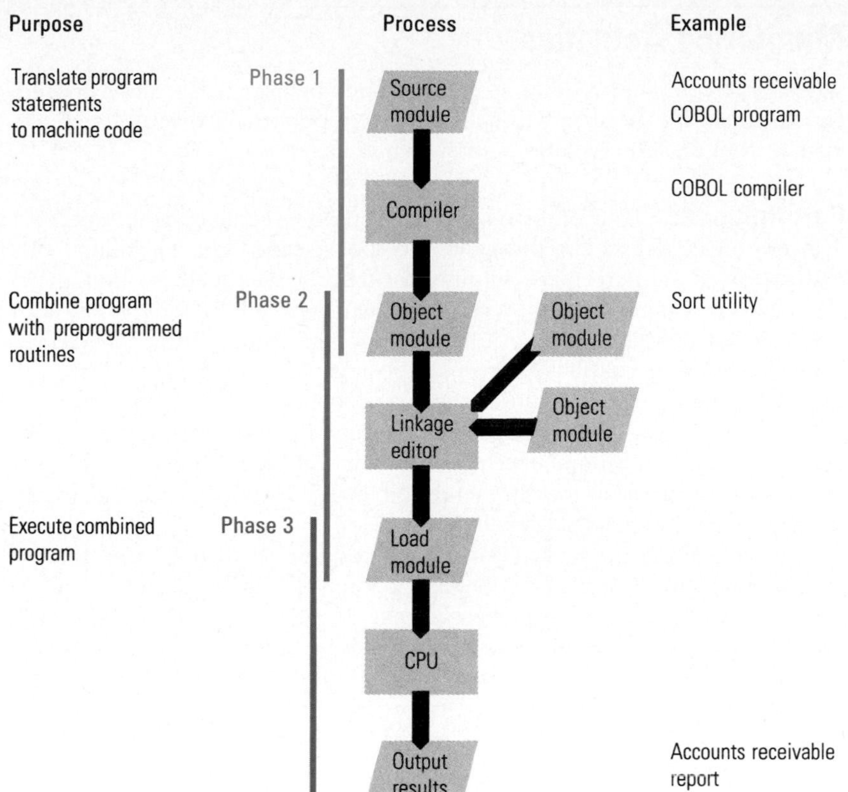

Exhibit 7.10
Phases in Running a Program

System Software. One of the functions of the OS is to manage the use of the system support software, such as compilers, linkage editors, and utilities (see Exhibit 7.10). To help you understand how these might be used, we'll first consider how an application program written in the COBOL computer language would be run.

The program would be submitted in the English-like statements of the COBOL computer language. These source statements would have to be translated into machine language. The OS calls on a system software module called a **COBOL compiler** to carry out this translation. The output of the compiler is called an **object module.** The COBOL program is called the **source module.**

Assume an accounts receivable COBOL program was written to produce a report that required company names to be sorted in alphabetical order. Instead of writing your own instructions for sorting, you could use a **sort utility,** which is stored on disk in machine language form. The OS now calls on another system software module called a **linkage editor** to link or combine your application program and the sort utility. The output is called a **load module,** which is in a form that can now be executed. When desired, it can be loaded into the CPU and processed, giving as output the accounts receivable report in alphabetical order.

From this example you can see that the OS not only has to control the flow of a program through various job steps, it also must manage the use of system support software such as compilers and utilities.

Monitoring Activities

When large computer systems are being shared by many users and managed for efficiency, it is necessary to monitor system performance and protect the system from unauthorized users or system errors.

Performance. Four of the major criteria used to judge computer performance are CPU utilization, throughput, response time, and reliability. **CPU utilization** is the percentage of time that the CPU is actually working. For expensive computer systems, it is very important that the CPU be kept busy and not stand idle, awaiting tasks. A CPU utilization of 50 percent is considered lightly loaded, whereas 80–90 percent is the target for a highly utilized system. Over 90 percent utilization causes significant reduction in response time.

A computer system's **throughput** is the number of programs completed per time period. In general, the higher the throughput, the greater the computer performance. This measure tends to be biased toward processing many small programs, rather than one long program.

From the user's point of view, a major criterion is **response time.** That is, with an interactive system, how long is the interval between a user's request and the computer's response? Often, response time is a second or two. However, the response time increases significantly, often to the point of being measured in minutes, when a system has CPU utilization over 90 percent.

The percentage of time that the computer is up relative to the time it is scheduled to be up and running is a measure of **reliability.** As computers have become more critical to organizational operations, it is quite common to expect reliability to be over 95 percent. For applications such as airline reservation systems and stock market transactions, reliability needs to be very close to 100 percent.

One of the functions of the computer staff is to monitor computer performance. By selecting the CPU scheduling scheme, changing priorities, adding more or faster computer resources such as memory, disks, etc., the staff can improve performance by alleviating bottlenecks.

Protection and Security. The increasing use of computers by multiple users and the shared use of primary memory and files brings the problem of accidental and purposeful abuse. A major function of the OS is to provide protection and security to minimize these possibilities.

Protection has been defined in terms of how access to programs and data stored in the computer is controlled once the user is using the computer. One of the initial concerns in sharing memory was that a user could accidentally write over or destroy parts of the operating system. This was prevented by locating the OS in a specific part of memory and allowing no user's program to address these locations. If, perchance, a user's program attempted to do so, the OS would abort that program. To keep a person from using data stored in another user's files, an access code can be set up to specify which individuals are allowed to access specific data. Notation can also show whether the program can only read the file, or whether it can write to it as well. Data protection will be discussed in more detail in Chapter 8, "File and Data Base Systems."

Security is defined in terms of the external threats from unauthorized users. One major problem here is authentication. That is, how does the operating system know that the user is who he or she purports to be? The most common approach is to use **passwords.** To sign on to a computer system, the user is required to supply a confidential sequence of alphanumeric characters, for example, T65RX2. If that password matches a valid password list stored in memory, the OS assumes the user is legitimate. The password can further be used to identify an access list, which specifies the rights the user has to view or change specific files.

Other possibilities include defining access rights by CRT. In other words, for a particular CRT located in a warehouse, the user, regardless of who it is, can only work on inventory records, and would not be allowed access to payroll records. This technique is often combined with time and date restrictions. That is, payroll files can't be worked on after 5:00 P.M., nor anytime on weekends.

The protection and security of systems is becoming increasingly important as computers become more critical to the daily operations of organizations. As we will discuss in Chapter 17, "Issues and Concerns," even with all the safeguards available, computer crime is, unfortunately, still on the rise.

TYPES OF OPERATING SYSTEMS

Having discussed the major functions of operating systems, let us consider the different types of operating systems that are being used.

Single Program

In the original operating systems, the complete computer system was made available to one program, which would be processed from start to finish. When programs are processed serially, this type of operation is called a batch-oriented operating system. That is, the first program is completed, and then the computer is ready to process the next program.

The primary difficulty with this type of approach is that major portions of the computer system are idle most of the time. While the card reader is reading in the program, the CPU and the printer are idle. When the CPU is processing the program job, the card reader is idle. For a computer system costing millions of dollars, as the mainframes did in the 1960s, it wasn't cost effective to have such low utilization of expensive resources.

Multiprogramming

The concept of multiprogramming was developed to take advantage of the significantly faster speed of the CPU in relationship to input, storage, and output devices. **Multiprogramming** means that two or more programs are being run concurrently by the computer system. This approach dramatically improved computer utilization.

In **concurrent** operations, at a given point in time, one program uses one computer resource while another program uses a different computer resource. For example, the computer could be doing an arithmetic calculation in the CPU for program 1, while data for program 2 were being read from magnetic tape. At the same time, the results of a third program could be printing out on the printer.

The basis for multiprogramming is **interrupt processing.** With event interrupts, the CPU processes a program until it requires an I/O operation. One possible multiprogramming sequence is as follows. The program being executed begins an I/O operation. While that I/O request is being handled by the card reader, disk, or output device, the CPU starts processing a second program. The CPU continues to process that second program until it needs to wait for an I/O event to occur. It then switches to processing the next program. Working in a round-robin fashion through the programs in process, the CPU will eventually get back to the first program. There, it will start processing where it left off, and processing will continue until the program is completed or another event interrupts the cycle.

Time-Sharing

Interactive systems were designed to allow direct communication between the user and the computer system. Combining the flexibility for users of the interactive approach with the computer efficiency of the multiprogramming concept led to **time-sharing** systems. These interactive, multiuser systems sequence tasks based on time slices, in contrast to the resource-based interruptions of batch-oriented systems.

Since each user's transaction tends to be short, time slices are allocated typically in milliseconds. Each user's program is put into a part of primary memory. The CPU works on one program for the allocated time slice, then switches to the next user's program. Because the CPU can execute millions of instructions per second, it can switch back and forth between different programs so rapidly that it appears to the many users that each of them has exclusive use of the computer. Large computer systems can accommodate hundreds of interactive users at a time. However, when the number of users increases to the point that resources such as the CPU and I/O devices are heavily utilized, the response time will no longer be immediate. Instead of receiving responses within seconds, delays are noticeable, and the response time can stretch to minutes (see Exhibit 7.11).

Most larger computer systems today offer both batch processing and time sharing to serve the different needs of users. Batch processing is ideal for production jobs such as the weekly payroll, the monthly sales report, the quarterly income statement, and semester grades. In contrast, programs used for airline reservations, automatic teller machines, word processing, and decision support systems are inherently interactive. Continuous response is necessary to meet a range of fluctuating and varying user needs.

To handle both batch and interactive jobs and meet their very different response time requirements, computer systems utilize the concept of **foreground/background processing.** These terms simply refer respectively to high- and low-priority jobs. In general, when the CPU is available, the OS will assign it to a foreground (high-priority) job if one is waiting on the CPU. Only when no foreground job is waiting on the CPU will a background job be processed. The actual mix of which interactive and batch jobs are run depends on the priority the users have set for each type. Thus, the high-priority interactive jobs are said to run in the foreground, and the low-priority batch jobs are said to run from the background.

Exhibit 7.11

In a time-sharing system, users in different locations can interact with the computer at the same time and run different applications. It appears to the many users that each of them has exclusive use of the computer.

Multiprocessors

So far, we have discussed processing done by a computer system with one CPU. But the tremendous demand for computing power, the need for increased reliability, and the decreasing price of hardware have led to the use of computer systems with multiple processors.

One of the early uses of multiple processors was in a master/slave relationship. Each slave processor was assigned a specific task, with one processor acting as the overall master control unit. This type of setup is used with remote job entry (RJE), where smaller processors aren't located next to the main computer, but rather are in a different building, or even in a distant city. The RJE processors are used to run card readers and line printers and to transfer jobs to and from the main computer. Multiple processors are also used in time-sharing systems, where smaller processors are typically used to handle all input and output tasks. Thus, the main CPU is freed from having to perform so many "housekeeping" tasks, allowing it to concentrate more on processing programs.

With organizations becoming increasingly dependent on computers to carry out their everyday tasks, a high degree of reliability has become paramount for certain industries. In the airline industry, for example, a major airline often uses two identical maxicomputers that are electrically connected. One computer will do interactive reservation processing, while the other can be assigned batch administrative tasks. In the event that the first computer failed, the second computer would take over and assume the interactive tasks. Batch processing would be suspended.

Tandem Corporation has commercially pioneered the concept of a single computer system that is designed for continuous operation—even if some components fail. This type of system is critical for organizations such as large international banks and stock market trading exchanges. Tandem uses a system with up to 16 processors, dual buses, shared memory, additional disks, multiple power supplies, and so on. If a hardware failure occurs, the OS senses this and automatically switches to an alternative electrical path and/or to a backup device. This action allows for continued operations. When repairs are necessary, removal and replacement of parts can be handled while the computer system continues to process work. Such a system is described as **fault-tolerant** (see Exhibit 7.12).

During normal operations, the multiple processors all work concurrently. None stand idle for use as backup support. If one of the processors fails, the OS shifts its workload to an alternative working processor. This results in the overall computer system now working at perhaps 90 percent of the normal rate, unlike most time-sharing systems, which have to shut down if they lose the host processor. **Fail-soft** is an industry term used to describe the system's ability to continue operation at a percentage of its normal rate, rather than shutting down altogether when a processor fails.

Exhibit 7.12

This fault-tolerant computer system is designed for continuous operation—even if some components fail. Tandem Computers' NonStop (TM) multiple processor computer systems provide support for very high-volume, online transaction processing applications with many terminals, communication lines, and large local or distributed data bases. Online transaction processing requires large information files that users must access continuously. These applications include bank deposits and withdrawals, funds transfer, hotel or airline reservations, order processing, retail sales, credit verification, inventory control, job flow control, stock trading, and medical records.

Virtual Machines

We have discussed the limited portability of application programs that are written for particular operating systems on a specific computer. In some of the more advanced computer systems, operating systems have been developed that are able to provide a **virtual machine** environment.

Within limits, each user is given the illusion that he or she is working with the very computer and OS environment that is needed to run an application program or work with the computer interactively. This is done by running different operating systems in different areas of memory, with the virtual machine OS controlling the other operating systems.

IBM's OS/VM (virtual machine) is a good example of this type of operating system. It runs on the latest IBM maxicomputer systems. It allows some users to work interactively with the computer, under the virtual storage operating system, while other users can run application programs designed for use with IBM operating systems from previous generations.

The advantage of a virtual machine approach is that one computer can be made to act as many different machines. Thus, the virtual machine can meet the specific needs of each user. It also helps eliminate the software compatibility problem, because it doesn't require that the older application software be rewritten or modified. Moreover, it enables management to take advantage of the latest computer technology and price/performance benefits.

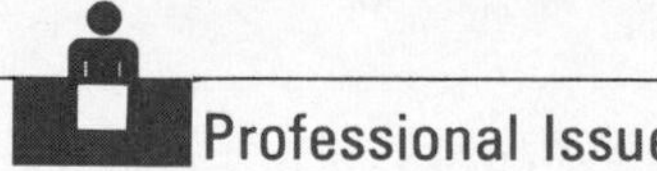

Professional Issue

Microcomputer Operating Systems

Historically, operating systems for microcomputers have been developed in a different way from those for the large maxicomputer systems. One difference has been the move directly into interactive and time-sharing systems. Most micro- and minicomputers have avoided strictly batch-oriented operating systems.

The major difference, however, has been the public orientation of microcomputer operating systems, as opposed to the proprietary single-vendor orientation of mini- and maxicomputer operating systems. For the larger computer systems, an operating system is generally developed by the manufacturer for use with its own computers only. Thus, there is an OS for use with IBM minicomputers only, a different OS for use with DEC minicomputers only, and so on. Developing the OS in this way allowed each computer manufacturer to tailor its OS to its own computer system characteristics.

However, because a manufacturer would not readily divulge detailed information on the internal workings of its OS, third-party hardware and software vendors couldn't easily design their offerings to "plug into" these computer systems. The net result was that users were forced to select peripheral equipment and application software from the manufacturer only.

With microcomputers, the total orientation has been one of unbundling all facets of hardware, software, training, financing, and even maintenance. Often, the user will get a microcomputer manufactured by one vendor and the disks from another vendor. The OS will come from someone else and the word processing or decision support software from still other independent vendors. Thus, microcomputers are sold more like stereo equipment, where a system's components can each be produced by a different vendor. Unfortunately, there isn't yet any standard way to connect a microcomputer's hardware and software together, as there is with stereos (see Exhibit 7.13).

Exhibit 7.13
Microcomputers are multivendor endeavors.

De facto Standard Operating Systems

Although an official committee has not specified standards, several defacto standards for operating systems have developed. A **defacto standard** is one that vendors informally accept, generally because it has come to dominate a market segment of the business.

For microcomputers with 8-bit processors, the OS developed by Digital Research called CP/M (Control Program for Microcomputers) has become the de facto standard. According to David Freedman of *Mini-Micro Systems,* this operating system is used on 100 different brands of microcomputers by over 500,000 users. Over 500 independent software vendors are making their products compatible with CP/M.

CP/M–80 was developed by Digital Research initially in 1974, and updated versions have been issued periodically. It is used with computers that use the Intel 8080, 8085, and Z–80 8-bit microprocessors, such as the Radio Shack TRS 80 Model III, Zenith Model 89, Vector Graphics Series 3, Osborne 1, and the Sony SMC–70. It is a single-user interactive system, and can process only one task at a time.

For the 16-bit microprocessors, the IBM PC has very quickly become a dominant force. The OS that IBM chose was the operating system developed by Microsoft. The IBM PC version is called PCDOS (Personal Computer Disk-Based Operating System), and is a variation of the MSDOS sold by Microsoft to computer vendors other than IBM.

Exhibit 7.14

Multitasking operating systems allow a user to be working concurrently on several different tasks.

MSDOS (*Microsoft Disk Operating System*) is designed for the 8086 and 8088 16-bit microprocessors, used in the IBM PC, DEC Rainbow, Televideo 1602, Wang PC, and Texas Instrument Professional Computer. This is a single-user interactive system that cannot do tasks concurrently. With many microcomputer systems, the user can't use the computer while the computer is printing. He or she has to wait until the print job is complete before using the CRT to do work on a spreadsheet program, for example. Operating systems that allow concurrent tasks are classified as **multitasking** (see Exhibit 7.14).

For those users who would like a multiuser environment for the IBM PC or some other 16-bit microcomputers, the Oasis–16 operating system has been developed. It is possible to have 32 concurrent users with this OS.

In the 32-bit microprocessor world, it is not clear yet what the dominant OS will be. However, many experts believe that the leading candidate will be some version of the UNIX operating systems developed by AT&T. The UNIX operating system was developed by Bell Lab. Western Electric, another subsidiary of AT&T, was chosen to license the product to other vendors. A variation of UNIX, called XENIX, has been developed by Microsoft. This OS is used with Radio Shack's Model 16 and other microcomputers based on the 68000 microprocessor. These UNIX-type operating systems are multiuser time-sharing systems.

Software Portability

The unbundled approach has led to a variety of choices for microcomputer operating systems. We have seen that some operating systems can be used on many different microcomputers. CP/M can be adapted to be used on any computer that is based on the 8080, 8085, or Z80 microprocessor chips. In turn, there is not just one operating system available for a particular microcomputer. The IBM PC, for example, can use tailored versions of PC DOS, CP/M–86, OASIS–16, USCD p–System, and XENIX.

The critical point is that application programs or software packages such as payroll, word processing, and spreadsheets are designed to be used with a specific operating system. In turn, most operating systems are designed for a particular computer. With some exceptions, the general rule is that application software is not portable. That is, it cannot be assumed that application software that is designed for one computer system will run on any other brand of computer system. This is true even when the two different computer systems use the same operating system and have identical microprocessors.

At present, the computer industry could be likened to a stereo market, where you would have to know the model of a given phonograph player before you could buy an album to play on it. Perhaps in ten years we will be able to buy or develop software that will run on any computer system.

Finally, many operating systems are now being implemented in **firmware**—permanently coded instructions within a ROM. These so-called software-on-silicon (SOS) chips are also being used to contain translators for high-level languages such as BASIC and FORTRAN. Hewlett-Packard, in its HP75 portable computer, has put a spreadsheet, mathematical programs, and a text formatter in a ROM chip. The SOS chip approach is effective for software that is relatively standard and is free of bugs so that it isn't going to change. It also is a means for distributing an updated version of the OS or other application and support software every year or so.

COMPUTERS AT WORK

Why Software Won't Run on All PC Clones

Manufacturers may claim their microcomputers are fully compatible with the IBM PC, but don't take their word for it.

When it comes to buying microcomputers, many businesses rely on the industry adage, "Nobody ever got fired for buying an IBM computer." After all, users can find security in the respected brand name, as well as the wide selection of peripherals and applications software.

But some vendors now hope to lure users away from the "safe" acquisition of an IBM Personal Computer (PC). These vendors sell microcomputers which have earned the industry nickname of "PC clones," computers which the vendors claim offer compatibility with the IBM PC.

More than two dozen vendors already make compatibility claims, ranging from use of the same microprocessor and operating system as the PC to the ability to use IBM-tailored software packages, memory, and peripheral boards without modification.

Why can't all software designed for the IBM PC be used on other components running the MSDOS operating system? The answer lies in the programming techniques used to develop the first generation of MSDOS software for the PC.

To achieve faster data transfer on the PC, some MSDOS programmers insert machine code sequences in their programs. While standard programming statements give instructions to the operating system, this code "bypasses" the operating system by directly addressing memory locations. However, the procedure makes the program hardware dependent.

Dr. Portia Isaacson, Future Computing's president, says few products on the market meet her strict definition of software compatibility, which includes running any software package designed for the PC with identical results. To many manufacturers, Isaacson says, IBM compatibility means use of a licensed version of MSDOS, which usually allows the running of at least some IBM software packages without modification.

"Manufacturers using only this meaning should call themselves MSDOS compatible, not IBM PC compatible," warns Christopher Larson, Microsoft's MSDOS product manager. But a few vendors use even this definition loosely.

Isaacson also believes that data compatibility is important. Data compatability means that data-file diskettes for a particular program can be moved between a PC and a compatible computer, even if both machines can't run the same program diskette.

Source: D. Stein, "Why Software Won't Run on All PC Clones," *Business Computer Systems,* July 1983, pp. 95–100.

SUMMARY

Application software is programs written to meet the needs of users. *System software* is a series of programs written to simplify the interface between the programmer and the computer hardware. System software is generally composed of an operating system, language translators and utilities, data management, and data communication systems.

The overall purpose of the *operating system* is to control the activities of the computer system. It serves as the traffic cop, directing and managing computer events. In addition, the OS provides a useful interface that allows the user to concentrate on what he or she wants to accomplish, rather than on the details of how the computer internally carries it out.

Three of the major functions of an OS are overall master control, resource management, and monitoring activities. A series of programs called a *supervisor* exercises master control of computer operations and coordinates the work within the computer system.

The supervisor initiates and controls the execution of jobs. This requires allocating computer resources and scheduling when they are to be used, a function known as *resource management.* Computer resources include the CPU, memory, input/output devices, and support software.

One of the primary computer resources that is shared is the CPU itself. The CPU can work on only one program at a time. But, because it is thousands of times faster than I/O devices or users working interactively with the system, it can be shared in a couple of different ways. With *event* interrupts, the CPU works on a program until there is an I/O request. With *time-slicing* interrupts, the CPU switches to the next program at the end of a fixed time period.

Once the CPU is to be switched, the CPU scheduling scheme is used to select the next program. The *first-come first-serve scheme* selects the job that has been waiting the longest. A *priority scheme* allows different programs to be selected, based on need. The highest priority program is selected next, regardless of whether other programs have been waiting longer.

With the move to multiuser computer systems came a need to share memory in more efficient ways. The allocation of memory is called *memory management.* In order to accommodate multiple programs in memory at one time, a way of allocating memory space and a means for moving programs in and out of memory had to be developed.

One allocation method is *fixed partitions,* in which primary memory is divided into sections of predefined size to accommodate user programs. To better handle a variety of programs of different sizes, *variable size partitions* are used. With this allocaton method, regions are defined dynamically, depending on the needs of a given program.

Swapping allows the OS to accommodate more programs at any one time than there are partitions or regions. This is accomplished by switching complete programs between primary memory and secondary storage. *Virtual memory* enables better memory management by keeping in primary memory only the active program instructions. The remainder of the program is kept on disk, available on demand.

When large computer systems are being shared by many users and managed for efficiency, it is necessary to monitor system performance and to protect the system from unauthorized users or system errors. One of the functions of the computer staff is to monitor computer performance. By selecting the CPU scheduling scheme, changing priorities, and adding more or faster computer resources, the staff can alleviate bottlenecks and improve performance.

CPU utilization, throughput, response time, and reliability are four major criteria used to judge *computer performance.* CPU *utilization* is the percentage of time that the CPU is actually working. A computer system's *throughput* is the number of programs completed per time period. From the user's point of view, a major criterion for interactive systems is *response time.* This is the interval between a user's request and the computer's response. The percentage of time that the computer is up relative to the time it is scheduled to be up and running is a measure of *reliability.*

Protection has been defined in terms of how access to programs and data stored in the computer is controlled once the user is using the computer. *Security* is defined in terms of the external threats from unauthorized users. One major problem is how the operating system authenticates that the user is who he or she purports to be. The most common approach is to use passwords.

There are several major design factors that can be used to distinguish among operating systems. Was the OS designed to be used primarily with *batch* or *interactive* processing jobs? Was it designed to accommodate *single* or *multiple users?* Was it designed for a specific computer or for a family of computers?

There are many different types of operating systems. The early OS made the complete computer system available to one program, which would be processed from start to finish. *Multiprogramming* means that two or more programs are being run concurrently by the computer. In *concurrent* operations, at a given point in time, one program will be using one computer resource while another program uses a different computer resource.

The basis for multiprogramming is *interrupt processing.* These batch-oriented systems have the CPU process a program until it must wait for an I/O event to occur. *Time-sharing* systems were designed to allow direct communication between the user and the computer system. These interactive, multiuser systems sequence tasks based on *time slices.*

The tremendous demand for computing power, the need for increased reliability, and the decreasing price of hardware have led to operating systems designed for use with computer systems that have *multiple processors.*

In some of the more advanced computer systems, operating systems have been developed that are able to provide a *virtual machine* environment. Within limits, each user is given the illusion that he or she is working with the very computer and OS needed to run an application program or work with the computer interactively.

A major difference between operating systems designed for microcomputers and those for mini- and maxicomputers is a *public,* rather than a *proprietary, orientation.* This unbundled approach has led to a variety of operating system choices for use on a specific microcomputer. Operating systems can also be adapted for use on different microcomputers.

While there hasn't been any official committee that has specified industry parameters, several de facto standards for microcomputer operating systems have developed. A *de facto standard* is one that vendors informally accept, generally because it has come to dominate a market segment of the business. For the 8-bit microcomputer, it is the CP/M operating system; for the 16-bit micro, it is the MSDOS; and for the 32-bit micro, UNIX appears to be the dominant OS. Many operating systems are now being implemented in *firmware,* as permanently coded instructions within a ROM.

A critical point to understand is that application programs or software packages such as payroll, word processing, and spreadsheet are designed to be used with a specific operating system. In turn, most operating systems are designed for use with a particular microprocessor. The general rule is that application software is not *portable.* That is, it cannot be used with just any computer system.

In the next chapter, we will discuss file and data base systems.

REVIEW QUESTIONS

1. Briefly describe the functions of the operating system.
2. Explain the major factors that are used to distinguish among operating systems.
3. Briefly describe the master control function of the operating system.
4. What computer resources must be allocated and controlled by the resource management portion of the operating system?
5. Explain the concept of virtual memory. What advantages does it offer?
6. The Excell Corporation's new CPU is extremely fast. In fact, the firm's CPU frequently has to wait for its printer to catch up before it can process more data. How might this problem be corrected without replacing the current printer?
7. Briefly describe the four major criteria used to evaluate computer performance.
8. What is the role of the operating system regarding the provision of protection and security?
9. What is multiprogramming? What are some advantages and disadvantages of this approach?
10. The Alphonso Company occasionally requires computerized data processing. When such needs are present, the firm could use the services of a large computer installation. However, management does not feel that the frequency of such requirements justifies the purchase of a computer system. How can the company meet its needs for occasional computing power?
11. What is a virtual machine? What are its advantages?
12. What is firmware? For what types of applications is it best suited?

CHAPTER 8
File and Data Base Systems

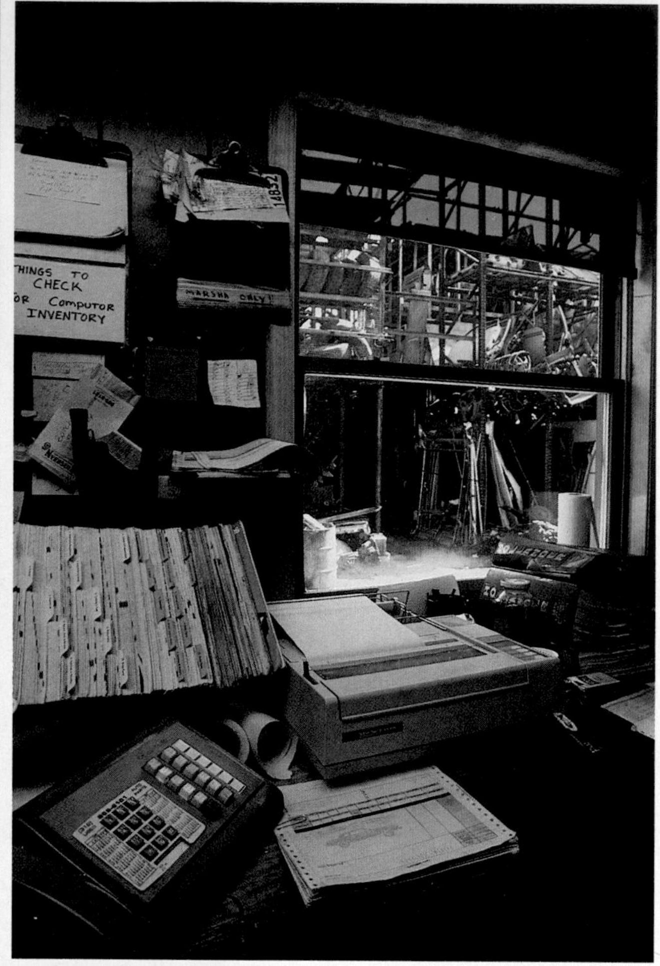

COMPUTERS AT WORK

Junkyards Aren't So Junky Anymore

Sealed in plastic, clearly labeled and laid out in neat rows along the rack, they are reminiscent of vegetables on display in a supermarket.

They are 500-pound engines pulled from wrecked automobiles, and they are for sale at Robertson's Auto Salvage in the southern Massachusetts town of Wareham. Robertson's, like much of the rest of the nation's $4 billion-a-year junkyard industry, is trying to upgrade its image.

The most noticeable change undoubtedly is the practice—now nearly universal—of dismantling used cars before sale. The days are gone when a junkyard owner would wave toward the acres of rusty heaps and say: "I think there's a wheel on the Chevy out in the corner there. If you can find it you can have it for $10."

Parts are removed, cleaned, tested and often displayed in bright, greaseless showrooms—frequently with a 90-day warranty attached. At Robertson's, salesmen in blazers and ties can show customers candy jars filled with used dome lights, axles for four-wheel-drive vehicles stored in cardboard tubes, and displays of windshield wiper motors.

In the warehouse, 600 plastic-wrapped engines—"It keeps them dry and the nuts and bolts intact," Robertson said—are stored on a three-tiered frame. Out back, hundreds of doors and "noses," the hood and front fender assembly, are displayed on numbered racks.

The industry has been changed by the use of computers, which prove invaluable to businesses that may stock more than 350 kinds of parts from countless automobile models. Robertson has a minicomputer that can tell him the location of every dismantled part he has, as well as the make, year and mileage of the car it was taken from.

Not only does this guide him in filling out his inventory when purchasing parts at salvage auctions, but it prevents the loss of sales because his staff did not know whether a part was in stock.

Source: P. Hemp, "Junkyards Polish Their Rusty Image," *The New York Times,* 30 August, 1983, p. D3.

So far, we have discussed computer hardware and the important roles played by application and operating software. Today we see information being used in a seemingly endless variety of ways, from inventory control in junkyards to sophisticated medical applications. Actually, it is only recently that organizations have begun to appreciate the importance of data and the ability to retrieve data easily to provide information. As much an asset as plant and equipment, skilled employees, and money are, careful management of data is essential.

In this chapter you will learn to do the following:

1. Explain the major purpose of data management software.
2. Specify the three ways files can be organized and be able to describe how they are accessed.
3. Explain the three primary data base organization models and the advantages and disadvantages of each.
4. Describe how a microcomputer data base management system can be used to answer management queries.
5. List the four criteria used to compare file and data base management systems.

THE ROLE OF DATA MANAGEMENT SOFTWARE

The primary role of data management software is to provide an easy way for the programmer to create and maintain files and retrieve data from them for use in developing information to meet users' needs. To understand this, you must first consider how data can be organized, and also learn more about data management functions.

An example you are familiar with—a phone book—is helpful for showing the basic concepts of data organization and how they affect the way a user can access data to answer questions.

In Exhibit 8.1 on page 202, a portion of the Local College phone directory is shown. Each of the characters would be represented within the computer by a byte such as eight bits in the EBCDIC or ASCII–8 code. A collection of related characters forms a **data item** or **field.** Employee name and phone extension are examples of data items. An occurrence of all data items is called a **record.** A **file** is a collection of similar types of records. In this particular case, the phone directory file contains the records of all the faculty and staff members of Local College.

This phone directory file is ordered on the key *employee name.* A **key** is a field that can be used to identify a record. A **primary key** is a field (or fields) that identifies a unique record. Organizations often have to use employee number or social security number as a primary key, since several people may have the same name.

A university would need many other files to conduct its daily business. There would be separate files for student grades, for courses offered, for personnel information, for payroll, and so on. An integrated collection of files is called a **data base.** We will discuss later the special characteristics that are necessary to make a data base more than just a group of files.

The way in which data are arranged is called **data organization.** This term refers to data items within a record, records within a file, or files within a data base. Accessing specific records and getting answers to various types of

Employee Name	Job Title	Building and Room Location	Telephone Extension
ANDAZOLA, Genevieve	Secretary, Financial Aid	1-308	0245
CARTER, Georgia	Secretary, Student Affairs	1-224	4716
DURBIN, Martina	Secretary, Counseling and Testing Services	1-110	4235
EKIZIAN, Olivia	Administrative Secretary, Student Affairs	1-224	4714
HART, Dr. Joseph T.	Director, Counseling and Testing	1-110B	4234
JACOBS, Harry M.	Director, Financial Aid	1-308	0244
JONES, Madelena	Administrative Assistant, Student Affairs	1-224	4715
SMITH, Rose	Secretary, Admissions and Records	1-104	4823
WELLS, Dr. Janet	Vice-President, Student Affairs	1-224	4713
YORK, Richard	Director, Admissions and Records	1-104	4822

Exhibit 8.1

A file made up of records ordered by key

questions may or may not be a simple, efficient process, depending upon the arrangement of the data. To illustrate, Exhibits 8.1 and 8.2a are two different data organizations of the phone directory file. In the first case, the records in the file are arranged in alphabetical order by the individual's last name. In the second case, the records are listed by function within the administrative hierarchy of the college. The indentation indicates administration levels. In both these examples, the data contained in each file are the same. However, there is a difference in how easily data within the files can be **accessed** or located.

Let's assume you want to find the phone number for a particular person, Rose Smith. If you knew her name, you could go to the alphabetical file and search through all the entries in it, in sequence. This would lead you, eventually, to entries beginning with the letter *S*, then to the Smith entries, and finally to the listing for Rose Smith. This is an example of a file that is organized in sequence on a key and is accessed sequentially. A file in which records are ordered in a particular sequence is called a sequential file. Often, the sequence is based on a primary key such as last name, employee number, or social security number.

When you look up an entry in a phone book using an alphabetical listing, you don't start looking on page one and continue through each entry, from Bob Able to Sue Bailey to Ed Cummins, until you come to Rose Smith. Instead of proceeding through each entry in sequence, you take advantage of the indexes printed at the top of each page. These are the first entry and the last entry that appear on that particular page, and they help you retrieve the appropriate data more quickly. These types of files are called indexed files.

Sequential files or indexed files are helpful when you know the primary key value. In our example, the primary key value is the employee name, Rose Smith. The file can be searched alphabetically until the record for Rose Smith is found. Then, that specific record is searched to find the desired data item, phone extension, and the data, 4823.

Exhibit 8.2a
A Listing of a Hierarchical Data Organization

	Telephone Extension	Building and Room Location
Vice-President, Student Affairs—Dr. Janet Wells	4713	1-224
Administrative Secretary—Olivia Ekizian	4714	1-224
Administrative Assistant—Madelena Jones	4715	1-224
Secretary—Georgia Carter	4716	1-224
Director, Admissions and Records—Richard York	4822	1-104
Secretary—Rose Smith	4823	1-104
Director, Counseling and Testing Services—Dr. Joseph T. Hart	4234	1-110B
Secretary—Martina Durbin	4235	1-110
Director, Financial Aid—Harry M. Jacobs	0244	1-308
Secretary—Genevieve Andazola	0245	1-308

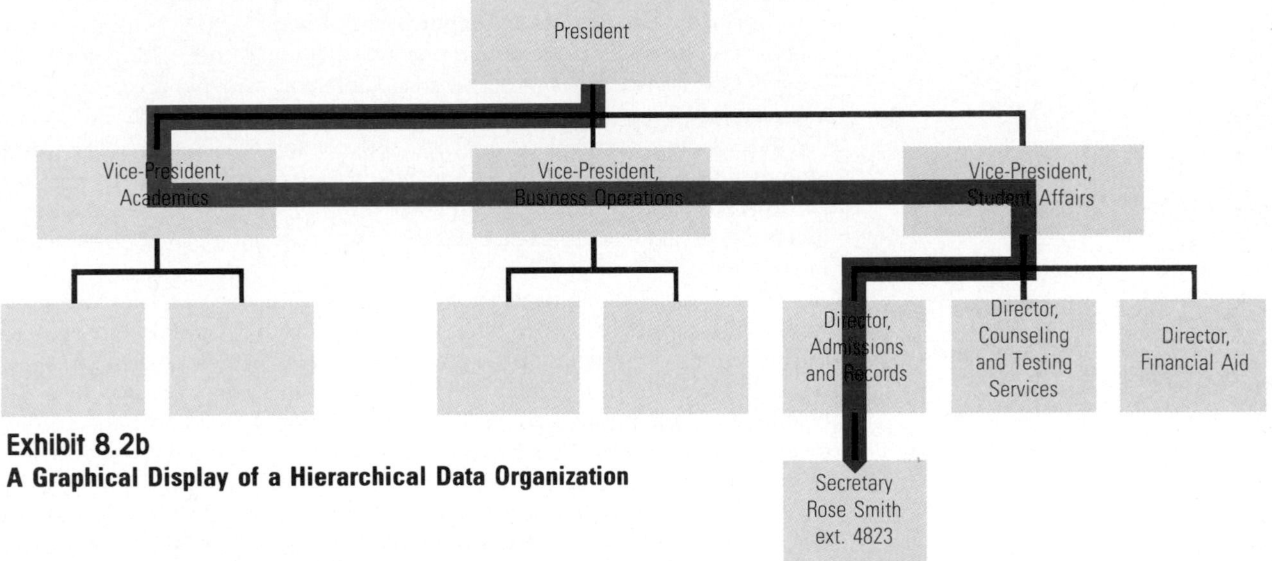

Exhibit 8.2b
A Graphical Display of a Hierarchical Data Organization

However, these methods of file organization would not be particularly useful for finding the phone number for the secretary of the director of admissions. If you wanted to search the file by function or job title, rather than by a person's name, you would find the data organization shown in Exhibit 8.2b more practical. It is ordered by function and shows the hierarchy associated with it.

To find the desired phone number, you would follow the path shown in Exhibit 8.2b. Beginning at the top administrative function, president, you then select the appropriate vice-president function from among vice-president of academics, vice-president of business operations, and vice-president of student affairs. Finding the student affairs box on the chart, you look at the titles of the directors that report to the vice-president of student affairs. Selecting the director of admissions and records, you look to the secretary's name. Here, you read that she is Rose Smith, and her phone extension is 4823. This is an example of a hierarchical data organization.

These illustrations are used to introduce you to the concept that data can be organized in many different ways. In this chapter, we will examine three major file organizations and three data base structures. The organization of files and data bases affects the ways in which information is retrieved and the types of questions that can be answered easily.

There are two primary reasons for needing to access data within a file or a data base: retrieval and updating. The purpose of having a data file is to be able to **retrieve** selected data from it for use in producing desired information. Depending on the application, it may be necessary to process the total file in some instances. In others, specific data records may be used. Either way, the data in the file are used by a program to produce the needed information.

Application programs cannot produce information that is any more accurate or current than the data within the file itself. **Updating** is the process whereby records are added, deleted, or modified within the file. By updating, the data are as accurate and current as needed. For example, with any type of reservation system, it is important to update the files continuously. For a student grade file, however, updating once a semester is usually sufficient, and often won't be done for several weeks after a term has ended.

A primary role of **data management software** is to provide an easier way for a programmer to create and maintain files and retrieve data from them. We will discuss two types of data management software: file access methods and data base management systems.

File access methods (FAM) are support software that enables a programmer to organize data into files and provides means for accessing data records. As we will see later, a particular type of FAM may be able to accommodate only sequential files, for example, whereas another FAM can handle index files.

Without the FAM, an application program that needed to retrieve a record would have to supply the operating system (OS) with the physical location of the desired record on the secondary device. That is, "Get data from cylinder 6, track 12, record 5" (see Exhibit 8.3A). File Access Methods were developed to enable a programmer to access data by having to specify only the record desired within a specific file, and thus not needing to know the physical details of storage. For example, in Exhibit 8.3B, the programmer could conceptually specify "Get Rose Smith's record in the Phone Directory File." The FAM would determine where the file was stored on disk and which record was Rose Smith's. The FAM would then issue a command to the OS to get the record. The OS would control when and how to retrieve the data record from secondary storage and place it in primary memory. The programmer would have written logic to retrieve the data item—the phone number extension—from that record for further processing.

Thus, using a FAM still requires the application programmer to be knowledgeable about the type of records that are used, and with which files they are associated. This is a distinct disadvantage, because it ties the program to a particular file structure and also forces the programmer to know more than he or she needs to in order to answer the question that was asked.

Another layer of data management software has been developed that is called a Data Base Management System (DBMS). One of its functions is to enable the programmer to be able to access data by having to specify only the data items that are needed. For example, in Exhibit 8.3C the instruction could be, "Get Rose Smith's phone number." The DBMS is responsible for determining which record contains phone numbers (a data item) and in which files these records are kept. It passes that information onto the FAM which, as before, translates that into a storage location.

The DBMS also allows much more complex data organization structures to be built than does FAM. This enables us to take advantage of relationships between records, which can shorten access time and allow more complex

Exhibit 8.3

A Conceptual View of the Role of Data Management Software

Without data management software, a programmer would need to know the disk address of the data needed. File access method software eases the task by requiring only the specification of the desired record and file. A data base management system requires that a programmer know only what data are desired—not the record or file with which they are associated.

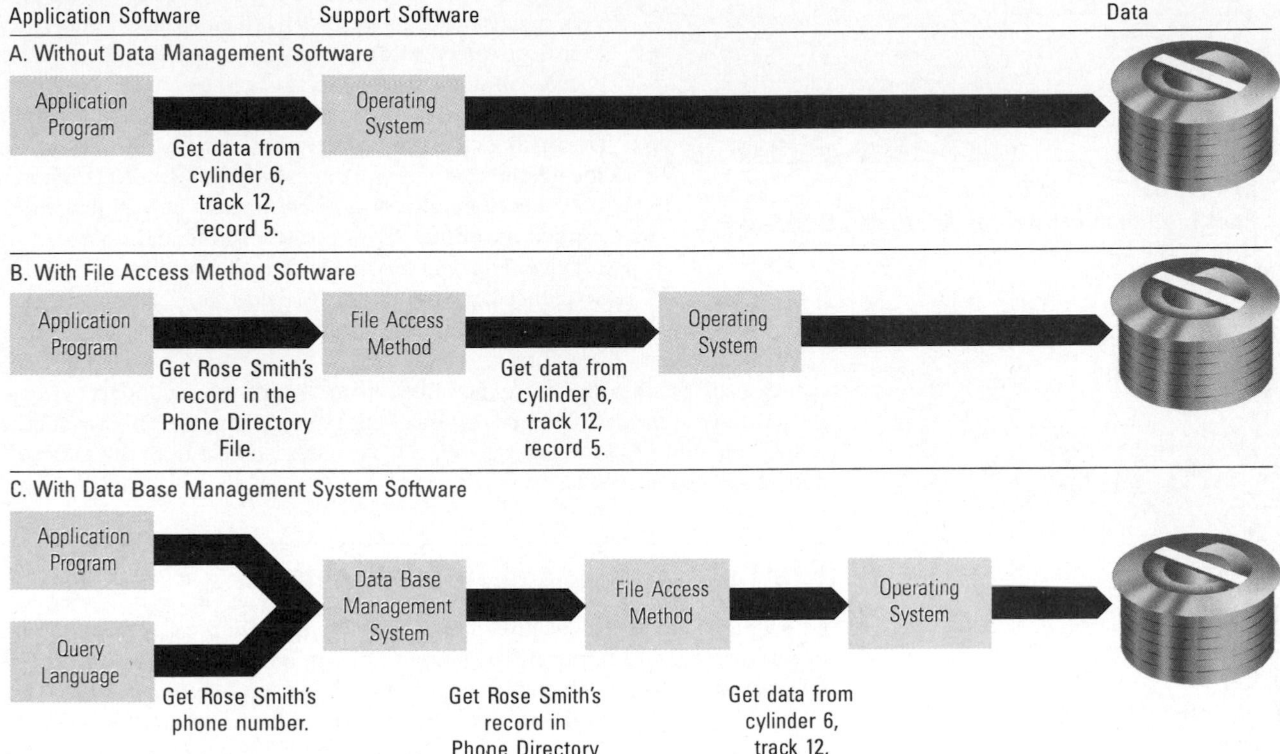

queries to be answered. The hierarchical data organization is an example of a data base structure that we will discuss. To aid in your understanding of the role of Data Management Software, we have taken a conceptual view of the functions that are performed. Actually, the file access methods are generally incorporated within the OS itself.

FILE SYSTEMS

We have seen that the main purpose of Data Managment Software is to enable programmers to concentrate more on the task of solving the user's problem and less on the physical details of how the computer actually locates and retrieves the data from secondary storage. But, to meet an organization's data processing needs, creation, manipulation, and updating of data are necessary. The primary means of storing data today is in files. These files are generally created and manipulated by a programmer writing an application program in a language such as COBOL, to be used in conjunction with the FAM and OS to produce the desired results. The means of providing file organization, access, and manipulation of data is called a **file system.**

File Organization

Access	Sequential	Indexed	Relative
Sequential			
Direct			

Exhibit 8.4
Possible Combinations for Accessing Different File Organizations

In this section we will look first at the various ways a file can be organized and accessed and how these affect the updating and retrieval of data. Then we will examine the ways in which data on several files can be shared. Next, we will contrast this with the DBMS, which is built to share data and provide easier ways to update and retrieve the data. These more expensive systems also provide means to access the data from either application programs or query languages that are easy for people who aren't computer experts to use.

There are several types of file systems, and they differ primarily in the file organization that they allow and the means they provide for accessing the data. Data records have been organized most commonly in business applications into three types of files: sequential, indexed, or relative. The data records within a file can be accessed in sequence or, when means provide for it, directly by specific record. Exhibit 8.4 shows the major combinations possible.

Not all combinations are possible on each type of secondary storage device. In Chapter 6 we learned that magnetic tape can provide only sequential access capability. On the other hand, disks can be used for both direct access and sequential access.

File Organization and Access Methods

Let's go through several examples to show how different file systems are used to do updating and retrieval. The simplest file organization is the **sequential file organization** in which the records are sequenced by primary key values. Using the payroll record introduced earlier, we will add an employee identification number to serve as the primary key (see Exhibit 8.5). To process the weekly payroll, we would locate the first record in the payroll file on the magnetic tape (0101 John Avery 550 40). This employee data would be read into the computer. The pay rate data would be multiplied by the hours worked, and the gross pay determined. Then the next record would be read (0351 Bill Jones 500 30), and so on. The records are being accessed sequentially. Sequential files are used primarily with batch processing applications, where most or all of the records on the file are needed each time the application is run.

Exhibit 8.5
Sequential File Organization
Data can be located only by reading records sequentially.

Some types of sequential file organization do not allow the updating of data records without copying the entire file. For example, a record cannot be added within a sequential file recorded on magnetic tape, since, to insert the record, all following records would have to "move down by one." Thus, the most practical approach when updating files on a tape is to rewrite all the records onto a new tape, while making the appropriate changes.

To envision how this would work, assume the changes shown in Exhibit 8.6 happened since the present payroll file was last updated. The present collection of payroll records is considered to be the old payroll master file. The transaction file includes all the changes that have

Update Action	Employee Name	Employee ID#	Reason
Change payrate to $9.00	Sally Wallis	0444	annual review
Delete record	John Avery	0101	retirement
Add record	Bob Green	7777	new hire

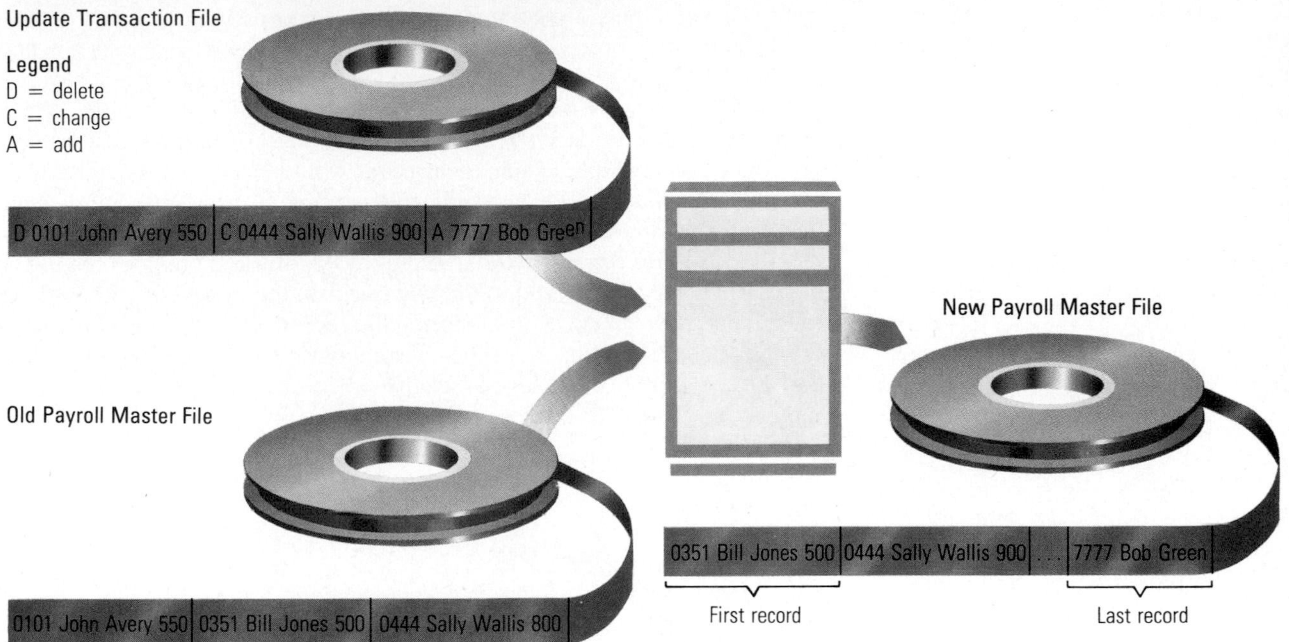

Exhibit 8.6
Master File Updating Process
An update transaction file would contain all the changes that have taken place since the last update. The present collection of payroll records is the old payroll master file. Each file would need to be sorted on the primary key *Employee ID.* By comparing the records on each tape file, a new payroll master file would be produced that incorporated the latest changes.

taken place since the last update. These changes must be applied to the old master file to produce a new (current) payroll master file.

To process these changes, the first step would be to sort each file into like order. Sorting could be based upon a primary key such as employee ID#, for example. Then the first record in the transaction file would be read in, and the key number noted. Next, the first record of the old master file would be read in, and its key noted.

If there wasn't a match, the record from the old master file would be recorded onto the new master file. When a match of key numbers did occur, a change such as a pay rate adjustment would be made and written onto the new file. A need to delete a record would result in that record not being written on the new file. A record would be added to the new master file in the appropriate sequence. The new master payroll file could then be used to process inquiries and develop payroll reports.

Another approach to file organization is called **index file organization.** This file is organized logically in sequence by key, and it has an index that specifies the correspondence between the key value and the disk location of the record. The index key shows the highest key value associated with a record held on a particular track. This approach is analogous to the alphabetical listing of the phone directory file, where the top of a page includes an index of the first and last entries appearing on the page.

Data can be retrieved from an index sequential file by directly locating a specific record through the use of the index, or by reading records sequentially. This flexibility enables both transaction and batch processing to be handled efficiently. For example, to answer a query by a counselor as to what grades Jerry Berry (student number 106) received last semester, a direct-access approach would be used. The index would first be searched by student identification number, and the appropriate track located. Then the records within that track would be searched sequentially until record 106 was found. Exhibit 8.7 illustrates this process.

To update the student files at the end of the semester, a sequential-access approach would be used since almost all records would be affected. Therefore, the record for the student with number 101 would be found, starting with the first record on track one. Then, each record would be read in sequence (105, 106, 119), checking for a match with student numbers on a sorted transaction file of updated grades.

Relative file organization arranges records by key, but does not use an index. The key value is used to directly calculate the relative record number (first, tenth, twenty-first, etc.) for storing the record. One of the disadvantages of large index files is that it is time-consuming to search the many indexes to find the appropriate disk address. Relative organization files are used for applications that require direct access and rapid response time.

Exhibit 8.7
A File Stored Sequentially with Index

Data can be retrieved from an index sequential file by locating a record through the use of an index or by reading records sequentially.

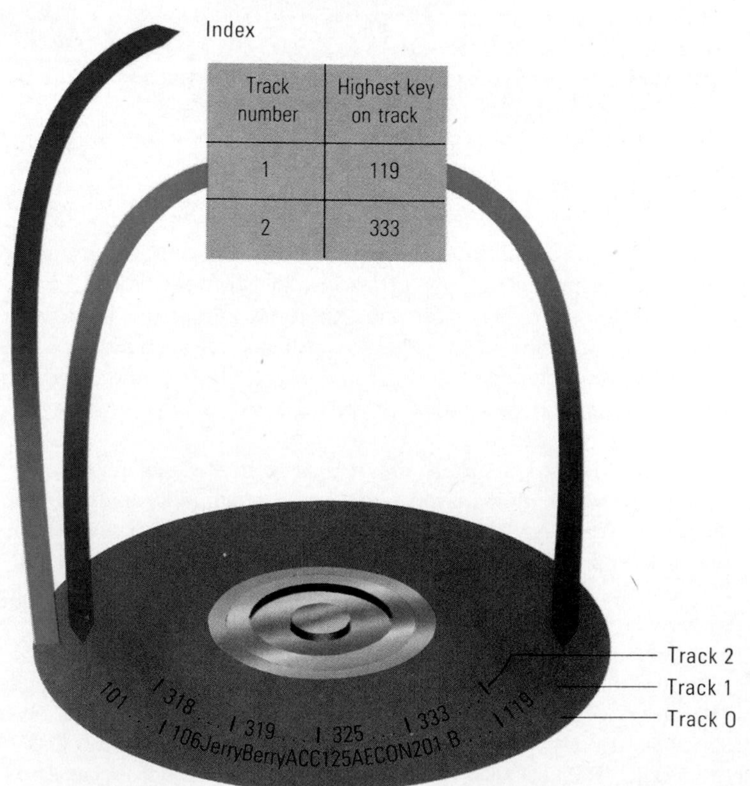

To see how this works, assume in an inventory example that part number is the key identifier and it is a three-digit number. Suppose we stock, at most, fifty types of parts during the year. If we were to allocate a disk address for each possible part number, much space would be wasted. Instead of 1000 storage locations (000–999), we really need only fifty. The problem, then, is how to use the three-digit part number as a key to identify which of the fifty disk addresses should be placed on the data record. Computer scientists have developed mathematical formulas called **hashing algorithms** to randomize this allocation.

One allocation approach used is the division/remainder method (see Exhibit 8.8). In our example, the part number identifier would be divided by the largest prime number less than the maximum number of records that will be needed. A **prime number** is a number not divisible by any other number than itself and 1. The largest prime number for 50 is 47. For part number 715, division by prime number 47 yields a remainder of 10. This record would be placed in the inventory file in the 10th record space. Part number 297 would be in the 15th space. Occasionally, this division/remainder method will yield the same remainder for different key values. These are called **synonyms.** In such instances, the second of these records to be stored is generally placed in the next available storage location.

To update a relative file is conceptually quite easy. To modify a record on the disk, the record is located by taking the key and dividing it by the largest prime number. The resulting remainder is used to determine the relative record location. That record is read into primary memory. The appropriate data elements are changed, and the complete record is written back to the same location. If a record is to be added, the relative address is calculated and the new record is placed in that space on the file, if no synonym record has already been recorded there.

We have seen that files are organized in three primary ways—as sequential, indexed, or relative files. Each approach has its own strengths and weaknesses. The processing requirements of the application determine which file design is best. The primary criterion for determining file design is whether the application is going to be used in batch- or transaction-processing mode. Batch processing generally uses sequential access. Transaction processing requires direct access, which can be handled by either relative or index files. Index file organization is a composite approach that can be used when both sequential and direct processing of a file are necessary for different applications.

Whether an activity should be using batch or transaction processing generally depends upon the response time needed, the currentness of data needed, the number of times records are to be added or deleted, and the percentage of records on the file that will be affected by the application programs. These trade-offs will be discussed in depth in Chapter 12, "System Development II."

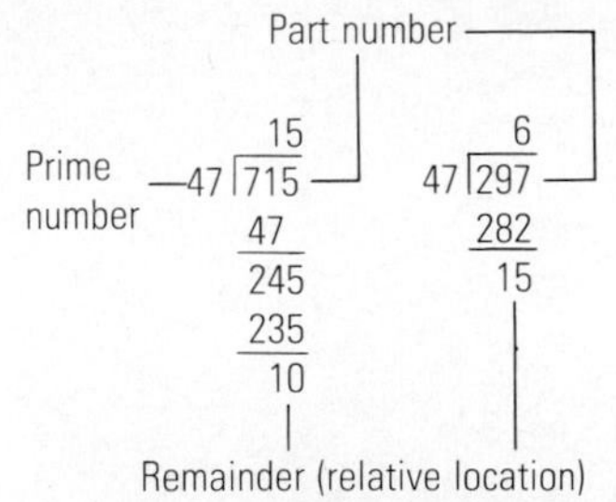

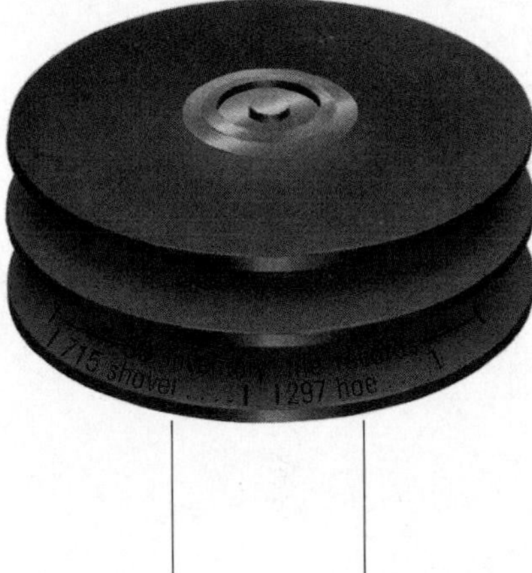

Exhibit 8.8
A File Stored by Key Value Calculation
The key value is used to directly calculate the relative record number for storing a record. The hashing algorithm used is the division/remainder method of randomizing this allocation. The part number is divided by the prime number, yielding a remainder that is used to determine the relative record location.

Sharing Files

So far, we have discussed the different ways that a file can be organized and accessed. File organization impacts the accessibility of data for retrieval and updating purposes. We have assumed that all the information that is needed for a particular program can be gotten by searching a specific file, but that isn't always true. What happens, for instance, if some additional data items are needed to answer a user's question?

Often, data that are needed for a given application are already in a file previously developed for a different application. Sometimes different data items contained on separate files may need to be combined to produce the necessary reports.

One way of doing this is to use a sort/merge routine. Suppose the Financial Aid department of a college had a requirement that each student receiving financial aid had to have a grade point average of at least a C for the year. They have asked that a program be written to make this check (see Exhibit 8.9).

There is a financial aid file containing the following information: student's name, identification number, local address, parents' annual income, and so on. There is also a student grade file, which the data processing department updates each semester. It contains each student's identification number, name, classes taken, grades earned, etc.

So, the information needed is already available in computer-readable form, though it is contained on separate tapes or disk packs. The financial aid file would first have to be sorted by student identification number, to match the sequence of the student grade file. Then, since only a percentage of students receive financial aid, a matching process would have to be initiated. When the student ID numbers match on both files, the data items needed from the record in each file would be processed. The result would be shown on the Financial Aid Student Grade Report. If any students listed on the financial aid file were not listed on the student grade file, an error list would have to be generated.

Exhibit 8.9
Sort/Merge Approach to Answering a Query

To answer a query that requires data stored in two separate files necessitates that the tape files be sorted first. The information is then merged based on key value.

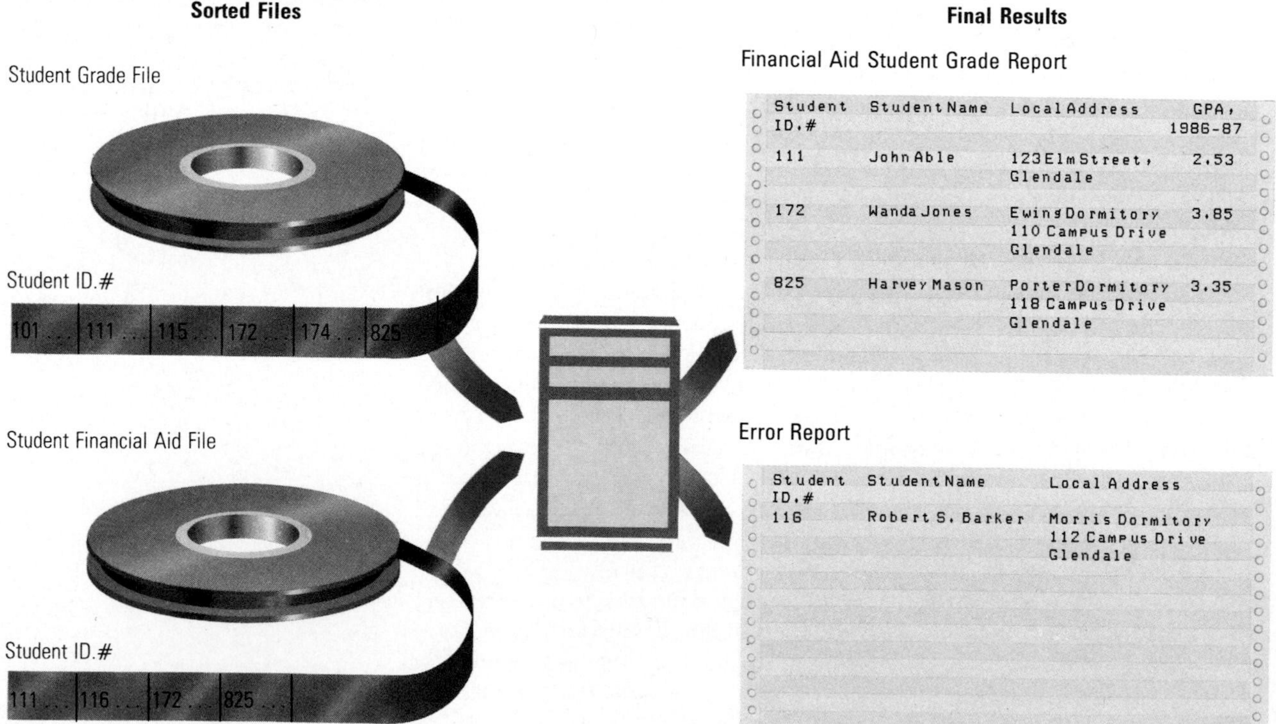

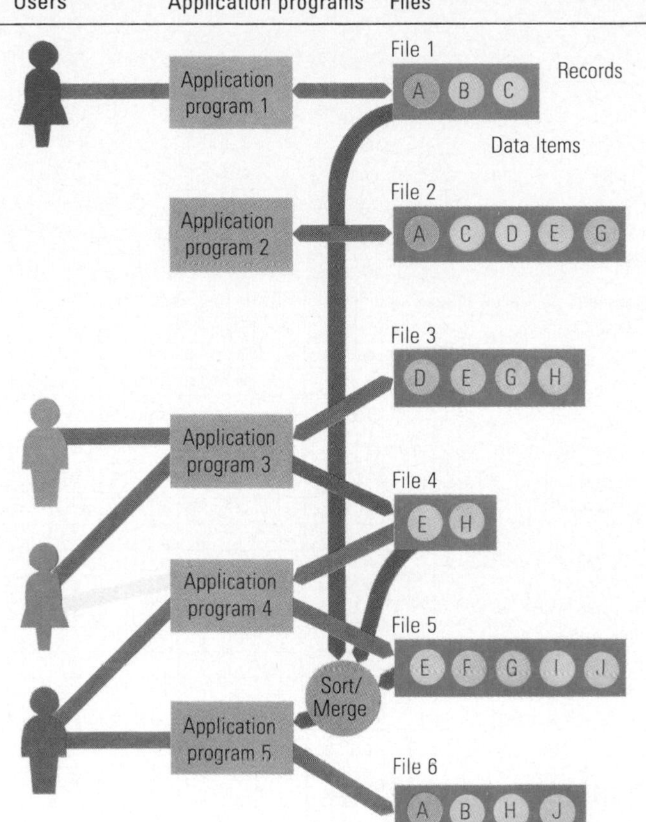

Exhibit 8.10

A system without a data base has much data redundancy, program overlap, and inflexibility.

Source: James Martin, *Principles of Data-Base Management*, © 1976, p. 37. Adapted by permission of Prentice-Hall, Inc., Englewood Cliffs, NJ.

Thus, the **sort/merge** method is a way of combining selected data items from several files to produce needed information. It is a common approach used in organizations that don't have the use of a data base. Exhibit 8.10 shows a generalization of this concept. The organization has many users who need information to accomplish their jobs. The data processing department has written programs for them to produce accounting reports (Application Program 1), information on sales analysis (Application Program 2), and so on. Ordinarily, an application program is written to produce each particular report. This results in an abundance of files that contain many of the same data items, creating much **data redundancy.** For example, data item E is used in four different files. Application Program 5 must use three files to produce the desired output.

Shown in Exhibit 8.11 on page 212 is a typical list of organizational reports and the data items that are on each. The sort/merge method is the primary way that relationships among these files have been handled. There are several distinct disadvantages to this approach, however. First, creating files by sort/merge requires a significant amount of computer resources and time to accomplish. Second, when updating data held in several different files, care must be taken to change all copies of a data item. Last, even if a needed data item is on an

Exhibit 8.11

Multiple input documents contain the same data items as those in various data files used to produce reports. A concern is that, when updating data held in several different files, *all* copies of a data item are changed. Also, it is unclear whether data items with the same name used in different contexts mean exactly the same thing.

Source: James Martin, *Principles of Data-Base Management,* © 1976, p. 41. Adapted by permission of Prentice-Hall, Inc., Englewood Cliffs, NJ.

Files, Reports, and Documents

Data Items	Order from Customer	Customer **File**	Warehouse Order	Warehouse Ticket	Invoice	Weekly Total Shipment **Report**	Weekly Item Shipment **Report**	Year-to-Date Shipment **Report**	Year-to-Date Item **Report**	Item **File**	Weekly Item Inventory **Report**	Inventory **File**	Branch **File**	Monthly Branch Summary	Year-to-Date Sales **Report**	Item On-Order **Report**	Total On-Order **Report**	Monthly Customer **Report**	Customer Payment	Accounts Receivable	Overdue Accounts	Overdue Notices
Customer Number	●	●	●		●													●	●	●	●	●
Customer Order Number	●		●		●														●	●	●	●
Item Number	●		●	●	●		●		●	●	●	●				●		●				●
Item Type and Size	●		●	●	●		●		●	●	●	●				●		●				●
Corporate Order Number			●	●	●		●											●		●	●	
Invoice Number					●														●	●	●	●
Branch Office Number	●				●								●	●	●		●	●		●	●	●
Customer Name	●	●			●									●				●	●	●	●	●
Item Name	●		●	●	●		●		●	●	●	●			●	●		●				●
Date of Invoice					●															●	●	●
Quantity Ordered	●		●	●	●				●		●	●				●		●				●
Quantity Shipped				●	●	●	●	●										●		●	●	●
Quantity Out of Stock				●	●	●	●	●	●		●							●				
Shipping Instructions			●	●	●																	
Code for Shipping			●	●	●																	
Customer Address		●			●																	
Branch Office Name	●	●			●								●	●	●		●	●				●
Branch Office Address	●				●								●									●
Price					●	●	●	●	●	●									●	●	●	●
Invoice Line Value					●															●	●	●
Discount Rate					●					●										●	●	●
Invoice Line Discount					●																	●
C.O.D. or Credit Code	●	●			●													●				●
Weekly Total of Item Shipped						●	●	●	●		●											
Weekly Value of Item Shipped						●	●	●	●													

existing file, it is not always clear that the meaning of a data element used in a given file is the same as you need, or is in the needed format. For example, does "price" refer to the retail price of an item, the wholesale price, or the discounted price given to special customers?

DATA BASE MANAGEMENT SYSTEMS

The development of data base management systems (DBMS), in the late 1960s for the large computers and the early 1980s for the microcomputers, has provided significant help in sharing and managing corporate data. The primary function of the DBMS is to enable users to establish the structure of the data base itself, which organizes data to be used in many different applications. Secondly, the DBMS facilitates the initial loading of the data into the data base and enables the user to easily update the data base. A third function is to provide an easy way for managers and staff personnel who are not computer experts, as well as programmers, to retrieve selected data items. Lastly, a DBMS must provide means for managing and protecting this organizational data, which is to be shared among many users.

Logical Versus Physical Views

The concept of a data base has emerged to provide a more effective way of sharing organizational data. In fact, it is a more uniform way of managing data as a critical organization resource. Conceptually, a **data base** is an integrated collection of data items that can be retrieved in any combination necessary to produce needed information. Programmers could write application programs in a language such as COBOL to directly extract data and develop overdue notices or weekly inventory reports, for example. Users, themselves, could make inquiries of the data by using Englishlike statements in a data base query language (see Exhibit 8.12). In contrast to the data base concept, file systems provide no integrated way of accessing, linking, or managing the data in a collection of files.

A major purpose of the DBMS is to divide the accessing of data into logical and physical concerns. The **logical** question refers to *what* data are needed to answer a variety of questions users might have. *How* those data should actually be positioned on the disk or be accessed is the **physical** question.

To accomplish this division, there must be a separation between the logic of the programs and queries and the physical placement and retrieval of the data on secondary storage devices. The significance of this separation is: (1) users now have a much easier way to visualize and use shared data; and (2) changes to the logic of programs and/or structure of shared data can be made without affecting each other.

Let's examine how this works. The logical description of the organization of the complete data base is referred to as a **schema.** It includes the name of the data items and specifies the relationship among them. A description of a particular subset of the total data base that is useful in answering a user's specific question is called a **subschema.** Each subschema is also called a **user's view.** In Exhibit 8.13 User A is using data items 3, 4, 5, 13, and 14, while User C views the data base to be composed

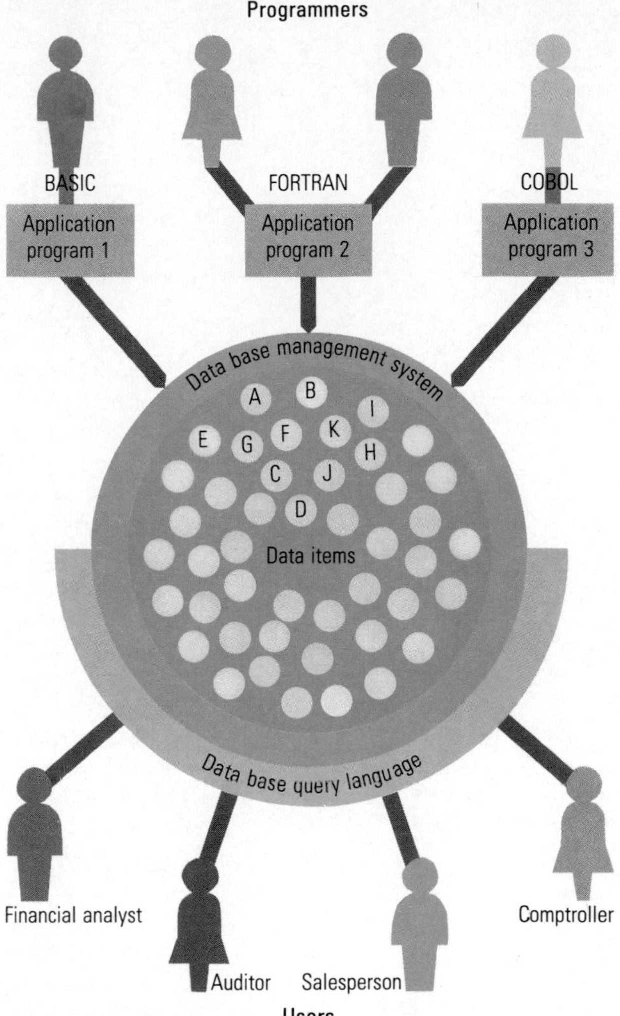

Exhibit 8.12
A Conceptual View of a Data Base System

Source: James Martin, *Principles of Data-Base Management,* © 1976, p. 38. Adapted by permission of Prentice-Hall, Inc., Englewood Cliffs, NJ.

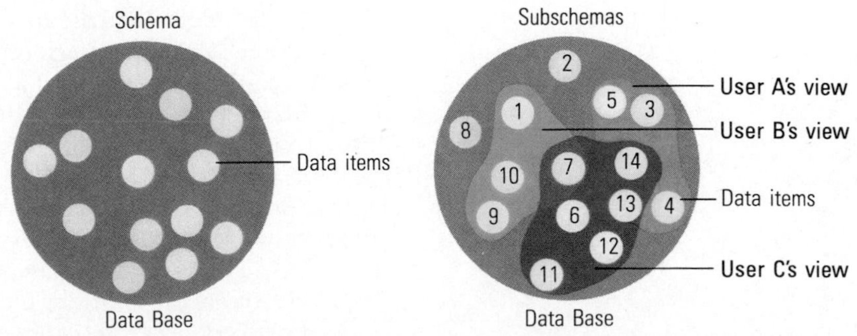

Exhibit 8.13

A data base can be defined to accommodate specific user views and as a means for limiting users' access to specific data.

of data items 6, 7, 11, 12, 13, and 14. The notion of a user's view allows each user to be concerned only with data that are of interest to him or her. From a security standpoint, a user's view can be implemented to keep unauthorized users from gaining access to specific data.

With the use of a file system, a programmer has to specify the next record that is needed. For example, a program to determine gross pay would be designed to request retrieval of the next employee's pay record. After the FAM and OS had retrieved and put that record in primary memory, the application program instructions would take the data items needed within the pay record—pay rate and hours worked—and perform the multiplication.

This approach requires that the size of the record and the number and order of data items be known and specified in the program. This is a **program data dependent** situation. The implication of this dependency is that if one of the fields within the employee record were to change, such as ZIP codes increasing from five to nine digits, all programs using this particular file would have to be rewritten to accommodate the change in record length. This is true even for those programs that do not use ZIP code, but use other data items in that record.

With a DBMS, the application program simply requests the specific data items that are needed, rather than the complete record. The data management software takes the logical request for pay rate and hours worked and issues the commands necessary to physically place those data items in primary memory. The net result is that, with the DBMS, this payroll program would not be affected by an increase in ZIP code length within the payroll record. **Program data independence** means that changes in either programs or data can be made without significantly affecting the other.

Data Base Organization Models

The three major models used for organizing a data base are hierarchical, network, and relational. A particular DBMS is generally designed to support only one of these models. An example of each kind of model is shown in Exhibit 8.14, representing data regarding major inventions by British and American individuals. The first model shows a hierarchical representation of the data. It is ordered by nationality, then major invention, then inventor's surname and given name.

How would this data base model be used to answer the query, "What British and American inventors are noted for their work on the computer?" The data base would be searched starting with the British side of the hierarchy, and then major inventions would be considered. Finding "computer," it would then note that Babbage, Charles was the inventor. Next, it would look at the American side of the data base hierarchy and trace a path to Mauchly, John.

The hierarchical data structure has a "one-to-many" relationship among the data records. This means that a higher-level data record, called a **parent,** can be related to one or more of the next lower-level records, each called a **child.** Thus, on the hierarchy in Exhibit 8.14, the British have three major inventions (children). Each invention or child, however, has only one nationality (parent). In a **hierarchical data base structure,** the relationship among records is always one to many. Each parent can have one or more children, but each child can have only one parent.

A different way of structuring the data is shown in the network model. With the network model, we can indicate explicitly through links that computers

Exhibit 8.14
The Three Most Common Data Base Organization Models

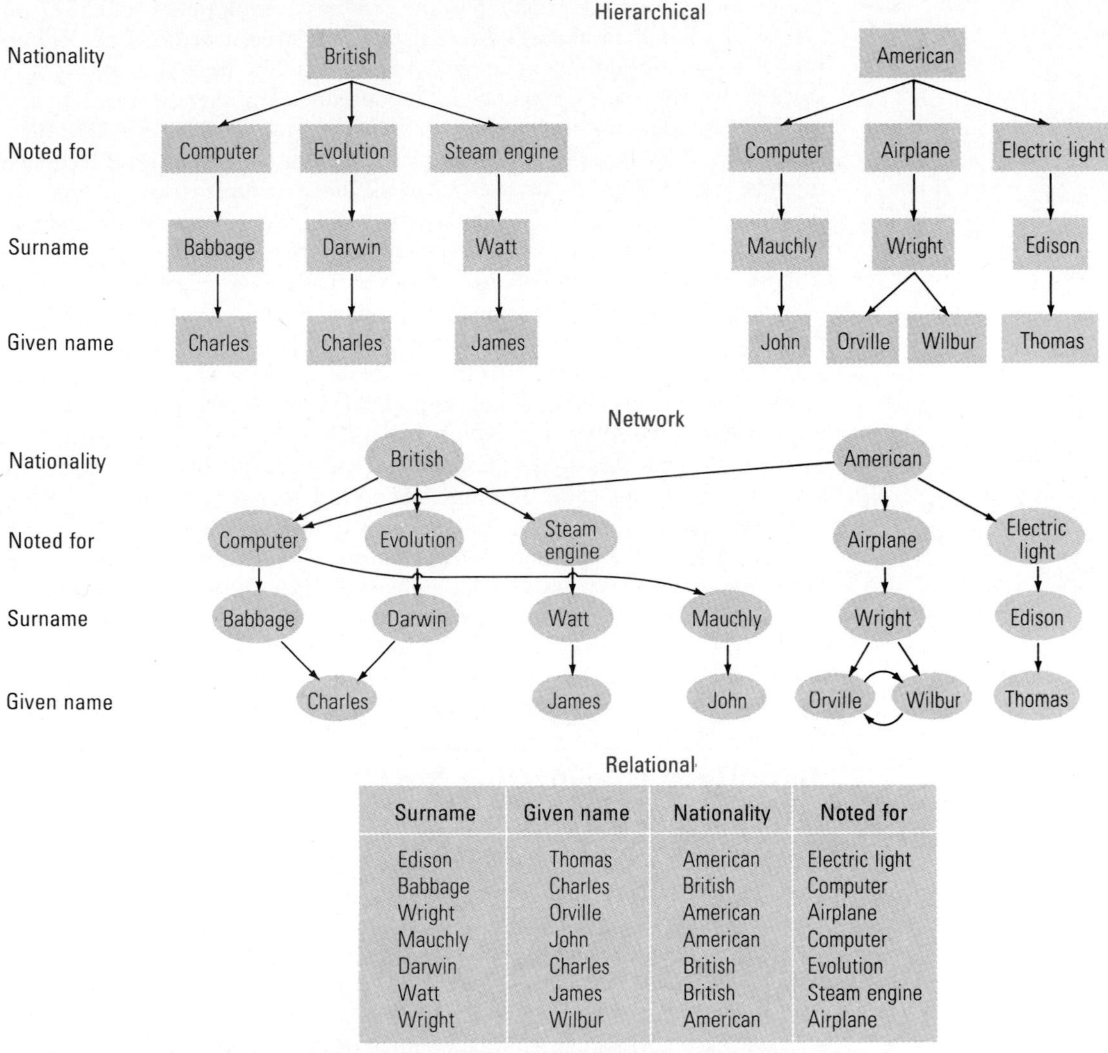

Surname	Given name	Nationality	Noted for
Edison	Thomas	American	Electric light
Babbage	Charles	British	Computer
Wright	Orville	American	Airplane
Mauchly	John	American	Computer
Darwin	Charles	British	Evolution
Watt	James	British	Steam engine
Wright	Wilbur	American	Airplane

Reprinted with permission, *High Technology* magazine, (December 1984). Copyright © 1984 by High Technology Publishing Corporation, 38 Commercial Wharf, Boston, MA 02110.

were a major invention of both British and American individuals. Thus, the child record "computer" has two parent records, "British" and "American." In turn, the British and Americans each have several children in addition to the record "computer." The **network data base structure** allows "many-to-many" relationships among parent and children records.

The third data base model is the relational model, and is based on presenting data in the form of tables or relations. In the table shown, surname and given name are used as the primary key. Each horizontal row is a record, and data items are shown in the columns. As we will see in a later section, "DBMS in Action," the **relational data base structure** shows relationships among records by linking tables together as needed.

Though we have used a simplified example, it is important to understand the implication that data can generally be shown in the three equivalent forms. Why have three data base models? Each has its particular strengths and weaknesses and needs to be matched to the data base requirements of an organization. The hierarchical data base is also called a tree structure. The network model allows the addition of lateral connections to the tree. The major advantages of the hierarchical and network models are economy and speed. In general, these models, in comparison to the relational model, have less data redundancy and allow faster access to the information. However, these data base models are complex to update, since all affected links must be reconfigured.

The major advantage of the relational model is that any combination of data in the data base can be easily retrieved. Links between data records (tables) can be established by user's commands as the need arises. This great flexibility allows the relational data base to be easily configured to answer new and unanticipated questions. In contrast, the hierarchical and network models require that the links be built into the design of the data base. Programs must follow established paths to find information. These paths or links are designed to quickly answer the typical questions that will be asked, but retrieval may be slow for questions that require accesses not supported by the built-in links.

Relational models are generally slower to access data in fairly large data bases. To answer the question about inventors of computers, a search through the complete table is necessary, looking at all entries of the data item "Noted for." With the hierarchical and network models, on the other hand, only a small percentage of entries had to be searched. To speed up access to data, relational models often use indexes for the most common search paths.

Historically, the hierarchical and network models were developed first. They are the major types used on maxicomputers. The relational data base model is a recent development used extensively on microcomputers, and is finding more and more applications on mini- and maxicomputers.

In looking at the diagrams of the three models, you probably felt most comfortable with the relational model. Your preference would probably be even stronger if there were thousands of entries, rather than the small number shown. We are used to seeing data in tables.

A trend is appearing that takes advantage of the ability to distinguish logical from physical structures of data. Since users are more comfortable with relational tables, the DBMS provides a relational look to the user. Internally, the DBMS translates the relational commands into a hierarchical or network model for structuring and retrieving the data from secondary storage. This dual approach allows us to make use of strengths of both humans and computers.

Data Base Administration

When important corporate data and computer resources are going to be shared among users with diverse interests, much time and thought must go toward balancing the often conflicting objectives of meeting user needs and making efficient use of computer systems. The **Data Base Administrator (DBA)** plays a key role in this effort. The DBA is (are) the person(s) acting as the keeper of the data base. The DBA ensures the effectiveness of data retrieval, the accuracy and confidentiality of data, and also keeps the physical data base

Exhibit 8.15
Authorization Rules for Accessing and Modifying a Data Base

Subject	Object	Action	Constraint
PGM OE104J	ORDER Record	Insert	Amount less than $500,000
Sally Smith	ORDER Record	Read	None
Payroll Dept	EMPLOYEE Record	Read	Hourly workers
Payroll Dept	EMPLOYEE Record	Modify	Hourly workers
Payroll Dept	EMPLOYEE Record	Insert	Hourly workers
Payroll Supv	EMPLOYEE Record	Delete	Hourly workers
Payroll Supv	Read Permission of EMPLOYEE Records	Grant	To payroll personnel only

running efficiently. As you can surmise, the DBA needs both technical and political skills to accommodate multiple users of a shared data base.

There are several important features that a DBMS should have to aid the DBA. The creation and maintenance of the data base structure is fundamental to the management of the DBMS. The complete description of the data base is contained in a **data dictionary.** This is used to identify the data elements, records, and relationships that will exist in the data base. In addition, schemas, subschemas, and programs are identified.

Since the data are being shared, it is important to determine who will be allowed access to any given data item and to establish modification rights. Exhibit 8.15 shows a set of authorization rules that specifically state who is allowed to do what with the various data records. For example, Sally Smith is authorized only to read the ORDER record. She can't modify it, nor can she add or delete data items within the record. In contrast, the application program PGM OE104J can make insertions to the ORDER record. This is true so long as the amount is less than $500,000. The payroll supervisor is the only one who can delete an employee record, and then only for hourly workers—not salaried employees. The payroll supervisor is also the only one who can grant the various actions (insert, delete, modify) to the records of payroll personnel. The critical point is that a user is allowed to do only a limited set of authorized actions, based on his or her password.

Support for auditing a data base is an important part of a DBMS where data are particularly sensitive or where possibilities for fraud exist. An **audit log** is a file where data on all operations performed by users of the data base are chronologically recorded. A typical entry in the audit log would include the following information for each transaction: the terminal used, the "log in" code the user used, the date and time, the data base, record, and field affected, and the old and new value of the data item. With an audit trail, the changing status of the data base can be tracked. Events can be reconstructed and suspicious outcomes can be traced. The use of audit logs in the detection of fraud and embezzlement is one of the major responsibilities of EDP auditors.

The sharing of data means that many applications will depend on the same data. This means that data integrity becomes even more critical when DBMS are used. Problems can be created by hardware and software errors. For example, a disk crashes, or a programmer writes a program that contains bugs that introduce errors into the data base. DBMS systems have been designed to recover from these kinds of failures. The most straightforward strategy is to periodically make a backup copy of the data base and keep a log of all transactions that occur from that point until the next backup copy is made. If the computer system were to fail, the transactions would then be reapplied against the backup copy of the data base to restore it to the state prior to the error. This **rollforward** strategy reconstructs the data base up to the time of failure. The major disadvantage to this approach is that it will take a significant amount of computer time to roll forward all the transactions.

When this form of recovery is too costly, the DBMS can utilize a different approach. The data base can be reconstructed by undoing all the incomplete changes that were in process at the time of failure. This backing out of incompleted transactions from the data base is called **rollback.** Processing can then be resumed using current transactions.

The DBA is concerned with monitoring DBMS performance and with evaluating potential changes to the design of the data base to make it more responsive to users' needs. It is hoped that when the data base structure was designed and first implemented, the users got quick response. But a data base has to evolve to reflect the changing nature of demand generated by the organization. New data items are added, additional security measures are taken, and more users need to access the data base. These are occurrences that generally cause the DBMS to become overloaded and to slow down.

The DBA uses performance monitors that are a combination of hardware and software. These monitors generate statistics on the utilization of data base resources as well as the CPU, primary memory, I/O channels, and secondary storage units. From this, specific data bottlenecks can be identified. Solutions may range from modifying the scheduling of applications so that certain jobs are run during slow periods, increasing the I/O speeds, allocating more primary memory to the DBMS, and even getting a more powerful computer system.

THE DBMS IN ACTION

There are many data base management systems available commercially. They extend from the sophisticated DBMS used to accommodate hundreds of users of many large, complex data bases on supermini- and mainframe computers to relatively simple data base management systems designed for single users on microcomputers.

The sophisticated DBMS, such as Cullinet's Integrated Data Management System (IDMS), which they proclaim to be the most powerful in the world, is generally based on hierarchical or network data base structures. The small- to medium-sized DBMS that runs on mini- and microcomputers is mainly a relational data base system. The differences revolve around computer efficiencies and user friendliness, rather than capabilities for updating and retrieving data.

The trend is toward a relational data base structure, because it gives the most flexibility to the user. Many experts believe that the user interface of future data base management systems will be based on relational concepts, regardless of the physical structure. The DBMS can then take that data base structure and translate it into whatever physical form will provide the greatest computer efficiency. It is for these reasons, plus the fact that relational data base management systems are on microcomputers, and will be the first DBMS you will most likely come in contact with, that we will concentrate our discussion on this particular form.

Exhibit 8.16
Relational Data Base

Salesperson Table

Name	City
Barker, Bob	Phoenix
Brown, Sally	Denver
Jones, Tim	Los Angeles
Patterson, Nancy	Dallas
Petro, Ramo	Phoenix
Smith, Barry	Chicago
Zulu, Wai	Los Angeles

Regions Table

City	Region
Los Angeles	1
Phoenix	1
Dallas	2
Denver	2
Chicago	3

Annual Sales Table

Name	Year	Sales
Barker, Bob	1984	155,000
Brown, Sally	1984	93,000
Jones, Tim	1984	60,000
Patterson, Nancy	1984	105,000
Petro, Ramo	1984	108,000
Smith, Barry	1984	70,000
Zulu, Wai	1984	70,000
Barker, Bob	1985	192,000
Brown, Sally	1985	115,000
Jones, Tim	1985	60,000
Patterson, Nancy	1985	145,000
Petro, Ramo	1985	93,000
Smith, Barry	1985	60,000
Zulu, Wai	1985	90,000

Relational MicroDBMS

Typical of the microcomputer, data base management systems are dBaseII and R:Base 4000. DBaseII is produced by Ashton-Tate, and is the leading seller. R:Base 4000 is sold by Microrim Corporation and owes its roots to a mainframe version, which was developed for Boeing Computer Services, called Relational Information Management (RIM). DBaseII and R:Base 4000 are relational data base management systems. They provide a language to create data base structures, perform data manipulation, and ensure data integrity.

How is the DBMS used to manipulate data? Each DBMS has its own name for commands, so we will use a generic version to show how this generally works. Retrieval of data in a form meaningful to a user is often the primary reason for having a DBMS. This facility is known as a **query language.** Commands are based on relational algebra. This is not algebra in the usual sense of that word, but rather is a way of combining and extracting data in relational tables. The primary commands are SELECT, JOIN, and PROJECT.

Exhibit 8.16 shows three relational tables. The first table lists the home office for each salesperson, the second classifies home offices into regions, and the third shows the annual sales for each salesperson for the years 1984 and 1985. Each table of data is known as a *relation.* In each table, the columns represent data items, and each row is a record, also called an occurrence.

How would we use these tables to answer the question "Which salesperson sold more then $100,000 in 1984?" We would state:

SELECT Name, Sales FROM Annual Sales
WHERE Sales GREATER THAN 100,000
AND Year EQUALS 1984

The result would be

Name	Sales
Barker, Bob	155,000
Patterson, Nancy	105,000
Petro, Ramo	108,000

The first line in the query language says to select the data items (columns) titled Name and Sales from the table called Annual Sales. The second line gives the conditions each record (row) must meet to be selected.

The next query is "Who are the salespersons in each region?" This information is not available from any single table. Therefore, we will have to build the new relationship we need.

JOIN Salesperson WITH Regions USING City

FORMING Salesperson-Regions

SORTED BY Region, ASCENDING

Since we needed data items from the Salesperson and the Regions tables, we joined them together on the common data item, City, to form a new table called Salesperson-Regions. The result gave us the names of the salespeople and their home offices, sorted by region in ascending order. From Exhibit 8.17, we can readily see, for example, that Barry Smith is the only salesperson working in Region 3.

Suppose the corporate vice-president of marketing wanted to know the dollar sales amounts for salespersons in region 1 in 1985. As you look at the three original tables, along with the new table built, the answer is not readily apparent. The key data items needed are sales data for 1985, name, and region 1. Thus, though all the data items to answer the question are available, they do not exist together in a single table.

In order to answer the marketing vice-president's query, the Salesperson-Regions table must be joined with the Annual Sales table, using Name as the common element. But this new table would have more data items than are needed. The PROJECT command is a way to build a table that is a subset of

Exhibit 8.17
Result of the JOIN Command

Salesperson/Regions Table

Name	City	Region
Jones, Tim	Los Angeles	1
Zulu, Wai	Los Angeles	1
Barker, Bob	Phoenix	1
Petro, Ramo	Phoenix	1
Patterson, Nancy	Dallas	2
Brown, Sally	Denver	2
Smith, Barry	Chicago	3

Name	1985	Region
Barker,Bob	192,000	1
Petro,Ramo	93,000	1
Zulu,Wai	90,000	1
Jones,Tim	60,000	1

Exhibit 8.18
Result of the PROJECT Command

another table. It also removes any duplicate columns and rows. Exhibit 8.18 shows the result of these operations.

Why have three tables, and then build and manipulate new tables from these? Instead, why not have one big table that combines all the data items? The answer is really a part of advanced data base theory, called normalization. The major purpose is to improve flexibility and data integrity. The details of how this is done are beyond the scope of this text. The basic concept, however, is to break a data base down into its fundamental relations. These tables serve as the basic building blocks that can be easily combined to form new tables when necessary. This allows users greater flexibility in answering queries, particularly those that are not anticipated when the data base is designed. Each fundamental table contains only data items that are directly related to its function. This minimizes the data maintenance problem by reducing data redundancy.

Through these examples, you can begin to see what a DBMS is, and how it can be used to answer queries. You may not be able to appreciate the power and ease of using a DBMS at this point, but after you write your first BASIC or COBOL program you will! It could take a couple of pages of instructions to answer these same queries in COBOL.

Accessing the Data Base

Data base management systems are useful to both end-users and application programmers, and there are several different means to access the data base. End-users such as managers and staff analysts often need to extract data from a data base to answer queries. We have seen how commands such as SELECT, JOIN, and PROJECT can be used to manipulate the relationships to answer queries. The **COMMAND MODE** allows the user to direct operations on the data base. There are commands for defining a data base, querying a relationship, doing computation, modifying the relationships, and generating a report.

Work has been done to make the interface even more natural for the end-user. For example, R:Base 4000 has a **natural language interface** called *CLOUT*, that allows the user to pose a question more as he or she would in talking with an associate, rather than by using formal commands. Thus, the first query using CLOUT could be posed as follows: "Give me the names of all persons with sales of more than $100,000 one year ago." Without CLOUT, the query would take this form: SELECT Name, Sales from Annual Sales WHERE Sales greater than 100,000 AND Year equals 1984.

The CLOUT software package has been programmed to look for key words in a sentence. In our query, these would be "names," "sold," "100,000," and "one year ago." CLOUT keeps track of key words and their synonyms that have been defined to the system. These are used to determine the meaning of the query and to select appropriate relationships and data items. In our example, "names" could mean persons, people, salespersons, and last names. CLOUT builds a profile of common user terminology. If it cannot match a key word to a synonym, CLOUT is programmed to ask the user to give another word, or to select from several choices that are probable synonyms. This is a simple application of some very exciting advances that are being made in the field of artificial intelligence, which will be discussed in Chapter 17, "Issues and Concerns."

Application programmers often need to reference key pieces of data for use in production runs such as an inventory report or a manufacturing vendor listing. However, application programming languages such as COBOL and FORTRAN, which were developed before data base management systems became available, do not have commands within their instruction set to take advantage of data base processing.

Some DBMS vendors have defined special data base language commands that can be used with certain high-level languages. The DBMS is then said to support a **host language.** The key idea is that with the use of a host language, the programmer can request the data items needed without having to know the physical organization of the data. This allows program-data independence. Typical commands would include FETCH, which retrieves data, MODIFY, which changes data, and DELETE, which deletes a record.

However, because these commands are not part of the high-level language itself, they cannot be translated by standard compilers (see Chapter 14, "Programming Languages"). Precompilers are needed to transform the special data base commands to their equivalent COBOL or FORTRAN instructions. The resulting code can then be translated by the standard compilers.

Professional Issue

File Systems Versus Data Base Management Systems

Now that we have explored some of the characteristics of file and data base systems, let's see how they compare on several major criteria: data, cost, risk, and personnel.

One of the major strengths of a DBMS is that it provides much greater access to organizational data through the use of host and query languages. The data base allows a significant reduction in data redundancy and provides for standard definition of data items and for control of the modification of records. This results in greater data integrity. The DBMS also provides for the separation of logical and physical concerns, which leads to program/data independence (see Exhibit 8.19).

Exhibit 8.19
A Comparison of File Systems and Data Base Management Systems

	File Systems	Data Base Management Systems
Data		
Access	limited	extensive
Redundancy	much	significant reduction
Integrity	little	great
Program	dependent	independent
Cost		
Data Management Software	less expensive	very expensive
Computer Hardware	less powerful computer	more powerful computer
Risk		
Failures	low	medium
Security	low	medium
Conversion	low	high
Personnel		
Computer Experts	programmers	programmer, DBA, technical specialist
Users	departmental	user groups

In contrast, when using a file system, there is much data redundancy. Access to data in several files is awkward and time-consuming. Further, there is little assurance that the same data items on different files are defined similarily or have been updated. This results in a lack of data integrity. Programs and data are dependent, meaning that a change in either can cause changes to be required in the other.

Data base management systems have some significant disadvantages, however. The sophisticated DBMS software designed to run on the larger computers costs hundreds of thousands of dollars—substantially more than the cost for file systems software. Generally, organizations considering purchasing a DBMS of this sophistication will have to move to a more powerful computer model. This is necessary in order to accommodate the large amount of primary memory the DBMS itself will occupy, as well as to ensure a quick response time to users' requests to compensate for the greater amount of time required to process the DBMS.

The biggest drawback of a DBMS, however, is the conversion effort required to move from a file-based system to a data base system. First the data base must be designed, and that entails forming a committee of user groups that need to work together to establish the critical data items, their definitions, and access privileges. Specialists must be hired to function as the data base administrator, and technical experts must be brought in for the DBMS software itself. Programmers and end-users must be trained in how to use the new DBMS.

In contrast, file systems have been used in organizations for years, and most programmers know how to use them. No lengthy coordination effort among many diverse user groups across the company is necessary. Rather, programmers can continue to work with users to develop programs that will meet their departmental information needs.

The strengths of centralization of the data and the ease of retrieving it also lead to one of the main drawbacks of a DBMS. The all-eggs-in-one-basket approach increases a company's vulnerability to failures of the data base system itself. All application programs and user requests using the DBMS cannot function until the system is corrected. Further, the centralization of the data can bring a wealth of well-organized company data to an intruder, if he or she can somehow penetrate the security system. The great overlap and chaos of individual file systems acts as a form of protection in this sense.

In summary, the major trade-off in deciding to use a DBMS rather than a file system is whether the benefits of greater access to more accurate and timely corporate data are worth the extensively higher costs of a more powerful computer system, expensive data management software, more specialized personnel, the higher risk associated with conversion efforts, and the widerspread impact of temporary failures of the DBMS system. Overall experience has been for companies to work toward using a DBMS as the foundation of their corporate data needs. This trend will continue to strengthen as new advances are made in improving the ease of interacting with the DBMS and as data base recovery and security protection schemes are improved.

Our comparison was made in relationship to organizations that have a need to share an extensive amount of corporate data. In these situations, medium- to large-size data base management systems make sense. But another trend is for a microcomputer DBMS that costs from several hundred to two thousand dollars to be used where there is a need to share a limited amount of data. This could be done in a small company, or in a division or department of a large company.

Future advancements include the linking of the mainframe DBMS with personal computers. Needed data are extracted from the DBMS and sent over communication links to a personal computer. The manager uses the data as input to the DBMS for querying, or as input to a spreadsheet to run a budget forecasting model, for example. We will talk more about how these communication links are set up in Chapter 9, "Data Communications."

COMPUTERS AT WORK

The PC Moves into Real Estate

The IBM Personal Computer has entered the real estate market in a big way. Across the United States, IBM PCs and XTs, as well as the PC compatibles, are showing up in real estate offices as the agents and brokers take advantage of the capabilities of desktop computing.

Computers have become increasingly common in the business of buying and selling property. From the individual real estate office, the Board of Realtors, and the Multiple Listing Service, to the title companies (which handle the legal aspects of sales) and financial institutions, computers are processing thousands of bits and bytes of information for real estate transactions.

The Board of Realtors is linked to a system called Real Trieve. The system allows real estate offices to access more than 2000 listings in the Multiple Listing Service.

Michael Baran, office manager of Gene O'Hagan Associates, a medium-sized real estate office in Santa Barbara, says that clients sitting in the office are impressed by the PCs ability to instantly search for property that meets the given specifications. To conduct a search with Real Trieve's online system, the agent signs on to the online system. A password is then entered, followed by specific information about the client.

Say, for example, that the agent wants to search a particular district of Santa Barbara, which the online system has designated as area 15. The client is looking for a three-bedroom home in a $150,000 to $200,000 price range. Now that the specifications have been given, the agent enters PRS (for Prospect Search), which initiates the search. The result is 22 matches.

This method of searching for property saves both the consumer and the real estate agent time. Details about the properties are listed in the printout: the number of bedrooms and bathrooms, the size of the garage, the number of stories (single or two-story), and such extras as a swimming pool, a spa, a family room, recreational vehicle parking, and wheelchair access. Also, for the agent's convenience, the listing office is given.

Real estate agents and brokers in Santa Barbara, California, are discovering the advantages of desktop computing, IBM style, for tracking residential sales and managing properties, among other tasks.

The online system has many other capabilities, some of which are listed below.

Residential analysis—Aimed at the first-time home buyer, this feature calculates the financial savings when tax breaks and equity build-up are taken into account.

Amortization schedules—This features enables the agent to show what the monthly mortgage payment will be, and how much of that payment applies to interest and principal, respectively. Year-end totals are also given.

Caravan lists—A list of properties to be shown. At any time, the agent can print out a list of properties to be shown for the week.

Comparative market analysis—With this report, an agent can show which properties have sold, which are currently on the market, and which listings have expired. The report can be used as a tool to generate computerized statistics that compare prices of a number of properties in a particular area, and are used to determine which ones are priced competitively.

Says Baran, "Using the IBM PC to do comps (the comparable searches) means we don't have to go through the Multiple Listings Book. What used to take hours to accomplish can now literally be done in minutes on the PC through the online system."

Source: B. Alvernaz, "The PC Moves Into Real Estate," *PC Magazine,* November 1983, pp. 491–96.

SUMMARY

The way in which data are arranged is termed *data organization.* Characters are represented by a byte generally in the EBCDIC or ASCII code within the computer. A collection of related characters forms a *data item* or *field.* An occurrence of all data items is called a *record.* A *file* is a collection of similar types of records. A *primary key* is a data item that has a unique value that can be used to identify a single record. An integrated collection of files is called a *data base.* Different data organizations affect how efficient it is to *access* or locate specific data records and what types of questions can be easily answered.

There are two primary reasons for needing to access data within a file or a data base. One is to be able to *retrieve* selected data to be used in producing desired information. The other is *updating,* the process by which records are added, deleted, or modified within the file.

The primary role of *data management software* is to provide an easier way for the programmer to create and maintain files and retrieve data from them. There are two levels of data management software: file access methods (FAM) and data base management systems (DBMS).

File access methods are support software that enables a programmer to organize data into files and provides means for accessing data records to be used in processing application programs. However, they provide a limited way of sharing data that are contained in more than one file.

There are several types of FAM, and they differ primarily in the file organization they allow and the means they provide for accessing the data. The simpliest file organization is the *sequential file organization* in which the records are sequenced by the primary key and are accessed in sequence. Another approach to file organization is called *indexed file organization.* This file is organized in logical sequence by key, and it has an index that shows the correspondence between the key value and the disk location of the record. *Relative file organization* arranges records relative to a key. This key value is used to directly calculate the disk address of a record.

Another layer of data management software has been developed, called a *data base management system (DBMS).* It is built to share data and provide easier ways to update and retrieve it. These more expensive systems also provide means to access the data from either application programs or query languages that are easy for personnel who are not computer experts to use.

The primary means of storing data today is in files. These files are generally created and manipulated by a programmer writing an application program in a language such as COBOL, to be used in conjunction with the FAM and OS to produce the desired results. The means of providing file organization, access, and manipulation of data is called a *file system.*

The concept of a data base has emerged to provide a more effective way of sharing organizational data. In fact, it is a more uniform way of managing data as a critical organization resource. Conceptually, a *data base* is an integrated collection of data items that can be retrieved in any combination necessary to produce needed information. In contrast, a file system provides no integrated way of accessing, linking, or managing the data contained in a collection of files.

A major purpose of the DBMS is to divide the accessing of data into logical and physical concerns. The *logical* question is concerned with what particular data are needed to answer a variety of questions users might have. Exactly how the data should actually reside on the disk or be accessed is the *physical* question. A DBMS allows programs and data to be more independent. *Program data independence* means that changes in either programs or data can be made without significantly affecting the other; In contrast, the use of a file system makes for *program data dependence.*

The logical description of the organization of the complete data base is called a *schema.* Description of a particular subset of the total data base that is useful in answering a user's particular question is called a *subschema.* Each subschema is also called a *user's view.*

The three major models for data base organization are: hierarchical, network, and relational. In a *hierarchical data base structure,* the relationship among records is always one to many. Each *parent,* or higher-level record, can have one or more children, but each *child,* or lower-level record, can have only one parent. *Network data base structure* allows "many-to-many" relationships among parent and children records. Also, it allows a record to be a child in more than one relationship. The third data base model is the relational model, and is based on presenting data in the form of tables or relations. The *relational data base structure* shows relationships among records by linking tables together as needed.

The keeper of the data base is called the *data base administrator (DBA).* The DBA ensures the effectiveness of data retrieval, the accuracy and confidentiality of data, and also keeps the physical data base running efficiently. The creation and maintenance of the data base structure is fundamental to the management of the DBMS. The *data dictionary* is used to identify the data elements, records, and relationships that will exist in the data base. In addition, schemas, subschemas, and programs are identified.

There are many data base management systems available commercially. They extend from the sophisticated DBMS used to accommodate hundreds of users of many large, complex data bases on supermini- and mainframe computers to relatively simple data base management systems designed for single users on microcomputers.

REVIEW QUESTIONS

Data base management systems are useful to both end-users and application programmers. The *COMMAND MODE* allows the user to direct the operations on the data base. There are commands for defining a data base, querying a relationship, doing computation, modifying a relationship, and generating a report. *Natural language interfaces* are available that allow the user to query a DBMS more as he or she would in talking with an associate, rather than by using formal commands. Some DBMS vendors have defined special data base language commands that can be used with certain high-level languages to access the DBMS. The DBMS is then said to support a *host language*.

Greater access to corporate data by programmers and end-users, reduction of data redundancy, and program/data independence are the major advantages of the DBMS, when compared to file systems. However, the DBMS also has some significant disadvantages. For one, the sophisticated DBMS software designed to run on the larger computers costs hundreds of thousands of dollars.

Also, organizations considering acquiring a DBMS of this sophistication may have to move to a more powerful computer model. This is to accommodate the large amount of primary memory the DBMS itself will occupy, as well as to ensure a quick response time to users' requests to compensate for the greater amount of time required to process the DBMS. The biggest drawback, however, is the conversion effort required to move from a file-based system to a data base system.

In the next chapter we will discuss telecommunication concepts that enable computer systems to communicate over long distances.

1. Briefly identify the three basic types of data organization discussed in the text in the phone directory examples. What are the advantages of each?
2. What are the two primary reasons for accessing data within a file or a data base?
3. Distinguish between file access methods (FAM) and data base management systems (DBMS). What is the purpose of data management software?
4. Briefly describe the sequential file approach. What problems are associated with this method?
5. Explain how an index file system works. What disadvantages are associated with this method?
6. How is a relative file system organized? What advantages are offered by this approach?
7. What ways are available to share data using file systems?
8. Briefly define *data base*. What logical and physical questions must be answered?
9. What are the three major models used in the organization of a data base? How many of these models can the typical data base use?
10. The Intel Corporation desires to create a data base system that will provide the greatest possible flexibility. Which of the three data base models would you recommend? Defend your position.
11. What features should a DBMS have in order to aid the data base administrator?
12. Briefly discuss the advantages/disadvantages of a DBMS versus file systems.

Chapter 9
Data Communications

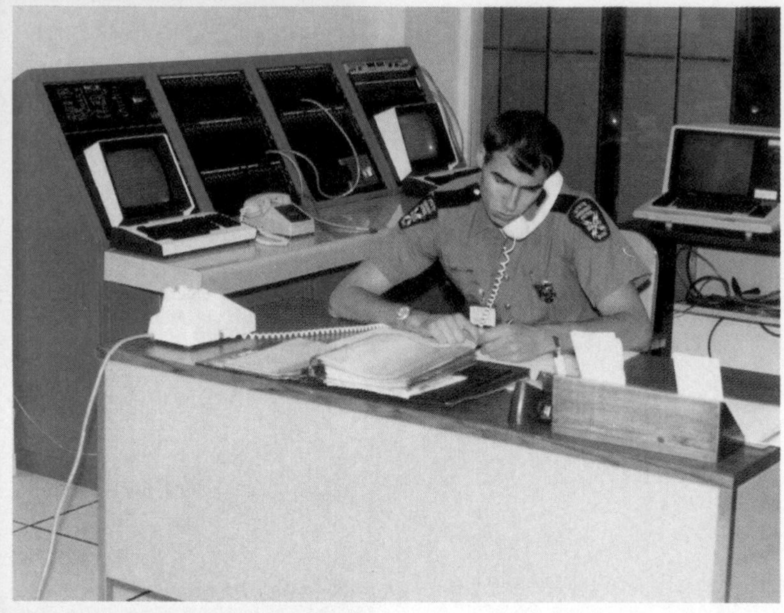

COMPUTERS AT WORK

Data Communication Aids Ohio Police in Doing Their Jobs

Ohio's acronym for its law enforcement system—LEADS (Law Enforcement Automated Data System)—is apt, since the state has been in the forefront of developing sophisticated systems for public safety. Nearly 1600 terminals at remote sites throughout Ohio are now linked via data communications lines to a large-scale Sperry-Univac 1100/83 computer system installed in the state office building in Columbus. The system supports a vast complex of communication lines—four high-speed data lines going to remote computers on the system in Cincinnati, Cleveland, Toledo, Cuyahoga County, and the Bureau of Motor Vehicles. Special communications circuits also connect the system with the FBI's National Crime Information Center (NCIC) in Washington, DC.

Stored in the Bureau of Motor Vehicles' portion of the data base is pertinent information on 7.4 million drivers' licenses and more than 8.5 million vehicle registrations in the state. The State Highway Patrol stores information in the data base on wants and warrants, stolen cars, stolen or lost license plates, and vehicles used in felonies. The success of the program is indicated by the statistics in reduction of auto theft.

Just as important is the system's ability to save the lives of troopers. By receiving information as to the status of a car before he actually stops the vehicle and confronts the driver, the trooper can be forewarned to take the necessary precautions to protect his life.

The computers are also used when applicants want to renew their licenses. Using the terminal, personnel can make a real-time check with the computer to ascertain that the person applying for license renewal is indeed qualified to drive and isn't under a suspension or revocation.

Previously, noted Donald Cort, data processing administrator of the Bureau of Motor Vehicles, the license would probably have been renewed, even though the person was ineligible, because of the time lag in getting information into the centralized system.

Under the old system, says Cort, information was entered into the computer under a batch program that could take a few days to process, and it might be 30–60 days before the information from the centralized system could effect a cancellation of the previously issued license.

Source: "DDP 'Nets' Violators in Ohio," *Data Management,* January 1981, pp. 24BB–24DD.

The ability to retrieve data from a centralized data base via remote terminals is a powerful tool for the Ohio State Highway Patrol. This tool is transforming both police work and administrative procedures, and similar dramatic effects can be seen in many businesses today. In this chapter we will discuss the hardware and communication software needed to send data between a computer and a terminal. The terminals may be directly attached to the computer, in the same building complex, or located across the country. In Chapter 16, "The Information Age Society," we will discuss the organizational applications of these concepts. In this chapter, you will learn to do the following:

1. Explain the differences in hardware and software needed to transmit data between the computer and both local and remote terminals.
2. List and describe the transmission media that are used in telecommunication and local area networks.
3. Explain why the telephone network is used as the primary way to communicate data between remote sites.
4. Describe what a local area network is, and the major functions it serves.
5. Specify the additional features an operating system must have in order to function as communication support software.

DATA COMMUNICATIONS FUNDAMENTALS

The movement of data from one location to another is called **data communication.** The types of communication hardware and support software that are necessary to move that data depend primarily on the distance involved. To move data within the computer itself, or to and from peripherals within a hundred feet radius, the only hardware needed are comparatively simple cables, and the only software needed are the standard operating systems.

If the peripherals are several miles away, or across the country, a telecommunications network such as the phone system of AT&T must be used to move data. **Telecommunications** refers to the transmission of data over long distances. This task requires extensive communication hardware and communication software. But data communication doesn't always occur over long distances. Recently, many organizations have realized the advantages of communicating data between microcomputers and shared peripherals within an office building. Such computer systems, called **local area networks,** require a moderate amount of communication hardware and software. In developing an understanding of what sending and receiving data involves, we will begin by discussing the fundamentals of data communication. Next, we will cover telecommunication and local area networks. With that background, we will then discuss the role of communication support software.

External Data Paths

Exhibit 9.1 on page 232 shows a typical microcomputer system, which includes input and output devices such as CRTs, disks, and printers that are used to send or receive data. **Terminal** is often used as a generic term for various input and output devices. The hardware linking the terminals and a computer are called **transmission media.**

Exhibit 9.1
Typical Microcomputer Setup
Special cables are used as transmission media to send and receive data between the computer and its input and output devices.

For microcomputers, the transmission media are generally cables. There is a printer cable linking the CPU and the printer, as there is a disk and a CRT cable. Let's look a little more closely at these cables. The CPU uses digital signals to communicate 1s and 0s. Typically, high voltage represents a 1, and low voltage represents a 0.

Data bits can be sent down the cable in a **serial** fashion, which means that one bit is sent after the other. Or, data can be transmitted in a **parallel** fashion, in which the eight bits that represent a character are sent simultaneously on eight parallel data paths. For distances less than 100 feet, parallel data transfer can be economically accomplished. One way of doing this is with flat-ribbon cables. The outlet where the cable is plugged into the computer is called an **input/output port.** The number of devices that can be connected to a computer is a function of the number of I/O ports (see Exhibit 9.2).

Serial and parallel connections require different types of I/O ports. The two de facto standards for microcomputers are called RS232–C and Centronics. For serial data transfer, the de facto standard is the RS232–C (Recommended Standard number 232 version C). It was developed by the Electronics Industries Association. The parallel standard is based on the connection used on the commercially successful Centronics printer, which popularized this approach to data transfer. Because different computers use different internal electronic

Exhibit 9.2
Serial and Parallel Data Transfer

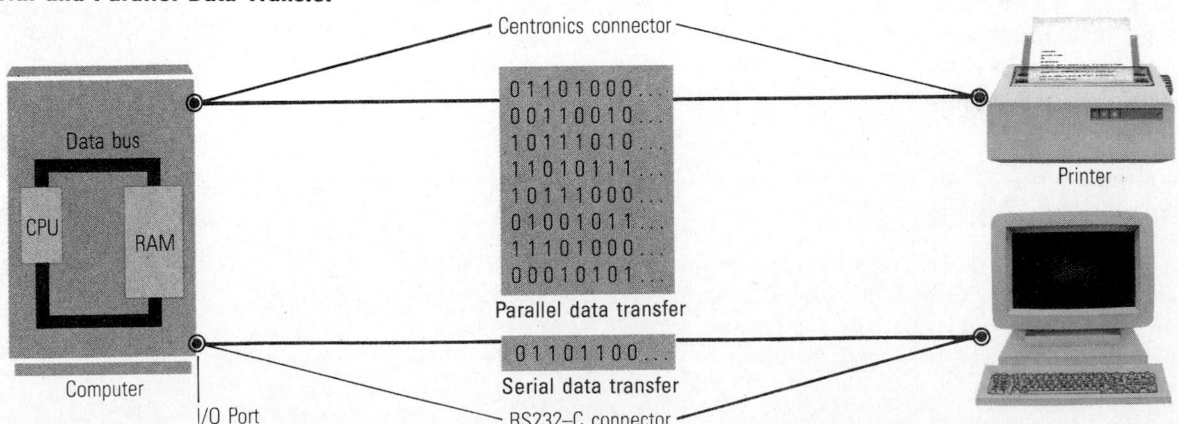

designs, but we wish to use the same I/O devices with these different computers, additional devices are needed to convert internal signals to communication signals. These devices, called interface units, are the topic of the next section.

Interface Units

The variety of input devices that exist is almost equaled by the variety of output and secondary storage devices in use. Some devices use serial data transfer, some use parallel data transfer. Some devices transfer data very quickly, some have slower data transfer rates. Sometimes these devices will not even use the same coding scheme (ASCII or EBCDIC). How can a computer communicate effectively with all these "nonstandard" devices now, and be prepared to deal in the future with an even greater variety of new technologies?

In some ways, this problem is like the problem of coordinating communication at the United Nations, where delegates speak a variety of languages. One solution would be to adopt a common language such as English or Russian or the neutral international language, Esperanto. This hasn't happened, however. Instead, the delegates depend on translators to smooth communication.

Since a standard data communication language has not evolved, the computer industry uses a similar translator approach. The translating device is called an **interface unit.** An interface unit is needed for each peripheral device, such as a disk, a CRT, or a printer. Each time a new device is added to the computer system, there must be an accompanying interface unit.

Exhibit 9.3 shows a typical interface board for attaching a printer to a microcomputer. These boards are also called *adapter boards.* One problem with this approach is that the number of devices that can be attached to a microcomputer is limited by the number of expansion slots provided for these boards. An **expansion slot** is made up of brackets to hold the board within the CPU housing and an opening for connecting the peripheral device. A second problem is that many of the interface units perform similar tasks. This results in

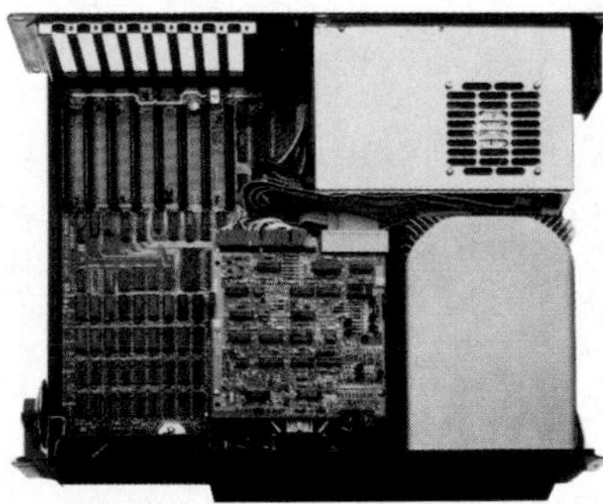

Exhibit 9.3
Interface, or adapter, boards are used to attach peripheral devices to microcomputers. Adapter boards fit into expansion slots in the CPU housing. The number of peripheral devices that can be attached to a particular microcomputer is limited by the number of expansion slots provided. The microcomputer shown has eight expansion slots.

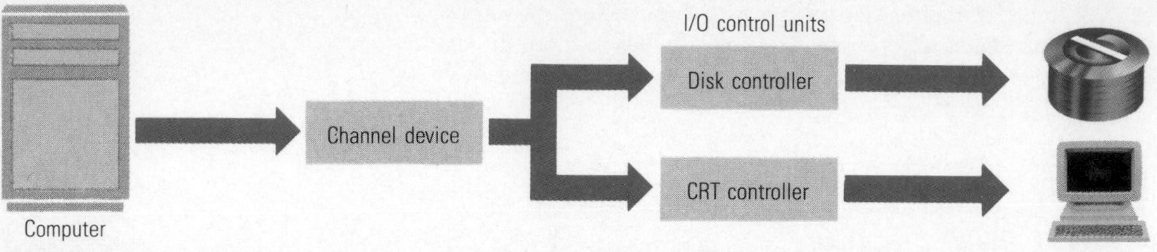

Exhibit 9.4
Input/Output Interface Units
With large computers, the interface function between the peripherals and the computer is often performed by a channel device and I/O control units. Common I/O tasks are performed by the channel device and device-specific tasks by disk and CRT controllers.

needless duplication of capabilities, and wastes limited expansion slots. To avoid this problem, some companies offer interface boards that combine several functions.

With some larger computer systems, the interface function is divided into common I/O tasks and device-specific tasks. Device-specific tasks are performed by an **I/O control unit** such as a disk controller. It is responsible for responding to a "READ data record" command by moving the read/write head over a specific track location on the disk, locating the record, and then reading the data. Thus, the disk controller has to be designed for the characteristics of the specific disk peripheral, and these characteristics vary greatly from vendor to vendor. I/O controllers for printers and monitors have similar requirements.

The common tasks are performed by a **channel device.** The channel device carries out the two major functions of counting and addressing. In counting, the channel device keeps track of how many bytes of data have been transferred. For example, when the operating system orders 256 bytes of data to be transferred from disk to RAM memory, the channel unit determines when that task has been completed. The goal of addressing is to be sure the data are loaded into the memory locations specified by the operating system.

These functions of counting and addressing can be performed by the CPU, and they generally are, for microcomputers. In larger, more expensive computer systems, efficiency is increased by "off loading" these tasks to a channel device. With large, maxicomputer systems, the channel device is often a specialized minicomputer. This frees the main CPU to continue with more important processing tasks, while data are being transferred by a channel and I/O controller. Exhibit 9.4 shows how I/O control units and channel devices are used in large computer systems.

TELECOMMUNICATION FUNDAMENTALS

So far, we have discussed data communication for stand-alone computer systems with local peripherals. How can data be transmitted to and from remote terminals located in different buildings or other regions of the country? Telecommunication, the transmission of data over long distances, is needed for these tasks. Conceptually, telecommunication uses the same principles as local data communication. The cables used for local communication, however, would not be effective for long distances.

There are two basic limitations to cables. First, there is a limit to the distance that data can be transferred over a cable, due to loss of signal strength. The electrons moving down the cable meet resistance, similar to what we recognize as friction, which causes the signal to diminish. In addition, there is background noise in the cable and its surrounding environment. The signal strength has to be loud enough to be differentiated from the noise. Just as in talking to someone in a noisy restaurant, you have to talk more loudly to be heard above the din, for distances greater than several hundred feet, *repeaters* are needed to amplify the electronic signal to overcome electrical resistance and background noise. A second problem would be to find a place to physically put all those cables. As more terminals were added, computer owners would have to string new cables themselves.

One way to avoid this tangle is to use what has been the primary means of remote voice communication—the telephone system. It is, after all, in place and working very well in North America. Since almost every work place and home has a telephone, electrically connecting one location to another is as simple as dialing the appropriate phone number and hooking the appropriate type of interface unit between the telephone and the computer. However, there is one major problem with using this system. The telephone network, which was invented and first built in the early 1900s, was designed for voice communication, not data communication. It is, in fact, slow and inefficient for transmitting data. To overcome these disadvantages, telecommunication now uses microwave communication channels, either land-based or satellite. We will explore some of the technical considerations for high-speed data telecommunication in the remainder of this chapter.

Carrier Signals

The human voice is made up of complex sound patterns that are combinations of sound waves. Like the music on your stereo, these patterns are composed of bass (low frequency) and treble (high frequency) sound waves. In addition to different frequencies, sound waves have varying amplitudes, or heights, that we hear as loud and soft sounds. These types of continuous sound waves are called **analog signals.** In contrast, the computer is limited to processing a discrete pattern of 1s and 0s, called **digital signals.** Digital signals are generated by on/off or high/low electrical signals. Exhibit 9.5 shows the difference between analog and digital signals.

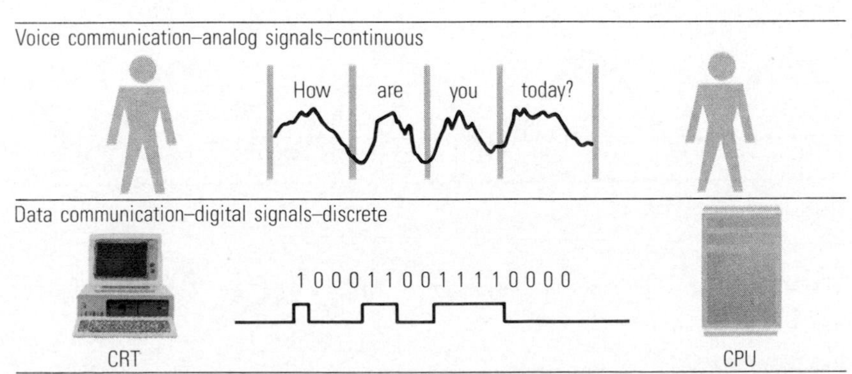

Exhibit 9.5
Voice and Data Communication Differences

People use their voices to communicate. The sounds they make are continuous analog wave patterns. In contrast, computers communicate data by the use of discrete digital signals.

The basic challenge, then, is to use the existing telephone network, which was designed to transmit analog signals, to transmit digital data. The solution is a hardware device that converts digital signals to analog signals. This device, called a **modem,** places a digital stream of data on top of an analog carrier signal.

A **carrier signal** is the basic analog signal used to transmit data over telecommunication lines. In a *modulating* process, this basic signal is modified by slight changes to either its amplitude or frequency to represent data. At the other end of the telephone line, a *demodulating* process occurs, in which another modem is used to separate the digital data (1s and 0s) from the carrier signal. Thus, the term *modem* refers to a device that can *MOD*ulate and *DEM*odulate signals.

This same process occurs when you tune your radio into a local radio station (see Exhibit 9.6). Each radio station is assigned a specific frequency, which refers to the frequency of its carrier signal. Assume your favorite station is at 690 on the AM dial. Six ninety means that the carrier signal has a frequency of 690,000 cycles per second. The radio station transmitter "piggybacks" the complex sound patterns representing music or talk on top of the carrier signal and sends them out over the airwaves. Since hundreds of radio stations are broadcasting at different frequencies, there is a mass of music in the air. When you tune your radio to 690 AM, only the carrier signal of 690,000 cycles is picked up. The tuner strips away the carrier signal and sends the music to your car radio speakers. As shown in Exhibit 9.7, modems work in the same way. Bits of data replace the radio music, and the carrier signals are limited to certain frequencies.

Exhibit 9.6
Modulating-Demodulating Music on a Radio Station

Music is "piggybacked" onto a carrier signal of a radio station. This modulated signal is sent out over the airwaves. By tuning your radio into the frequency of the carrier signal, 690,000 cps, the signal is demodulated and the music is received.

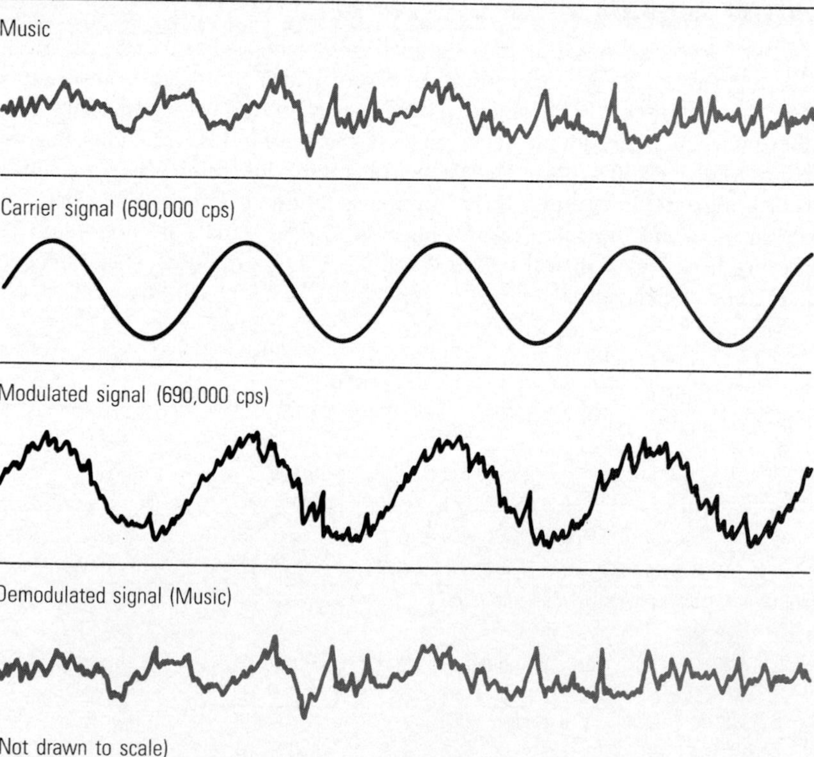

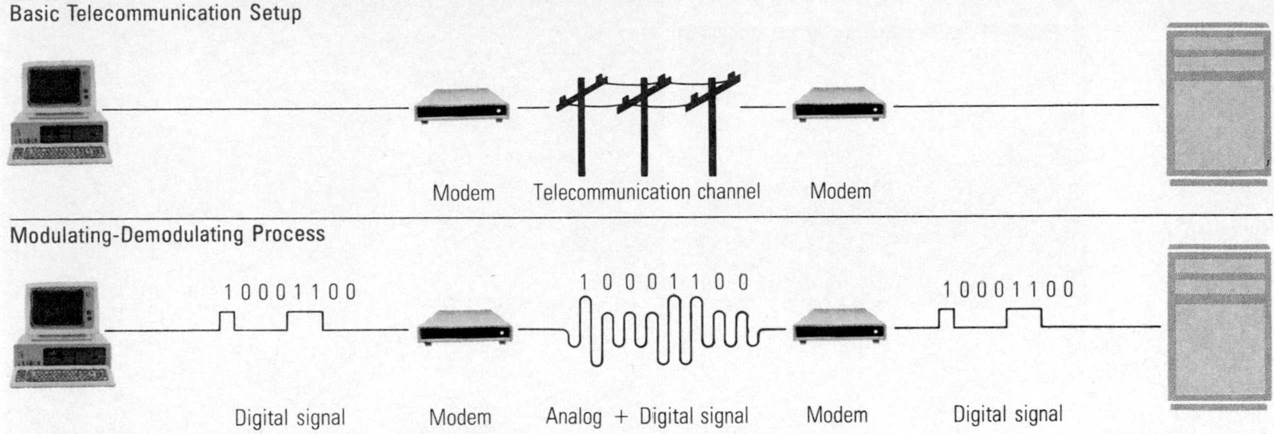

Exhibit 9.7
Data Communication Over a Telecommunication Channel
The discrete digital signal from the terminal is placed onto an analog carrier wave by the modem. At the other end of the telecommunication channel a modem demodulates the carrier signal and sends the digital information to the computer.

The frequency of the carrier signal partially determines the speed or **data rate** of a telecommunication link. This speed is usually measured in bits per second (bps). For example, a rate of 300 bps means that 300 data bits could be transmitted each second. Frequencies are stated in cycles per second (cps) or Hertz (Hz), in honor of one of the pioneers of electromagnetic theory.

To understand the relationship between carrier frequency and data rate, look again at Exhibit 9.7. The amplitude of the carrier wave is increased to signal a 1 and left unchanged to signal a 0. If the amplitude is increased or not increased just once each cycle, then the speed of transmitting data would be directly related to the frequency of the carrier signal. For a carrier wave with a frequency of 3000 cps, each cycle's change/no change in amplitude would signal a 1 or a 0, meaning that 3000 bits could be transmitted each second. When the amplitude can change once per cycle, then bps is equal to the **baud rate,** a term derived from the name of Émile Baudot, a pioneer in data communications. Thus, 300 baud are often referred to as 300 bps. The speed of modems is frequently described as 1200 baud or 9600 baud. To get much higher rates, engineers have devised ways to transmit several bits per cycle. In these cases, the usage of bps and baud interchangeably is incorrect.

There are two basic types of modems. One type is connected to the computer via a cable and to the telephone line via a standard phone jack. The other type of modem is the acoustic coupler, which is also attached to the computer by a cable. The body of the acoustic coupler contains molded rubber cups in which a telephone headset is cradled. The acoustic coupler converts bits of data into high and low pitch sounds that are "spoken" into the telephone mouthpiece. Thus, it provides an acoustic connection between the terminal and the telephone line. The advantage of the acoustic coupler is its portability. Its disadvantage is the amount of noise transmitted, which results in higher error rates. Exhibit 9.8 on page 238 shows each type of modem.

Exhibit 9.8

One type of modem connects to the computer via a cable and to the telephone line via a standard phone jack (left photos). The second type of modem, the acoustic coupler, cradles a telephone headset in molded rubber cups and connects to the computer via a cable (right).

Data Packets

To send data in a telecommunication network, start and stop information, origin and destination information, and error check bits must be added to the encoded data to form a **data packet.** These added data bits are used to aid in sending and receiving data, checking for errors, and for routing messages through a network of computers. The contents of a data packet are affected by the way data are transmitted. Data can be transmitted in either the asynchronous or synchronous mode. Exhibit 9.9 shows the differences between these two modes.

In the **asynchronous mode,** sometimes abbreviated as async, one character would be transmitted at a time. The data packet would contain a start bit to let the receiving unit know that a character is to follow. Then the packet would contain the bits representing the encoded character. The most popular code used in telecommunication is the seven-bit ASCII. Support software used for telecommunication would have translated the eight-bit code of ASCII–8 or EBCDIC into the seven-bit code of ASCII. Next would come an error check bit and a stop bit. The error check bit is used to make sure the data received were not garbled during transmission. The stop bit is used to signal the receiving unit that the complete character has been sent. This simple mode of transmission does not use origin and destination bits, thus it is used only for single-point-to-single-point transmission.

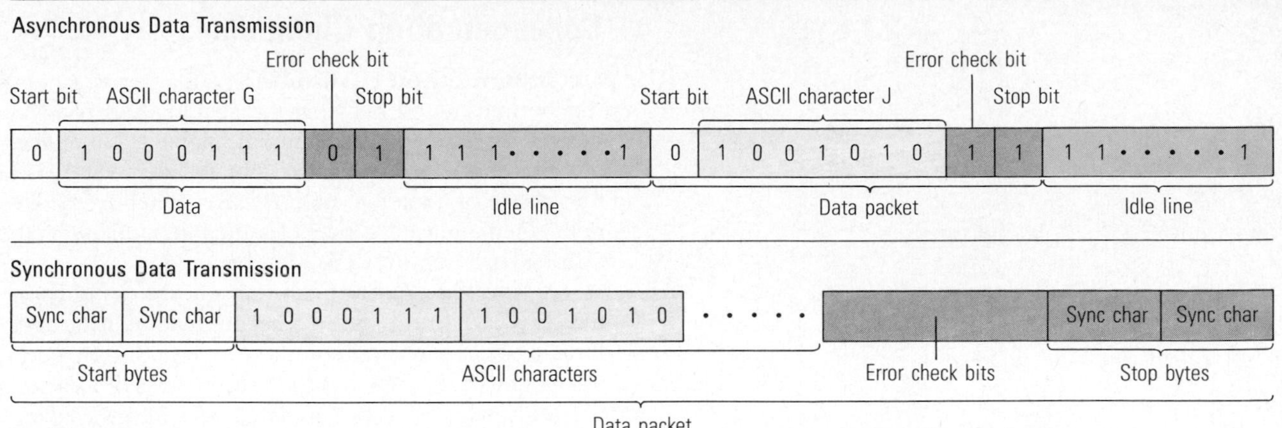

Exhibit 9.9
Asynchronous and Synchronous Data Transmission
In asynchronous data transmission, individual characters are sent. In synchronous data transmission, blocks of characters are sent. Data packets shown include start, stop, and error check information.

In asynchronous transmission, the commonly used error check method is a parity bit. A **parity bit** is an extra bit that makes the sum of bits representing a character either even or odd. In an even parity system, the sum of bits should be even. For example, in ASCII, the letter *G* is encoded as 1000111. Since the number of 1s is already an even number (4), the eighth bit is a 0 to give 10001110. Although the parity bit scheme cannot catch all errors, such as some double errors, its ability to catch most transmission errors has made it a standard feature.

The net result of adding start, stop, and error check bits is that each data packet would contain ten bits to transmit a single character via asynchronous transmission. Thus, a 1200 baud (bps) modem would be able to send about 120 characters each second. Asynchronous transmission is especially appropriate for low-speed data communication, such as a person working at a CRT. When compared to a computer, most people are relatively slow to enter data and respond.

The **synchronous** or **sync mode** of data transmission is used when large volumes of data are to be sent and speeds of thousands of characters per second are needed. In the synchronous mode, a block of hundreds of characters is sent in a data packet rather than on a character-by-character basis as with async. Each block is preceded by a sync byte or bytes to signal the start of the message, and is followed by an error check code and an ending sync byte or bytes. In synchronous transmission, the most common error check code is called **Cyclic Redundancy Coding (CRC).** This complex algorithm calculates a value by placing a different weight on each bit. Through this method, almost all transmission errors can be detected.

The synchronous mode might be used when the contents of a file are to be sent from a central computing facility to a remote site for printing. The obvious advantage of this mode is its speed and the reduced transmission costs for a given amount of data. Its disadvantages are the complexity and expense of the timing devices needed to synchronize transmission.

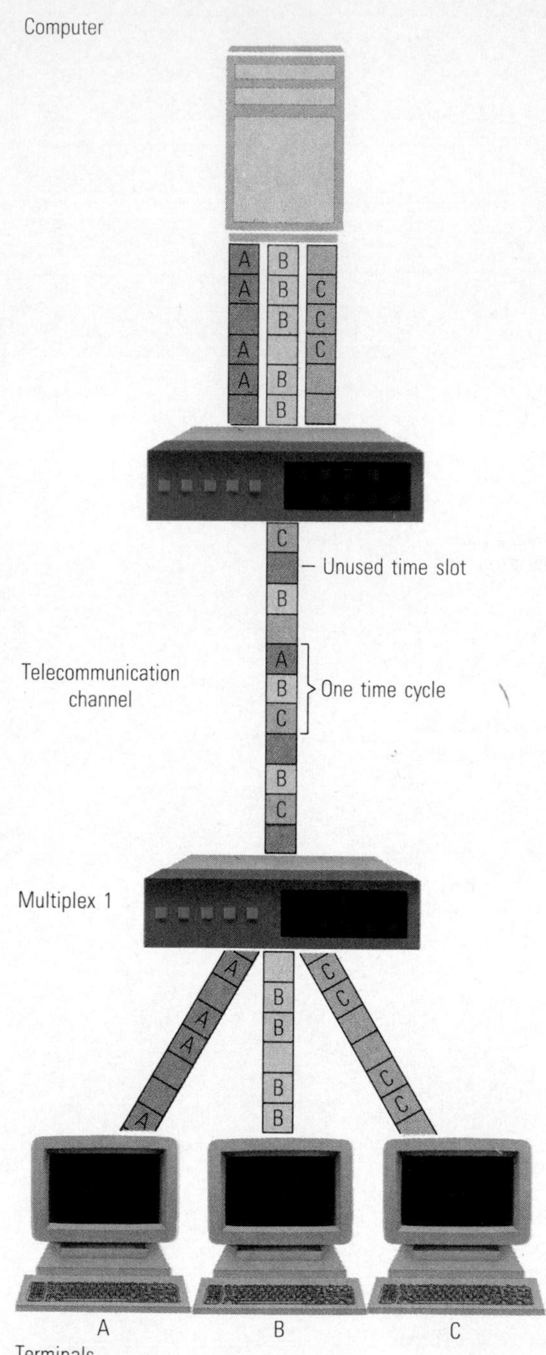

Exhibit 9.10
Time-Division Multiplexing
Multiplexers are used to send data from multiple terminals over one high-speed telecommunication channel to a computer. The sequence is reversed when the computer transmits to the terminals.

Communication Channels

A **communication channel** is a path along which data can be transmitted between the sending and receiving devices. Typically, in telecommunication the communication channel is a telephone line, but it could also be a land microwave or a satellite link. These channels, regardless of the medium used, can be classified as operating in the simplex, half-duplex, or full-duplex mode.

A **simplex channel** can transmit data in only one direction. While this is the cheapest mode, it has very limited use in telecommunication applications. However, it is now starting to be used in certain types of local area networks, which will be discussed later in this chapter.

A **half-duplex channel** can transmit data in either direction, but only one way at a time. This is the most common mode, and is used for data communication between the user at the terminal and the CPU. The user types in data, which are transmitted over the communication channel to the CPU. The CPU processes the data and then uses the same channel to respond to the user at the terminal.

A **full-duplex channel** allows data to be transmitted in both directions simultaneously. This is analogous to trucks carrying goods in both directions on a two-lane highway. For high-speed communication between computers and peripherals or computers and computers, this more costly communication method is warranted.

Multiplexers are used to make more efficient use of channels. A **multiplexer** is a piece of hardware that allows several communication signals to share the same channel. Multiplexing avoids two major sources of inefficiency. First, most interactive data communication is intermittent, meaning that a person enters data, then waits for a response. During these waits, the communication channel is not being used. Second, without multiplexing, adding another terminal would require a new channel. This expense could grow quickly if a company wants to accommodate many users on a time-shared computer.

There are two methods for sharing a communication channel: time and frequency division multiplexing. Exhibit 9.10 shows a picture of a multiplex system that is based on time divisions. The first multiplexer is used to take the slow-speed data from each terminal and distribute it onto a faster telecommunication channel. At the other end, a multiplexer separates the data and sends them to the correct computer I/O port. Another form of multiplexing, called frequency division, is based on sending data on different carrier frequencies within the communication channel.

The amount of information (total bits per second) a communication channel can transmit in a time period is a measure of its carrying capacity. In a way, this is analogous to water flowing in pipes. The amount of water a pipe can carry is measured in gallons per minute. Generally, pipes with greater diameter can carry more water faster.

With telecommunication media, the carrying capacity is a function of their bandwidth. Physical size of the medium, such as copper wire or optical fibers, is less important than its natural characteristics in determining the bandwidth. **Bandwidth** is the range of frequencies that can be used with a particular communication channel. The greater frequency range allows more subdivisions through multiplexing to carry multiple signals.

The bandwidth varies widely among the various media, and this affects the telecommunication applications that can be used with each medium. For example, the lines typically used in the telephone network are classified as **voice-grade lines.** They use a bandwidth of 2400 cycles per second to support one voice conversation. In contrast, a microwave link has a bandwidth of 2 GHz. A GHz, short for GigaHertz, is a billion cycles per second. Thus, the microwave link, through multiplexing, can transmit over 100,000 simultaneous voice conversations, or it can be used to transmit a hundred different color television programs.

TELECOMMUNICATION NETWORKS

There are several different ways to form a telecommunication network that connects a terminal located in city A to the computer system across the country in city B. Until recently, AT&T owned the most prevalent telecommunication channels in the United States, the telephone network. This network is the backbone of telecommunication today. The forced breakup of AT&T in 1984 is, however, expected to encourage significant alternatives to the telephone voice network. Before we discuss these implications, let's take a look at the reasons the telephone network has, is, and will continue to play such an important part in distant communication of data.

Telephone Network

Today there are close to half a billion telephones in the world. Each telephone can, in theory, be connected to any other phone through a series of mechanical and electronic relays. These relays switch the call from one electronic path to another, something like the switches that move railroad trains from track to track. To transmit data to a computer across the country, you could use this same telephone network. Assume that you are using an acoustic coupler in California. If you dial the number of the computer in New York City, the computer would "answer" the phone and send back a signal tone indicating it is ready to receive data. When you heard that tone, you would put the phone receiver into the cradle of an acoustic coupler and start keying the appropriate data. In essence, you would be having a data conversation with the computer over the telephone network in much the same way you would have a voice conversation. The only difference is that a set of modems is needed to make the digital/analog conversions.

We have already discussed some of the many drawbacks to using the public voice telephone network for data communication. First, the telephone network was designed for voice—not data—communication. This means that additional interface equipment, such as modems, is needed. It also means that the error rate is relatively high, and can increase as the data go through each switching office. Thus, it is critical to have a reliable way of checking important data for errors. Second, long-distance telephone charges are determined by the distance between two points and the time of day. Lastly, the maximum practical data rate is 4800 bps. This rate is not acceptable for corporate telecommunication needs.

For important data communication, such as sending nightly reports from supermarket point-of-sale terminals to central headquarters, a business can lease a **private line** from the telephone company. Such lines are reserved for the purpose of providing a permanent connection between point A and point B. Further, the lines have been conditioned to reduce noise and ensure a much lower error rate for data communication. Their data rate of 9600 bps is also faster than that of the public voice network. Of course, these lines cost more to use, meaning that only those companies with significant data traffic can justify the expense.

Transmission Media

The telephone switch network contains several different types of transmission media. Each telephone line that connects a home or business to the local switching office consists of pairs of copper wire. The regional and long-distance trunk lines were initially copper wires also. But the growing demand for more phones has required advanced technology, including media with greater bandwidths.

One alternative has been the use of high-frequency radio signals called **microwaves.** These microwave links provide high-capacity transmission of data or voice. They are used quite extensively in remote areas of the country,

Exhibit 9.11
Microwave Links

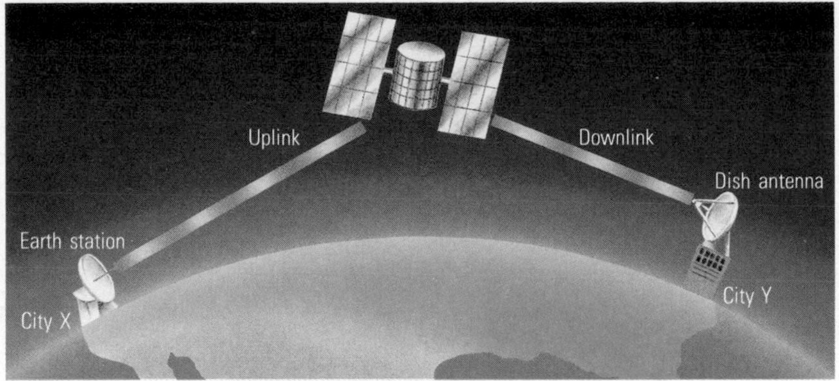

Exhibit 9.12
Satellite Telecommunication

and are now a cost-effective alternative to laying or stringing new line. The major disadvantage is that microwave is limited to line-of-sight transmission. No buildings or mountains can be between the microwave towers. A further problem is that the curvature of the earth limits the distance between stations to less than thirty miles. In addition to long-distance transmission, microwaves can be used by companies to transmit data between buildings in a downtown area. These leased, private microwave signals can carry data at speeds from 9600 to 56,000 bps. (see Exhibit 9.11).

Satellites placed in orbit by the space shuttle are also being used for data and voice communication. The most appropriate orbit for this type of communication satellite is called **geosynchronization.** In this type of orbit, the satellite is synchronized with the earth's rotation. Thus, the satellite appears to be stationary to an observer on earth. This means that fixed-dish antennas can be used in the earth stations that receive signals from the satellite. Such earth stations are cheaper than the more complex radar that must rotate to find and track satellites that are not "fixed" in a geosynchronized orbit.

A **communication satellite** is an electronic device that receives, amplifies, and transmits signals from space to earth. These satellites contain one or more transceivers, which are combined transmitters and receivers. On the *uplink,* data are sent from the earth station in City X to the satellite on a certain frequency. At the satellite, a transceiver is tuned to this frequency to receive the data. The transceiver then amplifies the signal and, on the *downlink,* transmits the data on another frequency to the antenna in City Y (see Exhibit 9.12).

Communication satellites are different from traditional point-to-point telecommunication links such as telephone lines and microwave in several significant ways. The major difference is that the cost of satellite transmission is independent of distance. That is, it costs the same to transmit data from Los Angeles to Tokyo as it does from Los Angeles to San Francisco. Second, satellite channels have very high capacities equivalent to 100,000 voice grade telephone lines, and they can transmit data at 50 million bps (Mbps). While it is initially very expensive to launch a satellite, its high data capacity and expected functional life of ten years makes the average cost for each circuit quite inexpensive.

Several of the disadvantages of using satellites include the initial high cost and sophistication required to build, launch, and maintain a communication satellite. Also, more complex circuitry is needed to handle propagation delay, the time the signal takes to complete the earth-to-satellite-to-earth circuit. These signals travel at the speed of light, 186,300 miles per second. If, however, the satellite is 23,000 miles away, the combined 46,000-mile round trip takes about one-fourth of a second. This is a substantial delay for computers functioning in millionths of seconds. Thus, compensating circuitry is needed to keep things synchronized.

One of the newest types of cable uses **fiber optics.** These are bundled strands of hair-thin fibers, each only two-thousandths of an inch thick (see Exhibit 9.13). Laser technology can be used to send an intense beam of highly focused light down these strands. The beam of light can be turned on and off at a rate of nearly one billion times per second. Thus, nearly 1 billion bits per second can be sent down a single optical fiber! The entire *Encyclopedia Britannica* could be transmitted in several seconds. Pacific Bell states that a bundle of fibers within a half-inch cable could handle 230,000 simultaneous voice conversations.

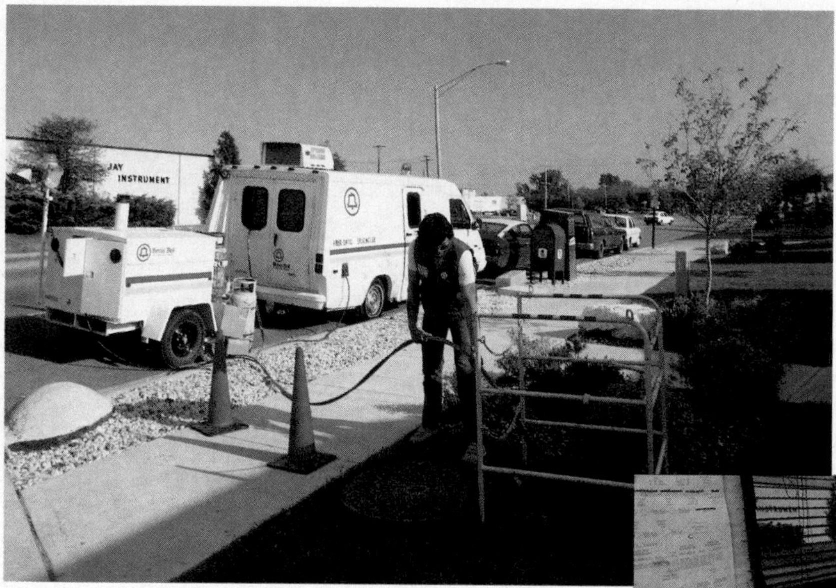

Exhibit 9.13

A telephone company technician pulls high-capacity, fiber-optic underground cable up into the splicing lab housed in the service truck. In splicing, each individual optical-fiber strand is placed in a slot as it is spliced to adjoining cable.

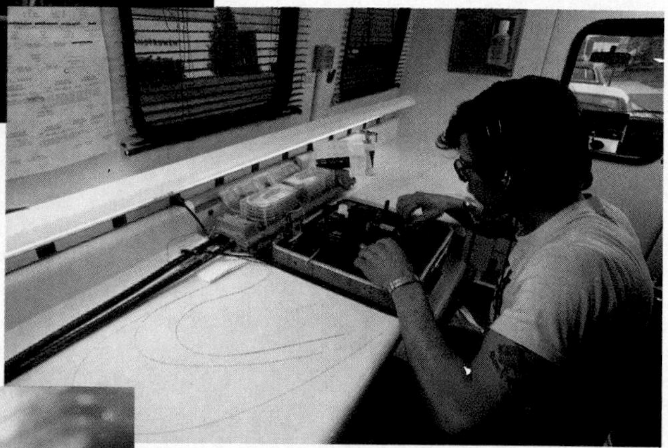

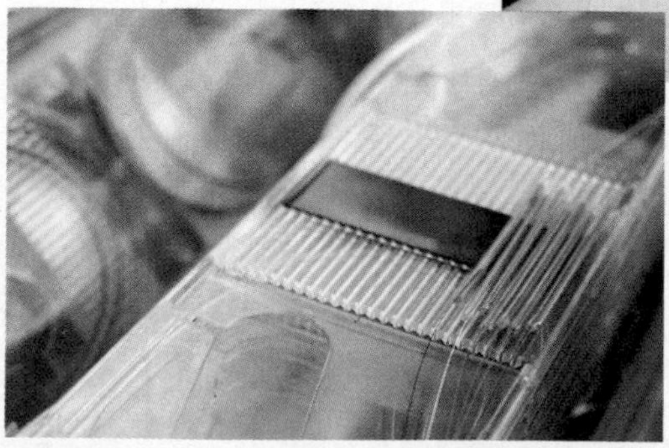

In addition to their significant carrying capacity, optical fibers are lightweight and have minimal electrical interference. Since fiber optics use photons, the basic unit of light, as opposed to electrons, they are not affected by electromagnetic forces which cause noise in electrical transmission. This allows greater distances between repeater stations. Optical fibers also used digital coding, which we'll discuss later in the chapter.

Most experts believe that fiber optics will revolutionize telecommunication where point-to-point cables are necessary. Pacific Bell first made extensive use of a fiber optic network to handle the complex communication needs of the 1984 Olympic Games held in Los Angeles. Several billion dollars are now being spent by AT&T and other organizations to build new long distance telephone networks using fiber optics that will become the backbone of the United States communication systems in the 1990s.

Telephone Voice Network Alternatives

The emergence of new technologies and the Federal Communication Commission's push for more competition in the telecommunication arena has led to a variety of alternatives to the telephone voice network. The use of satellites for commercial telecommunication began in the early 1960s with the development of COMSAT (Communication Satellite Corporation). In the 1970s, Western Union launched the Westar satellites and the Satellite Business Systems, a partnership of IBM, COMSAT, and Aetna, started operating a satellite communication network. At about the same time, the FCC allowed organizations other than the common carriers such as AT&T and GTE to offer land-based communication services. MCI and Sprint are two of the more successful companies offering long distance data and voice transmission services.

These developments, together with the 1984 breakup of AT&T, are sure to encourage many new options for meeting organizational and personal telecommunication needs. More and more telecommunication networks will be designed to meet the data communication requirements of high speed, digital, and low error-rate transmission.

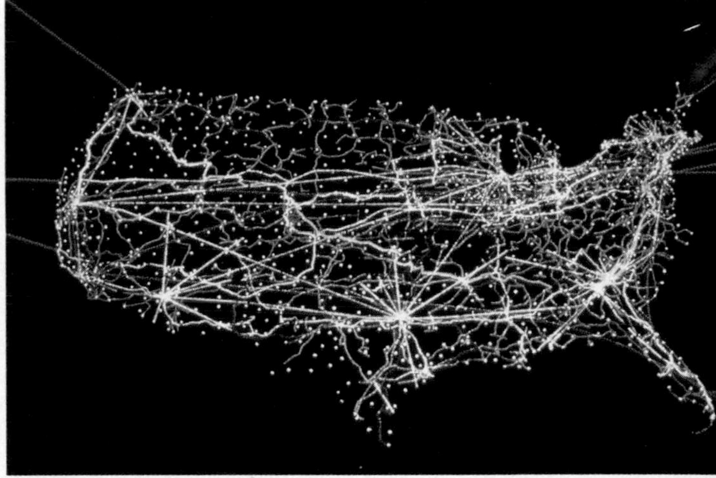

Exhibit 9.14
Telephone Network
To accommodate the increased emphasis of computer data communications, special digital networks have been created by AT&T.

It is likely that these new telecommunication networks will completely bypass the public voice telephone network. During the last fifteen to twenty years, the cost of computing has dropped dramatically, while the cost of using the telephone network has remained basically unchanged. This doesn't mean that AT&T will not continue to play a major role in future telecommunication. AT&T and the telephone operating companies have installed an all-digital network, called **dataphone ditigal service (DDS).** Digital networks can directly transmit the discrete digital signals of the computer. There is no need to convert these to continuous analog signals, as is required when sending computer data over the regular voice communication network. Additionally, digital networks can be used to carry any digitized information. Thus, DDS can be used to integrate data, voice, and video transmission. DDS uses high-speed paths to connect major cities within the United States (see Exhibit 9.14). Data rates range from 56K to 1.5 Mbps. Because the communication paths are digital, modems are not needed, and the error rates are significantly lower than with conventional phone lines. A disadvantage is that DDS connects only major cities at this time, although there are plans to extend the network in the future to many more locations. Also, DDS is more expensive to use.

We will be talking much more about the exciting developments and implications of these new communication technologies in Chapter 16, "The Information Age Society."

Professional Issue

Local Area Network

Another emerging form of data communication that is bypassing the telephone network can be found within the business office itself. Electronic pathways that connect various communication devices are called a **network.** When a network is confined to a building or office complex, it is called a **local area network** or **LAN.** LANs serve new needs based primarily on the evolving uses of microcomputers.

When professionals first purchased microcomputers, the attraction was stand-alone processing capability that enabled people to increase their individual productivity. A professional's equipment included a printer and, often, hard disk capability as well. As more and more people in organizations wanted their own microcomputers, it became evident that it was too costly to equip each user with a printer and hard disk capability. Ways of sharing expensive peripherals were explored.

As more users got their own microcomputers, they wanted to share data and information electronically. Instead of using word processing software to write a memo on a micro and a printer to produce a hard copy output to send through office mail, why not just send a message electronically to the appropriate microcomputer? A coworker could then read the memo and send a response electronically. This process is called electronic mail.

In addition, users realized the advantages of allowing only authorized access to important data files stored on other microcomputers. For example, assume the company accountant had developed such files and stored them in the hard disks of his or her microcomputer. If the vice-president of finance could electronically transfer a copy of that data to his or her microcomputer's hard disk, then that data could be used as input to an electronic spreadsheet for use in future planning.

Microcomputer users also realized they needed access to the data base held in the company's main computer, which might be a mini- or maxicomputer. If those data could be downloaded to microcomputers, users could be sure they were using the latest information in preparing accurate reports and projections. Once this link is established, the next step is to provide the means for downloading software programs.

Another emerging objective in many organizations is to connect computer equipment manufactured by different vendors. As organizations purchased microcomputer equipment during the late 1970s and 1980s, different departments usually bought different kinds of computer systems. Department A got IBM PCs, Department B went with Apples, and Department C acquired Datapoints. As long as microcomputers are used as stand-alone units, this isn't a major problem. However, once organizations needed to share resources or information electronically, the realization that computers from different vendors aren't compatible caused significant problems. In theory, LANs can overcome these incompatibility problems. So far, though, there has been limited success in connecting highly different computer systems.

The future importance of LANs becomes clearer in light of studies that show 70 to 80 percent of an organization's communication takes place within a local area. Most of that communication now occurs through written correspondence (interoffice mail) or voice conversation (intercom telephone network or face-to-face meetings). The projection is that LANs will replace most written and voice communication within an organization, as well as open exciting new ways of exchanging ideas. We will talk more of these applications in the discussion of office automation in Chapter 16, "The Information Age Society."

Topology

The term *topology* refers to the patterns formed when hardware devices are connected to form a network. The three most common network topologies used with LANs are the star, the bus, and the ring. Exhibit 9.15 on page 248 shows each of these topologies.

In the **star network topology,** each device is connected to a central unit. Any communication between one device and another goes through the central unit. The exhibit shows a typical configuration using microcomputers and peripherals. Each device is directly connected to the central communications controller, which is a microcomputer containing the interface cards and software to manage all data communication in this network. If a user at Microcomputer 2 wants to print out a memo on the letter-quality printer, Microcomputer 2 sends that request to the network controller. This central controller notifies Microcomputer 2 when that task is complete.

With the **bus network topology,** each device is connected to a common cable. Each component must have its own interface device. This is usually a circuit board or card, which plugs into one of the expansion slots. The card contains the hardware and software necessary to access the network. All communication takes place on the common cable or bus. The data are sent down the bus and are available to all devices. Each message must contain information identifying the destination device.

With the **ring network topology,** each terminal is connected to two others, forming a circle or ring. All communication between terminals follows a clockwise or counterclockwise pattern. The message goes from terminal to terminal until the designated device is reached.

Network Access

How do the many devices in a network gain access to the network to transmit their messages? The problem is similar to deciding who will speak at a large meeting. One access method is to ask individuals to raise their hands to be recognized by a group leader. With computer networks, the most common access methods are polling, token passing, and contention.

Polling is used primarily with the star network topology. Here, the central controller goes around the star in order, asking each terminal if it wishes to transmit. Under this method, once a device is given permission to transmit, no other device may use the communication link until that terminal is finished. Then the controller resumes polling the next device.

Exhibit 9.15
Three Common Network Topologies

Star Network

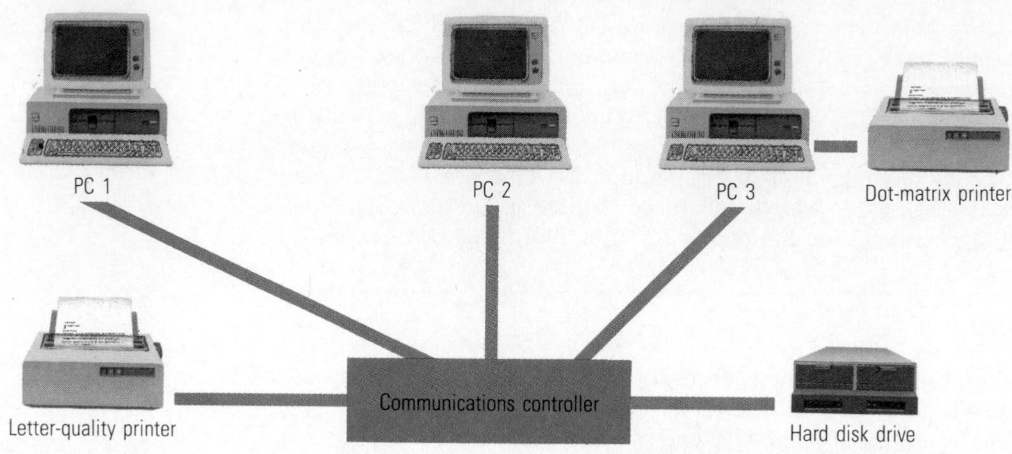

Bus Network

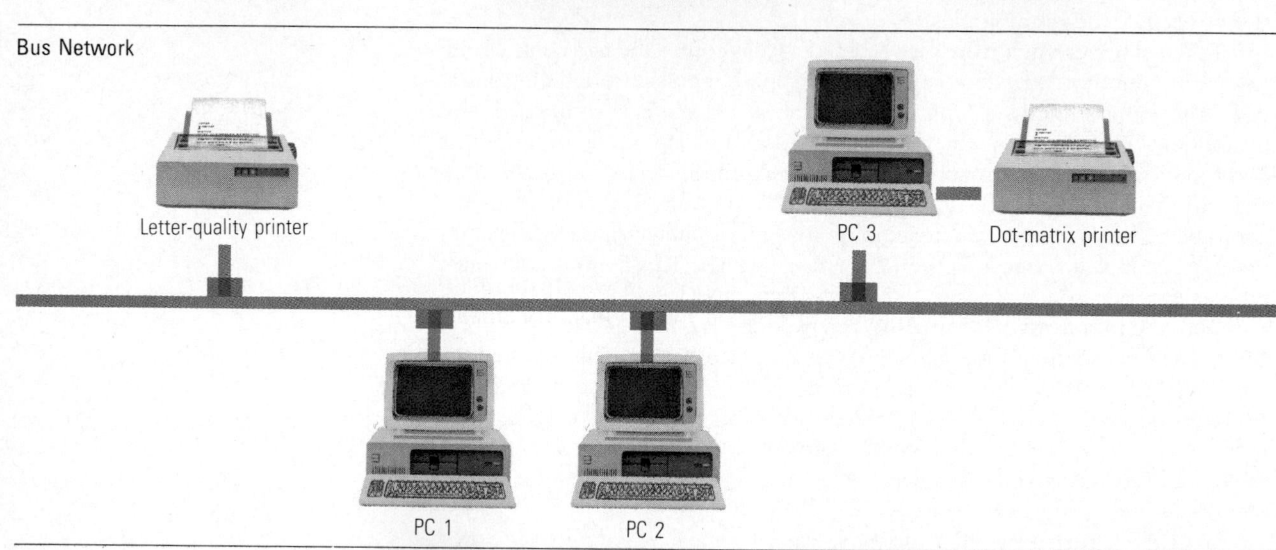

Ring Network

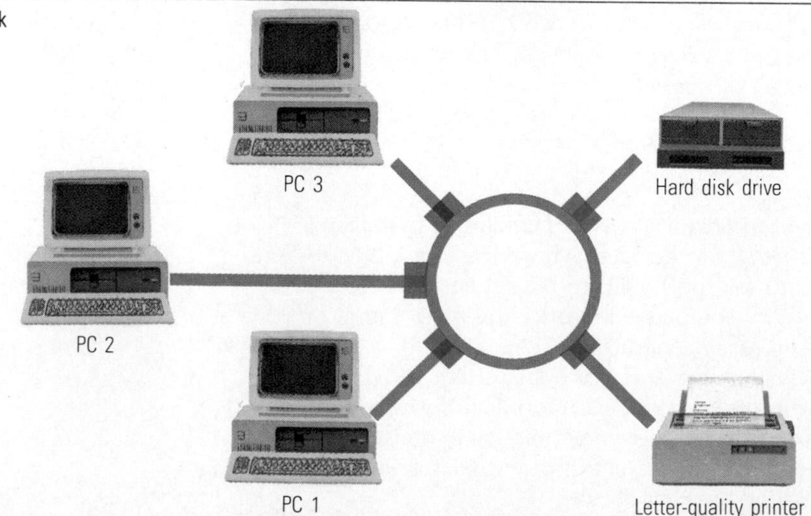

The access method called token passing is used primarily with ring networks. **Tokens** are defined bit patterns that are circulated around the network from device to device in the form of a data packet. The data packet has a source and destination address and room for a data message. If a terminal wants to transmit, it must wait until the token is passed to it. At that point, it takes the token and adds its message to the token, along with the address of the destination terminal. The token is now put back into the ring and sent to the next terminal. Each terminal, in turn, looks at the address to see if the message is for it. If it is not, the token is passed on. When the token reaches the destination device, the message is read from the data packet.

With the bus network, the common access method is **contention.** This approach is analogous to a meeting without a leader. Anybody can talk at any time, without having to be formally recognized. However, if this leads to two or more people speaking at the same time, all have to stop talking for a moment or two. Usually, one person will then start talking without contention from others.

Several contention methods are used in LAN, the most common being **carrier sense multiple access with collision detection (CSMA/CD).** What this means is that any of the devices connected to the bus can transmit when it needs to do so. There is no formal recognition as with polling or token passing. However, if more than one device tries to transmit at the same time, the resulting transmission "collision" will result in a garbled message.

The CSMA/CD is used to sense this collision. After a collision is detected, each of the transmitting devices stops briefly. Then each device is allowed to resume transmitting. If each device were instructed to back off 100 milliseconds, another collision would occur. So, instead of the same fixed time, a random time is set for each device.

The CSMA/CD approach is especially useful for LAN in which there is intermittent need to transmit. The XEROX Corporation, the originator of Ethernet, a bus network using CSMA/CD, claims that this contention approach works over 99 percent of the time without collision. Even on a heavily used LAN, with a modest number of devices, the implication is that only one or two collisions would occur a day.

Transmission Media

Several different types of wires or cables can be used to connect devices in a network to form a data path. The most common are twisted pairs, coaxial cable, and CATV (see Exhibit 9.16 on page 250).

Twisted pair wiring is the typical telephone cable used in your house. It is two individual copper wires that are twisted to give it physical strength. It is relatively cheap and has low installation and maintenance costs. A major disadvantage of twisted pair wiring for LAN, however, is that it is highly susceptible to electrical interference from within and outside the network. For higher interference immunity and also greater bandwidth capability, shielded twisted pair wiring is available at a slightly higher cost.

Coaxial cable is the most common transmission medium for LAN. Its major advantage is that it is sturdy enough to be laid in place as is. It doesn't require wiring conduits or mechanical support elements as does twisted pairs wiring. Thus, coaxial cable saves on installation cost and gives greater configuration flexibility. Because of its inherent construction, it has greater shielding,

Exhibit 9.16

Wires or cables are used to connect devices in a network to form a data path. The most common types are shown here: shielded twisted pairs (top left); coaxial cable (top right); coaxial cable for CATV (bottom left); and shielded internal twisted pairs (bottom right).

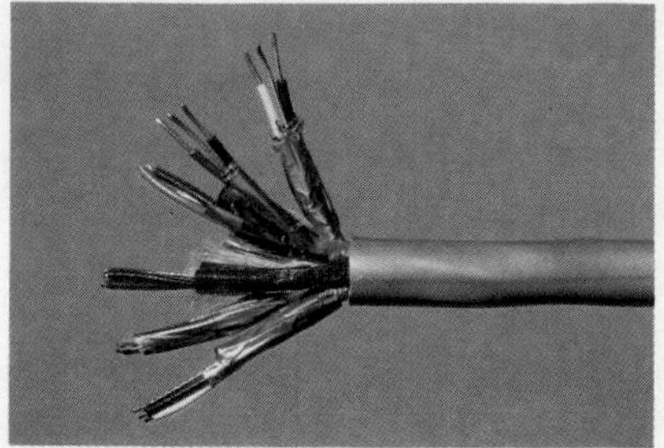

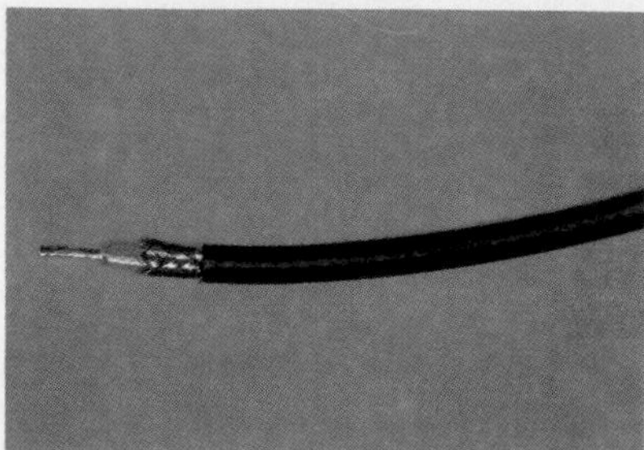

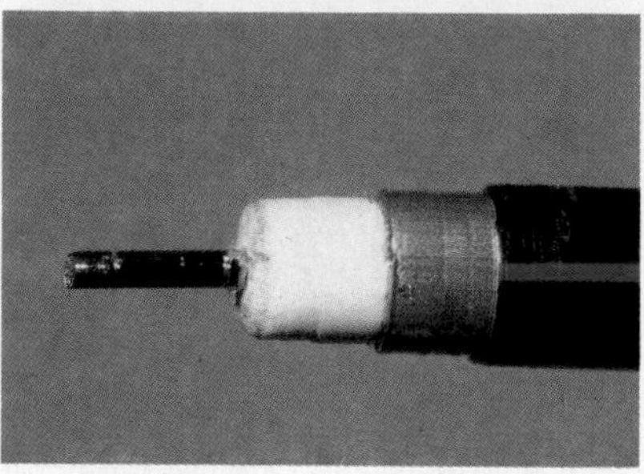

which makes possible much lower error rates. It costs about twice as much as unshielded twisted pair wire.

Another type of cable used with **cable television (CATV)** service has been designed to accommodate fifty television channels. It is an attractive transmission medium for LAN because its high capacity bandwidth can easily accommodate not only data, but also voice, images, and video.

Transmission media can be classified as being either baseband or broadband, depending on the size of the bandwidth. If the bandwidth of the medium will only accommodate sending one data stream at a time, it is called **baseband. Broadband** media can handle multiple data streams simultaneously. Twisted pairs and coaxial cables are examples of baseband media. Their advantages are that they are simpler and, since a digitized signal is sent, modems are not needed. The result is a less costly system. CATV is an example of a broadband medium. Its major disadvantage is its higher cost, due to more expensive cabling and the fact that modems have to be used with it.

LAN Characteristics

Now that we have discussed the basic aspects, let's review a summary chart of the cost, flexibility, growth, and capacity of various LAN configurations (see Exhibit 9.17).

Baseband has less capacity, but is much less costly than broadband. Broadband, because of its significant bandwidth, can accommodate more growth. The star network topology is the least costly, while the bus network gives the most flexibility, capacity, and growth possibilities. The ring topology is a compromise solution, since it is neither best nor worst on the specified criteria. The access method of polling is least costly, since the only intelligence needed is in the network controller, as opposed to access methods requiring each device to be "smart." The contention method gives the most flexibility, but doesn't have as much capacity as that of token passing. Polling has limited growth potential because of the higher overhead associated with this approach.

Connecting Networks

Exhibit 9.18 on page 252 shows a detailed look at how a LAN would be configured in one building and then interfaced with a LAN in an adjacent building. The top right section of the exhibit shows a LAN that has been placed in Building A. It is a bus network, since each microcomputer or peripheral is connected directly to what is mostly likely a coaxial cable. The boxes show the interface units. This exhibit also shows a disk server and a printer server. In general, a **server** is any device that interfaces a peripheral to a network and allows the sharing of that peripheral by other network units. For example, the disk server allows many microcomputers to share a common hard-disk drive. The disk server might itself be a microcomputer that handles accesses to the disk and partitions the hard disk into virtual diskettes. In Building A, only one person has a personal computer with a hard disk drive. The disk server allows extensive storage and common access to shared files for the network's other users.

	Least Cost	Most Flexibility	Most Growth	Most Capacity
Bandwidth				
Baseband	■	■		
Broadband			■	■
Topology				
Star	■			
Ring				
Bus		■	■	■
Access Method				
Polling	■			
Token Pass			■	■
CSMA		■	■	

Exhibit 9.17
Local Area Network Characteristics
Source: L. Jordon and B. Churchill, *Communication and Networking for the IBM PC* (Bowie, Maryland: Robert J. Brady Company, 1983), p. 118.

In Building B, another LAN is shown that also uses a bus topology and coaxial cable. A new feature is the mainframe computer system. Often, there is a need to upload or download data from a particular micro to the mainframe. This may involve two LANs that have different communication characteristics. A **gateway** is an interface device that provides the translations necessary to link two different types of networks.

The interface device that links the LAN in Building A with a similar LAN in Building B is called a **bridge.** This device increases the coverage and scope of a LAN by linking similar networks. It would enable the user of PC#2 to "talk" to PC#7. For communication to networks outside the local area, a communication server is used. The communication server functions in a way to share different speed modems, to accomplish the desired tasks.

ROLE OF COMMUNICATION SUPPORT SOFTWARE

Now that we have examined the considerations involved in data communication, telecommunication, and local area networks, let's look at the role that communication support software plays.

When we discussed operating systems in Chapter 7 and file and data base systems in Chapter 8, we concentrated on the functions this support software had to perform, such as controlling the flow of jobs and resources within the computer and providing access to specific data stored on disk or tape. We did not discuss the additional considerations necessary to accommodate remote terminals. This is the role of **communication support software (CSS).** In this section, we will discuss four of the major functions that communication

Exhibit 9.18
Office Complex LAN

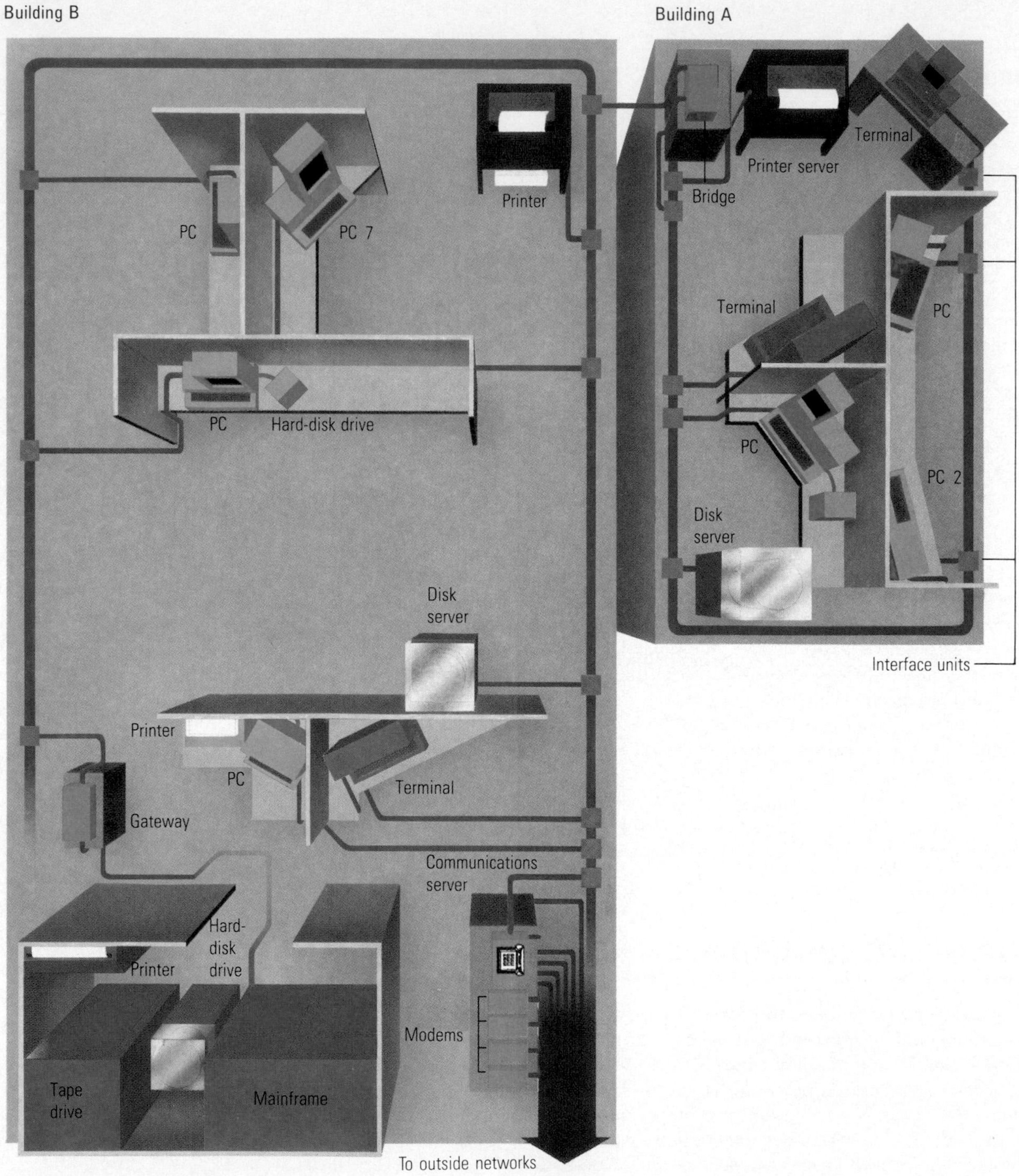

support software must provide: terminal access, protocols, error detection and correction, and security.

When there are many remote terminals connected to a computer system, what method is used to decide which one gets access to the computer? One of the major access methods used in telecommunication is polling. With the polling method, the communication software is responsible for querying each terminal in some specific order, such as round robin, to see if it has something to transmit. If it does not, the CSS goes on to the next terminal. After entering data, you hit the RETURN key, which serves as the signal that the terminal has something to transmit. When the computer system has something to transmit to a terminal, the CSS is used to select the correct terminal and determine if it is ready to receive data. When these conditions are met, the data are sent.

A second function of the CSS is to handle a variety of protocols. A **protocol** is a set of rules and procedures used for transmitting data between two hardware devices in a network. For example, before data can be exchanged between a terminal and a computer, the following must be established: Are the data that are to be sent asynchronous or synchronous? What format will the data packet be in (start and stop bits) and what kind of error-checking method is being used (parity or CRC)? Unfortunately, there are many different protocols in use today, with no universally accepted standard. Consequently, it is not always possible to communicate between a given terminal and any computer. However, as in other facets of the computer field, a small number of protocols are emerging as de facto standards.

In a previous section, we discussed the use of the parity and CRC methods of detecting errors in data transmission. With both methods, the CSS detects an error and responds with a signal to the terminal to retransmit the complete message. This form of error control ensures a high accuracy rate, but can require a significant amount of retransmission. The error rates are a function of the type of media used. Regular voice-grade lines have the highest error rates, whereas the all-digital networks have the lowest.

In those situations where high security is needed for transmitting sensitive organizational data across telecommunication paths, **data encryption** techniques can be used. These convert the data to be transmitted into a scrambled form. Unauthorized users who might somehow get to the data, but don't know the encryption key, would get meaningless data. Encryption keys must be very sophisticated schemes so they can't be easily deciphered. However, the underlying concept is not complicated. A simple encryption key could be to add 3 to each number and to descend 3 letters for each alphabetic letter.

Using this simple encryption key, the data would appear as shown.

the data	5	A	T	6	1	1
the encrypted data	8	D	W	9	4	4

The decryption process is just the reverse. Subtract 3 from each encrypted number and ascend 3 letters.

We have discussed several major functions that are needed to perform data communication. A major question is where the communication support software should be located to perform these tasks. One answer is to have the communication support software be a part of the operating system of the host computer. The newer time-sharing operating systems incorporate communication functions. For host computers using operating systems originally designed to support multiprogramming batch operations, add-on telecommunication software packages are available.

As we connect more and more remote terminals to a computer unit, the host computer has to spend an inordinate amount of time keeping track of which terminals are sending data, converting characters from serial to parallel format, error checking that data, and loading it into primary memory. This is all overhead, since the CPU isn't doing actual work or processing on a user's application. To alleviate this bottleneck, a **front-end processor** can be added. This is a micro- or minicomputer that functions as a specialized data communication handler to deal with these tasks. The CPU is free to concentrate on processing, under the assumption that the data are in place and are error-free.

The trend is to put more and more "intelligence" into the data network, in the form of multiplexers, front-end processors, computer switching devices and so forth. In this way, the complications caused by incompatible standards, protocols, and the wide variety of computers and terminals in use can be handled by the network itself. This provides a simpler, more universal way to meet telecommunication needs.

Federal Express Spends Millions for Its Telecommunications Networks

When Federal Express Corporation wanted to prove to the American public that the quickest route between any two points in the U.S. is through Memphis, corporate officials demanded an unerring communications network.

And they were willing to put dollars behind their demand. Today they spend $24 million annually on overall communications; about 20 percent of that sum is devoted to data communications.

The 10-year-old company, which in its 1983 fiscal year topped $1 billion in revenues for the first time, turned the problem of transporting a package overnight from point A to point B into a creative challenge. Federal Express is the originator of the "hub and spoke" concept of overnight delivery, a concept that at first glance seemed so improbable even the company's original investors balked.

Each one of the 200,000 packages to be delivered the next day, no matter its origin or destination, is flown to the "superhub" at the Memphis International Airport. While the city sleeps, 1300 employees sort the packages in the space of two hours. By 2 AM, each package is on a Federal Express jet chasing a 10:30 AM delivery deadline.

Dan Hinsley, Federal Express' director of communications and operations support, said the company is one of IBM's largest customers. Two of the company's four IBM mainframes in Memphis (two additional mainframes reside in Colorado Springs, Colorado, for backup and software development) are devoted to nothing but online data communications.

Operating under IBM's telecommunication support software, the two IBM 3081 computers handle two specific communication networks. One is dedicated to customer inquiries and customer support. The other is for internal information such as flight schedule and weather reports.

Approximately 6000 CRT terminals throughout the country transmit data through modems at speeds from 4800 bit/sec to 9600 bit/sec over 281 circuits, 250 of which are private leased lines. In all, over 150,000 circuit miles of telephone transmission are traversed by the Federal Express network.

The company uses 10 IBM 3705 front-end processors and one NCR Corporation Comten 3650 front-end processor for its Canadian operations.

Efforts to stay on top of constantly changing technology in communications include the installation of a Digitally Aided Dispatch System, which put a communications terminal in the company's courier vans. In addition, there is a plan to use the company's satellite network for a facsimilie service. Federal Express has also received permission from the Federal Communications Commission to build a digital termination system to act as backup to the local loop of telephone companies or perhaps as an electronic mail setup. The company is also looking at cellular radio.

Winn Stephenson, a director of telecommunications engineering and development, was quick to point out that these technologies will be implemented only after thorough examination. "We're not in technology for technology's sake," Stephenson said. "When something becomes cost-effective and makes sense, then we'll jump into it."

Source: K. Hafner, "Federal Express Puts Dollars—$24 Million—Behind Demand for Unerring Communications," *Computerworld,* 8 August, 1983, pp. 10–11.

SUMMARY

The movement of data from one location to another is called *data communication.* The types of communication hardware and support software necessary to move those data differ, depending primarily on the distance involved. *Terminal* is the generic name for the myriad of possible input and output devices. The hardware linking the terminals and a computer are called *transmission media.*

With a microcomputer, the transmission medium is generally a cable. The cable hooks to the computer at an *input/output port.* The number of devices that can be connected to a computer is a function of the number of I/O ports. A serial connection requires a different type of I/O port than does a parallel connection. The two de facto standards for microcomputers are called RS232–C and Centronics.

An *interface unit* is needed for each peripherial device to translate computer I/O commands into device-specific instructions. With some larger computer systems, the interface function is divided into common I/O tasks and device-specific tasks. Device-specific tasks are performed by an *I/O control unit* such as a disk controller. The common tasks are performed by a *channel device.* A channel unit is a common link between the computer and its peripheral.

Telecommunication is the transmission of data over long distances. The telephone voice network uses continuous frequency waves called *analog signals.* In contrast, the computer is limited to processing a discrete pattern of 1s and 0s called *digital signals.* A *modem* is a device that converts digital patterns to analog signals and allows the sending of computer data over telephone lines. A *carrier signal* is the basic signal used to transmit data over telecommunication links, and is modulated by slight changes to its amplitude or frequency to represent data.

The *data rate* or *speed* of a telecommunication link is the amount of data that can be sent per time period. It is measured in bits per second (bps). Frequencies are stated in cycles per second (cps) or Hertz (Hz). To be able to send data in a telecommunication network, start and stop information, origin and destination information, and error check bits must be added to the encoded data to form a *data packet.* These added data are used to aid in sending and receiving data, checking for errors, and for routing messages through a network.

In the *asynchronous* mode of data transmission, one character at a time is sent over the communication link. The *parity bit* method of error checking is used primary with Async. With the *synchronous* mode of data transmission, a block of characters is sent. Here, the most commonly used error-checking method is *Cyclic Redundancy Coding (CRC).*

A *communication channel* is the transmission medium that links the sending and receiving devices. Typically, in telecommunication the channel is a telephone line, but it could also be a microwave or satellite link. A *simplex* channel can transmit data in only one direction. A *half-duplex* channel is one where data can be transmitted in either direction, but only one way at a time. In a communication channel that is *full-duplex,* data can be transmitted in both directions simultaneously.

Multiplexing means having several communication signals share the same communication channel using time or frequency divisions. *Bandwidth* is the range of frequencies that can be used with a particular communication channel. It is used as a measure of information-carrying capacity.

Until recently, the owner of the telecommunication channels in the United States was primarily AT&T. The most common way to connect a remote terminal to a computer is by using the telephone network. This dial-up service uses relay switches to provide a temporary network connection between the two devices. A *private line* provides for a permanent connection between point A and B, for the exclusive use of an organization.

Inside the telephone switch network are different types of transmission media. Each telephone line that connects a home or business to the local switching office consists of pairs of copper wire. The regional and long-distance trunk lines were initially copper wires also. But as technology has advanced and the demand for phones has increased, media with greater bandwidth have been required.

One means to do this is the use of high-frequency radio signals called *microwaves.* These microwave links provide high-capacity transmission of data or voice. A *communication satellite* is an electronic device that relays signals between earth and space. The cost of satellite transmission is independent of distance. One of the latest types of cable is called *fiber optics,* which uses laser technology to modulate light waves.

The combination of the emergence of these new technologies and the push by the FCC for more competition in the telecommunication arena has led to a variety of alternatives to the telephone voice network. For example, AT&T's *dataphone digital service (DDS)* uses high-speed paths that connect major cities within the U.S. It can carry any digitized information—data, voice, or video.

Electronic pathways that connect the various communication devices are called a *network.* When that network is confined to a building or an office complex, it is designated as a *local area network.* It serves new needs that are based primarily on the evolving uses for microcomputers.

The pattern formed by the way devices are connected to form a network is called *topology.* The three most common network topologies used with LAN are the *star,* the *ring,* and the *bus.* With computer networks, the most common access methods are *polling, token passing,* and *contention.* There are several different types of wires or cables that can be used to connect devices in a network to form a data path. The most common are *twisted pairs, coaxial cable,* and *CATV.*

A *server* is any device that interfaces a peripheral to a network and allows the sharing of that peripheral by other network units. A *gateway* is an interface device that provides the translations necessary to link two different types of networks. *Bridges* are interface devices that link similar types of LAN networks.

The major functions that communication support software provides are terminal access, protocols, error detection and correction, and security. A *protocol* is a set of rules and procedures used for transmitting data between two hardware devices in a network.

In those situations where high security is needed for transmitting sensitive organizational data across telecommunication paths, *data encryption,* a technique for converting data to be transmitted into a scrambled form, can be used.

A major question is whether the communication support software should be located in the host computer or the data network itself. The trend is to put more and more intelligence in the network, in the form of multiplexers, front-end processors, and computer switching devices.

REVIEW QUESTIONS

1. Distinguish between data communications and telecommunications.
2. Explain the difference between serial and parallel transmission of data bits.
3. What is an interface unit? Why are such devices necessary?
4. What is a channel device? What are its two major functions?
5. The Zenon Corporation desires a means of transmitting data from remote terminals in each of its several regional branches to the mainframe located at corporate headquarters. A consultant has told them they must use the telephone communication network. Why? What alternatives are available?
6. How does a modem overcome the problems involved in the use of telephone lines for the transmission of data?
7. What is a data packet? Explain the difference between the asynchronous and the synchronous modes of transmission.
8. The Arrow Corporation needs the most efficient communication channel possible to allow numerous remote terminals located in its offices to access the mainframe. Which communication channel system would you suggest? Why?
9. What are fiber optics? What advantages do such systems offer?
10. Explain the LAN concept. Why are such systems increasing in popularity?
11. What is meant by the term *topology?* Briefly describe the three most common topologies in use today.
12. Briefly compare the most commonly used LAN configurations.

PART IV COMPUTER-BASED INFORMATION SYSTEMS

CHAPTER 10

Management Information Systems

COMPUTERS AT WORK

Selling Will Never Be the Same

Less than a year ago, Mike Reilly, Atlanta Bar Soap & Household Cleaning Products district manager, didn't know how to turn on a computer. Now, it's the first thing he does each morning when he gets to the office.

Just as with Reilly, the computer has become a day-to-day tool for many in the Procter & Gamble sales organization in a relatively short time. Computer knowledge and proficiency are growing in leaps. Five years ago, only a handful of field salespeople were familiar with computers; as of this printing, dozens of district managers have attended three-day computer training courses in Cincinnati.

Although Sales is continually exploring new computer applications, computers are already having a significant impact on selling techniques, communication and data analysis.

Mike Reilly is one of hundreds of P&G sales managers who have mastered the personal computer and use it as a selling tool. His appetite for computer proficiency was whetted after attending a Sales computer training course at the General Offices in January 1983.

The course didn't make him an instant expert, but it did give him enough knowledge to start puttering around with programs of his own. And the more he experimented, the more potential applications he began to see.

Source: G. Sanders, "Selling Will Never Be the Same," *Moonbeams,* November 1984, pp 13–15.

Mike Reilly is a good example of today's successful manager. By combining knowledge about his job and the computer's potential to support managers, Mike is developing applications to keep him "one step ahead of the competition." Mike and other Procter & Gamble managers are not alone in their ability to make use of the computer. Managers in all types of businesses are finding that good information systems can greatly improve their decision-making capabilities.

In this chapter you will learn how to do the following:

1. Explain what a management information system is.
2. Define and describe the two main roles of management information systems in business.
3. List the three levels of management, explain their business roles, and describe their information needs.
4. List the three types of business information systems and describe how each can serve as an MIS.
5. Explain what an MIS master plan is, what its components are, and why it is important to a firm's overall MIS design.
6. Explain what an MIS architecture is and why it is important to a firm's overall MIS design, and describe the three basic forms an MIS architecture can take.
7. Describe the MIS roles microcomputers can play in both small and large businesses.
8. Explain what a systems model of a business is and what it can accomplish.

COMPUTER SUPPORT OF MANAGEMENT

In 1980, when Barry Allen, John Hardy, and Susan Tate founded CompuStore, the world of microcomputers was still young. CompuStore, in fact, was the first store in the state to sell microcomputers to businesses rather than hobbyists.

Many of CompuStore's early customers were surprised to find that the owners did not use computers in managing their business. They had little need for a computer—together, Barry, John, and Susan performed all the necessary tasks. Each, over time, ordered the hardware and software products that were sold, unpacked shipments, stocked the small stockroom and the sales floor, waited on customers, and kept track of sales and expenses. Also, with the microcomputer industry in its infancy, only a small number of hardware and software products were offered for sale.

Since the owners personally ran the store, each kept up to date on all the firm's business activities. When a situation arose with which John was unfamiliar, he simply yelled over to either Barry or Susan to get the information he needed. Their management information came from accounting records, paper files of purchase orders and sales receipts, and lots of memos to each other.

All this has changed. CompuStore today is a major retail chain with eight locations, annual revenues of over $15 million, and close to 100 employees. On average, the chain carries over 200 hardware components, over 400 software packages, and a variety of supplies and publications. Rather than dealing only with "walk-in" customers, CompuStore now handles many corporate accounts.

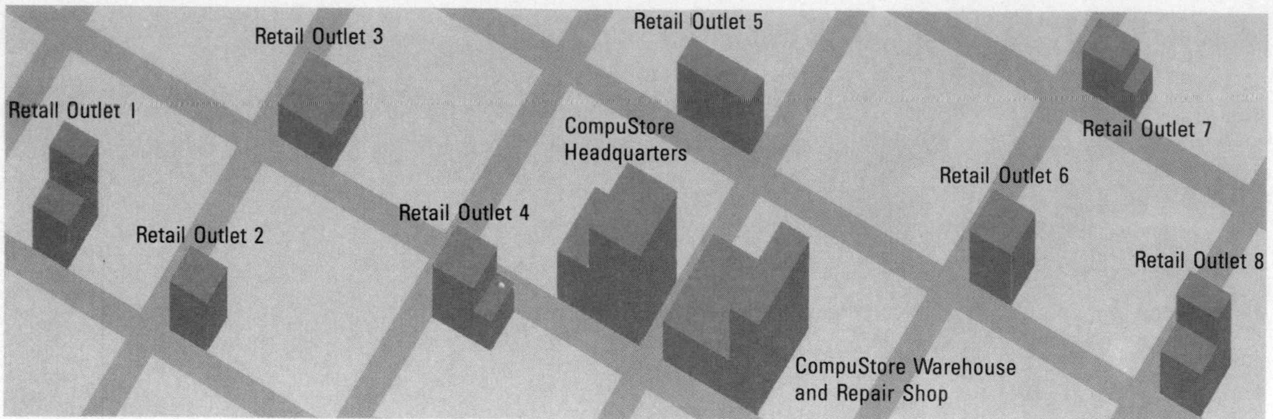

Exhibit 10.1

CompuStore has grown from a one-store business in 1980 to an eight-store chain today. This growth has made it more difficult for managers throughout the firm to fully grasp all of CompuStore's business activities.

In contrast with 1980, when it dealt with 15 suppliers, CompuStore now orders products from over 100 suppliers. Exhibit 10.1 depicts CompuStore's current facilities.

Barry is now the firm's president, John is vice-president for finance, and Susan is vice-president for marketing. Each owner now performs specialized duties. Most of the firm's other employees are also specialized. They include accountants, bookkeepers, a financial analyst, a marketing manager, a marketing analyst, an advertising manager, salespeople, a general manager, an office manager, store managers, secretaries, inventory clerks, buyers, purchasing clerks, computer technicians, a systems analyst, and a programmer.

While all this specialization has played a part in CompuStore's success, none of the firm's managers now has a complete grasp of the business. Problems arise in which John, for example, is not that familiar with all the issues. More often than not, Barry and Susan are of little help unless the issues involve activities they directly manage. Without computer support, John would have to track down employees who had the needed information or at least knew where to find it. If this took too much time, John would have to act without the information. When managers act without a good grasp of the situation, the result is often unsatisfactory. Important facts are ignored or forgotten, and mistakes occur.

With good computer support, John might be able to obtain needed information as easily as he did in 1980. With more computer support, he should be able to obtain information that wasn't available to him in 1980. Information systems that provide managers with information that enables them to perform their jobs quicker or better, or both, are called **management information systems,** or **MIS** for short.

The Role of MIS in a Business

The obvious role that MIS play in any business is to provide managers with the information they need to carry out their own duties. Barry Allen receives a monthly report summarizing CompuStore's profits on a store-by-store basis. This information enables him to assess a number of things, including CompuStore's various growth patterns and the retail outlets that might be having problems. John Hardy receives a weekly report that analyzes the firm's cash position. With this information, he can decide whether or not he will have to arrange loans for the business. Susan Tate receives a weekly report listing the fastest-selling items at each retail location. Knowing this, she can provide the firm's buyers with better directions regarding which product lines should be stressed.

A less obvious role that MIS play is to provide a means by which managers can coordinate activities taking place in different parts of a business. John Hardy estimated that CompuStore lost over $80,000 in 1984 because it failed to take advantage of volume discounts offered by some suppliers. If the firm's buyers could have been provided with monthly sales volumes by suppliers for specific products, these discounts might have been realized. Coordinating sales activities with buyer activities could result in better purchasing decisions.

Thus, there are two major roles of MIS in a business:

1. providing managers with information that enables them to carry out their own assigned duties
2. providing managers with information that enables them to better coordinate business activities

MIS cover a wide range of computer support for managers because of the variety of management positions that exist.

Levels of Business Management

One way of looking at different management positions is shown in Exhibit 10.2. **Operating managers** make sure that a business's day-to-day activities are performed. They direct and oversee workers, and they solve any immediate problems that arise. **Middle managers** make sure that business objectives are achieved. They make certain that operating managers are given enough resources (people, money, facilities, and supplies), they direct and oversee the work of operating managers, and they identify and react to major problems and opportunities. **Senior managers** make sure that the business will, over time, be successful. They decide on the type of customers to be served and the type of products to be offered, they provide the resources necessary for long-term success, and they decide how the business should be organized.

These three levels of business management have quite different **information needs.** As a result, an MIS designed for one level is unlikely to meet the needs of the other two. Managers have five types of information needs:

1. A need for *detailed* or *summarized* information.
2. A need for *more* or *less current* information.
3. A need for *past, present,* or *future* information.
4. A need for a *narrow* or *broad range* of information.
5. A need for *internal* or *external* information.

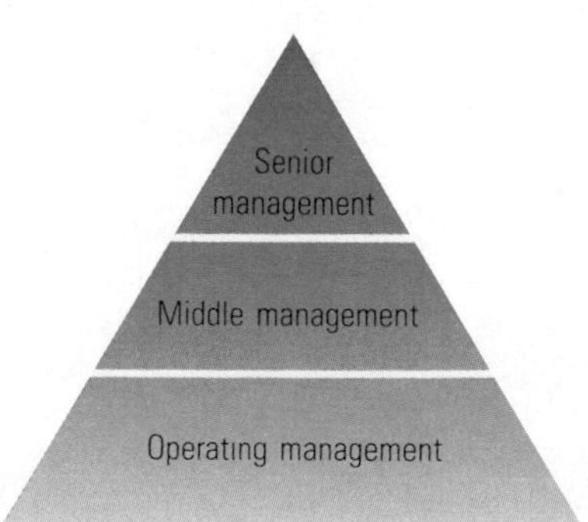

Exhibit 10.2

Most management positions fit one of three categories. Operating managers make sure day-to-day activities are performed. Middle managers make sure business objectives are achieved. Senior managers make sure the business continues to be successful over time.

Operating Management.

Connie Bledsoe is the store manager at CompuStore's Central Avenue store. She must manage the store's employees, keep track of daily sales receipts, keep track of products kept on the sales floor and in the stockroom, make sure that customer orders arrive on time, schedule store maintenance, and coordinate with the firm's advertising, warehouse, and repair shop staffs.

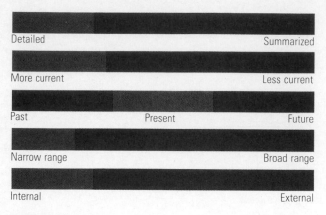

Exhibit 10.3

Operating managers need information that is detailed, current, concerned with the present, and focused on a narrow set of internal business activities.

Connie needs information that enables her to track store-related events as they occur. Such information tends to be detailed and current, is concerned with the present, and focuses rather narrowly on the internal activities of the Central Avenue store. Exhibit 10.3 summarizes these information needs.

Middle Management. Tim Scott is CompuStore's marketing manager. His primary duty is to see that the firm's sales goals are met. He works with Susan Tate to set sales targets, and then works with his marketing staff, the buyers, and the store managers to see that these sales targets are met.

Tim must have a good grasp of sales trends at each of the retail outlets, sales trends for each of the product lines, the extent to which the firm's marketing and advertising strategies are working, any problems in the warehouse or the repair shop that might be hurting sales, national sales trends, and sales trends for CompuStore's main competitors. In general, Tim needs a general picture of sales potential but a fairly detailed understanding of actual sales relative to sales targets. Such information tends to be aggregated over product categories and time so that trends can be observed. Exhibit 10.4 summarizes these information needs.

Senior Management. In her role as vice-president of marketing, Susan Tate is responsible for identifying exactly who CompuStore's customers are and what types of microcomputer products they are most likely to buy. She then works with Barry Allen, John Hardy, and Tim Scott in setting CompuStore's sales strategies and targets.

Susan needs to know how well CompuStore's sales are doing relative to its sales targets and in comparison with its major competitors. It is just as impor-

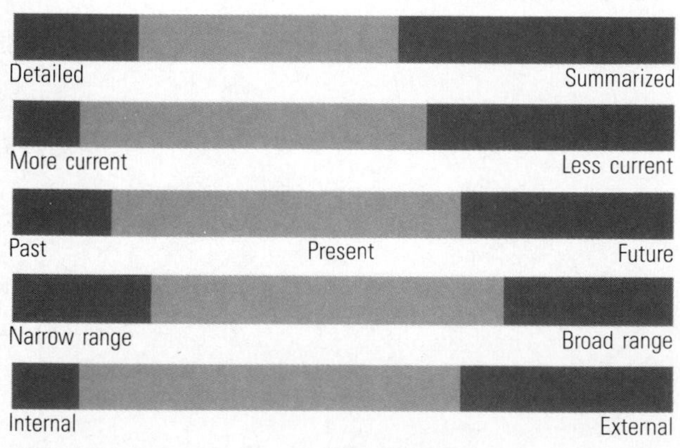

Exhibit 10.4

Middle managers need information that is aggregated but fairly current, that compares the present with the recent past, and that covers a broad range of internal business activities but only a narrow range of external business activities.

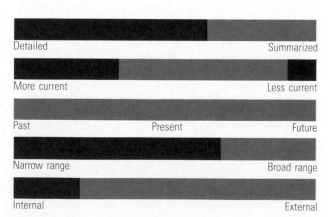

Exhibit 10.5

Senior managers need very summarized information that is aggregated over lengthy time periods, that covers the past, present, and future, and that includes a broad range of internal and external business activities.

tant, however, for her to follow nationwide microcomputer sales trends, to keep up with new technical developments, and to understand the general level of business activity in and around CompuStore's sales region. In order for Susan to deal with such a broad range of internal and external information, she needs information that is very summarized and aggregated over fairly long periods of time, and that covers the past and future as well as the present. Exhibit 10.5 summarizes these information needs.

Management Support Provided by Business Information Systems

Three types of business information systems were introduced and described in Chapter 2—transaction processing systems, information reporting systems, and decision support systems. Each type can produce useful management information. This is illustrated on page 266 by Computers at Work: "Chemical Bank Computers Drive Hard Bargains," which describes how business information systems are enabling Chemical Bank to solve a number of management headaches regarding its office supplies and services.

Generally, operating managers tend to make more use of transaction processing systems, middle managers tend to make more use of information reporting systems, and senior managers tend to make more use of decision support systems (see Exhibit 10.6). This is due to the nature of the information typically produced with each type of information system.

Transaction Processing Systems. Transaction processing systems record, process, store, and release data describing the day-to-day activities of a business. The management information produced by transaction processing systems usually takes the form of a listing of transactions, or business events, that have recently occurred or are scheduled to occur.

Consider a transaction processing system that captures daily sales activities at CompuStore's retail outlets. Three main sales activities are involved: customers ask for items that are in stock and then purchase them, customers ask for items that are not in stock but place future orders, and customers ask for items that are not in stock and then leave without purchasing them or placing future orders. This last sales activity is called a "lost sale."

Connie Bledsoe, Tim Scott, and Susan Tate could all make good use of outputs from this information system. If Connie were given a listing of future orders due in the next day, she could make sure that the ordered products were at the store. If some deliveries were delayed, Connie could at least call the customers, tell them about the delays, and inform them of the new delivery dates. Tim would be very interested in a listing of all lost sales over $100. With this information he could better forecast product sales volumes. Also, as lost sales are often a symptom of larger troubles, Tim might be able to spot a growing problem before it got out of hand. Susan would be very interested in the impact on CompuStore's sales whenever competitors opened up new retail stores. With this infor-

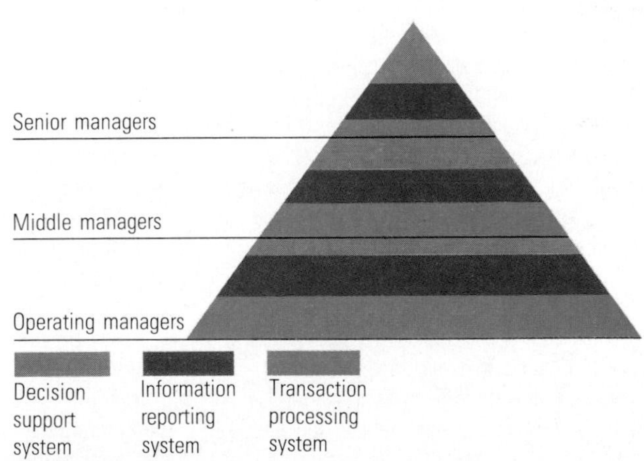

Exhibit 10.6

Each type of business information system can be used to produce management information. Generally, operating managers make more use of transaction processing systems, middle managers make more use of information reporting systems, and senior managers make more use of decision support systems.

COMPUTERS AT WORK

Chemical Bank Computers Drive Hard Bargains

To support 20,000 employees in 400 far-flung offices, New York City's giant Chemical Bank spends $125 million a year on blank forms, typewriters, spare light bulbs, and thousands of other supplies and services—most of which are requisitioned through a central purchasing department. As the bank has grown, however, the labor-intensive purchasing methods that served it well in the past have been taxed to the limit, causing endless management headaches.

But Chemical's migraines are subsiding these days, thanks to a sophisticated new computer setup called the materials management reporting system. MMRS, which can best be described as a kind of highly specialized decision support system, has automated many of the tasks that used to be done by hand—tracking warehouse inventory and analyzing vendor bids, for example. Moreover, by monitoring the performance of individual buyers and vendors, it is helping to weed out purchasing abuses and inefficiencies that were virtually impossible to detect in the past. In fact, after less than a year in operation, the $700,000 system has already paid for itself in cost savings.

MMRS is largely the creation of purchasing director David H. Offenberg, who joined the bank from Western Electric Company in 1975. The system he found at Chemical bore little resemblance to the one he was used to; it was, as he diplomatically puts it, "archaic." Consider, for example, a bank branch that needed a supply of checking account deposit slips. The manager would sign a requisition and dispatch it by interoffice mail to purchasing, where a clerk would record it and forward the order to either the bank's main Secaucus, N.J., warehouse or to one of six satellite warehouses in the New York area. There, another clerk would fill the order and return it by interoffice mail to the branch—if it was in stock, and all too often it wasn't. Recalls Offenberg: "We would send along an order, then find out three or four days later we couldn't get it."

The materials management reporting system was up and running last May, and in a matter of months has revolutionized the way Chemical Bank's purchasing department conducts its affairs. One obvious change is in the preparation of purchase orders. Instead of typing out all of the data about a product on a paper form, a clerk simply keys the item's code number into the computer. A complete description of the item appears on the terminal screen, so that the operator can double-check the order. "When you buy 250,000 corrugated cartons at one clip, and you key in a wrong digit, you're likely to get a number 3½ carton when you want an 8½," says Salvato, head of the purchasing department. "That can mean big trouble."

A computer at the warehouse keeps track of stock levels, and each evening dispatches a summary of the day's warehouse activity over telephone lines to a computer in the purchasing department. Buyers can then replenish supplies as necessary.

The computer monitors all purchase requests, looking for small orders that can be lumped together, thereby taking advantage of vendors' volume discounts. To further streamline the purchasing process, the system generates monthly and yearly product usage reports along with the names of successful and unsuccessful vendors. The purpose is to identify—and possibly eliminate from consideration—vendors that consistently submit unacceptable bids. Vendors are also evaluated by how well they perform over time. For example, the computer will flag a supplier that consisently delivers—and charges for—more than the quantity ordered. Although this practice is well known to purchasing agents, it is extremely difficult to detect with manual purchasing systems.

Buyers are also aided by a long-range planning program that digests information about market conditions and relates it to the bank's purchasing practices. For example, it may alert a buyer that paper prices are expected to skyrocket, so that the buyer can stockpile forms. The program will even help the buyer decide whether it pays to stockpile by calculating storage costs.

Source: J. Herrmann, "How Chemical Bank Uses Computers to Drive Hard Bargains," *Management Technology,* March 1984, pp. 42–46.

mation she could begin to assess whether or not CompuStore was losing sales to a competitor.

Transaction processing systems serve one other key MIS role. Most of the data in a firm's data base are captured by transaction processing systems. This data base is then accessed by information reporting systems and decision support systems to produce still more management information.

Exhibit 10.7 illustrates how the three transaction listings described above might be produced.

Information Reporting Systems. Information reporting systems retrieve data from a firm's data base to produce prespecified management reports. Usually the information output is quite different from the data that were initially captured. It is summarized, aggregated, and otherwise transformed to produce reports that enable managers to monitor business activities, spot problems and opportunities, and analyze specific issues.

Three types of reports can be produced. **Periodic reports** are distributed at regular intervals: daily, weekly, monthly, quarterly, or annually. What "triggers" the release of the report is the elapsing of the specified time period. Connie Bledsoe, for example, gets a weekly report that summarizes sales at the Central Avenue store across specific hardware and software products. With this information she is better able to place weekly and monthly product orders.

Exception reports are distributed only when an "exception" occurs, usually the missing of some business target. What actually triggers the report

Exhibit 10.7

Managers at all levels at CompuStore can use outputs from a transaction processing system that tracks sales activities at retail outlets.

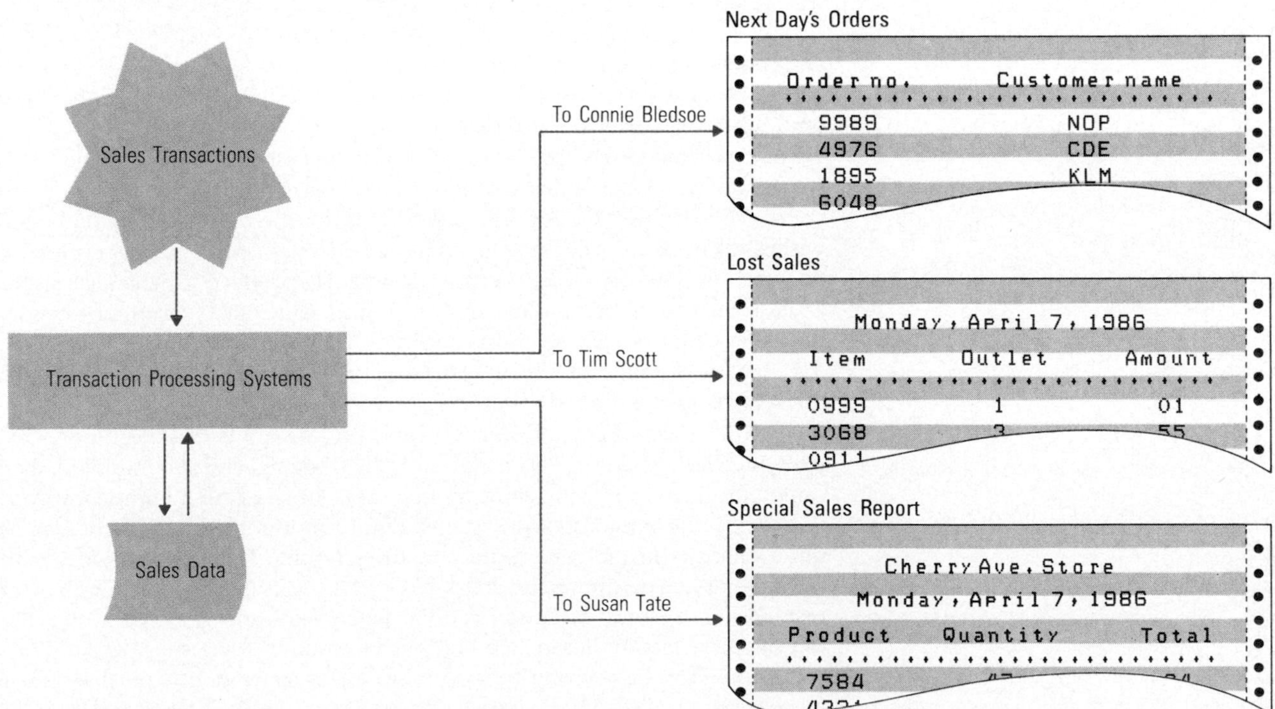

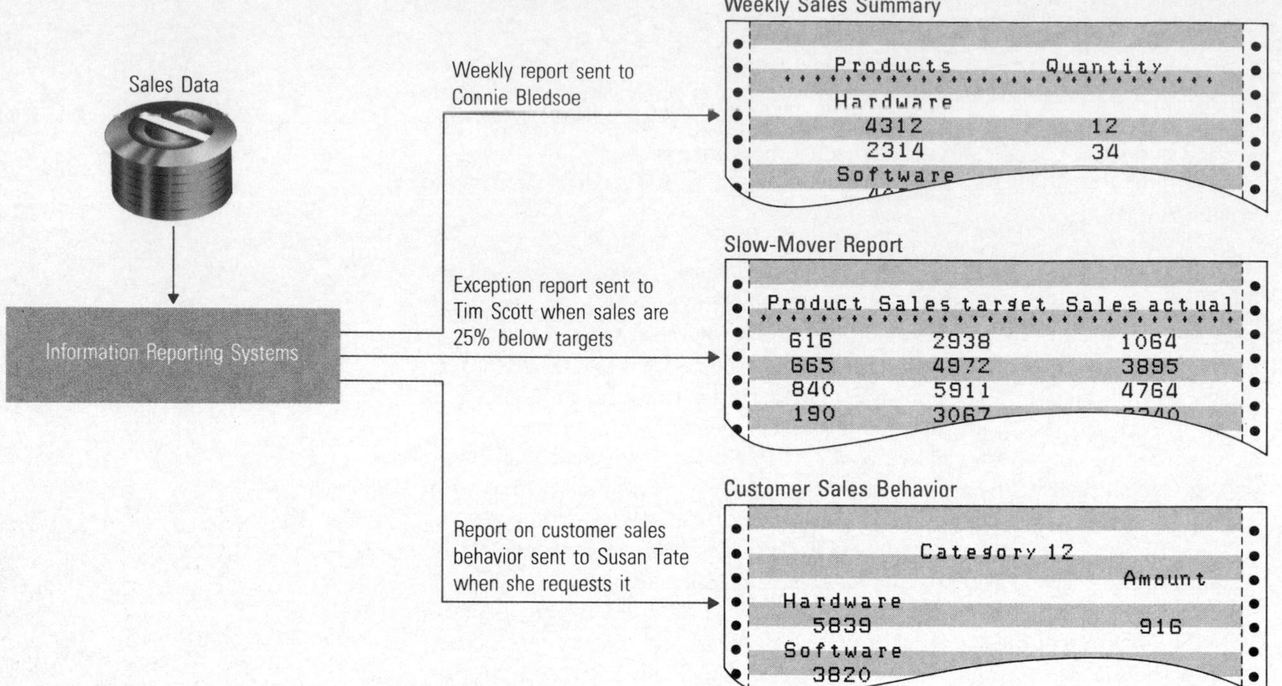

Exhibit 10.8

Managers at all levels at CompuStore can have prespecified reports produced from data retrieved from the firm's data base.

are processing rules that detect an exception. Tim Scott receives a special report whenever sales for any of the firm's hardware or software product lines are 25 percent under the forecast sales target.

Demand reports are distributed only when asked for by a manager. This typically occurs when a manager wishes to analyze a particular issue in more depth. What triggers the report is the request for the report. Susan Tate often wishes to check the recent buying behavior of certain customer categories. An information system was consequently designed to produce such an analysis for 15 customer categories. Susan simply gives the name of the customer category whose buying behavior she wishes to examine.

Exhibit 10.8 illustrates how sets of data base items are retrieved to produce the reports just described.

A key aspect of any information reporting system is that the reports are **prespecified.** As these reports are carefully designed and programmed, they can be produced very efficiently. It often takes long periods of time, however, to develop these information systems. Furthermore, managers often wish to make changes in the reports they receive. Connie Bledsoe may decide to expand her key hardware and software products lists from 10 to 20. Tim Scott may wish to receive exception reports when sales are 25 percent *over* the forecast sales targets. Susan Tate may wish to examine customer payment histories as well as their buying behaviors. Modifying a report requires that one or more programs be revised. Revising programs, as we shall see in Chapters 11 and 12, can be difficult and time consuming.

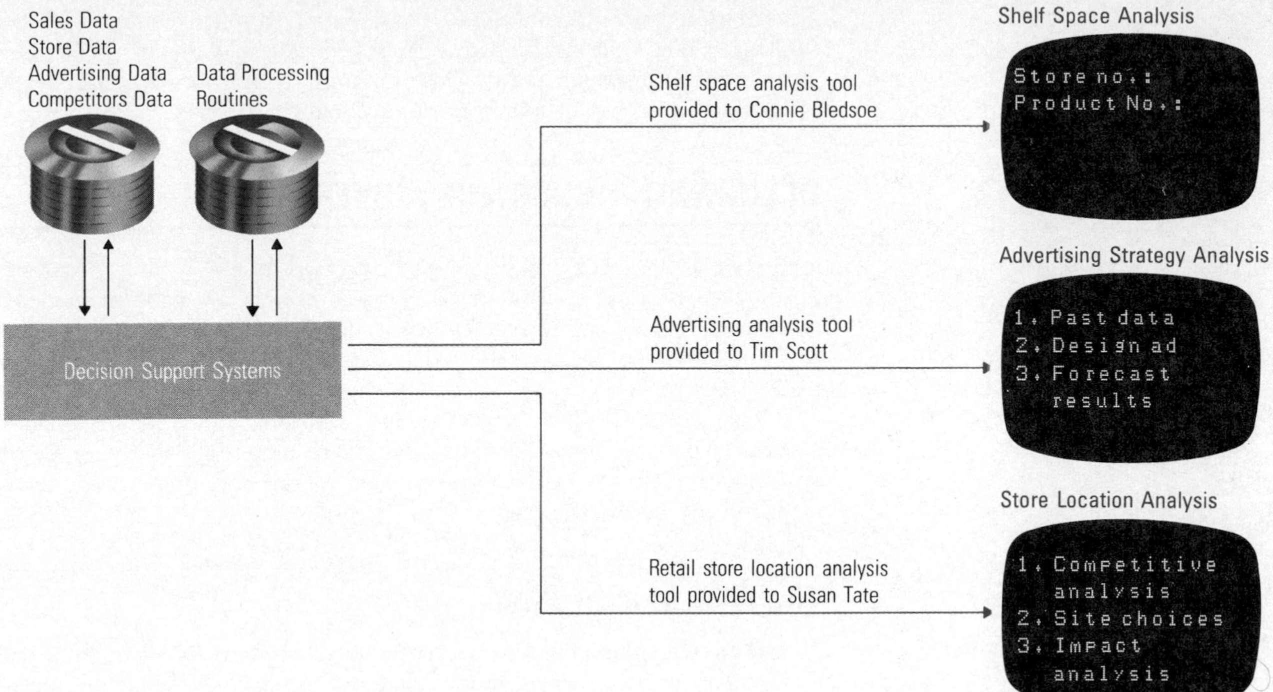

Exhibit 10.9

Managers at all levels at CompuStore can interact with a decision support system to produce ad hoc information outputs.

Decision Support Systems. Decision support systems allow managers to access and transform data on an *ad hoc* basis. The manager's information needs do not have to be specified in advance. Rather, the manager interacts with the decision support system to describe the data to be retrieved, the processing operations to be performed, and the output form.

With a decision support system, information can be provided for decisions that arise only occasionally or that have not previously arisen. Decision support systems are also used when a manager wishes to try out a number of decision alternatives, each of which might require changes in the data being retrieved, the processing operations performed, or the information released.

All CompuStore's managers could make use of decision support systems. Connie Bledsoe might wish to perform an analysis of product profit margins and sales floor shelf space to decide which products to place on display. Tim Scott might wish to analyze the relative effectiveness of different advertising strategies to decide how much to spend on radio, television, and newspaper ads. Susan Tate might wish to perform an analysis of sales trends for CompuStore and its major competitors to decide where to locate new retail outlets.

Exhibit 10.9 illustrates how sets of data base items are retrieved to produce the information outputs just described.

Decision support systems are powerful as well as flexible information systems. Few businesses today can afford to develop their own decision support software. However, software packages that can serve as **decision support**

system generators are available. A decision support system generator is used to develop a specific decision support system. The electronic spreadsheets introduced in Chapter 2 and described more fully in Chapter 15 are simple examples of a decision support system generator.

DESIGNING A BUSINESS'S OVERALL MIS

A business's MIS needs to serve all the firm's managers. For this to occur, the firm's data base must contain a broad range of data items. If information systems are developed on a piecemeal basis, such a data base will not exist. Data will tend to be haphazardly collected as specific requests for MIS support are made.

This piecemeal approach to MIS design can be avoided. Each information system being developed needs to be viewed in relation to all other information systems: those already in use, those currently under development, and those planned for future development.

The MIS Master Plan

An **MIS master plan** consists of descriptions of a business's current information systems as well as descriptions of and a development schedule for all future information systems. These descriptions should include the purpose and users of each information system, the data files being manipulated, linkages with other information systems, and the information system's current status. *Status* here refers to whether an information system is currently in use, being modified, under development, or planned for future development.

Putting together such a plan offers two major benefits. First, money can be saved. An MIS project proposed by one manager may be seen as similar to one already being used by another manager. Or the data needed for a new MIS project may be recognized as already available in the firm's data base. Taking full advantage of existing information systems provides many opportunities for lowering a business's total MIS costs. Second, ways to link information systems through the data being entered, stored, and released are much more apparent. By linking information systems, one can more easily coordinate business activities. When two information systems are developed in isolation, linking them later can be very difficult.

Exhibit 10.10 shows CompuStore's MIS plan as of March 31, 1984. It was soon after this plan had been distributed that Tim Scott first got his idea to generate information on the firm's customers. At first Tim was thinking only of questioning customers to see whether or not they had seen advertisements CompuStore was running. While looking over the MIS master plan, he noticed that a lot of point-of-sales information, such as date of sale, customer name, and items and quantity sold, was already being captured. Why not ask selected customers additional questions about their occupations, employers, salaries, and home addresses, he wondered. In return for filling out the questionnaire, a customer could qualify for a quarterly drawing for a software package. By combining the information obtained this way with that already being captured, CompuStore was able to establish a fairly detailed set of customer categories. Much of its market planning is now based on these categories.

An MIS master plan can thus serve a variety of purposes. It educates managers throughout a business about the information systems currently in use and those planned for future development. It stimulates managers to propose

Exhibit 10.10

CompuStore's MIS master plan sparked ideas for many MIS projects. By itemizing those information systems already being used as well as those planned for future use, managers throughout the business can be kept informed of the potential benefits of MIS.

1984	1985	1986
Accounting systems		Accounting (online)
Inventory (batch)	Inventory (online)	
Purchasing (batch)		Purchasing (online)
Billing (batch)		
Sales analysis (internal)	Sales analysis (internal and external)	
	Advertising reports	Advertising analysis

new MIS projects. It identifies those parts of a business that are and are not making use of computer technology. Finally, it can inform senior management of a firm's overall investment in computer technology.

The MIS Architecture

So far, our MIS discussions have focused on information outputs and on the importance of a firm's data base. It is easy to forget that other information processing activities, such as data entry and data processing, must also take place. It is also easy to overlook the fact that the location where these information processing activities take place can affect the ease with which managers access needed information, as well as the cost of these information systems. **MIS architecture** refers to where data entry, processing, storage and retrieval, and release actually occur.

MIS architectures normally take one of three forms: centralized, decentralized, and distributed. Exhibit 10.11 lists the main advantages of each.

Exhibit 10.11
Comparison of Centralized, Decentralized, and Distributed MIS Architectures

A centralized architecture is preferred when most of a business's activities are located at a central site. A decentralized architecture is best when a business's activities are located at multiple sites but generally do not require very tight control. A distributed architecture is best when a business's activities are located at multiple sites and require tight coordination.

MIS Architecture	Advantages
Centralized	specialized staff more sophisticated hardware and software hardware and software compatibility easier MIS integration
Decentralized	better able to meet "local" information needs of all managers better able to match hardware and software to actual business needs less sophisticated, easier to use hardware and software
Distributed	centralized advantages decentralized advantages improved manager access to all business information ability to share hardware and software

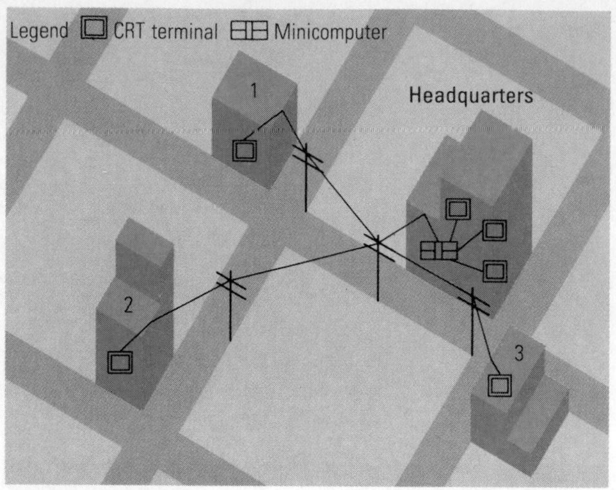

Exhibit 10.12

In 1982 CompuStore used a centralized MIS architecture. Note that all processing and storage occurs on the central computer system, but that some entry and release of data can occur via terminals located at the retail outlets.

Centralized Architecture. With a **centralized** architecture, all data processing and all data storage and retrieval are performed on a central computer system. Entry and release of data can occur either at the central facility or at other locations via terminals connected to the central computer system through communications lines.

In 1982 CompuStore's MIS architecture was centralized. At that time the firm consisted of three retail outlets and a headquarters building holding the central office, a warehouse, and a repair shop. A minicomputer located at the headquarters building was the firm's only computer system. Each retail store had a CRT that was linked through telephone lines to this central computer system. Exhibit 10.12 shows this arrangement.

A centralized MIS architecture offers a number of advantages over other forms (refer back to Exhibit 10.11). A firm can usually employ a more specialized computer staff and a more sophisticated hardware and software. With all hardware and software located at one site, it is less likely that hardware or software incompatibility problems will arise and more likely that MIS integration will occur.

There are two main drawbacks to a centralized MIS architecture. First, managers at remote locations may not feel that their information needs are being met very well. Some of this dissatisfaction might be due to delays in sending data inputs to the central site, in scheduling applications on a single computer system, and in sending information outputs to a firm's various business sites. Dissatisfaction might also arise because the centralized computer staff cannot be completely familiar with all business activities, especially those occurring at remote sites. Second, communications costs can become high when data and information flows over communications lines are heavy.

Decentralized Architecture. With a **decentralized** MIS architecture, multiple computer systems are located throughout a firm so that the information processing activities at each business location are handled "locally." These computer systems, however, are not connected.

By 1984 CompuStore had grown to include six retail outlets, a building containing the central warehouse and the repair shop, and a separate headquarters building. The firm's original minicomputer was still used at the central warehouse/repair shop site. The other seven business locations each had a terminal connected to the minicomputer and a microcomputer to handle some local information processing. The microcomputers were not connected to each other or to the minicomputer. Exhibit 10.13 shows this architecture.

A decentralized MIS architecture also offers a number of advantages (refer back to Exhibit 10.11). With computer systems located at each business location, the local information needs of all CompuStore's managers should be better met. Also, where these local needs do not require sophisticated computer support, less sophisticated computer systems can be used. Simpler computer systems tend to be easier to use and less expensive to operate.

A decentralized MIS architecture has one major drawback. Because these computer systems are not linked, they cannot electronically share the data each stores.

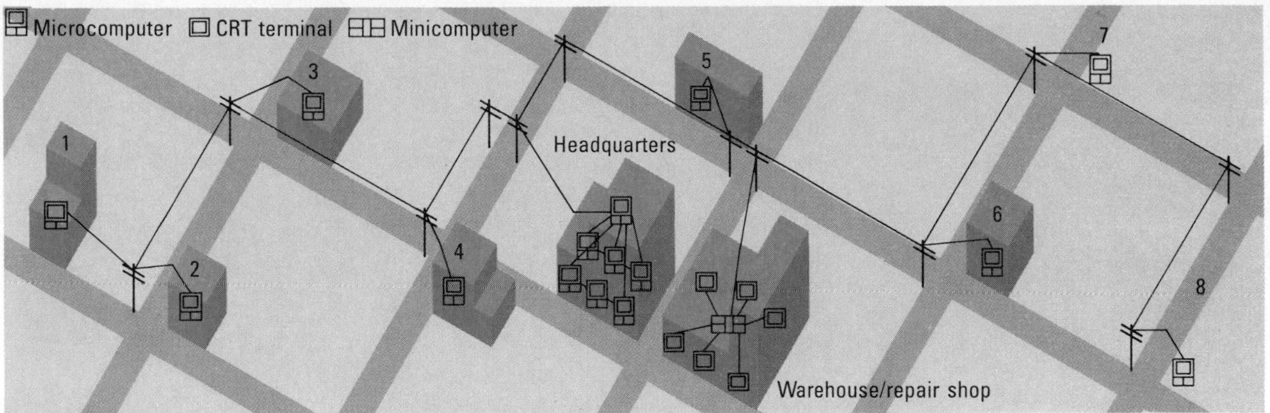

Exhibit 10.13

In 1984 CompuStore used a decentralized architecture. Note that information processing occurs at each business site but the various computer systems are not linked.

Distributed Architecture. With a **distributed** MIS architecture, multiple computer systems, connected in a computer network, are located throughout a firm. Local information processing is handled locally, and computer applications serving the entire business can be handled on central computer system. Most important, data stored on any one computer system can be electronically accessed by another computer system.

CompuStore today has eight retail locations along with the headquarters office and the warehouse/repair shop building. A new minicomputer is located at the warehouse/repair shop, microcomputers are used at each retail location, and seven microcomputers are used at the firm's headquarters. As the firm's computer systems are now linked, terminals are no longer used except at the warehouse/repair shop. Exhibit 10.14 shows this architecture.

Exhibit 10.14

Today CompuStore uses a distributed architecture. Note that all the firm's computer systems are linked so that each can access the data, peripheral devices, and software kept on the others.

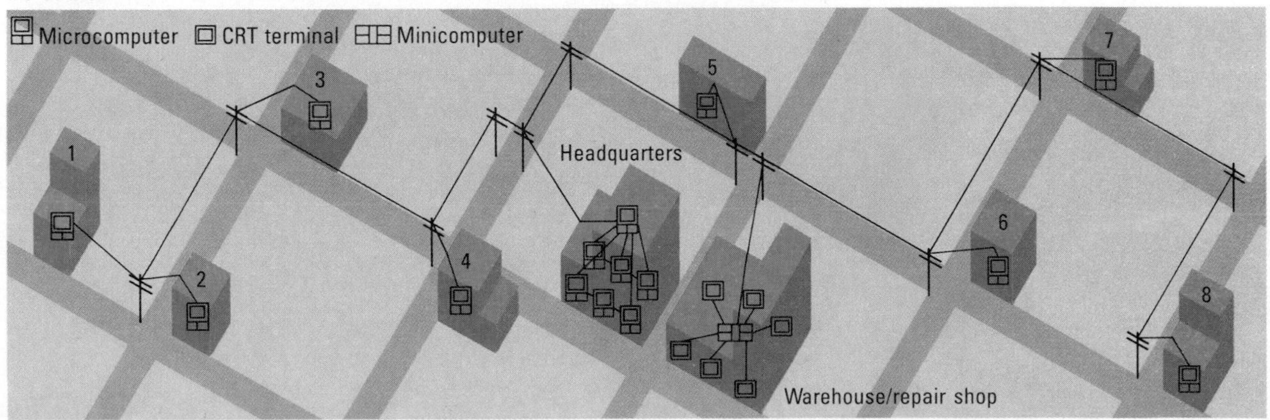

A distributed MIS architecture offers the advantages of both the centralized and decentralized architectures plus some additional advantages (refer back to Exhibit 10.11). Managers throughout the firm now have access to the data, peripheral devices, and software kept on any of a business's computer systems.

All these advantages of a distributed MIS architecture do have a cost. Developing and maintaining this MIS architecture requires a good deal of technical expertise, a lot of MIS planning and coordination, and the active involvement of all managers.

Professional Issue

Fitting Microcomputers into a Business's Overall MIS

Most people tend to think of the microcomputer only as a personal computer providing "personal support" tools. This is quite understandable. Exhibit 10.15, for example, shows that the most common microcomputer applications involve the personal computing software packages introduced in Chapter 2.

It is important to recognize that microcomputers are being used as important MIS tools in many businesses. With microcomputer hardware and software steadily improving, an increasing variety of business applications can be successfully placed on microcomputers. The MIS role of microcomputers, however, has tended to evolve differently in small and large businesses.

The MIS Role of Microcomputers in Small Businesses

Prior to the advent of the microcomputer, many businesses could not justify the expense of buying their own computer system. This was particularly true for small businesses. Data were processed manually or by a data processing service bureau.

The microcomputer's low cost now makes it practical for all businesses to acquire their own computer systems. Microcomputer use frequently evolves as follows:

1. The first applications placed on microcomputers are word processing and basic transaction processing systems, such as accounting, customer billing, and payroll.
2. As the amount of data stored on a microcomputer increases, it becomes possible to produce useful management reports. Sales analyses, inventory analyses, and budget planning are common applications. Personal computing by managers also begins.
3. As managers become experienced in their use of computers and as integrated data bases are built, more sophisticated information reporting systems and decision support systems are acquired or developed.
4. Finally, the microcomputers are electronically linked so that data, as well as other computer resources, can be shared by managers throughout the firm,

Computers at Work: "PCs in Napa Valley" describes microcomputer MIS use at Franciscan Vineyards, a small Napa Valley winemaker (see pages 276–77).

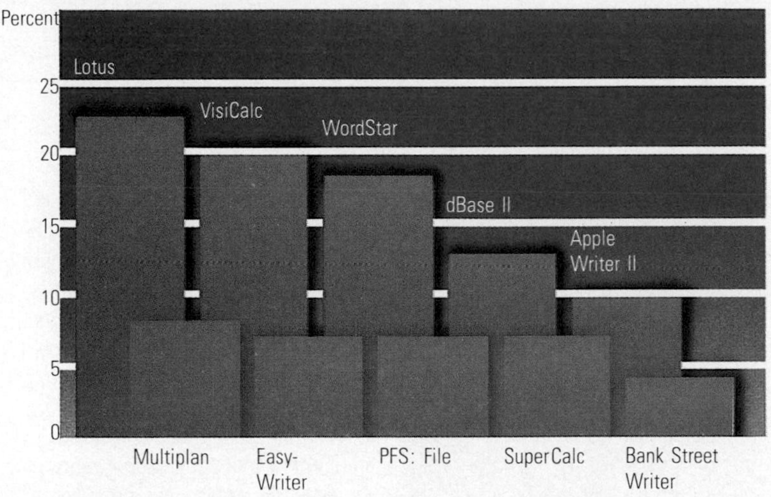

Exhibit 10.15
Software Packages Used
The most popular software for personal computers is Lotus 1–2–3, an integrated package with a usage rate of about 23 percent. The original spreadsheet package, VisiCalc, runs a close second. This survey found word processing and spreadsheet packages to be the applications chosen most often.

The MIS Role of Microcomputers in Large Businesses

Most large businesses are experienced users of minicomputers and maxicomputers prior to their first use of a microcomputer. However, these firms' managers may not be experienced computer users. Too often, few managers outside of the computer department are actually involved with MIS design.

One pleasant side effect of the installation of microcomputers in large businesses is that the ease of use of microcomputers motivates managers to experiment with computer use and to become more involved with MIS design. Microcomputer use typically evolves in a large business as follows:

1. The firm's basic transaction processing systems, many information reporting systems, and some decision support systems are already available on minicomputers and maxicomputers.
2. The first use of microcomputers usually occurs when managers outside the computer staff become aware of the advantages of personal computing. Most often this involves relatively simple decision support system applications using spreadsheet, graphics, and file management packages. Normally all data entry is performed by the manager using the microcomputer.
3. A common complaint soon raised involves the need to key data into the microcomputer, particularly when the data being entered come from a computer printout. The second phase of microcomputer MIS usage in larger organizations overcomes this data entry complaint. Three actions can be taken:
   a. Stand-alone microcomputers can be linked in a local area network so data, peripheral devices, and software can be shared.
   b. Communication links can be set up between the microcomputers and the larger computer systems so data can be downloaded and uploaded. **Downloading** data refers to retrieving some data from the data base maintained on a large computer system and sending it to a microcomputer for local storage and further analysis. **Uploading** data refers to sending data that have been captured and initially processed on a microcomputer to a data base maintained on a larger computer system.

PCs in Napa Valley

We walked the cool cement between the great aluminum tanks that rose above us like Greek columns. The rich and hearty smell of wine was everywhere. Outside, trucks filled with grapes waited in the heat. On the catwalk, 30 feet above, the winemaker was taking the temperature of the wine in the tanks—a doctor with a hospital full of patients.

"We trace the wine from the day it's crushed all the way to bottling," said Ken Robinson, Franciscan Vineyard's winemaker, still breathing heavily from his exertion as he directed me to the lab, where an IBM XT sat incongrously among countless vials and chemical contraptions.

After a couple of days, when the last grapes are delivered and crushed and he has had a chance to catch up on his sleep, Robinson sits down in front of the XT and begins the history of the 1984 vintage.

The Napa Valley wine region is blessed with a variety of good soils. Mountains protect the region, insuring hot days and few untimely storms. The nearby Pacific bays bring cool nights, lengthening the time for wine growing and developing. And though the famed wine regions of France may produce more truly great wines, even those vintners admit that they cannot match the consistently good wines produced in the Napa Valley.

The Napa winemakers are not content with their natural advantages, however. Only 85 miles from the Silicon Valley, Napa wineries are making computer technology part of the art, science and business of winemaking.

Two years ago, Franciscan Vineyards didn't have a single computer. Now, the firm has an XT, a PC equipped with a hard disk and a Compaq Plus portable that the president of the company brings home. Like many medium-sized wineries in the Napa Valley, Franciscan is using the PC to help document and direct the exacting process of winemaking. The PC is also aiding in more general business tasks such as accounting, inventory and budgeting.

Beth Hernandez is Franciscan's traffic manager. It's her job to keep track of the wine once it's produced. She does orders and invoicing on the hard-disk PC, using the Data Consulting Associates *Winery Information Management System.* "It's geared to the people who use it. It's challenging," she said. Hernandez likes numbers and enjoys the fact that when you "put the right 2s in you get 4."

Hernandez also does the inventory for the Wine Service Coop and the winery, and produces distributor reports and sales reports by variety. The pro-

gram is especially helpful with the state 703 report. The state requires a monthly report showing what wine has moved from one bonded (government-certified) cellar to another. But once wine is moved from a bonded cellar—for instance, when wine is shipped to a distributor—tax must be paid. The reports show these transfers and when the taxes are due.

Romantic as a vineyard may seem, it is still a business. As Franciscan's president and winemaker, it is Thomas Ferrell's job to make it a profitable one.

In search of a black bottom line, Ferrell created a spreadsheet using *Multiplan* and copied it for each of the vineyard's cost centers. He used it as a budget for the last four years and the future. The spreadsheet helped him to calculate the cost of goods sold; the number of cases and the cost of producing them. Using *Multiplan's* capability for merging the data from separate spreadsheets, the data from the separate cost centers could be folded into the balance and income statement. Then he could check the potential results of a change in a particular cost center. "It helps with priorities," said Ferrell.

Another *Multiplan* spreadsheet he created takes the crop estimate at a given time of the year and projects how many gallons the grapes would produce and how much space they would need. "We have 430 acres, and each vineyard has five or six varieties—that makes for 20 blocks, each one with different soil and grape variety. For each one we get a crop estimate." Each time the estimate changes, the program can recalculate the yield virtually simultaneously, Ferrell said. That way, employees know ahead of time whether they may have to sell grapes, juggle harvest dates, or in some way accommodate the yield.

Multiplan also helps Ferrell plan for the future. "Many wines are sold five years after they're harvested. If you plan on growth, you have to make more now for the future. But as your sales plan changes, you have to achieve a balance between inventory and production. You can't make too much wine or allow your inventory to grow too old."

Multiplan may be useful, but the ultimate program, said Ferrell, will be an expert system—a program that helps solve some of the problems of winemaking, such as, "How do you take quality aspects of winemaking, balance them with production and optimize?" Ferrell explained. "During harvest time, it's a question of juggling. You're moving wine from one tank to another, trying to optimize quality but you're always compromising." Most of the decisions are simple logic, he said, but they are so intertwined that you often don't see the consequences of a decision until it's too late.

Source: J. Littman, "PCs in Napa Valley," *PC Week,* 13 November, 1984, pp. 115–18.

c. Computer links can be set up between the microcomputers and **external data services** so that managers can gain access to the libraries of data provided by these data services. Exhibit 10.16 lists some popular external data services.

4. The final phase of microcomputer MIS usage in large organizations finds certain business applications being moved from larger computer systems to microcomputers. These applications tend to be relatively simple, such as billing and purchasing, and localized, which means they involve business

Exhibit 10.16
Ten Useful Data Bases for Executives

Name	Producer
ABI/INFORM **Content:** Citations, with abstracts, of worldwide literature in business professions **Uses:** Professional and management development in subjects from accounting to telecommunications; business environment **Sources:** Over 550 publications, primarily professional, e.g., *Harvard Business Review* **Updating:** Monthly	**Data Courier Inc.** 620 South Fifth Street, Louisville, Ky. 40202 (502) 582-4111, (800) 626-2823 **Distributors:** Bank Administration Institute, BRS, DATA-STAR, Dialog Information Services, ESA-IRS, ITT Dialcom, SDS Information Services
COMPENDEX **Content:** Citations, with abstracts, of worldwide literature in engineering and technology **Uses:** Product and production research, development, and design in subjects from aerospace to waterworks, including related subjects from construction materials to thermodynamics **Sources:** Approximately 2,000 professional journals plus miscellaneous publications of engineering societies and conferences **Updating:** Monthly	**Engineering Information Inc.** 345 E. 47th Street, New York, N.Y. 10017 (212) 705-7615, (800) 221-1044 **Distributors:** CEDOCAR, ESA-IRS, INKA Karlsruhe, Pergamon-Info-Line, SDS Information Services, Tsukuba University
COMPUSTAT **Content:** Company financial statistics 6,000 publicly held U.S. and some foreign corporations **Uses:** Investment management; mergers and acquisitions; corporate finance **Sources:** Company financial reports **Updating:** Weekly	**Standard & Poor's Compustat Services Inc.** 7400 St. Alton Court, Englewood, Colo. 80112 (303) 771-6510, (800) 525-8640 **Distibutors:** ADP Network Services, Boeing Computer Services, Chase Econometrics/Interactive Data, CitiShare, CompuServe, Data Resources, FactSet Data Systems, Management Decision Systems, Warner Computer Systems
DISCLOSURE II **Content:** Company financial statistics and edited text of company financial reports of 9,000 publicly held corporations **Uses:** Investment management; mergers and acquisitions; corporate finance; marketing **Sources:** Official company filings with Securities and Exchange Commission **Updating:** Weekly	**Disclosure** 5161 River Road, Bethesda, Md. 20816 (301) 951-1300, (800) 638-8076 **Distributors:** ADP Network Services, Bank Administration Institute, CompuServe Executive Information Service, Control Data Corporation/Business Information Services, Dialog, Dow Jones & Co., I. P. Sharp, Quotron Systems, Warner Computer Systems
DOW JONES NEWS **Content:** Edited business, economic, and political articles **Uses:** Investment management, mergers and acquisitions, corporate finance; marketing; public relations; news and issues management; business environment **Sources:** Most recent 90 days of Dow Jones News Wire ("broad tape"), *The Wall Street Journal, Barron's* **Updating:** Continuously, throughout the day	**Dow Jones & Co. Inc.** P.O. Box 300, Princeton, N.J. 08540 (609) 452-2000, (800) 257-5114 **Distributors:** Dow Jones & Co., ADP Financial Information Services, Bunker Ramo, Quotron Systems

Source: "Ten Useful Data Bases for Executives" from "OnLine Data Bases: The Facts You Want Are at Your Fingertips," *Management Technology,* November 1984, pp. 63–64.

activities located at the business site where the microcomputer is located. Data maintained in these "local" information systems are then electronically linked to other information systems that fit into the firm's overall MIS. The microcomputer thus serves as a local processing node in a distributed network.

On the following page Computers at Work: "PCs Are Woven into Company Plan" describes microcomputer MIS use at Levi Strauss & Company.

Name	Producer
NEXIS **Content:** Full text of current and past political, social, economic, business, and cultural news articles **Uses:** Marketing; public relations; advertising; investment management; mergers and acquisitions; corporate finance **Sources:** Over 60 wire services, newspapers, magazines, and newsletters, e.g., AP, *The New York Times, Business Week* **Updating:** Varies—within 12-48 hours for wire services, 24 hours for newspapers, one week for weeklies, three weeks for monthlies	**Mead Data Central** P.O. Box 933, Dayton, Ohio 45401 (800) 227-4908 **Distributor:** Mead Data Central
PTS PROMT **Content:** Citations, with abstracts, of worldwide literature in business and economic news **Uses:** Marketing; research and development; mergers and acquisitions; corporate finance; investment management **Sources:** Over 1,500 worldwide general news, business, and technical publications **Updating:** Weekly	**Predicasts Inc.** 11001 Cedar Avenue, Cleveland, Ohio 44106 (216) 795-3000, (800) 321-6388 **Distributors:** ADP Network Services, BRS, DATA-STAR, Dialog, VU/Text
THE REUTER MONITOR **Content:** Commodity, foreign exchange, and securities market statistics; edited text of current business, economic, and political news stories **Uses:** Commodity, foreign exchange, and securities trading; investment management; news management **Sources:** Most recent 24 hours of Reuters News Service **Updating:** Continuously on a daily basis	**Reuters Ltd.** 2 Wall Street, New York, N.Y. 10005 (212) 732-7800 **Distributor:** Reuters Ltd.
U.S. CENTRAL DATA BANK **Content:** Over 33,000 financial, economic, and demographic time series on the U.S. in the aggregate **Uses:** Macroeconomic forecasting and analysis; corporate financial forecasting and planning; marketing; investment management **Sources:** Government and private sources, e.g., Bureau of Economic Analysis, Census Bureau, Federal Reserve Board **Updating:** Varies by series	**Data Resources Inc. (DRI)** Data Products Division Headquarters 1750 K Street, N.W., Suite 1060 Washington, D.C. 20006 (202) 862-3760 **Distributor:** Data Resources
VALUE LINE DATA BASE II **Content:** Company and market financial statistics, earnings projections, accounting practices, and related statistical measures for approximately 1,700 publicly held U.S. corporations **Uses:** Investment management; mergers and acquisitions; corporate finance **Sources:** Financial reports and *Value Line Investment Survey* **Updating:** Varies by distributor	**Value Line Inc.** 711 Third Avenue, New York, N.Y. 10017 (212) 687-3965 **Distributors:** ADP Network Services, Chase Econometrics/Interactive Data, CompuServe, Data Resources, General Electric Information Services, Shaw Data Services, SLIGOS

PCs Are Woven into Company Plan

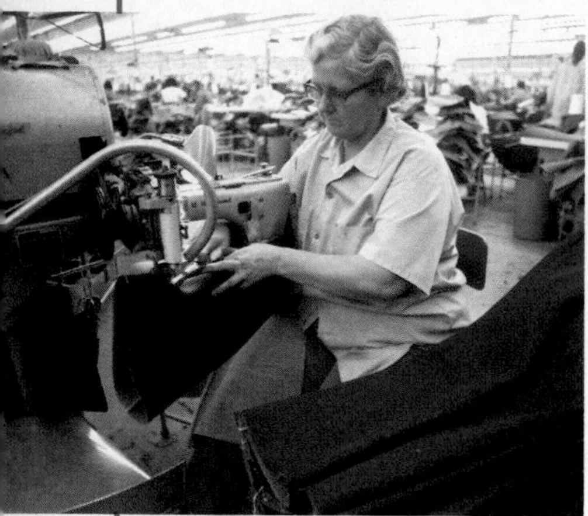

When a Bavarian-born dry goods peddler named Levi Strauss began selling canvas overalls to California's Gold Rush miners in 1850, the durable canvas pants were an immediate hit. Regular pants of the day kept wearing out from the rigors of the mining life, but Levi's tough overalls, made from his excess tent canvas, passed the test.

The miners weren't wearing blue jeans, though; they were wearing mostly brown jeans. It wasn't until the 1870s that Strauss dropped canvas and completed the switch to a rugged cotton fabric produced in Nîmes, France, called "serge de Nîmes." The name was shortened to denim in this country.

There was a problem of inconsistent color, at least in Levi's mind. In what must be one of the most farsighted business decisions in American history, Strauss figured he would dye all his denim indigo blue.

Today, selling jeans of all colors and a host of other clothing lines, Levi Strauss and Co. is the largest apparel maker in the Western world and possibly the entire world; company officials aren't sure about the clothing industry in the Soviet bloc. Still run by Levi's descendants, the company sells its products in more than 150 countries. Worldwide sales for 1983 exceeded $2.7 billion, with a work force of more than 45,000 employees.

But jeans aren't the only Blue at Levi Strauss. Since the company first began investing in IBM PCs, it has installed about 250 PC systems in its corporate offices and 120 more among the field sales force and distribution centers.

Applications for PCs have spread quickly through the company's new headquarters "campus" that was built near San Francisco's waterfront. Users range from secretarial support people right up to the president of the corporation. Division heads at Levi Strauss all have PCs, and there's an Executive Bulletin Board service so they can exchange information.

The role of the PC in productivity gains becomes even more important to the company over the next year or so as Levi Strauss and its competitors try to adjust to a flat jeans market that caused a significant drop in sales in 1984.

The first personal computers were brought into the company about 1981, recalled James Wilson, manager of microcomputer support in the firm's Information Resource Department. Those first machines were Apples, brought in by individual employees who had some computing experience or who just felt adventurous about computerizing some of their work.

About 1982, Levi Strauss made a corporate decision to standardize on IBM. The early Apple applications were converted to the company's new standard system—a PC XT with 256K bytes of main memory, one floppy disk and a 10-megabyte hard disk.

Initially, the PCs were used to perform many of the standard business tasks, such as word processing, spreadsheet and data base applications and communications with the mainframe.

Wilson said, however, that many individual employees have come up with more ideas for unique applications geared to the needs of their particular jobs.

PCs are also in place at the firm's six distribution centers, extending PC value to the field sales force and even to their customers, the retail shops that sell Levis.

Perhaps the most ambitious of these applications is the Retail Inventory Management System, or RIMS, developed in house. The program enables the company to provide, free of charge, a sophisticated inventory-management service to its retail customers. "We're proud of it," Wilson said. "We think it's a value-added service for our customers. Significantly, size is included in the system. We sell products at the size level. If a store doesn't have the proper sizes, and they're not keeping track of that, it can be a critical factor."

Before RIMS, a retailer had to keep that kind of inventory manually or on his own computer, if he had one; Levi Strauss couldn't do the job for him. The RIMS service makes things much easier for the retailers while costing them nothing.

Source: J. Greitzer, "PCs Are Woven into Company Plan," *PC Week,* 2 October, 1984, pp. 25–28.

A SYSTEMS APPROACH TO MIS DESIGN

MIS design requires a wide range of information. Business objectives, activities, opportunities, and problems must be known. The availability and possibilities of different computer technologies must be determined. The readiness of a firm's employees to accept and use computer technology must be assessed. This information is then combined to determine which information systems should be built, how they should be designed and developed, and how they can fit together into an overall MIS design.

Rarely does one person in a business have a firm grasp of all this information. Thus, a **project team** is usually formed when an MIS design and development effort is undertaken. Normally this team is composed of managers, information system users, and computer specialists.

The first thing that a project team needs to do is arrive at an overall understanding of what the different parts of the business do and how they act in a coordinated fashion to achieve the business's goals. This is a much more difficult task than it might initially seem. Consider the following three points:

1. Most managers have a good understanding of what their departments do but a much poorer understanding of what other departments do. Few managers in a business really understand how the entire firm operates.
2. While most managers understand how their own departments operate, they often have trouble explaining this to others.
3. People in different departments of a business often use terms that people in other departments may not understand. This "jargon" barrier can be quite difficult to overcome.

A technique that often solves these problems is to build a **systems model** of the business. A model is an alternative way of looking at some object such that the important relationships among the object's components can be more easily observed and understood. A business, even a small business, can be quite complex. Building a systems model of a business should accomplish two things. First, a simplified view of the business is achieved. Project team members should thus find it easier to develop an overall understanding of the business's basic activities. Second, this simplified view becomes a common frame of reference for all project team members. Communication among project team members should thus improve.

Systems Modeling Concepts

In its simplest form, a systems model is composed of **inputs, outputs,** and **processors.** Inputs are transformed by the processors into outputs, as shown in Exhibit 10.17A on page 282. Some examples of this include:

Workers and machinery in an automobile manufacturer transforming raw materials and parts into completed cars (Exhibit 10.17B),

Doctors, nurses, and equipment in a hospital transforming sick people into healthy people (Exhibit 10.17C),

Sales personnel and product displays in a retail store transforming customers with some desire for a product into customers who have purchased that product (Exhibit 10.17D).

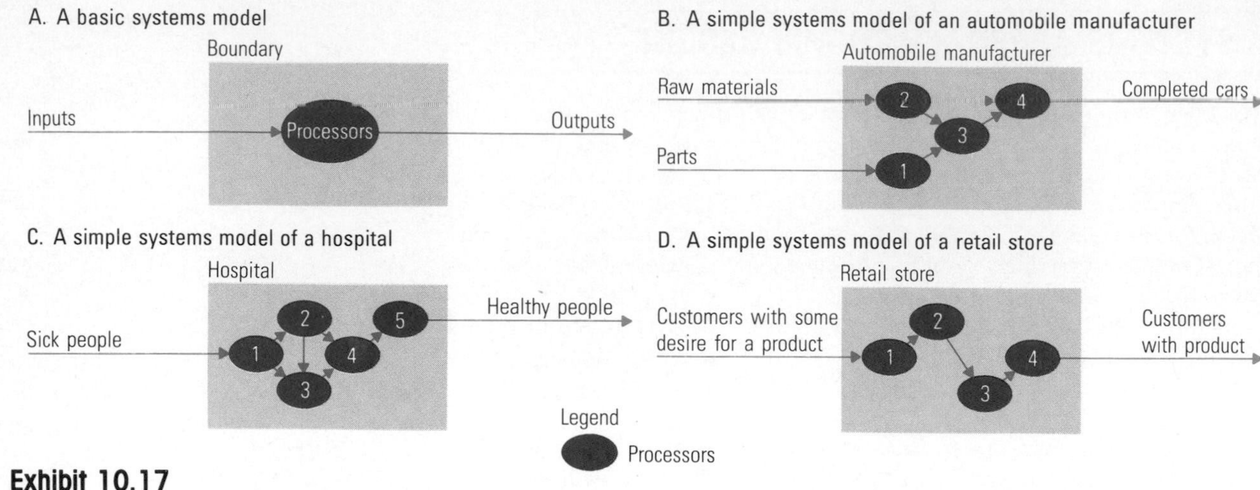

Exhibit 10.17

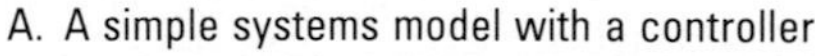

Note that the object being modeled consists only of the processors. Inputs come from the **environment** that surrounds the object and outputs are sent into this environment. A **boundary** separates the object from its environment. System boundaries are important because the events that occur at boundaries tend to be very important.

Processors that direct or coordinate other processors are called **controllers** (Exhibit 10.18A). Controllers collect **feedback** information about the processor activities they are controlling. When systems models of businesses are built, managers are the controllers. Exhibit 10.18B illustrates this using the systems model of an automobile manufacturer.

Exhibit 10.18

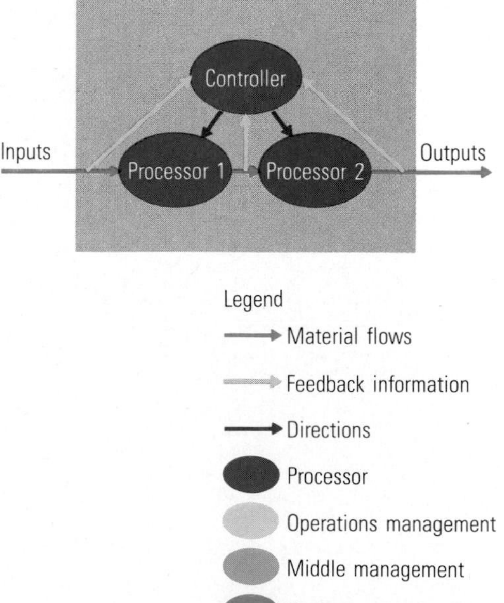

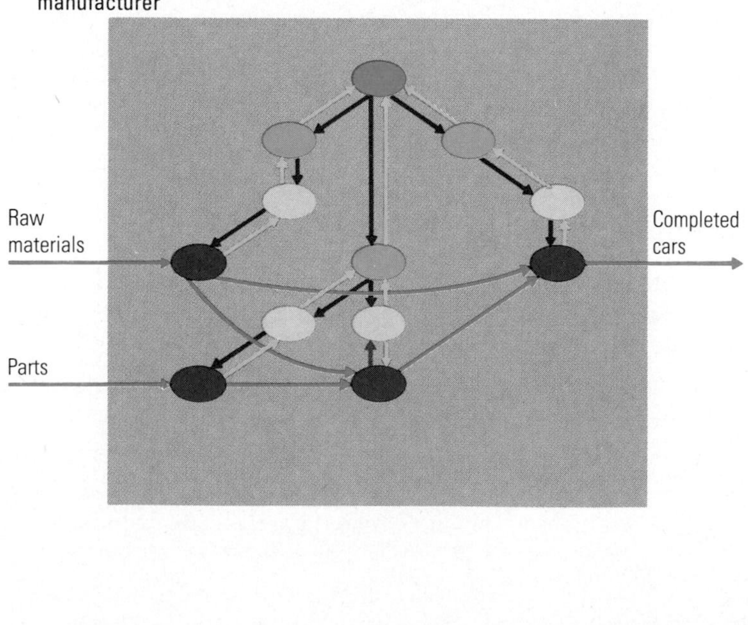

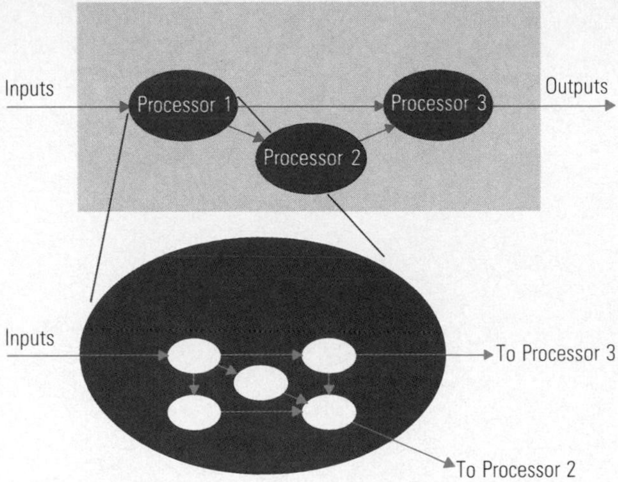

Exhibit 10.19

Each part of a systems model can itself be modeled as a system. This limited but more detailed view of the object being modeled is termed a *subsystem.*

A key idea in systems modeling is that of a **subsystem.** Any part of a system can itself be modeled as a system, or, more accurately, as a subsystem. Thus, it is possible to develop both an overall view of the object being modeled and detailed views of each of the object's important parts. This concept of a subsystem is illustrated in Exhibit 10.19.

A Systems Model of CompuStore

When a systems model of a business is built as part of an MIS project, the objective is to better understand the business's information processing activities. If a systems model's processors represent business activities rather than people or equipment, this improved understanding is more likely to occur.

CompuStore can be viewed as consisting of four main processors: a marketing activity, a warehousing activity, a sales activity, and an accounting activity. On page 284 Exhibit 10.20 illustrates a systems model of CompuStore. Notice that specific inputs and outputs are labeled on the flow lines that connect the various parts of the systems model. These represent flows of both materials and data. By modeling some of CompuStore's subsystems, one can obtain an even better understanding of the firm.

The marketing activity is comprised of three departments: market research, merchandising, and advertising. Market research collects information about customer needs and microcomputer technical trends. This information is used by the merchandising department along with sales and service data to decide which products should be offered to customers. The advertising department uses the sales plan developed by merchandising to promote the company's products to potential customers. Exhibit 10.21 models this subsystem on the following page.

The sales activity takes place at the retail outlets. Three main operations take place at each store: customer sales, store inventory, and store accounting. *Customer sales* involves the direct customer contact that produces sales. *Store inventory* refers to maintaining appropriate product stock levels at the retail outlet. *Store accounting* tracks the store's sales and expense data. Exhibit 10.22 models this subsystem on page 285.

Exhibit 10.20

An overall systems model of CompuStore

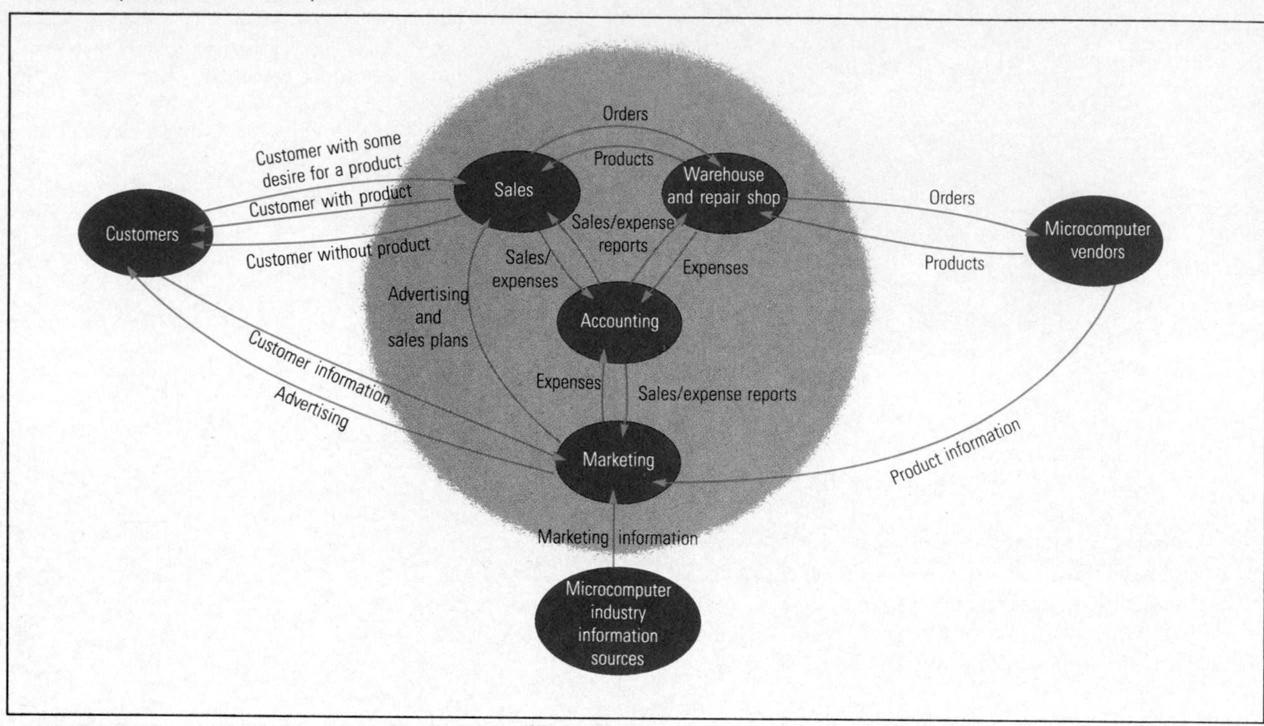

Exhibit 10.21

A systems model of CompuStore's marketing subsystem

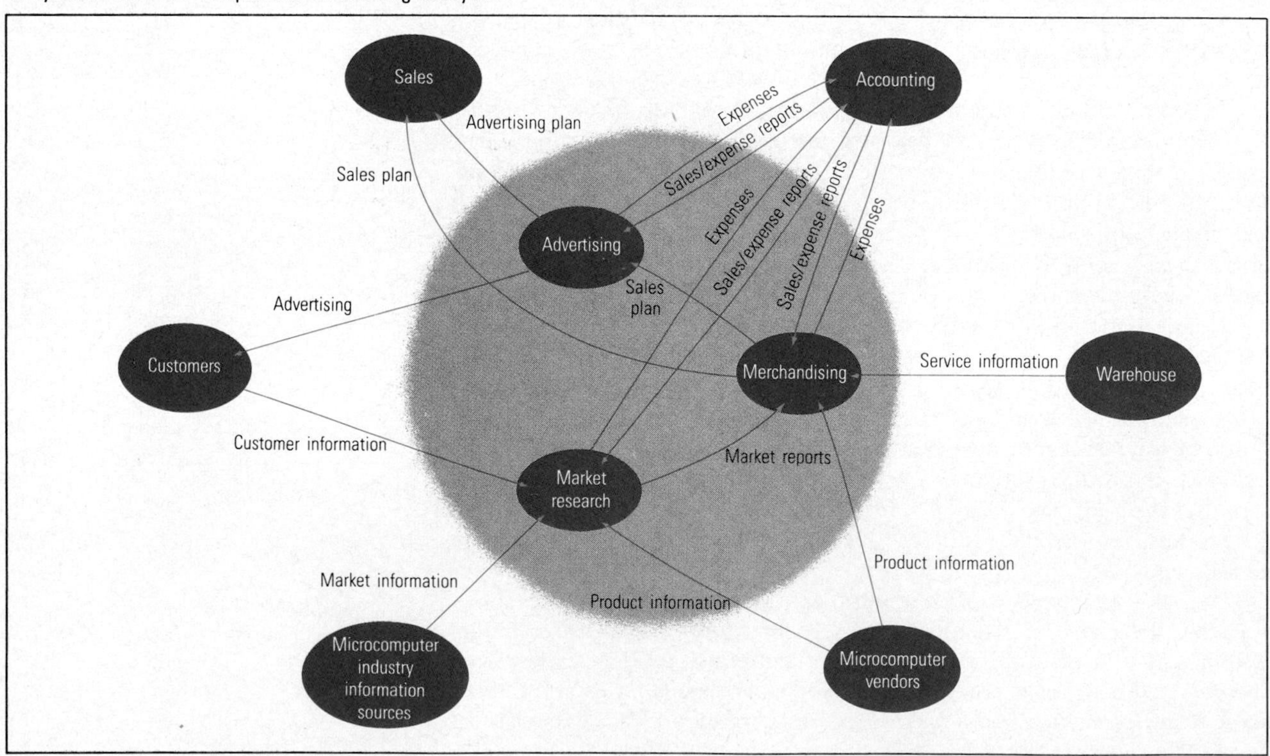

Exhibit 10.22

A systems model of CompuStore's sales subsystem

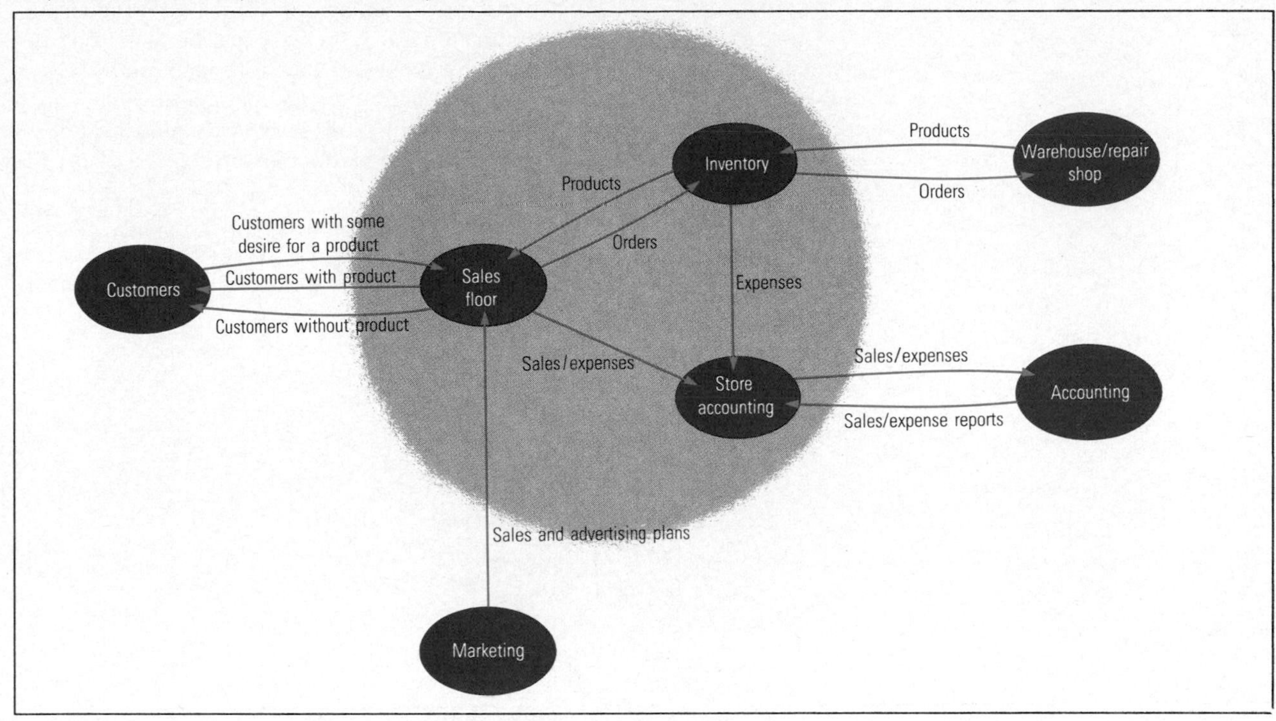

Exhibit 10.23

Adding a manager to the systems model of CompuStore's sales subsystem should result in some understanding of the store manager's information needs.

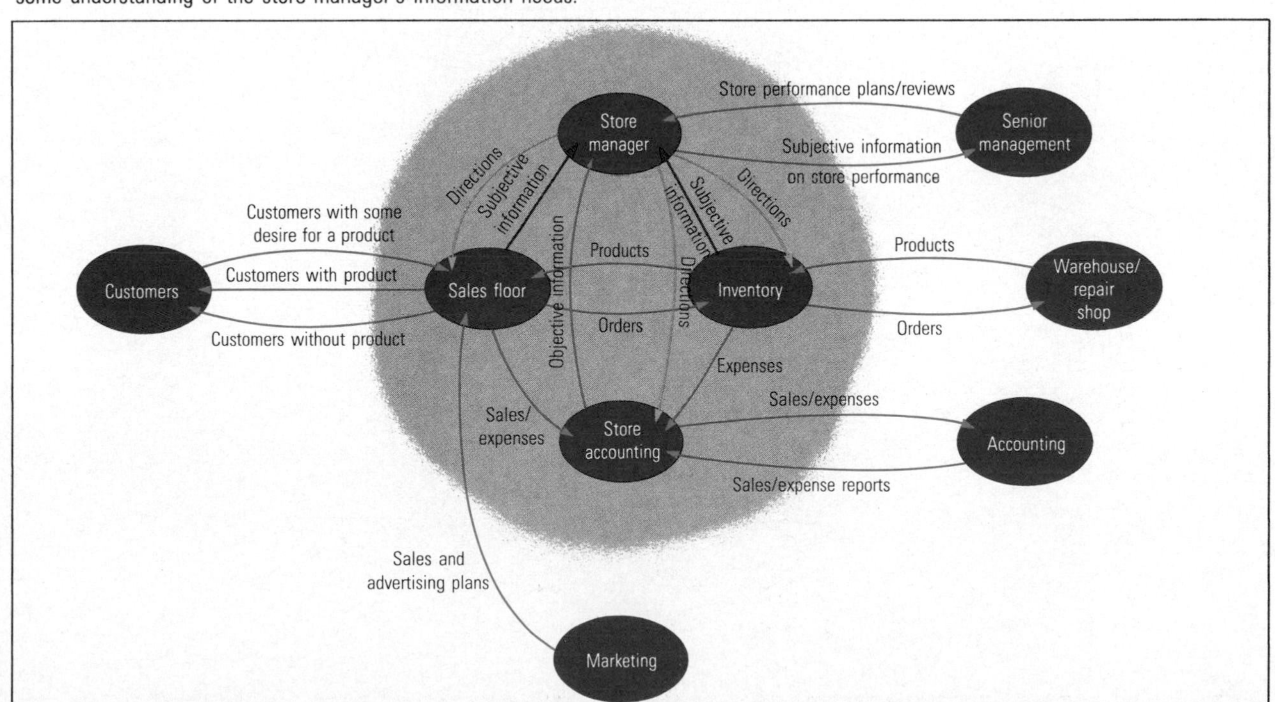

By adding a store manager, such as Susan Bledsoe, to the model of the sales subsystem, one can achieve an even better understanding of the firm's sales activities (see Exhibit 10.23 on the preceding page.) The lines to and from the store manager represent information flows, such as plans, budgets, reports, directions, and employee evaluations. Note that the store manager receives subjective information directly from the sales floor and the store inventory and objective information from store accounting. **Subjective information** refers to impressions and opinions, while **objective information** refers to data of a more quantitative nature.

A systems model of a business should produce a fairly comprehensive **information processing model** of the business. Data flows to and from a business's various activities are shown as well as information flows to and from its managers.

Innkeeper Picks PCS

By Mike Major

Ramada, with a gross income of about $1 billion, has 97,000 rooms in more than 600 inns and hotels. This makes it the world's third largest hotel company, and it also has the distinction of being the first company to use IBM PCs as reservation terminals.

"I believe that we're the leading users of PCs in the hotel industry," says Fred Miller, vice-president of reservations for Ramada Inns, Inc. "And our plans for the future are geared to both continuing and expanding that leadership."

Though Ramada is finding multiple uses for its more than 600 personal computers, Miller says, "The primary function of the units is booking reservations. Giving our hotel operators automated front offices is our highest priority."

PC involvement begins when a customer calls for a reservation via an 800 number. All relevant information, including name, address, credit card guarantee, price quote, and special requests such as a king-size bed, are recorded in an IBM mainframe computer in Phoenix. Information is stored under a confirmation room number and transferred to the hotel involved. Here it is printed out on the personal computer. "The data are stored in the mainframe in case the hotel misplaces the order," says Miller. "And now we're enhancing the process so that the hotel will print out the information on the reservation form, which means that all the guest has to do when he arrives is sign it."

The process is even simpler for travel agents and Ramada Pacesetter (frequent business traveler club) members. Pertinent information is filed on the computer so when clients call in, all the front desk has to do is ask for the Ramada Business Card or Pacesetter number. Automation does the rest.

Personal computers are linked not only with the main IBM 4341 computer in Phoenix, but also with those in the other reservation centers in Omaha, Toronto, London, and Frankfurt. Room availability inquiries, reservations, confirmations, cancellations, and updates can be made instantaneously anywhere throughout the system. Each computer is programmed with general information listings for every hotel in the Ramada system so front-desk personnel can quickly answer guests' questions about Ramada properties worldwide.

Two technical features allow the Ramada system to approximate the efficiency of a dedicated, multiuser system. According to Nick Bredimus, vice-president of the information services division, "We have a very effective communication protocol and use a communication concentrator at the front of our IBM 4341. This allows us a very rapid response time to dial-up terminals. Our dial-up network is unique in that it functions like a dedicated network, and this, of course, results in a substantial savings."

Bredimus says they've built a capability in the computer that allows it to be used for functions other than reservations, though it is available for the latter 100 percent of the time. "The operator can be working diligently from the supply catalog, but if a reservation comes in, the screen is frozen and the reservation transmitted. So, though the units are not multi-user, they are, in effect, multitasking."

Prior to the installation of the IBM PCs, Bredimus says, "Ramada worked with a homegrown system that we developed over 10 years ago. It wasn't appropriate for the eighties.

"We changed our main reservation system in December 1982. Our IBM-based system uses the airline control program operating system used by most major airlines and travel companies. Then we followed up with a replacement of all the terminals. It just happened that at the time we were looking for a replacement terminal, IBM announced its PC."

Ramada did not choose IBM automatically, however. An extensive evaluation took place that narrowed down top choices to Digital Equipment Corp., Texas Instruments, and IBM. "Fortunately for us, IBM, which we favored from the service standpoint, also had the best price." says Miller.

Ramada's reservations/communications program is unique, as is its labor forecasting program that projects the personnel requirements in restaurants, lounges, and other areas. Some of its other software is semi-custom written for the hotel industry. But many of the packages use standard Lotus 1-2-3 and similarly available business software.

Though the reservation terminal concept is the heart of the Ramada's PC system, there are already another 50 PCs installed for other purposes. One hundred machines are on order.

But the most sophisticated computerization in the world won't fulfill its promise if the people using it feel intimidated and are unable to use it properly. This is a potential problem that Ramada has anticipated. Bredimus says, "We put a tutorial system right into the software because it was designed for people who have no prior experience with computers. The software actually shows them what every key on the keyboard does."

BUILT-IN TUTORIAL TRAINS STAFF

Bredimus maintains that the tutorial, which novices can complete in two hours time, is "user friendly and foolproof." The PC leads the clerk through each step from the arrival of the guest to departure, prompting—in English—what is to be done next. For example, it tells the clerk to ask the guest's name (while a screen example demonstrates that it is to be entered as last name/first initial), as well as remind the clerk to thank the guest and ask if he/she needs any more reservations.

"We've worked hard to make our computerization smart," says Ramada's Miller. "A key area in this regard is that of security checks." When a new Ramada is built, the operator receives the PC in a carton. Once it's set up, the operator calls a control center that sends over the communications line the personalized information relevant to that hotel location, along with a security code. "Someone with an IBM at home couldn't get into our reservations data bank," says Miller. "Our software wouldn't accept the dial-in."

"We've worked hard to make our computerization smart."

Security codes are changed periodically. And every time the operator takes the computer off the reservations line to run another program, when he or she dials the central computer again, a clearance check is made before the operator can get back on line.

The smart computer not only takes charge of its own security, but also monitors its mistakes. A new release of software keeps track of failures, such as a communication error or printer problem. The statistics are kept within the PC, which can be queried by the main computer. "The property doesn't even know it's there," says Miller. "The smart computer does it itself."

Another ability the smart computer will provide in the near future is electronic mail. "All of the information a hotel needs to send to or receive from corporate headquarters or other units can be handled automatically," says Miller. "There will be a significant savings of postage and handling. The operator won't have to question the computer for news. He'll simply look at the screen at a particular time of day and the mail will be there."

A new program completed, but not yet installed, will soon provide automatic ordering of the wide variety of supplies needed to keep a hotel running efficiently. Already in place is the daily collecting of statistics regarding room occupancy. This makes it possible to better project labor needs. The more this program is run, the better the company will be able to forecast labor needs during busy or slack seasons.

PROMOTING WITH PCs

PCs also give a boost to promotional activities. At any time of day, individual properties can download promotional information to the mainframe regarding property improvements, lounge attractions, or community events. These updates are immediately available to all Ramada reservation offices worldwide.

The mailing list interfaces with word processing to send personalized mailings or tie-ins with golf tournaments or other events to travel agencies, corporate accounts, or individual guests.

The more timely tabulation of trends in room occupancy "allows us to react quicker with needed advertising," Miller says. "Also, the PCs give us valuable feedback on the effectiveness of local advertising."

Another service PCs will provide Ramada concerns the merchandising of rooms. "Such a system," Miller says, "would allow an operator to perform a sales trace over a period of time. Eventually benchmarks would present themselves."

These benchmarks would alert the operator when a certain business segment wasn't performing the way it should. "If a tour group wanted an extra 10 rooms at the last minute, the operator would be better equipped to decide whether or not he should sell the additional rooms at the discounted tour group rate, or hang onto them so they could be sold at the rack rate."

MILLION-DOLLAR SAVINGS

"Many of the things we're doing now would be impossible without the computer," says Miller. "For instance, we've just installed 28 PCs in the back office for budgeting. We prepare the spreadsheets, which are sent out to the individual hotels and returned with revisions. Before, our forecasting just was not timely. We would be operating for three months, six months, or sometimes a year with numbers we knew just were not valid."

"Many of the things we're doing now would be impossible without the computer."

Though most purchases require some justification, Miller says there are some situations, such as a request from a financial analyst, that require no further justification. "We just go ahead and buy one," Miller says, "for our conviction is so strong that productivity will be increased."

It's too early to say just how much the new IBM system will save Ramada in the long run, but some early estimates are in. Miller says, "Just putting the new system in place has resulted in a $1 million savings in communication costs, as well as maintenance and repair changes. Labor savings have not been used as a justification so far, but we know they're there."

Ramada's Bredimus believes that the purchasing program should save about two positions in each purchasing department. And Miller thinks that the automated front office should increase profitability by about 2 percent.

The PCs are in the process of being programmed to offer to all Ramada outlets the enhanced features currently available to only some of the bigger hotels through the larger, more expensive IBM Series I. These include fully automated guest accounting, which is very accurate for items like room and tax, telephone, and restaurant. "It also includes a guest history," says Miller. "If there has been a record of stays, we can respond to a preference for particular accommodations. We can block a room, like an airline seat assignment, for up to one and a half years. It's useful in providing superior service."

As Ramada moves into city centers with its new Renaissance hotels, the enhanced service made possible by the PCs will enable the company to broaden its appeal to the business community. The management's decision to install PCs at the front desk not only has lowered costs, it has given Ramada the power and flexibility to hold, and perhaps advance, its position in a highly competitive marketplace.

Source: M. Major, "Innkeeper Picks PCs," *Business Computing,* October 1984, pp. 46–48.

SUMMARY

Management information systems are information systems that provide managers with information that enables them to perform their jobs quicker or better, or both.

Management information systems perform two main business roles: they provide managers with information needed to carry out their own duties, and they provide managers with information needed to coordinate business activities.

There are three main levels of management. *Operating managers* make sure that day-to-day activities are performed. *Middle managers* make sure that business objectives are achieved. *Senior managers* make sure that the business continues to be successful over time.

These three levels of management tend to have different *information needs.* Information can be detailed or summarized, more or less current, focused on the past, the present, or the future, narrow or broad in scope, and internal or external.

Operating managers tend to need information that is detailed, current, concerned with the present, and focused on a narrow set of internal business activities.

Middle managers tend to need information that is aggregated but fairly current, that compares the present with the recent past, and that covers a broad range of internal business activities but only a narrow range of external business activities.

Senior managers need very summarized information that is aggregated over lengthy time periods, that covers the past, present, and future, and that covers a broad range of internal and external business activities.

Transaction processing systems, information reporting systems, and decision support systems can all produce useful management information.

Transaction processing systems produce listings of business events that have recently occurred or that are scheduled to occur. They also capture most of the data that are placed in a firm's data base.

Information reporting systems retrieve data from a data base and produce *prespecified* management reports. These reports can be produced on a *periodic* basis, when *exceptions* occur, and on *demand.*

Decision support systems allow managers to access and transform data on an *ad hoc* basis. Managers obtain the information they need by interacting with the decision support system to describe the data to be retrieved from a data base, the processing operations to be performed, and the form of the information being released. Software packages that can serve as *decision support system generators* are available today.

An *MIS master plan* lists all a business's current information systems as well as those that are planned for future development. This plan includes descriptions of each information system and the schedule for developing future information systems.

An MIS master plan serves two major purposes: it enables managers to take full advantage of a firm's existing information systems, and it promotes efforts to link a firm's information systems.

MIS architecture refers to the physical locations where data entry, processing, storage and retrieval, and release take place. By employing an appropriate MIS architecture, one can improve access to a firm's information systems and reduce the cost of these systems.

The three basic MIS architectures include a *centralized* form, a *decentralized* form, and a *distributed* form. A centralized architecture is best when most of a business's activities occur at the same site. A decentralized architecture is best when a business's activities occur at multiple sites but generally do not have to be coordinated very tightly. A distributed architecture is best when a business's activities are located at multiple sites and require tight coordination.

Microcomputers can serve an important MIS role in businesses. However, this MIS role of microcomputers is different in small and large businesses.

In small businesses, the microcomputer is often the first computer system acquired by a business. As a result, all a firm's information systems are provided through microcomputers.

In large businesses, most of a firm's information systems are provided through minicomputers and maxicomputers. Microcomputers primarily serve as personal computing tools and as gateways into these larger computer systems. They are also being used increasingly as local computer systems in a distributed MIS architecture.

A *systems model* of a business is an alternative way of looking at the business that makes it easier to observe and understand the important relationships among the business's various activities.

Systems models are composed of inputs, outputs, processors, controllers, and boundaries. *Inputs* are transformed by *processors* to produce *outputs.* The *boundary* separates the business being modeled from its *environment.* Inputs come from the environment, and outputs are sent to the environment. *Controllers* direct or coordinate processors using *feedback* information about the processors' activities.

A key idea in systems modeling is that any part of a system can itself be modeled as a system. This limited but more detailed view of the object being modeled is termed a *subsystem.*

Systems models of businesses are built to help the members of an MIS *project team* understand the basic activities of a business and to improve communication among project team members by serving as a common frame of reference.

A systems model of a business should produce a fairly comprehensive *information processing model* of the business. Data flows to and from the business's various activities are shown, as are information flows to and from its managers.

The next chapter will look at the steps normally followed in developing an information system, as well as some difficulties that can arise.

REVIEW QUESTIONS

1. What are the two major roles of MIS in a business?
2. Relate the five basic levels of business information to the three levels of business management.
3. What types of business information systems are most likely to be used by each level of management?
4. Briefly describe the three types of reports produced by information reporting systems.
5. The Alpha Corporation is considering the creation of an MIS. Why should it formulate an MIS plan first?
6. Briefly describe the three basic forms that may be employed in an MIS architecture.
7. Briefly describe the typical pattern in which microcomputer use evolves in a small firm.
8. How do microcomputers typically first appear in a larger firm?
9. How can the need to key data into a microcomputer be avoided?
10. Your superior has asked you to develop an overall MIS design. What questions must such a plan address and what types of information would you require in order to accomplish this task?
11. What is a *systems model?* How is systems modeling applied to the development of an MIS system?
12. How can the concept of modeling be used to provide detailed views of and insights into the configurations and interrelationships of the parts of that system?

CHAPTER 11

Systems Development I

COMPUTERS AT WORK

The Right Place at the Right Time

Training, for its customers and service personnel, was a major operation at Digital Telephone, an independent supplier of sophisticated private branch exchange (PBX) equipment. The company had just moved to larger offices. At the new quarters, an entire floor was devoted to its first in-house training center, complete with classrooms, audio-visual laboratories, and training rooms containing PBX systems. Digital Telephone previously held classes in various hotels located in cities near its customers.

The new facility and a class schedule twice as large as last year's left training manager Connie Cunningham with a giant headache: scheduling instructors, rooms, and equipment for 235 courses. She also had to communicate the inevitable schedule changes not only to instructors and students, but also to audio-visual equipment operators, caterers, and the housekeeping staff. She eventually found a cure in a microcomputer system and a contract that forced her dealer to learn to use and support the system while he taught her.

First, though, Cunningham tried using a large matrix diagram to match courses with instructors, dates, and rooms. She spent at least ten hours a week keeping the matrix up-to-date, to say nothing of the secretarial, reproduction, and mailing expenses required to notify everyone of the changes.

There had to be a way to automate at least part of the scheduling task, Cunningham reasoned, so she asked Stan Sitorius, an analyst from the company's information center, for help.

Source: J. T. Monk and K. M. Landis, "The Right Place at the Right Time," *Business Computer Systems,* October 1983, pp. 23–24.

For Connie Cunningham, being in "the right place at the right time" meant knowing where to go to for help in scheduling Digital Telephone's training classes. Working with Stan Sitorius, one of the firm's systems analysts, Connie was able to automate this time-consuming task. By investing about forty hours of her time and a little over $5000, Connie has saved Digital Telephone 400 to 500 person hours a year and decreased training materials expenditures by over 20 percent.

What did Connie and Stan do? Would you know what to do if you were in Connie's position? In this chapter and the next, we will be looking at the various activities involved in developing a business information system.

In this chapter, you will learn to do the following:

1. Define what is meant by a successful information system.
2. Define the terms *structured design, project management,* and *documentation* and discuss the importance of each in developing a successful information system.
3. Explain what is meant by the systems life cycle and list its five stages.
4. Explain why a systems analyst has to be concerned with "people issues" throughout the systems life cycle.
5. Describe the purpose of the systems analysis stage of the systems life cycle and list its three steps.

BUILDING A SUCCESSFUL INFORMATION SYSTEM

Jerry Lincoln had just been hired by Jan Hale, CompuStore's senior systems analyst, to serve as the firm's second systems analyst. Jerry had just come out of a meeting with Jan and was sitting in his office thinking over what Jan had said. Jerry had heard much the same message in school, but he was glad to have a reminder. This was his first professional job, and he was nervous about his first big system development assignment. What stuck most in his mind were Jan's words:

> *"Our job is to provide management with information systems that fit the business and that are used. Management really isn't concerned that we come up with the 'best' solution to a problem. Want they want is a solution that solves the problem at hand, and that does so at a reasonable cost and in a reasonable time frame. What I want you to do this first week is get to know what goes on here and who does what. I'll introduce you to top management. Then, go and meet some of the other managers and workers. It's important that you get to know them and that they get to know you. We'll talk about your assignment first thing next week."*

Jerry's boss had just given him sound advice on developing successful information systems. The term **systems development** refers to the complete set of activities performed in, first, designing and building an information system and, then, successfully introducing this information system into the business unit that will be using it. Normally, a systems analyst, such as Jerry Lincoln, is given the job of directing and performing much of this work.

Successful information systems have three major characteristics:

1. They perform a useful business function. Information systems can either perform business information processing tasks or support people performing such tasks. Chapter 2 discussed how you could identify business situa-

tions where information systems would be useful, and Chapter 10 described a number of ways in which information systems support business managers.

2. They are appropriate for the business. Information system designers must carefully match hardware and software to a business. Is the cost reasonable? Is the technology too sophisticated for a firm?
3. They are used. Information systems that are not used, that are underused, or that are misused can have damaging effects on a business and its employees. Will employees be able to use the information system? Will they want to use it? Will they make use of all its features?

It is also important to recognize that businesses, as well as their employees, change over time. A truly successful information system continues to serve a useful business function, to be appropriate to the business, and to be used long after the information system was first introduced.

Developing a successful information system is a challenging task that finds the systems analyst working with both computer technology and people to solve important business problems. In this chapter and the next, we will discuss the different activities you would be performing if you were to become a systems analyst.

Systems analysts spend much of their time communicating. They regularly talk with managers and workers to discover where information systems are needed, and they constantly interact with information system users and with computer specialists while developing an information system. You should now understand Jan Hale's remarks to Jerry Lincoln. In order to develop successful information systems for CompuStore, Jerry needs to have a good understanding of CompuStore's business activities as well as good working relationships with most of CompuStore's employees.

Many information systems, however, are not successful. This doesn't mean that they are not completed or are rarely used. Rather, it means that an information system failed to completely serve its intended business role, that it cost far more than was expected, or that its development took much longer than was anticipated. Studies of these sorts of "failures" indicate that events such as the following often occurred:

Major errors are discovered late in the development of an information system. A lot of the work already completed must then be "thrown away" and redone.

Two parts of an information system, which were worked on by different people, do not fit together as they should. More work must be performed to join the two parts together.

When users begin to work with an information system, they discover that the information system does not perform as expected. Often, the systems analyst misunderstood the user's earlier requests. Costly and time-consuming revisions must now be made to the information system.

All of these problems result from inadequate communication during systems development. We saw in Chapter 10 how building a systems model of a business could improve the communications among people working together as a team to produce a MIS design. Many other tools have been found to aid and improve system development communications. Three of these—structured design, project management, and documentation—are especially important, because their impact is felt across all system development activities.

Improving Communication with Structured Design

Structured design, also refered to as **top-down design,** is an approach to systems development that stresses the importance of reaching early agreement on an information system's major design decisions. Three main benefits arise when a complete, overall design of an information system exists at an early stage of systems development:

1. The purpose and scope of an information system are made clear to both the creators and the users of the information system.
2. Major design errors are caught early enough such that few, if any, development tasks need to be redone.
3. The people involved in systems development activities can see how the various parts of the information system fit together.

These benefits improve understanding and both speed and simplify system development. The structured design process emphasizes three design principles.

First, keep the overall design of an information system as simple as possible. If a "top-level" design is stated in general terms and refers only to the essential aspects of an information system, everyone will be able to understand the overall design. On the other hand, if a top-level design is too detailed, people tend to lose sight of the total design. This is referred to as **the principle of abstraction.**

Second, add detail to a design in small steps. Each new layer should explain in a clear and obvious manner how the prior layer will accomplish its purposes. If this is done, omitted parts of a design are more likely to be detected. This is referred to as **the principle of stepwise refinement.**

Third, the "bottom level" of a design should be made up only of small, single-purpose parts. Each of these well-defined parts is termed a **module.** Information systems designed in this way are far easier to understand, to develop, and to change at some future time. This is referred to as **the principle of modularity.**

Exhibit 11.1 on page 298 shows a structured design of an information system now being used by CompuStore's purchasing clerk for ordering hardware, software, magazines, books, and computer supplies. We will be looking at the development of this information system in more detail in Chapters 11 and 12.

Did you build any systems models while you were studying Chapter 10? If so, then you have already produced some structured designs. Your overall business model represents the top layer of your design, and your subsystems models represent lower layers of the design.

Improving Communication with Project Management

In developing an information system, a large number of tasks need to be performed. Information must be gathered about business activities, users, existing information systems, and computer technology. The costs and benefits of the information system need to be determined. The information system's hardware, software, and people components need to be designed. Next, hardware and software components are purchased, and programs might be written.

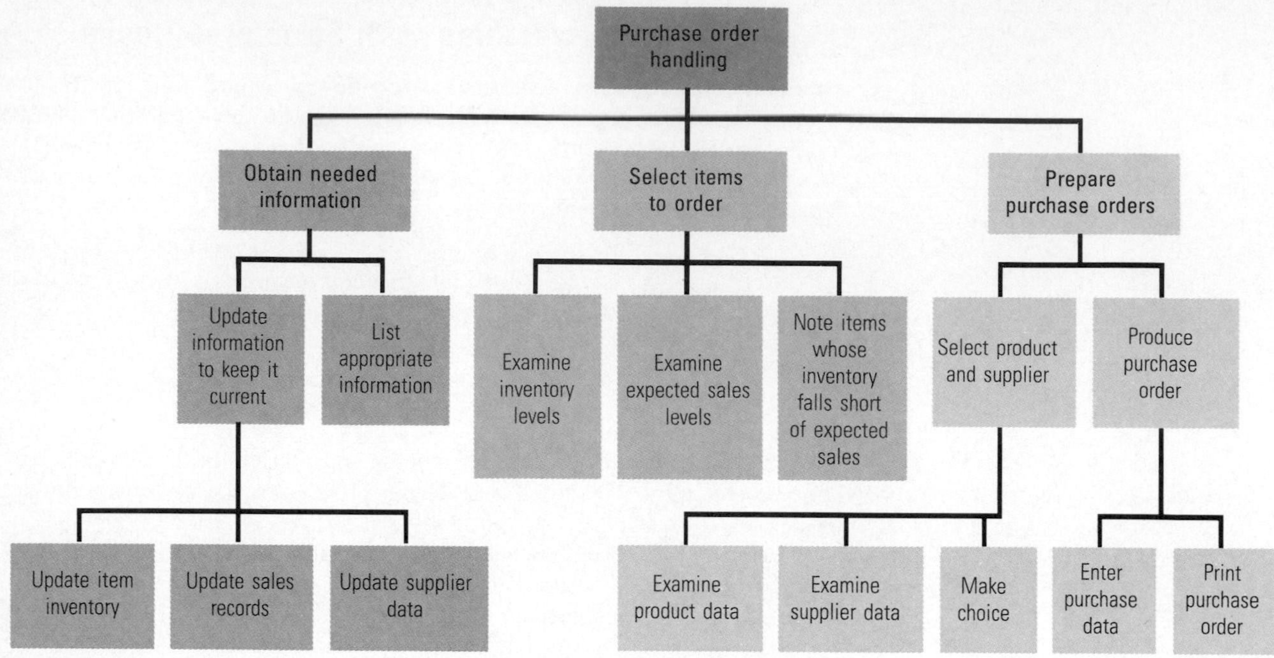

Exhibit 11.1

A structured design representing CompuStore's Purchasing Information System. The higher decision levels give an overview of the functions being performed, while the lower design levels give details on handling these functions.

Finally, the information system is introduced into the business departments where it will be used. Project management techniques can provide an effective means of coordinating all these tasks.

Because of the variety of skills required and the time-consuming nature of many of these tasks, most information systems are developed by project teams composed of both information system creators and users. With a large systems development project, many systems analysts, systems designers, programmers, and users would all be included on the project team. With a small project, a single systems analyst working with a single user might compose the entire team.

Often, the project team reports to a steering committee composed of senior managers. This steering committee approves the major decisions that arise during the project and resolves problems that the project team cannot handle on its own. The size and management level of this steering committee depends on the importance of the information system being developed.

Exhibit 11.2 shows the project team that CompuStore set up to develop its purchasing information system. Jerry Lincoln was assigned to serve as the team's leader, the project manager.

It is the **project manager's** job to plan and coordinate the tasks to be performed in a systems development project. This, itself, can be a major responsibility. When Jan Hale assigned the development of the purchasing information system to Jerry Lincoln, she gave him the following advice:

> *"A system development project can be a real headache if it is not managed well. The key idea is to let everyone know what they are supposed to do and when they are supposed to do it, let everyone know what other people are doing that affects them, and then keep current on how well every-*

one is coming along on their work. What you don't want are any surprises! You can usually work around problems as long as you know about them far enough in advance."

Successful project managers divide a project into small, well-defined tasks that have observable endpoints or **milestones.** With such tasks, it is possible to closely monitor a project's progress. If each of a task's milestones are being achieved as scheduled, then the entire project is likely to be completed on time.

Project management tools are available to help a systems analyst direct a systems development project. Two of the most common are the Gantt chart and the Program Evaluation Review Technique, PERT, for short. A **Gantt chart** specifies the timing of a series of tasks so that it is easy to see whether the tasks are being completed on schedule. A **PERT diagram,** on the other hand, shows the relationships among a project's tasks, as well as their timing. Exhibit 11.3 illustrates both of these tools.

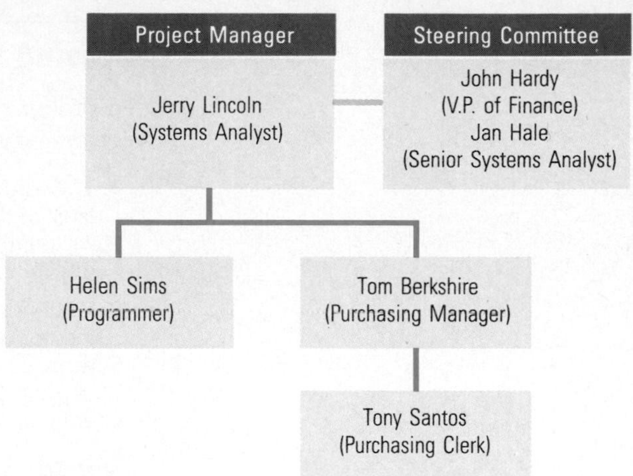

Exhibit 11.2

The project team used by CompuStore in developing the Purchasing Information System. Here, as is often the case, a systems analyst serves as the project manager.

Exhibit 11.3

A Gantt chart and a PERT diagram for preparing a pecan pie. The lines on the Gantt chart represent *planned* times. *Actual* times are then written over these to show whether a task is on schedule. The arrows on the PERT diagram indicate the tasks that precede each task. The numbers above the arrows are the time in minutes required for each task.

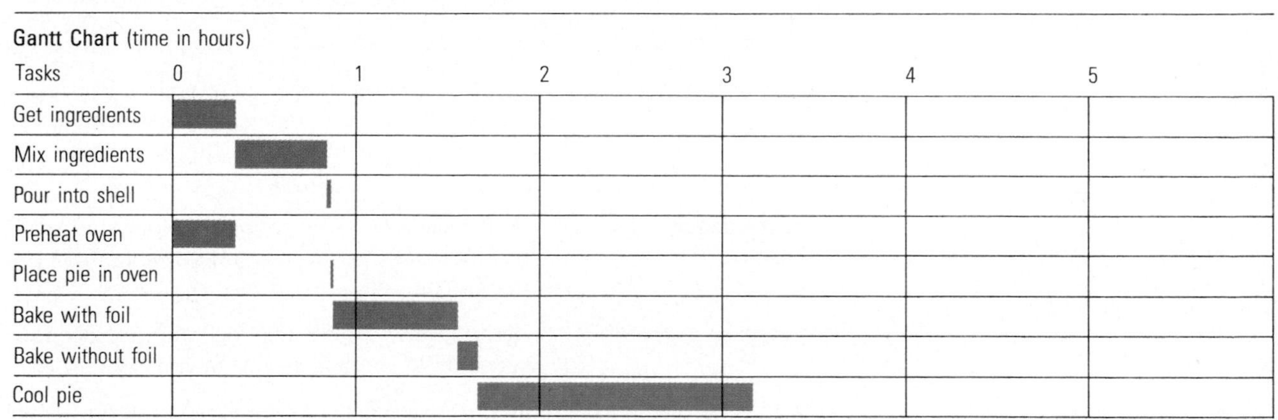

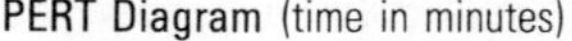

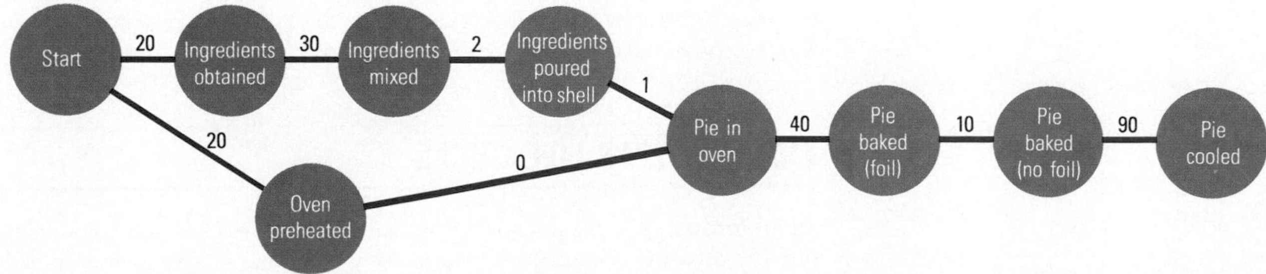

Improving Communication with Documentation

When project work is performed by many people over a lengthy period of time, two major problems can occur:

1. The work done by one person early in a project is used by another person later in the project. If the first person did not carefully describe what was accomplished and how it was accomplished, the second person may find it difficult to perform assigned tasks.
2. When a project covers a long time span, the particular people assigned to the project may change. Employees can be promoted, take jobs with other firms, or become ill for an extended period of time. If a detailed description of project work does not exist, a new person assigned to a project may find it difficult to complete a task begun by someone else.

Documentation, or permanent descriptions of the work performed during a systems development project, prevent the disruptions these communication problems could cause.

It is important that documentation be performed continuously throughout systems development. In a way, documentation should "unfold" in the same way a structured design evolves. Early documentation provides an overview of what is to be done, later documentation describes how things are done, and the final documentation describes the completed information system.

Five types of documentation are typically used in a systems development project:

project manual — a description of the work performed during a systems development project

systems manual — a complete description of an information system

users' manual — descriptions of a completed information system in terms that users can understand, as well as instructions regarding the use of the information system

programmers' manual — descriptions of all the program development work that took place during a systems development program

operators' manual — descriptions of all the operating procedures required in running an information system

Each of these will be described in more detail as the various systems development activities are covered in this chapter and the next.

The key thing to remember about documentation is that it must be written so that people can understand it. This does not always occur, as is vividly illustrated on pages 302–3 in Computers at Work: "Documenting an Infinite Number of Monkeys."

THE SYSTEMS LIFE CYCLE

All information systems initially start as an idea in someone's mind. For example, the idea for CompuStore's purchasing information system was initially raised when John Hardy, vice-president of finance, realized the firm lost over $80,000 in 1986 because of poor purchasing decisions. This idea is then transformed into a working information system that meets the business need that triggered the idea in the first place. The complete set of system development activities that produce an information system is known as the **systems life cycle.** The term *life cycle* refers to the notion that the initial idea for an information system gives birth to an information system, and that the systems development activities produce a common growth pattern through which the information system matures into a practical business tool.

There are five stages in the systems life cycle. Exhibit 11.4 provides an overview of these systems development activities.

The purpose of **systems analysis** is to analyze a business activity to assess the feasibility of a proposed information system and to determine how it should function. Since these analyses require an understanding of both busi-

Exhibit 11.4
The Five Stages of the Systems Life Cycle

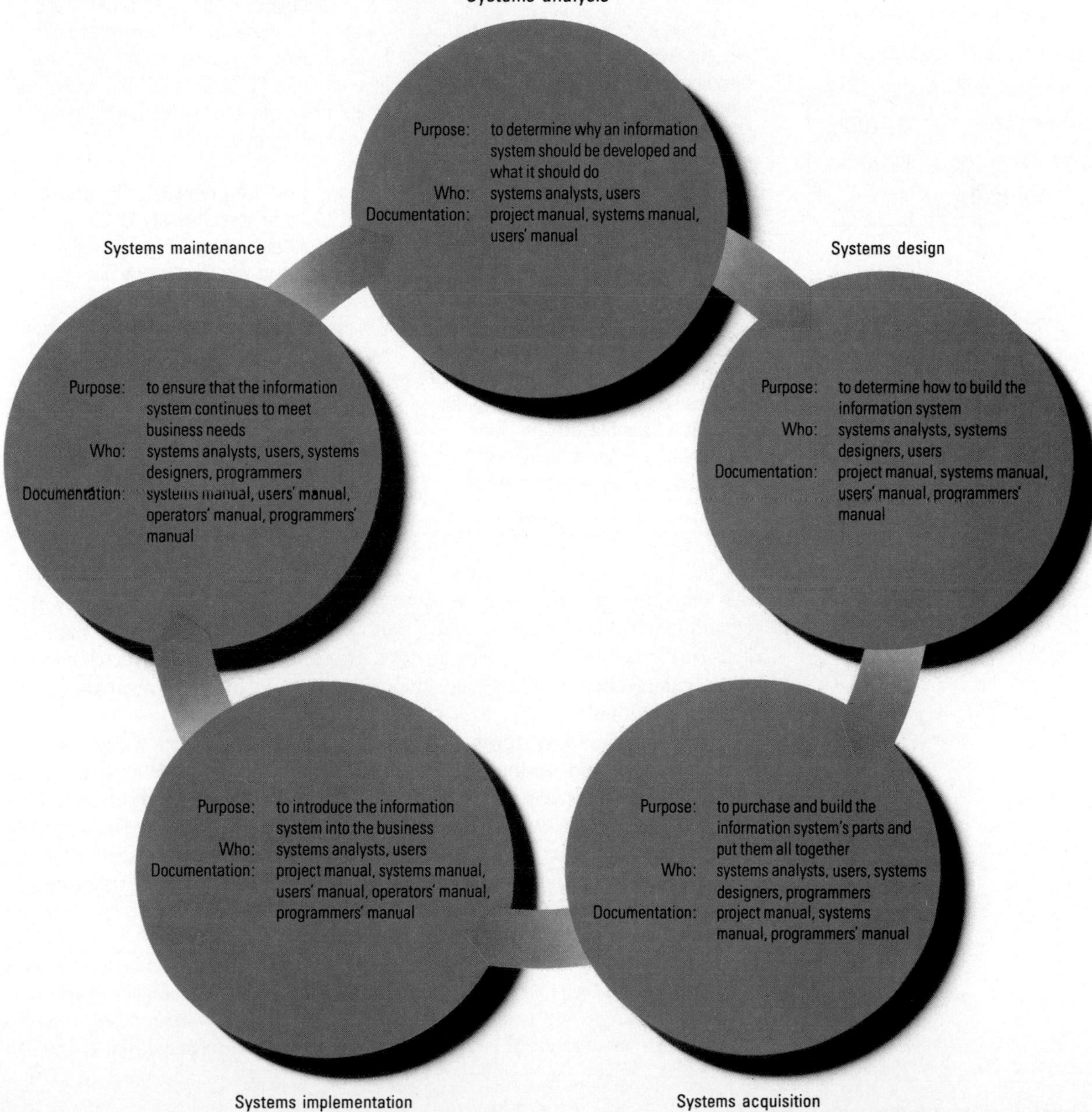

Systems analysis
Purpose: to determine why an information system should be developed and what it should do
Who: systems analysts, users
Documentation: project manual, systems manual, users' manual
Systems design
Purpose: to determine how to build the information system
Who: systems analysts, systems designers, users
Documentation: project manual, systems manual, users' manual, programmers' manual
Systems acquisition
Purpose: to purchase and build the information system's parts and put them all together
Who: systems analysts, users, systems designers, programmers
Documentation: project manual, systems manual, programmers' manual
Systems implementation
Purpose: to introduce the information system into the business
Who: systems analysts, users
Documentation: project manual, systems manual, users' manual, operators' manual, programmers' manual
Systems maintenance
Purpose: to ensure that the information system continues to meet business needs
Who: systems analysts, users, systems designers, programmers
Documentation: systems manual, users' manual, operators' manual, programmers' manual

COMPUTERS AT WORK

Documenting an Infinite Number of Monkeys

Help Wanted: Semiliterate, noncreative misspeller with gift for technobabble and an innate ability to complicate the simple and to oversimplify the difficult. Propensity for making blatant errors a plus. Word processing skills not necessary. Apply now at Personnel Office, SuperDuper Computer Software/Hardware Company.

Perhaps you haven't come across this ad, but you've surely encountered the end product. To adapt that most overused and unpleasant phrase, we are all too often victims of non-user-friendly "documentation." I think its authors are wrong from the very start: We would automatically be on friendlier territory if they'd start calling the things "manuals."

Writing a manual for a complex piece of work like a word processor or telecommunications program is considerably different from writing poetry, but there is still a fundamental need to communicate with the reader. Many of us who use microcomputers out of necessity have resorted to learning programs by experimentation: Just open the box, pop the disk in the drive, and explore. *When all else fails, read the manual.*

So how do these manuals get written? They sometimes make me think of Bob Newhart's classic comedy routine in which a scientist explains the theory of probability. It went something like this: If you put an infinite number of monkeys in front of an infinite number of typewriters and let them peck away for an infinite period of time, sooner or later one of them would produce a great masterpiece of literature.

"Eureka!" yells the scientist as she grabs a sheet of paper from one of the simian typists. "Listen to this!" 'To be, or not to be; that is the gzornnplatt.' "

I thought I might offer a few translations of some of the most egregious paragraphs from manuals written for—or at—the PC user. All of the examples are real; only the names have been changed to protect the guilty.

From a modem manual: The user has the ultimate responsibility to correct problems arising from harmful radio-frequency emissions for equipment under his control. If this equipment does cause interference to radio or television reception, which can be determined by turning the equipment off and on, the user is encouraged to try to correct the interference . . . All of these responsibilities and any others not mentioned are exclusively at the expense of the user.

ness activities and information system capabilities, they are normally performed by a team of systems analysts and users. The activities undertaken and decisions made during systems analysis are described in the three documentation manuals begun at this stage: the project manual, the systems manual, and the users' manual.

The purpose of **systems design** is to select the hardware and software components, as well as the operating procedures, needed to link these components in a way that will meet the information system's users' needs. The testing procedures to be used during the systems implementation stage are also selected. Systems designers often join the project team at this point to provide additional technical expertise. Descriptions of the information system's technical design are added to the project and systems manuals. Also, the programmers' manual is started at this time.

With most information systems, it is necessary to purchase hardware and software components to provide the information system detailed in the systems design stage. With other information systems, software may have to be developed from scratch. It is in the **systems acquisition** stage that hardware

Translation: Don't call us if your VisiCalc screen marches across your neighbor's Sony in the middle of the World Series. That's between you and the FCC. Fix it yourself.

From a Disk Copying Utility: Most computer software that is available from the IBM personal computer is copyrighted, trademarked, and protected under the laws of the United States of America. There are numerous moral and financial issues which you should be aware of when using the . . . utility . . .

Translation: Our lawyers made us run this.

From an expensive data base package: After our new manual went to print we found some typographical errors and we revised a few . . . commands. Enclosed are the corrected pages. Please insert them into this manual according to this substitution chart. Discard the old pages.

Translation: We didn't get around to proofreading the manual until we shipped the first 18,000 copies, so we received a couple hundred phone calls from users who said the program didn't work. We don't want to be bothered with inserting these new pages or reprinting the whole manual—what do you expect from a $495 product?

From a "Simple" Desktop Manager: String overflow—Seg XXXXXXXX PppOoo indicates a system failure which is usually the result of hardware error. It can also be caused by a damaged data base. If this error occurs you should record the name following "Seg," and the numbers which appear as pp and oo. You should then follow the procedures in section 20.2 and 20.1. If the problem can be reproduced with a new copy of . . . then you should communicate with technical support.

Translation: Hoo boy, do you have a problem! We sure hope it's in your computer and not our program. Check it out, will you? And thanks for beta-testing our product.

From a Utility Package: Print Spooler Module Update: If you try and run the spooler without having first created the Autoexec.Bat, the system will lock up and you must re-boot.

Translation: We call this an update so that you won't recognize that we made an horrendous mistake. And please tape this little slip of paper somewhere in the manual, won't you? We couldn't be bothered to do it ourselves.

From a famous word processor: ***Fatal Error F29: Rename Failure, System Failure, or you changed disks. These messages should not occur.

Translation: Go away son, you bother me.

Newhart, you were wrong. An infinite number of monkeys sitting at an infinite number of microcomputer keyboards couldn't write a great computer manual—merely the typical ones. Gzornnplatt!

Source: C. Sandler, "Documenting an Infinite Number of Monkeys," *PC Magazine,* August 1983, pp. 35–37.

and software are purchased and that programs are written. Programmers join the project team when software needs to be developed. Information on all the activities that do take place are added to the project, systems, and programmers' manuals.

The information system is introduced into the business during **systems implementation.** Most of this time is spent making sure that any anticipated problems regarding the use of the information system do not arise by careful testing, with training, and by developing an appropriate conversion strategy. This is typically performed by systems analysts and users. The users', operators', and project manuals are completed during this stage, and the systems and programmers' manuals are updated.

The majority of information systems need to be changed after they have been implemented. Most often, ideas for changes arise because errors are detected that prevent a business's information needs from being met or because these information needs change. **Systems maintenance** refers to the efforts taken to ensure that an information system, over time, continues to meet a business's information needs. Because a maintenance project is actually a

Exhibit 11.5

This pie chart illustrates the amount of labor hours that would typically be spent in each systems life-cycle stage for an average information systems project.

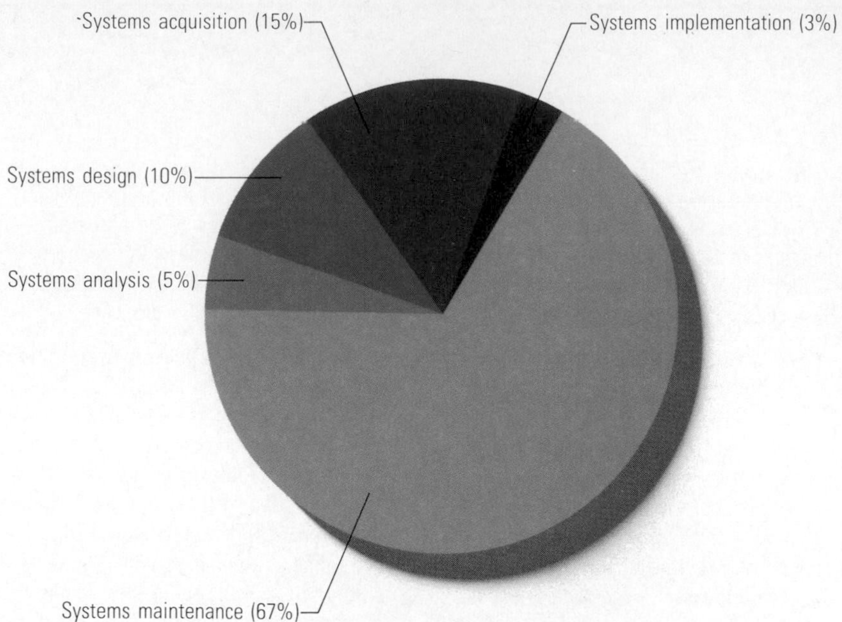

"mini" systems development project, it would not be unusual to find systems analysts, users, systems designers, and programmers all involved with systems maintenance tasks. The systems, users,' operators,' and programmers' manuals would be updated at the conclusion of each systems maintenance project.

These five systems life-cycle stages can consume quite different amounts of time. Exhibit 11.5 depicts the proportion of labor hours typically spent in each of the stages for an average information systems project. Some of the large amounts of time given to systems acquisition and systems maintenance may be avoided by paying attention to communications issues during the systems analysis and systems design stages.

Professional Issue

Cultivating the Human Touch

When Jan Hale first assigned the purchasing information system project to Jerry Lincoln, they spent all afternoon talking about what Jerry would be doing. While Jan did give Jerry an overview of CompuStore's existing information systems, "people issues" dominated their discussion:

Jerry: I understand why it's important for me to talk to purchasing department employees during the systems analysis. If I'm going to design an information system that is useful, I've got to find out what they need. Since I don't work in purchasing, I need to rely on these employees to tell me what they need.

Jan: You need to do even more than that, Jerry. We know that John Hardy wants this system badly, but you have to find out if the purchasing staff feels they need a new information system. If they don't, then you've got to explain how a new information system could help them. You won't get very far unless the users are motivated to work with you in defining their information needs. Don't forget, many of these people may feel that their jobs are threatened. Explain to them how their jobs will improve when the computer begins to do away with some boring and tedious parts of their jobs.

Second, you've got to help them tell you what they need. Many people find it hard to explain what their jobs involve. An important part of being a systems analyst is knowing when people are having difficulty expressing themselves and then helping them think through their work activities.

Jerry: Do I really need to be a psychologist? It sounds as if all this communicating will take a lot of time.

Jan: No, not a psychologist. More of a "street wise" business analyst. Understanding people, their attitudes, and their motivations are the important things. You're not trying to solve their personal problems.

Jerry: Well, once I get through the systems analysis, I'll be able to concentrate on the technical parts of the information system. That stage should go faster.

Jan: You're right in saying that. Many of the later systems development tasks are more technical than the systems analysis tasks. However, you can't forget about the people using the information systems. They are still the major focus of your job.

Jerry: I thought systems design involved choosing the right hardware devices and software options.

Jan: It does. But, it also involves making sure that the information system will be easy to use, accessible, and doesn't upset the routine of a department. Also, I've become very aware of ergonomics, the physiological aspects of using computer devices. Some types of CRT displays, for example, can reduce back strain as well as eye strain. Some of our people have complained of these problems.

Jerry: We did study ergonomics in school, but most of the studies about eye strain seemed inconclusive. I guess the important point is to think about how people will be using the equipment we purchase.

Jan: Yes, and also about how they'll work with the software we design.

Jerry: That takes us through systems acquisition. How about the last two stages of the life cycle? Don't tell me! Let me think about it on my own.

During systems implementation I've got to make sure that my implementation plan handles any problems that might arise. That means I have to identify who might not want to use the information system and give them some extra attention during training. Right?

Jan: You've got it! You've also got to make sure that the really critical business activities aren't disrupted more than is necessary.

Jerry: I'm having a problem with system maintenance. I can't think of anything. All I can think of are programmers programming!

Jan: Well, for one thing, systems maintenance can involve any of the systems development tasks. Everything we've covered so far applies. The main issue with systems maintenance, however, is knowing when an information system needs to be changed. In this case, you'll need to establish a close, long-lasting rapport with the purchasing department. You will need to interact with them on a continuing basis to become aware of any problems they are experiencing with the information system or any ideas that could improve it. In a way, part of you now belongs to the purchasing department!

Through this discussion, Jerry came to realize how important the "human touch" would be in each of the systems life-cycle stages. The job of a systems analyst, largely because of these people issues, remains much more of an art than a science.

Developing People-Oriented Skills

If you were to become a systems analyst, where would you pick up the skills you need to deal effectively with the people issues?

One obvious place is your college classes. Courses that cover human psychology, the behavior of groups, human social relations, and business management are ideal for acquiring some understanding of the human issues that surround systems development.

A second way to pick up these skills is to observe and talk with "seasoned" professionals such as Jan Hale. While you do not have to go through an apprenticeship to become a systems analyst, the lessons to be learned working under an expert can't be picked up from any book.

Finally, your own experiences can provide a wealth of insights into these human issues. Observe people's behaviors. Listen to their conversations. Question their actions. Try to see the world from others' perspectives. Find explanations for behaviors that don't make sense to you. Above all, keep an open mind about why people behave as they do.

Exhibit 11.6

User participation is needed in each of the systems life-cycle stages.

The Importance of User Participation

Information system users are included on project teams to ensure that people's concerns are handled in an appropriate manner. Throughout the systems life cycle, opportunities for user participation exist (see Exhibit 11.6). Experienced computer professionals take advantage of these opportunities for several reasons.

Most importantly, users can contribute both a practical knowledge of a business's activities and an in-depth understanding of their own work behaviors and relationships with coworkers or customers. User participation has two other benefits. First, working on a project team gives users a better idea of the potential of both business computing and personal computing. Second, contributing to the development of an information system often gives a user a feeling of personal attachment toward the information system. The enthusiasm such feelings generate is then passed on to other employees.

However, just like anything else, too much user participation can be a bad thing. Project management becomes harder as more people are assigned to a project team. The difficulty of coordinating and monitoring task assignments may simply overwhelm the project manager. Also, assigning users to work on an information systems project does take them away from their normal duties.

Determining the extent to which users should contribute to a systems development project is another one of the skills a systems analyst must acquire. The following guidelines can be used as a starting point in deciding the number of users to place on an information systems project team. User participation is generally more desirable when the following are true:

- Human-computer interaction is important.
- A large number of people are affected by the information system.
- The systems analyst lacks an understanding of the business activity being automated.
- The business activity being automated is very important.

SYSTEMS ANALYSIS

Three things are accomplished during the systems analysis stage (see Exhibit 11.7). First, the project is defined. Next, the project's feasibility is examined. Third, the nature of the information processing required of the information system being developed is described in detail.

Taken together, these three activities represent a user-oriented structured design of an information system. The *project definition* provides an overview of the information system. In order to arrive at estimates of benefits and costs in the *feasibility study,* rough descriptions of the information system's inputs and outputs, as well as a basic idea of how the information system will function, are needed. The final step, known as the *logical design,* provides a detailed description of the information system from a business, rather than a technical, perspective.

Exhibit 11.7

The aim of the systems analysis stage of the systems life cycle is to provide a clear direction for the remaining stages. Three primary activities are included in the systems analysis stage: project definition, feasibility study, and logical design.

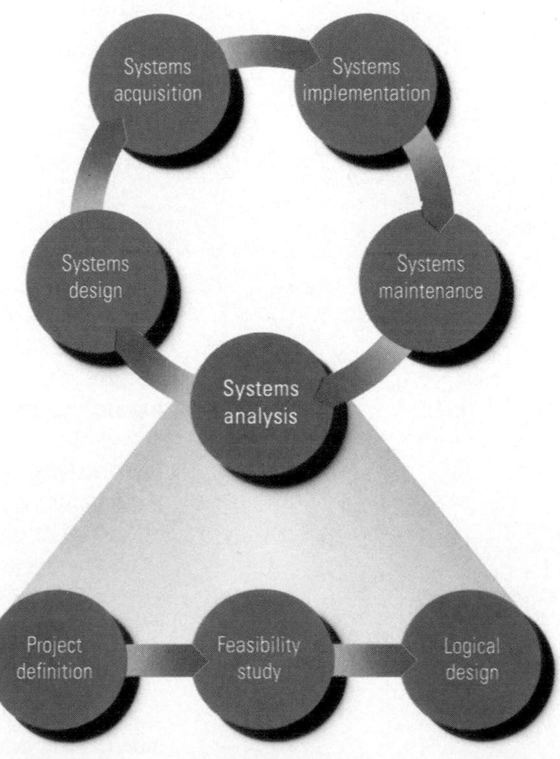

Step 1: Project Definition

The aim of **project definition** is to make the scope and purpose of the systems development project clear to everyone concerned with the information system. This includes project team members, all users, and top management.

In determining the scope of an information system, the business activities that are to be performed or supported are identified. A clear understanding of the purpose of an information system ties the project back to the business needs that motivated the project in the first place. If agreement is reached on an information system's scope and purpose at an early point in a project, then one of the major sources of systems development communication problems has been avoided.

On page 308, Exhibit 11.8 shows the project definition Jerry Lincoln prepared for the purchasing information system project. Jerry and Tom Berkshire, the purchasing manager, presented this project definition to Barry Allen and got his approval to go ahead with a feasibility study. Barry strictly refuses to provide funding for any project whose scope and purpose have not been approved by both the MIS department and the manager of the department in which the information system is to be used.

Exhibit 11.8
Project Definition for CompuStore's New Purchasing Information System

```
To:       John Hardy, V.P. of Finance
          Jan Hale, Senior Systems Analyst

From:     Jerry Lincoln, Project Manager
          Tom Berkshire, Purchasing Manager

Subject:  Project Definition, Proposed Purchasing Information System


Scope:  This information system supports purchasing clerks in ordering
products, prints purchase orders, and provides the purchasing manager
with monthly reports on the quality of the firm's purchasing
decisions.  Three data  files - a purchase order file, a vendor file,
and a product file - are maintained by the information system.

Purpose:  This information system is being developed for three main
reasons:  (1) to reduce the cost of purchased goods; (2) to reduce the
size of the product inventory; and (3) to reduce the number of lost
sales attributed to being "stocked-out" of a popular product.
```

Step 2: Feasibility Study

The main purpose of a **feasibility study,** also called a **systems survey** or a **preliminary investigation,** is to determine if an information system should be developed or not. This analysis examines the information system proposal from three perspectives:

Technical	Can the information system be developed?
Operational	If developed, will the information system be used?
Economic	Can the business afford the information system?

This final decision is usually based on a comparison of expected benefits and expected costs. If benefits exceed costs, then it makes sense to go ahead with the systems development project.

The project team prepares a report that describes the proposed information system, estimates its benefits and costs, and then makes a recommendation that either supports or does not support continuing with the project. However, the project's steering committee normally makes this *go/no go* decision.

In preparing its report, the project team produces a tentative information system design. To estimate benefits, they describe the information system's outputs. To estimate costs, the team identifies the hardware, software, operating procedures, and project plan needed to produce these outputs.

Estimating Project Benefits. Four categories of information system benefits were introduced in Chapter 2: cost-reducing benefits, cost-avoiding benefits, better products and services, and better management information. It is relatively easy to assign dollar values to the first two cost-related benefits. These, or very similar, costs are currently being incurred by a business. Thus, the systems analyst only has to look at past business records to estimate any cost savings. Such benefits are known as **tangible benefits.** It is generally much more difficult to assign dollar values to the latter two benefit categories. To estimate these **intangible benefits,** the systems analyst works with an information system's users to "predict the future."

Exhibit 11.9
Estimated Benefits of CompuStore's New Purchasing Information System

```
To:         John Hardy, V.P. of Finance
            Jan Hale, Senior Systems Analyst

From:       Jerry Lincoln, Project Manager
            Tom Berkshire, Purchasing Manager

Subject:    Estimated Benefits and Costs of CompuStore's
            New Purchasing Information System
----------------------------------------------------------------------

Cost-Reducing Benefits:

  * Reduce purchasing costs by reducing the cost of preparing a
    purchase order.  It currently takes a purchasing clerk ($8/hr.)
    30 minutes to prepare a purchase order.  With an online
    information system, this time is expected to be reduced to 5
    minutes.  Using an average of 80 purchase orders per week, this
    amounts to a savings of 80 x 52 x ($3.33), or $13,852.80 per
    year.  (There was other work the purchasing clerk could do.)

  * Reduce the cost of ordered goods by taking advantage of volume
    discounts.  The $80,000 amount previously calculated by John
    Hardy was used.

Cost-Avoiding Benefits:

  * Avoid hiring another purchasing clerk in 1988.  The cost of this
    clerk was estimated to be (52) x 40 x $8, or $16,640.

Better Service Benefits:

  * None identified.

Better Information Benefits:

  * Reduce total number of purchases by being able to better tie
    purchasing to sales patterns.  Intangible benefit.

  * Reduce lost sales by not stocking out of popular products.
    Luckily, Susan Tate had asked the retail stores to log all lost
    sales for a three-month period in 1985.  This amounted to
    $40,000.  Recognizing that this figure is likely too high, Jerry
    and Tom cut it in half.  Still, this results in an annual sales
    increase of $80,000.  Using an average profit margin of 40
    percent of sales, this works out to be a $32,000 benefit.

  * Reduce cost of ordered goods by locating a lower-priced supplier.
    Intangible benefit.
----------------------------------------------------------------------
```

Jerry Lincoln and Tom Berkshire tried to identify benefits in each of these four categories when they were preparing the purchasing information system's feasibility study. Exhibit 11.9 lists these benefits along with the dollar values assigned to them.

Estimating Project Costs. Four categories of information system costs were also introduced in Chapter 2: hardware costs, software costs, people costs, and operating costs. The hardware costs reflect the need to purchase, install, and maintain new hardware devices for the information system being developed. The software costs include the project's labor costs (project team members and consultants) and cost of purchasing or developing software. Generally, people costs refer to training expenses and the time users spend adjusting to their new work activities. Finally, operating costs cover the day-to-day computer, supplies, and labor expenses that arise with a working information system.

The information system design that Jerry and Tom initially selected for the purchasing information system used an intelligent terminal linked to a minicomputer at a warehouse. The only hardware needed was the terminal, which was to be tied directly to the minicomputer through a cable. Jerry and Tom did an investigation, but could not find a software package to meet their needs. Software development costs thus included a customized programming effort. Very little training or disruption costs were anticipated. Finally, the day-to-day operating costs included the following categories: CPU time, disk space, paper, and the labor associated with keeping data files current and preparing purchase orders. Exhibit 11.10 details the cost estimates that Jerry and Tom used.

Comparing Benefits and Costs. The identified benefits and costs result in positive and negative cash flows. The cash flows are examined on a year-by-year basis and then totaled. This analysis is shown in Exhibit 11.11. Notice the row with the title *discounted value.* This calculation accounts for the

Exhibit 11.10
Estimated Costs of CompuStore's New Purchasing Information System

```
To:        John Hardy, V.P. of Finance
           Jan Hale, Senior Systems Analyst

From:      Jerry Lincoln, Project Manager
           Tom Berkshire, Purchasing Manager

Subject:   Estimated Benefits and Costs of CompuStore's
           New Purchasing Information System

---------------------------------------------------------------------

Hardware Costs:

   * Intelligent Terminal:  $900

   * Cable:  $145

   * Installation:  $80

Software Costs:

   * Systems Development Cost:  8 man-months at $3000 per month, or
     $24,000

   * Software Maintenance Cost:  $10,000 per year (estimate)

People Costs:

   * Training:  2 man-days at $64 per day, or $128 (clerk)
                2 man-days at $150 per day, or $300 (trainer)

   * Disruption:  5 man-days at $64 per day, or $320

Operating Costs:

   * CPU:  1/2 hour per day at $60 per hour, or 52 x 5 x $30, or $7800
   per year

   * Disk Space:  1 million bytes at $.001 per byte per month, or
                  $12,000

   * Paper:  Not applicable as the price of manual vs. computer-
             printed order forms is comparable.

   * Labor:  5 hours per week keeping files current at $8 per hour, or
             5 x 52 x $8, or $2080

             7 hours per week preparing purchase orders at $8 per
             hour, or 7 x 52 x $8, or $2912

   ------------------------------------------------------------------
```

	1986	1987	1988	1989
BENEFITS				
purchase order preparation		13,852	13,852	13,852
volume discounts		80,000	80,000	80,000
hire additional clerk			16,640	16,640
reduce lost sales		32,000	32,000	32,000
total benefits		125,852	142,492	142,492
COSTS:				
hardware and installation	1,135			
systems development	24,800			
software maintenance		10,000	10,000	10,000
training and conversion	740			
operating expenses		24,392	24,292	24,292
total costs	26,675	34,392	34,392	34,392
NET VALUE (Benefits minus costs)	-26,675	91,460	108,100	108,100
DISCOUNTED VALUE (Minus 10% net value)	-26,675	82,314	87,561	78,805

NET PRESENT VALUE: $222,005

Exhibit 11.11

Benefit-Cost Analysis for CompuStore's New Purchasing Information System

Since the net present value of the project is positive, CompuStore should develop this information system. Note that the discount factor is 10 percent. This means it is believed that money will lose 10 percent of its current worth each year in the future.

fact that future dollars are worth less to a business than are current dollars due to factors such as inflation. Summing up the discounted values gives the *net present value* of the project. If the net present value figure is positive, as it is here, then the information system's benefits are greater than its costs. Given these results, CompuStore decided to develop the Purchasing Information System.

Developing the Project Plan. When the project's steering committee approved the purchasing information system, Jerry then put together a **project plan.** This plan listed the main tasks to be accomplished, identified who was to perform each task, and estimated the time and cost of each task.

Step 3: Logical Design

The objective of this final systems analysis step is to describe in detail the information processing requirements of the business activity being automated. This description, known as a **logical design** or **requirements specification,** should provide a complete picture of the information system from the user's viewpoint. The information system's purpose and objectives are stated in a fashion that links them back to the business problem that motivated the project. Inputs and outputs are shown, with their use explained in terms of the business activities being performed. Anticipated changes in these inputs and outputs are listed, along with explanations of the business changes that are likely to prompt these information system changes.

Many experts believe that the logical design is the single most important step in the systems life cycle. If this step is performed well, it can serve as a guide for all remaining systems development activities. However, if it is hurried or done haphazardly, the requirements specification that results is usually incomplete or inaccurate. When this occurs, information system "failures" similar to those mentioned at the beginning of this chapter are likely to arise.

Logical design involves five tasks:

1. Gather information about business activities and business information needs.
2. Analyze this information.
3. Develop the logical design.
4. Validate the logical design.
5. Review the feasibility study and project plan.

Information Gathering. A systems analyst gathers information about a business activity from both internal and external sources. Internal sources include employees and managers involved with the business activity, business documents associated with the activity (forms, standard operating procedures, training manuals, performance reports, problem reports, and budget reports), general business documents (financial reports, organization charts, job descriptions, and expansion plans), and related information systems documentation. External sources might include customers, suppliers, other businesses performing similar activities, computer vendors, magazines, books, and personal contacts who are knowledgeable about either the business activity involved or computer use. Developing access to each of these sources is an important part of a systems analyst's job.

Experienced systems analysts make use of a number of information-gathering techniques in working with these information sources. Documents, magazines, and books are read. Business activities are observed. Often, work rates and volumes are monitored and measured. The most important techniques, however, are those that are used to obtain information from people. Three of the most common techniques for gathering such information include diaries, interviews, and questionnaires.

One of the best ways to find out what employees or managers do in performing their work is to have them, or their secretaries, keep a diary of how they spend their time. You should understand how keeping a **diary** can be both time-consuming and disruptive. Use this technique sparingly and wisely! A poorly kept diary is useless to you, and frustrating the users can keep them from participating actively on the project.

The most important data-gathering skill for a systems analyst to develop is to learn how to be a successful interviewer. Exhibit 11.12 suggests some pointers for you to follow in becoming a skilled interviewer. In preparing for an **interview,** you should develop an interview plan and review the basic listening and observing skills. In carrying out the interview, be sure to allocate time to "warm up" the interviewee and "wind down" the interviewee. After the interview, carefully jot down extra details on what was said and review your own behavior, looking for ways to improve your interviewing skills.

Interviewing can be demanding for both the systems analyst and the interviewees. Often, there just isn't enough time to interview everyone you would like to interview. In these situations, developing a **questionnaire** that touches on key issues can be very useful. Developing good questionnaires, however, is not as easy as you might think. Will everyone interpret the questions in the same way? Will you be able to interpret the responses? Be sure to test your questionnaire out with a small sample of people. Often, it takes two or three such tests to develop a questionnaire that is really useful.

Exhibit 11.12
Tips for Developing Good Interviewing Skills

BEFORE THE INTERVIEW

Develop an interview plan:
Define the objectives of the interview.
Develop an interview outline.
Learn about the interviewees.
Prepare specific questions for each interviewee.

Review basic listening and observing skills:
Place yourself in interviewee's position.
Be aware of your own biases and remain neutral.
Give your full attention to the interviewee.
Listen for "hidden" meanings behind statements.
Watch for facial expressions, body language, and signs of nervousness.

DURING THE INTERVIEW

For the opening:
Use "small talk," perhaps discussing the weather or general company gossip, to develop a rapport with the interviewee.
Gain the interview's trust by being open about the information system and the interviewee's relationship with the information system.
Provide background on the purpose of the interview.

During the body of the interview:
Start off with broad issues, and then move to specific points.
Do not ask needless questions.
Do not suggest answers.
Talk with, not at, the interviewee.
Encourage more complete discussions of key issues.
Consider using a tape recorder or taking notes (with the interviewee's permission).
Avoid attacks, cross-examinations, or jargon.

For the closing:
Watch time closely; the length of the interview period should be reasonable.
Use some casual conversation to "wind down" the interview.
Leave on a pleasant note.

AFTER THE INTERVIEW

Take detailed notes on what was said.
Review the interview outline, and revise it appropriately.
Review your own behavior, noting where you could improve your interviewing skills.
Determine if a "follow-up" interview will be needed.

Analyzing Information. Another skill to be developed by a systems analyst involves learning how to "make sense" out of all the information that has been gathered. To determine a business's information needs, its objectives, activities, and problems must be understood. The analysis process should be similar to that you went through in systems modeling—identify essential elements and their relationships.

A number of tools and techniques are available to help you in analyzing this information. Developing a clear **narrative description** of a business activity or a user task is an ideal way to start. Work rates and volumes can be calculated and portrayed in tables and graphs to provide an understanding of growth trends. The relationships between existing business documents and existing information system inputs, data files, and outputs can be depicted through the use of grid charts. Exhibit 11.13 illustrates a **grid chart** that identifies the data files used with each major purchasing task. Developing **decision tables** can help you understand the important factors behind specific business or user actions. On page 314, Exhibit 11.14 illustrates a decision table that details the criteria CompuStore uses in selecting the vendor to buy a product from. Developing a data flow chart is a useful means of understanding the data processing activities required in handling a business task. A **data flow chart** is very similar to a systems model. Two major differences exist. First, only data and information flows are shown flowing among a system's elements. Second, data files are explicitly shown. Exhibit 11.15, on the following page, shows the data flow diagram that Jerry Lincoln developed to illustrate the data processing steps that occur in preparing a purchase order.

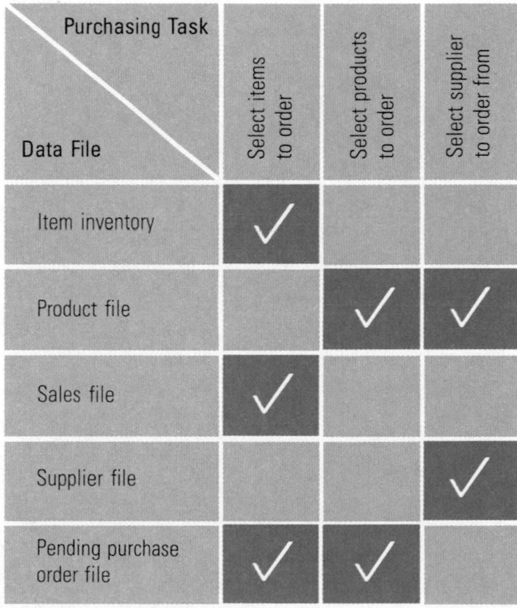

Purchasing Task / Data File	Select items to order	Select products to order	Select supplier to order from
Item inventory	✓		
Product file		✓	✓
Sales file	✓		
Supplier file			✓
Pending purchase order file	✓	✓	

Exhibit 11.13
This grid chart shows which data files are needed for each major purchasing task. The check marks in the chart's cells indicate that the data file in that row is used with the purchasing activity given in that column.

Exhibit 11.14

This decision table shows the decision rules the purchasing clerk follows in selecting a supplier. The three conditions that are the basis for this supplier decision are given either *Y* (yes) or *N* (no) answers. Below these conditions are three possible actions, and the action that should be taken is indicated with a check mark. Decision Rule 4 thus states: if a supplier has the lowest price, but has neither acceptable delivery times nor acceptable quality, then the clerk should not buy from that supplier.

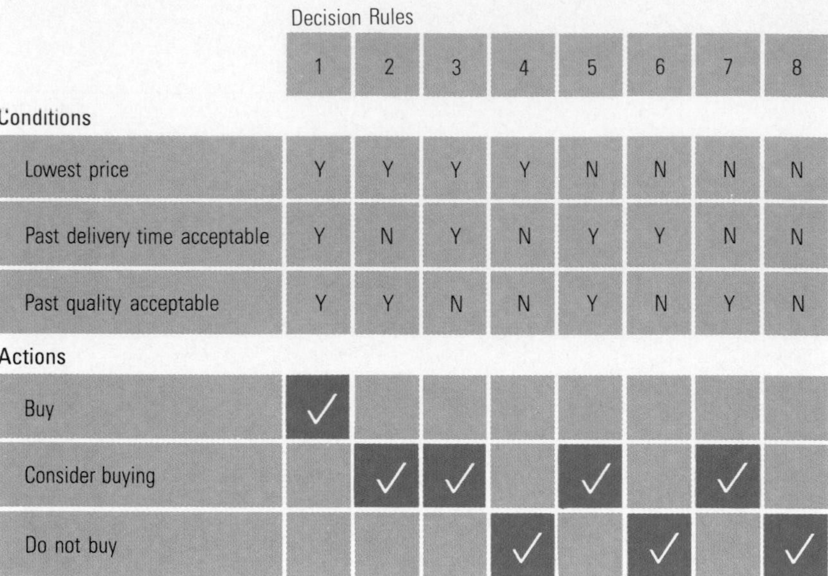

	Decision Rules 1	2	3	4	5	6	7	8
Conditions								
Lowest price	Y	Y	Y	Y	N	N	N	N
Past delivery time acceptable	Y	N	Y	N	Y	Y	N	N
Past quality acceptable	Y	Y	N	N	Y	N	Y	N
Actions								
Buy	✓							
Consider buying		✓	✓		✓		✓	
Do not buy				✓		✓		✓

Exhibit 11.15

This data flow diagram shows the data flows associated with the major purchasing tasks. The closed rectangles represent sources and destinations of data outside the purchasing function. The circles represent purchasing activities that involve information processing. The open rectangles represent data files. The arrows represent data flows.

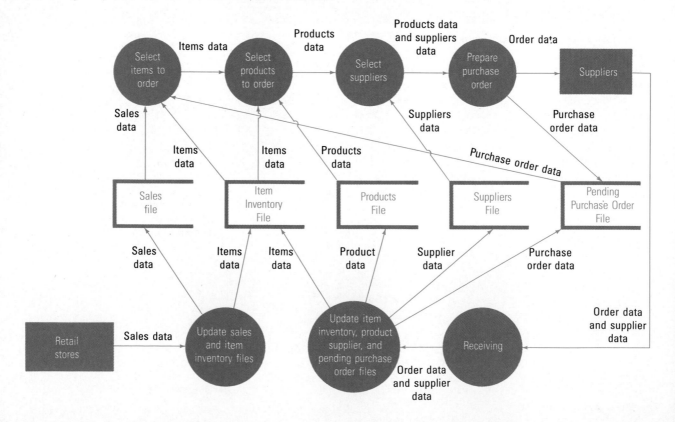

Developing the Logical Design. A systems analyst must make use of a number of skills in arriving at a logical design. The analyst blends together an understanding of business activities, user behaviors, computer technology, and information system design guidelines (to be discussed in Chapter 12) to propose a set of information system outputs that achieves the purpose and benefits stated in the project definition and feasibility study.

Two basic design strategies are used in developing a logical design:

Data-oriented The analyst first studies the day-to-day business activities as they are actually performed. Next, the analyst identifies existing problems and all required information processing operations. Finally, the analyst arrives at a logical design that solves the problems and handles all the information processing operations. As Exhibit 11.16a shows, the focus is on data that are to be processed by the information system.

Decision-oriented The analyst first talks with managers to determine the critical factors leading to business success and the key decisions they make in managing business activities. Next, the analyst identifies those critical information processing operations that directly impact or influence these key decisions. Finally, the analyst arrives at a logical design that handles these critical information processing operations. As Exhibit 11.16b shows, the focus here is on factors that are critical to the success of the business activity or task being handled by the information system.

Most systems analysts actually use both of these design strategies, placing a greater emphasis on a data-orientation with transaction processing systems and on a decision-orientation with information reporting systems and decision support systems.

Jerry Lincoln used both strategies in developing his logical design for the purchasing information system. A data orientation was ideal for tracing the steps needed to prepare a purchase order. However, a decision orientation

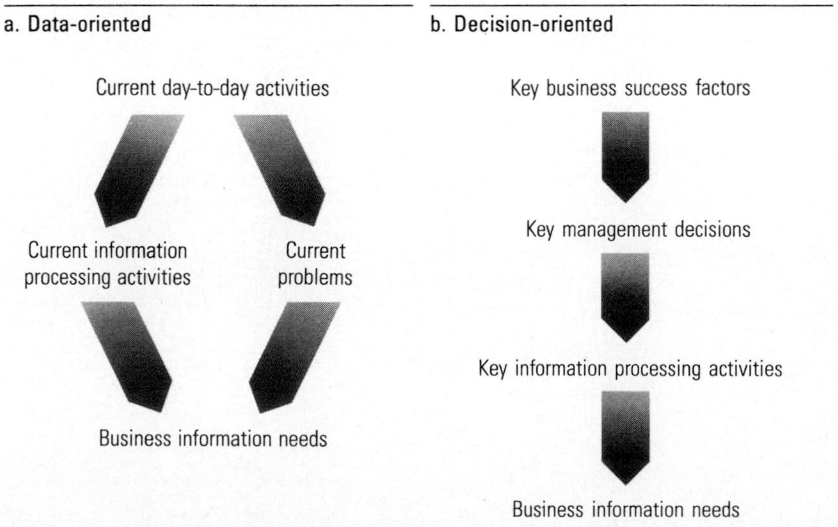

Exhibit 11.16

The data-oriented approach to logical design focuses on day-to-day business activities.The decision-oriented approach to logical design focuses on the managerial decisions critical to the business function being performed.

Exhibit 11.17

This CRT screen layout form shows a screen display that Jerry Lincoln felt would aid the purchasing director in selecting a supplier for a particular product. The heavy lines on the form indicate different sizes of CRT screens. The numbered columns across the top and the numbered rows down the left side of the form allowed Jerry to show precisely where information will appear on the CRT screen.

CRT LAYOUT FORM

PROGRAM NAME ______ PROGRAM IDENTIFICATION ______
PROGRAMMER ______ DATE ______ PAGE ______ OF ______

PRODUCT NUMBER: XXXX
PRODUCT DESCRIPTION: XXXXXXXXXXXXXXXXXXXXXXXXX

SUPPLIER NUMBER	NAME	PRICE	DISCOUNT	ON-TIME DELIVERY	REJECTION RATE
XXXX	XXXXXXXXXXXXXXXXXXXX	$XXXXX.XX	XXX.X %	XXX.X %	XXX.X %
XXXX	XXXXXXXXXXXXXXXXXXXX	$XXXXX.XX	XXX.X %	XXX.X %	XXX.X %
XXXX	XXXXXXXXXXXXXXXXXXXX	$XXXXX.XX	XXX.X %	XXX.X %	XXX.X %
XXXX	XXXXXXXXXXXXXXXXXXXX	$XXXXX.XX	XXX.X %	XXX.X %	XXX.X %
XXXX	XXXXXXXXXXXXXXXXXXXX	$XXXXX.XX	XXX.X %	XXX.X %	XXX.X %

DETAILS:

proved best in diagnosing and then presenting the factors to be considered in selecting suppliers.

Validating the Logical Design. After a logical design has been produced, the design should be reviewed by users as a check on its appropriateness. The systems analyst thus has to present this design to users in an easily understood manner.

A good way to communicate information system outputs and inputs to users is to produce examples of what the outputs and inputs will look like. **CRT screen layout forms** and **report layout forms,** for example, provide an easy way to show users how a CRT screen or a report might appear. Exhibit 11.17 shows the layout Jerry Lincoln prepared to show Tom Berkshire one of the CRT screen images he felt would help purchasing clerks select suppliers. Data flow diagrams are another excellent means of communicating a logical design to users. Finally, **systems flowcharts,** which depict the various hardware devices and media involved with a design, are a very useful way of showing users how the logical design will be physically implemented. Exhibit 11.18 shows the standard symbols used with system flowcharts and Exhibit 11.19 shows the systems flowchart that Jerry put together for Tom.

Exhibit 11.18
Standard System Flowchart Symbols

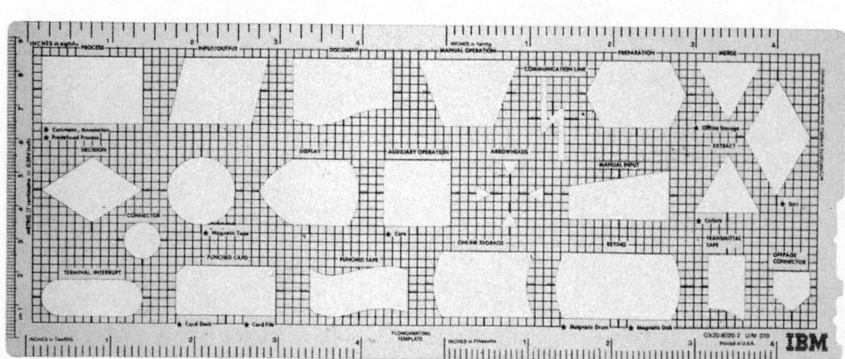

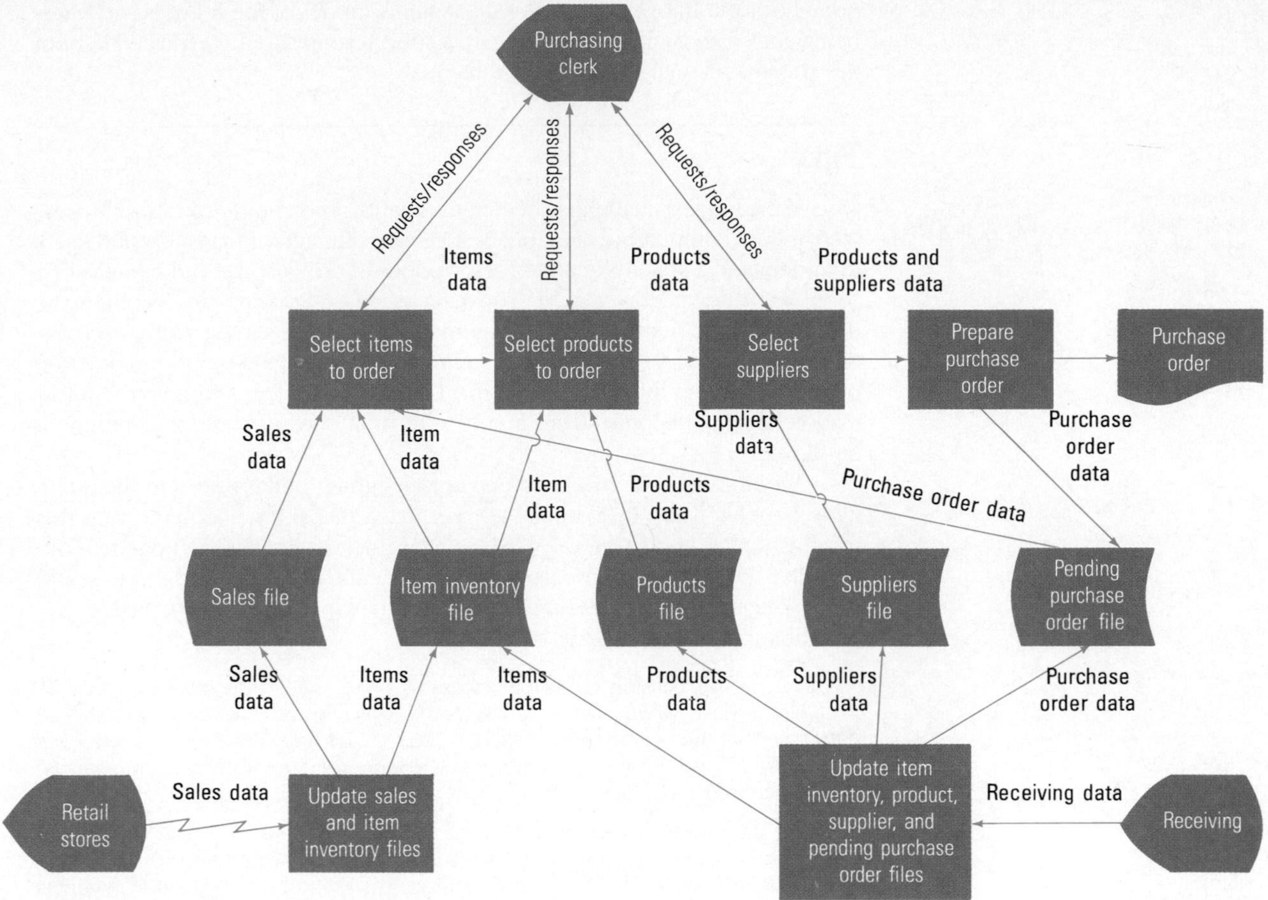

Exhibit 11.19

This systems flowchart shows the hardware devices that Jerry Lincoln believed should be used in handling the information processing associated with the logical design of Compu-Store's Purchasing Information System, shown in Exhibit 11.15.

Reviewing the Feasibility Study and the Project Plan. Systems analysts learn a great deal about an information system when they develop and then validate a logical design. Often, what they learn proves some of their earlier assumptions incorrect. Because of this learning, key decisions reached early in a project need to be reviewed throughout the project.

The conclusion of the logical design is a good time to take another look at the reasoning that went into the feasibility study and the project plan. Remember Jan Hale's advice—you don't want to get surprised late in a project.

Documentation

Three documentation manuals are begun during the systems analysis stage. Descriptions of a project's purpose and scope, all the details associated with its feasibility study, and an up-to-date version of the project plan should be placed in the project manual. A discussion of the motivations that prompted the development of the information system, a systems model of the business activities being automated, and the requirements specification should be placed in both the systems manual and the users' manual.

Tips

One of the biggest challenges of systems analysis is communicating with users who are not computer professionals. It is often difficult for managers and users to understand a systems analyst's descriptions of the purpose and benefits of a proposed information system. You can usually overcome this problem by using business-oriented descriptions and stating benefits in *measurable* terms. Review Exhibit 11.8 to see how Jerry Lincoln expressed the scope and purpose of the purchasing information system. This description should help the information system become clear in the minds of the purchasing department employees.

One of Jerry Lincoln's problems was assigning dollar values to the intangible benefits listed in Exhibit 11.9. Yet, most managers need and want this information. A good way to place dollar values on intangible benefits is to consider the secondary impacts of these benefits. In other words, you would carry your analysis forward until you reach tangible outcomes. Consider the two intangible benefits Jerry identified:

1. If the purchasing clerk has access to better sales information, decisions regarding when and how much to order should improve. This should reduce the overall number of purchase orders (possibly by 15 percent) and reduce the number of "emergency shipments" (possibly by as much as 80 percent).
2. If the purchasing clerk has access to better supplier information, CompuStore could consistently order from the suppliers with the lowest costs and highest reliability. This should reduce the overall price paid for products (possibly by as much as 20 percent). CompuStore could lower its customers' prices about 10 percent, and still increase its profitability by as much as 10 percent.

Using reasoning such as this, Jerry and Tom Berkshire can arrive at dollar values for the intangible benefits.

A final source of faulty communication may occur during the information gathering interviews. Managers and users have a tendency to start talking about computers and the information system outputs they are already receiving. Such a discussion tends to focus on current problems rather than future possibilities. Thus, managers and users might never mention an information need they incorrectly feel could not be met. A good strategy for avoiding this problem is to steer interviewees away from talking about computers or about their current information systems. Direct the conversation toward their work and toward business activities.

Gearing Up for Rapid Growth

Carol Lake, director of investor relations for Texasfirst, was overwhelmed with work. Like many managers she was asked to do a superlative job on an impossible timetable with a limited budget.

Texasfirst was a fast-growing Fortune 1000 petrochemical company. As an outstanding performer in a glamourous industry, it was attracting a lot of attention from investors and the financial community. Lake's job was to keep the two groups up-to-date on the company's operations and performance.

Lake saw the problem. She, her secretary and two administrative assistants sometimes worked 10-hour days, but, in the rush to get work done, procedures that had worked well before were breaking down now. Either she had to convince management to give her more staff, or she had to find some cost-effective way to automate her department.

Following prescribed company policies, Lake requested help from Texasfirst's central data processing department. Mary Phelan, an office systems analyst, was assigned to work with Lake.

Phelan began by diagramming department workflows to determine what activities were performed, which personnel were involved and how much time a given task required.

Lake had been classifying incoming requests according to source—existing stockholder, potential stockholder, financial press, industry analyst. Phelan's diagrams showed that the processing of each type of request followed a different path within the department.

Almost everyone asked for one or more financial documents—annual reports, Securities and Exchange Commission filings, press releases. Both current and potential stockholders also requested explanations of financial data, for example, details on how the company calculated inventory.

TWO ROADS DIVERGE

Information to fill most requests came from two sources: a file room and the company's mainframe computers. If publications were requested, one of Lake's assistants typed an order form and forwarded it to the file room. File clerks selected the correct materials and sent them to the mail room. If financial data were requested, Lake's assistant retrieved it from the central computer using a dedicated terminal and mailed it directly from her department. Unfortunately, as the number of requests increased, so did errors: lost order forms, materials in the wrong envelope, only parts of a request filled.

Lake directly handled requests for meetings or interviews with management. She would telephone an executive or his secretary to schedule an appointment. Inevitably her calls led to telephone tag, scheduling delays, and the risk of alienating an analyst.

Once Phelan had diagrammed this workflow, she requested computer-cost data for Lake's department from the controller's office. As part of its budgeting process, Texasfirst charged each department for its use of the corporate computer center, including hardware costs such as terminals and printers, computer time for processing departmental records and disk storage for departmental data.

WHICH WAY TO GO?

Phelan found that the terminal in investor relations had been purchased three years ago and was completely depreciated. Its maintenance cost was negligible, about $12 a month. Annual usage charges for getting and printing financial data from the central computer were about $25,000 a year. Data processing estimated that these charges would probably grow by about 20 percent a year, based on predicted increases in cost and usage.

Other related expenses for the department—word processing costs and special charges for things like graphics generation, slide production and telegrams—totalled at least $25,000 a year.

Armed with her workflow diagrams and this financial information, Phelan began her analysis: what system or systems would best solve the problems of Carol Lake's department at a reasonable cost?

Phelan came up with two alternatives. The first was to acquire an additional mainframe terminal that could be installed in the department for about $3400 including cabling costs. One problem, however, was the training time required. Each of the mainframe software packages had a different set of commands, keystrokes, and procedures. Given the heavy workloads of Lake's staff and the data processing people who could act as trainers, Phelan estimated that at least two additional employees would be needed to fill in during the training period. Total cost for this alternative—equipment, training, and personnel—would be at least $25,000 the first year, according to Phelan's calculations. This was in addition to the estimated $50,000 a year already charged to Lake's department by the corporate computer center.

The other option was to install microcomputers connected to the mainframe. These could serve as multifunction workstations, operating both as microcomputers and as mainframe terminals. Using standard, simple-to-learn software packages, Lake's administrative assistants could quickly produce orders for information by using a program called VersaForm from Applied Software Technology, Los Gatos, California, a data-base manager easily customized by the user. VersaForm allows the user to "paint" desired input and output forms on the display, and then creates and stores those forms.

TURN TO EFFICIENCY

Mary Phelan calculated the cost for the microcomputer option at approximately $50,000, including hardware, software, installation costs and training time. Both she and Carol Lake were convinced it was the best option. Phelan's analysis showed that it could quickly increase both the capacity and effectiveness of Lake's department, without requiring additional staff for at least four or five years.

Today both Lake and Texasfirst are convinced they made the right decision. Information provided by the investor relations department has improved in quality and quantity, while response time has been drastically reduced. That success has been translated into personal terms for Carol Lake: she is now a vice president of the corporation.

Source: J. T. Monk and K. M. Landis, "Gearing Up for Rapid Growth," *Business Computer Systems,* September 1983, pp. 45–46.

SUMMARY

Systems development refers to all the activities performed in designing, building, and introducing an information system. Systems analysts direct and perform much of this work.

Successful information systems perform a useful business function, are appropriate for the business, and are used.

Many information system failures can be traced to "communication" problems during systems development. Three systems development tools useful in preventing these problems are structured design, project management, and documentation.

Structured design is an approach to systems development that stresses the importance of reaching early agreement on an information system's major design decisions. This approach to information systems design is guided by the three *design principles of: abstraction, stepwise refinement,* and *modularity.*

Project management techniques provide an effective means of coordinating system development tasks. Project teams are set up to develop an information system, with a systems analyst usually serving as the project manager. Often, the project team reports to a top management steering committee. Project activities are broken into small, well-defined tasks whose completion represent project milestones. These activities are then monitored by using project management tools such as *Gantt charts* and *PERT diagrams.*

Documentation refers to permanent descriptions of the systems development activities and their outcomes. Five types of documentation are commonly used in a systems development project: a *project manual,* a *systems manual,* a *users' manual,* a *programmers' manual,* and an *operators' manual.*

The *systems life cycle* refers to the complete set of systems development activities normally involved in the development of an information system. There are five stages in the systems life cycle: systems analysis, systems design, systems acquisition, systems implementation, and systems maintenance.

The purpose of *systems analysis* is to assess the appropriateness of a proposed information system and to describe how the information system would function.

The purpose of *systems design* is to design the hardware and software components as well as the operating procedures to link these components to an information system's users.

The purpose of *systems acquisition* is to purchase hardware and software components and to write any needed programs.

The purpose of *systems implementation* is to introduce the developed information system into the business departments that will be using it.

The purpose of *systems maintenance* is to ensure that an information system, over time, continues to meet a business's information needs.

People issues need to be addressed during each of the systems life-cycle stages. Systems analysts can develop these needed people-oriented skills from college classes, from working with an experienced systems analyst, and from their own experiences. Having users participate actively on project teams is another means of making sure that people's concerns are handled in an appropriate manner.

Three major activities are performed during the systems analysis stage of the systems life cycle. During *project definition,* the scope and purpose of an information system are determined. During the *feasibility study,* a decision is made regarding whether or not the information system should be developed. During *logical design,* the business's information needs are described from the user's perspective.

The scope of an information system identifies the business activities that are to be performed or supported. The purpose of an information system ties the project back to the business needs that motivated the project in the first place.

The feasibility study should address three issues: the information system's technical feasibility, its operational feasibility, and its economic feasibility. The final *"go/no go"* decision is normally based on a comparison of the project's benefits and costs. Both *tangible and intangible* benefits and costs should be included.

The logical design produces a detailed description, known as a *requirements specification,* of the information system's inputs and outputs. Many experts believe the logical design is the most important step in the systems life cycle. Five tasks are involved in performing a logical design: gathering information, analyzing the information, developing the logical design, validating the logical design, and reviewing the feasibility study and the project plan.

A systems analyst gathers data from both internal and external sources. Common information-gathering techniques include reading relevant materials, observing business activities, measuring work rates and volumes, having users keep *diaries* or fill out *questionnaires,* and *interviewing* users and their managers.

Gathered information needs to be analyzed in order to derive a business's information needs. Common tools used are *narrative descriptions,* tables or graphs that summarize data, *grid charts, decision tables,* and *data flow charts.*

Logical designs can be developed following a *data-oriented* approach, a *decision-oriented* approach, or, as is usually the case, both approaches.

The logical design should be validated by users. In communicating the information system's inputs and outputs to users, the systems analyst can make use of *CRT screen and report layout forms, data flow diagrams,* and *systems flowcharts.*

Three documentation manuals are begun during the systems analysis stage—the project manual, the systems manual, and the users' manual.

In the next chapter, we will examine the remaining four stages of the systems life cycle.

REVIEW QUESTIONS

1. What is *systems development?* What three characteristics are shared by successful information systems?
2. Identify the three most common problems associated with unsuccessful information systems.
3. What is *structured design?* What major benefits does such an approach offer?
4. Briefly describe the three design principles embodied in the structured design approach.
5. The Alpha Corporation is preparing to embark on a systems development project. The firm is seeking tools to aid in the management of this activity. Discuss two project management tools Alpha may consider.
6. Briefly describe the five basic types of documentation used in a systems design project.
7. Briefly describe the five stages of the systems life cycle.
8. Briefly evaluate the advantages and disadvantages of user participation in systems development.
9. Briefly describe the three basic activities involved in systems analysis.
10. The Zephon Corporation is engaged in a systems development project. Management is of the opinion that all steps in the systems life-cycle process are equally important. Do you agree? Which step would you consider to be most important? Why?
11. Briefly describe the two basic design strategies used in developing a logical design. When is each most likely to be emphasized?
12. Identify the three types of documentation manuals that are begun during the systems analysis stage and briefly describe the information each would contain at the conclusion of this stage.

CHAPTER 12

Systems Development II

COMPUTERS AT WORK

Aetna Plans for "No-Fault" OA

In October 1980, Aetna Life & Casualty's senior management met to discuss the long-term impact of technology on Aetna's business. There was little disagreement that technology and office automation were playing an ever expanding role in business operations. But management also recognized that a critical factor in successfully applying such technology, then and in the future, would be the employees' ability and willingness to use it. If work was to be done in dramatically different ways, Aetna employees were going to be significantly affected. Senior management wanted to know what the impact would be and how they could make the introduction of technology a positive experience. They decided to create a unit that would assess the impact of technology on Aetna employees and develop programs and policies to address the issues found. The unit was called People/Technology Programs (P/TP).

Addressing the ergonomic and human factors that can arise when people must interact with machines is not an easy task anywhere. At Aetna, it is more complicated than at most companies because of the size of the organization.

Aetna Life & Casualty, based in Hartford, Connecticut, is the nation's largest investor-owned insurance and financial services institution, based on assets of $47 billion. The company's six divisions, including subsidiaries, employ 53,000 workers nationwide. Assisting these employees are 23 large-scale computer systems, processing approximately a half million transactions a day and supporting a network of about 12,000 visual display units (vdus). Combine these 12,000 vdus with about 2000 word processing and personal computer workstations and Aetna has a terminal-to-worker ratio of approximately one to three. By 1990, Aetna anticipates it will have one terminal for every worker it employs. P/TP was mandated to handle issues pertaining to both the personnel and the data processing departments, yet it does not clearly fall under the purview of either department. But because most of the knowledge and experience with technological issues at Aetna resides in the data processing areas, the unit reports to the company's vice-president of the Corporate Administration Division, the top information systems executive.

MANAGER IS KEY TO SUCCESS

The manager is the key to successfully handling the relationship between the worker and the work environment in the automated office. P/TP helps managers understand and manage the new workplace and the new problems and procedures that may accompany it. We encourage managers to become more involved with systems development than they traditionally have been, and more aware of the available technology. We are also concerned with the human issues involved in getting managers to use the new technology themselves.

Source: R. J. Telesca, "Aetna Plans for 'No-Fault' OA," *Datamation,* 15 April, 1984, pp. 93–100.

Aetna Life & Casualty clearly understands the importance of "people-issues" in systems development. Their People/Technology Program was formed because they recognize that information system success depends on a careful blend of technology and the needs of the people who will use it. It became impossible for them to separate business success from their employees' willingness to use technology effectively.

The key to Aetna's People/Technology Program is the firm's managers. All managers are expected to become involved with systems development activities. What goes on in systems development? In the last chapter, you learned the systems analysis stage of the systems life cycle. Here, you will focus on the remaining four stages. In this chapter, you will learn to do the following:

1. Describe the systems design stage of the systems life cycle and list its five steps.
2. Describe the systems acquisition stage of the systems life cycle and list its five steps.
3. Describe the systems implementation stage of the systems life cycle and list its three steps.
4. Describe the systems maintenance stage of the systems life cycle and list its two steps.
5. Explain how prototyping fits into the systems development process.

SYSTEMS DESIGN

Jerry Lincoln was a bit uneasy about his first systems design project. Actually, the systems analysis for CompuStore's Purchasing Information System had gone smoothly. Learning about people's work and helping them find solutions for problems had actually been fun. Jerry, however, did not consider himself a "computer jock." How was he supposed to put together the best possible technical design for the Purchasing Information System?

The **systems design stage** of the systems life cycle produces a physical design of the information system being developed. A **physical design** describes the hardware, software, and operating procedures that should enable an information system's logical design to become a reality.

While technical knowledge is important in systems design, the "human touch" cannot be overlooked. Jan Hale made this quite clear as she advised Jerry about the project:

> *"I'm not expecting you to come up with the 'best possible' design, Jerry. What I want is a 'workable' design, a design that fits the task, fits the firm, and fits the people. And the design shouldn't be out-of-date next year.*
>
> *You need to concern yourself with three things. First, use appropriate computer technology. Meet the information needs that are described in the requirements specification, but be sure that your design is affordable and compatible with our other equipment and the abilities of the users and that it makes use of up-to-date technology. Second, don't unnecessarily upset the firm or its employees. Maximize positive changes—changes that improve business operations or people's jobs. At the same time, minimize negative changes—changes that disturb business operations or the work environment. Third, make sure your design can grow with the business. Increases in work volumes, in staffing, or in the product line should be handled easily, as should changes in computer hardware.*
>
> *If your systems design meets these three objectives, we'll have a successful information system."*

Jerry's confidence returned while he was listening to Jan. He didn't have to be a technical expert to develop a physical design of the Purchasing Information System. What he needed was a knowledge of the basic technical alternatives, some sense of current hardware and software trends, and most important, a good understanding of the business and the information system's users. This need to constantly address both technical and people issues is precisely what makes the systems analyst's job such a challenging and rewarding career.

Five activities are performed during systems design (see Exhibit 12.1). The first three activities, output design, input design, and process design, produce the physical design. The last two activities, testing procedures and a review of the feasibility study and project plan, tie this physical design to the remaining systems development activities. The testing procedures designed in systems design will be used during the systems acquisition and systems implementation stages.

Step 1: Output Design

Information systems produce three types of outputs. Two of these have been discussed in detail in earlier chapters: business documents and management reports. The third type of output might be thought of as an electronic document, a business transaction sent from one computer system to another. CompuStore is thinking of transmitting purchase orders directly from their minicomputer to their suppliers' computers. This could reduce paperwork and improve the accuracy and speed of the purchasing process. Another business

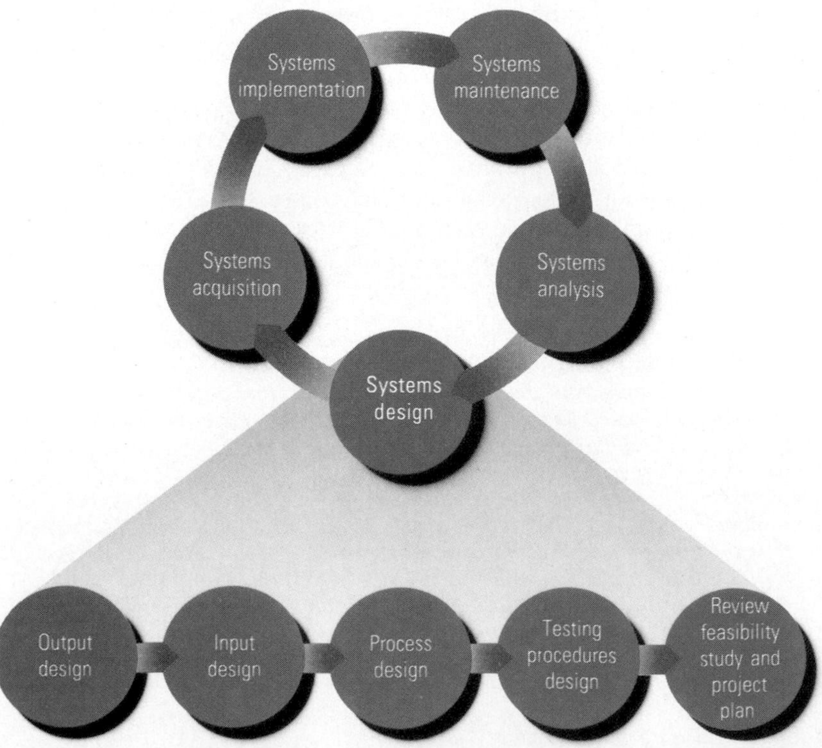

Exhibit 12.1

The systems design stage of the systems life cycle produces a detailed specification of the hardware and software components required to build an information system.

document might be considered a fourth type of output: the turnaround document. A **turnaround document** refers to a paper-based output, such as a bill or an order form, that is computer-readable.

All these outputs were described in detail during systems analysis. What, then, takes place in **output design?** First, the content and ease-of-use of these outputs are evaluated. Errors and omissions are corrected, and improvements are suggested. Second, needed hardware and software are identified and then described in terms of their information processing characteristics and costs.

How would you go about evaluating the outputs described in a logical design? The following approach is a good starting point: First, look at the information system's purpose and benefits and then decide whether the outputs are relevant. Are the data and information complete? Has anything been overlooked? Are all data and information needed? Are data and information being produced in a timely fashion? Could outputs be produced less frequently and still be effective?

Second, examine the documents and reports to determine if the data and information could be made more presentable. Are the data readable? Is the information usable? Can tabular information be replaced with charts or graphs? Could color be used to clarify a document or enhance a report? On the following page, Computers at Work: "Color Communicates" discusses some of the benefits that color can provide.

Third, check the accessibility of documents, reports, and the information system for users. Will access be difficult or inconvenient? If so, users may stay away from the information system. Will hard copy output be needed or will a CRT screen image be sufficient? Might users wish to access the information system immediately after looking at a document or a report? You should notice the common theme that runs through each of these considerations—an attention to "people issues."

Step 2: Input Design

Input design is concerned with the procedures followed in entering data into an information system. As with output design, the first task is to make sure that the input items specified in the logical design are complete and relevant. Are all the inputs required to produce each output present? Are all inputs being used to produce outputs? Once this has been done, three design issues remain: selecting a dialogue style, selecting a data entry procedure, and designing forms.

Dialogue Design. Dialogues refer to the interactive "conversations" between an information system and a user. Usually, this interaction takes place so that the user can "trigger," or select, an information processing action or enter data for processing or storage. Tony Santos, CompuStore's purchasing clerk, engages in both types of interaction with the Purchasing Information System. He triggers the actions to be performed, such as listing the current status of an inventory item or printing a purchase order, and he enters data, such as the name of the selected supplier or the quantity to be ordered.

The three most common dialogue styles are commands, menus, and prompts. These styles vary in the flexibility provided users and in the demands placed on users.

With the **command dialogue style,** each information system action is given a "tag," termed a command. To trigger an action, the user enters the

Color Communicates

Did you know:

red-appearing surfaces tend to "advance" toward the viewer? And blues "recede"?

color preferences change during the aging process? (Children prefer warmer colors, adults cooler.)

the human eye can discern roughly one million colors?

Color.

It's something we share and talk about as much as the weather. Yet it has an influence over human behavior that's sometimes simple, sometimes mysterious. There are certain combinations that almost all of us respond to positively, like the first blossoms of spring. But color can be something we debate as much as sports strategy or the merits of an investment.

With color, there are absolutes in terms of physics, light, and the chemicals that make up the dyes of inks and paints. But that's where the absolutes end.

A number of experiments have shown that we rarely see a color as a "pure" value. More often it is viewed in relation to its surroundings, cultural attributes, and our own physiological and psychological states at the moment of perception. (Anyone questioning the latter need only look into his or her closet. We all have a few items that make us say "Why in the world did I ever think this was attractive?")

In business communications, then, we might benefit from uncovering those factors that will aid us in using color to our advantage.

GAINING AN EDGE

In charts and graphs, annual reports, business letters, stationery, and CRT displays, the knowledgeable communicator has an edge. People can be moved by, or at least pay more atten-

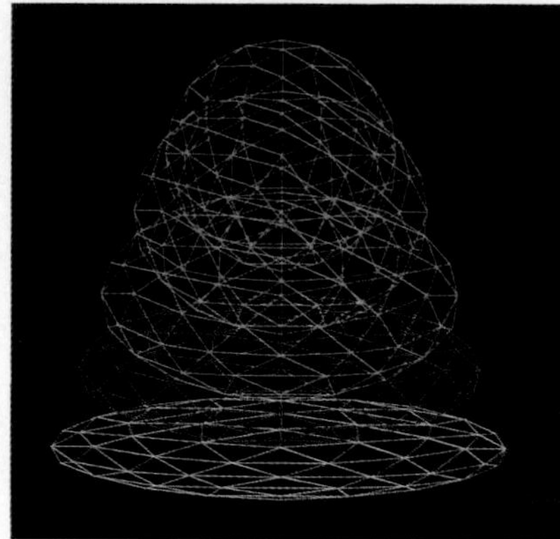

tion to, certain color combinations over others.

Steve Tharler, creative director of Cinamon Associates, a prominent Boston area direct mail consulting firm, says there are a great many things to take into consideration. "Insurance companies, for instance, generally stay away from using red and black together, because they connote injury and death to a number of people. Or when communicating with a western U.S. audience, it's best not to use browns, because they bring to mind dryness, bad crops."

In business letters (even when printed), Tharler continues, "a blue signature is usually taken more seriously; and a light blue reply envelope consistently draws a better response than any other color. This is currently so well established that light blue is practically automatic." Tharler emphasizes that nothing is always "true" in the use of color—at least not in direct mail. And what people respond to today is not necessarily what they will respond to tomorrow.

The Institute of Outdoor Advertising, a group naturally concerned with color legibility, offers a number of pointers for prospective users of color on a BIG scale. The most readable two-color combination for billboard and poster use is black on a yellow background. Next is black on white, yellow on black, white on black, blue on white, and white on blue. From there, more colors come into play, but readability declines. Of the eighteen combinations that provide "excellent" outdoor readability, yellow on bright pink finishes at number eighteen. (Let us give thanks.)

MAKE EVERY SLIDE A BILLBOARD

What applies to billboards may also apply to projected slides and presentations in general. Outdoor advertisers have always been forced to live by the "Less is More" theory of communication. After all, their readers have only a few seconds to see the message before they go whizzing by.

The main guideline of their genre, as is true for most effective communications, is simply this:

> Use fewer but more dramatic images, in fewer but more dramatic colors, with fewer but more dramatic words.

Think of each business graph or slide as a billboard, where your viewer should be able to grasp the main point at a glance.

Thus a choice selection of four colors, tastefully arranged and distributed, can be far more potent than fifteen colors used together. The more colors used, the more competition for your viewer's attention. Charts and graphs can often be "dense" enough without forcing your audience to "dig out" the profit line on a poorly designed, multihued graph. (Conversely, if the intention is to hide an unpleasant fact, by all means use a plentiful palette.)

Source: J. DiCocco, "How Color Communicates," *Business Computing,* July/August 1983, pp. 27-29.

appropriate command. Because the user actively directs the information system's actions, this style provides users the most flexibility. The user, however, has to remember the commands to use the information system. This can be difficult, especially when a large number of commands are available.

Commands vary in their form. Abbreviations, single words, and phrases are all used. Exhibit 12.2 illustrates the two extremes of abbreviations and phrases. While abbreviations require fewer keystrokes, they are often hard to remember. Phrases tend to be easier to remember, but keying a long series of characters can be slow and tedious.

With the **menu dialogue style,** the information system lists a series of actions and the user selects an action from this list. Often, menu options may lead to other menus until the action sought by a user is reached. Exhibit 12.3 illustrates the **main menu** from the Purchasing Information System.

With menus, the software limits the user's choice of action. Another disadvantage of menus is that it may take a long time to move through a series of menus. On the other hand, menus are easy to use. An inexperienced user can quickly begin to use an information system. No command list needs to be learned, and the menus inform users of the information system's basic capabilities.

The final dialogue style involves the use of *prompts,* simple instructions or questions posed to a user by the information system. If clear prompts are used, prompts require minimal effort on the part of users. However, users do lose considerable flexibility—the software dictates the sequence in which actions are taken. Exhibit 12.4 illustrates how prompts might be used with the Purchasing Information System.

Exhibit 12.2

The command dialogue style can vary in form. Abbreviations are easy to use, but hard to understand and remember. Phrases are easier to understand and remember, but can be inconvenient.

Abbreviations	Phrases
LSTS	LIST SUPPLIERS
LSTI	LIST INVENTORY ITEMS
FCSTS	FORECAST SALES
DSPS	DISPLAY SUPPLIER INFORMATION
DSPP	DISPLAY PRODUCT INFORMATION
PREPO	PREPARE PURCHASE ORDER
PRIPO	PRINT PURCHASE ORDER

Data Entry Design.

Data entry design refers to the manner in which data are initially entered into an information system. As discussed in Chapter 4, this normally occurs in one of two ways. In batch processing, data are trans-

```
Purchasing Information System
          Main Menu

1. Select items to order
2. Select products
3. Select suppliers
4. Prepare purchase order
5. Print purchase order

Select desired menu choice:
```

Exhibit 12.3

This main menu is the purchasing clerk's "entrance" into the Purchasing Information System. If Tony Santos were ready to select a supplier, he would enter a "3."

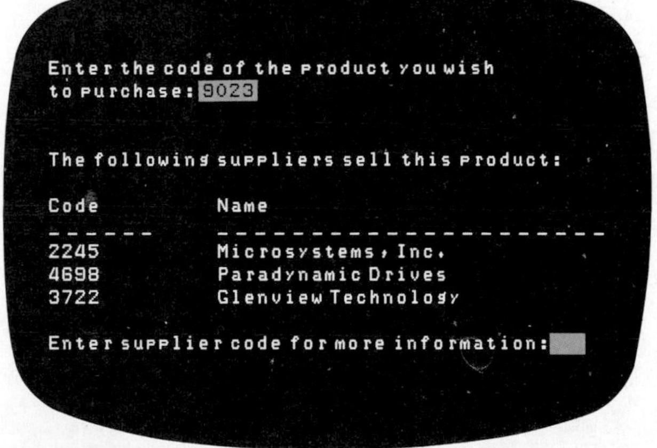

Exhibit 12.4

This CRT screen appears when main menu "3" is selected on the Purchasing Information System's main menu. Tony is first prompted to enter the code number of the product to be purchased. His response produces a list of suppliers who sell the product. To obtain information about a particular supplier, Tony simply enters the supplier's code.

formed into computer-readable form offline and then entered into the computer in a batch. Two basic types of batch processing exist. The first uses people and key-to-tape or key-to-disk devices in entering data. The second uses source data automation devices. In transaction processing, data are entered into the information system for immediate processing as each business transaction occurs. Data can be entered by a person working through a terminal or through source data automation devices. These various data entry approaches can produce large differences in the nature of the data that enter an information system, in the impact an information system has on business operations, and in an information system's cost.

Two key characteristics of data are integrity and currentness. **Data integrity,** or accuracy, is achieved in two ways: by preventing errors, or by detecting and then correcting them. Errors can be prevented by eliminating steps in data entry procedures, by simplifying data entry procedures, or by training the people performing data entry tasks. A number of techniques for detecting data entry errors were discussed in Chapter 8.

Data currentness, or timeliness, is achieved by entering data as soon as it is possible to do so. Jerry Lincoln's first thoughts about data currentness can best be summarized as "the more current the data, the better the information." Jan Hale explained that this isn't always the case:

> *"What you need to remember, Jerry, is that the important issue is the timeliness of information, not the currentness of data. If an information system produces monthly reports, it is not necessary to enter data as soon as they are captured. Entering data an hour, a day, a week, or even two weeks after they have been captured might be fine."*

Data entry can be very disruptive. Procedures that require employees to fill out forms or use a keyboard can take people away from their normal jobs. Not only does this interrupt their work, but it causes them to be careless as they enter data. As a result, automated data entry is almost always preferred. When employees must perform data entry tasks, make these tasks as close as possible to their normal work duties.

Data entry costs depend on the cost of labor and the cost of input devices. Exhibit 12.5 shows how these costs vary as data volumes increase. With low data volume, human data entry is normally less expensive, since inexpensive hardware is used. With high data volumes, automated data entry becomes less expensive, since the cost of the hardware can be spread over many data entry operations.

Exhibit 12.6 summarizes the performance of the different data entry procedures. Manual batch processing tends to be used when cost is more critical than are accuracy or currentness. With high data volumes, batch processing with source data automation input devices can reduce this cost even further while improving accuracy and being less disruptive. When currentness and accuracy are critical, transaction processing tends to be preferred. With high data volumes, transaction processing through source data automation can result in even higher performance.

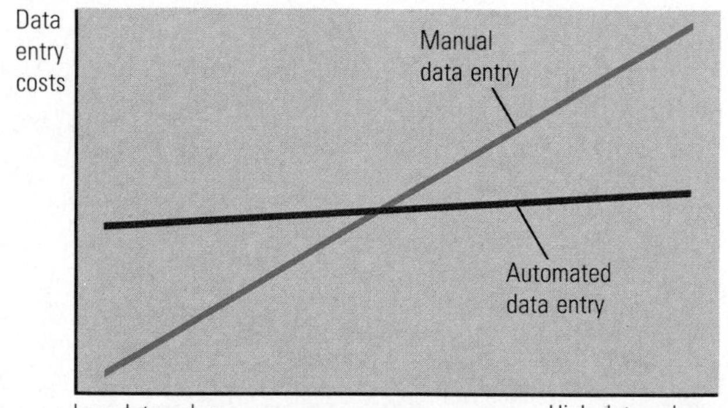

Exhibit 12.5

Automated data entry procedures usually require more expensive hardware than manual procedures use. Thus, manual data entry is usually less costly at low data volumes.

Exhibit 12.6

The different data entry procedures can result in quite different information systems. The accuracy and currentness of stored data and the extent to which the information system disrupts business operations will vary as will the cost of the information system.

	Produces accurate data	Produces current data	Disrupts normal procedures	Cost
Batch processing				
Manual	fair	fair	fair	good at most all volumes
Source data automation	best	fair	good	best at high volume; poor at low volume
Transaction processing				
Manual	good	good	fair	good at low volume; poor at high volume
Source data automation	best	best	good	poor at low volume; good at high volume

Forms Design. Businesses use many forms to track their day-to-day activities. Large businesses use thousands of forms. When a business form captures data that are to be entered into an information system, the form is called a *source document.* Fewer errors occur when well-designed forms are used. You can design good forms by following a few simple rules:

It should be easy to read or enter data on a form. Leave a lot of "white space" on the form.

Be sure to include instructions on the form.

Reduce the amount of data that need to be entered on a form by prerecording all data known ahead of time.

Most important, make sure that the data being collected need to be collected. Some collected data are never used, and data collected on one form have often already been collected on another form.

Step 3: Process Design

Most computer-generated business documents and management reports are produced from stored data. These data are transformed into outputs by programs. File design and software design are the main activities accomplished during process design.

File Design. File design includes five tasks. First, all data items to be stored are identified and organized into records and files. Second, any codes used to represent data values are designed. Third, file updating procedures are selected. Fourth, file access methods are selected. Fifth, file protection schemes are specified.

The first task, identifying and then grouping the data items to be stored in an information system, is the most important file design activity. Adding data items to an information system's data files late in the systems life cycle can be very costly. A major benefit of data base management systems is the ease with which such data file changes can be handled.

Exhibit 12.7

If an information system will access data already stored in a computer data file, the file design should list these data files and data items. The Purchasing Information System uses the data items shown from the sales, item inventory, and supplier data files.

Existing data file	Retrieved data items
Sales	item number sales totals for each of last 12 months
Item inventory	item number current inventory level suggested reorder point suggested reorder quantity
Supplier	supplier number supplier name supplier address average delivery time discount rate

Jerry Lincoln used five data files in designing CompuStore's Purchasing Information System: a sales file, an item inventory file, a products file, a suppliers file, and a pending purchase order file. Since the sales, item inventory, and suppliers files already existed, Jerry listed only the data that would be retrieved from these files. This is shown in Exhibit 12.7. The products and pending purchase order files were new. For these files, Jerry created a file layout chart and a data dictionary. A **file layout chart** shows how each record in a data file is organized, and a **data dictionary** defines the data items in this record. Exhibit 12.8 gives the file layout chart and data dictionary definitions that Jerry created for the pending purchase order file.

The second task in file design is designing the data codes. **Data codes** are used to reduce the amount of data being stored, to identify records in a data file, and to link data files together. For example, rather than place a supplier's name and address in the pending purchase order file, Jerry stored the supplier's code. Given this code, a program can retrieve the correct name and address when printing a purchase order. The most important rule to follow in designing a set of codes is to allow for the future expansion of the code. CompuStore's product and supplier codes, for example, allow for 9999 different products and 9999 different suppliers.

The third task in file design is choosing between the batch processing and transaction processing mode of updating data files. With batch processing, data describing recent business transactions are collected over a certain period of time, termed the **batching cycle.** Then the entire batch of transactions is

Exhibit 12.8

If an information system will require that new data files be created, the file design needs to describe these data files. A file layout chart indicates how data items are to be stored in a file. A data dictionary describes each of these data items. One of the new data files used by the Purchasing Information System is the pending purchase order file.

File layout chart

Position	Data item
1–5	purchase order number
7–10	supplier code
12–19	date of order
21–28	date order expected
30–33	product code (1st product ordered)
35–38	product quantity
40–43	product code (2nd product ordered)
45–48	product quantity
"	"
"	"
"	"
120–123	product code (10th product ordered)
125–128	product quantity

Data dictionary

Purchase order number	5-digit code identifying the purchase order. Begins at "10000" at beginning of each calendar year.
Supplier code	4-digit supplier code identifying the supplier from whom products are purchased.
Date of order	The date the purchase order was sent. Stored as MM-DD-YY.
Date order expected	The date the order is expected to be received from the supplier. Stored as MM-DD-YY.
Product code	A 4-digit product code identifying an ordered product
Product quantity	The quantity ordered for the product (up to 9999 units).

processed at once to update a data file. With transaction processing, data describing business transactions are entered into the information sytem as they occur. Thus, the data file is immediately updated.

In selecting an updating procedure, a trade-off is made between processing cost and data file currentness. The longer the batching cycle, the less expensive it is to update a data file. But, long batching cycles may result in out-of-date data files. Few business applications can justify the expense of immediate file updates. However, relatively current data files can be maintained by using short batching cycles.

The data files used in the Purchasing Information System varied in their currentness requirements. Jerry Lincoln accounted for this by using the following batching cycles: monthly for sales, every four hours for item inventory, monthly for products, weekly for suppliers, and daily for pending purchase orders. These batching cycles were chosen to mesh with the purchasing information needs described by Tony Santos and Tom Berkshire.

A fourth task during file design is choosing between the sequential, direct, and indexed sequential access methods. A key factor here is **data file activity,** the proportion of records in a file that are retrieved and processed. When file activity is high, sequential access is both less expensive and more timely than direct access. When file activity is low, the opposite is true. Searching through the complete item inventory file to compare item inventory levels with their reorder points is a high-activity task. However, retrieving a reorder quantity for a single item is a low-activity task. In this situation, the indexed sequential access method, which allows both sequential and direct access, is often the best choice.

The final task in file design is to protect an information system's data files. Why is this important? Jerry Lincoln remembers the advice his professor gave him when he first used a microcomputer:

> *"Be sure to back up your data and program files. It is fairly easy to replace hardware if it fails, is damaged, or is destroyed. It's almost impossible to replace data or program files that have been damaged or destroyed. The cost of the tape or disk is not important. Rather, it's all the work that went into creating and updating a data file or into writing a program that is valued. Along with the backup procedure, set up a recovery plan that uses these backups to get the information system running again."*

A business can be stopped dead if the data files and programs it depends on are suddenly not available for use.

Software Design. In software design, the programs needed to handle the various information processing activities are first described and then linked together. In preparing a software design, you need to be concerned with two things. First, make sure that all required information system outputs will be produced. Second, produce a software design that will be easy to maintain. The structured design principles introduced in the last chapter can help you achieve both of these aims.

The **Hierarchical Input-Process-Output technique,** or **HIPO,** is a very popular software design tool that can aid you in building a structured design and generating its documentation. The HIPO technique uses three kinds of diagrams: a visual table of contents, an overview diagram, and a detail diagram. The **visual table of contents** is similar to the structure chart introduced in the previous chapter. Its purpose is to show all the functions performed by the software and to refer to the overview and detail diagrams. **Overview diagrams** describe the input, process, and output of the main software

Exhibit 12.9

A HIPO visual table of contents for the Purchasing Information System. It shows all the functions performed by this information system.

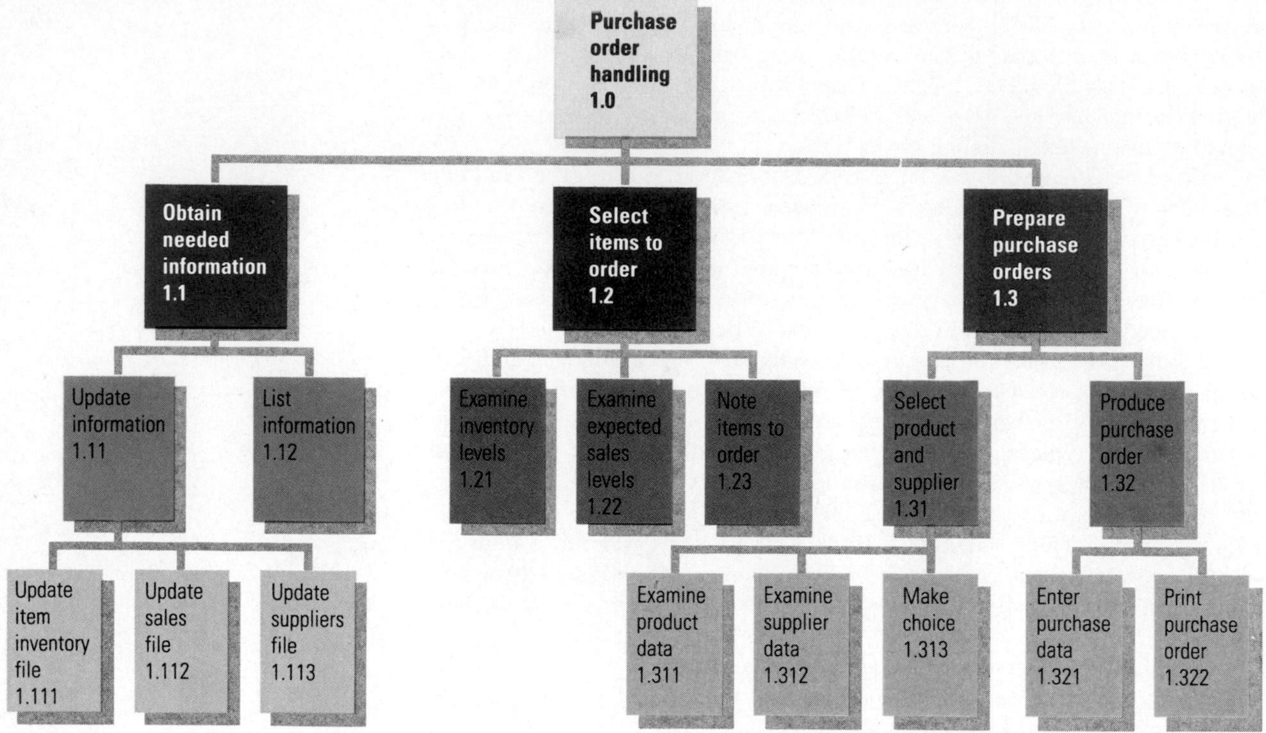

components. Thus, they provide a general knowledge of a component. **Detail diagrams** provide a more complete understanding of a software component's information processing activities. Often, overview diagrams are used to describe "top-level" components while detail diagrams are used to describe "bottom-level" components. Exhibits 12.9, 12.10, and 12.11 show some of the HIPO diagrams that Jerry Lincoln used in designing CompuStore's Purchasing Information System.

It is often hard for systems analysts to recognize errors in the software designs they build. The design technique known as a **structured walk-through** is a good way to overcome this problem. Here, a systems analyst "walks through" a design in front of other members of a project team. By having to explain your design to someone else, you often discover your mistakes. The advantage is that errors are caught before a programmer begins work.

Step 4: Testing Procedures Design

Information systems testing takes place in the systems acquisition and systems implementation stages. During systems acquisition, software packages that have been purchased and programs that have been written will be tested to make sure they perform as required. During systems implementation, all the hardware and software components will be joined together and tested to make sure the complete information system performs as required.

Exhibit 12.10

A HIPO overview diagram for the Purchasing Information System. It shows the inputs, processes, and outputs for a module of the information system. Here, the "scratch" file is a temporary file that holds the items to be ordered until the purchase order is prepared.

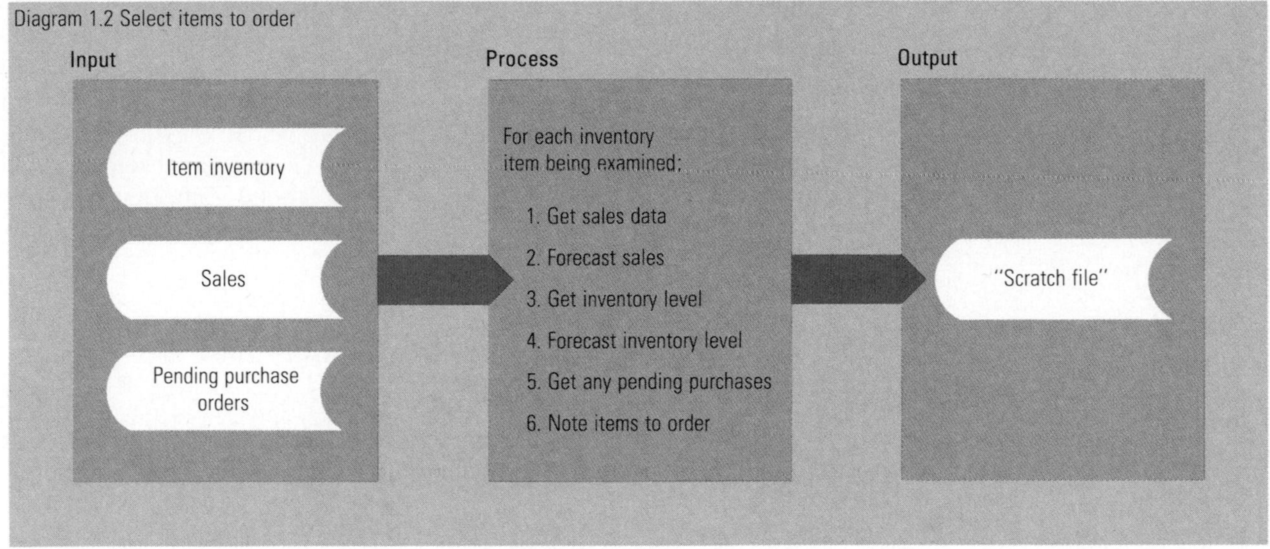

Exhibit 12.11

A HIPO detail diagram for the Purchasing Information System. It shows a detailed view of the processing that occurs in a module of the information system. The order flag is a program storage area temporarily marked to indicate whether the inventory item being processed is to be ordered.

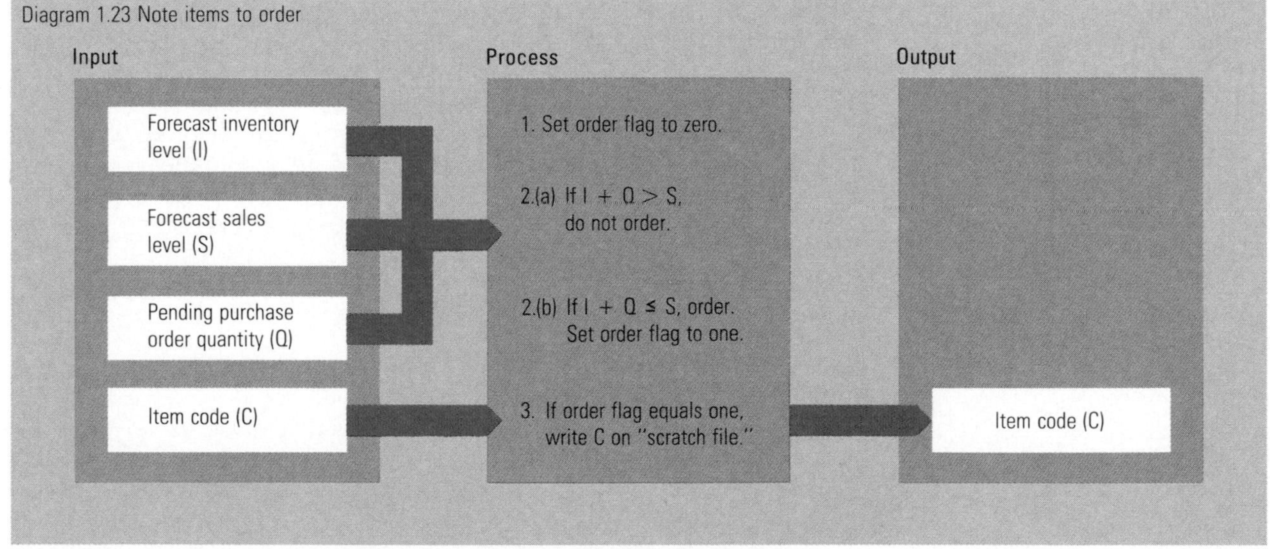

If testing procedures are not designed prior to these latter systems life-cycle stages, business pressure to "get the information system up and running" can force a hurried, incomplete set of testing procedures. The time taken to design a good set of testing procedures during the design stage is well worth it. Many headaches might be avoided, such as software failures, called "crashes," and angry users.

The key to a good set of testing procedures is the test data that will be used. Some of this test data is artificial and some is live. **Artificial test data,** created just for testing, usually assess how the software would react to extreme or unusual situations. **Live test data** are taken from existing business records and usually assess how the software would handle day-to-day situations. The best sets of test data seem to be built when systems analysts and users work together to create the set of test data.

Step 5: Review the Feasibility Study and the Project Plan

The various systems design activities should "peel away" some of the questions that initially cloud an information systems project. The size and complexity, and thus the difficulty, of the project should be more apparent. The degree of technical sophistication that will be required should now be known. The probable impacts of the information system on a business's operations should be clearer. The conclusion of the systems design stage provides another good time to reassess the project's feasibility study and project plan.

Documentation

The three manuals begun during systems analysis are updated during systems design. All systems design tasks are reported in the project manual, and the feasibility study and project plan sections of the manual are revised. Output, input, processing, and testing procedure design details are added to the systems manual. More complete descriptions of user input and output behaviors are also included in the users' manual. A fourth piece of documentation, the **programmers' manual,** is started during systems design. The programmers' manual consists of the information system's overall software design and brief descriptions of each of the programs that make up this design.

Tips

Be sure to carefully match an information system's dialogue style with user capabilities. Since most information systems serve both experienced and inexperienced users, two or more dialogue styles might be desirable. A common strategy today is to offer both menus and abbreviated commands. Inexperienced users can use the menus, and experienced users can bypass the menus and use the commands.

Design the information system to fit the task at hand, not the latest technology. Remember that the objective is to build a useful and appropriate information system that will be used.

Finally, the most useful rule of thumb in systems design is to eliminate steps or procedures whenever and wherever possible. Unnecessary operations allow errors to occur and increase processing time. "The simpler, the better" is usually a good procedure to follow.

SYSTEMS ACQUISITION

During the **systems acquisition stage** of the systems life cycle, hardware and software packages are purchased and customized software is developed. Five activities are normally involved (see Exhibit 12.12). First, a search is made to determine if software packages are likely to fit the physical design. Second, if needed, a process is put in place to purchase a software package. Third, if needed, a process is put in place to purchase new hardware devices. Fourth, if needed, a process is put in place to develop customized software. Fifth, the feasibility study and project plan are reviewed.

Step 1: Make the Software "Package Versus Customized" Decision

It is almost always better to use a software package than to customize your own software. The software package usually will cost less, be immediately available for use, contain few errors, and be of high overall quality. Two other benefits are also important. First, the software vendor will be improving the package. These new versions of the software are normally made available to existing customers for a nominal cost. Second, businesses that buy most of their software do not need a large programming staff.

The only good reason not to use a software package is that you cannot find a package that meets your information needs. Software vendors develop generalized packages that can be sold to a large number of firms. If your needs are unique, you may not be able to find a suitable package.

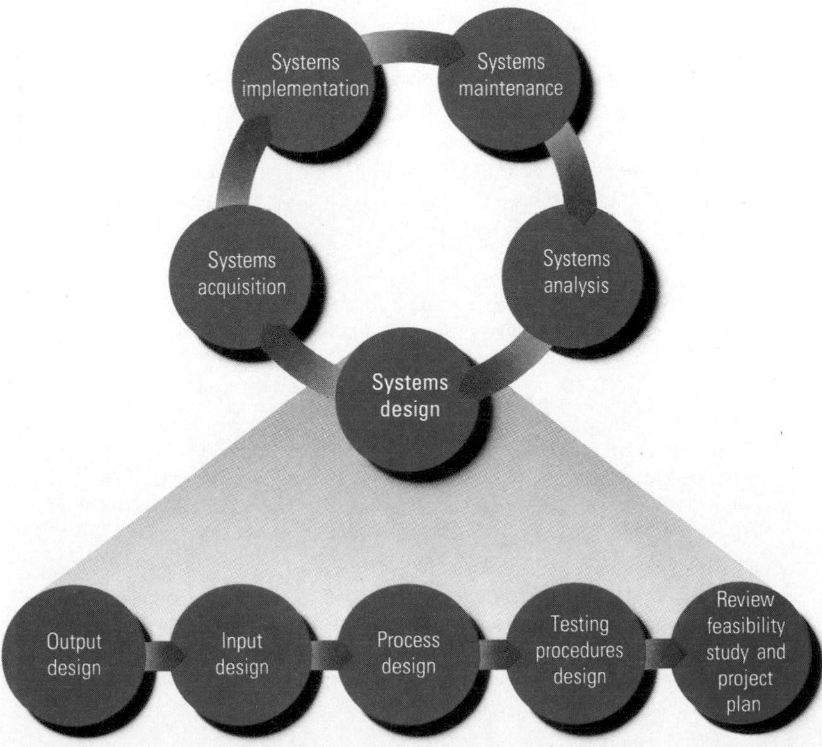

Exhibit 12.12
The systems acquisition stage of the systems life cycle obtains or builds the hardware and software components of an information system.

There are disadvantages to software packages. If you wish to modify a software package, the work must usually be done by the software vendor. The fees charged depend on the amount and complexity of the modifications, but they are usually high. If you modify the package yourself, the vendor may refuse to support the program. This means the vendor will no longer be responsible for any errors that arise. You may not want to be in this situation!

Another option does exist. You can change your business procedures to fit the software package. This option should be viewed with caution, however. In some cases such a change might improve business operations. In other cases there may be very good reasons for existing business procedures. In either case, systems implementation costs will increase if workers need to be trained in new procedures.

Step 2: Purchase Packaged Software

If the initial screening of software vendors indicates that existing software packages are suitable, then a process needs to be set in place to choose and purchase an appropriate package. The process Jan Hale follows is typical:

1. Identify the key performance factors of the software package you will be buying. Most often, these factors should parallel the output, input, and processing designs documented in the systems manual. Jan pays close attention to the forecast of likely information system changes. No one wants to solve today's problem with tomorrow's headache!
2. Identify the criteria to be used in selecting a package. In addition to meeting key performance factors, Jan feels it is important to consider the software vendor's track record and financial stability as well as the support the vendor can provide. And, as Jan is fond of saying, "Cost, sooner or later, does tend to enter the decision."
3. Prepare a formal statement that describes these selection criteria. This document is often referred to as a **Request for a Proposal** or an **RFP.** Jan feels that the time spent preparing such a document is a very good investment. When vendors know the "rules of the game," the whole process goes more smoothly.
4. Identify vendors and give them the RFP. Identifying vendors is one of the hardest tasks in purchasing a software package. There are thousands of potential sources of software packages. This includes software vendors, hardware vendors, mail-order houses, computer retailers, and consulting firms. Some consulting services even exist to help other firms locate suitable software packages. Jan spends a lot of time just keeping up with these various sources of software packages. In one of her recurring nightmares, she learns about a "perfect" package just after a great deal of time and money has been spent customizing an information system.
5. Work with vendors who have suitable packages to help them prepare a proposal. Vendors often need more information about a business and its software needs than is included in the RFP. This is particularly true when a package must be modified. Again, Jan feels this work is well worth the effort. The better the vendor proposals, the better her decisions.
6. Evaluate the vendors' bids and choose a software package. Jan has found it very useful to use a **package evaluation matrix** in comparing vendor proposals. Exhibit 12.13 shows the evaluation matrix Jan is currently using to select a new payroll and benefits software package. Jan rated each of these three packages on a one-to-ten scale, where a one means the package is bad

	(Weight)	Packages #1	#2	#3
Selection criteria				
Payroll processing	.3	8	6	10
Fringe benefit processing	.2	7	9	7
Handle expected 5-year growth	.2	3	10	10
Training provided	.1	10	8	8
Vendor reputation	.2	7	9	10
Overall score		6.8	8.2	9.2
Cost		$3000	$8500	$7000

Exhibit 12.13

An evaluation matrix is a useful tool for comparing software packages or hardware devices. The "weights" shown are Jan Hale's opinion of the importance of the five selection criteria. Each package rating is multiplied by these weights. Summing up the adjusted ratings results in an overall rating for each package.

and a ten means the package is superior. Jan arrived at these ratings by reading vendors' proposals, by studying documentation, and by talking with other firms who used each package.

7. Negotiate a contract with the vendor. This is a critical task. The contract should protect you if a vendor fails to produce what was promised. **Acceptance tests,** or tests that check on key performance factors, should be written into the contract. **Penalty payments** should also be placed in the contract to cover instances where software is delivered late or fails to perform as expected.

Depending on the situation, you might not always follow so formal a purchasing process. Even so, it is always important that you define performance factors and other important selection criteria. Choosing an unsuitable software package is the most common "computer mistake" being made today.

Step 3: Purchase Hardware

The physical design includes descriptions of all the new hardware to be acquired. Decisions about these hardware purchases should be delayed until you know how software will be acquired. As much as is possible, let the software drive your acquisition decisions. One of the main reasons for the success of the IBM PC was all the business software developed for it. However, there are exceptions to this rule. If you run an application on an existing computer system, you would only consider software packages available on that computer system. At other times, software and hardware may be purchased as a complete system from vendors known as **systems houses.** Once the hardware to be acquired is identified, a process similar to that given for purchasing software is followed.

Step 4: Develop Customized Software

Two choices exist when software is customized. A firm can contract the software development project to a consulting firm or have the software developed by its own programmers.

Contract programming has a number of advantages. If a consulting firm has experience in a certain area, their programmers will very possibly be able to develop a higher quality information system. They may even do it faster and at less expense than if it were done in-house. Contract programming, however, can be expensive.

If a business has its own staff of programmers, it usually is less expensive to have software developed in-house. Program development will be discussed in the next chapter.

Managing a large software development project can be a difficult job. Not only is it hard to monitor the work of programmers, but their programs must eventually fit together as defined by the software design. **Chief programmer teams** are often formed to ease this management task. The **chief programmer** is the project leader responsible for overall program design and coordination. The chief programmer works on the more difficult programming tasks. Working with the chief programmer are **senior** and **junior programmers.** The junior programmers are newly hired programmers given mostly simple programming jobs. A **technical secretary** keeps track of programs, files, testing procedures, documentation, and the like. Because each team member has a specialized role, it becomes much easier to both assign and monitor work.

Step 5: Review the Feasibility Study and the Project Plan

Once all software and hardware acquisition activities are completed, most of the initial systems development costs are known. Also, the project manager should now have a clear idea of what needs to be done during systems implementation and systems maintenance. This is a good time to reassess the feasibility study and the project plan.

Documentation

After the four ongoing documentation manuals are updated, they will be fairly complete. Exhibit 12.14 outlines the contents of the project, systems, users,' and programmers' manuals.

Tips

Always talk with more than one vendor when buying hardware or software. Not only are you exposed to a variety of products, but many vendors have a great deal of business computing experience. You can learn from them even if you don't buy their products.

Exhibit 12.14

At the conclusion of systems acquisition, the project, systems, users,' and programmers' manuals are almost complete.

Project manual	Systems manual	Users' manual	Programmers' manual
Purpose and scope	Purpose and scope	Purpose and scope	Software design
Feasibility study	Business systems model	User benefits	File designs
Project plan	Logical design	Inputs	Program descriptions
RFPs	Physical design	Outputs	
Vendor evaluation reports	Testing procedures	User instructions	
Contracts			

When a hardware or software purchase is important, it might be worthwhile to visit a lawyer experienced in computer contracting. Most vendors will ask you to sign a "standard" contract. For the most part, these contracts protect the vendor, not you. It just makes sense to have a lawyer look over the contract and suggest changes that could protect you.

SYSTEMS IMPLEMENTATION

The **systems implementation stage** has two main objectives. First, install the information system so that its benefits can be achieved. Second, do this in a manner that disrupts operations as little as possible. Three activities are performed to reach these objectives: systems testing, training, and conversion.

Systems implementation differs from the other systems life cycle stages in that its activities are not performed in sequence. Most often, they occur simultaneously (see Exhibit 12.15). A successful systems implementation, as seen on the following page in Computers at Work: "The Best-Laid Plans of Micros and Men," requires careful planning.

Systems Testing

The testing done in systems acquisition has three aims. First, tests are performed to make sure all the parts still work correctly once they are joined together. Second, tests are performed to make sure that any "electronic links" with other information systems work as expected. Third, tests are performed to make sure that all "people links" will work. These "people links" refer to user input and output procedures.

The first two sets of systems testing are usually the easiest. If good test data exist, the testing is a straightforward technical task. Checking the suitability of the "people links" is not as simple. Employees must be taken from their normal jobs, trained, and then observed as they perform the new work procedures.

Two systems testing methods frequently used in checking these "people links" are structured walkthroughs and pilot studies. Structured walkthroughs were introduced earlier in the text as a good means of reviewing a software design. They are also a very good way to have users go through input or output procedures step by step.

A **pilot study** is a little different from a structured walkthrough. Here, the information system is used "live," but in a controlled manner. When Jan Hale implemented the firm's point-of-sales data entry system, a pilot study was held at CompuStore's smallest retail outlet. It wasn't until Jan felt she had located all the snags with the data entry procedures that the information system was installed in the other stores.

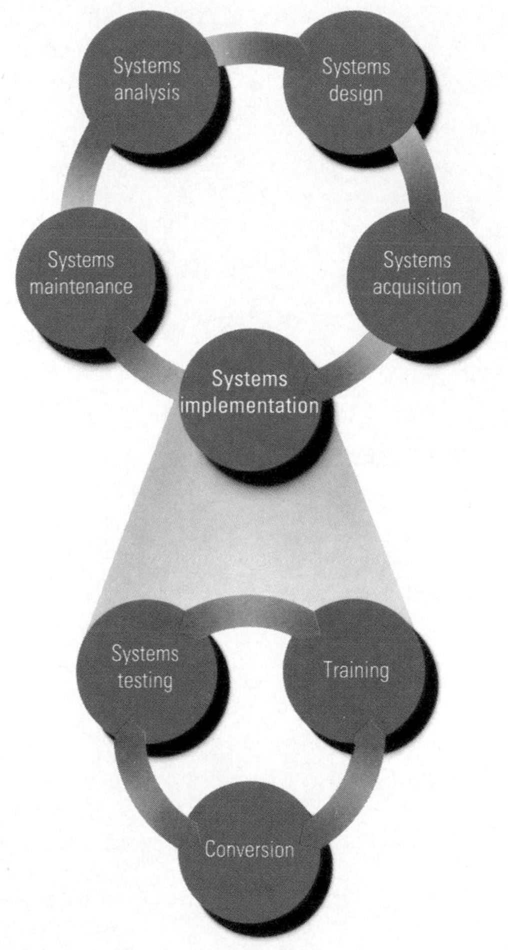

Exhibit 12.15
The systems implementation stage of the systems life cycle introduces the new information system into a business.

The Best-Laid Plans of Micros and Men

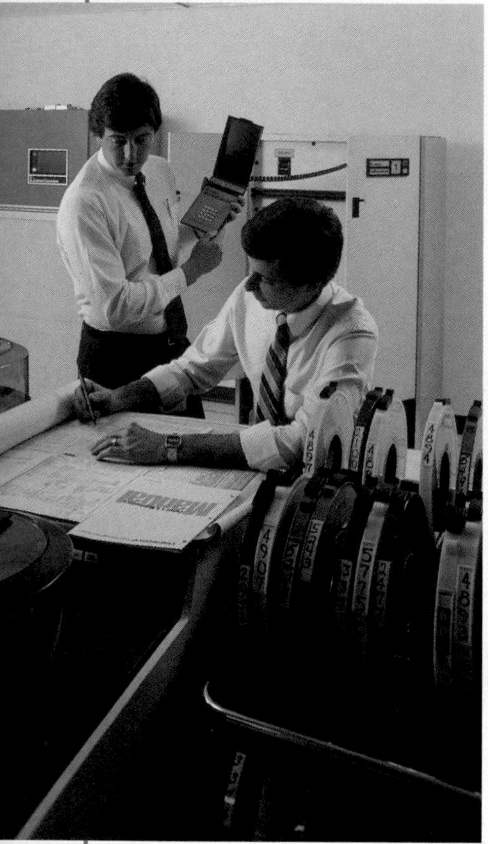

Rascomb, Inc. is a $50 million service organization. Using the large computer at its headquarters, in the 1970s the company initiated centralized automation of the management and financial information for its sixty-five locations. The system was state of the art at the time, but Rascomb's business environment changed dramatically. As it grew to eighty offices by mid-1980, it became clear that the system was no longer adequate.

Rascomb's chief financial officer (CFO) hired a consultant to review (1) the corporation's management information needs, (2) its current computer hardware, and (3) the available alternatives for meeting its needs. The consultant's recommendation—that Rascomb install a distributed computerized system in each of its eighty office locations at a total cost of $500,000—was accepted by Rascomb's top management.

After overseeing the acquisition of the best hardware and software, the CFO assigned his best technical people to the conversion and installation effort. Hardware and software functioned perfectly in the preinstallation tests carried out in early 1981. On May 1, the installation team met at the Westvale office, the initial conversion site.

During the first week, the team installed the computer and the system. It worked closely with office personnel for the next three weeks, teaching them how to use the system, then left Westvale on May 30, advising the CFO that the system was operational.

Delighted with the rapid progress, the CFO assigned the installation team to the Allston office for the next conversion. In a progress review with Rascomb executives, the CFO noted that the company's systems were finally being repositioned for the 1980s and declared that the conversion was going smoothly. But on June 15, the CFO received a frantic telephone call from the Westvale office director. Frustrated and angry, the director reported that:

> Operations were in turmoil;
>
> Office personnel did not understand the system's purpose, or how it worked;
>
> The computer room air-conditioning had twice overloaded and shut down—a disruption which also shut down the computer, lost considerable time, and forced the staff to re-input three full days of data;
>
> Managers were continuing to rely on old manual systems they considered reliable;
>
> Several managers commented, "We were really sold a bill of goods this time!"

The Westvale director stated the only option was to recommend shutting down the system until all the problems could be corrected. Since the installation team was now working at the Allston office, the CFO decided to personally investigate.

PICKING UP THE PIECES

After extensive meetings at Westvale, the CFO agreed that there were serious problems. He also realized that identical problems would occur at all the other offices as well if corrective action was not taken.

In a memo to top management, the CFO wrote that insufficient attention had been given to the *human factors* involved in installing and implementing the new system. Specifically, he noted:

> *Developing effective hardware and software had not been as difficult as anticipated.* Rascomb had devot-

ed a disproportionate amount of attention to issues which turned out to be quite manageable.

Distributed computers systems place heavy demands on new, inexperienced computer users. Installing screens at managers' desks brings people substantially closer to a computer than they ever dreamed. Success is thus totally dependent on those who are largely unskilled and inexperienced.

Bringing computer hardware into local offices adds responsibilities that they may not be able to handle. Rascomb's centralized computer was a well-run and properly staffed operation, but the local offices represented entirely different circumstances. Many locations where hardware was installed had neither the resources, nor the people, nor the commitment to handle it. Personnel may view the computer as an unpredictable, messy responsibility, in short, an obstacle to the real task of meeting operating targets.

To overcome local office trauma and reduce the risk of user rejection, the CFO offered five recommendations for successfully implementing Rascomb's distributed computerized system.

THE SOLUTION

Assemble the right installation team. Instead of relying on technical people, he suggested staffing the installation team primarily with nontechnical people who understand the business office environment, communicate well, and enjoy helping train others.

Research the local office before installation. Is one person in control? Is management committed to the success of the system? What do office personnel expect of the system? What are their skills? Is there anything in the office that might cause the system to fail?

Select a local system coordinator. This is a most critical and difficult decision. The coordinator must be able to learn the technical aspects of the system and assist users, be able to perform the job well, be respected by senior management, be committed to excellence, be enthusiastic about new things, and be in place for at least a full year after installation.

Establish realistic expectations. The system's sales effort must be a soft sell. The installation team's stake in the new system will affect the way it's presented and the way that presentation is perceived by the users.

Set up formal training to promote computer literacy. The CFO underscored that need. Computer literacy requires technical skills, realistic consensus expectations, and proper attitudes among users.

Rascomb's executive management group followed through on its CFO's five recommendations. Even so, the conversion of Rascomb's eighty offices to a distributed computerized system was a difficult undertaking. But, the people-based approach that evolved from recognizing the real issues substantially improved results.

Source: J. D. Krauss, "The Best-Laid Plans of Micros and Men," *Modern Office Technology,* March 1984, pp. 84–88.

Training

Before users can work with an information system, they must learn how to use it. A good training program covers an information system's overall purpose, its benefits to users, and all standard input and output procedures.

There are three basic training options. When there are only a few users, **one-on-one training** by a systems analyst is the standard training method. Because the systems analyst can personalize the training to each user, training can be brief and very effective. When there are many users, however, one-on-one training is too expensive.

Workshops, where groups of users are trained in a classroom setting, are a common training method when an information system has many users. Workshops are most effective when users are given access to a terminal or microcomputer so they can practice what they are being taught. Workshops can be taught by a firm's in-house staff or by consultants brought in to develop the training program. When an information system uses a popular software package, it is usually possible to send users to workshops developed and run by the package's vendor or by a consultant.

A training method growing in popularity involves **computer-aided instruction,** or **CAI.** With CAI, a program is developed that instructs users through an interactive dialogue. A major benefit of CAI training is that it is self-paced. Trainees can select the topics to be covered, the sequence in which topics are covered, and the pace at which training takes place.

Conversion

The purpose of most information system projects is to improve the manner in which a set of business activities are handled. The Purchasing Information System, for example, automates a manual means of preparing purchase orders. The term **conversion** refers to the manner in which a business converts from the "old" way of doing business to a "new way."

Conversion involves two steps. In the first step, existing data files need to be changed to fit the new information system. Thus, when moving from a manual to a computer-based way of handling work, all paper files need to be converted to computer-readable media. This can be a time-consuming task. In the second step, the new information system is physically introduced into the work place.

The aim of all conversion efforts is to introduce the new information system both quickly and smoothly. The problem that arises is that it is virtually impossible to develop an error-free information system. Errors lead to mistakes and failures, and these disrupt business operations. And, as information systems increase in size and complexity, the number of errors not caught before conversion increases.

Jerry Lincoln was proud of the Purchasing Information System. He had worked hard on it. Both Tom Berkshire and Tony Santos were excited about it. The day before Tony was to start using the new information system, Jerry scheduled a lunch meeting with Tom and Jan Hale. The following conversation took place:

Tom: Well, Jerry, tomorrow's the big day. I sure hope things go smoothly. With sales growing like they are, Tony really needs help in purchasing.

Jerry: I know, Tom. That's why Tony and I decided on a crash conversion.

Tom: Crash conversion? I don't like the sound of that.

Jerry: Don't worry, Tom. It's just a computer term. **Crash conversion** just means we'll be switching over directly from the old system to the new system. That way Tony can begin using the computer to prepare purchase orders tomorrow.

Tom: Sounds good.

Jan: Wait a second, you two. This is a pretty complex system, Jerry. Are you sure everything is going to work right from the start? What if errors get into some of the data files or some of the price calculations are wrong? Stop fidgeting, Tom! Jerry has done a professional job. It'll work. But, I'd rather be safe than sorry. Maybe you should try a parallel conversion, Jerry.

Tom: What do you mean by a parallel conversion?

Jan: With a **parallel conversion,** we run the old and the new systems together for awhile. This way, we can use results from the old system as a check on the new system.

Tom: That makes sense.

Jerry: Also, if the new system fails, the old system will still be there for Tony to use. The only problem is that we'll be doubling Tony's workload.

Jan: I don't think you'll need more than a week's parallel operation, Jerry. It shouldn't be too bad.

Tom: I can have my secretary, Sue, help Tony out if he gets backed up. I like this "parallel" idea, Jerry. Let's try it.

After the lunch, Jerry realized that he had let Tom's and Tony's enthusiasm cloud his thinking about the conversion.

A crash conversion is fine when converting a simple information system or when information system failures won't disrupt business operations. When an information system's failure might be disruptive, other conversion strategies should be used. The parallel strategy is one option. Another alternative is known as a **phased** conversion. Instead of going directly from the old system to the new system, the conversion is broken into smaller steps, or phases. Each phase can be done in either a crash or a parallel manner.

Documentation

The major documentation effort in systems implementation involves preparing the **operators' manual.** This manual provides a detailed description of an information system's operation from a technical point of view. Included in the operators' manual are: descriptions of the information system's purpose and scope; inputs, data files, and outputs; links with other information systems; and step-by-step operating procedures. Computer operators refer to this manual when an information system is actually executed on the computer system.

The project, systems, users,' and programmers' manuals need to be updated to include all relevant systems implementation activities and information system design changes. At the conclusion of this systems life cycle stage, the project manual is complete.

Tips

Never try to prove that an information system is error-free during systems testing. This is an impossible task. Instead, first check that the information system works for all standard types of processing. Then try to make the information system fail by testing "extreme" types of processing.

Training does not stop with the end of a conversion effort. Users will always be needing some help, and new users will be using the information system. The project plan should indicate how this recurring need for training will be met.

SYSTEMS MAINTENANCE

Building a business information system is like trying to hit a moving target. Businesses constantly change. Computer technology constantly changes. The **systems maintenance stage** of the systems life cycle covers the efforts taken to ensure that an information system continues to meet information needs. Two basic activities are involved: identifying the need to change the information system, and then making appropriate changes. Exhibit 12.16 shows that these activities are repeated throughout the "life" of an information system.

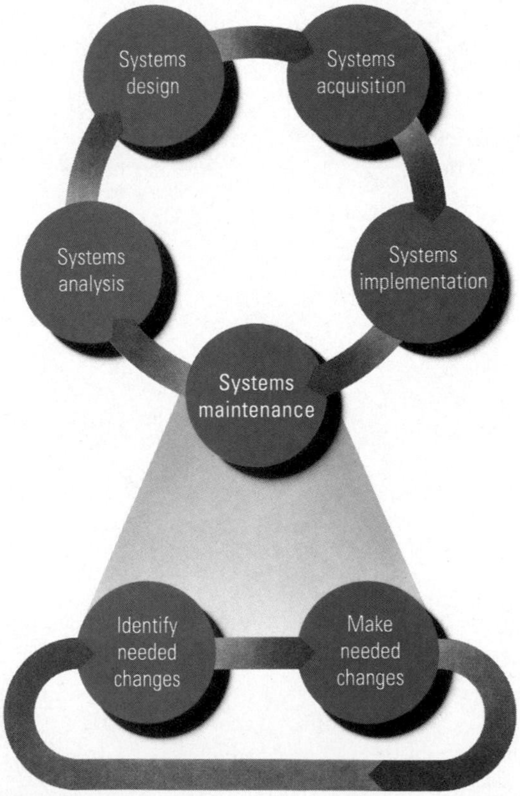

Exhibit 12.16

The systems maintenance stage of the systems life cycle ensures that an information system will continue to meet a business's information needs.

Step 1: Identify Needed Changes

Most firms use two strategies to identify desired information system changes. First, suggestions for business-related changes are gathered from users. Second, suggestions for technology-related changes are raised by the systems analyst.

If a systems analyst has established a good working relationship with users, the users should feel comfortable telling the systems analyst about their problems and their ideas for improving the information system. These conversations can occur spontaneously or during scheduled meetings. When there are too many users for the systems analyst to talk with each one, questionnaires can be distributed. Some of the questions to be raised include:

Have the business activities changed in any way?

Are the business activities being supported by the information system going smoothly?

Are the information system's objectives being achieved?

Is the information system being used?

Are users satisfied with the information they are receiving or with their access to the information system?

If systems analysts are expected to identify ways to technically improve a firm's information systems, they must be given ample time to study the performance of the information systems. Collecting measures of information system performance is very helpful. Examples of these measures include CPU processing time for batch applications and response time for interactive applications.

Step 2: Change the Information System

Systems maintenance projects are actually systems development projects. Most of these projects are small. Some, however, can be quite large. All the activities discussed in the first four systems life cycle stages are likely to be performed during the systems maintenance stage.

The obvious difference between initially developing an information system and maintaining that information system is that the information system already exists. If you are asked to change an existing information system, you must work with an existing design. This can lead to two types of problems. First, you may find it difficult to understand the existing design. It can be hard to understand your own software design, especially if you haven't looked at it recently. It can seem impossible at times to understand someone else's software design. While this problem will always exist, it can be lessened by following structured design principles and by carefully documenting systems development projects.

Second, you may find it difficult to determine how to change the existing design. If the initial software design did not anticipate the change, it can be extremely hard to implement the change. Again, this problem will always exist, but it can be lessened by following the structured design principles and being sure to clearly describe all likely future changes in the requirements specification.

As more and more changes are made to an information system, it becomes increasingly harder to make the changes. An initially "clean" design has become a very "messy" design. Sometimes it is better to completely rebuild, rather than change, the existing information system. Recognizing this point is another important systems analyst skill.

Documentation

Whenever changes are made to an existing information system, its four ongoing documentation manuals must be appropriately updated. The systems, users,' programmers,' and operators' manuals should always describe the current version of an information system.

It is very important that all changes be carefully documented. The most difficult maintenance task Jerry Lincoln had to perform was on the project in which the inventory control information system was changed from batch to transaction processing. It took him over two weeks to figure out how one module within the design worked. As it turned out, the consultant who had initially worked on the information system had failed to document an emergency modification. Jerry's troubles arose because the module's documentation did not match the programs currently running on the computer system.

Tips

You do not have to review all of a business's information systems on the same cycle. Generally, transaction processing systems require major changes every three to five years, information reporting systems every one to two years, and decision support systems every year.

Many firms tend to assign their most experienced systems analysts and programmers only to new systems development projects. As a result, these firms' systems maintenance projects are staffed with newly hired personnel. This is not a good practice to follow, however. Because systems maintenance can be difficult, some projects require experienced personnel. More importantly, a poorly done maintenance project only leads to future problems. At best, a firm's information systems will need to be rebuilt much sooner. Systems analysts and programmers should be assigned to new development and maintenance work on the basis of the skill and experience required for each project.

Professional Issue

Prototyping in Systems Development

Prototyping, or building a "quick and dirty" version of an information system, is one of today's hot topics in business computing. Using new software tools, it is possible for a systems analyst, a programmer, or a user to build a prototype of an information system in a short period of time.

A variety of software packages are available today for prototyping. Examples include **CRT screen generators, report generators,** and **data base management systems.** Certain prototyping tools, referred to as **application generators,** cover the full range of systems development activities. Computers at Work: "Three-Person DP Staff Backs $21 Million Firm" describes how one firm is making use of these software tools.

Advantages and Disadvantages of Prototyping

Prototyping has three main advantages. First, system development time is shortened. Second, the length of time a systems analyst must wait before getting user feedback about an information system is also reduced. Third, users can use the prototype to better grasp how they might best make use of a computer in their work.

There is also a disadvantage to prototyping. When a prototype is built, the gains that are obtained from cautiously stepping through each of the systems life cycle stages might be lost. These gains include a thorough understanding of the information system's benefits and costs, a detailed description of the business's information needs, an information system design that is easy to maintain, a well-tested information system, and a well-prepared group of users.

If used appropriately, prototyping offers many benefits. If used inappropriately, information system failures can result. The key is knowing where to apply the prototyping approach in systems development.

COMPUTERS AT WORK

Three-Person DP Staff Backs $21 Million Firm

How large a staff does it take to run the data processing center for a $21 million, 410-employee company?

Only three, according to DP specialist Robert Wilson of Chem-Tronics, Inc., a manufacturer of engine components for the aerospace industry.

The three programmer/analysts at Chem-Tronics have been neither overworked nor backlogged with requests since the department installed a COBOL program generator in October 1981. The generator has cut applications development time up to 200 percent, Wilson said.

"We do virtually all our screen and report formatting" with Bytek, Inc.'s Cogen generator, "together with file definitions and other more mundane tasks," Wilson explained. "In fact, only about 20 percent of the code we produce is still written by hand."

Wilson said that Cogen fills a gap between the National Cash Register Corporation package's capabilities and the corporation's special needs. "The information we require already resides in the data base," he said, "but we often need to sort, format, or display it in a different manner. In a sense, we use the generator as a querying system."

One query and report system developed for the company's aviation repair section took four weeks to finish. Wilson estimated that without Cogen, the job would have required three to four months.

Furthermore, Wilson said, the generator has allowed the DP department to remain small and responsive to users. "We are vertically oriented, with each member having an area of responsibility and a single programmer overseeing a project from start to finish," he said. "It's a much more satisfying arrangement."

Source: "Three-Person DP Staff Backs $21 Million Firm," *Computerworld,* 14 March, 1983, p. 35.

Guidelines for Prototyping

Prototyping is useful in two types of situations. First, it can help users express their information needs during systems analysis. Second, in certain situations it can replace the lengthy systems life cycle approach to systems development.

A Systems Analysis Aid. Users often find it hard to state their information needs. A major cause of this difficulty lies in the users' inability to "see" how they might use an information system. By providing a user with sample CRT screens or management reports, the user is able to "experience" the information system. If good software tools are available, user suggestions for improving a CRT screen or management report can quickly be tried out.

Prototyping as an aid to systems analysis is appropriate for any type of information system project. It is particularly well suited for applications that are new or involve poorly understood business activities.

As a Substitute for the Systems Life Cycle. An information system developed through prototyping can be thought of as always being in the systems maintenance stage of the systems life cycle. A "quick and dirty" initial design is implemented. Then, a constant series of small maintenance projects cause the information system to evolve into a useful business tool.

Prototyping as a substitute for the systems life cycle is not appropriate for many information system projects. When an information system will handle a critical business activity, the information system must work in a correct and reliable manner. A carefully managed systems life cycle approach to systems development is best. However, when the information system will serve a less critical business role, prototyping may work out fine. Information systems that are small, inexpensive, temporary, or to be used for "personal" rather than "business" computing are good candidates for prototyping.

Made-to-Measure Software

So you think your problem's unique. You've looked at what seem like thousands of packaged programs. The inventory control programs are close, but not close enough. The sales analysis programs give you 80 percent of the information you'd like to have, but they lack the all-important 20 percent that you *need* to have. You wonder whether anyone else in the word operates an order entry system the way you operate yours. The packaged programs just don't get the computer to do what you want it to do.

Try as you will, you've not been able to find an inventory control program that fits your business. What are you going to do? Let that new personal computer sit in the corner and gather dust?

J.H. Riesenberg and Associates, a small Cincinnati food brokerage firm, faced this problem a few years ago. Jerry Riesenberg, president, recalls: "It was a matter of either hiring more people and continuing to process tons of paperwork, or condensing that paperwork with a modern, more efficient method of handling data." His data requirements were specific. He needed an order entry system that would allow him to view data in a variety of ways. The data are constantly used to track orders. They are often used for sales analysis. They are sometimes used to understand, follow, and negotiate contracts. And they are also used for "bookings," which means tracing the activities of two or more files, comparing each of them, and adding updates where needed.

More specifically, data have to be traced by supplier, customer, product, and by volume of product to analyze sales trends on a constant basis. This information is also used to show the status of relations between customer and supplier.

Riesenberg and Associates employs eight people, including two part-time clerical workers. Titles seem to mean little in this modest office, where the telephone is usually answered by the person closest to it. Riesenberg points out: "We are responsible for gaining, processing, and shipping ingredients and commodities." He places emphasis on the word "We."

"We're a service company," Riesenberg says, "and we have to be able to communicate constantly with our customers and suppliers. As the communications channel to both, we must have the most up-to-date information. Quite simply, the better our communication system, the better we're going to service our customers. We don't physically do the shipping, but we make sure our customers receive their products when they ask for them."

Improving the method of handling orders was not an area where Riesenberg was willing to compromise. After all, this company (formerly Lampe Brothers) has a good track record which dated back to 1927. Timely information had always been the key to their success.

The generic packages offered by software vendors couldn't meet the challenge. Even the best of the packages would require that he rebuild his order entry system from the ground up. Instead, Riesenberg decided to commission customized programs for his operation. Riesenberg was lucky. He didn't have far to look in his search for a computer consultant who could develop the programs he needed. He just happened to have a brother-in-law who had been in the data-processing business for twenty years.

Bill Meyer knew very little about his brother-in-law's business. Meyer had served his apprenticeship in data processing working on mainframe systems. Much of his time had been spent as an applications programmer and systems analyst, before he was bitten by the personal-computer bug. A few years ago he dove into the newly emerging personal-computer field in earnest, and is now president of Micro Masters, a service and consulting company dealing in personal computers.

Meyer and Riesenberg, along with Bob Weigand, a computer programmer who had joined the project at Meyer's request, sat down and made a detailed blueprint of the system.

The first order of business was for the programmer to learn about the client's business. Meyer and Weigand took a crash course—"Everything You Always Wanted To Know About the Food Brokerage Business . . ."

Having so little knowledge of the other's business requires that a strong relationship of trust be established between the consultant and businessman before the project is too far along.

Beyond trust and the early information exchange, the development of customized software should include a number of checkpoints to be sure the program will give optimum performance. "We learned that we would have to reorganize our way of thinking about how an order was handled," Riesenberg says, "but we were involved in every step of the order entry program's development." Meyer and Weigand would design a section of the program and present it to Riesenberg with the following questions attached: "What do you think is wrong with this? What do you think is right with it?" This gave everyone an opportunity to amend the original design before it was put into the program. Several meetings were scheduled along the way, to be sure the program would reflect the information required for any given operation of the program's menu.

Meyer says, "It's imperative that the programmer and businessman agree (up front) what the essentials of the program will be. You start with, 'How do you do it now?' If a consultant doesn't ask that question, find another consultant." An equally important question is, "What don't you have in your present system that you'd like to have in your computerized system?" A good programmer will look for ways to give you not only speed and better organization, but also enhancements that were previously unthinkable.

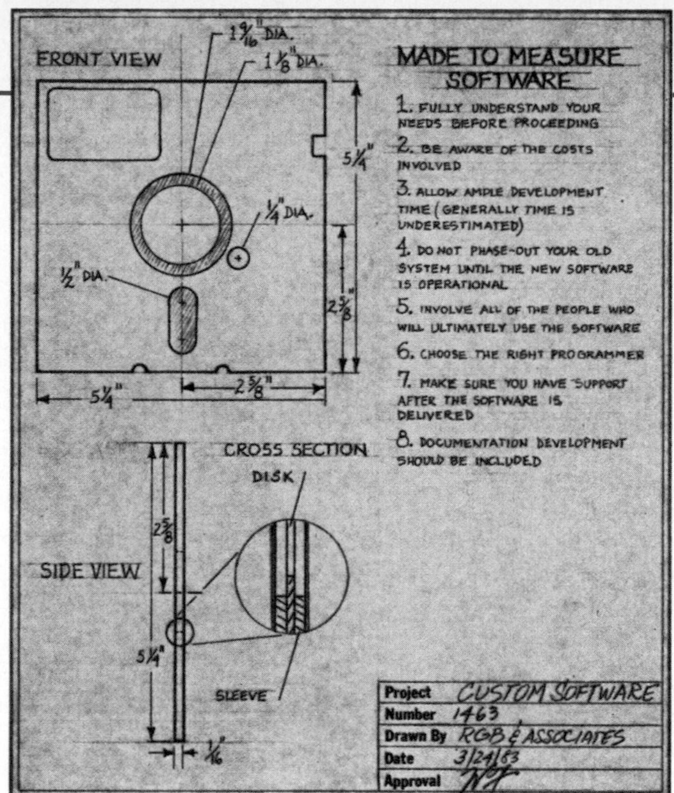

The customized programming has given Riesenberg and Associates an orderly system that handles the order entry process from the initial order to the time the invoice arrives, verifying that the order has been shipped. Before the computer was installed, the same information was spread throughout the office, over as many as five desks, and each step was processed manually.

Everybody in the office has access to, and regularly uses, the TRS–80 Microcomputer. The TRS–80, coupled with the customized programs, has replaced tons of paperwork.

Riesenberg admits the company still encounters an occasional error—"the human element," he calls it—but the system itself is so fail-safe that the computer regularly rejects information that isn't consistent with the standards they've defined. "That has added a level of control," he says, "that we didn't have before."

Mary Kob, who has been with the company four years, says, "At first I thought the idea of getting a computer to handle the order entry system was terrible. We had everything under control and here we were going to change the whole thing. But, the computer opened up my job. It's given me more responsibility because I can do more. The (customized) programming allows us to do everything exactly the way we want to do it. It lists everything we require, in the order that we need it. We're better organized and we access information faster. As opposed as I originally was to the new system, I realize I'd really miss it if we didn't have it now."

CHOOSING A CONSULTANT

Not everyone considering custom software for a personal computer is fortunate enough to have a computer consultant in the family. As the personal computer becomes more commonplace in business, there will be a corresponding increase in the number of computer consultants. Be that as as it may, how do you find the right one for you right now?

The first place to shop is at your local retail computer store. Most of them have a list of consultants, and a quick discussion with the store manager about your needs should be helpful. Be sure to ask for the names of at least two or three consultants. You'll want to interview more than one.

Many consultants get their work through referrals. When they've done a good job for someone, word gets around. Check with the local computer user's groups. You'll probably find more candidates than you've time to interview.

The universities and colleges are often helpful to the businessman in search of a consultant. Be sure to specify your needs and be forewarned that a first-year student programmer—though often cheaper—probably won't write programs as efficiently as will a full-time consultant. In this, it's a clear case of getting what you pay for. Read about operations that are similar to your business. You may find a programmer who's already written a custom system like the one you've been looking for.

"Don't hesitate to get a second opinion," programmer Bob Weigand adds. "It's like when the American Medical Association suggests you get a second doctor's opinion before you decide to have surgery. This is basically the same thing. The reason we need two opinions is because very few of us really understand medicine."

DON'T BE IMPATIENT

More than two months of development took place before Riesenberg got his first look at the customized order entry system. "We were all anticipating that day," he says. "We were going to plug it in, and right then and there we were going to solve all our problems." Well, that's not quite the way it works.

Creating custom software is like building a high-performance internal combustion engine. In other words, you tinker a little bit until you've got it running just so.

Once the custom software is fine-tuned and you're ready to roll, you're also going to have to deal with learning to use it. Again, the automobile serves as an example. Though all of Riesenberg's people were confident drivers, none had ever driven a high-performance racing car. Once they gained confidence in the computer, and their ability to use it, they had no qualms about getting out there on the track with Mario Andretti and A. J. Foyt.

Though happy with the end result, Riesenberg would make a few changes were he to do it all over again. "We didn't anticipate the future as well as we might have." The computer is presently equipped with two 5¼-inch floppy disk drives, and Riesenberg can see ahead to the time in the not too distant future when he'll need a hard-disk system. "Don't get yourself into a system that you're going to outgrow quickly," he warns. "Try to anticipate your future needs." Nevertheless, Riesenberg doesn't dwell on such oversights. His staff is putting the software to good use today and he'll cross the hard-disk hurdle when he comes to it.

THE BOTTOM LINE

How much can custom software contribute to a larger profit? Riesenberg expects that his answer to that question will be quite a tidy sum. His customized order entry system cost the company in the neighborhood of $5000. When compared to the prices of packaged software, that seems a sizable chunk of money. For instance, there are order entry programs on the shelf that retail for $250 to $600.

What possesses a person to spend more than eight times the amount of the most expensive packaged product on the market? Riesenberg responds: "When we turn the computer on, we're looking at an order entry system we developed.

"The manual handling of orders didn't make money for us," Riesenberg says. "The computer and the customized programming freed up time to pursue new orders and make new sales. When you're a small company, like we are, you've got to make the most of every individual's time."

Customized programming has made their system unique to their business. Because of this, the computer never forced them to change their way of doing business. On the contrary, they forced the computer to do business their way. Riesenberg is sure that it's the only way to go.

Source: D. Collopy, "Made-to-Measure Software," *Personal Computing,* April 1983, pp. 80–85 and 164.

SUMMARY

In *systems design* an information system's hardware, software, and operating procedures are specified.

Five activities are performed during systems design: *output design, input design, process design, testing procedures design,* and *reviewing the feasibility study and the project plan.*

In output design, the business documents and management reports to be produced by an information system are examined to make sure they are relevant, presentable, and accessible.

Input design is concerned with the procedures taken in entering data into a computer system. Input data items are examined to make sure they are complete and relevant. A *dialogue style* and a *data entry approach* are selected, and *forms* are designed.

The three most common dialogue styles are *commands, menus,* and *prompts.*

The two most common data entry procedures are batch processing and transaction processing. Each can be performed in a manual or fully automated manner.

Process design includes both *file design* and *software design.*

The following tasks are performed during file design: data to be stored are identified and organized, *codes* are designed, *file updating procedures* are selected, *file access methods* are determined, and *file protection schemes* are specified.

Two useful tools for describing how data items are stored in an information system are a *file layout chart* and a *data dictionary.*

The most common means of updating data files are through batch processing and transaction processing. With batch processing, files are updated at some regular interval, the length of which is termed a *batching cycle.* With transaction processing, files are immediately updated.

The three major file access methods are the sequential access, direct access, and indexed sequential access methods. A data file's *activity,* or the proportion of the file's records that are to be processed, is an important factor in selecting an access method.

In designing a file protection scheme, *backup* and *recovery procedures* are specified.

The aim in software design is to produce software that is correct, complete, and easily maintained. The structured design principles are helpful in achieving these aims. The *HIPO technique* and *structured walkthroughs* are useful tools in software design.

The key to designing a good set of testing procedures is selecting a good set of test data. Both *artificial* and *live* data items should be used.

The project, systems, and users' manuals are updated and the programmers' manual begun during systems design.

In *systems acquisition,* hardware and software packages are purchased, and customized software is developed.

It is almost always better to use a software package than to customize your own software. The only good reason not to buy a software package is when you cannot find one that meets your information needs. If a package requires a lot of modification, the cost may exceed that of customizing the software.

There are seven steps in purchasing hardware or software: identify key performance factors, identify selection criteria, prepare an RFP, identify vendors and give them the RFP, work with vendors who have suitable products to help them develop a proposal, evaluate the vendors' bids using an *evaluation matrix,* choose a product, and negotiate a contract with the vendor. This contract should include *acceptance tests* and *penalty payments.*

Sometimes, a total information system solution to a business problem can be purchased from a *systems house.*

In customizing software, a firm can contract the software development project to a consulting firm or have the software developed in-house. It is usually less expensive to have software developed by an in-house programming staff.

Managing a large software development programming project can be a difficult job. The use of *chief programming teams* can ease this management task.

The project, systems, users,' and programmers' manuals are all updated during systems acquisition.

During systems implementation a developed information system is introduced into the business unit that will use it. The two aims of systems implementation are to introduce the information system quickly but smoothly. This involves three activities: *systems testing, training,* and *conversion.*

Systems testing makes sure that the entire information system performs as required, that all electronic links function as expected, and that manual input and output procedures will work. *Structured walkthroughs* and *pilot studies* are useful techniques for having users go through input or output procedures step by step.

Training ensures that users are able to use an information system. Training options include *one-on-one training, workshops,* and *computer-aided instruction,* or *CAI.*

Conversion is the act of switching from an old way of handling a set of business activities to a new way. Two conversion steps are normally taken. First, data files are converted so they can be used with the new information system. Second, the new information system is physically introduced into the work place.

The three most common information system conversion strategies are the *crash, parallel,* and *phased strategies.*

The project, systems, users,' and programmers' manuals are updated during sytems implementation, and the *operators' manual* is produced. The project manual is now complete.

During *systems maintenance,* steps are taken to ensure that an information system continues to meet the business's information needs. Two activities are performed on a regular basis. First, needed information system changes are identified. Then, the information system is changed.

Two types of problems often arise with systems maintenance projects. It can be hard to figure out how the existing information system design works. And, it can be difficult to determine how to change this design. These problems can be reduced by following good systems development practices.

Recognizing when an information system should be rebuilt rather than changed is another important systems analyst skill.

The systems, user's, programmer's, and operator's manuals are updated during systems maintenance.

Prototyping refers to building a "quick and dirty" version of an information system. A variety of software tools, such as *CRT screen generators, report generators, data base management systems,* and *application generators,* are available today for prototyping.

Prototyping has three main benefits: systems development time is shortened; user feedback is obtained sooner; and users can use a prototype to understand how an information system might help them. The disadvantage of prototyping is that the gains made by cautiously stepping through the systems life cycle might be lost.

Prototyping can be used simply as an aid to systems analysis or as a substitute for the systems life cycle approach to systems development.

In the Special Feature that follows, many of the ideas about systems development introduced in this chapter and the last will be applied in describing the steps you might take in buying your own microcomputer.

REVIEW QUESTIONS

1. What are the five basic activities that must be performed during systems design?
2. The Apex Corporation is just embarking upon a systems design project. The firm knows that it should begin by evaluating the outputs of the proposed system. How should Apex approach this task?
3. Briefly compare the three most common dialogue styles used in computer systems.
4. What is meant by *data entry design?* Briefly describe the two basic approaches to data entry.
5. Briefly discuss the five major tasks involved in file design.
6. Briefly describe the HIPO approach to software design.
7. How can a firm create a good set of testing procedures?
8. The IfSo Corporation is undecided between purchasing software and creating customized software. How would you evaluate these two alternatives?
9. What steps are involved in choosing and purchasing an appropriate software package?
10. Briefly describe the two most common system testing methods.
11. What information should be covered in a good training program? Briefly describe the three basic training options.
12. What is prototyping? What advantages does it offer?

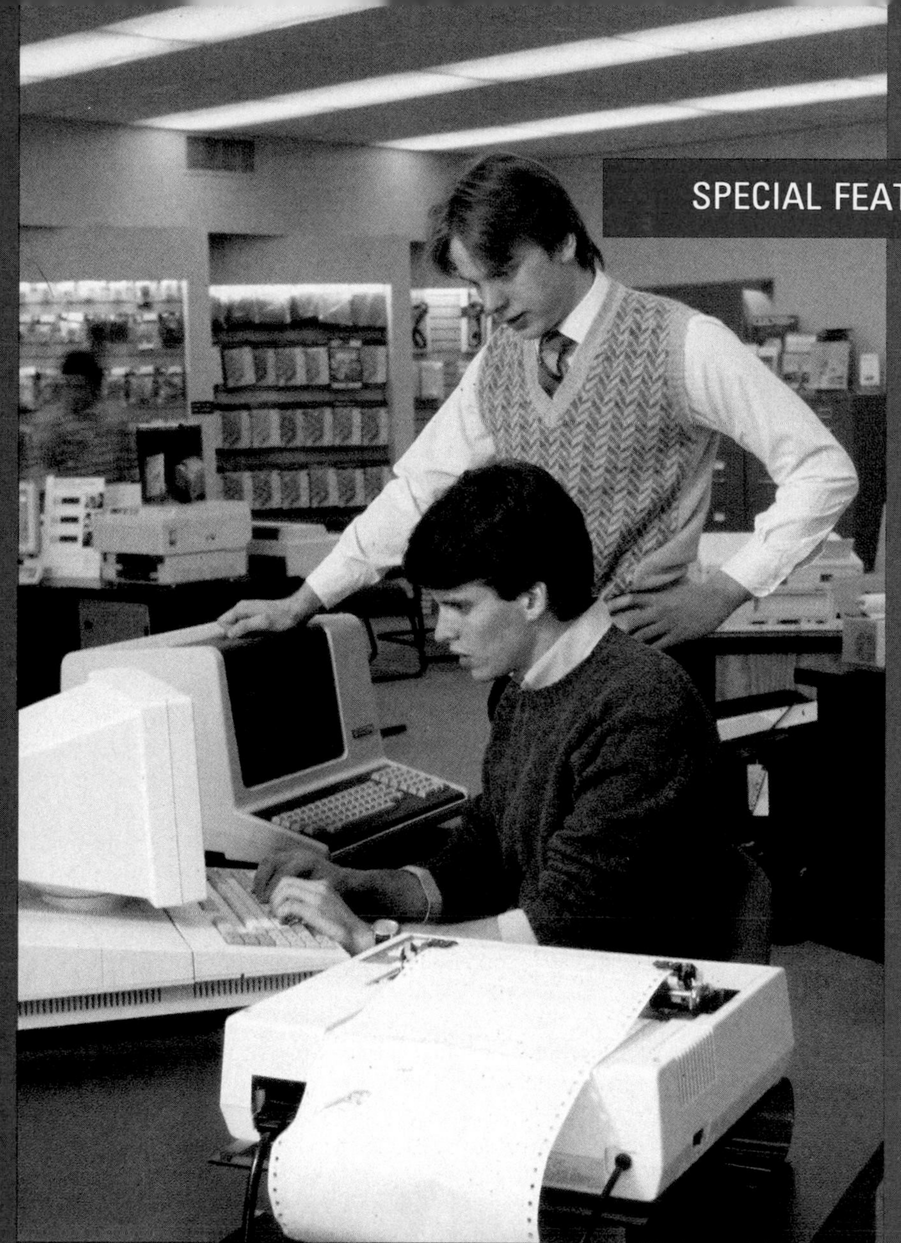

SPECIAL FEATURE

A Systems Approach to Selecting a Microcomputer

Many business students wonder which computer they should select. Taking a lesson from systems developers can help you in making your decision.

Like many students, Brent Hogan is a busy person. A second-year student at a community college, he intends to transfer to a four-year university and complete a bachelor's degree in business. He hasn't declared a major yet and is attempting to finish his general curriculum and basic introductory courses, including one on the use of computers. Brent also works part-time delivering auto parts and supplies twenty hours a week. Clearly, Brent has little free time to shop for a computer.

And yet, Brent is beginning to think a microcomputer could actually save him time. One reason Brent is thinking about buying a microcomputer is that everyone else, it seems, is considering buying a microcomputer. The computer course, television, magazines, friends, and relatives have all made him aware that anyone can own and operate a microcomputer. A friend of his, a computer science major at a nearby university, bought one last year, and his uncle, a writer on the East Coast, got one for Christmas.

As Brent sits at his desk struggling to type a paper, he remembers his computer text's discussion of word processing and the demonstration his professor arranged. He also remembers his uncle's delight with word processing and the ease with which he can write, revise, and print almost perfect final drafts. Brent also suspects that some of his accounting assignments would be easier to do on a microcomputer. Could the electronic spreadsheets many business professionals use help him do his accounting assignments?

A few years ago, neither college students, nor even most small businesses could consider such a purchase. But Brent has seen advertisements for microcomputers priced at around a thousand dollars. Brent has saved $800 and is willing to spend it on a microcomputer—if it will make his life easier and help him at school. Certainly, the ads promise that a microcomputer could do this. But before he spends his money, Brent wants to be sure.

By now, you may be eager to buy a microcomputer of your own. Yet, at the same time, you may also be unsure of yourself. Should you buy a microcomputer? If so, what kind? Through the following discussion, we want to show you how to use some systems development techniques to simplify your decision. Throughout, we'll be following Brent through his decision-making process, but the same techniques can easily be applied to your own decision.

As described in Chapters 11 and 12, systems development takes place in five stages: systems analysis, systems design, systems acquisition, systems implementation, and systems maintenance. These five stages make up the systems life cycle. Brent plans a career in business, and he values the logic that goes into systems development. But he is not sure how to apply this logic to his own decision. Does he need to prepare elaborate plans and forms? He decides to ask Amy, a friend of his who is a computer science major, for help. Amy plans to become a systems analyst, and she just bought a microcomputer last year. Amy agrees, and they make an appointment to meet the next afternoon.

Brent Amy, I need some advice. I think I need a microcomputer, but I don't know where to begin. We studied systems development in a computer class I'm taking, so I think I understand how computer professionals in a corporation would develop a system. But how do I go about deciding whether I should buy a microcomputer and what kind I should buy? Do I have to do systems flowcharts and all that?

Amy Not necessarily. The important thing about systems development is to match the technique to the situation. For example, your information processing needs probably aren't as complicated as those of most businesses. You may not need to use all of the tools a computer professional would use in making a choice. But you can still benefit from performing most of the activities that take place during systems analysis, systems design, and systems acquisition. Let's start with some user participation. What are the three tasks of systems analysis?

"I think I need a microcomputer, but I don't know where to begin."

Brent Well, first there is project definition, which lets everyone know what the user expects from the information system. Second is a feasibility study. That shows whether an information system can be developed technically, whether it will be used, and whether a business can afford to develop the system. Last is a logical design—basically a list of user requirements. It means that the system will be described in terms of the functions the user expects the system to perform. In systems design, computer professionals translate user requirements into specific input, processing, and output designs. So how do these steps apply to me?

Amy Start with project definition. What do you expect from a microcomputer? Or, put it another way; What kinds of problems do you think a microcomputer could solve for you?

Brent That's easy. My biggest problem is typing. I had four papers to write last term, and typing them—without mistakes—took as long as writing them. I tried a typing service once, but I won't do that again. I had to give them the draft four days before the actual deadline. And they still made mistakes. Some were my fault, but I still had to pay $1.50 a page.

Amy Let's make a list. Problem number one is typing. What else?

Brent Accounting. I think that will be my major, but the homework is driving me crazy. In most of the assignments, I have to prepare sample ledger entries or financial analyses on a spreadsheet. Some figures are given as part of the assignment, and then I have to calculate the figures that should appear on other parts of the spreadsheet. Usually, the figures are related by formulas like "profit = revenue − costs." Often I have to show what happens to the other figures when one basic figure, like revenue, is changed. Make a change—or mistake—in one entry and it always seems to affect other entries. I use up a lot of pencil erasers.

Amy Okay, problem two: mathematical calculations. An electronic spreadsheet should help you here. Are you taking any other courses that use a lot of calculations?

Brent Not right now, but I will probably take more accounting in the future.

Amy It's smart to try to anticipate your needs in the future. You really need to plan for them, as well as for the present. But let's finish with your present needs. Anything else?

Brent I keep thinking that I can use the terminals in the computing center. The problem is that I can never get a terminal when I am free. Working part-time really limits the hours I can go to the center. We had an orientation tour of the facilities, but I still need help in using them. The few times I tried to work at the center, I couldn't finish my assignment. If I had my own microcomputer, I could start whenever it was convenient, stop in the middle to go to work, and work as long as I needed to finish an assignment. That would really help.

Amy Yes, it does. I like having my own microcomputer. I used to spend a lot of nights waiting in line at the computing center, so I know what you go through. It seems problem number three is schedule and convenience, both important if you want to both go to school and hold down a part-time job. Anything else?

Brent I sure could have used a microcomputer last spring, when I was in charge of the alumni run. It was chaotic! I was up until 3 A.M. addressing mailers, and then I had to organize the entries. I'll probably be asked to help with it again. Could word processing be used in a situation like that, or do I need some sort of data management software?

Amy That's hard to say right now. Let's just list this as problem four, mailing list and organizing entries. Anything else?

Brent Not right now, but I know I will have other problems in the future. I'll be applying to four-year schools soon and some of them require autobiographies and essays. If I had word processing software, maybe I could write one autobiography and just use it again and again. And then I will have to write a résumé. Actually, I'm thinking I might try to get a better job next semester and I will need a résumé for that, too. And when I start my job, I know that having experience on a microcomputer will be a plus. I might want to have my own microcomputer at home, just in case I take a job with a small firm or don't have a microcomputer at the office. I guess this is the point where I start to get confused. If I just had to buy a microcomputer for now, I think it would be relatively simple. But I don't know for sure what my major will be or where I will be working even next year.

Amy In some ways, selecting a microcomputer for your own use is more complicated than developing an information system for a major corporation. You want to use the microcomputer to accomplish some very different tasks. And each task is like a different information system. But don't worry—that's the beauty of computers. They are general-purpose machines. Change the software, and you change the information the computer can produce. With the right software, one microcomputer can meet all your needs now and maybe even in the future.

I had trouble planning for the future, too. Since computers are going to be my career, I needed a powerful computer, but at a reasonable price. But because prices keep dropping every year, I really wondered if I should wait. The best advice I got was to weigh the benefit of having the microcomputer to use now versus the money I might save if I waited. I decided to buy, and I haven't regretted it. By planning and anticipating your future computing needs, I'm sure you'll make the right decision.

Let's sum up your "project definition." For now, you need a microcomputer to solve these problems: 1. typing papers; 2. tedious mathematical calculations; 3.

schedule/convenience; 4. running club mailing list and organizing entries. And for the future, you have "complete college applications, write and revise résumé, use on job." I think we're ready to do a feasibility study.

Brent The feasibility study confuses me a bit. I know that I can probably find a microcomputer that will solve my problems, and I know I will use it. That just leaves the big question: can I afford to buy a micro?

Amy Right. Some of the microcomputers cost a few hundred dollars, but many are awkward and slow for anything other than games or educational software. The kind of software you need may not even be available for the less-expensive microcomputers. Other microcomputers are as powerful as minicomputers, but their prices are usually over a thousand dollars, and often closer to three thousand. And you may want to buy peripherals, like a printer or modem. How much money do you have to spend? We could make out a statement of your finances. I know that helped me.

Brent I'm ahead of you there. I've been looking at this a lot lately. I could come up with over $1400 in cash, counting my tax refund, but that would totally deplete my emergency fund. I don't want to do that. But I've been thinking. I doubt that I could get a loan from a bank, but my church has a credit union, and so does the auto parts store. My savings are split between those two places. Usually, credit unions are pretty good about giving low-interest loans to members. Of course, if my parents co-sign, I might be able to get credit from a computer store, but I'd rather not do that. I might be able to get a loan from my uncle. He said he would help me if I ever needed it, and this might qualify.

Amy You might also ask at your school. One of the reasons I chose my computer was that my school was offering a student's discount on a model that met my current and probable future needs.

"Your goal now is to get an idea of what software and hardware are available."

Brent I'll do that. I also thought I might try making a down payment and monthly payments. So it looks like I might be able to afford a microcomputer. For right now, let's assume I can. What next?

Amy Next, you prepare your list of user requirements. That means you list the functions you need a microcomputer to perform for you. But before you do that, you need to get some more information. I can save you some work by telling you that word processing and electronic spreadsheet software would probably meet most of your current needs. But you need to do some reading and ask questions to make sure. Also, you'll find that there are lots of word processing packages and good spreadsheet packages. Each of them offers slightly different functions. You'll have to decide which functions are important to you.

One place you might start is your computer textbook. In looking through the table of contents I see that it has a lot of relevant information about microcomputers. For example, Chapter 2 and Chapter 15 both describe the most popular types of microcomputer software packages used in business. The sections on classifying computers and choosing printers and so on might also help you when you begin your "systems design" and "systems acquisition." But you also need to check some other sources.

One good source of free advice is microcomputer owners. Another is your school. Even though the computing center is always busy, sometimes they offer seminars on choosing a microcomputer. My school did. If nothing else, the computing center gives you the chance to experiment with various brands of software and hardware. You will want to do this before you make a final decision.

Another advantage of the campus computer center is that it may have resources usually available only to computer professionals. For example, our computer center subscribes to two services that rate hardware and software: Datapro Research and Auerbach. These services are expensive, but they publish books, newsletters, and updates regularly. I had to make an appointment to use these services, but they did help.

But you won't need to use these services just yet. Your goal now is to get an idea of what software and hardware are available.

Brent You keep mentioning software first. I don't have the microcomputer yet!

Amy Remember, the software determines what the microcomputer can do for you. You have to find out the functions software can offer to help you solve your problems.

Brent So where do I look, besides the text and maybe the computing center?

Amy You might get more relevant information from some of the computer magazines, especially the advertisements. *Personal Computing, Popular Computing, Creative Computing,* and *Business Computer Systems* are good because they're somewhat general. Other magazines are written for owners of particular computers, like *PC World* for IBM PC owners, *Compute* for Commodore owners, *Macworld* for Macintosh owners, and *A+* for Apple owners. I can lend you some of my issues, if you want them, or you can check at the library. Read some of the product reviews to get an idea of what professional computer reviewers look for, and study the ads to see what is available. You might also look for the annual and quarterly buying guides some of these magazines offer. They list all possible types of products with information about their features, requirements, and prices. The features are what you are interested in right now.

It's a good idea to check the *Readers' Guide to Periodical Literature* for articles that have appeared in general-interest magazines, like *Consumer Reports.* Articles written for a general audience sometimes give you a better overview of available features than articles written for specialized audiences. Another source is the *Business Periodicals Index.*

After you do some reading, you need to talk to other people. Ask micro owners what was important to them when they chose particular software. Or better yet, ask them what they don't like, and why. Most micro owners love to talk about that sort of thing. Another strategy is to go to a computer store. Tell the sales representative you think you want to buy a microcomputer and see what kinds of questions you are asked.

Brent Won't a sales representative be biased? What if I ask the wrong questions?

Amy Sales representatives may be biased, but a good computer store will try to meet your needs. And if the personnel aren't helpful before you buy, they probably won't be helpful after you give them your money. Don't worry about asking the wrong questions, either. When you are making a large purchase, there are no wrong questions. Let's get together in another two weeks. You'll have had time to do some research and we can go over your list of user requirements and your systems design.

Brent Wait a minute—how do I design a system?

Amy The user requirements describe the functions you need to perform. For example, you need to type four papers. So the function you require is easy correcting of typing mistakes. You might also want a program that could proofread your paper. Maybe you organize your paper as you write it and find that you want to reorder whole paragraphs. Then that is a function you need. Think about organizing the alumni run, and the other things you do for the running club. For instance, will you be mailing the newsletter and special announcements to members and alumni? The body of the letter or newsletter stays the same, but the name and address on each copy changes. So, addressing a mailing would be a function you'd require. Another function you might need is the ability to print papers and mailing labels.

When you are ready to do your systems design, you will translate the functions you require into the capabilities offered by existing software. And the type of software you will need will show you the type of hardware you will need to buy. For example, all software requires a minimum amount of primary memory, and some software requires two disk drives. These hardware requirements will play a major part in your choice of a microcomputer. Some functions will translate directly into hardware requirements. For example, the ability to print means you will need a printer. These general software and hardware requirements make up your systems design. In the systems acquisition stage, you'll be trying to choose among specific software packages and microcomputers.

Brent And by then I should know what I really need. Thanks for your help, Amy.

Brent asked the questions and did the research Amy had suggested. They met again, as arranged, two weeks after their first meeting.

Brent Amy, I think you'll be impressed. I have both user requirements and a system design down on paper. I still have some questions, though. You said I would probably need word processing and a spreadsheet, and I think you're right. I'm still not sure what kind of software I need to handle the running club work. A data base management system would be nice, but a mail merge package might work just as well. A mail merge package would let me maintain a list of names and addresses, plus some additional information like standings. Most packages would either let me print the list out by itself, as on mailing labels for the running club newsletter, or combine the names and addresses with a form letter to produce a customized letter. This could come in handy when I start applying to other schools or looking for a job after I graduate. But other than finding out about mail merge, it took me over a week to reach the conclusion you came to in five minutes: I definitely need word processing and an electronic spreadsheet. So what did I gain?

Amy A lot, Brent. By now, you are a lot more confident about the ways a microcomputer could help you. And you are able to make a more realistic prediction of how much you will have to spend for a microcomputer—software and hardware—that will meet your needs.

Brent So, this is a good time to review my "feasibility study" and "project plan."

Amy Right. You should do that on your own, because from this point, the decisions become pretty personal. I can give you my opinion, but when it comes to spending hard-earned cash, you'll want to make your own decisions.

Brent Let's assume I decide to go ahead. I'd be ready for "systems acquisition." Do I have to start my research all over again?

Amy Not at all. This is where all your effort begins to pay off. You will still have to do some research, but it will be more specific than before. In systems analysis, you went to your textbook, to magazines, to buyer's guides, and to computer stores just to get an idea of what was available. Now that you have a sense of what is available and what you need, you're ready to narrow your options. You're ready to evaluate specific features and prices.

Brent Actually, I started forming some opinions this past week. But the problem comes when I try to put the pieces together. One word processing package might sound good, but it is not available for the microcomputer I thought I wanted. Where do I start?

"Now that you have a sense of what is available and what you need, you're ready to narrow your options."

Amy Always start with your software. I brought along a software checklist that helped me when I started seriously shopping for my microcomputer system. You might find it helpful.

Brent How does this work?

Amy I made out a separate sheet for each type of software package I thought about buying. One of the entries you need to pay special attention to is the brand and model of microcomputer the package is offered for. This fact will have a big effect on your choice of a microcomputer. Ditto for the operating system required.

Brent Does that mean that I can choose any computer whose ads say it uses the "right" operating system for my software?

Amy Not necessarily. Because of legal restrictions, manufacturers often have to make minor changes to their products. These changes may cause software to perform differently, or not at all. This is what makes compatibility such a tricky issue for microcomputer buyers. There are at least a couple of ways to deal with this problem, though. First, you can buy the brand of microcomputer the software was written for. Second, you can identify the software you want and ask a computer store to demonstrate the software on the brand of microcomputer that is supposed to be compatible.

Brent So the software decisions I make start to limit some of my hardware choices.

Amy To some extent, yes. Some of the most popular software packages are available for a number of microcomputer brands and for the two most popular operating systems, CP/M and MSDOS. Getting back to the software checklist, minimum primary memory requirements are an important consideration. Some programs are very powerful, but they need a lot of primary memory. And primary memory is something you need to consider when you select a microcomputer.

Type of Software Package

Name				
Offered for which micros?				
Operating system?				
Memory requirements?				
Ease of use Reputation Personal experience				
Support Documentation Telephone hot line? Training? (free?)				
Special features				
Related packages				
Price Retail? Discount? Bundled? User-supported?				

Brent Since all of the software reviews give this information, I expect I can do a lot of shopping in the comfort of my own home. What about the software shopping list entry, "Ease of use: reputation and personal experience"?

Amy You can judge a software package's reputation from reviews and from talking to users. But to decide if you like the software, you have to try it out. This means going to the campus computer center or back to the store to see if it has the software you are considering. You won't be able to take the software home or use it for an unlimited amount of time, but most stores will help you try out a particular software package.

Brent To save time, I expect I should narrow my choices down to two or three packages before I ask for any demonstrations. When I get to that point, what should I be looking for?

Amy Several things. First, look over your user requirements to get an idea of the functions you will be using most often. Experiment with them. To use some functions, some software packages require that you hit several keys in sequence. Others require only one or two keystrokes. The difference may not seem significant until you spend several hours at your micro. After the third hour, you may appreciate the more convenient package.

Also, look at the way the software uses menus and commands. A menu saves you the labor of memorizing commands and options. Some software packages always show the menu. Others let you call the menu up only when you need it.

Brent I think I would want the menu there all the time.

Amy At first, you may. Most menus take up a significant portion of the screen, however. Once you learn some of the commands, you may decide you want to see more of your document or spreadsheet and not the menu. Look at the commands the software package uses, too. To save space in memory, most of the commands are made up of two or three letters. These commands should use mnemonics, memory cues that help you learn the commands, so you don't need the menus. For example, pressing a special key called the control key and the "d" key might tell the microcomputer to "delete" a character, word, or paragraph. If you memorize the command, you save the time spent giving the command for a menu and waiting for it to appear. And the sooner you learn the commands, the sooner you will feel comfortable with your software. That means that you will be able to concentrate on the problems you expect the micro to solve, not the hardware and software.

Brent So once I learn the package, I should be able to do more in less time. How much time should it take to learn a software package?

Amy It depends on you and the support you get from the manufacturer, the store, and other users. Be sure you look at the documentation when you take your "test drive." Some software packages now include tutorials with simple lessons to show you the basic functions. Others offer a telephone hot line with technical experts that will talk you through specific problems. Some stores will include a free orientation lesson in the price of a microcomputer purchase, while other stores charge for the lesson.

Brent So the time to investigate this is before I buy?

Amy Definitely. A final entry on the software checklist concerns features. For example, some word processing packages can handle footnotes and others cannot. You will have to rate this particular feature as essential, preferable, or optional. If you want to, you can assign each feature a numerical value and compare the software package scores.

Brent So I could make out a checklist entry for each package and then compare them side by side. Then I could arrange a test drive of just the packages that scored above a certain number. What does this entry on the shopping list mean: "related packages available"?

Amy When I was shopping for software, I wanted to look at some of the "integrated packages," like Lotus 1–2–3. An integrated package combines the equivalent of several software packages in one package. I changed the entry to "related packages available" when I found out that some software companies offer add-on packages. For example, WordStar has been a top-selling word processing package for years. You can also buy a related proofreading program called SpellStar, a related spreadsheet called CalcStar, and a related mail merge program called MailMerge. The advantage is that you can add packages as your budget allows and still have the convenience of knowing that your word processing package can print a spreadsheet in the middle of a page, if you need that capability.

Brent I might. I definitely know I am on a tight budget. I see you have some entries for comparison shopping. I've been looking at price all along. The mail-order houses seem to offer lower prices, but is it a good idea to order from them?

Amy It depends. There are a couple of issues to consider. One is the kind of support you need versus the kind of support the software company offers. Mail-order houses don't charge as much as retail stores, but they don't offer the same kind of support either. Another issue to consider is the fact that some retail stores will offer you a lower price if you buy the software bundled with the hardware.

You might also want to look into "user-supported software" or "public domain software." In the early days of microcomputers, almost everyone wrote and shared programs. Some software developers carry on that tradition. They will send you their program on a diskette and, if you like it, either ask you to send a modest sum or to buy their manual explaining how to use the program.

Brent That could really save me money. Some of the programs are really expensive. And I know that software companies prohibit borrowing programs from user to user.

"Once you've selected your software, you will know your hardware requirements."

Amy I can see their point. Some of these software packages take thousands of hours and many people to develop. They have a right to make money from their investment. The important point is that you need to choose software that will be valuable to you. And the value of software depends on the functions it performs for you. You may find a very inexpensive program that does everything you need.

Brent So once I've selected software that meets my needs, I'll be ready to "acquire" my hardware. I can see now that the software I choose will affect my hardware choices.

Amy That's right. Once you've selected your software, you will know your hardware requirements. In some cases, the software you choose will limit your hardware options to machines that use a particular operating system, such as CP/M or MSDOS. In a few cases, the same software package may be offered in slightly different versions for different operating systems. Choosing can be hard. There are literally thousands of software packages available for each of the most popular microcomputer operating systems.

Brent Since I'm going to major in business, am I limited in the kind of machine I buy?

Amy Not at all. Some business-oriented software packages are available for almost every type of microcomputer. You might also consider portable computers, or lap-top computers, or even notebook computers. These computers were designed for business professionals who are away from their offices. Most of these types of microcomputers are less expensive than the typical microcomputer, which can crowd the top of a desk. Some of the portables include a small monochrome monitor or CRT, a generous amount of primary memory, two disk drives, and a keyboard in a case that weighs around 35 pounds. The advantage is that you do not need to buy a monitor or disk drives, since these are included in the package. The disadvantage is that the manufacturer chooses these peripherals for you.

Brent So I need some way to systematically compare microcomputers.

Amy True. Here is another chart that helped me. I used it to compare the price of a basic microcomputer plus the options I needed. In some ways, buying a microcomputer is like buying a car. On some models, a certain feature may be standard. On other models, the same feature may mean an additional cost. And when you buy a computer, the little extras can add up fast. For example, most microcomputers will let you expand the size of memory up to certain limits, but that is an additional expense.

"How do I know a price is a good one?"

Brent Price is certainly important to me. I've been watching the newspaper for sales and so on. How do I know a price is a good one?

Amy One way is to know the manufacturer's suggested retail price. Another is to check the advertisements that mail-order houses run in the computer magazines. These can be a good reference, although most mail-order houses do not offer the kind of support I know I need. Also, some manufacturers and stores will combine or bundle a microcomputer with certain software packages. If you happen on the right combination, you can save a lot of money this way.

Brent That's good to know. What should I know about choosing a monitor?

Amy First, is the price of the monitor included in the price of the microcomputer? If it isn't, you may have to spend another two to four hundred dollars. Some microcomputers are designed to use a television set as a monitor, but there are drawbacks if you plan to use the microcomputer for complex applications. Second, you need to decide if you want a color or a monochrome monitor. A color

Hardware Cost Sheet

Brand/model				
Basic price Retail Discount				
Primary memory Amount included in basic price? Optional? price?				
Disk drives Number Size included in basic price? Optional? price?				
CRT Included? Optional? price?				
Keyboard Fixed? Detached? Tilts? Function keys? Number key pad?				
Other items needed? Printer? price? Modem? price?				
Total cost of hardware				

monitor is good if you want to do elaborate graphics or to play games. Some users feel that a monochrome monitor, whether it is green or amber, is easier on their eyes, however. The important issue here is choosing a monitor you will be comfortable with. After all, you may spend a lot of time staring at your spreadsheets.

The same goes for the keyboard. In most cases, you don't have a choice in the keyboard. However, if two microcomputers seem about equal, the keyboard's comfort might help you choose. For example, some keyboards are built into the housing of the computer itself. Other keyboards are attached to the computer processor by a coiled cord. This feature lets you move the keyboard to a convenient distance from the computer itself. Some keyboards tilt, which also makes them easier to use for long periods. Another useful feature is special keys for moving the cursor around the screen. Without cursor control keys, you may have to hit two or three separate keys. Some people like to use a mouse to do the same thing. A mouse, which is standard on the Macintosh, is a little box-like control on rollers. Roll the mouse to the left and the cursor moves to the left. Some keyboards offer an entire bank of special keys called function keys, which can be used just to enter commands, not data. For example, hitting a single function key may issue the same command as three letter keys hit in succession. Again, these are matters of convenience.

"If two microcomputers seem about equal, the keyboard's comfort might help you choose."

Brent What I'm interested in is the numeric keypad, the separate bank of keys that is laid out like the keyboard of a calculator. I'm sure I want this feature on my microcomputer. What about a printer? A computer is no use unless I can print the results of my spreadsheet.

Amy The printer was an important issue for me, too. I decided I was facing one basic question: did I need a dot matrix printer or a letter quality printer? Dot matrix means that each letter is formed of small dots, like the time and temperature signs outside a bank. A letter quality printer works more like a typewriter, but it is usually slower and more expensive than a dot matrix printer. An issue you'll want to consider is the width of your printer carriage. My printer accepts paper that is 8½ inches wide, but you may need a printer that accepts wider paper if you are going to be printing spreadsheets. In any case, your research will show you which features are available and important to you. Then you'll be able to make a decision.

Of course, you might be able to save some money by not buying a printer. If your equipment is compatible, you may be able to use a printer at your school's computing center. At my school, any student can use the computing center equipment to print a document for a small hourly charge and an additional charge per page. I printed a term paper for about five dollars.

Another purchase you need to plan for is supplies like diskettes and fanfold paper. You need to have plenty of diskettes, so that you can make backup copies of all your original software and important data files. You probably know that a backup should always be on a separate diskette, just in case something happens to your original. You can save some money by purchasing some of these supplies by mail through discount houses.

Brent I'm not certain just when I'll buy software and a microcomputer, but I think I have some good ideas for "systems implementation." The main task of systems implementation is training and starting to use the new system. After all, I'll have researched training while I am researching my possible purchase, so it should be easy to get my computer system operating.

Amy I hope so. You really should allow lots of time for familiarizing yourself with the software and the microcomputer. Sometimes I think computers are governed by Murphy's Law: "If anything can go wrong, it will." If you are hurrying or trying to meet a deadline, the chance you will make mistakes increases. And some mistakes can erase a lot of hard work.

And even if you do buy a microcomputer and printer, don't give up your typewriter. If your printer breaks down, your typewriter is a good backup. Also, you'll need your typewriter to fill out application forms. This is almost impossible to do with a microcomputer and printer.

Brent So I'm still facing the big decision: to buy or not to buy?

Amy No major purchase decision is easy. Anyway, if you have more questions, you can always get answers by checking either your textbook or magazines, or asking a sales representative at a computer store.

Major purchases are never easy, but Amy helped Brent see how a systems development approach could simplify his decision. We work with computers and are aware of the important role the microcomputer has played and will continue to play in the information society. That is why we have included several discussions of specific aspects of microcomputer hardware and software. For example, the text includes specific discussions on classifying computers (including microcomputers), on CRT devices, and on criteria that can be used to choose printers. Check the index under "microcomputer" to find these discussions.

CHAPTER 13

Program Development

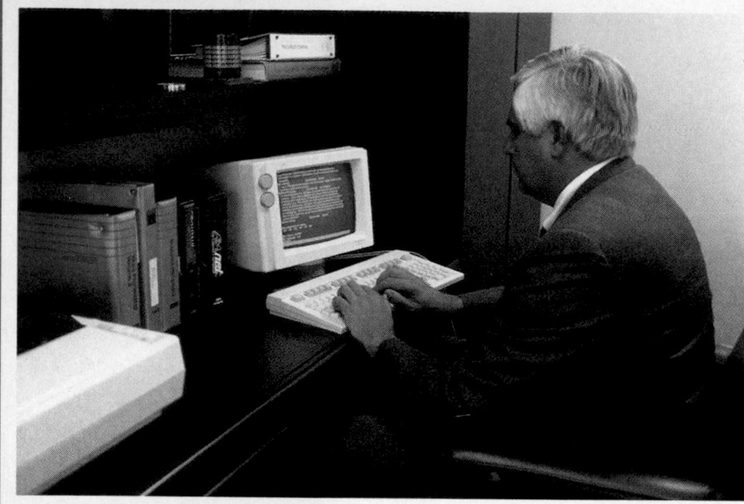

COMPUTERS AT WORK

Professionals Turn Programmers

Once programming was deemed a relentless, exacting chore performed by people who were often considered socially inept, who could only communicate in BASIC, COBOL, or assembly languages instead of plain English.

Now that's all changing. Professionals from all walks of life, ranging from doctors and lawyers to businessmen and teachers, are boasting about their newly developed programming prowess as if they had just mastered the skill of hang gliding or water skiing.

In fact, programming may well be the most intriguing intellectual sport since chess. Amateur software developers find it exciting, challenging, and sometimes addicting. Staying up round-the-clock debugging a line of code is not an uncommon occurrence among this enthusiastic throng of computerists.

Professionals lured into the hacker's habit fall eventually into one of three categories: those writing their own programs for work or pleasure; those touting dual careers as programmers/professionals; and those who have left their original vocations entirely to pursue a calling in software development.

The first case is the norm. It happens every day. Take the director of the American Bar Association, for instance. Attorney Tom Gonzer of Chicago, Illinois, has developed a program that evaluates lawsuits. Called Invalue, the software determines the economic impact of a suit on the basis of cost and other factors. "I don't consider myself an expert programmer by any means," he says humbly.

What is it about programming that keeps many a glassy-eyed user intensely glued to the terminal, oblivious while hours and almost days pass by? Those who are just getting used to sitting at a keyboard have yet to understand a neophyte software author's victory cry when a program is finally debugged. But for the programmer, such an act is the ultimate high, the seduction of challenge, and, for some, the only outlet to creativity.

From "Professionals Turn Programmers" by Kathy Chin, *InfoWorld,* February 6, 1984, pp. 82–84. Copyright © 1984 by Popular Computing Inc., a subsidiary of CW Communications, Inc. Reprinted from InfoWorld, 1060 Marsh Rd., Menlo Park, CA 94025.

You may find it rewarding to learn how to program even if you do not pursue an information systems career. For some people, programming is actually fun! And, like attorney Tom Gonzer, you might be able to develop a program that can help your work performance no matter which career field you enter. In this chapter, you will learn to do the following:

1. Explain how program development fits into the systems life cycle.
2. Describe the main goal in business programming and explain how it is achieved.
3. List the three types of activities that take place during the programming process.
4. Explain what is meant by the term *structured programming.*
5. Describe how flowcharts and pseudocodes are used in program development.
6. List the basic programming concepts that are made available in all programming languages.
7. Describe the standard program design for business computing.

THE NATURE OF PROGRAMMING

When Jan Hale began working at CompuStore, she was the firm's entire information systems staff. Her first information systems project began as a request from Susan Tate to analyze monthly sales data to identify buying trends. Susan gave Jan the project description shown in Exhibit 13.1 on the following page when they first discussed the project.

Jan thought this fairly simple systems development project would give her a good chance to show off her programming skills. Thinking about the programs she had written in college, Jan told Susan it would take less than a week to write the program. Susan was impressed. Two hours later Jan was sitting at a terminal keying in her program. Susan was even more impressed.

It took Jan over three weeks to finally get the program running. Susan was no longer impressed. Then, adding insult to injury, Susan complained that the reports were not what she had expected.

That same night Jan ran into a friend of hers, Terry Hill, at a meeting. Terry had graduated a few years ahead of Jan and worked as a systems analyst at a larger company.

Still feeling confused over the length of time it had taken her to develop the sales analysis information system, Jan described the project to Terry. After listening to Jan's story, Terry smiled and then explained: "You made two big mistakes, Jan. First, you thought the project was so easy that you could skip most of the systems life-cycle stages and jump right into program development. Second, instead of spending some time putting together a clear program design, you immediately started to write your program.

"I know you wanted to hurry and make a good impression on your first big assignment. However, the few days you saved by skipping the early systems analysis and design steps ended up costing you a couple of weeks of time."

This early experience had a big impact on Jan. She read a number of books on systems analysis, systems design, and program development, and she put these ideas into practice. Much of the advice Jan gave Jerry Lincoln in Chapters 11 and 12 had its roots in Jan's determination never to make these same mistakes again.

Exhibit 13.1

Susan Tate's initial description of the Customer Sales Analysis System

```
To:           Jan Hale

From:         Susan Tate

Subject:      Description of Customer Sales Analysis System

Project:      Customer Sales Analysis

Purpose:      Analyze one month of customer sales data to identify
              buying trends.

              Process monthly sales data to prepare reports giving
              customer and product trends for each store and for the
              entire company.

Input Data:   Month and Year

              Record of each sales transaction for the current month

                  Retail location code
                  Customer code
                  Product code
                  Amount of sale

              Data file containing sales summaries for all prior months
              of the current year

                  Total monthly sales by customer and product for all
                  prior months of the current year

Output
Information:  Report showing monthly sales trends for the entire firm
              and for each store

              Report showing monthly customer trends for the entire firm

              Report showing monthly product trends for the entire firm
```

Programming and the Systems Life Cycle

Programs are written during the **systems acquisition stage** of the systems life cycle (see Exhibit 13.2). Since systems analysis and systems design precede programming, the information system's output, input, file, and processing specifications should have already been determined as part of software design. Programming transforms these specifications into concrete outputs, inputs, and files.

The software design produced during systems design should identify the major functions involved in processing data to produce an information system's outputs. What is not detailed is exactly what processing operations will be performed and how they should be performed. This is the programmer's job.

Think of software design as a standard flight plan given to a World War II combat pilot. The flight plan describes a route to be flown, but the pilot still has to figure out the actual flight path he will take. Similarly, the software design is developed during systems analysis and design, while the programmer "plots" the actual course the computer will follow in meeting these specifications. Without the "flight plan" of software design, programmers are very likely to become lost and have to retrace their steps. This is what happened to Jan Hale and caused her four-day project to take three weeks.

These "flight plans" become even more important when many programmers work on a software development project. Today few programming projects involve a single programmer. All programmers working on a large project need direction for their own programming assignments, and their programs must fit together. Software design can both direct and coordinate the work of many programmers.

The Art of Programming

If you have never programmed a computer, you may not understand the satisfaction a programmer feels after completing a difficult programming task. But you may have felt the same kind of satisfaction if you have ever put together a 1000-piece jigsaw puzzle, solved a *New York Times* crossword puzzle, assembled something you bought as a kit, or finished a lengthy craft project. Now, have you ever gotten frustrated when your car wouldn't start, when your stereo went on the blink, or when your camera "froze up"? Think how satisfied you would have felt had you been able to fix the problem. Now combine the satisfaction you feel after solving a puzzle with the satisfaction of mastering a balky machine. This is what programmers enjoy about their work.

A programmer works with a fairly limited set of information processing capabilities. Some of these will be described later in this chapter and the next. However, the information processing requirements of most information systems are not simple. At times, figuring out a programming problem can be like trying to fit a size 8 foot into a size 7 shoe. Much of the enjoyment of programming comes when programmers, using their creativity and experience, are able to solve such problems. The "fun" part of programming, as with any creative activity, is seeing the finished "piece of art." With programming, this is a program that works!

Perhaps you can now begin to understand why Jan Hale immediately jumped into writing the sales analysis program. It takes a good deal of self-discipline for programmers to produce clear and complete designs before they begin writing their programs. In addition, programmers must learn and use the same communication techniques that are so important to successful systems development.

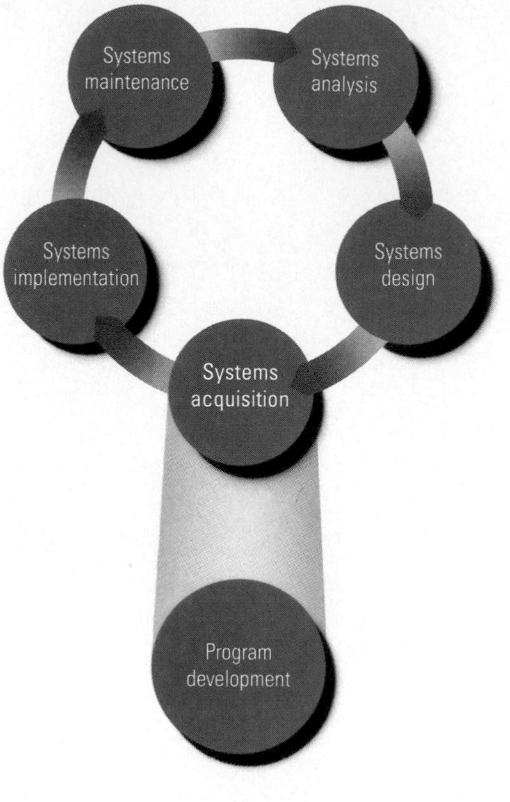

Exhibit 13.2
Program development takes place during the systems acquisition stage of the systems life cycle, after systems analysis and systems design. An overall information system design should exist before program development begins.

The techniques discussed in this chapter can help you avoid Jan Hale's experience with the sales analysis project. Whether you are developing your own programs or being asked to evaluate the work of professional programmers, you should be aware that following certain practices can prevent many programming problems and produces good results.

PROGRAM DEVELOPMENT

The main goal in business programming is to develop programs that are correct and maintainable. A **correct program** completely and accurately performs the information processing activities as specified in the systems design. A **maintainable program** can easily be changed at some future time. Interestingly, both these objectives are achieved in the same way: programs should be written so they are easily understood by people.

Jan Hale made this point very clear to Helen Sims, CompuStore's programmer, one day by writing the following message on the blackboard in Helen's office:

Programs are for people, *not for* computers!

Helen had been having trouble developing a program and had asked Jan to look at her program design. Jan couldn't make heads or tails of it. She saw bits and pieces, but couldn't get a handle on the program's overall logical flow. When Helen read Jan's message, she asked Jan what she meant:

Helen: I don't see your point, Jan. Computers run programs, not people.

Jan: Computers may run programs, but people write them. I can't follow your design at all. Can you?

Helen: Sure! Do you want me to explain it to you?

Jan: Not now. Hmm . . . you're working on some more important projects than this. Why don't I take all your notes and keep them for a week. You can explain your design to me then.

When Jan and Helen got together the next week, Helen had trouble explaining the design to Jan. She couldn't remember some of the things she had been doing, and her scratchy notes were just useless. Jan then explained: "If you have trouble figuring out the design, think of the trouble someone else would have. Produce designs and write programs that people can understand!"

Three benefits occur when you develop an understandable program. First, it is easier to resume work on a program you haven't worked on for a couple of days. Second, others can understand your program and give you some help with it. Third, it is far easier for you or another programmer to figure out how to modify the program in the future. The techniques discussed in this chapter are all geared toward helping you develop understandable programs.

The Program Development Process

Program development involves three distinct activities:

Program design Producing a clear, logical flow for a program's information processing operations.

Program coding Translating the program design into a program using a programming language.

Testing Checking the correctness of a program design and a program's code.

Most people think of program development as primarily program coding. Actually, coding accounts for the smallest amount of the total effort put into a programming project. Exhibit 13.3 shows the typical amount of time good programmers spend on each of these programming activities. Far more time is spent on both testing and designing than on coding.

Also, these three activities usually do not occur in a step-by-step manner. While program design always occurs first, programmers often move back and forth among the three activities (see Exhibit 13.4). Tests performed on a program design may indicate the need to make some design changes. Tests performed on a program code may indicate the need to make some code changes, some design changes, or both.

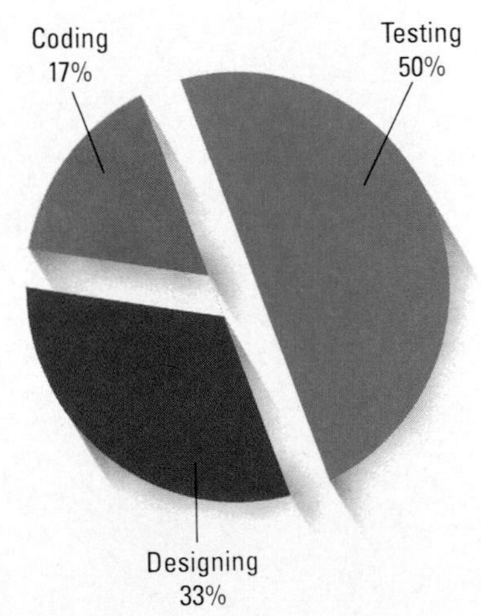

Exhibit 13.3

Good programmers actually spend very little time writing their programs. Much more time is spent designing their programs and checking their designs and codes.

Exhibit 13.4

Programming rarely takes place in a step-by-step manner. A lot of "backtracking" is usually observed as designs are improved and errors or omissions are detected and corrected.

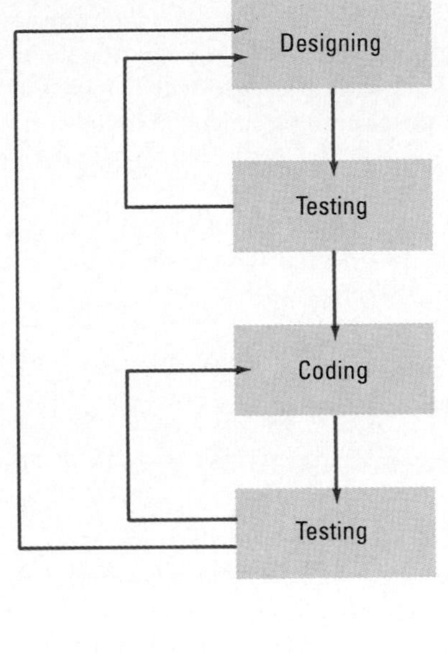

Exhibit 13.5

When a program design has a clear, logical structure, program segments do not overlap. Note that this is the case with the design for CompuStore's Customer Sales Analysis System.

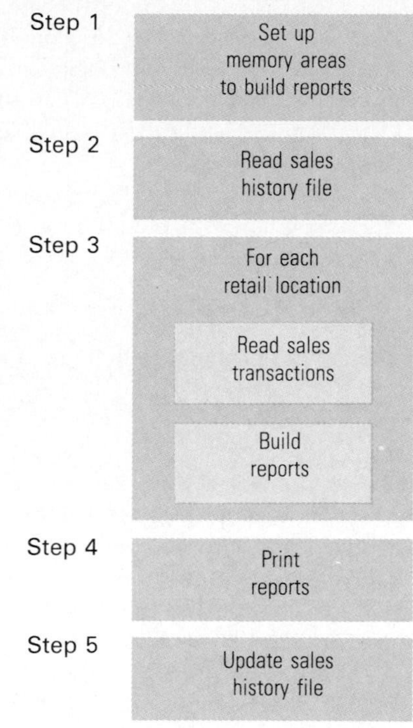

Design Program. Three steps are involved in program design. First, study the overall software design to make sure you understand the program's purpose and its relationship to any other programs that make up the information system being developed. Obtain answers to anything that is not clear before you start preparing a design. Second, think about different ways the program's design could be approached and compare their advantages and disadvantages. As a general rule, select the approach that seems easiest for someone else to understand. Third, produce a program design that has a clear, logical structure.

A design with a clear, logical structure is made up of a number of segments, each of which performs a well-defined information processing task. The program's logical flow should not jump randomly between segments, but should move through them in a straightforward manner. Exhibit 13.5 illustrates a clear, logical structure for a program design to handle CompuStore's sales analysis project. Note that program segments do not overlap.

Some programmers find it challenging to develop clever program designs that produce very efficient programs. Sometimes this is important because there are hardware limitations or because the business application must be executed extremely fast. The problem with "clever" program designs is that they often are difficult to understand. And much of the time, the extra efficiency is not really needed. Ideally, software should handle an information processing task in much the same way a person would handle the task.

Test Program Design. It is important to carefully check a program design before beginning coding. Usually this testing ensures that the design is both correct and complete. That is, it results in a program that will meet the information processing specifications set forth in the software design. It is far easier to correct or discard poor thoughts than poor code.

Code Program. If a good program design exists, coding is an almost mechanical task of translating, in a one-for-one fashion, each design step into a corresponding programming language statement. The ease with which this translation is done depends on both the programming language being used and the business application being developed. The next chapter discusses these issues.

Although it is not always possible, it is advisable to postpone selecting a programming language until the program design is fairly well set. This overcomes the tendency to use old programming habits, such as:

I always do it this way when I program in FORTRAN,

or to bend the problem to fit the programming langauge:

It's hard to do this in COBOL, so I'll change the report formats a little from what has been specified.

The programmer sooner or later has to consider the specific characteristics of the programming language that will be used. Still, easier-to-understand programs tend to result when these considerations are postponed. Try to avoid a programming language that does not support an excellent design. It is better to make a few changes in a good design than to start off with a poor design.

Test Program Coding. The testing of program coding is popularly referred to as **debugging.** Debugging is done for three main reasons: to make sure the program meets the processing requirements spelled out in the logical design, to locate and correct syntax errors, and to locate and correct logic errors. **Syntax errors** involve "grammatical" mistakes in using a programming language. **Logic errors,** on the other hand, indicate that the program design is incorrect. Logic errors are far more difficult to detect and correct than syntax errors.

Many program errors can be corrected by "handchecking" code prior to executing the program. Even so, errors will remain to be discovered when the program is executed using different sets of input data. These testing procedures and test data are developed during systems design.

Program Documentation

Programs are documented for two reasons: to improve communications among the people involved with a programming project and to make it easier for anyone who will have to use or understand the program in the future. In the early days of computer programming, documentation was usually prepared after a program had been developed. Such a practice has a number of drawbacks:

Important program design, coding, and testing issues are forgotten.

Documentation is usually incomplete because programmers tend to hurry through the task in order to start a new assignment.

The documentation might never be produced.

Today programmers are encouraged or required to produce documentation throughout the programming process (see Exhibit 13.6).

Program documentation should be both external and internal to the program code. **External program documentation** would be in each of the documentation manuals described in the chapters on systems development. **Internal program documentation** includes explanatory statements inserted directly into a program's code. All programming languages provide for internal documentation. Because it is so easy to forget to revise external documentation when program changes are made, internal documentation is extremely important.

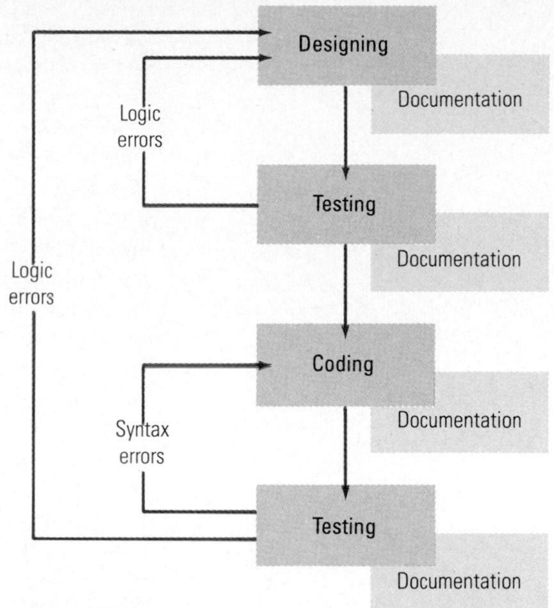

Exhibit 13.6

Documentation should occur throughout the programming process—not only upon completion of the program.

Programming Teams

While the "art of programming" is a creative activity, few of today's business programming projects involve a single programmer. As a result, most software is developed by programming teams, with each programmer assigned to develop one or more of the programs that make up the information system being developed. The size of these teams may vary from a couple of programmers to 10, 50, 100, or even 1000 or more.

With large programmer teams, management and communication problems become just as difficult as the program design, coding, and testing problems. The project mamagement techniques described in Chapter 11 and the chief programmer team described in Chapter 12 are often used in managing large teams of programmers.

Another problem that arises with programmer teams is that some programmers tend to view their programs in much the same way that artists view their work. Criticism of a program becomes a personal affront to the programmer's ability or creativity. This is troublesome because it is very useful to have programmers review each other's work. Errors can be located and program improvements can be suggested. This will not occur if programmers are reluctant to allow others to criticize their efforts. The overall performance of a programmer team can improve a great deal when team members freely criticize each other's work. This is referred to as **egoless programming.**

Two management techiques exist that can take advantage of egoless programming. One, the **structured walkthrough,** was introduced in our discussion of systems design. Here a programmer gets up in front of the other members of the programming team and "walks through" a program design, a set of code, or a testing strategy. The other tool is the **inspection team.** Here a select group of experienced programmers is trained in detecting common program design or coding errors. At regular intervals during a project, programmers explain the current version of their program to this team of inspectors. The inspection team identifies any errors the programmers have made and explains what must be done to correct them.

User Participation

Since programmers work from a well-defined set of software requirements, you might think there would be little need for them to interact with users. Remember, however, that the new information system does not exist during the systems analysis and systems design stages of the software life cycle. As a result, software requirements can be the result of a "best guess" effort. Thus, user participation continues to be important during program development.

One way to encourage user participation is prototyping, which produces a "quick and dirty" version of an information system. This strategy, first discussed in Chapter 12, can help programmers get user feedback. Experimenting with a prototype lets an information system's users see whether or not the information system's outputs are useful.

Similarly, periodically meeting with programmers to examine program inputs and outputs will help an information system's users visualize their use of the information system. These meetings are valuable in that both users and programmers can brainstorm about improving the information system. These meetings can also serve as another check on whether or not a program meets the software requirements.

The potential benefit of having users interact with programmers during program development will vary with each information systems project. The user participation guidelines for systems development apply here as well.

Ways to Design Good Programs

A program with a clear, logical structure is more likely to be correct and maintainable than a program without such a structure. The program design and code will both be easy to understand. As a result, the programmer should be able to detect errors and modify the program more easily, programming team members will be able to contribute to each other's programs, and users will be better able to follow what the programmer is doing.

How, then, can you produce a program design that has a clear, logical structure? The key is to think clearly and use good program design techniques. Computers at Work: "Attributes of an Ideal Programmer" should give you some idea of the kind of thought processes needed to design a good program. The remainder of this chapter will introduce you to a number of good program design techniques.

STRUCTURED PROGRAMMING

Structured design was introduced in Chapter 11 as an approach to systems development that produces an easily understood, overall information systems design. The ideas behind the structured design approach were actually introduced around 1970 to improve the programming process. The name given these ideas for producing an easily understood program design was **structured programming.** While structured programming is a recent arrival on the programming scene, good programmers have always tended to design their programs in this fashion. As with structured design, structured programming makes use of the principles of abstraction, modularity, and stepwise refinement.

Abstraction

A program design should begin with an overview of what is to done, rather than how it will be done. This top level of design should be expressed in "everyday" English.

COMPUTERS AT WORK

Attributes of an Ideal Programmer

Three and a half years ago, I was a newly minted MBA with a concentration in MIS and a burning desire to save the world from information overflow. It took about six months of working in a large corporate data processing organization for me to realize that I needed some technical background if I was going to be more than a casual participant in the systems development process. I made the decision, aided by several supportive managers, to learn how to program.

It was a frustrating experience initially. There were two hundred errors in my first program because I started my code in column seven instead of column eight.

But I did it. By the end of seven months, I had moved into a position of checking over the work of other programmers. A few months after that, I was given responsibility for several major installations of the new release of our system. And about fifteen months after I began my task, people started to ask me questions. I had arrived.

I don't regret those long hours spend hunched over an IBM 3278. My experience left me with very definite opinions about why I succeeded and what makes a programmer think like a programmer. There are four attributes typical of an ideal programmer:

Logical thought process. The ability to understand the logical flow of a program or system and to reason through a problem.

Problem-solving orientation. The ability to ask good questions and leverage available resources to solve the problem.

Determination. Never letting go until the problem is solved.

Technical knowledge. Understanding the basics about the language and/or system and knowing where to go for more technical information when required.

A good programmer can become a good programmer on any system. A technical background is, of course, invaluable, but what helps the most is having the orientation and the attitude of a proficient programmer.

Source: D. Zahay, "Programming Has Wide DP Application," *Computerworld,* 30 July, 1984, p. 43 and p. 49.

Jan Hale advised Helen Sims to ask herself the following questions about her initial program designs: Will other programmers be able to quickly check this design against the software specifications? More to the point, will users be able to read and understand the design? If the answer to either question is "No," the design probably needs more work.

Consider the customer sales analysis system mentioned at the beginning of the chapter. The initial design of this program might appear as follows:

enter and process the current months sales transactions

enter the sales summaries for prior months

build the monthly sales trends reports

build the customer and product reports

print the monthly sales trends reports

print the customer and product reports

update the sales summary file so that it contains the current month's sales data

This "abstract" program design is not some "fuzzy" view of the program, but rather a business-oriented look at the tasks to be performed.

What is gained from abstraction? Ideally, it results in a program design that almost anyone can understand. Thus, it should be easy to determine if the programmer left something out or misunderstood an aspect of the program's purpose or description.

Modularity

Programs should be made up of modules, or segments, that perform distinct processing tasks. Ideally, each of these modules should serve a single purpose. The initial design of the customer sales analysis project, for example, consists of two segments that handle data entry, two that build management reports, two that print these reports, and a final segment that updates a data file.

While it might not be that obvious, each of the program segments in the initial design for the customer sales analysis project has a distinct processing flow. This is important, as it helps the programmer produce an overall program design that has a clear, logical structure.

What is to be gained from modularity? First, highlighting a program's major processing tasks increases the understandability of the program. A quick glance at the program design is all that is needed to obtain a basic understanding of the program's purpose. Second, separating the program's processing tasks into single-purpose segments increases the maintainability of the program. Ideally, future program revisions will occur within one, or at most a few, of these segments. This greatly eases future efforts to revise the program.

Stepwise Refinement

Programs should be designed in levels, with the top level being user oriented and the bottom level being computer oriented. Ideally, "how to" processing details are postponed to lower design levels. This prevents a premature design for one program segment from limiting the design alternatives for other program segments. Good programmers move very slowly in refining their program designs.

Exhibit 13.7 uses the pecan pie recipe given in Chapter 3 to illustrate the stepwise refinement concept. Only the first two levels of the design are shown. Lower design levels are added until the tasks given parallel those actually performed by a baker making a pecan pie.

The lowest level of a program design similarly gives the computer operations that must occur for the program to accomplish its purpose. The bottom level of a program design should be given in terms of the processing capabilities of the programming language that will be used. When this is done, coding becomes a rather mechanical task.

To produce program designs that maintain a clear, logical structure throughout the design process, each program segment should exhibit a **single-entry, single-exit processing flow** (see Exhibit 13.8). As a result, a key rule in structured programming is to restrict processing flows, as much as possible, to the following patterns:

Sequential — The processing flow moves through a set of processing tasks in a step-by-step fashion.

Selection — Options often exist in a program's logic. Depending on input data, all the processing tasks may not always be performed. Also, depending on input data, a selection may be made among two or more ways of handling a processing task. Decision points thus exist in the processing flow that allow a way to skip over a processing task.

Exhibit 13.7

The pecan pie recipe from Chapter 3 can illustrate how a design evolves with stepwise refinement. Here only the first two levels of the design are given in terms of each of the actual steps a baker would take in making the pie.

Level 1

Step 1	get ingredients
Step 2	mix ingredients
Step 3	bake pie

Level 2

Step 1	gather ingredients get measuring aids measure ingredients
Step 2	prepare different mixtures combine mixtures pour into pastry shell complete pie
Step 3	prepare oven place pie in oven remove pie from oven cool pie

Iteration The term **iteration** refers to the need to cycle through a processing task or a set of processing tasks. Depending on input data, processing tasks are repeated a certain number of times or until some condition is met. A **condition** involves a test of the values of one or more data items.

Each of these flow patterns will be illustrated in more detail later in the chapter.

What is to be gained from stepwise refinement? It provides a means for programmers to routinely check the overall correctness of a program design as the design unfolds. Perhaps even more important, each higher layer of a design serves as a map to guide the design of the lower layers and to aid other programmers or users in understanding the more detailed, computer-oriented, lower design levels.

PROGRAM DESIGN TOOLS

With simple programs, it might be possible to "think the problem through" in your mind and then sketch out the complete design. Most programs, even seemingly simple ones, cannot be designed this way. It helps considerably to write an evolving program on paper or a CRT display screen and work on only a small part of the design at a time. This also lets you stop work on the design, store the partially completed version, and then return to it later.

Programmers tend to have their own preferences as to which program design tools work best. However, most companies are beginning to set stan-

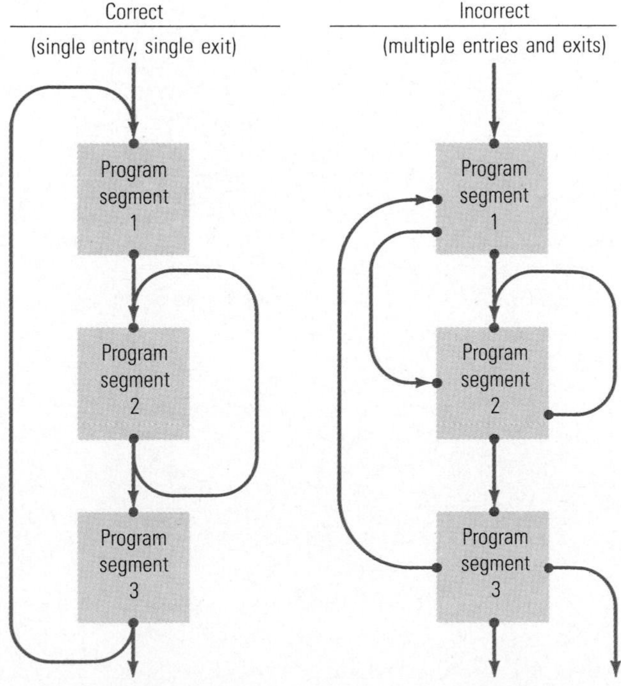

Exhibit 13.8
With a single-entry, single-exit processing flow, each program segment has a single entry point and a single exit point.

Exhibit 13.9
Standard Flowchart Symbols

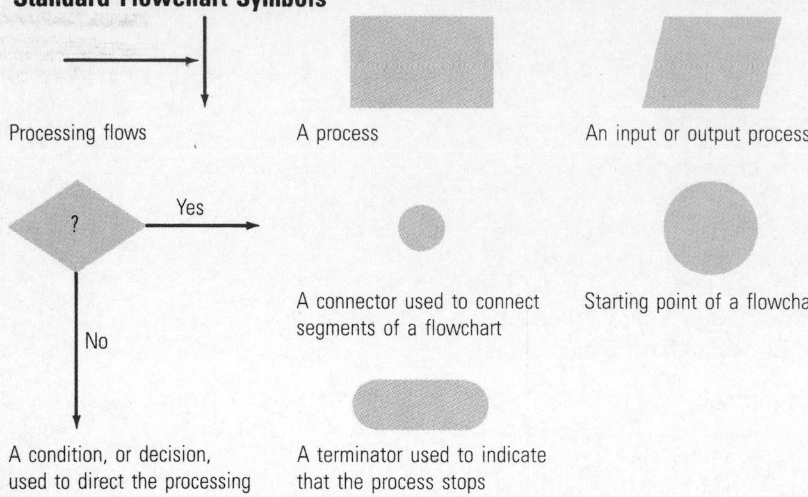

Exhibit 13.10
A flowchart indicating the steps a baker takes in making a pecan pie.

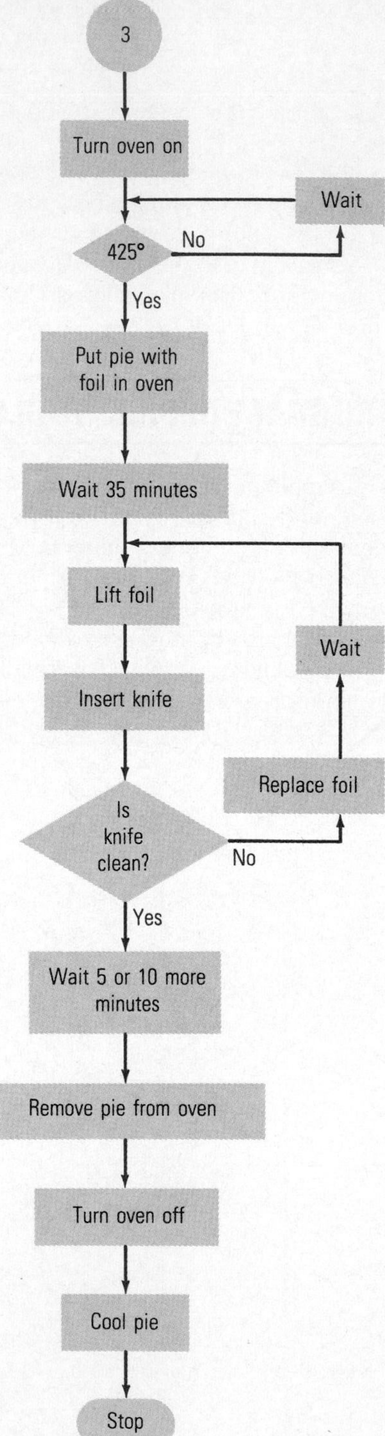

Exhibit 13.11
Compare this pseudocode version of the instructions for baking a pecan pie with the flowchart in Exhibit 13.10. Which do you find easier to follow and understand?

```
turn oven on
while (oven temperature is less than 425° F)
      wait
put pie with foil on top in oven
wait 35 minutes
repeat
            wait a few minutes
            lift foil
            insert knife and pull it out
            replace foil
      until (knife is clean)
remove foil
wait 5-10 minutes
turn oven off
cool pie
```

dards regarding the tools to be used in developing information systems. Communications regarding a systems development project are improved when standard tool sets are used.

Two of the more common program design tools are the flowchart and pseudocode. While both are used today, the pseudocode provides many advantages over flowcharts. These will be made clear as each of these tools is described.

Flowcharts

Flowcharts visually portray a program's processing flow by showing the operations to be performed, the order in which they are performed, and the conditions that affect this order. Exhibit 13.9 shows the standard flowchart symbols, while Exhibit 13.10 uses these symbols in a flowchart of the baking of a pecan pie.

Many programmers, especially those following the principles of structured programming, have become disenchanted with the use of flowcharts in program design for several reasons:

- Important design information, such as the program's logical structure, may be vague or missing.
- Flowcharts, by themselves, do not motivate good programming practices.
- Carelessly designed flowcharts can be very difficult to follow.
- Without sophisticated software, flowcharts cannot be drawn interactively using a computer. As a result, programmers must usually spend a good deal of extra time and effort to produce good flowcharts.
- To change a flowchart, one must usually completely redraw it.

Still, many people feel that flowcharts are a good way to show a program's main processing flows. As a result, flowcharts often appear in a program's documentation.

Pseudocodes

Pseudocodes reproduce a program design in everyday English and use indentations to represent the processing flow. Pseudocodes, initially introduced as a way to design structured programs, produce a very readable program design. Exhibit 13.11, for example, gives a pseudocode version of the flowchart in Exhibit 13.10.

Since a pseudocode program design requires no symbols other than the English language, programmers can interactively design their programs using word processing software. Not only does this help to shorten the time it takes to produce a program design, it also makes it very easy to make changes in a design.

The indentation standards of pseudocodes reflect the three structured programming processing flows introduced earlier in the chapter. In the descriptions that follow, each processing task could be replaced by a set of tasks.

Exhibit 13.12

A flowchart of the sequential processing flow pattern

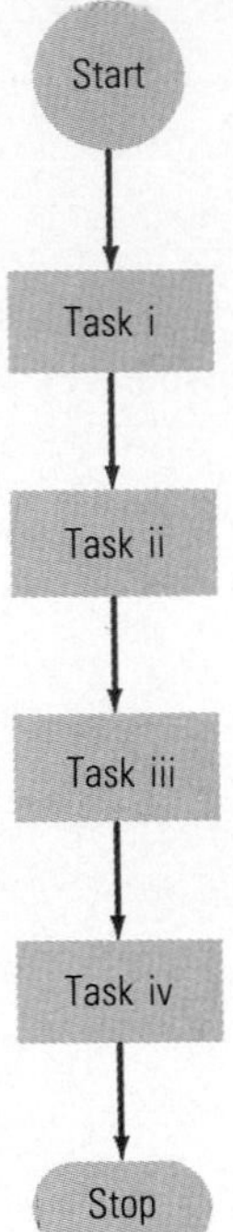

In the *sequential pattern,* processing tasks occur in the order they are listed. This is shown by placing each processing task at the same indentation level:

```
Task i
Task ii
Task iii
Task iv
```

Exhibit 13.12 is a flowchart that visually portrays this pattern.

The pecan pie assembly design shown in Exhibit 13.7 will be used to further illustrate how these processing flow patterns are represented in pseudocode. The "gather ingredients" step, for example, would be detailed as follows:

```
get a pastry shell
get butter
get sugar
get eggs
get salt
get vanilla
get dark corn syrup
get light corn syrup
get pecan halves
```

The *selection pattern* controls the execution of a particular processing task. Two distinct patterns tend to be used:

```
Task i
if (condition)
  then
      Task ii
Task iii
```

and

```
Task i
if (condition)
  then
      Task ii
  else
      Task iii
Task iv
```

The indentation is very important. Only tasks that follow one another at the same indentation level are executed in sequential order.

With the first selection pattern, the program will execute "Task i," then "Task ii" if the condition is met, and finally "Task iii." Exhibit 13.13 shows a flowchart of this pattern. The processing flow either executes or skips over "Task ii," depending on some condition. With the second selection pattern, the program will execute "Task i," then either "Task ii" or "Task iii," depending on some condition, and finally "Task iv." Exhibit 13.14 shows a flowchart of this pattern. The processing flow executes either "Task ii" or "Task iii," but not both.

When a recipe calls for a cup measure, the measuring device used depends on whether an ingredient is liquid or dry. Using the second selection pattern shown above, this would be detailed as follows:

```
if (ingredient is liquid)
  then
        pick up a 1-cup measuring cup
  else
        pick up a 1-cup measuring scoop
```

The *iteration pattern* is used to repeat a processing task. Two distinct patterns, again, are used. The first iteration pattern is termed a **dowhile loop.** The reason for calling this a loop should be obvious from Exhibit 13.15: program execution "loops" around the processing task being repeated. The pseudocode for this pattern is as follows:

```
Task i
while (condition)
      Task ii
Task iii
```

Here the program first executes "Task i," then tests to see if the condition is met. "Task ii' is repeatedly executed as long as this condition is met. As soon as the program detects that the condition is not met, it executes "Task iii." Note that the program tests for the condition before executing "Task ii."

The second iteration pattern is termed a **repeatuntil loop.** The pseudocode for this pattern is:

```
Task i
repeat
            Task ii
      until (condition)
Task  iii
```

Exhibit 13.13

A flowchart of the first selection flow pattern: a decision is made whether to perform Task ii.

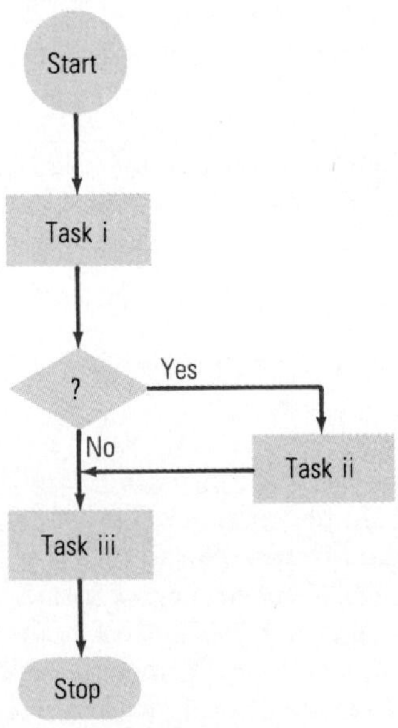

Exhibit 13.14

A flowchart of the second selection flow pattern: a decision is made to perform either Task ii or Task iii.

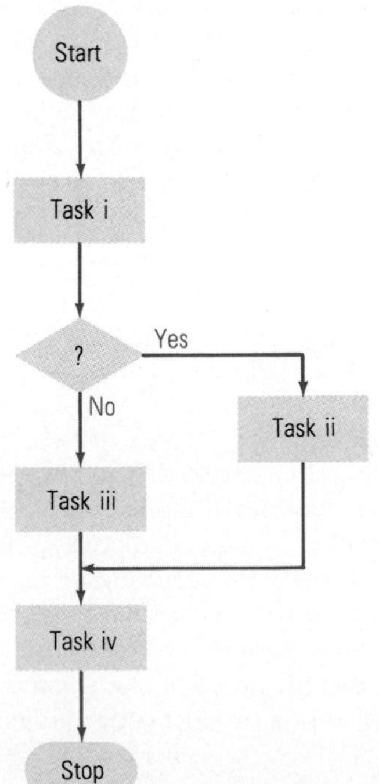

Exhibit 13.15

A flowchart of the "dowhile loop" iteration flow pattern: the condition test is made before Task ii is performed.

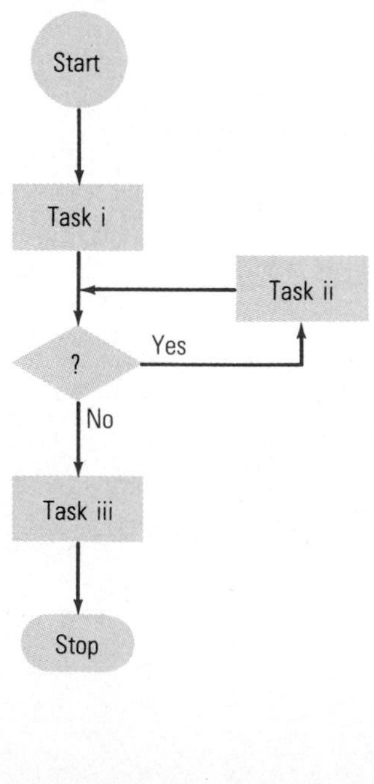

Exhibit 13.16

A flowchart of the "repeatuntil loop" iteration flow pattern: the condition test is made after Task ii is performed.

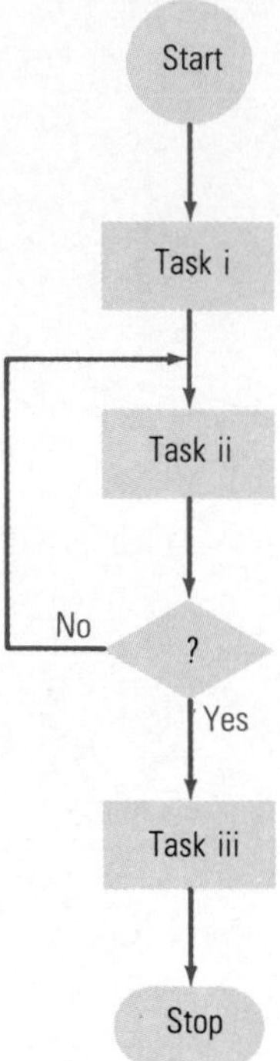

Again the program starts off by executing "Task i" and then "Task ii." After executing "Task ii," the program tests to see if the condition is met. As long as the condition is not met, "Task ii" will be repeatedly executed. As soon as the condition is met, the program executes "Task iii." Exhibit 13.16 depicts this pattern. Note that the condition is tested after "Task ii" is executed.

The major difference between these two iteration flow patterns is that "Task ii" may never be executed with the first pattern, but is always executed at least once with the second pattern. In choosing between the two patterns, use the one more natural for the task being performed.

True lovers of pecans might like to have three cups of pecans in their pecan pie. As a 1-cup scoop would be used to measure pecans, the following directions could be used to direct a baker in gathering the correct amount of pecans:

```
if (ingredient is liquid)
  then
       pick up a 1-cup measuring cup
  else
       pick up a 1-cup measuring scoop
repeat
          measure out 1 cup
          make a mark on a piece of paper
      until (there are three marks)
```

The second iteration pattern was used because it seemed more natural for the task at hand.

BASIC PROGRAMMING CONCEPTS

Most programming languages provide a similar set of basic processing operations. One secret of developing good programming practices is to learn the programming concepts behind these processing operations. Most programming assignments can be approached in a number of ways. However, not all these designs possess a clear, logical structure.

To produce a program design with a clear, logical structure, you need to use the programming concepts most appropriate to the processing tasks being performed. This basic understanding of programming involves some notions about data types, data structures, data operations, and processing flow control.

Data Types

For computer efficiency, different **data types** are physically stored within a computer system in different ways. Data items, for example, can be defined as either numeric or alphanumeric. **Numeric data items** refer to data that can be mathematically manipulated. Examples include the amount of a sale, the number of items entering or leaving an inventory, the number of hours an employee has worked, and the number of employees of a company. **Alphanumeric data items** refer to data that have no mathematical meaning. Examples include an employee's name, a customer's account number, a supplier's address, or a product code. While some alphanumeric data might be made up of numbers, or, more correctly, digits, they are not numeric data. Adding two customer account numbers does not produce a meaningful result.

Numeric data, in turn, can be defined as integer or real. **Integer numbers** cannot take on decimal values, while **real numbers** can be given such values. While it might be desirable to define the number of employees in a firm as an integer number, it might be desirable to define the number of hours each worked as a real number. If a person worked only part of an hour, an employer would not want to pay for an entire hour of work.

Data Structures

Data structures represent alternative ways a set of data items can be organized. One of the real tricks to producing a program design with a clear, logical structure is to use an appropriate data structure.

The simplest data structures are constants and variables. **Constants** are single memory locations whose contents do not change during program execution. **Variables** refer to single memory locations whose contents can change during program execution.

Consider the calculation of an employee's wage allowing "time-and-a-half" pay for overtime. Assuming a 40-hour workweek, one approach for handling this calculation is:

"regular" = "hours worked"
or
40 if "hours worked" is greater than 40
"overtime" = 0
or
("hours worked" − 40) if "hours worked" is greater than 40
"wage" = ("regular" × "rate") + (1.5 × "overtime" × "rate")

As "regular," "hours worked," "overtime," "wage," and "rate" are variables, they can take on different values for different employees. Since "40" and "1.5" are constants, they remain the same across all employees. Exhibit 13.17 gives a pseudocode design for this calculation.

One of the easiest ways to improve a program design is to use variables rather than constants. If a constant's value changes, the program design must be changed every time the constant is referenced. A program design usually does not change when a variable's value changes.

Three common but more complex data structures are records, files, and arrays. Records and files have been described earlier in this text. An **array** is a similar but more general way to link a number of data items. The simplest form of an array is a **one-dimensional array.** It may help you to think of this as a single row or column of data. Examples might include listings of employee names, product codes, or monthly sales totals (see Exhibit 13.18 on page 390). It is often much easier to process data items when they are organized as arrays rather than variables.

A more complex array is a **two-dimensional array,** also called a table. Think of a table as a square or rectangular set of data organized as rows and columns. Each cell of the table is referenced by its row and column indicators. On the following page, Exhibit 13.19 illustrates a data table that CompuStore uses in determining shipping charges. Given a shipment's weight and delivery

Exhibit 13.17

A pseudocode design for calculating an employee's wage: the Englishlike nature of this design makes it easy to check for errors.

```
get hours worked and rate
if hours worked ≤ 40
  then
      let regular = hours worked
      let overtime = 0
  else
      let regular = 40
      let overtime = hours worked − 40
let wage = (regular × rate) +
(1.5 × overtime × rate)
```

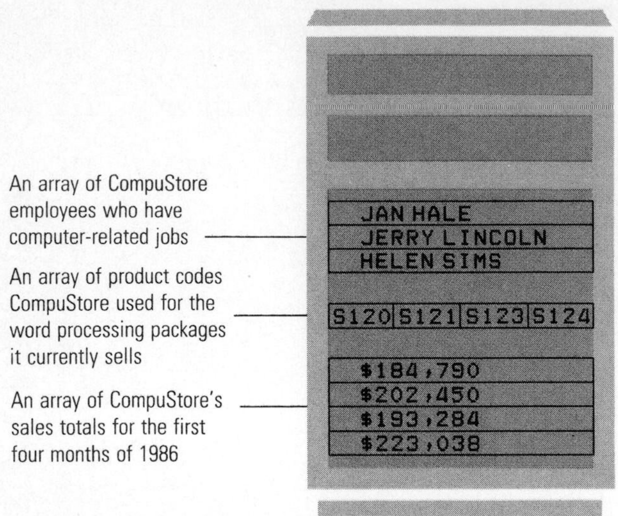

Exhibit 13.18

One-dimensional arrays are frequently used in business programming.

	Miles to Be Shipped			
	0-99	100-499	500-999	1000+
Pounds				
0-5	$0.50	$1.00	$1.75	$2.25
6-20	$2.00	$3.25	$4.00	$4.50
21-49	$3.00	$4.50	$5.75	$6.50
50+	$3.50	$5.00	$6.25	$7.00

Exhibit 13.19

Program designs can often be made simpler by using two-dimensional arrays. By storing shipping charges in such an array, one can easily assign these charges correctly.

distance, it is relatively easy to locate the cell that contains the appropriate shipping charge. This is a good example of how the appropriate use of arrays can simplify program designs.

Data Operations

There are five basic types of data operations: arithmetic, relational, logical, memory manipulation, and input/output. Exhibit 13.20 lists the standard arithmetic, relational, and logical operations. **Arithmetic operations** are used to perform calculations on numeric data. **Relational operations** and **logical operations** are applied to both numeric and alphanumeric data items in determining whether or not a particular condition exists.

Memory manipulation operations work directly on data structures. Most programming languages, for example, allow programmers to set up a data structure, move data items from one structure to another, and modify the items within a structure. **Input/output operations** are used to read data from input devices and secondary storage devices and to write data and information to secondary storage devices and output devices.

Processing Flow Controls

There are two disinct means of controlling processing flows. With **unconditional controls,** the program flow immediately "jumps" from one segment of a program to another. These controls are popularly referred to as **GOTO**s, as in "*go to* the fifth program segment." The haphazard use of GOTOs can make a program design very difficult to understand.

Conditional controls, on the other hand, direct the processing flow on the basis of certain conditions. The program flow "jumps" over or to a program segment only when a condition is met. The selection and iteration structured programming patterns make use of conditional controls.

Operation	Description
Arithmetic	
+	addition
−	subtraction
*	multiplication
/	division
** or ∧	exponentiation
Relational	
>	greater than
>= or ≥	greater than or equal to
<	less than
<= or ≤	less than or equal to
=	equal to
<> or ≠	not equal to
Logical	
AND	two conditions have to be met
OR	at least one of two conditions has to be met
NOT	the condition cannot be met

Exhibit 13.20

All programming languages provide a very similar set of standard arithmetic, relational, and logical processing operations. Programming languages may also provide additional processing operations.

Professional Issue

A Standard Program Design for Business Computing

Another secret of good program design involves recognizing when you can reuse all or part of a design you previously composed. A program design with a clear, logical structure deserves to be used over and over again when appropriate. Not only does this guarantee that the "new" design will be readable, it drastically shortens the amount of time needed to produce the design. Many business information systems follow a very similar processing flow. Exhibit 13.21 outlines this flow.

Initial processing serves two purposes. First, primary memory and secondary storage devices are readied for processing. Data structures are set up and, if needed, assigned starting values. The operating system is notified that data files are to be used as information system inputs and outputs. Second, output headings are produced. Many information system outputs are comprised of two parts: a **heading** and a **body.** For example, in a management report, the heading would include the title and various column headings, while the body would contain the information desired by the manager requesting the report.

Main processing performs what is normally thought of as the program's processing operations. Data items are entered from input or secondary storage devices. Error checking is performed as a check on the accuracy of these data items. Next, data are manipulated as required. Information system outputs in the form of documents and reports are produced. Data files maintained on secondary storage devices are updated. Finally, a check is made to determine if more data remain to be processed. If so, main processing continues. If not, main processing has been completed.

Final processing completes the program. Totals and summaries are calculated and printed. The operating system is informed that data files are no

Exhibit 13.21

Familiarity with this standard program design for business computing may help you in initially composing a design.

Initial Processing

Define data structures
Initialize data structures
Open data files
Print report headings

Main Processing

Enter a set of data
Edit data
Manipulate data
Produce outputs
Update data files
Check for more input data

Final Processing

Calculate totals and summaries
Print totals and summaries
Close files
Stop processing

longer needed. Finally the program terminates, at which time control of the computer systems is returned to the operating system.

One of CompuStore's most frequently used information systems can illustrate this standard processing flow. This relatively simple program checks the current status of customer accounts. This information system is used in two ways. The sales staff uses it to check a customer's credit history when the customer makes a large purchase on credit. The accounting staff uses it when responding to customers inquiring about their account balances. The user enters a customer account number when prompted to do so by the program. This CRT screen image is shown in Exhibit 13.22.

The program then searches through a customer account file for the record of the customer whose account number was entered. This record contains the ending account balance for the previous month, all the customer's purchase and payment transactions for the current month, and the customer's approved credit limit.

When the correct record is found, the current transactions are displayed on the CRT screen along with the previous month's balance, the current balance, and the approved credit limit. This is shown in Exhibit 13.23. After examining this information, the user either enters another customer account number or hits the "Q" key to stop the program.

The first two levels of the pseudocode design for this program are given in Exhibit 13.24. This is not a complete design, as more detail is needed for a number of the processing operations. Note that it does follow the standard processing flow shown in Exhibit 13.21 on page 391.

The initial part of the program design opens the customer account file and displays the input screen image. This prompts the user for a customer account number. The main part of the program design contains most of the processing that will occur in the program. A customer account number is entered and then checked to make sure it is a valid number. Next, the customer account file is searched for the entered account number. Once the correct record is located, the customer's credit limit, previous balance, and current transactions are dis-

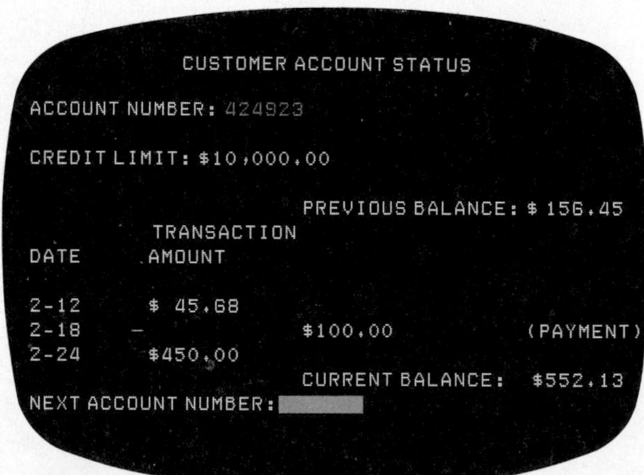

Exhibit 13.22

The initial CRT screen display for CompuStore's Customer Account Status Information System: the user is being prompted for a customer account number.

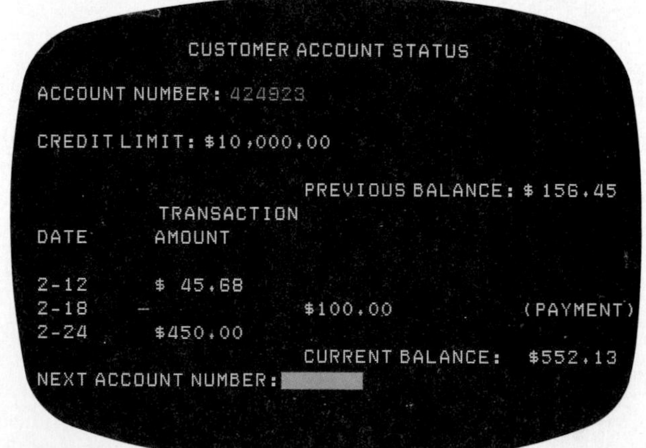

Exhibit 13.23

The full CRT screen display for the Customer Account Status Information System: information is displayed for the customer whose account number is 424923 and the user is being prompted by another customer account number.

Exhibit 13.24

The first two levels of a pseudocode design for the Customer Account Status Information System: the second design level only "refines" the second phase of the program design.

Level 1

```
Phase 1   open customer file
          display input screen image

Phase 2   enter customer account number
          check validity of account number
          locate customer record
          calculate current balance
          display output screen image
          determine if there are more accounts to check

Phase 3   close customer file
```

Level 2

```
Phase 1   open customer file
          display input screen image

Phase 2   while (there are accounts to check)
               enter customer account number
               check validity of account number
               repeat
                         input record from customer file
                    until (match customer number)
               display credit limit
               display previous balance
               print column headings
               repeat
                         get transaction
                         display transaction
                         accumulate total
                    until (no more transactions)
               calculate current balance
               display current balance

Phase 3   close customer file
```

played on the output screen image. The current balance is calculated and also displayed. Finally, the user is prompted for another customer account number by the prompt in the lower lefthand corner of the CRT screen. The final part of the program design begins when the user enters a "Q" in response to the prompt asking for another account number. The customer account file is closed and the program stops.

Note how important the "dowhile" and "repeatuntil" loops are to this program design. The "dowhile" loop controls the main part of the program design by checking to see if there are more customer accounts to check. As long as the user enters a customer account number in response to the prompt, the main processing program segment will be repeated. The "repeatuntil" loops serve as two of the program segments that give the design its clear, logical structure. The first "repeatuntil" loop searches through the customer account file for a particular customer account number. The search continues until a match is achieved. The match indicates that the correct customer record has been found. The second "repeatuntil" loop processes each of the account transactions in the data record. When all the transactions have been processed and displayed, the current balance is ready to be displayed.

The $2 Sure Thing

My friend Ralph and I were two of the very few liberal arts students who dared enter the world of computers back then. It was mostly a matter of curiosity, for everyone knew that writers and business people and other non-technical people would never use a computer. That's why you hired a computer programmer and a computer operator and a systems analyst and a team of consultants. There was something about computer people that was, well, different from you and me.

So there we were, squeezed in among the engineering and math types in "Introduction to Programming" in the temple of computing called "Machinery Hall." I am not going to attempt to demean the personal qualities of the rest of the class. (For one thing, they're all probably making much more money than I am today.) But let me just say that Ralph and I were the only ones present without a plastic pocket pen protector and in possession of glasses that were not held together at the bridge by a piece of electrical tape.

Well, it happened in September, some 15 years or so ago, that a horse—his name was blissfully departed from memory—came out of nowhere in a cheap claiming race somewhere and paid $442.87 on a $2 win ticket. That seemed like an awful lot of money to us, impoverished college students that we were. Knowing absolutely nothing about horses and racing, a few of us stumbled across a copy of *The Racing Form* in the trash outside an English professor's office.

In case you've never seen *The Racing Form,* this daily newspaper is just packed with numbers and ratings and timings. You can find out where a horse has been racing, from what post position it started, where it was at the first quarter, at the halfway point, at the top of the stretch, and at the finish line. You can learn about the weight carried (jockey plus compensating lead packets); about the purses won; about a horse's parentage. It is a daily update to a massive data base.

Our final assignment for Introduction to Programming was to write a Serious Program. The rest of the class worked on exciting things like The Sieve of Eratosthenes, calculating pi to 10,000 places and figuring out the fifteenth Perfect Number. Ralph and I set out to write a horse-racing handicapping program for Vernon Downs.

The program was, in retrospect, a very simple one, although it hardly seemed so at the time. Every horse had a card of its own. We put on it its total winnings, its number of wins, places, and shows, its "Speed Rating" (about which we understood nothing, but the number *sounded* very significant), and a few other factors. We asked the program to divide the number of starts by the number of wins, calculate the average payoff, factor in the Speed Rating somehow, and then print out the value of X. The highest rating would be the IBM 360's prediction of the winner.

The first eight times we tried to run our thick pack of punchcards we got no further than the twelfth card. We tried double-teaming, each debugging a different part of the program, and that pushed us to the fortieth line. And then finally, just five days before our term project was due, the printout we received included a full run of the program, without errors, and with a nice, confident prediction based on that afternoon's racing program: Number 5, on the nose, in the sixth. Well, we could hardly wait until the Sports Final edition of the newspaper made its way to the neighborhood candy store. There, in plain black type, was red-letter news: The winner of the sixth race was Number 5, paying $17.80 for a $2 bet. We were cautiously giddy.

We ran back to Machinery Hall and knocked out another set of punch cards for the next day's fourth race and then fed it into the card reader. Twelve hours later we stood anxiously at the printout bins. A nice, one-page printout awaited us: Number 5 to win, it advised. And yes, Number 5 won. We were now seriously giddy.

It was not yet time to head for our neighborhood bookie. To begin with, it was Thursday already, and our project was due in the professor's office the next day. There was one more test—a big stakes race down at Belmont. We scoured *The Racing Form* and put in every variable we could find. We ran the cards through the reader and retreated to our apartments to stew, visions of fists full of winning tickets dancing in our brains.

Well, we picked up the printout right around post time, and dashed over to the campus radio station and stood around the AP sports ticker. We were a little bit skeptical, because once again the computer had selected Number 5. Well, the probability factor seemed so remote, but somehow as the horses came around the final turn and into the top of the stretch, Number 5 broke from the back of the field and charged past the grandstand to win an upset victory. We were well past giddy now, but we somehow managed to pull together a printout of our program and a short, modest summary of our achievements and deliver it to the professor. Saturday we were going to the track.

At 11 PM that night, the phone rang. It was a solemn Ralph: "I have a little problem," he began. "I dropped the shoe box and the cards got all jumbled." I laughed. "That's no problem. Just use the printout of the program to put them back in order," I said.

"I did that," Ralph said ominously. "Do you want to guess what I found?" There was a long pause and Ralph pushed on unasked: "I found an extra card just before the print statement. It wasn't one of ours. It said, 'X = 5'."

It took just a few moments for the import of Ralph's statement to sink in. After all of our computations, and after each horse had been assigned a rating, this infiltrating card was resetting the final X variable to 5, the same number we had seen as our program's pick for all three races.

Visions of fists full of winning tickets were dancing in our brains.

We met down at Machinery Hall at midnight. Ralph clutched the shoe box to his breast, the offending extra card waving accusingly in his left hand. As chance would have it, the computing center was very quiet that night and we somehow managed to hit a sweet spot in time when our program could be read into the computer and the printout returned to the rack in 20 minutes or so.

We resubmitted the cards for the stakes race at Belmont. The computer picked the Number 8 horse, a filly that barely managed to complete the mile-and-an-eighth. We put in the cards for the sixth at Vernon: Number 3 the program said. Number 3 had balked coming out of the gate and then had struggled gamely to come in eighth. We tried the fourth from Vernon: The computer boldly declared the Number 1 horse a $2 Sure Thing. According to the newspaper, that horse had tied for sixth, and then only because two horses in front of him had been disqualified.

We struggled on wearily through most of the night, never again picking a winner. Things had been so much simpler when our program had reported false results. And that is the story of why I never made my fortune as a racing handicapper . . . or as a computer programmer.

Source: C. Sandler, "The $2 Sure Thing," *PC Magazine*, September 1983, pp. 41-46.

SUMMARY

Program development takes place in the systems acquisition stage of the systems life cycle. The preceding systems analysis and systems design stages should have determined a set of software requirements that describe the program's outputs, inputs, files, and processing functions. These software requirements direct and guide the program development process.

Good communications are just as important to program development as they are to systems development. Many programming techniques and tools have been developed to improve communications among the people involved with a programming project.

The goal in business programming is to develop programs that are correct and maintainable. A *correct program* completely and accurately performs the information processing activities laid out in the systems design. A *maintainable program* can easily be changed at some future time. Writing understandable programs helps achieve both of these objectives.

Programming involves three distinct activities. *Program design* provides a clear, logical structure to a program. A design with a clear, logical structure is made up of a number of *modules* or segments, each of which performs a well-defined task. *Program coding* translates a program design into a program using a programming language. If a good program design exists, coding is an almost mechanical task. Whenever possible, it is best to postpone selecting a programming language until the program design is complete. *Testing,* commonly termed *debugging,* checks the correctness of a program's design and code. Both *syntax errors* and *logical errors* are located and corrected. While program design always occurs first, most programmers move back and forth among these three programming activities.

A program should be documented throughout the programming process. This documentation should be both *external* and *internal* to the program code.

Most of today's business programming projects are performed by *programming teams.* Effective project management is very important. *Chief programming teams* are used. Also, an effort is made to encourage *egoless programming,* in which programmers freely criticize each other's work. Some of the techniques used are the *structured walkthrough* and the *inspection team.*

It is also helpful for a programmer to periodically interact with a program's users to exchange ideas on the program's inputs and outputs.

Structured programming refers to an approach to program design that results in a clear, logical design structure. As with structured design, structured programming makes use of the principles of *abstraction, modularity,* and *stepwise refinement.*

One major goal of structured programming is to design programs that follow a *single-entry, single-exit processing flow.* This is accomplished by restricting most processing flows to one of three patterns: the *sequential, selection,* and *iteration* flow patterns. There are two forms of the iteration flow pattern, a *dowhile loop* and a *repeatuntil loop.*

The two most common program design tools are the flowchart and pseudocode. *Flowcharts* visually portray a program's processing flow by showing the operations to be performed, the order in which they will be performed, and the conditions that affect this order. Many programmers, especially those following the principles of structured programming, have become disenchanted with the use of flowcharts in program design. With *pseudocodes,* programs are designed in everyday English, with processing flow shown by indenting the English phrases in a standard way. Not only is it easy to follow the structured programming principles with pseudocodes, programs can be designed interactively using word processing software.

Most programming languages make a similar set of basic processing operations available to a programmer. One secret of developing good programming practices is to learn the programming concepts behind these processing operations.

Data types represent alternative ways data are physically stored within a computer system. Two common sets of data types include *numeric* and *alphanumeric data* and *integer* and *real data.*

Data structures represent alternative ways a set of data can be organized. The simplest data structures are constants and variables. *Constants* are single memory locations whose contents do not change during program execution. *Variables* are single memory locations whose contents can change. Three other common data structures are records, files, and arrays. An *array* links a number of data items. *One-dimensional arrays* can be thought of as rows or columns of data. *Two-dimensional arrays* can be thought of as tables of data.

There are five basic types of *data operations. Arithmetic operations* perform calculations on numeric data. *Relational* and *logical operations* determine whether or not a particular condition exists. *Memory manipulation operations* work directly on data structures. *Input/output operations* read and write data.

Processing flow controls direct the order in which a program performs its processing operations. With *unconditional controls,* popularly termed *"gotos,"* the program flow immediately "jumps" from one program segment to another. With *conditional controls,* the program flow "jumps" over or to a program segment only when a condition is met.

Many business information systems follow a standard processing flow with three main program segments. *Initial processing* readies the computer system for processing and produces output *headings. Main processing* performs what is normally thought of as the program's processing operations; data are entered and processed, and information systems outputs are produced. *Final processing* completes the processing by calculating and printing summary outputs and releasing any computer system devices that were used.

In the next chapter we will look more closely at the six main programming languages used to develop business programs.

REVIEW QUESTIONS

1. At what point in the systems life cycle are programs written? Why?
2. Identify and briefly discuss the two major goals of business programming.
3. Briefly describe the three activities that comprise the programming process. Do these activities really occur in a step-by-step fashion? Explain.
4. The Alpha Corporation has just completed the coding of a rather complex programming project. Management is considering the immediate utilization of the resulting programs. Would you support such a decision? Explain your position.
5. What problems might arise with the use of programming teams? How can such problems be overcome?
6. Should user participation be sought in the programming activity? If so, how can this be accomplished?
7. Briefly describe the basic principles used in structured programming.
8. How can a clear, logical structure be maintained when using structured programming? Briefly describe the major processing flow patterns employed to maintain logical structure.
9. Briefly discuss the two most common program design tools used today.
10. Jon Smythe is creating a program in which several processing tasks must be repeated. How can this be most efficiently accomplished?
11. What are data structures? Briefly describe the more commonly used data structures.
12. Briefly discuss the five basic types of data operations.

PART V APPLICATIONS SOFTWARE

CHAPTER 14
Programming Languages

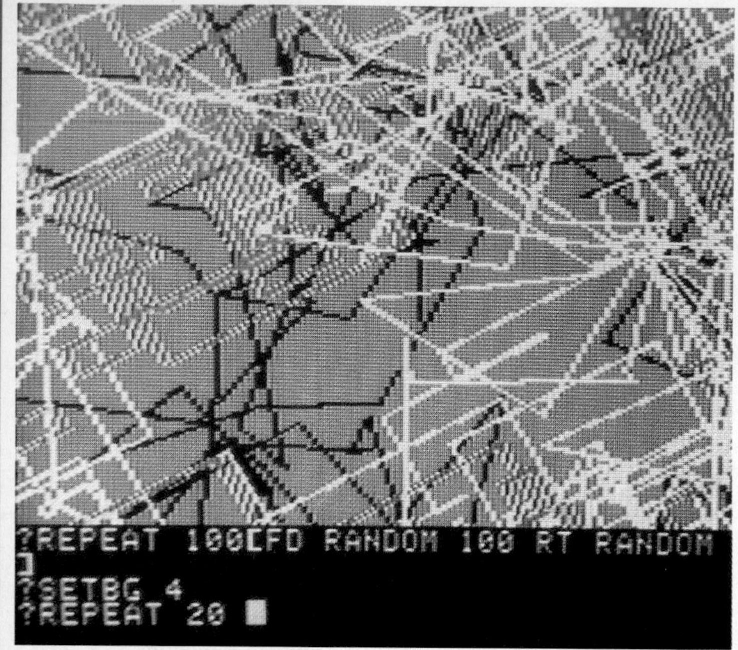
?REPEAT 100[FD RANDOM 100 RT RANDOM
]
?SETBG 4
?REPEAT 20

COMPUTERS AT WORK

Division of Labor Makes Sense

Do you do your own dry cleaning? Do you make your own shoes? Do you attempt to create your own laundry detergent?

A society that is economically successful is predicated on a division of labor; each person produces a different valuable service or product. Computer software and programming are not exempt from this principle called the division of labor.

Developing computer programs is a challenging and enticing activity. Unfortunately, there is a big difference between developing programs and developing good, accurate programs. Developing good programs; those in which you have confidence, is extremely time consuming.

If you can't program a computer, don't worry; you'll never have to. If you are just beginning to learn programming, be sure you have a good reason to invest your time studying about software development. Programming will not save you time or money. If you program, you should enjoy it as a hobby for its own sake or view it as an employment opportunity. If you insist on programming, become a skilled craftsman and take pride in your work. Learn about the language and utility tools available.

From "Digital Dialects" by Charles Kelley. Reprinted by permission of *PC World* from Volume 1, Issue 2, published at 555 De Haro Street, San Francisco, CA 94107.

As this chapter's opening excerpt makes clear, few people today need to write their own computer programs. Software packages are sure to meet most information processing needs. Even so, it is important for you to become familiar with the major programming languages. Regardless of our chosen careers, many of us are likely to be involved with determining the programming languages in which information system applications should be written.

In this chapter, you will learn how to do the following:

1. Describe the differences among the three levels of programming languages.
2. List and explain eight features useful in comparing programming languages.
3. List the six most popular programming languages and discuss their strengths and weaknesses.
4. Describe three programming languages of the future.
5. List six factors important in selecting a programming language.

PROGRAMMING LANGUAGE LEVELS

For a program design to be implemented, it must be coded in a language "understood" by the computer system on which the program is to be executed. Programming languages serve as the means by which a programmer communicates a program design to a computer system.

The fundamental language for every computer is a set of electrical impulses, or sequences of "0s" and "1s." The circuitry of most CPUs allows only a limited set of processing operations, which are directed by program instructions in **machine language,** or "0" and "1" form. A program must be in machine language to direct the CPU in processing a set of data.

The first electronic computers were actually coded in machine language, a very tedious chore. Programmers not only had to be "hardware experts," they had to "think" like a computer as well. Steps were soon taken to develop people-oriented programming languages, so few people code in machine language today.

Three levels of programming languages are in common use: **assembly languages, high-level languages,** and **very-high-level languages.** Assembly languages were developed in the early 1950s, high-level languages in the mid-1950s, and very-high-level languages in the mid-1970s. Each higher-level programming language makes coding a little easier. This evolution in programming languages is shown in Exhibit 14.1 on the following page.

As most programs are not coded in machine language, they are translated into machine language by systems software (see Exhibit 14.2 on page 402). The initial version of a program is called the **source code** and the machine language version is called the **object code.** Listings of the source code and source code errors are usually produced along with the object code. These error listings are very important in debugging a program.

With assembly languages, an **assembler** performs the translation. With high-level languages, the translation is performed by a **compiler** or **interpreter.** A compiler translates the entire program but does not execute the source code. Normally, a very efficient object code is produced. An interpreter translates a program one statement at a time and executes the statement before translating the next statement. Since programmers can follow the execution of their programs in a step-by-step fashion, interpreters can be very helpful when debugging a program. Executing a program through an interpreter, however,

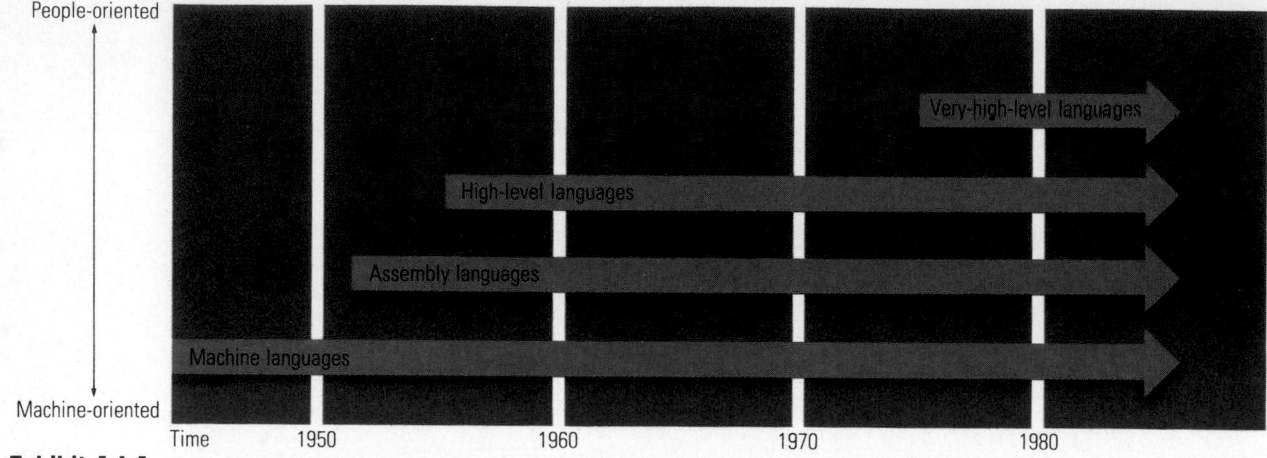

Exhibit 14.1

Levels of programming languages have been developed to ease the programming task. Each higher programming language level is more people-oriented than the lower ones.

Exhibit 14.2

Systems software translates a program's source code into its object code. Programmers create the source code, while the object code is the machine language version of the program used to direct the CPU's operation.

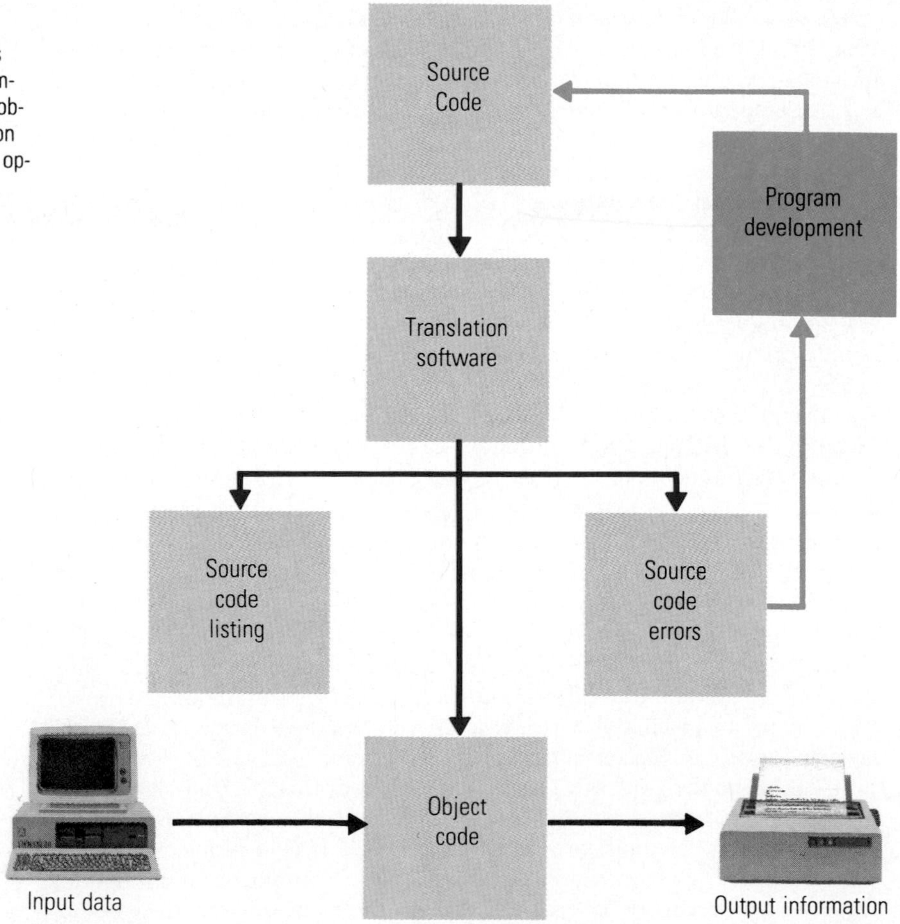

Source Code

Program development

Translation software

Source code listing

Source code errors

Object code

Input data

Output information

is slower than with a compiler. A compiled instruction might take a few microseconds to execute, while the same instruction might require thousands of microseconds to execute through an interpreter. No specific name has been given the translation software associated with very-high-level languages.

With long programs, translating a source code into an object code can take a fairly long time. As a result, a program's source and object codes are both stored in secondary storage. The object code can be retrieved and executed without having to be translated. The source code is available for retrieval in case the program needs to be revised.

Assembly Languages

Assembly languages were developed to relieve the tedium and reduce the errors of machine language programming. They can be a fairly readable form of machine language—primary memory locations, CPU registers, and CPU processing operations are represented by abbreviated names, rather than "0s" and "1s." However, each assembly language statement still translates into a specific machine language instruction.

Some assembly language programs are quite easy to follow. For example, Exhibit 14.3 shows an IBM PC assembly language program that sums up the integers 1 through 10. Most assembly language programs, such as that in Exhibit 14.4, are not so easily understood. This assembly language program, which makes use of special features of the IBM PC's operating system, prints out the word "HELLO" on a CRT screen.

```
Line     Program
number   statements
------   ------------
100      MOV CX,1
101      MOV AX,0
102      ADD AX,CX
103      INC CX
104      CMP CX,0A
105      JBE 102
106      NOP
```

Exhibit 14.3

This IBM PC assembly language program sums the integers 1 through 10. The CPU register "CX" holds a value to be added and the CPU register "AX" holds the accumulated sum. The "0A" in line number 104 is the hexadecimal representation of the decimal "10." Line 100 moves a "1" into "CX." Line 101 moves a "0" into "AX." Line 102 adds "CX" to "AX." Line 103 increases "CX" by "1" (a "1" is added to the current value of "CX"). Line 104 compares "CX" with the value "10." Line 105 directs the program to "jump back" to line 102 as long as "CX" is less than or equal to "10." Line 106 contains a "no operation" instruction that ends the program.

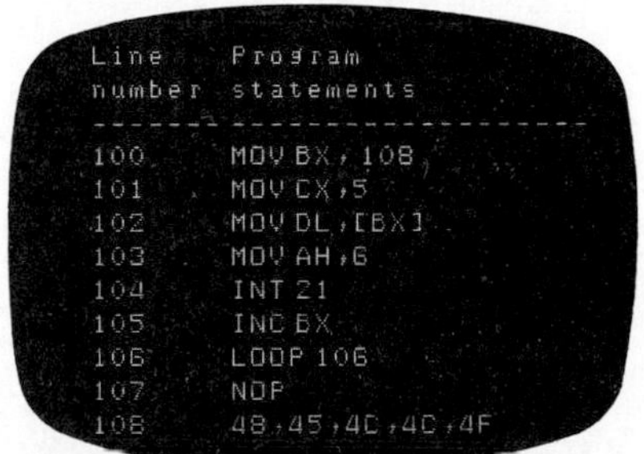

Line number
Program statements
100 MOV BX,108
101 MOV CX,5
102 MOV DL,[BX]
103 MOV AH,6
104 INT 21
105 INC BX
106 LOOP 106
107 NOP
108 48,45,4C,4C,4F

Exhibit 14.4

This IBM PC assembly language program prints "HELLO" on a CRT screen. CPU register "BX" is used to indicate the character to be displayed on the screen. CPU register "CX" works with the "LOOP" operation. CPU register "DL" is reserved to be used with IBM PC's operating system "interrupt 21" operation. CPU register "AH" is reserved for use with special input/output operations. The numbers given in line 108 are ASCII codes for the characters "H," "E," "L," "L," and "O." Line 100 points "BX" at the first character given in line 108. Line 101 moves a "5" into "CX," indicating that five iterations will be made through the "LOOP" operation. Line 102 moves the character being pointed at by "BX" into "DL." Line 103 moves a "6" into "AH," indicating that an operating system "function 6," or CRT display activity, will occur. Line 104 executes the "interrupt 21" operation, which displays the character stored in "DL." Line 105 increases "BX" by "1," thereby pointing to the next character in line 108. Line 106 loops back to line 101. Line 107 contains a "no operation" instruction that ends the program.

Helen Sims, CompuStore's programmer, was attending classes part-time in working toward a bachelor's degree in information systems. One semester she became very excited about an assembly language programming class she was taking. She was especially proud of how fast her programs were.

At the same time, Helen and Jerry Lincoln were working on a project to add an interactive inquiry capability to CompuStore's inventory control system. Helen had an inspiration. Why not code the revisions in assembly language to make the information system more efficient? Jerry quickly put a damper on Helen's idea.

Jerry: While you can code a much more efficient program by using assembly language, you need to consider a number of other factors. First, your attention will be directed toward the computer system as much as toward the inventory control system revisions. Our main objective is to get the new version of this information system up and running. Second, when you code in assembly language, you have to take care of every little detail yourself. Third, assemblers provide very little error protection compared with compilers and interpreters. Just about everything you code, whether it's correct or incorrect, will be executed. Finally, the relatively "free form" nature of assembly-level programming won't encourage you to follow good programming practices. If we code in assembly language, coding will be harder and take longer than if we use a high-level programming language. And it will probably be very difficult to make future changes in our revisions. We'll just be a lot better off using a high-level language.

Helen: Then I don't understand why I'm taking this course!

Jerry: Aren't you learning a lot about how computers work?

Helen: Yes.

Jerry: Anyway, some programs do need the extra bit of capability or efficiency that assembly language can provide. Most systems software programs, for example, have many assembly language modules. You're not wasting your time. If you were, Jan wouldn't have recommended that the company pick up your tuition for the course!

High-Level Languages

A high-level language consists of a set of predefined commands that are combined according to a tightly specified syntax. The processing commands made available to a programmer are most often oriented toward a certain type of information processing. Still, these commands are general enough that they can be used with almost any information processing problem. The **syntax** is a set of rules, similar to rules of grammar, that the programmer follows in coding the commands.

The disadvantages of assembly language programming are overcome in the following way:

1. As the programming language commands are "problem-oriented" rather than "machine-oriented," the programmer can concentrate on solving information processing problems.

2. Most programming language commands translate into multiple machine language instructions. The translation software actually handles many of the hardware and systems software details involved with information processing.

3. While having translation software handle some processing details lessens the programmer's control over the computer system, it reduces the chance that the programmer will use a hardware device or systems software feature incorrectly. The translation software also locates syntax errors.
4. The requirement that programmers follow a strict syntax can result in a program code that is quite easy to understand. Generally this occurs only when the syntax has been designed to encourage good programming practices.

As a result, program coding usually proceeds much faster with high-level languages. We will cover the six high-level programming languages most often used in business computing later in this chapter.

Coding in a high-level language is certainly easier than coding in assembly language. Much training, however, is still required for a person to become proficient in a high-level programming language. Furthermore, it still takes a fairly long time to code a set of commands that completely describes how the required information processing tasks are to be handled.

Very-High-Level Languages

Very-high-level languages also consist of a set of predefined commands that are combined according to a tightly specified syntax. These languages differ from high-level languages in two major ways. First, the translation software performs most of the details involved with handling information processing tasks. Second, the commands are such that the programmer need only specify what tasks are to be performed, rather than how they are to be performed. Stated simply, they provide a comfortable degree of information processing support.

Very-high-level programming languages are very easy to use and require little training. Both users and computer specialists can develop application software with these programming languages. We will look at very-high-level programming languages in more detail in Chapter 15.

To reap the benefits of very-high-level programming languages, the programmer gives up a lot of control over how information processing tasks are handled. A very-high-level language is tailored to a rather narrow set of information processing tasks. As long as the problem being worked on fits with this set of information processing capabilities, coding proceeds quickly and smoothly. When the information processing capabilities are not appropriate to a problem, coding can be difficult, if not impossible.

As you have seen, the three language levels offer quite different capabilities to programmers. Now let's look at these differences in more detail. Later we will see how these language features can help you understand the strengths and weaknesses of different programming languages.

PROGRAMMING LANGUAGE FEATURES

Hundreds of programming languages have been developed across all three language levels. Some were successful and are in common use today, many others have not been so successful. What makes some programming languages more successful than others? More important, what should you be looking for in a programming language?

Every programming language is designed to achieve certain goals. These goals can be thought of as the design features of the language. The more successful languages are those whose design features were found useful by a large number of programmers. While many features have been incorporated into programming languages, eight are particularly helpful in comparing the strengths and weaknesses of different programming languages.

General-Purpose Programming Languages

General-purpose programming languages provide a set of processing capabilities that can be applied to most information processing problems. **Special-purpose programming languages** focus on a particular type of information processing problem. While it is easier to handle any processing task with a programming language designed for the task, that language might not be very helpful in other situations.

It can be difficult to produce high-quality graphic displays with most general-purpose programming languages. Such displays could be produced quite easily with a graphics-oriented programming language. However, it might be very hard to develop even a relatively simple payroll program with a specialized graphics programming language.

Assembly language is the most general purpose of the language levels. A skilled assembly language programmer can handle any type of processing task. The commands available with most high-level languages are flexible enough that these languages can also handle most processing tasks. Very-high-level languages, however, make use of quite specialized commands.

Hardware Control

Programming languages that give a programmer extensive **hardware control** provide commands that operate directly on primary memory, CPU registers, secondary storage devices, input devices, and output devices. With such capabilities, a programmer can improve an information system's performance by using a computer's hardware and systems software features.

The speed with which an information system's users enter data and retrieve information through a CRT can be increased if the programmer can directly manipulate a primary memory region used by a computer's operating system to represent the CRT's display screen. However, a programmer has to know a lot about the computer's hardware to "build" a display screen in this fashion. Also, program development time is likely to take longer than when a programming language's translation software controls how data and information are sent to and from a CRT.

Since programmers work at the "level of the machine" with assembly language, they have extensive control of the computer systems hardware devices and systems software. Some high-level languages provide commands that provide access to some hardware devices and systems software components. Very-high-level languages "hide" all these technical details.

Interactive Programming

With **interactive programming languages,** the programmer directly interacts with a computer during program development. This interaction is achieved by using an interpreter rather than a compiler to translate source code into object code. The immediate feedback that results is useful in locating and correcting both syntax and logic errors.

The main disadvantages of interactive, or interpreted, languages are that they execute more slowly than compiled languages and they can be an inefficient way to handle large volumes of data. How would you like to enter 100 data values through a keyboard, have the interpreter stop the program because of a syntax error, and then be told that you have to enter all 100 data values again? It might be better to store the 100 values in a data file to be used over and over again as the program is rerun. Also, the temptation to hurry a program design so that coding can begin is hard to resist with an interactive programming language.

Control Structure Sophistication

As discussed in Chapter 13, program designs possessing a clear, logical structure result in programs that take less development time, have fewer errors, and are easier to maintain. Programming languages that offer **sophisticated control structures** that follow the structured programming concepts produce a code that is easy to understand. In Computers at Work: "Can You Understand This Program?" such readability is illustrated (see page 408). The Modula–2 programming language will be discussed later in this chapter.

Most of the newer high-level languages provide very sophisticated control structures. As very-high-level languages do not depict logical processing flows, they have little need for sophisticated control structures.

Data Structure Sophistication

Programming becomes much easier when the programmer can work with data types and structures that naturally fit the processing tasks being performed. It could be hard to set up a table of data and then retrieve values from it if the programming language lacked this data structure. Commonly used data types and structures were introduced in Chapter 13. Programming languages with more **sophisticated data structures** enable programmers to work with many data types and structures.

Most of the newer high-level programming languages also provide for sophisticated data structures. The very-high-level programming languages usually provide a small set of data structures that are very useful for the processing tasks being handled.

Nonprocedural Commands

Nonprocedural commands allow programmers to describe what processing is to occur, rather than requiring them to detail *how* processing will occur. Programmers "paint pictures" of display screens, records in data files, and reports. Then translation software provides the detailed processing operations.

It often is easier and quicker to develop business applications with nonprocedural programming languages. This only occurs, however, when a language's commands match the processing to be performed.

The only programming languages with many nonprocedural commands are the very-high-level languages.

Can You Understand This Program?

Modula-2 programs have an Englishlike readability that can be self-documenting. Shown is an excerpt from an actual program that "tells a story" and illustrates Modula-2's clear control flow, conspicuous key words, and conducive identifiers.

For more information on Modula-2, consult the contact designated by the program. ETH Zurich is the University in Switzerland in which Niklaus Wirth created Pascal and Modula-2. The Modula Research Institute is a nonprofit group affiliated with Brigham Young University, Provo, Utah. Volition Systems, Del Mar, Calif., offers Modula-2 compilers and support systems.

Source: A. W. Brown and R. E. Gleaves, "Modula-2: Pascal's Powerful Heir," *Mini-Micro Systems,* pp. 183–86.

```
BEGIN
  IF YourLanguage = Modula2 THEN
    LOOP
      Success;
    END
  ELSIF WantToUseModula2 THEN
    CASE YourProcessor OF
      6502, 68000, 8080, 8086, 9900, Alp2, AppleII:
        Contact: = VolitionSystems;
      PDP11, Lilith:
        IF Location = USA
          THEN Contact: = ModulaResearchInstitute
          ELSE Contact: = ETHZurich
        END
      ELSE
        REPEAT
          Contact: = ETHZurich;
          Contact: = ModulaResearchInstitute;
          Contact: = VolitionSystems;
        UNTIL Satisfied;
    END
  ELSE
    WHILE NOT Investigating (Modula2) DO
      Suffer; Suffer; Suffer
    END
  END
END ControlStructures.
```

Easy-to-Use Language

In programming, an **easy-to-use language** is always preferred to one that is not. Easy-to-use programming languages can be learned quickly, allow programmers to develop simple programs very quickly, and result in very readable programs. As a general rule, the programming languages that are easy to use have an Englishlike syntax and a small number of commands.

The very-high-level languages are specifically designed to be easy to use. Some of the high-level languages are fairly easy to use.

Standardization

Each computer system's object code is unique. Translation software must thus be developed specifically for each computer system. A programming language's syntax rules and commands may or may not be similar across the versions developed for different computer systems. When the different versions are the same, the language is said to be **standardized.**

Programming language standardization may occur officially or unofficially. In the United States, the American National Standards Institute (ANSI) sets official computer standards. Unofficial standards are set when a particular version becomes so popular that most other vendors copy it.

The advantage of standardized programming languages is that the source code is similar across its different versions. As a result, it is fairly easy to execute a program written for one computer system on another computer system—the source code is simply processed by translation software developed for the second computer system. When this occurs, the program is said to be **portable.**

A number of the high-level programming languages have officially been standardized and most of them, to some extent at least, have unofficial standard versions. Very-high-level languages are too new for a standardization effort to have taken place. However, the market success of certain software packages, such as Lotus 1–2–3, are beginning to create some unofficial standards. As an assembly language's commands represent the CPU's processing circuitry, this language level cannot be standardized.

Comparing the Language Levels

Exhibit 14.5 rates the three language levels on these eight language features. This comparison should provide you with some insight into when the various levels should be used.

When high efficiency is critical, the power and flexibility of assembly languages are very attractive. As a result, most systems software is partially written in assembly language.

The portability and maintainability of programs written in high-level languages make this language level attractive for developing the information systems that handle a business's day-to-day activities. Also, some high-level languages provide programmers with a great deal of power and flexibility. This,

Feature	Assembly Language	High-Level Language	Very-High-Level Language
General-purpose programming			
Hardware control			
Interactive programming			
Control structures sophistication			
Data structures sophistication			
Nonprocedural commands			
Easy-to-use language			
Standardization			

Note: ▬ means that the language level usually exhibits the feature.
▬ means that the language level sometimes or partially exhibits the feature.

Exhibit 14.5

The strengths and weaknesses of the three programming language levels become apparent when they are compared across the eight language features.

combined with the fact that high-level languages are fairly easy to use, has resulted in this language level's being increasingly used to develop systems software.

Since very-high-level languages are so easy to use, many business applications are now being developed at this language level. These programming languages, however, can only be applied to a narrow range of problems and are not portable. As a result, very-high-level languages are being used primarily to develop relatively small, management-oriented applications.

Most business information systems have been developed using high-level languages. How exactly does one select among the various high-level languages? The next two sections should enable you to make such decisions. First, the six most popular high-level programming languages are described; then decision criteria commonly used in choosing among these six languages are discussed.

SURVEY OF POPULAR HIGH-LEVEL LANGUAGES

Exhibit 14.6 shows the approximate proportion of business information systems written in each of the seven most popular high-level programming languages. COBOL remains the programming language for most business information systems.

As Computers at Work: "What's in a Name?" points out, you can discover a great deal about programming languages by studying their names and origins (see page 412). This chapter will go beyond that, however, and take a more professional approach. First, the eight language features will be used to indi-

Exhibit 14.6

The six programming languages discussed in this chapter account for most of the business information systems in use today.

Large sites (Staff greater than or equal to 20) **Small sites** (Staff fewer than 20)

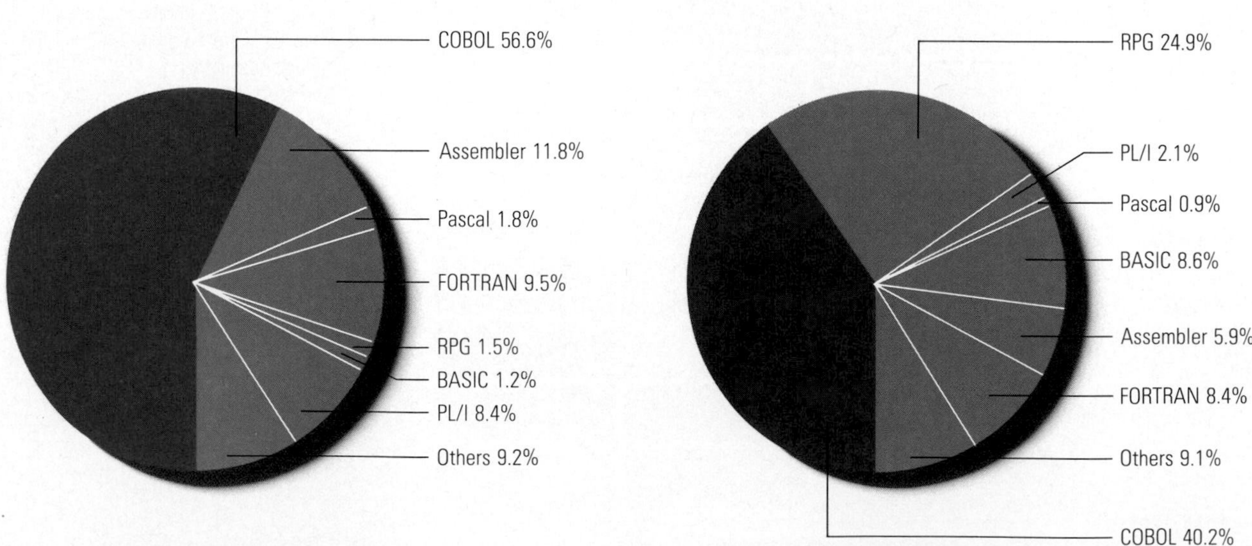

cate the strengths and weaknesses of each language. Second, these strengths and weaknesses will be shown through an illustration of how each language handles a typical business information processing problem. More information on these programming languages and the people associated with their development is given in Appendix A, "History of the Computer."

The business information processing task involves one small part of the inventory control project that Helen Sims and Jerry Lincoln worked on. The task is to produce the CRT display screen shown in Exhibit 14.7 using the item inventory file whose layout is shown in Exhibit 14.8. Two steps are required. First, the user is prompted to enter an item number. Second, all the inventory status information is displayed. Exhibit 14.9 gives a pseudocode design for this program.

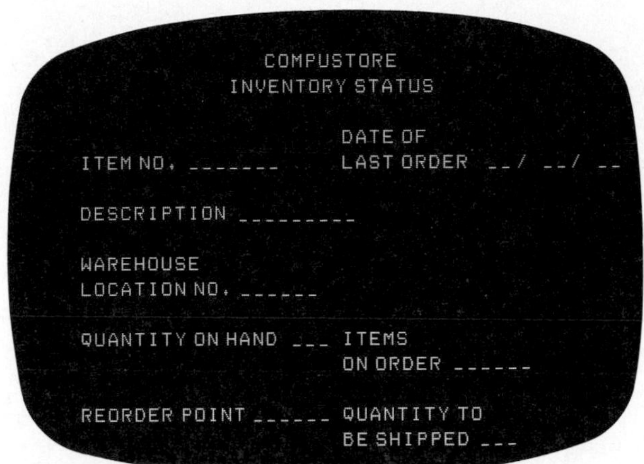

Exhibit 14.7

One of the display screens used in the interactive version of CompuStore's inventory control system

ITEM INVENTORY FILE

Field name	Field size	Field type
item number	6 bytes	numeric
item description	15 bytes	alphanumeric
warehouse location	6 bytes	alphanumeric
date of last order	6 bytes	alphanumeric
quantity on hand	5 bytes	numeric
quantity on order	5 bytes	numeric
reorder point	5 bytes	numeric
quantity to be shipped	5 bytes	numeric

Exhibit 14.8

The inventory information to be displayed on the CRT screen comes from CompuStore's item inventory file. This file layout describes the file.

Exhibit 14.9

A pseudocode design for a program that retrieves information from the item inventory file and displays the information on a CRT screen.

```
open item inventory file

print screen heading

repeat
       prompt user for an input item
       repeat
              read a data record from the file
              until (match desired item)

       display item information on screen
       until (no more input items)

close item inventory file
```

FORTRAN

FORTRAN, which stands for **FOR**mula **TRAN**slation was developed by IBM and came into general use in 1956. Its designers' main goals were to provide an easier way of writing scientific and engineering programs, to simplify the processing of large quantities of numeric data, and to produce efficient object codes.

Strengths. Almost any type of mathematical or business problem can be solved with FORTRAN. While only a few data structures are provided, they include the data structures most commonly used for scientific and engineering problem solving. Because FORTRAN is made up of a few fairly Englishlike commands, it is relatively easy to learn. Since FORTRAN has been standardized, it is possible to develop quite portable programs by limiting oneself to these official standards.

Weaknesses. While FORTRAN can be used for almost any type of information processing task, input and output processing, as well as the handling of alphanumeric data, can be cumbersome, inflexible, and slow. As a result, few business applications are written in FORTRAN. Early versions of the language did not provide very sophisticated control structures. However, FORTRAN 77, the latest standard, does provide some structured programming logical flow patterns. Finally, even though FORTRAN is easy to learn, its syntax rules are very strict. It is easy to make errors when keying in programs or choosing names for a program's variables that cause the program not to execute or, worse, to result in execution errors.

An Example. Exhibit 14.10 lists a FORTRAN program that produces the screen display shown in Exhibit 14.7. While the program is short and the processing flow relatively clear, it can be difficult to see how data are moved from the item inventory file to the CRT screen. The key is knowing that "FORMAT" statements indicate how data are stored, printed, or displayed. Thus, the "READ" statement 950 retrieves one data record from the file using "FORMAT 1080." The other "FORMAT" statements along with the "PRINT" statements display prompts, messages, or headings on the CRT screen.

One reason it is difficult to understand a FORTRAN program is the syntax rules used in naming the program's variables. While "ITEM" is easy to understand, what is "IWHLC" or "IQTSH"? Since you already know what this program is doing, you might correctly guess that these refer to "warehouse location" and "quantity to be shipped." Most FORTRAN programs require extensive internal documentation to be truly readable.

COMPUTERS AT WORK

What's in a Name?

I have a theory that you can tell a great deal about a computer language just from studying its name and its origin.

BASIC, like its name, is a simple, basic language. Pascal, named after the French philosopher, is more philosophical than practical in orientation. LISP is really Lots of Irritating Single Parentheses.

Finally, the Department of Defense (big and ungainly with many jobs and classifications) has given us Ada, a language with no apparent end in sight. Ada, which looks like a defense contract cost overrun for software, is named for Ada Augusta Lovelace, who programmed the first analytical engine (never built because the technology was lacking in Charles Babbage's time). The Department of Defense has created Ada as the ultimate language with something for everyone. The question is, can today's technology support it?

Finally, there is C. The language is just like its name: brief (no computer language name could be shorter), powerful, and elegant.

Source: T. A. Ward, "Power and Elegance," *Microcomputing,* August 1984, pp. 76–80.

COBOL

COBOL, which stands for **CO**mmon **B**usiness-**O**riented **L**anguage, came into general use in 1960 as the result of a Department of Defense initiative to obtain a business-oriented programming language that would produce portable and easily maintained programs. COBOL is an extremely successful programming language—more than half of today's business information systems are written in it.

Exhibit 14.10

A FORTRAN program for displaying information from the item inventory file on a CRT screen: this program is written in FORTRAN 77 on a Digital Equipment Corporation VAX minicomputer.

```
C         FORTRAN PROGRAM
C         SCREEN INQUIRY FOR COMPUSTORE
          INTEGER MO,DA,YR
          CHARACTER ANS*1
          REAL ITEMNO
  900     OPEN(UNIT=9,FILE='INV.DAT',ACCESS='SEQUENTIAL',STATUS='OLD')           {open file}
          PRINT 1000
 1000     FORMAT('1',31X,'COMPUSTORE')
          PRINT 1010                                                             {print screen headings}
 1010     FORMAT(27X,'INVENTORY STATUS INQUIRY')
          PRINT 1020
 1020     FORMAT('$',25X,'ENTER ITEM NO.?')
          READ *,ITEMNO                                                          {prompt for an item}
          PRINT 1000
          PRINT 1040
 1040     FORMAT(33X,'FINISHED GOODS')
          PRINT 1050
 1050     FORMAT(32X,'INVENTORY STATUS')
  950     READ(UNIT=9,FMT=1080,END=960)ITEM,DESC,IWHLC,IDLMO,IDLDA,IDLYR,        {read...until(match on item)}
      $        IONHND,IFGOR,IROPT,IQTSH
 1080     FORMAT(I6,A15,I6,3I2,4I5)
          IF (ITEMNO .EQ. ITEM) THEN
            PRINT 1085
            PRINT 1090,ITEM,IDLMO,IDLDA,IDLYR
            PRINT 1100,DESC                                                      {display item information}
            PRINT 1110
            PRINT 1120,IWHLC
            PRINT 1130,IONHND
            PRINT 1140,IFGOR
            PRINT 1150,IROPT
            PRINT 1160,IQTSH
          ELSE
          ENDIF
          GO TO 950
  960     PRINT 1170
          READ *,ANS
          IF (ANS .EQ. 'Y') THEN                                                 {repeat...until(no more items)}
             CLOSE (UNIT=9)                                                      {close file}
             GO TO 900
          ELSE
          ENDIF
 1085     FORMAT(47X,'DATE OF')
 1090     FORMAT(4X,'ITEM NO.',2X,I6,27X,'LAST ORDER',2X,I2,'/',I2,'/',I2)
 1100     FORMAT(/4X,'DESCRIPTION',2X,15A)
 1110     FORMAT(/4X,'WAREHOUSE')
 1120     FORMAT(4X,'LOCATION NO.',2X,I6)
 1130     FPR,AT(/4X,'QUANTITY ON-HAND',2X,I5,20X,'FINISHED GOODS')
 1140     FORMAT(47X,'ON ORDER',2X,I5)
 1150     FORMAT(/4X,'RE-ORDER POINT',2X,I5,22X,'QUANTITY TO BE')
 1160     FORMAT(47X,'SHIPPED',2X,I5)
 1170     FORMAT('$','DO YOU WISH TO SELECT ANOTHER ITEM (Y OR N)?')
          END
```

Strengths. COBOL is very good at what it does—processing large data files and performing repetitive data processing tasks such as payroll and customer billing. This is largely due to the way COBOL handles business-oriented data structures such as records, files, and tables. Also, COBOL's wordy, Englishlike syntax can produce codes that are fairly easy for managers, as well as computer professionals, to understand. Finally, perhaps more than any other higher-level programming language, COBOL's different versions generally do conform to the official standards for the language.

Weaknesses. While COBOL is very good at many business computing tasks, other types of processing tasks can be quite awkward. Complex mathematical operations, for example, are very difficult to perform in COBOL. COBOL's wordy syntax can also lead to problems. While it is easy to develop a simple COBOL program, it can take a long time to write complex programs. And if programmers are not careful, the syntax can become confusing to anyone but an experienced COBOL programmer.

An Example. Exhibit 14.11 lists a COBOL program that handles the item inventory file task. At first glance, a COBOL program can appear very imposing. With a little explanation, however, the program's parts should begin to make sense.

All COBOL programs have four major divisions. An "identification" division (lines 1–2) is used to identify the purpose and author of the program. An "environment" division (lines 3–9) describes any needed hardware devices. The "data" division (lines 10–92) lays out all the data structures that will be used. Here the data file (lines 12–25) and various screen displays (lines 31–92) are described in great detail. Finally, a "procedure" division (lines 93–117) provides the program's processing flow. Note how well the procedure division matches with the pseudocode design in Exhibit 14.9. The readability of the procedure division along with the great detail of the data division are the major reasons COBOL programs can be relatively easy to maintain.

Exhibit 14.11

A COBOL program for displaying information from the item inventory file on a CRT screen: this program is written in IBM COBOL on an IBM PC.

```
 1        IDENTIFICATION DIVISION.
 2        PROGRAM-ID.
 3        ENVIRONMENT DIVISION.
 4        INPUT-OUTPUT SECTION.
 5        FILE-CONTROL.
 6             SELECT MASTER-FILE ASSIGN TO DISK
 7             ACCESS MODE IS RANDOM
 8             ORGANIZATION IS INDEXED
 9             RECORD KEY IS ITEM-NO.
10        DATA DIVISION.
11        FILE SECTION.
12        FD MASTER-FILE
13            LABEL RECORDS ARE STANDARD
14            VALUE OF FILE-ID IS "INPUT.DAT".
15        01 MASTER-REC.
16            02 ITEM-NO                      PIC 9(6).
17            02 DESCRIPTION                  PIC X(15).
18            02 WHSE-NO                      PIC 9(6).
19            02 ON-HAND                      PIC 9(6).
20            02 RE-ORDERPT                   PIC 9(6).
21            02 ITEM                         PIC 9(6).
22            02 QT-SHIP                      PIC 9(5).
23            02 MONTH                        PIC 99.
24            02 DAY                          PIC 99.
25            02 YEAR                         PIC 99.
26        WORKING-STORAGE SECTION.
27        01 WORK-AREAS.
28            02 ITEM-NO2                     PIC 9(6).
29            02 ANS                          PIC X.
30        LINKAGE SECTION.
31        SCREEN SECTION.
32        01 INQUIRY-SCREEN.
33            02 BLANK SCREEN.
34            02 REVERSE-VIDEO
35               LINE 1 COLUMN 35
36               VALUE "COMPUSTORE".
37            02 REVERSE-VIDEO
38               LINE 3 COLUMN 36
39               VALUE "STATUS INQUIRY".
40            02 LINE 7 COLUMN 5 VALUE "Item No".
41            02 LINE 7 COLUMN 14             PIC 9(6)
42                                            USING ITEM-NO.
43            02 LINE 9 COLUMN 19             PIC X(15)
44                                            USING DESCRIPTION.
45            02 LINE 9 COLUMN 5              VALUE "Description".
46            02 LINE 11 COLUMN 5             VALUE "Warehouse".
47            02 LINE 12 COLUMN 19            PIC 9(6)
48                                            USING WHSE-NO.
49            02 LINE 12 COLUMN 5             VALUE "Location No".
50            02 LINE 14 COLUMN 23            PIC 9(6)
51                                            USING ON-HAND.
52            02 LINE 14 COLUMN 5             VALUE "Quantity On-Hand".
53            02 LINE 16 COLUMN 20            PIC 9(6)
54                                            USING RE-ORDERPT.
55            02 LINE 16 COLUMN 5             VALUE "Re-order Point".
56            02 LINE 7 COLUMN 50             VALUE "Date of".
```

BASIC

BASIC, which stands for **B**eginner's **A**ll-purpose **S**ymbolic **I**nstruction **C**ode, was developed by John Kemeny and Thomas Kurtz of Dartmouth College and made available for general use in 1964. The design goals emphasized by Kemeny and Kurtz reflected their desire to develop an interactive programming language that would be easy for students to learn and to use.

Strengths. BASIC is a "Jack-of-all-trades" language, able to handle just about any processing task but excelling at few. Its strength lies in the ease with which it can be learned and used. It has only a few commands, the purposes of which are self-evident, and it handles many programming details for the programmer. As intended by Kemeny and Kurtz, BASIC is a very popular language for teaching people how to program. Also, the relatively small size of BASIC compilers and interpreters has resulted in BASIC's becoming the universal microcomputer programming language.

```
           02 LINE 8 COLUMN 50           VALUE "Last Order".
           02 LINE 8 COLUMN 65           PIC 99
                                         USING MONTH.
           02 LINE 8 COLUMN 67           VALUE "/".
           02 LINE 8 COLUMN 68           PIC 99
                                         USING DAY.
           02 LINE 8 COLUMN 70           VALUE "/".
           02 LINE 8 COLUMN 71           PIC 99
                                         USING YEAR.
           02 LINE 10 COLUMN 50          VALUE "Items".
           02 LINE 11 COLUMN 50          VALUE "On Order".
           02 LINE 11 COLUMN 65          PIC 9(6)
                                         USING ITEM.
           02 LINE 15 COLUMN 50          VALUE "Quantity to be".
           02 LINE 16 COLUMN 50          VALUE "Shipped".
           02 LINE 16 COLUMN 65          PIC 9(5)
                                         USING QT-SHIP.
       01 ASK-SCREEN.
           02 LINE 24 COLUMN 30
                                 VALUE "More Item Inquires <Y/N>".
           02 LINE 24 COLUMN 56          PIC X TO ANS.
       01 ERROR-SCREEN.
           02 BLANK SCREEN.
           02 LINE 12 COLUMN 32
                                VALUE "Cannot locate by item no ".
           02 LINE 12 COLUMN 58          PIC 9(6)
                                         USING ITEM-NO.
       01 ERROR1-SCREEN.
           02 LINE 13 COLUMN 28
               VALUE "Would you like to try again or quit <T/Q>".
           02 LINE 13 COLUMN 70          PIC X TO ANS.
       01 ITEM-SCREEN.
           02 BLANK SCREEN.
           02 LINE 12 COLUMN 30
               VALUE "Input ITEM-NO <999999> TO EXIT>".
           02 LINE 12 COLUMN 61          PIC 9(6) TO ITEM-NO.
       PROCEDURE DIVISION.
       CALC-RTN.
           OPEN INPUT MASTER-FILE.                                       {open file}
           DISPLAY ITEM-SCREEN.
           ACCEPT ITEM-SCREEN.
           IF ITEM-NO=999999 CLOSE MASTER-FILE
             STOP RUN.
           READ MASTER-FILE INVALID KEY CLOSE MASTER-FILE                {read...until(match on item)}
               PERFORM ERROR-RTN.
           DISPLAY INQUIRY-SCREEN.                                       {print item information}
               DISPLAY ASK-SCREEN
               ACCEPT ASK-SCREEN                                         {enter item}
           IF ANS IS EQUAL TO "Y" CLOSE MASTER-FILE                      {repeat...until(no more items)}
               GO TO CALC-RTN.
           CLOSE MASTER-FILE.                                            {close file}
           STOP RUN.
       ERROR-RTN.
           DISPLAY ERROR-SCREEN.
           DISPLAY ERROR1-SCREEN.
           ACCEPT ERROR1-SCREEN.
           IF ANS="T" PERFORM CALC-RTN.
           DISPLAY ASK-SCREEN.
           ACCEPT ASK-SCREEN.
           IF ANS="Y" PERFORM CALC-RTN.
           STOP RUN.
```

Weaknesses. BASIC's greatest weakness is its limited control and data structures. This, combined with a limited set of syntax rules for naming variables, can result in a program code that is extremely hard to understand. It is easy not to practice good programming practices in BASIC! Another of BASIC's weaknesses is that the official ANSI standard for BASIC is so limited that almost every version of the language extends the standard. As a result, BASIC programs are not that portable, despite the many computer systems that have BASIC compilers and interpreters. These weaknesses are being overcome in many newer versions of the language. At the end of the chapter, Computers at Work: "In Quest of True BASIC" describes the current efforts of Kemeny and Kurtz to improve the BASIC programming language.

An Example. Exhibit 14.12 gives a BASIC program for the item inventory file task. BASIC's strengths and weaknesses are clearly seen with this example. The program makes use of very few commands and is quite short. However, it is initially difficult to follow even this simple program's logical flow.

The key to understanding the program lies in knowing that the "LOCATE" command displays messages and information on a CRT screen. Lines 60–90 initialize the CRT screen and prompt the user for an item. Line 150 retrieves a record from the item inventory file. Line 160 tests the retrieved record to

Exhibit 14.12

A BASIC program for displaying information from the item inventory file on a CRT screen: this program is written in IBM Microsoft BASIC on an IBM PC.

```
30     REM BASIC PROGRAM
40     REM COMPUSTORE INQUIRY PROGRAM
50     REM
60     CLS:SCREEN 2:KEY OFF
70     LINE (1,1)-(620,200),,B
80     LOCATE 4,29:PRINT "COMPUSTORE"
90     LOCATE 5,23:PRINT "ITEM STATUS INQUIRY"                                  {print screen headings}
100    LOCATE 6,23:PRINT  "-------------------"
110    LOCATE 10,13:INPUT "ENTER ITEM NUMBER                    ";XXXX          {prompt for an item}
140    OPEN "INV.DAT" FOR INPUT AS #1                                           {open file}
150    INPUT #1,ITEM,DESC$,WLNO,DORD,ONHD,FGOR,REPT,QSH                         {read...until(match on item)}
160    IF XXXX=ITEM THEN 190
170    IF EOF(1) THEN 470
180    GOTO 150
190    CLS:SCREEN 2:KEY OFF
200    LINE (1,1)-(620,200),,B
210    LOCATE 2,33:PRINT "COMPUSTORE"
230    LOCATE 4,31:PRINT "INVENTORY STATUS"
240    LOCATE 5,31:PRINT "----------------"
270    LOCATE 7,7:PRINT USING "ITEM NUMBER:     ######";ITEM
280    LOCATE 10,7:PRINT USING "DESCRIPTION:     \                 \";DESC$
290    LOCATE 13,7:PRINT "WAREHOUSE"
300    LOCATE 14,7:PRINT USING "LOCATION NO:     ######";WLNO
310    LOCATE 17,7:PRINT "QUANTITY"
320    LOCATE 18,7:PRINT USING "ON-HAND:           #####";ONHD                  {display item information}
330    LOCATE 21,7:PRINT "RE-ORDER"
340    LOCATE 22,7:PRINT USING "POINT:             #####";REPT
350    LOCATE 17,50:PRINT "ITEMS"
360    LOCATE 18,50:PRINT USING "ON ORDER:          #####";FGOR
370    LOCATE 21,50:PRINT "QUANTITY TO"
380    LOCATE 22,50:PRINT USING "BE SHIPPED:        #####";QSH
390    LOCATE 10,50:PRINT "DATE OF"
400    LOCATE 11,50:PRINT USING "LAST ORDER:      ######";DORD
410    LOCATE 24,13:INPUT "WOULD YOU LIKE TO INQUIRE ABOAUT A DIFFERENT ITEM";ANS$
420    IF ANS$="N" OR ANS$="NO" THEN 520
430    IF ANS$="Y" OR ANS$="YES" THEN 440 ELSE 410                              {repeat ... until (no more items)}
440    CLOSE #1                                                                 {close file}
450    GOTO 60
460    END
470    LOCATE 23,25:PRINT "ITEM NUMBER NOT FOUND"
480    LOCATE 24,14:INPUT "DO YOU WISH TO SELECT ANOTHER ITEM(Y OR N)";ANS$
490    IF ANS$="N" OR ANS$="N" THEN 520
500    IF ANS$="Y" OR ANS$="YES" THEN 510 ELSE 480
510    CLOSE #1:GOTO 60
520    CLS:LINE (1,1)-(620,200),,B
530    END
```

determine if it contains the desired inventory item. Lines 210–400 display the retrieved information on the CRT screen.

PL/I

PL/I, which stands for **P**rogramming **L**anguage **I,** was developed by IBM and made available for use in 1964. IBM's goals in designing PL/I were almost the opposite of those that guided the design of the BASIC programming language. IBM desired a programming language that would provide extensive yet flexible support for all types of information processing tasks. For the most part, PL/I meets these rather ambitious goals.

Strengths. PL/I is perhaps the best example of a general-purpose programming language. It almost achieves the claim of being "all things for all people." Its huge set of commands cover a wide variety of processing tasks—complex mathematics, text processing, large volumes of input and output activity, and so on. In addition, it provides for most structured programming control structures and offers programmers a variety of data structures useful in both scientific and business computing.

Weaknesses. Despite PL/I's strengths, it has never achieved the success IBM sought. Its many capabilities are partly to blame. Because it is one of the largest, most complex programming languages ever developed, a skilled programmer is required to learn and make use of all PL/I's capabilities. A more important problem, however, lies with the huge number of FORTRAN and COBOL programs that exist and the large number of programmers skilled in FORTRAN and COBOL programming. As Computers at Work: "Gimme That Old-Time Language" describes, in "tongue-in-cheek" style, many firms and programmers simply could not be convinced that it was worth their effort to switch to a new programming language (see page 419).

An Example. On page 418, Exhibit 14.13 lists a PL/I program to handle the inventory file task. As with COBOL, the programmer must carefully define the data structures used. Lines 13–22 lay out the item inventory file. Separating data definitions from a program's logical flow makes it easier to both understand and maintain a program. The structured nature of the logical flow (the key elements of which are given in lines 37–68) makes it fairly easy to follow the processing operations that will take place. With PL/I, the "PUT" statement displays information on the CRT screen. One of the more undecipherable statements in this program is "PUT LIST ('^C')." This simply blanks the CRT screen.

RPG

RPG, which stands for **R**eport **P**rogram **G**enerator, was developed by IBM and made available for general use in 1964. IBM's aim in developing the language was to ease the effort required of small businesses in switching their data processing from punched card equipment to electronic computers. As a result, the goals of RPG's designers were to produce a language that duplicated punched card data processing procedures and that could be learned easily by people without any prior programming experience.

Exhibit 14.13

A PL/I program for displaying information from the item inventory file on a CRT screen: this program is written in Digital Research PL/I–80.

```
INQUIRE:
   PROCEDURE OPTIONS(MAIN);
/*
     RETRIEVE INVENTORY RECORDS FOR DISPLAY
                                                              */
%REPLACE
   TRUE BY '1'B,
   FALSE BY '0'B;
DCL
    1 INVEN_RECORD STATIC,
       2 ITEM_NO        FIXED BINARY(7),
       2 ITEM_DESC      CHARACTER(15) VARYING,
       2 LAST_ORDER     CHARACTER(8) VARYING,
       2 WHSE_LOC       FIXED DECIMAL(7),
       2 QTY_ON_HAND    FIXED DECIMAL(5),
       2 QTY_ON_ORDER   FIXED DECIMAL(5),
       2 ORDER_POINT    FIXED DECIMAL(5),
       2 QTY_TO_SHIP    FIXED DECIMAL(5);
DCL
   INPUT FILE;
DCL
   FILENAME CHARACTER(14) VARYING;
DCL
   END_OF_SECCESION BIT(1) STATIC INITIAL(FALSE);
PUT LIST('^C');
PUT LIST ('INVENTORY INQUIRY--FILE NAME:');
GET LIST (FILENAME);
PUT LIST ('^C');
OPEN FILE(INPUT) RECORD INPUT DIRECT KEYED ENV(F128)) TITLE(FILENAME);           {open file}
   DO WHILE (^END_OF_SESSION);
      PUT SKIP(3) LIST('ITEM: ');
      GET LIST(ITEM_NO);                                                         {enter item}
      END_OF_SESSION = (ITEM_NO = 0);
IF ^END_OF_SESSION THEN
DO;                                                                              {repeat...until(no more items)
  /* RETRIEVE THE NEXT RECORD */
  READ FILE(INPUT) INTO(INVEN_RECORD) KEY(ITEM_NO);                              {read...until(match on item)}
  /* CLEAR SCREEN AND DISPLAY THIS ONE */
  PUT LIST('^C');
  PUT SKIP(2) EDIT('COMPUTSTORE')                   (COLUMN(32),A);
  PUT SKIP(1) EDIT('Inventory Status')              (COLUMN(32),A);              {print headings}
  PUT SKIP(3) EDIT('Item Number:',ITEM_NO)          (COLUMN(3),A,COLUMN(20),F(7));
  PUT         EDIT('DATE OF')                       (COLUMN(45),A);
  PUT SKIP(1) EDIT('Last Order:',LAST_ORDER)        (COLUMN(45),A,COLUMN(60),A); {print item information}
  PUT SKIP(1) EDIT('Description:',ITEM_DESC)        (COLUMN(3),A,COLUMN(20),A);
  PUT SKIP(2) EDIT('Warehouse')                     (COLUMN(3),A);
  PUT SKIP(1) EDIT('Location No:',WHSE_LOC)         (COLUMN(3),A,COLUMN(20),A);
  PUT SKIP(2) EDIT('Quantity on Hand:',QTY_ON_HAND) (COLUMN(3),A,COLUMN(20),F(5));
  PUT SKIP(1) EDIT('On Order: ',QTY_ON_ORDER)       (COLUMN(46),A,COLUMN(60),F(5));
  PUT SKIP(2) EDIT('Re-Order Point:',ORDER_POINT)   (COLUMN(3),A,COLUMN(20),F(5));
  PUT         EDIT("Quantity to be')                (COLUMN(45),A);
  PUT SKIP(1) EDIT('Shipped:',QTY_TO_SHIP)          (COLUMN(45),A,COLUMN(60),F(5));
END;
END;
END INQUIRE;
```

Strengths. RPG's greatest strength lies in the ease with which it can be learned by people who know very little about computers or programming. "Programs" are coded by filling out forms to specify the layout of data files, input records, reports, and CRT screen displays as well as processing operations. As a result, RPG provides good data structures for standard business computing applications, such as payroll and customer billing.

Weaknesses. The "form filling" nature of RPG coding does have its disadvantages. While some current versions of the language go beyond the language's original purposes, many versions are quite inflexible. To a large

Gimme That Old-Time Language

You've heard, of course, of FORTRAN and COBOL. If there was a popularity contest for programming languages where votes were tallied based on the accumulated height of listings of programs written in each language, FORTRAN and COBOL would win stratospherically. In fact, I'd hate to get hit on the head if the COBOL stack ever toppled over.

Now, one of the reasons that FORTRAN and COBOL have remained popular for over thirty years is that they do the job. If you have a program to write in the scientific or commercial domain, there is no question but that FORTRAN or COBOL have the facilities to make it possible.

As better languages have developed in the programming world, programmers have tended to develop an emotional attachment to some of them. Whether they *should* have is a question for another story at another time. The fact of the matter is FORTRAN and COBOL have survived the best of the technical attempts to dislodge them.

"He beat off each new wave with the conviction that God, Uncle Sam, and FORTRAN were all on his side."

In addition to general capability, there is another reason why FORTRAN and COBOL remain popular. The reason is Inertia (note the capital "I"). Inertia is that old-time religious force which says, "If it was good enough for Mother, it's good enough for me." That inertia can come at either the technical level, the management level, or both. This is a story about the latter.

Kip D. Brakon is an old-time manager from the old-time religious school. Not only do all his programmers uses FORTRAN, they use FORTRAN IV. Kip is not at all sure about this new-fangled FORTRAN 77 stuff. In fact, he's not even sure it was worth switching away from FORTRAN II. After all, he wrote a lot of trajectory programs for lunar probes in FORTRAN II, he is proud of telling people, and it never failed him. The general feeling among the younger set in Kip's group is that if he still had the chance, he'd probably still drive a Model A to work.

As the years rolled by, Kip took a lot of heat from college new hires about better languages. He beat off each new wave with the conviction that God, Uncle Sam, and FORTRAN were all on his side. But still, the opposition gradually got tougher. Finally, with the advent of the Pascal wave, Kip blew his cool. The pressure simply got to him. He decided to strike back. With Kip, that meant issuing a "put up or shut up" challenge.

The challenge took the form of a memo to all of Kip's subordinates, managers, and managee. It went something like this:

"As you know, Pascal is becoming increasingly popular among new programmers. This is not surprising; many higher-order programming languages have captured the fancy of the technical *avant garde,* and many more will in the future. Perhaps Pascal will eventually supplant FORTRAN. But if past prognoses are any guide, the likelihood of correctly predicting FORTRAN's successor is remote. Therefore, I am issuing the following guidance.

"For computer programs targeted for multiuser production usage, only COBOL or FORTRAN should be used unless there is a specific cost-performance reason, approved by management, to do otherwise. An acceptable exemption from the above is that *any* language may be used if a 35 percent reduction in the program's development and maintenance costs can be expected, *and* if the program's execution costs are no higher as a result, *and* if the sponsoring organization commits to relinquishing computing budget equivalent to 35 percent."

"So . . . how are FORTRAN and COBOL doing where *you* work?"

"There," said Kip to no one in particular as he finished the memo, "that should cool them off." Because, as Kip well knew, no one had any data of high enough quality in his shop to prove *any* kind of percentage improvement over anything, let alone 35 percent. And even if they did, they still wouldn't risk the budget contraction. Under the guise of fairness, Kip knew, his memo was actually a door slam.

So . . . how are FORTRAN and COBOL doing where *you* work? If they're still in force, I'll bet there's someone like Kip D. Brakon fighting progress behind the scenes at your place, too!

Source: R. Glass, "Gimme That Old-Time Language," *Software News,* September 1983, p. 7.

Exhibit 14.14

Some of the forms used in an RPG program for displaying information from the item inventory file on a CRT screen: this program is written in RPG II for an IBM System 36 minicomputer.

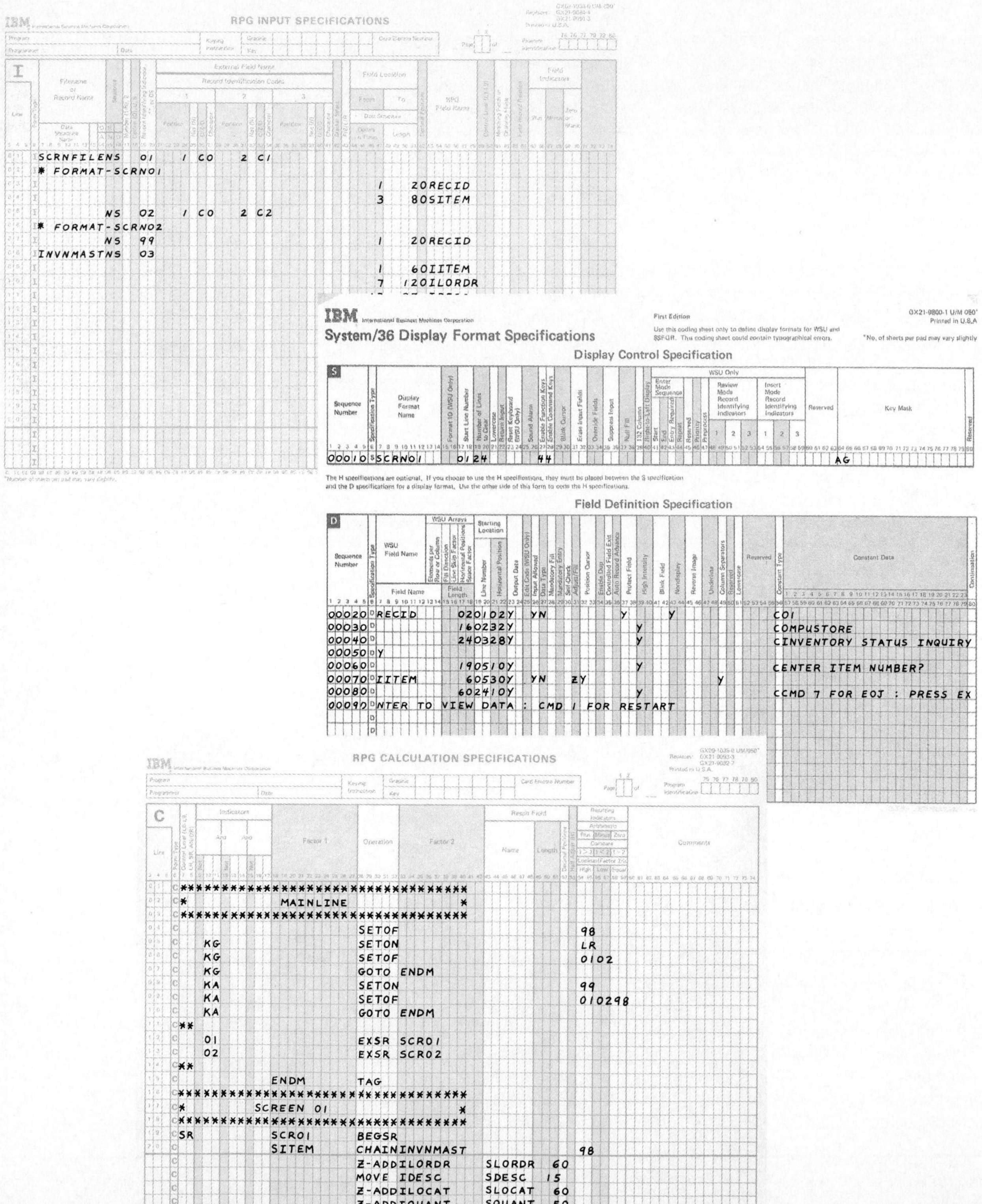

IBM RPG INPUT SPECIFICATIONS

```
ISCRNFILENS  01    1 CO   2 C1
I* FORMAT-SCRN01
I                                        1   20RECID
I                                        3   80SITEM
I          NS  02    1 CO   2 C2
I* FORMAT-SCRN02
I          NS  99                        1   20RECID
IINVNMASTNS  03
I                                        1   60IITEM
I                                        7  120ILORDR
```

IBM International Business Machines Corporation
System/36 Display Format Specifications

Display Control Specification

```
00010 S SCRN01      0124        44                                  AG
```

The H specifications are optional. If you choose to use the H specifications, they must be placed between the S specification and the D specifications for a display format. Use the other side of this form to code the H specifications.

Field Definition Specification

```
00020 D RECID      020102Y  YN         Y   Y      C01
00030 D            160232Y             Y          COMPUSTORE
00040 D            240328Y             Y          CINVENTORY STATUS INQUIRY
00050 D Y
00060 D            190510Y             Y          CENTER ITEM NUMBER?
00070 D IITEM       60530Y  YN    ZY        Y
00080 D             602410Y            Y          CCMD 7 FOR EOJ : PRESS EX
00090 D NTER TO VIEW DATA : CMD 1 FOR RESTART
```

IBM RPG CALCULATION SPECIFICATIONS

```
C*****************************************
C*              MAINLINE                 *
C*****************************************
C                     SETOF                     98
C   KG                SETON                     LR
C   KG                SETOF                     0102
C   KG                GOTO ENDM
C   KA                SETON                     99
C   KA                SETOF                     010298
C   KA                GOTO ENDM
C**
C   01                EXSR SCR01
C   02                EXSR SCR02
C**
C           ENDM      TAG
C*****************************************
C*        SCREEN 01                      *
C*****************************************
CSR         SCR01     BEGSR
C           SITEM     CHAININVNMAST             98
C                     Z-ADDILORDR    SLORDR  60
C                     MOVE IDESC     SDESC  15
C                     Z-ADDILOCAT    SLOCAT  60
C                     Z-ADDIQUANT    SQUANT  50
```

degree, this inflexibility arises because of the very limited set of control structures made available for directing processing operations. Also, while coding via forms does ease the learning process, RPG's source code is very difficult to understand for someone who knows little about RPG.

An Example. Exhibit 14.14 shows some of the forms used in an RPG program that handles the item inventory file task. The "program" simply consists of filled-out forms. The "I" form defines input records from the item inventory file. The "S" and "D" forms define the various CRT screen images used with the program. Finally, the "C" form defines the processing logic that ties everything together.

Pascal

Pascal, named for the French inventor of the mechanical calculator, was developed by Niklaus Wirth, a Swiss computer science professor. It was made available for general use in 1971. Professor Wirth's main design goal was to develop a language for teaching structured programming concepts. In addition, he wanted a programming language that would provide a powerful set of information processing capabilities but still be easy to learn.

Strengths. Pascal's greatest strength is the sophistication of its control structures and data structures. Programmers are encouraged to follow the structured programming concepts through the language's commands and syntax. As a result, Pascal code usually possesses a very clear, logical structure. In addition to providing many standard data structures, Pascal allows programmers to define new data structures to be used in their programs. Also, like BASIC, Pascal uses relatively few commands. As a result, one can write simple programs with very little training. Finally, Pascal's popularity as a teaching language has made it widely available.

Weaknesses. While Pascal was designed to serve as a general-purpose programming language, its relatively weak input, output, and file-handling capabilities have limited its use for business computing. Pascal's highly structured but terse syntax can also prove a liability at times. It can be difficult to understand a program's processing flow if the program has not been documented very well.

An Example. On the following page, Exhibit 14.15 lists a Pascal program that handles the inventory file inquiry task. Pascal's "bookkeeping" demands and terse but strict syntax result in a code that is difficult to understand unless you understand the Pascal language. All data structures must be very carefully described. Lines 3–33 define the different data structures used in the program. Pascal "hides" the programmer from many of the details for processing inputs and outputs (see lines 35–43 and lines 65–78). While this makes it easier for the programmer to concentrate on a program's logical structure, it makes it harder to learn and follow Pascal code. This program's actual processing operations occur in lines 53–93. By ignoring the statements that link retrieved data items to previously defined data structures (lines 65–72) and those involved with displaying these data on the CRT screen (lines 73–91), you should see just how concise Pascal code can be.

Exhibit 14.15

A Pascal program for displaying information from the item inventory file on a CRT screen: this program is written in JRT Pascal for a Zenith Z–100 microcomputer.

```
PROGRAM inventory;

TYPE
    key_t = ARRAY[1..256] of CHAR;
    rec_t = ARRAY[1..2048] of CHAR;
    ctrl_rec = RECORD
        c_1:ARRAY[1..4] of INTEGER;
        rec_size : INTEGER;
        c_2 : INTEGER;
        key_size : INTEGER;
        END;
index_record = RECORD
        disk : CHAR;
        filename : ARRAY[1..8] of CHAR;
        return_code : INTEGER;
        res_: INTEGER;
        ct1 : ^ctrl_rec;
        reserved : ARRAY[1..196] of CHAR;
        END;

VAR
    key : key_t;
    rec : rec_t;
    cmd : CHAR;
    ir : index record;
    tem_d : ARRAY[1..2048] of CHAR;
    description : ARRAY[1..15] of CHAR;
    last_order : ARRAY[1..8] of CHAR;
    whse_loc : ARRAY[1..7] of CHAR;
    quan_on_hand : ARRAY[1..5] of CHAR;
    on_order : ARRAY[1..5] of CHAR;
    reorder-point : ARRAY[1..5] of CHAR;
    quan-ship : ARRAY[1..5] of CHAR;

PROCEDURE INDEX0 (command : CHAR;
            var key : key_t;
            var rec : rec_t;
            var ir : index_record );extern;

PROCEDURE INDEX1 (command : CHAR;
            var key : key_t;
            var rec : rec_t;
            var ir  : index_record );extern;

BEGIN
ir := ' ';
cmd := '0';
WRITE('Disk: ');
READLN(ir,disk);
WRITE('File: ');
READLN(ir,filename);                                        {open file}
INDEX0(cmd,key,rec,ir);
REPEAT                                                      {repeat...until(no more items)}
        key :=' ';
        rec :=' ';
        cmd :='R';
        WRITE('Next Item: ');                               {prompt for an item}
        READLN(key);                                        {read...until(match on item)}
        key := UPCASE(key);
        INDEX0(cmd, key, rec, ir);
        IF (ir.return_code <> 0) THEN
              BEGIN
              WRITELN('Error: ',ir.return_code);
              END;
tem_d := copy(rec, ir.ctl^.key_size + 1,ir.ctl^.rec_size - ir.ctl^.key_size);
last_order := copy(tem_d,1,15);
description := copy(tem_d,16,8);                            {display item information}
whse_loc := copy(tem_d,24,7);
quan_on_hand := copy(tem_d,31,5);
on_order := copy(tem_d,36,5);
reorder_point := copy(tem_d,41,5);
quan_ship := copy(tem_c,46,5);
WRITELN('                                   Compustore');
WRITELN('                                 Inventory Status");
WRITELN;
WRITELN;
WRITELN(' Item No: '.copy(rec, 1,ir.ctl^.key_size),'                 Date of');
WRITELN('                                     Last Order: ',last_order);
WRITELN(' Description: ', description);
WRITELN;
WRITELN(' Warehouse');
WRITELN(' Location: ',whse_loc);
WRITELN;
WRITELN(' Quantity On Hand: ',quan_on_hand,'                Items');
WRITELN('                                     On Order: ',on_order);
WRITELN;
WRITELN(' Re-order Point: ',reorder_point,'                      Quantity to be');
WRITELN('                                         Shipped: ',quan_ship);
WRITELN;
WRITELN;
UNTIL (key = 'END');
END
```

Some New Languages

New programming languages are still being designed. Three recently developed languages have gained a lot of support throughout the computer industry. It is too early to know if Ada, C, or Modula-2 will obtain the success of FORTRAN, COBOL, or BASIC, but the future of these languages looks bright.

Ada. Like COBOL, the development of **Ada** was supported by the Department of Defense to build large, reliable, yet efficient military software. The major goals of Ada's designers were to provide programmers with sophisticated control and data structures and to provide commands that directly operated on hardware devices. These design features have resulted in Ada's being a very complex but powerful programming language.

Currently, Ada is primarily used to develop information systems that control and direct military weapons systems. Its strengths suggest that it will also be a very good language for nonmilitary computer applications demanding very high levels of efficiency and reliability. Likely applications include air traffic control, hospital patient monitoring, manufacturing control, and electronic banking.

C. Bell Laboratories developed the **C** language to use in building systems software. C was created by combining some features of assembly languages and high-level languages. It produces very efficient programs that are easy to maintain.

C combines the advantages of assembly and high-level languages. It offers programmers extensive control of a computer system's hardware devices, provides some very sophisticated control and data structures, but remains a very concise language. These strengths lead directly to C's major weakness: skilled programmers are needed to develop, or even to understand, C programs.

Today C is primarily used to develop systems software for minicomputers and microcomputers. However, some business applications are beginning to be developed in C.

Modula-2. Niklaus Wirth, Pascal's developer, designed **Modula-2** to improve Pascal. On the following page, Computers at Work: "The Maestro of Modula-2" discusses Professor Wirth's many accomplishments.

Modula-2 corrects Pascal's flaws and adds some new features. Wirth's main aim was to rewrite Pascal so it could serve as an applications software development tool as well as a teaching tool. Some key enhancements to Pascal include the capabilities to better handle business data processing tasks, to directly control hardware, and to improve program modularity. As Modula-2 becomes better known and more widely available, it may very well become a successful programming language for business computing.

Professional Issue

Selecting a High-Level Programming Language

If you remember, Jerry Lincoln had convinced Helen Sims that assembly language would not be the appropriate language level to use in revising CompuStore's inventory control system. But they still hadn't decided which high-level language to use.

COMPUTERS AT WORK

The Maestro of Modula-2

Professor Niklaus Wirth doesn't regard a programming language as a "language" at all.

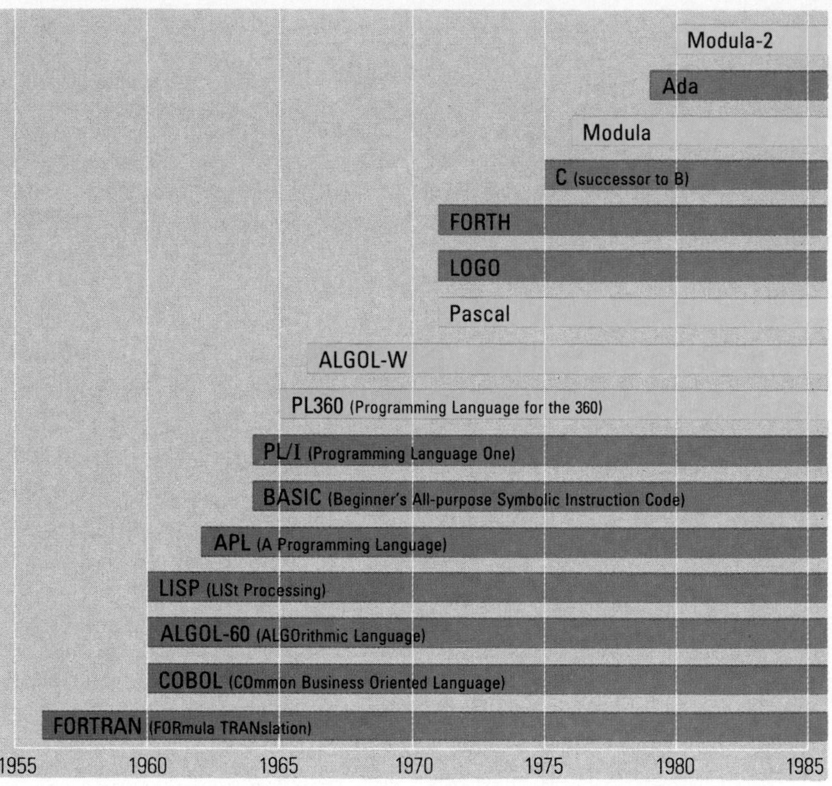

In November 1982, 20 pioneering computer scientists were initiated into the Computer Industry Hall of Fame. The list of Hall of Famers spanned the industry from head to toe, from Thomas Watson, Sr., the grand-patriarch of IBM, to Bill Gates, the guru of Microsoft, to Steve Jobs, the rootstock of Apple. While the computing community could readily identify most of these innovators with landmark discoveries or corporate entities, one academician stood out for obscurity rather than notoriety.

Niklaus K. Wirth holds no patents in silicon circuitry. He never entrepreneured a high-tech firm. Instead, his contribution to computing rests in slim scholarly reports brimming with Greek symbols and mathematical notation. Over the past twenty years, these reports have defined no less than five programming languages, and have earned the Swiss professor the title of "Father of Structured Languages."

Ironically, the master of computer linguistics doesn't regard a programming language as a "language" at all. He shies away from the popular notion that a language is a medium of communication between human and machine. Rather, he sees it as an abstract tool for construction of computing machinery. "In my opinion," said Wirth, "the term *programming language* is still chosen and misleading. *Program notation* would be eminently more appropriate."

Source: E. Joyce, "The Making of Modula-2," *PC Magazine,* 3 April, 1984, pp. 177–81.

Helen: Well, Jerry, what language should we use? One of my instructors says Pascal is the best language around today. Should we use Pascal?

Jerry: Pascal's a good language, but so are a number of others. Some firms have strict standards that determine which programming languages are to be used. We're a bit more informal here. Jan Hale wants us to study the situation and then select the language that is most appropriate.

Helen: What should we be looking at, specifically?

Jerry: There are a number of things that need to be considered—the nature and performance objectives of a program, language availability and portability, and program development and maintenance needs. Choosing a language that's wrong for the situation can make programming a trial rather than enjoyable work.

As Jerry Hale said, a number of factors need to be considered in selecting a programming language. Let's take a more detailed look at those Jerry mentioned.

The Nature of the Program. Business programming covers a wide variety of processing tasks. While many business programs emphasize file processing, programs in applications such as sales forecasting are very similar to scientific or engineering programs. Selecting a language designed to handle the type of information processing being performed can both ease program development efforts and result in better computer applications.

The Performance Objectives of the Program. Program performance objectives vary a lot more than you might initially think. Efficiency is extremely important for programs that run continuously and require fast response times. An example would be the programs used in airline reservation systems. Efficiency, however, is not that important with programs that are seldom used or for which response time is not crucial. An example might be a firm's quarterly financial report.

The Availability of a Language. A programming language cannot be used if it is not available on your computer system. Similarly, it would be far more difficult to develop a program in a new programming language than in a language you already knew. Even though a programming language might be ideal in terms of a program's nature and performance objectives, it might be impossible or infeasible to use the language.

The Portability of a Language. If a program were developed in a language with no official standard or in a nonstandard version of a standardized language, it might have to be changed before it could be run on a different computer system or even on a different operating system with the same computer system. You should ask yourself, are any equipment or systems software changes planned in the future? Will the program be used on more than one computer system?

Program Development Needs. Business needs often place limits on the amount of money or time available for a programming project, as well as on the skill level of the programmers assigned to the project. When money, time, or programmer expertise is lacking, then programming languages that are easy to use become very attractive.

Program Maintenance Needs. If frequent modifications are expected, a programmer unfamiliar with a program must be able to understand its processing flow. Programming languages that are Englishlike, that separate data descriptions from processing operations, and that support structured programming concepts are generally easier to understand than languages that lack these features.

An Example: Making a Selection

By using these factors, Helen and Jerry were able to select a programming language without too much trouble.

Helen: It seems clear to me that this revision in the inventory control system involves business processing rather than scientific processing. Right?

Jerry: Yes. Most of the time we'll just be moving data from disk to primary memory and from primary memory to a CRT screen. Well, what does that mean in terms of an appropriate programming language?

Helen: I guess it means we won't be using FORTRAN or Pascal.

Let's see . . . what was next? . . . Just how important is program efficiency,

Jerry? Since this program will run interactively, I guess response time is crucial.

Jerry: It's true that we don't want slow response. However, there won't be that many users on the computer system at the same time. We shouldn't have to do anything fancy to achieve adequate response time. COBOL, BASIC, PL/I and RPG would all be fine.

Helen: But we don't have PL/I or RPG available on our computer system. I guess they're eliminated.

Jerry: Not necessarily. If the program were important enough and if either PL/I or RPG were clearly the best programming language to use, I'm sure Jan would let us acquire it. In this case, however, they are both eliminated.

That leaves COBOL and BASIC. As we don't expect to be changing our computer system any time in the future, portability really isn't an issue. COBOL and BASIC are both widely available anyway. And while COBOL is a more standardized language, it is fairly easy to convert a carefully written BASIC program.

Helen: That leaves us with program development and program maintenance needs. The project schedule Jan put together doesn't look too bad. So we're still left with COBOL and BASIC.

This is the fourth major revision in the inventory control system. I guess we should be concerned about program maintenance.

Jerry: I agree. Which of the two programming languages usually results in programs that are easier to maintain?

Helen: I'd say COBOL.

Jerry: That's my feeling, too. Let's go see if Jan agrees with our choice.

In Quest of True BASIC

Dartmouth College's colonial brick buildings rest secluded among wooded New Hampshire hills as the northernmost outpost of the Ivy League. There, in 1964, two professors in the mathematics department, John Kemeny and Thomas Kurtz, invented a computer language for their students. They called it the Beginners' All-purpose Symbolic Instruction Code.

Today, BASIC is not only the most widely used computer language, it has become one of the major world languages. More people are conversant with BASIC than speak Norwegian, Swedish, and Danish combined.

The spread of BASIC was due in large part to the personal computer explosion. While personal computer BASIC was making converts among the general public, BASIC continued to evolve at Dartmouth in its original time-sharing, mainframe-based environment. This "Dartmouth BASIC" developed most of the features of a modern, structured programming language. Many of the features of Dartmouth BASIC found their way into a set of standards for the BASIC language that is currently being proposed by a committee of the American National Standards Institute (ANSI). This proposed ANS BASIC is quite different from the Microsoft-produced BASIC and BASICA that IBM distributes for the PC.

Kemeny and Kurtz, who are still on the Dartmouth faculty, have supervised the development of an ANS BASIC for the PC, which they are calling True BASIC.

PC World Editor-in-Chief Andrew Fluegelman traveled to Hanover, New Hampshire, to speak with Kemeny and Kurtz about their contributions to computing. The following is an edited version of that conversation.

PCW: What was the state of computing back in 1964?

Kemeny: Everything was done in batch processing. There are now some systems that have what is called "batch processing," but they are nothing like what computers were like back then.

People would punch their programs on IBM cards and submit them to a computer operator. The operator would collect the cards for hundreds of programs and feed them to the computer in a "batch." When all the batch jobs were completed, it was time for the next feeding of the computer. You got only one, maybe two, shots a day at running a revised version of your program. John McCarthy, the artificial intelligence expert at MIT, who was a very good programmer, said that it used to take him two weeks to debug a program.

The limitations of batch processing were the dominant factors we were battling. Computers were very expensive and most computer center operators figured people were cheaper. The whole philosophy was that you mustn't waste unnecessary computer time. And that situation made the computing environment impossible as a teaching or research environment.

PCW: So what was your response to that situation?

Kurtz: I had reached the conclusion that it was possible to design a computing environment that would be palatable for students so that they could get their answers fairly quickly. That was one ingredient.

The second ingredient was this notion of time-sharing, which had been invented at MIT in 1959 in a research environment. There was no cost/benefit analysis. We just decided to do it.

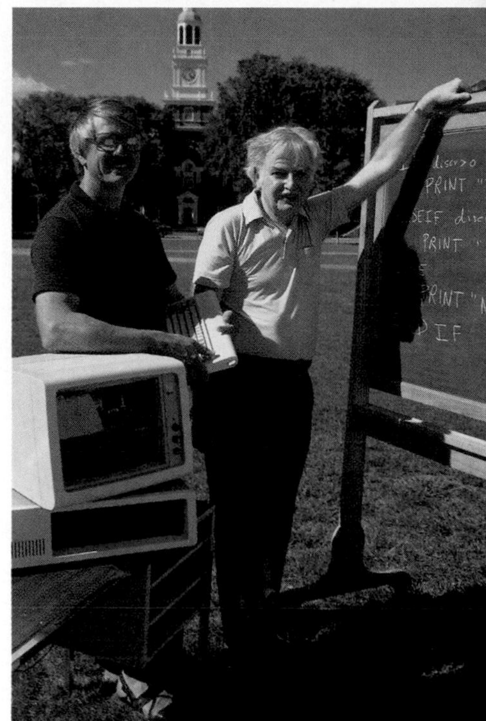

Kemeny: It was perfectly obvious to both of us that time-sharing would be a vastly superior environment for teaching. We could give each student the ability to communicate directly with the computer—with the illusion that it was just sitting there waiting to serve.

Kurtz: There was one other important component—the open-access principle, which was that students and faculty members shouldn't have to pay for or get permission to use computing time.

Kemeny: It was a rather radical decision at the time. The analogy that Tom came up with was the college library, and I used that analogy in presenting the notion of free computer time to the college trustees at a time when all educational institutions were under tremendous financial pressures.

We proposed that computer time should be a central collegewide facility, much like the library, to be used for everything from course work to research to recreation—as a library is. Once I had convinced them of the reasonableness of the analogy, I asked them, "Would you charge a student to take a book out of the library?" That analogy worked every single time, and it's a perfectly good analogy. Even now, computer center costs run about the same as library costs.

PCW: How did BASIC fit in?

Kurtz: We decided to develop BASIC because we needed an easy language that students could learn quickly and that was appropriate to the system we were creating.

Kemeny: I just knew that we could do much better than FORTRAN, and in a way, the fact that BASIC was not the first general-purpose language gave us an advantage.

PCW: Time-sharing and open access and BASIC were obviously key elements in the democratization of computing. What were the innovations of BASIC that made computing more accessible?

Kurtz: We wanted to get rid of the elements of a computer language that would not be obvious to students. For example, the difference between integers and floating point numbers was built into FORTRAN. But to the ordinary person, a number is a number. So we made the decision to have a single number type.

Kemeny: Take the following example: A student will understand that 2 is an integer and that 3 is an integer, but a student who is nervous and who is writing his or her first program may not remember that when you divide 2 by 3 you're going to get a different kind of number. That sort of thing is a tremendous psychological barrier to programming.

Kurtz: BASIC's input and output were new. Almost anything you typed for a number was legal, and you didn't have to worry about format on output.

Kemeny: Just having an INPUT statement was an innovation. BASIC was the first language that was designed for interactive rather than batch processing. Several features of the language were developed because we knew that students would be sitting at a terminal rather than handing a computer center operator a batch of cards.

"Many people criticize BASIC for its lack of structure."

PCW: Many people criticize BASIC for its lack of structure. When and how were structured program features added?

Kurtz: The structured programming boom came around the middle seventies. Some work had been done earlier than that, but it hit this campus around 1974–1975. We began experimenting with a version of BASIC called SBASIC, for Structured BASIC. The person mainly responsible for that was Professor Stephen Garland.

PCW: That was in 1975—the year that Bill Gates and Paul Allen wrote a version of BASIC for the Altair. What was your reaction to that?

Kurtz: To be honest, I didn't have any reaction in 1975. I didn't look at BASIC on any personal computer until about three years ago when I had occasion to use an Apple. The reason for that is that we've always had such a friendly and convenient time-sharing system here at Dartmouth that there was never any cause to go outside.

PCW: And what was your reaction when you saw BASIC on the Apple?

Kurtz: Well, of course, I was appalled at what I saw.

PCW: What was appalling?

Kurtz: The most obvious deficiency was the lack of structured features and the reliance on line numbers. Many of the problems have been corrected in subsequent implementations on the PC, but the lack of structured programming still remains.

Kemeny: I was horrified by the fact that microcomputer BASICs insisted on changing your entire program to capital letters.

PCW: Do you regret that BASIC was allowed to slip out into the world in imperfect or corrupted form?

Kurtz: I don't personally, because I don't know that I could have done anything to improve the situation. The popularization of BASIC happened because of the completely laissez-faire situation.

Right now, the real question is whether we, together with the ANSI standard, can bring the language back.

Kemeny: The first time I really became aware of the problem was when the College Board made its decision that the language it would use on the advanced college placement exam in computing would be Pascal. The irony is that the chairman of the College Board committee was the same Professor Garland who had been responsible for getting all of us on campus to program in Structured BASIC.

Almost all of the high-school teachers pushed for BASIC, because that was the language that they all knew. Steve Garland himself pushed for BASIC. But then the committee asked the question, "Which version of BASIC should we choose?" They surveyed all the available versions of BASIC and ended up not choosing any of them, and that's how they finally chose Pascal. But the board did say that if and when acceptable structured versions of BASIC became available for personal computers, they would consider BASIC.

I was furious when I heard that decision, and that motivated me to become interested in getting somebody to write a really good version of BASIC for microcomputers. It took us a year or so to decide that we ought to be part of that "somebody."

PCW: Do you think that True BASIC will be able to set a new standard?

Kurtz: This may be looking at the world through rose-colored glasses, but from the initial reception that we're getting, I feel confident that this is going to turn things around.

Kemeny: I feel really good about the ANSI standard. Having experienced what happened to the original BASIC on microcomputers, I have this nightmare that someone will write a truly bastardized version of ANS BASIC and that *it* will become the standard. In a way, I see True BASIC as a preemptive strike to try to maintain the integrity of the ANSI standard.

Kurtz: Once our product appears, I hope it will be very hard for people to come out with shoddy versions of BASIC. One of our altruistic goals is to improve the quality of computing that is available for education at all levels.

Kemeny: Of course, we'd love to make some money also—we've put a heck of a lot of work into it. I do hope to make very sure that no one's going to beat us with a bad implementation. But if it should turn out that someone comes out with a better ANS standard version, I think we still will have made a major contribution to education.

From "In Quest of True BASIC" by Andrew Fluegelman. Reprinted by permission of *PC World* from Volume 2, Issue 12 (November 1984) published at 555 De Haro Street, San Francisco, CA 94107.

SUMMARY

Programming languages serve as the means by which a programmer communicates a program design to a computer system. Three levels of programming languages are in common use: *assembly languages, high-level languages,* and *very high-level languages.*

As most programs are not coded in machine language, they are translated into machine language by systems software. The initial version of a program is called the *source code* and the translated version is called the *object code.* With assembly languages, an *assembler* performs this translation. With high-level languages, *compilers* or *interpreters* perform the translation. A compiler translates a program all at once, but does not execute it. An interpreter translates a program one statement at a time and then executes it prior to translating the next statement.

Assembly languages, which were developed to relieve the tedium and reduce the errors of machine language programs, are essentially a more readable form of machine language. High-level languages have more powerful commands that are "problem-oriented" rather than "machine-oriented" and that translate into multiple machine language instructions. Very-high-level languages consist of even more powerful commands that enable programmers to specify what processing tasks are to be performed, rather than how the tasks are to be performed. However, programmers lose some control over the manner in which processing occurs as they make use of each higher level of programming language.

Every programming language is designed to achieve certain goals. These goals represent the design features of the language. Eight design features are particularly useful in comparing the strengths and weaknesses of different programming languages: the extent to which language is *general-purpose,* provides for *hardware control,* is *interactive,* provides *sophisticated control structures* and *sophisticated data structures,* is *nonprocedural,* is *easy to use,* and is *standardized.*

The six most popular high-level languages used for business programming are *FORTRAN, COBOL, BASIC, PL/I, RPG,* and *Pascal.* FORTRAN is primarily used for scientific and engineering problem solving. COBOL is a business-oriented language that is well suited for processing large data files and handling repetitive data processing operations. BASIC is a general-purpose programming language that is very easy to learn and to use. PL/I is a more powerful, but also more complex, general-purpose programming language. RPG is an easy-to-learn, business-oriented language that is well suited to repetitive data processing operations. Pascal is a general-purpose programming language that offers very sophisticated control and data structures.

Three new high-level languages that are likely to be successful are *Ada, C,* and *Modula-2.*

Six factors should be considered in selecting a programming language for a particular programming project: the nature and performance objectives of the program, the availability and portability of the language, and program development and maintenance needs.

In the next chapter we will see how very-high-level languages are enabling managers and other users to develop business applications by themselves.

REVIEW QUESTIONS

1. Briefly describe the three levels of programming languages in use today.
2. Compare general-purpose and special-purpose programming languages.
3. What are hardware control features of program languages?
4. What is meant by the interactive feature of a programming language?
5. Discuss the advantages offered by sophisticated control structures.
6. Briefly describe the three basic data structures utilized by higher programming languages.
7. Under what conditions are assembly, high-level, and very-high-level programming languages each most likely to be used?
8. Janet Paxton is developing a program to handle her firm's payroll and customer billing operations. Which language is Janet most likely to choose for this purpose? Why?
9. Why is BASIC called a "Jack-of-all-trades" language? What advantages and disadvantages does it offer?
10. In view of the many advantages offered by PL/I, why has it never achieved the success hoped for by IBM?
11. Briefly discuss the three "new" languages described in the text.
12. Jim Hasboro must select a high-level language for use in his firm. What factors should he consider in making his choice?

CHAPTER 15

Application Development Without Programmers

COMPUTERS AT WORK

IBM PCs Create a Winning Formula

When you are part of a business unit responsible for deciding whether your company should build a new plant, you need to do a lot more than analyze historical data. You must be able to plan what the company should do and then show what the results of that plan would be if it were implemented.

As manager of planning for chemical giant Ciba-Geigy Corporation's resins department, William Walsh is in this position. He must ensure that personnel in the resin department's market centers analyze the growth rates expected in their segment of the industry, study the corresponding economic result of changes in product mix, and gauge the effect of new product introductions.

Before IBM PCs were introduced into his department, there were two ways for Walsh's groups to get reports based on this analysis. His staff could do the reports manually or make a formal request to the department to set up the reports using mainframe software.

Walsh tended to do the reports manually because it was faster than explaining what was required to a programmer who did not understand Walsh's part of the business.

Using IBM PCs and Lotus Development Corporation's *1-2-3,* resins department market center personnel now can plan separately and then do the consolidation required for department-level analysis. As Walsh explains it, "The person who is doing the programs is now part of the business."

Walsh spends about 40 percent of his time working on the IBM PC to develop action programs and current marketing awareness programs, and he is typical of the large number of Ciba-Geigy end-users who are taking advantage of the independence personal computers can provide.

Source: L. Paul, "IBM PCs Create Winning Formula," *PC Week,* 6 March, 1984, pp. 26–27 and 32.

The growth of business computing in many organizations has outstripped the capabilities of computer staffs. Other organizations, particularly smaller firms, cannot afford a skilled computer staff. Today, however, many business professionals, such as William Walsh of Ciba-Geigy, are developing their own computer applications. Even if you do not pursue an information systems career, you may well find yourself "programming" during your professional life. In this chapter, you will learn to do the following:

1. Explain what "end-user computing" is and describe how it differs from the traditional systems development process.
2. Describe the differences between mainframe and microcomputer end-user tools.
3. List four strategies for accessing mainframe data from a microcomputer.
4. Describe four types of end-user tools.
5. Describe two approaches by which software vendors are providing business professionals with multipurpose end-user tools.
6. Explain what "desktop organizers" are.
7. List the two types of facilities used in promoting and managing end-user computing.

END-USER COMPUTING

Jan Lincoln and Jerry Hale were telling Helen Sims about the "good old days" over coffee.

Jerry: You've sure got it easy now, Helen. Computers are as common as phones in many businesses today. Everyone knows about them. Most business professionals use them on a daily basis. When you want to talk with a manager about an idea you have to improve an information system, you don't think twice about it. You just go and do it.

Jan, tell her what it was like when they were the "good guys" and we were the "bad guys."

Jan: Back in the 1970s, information systems departments couldn't keep up with management's demands to develop new information systems. Since most firms by this time had implemented a number of information systems, managers were becoming aware of a growing mass of information being stored on their firms' computer systems. Looking back, it seems like requests for projects arose on a daily basis.

Helen: But wasn't that good? It means that management recognized the value of business computing.

Jerry: Not when you couldn't meet the demand. Management got frustrated. We got frustrated. It was like spinning your car's wheels on ice—we used up a lot of energy but were not getting very far.

Helen: I still don't understand what the problem was.

Jan: To begin with, there just weren't very many of us "information systems people" around. And most of the time we were maintaining existing applications rather than working on new ones. New projects were **backlogged,** or put on long waiting lists, in most firms.

Helen: What happened to change the situation?

Jan: Advances in hardware and software enabled users to perform many of the systems development activities normally performed by systems analysts and programmers. As a result, users began to develop some of their applications by themselves—the era of **end-user computing** had begun.

A Crisis in Business Computing

Business computing had reached a crisis in the mid-1970s for many firms. A "new breed" of business professional, one aware of the potential of computers, was beginning to enter the work force. As a result, requests for new information systems projects increased. However, the computer staffs in most firms were hard pressed just to keep the existing computer applications running smoothly.

The backlog of "postponed" information systems projects was growing larger and larger. In some firms, this backlog was talked about in terms of "man-centuries" of systems development. (One man-century of work would keep a single systems analyst or programmer busy for 100 years.) It was not that unusual for a marketing manager, for example, to be told that the new sales reporting system being requested would be scheduled for development in three or four years. As you might expect, the marketing manager would not be very happy—such reports are needed now, not three or four years in the future!

This **visible backlog** was actually small compared to the **invisible backlog** of projects that were needed but never proposed.

In small firms the situation was even worse. Most small firms could not employ many, if any, systems analysts or programmers. As a result, they had to meet most of their information needs through software packages. This caused few problems with standard computer applications such as accounting and inventory control. However, when a small business wished to go beyond these standard applications, few options existed. As we learned in Chapter 12, customizing software can be quite expensive.

The Solution: Very-High-Level Languages and Microcomputers

Two advances in computer technology provided the solution to this crisis.

First, very-high-level languages began to be developed in the mid-1970s. As discussed in Chapter 14, these programming languages are easy to learn but designed to handle a specific type of information processing problem. By using these very-high-level languages, some business professionals began to develop their own information systems.

Very-high-level languages make good **end-user tools** for three reasons. First, a business professional who knows little about software development can begin to produce useful information in a few hours. Second, to a large extent the business professional describes what is to be produced, rather than the detailed information processing steps actually required. Third, the business professional need not know much about the computer's operating system. In short, the business professional can focus on the problem being solved, rather than on the details of program development.

The second advance was the microcomputer, which was developed in the late 1970s. As described in Chapter 2, the use of microcomputers in business has mushroomed during the 1980s. A driving force behind this growth has been the large number of quality business software packages, many of which are suitable for end-user computing. Today, very-high-level languages are available to all business professionals, and end-user computing has become commonplace in many firms.

With end-user computing, business professionals perform the system development activities traditionally performed by systems analysts and programmers. Exhibit 15.1 depicts the differences between the traditional systems development process and end-user computing. With the systems life cycle approach to systems development, the user influences information systems design indirectly through a systems analyst. With end-user computing, the user influences information system design directly by using a very-high-level language to build the information system.

You should also notice two other things about end-user computing. First, the systems design and systems implementation stages disappear. Hardware and software designs disappear since they are "built" into the very-high-level language. Implementation disappears because users can begin to use their information system as it is being developed. Second, systems analysis, acquisition, and maintenance occur more or less at the same time. Users determine

Exhibit 15.1

End-user computing differs considerably from the traditional systems development process. With end-user computing, two systems life-cycle stages disappear and the other three stages take place simultaneously.

Traditional Systems Development — Versus — End-User Computing

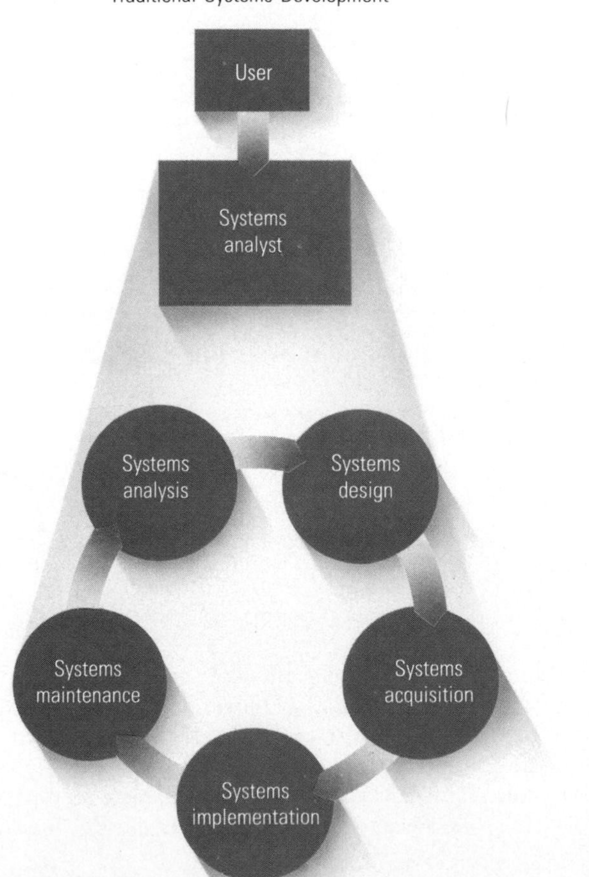

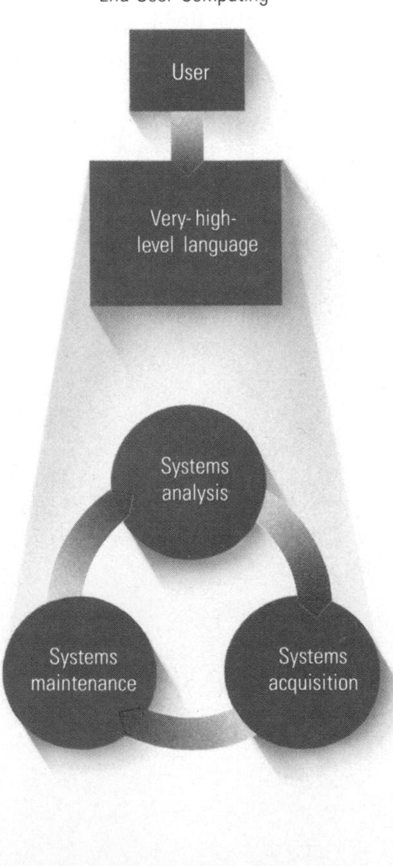

their needs by experimenting with partially built programs, and these experiments suggest revisions that overcome errors or add improved features.

End-user computing offers two obvious benefits to a business—information systems can be developed quickly and inexpensively, and the application backlog is reduced. Two less obvious benefits are even more important. First, better information systems often result. Second, business professionals are more apt to use an information system that they have developed.

It is also important to recognize the potential hazards of end-user computing:

Many users are unable to determine their information requirements without the aid of a skilled systems analyst.

Many users are insensitive to the need to test and document software, to validate input data, and to back up the results of processing operations.

If users develop applications without finding out what information systems already exist, a lot of "reinventing the wheel" can occur.

Many computer applications require the use of data already stored in a firm's computer systems. If users cannot access these data through a very-high-level language, the potential benefit of end-user computing is limited.

Private collections of data, accessible only by the individuals who created them, tend to arise.

End-user computing, to be effective, must be well managed. Appropriate end-user tools in the form of very-high-level languages must be made available and users must be trained in their use. As you might expect, some end-user tools are more appropriate for certain types of information problems than are others. Furthermore, users need to be able to access data already captured and stored on a firm's computer systems.

You will be introduced to a number of end-user tools later in this chapter. However, as these tools are available for both mainframe computers and microcomputers, we shall first look at the differences between end-user computing on mainframes and on microcomputers.

MAINFRAMES VERSUS MICROCOMPUTERS

All end-user tools provide business professionals with the same basic capabilitites:

A set of commands to describe the information outputs to be produced.

A set of commands to describe and manipulate the data structures that contain data from which information is to be produced.

A set of commands to describe the processing operations that convert raw data into information outputs.

These tools are available on both mainframe computers and microcomputers.

Because mainframe computers have larger and faster central processors, mainframe end-user tools can be used to develop bigger and more sophisticated programs than can microcomputer end-user tools. Also, because of the larger capacity of mainframe secondary storage devices, mainframe end-user tools gain direct access to much larger data files than are available with microcomputer end-user tools. Thus, one advantage of mainframe end-user computing is that larger, more complex problems can be tackled. The larger capacity of mainframe end-user tools is one issue to consider in choosing between mainframe and microcomputer end-user tools.

Two other mainframe/microcomputer issues need to be addressed in selecting appropriate end-user tools. First, the costs of end-user computing via mainframes or microcomputers can be quite different. Second, the need to link mainframes and microcomputers for end-user computing is becoming increasingly important. We will look at both issues in more depth.

Cost Considerations

Business professionals actually have three ways to access and use end-user tools (see Exhibit 15.2): through a CRT to an **in-house mainframe;** through a CRT to an **external mainframe,** and through a microcomputer. Mainframe access, no matter whether you access your own mainframe or another firm's, normally occurs via a time-sharing operating system (discussed in Chapter 7). In learning about the computer industry in Chapter 18, you will see that it is possible to "buy computer time" from other companies.

End-user tools are available for most mainframes as well as for many minicomputers. Prices can range from as little as $10,000 to well over $100,000. While these prices may seem high, a large number of business professionals can use the same package via online terminal access. The cost per user, thus, is lower. However, since mainframe users share a computer system's processing power with other applications, computer system response time can be poor. Also, not all businesses can afford to acquire an in-house mainframe or minicomputer.

Business professionals in firms without their own mainframes can access end-user tools made available by a time-sharing service. The fee they pay depends solely on their actual use of the tool. It normally includes a fixed fee for each session plus a variable amount that reflects the computer system resources, such as CPU time and disk storage space, actually used. While such charges might be low for a firm making little use of an end-user tool, they can grow quickly as usage increases. For example, monthly charges of $10,000 or more are not uncommon for firms making heavy use of a time-sharing service's end-user tools.

Microcomputers provide, at first glance, a low-cost alternative to mainframe end-user tools. For less than $5000, a business professional can have unlimited use of a microcomputer end-user tool. If the microcomputer sits on the business professional's desk, system availability and response time can both be very good. However, when this $5000 is multiplied by 50 or 100 or 500 to account for the total number of business professionals in a company, the cost begins to balloon. Most microcomputer software vendors require that firms buy one copy of software for each microcomputer on which the firms wish to run the software. Today many firms are balking at this policy and investigating whether the software vendors allow site licenses. With a **site license,** a firm pays a flat fee and then can copy the software and run it on a

Exhibit 15.2

End-user tools are made available to business professionals through an online CRT to an in-house mainframe, through an online CRT to a time-sharing service's mainframe, and through a microcomputer.

large number of microcomputers. Such "sharing" of software also allows a number of business professionals whose microcomputers are linked through a local area network, or LAN, to access and use a single copy of a software package.

The following discussion between Jan Hale and Susan Tate illustrates some of the issues that need to be raised in deciding between mainframe or microcomputer end-user tools:

Susan: Jan, we need some easier way of developing and modifying our marketing reports. Knowing how busy Jerry, Helen, and you are, I'm reluctant to keep bothering you with these little tasks. But we do need the reports. Any solutions?

Jan: First of all, Susan, we certainly don't mind helping you. That's our job! However, you could get your reports finished more quickly if you and your staff started doing some of the projects yourselves.

Susan: We're not programmers!

Jan: With some of the software around today, you don't have to be a programmer to develop business applications. In fact, the marketing reports you're talking about are exactly the type of applications best suited for this software. What we need to decide first is whether we should get a package that runs off the minicomputer or off a microcomputer. How many microcomputers does the marketing department have now?

Susan: Two. I've got one, and the staff uses another one. We've also got access to a CRT linked to the firm's minicomputer.

Jan: Given that, I've got four other questions. First, are the data you need currently stored in the minicomputer? Second, how complicated is the data analysis you need to do? Third, how often will you perform these marketing analyses? Fourth, how many other people in the firm will be doing similar analyses on the same data?

Susan: Some of the data I need are on the minicomputer, but not much. And what I need is already being printed on other reports.

The marketing analysis is fairly simple. It's mostly summing across different products and market segments.

Altogether, we do this type of analysis about five to six hours a day. Of course, this timing will vary from day to day.

Finally, I really can't think of anyone outside our department who would be doing this type of analysis on these data.

Jan: Well, from what you say it seems that your best bet would be to acquire a microcomputer package. Let's go look at some product reviews I've been saving.

Mainframe–Microcomputer Links

As with Susan Tate's marketing reports, much end-user computing today occurs on microcomputers. Much of this, however, can best be described as **stand-alone use.** That is, the microcomputer users create and use private data bases.

One of the first complaints voiced by business professionals about stand-alone end-user computing is the time they spend entering data. This is particularly frustrating when the data being entered are stored in a mainframe data base or on someone else's microcomputer. Requests soon arise to electronically capture these data.

One way to electronically share data files is to link microcomputers through a LAN. Then a user working with an end-user tool on one microcomputer can access data files that have been organized specifically for the tool and stored on any of the other microcomputers attached to the LAN.

The problem becomes more difficult when the desired data are stored in a mainframe data base. While requests to access these data from a microcomputer may seem very reasonable to a business professional, they are often dreaded by information systems managers for several reasons:

Data are often stored differently on mainframes and on microcomputers. This is very much the case with IBM computers. Special programs must be developed to transfer data between mainframes and microcomputers.

Some microcomputer end-user tools store data in specialized data structures. As a result, special translation programs are needed even after the data have been transferred from a mainframe to a microcomputer.

Mainframe data bases represent the lifeblood of a business. Sales orders, part and product inventories, customer lists, employee records, and all accounting and financial records are maintained in these data bases. If these data were inadvertently changed or destroyed, the results could be disastrous.

Finally, it is important for businesses to protect their data. The potential for computer security problems increases whenever new access paths to data are opened. We shall look at these security problems more closely in Chapter 17.

Even with these difficulties, firms are beginning to find ways of forming effective mainframe–microcomputer links.

Four common strategies for accessing mainframe data from a microcomputer are pictured in Exhibit 15.3 on the following page. The easiest type of mainframe-microcomputer link involves using the microcomputer as an online CRT, accessing the mainframe, and then using a mainframe end-user tool. Another fairly simple link involves retrieving data off a mainframe and storing them on a diskette. The diskette is then delivered to the business professional desiring access to the data, who accesses them with an appropriate microcomputer end-user tool. A third strategy uses software on a mainframe to translate a data file to a form usable by the microcomputer end-user tool and then transmits the data over a communications line to the microcomputer. A number of software vendors are beginning to provide such translation software. A final strategy makes use of an end-user tool that is available in both a mainframe and microcomputer form. Here data stored on a mainframe computer and accessed through a mainframe end-user tool can be downloaded to a microcomputer to be accessed by the microcomputer version of the tool.

END-USER TOOLS

It should not surprise you that the four common types of end-user tools are basically the same as the four personal computing software packages introduced in Chapter 2. Personal computing *is* end-user computing. However, a slightly different set of terms is used to refer to these tools in order to emphasize the information outputs each tool produces.

Exhibit 15.3

Today business professionals are accessing mainframe data from microcomputers by using the microcomputer as a CRT, by physically passing a diskette, by using mainframe translation software, and by using both mainframe and microcomputer versions of an end-user tool.

Financial Analysis Tools

Accountants and financial analysts have long used paper spreadsheets for preparing budgets, income statements, balance sheets, and other financial reports. As described in Chapter 2, spreadsheets are composed of cells made by intersecting rows and columns. In a spreadsheet, rows usually represent different financial entries while columns represent some measure of time, such as months or years. This is illustrated in Exhibit 15.4. Here the profitability of a product is being examined over a three-year period, assuming 5 percent growth in sales and 8 percent inflation.

An electronic spreadsheet works in a similar fashion. Exhibit 15.5 shows the standard format of most spreadsheet packages. The spreadsheet itself is the table in the middle of the screen display. Rows are indicated by numbers and columns are indicated by letters. The programmer moves from cell to cell by moving the cursor. One of three things can be entered into these spreadsheet cells:

Text — Used to list financial entries, prepare report headings, and document the spreadsheet.

Numbers — Used to give a numeric value to a cell.

Formulas — Used to operate on the contents of one or more cells.

The two lines above the spreadsheet are important. The top line shows the *contents* of the cell currently "pointed at" by the cursor. The second line is a "prompt" line, where menu items are displayed and user commands and spreadsheet entries are listed.

		1985	1986	1987
1	Price	50	50	50
2	Sales Volume	100000		
3	@ 5% growth	100000	105000	110250
4	Revenue	5000000	5250000	5512500
5	Cost of Goods Sold	3000000		
6	Cost-of-Goods-Sold rate	60%		
7	@ 8% inflation	.60	.648	.700
8	Cost of Goods Sold	3000000	3402000	3858750
9	Overhead	500000		
10	overhead rate	10%		
11	@8% inflation	.1	.108	.117
12	Overhead	500000	567000	644963
13	Income	1500000	1281000	1008787
14	Taxes (@45%)	675000	576450	453954
15				
16	Net income	825000	704550	554833
17				
18				
19				
20				
21				
22				

SALES FORECAST 1987

	ACTUAL Q1 SALES	ACTUAL Q2 SALES	PROJECTED Q3 SALES	PROJECTED Q4 SALES	PROJECTED YR TOTALS	PROJECTED Q1 1988
Rep #1	10200	11495	11546	30560	63802	11900
Rep #2	30450	34317	34469	31200	130437	[illegible]
Rep #3	26912	30330	30464	37900	125606	21665
Rep #4	8200	9241	9282	14340	41064	7239
Rep #5	12500	14080	14158	9840	49770	8114
Totals	88262	99471	99913	123840	410606	

Prep By Sterno

Exhibit 15.4

This handwritten financial spreadsheet examines the profitability of some product over a three-year period. The financial analyst preparing such a spreadsheet would likely use a hand calculator to do the arithmetic.

Exhibit 15.5

A spreadsheet display using VisiCalc

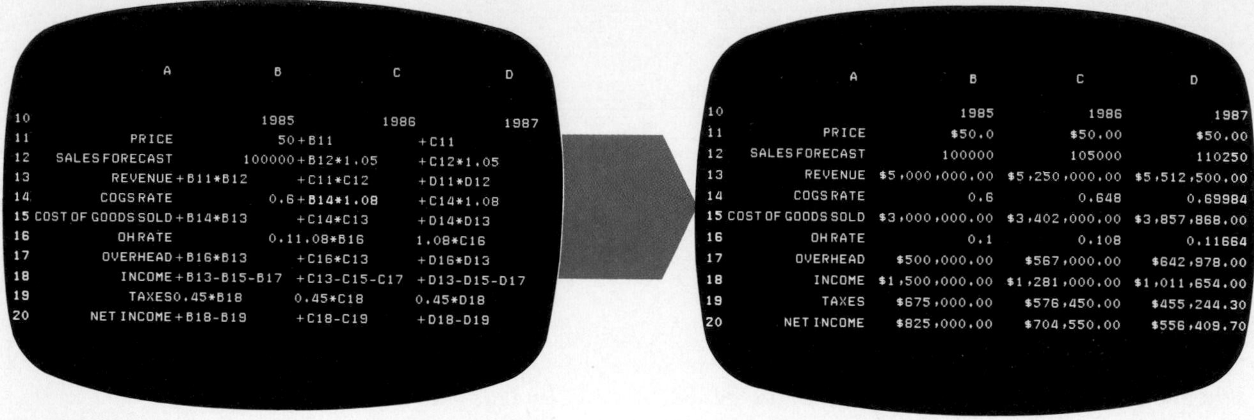

Exhibit 15.6

An electronic spreadsheet model for the handwritten spreadsheet in Exhibit 15.4: the left screen gives cell values and the right screen gives cell contents.

A spreadsheet model is "programmed" by filling appropriate cells, copying cells, and preparing appropriate report headings. This process is actually quite similar to the way a hand-prepared spreadsheet is produced. To print a report, the segment of the spreadsheet containing the report is printed.

Exhibit 15.6 shows an electronic spreadsheet model for the manually prepared spreadsheet in Exhibit 15.4. Note the difference between a cell's value and its contents. The **value** is the report that is printed; the contents represent the program that produces the report.

The advantage of using an electronic spreadsheet lies in the ease and speed with which it can be modified. Computers at Work: "Making Decisions Quicker and Better" illustrates these benefits (see page 444).

While spreadsheet models were first used by accountants and financial analysts, they are used by all types of managers today. Susan Tate, for example, could easily use an electronic spreadsheet to analyze marketing data. The rows of her spreadsheet models could represent product sales growth and profitability, and the columns could represent years, customer groups, retail stores, or competing firms.

Some types of financial analysis are too complicated for spreadsheet modeling. Most often this increased complexity is due to a need to perform very sophisticated mathematical operations. A **financial modeling system** is an end-user tool that can perform financial analyses that are too complicated for an electronic spreadsheet. Exhibit 15.7 illustrates such a tool.

As an example, consider the analysis performed in the spreadsheet model in Exhibit 15.5. These calculations can be given in the form of mathematical equations, or a "financial model":

Price = ?
Sales forecast = 100,000 units
Revenue = sales forecast X price
Cost of goods sold = 60% of revenue
Overhead = 5% of revenue
Income = revenue − cost of goods sold − overhead
Taxes = 45% of income
Net income = income − taxes

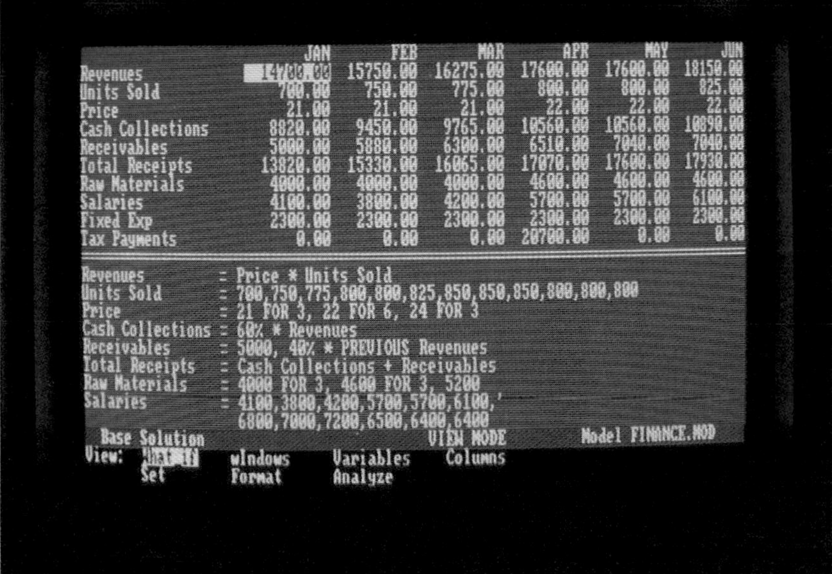

Exhibit 15.7

A financial modeling system performs financial analysis too complicated for an electronic spreadsheet.

Many types of analysis could then be performed to examine the product's profitability. Different prices could be used to see how competitive pricing might affect net income. Also, the impact of different growth and inflation rates could be explored. Each of these analyses simply extends the model given above. Exhibit 15.8 illustrates how a financial modeling system could be used to assess a product's profitability for different price alternatives.

Text Generation Tools

You may not think of text-generating software as an end-user tool. However, many business professionals spend much more time preparing memorandums, letters, and reports than they spend in financial analysis and other forms of "number-crunching." Tools that enable these people to express themselves better and faster can be invaluable. Computers at Work: "Relax and Write" describes some benefits of text generation tools (see page 446).

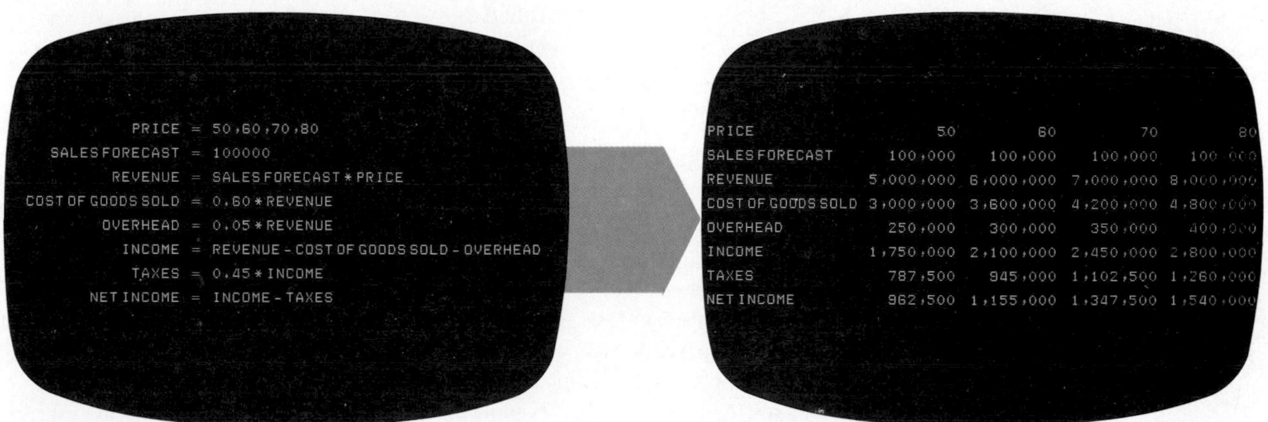

Exhibit 15.8

The "programming" statements used with most financial modeling systems are a series of formulas relating the variables and constants in a particular model.

COMPUTERS AT WORK

Making Decisions Quicker and Better

Three years ago Intec was fighting a worldwide business recession, and we needed to keep a tighter, week-to-week rein on the business. It so happened that one of our engineers had bought an Apple II and fooled around with it—but then just left it sitting there. One day the president called me into his office and said, "Come on, let's go. Let's use this machine."

We quickly built a cash-flow model of the company on our Apple, using VisiCalc spreadsheets. I worked right along with the president of the company, and we ran through a number of "what if" scenarios.

What if orders for January go to $2,000,000?

What if product mix and gross margins change?

What if we reduce overhead?

What if our receivables get extended by "x" number of days?

What if we reduce our prices by 25 percent?

We explored all of these conditions daily—after all, marketing drove the whole model and kept us busy.

The most valuable thing about the personal computer was that it allowed all of the top managers to become very personally involved in the situations we analyzed, and get the answers before the bad news kicked us in the butt. It could simulate the business—and look at the future—before reality hit us. We'd pick the most likely scenario and go with it. We just made decisions better.

Source: B. Denoyer and B. Yeager, "Modeling Cash Flow on Your Personal Computer," *Management Technology,* February 1984, pp. 27–28.

The most visible tool used for text generation is the *word processor.* These software packages provide four basic capabilities:

Text editing	Enables a user to insert, move, locate, modify, and delete text. Operations can be directed at characters, words, sentences, paragraphs, pages, and entire documents.
Text formatting	Enables a user to easily specify and modify the manner in which text is to be presented. Some common formatting actions include tab setting to indent lines and columns, paragraph **justification** to obtain fixed paragraph borders, and text **highlighting,** such as underlining, italics, and reverse-screen video.
Document management	Enables a user to save, retrieve, and delete full or partial documents.
Document printing	Enables a user to print single or multiple copies of a document.

Advanced word processing features include commands to handle footnotes, page headers and footers (text placed at the very top or bottom of every page of a document), superscripts, and subscripts, and to automatically produce a table of contents or an index.

Many word processing vendors also offer very useful "add-on" packages to their word processing software. **Spelling checkers** make use of online dictionaries to locate spelling errors. **Thesaurus programs** provide an online thesaurus. **Style checkers** analyze a document to locate and correct grammar or punctuation errors and to suggest ways of improving writing style. Finally, **mail-merge programs** link documents with address lists to "mass mail" letters.

Word processing packages are perhaps the most specialized very-high-level languages that exist today. Language commands are tied so closely to processing operations and are so easy to learn and use that it is hard to think of word processing as a "programming" activity (see Exhibit 15.9).

Would a top manager like Susan Tate use a word processor? This largely depends on Susan's preferences . . . as well as her ability to type! Today some managers do use word processors to produce much of their own text. Others prefer to give their secretaries handwritten or dictated first drafts and then handle all subsequent drafts themselves. Many others do little, if any, of their own text generation.

Business professionals are also beginning to use a new type of text generation tool, popularly referred to as **thoughtware.** These software packages take two basic forms. One type helps users develop and outline their thoughts prior to preparing a textual document. The other type provides a free-form data base in which ideas, facts, and reference materials can be saved and then retrieved via Englishlike retrieval cues. Exhibit 15.10 illustrates such packages.

Presentation Graphics Tools

Most businesses produce **presentation graphics,** or tables, charts, and pictures, by using their own graphic arts department or a graphic arts firm. However, the expense and time delays associated with such services have kept many managers from using this very effective means of presenting information.

Exhibit 15.9

In word processing packages, language commands are easy to learn and use.

Exhibit 15.10

"Free-form" software allows business professionals to develop and outline creative management ideas.

Relax and Write

"The idea," Bernard Malamud once said about writing, "is to get the pencil moving quickly." For many executives and professionals, however, a blank sheet of paper or a blank computer screen immediately produces hardening of the arteries in the hands. Sweat accumulates on the forehead much more quickly than words do on the page. If the report is due tomorrow, you could probably cut the tension with a knife.

If this sounds familiar, take heart. Your IBM PC, a good word processing program, and this column will get you going. I realize this may sound unreasonably optimistic, but it has frequently been observed that writers must be optimists to sit down in front of a pile of blank sheets intending to fill them with intelligent and interesting words. So relax and join the club.

This optimism is not meant to encourage magical thinking about the power of a keyboard and monitor. Tools, even great ones, don't rate that sort of blind devotion. A PC and a word processing program can't provide the words if you don't have them to begin with. Often, what you really lack while sitting in front of that blank page is not the right word, but the right tune. Good writing, like good music, always contains that most essential ingredient—rhythm.

Most of us know the rhythm of our writing "voice" as well as we know the sound of ourselves speaking. But we rarely find that rhythm at the beginning of a writing session. Like a car engine on a cold morning, your written words seem awkward and shaky until you warm up and get in gear. Many writers lose confidence during that cold start, however, and the most enthusiastic effort can grind to a screeching halt.

A word processor gets you over that hurdle by making your initial mistakes trivial and irrelevant. You don't make fewer of them—you just stop caring about the ones you do make because correcting them later will be easy. With the compulsive worrying out of the way, it's likely you'll find your writing voice's natural rhythm.

Overcoming that worry won't happen overnight, even with the most sophisticated word processor. A lifetime of compulsive advice has drilled into your writing conscience the need to organize your thoughts clearly before you write. Some people never get past this. Take Philip Roth's fictional author in *The Ghost Writer,* for example. He writes a sentence every morning, takes a walk, then turns the sentence around before breaking for lunch. Now, if you're getting paid $100 a word or you have a patient boss, that method may work for you. In the real world, however, things have to move faster.

GETTING OUT OF THE STARTING BLOCKS

It's in that real world of professional and business writing that traditional notions about translating thoughts into words can really cripple you. According to Peter Elbow, author of two terrific books on the psychology of writing, the quest for the *perfect first sentence* leads to unrealistically high expectations. Every time you strike a key you are disappointed. What happened to all those clever ideas as they moved from your mind to your fingers? Could they possibly be so poorly preserved they get stale as soon as they hit the air?

> ". . . the quest for the perfect first sentence leads to unrealistically high expectations."

Most likely, those great ideas don't die a natural death. You kill them before they have a chance to see the light of day. Inside all of us, it seems, are two literary figures: a writer and a critic. As soon as we start to write, the critic begins to disapprove of our choice of adjectives, sentence structure, and conclusions. The writer wants to swing into action, but the critic is instantaneously editing every thought, seeking perfection. Nothing happens, or so little happens that it feels as if we'll never complete the assignment. It's all downhill from there.

The way to keep great ideas alive is to just start writing. That's what Elbow recommends: "Make some words, whatever they are, and then grab hold of that line, and reel in as hard as you can." Easier said than done. With a pen and a large yellow pad, or a typewriter, you are haunted by a vision of the major surgery that awaits you if you don't come up with a perfect first draft. Here's how it's described in Strunk and White's classic *Elements of Style:*

[Cut] it to pieces and [fit] the pieces together in a better order. If the work merely needs shortening, a pencil is the most useful tool; but if it needs rearranging, or stirring up, scissors should be brought into play. Do not be afraid to seize whatever you have written and cut it to ribbons. . . .

As good as that advice seems, I could never quite put together that two-pronged approach to less painful writing—start fast and don't look back till you run out of steam; then recklessly revise and rewrite. That is, I couldn't do it until I started using a PC and a word processing program. Those were the tools I needed to put into practice the attitude Strunk and White were suggesting.

In fact, even if my first word processing software had contained nothing more than a delete and an insert feature, it would have been a leap into the 21st century when compared to my electric typewriter and its companion bottle of correction fluid. Then throw in the capacity to move a section of text from one place to another in seconds, or a search-and-replace feature that lets you change the 50 occurrences of "SuperSoap" to "WonderBar" an hour before the board of directors meeting. Thereafter, creating a professional document becomes a lot more like satisfying labor and a lot less like picking lint off a blue wool blazer.

AND WHISTLES AND BELLS TO BOOT

Software writing tools, however, have developed well beyond that simple level. You can hop all over a 100-page document with a few keystrokes, create perfectly balanced columns of text, underline and boldface words on screen, or center any line of text by pressing a key. You can whimsically kill entire unwanted paragraphs and watch the rest of your document close ranks as if the deleted text had never been there. And, finally, you can do all of this to one of your pieces of writing while simultaneously printing out another at 300 or 400 words per minute.

Remember footnotes in college term papers and how you had to plan to make sure you were leaving exactly the right amount of space at the bottom of the page? The word processor I am using to write this article makes footnoting a simple and elegant process. I do the writing and it does the measuring and fitting. Some programs will even generate an index and a table of contents.

"I do the writing and it does the measuring and fitting."

After all that work has been done, a spelling program will check for typographical errors, so you soon learn not to waste time watching for those errors as you work. Punctuation and style programs have also appeared. They make sure you haven't missed a "the the" or a "wOrd," and they even point out commonly misused expressions you *commonly misused* in your report or article.

Separating myth from reality in the marketing-driven computer industry is not always easy, and word processing is no exception. You don't have to throw out all your pens and paper just because a PC is sitting on your desk.

In fact, a word processing program is a computerized writing aid, not a gee-whiz electronic miracle. Many of the currently available word processors are easy to master. All of them can eliminate the more prominent roadblocks that stand between ethereal ideas in your mind and the clear, vigorous expression of those ideas on paper. When you are writing, whatever works best for you is best for you.

Source: C. Spezzano, "Thinking and Writing with a PC," *Business Computing,* June 1984, pp. 67–68.

COMPUTERS AT WORK

A Graphics Master

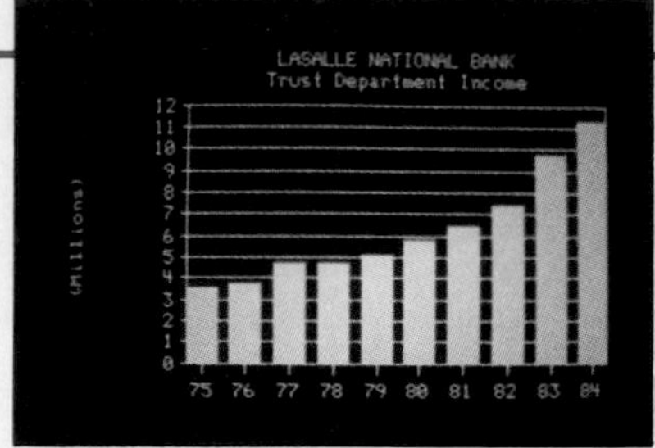

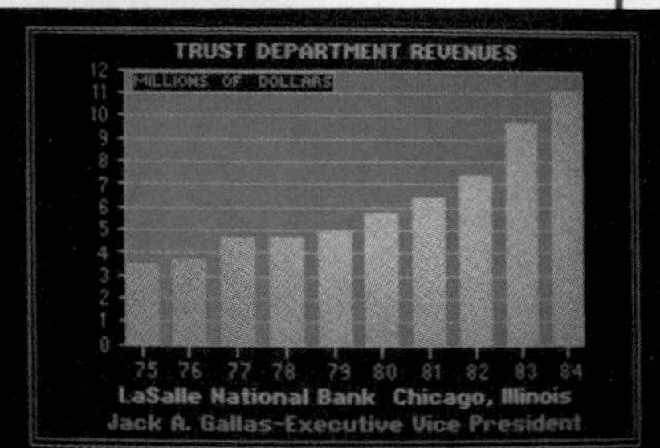

Ray Jacobson, vice-president and auditor for LaSalle National Bank in Chicago, takes his graphics seriously. The seasoned executive regularly uses eight different IBM PC graphics programs to create various charts, diagrams, and signs. He turns them into photographic slides, overhead transparencies, and images on paper. The material invariably finds its way into management reports, employee training classes, a newsletter sent to bank customers, and meetings of the bank's board of directors.

Why eight programs? Jacobson takes pride in making his graphics look as professional as possible. One piece of software offers a wider selection of text fonts; another makes more attractive line charts; another yields better colors. Jacobson mixes and matches capabilities to create artistic-looking material to show to others—in the parlance, presentation graphics.

One of his favorite tools for that purpose is Grafix Partner by Brightbill Roberts of Syracuse, New York. Grafix Partner lets Jacobson take data or a chart produced with Lotus 1-2-3 and gussy it up until it appears just the way he wants it.

From "The New Look of Presentations" by Doran Howitt, *InfoWorld,* December 24, 1984, pp. 28–31. Copyright © 1984 by Popular Computing, Inc., a subsidiary of CW Communications, Inc. Reprinted from InfoWorld, 1060 Marsh Rd., Menlo Park, CA 94025.

Graphic presentation tools, as described in Computers at Work: "A Graphics Master," provide the business professional with an attractive alternative to professional graphics services. Exhibit 15.11 illustrates some of the graphics that can be generated with these end-user tools.

Most presentation graphics tools provide users with a series of menus and prompts with which to create graphic outputs. Exhibit 15.12 illustrates such a dialogue along with the bar chart that is being specified.

Susan Tate's marketing staff could make very good use of a presentation graphics tool. Marketing offers many opportunities for the creative use of business graphics to display information about sales, product, or customer trends, about competitors, and about advertising effectiveness. Susan's marketing staff might even be able to produce some exciting displays that advertise the hardware and software products CompuStore sells!

Report Generation Tools

Report generation tools, not to be confused with the RPG high-level programming language, were the first end-user tools. With the early report generators, developed for mainframes in the mid-1960s, users filled out forms to describe the reports to be printed. These forms were then keypunched and run in a batch mode to produce reports.

Today's report generators are much easier to use. Users can interactively define data files, enter and manipulate data, and produce reports. Many possess quite Englishlike query languages. On page 450, Exhibit 15.13 gives an exam-

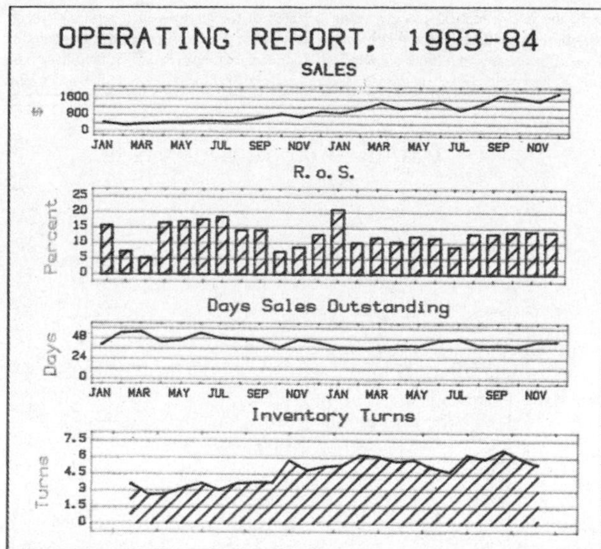

Exhibit 15.11

Graftalk, a popular business graphics package, combines four separate charts on one page to illustrate business activity over time.

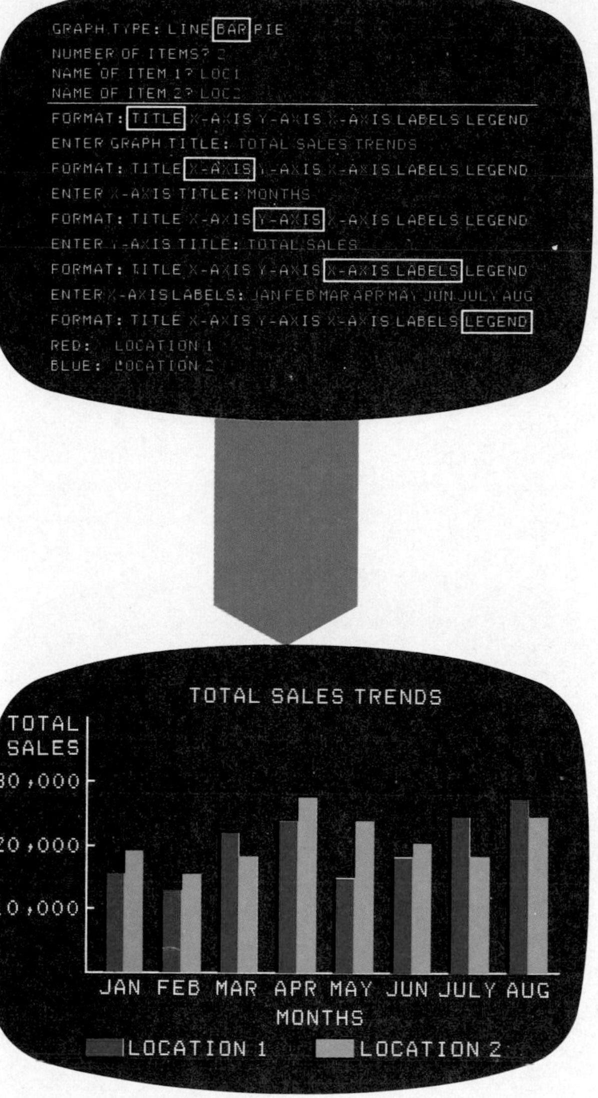

Exhibit 15.12

Most presentation graphics tools provide the user with a series of menus and prompts with which to specify graphics outputs. "LOC1" and "LOC2" are variable names referring to two arrays holding the values to be shown in bar chart form.

ple of the typical dialogue used to generate a report, while Exhibit 15.14 illustrates a sample query into a data file. Computers at Work: "Putting Trains on the Right Track" describes some benefits of using these tools.

Report generation tools typically take the form of user-oriented file management systems and data base management systems, which were described in detail in Chapter 8. These software packages are widely available for most mainframe computer and microcomputer systems.

Given the existence of the needed data files, Susan Tate's marketing staff could use such tools to generate many marketing reports. Some useful reports might be monthly comparisons of product sales for each of the retail stores and month-to-month trends regarding products and customers. An almost limitless variety of inquiries into the data files, such as checking sales during a special promotion, would also be possible.

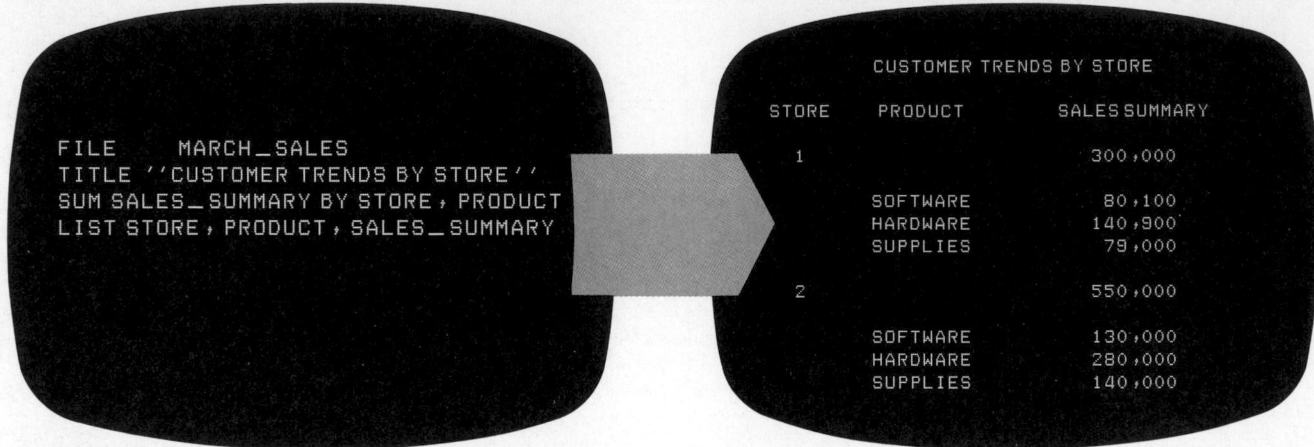

Exhibit 15.13

The dialogue used with most report generation tools is very Englishlike. The data file "March Sales" has already been defined, as have the different stores and products.

SUM AND DISPLAY SALES IN MARCH_SALES
FOR STORE ''1'' AND PRODUCT ''HARDWARE''
MARCH_SALES FOR STORE 1, PRODUCT HARDWARE: 140,900

Exhibit 15.14

The dialogue used for inquiring into a data file is also very Englishlike. This example uses the data file from Exhibit 15.13.

MULTIPURPOSE TOOLS

A current trend with today's end-user computing involves providing a business professional with access to a number of tools at the same time. The idea is to allow a business professional to process a set of data in a variety of ways without having to regularly exit to the operating system and begin a new program.

Why might this be useful? Consider how nice it would be if Susan Tate could build a spreadsheet model using data stored in a data base, produce some charts from the spreadsheet results, and then embed the charts in a report she was preparing. Data would need to be entered only once. Even better, any changes that occurred to data items in the data file would automatically "perk" through the information outputs she had created—the spreadsheet model, the charts, and the report.

COMPUTERS AT WORK

Putting Trains on the Right Track

Accessing the mainframe's data base was the No. 1 usage that Dennis Bailey wanted for his firm's system.

The assistant vice-president of systems for the Missouri-Kansas-Texas Railroad Company, based here and popularly known as "Katy," barely considered micros for his user-oriented system.

"I wanted everybody on the system to have access to the same data base," Bailey explained. "You still can't do that as easily with a micro."

"The way we're doing it, when a user gets a terminal, he or she gets the 1100," he added, referring to the mainframe, a Sperry Corporation "1100/60."

"It would be crazy to build a data base on a micro for each user. And micros just don't have the capacity to do it."

What Bailey did choose was Sperry's Mapper system, a user-programmable package.

The main problem was teaching people to use it, Bailey said. "Being a railroad company, we have employees who have been around here for thirty-five to forty years. It's not easy to take away their pencil and paper."

So, a Mapper coordinating team, made up of three users ("We did not use anyone out of the programming staff," according to Bailey), was set up. "It's supposed to be a user system, so I wanted to see if that was so."

The team's job is to show users how to work the terminal for their own advantage. "The team shows them how to use it. They help install it, they teach them how to do one or two things with it, then they let them play with it for a month or so and then come back to see how they're doing, and then they show them some fine-tuning and more applications," said Bailey.

The system today has about 200 users. Total costs for the 1100/60 system, including hardware, software, and personnel, are about $40,000 a month. And cost savings from the data, from top executives to clerks, already have reduced expenses some $100,000 a month, for a net savings of about $60,000 monthly. A few examples:

The system now rates bills, formerly handled manually with heavy overtime. This saves the waybill department about 400 hours a month, or $4800 at $12 an hour.

In customer accounting, using system displays instead of printouts to work with freight receivables saves 344 hours a month.

In corporate accounting, analyzing vouchers via the report generator saves about 60 hours a month, compared to manual processing of the past.

And in purchasing, handling inventory control now saves 172 hours a month. Also, the system has reduced inventory about $60,000 a year.

Source: " 'Mapper' Puts Trains on Right Track," *Management Information Systems Week,* 7 September, 1983, pp. 20–21.

Software vendors are using two basic approaches to provide such multipurpose tools: **integrated software** and a **software integrator.** We will describe each, and also introduce you to another multipurpose tool, the **desktop organizer.**

Integrated Software

The intent with **integrated software** is to allow users to apply a very similar set of commands to manipulate data without having to enter any data item more than once. The information processing functions most commonly included in integrated software packages are spreadsheets, word processors, business graphics, and data management. Each tool can be displayed in its own window on the CRT screen, and data values can be moved from one window to another.

Exhibit 15.15

Integrated software packages base all tools on one major tool. In the case of Lotus 1–2–3, spreadsheet, graphics, and data management functions all spring from an underlying master spreadsheet.

Adaptation of Figure 1, p. 74. Reprinted by permission of *PC World* from Volume 2, Issue 11, (October 1984) published at 555 De Haro Street, San Francisco, CA 94107.

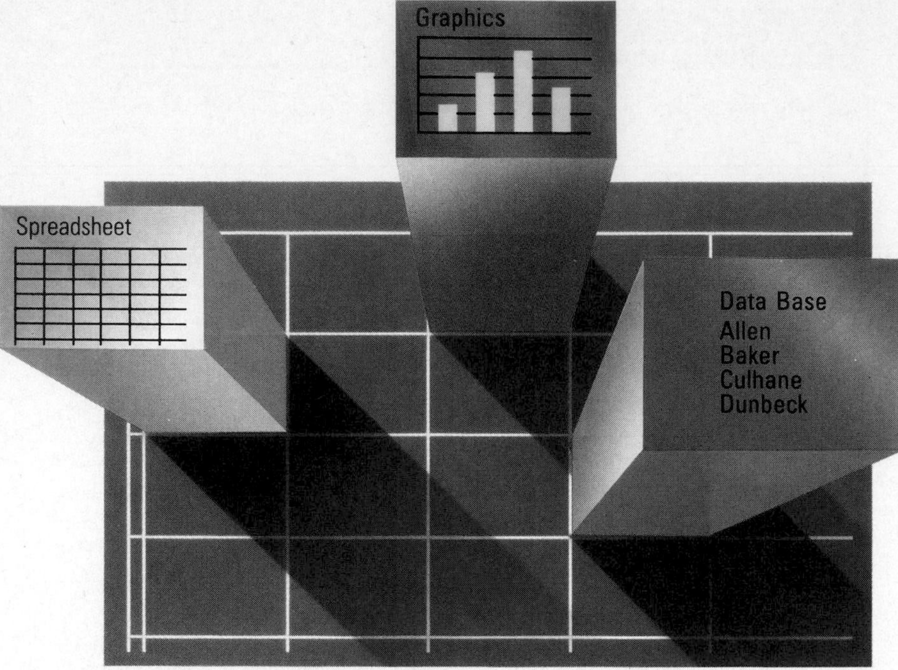

The first successful integrated software package was Lotus 1-2-3, which combines spreadsheet modeling, business graphics, and data management. As shown in Exhibit 15.15, Lotus 1-2-3 uses a master spreadsheet to organize data elements. Two of the newer integrated packages are Symphony and Framework (see Exhibits 15.16 and 15.17). Symphony, which added word processing and communications capabilities to Lotus 1-2-3, is still organized around a master spreadsheet. Framework is organized around the concept of a "frame," which can hold an outline, a spreadsheet, a data base, or other frames.

As all the functions of integrated software must fit within the computer system's primary memory, these functions are generally slower and less capable than those provided with single-purpose software packages. Still, a capa-

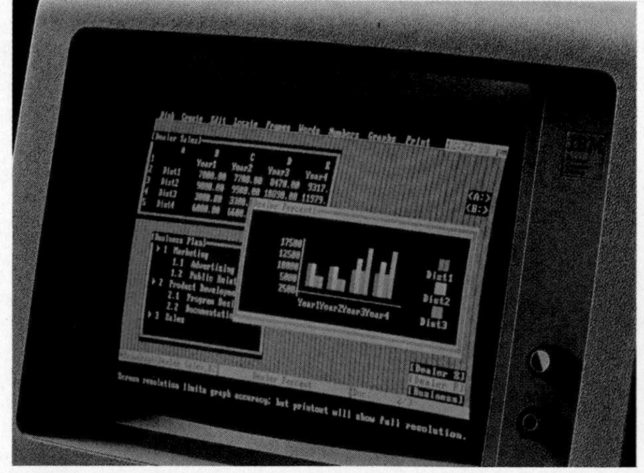

Exhibit 15.16

A display screen from Symphony, an integrated software package.

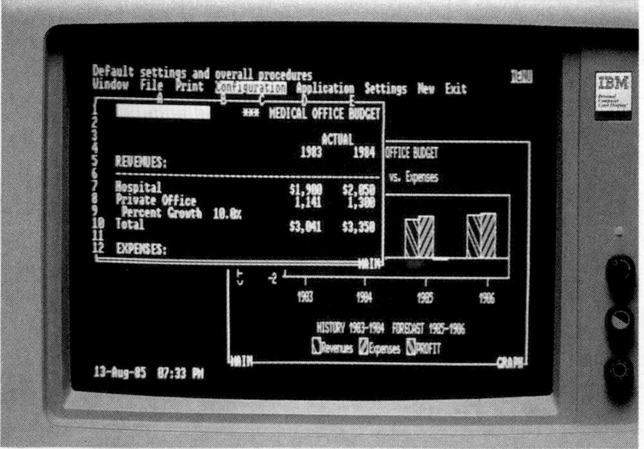

Exhibit 15.17

A display screen from Framework, integrated software organized in "frames" that can contain a spreadsheet, a graph, or an outline of these elements.

bility to easily move data back and forth between different functions is very desirable to a business professional who regularly makes use of these functions.

Some software vendors are taking another approach with integrated software. Rather than placing multiple functions within a package, they are developing "families" of single-function tools that can share data files (see Exhibit 15.18). While this approach does not produce a set of tools as tightly integrated as Lotus, Symphony, and Framework, the individual packages are often faster and more sophisticated.

Software Integrators

The second approach for providing business professionals with a set of multipurpose tools is through a **window manager** that sits between the tools and the operating system. Window managers allow users to execute a number of applications at the same time, to view each application in its own window, to change the size of the windows, and to move data values between the windows.

What distinguishes these system integrators from integrated systems is that the former work with single-purpose tools. Thus, users have the best of both worlds—they can work with powerful single-purpose tools or a favorite tool but still integrate their end-user applications.

Certain system integrators require that the single-purpose tools be modified to run under the system integrator (see Exhibit 15.19, p. 454); others, however, can work with any tool (see Exhibit 15.20, p. 454).

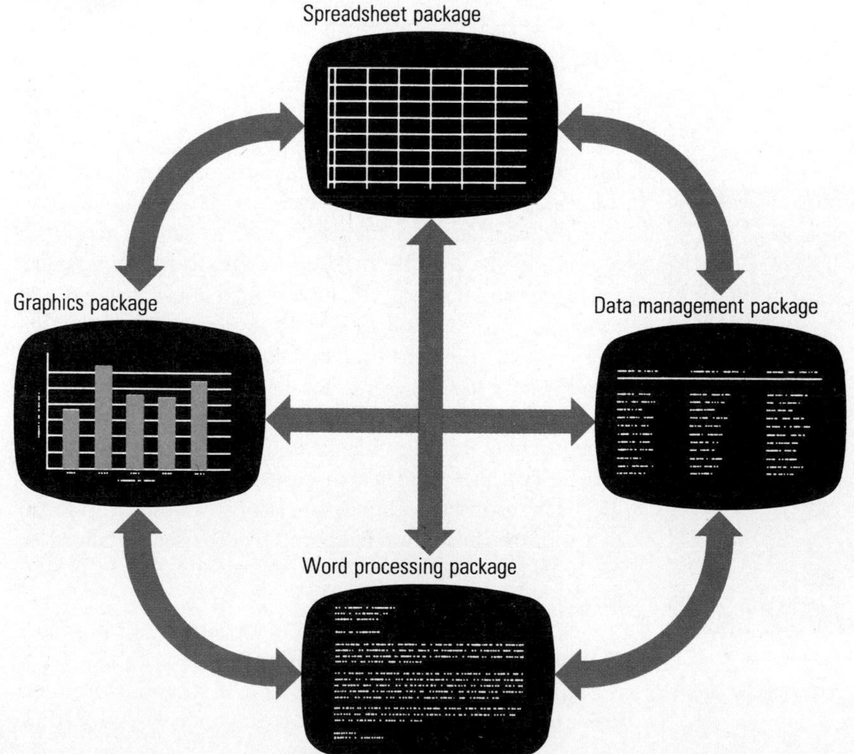

Exhibit 15.18

Rather than offering multiple tools within a single tightly integrated software package, a family of single-purpose packages can provide a user with a loosely integrated set of end-user tools. Each package can read data files created by other family members.

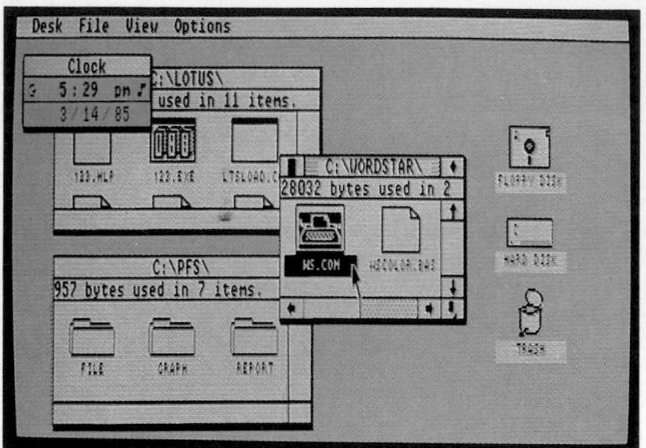

Exhibit 15.19

With some window managers, application software must be specially modified if it is to execute within the operating system.

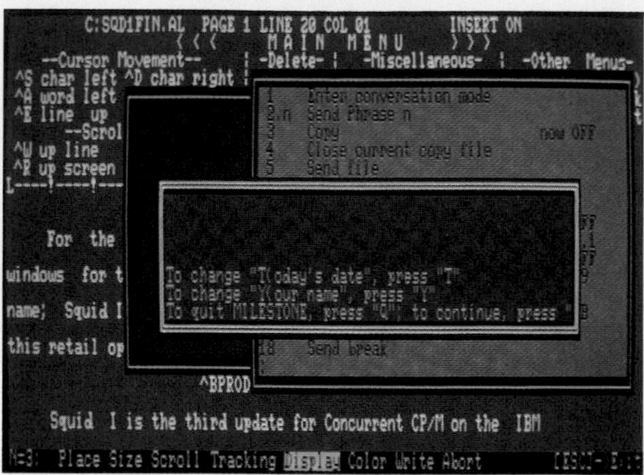

Exhibit 15.20

With other window managers, application software does not have to be modified to execute within the operating system.

Because the technology is relatively new, window managers have not been that successful. Fitting applications into windows strains the speed and capacity of today's microcomputers. They require microcomputer systems with hard disks and large amounts of primary memory, but are still relatively slow. As the technology improves and microcomputers become even more powerful, window managers are likely to achieve the success that was initially predicted for them.

Desktop Organizers

When managers such as Susan Tate begin to spend a large portion of their time working with microcomputer end-user tools, interruptions that take them away from their microcomputers can be frustrating. Often the smaller the interruption, such as making a phone call or writing a memo, the greater the frustration. **Desktop organizers** are integrated packages that allow a business professional to juggle several small tasks without leaving the big tasks that are executing on their microcomputers.

These software packages share a number of traits (see Exhibit 15.21). First, they replace common office tools such as Rolodex files, calendars, notepads, calculators, telephones, and alarm clocks. Second, they stay in the background of other applications, waiting to pop up in a window only when triggered by the user. Finally, they are inexpensive. Many are priced in the $50–$100 range.

Why are desktop organizers becoming so popular? The main reason is that they fill a real need of many business professionals. Desktop organizers handle the little tasks that recur throughout a manager's workday, thus

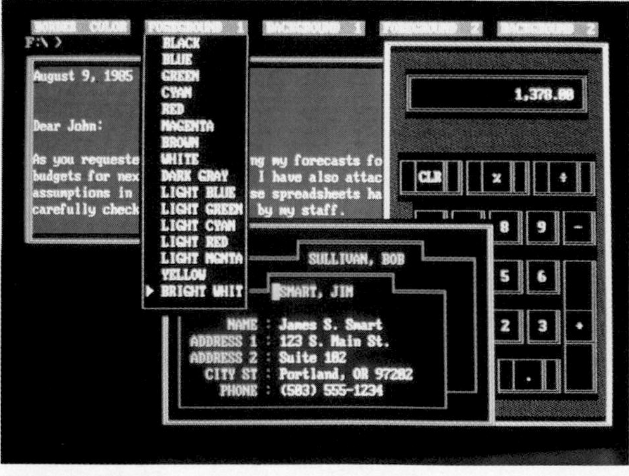

Exhibit 15.21

Desktop organizers can execute a number of useful functions, such as performing calculations and retrieving addresses.

increasing on-the-job productivity. They also keep these tasks and the associated paperwork in one place, rather than scattered all over a manager's desk and office.

Professional Issue

Promoting and Managing End-User Computing

End-user computing can provide numerous benefits to a business. Inappropriate end-user computing, however, can be disruptive and expensive. By actively promoting and managing end-user computing, a firm can increase the benefits it receives from end-user computing and prevent many potential disadvantages.

A good way to manage end-user computing is to set up a facility with end-user tools that is staffed by end-user computing specialists who first train and then support business professionals in their computing efforts. Such a facility is usually termed an **information center** when it is directed toward mainframe end-user computing and a **personal computer support center** when it is directed toward microcomputer end-user computing. We will adopt these terms here.

Information Center

The primary objective of an information center is to give business professionals access to mainframe data bases through mainframe end-user tools. The following services are typically provided:

Access to and training with end-user tools,

Access to terminals,

Assistance in accessing and storing data,

Advice on how particular business problems might best be solved through end-user computing,

Assistance in using end-user tools,

Maintenance of catalogues of available data and previously developed end-user applications.

On the following page, Computers at Work: "Resources for Mid-Sized Applications" describes the successes being achieved with one information center.

Personal Computer Support Center

There are two main objectives in establishing most personal computer support centers: to help business professionals acquire microcomputers for their offices and homes, and to prevent the uncontrolled influx of microcomputers into a business. The first objective is achieved by encouraging business professionals to experiment with and then use microcomputers. The second is achieved by limiting the variety of microcomputer hardware and software being used in a firm. It is difficult for a business to provide its employees with a

COMPUTERS AT WORK

Resources for Mid-Sized Applications

The information center serving the aircraft division of Northrop Corporation, a manufacturing company in Hawthorne, California, that handles mostly government contracts, follows the "traditional" IBM mainframe path.

"Data processing just couldn't meet end-user demand," says Tom McNeill, Northrop's manager for technical systems administration. "Smaller to mid-sized applications weren't getting done, things that users could really do themselves, given the right resources." These tasks included statistical analysis, budgeting, and labor reports.

Northrop's information center, approximately a year old, began as a highly successful pilot program in the engineering department. The pilot program saved the company some $820,000 in applications development, money that would ordinarily have been spent for data processing time, resources, and staff.

Northrop's center now serves about 150 users, a number that McNeill says is growing rapidly.

"Everyone from secretaries to managers, including technical engineers, engineering planners, and finance controllers, uses the center. People love it," McNeill says. "We've got one guy who practically lives here. We find him there late at night. Often, if I call at 6:30 in the morning, he'll answer. The information center is to him what video game arcades are to other people."

McNeill says that one of the biggest uses for the information center is business graphics, a capability data processing didn't have before. Other uses include report generation (a major application for graphics, especially charts), downloading of data from the corporate data base for summary and manipulation, and financial planning and modeling. At the information center, users can also maintain their own data bases, which they update and use for report generation.

Source: A. E. Smith, "Northrop: Resources for Mid-Sized Applications" in "A Concept Comes of Age," *Business Computer Systems,* November 1983, pp. 173–78 and 183–84.

high level of microcomputer support without identifying microcomputer hardware and software products that are recommended by the personal computer support center.

As with information centers, personal computer support centers typically offer a wide range of services:

Helping employees select and purchase microcomputer hardware and software,

Arranging discount purchase programs with microcomputer vendors,

Training employees in the use of microcomputers,

Keeping employees informed about new microcomputer products,

Consulting with employees on their microcomputer applications,

Helping employees access and download mainframe data bases,

Maintaining catalogues of all developed microcomputer applications,

Repairing microcomputer hardware,

Providing supplies and replacement parts.

Computers at Work: "The Computer Store at the Office" describes the types of activities performed in one personal computer support center.

The Computer Store at the Office

The eighteenth-story window next to Judith Larson's shoulder frames a panoramic view up the Charles River toward Cambridge and the Harvard campus, but the young banker doesn't take her eyes off the IBM Personal Computer monitor as she cranks in data on a VisiCalc template. "I'm just doing a 'snapshot' of how our thirty-five local retail branches stood at the end of December," she explains.

Her concentration on this financial data is hardly unique for a staff member of the First National Bank of Boston. What is unusual is her location: the personal computing center established by the bank in its red granite headquarters in Boston's financial district. Larson is using one of five microcomputers designed to introduce employees to the power of disks and chips.

The bank's Professional Computing Center gives employees a chance to "test drive" PCs, Apples, and TRS–80s, and to sample a variety of software packages, all under the tutelage of experienced personnel from the firm's Information Systems and Services Division. As John McCarthy, assistant vice-president of the division, puts it, "We're just fighting for rationality in a crazy, everybody-needs-a-PC world."

When a bank employee comes to the center for advice about using computers, one of several consultants begins by determining the person's computing needs. "It may be that what someone wants to do—word processing, for example—can be done better on the Wang system existing throughout the bank," McCarthy points out, "or perhaps our mainframe programs are more appropriate."

If a PC can do the desired job, however, the employee is coached on using the machine and the necessary programs. Once the employee is familiar with the hardware and software, he or she can borrow one of the center's computers. "We also have a loan program," McCarthy adds, "so employees can take a PC to their office here or in the branches for a couple of days or home on the weekends."

FROM LEARNING TO OWNING

The bank's encouraging employees to use microcomputers is not limited to a few days with a borrowed machine, however. First National has established discount buying arrangements for hardware and software with some Boston-area vendors, and the center's staff will make the arrangements for purchases by departments or individual employees. In this way employees can take advantage of the bank's discounts, which range from 7 to 20 percent, when they buy their own computers.

MATCHING COMPUTERS TO TASKS

The center's consultants also evaluate new software for suitability in the banking industry. Spreadsheet programs—which permit a quick look at repetitive or unique "what if" financial issues—are an ideal tool for banking, McCarthy notes.

"Our bank has historically financed creative projects such as Hollywood movies, record industry deals, and cable television facilities," he states. "Each of these calls for a unique set of financial variables, and if a loan officer can run these proposals through VisiCalc, for example, it increases that person's efficiency or allows him or her to ask more creative questions of the project. One loan officer recently told me he spent twelve hours on a VisiCalc model for a project that used to take him five weeks."

As the center has gained popularity within the bank, McCarthy's staff has added other computer capabilities. Two of the newest components are a stand-alone color graphics system and a link via two terminals to the bank's mainframe computers. At present the center's PCs are not being used as terminals for the mainframes, as McCarthy explains.

"There are serious security issues to be resolved and substantial upfront costs to install access ports. In most instances the host programs would need to be rewritten somewhat to allow that communication. We don't exclude mainframe access, but we're waiting for a good project proposal to come along to justify it."

The telecommunications capability of the PCs recently came in handy, however, according to Ed Care, one of the center's systems analysts. "Our Human Resources Department recently used the PC to scan the resumes of upcoming graduates from the Harvard Business School. They just hooked up to Harvard's data base, reviewed the resumes, and decided who they wanted to invite for interviews."

From "The Computer Store at the Office" by J. T. Johnson. Reprinted by permission of *PC World* from Volume 1, Issue 2, published at 555 De Haro Street, San Francisco, CA 94107.

Personal computer support centers take a variety of forms. Some firms with information centers simply add these activities to those already given the information center staff; others separate the two facilities for managing end-user computing. Some personal computer support centers in large businesses have staffs of twenty or more people; others are staffed by one or two people. Some small firms, like CompuStore, make these duties a part-time assignment for a single employee.

How American Express Saves with PC XTs

Do you remember what he looks like? The tough cop, kind-eyed and fedora-clad, lurks behind curtains at operas and airports. "Don't leave home without them!" he exhorts, meaning the traveler's checks backed by the pillar of the financial community, American Express. Can the company that promotes the tough but kind image itself maintain a similar stance toward its own internal operations, cutting costs while providing high-quality services to both employees and customers?

At Amex's Human Resource Systems Department in the New York corporate headquarters, managers are cutting costs and maintaining a lean and security-conscious profile by using PCs to decentralize record keeping and report writing. The strategy is reducing the unit's reliance on the corporate mainframe for generating reports.

"Our general philosophy is that we're decentralizing many functions," says Walter Whitt, vice-president of headquarter personnel and employee relations. "A major reason for going to the personal computer is cost. Within our department, on an annual basis we'll reduce our operating costs by about $120,000 to $150,000. With a personal computer-based information retrieval package, we move from a complicated search-writing language on a mainframe to a simpler language. That move enables our personnel generalists to access data on the PC, which gives us our second major benefit."

Human Resource's central strategy involves linking an already existing personnel information system on several IBM and DEC mainframes to three IBM PC XTs equipped with PC/Focus, a data base manager and application development tool. The Focus package by Information Builders, Inc. (New York, N.Y.), offers a screen manager and report writer, enabling personnel managers to develop selected employee data bases on hard disk or to write queries that extract personnel files from the mainframe. This package lets you manipulate and execute large chunks of data, as well as reports, on the XT. Focus files are encrypted to ensure limited and secure access.

Corporate Human Resource Systems, Whitt's department, shares responsibility for keeping track of 25,000 American Express employee files with 10 personnel offices around the country. Amex's subsidiaries maintain separate personnel records. Whitt's department has had the additional task of developing microcomputing applications: among them, a master file on about 1000 corporate headquarter employees. This strategy, Whitt says, "reduces operating costs because we're no longer running those searches on our central processing unit."

Indeed, all current data on corporate headquarter employees is compiled on the XT's hard disk, which authorized personnel management can access. Details of salary, job classification, eligibility for bonuses, benefits, selected medical information, and demographics are sorted and extracted using PC/Focus's data base management capabilities.

Personnel management can then print out any number of customized reports on benefits, compensation, recruitment, EEO (Equal Employment Opportunity), training, and management development. Amex uses such reports to track employee talent, determine salary and benefits structures, and forecast the effects of proposed policy changes on employee populations.

"We're doing almost all our master file searches with PC/Focus," says Claire Lichack, manager of human resource systems operations in the corporate division. She is responsible for researching and implementing new PC applications in the personnel area.

The corporate historical files will be converted to the XT next year. "We have an XT in the medical department now and one in employee relations," she says. "All these applications are being created with PC/Focus. It seems to be the answer for us."

The answer, though, grew out of a series of frustrations and uncontained costs. Amex's personnel divisions, Lichack says, had been tasked in the early 1980s with producing literally hundreds of reports each month. They used the company's IBM mainframe and a batch report generator package that had been installed in 1978.

"In 1982 we were experiencing very large costs to create these reports," Lichack says. "Part of the problem was that people in personnel weren't that familiar with the report generator on the mainframe. They were using inefficient coding techniques, and we didn't have the most efficient methods in place for doing batch searches. So we started to look into the possibility of getting another report generator. That was like chasing the Holy Grail.

"At the time we were making decisions about mainframe alternatives, we were also deciding to look into personal computers to see if they would be used for information retrieval. And that was the only thing we were looking at," Lichack notes. "If PCs could do information retrieval, we could really cut costs."

Her search for the right PC and software proved less quixotic than the mainframe software search. "We were basing the choice of personal computers on the software—software and communications," she says. "I wasn't about to buy a machine and then go looking around for software to run on it. I wanted to find the software first, then base the hardware decision on that."

Her strategy very quickly narrowed the search to IBM PCs and Apples, both of which run a variety of data base management software. Lichack believes she was lucky that there were so few significant players in the market—and in Amex corporate headquarters.

"In house we had Apples and IBM PCs," Lichack recalls. "I didn't have to look at TRS-80s or Ataris or anything else. And I knew we wanted to get to the mainframe data." That immediately imposed constraints on her choices.

"There were a lot of claims at the time by various vendors that they had an Apple link to the IBM mainframe," Lichack says. "I checked into a few of these claims, but nothing proved out." She decided to recommend the IBM PC at a time, "when it wasn't clear that IBM would be the winner." Amex did not form a company-wide policy on personal computers until late 1983, when it chose IBM PCs.

Lichack's decision was a fortuitous one. Soon after the decision, Information Builders announced PC/Focus for the IBM XT. "PC/Focus seemed to be the answer to our problem because it was very similar to mainframe Focus. It offered similar coding and most of the features of the mainframe package." To Lichack, PC/Focus was a bargain at $1595 per package. It was capable of writing report queries and executing them on the XT or using Amex's existing personnel file on the mainframe.

Walter Whitt saw an immediate benefit. The prospect of separate files, and easier access to files on the XT, meant more direct and responsible reporting. "Now someone such as myself, my secretary, or one of my managers in personnel can ask the computer for data when normally we'd have to go to Claire [Lichack] and her folks. About five people [out of an 11-person human resource department] use it now as compared to one person in the past."

"I've done demos with executives who've never touched a computer before and they can produce simple reports [using PC/Focus] right away," Lichack reports. The software provides a relational data base; a single, straight-path data base is also available.

You can transfer Focus files to other software such as Lotus. "If I have Lotus, I can take the data and put it in a Lotus 1-2-3 or Symphony format," Lichack says. "If you have software that has DIF [data interchange format] files, then you can take the data from your PC/Focus report, format it in DIF and feed it into those files. There are a lot of options."

When Lichack wants to sort data, she enters a request on Focus. "A window appears with field names. The request can tell the system, for example, how you want it to sort a report—alphabetically or by some other measure. Once the sorting strategies are designated, Focus will extract the data requested and produce a report.

Lichack and Whitt say that applications are being developed on PCs to track employee assistance programs and a special employee "expressline"—a PC-based communication system for employees and managers. Lichack will further consolidate corporate employee records by incorporating historical files on the XT next year.

Amex as a whole is still tied to networked systems—nine major information processing centers and six worldwide data and timesharing networks. The number of PCs is small when compared with the 17,000 terminals Amex uses internally.

"But in our own department," says Whitt, "we've begun to revolutionize our process. By operating on our own PC system, we've reduced costs."

Source: A. Emmett, "How American Express Saves with PC XTs," *Business Computing,* December 1984, pp. 23–26.

SUMMARY

Business computing reached a crisis in the mid-1970s as the *visible* and *invisible backlogs* of new information systems projects grew very large. Two advances in computer technology, very-high-level languages and microcomputers, provided many business professionals with *end-user tools* that enabled them to develop some of their own computer applications. In this way the era of end-user computing began.

With *end-user computing,* business professionals take on the systems development activities traditionally performed by systems analysts and programmers. The systems design and implementation stages disappear, while the systems analysis, acquisition, and maintenance stages occur more or less at the same time.

End-user computing has a number of benefits. Information systems are developed quickly and inexpensively. The application backlog is reduced. Better information systems often result. Finally, users are more apt to use an information system that they have developed. However, there are also some potential hazards. Many users are unable to determine their information needs. Many are insensitive to the need for information systems testing and controls. "Reinventing the wheel" can occur. Users unable to access needed data stored on a firm's computer systems gain little from end-user computing. Finally, end-user computing can promote the creation of private collections of data.

End-user computing must be well managed. Appropriate tools must be made available. Users must be trained in their use. Moreover, users must be able to access data already stored on a firm's computer systems.

All end-user tools provide commands that describe information outputs, describe and manipulate data, and describe processing operations. These tools are available on both mainframes and microcomputers. Generally, mainframe end-user tools can handle larger, more complex problems than microcomputer end-user tools.

Business professionals access and use end-user tools in three major ways: through time-sharing with an *in-house mainframe,* through time-sharing with an *external mainframe,* and through a microcomputer. The cost of these alternatives can vary widely, depending on the price of a tool and the number of people using it. One way to lower the cost of providing microcomputer end-user tools to a large number of users is to negotiate a *site license* from a software vendor.

Much end-user computing on microcomputers begins as *stand-alone use,* with business professionals creating private data bases. An early complaint with stand-alone end-user computing is the time these users must spend entering data, especially when the data exist in a mainframe data base or on someone else's microcomputer.

Sharing data files through local area networks is one way to solve the problem of users having to reenter data. The other solution involves establishing links between a firm's microcomputers and its mainframes. The easiest type of link is using a microcomputer as an online CRT. Another fairly simple link uses a diskette to transfer the data. A third strategy is to use special software that translates mainframe data files to a form usable by the microcomputer end-user tool. A final strategy makes use of an end-user tool available in both mainframe and microcomputer versions.

There are four main types of end-user tools: *financial analysis tools, text generation tools, presentation graphics tools,* and *report generation tools.*

The financial analysis tools include *electronic spreadsheets* and *financial modeling systems.* With electronic spreadsheets, models are built by entering text, numbers, and formulas into cells. These cell *contents* are the operations that produce the cell *values,* or information outputs. Some types of financial analysis are too complicated for spreadsheet modeling. Financial modeling systems can handle these more sophisticated modeling problems.

The text generation tools include *word processors* and *thoughtware.* All word processing software provide for text editing, text formatting, document management, and document printing. Other word processors provide more advanced features, and some software vendors provide "add-on" packages such as *spelling checkers, thesaurus programs, style checkers,* and *mail-merge* programs. Thoughtware comes in two basic forms: outlining software and free-form data base software.

Presentation graphics tools enable users to produce tables, charts, and pictures for public display.

Report generation tools enable users to define data files, to enter and manipulate data, to produce reports, and to make inquiries into a data file.

A current trend with today's end-user tools is to provide a business professional with access to a number of tools at the same time. There are two basic approaches for providing multipurpose tools: *integrated software* and *software integrators.*

With integrated software, users apply similar sets of commands to manipulate data with a variety of end-user tools without having to enter any data item more than once. Each tool can be displayed in its own window on the CRT screen, and data values can be moved from one window to another. While integrated software is very useful, the tools provided with these packages are generally slower and less powerful than those of single-purpose software packages.

With software integrators, a *window manager* that sits between single-purpose end-user tools and the operating system allows users to execute a number of applications at the same time, to view each application in its own window, to change the size of the windows, and to move data values between the windows. Fitting a number of applications into windows does strain the speed and capacity of today's microcomputers. Thus, software integrators tend to require hard disks and a large amount of primary memory, and they are still relatively slow.

A recently introduced integrated software package is the *desktop organizer.* This package provides the business professional with a number of tools to handle the small tasks that occur throughout a manager's workday, replacing Rolodex files, calendars, notepads, calculators, telephones, and alarm clocks. One of the best features of desktop organizers is that they stay in the background of other applications, popping up only when triggered by the user.

A very good way to manage end-user computing is to provide a facility with end-user tools that is staffed by end-user computing specialists to train and support business professionals in end-user computing. Such a facility is usually termed an *information center* when it is directed toward mainframe end-user computing and a *personal computer support center* when it is directed toward microcomputer end-user computing.

In the next part of the text, we will look at some of the ways information systems are affecting our society and at the computer industry.

REVIEW QUESTIONS

1. Briefly explain the causes and significance of the business computing crisis of the mid-1970s.
2. How has computer technology provided solutions to the business computing crisis? What hazards are involved in end-user computing?
3. The Apex Corporation is deciding on the best way to meet the end-user computing needs of its business professionals. At present, the firm is undecided between emphasizing mainframe or microcomputer end-user tools. What issues should be considered in making the final choice?
4. Why would information systems managers dread, or even resist, mainframe information requests from stand-alone end-users in their firm? How may mainframe-microcomputer links be formed?
5. Briefly describe the four most common types of end-user computing tools in use today.
6. The Cyclops Corporation desires to allow its executives to utilize a number of computing tools at the same time. What approaches might the firm consider?
7. Briefly describe the concept of integrated software. What advantages does such an approach offer?
8. What is a software integrator? How does this approach differ from integrated systems?
9. Briefly explain the concept of desktop organizers. Why have such programs become popular?
10. What two approaches may a firm adopt to manage end-user computing? How are the two distinguished?
11. Briefly describe the purpose and services of an information center.
12. What purposes and services are typically associated with a personal computer support center?

PART VI COMPUTERS AND SOCIETY

CHAPTER 16

The Information Age Society

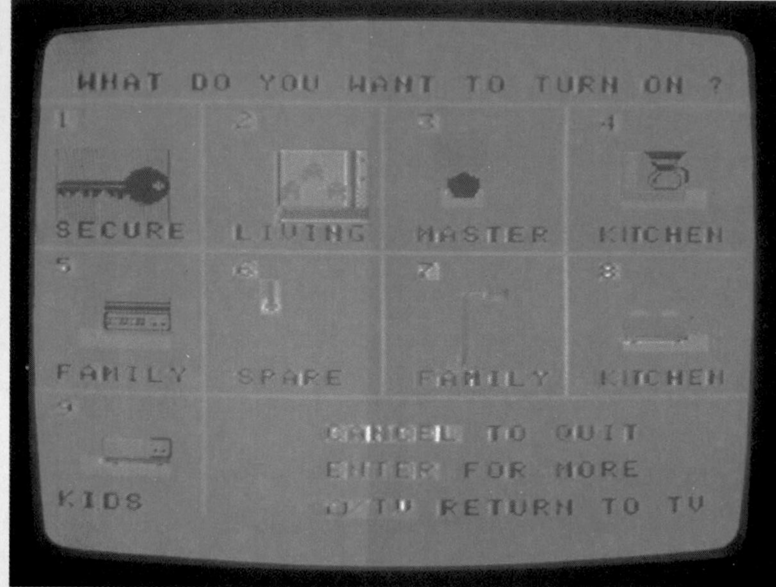

COMPUTERS AT WORK

Welcome to Xanadu

Tour Xanadu, a prototype home of the future, and sample the computerized home of tomorrow.

Imagine yourself in a house that has a brain—a house you can talk to, a house where every room adjusts to your changing moods, a house that is also a servant, counselor, and friend to every member of your family. A science-fiction tale of the far future? Not at all. The idea of the "intelligent house" has been around for years, and today's "architronics"—the application of computer technology to architecture—is transforming that idea into reality.

Prototype "homes of the future" are open to the public at several locations. In them you will find many applications of electronics to family living that may become commonplace within a few years. You will also see gadgets and gimmicks that are likely to remain costly luxuries for decades, and others that will probably be outdated in a few months. No model home can accurately depict the "best" or even the "most probable" lifestyle of the future. There are too many uncertainties—too many unrecognized problems and undiscovered opportunities ahead for anyone to build the definitive House of Tomorrow today.

But you can explore alternative lifestyles—compare different house designs and computer applications to find out which combinations of old and new, traditional and modern, flexible and solid, inner-focused and community-minded, high tech and handmade, automatic and labor-intensive best match your tastes, ambitions, and interests.

The Xanadu House, located just outside Orlando, Florida, is designed to showcase some of the options that architronics will add to family and home life in the 1990s. Although conceived as the luxury home of a wealthy family in the mid-1990s, Xanadu's various computer-enhanced security, telecommunications, energy monitoring, entertainment, and climate control systems are all adaptable for use in far smaller and less expensive houses.

The electronic equipment in these houses is more elaborate than can be easily found today. But talking computers, a self-selecting telecommunications center—an "electronic hearth"—and the various computer-activated sensors and control systems that regulate energy, lighting, etc., are all plausible extensions of existing technologies, and in many cases can be bought or custom-built today.

Source: R. Mason, "A Day at Xanadu," *The Futurist,* February 1984, pp. 17–18.

The day when computers control our homes, supervising tasks ranging from heating and security to our diet, exercise, and work habits, is still in the future. But computers are causing and will continue to cause vast changes in our lives. So far, we have focused on the changes computers have made in the world of business. Here we want to explore some of the broader changes computers are causing and will continue to cause in our society. In this chapter, you will learn to do the following:

1. Give an overview of the computer technologies now available for use in the office.
2. Discuss how computers are increasing the efficiency of modern factories through computer-aided manufacturing, design, and engineering.
3. Describe the number and kinds of telecommunication services now available.
4. Explain the information services now or soon available in the home.
5. Describe how, through telecommuting, the work place of the future for many may be the home.

OFFICE AUTOMATION

Since the advent of the early typewriters in the 1850s, machines have played an increasingly important role in the offices of business, industry, and government. In the 1900s the Morse telegraph, Edison's dictating machine, and the Bell telephone were added. More recent additions were adding machines, copiers, tape recorders, and electric typewriters.

In the 1960s organizations began to use the newly developed large central computers, primarily for accounting. A decade later, the remote terminal allowed data to be entered and received from a large computer, which was often far away. In the 1970s and early 1980s the microcomputer burst on the scene. It began to significantly change the complexion of the office in terms of how work is done and the social patterns of the employees.

Why this increase in automation? To understand, let's take a closer look at office work. Here people read, think, write, and communicate. Proposals are considered; money is collected and spent; and organizations are managed. The key ingredient in these activities is information. More and more companies need and value any tool or technique that will increase their efficiency in gathering, storing, retrieving, manipulating, and distributing information.

This is one aspect of the need for automation. Another is the fact that information workers, who are primarily office workers, are becoming an increasingly large part of the work force. Today there are over 60 million white-collar workers, including professional and technical workers as well as clerical and sales people. The majority of these knowledge workers are represented in the Information Sector, which in 1980 was about half of the total work force in the United States. On the following page, Exhibit 16.1 shows the composition of this group and its projected growth in the rest of this century. Supplying these workers the tools and information they need to work efficiently is a crucial task for all successful organizations.

Major companies such as AT&T, IBM, and Wang have declared that their futures are based on the assumption that this move toward "office automation" is only beginning. They predict that the "office of the future" will be the cornerstone of a large industry devoted to supplying increased automation to a

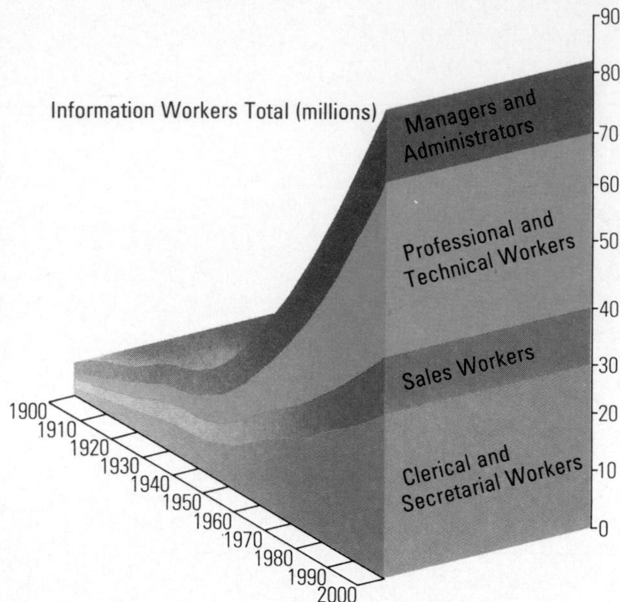

Exhibit 16.1
Information Workers' Growth
The demand for information workers has increased dramatically since the 1950s. Most white-collar workers work in office environments. Their productivity is critical to an information age society.

growing number of white-collar workers. As we will see, the information age office will provide computing tools that simplify and streamline traditional office work. These tools include word processing, electronic mail, voice mail, facsimile, teleconferencing, and other forms of administrative support. The automated office will also routinely include tools for end-user computing. These tools will allow workers to effectively perform complex tasks that might not be attempted without computer support.

Word Processing

Word processing, a computerized way of creating, editing, and filing memos, letters, and reports, is really not much more complicated than using a typewriter. Word processing is available either in dedicated systems or as a software package for personal computers. The real advantage of word processing comes from the ability to correct errors and make even major revisions with just a few keystrokes. In the past, a major proposal or sensitive document might have had to be completely retyped several times as each level of management made changes and corrections. With word processing, only the changes need to be rekeyed, and then the revised document can be printed quickly and cleanly. These documents can then be electronically filed on disk and easily retrieved.

In addition, most word processing packages offer online dictionaries that check spelling and hyphenation. Other software packages offer the option of mail merge. **Mail merge** is a general term for packages that allow users to maintain a mailing list of names and addresses and certain other information, such as hobbies or birth date. These names and addresses can be subdivided into groups, such as all customers who live in Boston. Or they can be reordered by zip code instead of last name. The list can be printed out by itself, or individual names and addresses can be incorporated into a form letter to create hundreds of customized letters in the time that might have been devoted to writing and editing the original form letter. In addition, software packages that check grammar are available and still undergoing development.

The net result is that the cumbersome, expensive process of preparing written documents is streamlined. With word processing, information workers are able to concentrate on information and not the mechanics of producing that information.

Electronic Mail

The time saved by preparing a document with word processing can easily be lost while that same document snakes its way through interoffice mail. These delays are even more frustrating when a number of workers have workstations supplied with a microcomputer and software packages like word processing.

Exhibit 16.2
Electronic Mail

These workers need and soon want the convenience of exchanging documents electronically. This is the idea behind electronic mail and local area networks, described in more detail in Chapter 9, "Data Communications." This technology also allows workers to access electronic "file folders" of information created and stored in different locations without physically moving either themselves or the files.

In addition to exchanging documents, local area networks can be used to send memos or letters. It is estimated that 70 percent of all business phone calls are not completed. The other person is out of town, in a meeting, or on another line. The result is "telephone tag," a series of short messages left with secretaries because the original message is too complex to easily explain. Much of this wasted effort could be replaced by electronic mail, where detailed messages can be left in an electronic mailbox (see Exhibit 16.2).

When the other person has time to review the accumulated messages, he or she can call them up on the CRT screen and take appropriate action. This could include sending a reply by electronic mail. Electronic mail is particularly attractive to organizations with offices across the United States or around the world. Here time zone differences can shrink the number of office hours you have in common with another party.

Voice Mail

A recent alternative to typing messages on a terminal and sending them by electronic mail is voice mail. As with an answering machine, a message is created by speaking into a phone terminal. Unlike an answering machine, which records a vocal message, **voice mail** uses a digitized form of the spoken message. This message can be stored on a disk and delivered at a later time to one or more phones. For example, you may want a message to be available to ten other parties at 2 P.M. local time, yet you want to leave the message at your convenience—at 6 A.M. This is possible with a feature called "store and forward." You will have to record the message only one time and then will enter a distribution list of phone numbers. Voice mail will do the rest.

An advanced feature is the ability to annotate a voice message. That is, assume you got a message from someone who works for you. You could add your comment to the "end" of this message and send both messages to your boss, who is on vacation in Bermuda. The boss could retrieve the voice mail at a convenient time and hear both the original message and your reaction. In addition, the boss could also retrieve voice mail from a different phone. Assume, for example, the boss decides to go to dinner without returning to the hotel to check for messages. A single call to the phone number left with you could forward the day's voice mail to the pay phone at the restaurant.

Both electronic and voice mail allow messages to be stamped for time and date of origin. In addition, these systems can verify that a party has received the message and record the time the message was received.

Facsimile

Facsimile (FAX) machines can be used to transmit nonelectronic documents electronically. In essence, these machines transform a photocopy of the document into a digitized form. The result can then be sent over telecommunication paths, just like other electronic mail. The FAX machine at the other end translates the digitized code back into an image. FAX machines can be used to send charts and photographs, as well as text or data. They can even be used to send signatures, which would be especially useful when authorization needs to be verified. In high-volume operations, a letter-sized document can be sent in under a minute and would cost around forty cents. In addition, FAX transmission allows certain security measures, like encryption, the "scrambling" of electronic data to prevent electronic "eavesdropping." Because of these advantages FAX transmission will replace regular and electronic mail for certain types of business communication.

Teleconferencing

Word processing, electronic mail, voice mail, and facsimile are all methods of one-way communication between users separated by time or distance. These tools will satisfy a surprisingly large percentage of white-collar workers' communication needs. But what about those occasions when two or more individuals in widely separated locations need two-way communication?

A telephone conference call is one obvious solution. But when visual cues are also important, **teleconferencing,** or electronic meetings, are a better solution. Video images of the activities at each location are sent over telecommunication paths, along with verbal messages. Full video conferencing includes transmission of full-motion video images and audio of both parties in "real time," meaning as the events are happening. This closely simulates what would take place if all parties were in the same room. Exhibit 16.3 shows a typical teleconferencing layout.

Atlantic Richfield has a private video teleconferencing system, ARCOVision, linking their offices in seven cities. It provides full-motion color video with life-size projection. The system cost $17 million to develop, but ARCO executives believe it will pay for itself within two years. Only a portion of the

Exhibit 16.3
A Teleconferencing Facility

payback will come from reduced travel expenses. ARCO feels that the ability to "meet" as a group and arrive at faster decisions gives them an important competitive edge.

Full video conferencing is, at this time, still very expensive and available only at certain locations. For example, AT&T offers video conferencing facilities in many major cities. To use this service, parties have to go to their local AT&T "video booths." Expensive and somewhat inconvenient as this service is, it is often cheaper and less time-consuming than flying several executives across country for a comparatively simple meeting.

Video conferencing is also offered by some hotel chains, like Holiday Inn. These facilities can be used to assemble large groups of people at various locations around the country to hear, for example, a real-time presentation by a company president. Television cameras set up to scan the audience allow questions and answers to be submitted from the floor and transmitted simultaneously to all viewing locations. Incidentally, several professional conferences are now offering sessions through teleconferencing, but with limited success. Apparently the sessions are just one attraction of these conferences. Others include opportunities for hands-on sampling of new products and techniques, visits with professional colleagues, and the sights and sounds of a different city.

Administrative Support

The automated office will also include a number of electronic tools to help manage time and resources. Among these tools will be electronic calendars. As one looks at what managerial and professional people do during a workday, it becomes clear that a significant percentage of their time is spent in scheduled meetings of two, ten, or even more people. The personal calendar is a necessary tool for clarifying time commitments vs. "open" hours or days. These activities can also be monitored through electronic calendars. There are a variety of formats, including the month-at-a-glance type.

Some of these calendars are available for personal computers as part of software packages called "desktop organizers." These packages were discussed in Chapter 15, "Application Development Without Programmers." Others are part of more sophisticated software packages used with mainframe computers or in local area networks. An advantage of the electronic calendars found in these more sophisticated systems is that they can be called up by a project manager who needs to schedule a meeting of several people. Software routines are available to highlight the "open" times common to all these people. The project manager can then "pencil" in the next meeting on each person's calendar.

Additional support items include online company telephone directories. These packages offer the ability to search the directory by name, department, or function. Tickler files, to remind the person of certain deadlines, are also available.

End-User Computing

In addition to computer support of routine tasks, many workers will also have access to the tools of end-user computing. These tools, discussed in more detail in Chapter 15, "Application Development Without Programmers," will include electronic spreadsheets, word processing packages, and graphics packages. This type of support is quite readily available on personal microcomputers. The trend, however, is to link microcomputers through a local area network within the automated office, allowing various data files and graphical output to be easily retrieved by any authorized user in the office.

In addition, many managers will have the ability to access data bases and other files held in the company's main computer. With this ability they can customize a decision support system that will supplement the information systems offered by the data processing center. These personalized decision support systems will allow them to make queries or ad hoc reports without the delay of making a formal request to the data processing department. Data downloaded from the main data base can also be used in electronic spreadsheets to speed and improve forecasting decisions.

Exhibit 16.4

Offices of the future will need many types of electronic equipment to conduct the business of creating, storing, manipulating, and exchanging information in innovative new ways.

Movement to the Information Age Office

The tools of word processing, electronic and voice mail, teleconferencing, administrative support, and end-user computing, if implemented successfully, will change the office significantly. The office of the future will be heavily equipped with electronic machines (see Exhibit 16.4). But even more importantly, how the office conducts its business of creating, storing, manipulating, and exchanging information will change.

For example, let's take a look at an insurance company before office automation. In this type of office, work focuses on processing transactions of new policies, sending out bills, collecting and crediting payments, and processing claims. For efficiency, these offices are generally set up as a production line (see Exhibit 16.5). Each workstation handles a particular type of transaction or is involved in checking the accuracy of entries or calculations. These activities could be input logging, validation, journal updating, exceptions, reconciliation, posting, and output logging.

Tasks are fragmented and standardized. This assembly-line approach is quite efficient in processing large volumes of transactions in a routine fashion. A customer inquiry can, however, cause major disruptions. Trying to locate the customer file in the "assembly line" is often close to impossible. Another disadvantage is that the currentness of the information is always less than up-to-date, because the file can only be updated after it has been through the entire "assembly line." Any type of reports generated by a management infor-

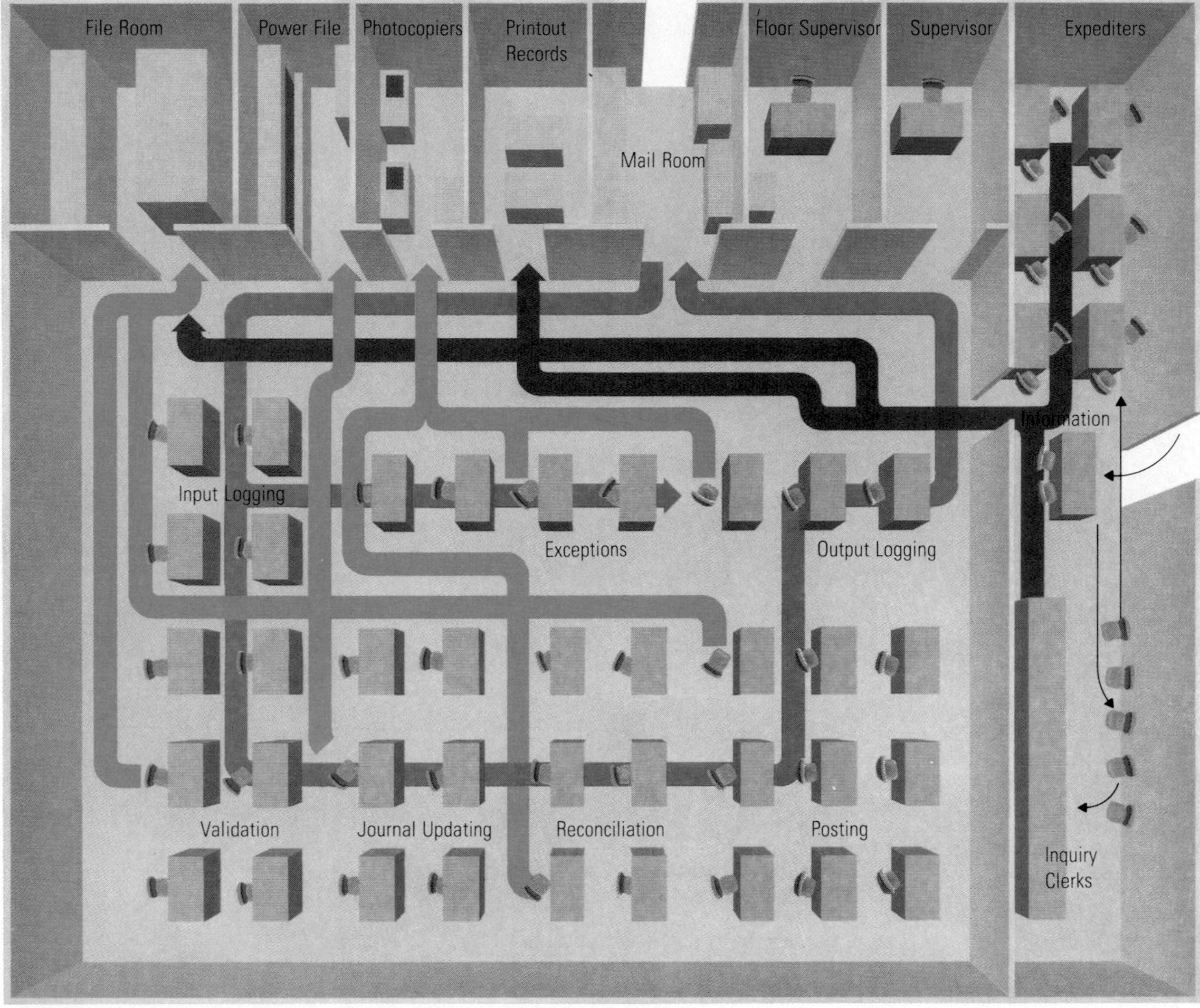

Exhibit 16.5

The industrial office—essentially a production line—has been favored for operations handling a large number of transactions, as in this claims-adjustment department of an insurance company. Tasks are fragmented and standardized. Documents are carried from the mail room to the beginning of the production line and eventually emerge at the other end; the flow is indicated by the color arrows. Successive groups of clerks carry out incremental steps in the processing of a claim; in general they leave their desks only to retrieve files or to examine computer printouts. If clients make inquiries, they are dealt with by clerks who may be able in time to answer a specific question but can seldom follow through to solve a problem. The work is usually dull. The flow of information is slow and the service is poor.

From "The Mechanization of Office Work" by Vincent E. Giuliano. Copyright © 1982 by Scientific American, Inc. All rights reserved.

mation system would have to be compiled periodically. It would be too much effort to assemble the data manually, and the data processing staff would need months to prepare programs to handle special requests.

Automating the office can result in an "Information-Age Office" (see Exhibit 16.6 on page 472). Each adjuster would have a computer workstation connected electronically to the host computer, which would provide ready access to customer files. Alternatively, the workstations could be personal

Exhibit 16.6

The information age office exploits new technology to preserve the values of the preindustrial office while handling a large volume of complex information. The drawing shows an information age claims-adjustment department. Each adjuster occupies a workstation, which is linked (color lines) to a computer that maintains and continuously updates all client records. Each adjuster can therefore operate as an account manager, handling all operations for a few clients rather than one repetitive operation for a large number of clients. Necessary actions can be taken immediately. Forms are updated and letters are written at the same workstation that gives access to stored data, and the forms and letters can be printed automatically. The same facilities are available to adjusters visiting a client's home or working in one of the company's field offices. The work is more interesting, service to clients is improved, and costs are reduced.

From "The Mechanization of Office Work" by Vincent E. Giuliano. Copyright © 1982 by Scientific American, Inc. All rights reserved.

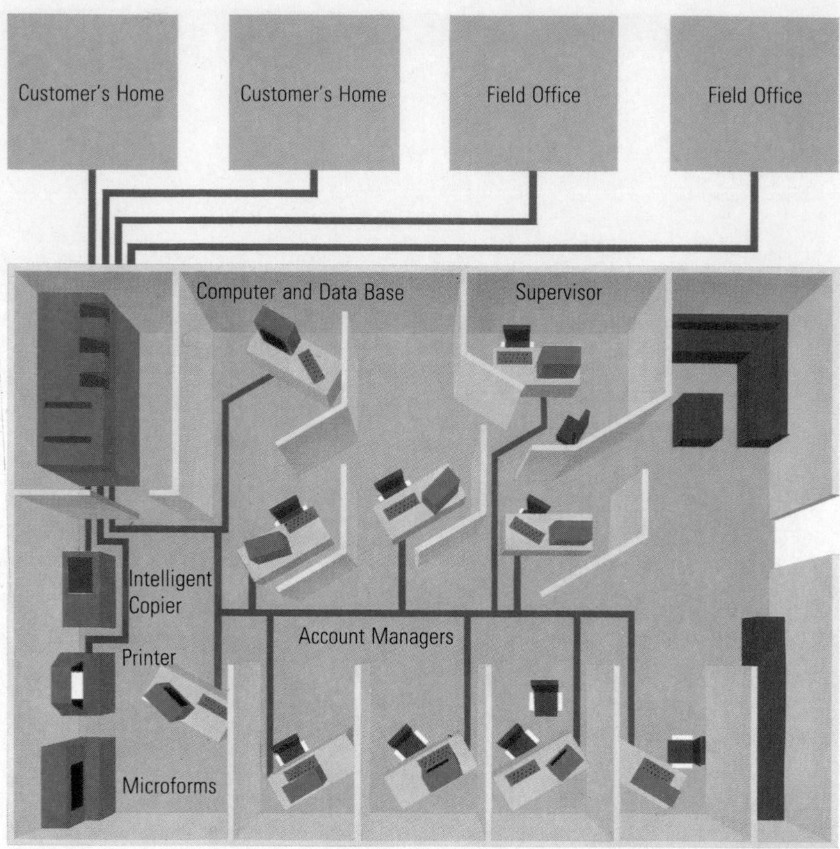

microcomputers, which are interconnected by a local area network and also connected to a central host computer.

The important point is that the adjuster can process the claims of a few clients and update their records as necessary. The adjuster is responsible for all aspects of a few client's records, as opposed to doing a few tasks on the records of many customers. In this way the client records are very timely, since there is no "work-in-progress."

Inquiries are handled quite easily, since the data are online electronically and a data base retrieval facility has been provided. Ad hoc queries by managers can draw upon the same data base without any manual manipulating or rekeying of the basic data. Software routines can be used to extract the appropriate data from the data base, which then can be used as input to various decision support systems.

FACTORY AUTOMATION

Office automation has been closely paralleled by movements to automate the factory. In the smokestack industries of steel, machine tools, textiles, and tires, especially, the use of advances in computer and machine technologies has been important in competing against companies that control costs by using the cheaper labor of Asian countries. Factory automation includes computer-aided manufacturing, computer-aided design, and computer-aided engineering.

Computer-Aided Manufacturing

Computer-aided manufacturing (CAM) uses computers to control the machines used in manufacturing. Computer-based factory automation began in the 1950s with the numerically controlled or N/C tools. These lathes and milling, drilling, and boring machines were controlled by punched paper tapes, similar to the music rolls used to control old player pianos. Today the same types of machines are controlled by microcomputer software instructions.

Exhibit 16.7 shows an example of a **flexible manufacturing system.** Here a set of machine tools are used to produce a variety of metal parts automatically. Each machine is driven by instructions from its individual microcomputer. In turn, each microcomputer is connected in a hierarchy to a minicomputer, which also controls the conveyor belt. The minicomputer determines the overall sequence of operations to be performed in tooling a partic-

Exhibit 16.7

The flexible manufacturing system is an automated set of programmable machine tools for metalworking. The machines are controlled by a hierarchy of computers and are linked by a conveyor that carries workpieces from one piece to the next. The minicomputer determines the overall sequence of operations to be carried out on each workpiece. When the workpiece reaches a machine, the minicomputer also directs the machine to select a cutting tool and "downloads" a program into a smaller microcomputer that controls the cutting path of the tool. Flexible manufacturing systems have now been built that can run for hours without intervention. Parts to be machined are loaded at the entry to the system during the first shift, and the system operates throughout the second and third shifts. Setup times are so reduced that such a system may be able to manufacture 100 randomly selected rotational parts in 72 hours.

From "The Mechanization of Design and Manufacturing" by Thomas G. Gunn. Copyright © 1982 by Scientific American, Inc. All rights reserved.

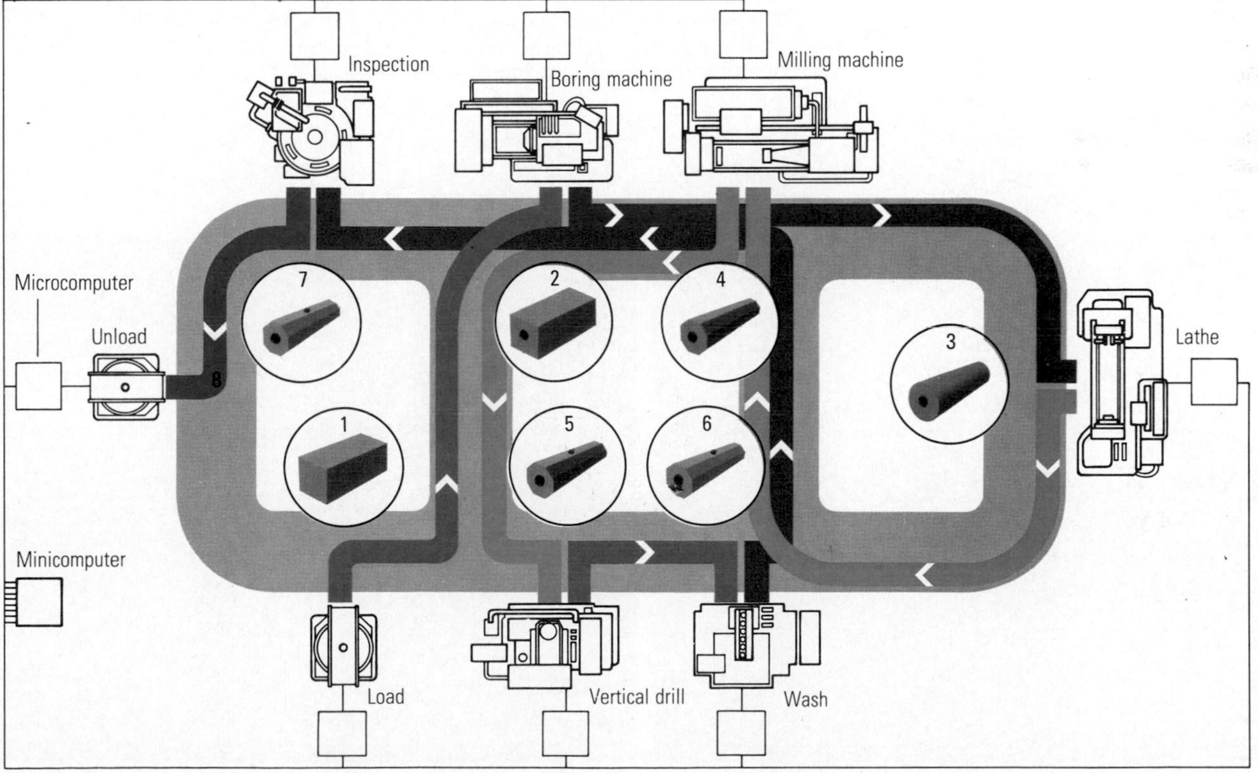

ular piece. As the computer-controlled conveyor belt delivers each piece to a particular machine, the minicomputer downloads a program into the microcomputer that controls that tool. Ordering the machines to produce a different type of part is as simple as changing the programs downloaded into each microcomputer. Flexible manufacturing systems have been built that can run for hours without human intervention, manufacturing a wide variety of parts.

Another type of computer programmable machine is called a robot. When the word *robot* is used most people think of something like R2D2 in *Star Wars*. But real robots are much more primitive. In their simplest form, **robots** are any mechanical devices that can be programmed to perform useful tasks involving manipulation and/or mobility. The two major types of robots used in industry today are materials handling machines and industrial robots.

In the 1970s computer science technology was applied to materials handling machines. Automatic storage and retrieval systems were programmed to transfer pallets of materials to or from storage racks or bins. For example, a part needed on the assembly line would be identified by part number. The computer would search its data base to determine the part's location. A computer-generated command would then shuttle the materials-handling machine to the correct storage location, where it would retrieve the needed part and deliver it to the assembly line.

An industrial robot is a device that can be programmed to move some gripper or tool through space to accomplish a useful industrial task. Human operators can use a variety of methods to teach robots to perform certain repetitive tasks. These include leading the robot through the desired positions by using a teaching box, or physically moving the robot's arm through the required motions, or designing software programs that control the robot's actions (see Exhibit 16.8).

This simple procedure is adequate for performing a surprising number of industrial tasks, such as spray painting, loading and unloading machine tools

Exhibit 16.8
Industrial Robots

A variety of methods can be used to teach robots to perform specific tasks (left). The lighted control panel monitors the robots in this auto assembly plant (right).

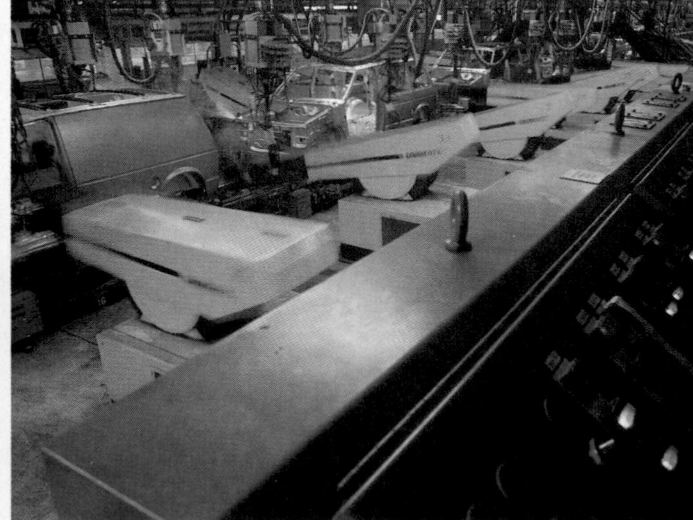

and presses, and performing a wide variety of materials-handling tasks. Robots have proved to be especially useful in simple, repetitive tasks like arc welding automobile bodies. For human workers, arc welding is a hot, dirty, unpleasant job requiring heavy protective clothing as shelter from showers of hot sparks and choking smoke. Typically, a human welder cannot keep a torch on the work more than 30 percent of the time. But a robot welder can keep its torch on the work 90 percent of the time, with only brief breaks required to move materials into position. Thus, even though the robot cannot weld any faster than a human, it can turn out about three times as much work.

The great majority of industrial tasks are still, however, beyond the capacities of current robot technology. Tasks are either too complex and unstructured, or they depend on the ability to see, feel, and adapt to changing circumstances.

Computer-Aided Design

Computer-aided design (CAD) is the use of a computer graphics terminal in product design. Designers are no longer limited to drawings of the top, side, and front views of a design, which were so laborously prepared by draftsmen using the manual tools of T-squares, compasses, pens, and pencils.

In fact, a designer using combinations of menus and light pens can easily generate these same views quickly on a computer display screen. In addition, the designer can rotate the part design on the computer screen along any axis, can zoom in close to see details, or can back off to see the whole object. With a few keystrokes, the designer can quickly and effortlessly change the scale of any drawing. Or a sequence of commands can divide the design into various segments or parts. If this overall design is to mesh with other parts to form a larger assemblage, those parts can be added to the design at the appropriate places. Each design image on the screen can be easily changed and then stored. When needed, a perfect set of engineering drawings can be printed by a plotter.

These engineering drawings are essential to producing the detailed programs that control each machine in a flexible manufacturing system. Efficiency would improve if these instructions could be generated as a by-product of the computerized design process. Once a design was finalized, algorithms could translate that design into programming instructions for each of the machines needed to manufacture the newly designed product. This coordination of computer-aided design and manufacturing, called CAD/CAM, is currently being developed.

Computer-Aided Engineering

CAD/CAM provides a very sophisticated way of seeing various views of a design and then generating appropriate engineering drawings and machine instructions. **Computer-aided engineering (CAE)** allows designers and engineers to use computers to test their designs. How, for example, will an airplane wing withstand the stress of flying at six hundred miles per hour? How will the metal react to the significant variations of temperature found when flying in the cold of 30,000 feet or the heat close to the surface of the desert?

Before CAE the primary way to test designs was to build a prototype and subject it to these conditions. With CAE, the computer is used to simulate mechanical stress conditions, temperature fluctuations, and so on. General Motors has used CAE for many of their auto part designs. They feel that the on-screen testing of a part has worked well and saved them significant amounts of time and money. They feel this computer process gives them a good idea of what a part is going to weigh, how strong and stiff it will be, and how well it will perform. As they state, CAE lets them fix parts before the car is even built.

Movement to the Information Age Factory

While individual robots can make some contribution to the increased productivity of a manufacturing plant, significant gains can only come when the many activities of a factory can be coordinated to respond to continually changing product demand. This will require the development of a factory information system.

Let's first look at a simple example of how this could be applied to the task of painting cars (see Exhibit 16.9). This assembly line uses a series of robots to paint the sides and roofs of a variety of car models. The management question becomes how to program these robots when the car models and appropriate colors change in an unpredictable pattern. Each of the robots has a machine controller, which could be a microcomputer, that uses software instructions to direct when the robot is to paint, what color is to be used, and what car model paint routine is to be used.

At the start of the production line, a model-recognition sensor reads identification codes, such as bar codes on the car itself. This information is sent to the main computer, which checks the data base to determine the car model and body style. The car model and body style, such as two-door or convertible, determine the painting routine. Information about car model and body style is then compared to the plant schedule showing how many cars of that model and body type are to be blue, green, red, and so on versus how many cars have already been painted in each color so far this day or week. Based on this comparison, the main computer sends instructions to the appropriate robots.

This integrated system, combined with local area networks and other telecommunication links, allows the plant to remain very flexible. For example, assume market research has just received a study showing consumer's color preference for Model X has shifted from green to red. This information could be programmed into the plant schedule, and the paint assembly line could be modified quite easily.

Another major aspect of the modern factory is the overall production planning. This planning drives the master production schedule, which in turn establishes the conditions for materials requirement planning. This is a complex task, but an example may show why information in general, and the factory information system specifically, is the key to the factory of the future.

Materials requirement planning (MRP) uses the computer to schedule purchases and deliveries of the parts needed to meet the master production schedule. The goal is to make certain materials are available when needed without diverting company funds to excess inventory and warehousing costs. The back-scheduling algorithm is a relatively simple way of performing this task. The finished product is broken down into its component parts, such as six shelves, four vertical supports, twenty-four shelf supports, twenty-four bolts, and so on. These parts can be further divided into those that can be purchased from outside vendors and those that are to be produced in-house. A back

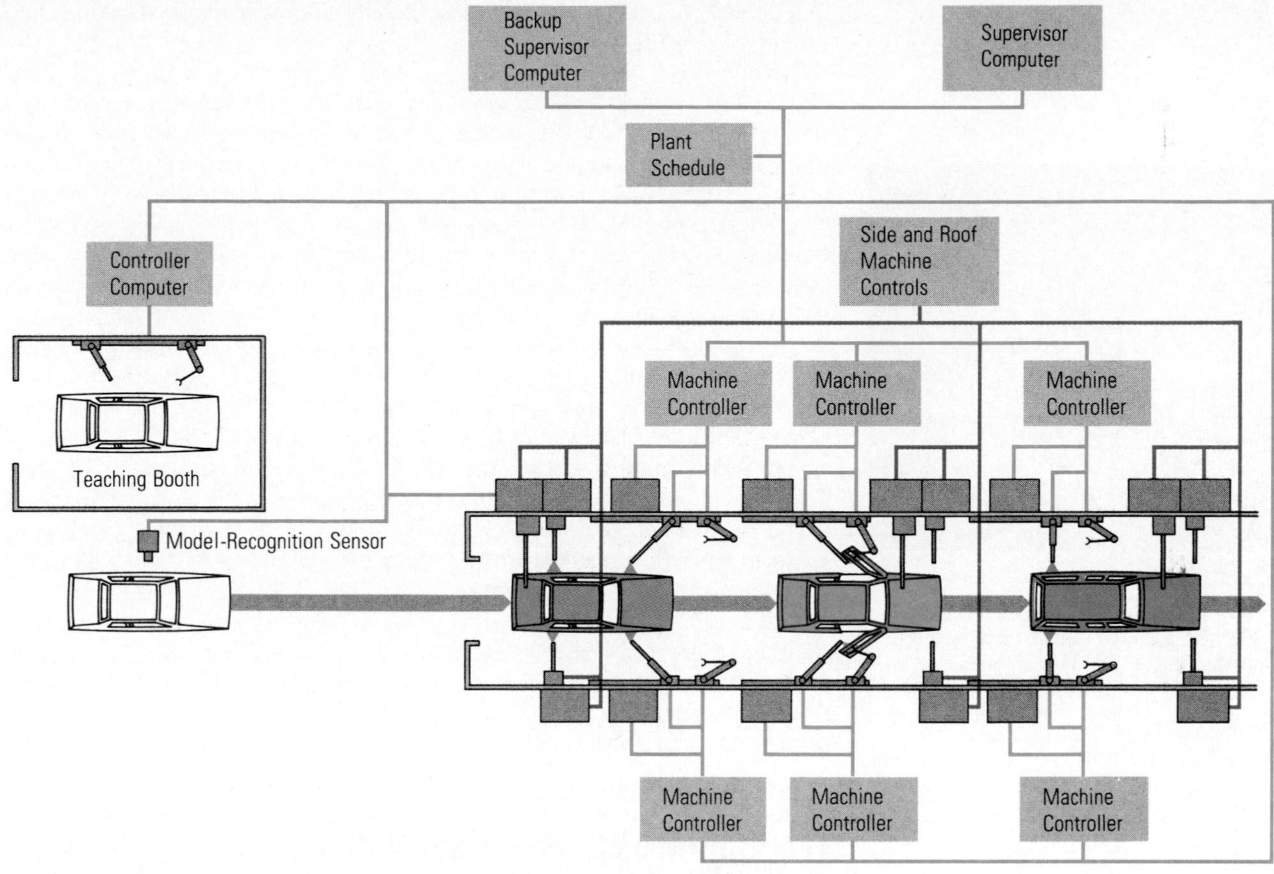

Exhibit 16.9

The total mechanization of a new system for the spray painting of the bodies of cars and light trucks makes it possible to remove all human workers from a particularly onerous industrial task. This diagram shows the control hierarchy for the Numerically Controlled Paint System, which has been developed over the past seven years by the General Motors Corporation; the system has recently been installed at the GM assembly plant in Doraville, Georgia. The present system consists of three pairs of automatic, fixed-stroke, roof and side sprayers of a type already in wide use for such painting operations, five pairs of numerically controlled paint machines (four pairs equipped with door-opening devices), and an offline teaching booth that houses another numerically controlled painter with its associated door opener. (The number of painting stations is expected to vary from plant to plant; one system currently installed has eighteen of the new machines.) The numerically controlled painter is a seven-axis device, hydraulically driven and servomechanically controlled. Its function is to paint all external body surfaces and various internal surfaces not covered by the roof and side sprayers. The machine's reach enables it to paint bodies of all sizes, ranging from subcompacts to full-size sedans, station wagons, and pickup trucks. The painter's companion, the door opener, has two servocontrolled axes and one pneumatic axis. The supervisor computer tracks each car through the painting booth and sends the correct path data to each machine controller at the proper time. A body-recognition system identifies each body as it enters the painting booth. The recorded information is sent to the supervisor computer and is checked against the plant schedule to determine the car's color and other options. In order to "teach" the painter a new routine, a worker in the offline teaching booth grasps a handle attached to the end of the teaching painter's arm and leads the spray guns through the appropriate paint paths, recording positions along the way and signaling "on" and "off" points. The resulting data are then stored in the system's computer.

From "The Mechanization of Work" by Eli Ginzberg. Copyright © 1982 by Scientific American, Inc. All rights reserved.

schedule is projected for each subpart, and the appropriate purchase and shop orders are given.

While this calculation may seem straightforward for a simple product, imagine the nightmare of fast, accurate materials requirement planning for a product with 10,000 parts. Then imagine the complication of daily adjustments to the production schedule. If production needs to jump from 10,000 to 20,000 units overnight, can the right number of parts be made available? Without a computer, these calculations and adjustments would be physically impossible. But this computerization needs to be supported by a good factory information system, which would supply accurate, timely information on inventory levels and required manufacturing lead times.

Exhibit 16.10

A technician monitors dishwasher production from a computer console at a refurbished General Electric plant in Louisville. The production line can easily be reprogrammed to make any of fifteen dishwasher models.

The factory of the future will be a computer- and information-intensive facility with a highly skilled work force. At the heart of the factory will be a computer-integrated manufacturing system that will coordinate product design, planning, and manufacturing in a way that will maximize efficiency.

In the Japanese vision, the factory of the future will be made up of glass-enclosed, air-conditioned, sound-protected worker areas, and workers will spend much of their time at computer terminals. In many ways, the work environment will become more like that of the typical office. There will still be noisy, dangerous processes, but these will be taken over by computer-controlled machines and robots. Factory workers will need fewer manual and craft skills and more technical and analytical skills. This shift in the nature of factory work will mean a further shift in the proportion of blue-collar and white-collar workers. As shown in Exhibit 16.10, the factory of the future already exists in this country and should become more common in the future.

TELECOMMUNICATION SERVICES

Many aspects of the office and factory of the future—from electronic and voice mail to teleconferencing and corporate changes to plant production schedules—will depend on the availability of sophisticated telecommunication services. This will, in turn, require a revolution in the way telecommunication services are provided in this country and around the world. In the last ten years, significant regulatory and technological changes have helped make these dreams real. In the rest of this section, we want to look first at these changes and then at the resulting data networks and information utilities now available to business and home users.

Regulatory Changes

The commercial use of communication services like the telegraph and the telephone have long been regulated by the Federal Communications Commission (FCC). Companies the FCC has authorized to provide certain types of communication services to the general public in this country are called **common carriers.** In the past, common carriers have included AT&T, GTE, and Western Union. In return for meeting regulations designed to protect the public, these companies were, in essence, allowed to operate as monopolies.

During the last fifteen years, a variety of government actions have introduced major changes to the concept of a regulated monopoly in this country. Starting in 1968, the Caterfone decision allowed nonregulated companies to provide devices that could be connected to the AT&T telephone network. This paved the way for the development and use of modems.

In the early 1970s, noncommon carriers were authorized to provide terrestrial (land) communication services that competed directly with AT&T. Companies like MCI began to provide long-distance voice phone service. Later MCI and Southern Pacific Railroad (SPRINT) each provided special communication lines designed to send data.

COMSAT was organized as a quasi-regulated company to provide the specialized services associated with launching and maintaining communication satellites. In the early 1970s, the FCC determined that any company should be able to own and operate domestic communication satellites. This ruling encouraged RCA, Hughes Aircraft Company, Western Union, and SBC to get into the satellite communication business. SBC, the Satellite Business Corporation, was a joint venture of Aetna, COMSAT, and IBM, but COMSAT dropped out in 1984.

In 1984 the breakup of AT&T was finalized. One of the major implications of this ruling is that competition in the communication field has intensified. Equally important, AT&T, which had been limited to providing only communication services, was now free to enter other businesses. AT&T decided to aggressively pursue many of the lucrative segments of the computer market. In fact, AT&T states that their long-distance telephone network is the largest computer system in the world. Given this expertise and the growing importance of hardware and software in telecommunications, this is a logical move.

Technological Advances

Three technological advances have played a major role in improving telecommunication services. First are the advances in telecommunications media. As discussed in Chapter 9, "Data Communications," the move from copper phone lines to microwave, satellite, and optical fibers has significantly increased the bandwidth or carrying capacity of telecommunication paths. For example, standard voice-grade lines used in the telephone network can move data at a rate of hundreds of words per second. A satellite link, in contrast, provides the capability of transmitting hundreds of thousands, if not millions, of words per second.

A second advance has been made in the ability to digitize voice, photographs, television pictures, images, and graphs, in addition to data. That is, each type of format can be translated to a bit format and then later retranslated to the original format. This allows a single telecommunications network to serve all these needs, as opposed to requiring a separate type of network to communicate voice, facsimile, video, and so on.

The last major technological advancement has been the computer itself. Great strides have been made in increasing hardware and software performance, while lowering cost and decreasing size. This has led to the computer's use in all aspects of telecommunications.

Data Networks

Organizations need a way to communicate data between headquarters and branch offices that is effective and can be cost justified. Initially, these data networks were based on the telephone network provided by AT&T. This was

Exhibit 16.11
***The Wall Street Journal's* Satellite Network**

The Wall Street Journal is an example of an organization that is using a satellite telecommunications network to distribute information. Besides the satellite, the network is made up of transmitting and receiving earth stations around the United States. The newspaper's editorial staff in New York selects, edits, and processes the business news and information to be printed that day. This information is then transmitted via satellite to regional printing plants in the United States. Laser technology is used there to convert the electronic signals into printing plates. This system allows the newspaper to centralize its primary information processing and geographically disperse the printing and distribution of that information.

Reproduced by permission of *The Wall Street Journal*.

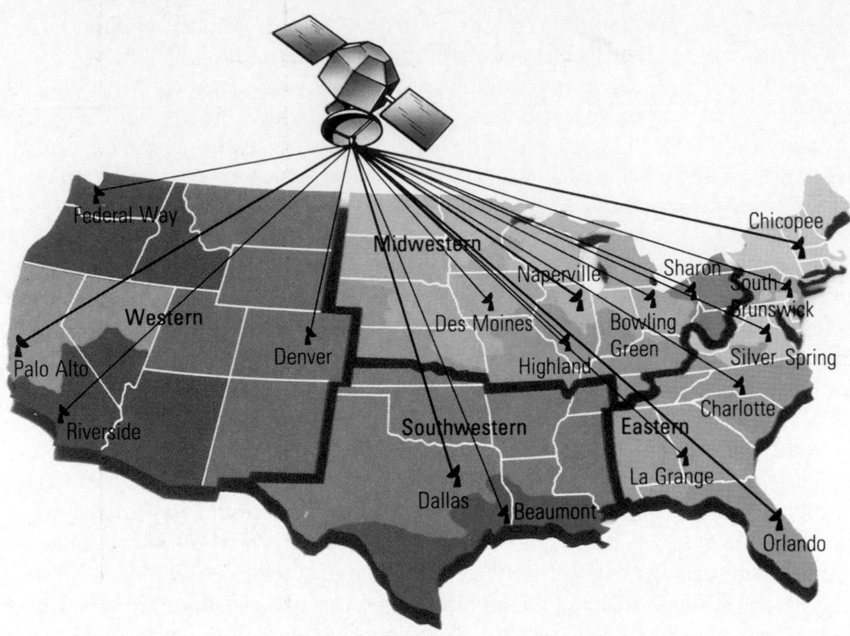

often an expensive option, since it involved lengthy long-distance telephone calls between company computers. Also, the telephone lines were often busy. Organizations that needed to transmit large volumes of data or sensitive data often decided to lease a set of conditioned lines from AT&T for their exclusive use. These private data networks took on many different forms, as satellites and microwave links became available (see Exhibit 16.11).

Public data networks were formed to meet the needs of organizations for whom private data networks were not feasible. These data networks, like GTE's Telenet and Tymshare's Tymnet, are classified as **value-added networks (VANs).**

To understand what this means, let's first understand what common carriers like AT&T have provided. They have offered a telephone network for voice communication that crisscrosses the United States and connects to other networks around the world. Through modems, this network can also be used for data communication. VANs like Telenet have leased a set of communication lines from AT&T to form a data network that covers selected areas of the country. VANs have then added the computer services needed to provide the capability of electronic and voice mail, information retrieval services, timesharing and distributed data processing (DDP).

In other words, AT&T has provided the electronic highways across the country. The VANs have leased many of these highways and provided the "trucks" that travel these electronic highways, carrying many different types of goods (data, messages, video). As an individual or organization, you only have to pay for the services that you use, as opposed to having to build your own roads or pay for the full cost of leased lines that are not fully used.

Information Utilities

Some very resourceful companies have taken advantage of the recent advances in VANs, microcomputers, and data bases to form information utilities. An **information utility,** like the electric or gas company, supplies its utility—

information—to homes or offices in return for a fee. In many ways, these services integrate computer and telecommunications technology. Subscribers can use computer terminals to access information stored in the utility's data base. This means that subscribers can perform extensive research quickly and easily from their homes or offices. The idea of using a computer for these personal services is not a futuristic notion. These services are available today, and have, in fact, been available since 1979.

Because they are changing so rapidly, it is hard to generalize about the charges for these services. Typically, subscribers must pay a one-time registration fee of around one hundred dollars or an annual charge of twenty-five dollars. "Connect time," the amount of time a user spends accessing a data base, costs around eighteen dollars an hour during prime time (7 A.M. to 6 P.M.) and between four to six dollars an hour during nights and weekends. In addition, subscribers must pay any telephone charges. In return, they gain access to a wealth of information.

For example, The Source is an information utility that has contracted for the access rights to a set of data bases, set up a nationwide telecommunication network, and is now selling the service of easy computer-based access to this online information. Home and business users equipped with a microcomputer, a modem, communication software, a telephone line, and a subscription to The Source can access any of these data bases through The Source. Exhibit 16.12 shows a sampling of other information utilities. Some others were shown in Chapter 10, "Management Information Systems."

Exhibit 16.12
Representative Information Utilities Services

Producing Company	Product or Service	Product or Service Description
Dialog Information Services, Inc. Palo Alto, California	Dialog	Online access to 170 data bases from many sources on a wide variety of subjects
Mead Data Central New York, New York	Nexis	Online access to full text from more than 50 publications and wire services
Dun & Bradstreet, Inc. Parsippany, New Jersey	Dunsprint	Online access to D&B financial reports on U.S. businesses
Viewdata Corp. of America, Inc. Miami, Florida	Viewtron	Videotex offering of news, data bases, entertainment, and financial services
Standard & Poor's Corp. Englewood, Colorado	CompuStat	Online access to financial reports on U.S. and Canadian businesses and financial institutions
Source Telecomputing Corp. McLean, Virginia	The Source	Online access to a variety of business and consumer-oriented data bases and computer services
The Bureau of National Affairs, Inc. (BNA) Washington, D.C.	Laborlaw	Online access to information on federal and state judicial and administrative decisions on labor and employment
Official Airlines Guides, Inc. Oak Brook, Illinois	OAG Electronic Edition	Online access to North American and international airline schedules
Congressional Information Service, Inc.	American Statistics Index (ASI)	Citations and abstracts to U.S. government statistical documents available online and in print
Economic Information Systems, Inc. New York, New York	X/Market	Online access to information on sales and purchases of U.S. businesses
Dow Jones & Co., Inc. Princeton, New Jersey	Dow Jones News	Online access to full text of the Wall Street Journal and other business news publications
CompuServe, Inc. Columbus, Ohio	CompuServe	Online access to a variety of business and consumer-oriented data bases and computer services

Source: "External Data Sources: In Depth," *Computerworld,* April 1984, p. 7.

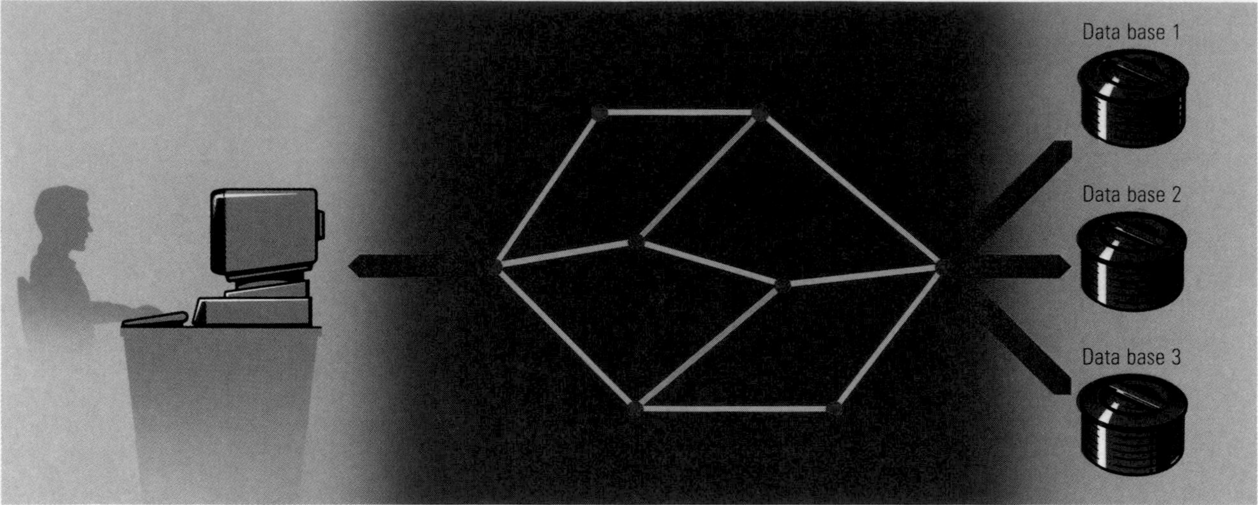

Exhibit 16.13

Information utilities often use value-added networks (VANs) to provide subscribers with access to data bases owned by various information providers.

Sometimes the information utility does not want to get into the telecommunication network business, and therefore acquires the services of a VAN, such as Telenet (see Exhibit 16.13). The advantage to the home user is that this generally increases the coverage of the network and often provides access through a local phone number. With some of the information services, access requires a long-distance call. These toll charges can be quite expensive, especially during normal business hours.

Most existing information utilities supply text alone. An emerging competitive service, called **videotex,** combines graphics and text. The proponents of videotex believe that this combination will be essential for services like teleshopping and travel planning. Eventually, they feel online subscribers will need and want television-quality images.

The videotex interface is provided by a special microprocessor that receives and sends video images across the same paths as cable television. The problem is that the videotex image will not show directly on your television or personal computer. Rather, a videotex monitor is necessary. Hardware and software advances may soon allow people to use their microcomputer monitors to display videotex, and some manufacturers are including videotex adapters in their new television sets.

The Knight-Ridder newspaper chain is selling this type of information service to Miami-area households, and the Times-Mirror newspaper company has similar plans for selected areas of Los Angeles. Exhibit 16.14 shows some sample videotex displays. Videotex services include local news and weather, electronic shopping at local stores, televised greeting cards and messages, and video games. The videotex services tend to emphasize local services, whereas the information utilities are usually national in scope. Videotex does, however, provide access to some national information services, such as the Official Airline Guide and Dow Jones stock quotations.

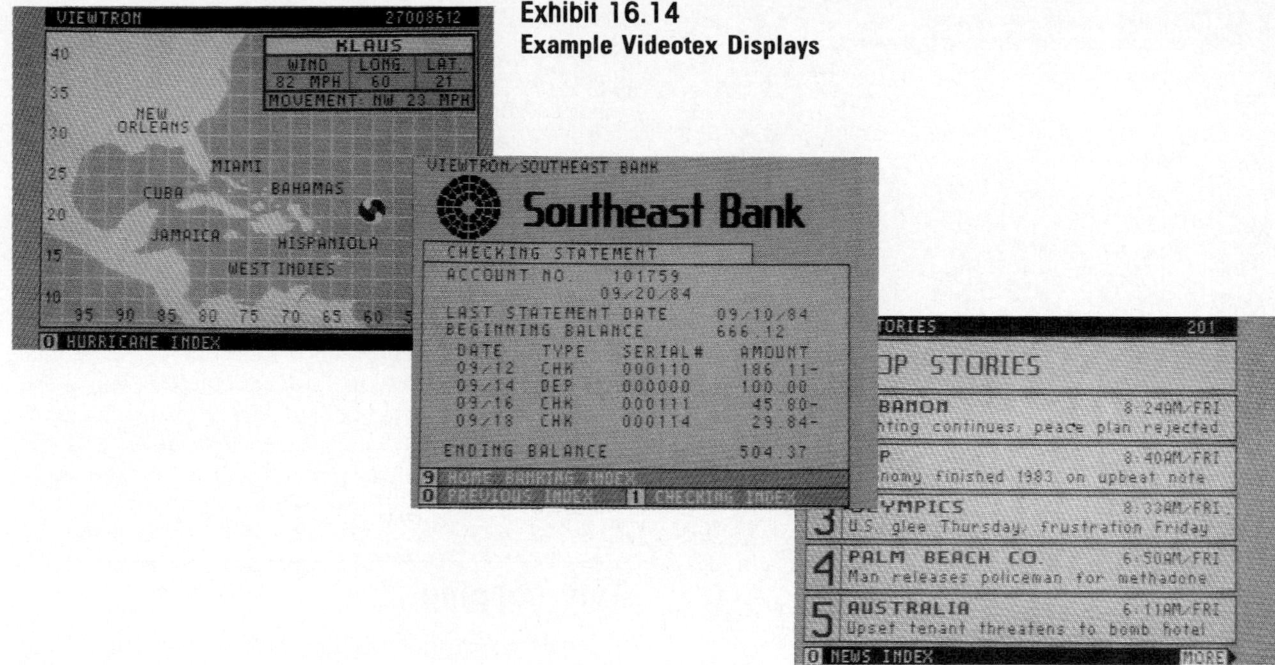

Exhibit 16.14
Example Videotex Displays

HOME INFORMATION SERVICES

As in the office and factory, the computer will be used in a variety of ways in the home. Some home applications include:

> Personal services: By using a computer to gain access to an information utility, people will have the convenience of electronic mail, banking, and shopping, including travel and entertainment planning.
>
> Computer-assisted education: Students of any age will have access to electronic learning games with graphics approaching the quality of arcade games.
>
> Control of home systems: A computer can be programmed to monitor and adjust heating and air conditioning based on variations in temperature, time of day, and other variables. The same computer can be used to monitor and control major appliances.
>
> Security: Through a system of sensors, the computer can detect dangers and can respond by activating safety measures, like a sprinkler system, and by activating various alarms either in the home or in the police or fire station.

Many of these applications are available today. Others can be seen in houses of the future, such as the Xanadu home described in this chapter's opening application. In this chapter, we will concentrate on the personal services information utilities offer.

Travel and Entertainment Planning

The data bases of the Official Airline Guide's (OAG) flight schedules, Cineman's movie reviews, and Mobil's restaurant guide could be used for travel and entertainment planning. These data bases can be accessed through a variety of

DATA TRAVEL gets you a room, a flight and a car anywhere in the world.
AIRWAYS
WORLD
The Source can provide you with flight information and make your reservations for travel just about anywhere.
If you would like to make reservations for flights, hotels, rental cars, etc., you simply join the Source's Travel Club.™ Just type DATA TRAVEL and you'll get all the details. Travel Club membership is free to all Source subscribers.
All Travel Club members automatically become eligible for a wide range of money-saving travel packages. Find out the latest package information by typing TOURS. If you're worried about any unusual weather conditions or transportation strikes find out about them by typing DATA ALERT.
If you make reservations more than three days before your departure, tickets will be sent to your office. After that, the Travel Club will have them waiting for you at the airport.
The Travel Club will make your business travel easier and more efficient than you ever thought possible.
How to find an air schedule.
If you want to know about flights from Boston to Cleveland, type AIRSCHED-D (for domestic). The system will prompt you for departure and destination cities. You then type BOSTON, MA/CLEVELAND, OH. The Source will respond with:
FROM: BOSTON, MA
TO: CLEVELAND, OH
DEPART APT ARRIVE APT FLIGHT
01:00P 02:40P C NW 0047
02:10P 03:57P C UA 0385
05:50P 07:31P C NW 0295
07:05P 08:53P C UA 0959
CLASS DAYS MEALS PLANE STPS
FY 1234567 S S 72S 0
YBH 1234567 737 0
FY 1234567 D D 72S 0
YBH 12345 7 D D 737 0

Exhibit 16.15

The Source provides flight information and makes reservations for travel worldwide.

information utilities. For example, you could use The Source to get flight information and reservations for flights and rental cars. Exhibit 16.15 shows the procedure for requesting flight information.

To determine what restaurants are available in Chicago or any of 5000 other cities in North America, you can call up the dining data base. This is an electronic guide that can be searched by city and by cuisine. For example, you can request and receive a printout of all French restaurants in Chicago. Further, the Mobil Travel Guide provides an overall rating of the restaurants (one to five stars), along with helpful information on prices, hours, entertainment, and credit cards accepted. If you finish dinner early, you can get help in deciding which movie to see by consulting the Cineman Movie Reviews. This service reviews fifty current movies and is updated every Friday.

Teleshopping

Through information utilities such as The Source and CompuServe, you can use your personal computer to shop at home (see below). Comp-U-Store, located in Connecticut, offers price quotes for over 50,000 brand name products from over two hundred companies. Products such as major appliances, televisions, stereos, videocassette recorders, and cameras with brand names such as GE, Canon, Maytag, Sony, and Zenith are available through this service. When several dealers handle the same product, the computer will search for and display the name of the merchant offering the lowest price. All prices quoted include shipping, handling costs, and applicable taxes. Price discounts of 40 percent are quite common. The subscriber can then order the merchandise at the quoted price and charge it to a major credit card. The item is shipped directly to the member.

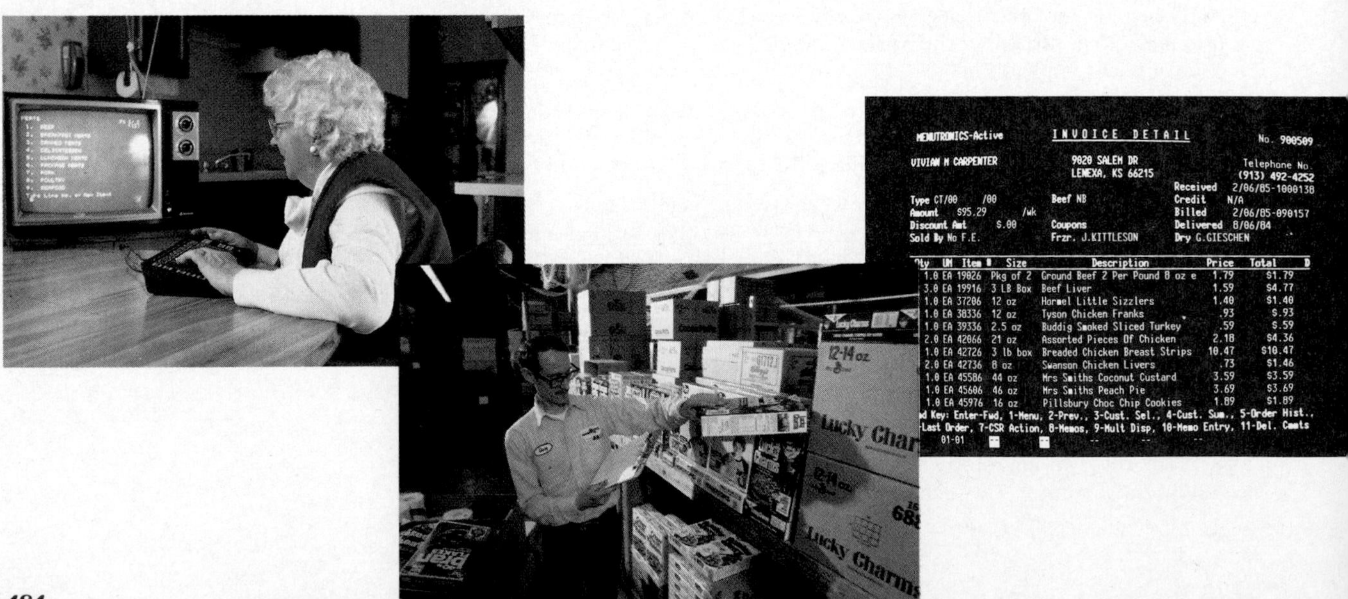

This form of the computerized mail order works well when you know specifically what you want, such as Magnavox videocassette recorder model 316. But how can teleshopping help you when you are still making up your mind? Electronic catalogs now available show individual models and product specifications. At some point in the near future, more information will be available online to help you. For example, videotex services would allow you to request more information about how a product works. Then a short videotape would be played showing the special features of the camera or lawn mower. Product evaluations, like those provided by *Consumer Reports,* could also be online. These could be searched to find an abstract of the major findings, or you could even get the full article printed out on your printer.

Electronic Banking

CompuServe also gives you access to electronic banking, banking you perform by computer from the convenience of your home or office. For example, the United American Bank of Knoxville, Tennessee lets you use your CompuServe account to access checking, savings, and credit card accounts.

Through a menu process you would be able to instruct the bank to pay particular creditors a certain amount on a specific date. Eventually, you may be able to create a standing order to pay recurring bills, such as a house or car payment. At any time you desire, you can check the current status of your various accounts. Exhibit 16.16 shows the menu for this process (A), as well as a sample display screen showing a current checking account balance (B).

Exhibit 16.16

CompuServe gives a user access to electronic banking services using his or her personal computer in the home or the office. The menu for this process is shown.

A

B

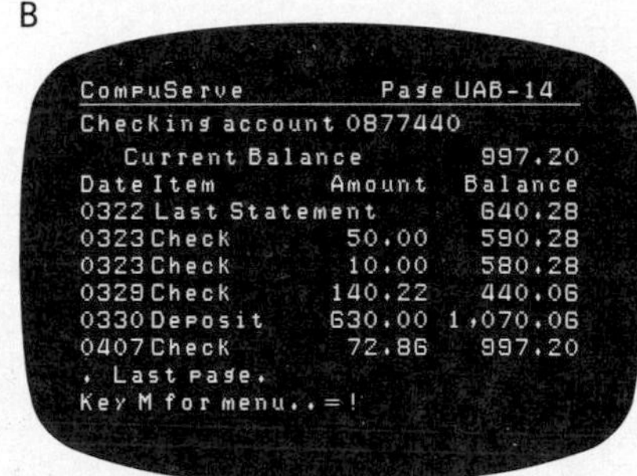

Financial Planning

An extension of the convenience provided by electronic banking is the ability to use information services and your microcomputer to make investment decisions. On the following page, Exhibit 16.17B shows how electronic banking services can let you monitor rapidly fluctuating interest rates for savings accounts, certificates of deposit, and other investments. Exhibit 16.17A shows the menu for this process. Based on this information, you can use electronic services to move your money from one type of savings account to another.

For more sophisticated investment decisions, one could subscribe to the Dow Jones News Service (DJNS). Through this service, you can get immediate online access to the complete text of the Dow Jones publications, *Wall Street*

A

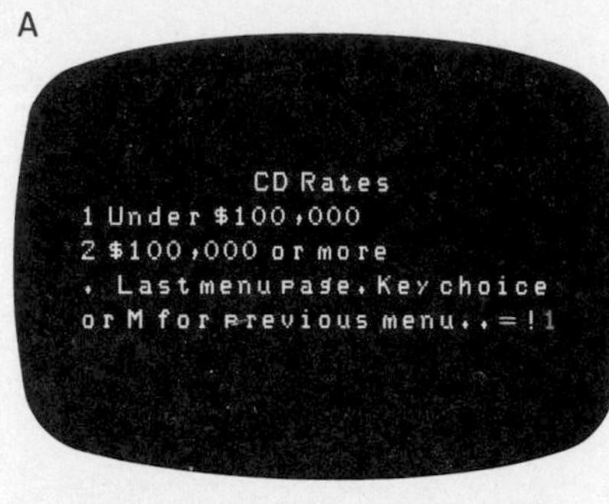

B

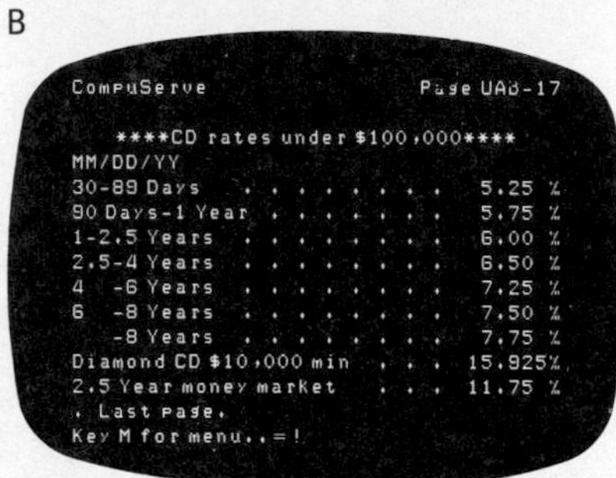

Exhibit 16.17

Electronic banking services allow individuals to monitor fluctuating interest rates for investments.

Week and *Barron's*. This includes business and economic news, stock quotations, financial and investment services, and general information services.

Users can first screen headlines and summaries of major stories that appeared during the last ninety days and then request a printout of the full text of specific articles. This service gives you access to information almost as soon as it is filed by Dow Jones reporters. Research reports done by the Merrill Lynch Research Service are also available through the DJNS.

The Dow Jones Quotes gives you current quotes fifteen minutes after they are brought to the stock floor, as well as historical quotes for the last year and historical Dow Jones Averages. In addition, more detailed financial statements are available, including those registered with the Securities and Exchange Commission (SEC).

With the appropriate software packages, this basic financial data can be entered into an electronic spreadsheet, such as Lotus 1-2-3. Then you could manipulate the data to explore the possible outcomes of various investment strategies.

Correspondence

The major information utilities offer several ways to achieve electronic correspondence, ranging from bulletin boards to electronic mail to computer conferencing.

Computer bulletin board systems, often referred to as "BBSs," allow users across the country to exchange announcements, comments, computer programs, and other information. There may be over five hundred BBSs operating in North America. Some of the special interest BBSs are Genealogy Interest Group, Astronomy, Computer-Dial-a-Joke, and People's Message System. There is Compuserve's CB Simulator, where people chat via their keyboard using CB "handles" and lingo, while jumping from channel to channel meeting new people.

Electronic mail for the home functions much like electronic mail for the office. One example of what is available is provided through MCI electronic services. MCI Mail allows one subscriber to send mail electronically to another instantaneously. A four-hour and overnight delivery service lets subscribers send electronic mail to people without computers. Once the electronic mail is received by MCI, it is printed, and the hard copy is delivered via overnight courier or the U.S. Post Office service.

Most information utilities offer computer conferencing, a special form of teleconferencing, which allows several parties to conduct an ongoing on-screen dialogue about a subject of mutual interest. These can be public or private. For example, several researchers around the country may want to exchange ideas on microcomputer software packages. Through a private computer conference, one person can present certain ideas. Anybody who is on the eligible list and finds the dialogue interesting can get a printout or add comments.

Unlike a real-time conversation, each respondent can read the comments and provide their response when they see fit—minutes, hours, or days later. If you ever search the list of active public computer conferences, you may find one that has been going on for a month. You can get a printout of all conversation to date.

People will leave the conference and others will join as their interest in the topic changes. Sometimes several people will find they want to pursue a subtopic within the general subject area. They can form another computer conference for people who are interested in this subtopic. The original conference can go on for days, weeks, or even months.

Research

Most of the information utilities are designed to provide information on a wide range of topics, but without much depth. Generally, this is adequate since most home researchers want only a specific fact or a capsule summary of an article. But some occasions, like a term paper or extensive investment analysis, require in-depth research. For these occasions, there are information services like DIALOG, BRS, and ORBIT.

DIALOG, the largest of the three, is owned by Lockheed. Through DIALOG, users can access over one hundred seventy-five encyclopedic data bases and over 55 million units of information or records. Typical data bases represented include the *Academic American Encyclopedia, Books in Print, Reader's Guide to Periodic Literature, International Software Directory,* MEDLINE, CLAIMS, *Federal Index,* and the *Dissertation Index.*

Through other data base services you can gain access to the full text of the *New York Times* newspaper, and also magazines such as *Business Week, Harvard Business Review, Foreign Policy, Scientific American, Consumer Reports, Sports Illustrated, Time, U.S. News & World Report,* and *Variety,* as well as specialized newsletters drawn from nearly thirty different industry groups and interest areas.

Until recently encyclopedic data bases have been available only to librarians and professional researchers of large organizations that could justify the costly equipment needed to access them. Now, through the microcomputer and telecommunication, you can access many of the research indexes once available only in libraries—from your living room. The key differences are that the indexes are available online and that the computer will use the key words you specify to search the data base. The advantages are speed and money. A typical search would take less than five minutes and cost less than $2.00.

Professional Issue

Telecommuting

As you read our discussion of the office and home of the future, you may have wondered if the two could be combined. Why couldn't you just work at home and use your computer to send or receive information as needed? Jack Nilles, now of the Center for Futures Research at the University of Southern California, proposed this concept in 1976, when he coined the word **telecommuting.**

Through the use of the company's private data network and/or information utilities, the telecommuter could work at home using a microcomputer. When data was needed from the company's central database, a micro/mainframe link could be used to extract the appropriate data and have it sent over the telecommunication link to the microcomputer.

Conversely, finished projects could be distributed to the appropriate people through a telecommunication network. Bosses would always be able to send the telecommuter messages through electronic or voice mail service. A home equipped for telecommuting is often called "the electronic cottage."

Actually, there is no reason a "virtual office" cannot be set up for jobs like computer programmer, financial analyst, or professional writer. Furthermore, a combination of portable computers and telecommunications services can let you set up a virtual office anywhere—a client's office, your own home, a friend's home, a hotel room, or the airport. With the new mobile cellular phone, you could even use voice-activated commands and computer-generated voice output to carry on business without taking your eyes off the road.

Nilles predicts that about 10 percent of the work force will become telecommuters by the year 2000. Most telecommuters will probably not work exclusively at home. Rather they would work at home two or three days a week. Studies have shown that some mixture of work at home and in the office seems necessary to meet the important psychological, social, and political requirements of today's work environment. Further, some individuals thrive in this type of environment and others find it very unsatisfying personally. Lastly, only certain types of jobs lend themselves to "working away." In Computers at Work: "High-Tech Nomad," you can read about a writer who is already telecommuting while he tours our nation on a bicycle.

High-Tech Nomad

A portable computer fuels a bicycle odyssey across America.

Since September of last year, I have lived on a recumbent bicycle—an eight-foot-long, high-tech extravaganza that combines the latest in human-powered vehicle research, portable computers, and solar power technology. It's my home, with the three-bedroom ranch in suburbia now just a memory. But beyond that, it's my office as well; as I pedal a 14,000-mile loop around the United States, I am maintaining a full-time freelance writing profession. Thanks to a carefully integrated network of support facilities, I can present the illusion of geographic stability when the need arises—and simultaneously juggle book and article manuscripts while having the adventure of a lifetime.

Those support facilities comprise a widely applicable technological infrastructure for almost any kind of information business—on the road.

TELECOMMUTING

There has been a lot of talk in the last decade about the "electronic cottage," or "telecommuting." According to this theory, the availability of personal computers would eliminate the need for people to remain entombed in an office. They can take their work home and commute electronically. But while the world has debated the viability of the electronic cottage, the technology on which it is based has continued to develop. It is becoming clear that one can work *anywhere,* not just at home.

So let's look at the essential ingredients of a nomadic business, and then see how they have come together to make my own high-tech adventure possible.

THE PORTABLE OFFICE

Perhaps the most obvious component is the portable computer—in my case, a Radio Shack Model 100. This four-pound machine is now viewed as a "transition product" that will tide us over until the *really* robust portables start showing up. But even with its limitations, it is at least as much responsible for this trip's success as is my bicycle. How else could I be spending this sunny winter afternoon pattering away on Broward Beach, the prime sunbathing spot for dorm residents at the University of Florida?

Of course there's an obvious problem: file storage. A stand-alone Model 100 would hardly go very far toward maintaining a serious writing business. The memory would fill up halfway through the first feature-length article, and that would be the end of it. There *is* the unaesthetic and crude alternative of audiocassette storage, of course, and a Model 100-sized dual-drive 3½-inch disk system with a CP/M file server is being created for me by Micromax as another solution to the problem. But the easiest method is the daily use of the second component, the Compuserve network.

THE NETWORK

My original reason for getting a Compuserve account (70007,362 here—pleased to meetcha) was simply to communicate with my assistant. This it accomplishes very neatly, but over the months I've been acquiring additional dedicated accounts as well—one for file storage, another for transferring manuscripts, another to support an online publishing venture, and a couple more for CB, and tinkering, and E-mail, and the special interest groups, and. . . .

Yes. That's what happens. The network ends up becoming dramatically useful in an enterprise like this, not only for the low-cost business communications that it provides but also for the maintenance of something approaching a stable social life. Even in a nodeless burg in the middle of nowhere, I can sign on to the CB simulator and find friends: "Hey Wordy! Where U B tonite?"

The combination of the portable computer and Compuserve, incidentally, offers occasional entertainment in my encounters with the public. I have become an agent of future shock. In Christiansburg, Ohio, I pulled up to the town's only pay phone and dismounted. The bike gleamed; the Solarex photovoltaics were tilted to face the October sun. I sat crosslegged on the concrete with the Model 100 before me, dialed Compuserve's number, and proceeded to upload a text file to my assistant in Columbus.

A dusty pickup truck rattled to a stop beside me, and an even dustier farmer squeaked open the door and stepped out. He walked slowly around the bike, quietly assimilating it, all the while thoughtfully chawin' tobacco. Finally he squinted at me and spoke.

"Are yew with NASA?"

THE HOME BASE

The third component in this nomadic business is a stationary office located in Columbus, Ohio. Should I ever need to present the illusion of stability, there is my established address—no small consideration when pedaling a bicycle around the planet. The office contains a Micromax CP/M system with a USR Password modem, a copier, files, books, and all the clutter one normally expects to find in a writing office. It also contains Kacy, my interface with the universe.

Yes, knitting all this together is a human being, still a necessary ingredient despite the wondrous technology I've already described. Kacy handles mail, deals with the phone, manages the business, edits text, coordinates research, monitors the flow of money, and generally keeps everything under control—something that is otherwise maddeningly difficult to do when traveling. In return for all this, she receives a percentage of the business's income, inducing her to share my own motivation and crack the whip when the distractions of life on the road begin to eclipse work-in-progress.

Given all this, the basic infrastructure of a business exists. All that remains is for me to generate copy now and again so we can eat.

Doing that is quite straightforward, assuming I can marshal the motivation to work. An article (like this one) begins its life in the Model 100 wherever I happen to be. It's massaged, modified, and manipulated, then shipped off with a flourish via the first available telephone, pay or otherwise. It is transmitted, not directly to Kacy, but into a work area on Compuserve cryptically called "PCP" (for Primary Communication Path).

There it sits until Kacy signs on and finds to her relief that I *have* been working after all. She downloads the article through a USR Password modem into the "base system," then sets to work fine-tuning it with Wordstar. At some point, she deems it shippable and generates a clean manuscript.

From there, it can go one of two ways. More and more publishers welcome electronic submission of manuscripts—it's much less work for everybody involved and reduces the potential for human error. In these cases, she retransmits the text, either through Compuserve or directly into the publisher's own computer system. Some magazines still prefer traditional paper submissions, so for these she simply generates a hard copy and sends it to the appropriate address.

If all goes well, the article will eventually generate a bit of money. Meanwhile, of course, I have been spending furiously on the road. This calls for some cash management since we are, in the manner of most small freelance businesses, always performing a financial juggling act. This is another of Kacy's jobs; she does battle while I strategize from a safe distance.

THE BIKE

The bike itself—which I have come to call my *Winnebiko* in honor of its 135-pound load—is something of a tour de force of high-tech self-sufficiency. It can be broken down into four major components: bicycle, electronics package, office, and bedroom.

Bicycle: the conveyance upon which everything else depends is a custom-made recumbent bicycle, built to my specifications by Franklin Frames of Columbus, Ohio. Over eight feet long from fairing to stern, it is a one-of-a-kind machine specifically designed for this trip. With its eighteen-speed wide-range derailleur, drum brake, underseat steering, and unique frame geometry, this alone is a traffic-stopper.

Electronics Package: the first thing one is likely to notice upon peering at the machine is the array of solar panels on their ball-and-socket mount. These generate about five watts in full sun and charge the twelve-volt, four-amp-hour nickel-cadmium battery pack that in turn powers everything else. The computer is a very minor load—it will happily run for hours on its internal AA batteries when not plugged into the wall or the bike.

The major loads include a quartz-halogen sealed-beam headlight, a taillight and yellow flasher, a xenon strobe atop the flagpole, a CB radio for emergencies, a pager-type vibration-sensitive security system, a fluorescent tent light, and a yacht horn.

Office: the major component of the office, of course, is the Model 100, but it is augmented by a microcassette recorder with a remote microphone for dictation on the road, and a small assortment of file folders, stationery, etc. All that fits in a soft briefcase that packs atop the touring gear.

Bedroom: finally, there are the components that allow me to be reasonably dry and comfortable wherever I happen to be. Included are a dome tent, stove, the usual camping gear, stereo, rainsuit, and clothes.

Needless to say after all this rhapsodizing, the system is working well. Work gets done, and life is a study in sheer exuberance, touched with madness, yet tempered by the realities of business. I lay over here and there to catch up on overdue projects—sometimes for weeks—and then the tires start to itch. The only cure is a good piece of asphalt.

So I say my good-byes, pack the office onto the bike, and pedal off once again, unfettered, seeking adventure, a nomad of the information age. It *is* a liberating technology, and it's getting better all the time.

Source: S. K. Roberts, "High-Tech Nomad," *Popular Computing,* August 1984, pp. 116–22.

SUMMARY

Office automation began in the 1850s with the introduction of the typewriter and continues today with the growing use of computers in the office. Office automation will continue for two reasons. First, workers need efficient ways to manage information. Second, the number of white-collar workers continues to increase.

The automated office will include computing tools like word processing, electronic mail, voice mail, facsimile, teleconferencing, and administrative support that streamline and simplify traditional tasks. Workers will also have access to the tools of end-user computing.

Word processing, a computerized way of creating, editing, and filing documents, simplifies the task of making corrections, major revisions, and clean final copies. Online dictionaries, proofreading, and *mail merge* programs aid in maintaining mailing lists and generating customized form letters. Software packages that check grammar are also available. The net result is that the cumbersome, expensive process of preparing business documents is simplified.

Electronic mail saves time by letting workers exchange documents, memos, and letters electronically through microcomputers connected by a local area network. Workers can also use electronic mail to access electronic files of information.

Voice mail uses a digitized form of the spoken message that can be stored on a disk and delivered electronically to one or more phones at a specified time. In addition, voice messages can be annotated, forwarded to other telephones, and verified as to time and date of delivery.

A *Facsimile (FAX) machine* transforms a nonelectronic document into a digitized form that can be sent over telecommunication paths to another FAX machine, where it is translated back into an image on paper. An advantage of FAX transmission is that it allows certain security measures, like encryption.

Teleconferencing uses telecommunications paths to transmit real-time audio and full-motion video images that allow workers in geographically dispersed locations to attend meetings. Although this service is expensive and still not widely available, it is often cheaper than the travel expenses needed to arrange face-to-face meetings.

Administrative support in the automated office will include electronic calendars, online telephone directories, and "tickler" files.

Workers in automated offices will also have access to the tools of end-user computing. Although these tools are now widely available on microcomputers, the trend is to link microcomputers through local area networks. In addition, many managers may have access to data bases and other files held in the company's main computer, an ability that will allow them to customize information for decisions without the help of the data processing department.

In traditionally organized offices, an assembly-line approach means that tasks are fragmented and standardized. In addition, data is always less than up-to-date. In the Information Age Office, computer support would allow workers to handle an entire task. Information would be very timely and inquiries could be handled easily.

The factory of the future will use computer-aided manufacturing, computer-aided design, and computer-aided engineering.

Computer-aided manufacturing (CAM) uses computers to control factory machines. In *flexible manufacturing systems,* a hierarchy of computers control factory machines and the movement of materials from machine to machine. *Robots* are any mechanical device that can be programmed to perform tasks involving manipulation or movement. Robots are used for materials handling and for repetitive tasks like arc welding and spray painting.

Computer-aided design (CAD), the use of computer graphics terminals in product design, allows designers to quickly generate engineering drawings. In addition, the designer can rotate the image, change its scale, and zoom in on specific aspects. The resulting engineering drawings can be stored electronically and used to produce the programs that control each machine in a flexible manufacturing system. This process of integrating computer-aided design and manufacturing is called CAD/CAM.

Computer-aided engineering (CAE) allows designers and engineers to use computers to test their designs without building prototypes.

The major advances in factory productivity will come from factory information systems, which will coordinate the design, engineering, production planning, and manufacturing of goods.

Many aspects of the office and factory of the future will depend on sophisticated telecommunication services. A variety of government actions have ended the monopoly of *common carriers,* companies licensed by the FCC to provide certain types of telecommunication services to the general public. As a result, there are now new sources of telecommunication services such as MCI, SPRINT, and COMSAT. There have been technological advances in telecommunication media such as fiber optics and communication satellites and the ability to digitize voice, data, and images. The merging of computer and communication technology is used in forming *value-added networks.* These are basic communication networks that have had computer services added to them such as electronic mail and information retrieval capabilities.

Information utilities provide ready access to information for teleshopping, electronic banking, financial and travel planning, correspondence, and research. *Videotex* is an emerging type of information utility that uses cable television and a special videotex monitor to combine graphics and text. Information utilities can be accessed from the office or from the home.

In *telecommuting,* workers would use a private data network or information utilities to work at home several days a week. A home so equipped is often referred to as a "electronic cottage," although portable computers and telecommunication services will allow workers to set up "virtual offices" at almost any location.

In the next chapter, we will look at some of the issues and concerns we will have to face in the information society.

REVIEW QUESTIONS

1. Briefly discuss the major factors that have accounted for the increase in office automation.
2. What is meant by the term *electronic mail?* What advantage does it offer?
3. Briefly describe several possible applications for facsimile machines in business.
4. The Altoona Corporation has a far-flung sales force. The company feels that sales performance could be improved by regular sales meetings to share problems and ideas, but cannot afford to bring the sales force to headquarters frequently. How can Altoona solve this problem?
5. How can the computer aid in manufacturing?
6. Briefly describe the benefits offered by CAD.
7. The In-Tech Corporation has traditionally tested new products by building prototypes. How might this task be accomplished more economically and efficiently?
8. Briefly discuss the role of computerized material requirement planning in the modern firm.
9. Describe the three technological advances that have made improved telecommunications possible.
10. What are *data networks?* What advantages do such systems offer?
11. Briefly summarize the major home information services that are, or will be, available for use by the owner of home computer systems.
12. What is *telecommuting?* How might it change work patterns in the future?

PART VI COMPUTERS AND SOCIETY

CHAPTER 17
Issues and Concerns

COMPUTERS AT WORK

Biometrics Has a Touch for Spotting Phonies

A tiny new industry is putting unique personal characteristics into digital electronic devices that make faking an I.D. tough.

While poets have long extolled the uniqueness of each individual, biometrics technology is making a business out of it. Biometrics is the science of taking a biological characteristic, such as a fingerprint, and quantifying it. Devices that can do this are being installed at military bases and other places that now employ guards to screen admissions. Eventually, biometrics may be economical enough to use in verifying the identity of bank customers.

The virtues of biometrics are clear. I.D. cards and credit cards can be filched or forged, and identification numbers can be forgotten by their owners or found out by strangers. But nobody can palm off his fingerprints as someone else's.

Biometrics is still an infant industry, with scarcely $5 million in factory sales last year. But Joseph P. Freeman, whose market research firm in Newtown, Connecticut, tracks the security business, projects sales of about $100 million a year by 1990. Freeman believes biometric devices will make their first big inroads by replacing guards who check photo badges in high-security areas.

Fingermatrix of White Plains, New York, is shipping a product that will guard access to a U.S. naval intelligence command post in Norfolk, Virginia. Bolstered by this invention, the stock of Fingermatrix, which sold at $4.75 a share a year ago, recently traded at $7.25. Yet the nine-year-old company has yet to make a dime: it lost $4 million on sales of $110,000 in fiscal 1984.

The device, which scans fingerprints, is user-friendly. A person puts his finger, any finger, in a slot on a scanning machine (see picture). Within five seconds a microprocessor translates the print into digital code—256 bytes per finger—and matches it against codes stored in the computer's memory.

Other ways of fingering the good guys come from two California companies, Stellar Systems of San Jose and Identix Inc. of Palo Alto. A subsidiary of Wackenhut, which sells guard services and security systems, Stellar markets a product that recognizes a person's hand when it is placed on a scanning device. The University of Georgia is using Stellar machines to identify students eligible to eat in its cafeterias. Identix, founded in 1982, raised $2.25 million to develop a fingerprint device. Early this year the FBI bought a system to control access to, of all places, an area where fingerprints are processed.

Another biometrics technique relies on scanning blood vessels in the retina. A device that uses this method is produced by Eye-dentify Inc., based in Beaverton, Oregon. The product is a machine fitted with what looks like a pair of binoculars. A person simply looks into the eyepieces and presses a button. Identification is quicker than you can say Sherlock Holmes.

At $7000 to $10,800 each, the various biometric devices are cheaper than guards but are too costly to install at every automated teller machine or cash register. Fingermatrix thinks that if its machine were mass-produced, the price would drop from $10,000 to perhaps $3500 and eventually go lower. It would need to. Some bankers say $2000 is the most they would pay; others say $500 would be tops.

Source: E. J. Tracy, "Biometrics Has a Touch for Spotting Phonies," *Fortune,* 15 April, 1985, p. 105.

In the last chapter, we discussed some of the benefits we can look forward to in the information society. But some people are concerned that every benefit will have a cost. The benefit of efficiency introduced by computers at work, for example, may be offset by increased unemployment or unforseen health hazards. Already we have learned that advanced computer-based information systems are open to electronic forms of old-fashioned crimes, like bank robbery and forgery. Some of these problems can be overcome by more technology, such as identification systems based on biometrics. Other problems involve ethical, not technological, issues. In this chapter, we want to discuss some of the issues and concerns that must be faced in the information society. Here, you will learn to do the following:

1. Discuss why the transition to the information society is having a major impact on people in the work force and how individuals can adapt.
2. Explain the physical, mental, and social problems some computer users are experiencing and the proposed solutions.
3. Discuss the ways technological advances are being used by private and government agencies to affect our personal privacy.
4. Describe the problem of computer crime and methods for protecting computer systems, programs, and data.
5. Discuss some of the research that may make computers more intelligent and its implications for user-computer interaction.

THE TRANSITION TO THE INFORMATION SOCIETY

One of the most important themes of this text has been the increasingly important roles information and computers are playing in our society. This trend has been noted by many social commentators, including John Naisbitt, author of *Megatrends,* and Alvin Toffler, author of *The Third Wave.* In his book, Toffler discusses the basis of the United States economy in terms of three "waves." Initially, the United States economy was based on agriculture. The industrial revolution—the "second wave"—began in the 1880s. The "third wave" will be the information society. These waves are reflected in the types of jobs available to workers.

On the following page, Exhibit 17.1 shows the dramatic shifts registered in the composition of the work force between 1800 and today and projects its composition through the year 2000. Important turning points have been 1880, when only 50 percent of the work force was involved in agriculture, 1920, when over 50 percent of workers were in industry, and around 1980, when over 50 percent of all workers were classified as "information" workers. What do these trends mean to today's workers, especially those in agricultural and industrial jobs? In the next section, we want to discuss some types of jobs that are being lost. Then we will discuss some of our options for helping workers who have lost jobs to automation.

The Problem: Displaced Workers

In today's factory, more and more of the routine, well-structured tasks are being performed by robots. In some cases workers might welcome this trend, since the robots are being used for either very monotonous or dangerous

Exhibit 17.1

There have been dramatic changes in the composition of the work force in the United States over the last two hundred years. Important turning points occurred around 1880, when only 50 percent of the work force worked in agriculture; around 1920, when over 50 percent of workers were in industry; and around 1980, when over 50 percent of all workers were classified as "information" workers.

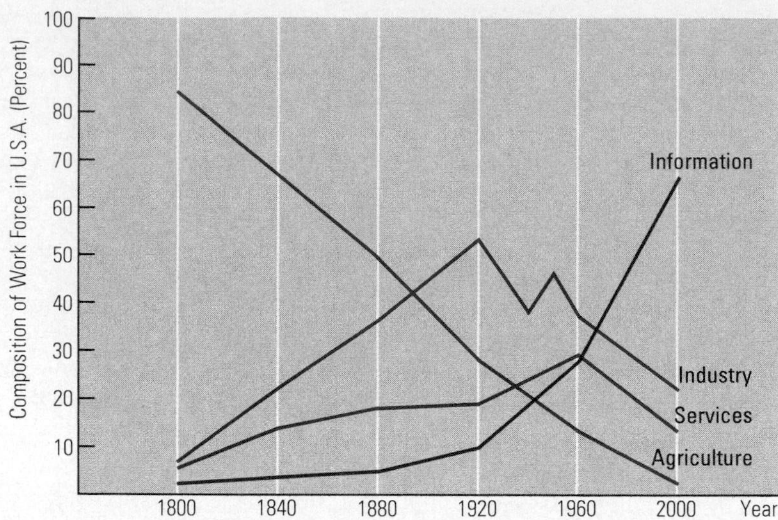

tasks. But one robot can replace six workers. The 6000 robots in use in the U.S. in 1984 are expected to grow to 200,000 in 1990 and to a million in the year 2000. This implies millions of displaced workers.

In the automated office, word processors, electronic mail, and end-user computing will reduce the need for workers whose skills are limited to typing, filing, and mail delivery. By 1990, it is predicted that 25 percent of all office jobs will be fully automated. The ready availability of effective software will allow a smaller number of people to do the same amount of work. But what about the bookkeepers and accounts receivable clerks that used to be needed?

As you go to the grocery store, fill your car with gasoline, and deposit and withdraw money from the bank, you can see more and more computerization. The implications are clear. The gasoline stations with computerized pumps have fewer attendants. Given the public acceptance of automatic teller machines (ATMs), banks are slowly reducing the number of tellers. Grocery stores that can check out more shoppers more accurately with computerized scanners need fewer checkout clerks.

Is computerization having a good or bad impact on society? In many ways the answer depends on your perspective. If you are the bank clerk replaced by an automatic teller machine, you probably feel that computers are bad. If you use an ATM, you may be convinced that ATMs are great. Similarly, the factory worker who may be replaced by a robot often resents the computer and fears permanent unemployment. But car buyers may feel the increased quality and reduced prices brought about by automation are long overdue. And, if you are one of the people hired to repair or program the robots, this type of automation is good.

From a societal viewpoint, does automation decrease or increase the total number of jobs? Obviously, new jobs will be created for robot and computer designers and repairers, as well as for programmers and related occupations. But will these new jobs offset the number of jobs lost to automation? The answer is not clear. What is clear is that a significant portion of the work force will be replaced by automation. What should we do?

The Options

One option is not to introduce any form of computerization to our offices or factories. In this way, no jobs will be lost. Unfortunately, this is not a realistic option in a highly competitive world economy. The United States auto industry, for example, has suffered in competition with highly automated foreign manufacturers. Foreign makes have, in essence, captured the market for small- and medium-sized cars. While American manufacturers have employed highly paid workers in basically unautomated factories, the Japanese have proved they can produce high-quality, reliable products at generally lower prices. As James Baker, Executive Vice-President of General Electric has said, "We in America must either automate, emigrate, or evaporate."

A second option is to become more competitive by quickly automating offices and factories. At the same time, we must recognize the economic and social consequences for workers and local communities. Computers at Work: "A New Bill of Rights" is a proposal from union leaders who recognize the need for automation but hope to protect their workers (see page 498). Companies employing workers about to be replaced by automation can: (1) allow workers to retire early; (2) share the cost savings of automation with workers so they can work fewer hours for the same pay; or (3) retrain workers.

Retrained workers could probably find employment. General Motors now classifies just 16 percent of their work force as skilled tradespersons, such as technicians, inspectors, and monitors. But, by the year 2000, GM predicts that number will swell to 50 percent. Other surveys have indicated the need for more highly trained personnel such as engineers, technicians, computer specialists, and managers with basic technical skills.

Clearly, educational programs for both children and adults will play an important part in creating a work force with computing literacy. Some of the techniques currently used in today's elementary and high schools might be adapted for adult education. For example, **computer-assisted instruction (CAI),** now used for drill and practice in mathematics, English, and foreign languages, might be used to teach workers useful computer skills like keyboarding or word processing. **Computer-based learning (CBL),** which simulates or models actual situations, is another technique that might be adapted to retraining workers. One application of CBL in schools allows students to perform traditional laboratory experiments in chemistry without the risk or expense of combining and heating chemicals. This same technique might be used to retrain workers by modeling or simulating industrial applications of computer technology. Exhibit 17.2 shows some ways optical discs or, in commercial terms, "videodiscs" can be used in retraining workers.

Exhibit 17.2

Teaching technologies based on videodisc systems offer a way to train employees more rapidly, more economically, and more enjoyably than in traditional classroom methods. Mariners learn to navigate on this simulated ship's bridge at the Maritime Institute of Technology in Maryland. Harbor lights are projected on a circular screen that surrounds the bridge.

Those outside the traditional education scene have many avenues for learning about computers, their operation, and their roles in the information society. These include industrial and government retraining programs meant to teach workers the skills needed for technical jobs. We will be talking about some of these programs in the next chapter.

But what about the workers who cannot learn these new skills? They may not have the educational background for retraining as technical workers. Some of these workers have twenty to thirty years of experience in declining industries. Under ordinary circumstances, they might have expected to work another ten to fifteen years before retiring. One rather unsatisfying solution is to train

A New Bill of Rights

This is the text of the Workers' Technology Bill of Rights of the International Association of Machinists and Aerospace Workers:

I. New technology should be used in a way that does not decrease jobs, but creates or maintains jobs and promotes community-wide and national full employment.

II. Unit cost savings and labor productivity gains resulting from the use of new technology shall be shared with the production workers at the local level and shall not be permitted to accrue solely for the gain of capital, management, and shareholders. Increased leisure time resulting from technology shall result in no loss of real income or decline in living standards.

III. Since the greater part of the local, state, and national tax revenues comes from taxes on labor, communities and the nation have the right to require employers to pay a robot tax, as a replacement tax, on all machinery, equipment, and production systems that displace workers and cause unemployment.

IV. New technology shall improve the conditions of work and shall enhance and expand the opportunities for knowledge, skills, and compensation of workers. Displaced workers shall not be penalized with loss of income and shall be entitled to training and retraining.

V. New technology shall be used to develop the U.S. industrial base, consistent with the full employment goal, before it is licensed or exported abroad.

VI. New technology shall be evaluated in terms of worker safety and health and shall not be destructive of the workplace environment, nor shall it be used at the same expense of the community's natural environment.

VII. Workers, through their trade unions and bargaining units, shall have an absolute right to participate in all phases of management deliberations and decisions that lead or could lead to the introduction of new technology or the changing of the workplace system design, work processes or procedures for doing work, including the shutdown or transfer of work, capital, plant, and capital.

VIII. Workers shall have the right to monitor control room centers and control stations. The new technology shall not be used to monitor, measure, or otherwise control the work practices and the work standards of individual workers, at the point of work.

IX. Storage of an individual worker's personal data and information file by the employer shall be tightly controlled and the collection and/or release and dissemination of information with respect to race, religious or political activities and beliefs, records of physical and mental health, and mental disorders and treatments, records of arrests and felony charges or convictions, information concerning sexual preferences and conduct, information concerning internal and private family matters, and information regarding an individual's financial condition or credit worthiness shall not be permitted, except in rare instances related to health, and then only after a consultation with a family or union-appointed physician, psychiatrist, or member of the clergy. The right of the individual workers to inspect their own data file shall at all times be absolute and open to him or her.

X. When the new technology is employed in the production of military goods and services, workers, through their trade union and bargaining agent, have a right to bargain with management over the establishment of Alternative Production Committees, which shall design ways to adopt that technology to socially useful production and products in the civilian sector of the economy.

Courtesy International Association of Machinists and Aerospace Workers

these workers to fill the growing demand for service jobs, such as janitors and waitresses. Forecasts indicate these jobs will grow faster in number than computer-related jobs. The problem is that service jobs, while useful, do not pay very high wages and have limited benefits. This limited earning potential compounds the problems of factory workers who have been used to substantial earning power. For some workers such a radical change may seem unthinkable. Yet it may be their only option.

WORKER HEALTH

Increased productivity is one of the positive side effects of using computers in offices and factories. Among the negative side effects are health problems computer users have either experienced or worried about.

Physical and Mental Problems

In the late 1970s, widely circulated rumors linked too many hours in front of a video display terminal with an increased risk of cataracts. Medical studies refuted these rumors. Then concern spread about the unusual number of birth defects occurring among babies born after their mothers had worked at one company's VDTs during their pregnancies. A report published by the U.S. National Institute of Occupational Safety and Health (NIOSH) showed no connection between the birth defects and the amount of radiation given off by computer terminals. Labor groups disagreed with this conclusion, and in 1985 NIOSH embarked on a more extensive two-year study specifically of this pregnancy-related issue as well as the effects of CRT radiation in general. But all interest groups agreed with the NIOSH study conclusions that working long hours at a computer was associated with eyestrain, headaches, nausea, lower and upper back pain, and stress.

What are the physical and psychological factors that might be responsible for these problems? In most cases they can be linked to inadequate working conditions, including poorly designed worker-computer interfaces, the wrong type of lighting, and uncomfortable chairs.

What about stress? In many ways computer-related stress depends on the type of job you have. If you are working as a data-entry or order-processing clerk, your stress comes primarily from the constant interaction with the computer. You are expected to perform at a high level of proficiency at an "assembly line" pace. In some companies the computer is used as a "watch dog" to monitor worker productivity, error rate, and hours worked. There is little chance to "get away" from the computer and reduce tension by socializing or talking with fellow workers about routine work matters.

While computer professionals experience many of the same physical problems as other computer users, stress is often their biggest problem. Stress for professionals has different causes than stress for clerical workers. Professional jobs, for example, require continual creativity under tight deadlines. There is always a backlog of applications to be developed, and each always seems to take longer than the time allocated. Computer professionals often feel they are never caught up with their work.

Another source of professional stress is the constant change in the computer field. The computer field is an exciting one, with its rapid growth and technological advancements, but these conditions can also cause stress as the computer professional tries to cope with rapid change. You are forced to learn increasing amounts of information to stay current with the general development of the computer field and your specific applications or specialties.

The lack of standards in hardware and software compounds the learning problem, and causes much unnecessary frustration. Because there is no standardization, for example, each new computer language and each new word processing, spreadsheet, and data base management package requires that you learn different commands and procedures to perform the same functions. Even more confusion and stress arise when the same command causes highly different results in two different software languages. For example, in one language, the command "Quit" may end your session, saving your files and logging off the computer. In another language, "Quit" may cause your files to be destroyed.

One of the subtle effects of the increasingly capable software packages and programming languages available with portable and personal computers is that the dividing line between work and play becomes vague. This is especially true for telecommuters. Managers and computer professionals in these situations don't have a well-defined, "nine-to-five" office job where it is clear what work is and where it should be done. The computer is always present and never gets tired. Its restless electronic screen poses a constant visible challenge.

In addition to fusing work and play, working with computers can lead to social isolation. High levels of performance often require significant blocks of quiet, uninterrupted time. Much of the professional's workday is spent interacting with the computer itself. Electronic mail further reduces the opportunity for face-to-face contact with co-workers.

While the fear of computers is well-publicized, little is said about those people who have a love of computers and what they can do. Hackers are people who see the computer as a combination of tool, toy, and lover. The thrill of working with the computer becomes an addiction. People have been known to work with the computer for sixteen, twenty-four, even forty-eight hours straight and longer, without eating or sleeping. In situations without real project deadlines, the computer may become the person's artificial world. This is extreme behavior, and most people are starting to recognize that it is as significant a problem as a dread of computing.

A Solution: Ergonomics

What is being done to help users cope with these physical, mental, and social problems? *Ergonomics* is the science of adapting machines to people. Ergonomics determines how computers, the work itself, and the work environment can be better designed to accommodate workers' needs and concerns, while enabling them to attain high levels of productivity. Ergonomic studies have shown the best physical arrangement for people using computers for any length of time (see Exhibit 17.3). The type of chair, the distance from worker to VDT, and the ability to adjust all components can ease back pains and reduce fatigue.

Some users feel the eye fatigue associated with traditional black-and-white or green-and-black cathode-ray-tube displays can be eased by switching to amber-and-black screens. Others feel that flat-panel displays, which eliminate the flickering common to CRTs, should significantly reduce eye fatigue. Ergo-

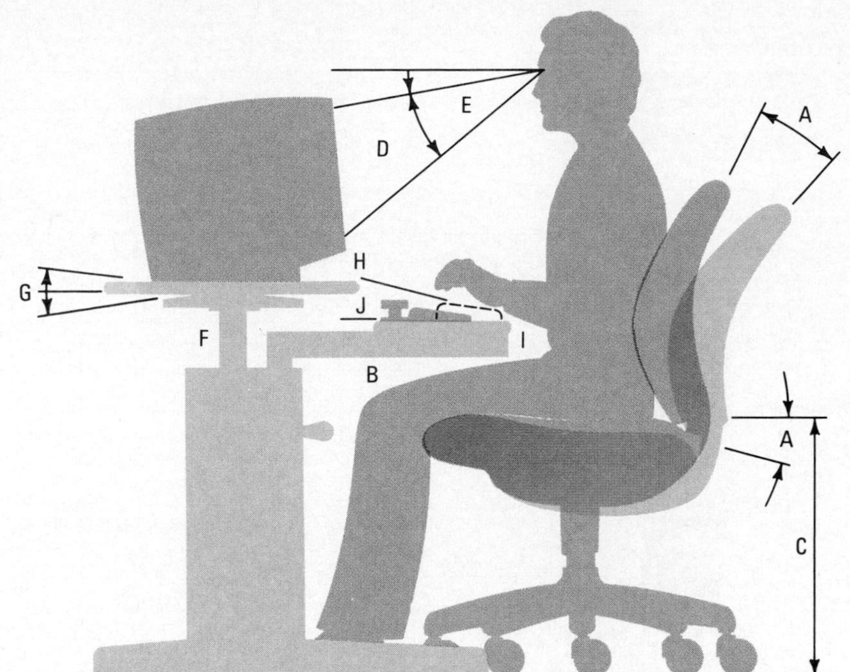

Exhibit 17.3
An Ergonomic Workstation
A. Synchronized seat and back movement (tilt range: back 16 degrees, seat 8 degrees; seat automatically tilts 1 degree for each 2 degrees the back tilts); B. Front edge pitch adjustment range: 3 degrees; C. Seat height adjustment: 17 to 21 inches; D. Normal eye-to-screen viewing range: 18 to 22 inches; E. vertical viewing angle comfort range to minimize eye, neck, and shoulder fatigue: 30 degrees (VDT height should be adjusted so viewing range starts 10 degrees below "horizon line" level); F. VDT screen height adjustment: 22–3/8 to 32–3/4 inches; G. Screen angle adjustment: ±7 degrees; H. Keyboard-to-screen adjustment: 0 to 7–1/2 inches; I. Keyboard height adjustment: 22–7/8 to 32–1/4 inches; J. Keyboard angle adjustment: 0 to 15 degrees.

nomics also studies office lighting. Because too much light from overhead or from windows causes glare on computer screens, computer workers are often more comfortable with light levels much lower than normal. Sometimes filters can be placed over computer screens to reduce glare and improve contrast.

Exhibit 17.4 shows a work area designed to give the computer professional both quiet and a correct physical environment (see page 502). In addition, it allows face-to-face meetings with other workers when needed. This exhibit also shows other aspects of office design considered by ergonomics.

Ergonomics is only now beginning to address the psychological problems of stress and overwork. Somebody has suggested that all personal computers should be sold with a warning sticker, "Computer use may be harmful to your personal and social life!" Alan J. Fridlund, a clinical psychophysiologist and avid personal computer user, suggests some more specific strategies in "Information Toxicity," an article that appeared in *PC World* magazine in November 1983. First, decide beforehand how much time you are going to spend on a task. When that time elapses, quit. Second, decide ahead of time the level of perfection you want to attain. Don't keep doing "what if" scenarios because they are so easy to do. Third, after you accomplish small goals, reward yourself with "fun" activities that are not connected with the computer, such as going to the beach or gardening. And fourth, plan activities each day that have nothing to do with computers.

If you do make computers a part of your life, these suggestions may help you keep your world in better balance. Unfortunately, little work has been done for those hackers who have an extreme and unhealthy love of computing. Maybe some of these people will decide they need a self-help group, "Computer Anonymous," similar to Weight Watchers or Alcoholics Anonymous.

Exhibit 17.4
An Ergonomically Designed Office Work Area

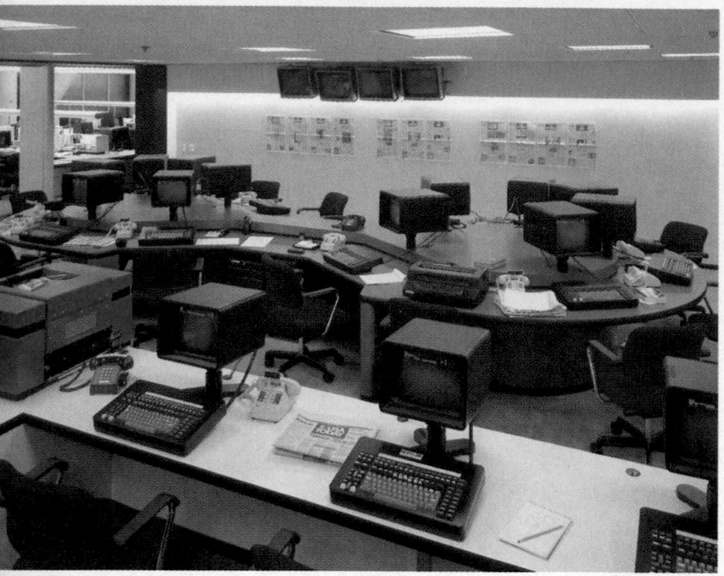

Furnishings	Chairs and work surfaces that adjust easily. Surfaces that hold keyboards should be lower than writing surfaces. Space design allows workers entering information from documents into the computer system to put such source documents in a convenient, well-lighted place.
Storage	Storage areas are easily accessible. Walls are utilized for overhead storage within the user's reach.
Lighting	General lighting is indirect or at least subdued to minimize glare. "Task lighting" is installed directly over work surfaces.
Visual display terminals	Screens adjust to minimize glare. Keyboards tilt upward or even adjust to the angle the user desires. Some keyboards are placed in drawers that can be stored when the terminal is not in use. Screen and keyboard should be separate units.

From "Ergonomics" by Juanita Darling, *The Register,* August 19, 1984. Reprinted by permission of The Orange County Register, Orange County, California.

PRIVACY

One of the keystones of an information society is the ability to collect and disseminate information efficiently. This in turn means that information will be stored in computer data bases. The office, factory, and home information systems that we discussed in the last chapter depend on this. Online encylopedias should be a big help in searching for facts. Checking the inventory data base for the location of parts and sending a robot to retrieve them is an important aspect of factory automation. But what about computerizing personnel files at the office? What about the information that is held in your medical records? What about your income and credit payment history? When does this pooling of personal information violate personal privacy?

While information in any computerized data base should be accurate and secure against unauthorized use, personal information demands extra care. Its entry in a data base opens the door to abuse of one of the fundamental protections offered by our Constitution, the right to personal privacy. **Privacy** might be loosely defined as the right to be left alone.

But several technological advances are being used in ways that may threaten our privacy. First, mass storage devices and data retrieval systems allow large data bases to be stored online relatively cheaply. This has allowed a tremendous increase in the number of computerized data bases holding personal information. For example, financial institutions have records of the number, type, and activities of savings and checking accounts we have. Government agencies have data on the types of cars and real estate we own, where we live, and our current and past spouses. Schools have detailed information on the results of aptitude tests required for admissions, courses taken and grades received, as well as educational degrees granted. Exhibit 17.5 shows some of the types of data bases that hold personal information. How many might contain personal data about you?

Exhibit 17.5
Data Bases Containing Personal Information

Police
FBI
Security clearances
Police information systems

Regulatory
Tax
Licensing
Vehicles

Planning
Property owners
Vehicles
Economic data
Business information

Welfare
Medical
Educational
Veterans
Job openings and unemployment

Financial
Credit bureaus
Savings and loan associations
Banks

Market
Mailing lists
Customer data
Prospect data

Organizational
Personnel files
Membership lists
Professional bodies
Armed forces
Corporation employee dossiers recording intelligence, aptitude, and personality tests, and appraisals and attitudes

Social
Computerized dating
Marriage bureaus
Hobbyist data

Research
Medical case histories
Drug usage
Psychiatric and mental health records

Travel
Airline reservations with full passenger details
Hotel reservations
Car rentals

Service
Libraries
Information-retrieval profiles
Insurance records

Qualifications
Education records
Professional expertise
Membership of professional groups
Results of IQ and aptitude tests

Source: James Martin, *Telemetic Society: A Challenge for Tomorrow,* © 1981, pp. 200–201. Reprinted by permission of Prentice-Hall, Inc., Englewood Cliffs, N.J.

Second, telecommunication networks allow the quick exchange of data between computerized data bases across the country and around the world. This has allowed the development of online information services like credit bureaus, employment search services, and the FBI's National Crime Information Center.

Information Privacy

When they apply for a loan, most people can see the necessity of allowing a credit check to verify their employment, income, and credit history. But what if the credit history contained information on your ethnic background and whether you were married or living with someone? Should an auto insurance company be able to purchase files listing names, addresses, type of cars owned, and car license expiration dates from the Department of Motor Vehicles? Should the police be able to question or arrest you on the basis of information checks made against your file in the Police Information Bank? Would you feel differently if you knew that independent checks of these files have shown that up to 20 percent of these records contain inaccuracies, including unfounded charges that should have been destroyed but were not?

Protection against these types of abuses, called **information privacy,** has three aspects: the data collected, their accuracy, and their release. Only those data that are relevant and necessary to a decision should be collected. The records that are collected should be accurate and kept up-to-date. An individual should have the opportunity to inspect any records and have inaccurate or misleading information corrected. *Confidentiality* means that people must consent to the release of information and that they have the right to know what information will be released to third parties.

What progress has been made in ensuring information privacy? In the private sector, retail credit bureaus maintain files on over 150 million Americans. The Fair Credit Reporting Act specifies the protection consumers have in terms of inspecting, questioning, and correcting their own credit files. Many industries have also established their own codes of ethics. For credit reporting agencies, this means that only the individual's payment record on credit transactions is given. Evaluations such as "slow payer" or personal data such as religion, ethnic background, and life-style are not collected.

Record collection by federal agencies is covered by the Privacy Act of 1974. This legislation specifies the type of records that can be kept, who has access to the information, and the rules of conduct. Exhibit 17.6, The Privacy Act Statement in the Selective Service Registration, specifies why the information is being collected and who can use it for what purposes.

Concerns

As you read the last sentence of the Selective Service registration, you will note that you have no choice but to provide the information requested. Similarly, if you apply for medical insurance, you must sign a waiver releasing information or you will be refused coverage. Government and private companies have managed to get to the information they need and want, while not always adhering to the spirit of the law.

Another threat to privacy comes from the telecommunication equivalent of "junk mail." Some businesses are now using telecommunications and computer voice synthesis to conduct "door-to-door sales" by telephone. These businesses begin by buying a mailing list of people who might be interested in their products. A likely source for these lists is magazine publishers, who often survey readers on their ages, interests, and income. The companies then program a computer to match names on the mailing list with another computer file containing local telephone directories. When the computer finds a match, it dials the phone number periodically until the party answers. Then the computer proceeds to deliver a prerecorded sales pitch. If privacy is the right to be left alone, this application definitely has the potential for harassment.

Exhibit 17.6
The Privacy Act Statement in the Selective Service Registration Regulations

The Military Selective Service Act, Selective Service Regulations, and the President's Proclamation on Registration require that you provide the indicated information, including your Social Security Account Number.

The principal purpose of the required information is to establish or verify your registration with the Selective Service System. This information may be furnished to the following agencies for the purposes stated:

Department of Defense—for exchange of information concerning registration, classification, enlistment, examination, and induction of individuals, and identification of prospects for recruiting.

Department of Transportation—for identification of recruiting prospects for the U.S. Coast Guard.

Alternative service employers—for exchange of information with employers regarding a registrant who is a conscientious objector for the purpose of placement and supervision of performance of alternative service in lieu of induction into military service.

Department of Justice—for review and processing violations of the Military Selective Service Act, or for perjury, and for defense of a civil action arising from administrative processing under such Act.

Federal Bureau of Investigation—for location of an individual when suspected of violation of the Military Selective Service Act.

Immigration and Naturalization Service—to provide information for use in determining an individual's compliance with the Immigration and Nationality Act.

Department of State—for determination of an alien's eligibility for possible entry into the United States and United States citizenship.

Office of Veterans' Reemployment Rights, United States Department of Labor—to assist veterans in need of information concerning reemployment rights.

Department of Health and Human Services—for location of parents pursuant to the Child Support Enforcement Act.

General Public—Registrant's Name, Selective Service Number, Date of Birth and Classification, Military Selective Service Act, Section 6, 50 U.S.C. App. 456.

Your failure to provide the required information may violate the Military Selective Service Act. Conviction of such violation may result in imprisonment for not more than five years or a fine of not more than $10,000 or both imprisonment and fine.

A much broader concern involves Project Match. The federal government is using its extensive data bases to match records held in various department's files in ways that were never intended. For example, the Selective Service System has cross-checked draft registration records with Social Security and motor-vehicle records to apprehend young men who have failed to register. In an effort to locate illegal aliens, the Federal Immigration and Naturalization Service sought access to the New York City Board of Education's computerized file of information about one million students with the goal of compiling a list of households with Spanish surnames. The Internal Revenue Service matches "life-style" data maintained by various business information services with its own internal files. Tax audits are triggered for those people reporting an income "too low" to support their actual life-styles.

It has been argued that Project Match has a valid goal. Few people would question the value of catching people who are cheating on their income taxes, not registering for the draft, or collecting welfare benefits illegally. But many people are concerned that programs like Project Match may be the first steps towards establishing a "Big Brother," the all-powerful surveillance system described in George Orwell's novel, *1984*. What if we allow Project Match to access data held by the information utilities, the telephone company, magazine publishers, credit bureaus, and banks? It is certainly possible that through these records a fairly complete, if not always accurate, picture of our life-styles, our friendships, and even our business associations could be gathered.

It is unlikely that "Big Brother" will be watching us in the near future. But the potential is there. Groups like the American Civil Liberties Union believe that the legal protection of the Privacy Act has become outmoded by new advances in computer technology. Computers at Work: "Silent Watchers" is an editorial from a professional journal that voices some of these concerns (see page 506). Democracy will continue to require a delicate balance between the benefits of providing information for reasoned decisions and the threat to individual privacy.

COMPUTER CRIME

As our society becomes more and more dependent on the computer, and information is recognized as a valuable resource, computers and the information stored in them become logical targets for illegal activities. **Computer crime** is the generic term for all illegal acts that involve the computer in some way. Actually, not all computer crimes are new or exotic. In some cases, hardware and software are simply new targets of thieves or vandals. In others, the computer replaces the bank robber's gun. In still other cases, the computer becomes an accomplice in "white-collar crimes" like fraud. We will give examples of the following types of computer crime: theft of computer hardware, software, and secrets; abuse of computer services; financial fraud; vandalism; and theft of data bases.

Theft of Computer Hardware, Software, and Trade Secrets

Computer hardware such as tape drives, printers, and even the CPU have always been valuable items, which individuals could steal and resell. However, the general security offered by the centralized computer facilities housing the

COMPUTERS AT WORK

Silent Watchers

For several years, government agencies have been matching various computer files to identify persons improperly receiving government benefits. Although the practice probably violates the 1974 Privacy Act, it has continued with little public notice, partly because the targets have been low-income citizens, such as welfare recipients, whose rights are of little concern to most Americans. Now the matching is moving to the big time: The Internal Revenue Service will be testing a match program that checks up on every U.S. citizen and zeros in on affluent ones in particular.

The IRS, hungry for increased revenues, said it plans to test the feasibility of matching its files against commercial lists of U.S. residents, ordered by address and income. If the IRS master file does not contain the name and address of someone judged to have a high income, the agency will assume that person has failed to file a tax return and begin an investigation.

Put another way, while you sleep, the IRS will be surveilling your lifestyle. Do you own an expensive car? Do you live in a neighborhood of above-average wage earners? Based on this and other data, the IRS will be using a statistical profile to gauge your income and make enforcement decisions from the profiles. Some third-party list broker will make a subjective, unsubstantiated decision about your income, and the IRS will launch an investigation against you if its records do not correspond to that data.

Of course you will be given a chance to defend yourself, and that's just what it will be—a defense against charges brought by nameless third parties whom you have never seen or to whom you have never talked. You will be considered guilty until you prove yourself innocent, and the evidence against you will possibly be self-incriminating information you supplied to various agencies with no idea it would be used against you.

It is bad enough when buying a car, paying local property taxes and answering U.S. Department of the Census questionnaires lead to an avalanche of junk mail targeted your way by commercial mailing address brokers who collect data from such sources. But when that same action can lead to possible IRS investigation, something is seriously out of whack.

The IRS argues it is only using publicly available data. That may be true, but the availability of the data has no bearing on whether it is reasonable or legal to use it for criminal investigations. This is nothing more than high-tech rumor mongering. And the rumors have nothing to do with whether you have paid your taxes. No, the rumors have to do with the way you live.

In an age of surveillance, it is dangerous to stand out, even if it is just for having an expensive automobile. We can only hope the IRS plan is not a sign of things to come, of a time when conformity is the only safety from the silent watchers in government agencies.

Based on recent congressional actions to limit the surveillance and computer capabilities of the IRS, we can only assume this plan would not be approved if the IRS had to ask for the money to develop its own profile information and had to get access to Census and local and state tax records on its own rather than purchasing this information cheaply from commercial sources. We hope Congress will look carefully at this program to see whether it violates the privacy directives now governing IRS operations.

Source: Editorial, *Computerworld,* 12 September, 1983, p. 90.

mainframes or minicomputers meant that criminals had to be fairly ingenious to remove the large and bulky computer equipment. The appearance of small, lightweight microcomputers on desktops throughout an organization greatly simplified this type of theft.

Computer software is also a valuable and vulnerable target of theft. Most proprietary software for microcomputers has been sold on highly portable and easily copied diskettes. Users have a legitimate need to protect valuable software by making backup copies, but it is just as easy to make extra copies to be shared among business associates, given to friends, or sold to other potential users. This practice, called **software piracy,** is becoming a major concern of software companies. It has been estimated that, for the most popular software packages, two out of every three copies have been made illegally. While the microcomputer has highlighted the software piracy problem, software for larger computers is an equally attractive target for thieves. Some of these sophisticated programs can cost several hundred thousand dollars.

Trade secrets have long been the targets of industrial espionage. In the highly competitive computer industry, technological breakthroughs, such as the design for an advanced CPU, optical disk, or operating system, are often the key to attaining and maintaining leadership. IBM, a leader in the computer field and dominant in the maxicomputer market, has been the target of several publicized attempts at industrial espionage. In 1982, employees of two Japanese companies, Mitsubishi and Hitachi, were indicted in separate plots to steal IBM trade secrets. An FBI "sting" operation caught these employees engaged in industrial espionage. Their shopping list for information included documents describing the design and manufacture of IBM's latest mainframe CPUs, operating systems, disk controllers, and diagnostic programs.

Abuse of Computer Services

Telecommunications offer the invaluable benefits of access to sophisticated computer systems. This technology can, however, be abused by unauthorized users. In 1983, newspapers headlined the story of the "Milwaukee Gang," a group of teenagers who were able to gain access to over sixty computer systems across this country. These included the computer systems of a bank, cancer research lab, and the nuclear weapons facility in Los Alamos, New Mexico. Using home computers, they accessed time-share computers with phone numbers available through public electronic bulletin boards. Sometimes the bulletin boards had the appropriate passwords, but more often the kids guessed at them or used the computer to cycle through randomly generated passwords.

Officials stated that the teenagers did not gain entry to confidential, classified, or critical data. But some people were reminded of the "prank" when the movie *Wargames* was released. *Wargames* tells the story of a teenage computer whiz who gains access to a Defense Department computer and almost starts a nuclear war. Although computer experts rushed to poke holes in the plot, others feel that sophisticated computer installations take too little care in protecting against unauthorized telecommunication access.

In other cases of abuse of computer services, employees sometimes use the company computer for personal projects. For example, a computer programmer employed by a school board used the school's computer to develop a racehorse handicapping system. In other cases employees have developed computer games or application software, which they can sell commercially for personal profit.

Financial Fraud

Computers have often been used in **fraud,** the use of deceit to gain valuables. The largest financial fraud to date has been the Equity Funding case, which involved several hundred million dollars. Equity Funding Corporation of America had subsidiary companies involved with investment programs, mutual funds, and insurance policies. Certain company officials used the computer to create imaginary new life insurance policies. Eventually, over 50,000 fraudulent policies were issued. To give the picture of realism, the computer was programmed to fabricate the appropriate number of cancellations, lapses, and deaths that might be expected to occur among actual policies. To keep the "books in order" when outside audits were to be performed, the computer was used to shift assets from subsidiary to subsidiary as needed. This type of juggling went on for over ten years!

In another case, Stanley Rifkin was a computer consultant retained by the Security Pacific Bank of California. He used his position to eavesdrop on the electronic funds transfer wire room of the bank. This enabled him to obtain a code that would allow him to manipulate the bank's computerized electronic funds transfer system. He transferred $10 million from Security Pacific to a Swiss bank account. Later he converted the cash to diamonds. Rifkin was caught when he returned to this country and bragged about his exploits.

Vandalism

Political dissidents have conducted assaults on computer installations, often causing extensive damage. Acts of physical violence have included shooting a computer with a revolver, flooding the computer room, or setting fire to a computer installation.

But more subtle methods have also been used. One fired employee erased valuable company records by walking through the data storage area with a powerful electromagnet. Software programming, so-called "logic bombs," have also been used to disable or destroy valuable programs or data after an employee has left the company. For instance, an employee who had programmed most of the company's financial software anticipated being fired because of a personality conflict with the company owner. To ensure his revenge, he planted a query in the program code for duplicating disks. If this query was not answered correctly, it would trigger automatic erasure of the master disk. The first time someone tried to run the disk, the company lost the master payroll file for the chain's two hundred fifty employees and the file containing postings to the general ledger.

Theft of Data Bases

A company's computer-based information is often a valuable resource to the company itself, to its competitors, and to the individuals who might be profiled in the data base. In Europe, Rodney Cox "kidnapped" both his company's financial tape and disk files, and their backup copies. He held about six hundred tapes and fifty disks for a ransom of $500,000. He was eventually caught when he went to pick up the money.

TRW, one of the largest credit-rating companies in the United States, was another victim. The company collects and disseminates credit information on over 50 million individuals. Based on information in its data base, TRW advises its clients about customers who may be bad credit risks. TRW's clients include banks, retail stores, several leasing establishments, and concerns such as American Express, MasterCard, Visa, and Sears.

Six company employees, including a key TRW clerk in the consumer-relations department, decided they could sell good credit ratings for cash. People with bad credit ratings were identified by the computer. Selected people were then approached by the TRW employees, who offered a "clean bill of health" in return for a "management fee." The principal victims of this fraud were TRW's clients, who acted on false credit information. It is easy to see that manipulation of information records could be extended to school grades, aptitude test scores, and police files of arrests or warrants. How much of this goes on is unknown, but the potential for abuse is great.

PREVENTION AND PROTECTION AGAINST LOSS

How big a problem are computer crime and software piracy? No one really knows, because very few computer crimes are ever detected, let alone prosecuted. However, the Research Institute of America has estimated that about $70 billion is lost each year to white-collar computer-related crime. Most experts believe that the problem can only get worse, due to the significant increase in the number of computers sold, the growing automation of business activities, and the spread of computing literacy. So the problem is a serious one. What can be done to prevent or at least minimize the problem? In the rest of this section, we will discuss three solutions, computer security, computer crime legislation, and improved computer ethics.

Computer Security

Most organizations have sought protection through increased computer security. **Computer security** is defined as those safeguards taken to protect a computer system and data from unauthorized access or damage either by deliberate or accidental means. In this section, we will first discuss measures intended to protect against deliberate and accidental loss. Then we will discuss the special field of EDP auditing.

During the last twenty years, most organizations have protected their large computers by controlling either physical access to the main computer room or by controlling logical access to programs and data. For example, large computer systems have been housed in a central location along with online disk drives and offline disk and tape storage. Authorized personnel were granted physical access by security guards who matched photo-identification badges to authorization lists or by computer-readable identifications, such as finger print, voice recognition, or access door combination.

Access to programs and data storage from remote time-sharing terminals was controlled by passwords and account numbers. Operating systems allowed valid users access to only certain programs and data records and limited the type of actions that could take place. This arrangement provides a reasonable level of protection, as long as authorized users don't share passwords, let unauthorized users see them, or use obvious passwords like their initials or birthday. This type of protection would have prevented many of the cases of unauthorized access reported in the press.

Additional mechanisms include logging a person off the terminal after a certain number of invalid passwords have been entered. Some telecommunication systems have a call back feature. When a user logs on, the computer consults a software table that identifies the user and the phone number he or she is authorized to call from. The computer then breaks the connection and calls the user back at the authorized phone number. This prevents access from unauthorized phones. Its disadvantages are that it restricts the mobility of authorized users and forces the computer center to pay for the return calls.

The recent popularity of microcomputers has added to the security headaches of the data processing manager. Personal computers are generally found throughout a corporation, not located in one central location that can be locked and guarded. To minimize theft of these "transportable" microcomputers, corporations often use devices that lock the computer to the desk (see Exhibit 17.7 on page 510). Locks are also used to keep unauthorized users from turning on the computer. Sometimes alarms are installed on personal com-

How Experts Protect Business Equipment
ANCHOR PAD makes it easy to protect against devastating burglary losses that claim over one billion dollars of business equipment yearly.
With ANCHOR PADS theft-stopping power of over 6,000 pounds . . . your computers, typewriters, terminals, video machines, calculators, medical and laboratory equipment are virtually 100% secure.
ANCHOR PADS can protect ten machines for about the cost of replacing one stolen typewriter or computer.
APi
ANCHOR PAD INTERNATIONAL

Exhibit 17.7

The Anchor Pad antitheft device is used to secure computers, typewriters, and other valuable office equipment to a desktop or workspace. Burglary losses claim over one billion dollars of business equipment annually.

Exhibit 17.8

The Semiconductor Key

To secure software, an electronic semiconductor key can be used. Software vendors program the key with their own codes and a matching code is embedded in the software package. The program can be run only if the semiconductor key is inserted into a special socket installed on the computer.

puters, so that any movement will immediately notify the police. With the appropriate key or combination, the computers can be unlocked and moved.

Personal computer software and data are not so easy to protect. Generally, there have been few or no security measures. Software piracy and the relative ease of copying and swapping software diskettes is a real threat to security. One form of protection is the Prolok Magic diskette system. It creates a unique "fingerprint" on each diskette, and encrypts the software program so that it is tied to the presence of this fingerprint. The result is that the software program can be run only when the related Prolok-formatted diskette is mounted on the default drive. Thus, users can make as many backup copies as needed to protect the program from normal accidents. These copies would, however, be inoperable without the Prolok-formatted diskette. This approach has proved to be very effective, except that some companies do sell software that would allow unauthorized users to duplicate the unique "fingerprint." Another security technique is a semiconductor key (see Exhibit 17.8)

The personal computer's threat to confidential data may be a more serious problem for individual companies than software piracy. The great attraction of the personal computer has been its availability, its ease of use, and, in many cases, its portability. Managers, the people we have urged to use microcomputers in decision support systems, data base queries, and electronic mail, often have access to highly confidential data. Now think for a moment about all the diskettes executives use in their office microcomputer or in portable microcomputers in airports or hotel rooms. These diskettes often contain some of the company's most sensitive data. In the case of electronic mail or word processing, these applications are useful because they allow fast delivery of important responses and sensitive data. But these messages are not encoded, so they would be very easy to read if they got into the wrong hands.

Many of these problems can be minimized if users are made aware of the potential seriousness of security problems. Protective measures can be taken. Diskettes can be locked up at the end of the workday. Workers can use shredders to destroy all preliminary printouts, instead of leaving them in wastebaskets, where they could be retrieved by unauthorized personnel. In addition, microcomputer data base management systems now under development offer the password and access code protection of data base management systems for large computers.

While deliberate acts receive much of the press coverage, accidental loss due to natural disasters or other uncontrollable situations is equally dangerous. "Acts of God," such as earthquakes, tornadoes, hurricanes, and floods, have caused significant losses to data processing installations. Electrical power and communication line failures due to brownouts or blackouts can cause problems. Also, power surges, sudden increases in voltage levels, can cause computer components to burn out. Lightning and thunderstorms can cause havoc with telecommunication links, but generally these cause temporary disruptions, as opposed to physical damage. Water pipes bursting, fires spreading from other buildings, even airplanes crashing into the center, and other more exotic chance happenings cause great loss to computer centers each year.

To protect against fire, companies can surround their computer rooms with fire walls and install automatic smoke, heat, and fire detection systems, plus some combination of handheld fire extinguishers and automatic dry and wet sprinkler systems. Flood damage can be minimized by building the computer room on raised flooring that will allow quick drainage. In the case of power outages, computer rooms can be equipped with the capability to switch from electricity from a public utility to an uninterruptible power supply (UPS) or a standby generator. In addition, audible alarm systems can signal danger to workers in the immediate area, and silent alarm systems can signal police or fire officials. Unauthorized personnel can be denied access by either a guard, various identification card readers, or closed-circuit television cameras. No organization can afford to be fully protected against every possible eventuality. Instead, organizations must determine the probability some accident will happen, the potential loss, and the cost of protecting its computer and data from that accident.

In addition to providing a reasonable protection level, it is also very important to have a disaster recovery plan. Such a plan would cover the actions to be taken by specific personnel to resume running critical applications and move toward restoration of all data processing operations. These measures could involve switching to an alternative computer system or retrieving backup programs and data from an offsite storage area.

Computer security has become such a concern to organizations that a special field has emerged to address these issues. **Electronic data processing auditing (EDP auditing)** is concerned with the prevention, detection, and correction of deliberate and accidental loss to computer systems, programs, and data. Because computer crimes, especially financial fraud, are a special concern, EDP auditors have to have a solid background in financial accounting along with computer knowledge.

In addition, EDP auditors are trained in methods of physical security and disaster recovery. Special auditing software is available to detect deliberate and accidental actions against a company's programs and data. But more and more, EDP auditors are taking steps to prevent losses by becoming part of the systems development team. This ensures that proper security measures are incorporated into application programs as they are being developed.

Computer Crime Legislation

In addition to the computer security measures that are or should be adopted by organizations, what other deterrents are being put forth? Legislation is slowly, but surely, being enacted to respond to deliberate acts by computer criminals. In 1978, the state of Florida passed the first computer crime bill in the nation. Since then over eighteen states have enacted computer crime laws. In recent years a host of bills have been introduced to Congress, but as of this date, not one has become federal legislation.

There are a number of reasons for this. First, many people feel that computer crime is not a special or exotic type of crime. Computer crime, they argue, can be prosecuted under existing laws. That is, fraud or embezzlement is illegal whether or not it was committed with a computer. Second, others believe that the new state laws will be sufficient to handle the problem. A third reason is the difficulty in wording new legislation in a way that will keep pace with computer technology.

However, one of the problems of applying existing laws to computer crimes is shown by a 1981 Supreme Court ruling that a person who steals a magnetic tape containing valuable programs or data could be prosecuted only for the cost of the tape itself. In the eyes of the law, the theft involved only a twenty-dollar tape, even if the magnetic tape contained a proprietary software program with a price of a million dollars. Existing legal statutes recognize only tangible value, and electronic impulses were not considered property. It took three or four more years of court cases before a landmark decision was made recognizing data and programs as valuable resources, even when in electronic form. For these reasons many people are recommending that careful legislative action be take to write federal crime laws that will deter and help prosecute criminals in the information age. These laws would focus on information and not just computer technology.

Another problem of applying existing laws to computer crimes involves the legal definitions of computer products. Under present law the source code of computer software is protected by copyright law. However, the machine language version is not. Furthermore, if that software is in a ROM chip, it is considered part of the machine. Thus its maker's rights should be protected by a patent. These distinctions were the basis of the precedent-setting legal case of Apple vs. Franklin. Apple Computer, Incorporated has been a leading manufacturer of microcomputers. One reason for the popularity of Apple computers was the availability of a large collection of application software. If competitors could make sure their machines were Apple-compatible, they could capitalize on this ready-made software without the expense of developing their own software. Compatible microcomputers use different designs but can run the same application software.

The Franklin Computer Corporation allegedly developed a microcomputer that was an Apple clone. To ensure software compatibility with the Apple microcomputer, Franklin did not take the usual path of writing a compatible operating system. Instead, Franklin copied the Apple operating system, which was held in a ROM chip. Apple sued, lost, and appealed. The ruling from the Court of Appeals, that Franklin's action was illegal, seemed to indicate all software was covered by copyright law, whatever its form. The issue may not be settled, however, as Franklin and its lawyers may appeal the case to the Supreme Court.

Ethics

While the movie *Wargames* and real-life examples of computer break-ins have focused attention on external threats to computer security, the truth is that company employees pose a greater threat to corporate data. About 75 percent of computer crime is committed by these employees. Insiders who have extended, if limited, access to a system and who know company procedures find it much easier to identify system vulnerabilities than unauthorized users from outside the company. A dishonest programmer can bypass controls and surreptitiously enter information into the system, authorizing personal transactions. This means that, in addition to computer security measures and crime legislation, employers need to carefully screen the people hired or trained as computer users. Further, it is important to educate company employees on proper computer usage and ethics.

In recent years the computer professional societies have moved to develop codes of ethics that would guide the everyday conduct of computer professionals. Computers at Work: "Ethics for a New Age" shows the standards proposed by DPMA as part of their code of ethics (see page 514). While it was aimed at computer professionals, it should be helpful to all computer users.

ARTIFICIAL INTELLIGENCE

As we have been discussing computer technology and its uses in payroll systems, computer art, or even robotics, we have in fact been talking about a marvelous, but "dumb" machine. For all its wonders, the computer is really just a machine that carries out instructions in a fast, accurate, and efficient way. The thought that directs the computer's actions belong to its programmers and users. But will we eventually build a computer that can think? This question is studied by a branch of computer science called artificial intelligence. The term **artificial** means that the intelligence is exhibited by a machine, while **intelligence** refers to human characteristics like reasoning, learning, and problem-solving abilities. In the rest of this section we will first discuss efforts to give existing computers intelligence through heuristics, learning, and expert systems. Then we will discuss the Japanese project to develop a fifth generation computer. Finally, we will discuss some of the implications of this research in artificial intelligence.

Heuristics and Expert Systems

Let's take some examples of human reasoning and problem solving and see if computers can also do them. If they can, the conclusion, as far as AI is concerned, is that the computer must be intelligent. First, we need to determine what tasks we would consider "intelligent."

What about the task of searching forty pages of text for all the misspelled words? Microcomputer word processing packages with dictionaries can complete this task quite effectively. The computer's technique is to compare the bit pattern representing each word to the bit patterns for all words in the dictionary. When there is no match, the computer highlights the potentially misspelled word. Does this task require intelligence? Probably not; tedious but simple right or wrong matching is sufficient.

COMPUTERS AT WORK

Ethics for a New Age

This is the Code of Ethics and Standards of Conduct approved by the Data Processing Management Association (DPMA):

CODE OF ETHICS

I acknowledge:

That I have an obligation to management, therefore, I shall promote the understanding of information processing methods and procedures to management using every resource at my command.

That I have an obligation to my fellow members, therefore, I shall uphold the high ideals of DPMA as outlined in its International Bylaws. Further, I shall cooperate with my fellow members and shall treat them with honesty and respect at all times.

That I have an obligation to society and will participate to the best of my ability in the dissemination of knowledge pertaining to the general development and understanding of information processing. Further, I shall not use knowledge of a confidential nature to further my personal interest, nor shall I violate the privacy and confidentiality of information entrusted to me or to which I may gain access.

That I have an obligation to my employer whose trust I hold, therefore, I shall endeavor to discharge this obligation to the best of my ability, to guard my employer's interests, and to advise him or her wisely and honestly.

That I have an obligation to my country, therefore, in my personal, business and social contacts, I shall uphold my nation and shall honor the chosen way of life of my fellow citizens.

I accept these obligations as a personal responsibility and as a member of this association. I shall actively discharge these obligations and I dedicate myself to that end.

STANDARDS OF CONDUCT

These standards expand on the Code of Ethics by providing specific statements of behavior in support of each element of the Code. They are not objectives to be strived for, they are rules that no true professional will violate. It is first of all expected that information processing professionals will abide by the appropriate laws of their country and community. The following standards address tenets that apply to the profession.

In Recognition of My Obligation to Management I Shall:

- Keep my personal knowledge up-to-date and insure that proper expertise is available when needed.
- Share my knowledge with others and present factual and objective information to management to the best of my ability.
- Accept full responsibility for work that I perform.
- Not misuse the authority entrusted to me.
- Not misrepresent or withhold information concerning the capabilities of equipment, software, or systems.

But what about a computer that can perform highly logical tasks like solving mathematical theorems or playing logic games like tic-tac-toe, checkers, backgammon, or chess? Is this computer showing "intelligence"? Before you answer let's see how the computer might perform these tasks.

One way to "teach" the computer to play tic-tac-toe would be to direct the computer to play each of the nine opening moves for X. For each opening move, the computer can be directed to consider the remaining options for O, then each of the remaining options for X, and so on until the game ends in a win, draw, or loss for O. Once all the possible outcomes are delineated, the computer would be programmed to respond with the best strategy to ensure at least a draw and possibly a win.

This brute-force approach of searching all possible outcomes break downs quickly as the type of games played become more complex. In chess, for example, each player must plan at least three or four moves in the future, considering the opponent's options as well. A computer using the same strat-

- Not take advantage of the lack of knowledge or inexperience on the part of others.

In Recognition of My Obligation to My Fellow Members and the Profession I Shall:

- Be honest in all my professional relationships.
- Take appropriate action in regard to any illegal or unethical practices that come to my attention. However, I will bring charges against any person only when I have reasonable basis for believing in the truth of the allegations and without regard to personal interest.
- Endeavor to share my special knowledge.
- Cooperate with others in achieving understanding and in identifying problems.
- Not use or take credit for the work of others without specific acknowledgment and authorization.
- Not take advantage of the lack of knowledge or inexperience on the part of others for personal gain.

In Recognition of My Obligation to Society I Shall:

- Protect the privacy and confidentiality of all information entrusted to me.
- Use my skill and knowledge to inform the public in all areas of my expertise.
- To the best of my ability, insure that the products of my work are used in a socially responsible way.
- Support, respect and abide by the appropriate local, state, provincial, and federal laws.
- Never misrepresent or withhold information that is germane to a problem or situation of public concern nor will I allow any such known information to remain unchallenged.
- Not use knowledge of a confidential or personal nature in any unauthorized manner or to achieve personal gain.

In Recognition of My Obligation to My Employer I Shall:

- Make every effort to ensure that I have the most current knowledge and that the proper expertise is available when needed.
- Avoid conflict of interest and insure that my employer is aware of any potential conflicts.
- Present a fair, honest, and objective viewpoint.
- Protect the proper interests of my employer at all times.
- Protect the privacy and confidentiality of all information entrusted to me.
- Not misrepresent or withhold information that is germane to the situation.
- Not attempt to use the resources of my employer for personal gain or for any purpose without proper approval.
- Not exploit the weakness of a computer system for personal gain or personal satisfaction.

Source: *Data Management,* December 1982, p. 31.

egy it used to "learn" tic-tac-toe would have to consider billions times billions of possibilities. Even the fastest computers would need years to play a game involving this kind of exhaustive search. Thus, a different strategy, called *heuristics,* is used. **Heuristics** are "rules of thumb" or general guidelines that help narrow the options that must be considered. For example, heuristics in chess might be "try to control the center of the board" or "it is generally more important to capture a castle than a knight."

Computers programmed with these heuristics and the ability to plan and evaluate several moves and countermoves have accomplished some very impressive results. In 1979 a computer defeated the world backgammon champion. Presently, the most powerful chess program is Belle, which was developed at Bell Labs. It plays at the expert level, which is just below masters. This means a computer can already defeat 99 percent of human players at what has always been considered a thinking game.

Computers can also exhibit learning. That is, they can gain from experience. For example, given the rule that it is more important to capture some pieces than others, some experts have assigned point values to the chess pieces. The queen could be worth ten points, the castle seven, down to the pawns, which might each be worth one point. The computer could play thousands of chess games, and record the outcomes. Based on this experience, the computer might refine the point system, assigning the Queen twelve points and the castle five points. By being able to constantly reevaluate the general rules, the computer is able to develop more effective guidelines. Don't people become good chess players by going through similar learning experiences?

The concept of heuristics has been extended from games to business and medical applications. These new applications are called **expert systems.** The foundation of an expert system is a knowledge base, a collection of rules or heuristics an expert might have about a particular type of problem. A knowledge base for auto care would include rules such as, "IF a car has been driven more than 5000 miles since the last service, THEN change the oil and lube." For medical care, a knowledge base might include the rule, "IF the patient has a runny nose and a fever, THEN the patient is likely to have a cold." Another rule might be, "IF the patient has a cold, THEN prescribe two aspirin and bed rest."

The second part of an expert system is the means to combine rules in the knowledge base to make a logical conclusion, or **inference.** In our simple medical example, the computer could determine that a patient with a runny nose and a fever should be sent to bed and given two aspirins. Exhibit 17.9 shows an example of a more sophisticated inference.

The third part of an expert system is a problem-solving strategy. If, for example, the knowledge base contains 2000 rules on colds, flu, and stomachaches, how would the expert system decide which ones were appropriate and how they should be linked? One form of problem-solving would ask the

Exhibit 17.9

A Computer-Made Inference

Equipping computers with everyday knowledge is the secret of making them smart. One program, Boris, calls on a considerable store of knowledge about such diverse matters as human motivations, restaurants, marriage, divorce, and litigation to gain a detailed understanding of stories it is fed dealing with these topics. The questions and answers shown are a test of Boris's understanding of the following segment of a much longer story: "George was having lunch with another teacher when the waitress knocked a glass of Coke on him. George was very annoyed and left, refusing to pay his check." Note Boris's talent for inferring things never explicitly stated, such as the waitress's bad service being the reason for George's refusal to pay.

Q: What happened at the restaurant?
A: The waitress spilled Coke on George, so he refused to pay.

Q: Where did George have lunch?
A: At a restaurant.

Q: When was George grading homework?
A: At the restaurant.

Q: Why did the waitress spill the Coke on George?
A: She did it by accident.

Q: Who was George eating with at the restaurant?
A: A teacher.

Q: What was George doing at the restaurant?
A: Having lunch and grading homework.

Q: Did George pay at the restaurant?
A: No. The waitress had given George bad service.

COMPUTERS AT WORK

Utah Facility Relies on Help

The Help system is pervasive at the Latter Day Saints Hospital (LDS) in Salt Lake City.

Electrocardiograms (EKG), which test for heart ailments, are input directly from the EKG machine into the Help computer and, within seconds, are analyzed and provided to the attending physician's terminal. Blood gas readings, which tell of heart ailments and test respiratory functions, are also entered directly to the Help computer from the testing machine.

"It's as though [the doctor] were consulting with others as soon as he gets back from the lab," said Dr. Homer Warner, leader of the team of LDS and University of Utah School of Medicine physicians that developed the system. Warner is chairman of the hospital's department of biophysics and the school of medicine's department of biophysics and computing.

When a doctor at LDS orders x-rays for his patient, the Help system considers all the data regarding the patient in question and advises the doctor as to which x-rays will be needed and even what the x-rays might find, Warner explained. A similar course of action occurs when the Help system responds to a doctor's prescription for drugs. The Help system reminds the doctor of the drug's potential side effects, considers the patient's other data and can recommend that lower dosages be administered or that the drug not be used at all.

Such an extensive data base requires a massive storage capacity and extensive hardware. LDS houses its Help system on six Tandem Computer, Inc., Nonstop II CPUs, with 1.3 billion bytes of disk storage and 250 terminals.

The only hang-up with Help at LDS, Warner said, is that it has come to play a key role in the work of physicians there. When the hospital shut down Help a few years ago to reconfigure its computer system Warner said, LDS doctors took a vacation from performing surgery for two weeks until the Help system came back online.

Source: "Utah Facility Relies on Help," Computerworld, 9 July, 1984, p. 18.

patient or doctor a series of questions. Does the patient have a fever? Depending on whether the answer is yes or no, another question would be asked. A form of "twenty questions" would be used to determine a diagnosis. If more information is needed at various points in the questioning, the computer could suggest additional tests or X rays.

Expert systems presently in use include MYCIN, which diagnoses infectious diseases and recommends appropriate drugs, PROSPECTOR, which aids geologists in evaluating mineral sites for potential deposits, and XCON, which is used at DEC to configure minicomputers to meet customer requirements. TAD, a tax advisor system, may soon be available at local offices of H&R Block. This expert system would be used to search the myriad federal income tax regulations, advise the user on what income must be reported and which deductions are applicable, and even complete the IRS tax forms. Computers at Work: "Utah Facility Relies on Help" describes another expert system.

Japan's Fifth Generation Computing Project

How important will artificial intelligence and expert systems become? The answer is controversial, but the Japanese believe this research will help make knowledge as important in the twenty-first century as oil has been in this century. They are devoting billions of dollars to a project of The Institute for New Generation Computer Technology (ICOT). Its complexity and the Japanese government's commitment to the research have led some to compare this

Exhibit 17.10
Components of the Fifth Generation Computer

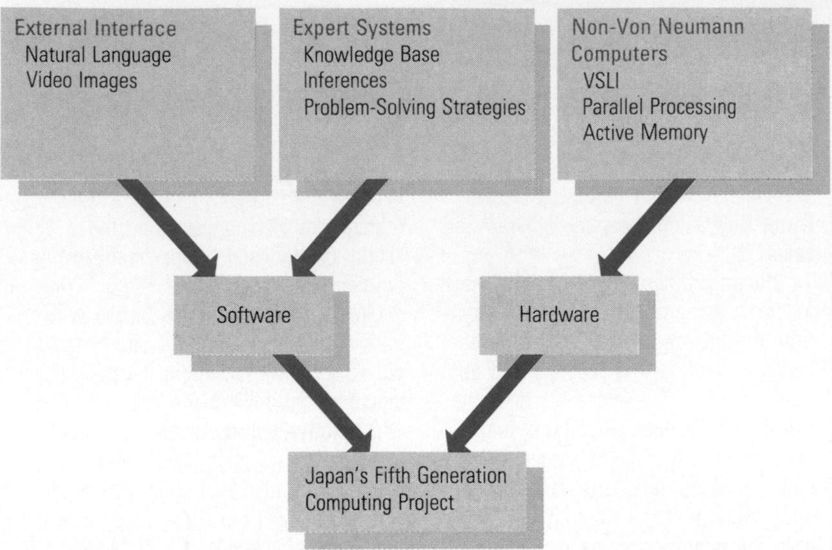

project to our space shuttle. Another term for this project is the **fifth generation computer.** As described in Appendix A, "The History of the Computer," key developments in computer technology have been used to divide computer history into four generations. The fifth generation computers would involve three parts: expert systems, computer hardware with a non-Von Neumann architecture, and external interfaces (see Exhibit 17.10).

The expert systems in fifth generation computers would be similar to current expert systems in that they would contain knowledge bases, the ability to make inferences, and problem-solving strategies. The difference between current expert systems and the Japanese vision lies in the number of rules contained in each knowledge base. Today most expert systems are based on 200 to 2000 rules; fifth generation systems would contain as many as 200,000 rules.

Expert systems of this increased complexity will require the building of significantly different types of computers. First, the memory requirements will be massive. Exhibit 17.11 shows how memory requirements might be reduced.

Exhibit 17.11

"Active" memories composed of tiny processors acting in parallel can perform mental feats much faster than conventional serial computers. Given the task of identifying a gray animal, the serial machine might bring items one by one from the memory's list of "gray things" into the central processing unit and match them against items in the "animal" list. In this example, the maximum number of comparisons needed to find "elephant" is sixteen, but the number increases with the number of objects in memory.

By contrast, an active memory takes the same amount of time no matter how many objects are stored. It consists of "nodes" (colored blocks) connected by "links" (tan bars). Both can perform simple processing functions in response to commands sent by the CPU over the black wires.

To identify a gray animal, the CPU could tell all the links simultaneously, "If you have the symbol 'animal' on one of your ends, set the number 1 at the other end." Then the CPU could say, "If you have the symbol 'gray' on one end, set a 2 on the other end." The final command, "All nodes that have both a 1 and 2, report your identity to the CPU." The only node responding in this instance would be "elephant." The number of commands, three, would stay the same no matter how many objects were stored in memory.

Exhibit 17.11

(See caption on page 518.)

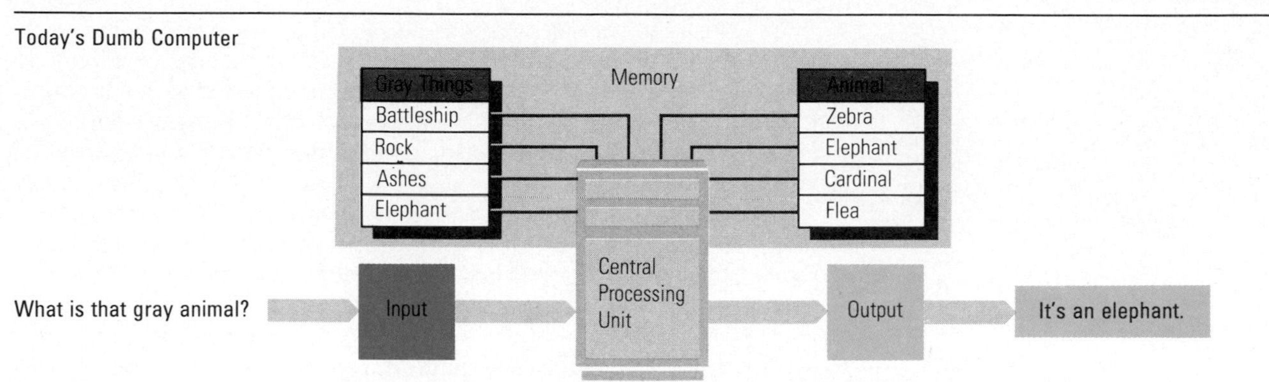

Tomorrow's Smart Computer

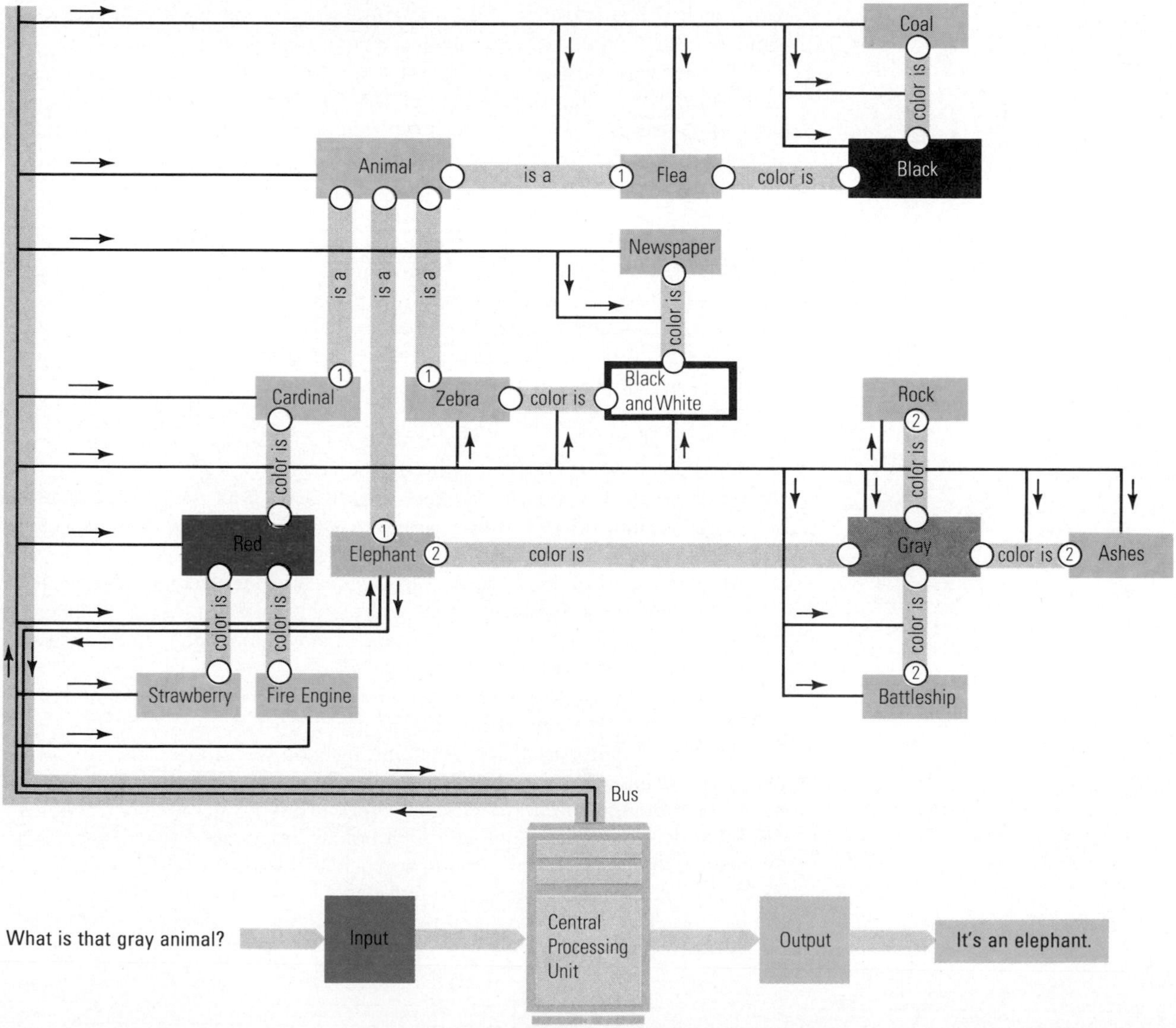

Coal
color is
Animal
is a
1 Flea
color is
Black
Newspaper
is a
is a
is a
color is
1 Cardinal
1 Zebra
color is
Black and White
Rock
2
color is
color is
Red
1
Elephant 2
color is
Gray
color is 2 Ashes
color is
color is
color is
2
Strawberry
Fire Engine
Battleship
Bus

What is that gray animal?
Input
Central Processing Unit
Output
It's an elephant.

Even though a more compact way of relating facts and rules will be used, primary memory requirements may be several thousand times larger than with present supercomputers.

If people are to get quick responses from expert systems, very fast computer systems will be needed to carry on dialogs, search the massive amount of knowledge stored, and make the many inferences required to reach useful conclusions. But we are approaching the limits of our present computers, which are based on the von Neumann architecture discussed in Chapter 3, "The Central Processing Unit."

As we discussed in that chapter, the von Neumann architecture is used in digital computers that use program instructions stored in primary memory to sequence operations performed by a single central processing unit. While the electronic components have moved from vacuum tubes to transistors to integrated circuits, the functions they carry out have remained basically the same. Fifth generation computing will require true parallel processing, which will probably involve millions of small central processing units operating in parallel. These computers will be much more complex than today's supercomputers, which contain several processor chips working on parts of a problem simultaneously, while under control of a central processor.

The last hardware breakthrough that will be required will be superchips built to hold 10 million transistor components. This technology, called very-large-scale integration (VLSI), will require new means of designing and manufacturing chips, since the present large-scale integration can hold "only" around 100,000 transistors.

If expert systems in fifth generation computers are to be useful as computerized advisors, we will also need a much different user-machine interface than we presently have. Keying, pointing, and even speaking have been limited to very structured dialogs. Users have, up to this point, had to learn the "language" of the computer. One of the major goals of fifth generation computing is to produce a natural language interface. A **natural language interface** would allow experts and nonexperts to speak in the language that is most familiar and most comfortable for them. Nonexperts would be able to conduct dialogs in English, Japanese, or Spanish that would seem as natural as talking to another human being. Experts in fields like chemistry would be able to use their more formal technical language directly. The importance of a natural language interface is that it shifts the burden of understanding from us to the computer.

The other part of the interface capability is a robot-machine interface. As robots become more intelligent, they will need to take in pictures or images that provide data about their environment. This will mean they need a vision system, such as a television camera.

Whether the Japanese will be successful in their projects is unknown. It will require significant breakthroughs in hardware and software technology. But the impact even partial success might have on world leadership in commerce is causing organizations within the United States and Europe to scramble to assemble similar efforts. One of the major ventures in the United States is the Microelectronics and Computer Technology Corporation (MCC). This is a joint research effort of twenty-one firms such as Boeing, Control Data Corporation, Kodak, 3M, and Motorola, in fifth generation computing. Of interest is the fact that IBM chose not to join this effort but rather continues on with its own proprietary research.

Implications

What are the implications of successfully developing fifth generation computing? It would extend our "mind power" as far as the Industrial Revolution extended our muscle power. AI expert, Edward Feigenbaum, writing with Pamela McCorduck, makes this judgment in *The Fifth Generation* (Addison-Wesley, 1983):

> *The change from the speed of walking—about four miles an hour—to the speed of automobiles—about forty miles per hour—was an order-of-magnitude change that, while it didn't represent so very much in numbers, has transformed our lives utterly. The next great order-of-magnitude change, from the automobile to jet planes that travel at four hundred miles per hour, has made an equivalent transformation in our lives. This is central to what the Japanese plan for their new generation of computers: quantitative changes in computing speed, power, and reasoning that must make qualitative changes in our lives we can barely foresee. As for the computers that most of us are familiar with right now, they aren't horseless carriages. They're no more than bicycles.*

Maybe even more important, truly intelligent computers would change the way we think about ourselves. Would this be the twenty-first century version of Copernicus's discovery that the earth is not the center of the world? Or would it be more like the discovery that people are not the only intelligent beings on earth?

To extend this thought one step further, if we build and use intelligent computers as our assistants, can we be sure they won't become more intelligent than us and eventually take control? This was the threat described in the movie *2001,* in which an intelligent computer, HAL, tried to control the crew of a sensitive space mission. In *Machines Who Think* (Freeman Publishing, 1979), Pamela McCorduck quotes Edward Fredkin of the Massachusetts Institute of Technology as saying, "It is very hard to have a machine that is a million times smarter than you as your slave."

This whole line of thinking is very controversial, even among experts in artificial intelligence. Even if the fifth generation research succeeds, many believe it would mean a very small advance toward the true intelligence that we humans have. In *What Computers Can't Do* (Harper & Row, 1972), philosopher Hubert Dreyfus argues that the whole AI movement will collapse since it is based on the false assumption that all important human expertise and intelligence can ultimately be analyzed as a set of rules and principles. He compares the AI endeavor to a man climbing a tree to get to the moon. Excellent progress is made at the beginning, but the project quickly gets harder and soon peters out completely at the topmost branches.

OA No Panacea for Economic Ills

An editorial by John B. Dykeman, Associate Publisher/Editorial Director, *Modern Office Procedures*

The emergence of high-technology industries, such as office automation (OA) and computing, has created the misguided impression that they will relieve our nation's unemployment problems and poor economic climate. High technology represents the fastest growing segment in our economy. It has created new jobs, and over the long haul it will improve our lot. In the next few years, however, we still can look forward to a gradual and somewhat painful reshaping and readjustment within the U.S. labor market. So let's not expect computer technology and office automation to be the cure-all.

Most unemployment today stems from the demise of the Second Wave (manufacturing) industries. More than 10 million are out of work in the U.S.; more than 30 million in all the Western countries. To be hard-nosed about it, many of the jobs they had will not return, predicts author Alvin Toffler. Some have moved offshore, some have been automated, and others upgraded.

The choice, then, at least in the short run, is retraining or retirement. Retraining is by no means a total solution, but at least a helpful and much needed Band-Aid. Proposals by well-meaning public figures call for simply retraining huge segments of today's unemployed (with obsolete industrial skills) with new skills in office automation, computing, programming, and other related high-tech activity. From a practical standpoint, only a handful of our 10-million-plus unemployed can quickly be absorbed under such programs. How many former industrial workers will be willing to retrain and re-enter the work force at near-entry level jobs after having earned $25,000 to $45,000 per year? And how many retrained workers can you move from Allentown to Silicon Valley, or how much work can be moved in the opposite direction? And who will come up with the funding?

While office automation and other high-tech activities will continue to spawn new jobs, they may not necessarily generate them at the same growth rate in a white-collar work force, now 54 percent of the total. Automation has changed the work force composition by reducing many clerical "drone" jobs. The ranks of technical and professional "knowledge" workers are swelling, and their productivity expands with the aid of automated tools of information processing. As Toffler points out in *Previews and Premises* (William Morrow & Co., New York, $11.95): "The key to future work is the recognition that routine, repetitive, and fragmented work is no longer efficient. It is already outmoded in high-technology nations." We are now in a custom, de-massified production society, he asserts. Toffler aptly sums it up this way: "Instead of extending brute force, the new technologies extend mental power."

The point: high-tech and office automation are not the total cure but perhaps part of it. OA is the means to an end, and never the end product itself, at least in the user community. Jobs will grow only when OA enables an organization to utilize information to produce products more effectively, competitively, and profitably.

High-tech will ultimately contribute to our national well-being. Meanwhile, everyone is aware of the problems, but the solutions have been mostly lip service. Let's not believe that high-tech can solve it all.

Source: J. B. Dykeman, "OA No Panacea for Economic Ills," *Modern Office Procedures,* July 1983.

SUMMARY

Many people are concerned that each benefit of the Information Society will have a corresponding cost. Some problems can be overcome by more technology, but some involve ethical issues.

Social commentators have noted the growing importance of information and predict that information will replace industry as the basis of our economy. This transition is reflected in the type of jobs available to workers.

The growing use of computers in factories, offices, and stores means that there are fewer and fewer jobs for workers without technical skills. New jobs will be created for robot designers and other information workers, but it is not clear whether these new jobs will offset the number of jobs lost to automation.

As a society, we have some options for dealing with the problem of displaced workers. One option is to stop introducing computers into our offices and factories. However, businesses that compete in the world economy need the economies that result from computerization.

A second option is to become more competitive by computerizing quickly. At the same time, employers can help displaced workers by allowing them to retire early, by sharing the cost savings of automation with workers, or by retraining workers. Retrained workers could probably find employment, since several sources predict a growing demand for highly skilled workers.

Techniques used in today's schools can also be used to retrain workers. These techniques include *computer-assisted instruction (CAI)*, which uses the computer to drill students and *computer-based learning (CBL)*, which uses the computer to simulate actual situations. Workers outside the traditional education scene have many avenues for learning about computers, including industrial and government retraining programs.

Workers who cannot learn new technical skills may be forced to take service jobs. Although the demand for these jobs is growing, these jobs pay low wages and have limited benefits. The result is that these workers may be forced to take substantial pay cuts.

Among the negative side effects of using computers in offices and factories are health problems computer users have either experienced or worried about. Medical studies have refuted many concerns about increased risks of cataracts and birth defects associated with working at video display terminals, but many labor groups are not convinced. A NIOSH study did, however, associate such work with eyestrain, headaches, nausea, lower and upper back pain, and stress.

Physical factors that might be responsible include inadequate working conditions, such as poorly designed worker-computer interfaces, poor lighting, and uncomfortable chairs.

The causes of stress depend on the type of job you have. For data-entry and order-processing clerks, stress comes from constant interaction with the computer and an "assembly line" pace. In some cases, the computer is used as a "watchdog."

While computer professionals experience physical problems, their biggest problem is often stress from the need to be creative under tight deadlines, the backlog of work, and the amount of time actually required by tasks. Constant change and the lack of standards in the computer field is another source of professional stress. Telecommuters, managers, and hackers also face the temptation to overwork and the problem of social isolation.

Ergonomics, the science of adapting machines to people, determines how computers, work, and the work environment can be redesigned for worker comfort and productivity. It involves the design of office furniture, hardware, and office lighting. Ergonomics is only now beginning to address the psychological problems of stress and overwork.

The need to collect, store, and disseminate information can conflict with the right to privacy. *Privacy* might be loosely defined as the right to be left alone. While information in any computerized data base should be accurate and secure, personal information requires extra care.

Mass storage devices, data retrieval systems, and telecommunication networks are being used in unintended ways to collect personal information in huge data bases. The kind and amount of information that is stored has a significant impact on personal privacy. In addition, independent checks have shown that up to 20 percent of these records contain inaccuracies, including unfounded charges that should have been destroyed but were not.

Information privacy, protection from these abuses, has three aspects: collect only data that is relevant and necessary to a decision; keep records accurate and up-to-date; allow individuals the right to inspect, correct, and control the release of personal information.

The Fair Credit Reporting Act specifies the protection consumers have to inspect, question, and correct their own credit files. In addition, many industries have established their own codes of ethics. Record collection by federal agencies is covered by the Privacy Act of 1974.

Concerns for privacy remain, because individuals are often forced to waive their rights to privacy, either by government law or by company policies that refuse service to customers who withhold personal information. Another threat to privacy comes from the telecommunication equivalent of "junk mail," in which computers are used in telephone sales. A more serious concern involves Project Match, the federal government's plan to cross-index its various computerized data bases to catch young men who do not register for the draft, tax evaders, and illegal aliens. To many, Project Watch sounds like "Big Brother" in *1984.* Groups like the American Civil Liberties Union believe that the legal protection of the Privacy Act has become outmoded by new advances in computer technology.

Their value makes computers and the information stored in them logical targets for *computer crime,* a generic term for all illegal acts that involve the computer in some way. One aspect of computer crime is the theft of computer hardware and software, a special problem with personal computers in use throughout companies. Stealing software by making additional, unauthorized copies is known as *software piracy.* Trade secrets are also attractive to thieves.

Telecommunication services can be abused by unauthorized users, who manage to find or guess passwords to computer systems in banks, hospitals, and military installations. In other cases, employees have used the company computer for personal projects.

Computers have also been used in *fraud,* the use of deceit to gain valuables. In these crimes, the computer is used to create and manipulate insurance policies, bank accounts, and other "electronic files" of value.

Vandalism committed by political dissidents include shooting the computer and flooding the computer room. More subtle methods involve exposing computer data to powerful electromagnets and "logic bombs."

In some cases, the information in a data base is stolen or misused. In one case, an employee "kidnapped" the company's financial tapes and disks. In another, TRW employees manipulated credit ratings in return for "management fees."

Although no one knows the extent of computer crime and software piracy, the Research Institute of America has estimated that about $70 billion is lost each year to white-collar computer-related crime.

Most organizations have sought protection through increased *computer security,* measures taken to protect a computer system and data from unauthorized access or damage either by deliberate or accidental means. Physical access can be controlled by locating large computers in central locations and granting physical access by security guards or by computer-readable identifications. Logical access can be controlled by passwords and account numbers and by limiting user access to certain programs and records. Personal computer hardware can be protected by locks and alarms, while software can be protected by measures like semiconductor keys. Data security can be improved by making users aware of its importance.

Computer security within the computer room also includes measures meant to protect against "Acts of God," like fires and floods. In addition to providing a reasonable level of protection, companies also need disaster recovery plans. These measures are often among the duties of *electronic data processing (EDP) auditing.* EDP auditors are often included on systems development teams.

Legislation is slowly being enacted to respond to computer crime. Many people resist federal legislation, however, on the basis that computer crimes are not different from other crimes. Also, some feel that state laws will handle the problem. And other feel that it would be too difficult to word new legislation in a way that would keep pace with technology. One problem with these views is that existing legislation does not recognize the value of information, an intangible good.

About 75 percent of all computer crime is committed by company employees. For this reason, professional organizations have tried to educate employees about proper computer usage and establish codes of ethics.

Artificial intelligence, a branch of computer science, attempts to create computers with the human characteristics of reasoning, learning, and problem-solving abilities.

Heuristics, "rules of thumb" or general guidelines that can be used to narrow the options that must be considered, have been used to make computers excellent players of chess and other logic games. These computers can exhibit learning and use problem-solving strategies.

Heuristics can be used in *expert systems,* which combine a knowledge base with methods for making inferences and problem-solving strategies.

Fifth generation computing would involve expert systems much more vast than today's expert systems, huge memory capacities, parallel processing, very-large-scale integration (VLSI) superchips, and a *natural language* user-computer interface, as well as a robot-machine interface.

If successful, these computer systems would greatly extend our "mind power." It might also change the way we think about ourselves. In the next chapter, we will look at the computer industry as it is today, as well as computer careers.

REVIEW QUESTIONS

1. Briefly summarize the lessons to be learned from Toffler's *The 3rd Wave.*
2. What strategies can this country use to deal with the problems posed by the information age? Which strategy would you suggest?
3. What physical and mental problems have been associated with the automation of offices and factories?
4. What is *ergonomics?* What role does it play in the computer age?
5. Briefly summarize the threats to personal privacy posed by technological advances.
6. Jan Lewis and Paul Mason are living together. Paul has a poor credit record. Jan has just applied for a loan from a very conservative bank. How might her application be affected by computerized information banks? On what protection(s) can Jan and Paul rely?
7. What concerns for technology abuse exist today? Does the government really provide protection?
8. What is *computer crime?* What forms may it take?
9. Briefly summarize the ways in which computer crime may be minimized or prevented.
10. What is *artificial intelligence?* Briefly evaluate its potential benefits and threats.
11. What are *heuristics?* How does this concept apply to computers?
12. What is an *expert system?* What kinds of applications does it have?

CHAPTER 18

The Computer and Information Industry

COMPUTERS AT WORK

The Hard Sell Comes to Software

The folks who brought you soap and soft drinks are now marketing the programs for your personal computer. It's an expensive game that favors the biggest players.

The television commercial looks like a compilation of *Close Encounters* outtakes: a casually dressed but serious threesome strides through the mist. Reaching their destination, they stop awestruck before a hologramlike cube that cradles a product name. "Framework," says a voice-over in ominous tones, "for thinkers."

Is this any way to sell business software for personal computers? Ashton-Tate, the maker of Framework, apparently thinks so. The company bought about $4 million worth of local and cable television time during the Democratic Convention and the Olympics to run this commercial. Lotus Development Corp., another major microcomputer software publisher, spent about the same amount touting its newest product, Symphony, on network TV during the Summer Games.

The clamor to capture the TV viewer's attention is just the latest—and most expensive—sign that hard sell is coming to software. The market for microcomputer business software—programs used mostly in the office for tasks like spreadsheet analysis, word processing, and data-base management—will reach $1.8 billion in sales this year and is expected to double by 1988. But with perhaps 2000 companies producing business software, the market is so fragmented that even the big players, such as Lotus and Ashton-Tate, have sales of $100 million or less.

The software companies are experimenting with an array of marketing techniques that they hope will propel them to the top of this highly charged industry. They are advertising on television and in newspapers, magazines, and catalogs, and selling through direct mail. They are courting dealers and offering consumers coupons, trial samples, and even trade-ins on older models. All the money and effort have one simple aim: to make the software name known.

That won't come cheap. At some software companies, marketing costs—advertising, promotion, sales support, and distribution—are now the single largest expense, bigger even than research and development. At Lotus, marketing costs for the launch of Symphony and spending to promote the best-selling spreadsheet program, 1-2-3, will probably amount to 20 percent of total revenues. Companies that don't pay up to get in on the action won't get their products on retailers' shelves and may ultimately fade away. "The days of writing a hit program, dumping it into distribution, and making an instant killing are over," says Jim Manzi, Lotus's vice-president of marketing and sales.

Joseph Levy of International Data Corp. and others predict that eventually the software business will be running the computer industry. Says he, "People will figure out what they want to do, have the retailer show them the various packages, and then decide what kind of computer to buy." Between now and then, millions more dollars will go into marketing. Software ads seem destined to become commonplace on TV, and software publishers will come up with more inventive ways to flog their brands.

Source: M. McComas, "The Hard Sell Comes to Software," *Fortune,* 17 September, 1984, pp. 59–64.

As the opening application shows, marketing—for both hardware and software—will become more important as the information segment of our economy continues to grow. In this chapter, we want to discuss several aspects of this growing field. In addition, we want to discuss some of the careers you may find in this growing industry. In this chapter, you will learn to do the following:

1. Describe the dominant manufacturers in the maxi-, mini-, micro-, and supercomputer markets.
2. Discuss how the software industry has developed to meet emerging needs for software packages.
3. List the leaders in the computer service industry and explain their roles in bringing computing power to organizations.
4. Explain the distribution channels that have developed to service organizational, professional, and home users of computer systems.
5. List the major ways people are getting information about computer systems and how to use them effectively.
6. Describe the computer professional jobs and their educational requirements.

THE COMPUTER AND INFORMATION INDUSTRY: AN OVERVIEW

The history of the computer and information industry has been marked by technological change and rapid growth. In Appendix A, "The History of the Computer," we show you how the technology used by today's leading companies developed. In this chapter, we want to give you an overview of the companies now leading the computer and information industry. To do this, we have researched industry sources to provide you the most current information available when this text was in preparation. These same industry sources can be consulted for updated information you may need as you plan your education and career.

The computer and information industry is made up of organizations that emphasize computer hardware manufacturing. Some companies, such as IBM, manufacture maxi-, mini-, micro-, and supercomputers. Other computer manufacturers, such as Apple Computer, produce only microcomputers. A growing number of companies, however, specialize in producing software packages. For example, Lotus Development Corporation is the producer of the software packages of 1–2–3, Symphony, and Jazz for the personal computer market. Other companies, such as ADP, provide computing services, such as general accounting and computerized payroll, to over 100,000 businesses.

At one time computer hardware and software could be purchased only from the computer manufacturer. The distribution channels are much more varied now. A recent phenomenon is the computer store, now common in shopping centers and malls. Lastly, there are many small businesses, vendors, and consultants who provide information and training in using computers and gaining access to electronic information.

On the following page, Exhibit 18.1 lists the top fifty companies in the world's computer and information industry. You will recognize many of the names. Of special interest is Fujitsu (number 6), which is the leading company not based in the United States. Another notable entry is AT&T (number 18). In

Exhibit 18.1
The Top Fifty Companies in the Computer and Information Industry

1984 Rank	Company	1984 Total Revenue	1984 DP Revenue*	1984 Rank	Company	1984 Total Revenue	1984 DP Revenue*
1	International Business Machines	$45,937.0	$44,292.0	26	N. V. Philips Gloeilampenfabrieken	$ 5,221.2	1,090.3
2	Digital Equipment Corp.	6,230.0	6,230.0	27	Northern Telecom Inc.	3,330.0	1,050.0
3	Burroughs Corp.	4,875.6	4,500.0	28	McDonnell Douglas Corp.	9,662.6	982.8
4	Control Data Corp.	5,026.9	3,755.5	29	Automatic Data Processing Inc.	958.3	958.3
5	NCR Corp.	4,074.3	3,670.0	30	Oki Electric Industry Co. Ltd.	1,738.6	899.8
6	Fujitsu Ltd.	6,440.7	3,499.3	31	General Electric Co.	27,950.0	865.0
7	Sperry Corp.	5,370.0	3,473.9	32	Texas Instruments Inc.	5,741.6	860.0
8	Hewlett-Packard Co.	6,297.0	3,400.0	33	Mitsubishi Electric Corp.	7,329.5	817.0
9	NEC Corp.	7,594.3	2,799.4	34	Storage Technology Corp.	808.0	808.0
10	Siemens AG	16,076.8	2,789.5	35	General Motors Corp.	83,889.9	786.1
11	Wang Laboratories Inc.	2,421.1	2,420.7	36	Amdahl Corp.	779.4	779.4
12	Hitachi Ltd.	21,048.2	2,199.5	37	Harris Corp.	2,187.7	730.0
13	Ing. C. Olivetti & Co. S.P.A.	2,891.9	2,012.4	38	Tandy Corp.	2,794.7	719.1
14	Apple Computer Corp.	1,897.9	1,897.9	39	Computer Sciences Corp.	709.6	709.6
15	Honeywell Inc.	6,073.6	1,825.0	40	Prime Computer Inc.	642.8	642.8
16	Groupe Bull	1,555.6	1,555.6	41	ITT Corp.	12,700.9	640.0
17	Xerox Corp.	8,791.6	1,518.0	42	Triumph Adler AG	807.0	631.6
18	AT&T Co.	33,200.0	1,340.0	43	Motorola Inc.	5,534.0	618.0
19	Data General Corp.	1,229.7	1,229.7	44	Datapoint Corp.	589.2	589.2
20	ICL	1,222.7	1,222.7	45	Tandem Computers Inc.	565.9	565.9
21	Nixdorf Computer AG	1,147.4	1,147.4	46	Computervision Corp.	556.3	556.3
22	Toshiba Corp.	13,891.8	1,136.6	47	National Semiconductor	1,818.0	550.0
23	Commodore International Ltd.	1,189.5	1,129.5	48	Dataproducts Corp.	484.5	484.5
24	L. M. Ericsson	3,545.1	1,123.3	49	C. Itoh Electronics Inc.**	531.1	443.1
25	TRW Inc.	6,061.7	1,105.0	50	Telex Corp.	523.8	442.7

*Ranking is by data-processing revenue in millions.
**U.S. operations only.

Source: P. Archbold and J. Verity, "The Datamation 100," *Datamation,* 1 June, 1985, p. 50.

1984, the FCC allowed AT&T to sell computers in addition to its extensive data communication facilities. The position of Apple Computer (number 14) is evidence of the impact of microcomputers in this industry. Lastly, note that General Motors (number 35) has entered the field through its acquisition of Electronic Data Systems, a leading computer services corporation.

Another way of looking at the relative importance of various aspects of this industry is to see how business organizations allocate their data processing budgets. The data processing budget for large organizations is typically 1 to 2 percent of company sales. In very information-intense corporations this figure can increase to 5 or 6 percent. These budgets are generally divided among computer hardware (37 percent), software packages (13 percent), supplies and miscellaneous expenses (10 percent), and computer personnel (about 40 percent). It may be helpful to keep these budgetary proportions in mind as we discuss various aspects of the computer and information industry and computer careers.

Computer Hardware Manufacturers

In the United States, business and government investments in computers have grown from around $7 billion in 1960 to over $100 billion in 1985. Coupled with this heavy investment is the tremendous increase in computer performance per dollar brought about by advances in technology. The net result is over a 1000-time increase in the value of computing power purchased during the last twenty-five years.

Who are the key manufacturers providing this computer power? The answer depends on whether we are talking maxi-, mini-, micro-, or supercomputer systems. But clearly, the primary force in the computer field has, is, and will continue to be IBM. Appendix A, "The History of the Computer," will help you understand how IBM achieved this position. Here, we want to overview the leaders in each of the major segments of the hardware industry.

Maxicomputers

For most of the history of the computer industry, maxicomputers, also known as mainframe computers, have been the primary segment of the hardware market. The dominant manufacturer is IBM. As seen in Exhibit 18.2, IBM's 1984 mainframe revenues were almost double the combined revenues of all other mainframe manufacturers. Estimates of IBM's market share in this segment range from 70 to 90 percent.

The other manufacturers in this segment of the hardware market simply lack the financial resources to compete directly with IBM. IBM's dominance does not necessarily imply they make better computer systems than Burroughs or Control Data Corporation. Rather, IBM's dominance results from a superb combination of manufacturing ability, marketing strength, maintenance and service, and research and development efforts.

Many people believe that only organizations outside the traditional computer field will be able to challenge IBM's leadership. Two likely candidates are Fujitsu and AT&T. Fujitsu, the largest computer manufacturer in Japan, is an international organization with the resources to compete with IBM in many segments of the computer industry. Fujitsu has entered the American market by acquiring a half interest in Amdahl, a manufacturer of IBM-compatible mainframe computers, and by producing their own IBM PC-compatible microcomputer. A second source of competition may be AT&T. In 1984, the federal government broke up AT&T. This action allowed former divisions of this massive organization to compete directly in the computer field. In a major computer show in April 1984, AT&T showed a full range of micro- to minicomputer systems, demonstrating its determination to compete aggressively in this field.

Exhibit 18.2
The Top Mainframe Manufacturers, Ranked by Mainframe Revenues in Millions of Dollars

Company	1984	1983	1982
IBM	13,131	11,444	10,662
Sperry Corp.	1,451	1,301	729
Burroughs Corp.	1,450	1,300	2,000
NCR Corp.	1,345	1,000	1,100
Control Data Corp.	813	775	705
Honeywell Inc.	665	630	1,060
Amdahl Corp.	400	571	412
National Semiconductor	250	201	175

Source: P. Archbold and J. Verity, "The Datamation 100," *Datamation,* 1 June, 1984, p. 50 and 1 June, 1985, pp. 37–182.

Minicomputers

In the minicomputer field Digital Equipment Corporation (DEC) and Data General have been the pioneers, with DEC being the dominant manufacturer for many years. However, IBM has entered this market with their System 34 and the recently added Systems 36, 38, and Series 1 minicomputers. These later computer systems have changed the market standings, and now IBM has taken the revenue lead (see Exhibit 18.3). DEC, however, has the largest installed base of minicomputers and was expected to sell almost 20 percent more computer systems than IBM did in 1985.

The difference in leadership based on revenues and on number of computers sold can be traced to the higher prices IBM charges. The average price of an IBM minicomputer is $217,000, versus $46,000 for a DEC minicomputer. This in turn reflects the fact that IBM sells complete computer systems (computer, peripherals, and software) to businesses. In contrast, DEC tends to sell "stripped down" models. These are either purchased by dealers, who add their own peripherals or proprietary software and resell the system, or the DEC minicomputers are used as data communication processors.

With aggressive minicomputer manufacturers such as DEC, Wang, Hewlett-Packard, and Prime in this field, it is not expected that IBM will be able to dominate this segment as it dominates the mainframe market.

Exhibit 18.3

The Top Minicomputer Manufacturers, Ranked by Minicomputer Revenues in Millions of Dollars

Company	1984	1983
IBM	3,000	2,627
Digital Equipment Corp.	1,527	1,000
Wang Laboratories Inc.	970	892.9
Hewlett-Packard Co.	950	735.3
Data General Corp.	840	706
Burroughs Corp.	700	650
Olivetti	540.1	490.5
Prime Computer Inc.	479.1	416.5
Tandem Computer Inc.	477.1	387.4
Toshiba Corp.	421	378.9

Source: P. Archbold and J. Verity, "The Datamation 100," *Datamation,* 1 June, 1985, p. 38.

Microcomputers

Between 1978 and 1982, when the microcomputer was first used in homes, schools, and businesses, Apple, Commodore, and Radio Shack (Tandy) were the primary manufacturers. IBM offered a small business computer series called the 5100 at that time, but it was overpriced and technically obsolete. IBM's effort to market this equipment for business applications was ineffective against the technically superior Apple and Radio Shack microcomputer systems.

This all changed in August 1981, when IBM entered the personal computer field with the IBM PC. This microcomputer, which offered a technically current 16-bit processor and good software, was marketed through computer stores and business product centers. By the end of 1982, IBM was number two in sales, took the lead in 1983, and by 1984 had close to a 50 percent share of the professional market (see Exhibit 18.4).

The personal computer market is really made up of several different market segments: business and professional users, home users, scientific users, and educational users. Several companies are strong in different segments. Commodore presently is dominant in the home market with the Apple II series showing strong. IBM's entry, the IBM PC Jr., fell on hard times and was withdrawn. The Apple II series and various models from Tandy (Radio Shack) are doing best in the kindergarten through high school educational market since Texas Instruments has dropped out. DEC, Hewlett-Packard, and IBM share the scientific market about equally. But overall, and for the professional market especially, the IBM PC along with the MSDOS operating system has become the de facto standard for microcomputers. By 1985, IBM had established a 60 to 70 percent market share. With the exception of Apple, almost every other major competitor in this market had developed a computer model that was "IBM PC compatible."

The innovator, Apple, felt that it could maintain its lead by continuing to be unique rather than by becoming an IBM clone. In 1983, Apple introduced the Lisa microcomputer, which featured a user interface based on a graphic (icon) approach. This computer system was aimed at the professional and managerial level of Fortune 500 companies. While the new user interface received rave reviews for its usefulness, the $10,000 price tag and lack of application software led to less-than-spectacular sales. A year later, Apple introduced the next edition of the icon approach, the Macintosh. This competitively priced microcomputer was aimed at the professional, home, and school markets. Sales were excellent in these markets. But if the Macintosh was going to succeed in the corporate market, Apple Computer had to develop a way to link Macintoshes, as it has done through the Macintosh Office. Secondly, Apple had to acknowledge the presence of IBM mainframes and develop ways to connect the Macintosh to them (see Exhibit 18.5 on page 534). Interestingly, an independent company, Dayne Communication, has developed an external attachment to the Macintosh that allows it to run MSDOS programs used with the IBM PC computers. It is called MacCharlie.

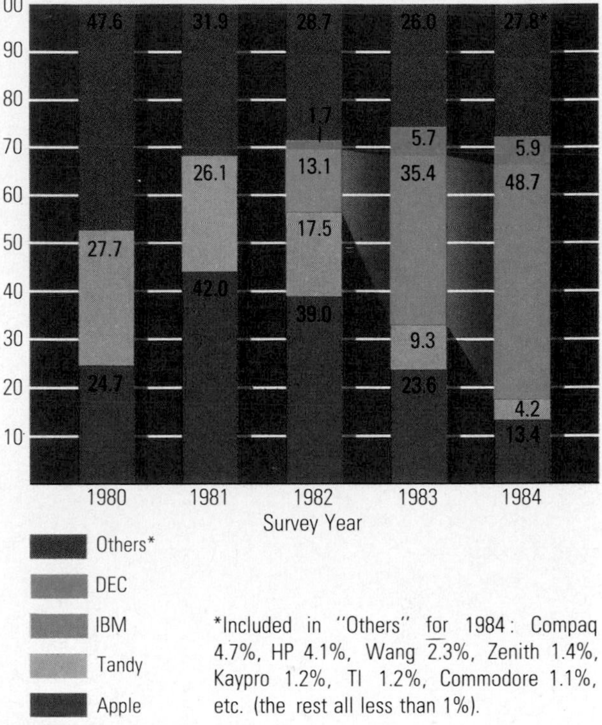

Exhibit 18.4
The Top Microcomputer Manufacturers for the Corporate Market

Supercomputers

The supercomputer market is supplied by two major companies, Cray Research Inc. and Control Data Corporation (CDC). These companies make large-scale scientific computers, which are used by organizations doing work in the fields of weather, seismic research, aerospace, biomedicine, and movie special effects (*Star Wars*). This market consists of about two hundred of the most prestigious users worldwide, and their computer needs are expected to grow at a rate of 40 percent per year.

Seymour Cray, one of the leading designers of supercomputers, led CDC's efforts in this area for many years (see Exhibit 18.6 on page 534). In 1972 he left to form his own company, Cray Research. The Cray supercomputer series has been and is expected to continue to be dominant, although several other companies have recently begun to plan products for this market.

Fifteen years ago IBM was a major supplier of supercomputers, but decided to focus its energies on other markets. Although IBM is not a factor in today's supercomputer market, there is speculation that IBM may reenter this segment and compete aggressively in the near future. However, the greatest potential competition will probably come from the Japanese and their fifth generation computer project.

IBM is finally talking to us.

And we're finally talking to them.

Thanks to The Macintosh™ Office.

Using our AppleLine protocol converter and MacTerminal™ software, Macintosh can speak IBM® 3270 like a native. Not to mention DEC® VT100,™ VT52™ and TTY.

In English, that means you can find almost anything that's stored in your company's mainframe. Just the same as if your Macintosh was an IBM terminal.

Say, for instance, you want to know how sales are going as of yesterday. Where your inventory stands. Or if receivables are staying ahead of payables.

With a Macintosh on your desk, all that information is right at your fingertip. Even if your mainframe's on the other side of the building. Or the other side of the world.

Now if you think that's impressive, you haven't read anything yet.

Once you've located the data you want, you can "cut" it out of the mainframe and "paste" it directly into a spreadsheet program like Lotus® Jazz™* Or Microsoft® Multiplan® Then turn the numbers into a chart with a business graphics program. Such as Microsoft Chart. And last, but certainly not least, print out a publication-quality report, memo or presentation with our LaserWriter printer.

Total elapsed time: about 20 minutes.

And if you need to know something that's not in your mainframe—like up-to-the-minute stock quotes—you can use MacTerminal and an Apple Modem to tap into a number of commercial information services. Including Dow Jones News/Retrieval® NEXIS® LEXIS® And The Official Airline Guide® So you can use Macintosh for everything from scanning *The Wall Street Journal* to making airline reservations.

In The Macintosh Office, workgroups of 5 to 25 people will talk to each other over our AppleTalk™ Personal Network.

All of which means you should finally be talking to us.

Call 800-446-3000, and we'll tell you more about how well The Macintosh Office will fit into the one you're in now.

Even if there's a big blue box in one corner.

The Macintosh Office

Exhibit 18.5

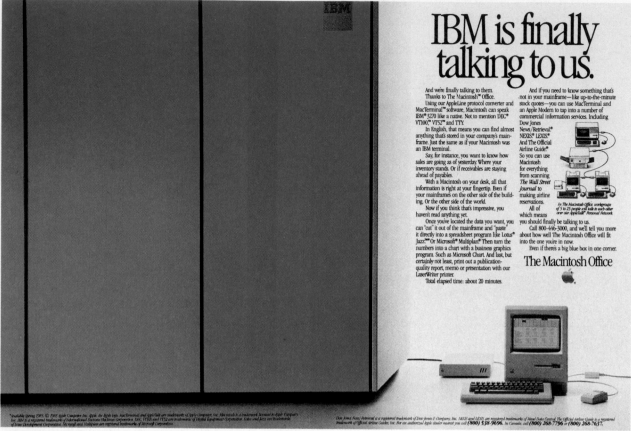

Apple had to acknowledge the presence of IBM mainframes and develop ways to connect the Macintosh to them.

Exhibit 18.6

Seymour Cray is one of the leading designers of supercomputers. The Cray 2 is the latest and most powerful of the supercomputers.

THE SOFTWARE PACKAGE INDUSTRY

As important as computer hardware is, the key to a successful computer system is the software. The two primary approaches to acquiring application programs are customized programming or buying a software package. The advantages and disadvantages of these approaches were discussed in Chapter 12, "Systems Development II."

It is forecast that the data processing budget for most companies will increasingly be devoted to the development and acquisition of software. Although hardware sales are expected to double over the next five years, hardware costs are decreasing, meaning that companies can spend less money to buy the more powerful maxi- and minicomputers needed to meet the growing demand for information. At the same time, however, the salaries of data processing personnel will continue to rise. Thus, companies will acquire software packages to clear the growing backlog of requests for application software and to meet the demand for end-user computing tools. Sales of software packages are expected to grow at twice the rate of hardware sales and be a 40 billion dollar industry by 1989.

The software package industry is composed of three major segments: systems support software, applications software, and end-user software (see Exhibit 18.7). Systems support software is composed of operating systems, language translators, sorting packages, telecommunication packages, and data base management systems. The mainframe, minicomputer, and microcomputer market for this software is about 30 percent of total software sales. This software has been supplied primarily by the mainframe vendors such as IBM, with the independent software companies providing about one-third. The top independent companies supplying systems support software for larger computer systems include Cullinet Software, Applied Data Research, Pansophic Systems, and Cincomm Systems, while Digital Research and Microsoft are among the many companies supplying system support software for microcomputers.

Applications software packages for all sizes of computer systems comprise about 40 percent of the total market. The applications have traditionally been accounting, payroll, and inventory control packages. The major growth areas are now electronic mail, purchasing management, material requirement planning (MRP), and master production scheduling. IBM, DEC, and Hewlett-Packard are major suppliers of this software. The major independent software companies are Management Science America (MSA), McCormack & Dodge, and Informatics General.

End-user software includes word processing, spreadsheets, data base management, financial analysis, statistical packages, and the like. This market is presently 30 percent of the overall industry, but is expected to continue to increase in importance to satisfy end-user computing needs. Lotus Development Corporation, Micropro International, and Ashton-Tate are major companies in this segment of the microcomputer software industry, while companies such as SAS Institute and Execucom supply similar tools for the larger computer systems. Many of the major companies who have been successful in the mainframe software field are now trying to adapt their software for microcomputers, but with mixed success.

Exhibit 18.7
Major Segments of the Software Package Industry

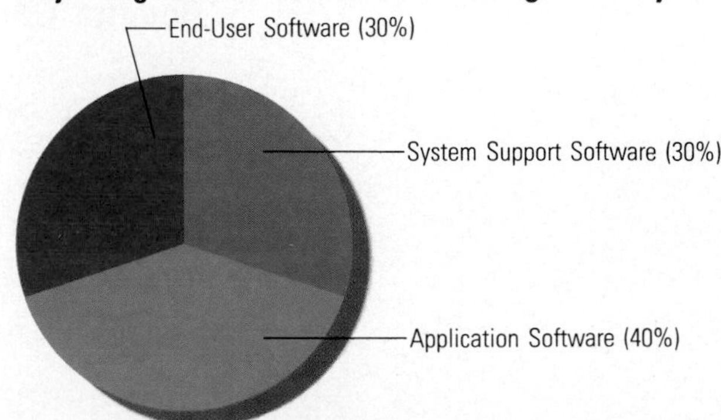

Exhibit 18.8
The Most Common Workplace Applications for Personal Computers

Reprinted with permission of *Datamation®* magazine. Copyright © by Technical Publishing Company, A Dun & Bradstreet Company, 1984—all rights reserved.

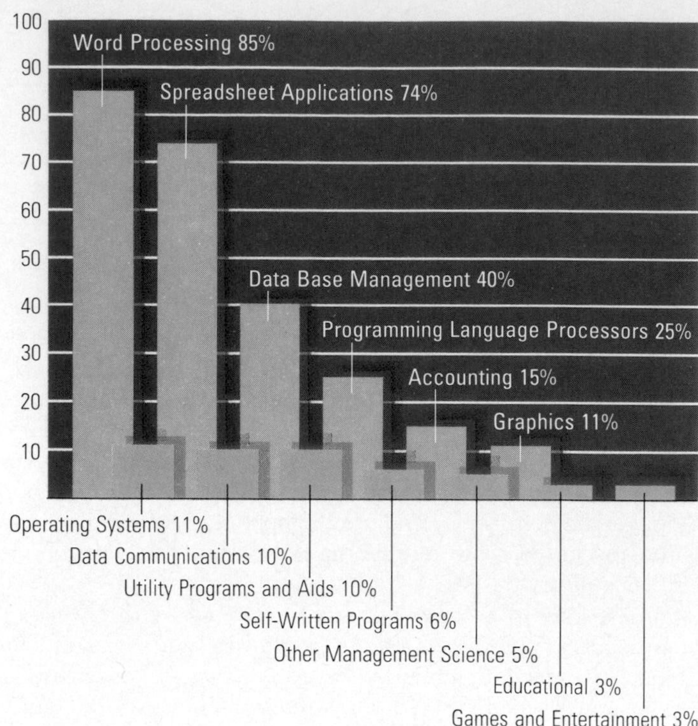

Exhibit 18.8 shows the results of a survey about the types of software packages most commonly used with personal computers. Clearly, the most common applications are for word processing and spreadsheets, with data base management systems used by 40 percent of the people.

THE COMPUTER SERVICES INDUSTRY

A very large segment of the computer and information industry is made up of companies that provide computer services to organizations. These can be classified as remote computer services, network services, and facilities management.

Remote Computing Services

Remote computing services (RCS) can take several different forms. In the service bureau approach, the client business would prepare data entry forms, such as payroll sheets, which would be picked up by courier. These forms would be keypunched by the service bureau personnel and run on the service bureau computer. The resulting printouts or payroll checks would be returned by courier to the company. The overall process usually takes several days.

With the advent of telecommunication links, a terminal can now be placed at the client's business location. A data entry clerk can key the data into the CRT following menus and "electronic forms." The input data are then captured and stored in a data base. Later the data are processed on the service bureau's computer using their proprietary software package. The results can then be returned by courier or sent to a remote printer located at the client's site.

For more interactive operations, such as specialized engineering and scientific packages, or to access a particular data base, remote computer services can be set up to act just like a remote time-sharing service. Some of the better-known companies offering remote computer services are Boeing, General Electric, and McAuto. Telecommunication allows users to access the time-share computers by terminals located at their own sites. The only difference is that the main computer is not owned by the user's company. Instead it is owned and operated by the remote computing service.

Three key factors make this approach attractive to several million users. First, remote computer services provide effective computing service at a lower cost than the client business could get with its own computer system. Second, the remote computing service has technical experts who specialize in specific industries and are therefore able to advise users and provide solutions to their problems. Third, remote computing services can offer specialized application software at a nominal charge, since any development costs can be divided among many customers.

Automatic Data Processing (ADP) is one of the leading firms in the computer services industry. While it is best known for its payroll software packages, ADP provides additional accounting services to over 700,000 clients. ADP provides financial services to bank and thrift institutions for loan processing, savings accounts, check processing, and cash management. Among its many other services, ADP provides a computerized data base for use in estimating insurance claims for collision repairs. This includes part descriptions, part prices, and labor costs involved in repairing over 2000 foreign and domestic cars.

Network Services

Network services are another facet of the computer services industry. A number of companies have established their own data communication networks. Several of the major companies are Tymshare (Tymnet), Computer Sciences Corporation (Infonet), and Control Data (Cybernet).

For example, users can gain access to Tymnet from over two hundred cities in North America, as well as parts of Europe via transatlantic cable. This access allows users to communicate with each other via electronic mail and message service. Generally, the connect charge is based on local call rates and thus is effectively independent of distance to either the other party, data base, or proprietary software. In addition, Tymshare can provide electronic funds transfer (EFT). This company has a significant presence in bank credit-card processing, credit authorization, and point-of-sale merchant service.

One of the emerging uses for this type of network service is shown by Telesun. *Telesun* stands for *Tele*communication *S*oftware *U*ser's *N*etwork. Its purpose is to provide an economical way to "rent" applications software. One of the advantages of remote computer services is that clients have to pay only local telephone rates. The disadvantage is that the total charge is based on how long they are connected to the network. With Telesun, the proprietary software is downloaded to the disk system of the client's microcomputer. This generally takes less than three minutes. There are no more connect charges to the network, and only a one-time access fee of about fifty cents to cover services and royalties. There is a monthly subscription fee of around twenty-five dollars.

Interestingly, clients can run the proprietary software on their present computers as many times as they want, so long as they don't turn the computer system off or exit the program. But, if any type of copy commands are entered, the program is rendered unusable.

Facilities Management

Another facet of the computer services market is that of **facilities management.** Here, a service company contracts to run an organization's local computer system and provide the professional services necessary to handle data processing needs. For an analogy, this would be like renting a computer and data processing department. Contracts typically run for several years and then are opened for bids once again.

Government agencies at the federal, state, county, and city levels are among the largest users of facilities management. Two of the major firms in this field are Electronic Data Systems (EDS) and Computer Sciences Corporation (CSC). CSC does the majority of its work with NASA and defense contractors such as the Navy. In 1982, EDS was awarded a half-billion-dollar contract by the U.S. Army. This was the largest contract in the history of the computer services industry. The project involved revamping the Army's information processing capabilities of stand-alone computers at forty-seven military bases into an integrated nationwide computer network. EDS is also involved in projects such as processing medical insurance claims for Blue Cross/Blue Shield.

The future of the computer services market is mixed, although many forecasts indicate a 20 to 25 percent growth rate over the next five years. The areas of highest potential will continue to be transaction processing, such as electronic funds transfer and point-of-sale data collection, and more specialized applications such as payroll and financial accounting services for specialized industries. Less potential is shown for forecasting applications, many of which can be taken over by users working with microcomputer packages. However, for large data base work, connecting microcomputers to remote computer service data bases through telecommunication lines is still attractive.

Significant changes in the computer services industry are forthcoming. One force that is reducing the attractiveness of this industry is the decreasing cost of mini- and microcomputers. Another is the introduction of effective and relatively inexpensive software packages. This will result in more organizations acquiring their own in-house computers. In addition, it is likely that IBM will reenter this market. As a result of an antitrust suit filed by CDC, IBM voluntarily agreed in 1975 to abandon this market for at least five years. Since the U.S. Justice Department dropped other antitrust cases against IBM in 1982, it seems reasonable that IBM will soon resume offering computer services. Another likely entrant into the processing services market is AT&T. Since they already have a very expensive telecommunication network in place, providing additional computing services should be relatively easy.

DISTRIBUTION CHANNELS

At one time, the only way to buy a computer was to contact the original manufacturer. The microcomputer, however, has led to significantly new avenues for acquiring computers, peripherals, and software. Today, distribution channels include a variety of retail outlets and systems houses, as well as manufacturer direct sales.

Retail Outlets

Since their appearance in the late 1970s, computer stores have shown rapid growth. Approximately two out of every three microcomputers are now purchased from a computer store. Computerland, the largest franchise, has over four hundred stores around the country. Businessland, one of the newer chains, caters to businesses rather than to home users. It is estimated that the number of computer stores, franchised and independent, will be over 6000 by 1987 (see Exhibit 18.9).

Computer stores owned by computer vendors, such as Tandy, IBM, and DEC, operate in a slightly different way from operations such as Computerland. Generally, the vendor-owned store features only its own equipment. Tandy computer stores feature only Radio Shack computers. Other stores, such as Xerox, may feature not only their own equipment, but also complementary equipment from other vendors. An additional difference is that Computerland features computers, while vendor-owned stores tend to sell other office equipment, such as typewriters, office copiers, and word processing equipment.

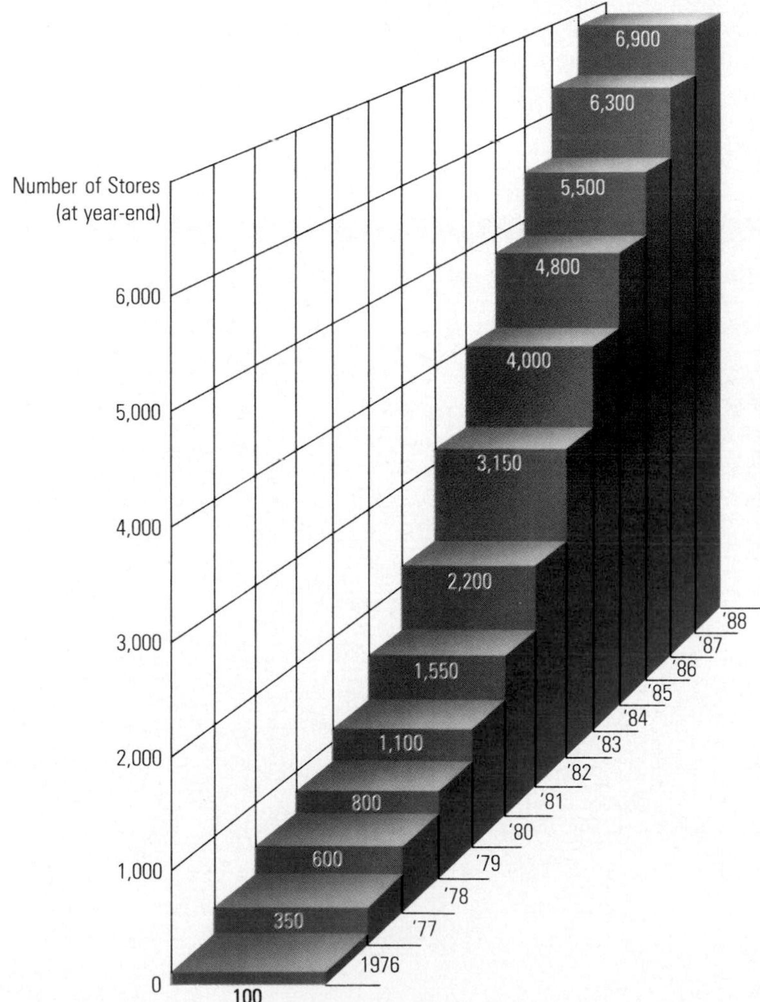

Exhibit 18.9
Projected Computer Store Growth

Computer stores of both types also sell software packages, and many have classrooms for conducting training sessions. Many stores are also able to repair the hardware they sell. For the business or home user, computer stores are evolving into a one-stop center for fulfilling the microcomputer user's needs.

Because software is the key to successful use of computer systems, several entrepreneurs felt there was a market for retail outlets that sell nothing but a great variety of software for a wide range of microcomputer systems. One of the largest software stores is the Softwaire Centre, which has outlets across the country. In addition to offering software for business, education, and entertainment, the outlets stock an extensive offering of computer books and magazines.

Competing with the computer and software stores are the mail-order houses. Their advertisements can be found in most computer magazines. Mail-orders houses sell computers, peripherals, and software packages at discount prices. Some even specialize in software. The future of these companies is in question, since many computer vendors feel that mail-order houses do not offer the follow-up support needed for either hardware or software sales. Apple and Hewlett-Packard have formally discontinued mail-order sales of their products, and a few software suppliers are taking similar action. A representative advertisement is shown in Exhibit 18.10.

A variation of the mail-order house will be the electronic delivery of software over telecommunication paths. Software could be sold this way by the software publishers themselves. By reducing the markup added by retailers, this might be one way to reduce prices and still allow software publishers to provide after-sales service.

Exhibit 18.10
A Representative Computer Mail-Order Advertisement

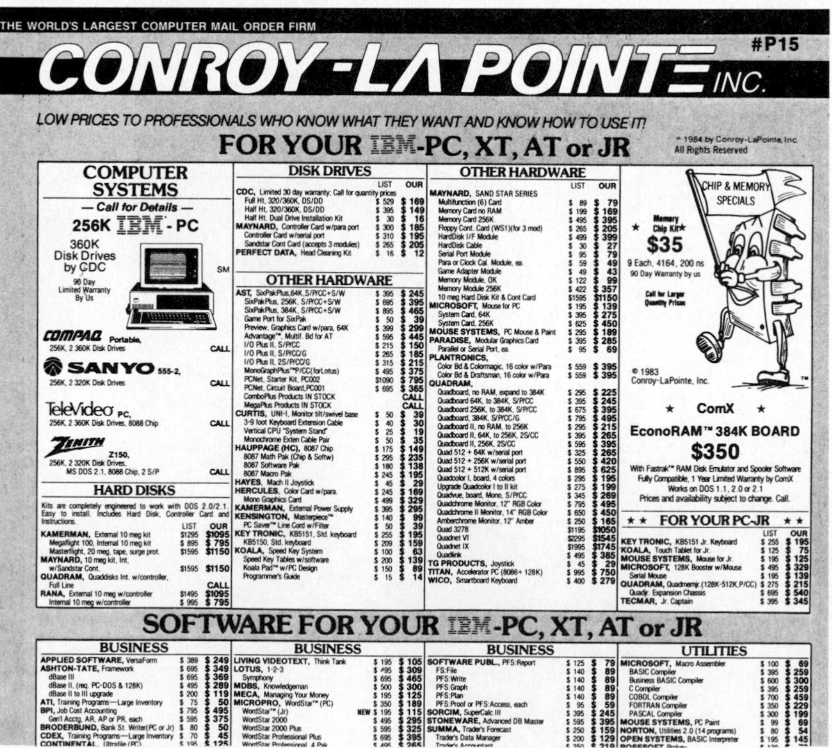

For the home computer user, mass merchandisers such as Toys 'R' Us and K mart offer such microcomputers as the Atari and Commodore series. Software packages for word processing, spreadsheets, games and education are available through these stores at prices comparable to those of videogames.

For microcomputer users within large organizations, many companies are adding their own in-company stores. Such stores are often run under the guidance of an organization's data processing department. Their purpose is to support end-user computing. By offering several types of hardware and software packages that are compatible with a company's mainframe (central) computer, the stores offer users a range of choices that will meet professional needs. Often, in-company store personnel can help with employee training and, when necessary, develop custom software or tailor software packages.

Systems Houses

Systems houses are full-service computer dealers that integrate hardware and software into a completely packaged or turnkey solution for applications in specific industries. Often a systems house develops an original software package for a specific client. Such a package is called a proprietary package. An example might be an accounting and billing package especially suited to the needs of a doctor's office. The systems house selects computer hardware that is most suitable to the proprietary software and offers the combination along with training for the doctor's employees. Thus, the systems house offers a complete solution to the doctor's computer needs now and in the future. This later point distinguishes the systems house from computer stores and other retail outlets.

Sophisticated proprietary software packages can cost millions of dollars to develop. Their advantage is that it is relatively easy to tailor the same basic program to meet the same, yet slightly different, needs of other doctors' offices and to resell the altered software with additional turnkey systems. Thus the expense of developing these proprietary packages can be divided among several clients. Yet the tailoring allows the software to "fit" each client's needs better than off-the-shelf packages. This industry is described in more detail in Computers at Work: "Pitching Computers to Small Business," which appears at the end of this chapter.

Manufacturer Direct Sales

Fortune 1000 businesses and large government agencies meet their computer needs in several different ways. The primary way has been to purchase computer hardware directly from computer manufacturers such as IBM, NCR, and CDC. For mainframe and large minicomputer systems, which cost between $100,000 and $1 million, the profit margin was such that the computer vendor could afford to "go to the customer" and do the systems development necessary to help the customer decide what size computer was needed.

Application software was generally written by the in-house data processing staff. However, as the sophistication and usefulness of software packages have developed, more and more organizations are first considering whether their needs can be met with a package. If they cannot, then they will consider developing something themselves in-house.

Most microcomputers and their software packages sell for hundreds or, at most, several thousand dollars. For these items, the profit margin is so small that vendors cannot afford to "go to the customer" and perform systems development services. This has, in turn, led to the boom in computer stores. The exception occurs when a Fortune 1000 company decides it will provide its employees with microcomputers. When a large insurance company decides to buy 3000 IBM PCs or a major university wants to buy 6500 Macintoshes, then the potential profit demands personal attention from the vendor. Computer vendors have established direct sales teams to service national accounts. This ensures these prime customers the technical support they need and also allows them "fleet" discounts.

INFORMATION PROVIDERS

As the computer has become more and more pervasive at all levels of our society, there is a need for more information about how computer systems work, how to compare and select hardware and software systems, and how people, businesses, and educational organizations are using them. Information is provided by literature, by seminars and courses, by conferences, and by research firms.

Literature

One of the major new sources of answers to the computer user's questions has been computer magazines. The major computer magazines had a combined circulation of over 66 million copies. That is a lot of information available to users (see Exhibit 18.11). First in circulation is *Computerworld,* a weekly newspaper for computer professionals. Sometimes called "The Wall Street Journal" of computing, *Computerworld* reports on the major events and products in the computer community. Other leading magazines are *MIS Week, Byte, PC World,* and *Datamation.*

Over two-thirds of the top twenty-five computer magazines are aimed at the microcomputer audience. Twenty of these magazines have been started within the last ten years. In addition to these popular magazines, there are many professional and academic journals. Several of the more influential ones are published by computer societies such as the Society for Information Management (SIM), Association of Computer Machinery (ACM), Institute of Electrical and Electronic Engineers (IEEE), and the Data Processing Management Association (DPMA). Additionally, there is a host of journals that address special topic areas such as computer education, data base systems, and telecommunication.

Within the last five years, trade book publishers have made a major effort to meet the demand for professional and educational computer books, one of the fastest growing subject areas. Some of these publishers, such as Sybex, specialize in computer books. B. Dalton, one of the largest book distributors, has stated that books on computers have replaced romantic novels as the best-selling topics. Once hidden in the back areas of the store, computer science books now are displayed prominently. A similar boom has occurred in textbooks, since almost all colleges offer some type of computer science degree. Many high schools also offer computer courses.

Exhibit 18.11

Computer magazines and journals are a good source of information on products and major events in the computer community.

Seminars and Courses

Computer book publishing is complemented by the thousands of seminars now conducted around the country. Seminar topics include personal computer hardware, operating systems, telecommunications, local area networks, and systems analysis and design. There are also "hands-on" seminars on operating a microcomputer or using a popular speadsheet or data base package.

Typically these seminars are presented in major cities at prominent hotels with special conference and dining facilities. These seminars may last one, two, three, or five days, depending on the subject matter and the intended audience. The daily cost for seminars aimed at business professionals averages around $250 to $350.

Exhibit 18.12

Courses and seminars are important sources for learning about computers and information systems.

Seminars for microcomputer home users are more typically sponsored by and presented at computer stores. These seminars usually offer "hands-on" experience, as opposed to in-depth knowledge. Generally, the classes are conducted on Saturday mornings or weekday nights for three or four hours. A price of about $40 to $60 is typical (see Exhibit 18.12).

For the person who wants a more academic instruction in the computer field, almost all community colleges and universities offer classes on different aspects of computing. Many now offer courses leading to a degree in the computer field.

New avenues of computer education include **telecourses,** computer seminars at a distance, and software tutorials. Major computer literacy courses are shown on public television and can be purchased on videotape by colleges and industrial groups. Two of the major producers of telecourses are the Southern California Community College TV Consortium and Ontario (Canada) TV. For businesses, Deltak and Edutronics have developed videotapes on specific subject matter such as system analyses, structured programming, and EDP auditing.

A new form of education is offered by the New Jersey Institute of Technology. Here, participatory seminars are conducted via computer telecommunication. Using your microcomputer or computer terminal, you access a com-

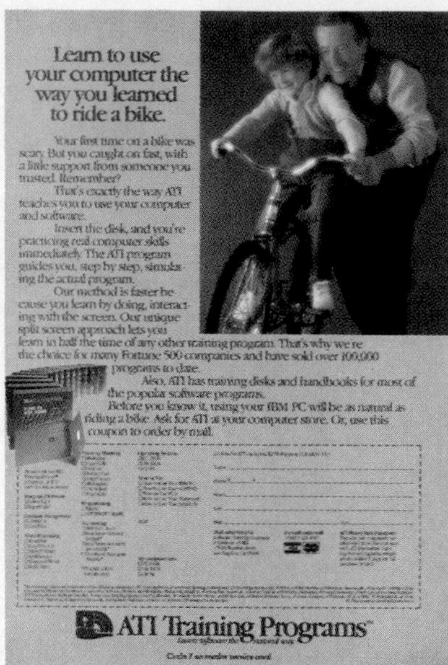

Learn to use your computer the way you learned to ride a bike.
Your first time on a bike was scary. But you caught on fast, with a little support from someone you trusted. Remember?
That's exactly the way ATI teaches you to use your computer and software.
Insert the disk, and you're practicing real computer skills immediately. The ATI program guides you, step by step, simulating the actual program.
Our method is faster because you learn by doing, interacting with the screen. Our unique split screen approach lets you learn in half the time of any other training program. That's why we're the choice for many Fortune 500 companies and have sold over 100,000 programs to date.
Also, ATI has training disks and handbooks for most of the popular software programs.
Before you know it, using your IBM PC will be as natural as riding a bike. Ask for ATI at your computer store. Or, use this coupon to order by mail.
ATI Training Programs

Exhibit 18.13

American Training International (ATI) is one of many firms now offering software tutorials.

puterized conferencing system. You can participate in online sessions or ask and answer questions of the instructor and other seminar participants at any hour of the day or week, without ever having to leave your home. Seminars are given on topics such as Apple BASIC, CP/M, local area networks, Pascal programming, and technological forecasting.

Many firms are now offering software tutorials on installing and using a computer, writing programs, or using a specific software package or operating system. Among the prominent firms in this training field are American Training International (ATI) and Cdex. Both provide software tutorials that include sample exercises and step-by-step instructions on disk (see Exhibit 18.13).

Conferences

To keep up with new hardware and software offerings, many people attend computer conferences. One of the largest is the National Computer Conference (NCC), which usually takes place in late spring of each year (see Exhibit 18.14). Over 100,000 people go to this conference to attend seminars and see a mind-boggling array of hardware and software exhibits. The conference attendance has increased to the point that it has outgrown almost all the possible convention sites, including the Houston Astrodome.

The growth of the NCC would be less amazing if it were the one and only major computer conference each year. But it is just one of hundreds of conferences given about various facets of the computer field. More than ten of these conferences draw over 30,000 to 50,000 people each year. In fact, promoters of SOFTCON (a software-only conference) were recently complaining because the attendance was only 20,000!

However, if you ever have the opportunity to attend one of these large conferences, you will quickly note that it is more like a zoo than a place to get any in-depth knowledge or answers to your specific questions. Promoters have noticed this and decided that there is an alternative way to inform prospective buyers of computer solutions available to them.

Exhibit 18.14

Hardware and software exhibits attract crowds of people interested in keeping up with the newest offerings.

The latest form of conference is the "permanent" one available at computer marts in major locations around the country. In 1983, a business product center was opened as part of Chicago's Merchandise Mart. During the next several years marts are scheduled to open in Los Angeles, Dallas, Boston, New York City, and Toronto.

The Dallas Informart is typical of these centers (see Exhibit 18.15). The plan is to have about three hundred exhibits, plus special events scheduled around end-user themes such as local area networking or the use of microcomputers in large organizations. At other times the theme will be on **vertical markets**—the supplying of information systems to specific fields, such as insurance, medical practices, or financial institutions. The promoters hope to offer a full schedule of computer seminars throughout the year. The goal is to provide quality information to prospective buyers in a more relaxed environment.

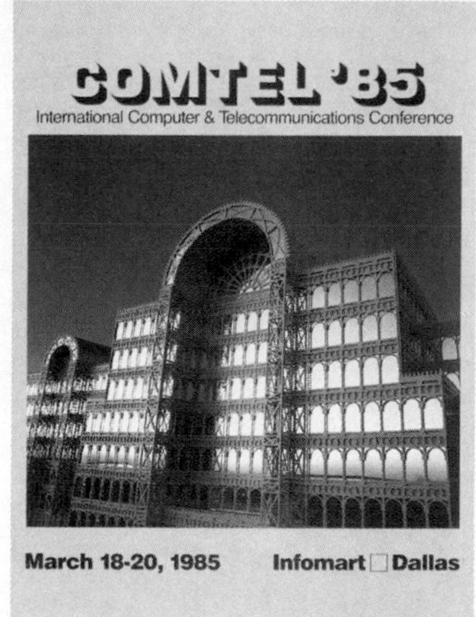

COMTEL '85
International Computer & Telecommunications Conference
March 18-20, 1985
Infomart Dallas

Exhibit 18.15

This computer conference brochure depicts the Dallas Infomart.

Research Firms

A number of firms will write research reports for organizations needing in-depth information on advanced topics within the computer field. These firms also distribute newsletters, conduct seminars, and do consulting. Two of the better-known research firms are Datapro and Auerbach. Datapro is an organization best known for evaluating computer equipment and compiling specifications. Auerbach has developed reports on important topics in the various fields of computing such as hardware, data processing management, EDP auditing, and telecommunication. They also condense their reports into ten- to twenty-page synopses written for management.

Firms that conduct market research on emerging areas within the computer field include Dataquest, Gnostic Concepts, and Gartner Group. Organizations are willing to pay around a $10,000 subscription fee to gain access to these research findings. In return, they get (1) an independent view of a topic area, which may or may not confirm the findings of their in-house research team and/or (2) a general understanding of an emerging market, which will allow their research team to focus its efforts.

International Data Corporation (IDC) shares some of its general findings in "white papers," which they present in *Fortune* each year. Generally, January's report is on the personal computer field, March's report is on business telecommunications, and June's report is on office automation. The rising star of the research firms on topics related to the microcomputer field is Future Computing, Inc. Its research on computer store sales, personal computer market shares, and future projections is continually referenced in the computer magazines.

COMPUTER CAREERS

As you have learned more about computers and their impact on our society, you may have considered a career as a computer professional. In this section we will discuss professional positions, how they fit into organizations, some typical salary ranges, and where most of the jobs are located geographically. With that background, we will then cover some of the formal education preparation that is available to help you succeed in this field.

The Data Processing Department

We can see some of the major jobs within the computer field if we look at the typical organization of a data processing department in many larger organizations (see Exhibit 18.16). Here, computer professionals are organized into four main groups. The computer operations group is responsible for keeping the large computer system and its peripherals operating. This would include the daily operation of the computer, hanging magnetic tapes and mounting disk packs, maintenance, and keeping the necessary supplies in order. In larger organizations, operations would include the mainframe computer system, plus telecommunications and the care of microcomputers located throughout the organization.

The technical support group functions as the experts on the system support software. These are people who are knowledgeable about the operating systems, the data communication and network connections, and the technical aspects of data base management systems. They also understand the detailed operation of the computer hardware.

The application development group is composed of programmers and analysts. They work with users to determine the problems users want solved and when computer solutions are appropriate. Further, they develop application software or buy software packages to meet users' needs.

The newest group staffs the information center. Information centers have been developed to help business professionals use personal computers and the tools of end-user computing. Since these managers and staff members are not computer professionals, they often want advice from computer professionals on the choice of microcomputer and software that will best meet their needs. Generally they also need training on how to use the computer and the software. Additionally, they need to know how to access data held in the mainframe data base.

Exhibit 18.16
Data Processing Department Organization

Large data processing departments typically include groups responsible for computer operations, technical support, applications development, and the information center.

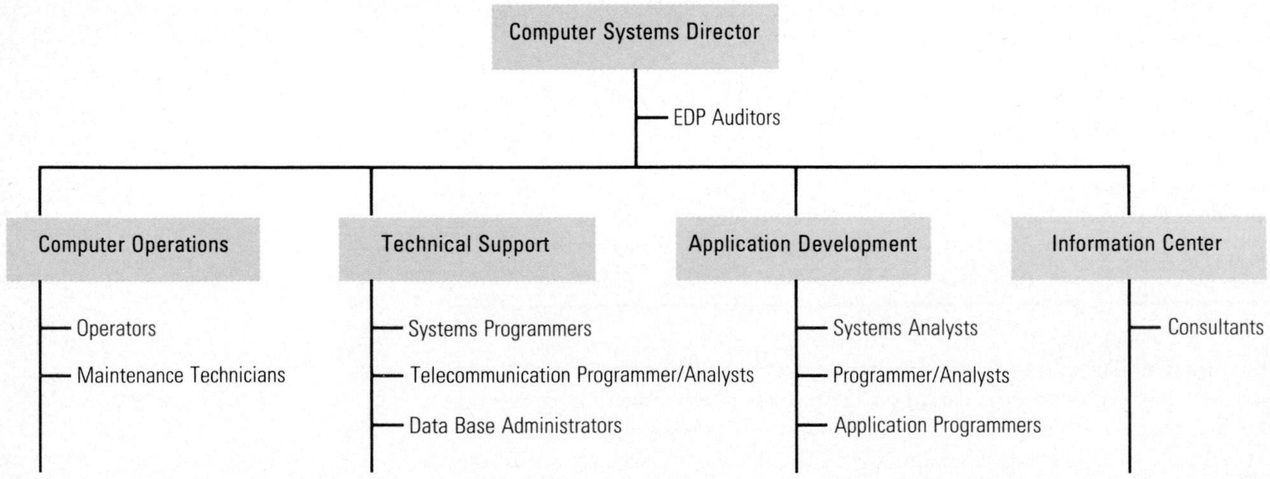

Computer Professionals

The types of computer jobs that are available within the data processing department vary with the size of the company and how far the company has progressed in their computing sophistication. Exhibit 18.16 shows some typical job titles found in each of the four areas of data processing. Generally, the computer operations area is composed of **computer operators** who are responsible for the operation of a large computer system for a particular work shift. **Maintenance technicians** are available to do routine maintenance and make minor repairs. For more extensive work, service representatives of the computer manufacturer are called in. People within computer operations have had formal training in their speciality, but are not required to have a college degree.

In the technical support area, typical job titles include system programmer, telecommunication analyst, and data base specialist. The **system programmer** is responsible for creating or maintaining operating systems, data base software, and language translators. **Telecommunication programmers/analysts** write or modify data communication software, or design or evaluate telecommunication or local area networks. The **data base administrator** designs and controls the use of an organization's common computerized data. This could include working with users to establish common data needs, interfacing with data base management software, and ensuring there are effective security and control procedures.

People in the technical support area require at least a bachelor level degree in the computer science area. Often graduate education is required in a technical specialty offering a master's degree. A solid mathematical background is a necessity for technical specialists.

Application development is generally composed of individuals classified as application programmers or systems analysts. **Application programmers** design, code, and test computer programs to meet specific user needs. **Systems analysts** work with the user to establish the user's needs. The analyst, a liaison between the user and the programming staff, functions to translate the user's problem needs into a set of programming requirements. These requirements are then used by the programmer to develop a set of computer programs that will meet the user's needs.

Often people function as both programmers and analysts and thus the job title "programmer/analyst" is common. Application development people need a bachelor's degree in a business-oriented computer program. For any analyst work, a strong set of communication skills is necessary, along with a good background in business concepts.

The information center is an emerging department, and it is not clear at this point what job title its staff will have. The generic title is **consultant,** which conveys the focus of the position. This person acts as an advisor, performs liaison functions, and conducts training sessions for end users. In the advisor role, the consultant discusses which microcomputer and software packages would best solve the user's problems. If the user's needs would be better served by a customized program, the consultant would act as a liaison between the application development group and the user. To help the user become productive quickly, information center consultants would conduct group training sessions or select appropriate instructional videotapes or software tutorials.

Information Center staff need at least a bachelor's degree. They also need a good blend of education in computers, business and training skills. This position requires a knowledge of data base and decision support concepts, and a solid background in evaluation methodologies and microcomputer hardware and software. Most importantly, these people need to be effective in communicating ideas, leading groups, and making people feel comfortable in learning new skills.

For the most part the jobs we have described are entry-level positions. As you gain more experience, there are promotion opportunities in each of the functional areas. Moving from a junior to senior position generally requires that you assume a leadership role. Project leaders accomplish project goals by organizing a group of users and technical specialists from each of the data processing areas.

More and more organizations are requiring the services of an electronic data processing (EDP) auditor. As we have discussed, the needs for security and privacy are important factors in the operations of computer systems. EDP auditors need a solid background in accounting and data processing. At least a bachelor's degree is required, and some universities are now offering graduate programs in this increasingly important position.

The highest position within the data processing department is the **computer systems director.** This person has overall responsibility for data center operations, technical support of computer information systems, development of new application software, and interfacing with end-user computing. This individual generally will have a technical degree and many years of data processing experience. In large companies the director will also need a Master of Business Administration (MBA) degree or the equivalent. This degree will provide an overview of data processing's role in the business organization.

A recent development in the computer profession is the emergence of a position, **vice-president of management information systems,** a senior executive who is responsible for all corporate information systems. He or she is responsible for long-range planning, budgeting, and data processing operations. This executive must have a broad understanding of how the organization functions and what makes it successful in its industry. A master's degree (MBA) is necessary, along with good strategic planning skills and a broad technical understanding of the computer and information field.

We have given you an indication of the types of jobs that are available for computer professionals and the education necessary. In Exhibit 18.17, we show a portion of the 1985 Source EDP Salary Survey. The Source EDP is a personnel service for data processing professionals. As you can see, salaries are a function of speciality and years of experience. Management positions, such as computing systems director, are further classified by the size of the installation. In general, "large" means a mainframe computer setup with more than forty people on the data processing staff. "Small" is a minicomputer system with less than ten people.

While there are jobs in almost all locations, some geographic areas clearly have greater demand for computer professionals. The computer job market is concentrated in cities such as San Francisco (Silicon Valley), Los Angeles, Dallas/Ft. Worth, Miami, New York City, and Boston (see Exhibit 18.18 on page 550). Salaries in the computer field are a function of supply and demand. The forecast for the next ten years is that the demand for almost all the computer professional jobs that we have discussed will outstrip the supply.

Exhibit 18.17
Professional Compensation: Some Representative 1985 Data

1. Nonmanagement Positions (Salary according to length of experience in the profession)	Annual Compensation ($000)		
	15th Percentile	Median	85th Percentile
Commercial Programmers and Programmer Analysts			
1 year-2 years	19.9	25.6	30.8
2-years-5-years	24.0	30.5	36.5
Over 5 years	27.6	35.5	40.8
Engineering/Scientific Programmers and Programmer Analysts			
1 year-2 years	21.7	26.0	33.0
2 years-5 years	26.6	31.9	38.8
Over 5 years	33.3	37.9	47.3
Systems (Software) Programmers			
1 year-2 years	23.5	30.6	39.6
2 years-4 years	27.2	35.5	45.9
4 years-7 years	34.4	43.0	52.6
Over 7 years	35.0	44.4	54.4
Data Base Administrators/Specialists			
1 year-2 years	23.0	29.3	40.6
2 years-4 years	27.5	37.4	43.2
4 years-7 years	35.5	43.9	54.0
Over 7 years	35.8	45.3	55.8
Data Communications Programmers and Programmer Analysts			
1 year-2 years	24.5	30.6	36.6
2 years-5 years	26.9	36.2	44.8
Over 5 years	34.0	43.1	49.9
EDP Auditors			
1 year-2 years	22.6	26.6	34.6
2 years-4 years	26.5	33.7	39.4
4 years-7 years	33.1	41.9	50.0
Over 7 years	34.3	43.9	50.8
Senior Analysts, Project Leaders, and Consultants			
2 years-4-years	27.6	34.4	41.2
4 years-7 years	31.7	39.1	47.1
Over 7 years	36.0	44.2	60.3
Computer Operators			
1 year-2 years	15.1	17.8	21.7
2 years-5 years	18.2	20.5	23.6
Over 5 years	21.2	25.8	30.5
2. Management Positions (Salary according to size of computer system or staff managed)			
Computing Systems Directors			
Small	35.6	44.1	54.8
Medium	43.5	56.9	65.4
Large	55.6	71.5	97.2
3. Sales Positions			
Sales Representatives			
Services	30.6	48.6	82.3
Hardware Products	36.2	50.3	84.7
Software Products	40.7	55.4	89.0

Source: "The 1985 Salary Survey," The Source EDP Personnel Service.

Exhibit 18.18
Major Computer Job Markets

Reprinted with permission of Integrated Software Systems Corporation, San Diego, California.

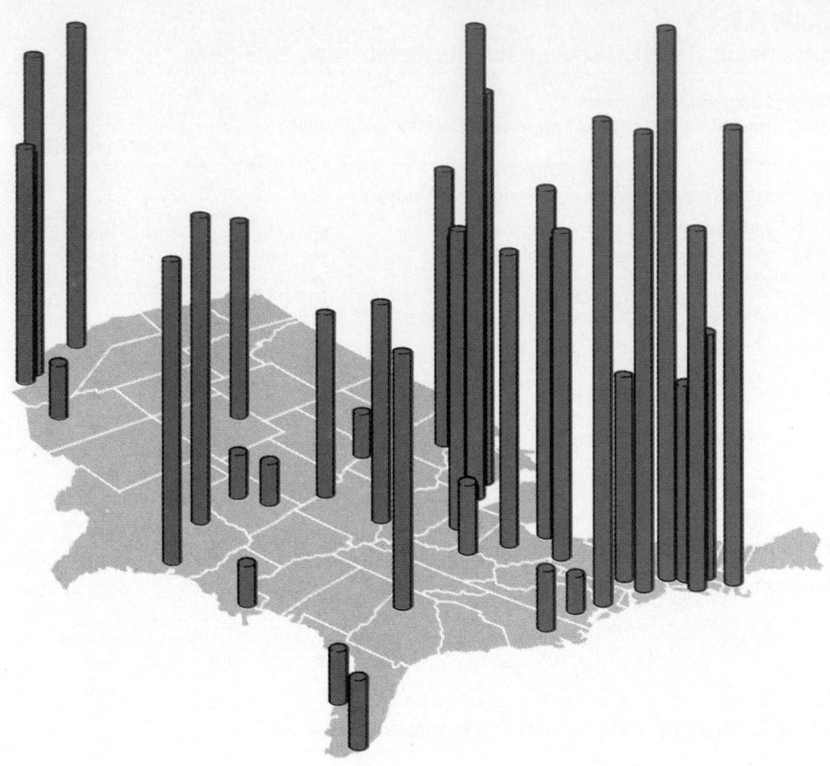

Formal Education

What avenues are available to people who want to become computer professionals? For people who want to become involved with computer operations, proprietary schools (vocational/technical) and community colleges often provide the required education. With continued education, computer operators may be able to become junior programmers.

The positions of programmer, analyst, and data base specialist require a formal college education. Most community colleges now offer courses in computer education, and many have associate degree programs in the computer field. Many universities offer four-year degrees in computer science.

While people outside the profession refer to these educational programs by the generic term, *computer science,* three distinct fields have emerged. Becoming aware of these distinctions will help you prepare for the computer position you want. The three major educational program areas are computer information systems, computer science, and computer engineering. Exhibit 18.19 shows a typical curriculum for each program area. **Computer information systems** educational programs are generally located in the school of business and emphasize the programmer and analyst skills. A strong background in the business core subjects such as accounting, finance, marketing, management science, and management are emphasized to complement the computer skills. People from these programs would be trained for entry into applications development and information center positions.

Exhibit 18.19

A Typical Curriculum for Computer Information Systems, Computer Science, and Computer Engineering

	Computer Information Systems (CIS)	Computer Science (CS)	Computer Engineering (CE)
Major	Introduction to CIS COBOL Programming Advanced COBOL Programming Systems Analysis System Design Data Base Programming Systems Development Project Information Resource Management	Fundamentals of Computer Science Computer Logic PASCAL Programming Data Structures Assembly Language Programming Computer Organization Programming Languages Operating Systems	Introduction to Digital Systems Network Theory Linear Active Circuit Design Communication Systems Analysis and Design of Computer Architecture Analysis and Design of Microprocessors Theory and Design of Operating Systems Advanced Logic Design
Support	Accounting Production Management Statistics Organizational Behavior Economics Marketing Business Finance Management Policies	Computer Electronics Advanced Computer Electronics Analytic Geometry Calculus Linear Algebra Calculus of Several Variables General Physics Applied Probability Theory	General Chemistry Analytic Geometry Calculus Calculus of Several Variables Differential Equations Vector Statics Vector Dynamics Material Sciences

The **computer science** programs are generally located in the school of science. These programs place emphasis on programming, computer hardware, and systems software skills. A strong background in mathematics complements this technical program. These graduates would primarily go to the technical support staff and possibly to the application development team.

We have not discussed the career positions for **computer engineers,** people who design computer hardware. Computer engineering programs are located in the school of engineering and emphasize the theory of electronics as it applies to computers. A strong background in mathematics, physics, and engineering is needed to supplement the technical knowledge of computer circuitry.

To prepare oneself for the position of computer center director or vice-president of information systems, one can attend graduate level programs offered under the title of Management Information Systems. The possibilities include a general MBA degree with an option in MIS, or a master's degree in MIS, now offered by many schools.

Pitching Computers to Small Business

Here's how: Find an industry—say, commercial printing or auto parts wholesaling. Design a system to solve its unique problems. Train a specialized sales force, go to conventions, and advertise in trade publications. And you can join the move to "vertical marketing."

The hottest thing in the computer business isn't a tinier microchip or a faster supercomputer. It's a strategy called vertical marketing: selling computer systems tailored to the unique needs of particular industries. Heavy hitters, including Apple, Wang, and McDonnell Douglas, look to vertical marketing for much of their future growth. So do hundreds of smaller and newer companies. Says Larry J. Wells, vice-president of Citicorp's venture capital subsidiary, "Vertical marketing is a hot term right now, the buzzword of business plans."

Like most buzzwords, this one is mightily abused. Classically, vertical marketing starts with picking an industry and designing a computer system—with special software and sometimes hardware—that solves critical problems that crop up only in that industry. The strategy includes techniques that are laudable for just about any kind of selling: marketing through special industry channels, training salespeople to know more about the business than its practitioners, and providing customers cradle-to-grave service.

True vertical marketing can be a good foxhole. It serves a particular industry top to bottom rather than cutting horizontally across many industries. Price wars and head-to-head selling in the roughly $50-billion-a-year horizontal market for general-purpose computers keep getting bloodier. God is on the side of the big battalions that produce at the lowest cost, above all, IBM. The allure of vertical marketing for IBM's competitors is that success depends more on a specialized knowledge of customers than on economies of scale.

Vertical marketing also brings computer technology to thousands of new customers. A minicomputer system for running a factory or automating a law office cost around $150,000 a few years ago; today a microcomputer system of similar power fetches about $15,000. Software programs tailored to an industry's special needs, once luxuries that only giant corporations could afford, are available to anyone with a few thousand dollars to spend.

Yet less than one-tenth of the 3.2 million U.S. businesses with fewer than fifty employees own any sort of computer, according to a recent survey by Dataquest, a California market research firm. Marketing computer systems to these relatively small businesses is expensive. They need a lot of persuasion before they'll ante up for a system, and much hand-holding after the sale to get the system working properly. Selling and service cost so much that anyone trying to serve small businesses must charge customers two to three times the market price of a basic computer to even hope to turn a profit. That's where vertical marketing comes in. A computer company can shave costs by focusing on a particular industry and marketing through trade publications, trade shows, and word of mouth; the company can charge premium prices for systems that solve the critical problems unique to an industry.

A pioneer in vertical marketing and a model for other companies is Triad Systems of Sunnyvale, California. Three friends—hence Triad—founded the company in 1972. Now public, Triad squeezed $4.8 million in earnings out of $120 million in sales for the fiscal year ended last September, mainly by solving the hideously complex inventory problems of automotive parts wholesalers. A typical wholesaler stocks 20,000 parts and finances inventory with hefty credit from suppliers. The key to profits is managing inventory.

Triad's first product, the Triad 3, was designed to record every sale. Special software enabled the wholesaler to analyze that information—say, by finding the ten fastest-moving items and the ten slowest—and to project the financial results of changing inventory mix and prices. Wholesalers who bought the system found, on average, that they could cut inventories 10 percent, turn their inventories over twice as often, and add two percentage points or so to their net profit margins.

Triad has built on its experience to solve many other problems for wholesalers. For example, wholesalers charge so many different prices—depending on the brand and on what kind of customer is buying—that the counterworkers writing up the orders get confused. A Triad program called a pricing matrix tells the counterperson how much to charge a particular class of customer for a certain type and brand of product. Accurate pricing can more than double a wholesaler's profitability, from about 3.5 percent to some 7.5 percent on sales before taxes.

Finding vertical markets is easy. "There are hundreds of vertical markets that you can define just by going to the government's three-digit standard industrial classifications," explains Larry Dietz, a veteran consultant who is helping start a newsletter, the *Vertical Market Report.* The hard part, Dietz adds, is finding a market where you can make a profit. The biggest and richest ones—banking and insurance, for example—already are served by the likes of IBM and Burroughs.

Dietz divides vertical markets into "herd" markets and niche markets. Typical herds—dentists, lawyers, and accountants—have drawn hundreds of competitors. The nichiest of niche markets are too small, too poor, or too hard to reach to produce a profit.

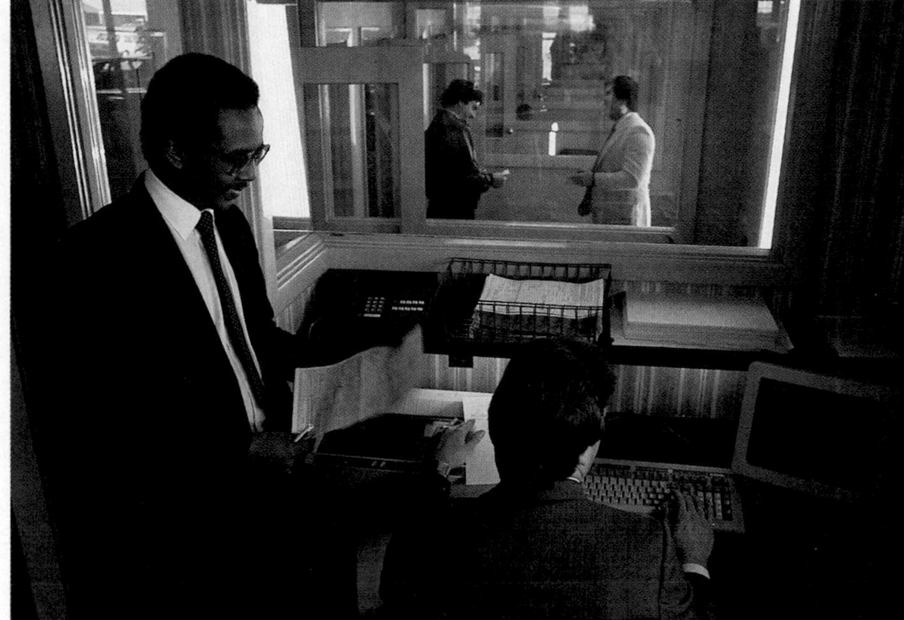

Vertical marketers are especially vulnerable to the rise and fall of their customers. The 1982–83 recession produced record bankruptcies among parts jobbers, so Triad's fortunes sank. Yet trying to diversify into other industries is difficult. Little of what a company learns about one industry can be effectively transferred to another.

A more profitable way for vertical marketers to grow may be to continue elaborating on their experience in one industry. A powerful way to do that is to create a new kind of service: vertical information networks. Automatic Data Processing keeps track of inventory for over 6000 auto dealers. With its knowledge of their inventories, ADP markets itself as a clearinghouse to help, say, a Chevrolet dealer who has run out of carburetors locate a dealer with an oversupply. Triad, which collects price changes from auto parts manufacturers, charges for updating wholesalers' computers over the telephone. Informatics has set up a network that allows a drugstore's computer to automatically reorder health and beauty aids.

Vertical information networks like these could become the crowning achievement of today's vertical marketing companies. Like telephone systems, information networks are highly profitable for dominant competitors, and almost impossible for johnny-come-latelies to create. They demonstrate the vertical marketer's maxim: the money is in knowing the industry.

Source: B. Uttal, "Pitching Computers to Small Business," *Fortune,* 1 April, 1985, pp. 95–104.

SUMMARY

The leading hardware manufacturers vary, depending on whether we are talking about mainframe, mini-, micro-, or supercomputer systems. In general IBM has, is, and will continue to dominate computer hardware sales. IBM has been a leader in the mainframe market for at least twenty years, due to a combination of manufacturing ability, marketing strength, maintenance and service, and research and development efforts. The most likely sources of competition are thought to be Fujitsu and AT&T.

Digital Equipment Corporation (DEC) and Data General pioneered the minicomputer market, and DEC has led in sales for many years. IBM, a comparatively recent entry, leads in revenues, however, since it charges higher prices for its complete information systems. DEC, in contrast, sells stripped-down models to suppliers who add their own software and peripherals and resell the resulting computer system.

Between 1978 and 1982, Apple, Commodore, and Radio Shack were the primary manufacturers of microcomputers. In 1981, however, IBM introduced the IBM PC and a year later was second in sales. The personal computer market is actually made up of several segments: the business and professional users, home users, scientific users, and educational users. Most computer manufacturers have chosen to create machines compatible with the IBM PC, while Apple has focused its energies on the Lisa and Macintosh.

The supercomputer market is supplied by Cray Research Inc. and Control Data Corporation (CDC). Their customers include organizations working in weather, seismic research, aerospace, biomedicine, and special movie effects. Seymour Cray, once a designer for CDC, left to form Cray Research Inc. in 1972. Although Cray leads in sales and is expected to continue to do so, competition is emerging from companies like IBM and Japan's fifth generation computing project.

It is predicted that data processing budgets will be increasingly devoted to the development and acquisition of software. Software packages will become an important way of meeting the demand for applications and end-user computing tools. The software package industry is composed of segments for system support software, application software, and software tools.

The computer services industry functions to provide remote computing services, network services, or *facilities management,* the complete management of the data processing facility.

The way organizations and individuals acquire computer hardware and software has changed significantly with the advent of the microcomputer. Retail outlets such as computer stores, mail-order houses, and mass-merchandisers have made these products available to businesses, professionals, and home users.

Medium to large organizations can still be serviced directly by *systems houses* and direct sale units of the computer manufacturer.

To provide information about computer systems magazines, books, seminars, classes, and software tutorials have emerged. To keep abreast of the latest in computer hardware and software offerings "traveling" conferences and "permanent" computer marts have evolved.

For organizations that need more in-depth knowledge of emerging computer areas, research firms offer newsletters, research reports, and consulting.

Primarily, computer professional careers within organizations will be in computer operations, technical support, application development, and information centers. Salaries in these career areas are a function of job position, geographic location, and supply/demand conditions. Formal education is available through trade and technical schools, through community colleges, and through universities.

Educational programs can be divided into the areas of *computer information systems, computer science,* and *computer engineering.* In addition, one can acquire an MBA with a concentration in MIS or a master's degree in MIS.

REVIEW QUESTIONS

1. Which firm is the "power" in the mainframe segment of the computer market? What firms are most likely to be able to challenge the leader?
2. Briefly summarize the position of IBM in the various markets in which it is active.
3. What is the primary factor in the success of a computer system? How will this impact upon business?
4. Briefly describe the types of firms that compose the computer service and information industry.
5. Jack Stewart is considering opening a retail outlet for computers and software. How would you evaluate his chances for success?
6. How has the computer "explosion" affected the publishing industry?
7. Evaluate the "participatory seminar" as a form of computer training and information.
8. Beta Corporation is in need of current, in-depth information concerning advanced computer topics. What source would you suggest?
9. Briefly describe the way in which data processing departments are evolving.
10. What are the responsibilities of the Computer Systems Director?
11. How have recent organizational changes documented the increasing importance of data processing in business?
12. What are considered to be "large" and "small" computer installations in today's organizations?

APPENDIX

APPENDIX A
The History of the Computer

COMPUTERS AT WORK

Computing on Target

On a gray and windy morning in March 1943, a young army officer bounded up a staircase in the University of Pennsylvania's Moore School of Electrical Engineering, seeking a man who might know how to resolve his dilemma. Six months earlier, Lieut. Herman H. Goldstine had come to Philadelphia to oversee a cadre of civilians working on ballistics problems for the Proving Ground in Aberdeen, Maryland. The solutions to those problems would eventually save precious time in combat. Just a slight change in wind direction, a drop in temperature, or even a switch to another type of ammunition can draw a well-sighted gun off target. When this happens, a glance at firing tables, sometimes bound in a handy little book, enables a gun commander to find the new and correct angle of elevation quickly and to resume firing.

Now that America's war industries were moving into high gear, more large guns were rolling off production lines. But completing the firing tables for them required a staggering number of long calculations, and the army's main computation center at Aberdeen and the substation in the Moore School were hard pressed to keep pace. There was also mounting concern that there might not be enough qualified people around to do the computing for the additional armament to be produced later in the war. Clearly, something had to be done to erase the specter of huge guns stored and silent in depots because no one had supplied the data to aim and fire them. Goldstine's mission was to help prevent this from happening and to accelerate the work of the computers, as they were called, in the Moore School contingent. But there were limits. Goldstine knew that calculations could not be hurried at the expense of accuracy. Yet, if output did not increase, he feared that his unit would never be able to satisfy the growing demand for more firing tables.

Then came the discovery, quite by chance, that a professor at the Moore School had been trying to sell a bizarre, but intriguing, idea: A machine without moving parts (an electronic computer, he said) could easily surpass the combined outputs of thousands of mechanical calculators. The man whom Goldstine sought that morning was John W. Mauchly, a thirty-six-year-old physicist.

Source: H. Wulforst, "The Project to Develop the ENIAC Begins," *Breakthrough to the Computer Age* (New York: Charles Scribner's Sons, 1982), pp. 1–2.

Today's computer technologies and uses reflect centuries of farfetched ideas and persistent hard work by many people. Often, these curious inventions were not immediately recognized as important or practical. For example, John Mauchly's plan to develop the first general-purpose electronic computer was not taken seriously—until a young army officer named Herman Goldstein saw this bizarre idea as a solution to a critical problem for the United States during World War II.

Tracing the history of the computer is useful for many reasons. First, it reveals the close connection between advances in computer technology and the real-world problems these advances solved. Second, it introduces you to the fascinating men and women who conceived and developed the computer's marvels. Third, it will increase your understanding of computer systems in use today. Finally, this history illustrates a number of the issues and trends important to a productive use of computers in business today. Though it isn't possible to list and discuss all the people and events that have contributed to the computer's development, this chapter explores the most significant contributions to business computing.

In this chapter, you will learn to do the following:

1. List and describe some of the early devices and major events that led to the development of the computer and to the use of computers in business.
2. Explain what is meant by the phrase "computer generation" and list the technological advance that brought about each new generation of computers.
3. List the key hardware and software features, as well as the main uses and users, of each of the four computer generations.
4. List and explain three issues that often arise when computer technology is introduced into a business.
5. List and describe three computer technology trends.

THE DAWN OF THE COMPUTER AGE

500 BC The abacus is invented.

100 AD Paper is invented.

1458 AD Johann Gutenberg invents the printing press.

Exhibit A.1
The abacus is still used, though it doesn't allow long-term information storage.

In the history of our effort to develop machines to process and store information, progress was once measured in centuries rather than years or decades. The abacus, a device of counting beads strung on rods, was used for many years to calculate and store the intermediate results of mental arithmetic. Although the abacus is still widely used, it does not provide long-term storage of information. In using the abacus one must destroy the results of past calculations (see Exhibit A.1). As a result, most "information processing" had to occur orally.

Almost six centuries would pass before information could be preserved on paper by specially trained scribes. For another fourteen centuries, knowledge would remain a private good available to only a select few. The labor required to produce handwritten manuscripts limited the number of books produced and made them incredibly expensive. In fact, books were so valuable that they were carefully guarded in libraries.

The printing press changed this. In the fifty years that followed its invention, over 10 million books were distributed. Still, it wasn't until the 19th century, when mass production greatly reduced book prices, that information became a true public good.

Calculating Machines Are Invented

1642 Blaise Pascal develops the mechanical calculator.

1676 Gottfried Leibnitz improves Pascal's calculator.

1801 Joseph Jacquard invents an automated loom "programmed" by punched cards.

1822 Charles Babbage develops the Difference Engine.

1833 Babbage outlines plans for the Analytical Engine, a general-purpose computer.

Blaise Pascal faced a tedious problem. His father, a French tax commissioner, had enlisted his help in reorganizing a provincial tax structure. Blaise spent hours laboriously calculating and recalculating the taxes owed by each citizen. And he was not alone in his labors. The spreading influence of commerce and government during the 15th, 16th, and 17th centuries had created a growing demand for lists, inventories, ledgers, and public records. Collecting this information required that countless hours be spent performing calculations and creating and updating records, and the occupation of clerk developed to meet this need.

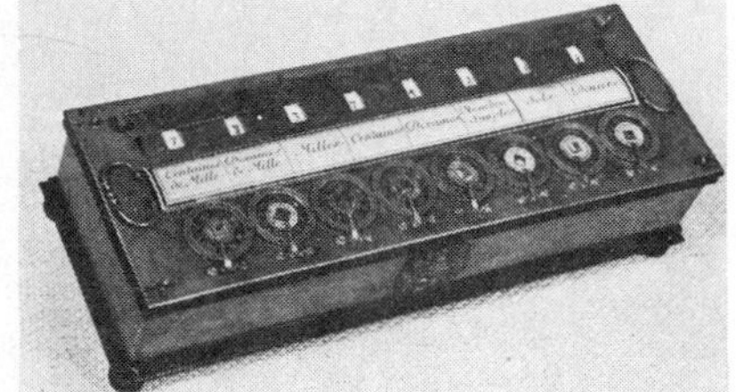

The Pascaline

But Pascal believed there had to be a better way to do such tedious work. He built the **Pascaline,** a mechanical calculator that performed addition and subtraction in a manner similar to a car's odometer. The operator entered numbers on sets of dials, and their sums and differences were mechanically calculated by the movements of interconnecting metal gears. Pascal failed in his attempts to market his machine, however. Because the technology used to create metal gears was still crude, the calculator's gearing mechanism needed constant repair, and Pascal himself made all repairs. It was actually more expensive to have clerks perform calculations with the Pascaline than to perform them by hand. And though the Pascaline's main benefit was that it made life easier for clerks, the clerks resented the Pascaline, viewing it as a job threat. Once the clerks spoke out against the machine, no incentives remained to prompt business and government administrators to purchase the calculator.

Gottfried Leibnitz improved Pascal's calculator by adding additional gearing that performed multiplication and division, but he never attempted to market his calculator, the **Leibnitz Wheel.** His work was driven by a philosophical view that it was "unworthy" for people to spend hours doing work that could be performed by a machine. It is unlikely that the Leibnitz wheel would have been a commercial success anyway, due to the poor mechanical devices available and the lack of any real demand for automating calculation. It wasn't until 1820 that a mechanical calculator, the **Thomas Arithmometer,** became a commercial success.

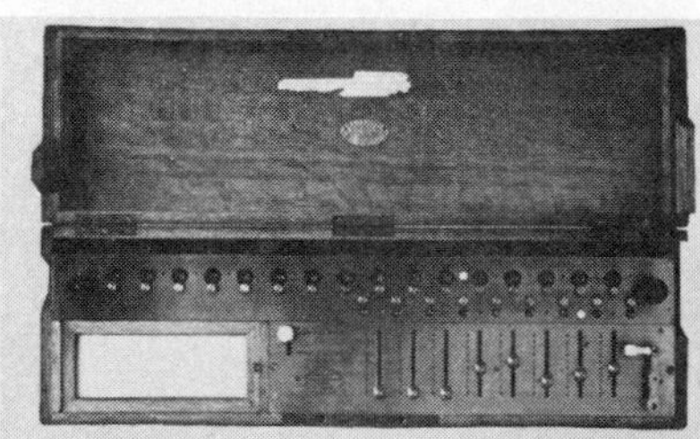

The Thomas Arithmometer

The next major development in the history of computing affected the weaving industry. Weaving was a craft of artisans, and weavers spent years developing their skill at the loom. But one inventor, Joseph Jacquard, saw that a weaver manually operating a loom was actually repeating the same movements over and over again. Couldn't the machine, he thought, be directed to

The Jacquard loom

perform the repetitive operations by itself? If the weaving could be automated, unskilled workers could produce more cloth faster, fewer workers would be needed, and profits would increase.

Jacquard's ingenious solution, the **Jacquard loom,** directed the movement of needles, thread, and fabric via a series of cards with holes punched in them. Stated simply, if a needle went through a hole, the thread was raised and appeared on the upper surface of the fabric. If the needle did not engage a hole, the thread remained in place and passed to the underside of the fabric. With colored thread being "input" to the loom and a series of punched cards as a "program," the loom automatically "output" a cloth pattern.

Jacquard's loom was an immediate success. By 1812, there were over 11,000 Jacquard looms in France. By 1834, there were over 30,000 Jacquard looms in Lyons, France, alone. However, as might be expected, not everyone was happy about the Jacquard loom. Cloth factories were hiring less-skilled workers at lower wages whose primary duties were to load the looms and position the sets of punched cards. In some cities, riots occurred when weavers resisted the introduction of the Jacquard Loom. Nonetheless, the economic advantages gained from using the loom insured its success.

The idea of using a series of punched cards to direct the operation of a machine eventually caught the attention of a Cambridge University professor, Charles Babbage. Like all mathematicians and scientists of his day, Babbage used large tables of numbers that were the results of mathematical computations. Much time and effort were spent in creating accurate mathematical tables, and Babbage became obsessed with the notion of using a calculating machine to produce them.

Babbage built his **Difference Engine,** a calculator able to compute the values of polynomial equations to six decimal places, in 1822. A polynomial equation takes the form:

$$y = a + bx + cx^2 + dx^3 + \dots$$

This device used gearing similar to that of the early mechanical calculators. Babbage, however, was not content with his invention. It was a **special-purpose computing machine,** able to perform only one type of calculation. It did not seem right to Babbage that different computing machines were needed for different types of calculations, so he decided to build a **general-purpose computing machine.**

Charles Babbage and his Difference Engine

Babbage obtained a government grant—one of the first research grants ever recorded—to pursue his goal. In 1833, Babbage outlined the plans for the **Analytical Engine,** a steam-driven calculator able to perform 60 additions a minute, to store more than 1000 numbers of 50 decimals each, and to handle any type of mathematical problem.

Babbage's plans for the Analytical Engine far surpassed all the work that had gone before him. Had it been completed, the Analytical Engine would have incorporated many of the features found in the computer systems of the 1940s and 1950s. For example:

A "mill," or logic center, would manipulate data values based on instructions, or a program, that could be changed at will.

A "store," or memory, would hold intermediate results.

The computer would have the ability to base current operations on the results of prior operations.

Punched cards would hold the data to be processed and the instructions directing the processing.

Although a few prototypes were built, Babbage's dreams of a general-purpose computing machine were never realized. His efforts, and those of his son after Babbage's death, were plagued by the machinists' inability to produce precision parts. Also, Babbage was driven by his dreams, not the practical need for large-scale computation. In fact, it was not until World War II that the benefits of large-scale computation were generally recognized. An idealist, Babbage could never bring himself to "finalize" his plans. Babbage would come up with new part designs and have them manufactured, only to redesign them again. The conditions were not yet ripe for the development of a general-purpose computer.

Babbage's Analytical Engine was reported on by his friend and colleague, Ada Augusta, Countess of Lovelace. Computers at Work: "Ada, Countess of Lovelace" describes this fascinating woman.

Office Automation Begins

1837 Samuel Morse applies for a patent on his telegraph.

1844 Morse transmits the first telegraph message.

1867 Christopher Sholes begins his work on the typewriter.

1873 E. Remington & Sons acquires Sholes' typewriter and successfully markets it.

1876 Alexander Graham Bell invents the telephone.

Exhibit A.2

The development of Morse code showed how complex messages could be represented with only two symbols, the "dot" and the "dash."

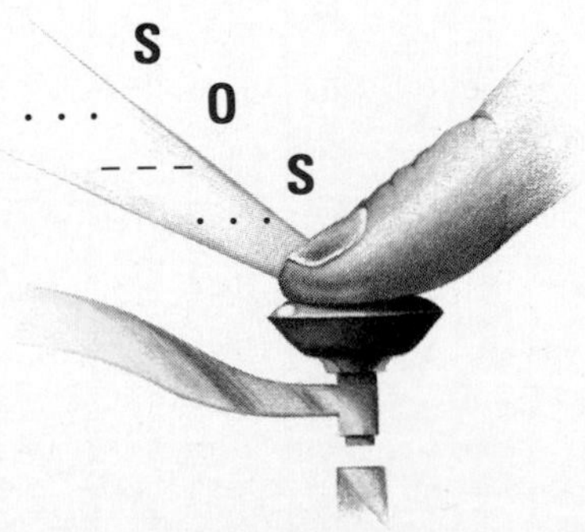

During the 19th century, the U.S. economy was transformed from one based on agriculture to one based on industry. Credit is usually given to the rush of advances that occurred in industrial machinery and transportation. What few people realize is that the changes that took place in the business office had an impact as well.

At the beginning of the 19th century, most businesses were small firms serving local markets. The difficulties of processing business paperwork with pen and ink and of buying and selling over long distances discouraged firms from expanding. By the end of the 19th century, however, the telegraph, the telephone, and the typewriter had eliminated these barriers. As a result, many

COMPUTERS AT WORK

Ada, Countess of Lovelace

She was a strange combination of beauty and intelligence, sophistication and naiveté, this slim dark-haired woman after whom the new programming language *Ada* is named. This honor underlines the fact that Ada Augusta, the Countess of Lovelace, was the first woman to make her mark in the field of computers—and this in the first half of the nineteenth century, 140 years ago.

Her reputation rests on the notes she added to her translation of Count Luigi Federico Menabrea's article on Charles Babbage's analytical engine. Menabrea, an Italian mathematician and officer in the Military Engineers who later became prime minister of Italy, had heard Babbage's talks on his engine in Turin in 1840. It is largely due to his paper and Lady Lovelace's notes that we have a good picture of Babbage's planned machine. Lady Lovelace's achievement is all the more remarkable since in her day women were literally not to be "heard" outside of the family circle, in such areas as scientific research.

As the daughter of the "great poet" Lord Byron, Ada had been of interest to many persons even before her ability as a mathematician had become known. Lord Byron's popularity as a poet had made his name a household word.

Handsome, talented, and unconventional, his marriage to the intellectual, righteous Anne Isabella Milbanke had been a disaster from the beginning. Small wonder that they separated a little over a month after Ada's birth. She was born in London on 10 December 1815, and was named Ada Augusta Byron.

Ada was raised by her mother, who fortunately fostered her mathematical interests. As mathematics and scientific subjects were not considered necessary in the schools for young ladies, it was perhaps just as well that Ada never attended any school or university, but was educated through governesses, tutors, and considerable self-study.

Ada met Charles Babbage in 1833 at one of the parties she attended after being presented at Court. He invited her and her mother to see his difference engine. After listening to him explain it, Lady Byron wrote to a friend: "There was a sublimity in the views thus opened of the ultimate results of intellectual power." Ada was fascinated by the machine and "saw the great beauty of the invention." Her reaction naturally pleased Babbage, and subsequently they became friends.

Throughout her life Lady Lovelace carried on scientific discussions with other respected scientists, such as Sir John Herschel and Michael Faraday (who pleased Ada by admiring the "elasticity" of her intellect). Among others with whom she enjoyed talking over ideas were Charles Dickens, Andrew Crosse (experiments in electricity), and Sir David Brewster (optics and polarized light). It is clear that she had an unusually capable mind and was respected for it by her contemporaries.

Source: V. R. Huskey and H. D. Huskey, "Ada, Countess of Lovelace, and Her Contribution to Computing," *Abacus,* Winter 1984, pp. 22–29.

large businesses could market and sell their products nationwide. Without these advances, the industrial society might never have come about.

Samuel Morse's invention of the telegraph was a key factor. Customers, suppliers, and branch offices could now be located far from a firm's main offices, factories, and warehouses. Also, the telegraph was faster than mailing information on paper. In addition, the development of Morse code showed how complex messages could be represented with only two symbols, the "dot" and the "dash" (see Exhibit A.2, opposite). As discussed in Chapter 3, today's computers use a similar method of coding data.

But it took an 1845 British news story to change the popular view of long-distance communication. After committing a murder west of London, a criminal thought he had made a clean escape by boarding a train to London.

The police, however, sent a telegram describing the murderer to the London police. The criminal was arrested as soon as he stepped off the train.

With Alexander Graham Bell's invention of the telephone, attitudes about communication changed even more. The convenience of telephone contact allowed a firm to have its managers located in adjoining offices, in different buildings at the same site, or in neighboring cities. This marked the beginning of business's growing dependence on its communications and information processing systems.

Surprising as it may seem, the typewriter was not accepted into the office as quickly as the telegraph or the telephone. As described in Computers at Work: "A Brief History of the Typewriter," it seemed, at the time of its invention, there was no practical need for swift written communication. A number of circumstances had changed this situation by the late 1880s. Business had become dependent upon the rapid communication of the telegraph and the telephone. Also, larger businesses were generating more written materials. In addition, the early typewriters' technical problems had been solved, and more people realized the value of producing high-quality business documents quickly. By the 1890s, over a million typewriters had been sold.

Alexander Graham Bell, making the first telephone call between New York and Chicago

Automated Data Processing Begins

1878 James Ritty develops the cash register.

1879 Thomas A. Edison invents the incandescent light bulb.

1885 Dorr E. Felt develops a key-driven calculating machine.

1890 Herman Hollerith develops an electromechanical tabulating machine to count the 1890 census.

1896 Hollerith leaves the Bureau of the Census to form his own company. This firm eventually becomes IBM. Guglielmo Marconi invents the radio.

1911 Hollerith's successor at the Bureau of the Census, James Powers, forms another company to sell punched-card equipment. This firm eventually merges with Remington Rand.

1914 James F. Smathers invents the electric typewriter.

1914 Thomas Watson, Sr., joins Hollerith's firm.

1915 Coast-to-coast telephone communication first takes place.

1930 The electric typewriter becomes a commercial success.

U.S. industry flourished in the late 19th and early 20th centuries, and with it the paperwork performed in offices. A new industry sprang up to sell equipment and supplies used in the office. Three business machines, in particular, were perfected during this period: the cash register, the adding machine, and punched-card processing equipment.

On a trip to Europe on an ocean liner, James Ritty watched a gauge that counted the revolutions of the ship's propeller. Why couldn't a similar machine, he thought, be used to record transactions in his business? When he returned home, Ritty and his brother John developed what was to become the first cash register, "Ritty's Incorruptible Cashier." In 1882, Ritty sold his business to Jacob H. Eckert for $1000, and the National Manufacturing Company was begun. A cash drawer and bell were soon added to Ritty's machine. The

A Brief History of the Typewriter

The man who invented the typewriter did not want to invent it; the company that first made it did not want to make it; when it got to market, hardly anyone bought it. When it finally caught on, it became boringly commonplace.

The inventor was Christopher Latham Sholes of Milwaukee (see below), collector of customs for the port of Milwaukee, and amateur inventor. His experiments began in 1867 in a machine shop as suitable for developing an intricate writing machine, noted one contemporary, "as a blacksmith's for making a watch." Sholes gave up often.

An obligation for swift communications finally supplied a rationale for writing machines.

His financial backer, James Densmore, browbeat Sholes into continuing. In 1873 a workable model was presented to E. Remington & Sons, gun manufacturers. Remington's production capacities had been swollen by the Civil War, and sewing machines took up the postwar slack. From the standpoint of factory equipment, sewing and writing machines had much in common.

What they lacked in common, in Philo Remington's opinion, was a market. Fortunately, assisting Sholes was George Washington Newton Yost, remembered as a smooth salesman. Remington was swayed by Yost's eloquent presentation and signed a contract to manufacture 1,000 Type Writers.

"The writing machine is to the pen what the sewing machine is to the needle," the manufacturers told an uninitiated public. To reinforce the point, they mounted the device on a sewing-machine stand, complete with foot treadle for carriage return. They even decorated it like contemporary sewing machines, with flowers and pastoral scenes. "An ornament to any parlour," they boasted. Sales agents—including Western Electric for a time—tried to ornament the parlors of America. They failed consistently.

One problem was that the machine had capital letters only. Another was that the printing was done on the underside of the platen, where it could not be seen. Worst was the resemblance of its product to printed matter. "I can read writin'," complained one field salesman, indignant that his boss seemed to think his letters required the attention of a compositor.

And Mark Twain, an early purchaser, was "wont to swear" because people ignored the content of his letters and asked how he got them printed. A "curiosity-breeding little joker" was his dismissal of the Type Writer.

But by the mid-1880s, the white-collar world became mechanized, as the blue-collar world had a generation earlier. Bell's telephone, Edison's dictating machine, in-house telegraphs and ticker tapes all established a mechanical context—and an obligation for swift communications—that finally supplied a rationale for writing machines. By the 1890s, about a million typewriters had been sold.

But a million extra men weren't available to operate the typewriters. So employers overthrew rules of Victorian propriety and brought in women. To the dual percussions of tongues clucking and type bars pounding, the white-collar career woman was born.

Source: D. Sutherland, "A Brief History of the Typewriter," in A. Solomon, "Remember This?" *Inc.*, October 1982, pp. 63–68 and 70.

Dorr E. Felt's key-driven adding machine

next owner of the firm was John Patterson, who changed the name of the company to National Cash Register (NCR).

Dorr E. Felt developed the first key-driven adding machine that effectively handled calculations containing digits. However, Felt's machine had one major problem; while key input was easy to use, output consisted of pin holes in paper. William Burroughs improved Felt's adding machine by using a paper printer. Burroughs' firm, originally named the American Arithmometer Company, began producing its own adding machine in 1890.

But the adding machine and the cash register, while important business inventions, only refined the calculating machines developed much earlier. The invention that drastically changed the nature of business data processing was the **electromechanical tabulator** developed by Herman Hollerith.

Hollerith worked at the Bureau of the Census while the 1880 census was counted. It took nearly seven years to complete this task. At that rate, the 1900 census would begin before the 1890 census was completed.

The Census Bureau announced a contest to select a new counting technique for the 1890 census. Three finalists were selected and given a problem to complete. Two of the competitors took fifty-five hours and forty-four hours, respectively, to complete the problem. Hollerith's invention, the **tabulating machine,** completed the problem in five and a half hours. Needless to say, the tabulating machine was used in the 1890 census. The first count was available in six weeks, and the entire census was completed in about three years.

Early Burroughs adding machines in use

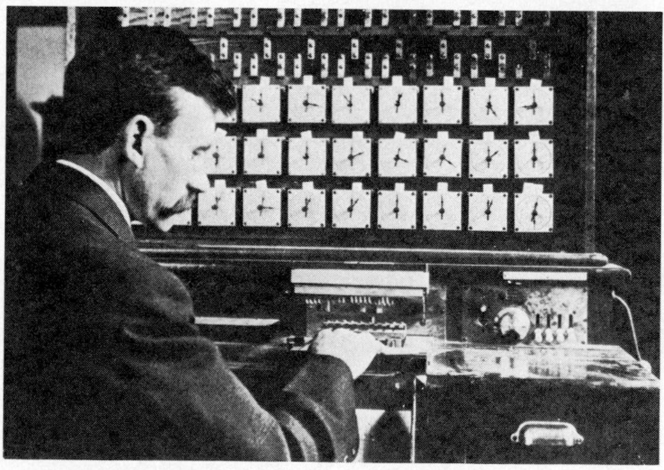

Hollerith's tabulator in use at the Bureau of the Census

In Hollerith's machine, data was represented by holes punched in cards. The cards were read by an electromechanical scanner. This scanner had pins which were lowered onto a card. If a pin went through a hole, it touched a pan of mercury, completing an electrical circuit, which moved a counting dial by one unit. Hollerith used electrical relays to handle this counting procedure. A relay is a wire coil wound around an iron core. A pulse of electricity through the coil briefly magnetizes the core, making it attract a thin metal strip and, hence, nudging a dial by one unit. The same basic principle is used with the telegraph key. Each dial could represent up to 10,000 units.

Hollerith was not familiar with either Jacquard's or Babbage's use of punched cards. As the story goes, he got his idea to use punched cards from watching a railroad conductor punch holes in tickets. Regardless of where the idea came from, the punched card was the key to his tabulating machine. Punched cards could be stored and reused over and over. Data needed to be entered only once, even when it was used in many different calculations.

Hollerith perfected his tabulating machine only a short time after Babbage failed. Why? First, improved machining and manufacturing produced essential parts precisely. Second, electricity had been harnessed. Third, business recognized the growing volume of business transactions as a problem. Finally, the census contest motivated Hollerith to solve a real problem within a limited time period.

Hollerith left the Census Bureau in 1896 to manufacture and sell his tabulating machine. His firm, the Tabulating Machine Company, started the **punched-card equipment** industry. In 1911, the Tabulating Machine Company merged with three other firms to form the Computer-Tabulating-Recording Company (CTR). In 1914, Thomas Watson, Sr., joined CTR as general manager and became president the following year. Watson later changed the name of CTR to International Business Machines (IBM). On page A–12 Computers at Work: "A Formidable Competitor" describes Watson's intense approach to business, which perhaps more than anything else established the corporate culture that has led IBM to dominate the business computing market.

Hollerith's successor at the Bureau of the Census, James Powers, eventually formed his own data processing business to compete against CTR. The Powers Accounting Machine Company was merged into Remington Rand, later to be IBM's strongest competitor in the 1950s.

Other events during this time period would prove important to business computing. Thomas A. Edison's invention of the light bulb not only made electric power a public good, but also started a line of research that eventually led to the **vacuum tube,** a critical component of the first electronic computers. Advances were also made in the field of communications. Marconi's invention of the radio would lead to other advances in "wireless" communication, even further expanding business communication capabilities. AT&T, using the vacuum tube, provided businesses with coast-to-coast voice communications. Finally, Electromagnetic Typewriters, the first firm to achieve commercial success with the electric typewriter, became a part of IBM in 1933.

Thomas A. Edison

Early vacuum tubes

COMPUTERS AT WORK

A Formidable Competitor

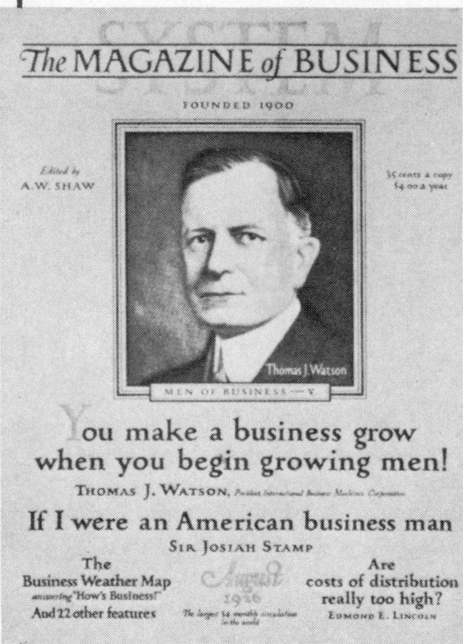

Thomas J. Watson's motto was *THINK;* and he made a lot of people, in particular his competitors, think long and hard. Actually he was more inclined to get out and hustle than to sit and think.

In 1892 Watson took a job as a bookkeeper in a butcher shop in Elmira, New York. Like other geniuses, he found manual bookkeeping painful. He gave it up for a congenial job—selling pianos, organs, and sewing machines. He liked being a one-man operation—manager, accountant, and deliveryman all in one. In 1894 he moved to Buffalo and eventually became a salesman for the National Cash Register Company.

The NCR had a problem: other companies were reconditioning and selling used NCR machines, which were in competition with new cash registers. John H. Patterson, NCR's president, decided to organize a secret subsidiary to take over the used cash register business.

Patterson picked Watson out of 400 salesmen to head his new subsidiary. Watson was given a million dollars to spend without having to account for its allocation. He proved to be an able guerrilla fighter; he opened up stores near those of the competition, undersold them, and lured away their salesmen. The competition was soon as dead as a doornail, and at age 33 Watson was the third man at NCR. At first Watson was Patterson's favorite, but like Lucifer, he aspired too high and aroused Patterson's jealousy. He was fired.

Watson then took a job as manager of Hollerith's ailing Computing-Tabulating-Recording Company (CTR). In three months he was president. He shortly negotiated an agreement with a major competitor, the Powers Accounting Machine Company. In six years CTR's gross income went from $4 million to almost $14 million. In the recession of 1921, however, annual sales fell to $3.5 million. With the astute backing of Alexander H. Hemphill, president of the Guaranty Trust Company, Watson expanded the business beyond just tabulating machines, and times got better. In his decade with the company Watson had sparked the development of better equipment—a tabulating printer, an efficient keypunch, a horizontal sorter. In 1924 the name of the company was changed to International Business Machines.

Watson was a man of violent temper and iron whim who would promote or fire a man on impulse.

The depression of the thirties slowed Watson little. Instead of curtailing production and the payroll, he kept on building up a huge surplus inventory. It was a gamble that paid off. Soon IBM got the contract to process the data for the Social Security System when it was established in 1935, and World War II brought a new flood of government business. Watson was also responsible for building IBM's matchless sales organization.

Watson became a public figure, the first of a new breed, the socially conscious industrialist, and he tried to put Roosevelt's New Deal across to businessmen. As a lifelong Democrat, he could have been an ambassador, but chose to become a kind of unofficial ambassador in international circles—to the incidental benefit of IBM.

Source: M. Harmon, "Electromechanical and Electrical Computers," in *Stretching Man's Mind: A History of Data Processing* (New York: Mason/Charter Publishers, Inc., 1975), pp. 114–16.

The General-Purpose Computer Is Developed

1930 Vannevar Bush develops a large-scale mechanical computer at MIT.

1937–38 George Stibitz and Samuel Williams at Bell Labs develop a small electronic computer using telephone relays as the basic electronic component.

1937–44 Howard Aiken develops an electromechanical computer at Harvard University.

1939 John Vincent Atanasoff and Clifford Berry of Iowa State College develop a small special-purpose vacuum tube computer.

1941–45 Alan Turing and other British scientists develop the Collossus, a large special-purpose electronic computer.

1943–46 J. Presper Eckert, Jr., and John William Mauchly develop the ENIAC, the first large general-purpose computer, at the University of Pennsylvania.

1944 John von Neuman, working on the plans for the ENIAC's immediate successor, defines the basic computer architecture to be used for the next forty years.

1946 Eckert and Mauchly form their own company to build and market the UNIVAC computer.

1947 William Schockley, Walter Brattain, and John Bardeen invent the transistor at Bell Labs.

1950 The Whirlwind computer is built at MIT.

A true need for large-scale computation did not arise until the 1930s, when research scientists began to require many extensive calculations. One of the first scientists to develop a large-scale computer was Vannevar Bush, Dean of Engineering at the Massachusetts Institute of Technology. He led a three-year effort to build a special-purpose mechanical computer, called the **Differential Analyzer,** for use in calculating complex differential equations.

Vannevar Bush and the Differential Analyzer

A similar motive prompted Howard Aiken of Harvard to develop a large-scale general-purpose computer (see page A–14). His doctoral work on the laws of space led him to hand-calculate thousands of nonlinear equations. After this experience, Aiken knew there had to be a better way to handle such calculations. However, as a practical scientist, Aiken recognized the huge cost of developing such a machine, so he looked for someone to sponsor his work.

Aiken first approached the Monroe Calculating Company, but his request for financial backing was denied. He then went to IBM and met with Thomas Watson, Sr. Eventually, IBM and the Navy Department jointly sponsored the development of Aiken's computer, the Automatic Sequence Controlled Calculator. Later, the name was changed to the **Harvard Mark I.** The machine was built by IBM engineers and delivered to Harvard in 1944, where it was used for over nineteen years (see page A–14). It cost just under $500,000.

One of the Naval officers assigned to the Mark I, Grace Hopper has made countless contributions to computer programming (see page A–14). An early contribution occurred one day when a Mark I program did not work. As it turned out, the problem was not with her program; a dead moth had created a short circuit in the computer. Programming problems from then on have been referred to as "bugs."

Howard Aiken

The Harvard Mark I

Grace Hopper

The first electronic computer was built by George Stibitz and Samuel Williams at Bell Labs. The **Complex Calculator** was a small special-purpose computer that used telephone relays for its electronic storage components. Stibitz later told Bell Labs executives that he could build a general-purpose relay computer for $50,000. Their response: Who would want to spend $50,000 to calculate?

Stibitz tested his first ideas for a computer in his kitchen, using a breadboard, tobacco cans, a dry-cell battery, and flashlight bulbs. This very simple computer, which could only add two numbers together, is referred to as the "Kitchen Table Computer" in Bell's annals.

In 1940, Stibitz made another contribution to computing when he demonstrated his Complex Calculator to scientists attending a meeting at Dartmouth College in New Hampshire. Stibitz and his computer were in New York City. Unable to attend the Dartmouth meeting, Stibitz used phone lines to hook his computer to a teletype terminal at Dartmouth. This was the first instance of a computer being used from a remote location.

George Stibitz

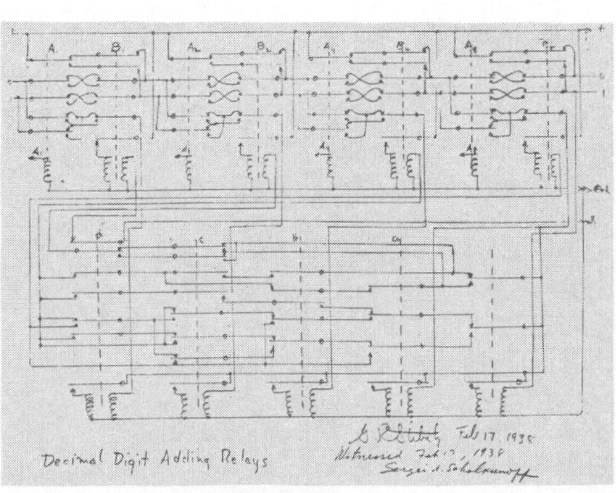

Plans for the Complex Calculator

John Vincent Atanasoff and his graduate students at Iowa State College were involved in complex mathematical research. Tired of making tedious calculations by hand, Atanasoff hit upon the notion of using an electronic computer for these calculations. His design did not progress very far for a couple of years, until one evening in the winter of 1937. Atanasoff went back to his office after dinner to work on his computer plans, but as was usually the case, no ideas came to him. Frustrated, he got into his car and raced over the highways of Iowa. Just over the border into Illinois, Atanasoff pulled onto a side road and came upon a tavern. There, after a couple of drinks, the plans for his computer came quickly.

Two key decisions that Atanasoff made that evening were to use vacuum tubes as the primary electronic component and to use the binary number system. As discussed in Chapter 3, the **binary number system** uses the symbols 0 and 1 to represent all numbers. Vacuum tubes provided an extremely fast means of processing data, and using binary numbers reduced the complexity of the electronic circuits.

Atanasoff and Clifford Berry, a graduate student, developed a prototype model of Atanasoff's computer and called it the **ABC Computer** for Atanasoff-Berry Computer. A small, special-purpose computer, the *ABC* was fully electronic. Unfortunately, the project was halted by insufficient funding and Atanasoff's departure to serve at the U.S. Naval Ordnance Laboratory during World War II.

One of the best-kept secrets of World War II involved a computer known as the **Colossus,** developed by a group of British scientists led by mathematician Alan Turing. Even today, most of the information about this project has never been released. What *is* known is that a large-scale electronic computer was developed to break the German military code system. The special-purpose Colossus, which may very well have been the first successful large electronic computer, was built in 1943 and played a vital role for the military in breaking the German code.

John V. Atanasoff

The ABC Computer

The Colossus

Like Bush, Aiken, and Atanasoff, John Mauchly was in need of a large-scale computing device to aid him in his research. In 1941, Mauchly went to the Moore School of Engineering at the University of Pennsylvania for a refresher course in electronics. There he met J. Presper Eckert, Jr., a graduate assistant for a laboratory course Mauchly was required to take. As Mauchly already had a Ph.D. in physics, he and Eckert spent most of their time in the lab talking about Mauchly's idea of building a computer. In time, the fact that they were unable to interest anyone else in their project didn't matter, because the war effort drew many of the Moore School faculty members from the university and allowed both Eckert and Mauchly to obtain faculty positions.

It was through the Moore School of Engineering that the U.S. Army sought Mauchly's help in designing a machine that could quickly perform the many calculations required to produce accurate gunnery tables. Even with over two hundred human "computers" performing these calculations, a growing backlog of work left many new weapons useless.

J. Presper Eckert, Jr., and John W. Mauchly (shown foreground left and center, respectively) with the ENIAC

With both the financial backing of the U.S. Army and the engineering talent of the Moore School, Eckert and Mauchly developed the **ENIAC,** the Electronic Numerical Integrator and Computer. It was the first large general-purpose electronic computer. The usefulness of the ENIAC was shown immediately, on one of its early test runs, when the computer took only two hours to solve a nuclear physics problem that would have required one hundred years of hand calculation by a physicist.

The key to the ENIAC's computational speed was its use of vacuum tubes. Eckert and Mauchly took a great risk in using vacuum tubes. Consider the problems they faced. The ENIAC used over 18,000 tubes, each operating at speeds of around 100,000 pulses a second. A chance for an error to occur due to tube failure, mostly because of overheating, arose every 10 microseconds. In a single second, almost two billion chances for errors arose.

Eckert and Mauchly resigned from the University of Pennsylvania in 1946 to form their own company to build the UNIVAC I computer, the Universal Automatic Computer. Their firm, always on the brink of bankruptcy, was eventually sold to the Remington Rand Corporation in 1950. Remington Rand also bought the rights to the ENIAC patent.

In the early seventies, Honeywell challenged the patent in a bitter court battle. During the trial, Honeywell lawyers revealed that Mauchly had visited Atanasoff in 1941 for long talks about his design. In 1973, the federal judge ruled the ENIAC patent invalid, concluding "Eckert and Mauchly did not themselves first invent the automatic electronic digital computer, but instead derived the subject matter from one Dr. John Vincent Atanasoff." Ironically, few computer scientists had known of Atanasoff's work before the trial, so the decision was a controversial one. In spite of the outcome, many people feel the court's decision does not cloud the contribution of Mauchly and Eckert, the team who led the effort to build the ENIAC.

While the ENIAC was faster than any calculating machine built before it, changing its program was very slow work. The ENIAC was "programmed" by wiring by hand circuit boards that linked the computer's components. This limitation discouraged applications other than massive computations, and led to the design of the **EDVAC,** the Electronic Discrete Variable Automatic Computer, ENIAC's successor.

The guiding light behind the EDVAC was mathematician John von Neuman. Von Neuman's insights into the operation of an electronic computer laid the groundwork for computer design over the next forty years. The architecture, or design, of today's computer is still referred to as a **von Neuman architecture.** This design includes the following:

Bell Lab scientists John Bardeen (left), William Shockley (seated), and Walter Brattain (right)

The Whirlwind

An arithmetic-logic unit handles mathematical and logic operations.

A control unit directs the proper sequencing of a computer's instructions.

An internal, or primary, memory temporarily holds data and programs.

Input and output devices move data into and from the computer system.

An outside recording, or secondary storage, device permanently holds data and programs.

These devices are the same devices introduced in Chapter 1.

Von Neuman's major contribution to computing was his concept that both data and programs should be stored in primary memory. Not only does a stored program do away with lengthy program setups, it allows full advantage of the speed of electronic components.

Two final important technological developments of this era grew out of research on radar systems. First, the unreliability of vacuum tubes led AT&T, among others, to search for better technology. The resulting improved technology was the **transistor.** Its inventors, Bell Lab scientists William Shockley, Walter Brattain, and John Bardeen, were awarded a Nobel prize in 1956. Second, the **Whirlwind computer** was built at MIT in 1959 to control radar installations. This computer was so big, people could walk through its control unit. The importance of the Whirlwind, however, lay not in its size, but in the research that went into its development. Two of its more notable advances included using a CRT for operator interactions and a new, faster primary memory technology called core memory. A **core memory** consists of tiny metal doughnuts, or cores, that can be magnetized in one direction or another (see Exhibit A.3). The difference in direction is used to reflect a 0 or 1. Core memory was the main form of primary memory in the latter 1950s and throughout the 1960s.

While the electronic computer was now a reality, few people aside from Eckert and Mauchly believed a market existed for computers outside of the scientific community. Aiken is believed to have said that only six computers would ever be sold, while Thomas Watson, Sr., allowed that as many as fifty computers would be sold. Although Watson supported the development of the Harvard Mark I, he viewed the computer as interesting, but too unwieldy, exotic, and expensive an experiment to replace adding machines and punched-card equipment in offices.

Exhibit A.3
Core Memory

OFF

Current passes through the wire in one direction. The core is magnetized as "off," represented by a zero.

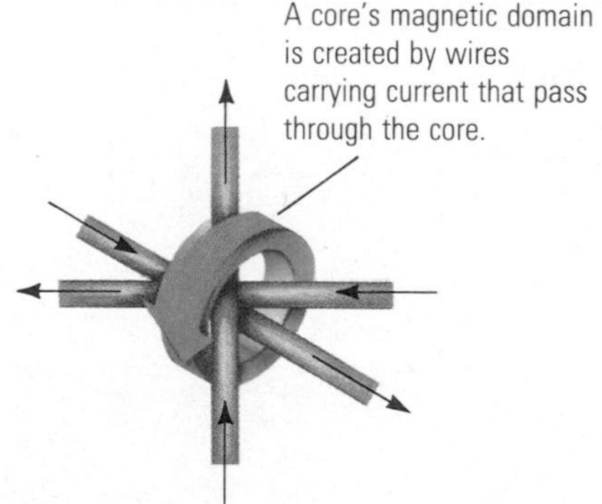

A core's magnetic domain is created by wires carrying current that pass through the core.

ON

Current passes through the wire in the opposite direction. The core is magnetized as "on," represented by a one.

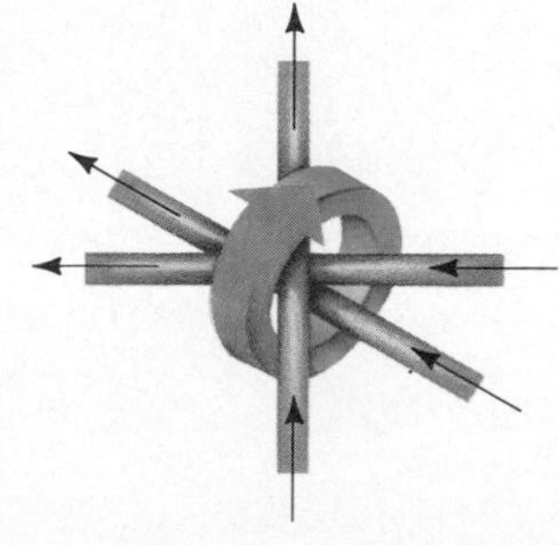

THE COMPUTER AGE

Computer technology has gone through many changes since 1950. Exhibit A.4 shows the impacts of these advances on business computing. Had automobile development paralleled the computer's development, today's luxury cars would cost $50, travel at 700 miles per hour, and get over 1000 miles per gallon. These changes are often divided into **computer generations,** based upon the main electronic component used. The first generation of computers (1951–58) used the vacuum tube, while the second generation (1959–63) used the transistor. In the third generation (1964–70), integrated circuits or "chips" were introduced. In the fourth generation (1971–present), the chips have become smaller and more complex. For the remainder of this chapter, we will discuss these computer generations.

The First Generation

The vacuum tube was the primary electronic element used in first generation computers. These early computers, while useful, were still quite unreliable. Vacuum tubes generated so much heat that water cooling was necessary. Even with these cooling systems, computers were in constant need of repair. The bigger a computer was, the more tubes it had, and the sooner it would fail.

Despite these technological obstacles, the computer industry was beginning to take shape. Remington Rand delivered the first UNIVAC 1 to the U.S. Bureau of the Census in 1951. This marked the first time an electronic computer had been built for a data processing application rather than a military one. By 1952, the Census Bureau had obtained three UNIVACS, which displaced much of the punched-card equipment that IBM had sold the Bureau. IBM was forced to take a hard look at this new data processing technology. Thomas Watson, Jr., IBM's new president, directed IBM toward electronic computers and away from electromechanical punched-card equipment.

The use of the UNIVAC 1 by the Columbia Broadcasting System (CBS) to project the winner of the 1952 presidential election brought the electronic computer to the attention of the U.S. public. On election eve, the UNIVAC projected that Eisenhower would win by a landslide. Because all the experts had predicted a close election, Remington Rand's staff thought there was an error in the computer program. They stalled CBS and began to make changes to the program. When they had "improved" the program to the point where Eisenhower would win by only a slim margin, the projection was released to CBS. By 11:00 P.M., voting results indicated an Eisenhower landslide! When this story spread, the computer's image as an electronic "brain" was formed.

A third important event of this period was an antitrust action by the U.S. Department of Justice against AT&T. In 1956, AT&T was barred from having anything to do with the computer market. However, this did not prevent AT&T from using or making computers for its own use.

Exhibit A.4

Performance differences for representative computers from each succeeding computer generation. In each case, the computer system is handling the same data processing problem.

Year	Generation	Cost to Perform the Problem	Processing Time
1955	1	$15.00	6 Hours
1960	2	$ 2.50	45 Seconds
1965	3	$ .50	30 Seconds
1975	4	$ .20	5 Seconds
1985	4½	$ .05	1 Second

A vacuum tube circuit

J. Presper Eckert, Jr., (center) and Walter Cronkite (right) look on as the UNIVAC counts votes for the 1952 presidential election.

Hardware. First generation computers used vacuum tubes for data storage in ALU and CU circuits, as well as in primary memory. By the end of this era, the faster magnetic cores were being used for primary memory. Data and programs were entered most often by punched cards; computer output was produced either on cards or on paper. Cards were the primary form of secondary storage, but by the end of this time period, magnetic tapes were commonly used for secondary storage.

Work to improve the transistor continued throughout the 1950s. Much of this effort was funded by the U.S. government, which used electronics in the Cold War and in the space program. Transistor manufacturing was still more art than science, however. And engineers of the day, trained to use vacuum tubes, were slow to switch to transistors. After using the larger vacuum tube, working with transistors was rather like doing surgery on the head of a pin. But by 1958, advances in transistors were bringing the first computer generation to an end.

Another important technical event took place in 1958. The leading electronic circuit technology at that time stacked components on top of one another, like dishes, with connecting wires running up through holes cut through the components. Jack Kilby at Texas Instruments wondered if it would be possible to build an entire circuit within a single piece of material, rather than stacking the components. His research led to the development of the **integrated circuit.** A few months later, Robert Noyce at Fairchild Semiconductor also developed an integrated circuit along with a greatly improved manufacturing method.

Software. First generation computers had very skimpy, if any, operating systems. Instead, a human operator loaded a stack of cards containing a program and data, which were processed as a batch. Military computers, such as the SAGE air defense system, led to new systems software able to handle remote data entry and to link computer systems together in networks.

The major software advances involved programming languages. As described in Chapter 3, all computers are directed by **machine language**

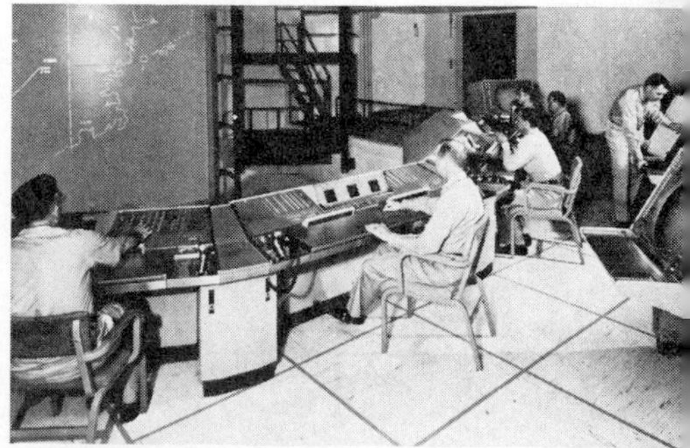

The SAGE U.S. air defense system

1951–58

The First Generation

1951 The UNIVAC 1 is delivered to the U.S. Census Bureau.

1952 Thomas Watson, Jr., becomes president of IBM.

1953 J. Lyons and Sons company, a chain of British corner tea shops, builds its own electronic computer.

1954 General Electric Company becomes the first private firm in the U.S. to take delivery of a computer, a UNIVAC 1.

1954 John Backus of IBM begins designing FORTRAN, the first high-level programming language.

1955 IBM begins delivery of its 705 business computer.

1955 The SAGE air defense system is installed.

1956 Grace Hopper develops a business-oriented programming language, FLOW-MATIC.

1956 John McCarthy at MIT begins to design LISP, the first programming language aimed at artificial intelligence applications.

1956 AT&T is barred from competing in the computer industry.

1958 Jack Kilby at Texas Instruments builds the first integrated circuit.

instructions. Here, each instruction takes the form of a series of **binary digits.** The very first computers, such as the ENIAC, were actually directly programmed in machine language, which was very difficult and time consuming. By the early 1950s, though, most programming was being done in **assembly languages,** in which abbreviations replaced the binary digits of machine language. Assembly language programs are then "translated" to machine language instructions by systems software known as an **assembler.** Because these abbreviations are easier to remember and use than binary digits, programming is much easier. Both machine and assembly languages require programmers to work at the level of a computer's electronic circuitry. Programmers have to understand both the problem they are solving and details about computer hardware.

Prior to 1954, all programming was done in either machine or assembly language, and programmers rightly regarded their work as a complex, creative job. These programmers, in general, were convinced that programming could not be automated. Simply too many shortcomings in the hardware had to be overcome by programming skill. As a result, the cost of programming was usually as great as the cost of hardware.

In 1954, a group of IBM scientists led by John Backús began work on the design of a **high-level programming language** for scientific computing. This design was called **FORTRAN,** short for *For*mula *Tran*slation. With high-level programming languages, program instructions are directed toward the problem being solved rather than the computer on which the program is run. As a result, a single program instruction may represent a series of machine language instructions. As you might expect, programming with a high-level language is not only easier, it is much faster. Exhibit A.5 illustrates some differences among machine, assembly, and high-level programming languages. The drawback of high-level languages is that they have to be "translated" into machine language. This is performed, as shown in Exhibit A.6, by a systems software program called a **compiler.**

When FORTRAN first became available, many programmers refused to use it. They did not believe that a compiler could produce efficient machine language versions of their programs. Luckily, the FORTRAN designers had anticipated this reaction. Their primary goal in developing FORTRAN was to produce an efficient machine language translation. This early decision was a major factor in FORTRAN's success and aided the rapid acceptance of high-

Exhibit A.5

Differences among machine language, assembly language, and a high-level language. The task used to illustrate these different forms of programming is the addition of one variable to another variable.

Language Form	Language Translation
Machine language 011011 0110 011100 0111 110001 0110 100 010101 0110	No translation is needed.
Assembly language FX B FY C ADA X Y STA B	These assembly language statements must be translated into machine language. Each assembly language statement will translate into one machine language statement.
High-level language LET B = B + C	This BASIC statement must be translated into machine language. This one BASIC statement will translate into four machine language statements.

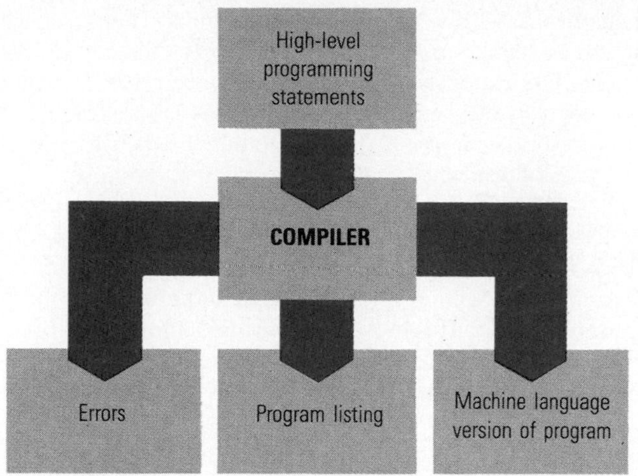

Exhibit A.6

A systems software program called a *compiler* translates programming statements written in a high-level language to the instructions that will actually run on the computer system.

level programming languages in general. FORTRAN was available by 1956 and in general use by 1957. By the end of the 1950s, over two hundred other high-level programming languages had been developed.

Uses and Users. All earlier computing had involved scientific or large-scale computing. Within this first generation of computers, however, business computing began. By the end of the 1950s, many large firms had begun to develop their basic transaction processing systems, such as payroll, billing, and inventory control.

The first firm believed to have used an electronic computer for business applications was J. Lyons and Sons, a chain of British tea shops. Some of the employees actually built the firm's computer! The firm's computer group broke away to become *ICL,* short for International Computers, Limited, which today is Europe's leading computer manufacturer. In the United States, General Electric was the first firm to purchase an electronic computer.

IBM's development in 1955 of the very successful 705 series of business computers proved to be an important milestone in the history of computers. IBM had finally caught up to and even surpassed Remington Rand's electronic computers.

First generation computer users were not computer scientists. None existed! These first users were scientists, engineers, and business people who saw the advantage of using computers and taught themselves to write the necessary programs. **End-user computing,** in which computer users develop their own information systems, flourished out of necessity. The increasing complexity of computer systems soon discouraged this early era of end-user computing.

The Second Generation

The appearance in 1959 of the first **transistorized computer systems** launched the second generation of computers. The continuing trend toward smaller, faster, more reliable, and less expensive computers was started. One year later, Digital Equipment Corporation, or DEC, introduced the first minicomputer, the **PDP–1.** The first minicomputers differed from regular computer systems in a number of ways. Not only were they smaller, they were built to

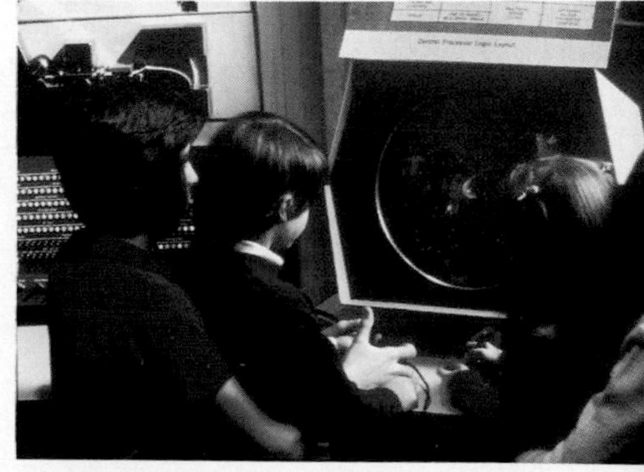

The first video game used the PDP-1, the first minicomputer.

1959–63

The Second Generation

1959 IBM introduces a transistorized computer, the IBM 1401.

1960 Grace Hopper and others design the COBOL programming language.

1960 Digital Equipment Corporation introduces the PDP–1, the first minicomputer.

1960 The Rand Corporation develops the first interactive computing system.

1961 IBM begins working on the System 360 family of computer systems.

1962 The Telstar communications satellite is launched.

1962 IBM and American Airlines develop the SABRE reservation system.

1963 John Kemeny and Thomas Kurtz develop the BASIC programming language.

1963 IBM begins to design the PL/1 programming language.

serve special purposes. They were very rugged, unlike their predecessors, and could function in harsh surroundings, with fewer climate controls needed. Also, they were less expensive. With these improvements, computer systems began to be used in new environments, such as laboratories and factories. Thus, the minicomputer not only opened up new markets for electronic computers, it also introduced the computer to new uses and users.

Two other events in this era were to greatly affect the future of business computing. First, IBM began work on its **System 360 Series** of computers, an immense project that would represent one of the most important events in the history of computing. Second, the launching of **Telstar** led the way to the communications satellite. This meant that business information processing was no longer "tied" to earth. Just as the telephone enabled firms to operate nationwide, communication satellites allowed firms to operate worldwide.

Hardware. Though second generation computers used transistors for most processing circuitry, magnetic cores were still used for primary memory. Most data and programs were entered into the computer from magnetic tape. Often, however, data would first be punched on cards and then copied onto tapes to speed data entry. Similarly, output was often directed to tape to be printed onto paper later. While magnetic tapes were the most common secondary storage devices, magnetic disks did appear toward the end of this era.

Software. The first real operating systems appeared during this second generation of computer development. Besides improving computer system efficiency, these operating systems brought about new forms of data processing, such as interactive processing, real-time processing, and time-sharing. With **interactive processing,** users could carry on a dialogue with the computer. With **real-time computing,** events could be captured and processed as

The IBM System 360 Series played an important role in the history of computing.

Telstar led the way to the communications satellite.

they occurred. With **time-sharing,** many people could use a computer system at the same time. For example, the SABRE reservation system, developed by IBM and American Airlines, allowed reservation clerks to interactively review or update a flight's data file as reservations were being made.

Developments in programming languages also occurred. First, the U.S. Department of Defense sponsored a meeting to develop a business-oriented programming language that could be used by all its agencies on different computers. This resulted in the design of the *Co*mmon *B*usiness-*O*riented *L*anguage, better known as **COBOL.** Second, two professors at Dartmouth College, John Kemeny and Thomas Kurtz, wanted to make computing available to all Dartmouth students. To achieve this, they needed an interactive programming language that was easy to learn and easy to use. Their work resulted in the *B*eginners *A*ll-purpose *S*ymbolic *I*nstruction *C*ode, or **BASIC.** Finally, IBM began to develop a programming language able to handle both scientific and business data processing. At this time, scientific programs were written in FORTRAN, and business programs were written in COBOL. Few programmers knew both languages. This project resulted in the design of **PL/1,** or *P*rogramming *L*anguage One.

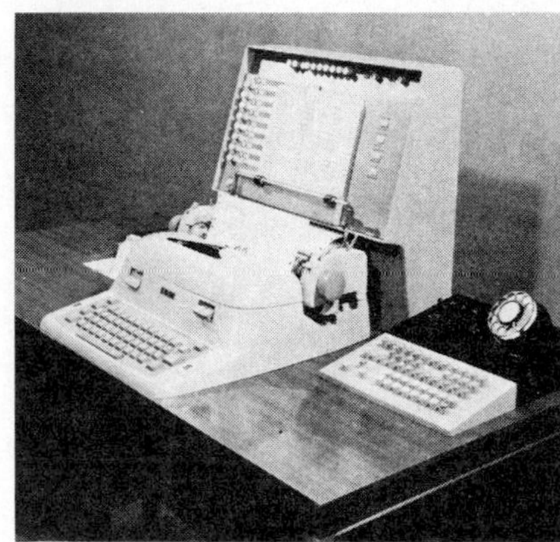

The SABRE reservation system for airline passengers

Uses and Users. All types of businesses were now using electronic computers for transaction processing. Some information reporting systems were being developed to provide managers with useful information from the growing data bases being created by these transaction processing systems.

Even though information systems were now common in many firms, not many employees actually came in contact with a computer. Data were usually recorded on paper and sent to the computer department for processing. Similarly, output was distributed by the computer department to users. Only computer specialists worked directly with the computer.

Computer systems had already become too complex for most users. Users explained their needs to programmers, who then developed application programs. Most programmers and other computer specialists obtained their computer skills from "on-the-job-training," usually through the military. Colleges and universities had not yet begun to offer degrees, or even many courses, in computer science or information systems.

The Third Generation

In 1964, IBM introduced the six computers that made up the System/360 series of computer systems. These six computers used designs similar enough to allow a program written for one machine to run on another. The computers differed mainly in the capacity of their primary memory. At the same time, IBM introduced another 150 related products. The impact of these innovations on the computer industry was tremendous. First, the "life" of a computer system was extended, since a firm buying a System 360 computer could "grow" into larger members of the series as its information processing needs increased. More importantly, firms could make this move without rewriting their software, an enormous savings of both time and money. This was a powerful incentive to choose and continue to use IBM equipment. Second, the operating system became the key component of a computer system. With software controlling all aspects of a computer's operation, efficiencies improved and failures were less frequent. As a result, firms became more willing to depend on computer systems to handle all their information processing needs.

The magnetic tape Selectric typewriter

Three other events important to business computing occurred during this era. First, the development of the **magnetic tape Selectric typewriter** made it possible for typists to store and retrieve documents. This was a major step toward today's **word processing systems,** and it opened the office market to electronic computers. Second, DEC's success with its **PDP–8 minicomputer** spurred other firms to enter the minicomputer segment of the computer industry. Finally, responding to possible U.S. Department of Justice antitrust actions, IBM "unbundled" its software. IBM previously charged customers a single price for its computer systems, which were made up of IBM hardware and IBM software. Other hardware vendors believed this unfair because they could not compete with IBM in developing both hardware and software. Joining the protest, software vendors, such as Computer Sciences Corporation, argued that there were few incentives for IBM's customers to purchase non-IBM software. Perhaps the competing vendors' protests were justified, because, after IBM unbundled its software, many new hardware and software products did appear.

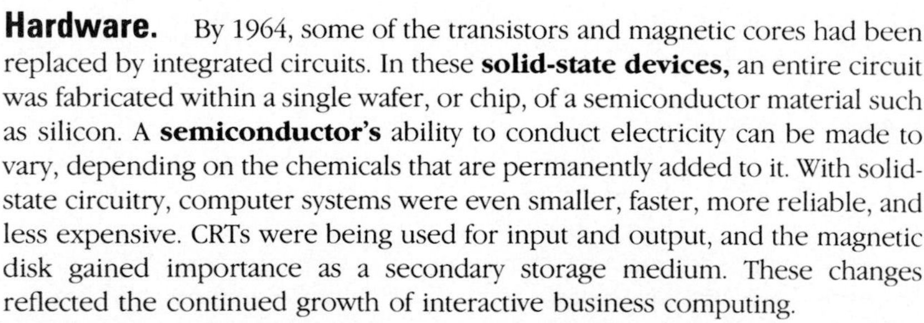

Hardware. By 1964, some of the transistors and magnetic cores had been replaced by integrated circuits. In these **solid-state devices,** an entire circuit was fabricated within a single wafer, or chip, of a semiconductor material such as silicon. A **semiconductor's** ability to conduct electricity can be made to vary, depending on the chemicals that are permanently added to it. With solid-state circuitry, computer systems were even smaller, faster, more reliable, and less expensive. CRTs were being used for input and output, and the magnetic disk gained importance as a secondary storage medium. These changes reflected the continued growth of interactive business computing.

Software. Operating systems continued to grow in power. Both interactive and remote business computing were now common. More programming languages were also developed. For example, IBM developed **RPG,** or *R*eport *P*rogram *G*enerator, to aid small businesses switching from punched cards to electronic computers. With a minimum of training, a small firm's employees could duplicate the firm's existing data processing procedures on a small computer system. In 1971, Nicholas Wirth developed the **Pascal** language, named in honor of Blaise Pascal. This was the first programming language to use **structured programming** concepts, an approach to program design that is covered in Part v of this text.

Uses and Users. Data input and output were now being performed by clerical employees rather than computer specialists, and the result was faster processing and fewer errors. It makes sense that a purchasing clerk entering a purchase order is more likely to catch an error than someone knowing little about the items being ordered. Also, information systems were being integrated, meaning that the outputs of some information systems became the inputs to other information systems. For example, an order entry system might have access to stock levels maintained by an inventory control system. A manufacturing scheduling system might have access to stock levels maintained by an inventory control system and the equipment statuses as registered by a shop floor control system. Finally, a wide range of information reporting systems were being developed at this time to support a firm's managers and other professional employees.

With interactive computing, users began to regain a more direct relationship with the computer that had been lost during the second generation of computer development. However, the increased complexity of computer and information systems now limited direct user involvement to input and output tasks. Application design and development, along with computer management and operation, remained the responsibility of computer specialists.

It wasn't until this time that college and university graduates could obtain degrees in computer science and information systems. Computing literacy was beginning to take root, and computer education was not limited to colleges and universities. Elementary and high schools began to introduce students to computing. As seen on the following page in Computers at Work: "Beginning a New Generation," a new computer user/specialist was emerging. Many of the major events of the fourth generation of computers would be led by people who, having grown up with computers, found computing to be a natural and positive force in their lives.

1964–70

The Third Generation

1964 IBM introduces the System 360 series of computer systems.

1964 IBM introduces the magnetic card Selectric typewriter.

1964 IBM introduces the RPG programming language.

1965 DEC introduces the PDP-8 minicomputer.

1968 Computer Sciences Corporation becomes the first software company to be listed on the New York Stock Exchange.

1969 IBM "unbundles" its software from its hardware.

1970 Nicholas Wirth develops the Pascal programming language.

The Fourth Generation

Instead of having one simple electronic circuit in a silicon chip, **large-scale integration (LSI)** technology places many circuits within a single chip. During this fourth generation of computing, LSI technology has improved to where first hundreds, then thousands, and now hundreds of thousands of electronic components are manufactured as a single chip. The term **very-large-scale integration (VLSI)** is used when referring to these very high chip densities. With LSI and VLSI technologies, computers have become even smaller, faster, more reliable, and less expensive.

A key achievement of this fourth generation of computers was the development in 1971 of the microprocessor. In the summer of 1969, Busicom, a now defunct Japanese calculator manufacturer, approached Intel with a contract to design a set of chips for a new family of calculators. At least twelve chips were required in Busicom's initial plans. Ted Hoff, Jr., was assigned to the Busicom project. Hoff, who used a PDP-8 in his design work, wondered why the electronics for the calculator were more complex than those in the PDP-8.

Ted Hoff, Jr.

COMPUTERS AT WORK

Beginning a New Generation

In the late 1960s a group of Seattle teenagers met each afternoon outside Lakeside High, the private suburban high school they attended, and biked to the offices of a local company. Although the company's employees were going home for the evening and the firm was officially closing, the boys were just getting started. They thought of themselves as an unofficial night shift. Every night they worked till long after dark, pounding the keys of the company's DEC (Digital Equipment Corporation) computer, while dining on carry-out pizza and soft drinks.

The leaders of the group were an unusual pair. More than any of the others, they were fascinated by computers; in fact, this fascination had earned them the label "computer nuts" among their classmates. Paul Allen, a soft-spoken 15-year-old, would have paid for the chance to work on the machines. His friend Bill Gates, 13 years old and looking even younger, was proud of his abilities in mathematics and was hooked on programming.

Gates, Allen, and the others had been hired—"allowed" might be a better word, since they worked for the fun of it, without pay—to find errors in the computer's programming. Computer Center Corporation (the boys called it C Cubed) was happy to have them around. According to the terms of C Cubed's contract with DEC, as long as C Cubed could show DEC that DEC's programs had bugs (errors that caused the programs to malfunction or "crash"), C Cubed didn't have to pay DEC for using the computer. The kids were postponing the day when C Cubed had to pay its bill to DEC.

"More than any of the others, they were fascinated by computers . . . ."

The DEC programs were new and complex, and there was nothing surprising in the fact that they were not entirely error-free. DEC's arrangement with C Cubed was a common technique for tracking down the subtlest bugs in such complex programs, and the kids found plenty of bugs in the next six months, with young Bill Gates finding more than his share. The *Problem Report Book,* as the boys labeled the journal of their discoveries, grew to 300 pages. Finally DEC called a halt, telling C Cubed, as Gates later recalled it, "Look, these guys are going to find bugs forever."

Allen and Gates stayed on for some months at C Cubed after the other boys left, and eventually drew pay for their work. The computer they worked on was a marvel of modern engineering. DEC had pioneered the concept of the minicomputer, which changed the computer from a wall of circuitry affordable by only the federal government and the largest companies into a box the size of a refrigerator, a machine that medium-sized offices, factories, and academic departments could afford. But the minicomputer was just a step on the path of miniaturization that would lead to the personal computer. Allen and Gates, loving their work at C Cubed, found themselves dreaming of the day when they would own their own computers. "It's going to happen," Paul Allen used to tell his friend.

Source: P. Freiberger and M. Swaine, *Fire in the Valley* (Berkeley, California: Osborne/McGraw-Hill, Inc., 1984), pp. xii-xiii.

Working with fellow engineers Frederico Faggin and Stan Mazor, Hoff whittled the twelve chips down to four, one of which, the **Intel 4004 microprocessor,** contained all the logic and control circuits. By today's standards, the 4004 was very primitive. Its development, nonetheless, did reshape modern electronics and the computer industry. Intel's earliest microprocessors, the 4004 and the 8008, were designed for special purposes. In 1974, Intel developed the **Intel 8080,** a microprocessor suited for general-purpose computing.

MITS, Inc., a small New Mexico instrument firm, soon developed the first commercially successful microcomputer, the **Altair.** Electronic computers suddenly became affordable. Although the price of a single Intel 8080 chip was

The Intel 4004 microprocessor

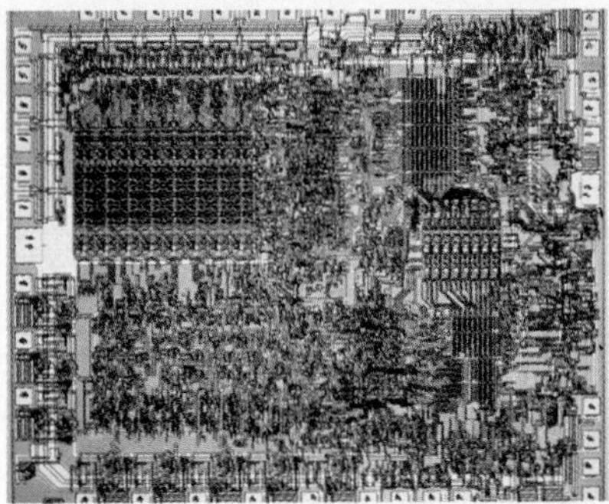
The Intel 8080 microprocessor

close to $400, MITS bought them for less than $100 and was able to sell the Altair in kit form for as little as $439.

But the microcomputer did not become a household word until Steve Jobs and Steve Wozniak formed Apple Corporation in 1977 to build and sell **Apple II** computers. Computers at Work: "Turning Apples into Gold" provides some background on the early days of Apple Corporation (see page A–31). Apple microcomputers were used by many hobbyists and educators, but by relatively few business professionals. The world of business had not yet accepted the microcomputer.

The Altair 8800 kit computer

Tandy Corporation's **TRS-80 Model II** opened the business world to the microcomputer in 1979. Two years later, the **IBM PC** met with overwhelming acceptance by businesses, and the microcomputer market exploded.

Managers and professionals have come to depend on their microcomputers to the same degree that businesses rely on larger computer systems. Portable microcomputers, beginning with the **Osborne 1,** and continuing with "notebook" computers such as the **Workslate,** even allow employees to take their computers along with them when attending meetings or visiting customers and clients.

The TRS–80 Model II

The IBM PC

An office computer system by Wang

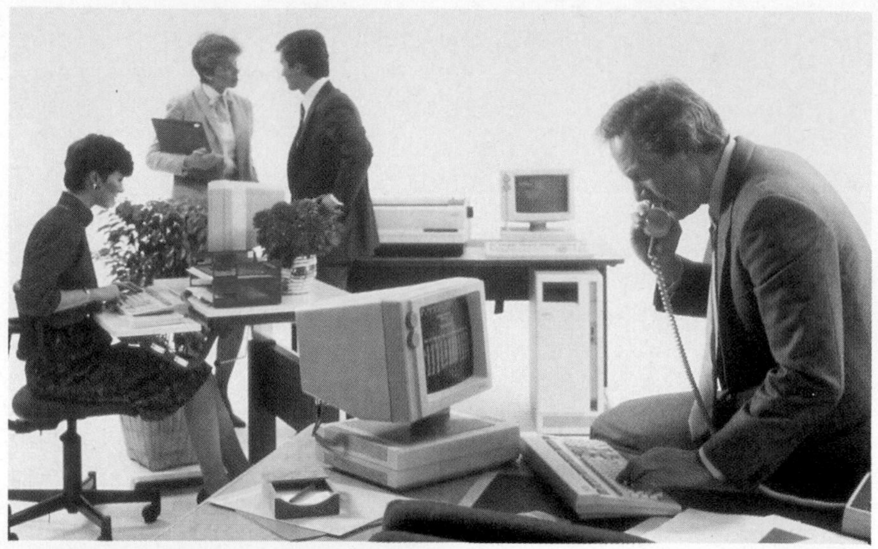

AT&T announces its entry into the computer industry

Apple's Lisa microcomputer

Apple's Macintosh microcomputer

While hardware advances brought about the microcomputer, the usefulness of its software was the major factor that thrust the microcomputer into the business world. Electronic spreadsheet and word processing software provided immediate benefits to business users. As a result, **VisiCalc** was responsible for many Apple II sales to businesses, and **Lotus 1-2-3** had much to do with the early success of the IBM PC.

Two other key computer industry developments occurred during this fourth generation. First, the office systems and computer systems industries merged. This merger began slowly, as word processing firms added electronic components to their products. Today's office automation firms, such as Wang, now sell general-purpose computer systems, and most computer manufacturers sell office automation software for their general-purpose computer systems. Second, the Justice Department dropped its antitrust case against IBM, deregulated the communications industry, and allowed AT&T to enter the computer industry. While it is too soon to assess the impacts of these actions, it's likely that most businesses will benefit from the new products and services that result from an even more competitive computer industry.

Hardware. With VLSI technologies, computer processor speeds and primary memory capacities have greatly increased. Small computers are now able to handle tasks previously performed only by large computers. While a variety of input and output devices are used, CRT input and paper output remain the major means of entering and receiving information. Magnetic disks are by far the most common secondary storage device.

Software. The operating systems on today's larger computers are extremely sophisticated. Microcomputer operating systems, such as Digital Research's **CP/M** and Microsoft's **MSDOS,** are comparable to those on second-generation computers that were intended to serve an entire business. With primary memory sizes and processor speeds increasing, more powerful microcomputer operating systems, such as AT&T's **UNIX,** are beginning to appear.

While microcomputer operating systems have lagged behind those available on larger computer systems, advances in application software have been led by microcomputer software. Microcomputer software is much more "user friendly" than is maxicomputer or minicomputer software. The early research on Xerox's Smalltalk project, for example, has been used by the software designers of Apple's **Lisa** and Macintosh microcomputers, but not by software designers for larger computer systems.

One final software issue of importance has been the development of the **ADA** programming language. Just as the U.S. Department of Defense sponsored the design of COBOL to reduce the costs of military data processing, the skyrocketing costs of weapons systems software motivated the Department of Defense to sponsor another design effort in 1975. This new language, named after Charles Babbage's friend and colleague, Ada Augusta Lovelace, is modeled after the Pascal programming language. It is too early to tell whether or not ADA will become as important to business computing as did COBOL.

Uses and Users. Computer-based information systems now handle all aspects of business activities. Many firms have become totally dependent on their computers. In these firms, business transactions are often automatically handled through information systems. The increasing use of decision support

1971–Present

The Fourth Generation

1971 Ted Hoff of Intel develops the first microprocessor, the Intel 4004.

1971 Lexitron introduces a CRT-based word processor.

1973 Xerox develops the Smalltalk, the first "user-friendly" software.

1974 Intel develops a general-purpose microprocessor, the Intel 8080.

1975 MITS, Inc., develops Altair, the first commercially successful personal computer.

1975 Paul Allen and Bill Gates form Microsoft Corporation.

1975 The U.S. Department of Defense sponsors the effort to design the ADA programming language.

1976 Gary Kildall forms Digital Research to sell CP/M, the first commercially successful microcomputer operating system.

1976 Wang introduces a multiuser word processing computer system.

1976 Michael Schrayer develops Electric Pencil, the first microcomputer word processing software.

1977 Steve Jobs and Steve Wozniak form Apple Corporation.

1979 Dan Bricklin and Dan Fylstra develop VisiCalc, the first electronic spreadsheet.

1979 Seymour Rubenstein of MicroPro develops WordStar, the first commercially successful microcomputer word processing software.

1979 Tandy Corporation introduces the TRS-80 Model II, the first commercially successful business microcomputer.

1980 The U.S. Department of Justice deregulates the communications industry.

1981 IBM introduces its personal computer, the IBM PC.

1981 Adam Osborne introduces the Osborne 1, the first portable microcomputer.

continued

1982 The U.S. Department of Justice drops its antitrust suit against IBM.

1983 The U.S. Department of Justice allows AT&T to compete in the computer industry.

1983 Apple introduces the Lisa, a microcomputer.

1984 Apple introduces the Macintosh, a microcomputer.

systems means that many key business decisions are also being made on the basis of computer output. It seems the computer has a place in a corporate boardroom, as well as in an accountant's office.

Improvements in both systems software and applications software have allowed users to become involved with all aspects of business computing. Employees are performing their day-to-day tasks with or through a computer system. Managers and other professional employees are working with spreadsheet, file management, and graphics software to design and develop computer applications without the aid of computer specialists. Managers are buying hardware and software, and then managing the computer operations in their own departments. Computer specialists today are becoming true experts who work only on the complex aspects of business computing.

Professional Issue

Lessons from History

As you read through this chapter, you may have noticed some common themes in the reaction of people to new technologies. While technologies change drastically over time, there seem to be predictable similarities in the ways in which people and businesses reacted to new technology prior to the development of the computer and through the generations of computer evolution. You can learn a lot about when and how a business can successfully introduce new computer technologies from these early failures and successes. You may have also noticed certain trends in computer technologies. One of the best ways to forecast the future is to understand the past.

Dealing with Technical Change

A new technology's practical use always lags behind its development. There are a number of reasons for this:

A new technology usually does not work very well when it first appears. As a result, few people are willing to risk using it.

Few people understand the practical potential of a new technology.

New technologies are usually expensive when first introduced. Since few people understand the technology, and the risk of failure is high, demand for the technology is low.

We have seen this occur with the Pascaline, the Leibnitz Wheel, and Babbages's Analytical Engine. This trend is also apparent in the history of the typewriter. In each case, the technology was not supported until it was recognized as a solution to a real problem, until its reliability was improved, and until its manufacturing costs declined.

We have also seen that new technologies are often resisted when they first appear. By nature, most people simply do not welcome change. When a new technology forces the change, our tendency to resist often increases. From the employees' point of view, the reasons are quite clear:

COMPUTERS AT WORK

Turning Apples into Gold

In Silicon Valley, two young engineers who may rightly be called true children of the microprocessor had gotten together to form a new home computer company. Steven Jobs and Stephen Wozniak grew up in Silicon Valley, met in the eighth grade, and attended high school together in Santa Clara. They were teenagers when the microprocessor was invented. Jobs was born the year William Shockley brought the transistor to Palo Alto. Wozniak, whose father worked for Lockheed Missiles and Space Company, started tinkering with computers in the fourth grade. After high school Stephen Wozniak went on to the University of Colorado and Steven Jobs knocked around for a while overseas. Eventually, they both ended up back in Silicon Valley, Wozniak with Hewlett-Packard and Jobs with Atari.

In 1976 the two got together again, fell in with a local computer club and indulged in the ever-popular California pastime of garage shop tinkering. They built a few basic microcomputer circuit boards and started selling them. In the best hacker tradition, they built a few finished home computers for themselves as well. Fellow computer freaks took a look and were interested. From then on, Jobs and Wozniak were in business. To bankroll their new enterprise, Jobs sold his Volkswagen bus and Wozniak his Hewlett-Packard H-P 65 calculator. They managed to secure thirty days' worth of credit and a few thousand dollars from an electronics distributor, and finally talked Intel's advertising and public relations firm, Regis McKenna, Inc., into promoting them with only a promise of future payment. (Since Intel did not make home computers and the two young men did not plan to make chips, there was no competitive conflict.) Finally, recognizing their own lack of marketing expertise, "the two Steves" talked former Intel marketing manager Mike Markkula into joining the uncertain venture. Markkula, a thirty-four-year-old valley veteran at the time, gave an aura of corporate authenticity and some personal financing to the new company, which was incorporated in early 1977. They called it Apple Computer, in commemoration of Steven Jobs's apple-picking summers in the Northwest. They began setting up distributorships and shipping the home computers. Apple Computer immediately caught the attention of venture capitalists.

Working at Apple in the early days was like riding a rocket. Sales zoomed from essentially zero in 1976 to $100 million in 1980. Jobs and Wozniak, during the same four years, went from part-time hackers assembling computers to the blare of rock music in Silicon Valley garages, to the microcomputer darlings of Wall Street. In late 1980, Apple Computer went public in one of the most successful high-technology stock offerings ever staged. When it was over, Steven Jobs's block of shares was worth, at the public offering price, roughly $165 million. The stock owned by Stephen Wozniak was valued at about $88 million. Jobs was twenty-five years old. Wozniak was twenty-eight. Still more silicon, in the hands of the young, had turned to gold.

Source: D. Hanson, *The New Alchemists* (Boston: Little, Brown & Company, 1982), pp. 207–209.

The employees are comfortable with the current technology.

The employees' status and position are often tied to their knowledge of the current technology.

The employees do not understand the new technology.

The employees cannot visualize what their working lives will be like with the new technology.

While few modern workers would follow the example of the weavers who rioted in protest of Jacquard's loom, many people do feel threatened by the idea of using a computer. Such feelings can be overcome by educating people, by slowing the rate of change that actually takes place, and by "adjusting" the new technology to address employee concerns.

We have also seen that the first successful use of a new technology tends to follow a similar chain of events:

A technology's major problems have been overcome and it is reliable.

A business problem or opportunity builds pressure to use the new technology.

Other needed technologies are reliable and available.

To the public, it may seem as though new technologies often arise by chance. We have seen, however, the effect of real-world problems and deadlines on Herman Hollerith, the inventor of the electromechanical tabulator. And the pressing problems of World War II provided support for the research team led by Eckert and Mauchly, who developed the first large, general-purpose electronic computer that actually worked.

Computer Technology Trends

Three technological trends recur throughout the computer's history:

1. The time between the development of a new technology and its practical use is becoming shorter.
2. Computer systems are becoming more intelligent.
3. Computer technology is being made available to more people.

Each of these trends is important for a number of reasons.

As new computer technologies become useful shortly after their development, businesses and their employees face increased pressures. They must keep abreast of new technical developments, and they find themselves having to adjust to technical change on a fairly regular basis.

Intelligent computers are increasingly able to perform more and more of a business's information processing tasks. Many routine tasks can now be handled without human assistance, and more sophisticated tasks are also being trusted to the computer. Business policies on how to best use computers, including when to create human-computer information processing teams, need to be rethought more frequently.

As computer systems become less expensive and easier to use, a larger portion of a firm's employees are becoming computer users. This change affects hiring, promoting, and even career paths for employees. Personnel policies should be revised to reflect this trend.

Learning about the history of the development of computers will not provide you with all the answers on people's reaction to change. Studying this material can, however, give you a general understanding of what can happen and why it happens. The abilities to anticipate needs, to understand people's natural aversion to change, and to develop products that fill real needs are essential ingredients for successful business computing.

The First Portable Computer

History is the last thing that comes to mind when we think of computers. Computers are synonymous with change and obsolescence. Many of us who have grown up with or adapted quickly to computers have forgotten what life was like in the stone age of the typewriter and the hand-held calculator. We sit before our personal computers and, like the man driving a Cadillac, have no idea of what life was like in a Model T with its hand-cranked engine and other curious features.

In 1973, when hand-held calculators were becoming popular, the concept of a portable personal computer did not exist; nor was there a reason why anyone would want such a machine. This was unimportant to Dr. Paul Friedl of the Palo Alto IBM Scientific Center.

Not all computers are built by whiz kids who retire at 30 to live off their investments. Dr. Friedl is 50, a family man with three sons and a daughter about to be married. Friedl did not spend his youth playing video games or punching computer keyboards. Those technologies were years in the future. He played baseball.

Friedl became acquainted with computers in an informal way. He studied chemical engineering at the Case Institute of Technology, earning his Ph.D. in 1960. One day, as he relates it, "I found a notice on the board that there was going to be a demonstration of an electronic computer. It was an analog computer, and afterward I thought I knew all about computers. Much to my confusion, the next week there was a demonstration of yet another computer—the digital computer." That computer was an IBM 650, and it caught Friedl's fancy.

Friedl began taking computer classes but rarely saw a computer. Students did everything at a desk. They wrote the program and hand-debugged it, all with a graduate student peering over their shoulders. When they finally thought they had the program right, they took it up to their favorite keypunch operator who checked it again and then said something like, "Yeah, that should work." Then, as Friedl says, "The great day came when they would even let you into the same room with the machine. You approached it like the Wizard of Oz—big doors opening up, fans going, tapes spinning, and lots of noise. Then someone took your card, put it into the hopper, and hit the button. The machine went 'chun, chun, chun' and the computer operator said, 'Well, that's the right answer . . . next.' I said, 'Wait a minute, you mean it's done already?' 'Sure, why not?' " Friedl was hooked.

His friends could never understand why he spent so much time with the computer. They asked why he wasn't boiling oil, pulverizing atoms, or doing something "modern." Instead, he started developing a specialty in computers and became interested in the potential of using the computer for process control in chemical engineering.

Friedl never forgot that IBM Wizard of Oz. After graduating he went to work for IBM Advanced System Development, joining a new group that was studying process control. Prophetically, because of the success of his process control work and long before a personal computer even existed, Friedl became known as Mr. PC.

In December 1972 Friedl was sitting in for his boss when he received a call from the IBM General Systems Division in Atlanta. General Systems wanted to see if it could raise the visibility of APL (A Programming Language) in its division product line. Friedl's name had been advanced as someone who knew about microcomputers. Two executives flew out to California the next day to ask Friedl if he could come up with something using APL. "We don't exactly know what," they said, "maybe something similar to a hand-held calculator." When Friedl told them that he would love to work on the project, they asked when he could come back with a proposal. He said one month.

Friedl had the notion of a portable personal microcomputer, but it wasn't going to be easy to get the most out of a full-fledged high-level language like APL. The technology didn't seem ready. What was needed was a display, keyboard, printer, and a magnetic data storage device. At this time there were no floppy disks, just big bulky tape drives, and the idea of a portable display was rare.

IBM manufactured a suitable processor, the PALM microcontroller that was designed to control other elements of a microcomputer. It offered Friedl the flexibility he would need to make an all-purpose machine, incorporating within its architecture the notion of an integrated TV display. He used a standard IBM keyboard and 64K of RAM (more memory than many of today's computers). Curiously enough, the memory cards were called Snoopy Cards, and since they were 16K each, only four were needed. The last basic piece of hardware was a new I/O card that allowed the computer to hook up to a printer, audio cassette recorder, and keyboard.

On January 22, 1973, with his ideas sketched on paper, Friedl took his plan for a portable computer to Atlanta. He told IBM executives that the only way to demonstrate the feasibility and uses of a portable computer would be to build one. When asked how long it would take, Friedl said six months.

At 30,000 feet, on the plane back to California, Friedl began to wonder what he had gotten himself into. He already

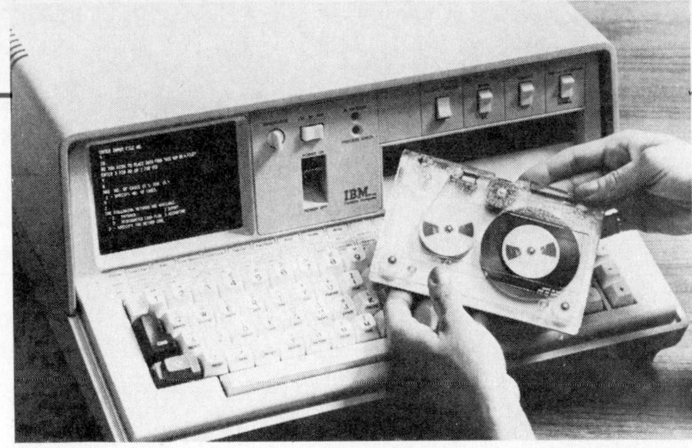

had a full-time job, yet he had just agreed to build something that had never been built before. "I was excited about the project, but I can't figure out why I said six months. I didn't have a single worker or the assurance that it could be built in two years, let alone six months."

Not only was Friedl blessed with available technology, he was also fortunate to have a tremendous team. Joe George had recently joined the staff of an IBM knight, Roy Harper (IBM "knights" a few of its exalted workers, allowing them to work on virtually any technical project, or "dragon," they wish). Because the knight was between dragons, George was able to work with Driedl. In only two weeks Friedl rounded up five engineers and five programmers. The project was christened SCAMP (Special Computer APL Machine Portable).

That was only the beginning. As Friedl says, "Once everyone else was busy making the system, I started thinking, 'so what! Why would anyone want such a thing? What possible use could a manager have for a portable microcomputer?' I was trying to figure out how to make it more than just a magical black box.

"I was thinking about six months into the future, when SCAMP would be sitting on the executives' desks. I realized that I never wanted them to be faced with a blank screen. The system should tell you all the possible choices you can make. I wanted menus, so that someone who had never used a computer could read the choices, make their decision, and then press the appropriate key. Originally, I thought up four or five possible applications, such as computer-aided instruction, project planning, and financial analysis." Friedl even developed word processing, but the APL implementation of the word processing was, as Friedl says, "horrendously slow." Instead, he created what was probably the first electronic spreadsheet.

Six months after his promise, virtually to the day, Friedl and Joe George were on a plane to Atlanta taking the world's first portable computer on its maiden voyage. While Friedl had planned well ahead for this day, it wasn't until he saw the executives staring up at him from the conference table that he realized the enormity of his task. Says Friedl, "I had planned numerous applications for the executives to do on SCAMP. Talk about apprehension. These poor people had either never had typing or the skill had evaporated. And then, all of a sudden, to have something thrust at you—here is the keyboard—and your peers waiting for the slightest mistake. It was terrifying for some of these executives. All they had to do was press a letter or number, but there were questions such as, 'Where is the A key?' One man broke into a sweat when I asked him to type his name."

People had difficulty understanding SCAMP. Friedl remembers one executive saying, "Gee, that thing almost does what a computer does!" Says Friedl, "We had to convince him that it was indeed a computer."

Despite all its triumphs, SCAMP was almost thrown out with the trash. When the project was finished, Friedl went on with his work and forgot all about the wooden-encased computer that had consumed his life for over six months. He became curious about the whereabouts of SCAMP when a colleague showed him an article proclaiming that the 5100 was the world's first truly portable computer. What the writer didn't know was that the portable computer technology of the 5100 evolved from SCAMP. Says Friedl, "I always felt the work we had done was worthwhile. But with the explosive growth of personal computers, suddenly I thought that perhaps we had played some historical role in that popular movement."

Friedl called up the Los Gatos lab and asked if SCAMP was still there. IBM technicians told him that it was, and if he wanted it he had better come quickly because they were just about to throw out a lot of junk. "I jumped in my car and drove over there. We searched back in the corner of the lab and finally found SCAMP covered with dust and cobwebs behind a work bench. After all that time, we plugged it in and it started right up, a tribute to all the fine people who worked on the project."

And so SCAMP was born, the father of the 5100 and grandfather of the IBM PC. Although SCAMP was based on a technology that preceded the age of floppy drives and 16-bit processors, the lineage is clear. Sometime when you're feeling nostalgic, look at the back of your PC. Right above the power plug are the numbers 5150, child of the 5100, grandchild of SCAMP.

From "The First Portable Computer" by Johnathan Littman. Reprinted by permission of *PC World,* (October 1983) published at 555 De Haro Street, San Francisco, CA 94107.

SUMMARY

The earliest technologies used to process and store information included the *abacus, paper,* and the *printing press.* These technologies, for the most part, had little impact on the common man. It wasn't until the 19th century, when mass production greatly reduced book prices, that information became a public good.

A number of scientists built mechanical "calculating machines" during the 15th, 16th, 17th and 18th centuries. Two of the more famous scientists were *Blaise Pascal* and *Gottfried Leibnitz.* Their efforts were plagued by two problems—an inability to obtain precisely machined parts and no real public demand for a machine that automated calculating. It wasn't until 1820 that a mechanical calculator, the *Thomas Arithmometer,* became a commercial success.

One of the key early developments in computing was *Joseph Jacquard's* use of punched cards to control looms in the weaving industry. This idea of using punched cards to direct the operation of a machine eventually led *Charles Babbage* to develop his *Difference Engine* and to outline the plans of his *Analytical Engine,* the first design of a general-purpose computing machine. Unlike the *Jacquard Loom,* Babbage's computing machines never achieved commercial success, with mechanical problems and no real demand for automated computing still the reasons. Most of what we now know about Babbage's machines was reported by *Ada Augusta, Countess of Lovelace,* who is often referred to as the world's first programmer.

The expansion of American businesses during the late 19th and early 20th centuries was largely due to a number of advances in the manner business information could be processed. The *telegraph* and the *telephone* made long-distance communication an everyday occurrence. The *typewriter,* the *cash register,* and the *adding machine* enabled businesses to keep up with the increased volume of business transactions.

It was *Herman Hollerith's* invention of the *tabulating machine,* however, that really began the business data processing industry. By storing data on punched cards, the same data could be processed over and over again to serve a variety of business uses. Hollerith eventually formed his own business to sell his tabulating machine. *Thomas Watson, Sr.,* became president of Holerith's firm in 1914, and later changed its name to *International Business Machines, or IBM.*

The first attempts to build automated computing machines occurred during the 1930s in response to a growing need in scientific and engineering research to perform massive amounts of computations. Two successful electromechanical computing machines were *Vannevar Bush's* special-purpose computer and *Howard Aiken's* general-purpose computer.

The first fully electronic, general-purpose computers were *John Atanasoff's* prototype version of the *ABC Computer* and *John Mauchly's* and *J. Presper Eckert's ENIAC.* Both of these computers were built using *vacuum tube* technology. Mauchly and Eckert eventually formed their own company to build the *UNIVAC* computer.

The ENIAC's successor, the *EDVAC,* was the first computer to utilize the *stored-program concept.* The EDVAC's design, which was developed by *John von Neuman,* laid the groundwork for computer design over the next forty years. This basic design is still referred to as a *von Neuman architecture.*

Electronic technologies have gone through a number of improvements since the days of these early computers. With each major change, the power of computer systems increased dramatically. It has become commonplace to refer to each transition to a new electronic technology as a *computer generation.*

The vacuum tube was the primary electronic component used in *first generation* computers. Vacuum tubes were used for the computer system's processing and storage circuitry. Data input was through cards, and data output was produced on either paper or cards. By the end of the first generation, *magnetic core* was used for primary memory, while *magnetic tapes* were used for secondary memory. The major software advance that occurred with first generation computers was the development of *high-level* programming languages, such as *FORTRAN.* Business computing was just getting underway during this first generation of computers. As few computer specialists were around at this time, most computer use was performed directly by the users themselves.

The *transistor* was the primary electronic component used in *second generation* computers. These small, but reliable, electronic devices led to the development of new electronic hardware, including the *minicomputer* and the *communications satellite.* Second generation computer systems used transistors for processing circuitry, magnetic cores for memory, and magnetic tapes for data input, output, and secondary storage. The first operating systems appeared, and with them new forms of data processing such as *interactive processing, real-time computing,* and *time-sharing.* More high-level programming languages were developed, including *COBOL, BASIC,* and *PL/1.* While business computing had now become commonplace, management applications were just beginning. With computer systems too complex for most users, computer specialists began to handle most data processing activities.

The *integrated circuit* became the primary electronic component used in *third generation* computers. Among the first of the third generation computers were the various members of IBM's System 360 series of computers. *Solid state* circuitry was used for processing circuits and for primary memories, *CRTs* served as input and output devices, and *magnetic disks* gained importance as secondary storage. The operating system was the dominant component within a computer system at this time, as it controlled most operations. Other high-level programming languages were introduced, including *RPG* and *Pascal*. Business information systems were *integrated* through the use of common input and output data files. Management applications were now routine. Computer users, while not directing data processing operations, frequently handled input and output tasks. Most information processing activities, however, remained the domain of computer specialists, who were now being trained in colleges and universities.

Large-scale integration (LSI) and *very-large-scale integration (VLSI)* are the primary electronic components of *fourth generation* computers. Hundreds of thousands of electronic circuits now reside on a single silicon chip. The most important electronic device developed during this computer generation has been the *microprocessor,* which led to the development of the *microcomputer.* While microcomputer hardware and operating systems have lagged behind those of larger computer systems, *user friendly* microcomputer applications software has begun to lead the software industry. Computer-based information systems now handle all aspects of business activities, from the automatic handling of day-to-day business transactions to supporting key top-management business decisions. Computer users are again involved with all aspects of business computing.

People and business react to new technologies in three common ways. First, the practical use of new technologies always lags behind their development. Second, new technologies are often resisted when they first appear. Third, the successful use of a new technology tends to follow a set chain of events: the technology becomes reliable; a business problem builds pressure, making it necessary to use the technology; and other needed technologies are both reliable and available.

Three technological trends recurred throughout the computer's history. First, the time between the development of a new technology and its practical use is becoming shorter. Second, computer systems are becoming more intelligent. Third, computer technology is being made available to more people.

REVIEW QUESTIONS

1. The abacus is one of the oldest means of information processing still in use. What are its limitations? How did the invention of paper, and later the printing press, help solve these problems?
2. Briefly describe the efforts of Pascal and Leibnitz. What was the significance of Jacquard's loom? Briefly describe the contributions of Charles Babbage.
3. Briefly trace the roots of automated data processing.
4. What was *Colossus?* What other early computer was largely financed by the military?
5. What was *EDVAC?* Briefly discuss the von Neuman architecture developed for this machine.
6. Upon what are the various computer generations based? Briefly trace the first four computer generations.
7. Briefly trace the advances made in programming languages from the early use of machine languages to the present.
8. What major events occurred during the Second Generation of computers?
9. Briefly describe the most significant developments of the Third Generation of computers.
10. What development ushered in the Fourth Generation of computers? What was the significance of this development?
11. Why do applications for a new technology tend to lag behind its appearance? What characteristics mark its first successful use?
12. Briefly discuss the three trends that have recurred throughout the technological history of the computer.

Appendix B

Arithmetic Operations and Number Systems

In Chapter 3, "The Central Processing Unit," we discussed the binary nature of computer systems. The chapter covered how numeric data can be represented in the binary number system and how alphanumeric data are represented in character codes such as EBCDIC and ASCII. In this appendix we show how arithmetic operations are performed on binary numbers. Also, we expand our knowledge of number systems beyond base 2 (binary) and base 10 (decimal) to include base 8 (octal) and base 16 (hexadecimal). We explain why different number systems are used and how to convert from one system to another.

BINARY ARITHMETIC

The fundamental arithmetic operations of addition, subtraction, multiplication, and division using the binary system have certain similarities to the more familiar decimal system. To aid in our discussion as we move from one number system to another, we will first set up a notation.

We can designate a number as being in a particular base system by using a subscript to the *lower* right side of the number. For example 125_{10} is the number 125 in the base 10 (decimal) number system. The number 1011_2 is in the base 2 (binary) number system. We can also talk about place values and show these by using superscript at the *upper* right side of the number. For example, the place value 10^3 would stand for numbers in the thousands, whereas 2^3 would equal values of eight.

With this introduction let us look at binary addition. The rules are:

$$0 + 0 = 0$$
$$0 + 1 = 1$$
$$1 + 0 = 1$$
$$1 + 1 = 10$$

As we discuss binary arithmetic, we also give comparable decimal numbers so that you recall the basic fundamentals of arithmetic operations and then compare how binary operations are similar or different.

Let us add some numbers in base 10 and in base 2 to see how this works (Exhibit B.1). Adding 10 + 4 in base 10 equals 14_{10}, and in base 2 gives the binary result 1110_2. Exhibit B.5 is a table that allows you to convert easily between decimal and binary numbers as we work through these examples. Adding 7 and 5 involves the use of a carry, as does the binary addition of these numbers. To make it easier to follow the additions and later the discussion on subtraction, we will put the carries below rather than above the numbers.

Exhibit B.1
Decimal and Binary Addition

Base 10		Base 2	
10		1010	
+ 4		+ 0100	
14		1110	
1	(This small number is a reminder to carry.)	111	(These small numbers are a reminder to carry.)
23		0111	
+ 9		+ 0101	
32		1100	

Binary subtraction can be performed like subtraction of decimal numbers. Starting with the digit on the extreme right, each digit of the subtrahend is subtracted from the corresponding digit in the minuend. If the subtrahend digit is larger, then one must be borrowed from the next higher place value. The result of the complete subtraction is known as the difference.

With computers however, binary subtraction is actually done by complement addition. A **complement** of a number is that value which must be added to it to get its number base. For example, in the decimal system the 10's complement of 8 is 2, because 8 plus 2 equals 10. The 10's complement of 4 is 6, and so on.

Complement addition can be used to attain the same results as with regular subtraction. For example, to perform the arithmetic operation $9 - 3$, we could convert this subtraction to an addition by using the 10's complement of 3, which is 7, and adding it to 9. The result is 16 and any carry is discarded, leaving the answer 6. So $9 - 3 = 9 + 7 = 16 = 6$. Let us do one more. $8 - 6 = 8 + 4 = 12 = 2$.

You're probably thinking, why go through all this? The reason is that a unique property of binary numbers allows the determination of the 2's complement to be very simple, a fact that has important implications for simplifying computer circuit design. All bits in the subtrahend are merely switched to their opposite value. That is, 0s become 1s and 1s become 0s. A binary 1 is added to this converted subtrahend to form the 2's complement. This complement then can be added to the minuend. Any extra carry digit in the resulting addition is discarded, just as in the 10's complement examples (Exhibit B.2).

To subtract 3 from 7 in the binary system, first the 2's complement of the subtrahend is determined. This is, 0011 is switched to 1100 and then a binary 1 is added, giving 1101. This number is then added to the minuend 0111_2 and the resulting extra carry digit is discarded. The complement addition answer is 0100_2 or 4_{10}.

What happens if you try to subtract, say, 6 from 3, giving a negative result, −3? In complement addition, the lack of any carry digit implies a negative number. You simply take the resulting complement addition number, determine its complement, and place a negative sign in front of it.

Exhibit B.2
Subtraction and Complement Addition

Base 10		Base 2
7	←(minuend)→	0111
− 3	←(subtrahend)→	− 0011
4	←(difference)→	0100

Subtraction

Base 10		Base 2	
7		0111	
+ 7	(ten's complement)	+ 1101	(two's complement)
(X)4	(carry digit discarded)	1010	
		1 1	(carry)
		(X)0100	(carry digit discarded)

Complement Addition

Exhibit B.3
Complement Addition with Negative Answers

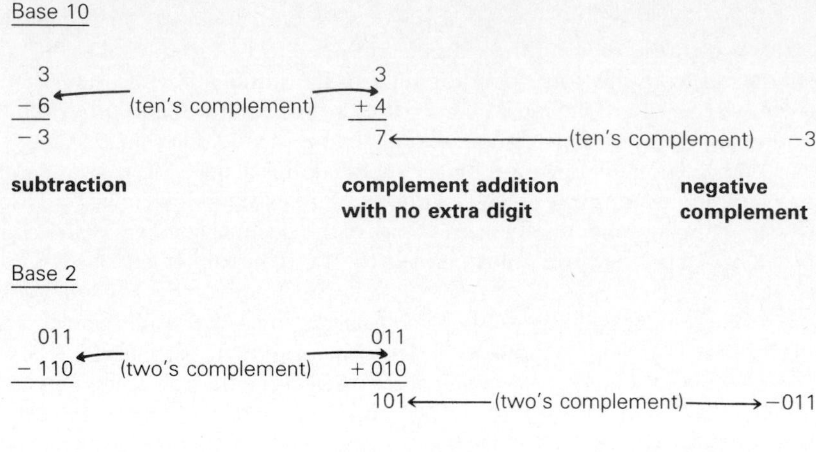

For example $3 - 6 = 3 + 4 = 7$. There is no carry digit, therefore determine the 10's complement of 7, which is 3. The answer, then, is -3. The binary complement addition resulted in 101_2 with no carry digit. The complement of 101_2 is 010 plus 1 or 011. The answer then is -011_2, which is -3 in the decimal system (Exhibit B.3).

This all seems like a very roundabout way of performing subtraction, and it is. But the reason for this operation is to simplify circuit design. Instead of having special circuits for addition, others for subtraction, and still others for multiplication and division, a set of adder circuits can be used as the basis for each of these arithmetic operations. As a result, circuit design is less complex and less costly since there are fewer parts. Because the computer can perform operations so quickly, this roundabout approach does not result in excessive time delays.

Let us now look at how multiplication is performed. The rules of binary multiplication are:

$$0 \times 0 = 0$$

$$0 \times 1 = 0$$

$$1 \times 0 = 0$$

$$1 \times 1 = 1$$

Exhibit B.4 shows the decimal and binary multiplication of $9 \times 12 = 108_{10}$. Notice that in the binary system a 0 in the multiplier results in 0s in the intermediate results. A multiplication by 1 results in the multiplicand being repeated and shifted to the left. The number of columns to be shifted is a function of what place value the 1 is in.

Therefore, binary multiplication can be performed by shifting the multiplicand to the left the number of times equal to the place value of the 1 in the multiplier. These shifted results can then be added using regular adder circuits. Verify these concepts multiplying 7 times 11 in binary.

As it turns out, division is the opposite of multiplication. Instead of shifting the multiplier left and adding the intermediate results, division is performed by shifting the divisor right and subtracting it from the quotient initially and

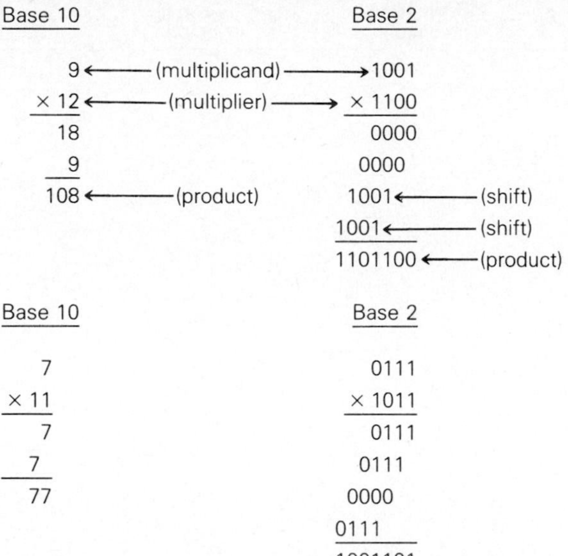

Exhibit B.4
Decimal and Binary Multiplication

then from each intermediate remainder. The subtraction would actually be performed by using the 2's complement addition method. We will leave this as an exercise for you to prove.

Higher-level mathematical operations are performed by using the basic operations that we have covered. For example, exponentiation is just a form of multiplication; that is, 2^3 can be performed by multiplying 2 times itself 3 times: $2^3 = 2 \times 2 \times 2$. Each multiplication can be performed by shifts and by using the adder circuits.

In summary, we have shown you how to do some basic binary arithmetic. We have also given you a basis for understanding how computers perform these arithmetic operations to take advantage of simpler circuit design.

NUMBER SYSTEMS

So far we have limited our discussion of numbering systems to binary (base 2) and decimal (base 10). However, there are two others you should know: octal (base 8) and hexadecimal (base 16).

We use the latter two number systems primarily as a shorthand notation that is easier for human comprehension than the long string of 1s and 0s used in the computer. We first describe these systems and then discuss why and how they are used.

The **octal** number system uses eight symbols, 0 through 7. As seen in Exhibit B.5, eight symbols can be accommodated in three bits since $2^3 = 8$. After the symbol 7, the count starts over with the next place value ...... 10, 11, through 17. The **hexadecimal** number system uses sixteen symbols, 0 through 9 and A through F. Sixteen symbols can be represented with four bits since $2^4 = 16$.

As you can see from this chart, the decimal number 5 can be represented by 0101 in base 2, 5 in base 8, and 5 in base 16. The decimal number 15 is 1111 in base 2, 17 in base 8, and F in base 16.

Exhibit B.5
Number Systems

Base 2 (binary)	Base 10 (decimal)	Base 8 (octal)	Base 16 (hexadecimal)
0000	0	0	0
0001	1	1	1
0010	2	2	2
0011	3	3	3
0100	4	4	4
0101	5	5	5
0110	6	6	6
0111	7	7	7
1000	8	10	8
1001	9	11	9
1010	10	12	A
1011	11	13	B
1100	12	14	C
1101	13	15	D
1110	14	16	E
1111	15	17	F
10000	16	20	10
10001	17	21	11
10010	18	22	12
10011	19	23	13
10100	20	24	14

Let's see how we can convert mathematically from one number system to another. Several methods can be used to convert a number in base 10 to one in another base. The method we explain is performing **successive place value division.**

Start with the highest place value divisor that does not exceed the base 10 dividend number. Divide that number into the dividend. The multipler is placed in the quotient. The product is subtracted from the dividend. The resulting remainder is then divided by the next lowest place value and so on until the lowest place value is accounted for. The quotient is the equivalent number in the new base number system.

To see how this works, let us determine the base 2 equivalent of 11_{10}. The dividend eleven is divided by the largest base 2 place value that does not exceed 11, which is 8, or 2^3. Eight goes into 11 once. The remainder of 3 is then divided by 2^2, or 4. Since 4 exceeds 3, we place a 0 in the quotient. Then we divide the remainder by 2^1 and, finally, 2^0. The final quotient of 1011 is the binary equivalent of 11^{10}. Shown on the right side of Exhibit B.6 is the expanded form discussed in Chapter 3 that can be used for converting base 2 numbers to base 10.

What would be the binary equivalent of 92_{10}? Here the initial divisor would be 64 or 2^6 (Exhibit B.7). In this example note that the remainder goes to 0 after dividing by 2^2. You still have to continue dividing for all lower place values. In this case that would be 2^1 and 2^0.

The same approach is used to convert the base 10 number 92 to its base 8 equivalent. This time place values of 8 are used. The initial division is started with 64 or 8^2. The resulting quotient is 134_8. To check the answer, the quotient 134_8 can be multiplied by its appropriate place value and the results added.

Exhibit B.6
Conversion Between Base 10 and Base 2

Base 10 to Base 2	Base 2 to Base 10
1011 ← (quotient)	
2^3 8) 11 ← (dividend)	$1 \times 2^3 = 8$
8	
2^2 4) 3 ← (intermediate remainder)	$0 \times 2^2 = 0$
0	
2^1 2) 3	$1 \times 2^1 = 2$
2	
2^0 1) 1	$1 \times 2^0 = 1$
1	
0 ← (final remainder)	11

Exhibit B.7
Conversion Between Base 10 and Other Number Systems

Base 10 to Base 2	Base 2 to Base 10
1011100	
2^6 64) 92	$1 \times 2^6 = 64$
64	
2^5 32) 28	$0 \times 2^5 = 0$
0	
2^4 16) 28	$1 \times 2^4 = 16$
16	
2^3 8) 12	$1 \times 2^3 = 8$
8	
2^2 4) 4	$1 \times 2^2 = 4$
4	
2^1 2) 0	$0 \times 2^1 = 0$
0	
2^0 1) 0	$0 \times 2^0 = 0$
0	
0	92

Base 10 to Base 8	Base 8 to Base 10
134	
8^2 64) 92	$1 \times 8^2 = 64$
64	
8^1 8) 28	$3 \times 8^1 = 24$
24	
8^0 1) 4	$4 \times 8^0 = 4$
4	92
0	

Base 10 to Base 16	Base 16 to Base 10
5C	
16^1 16) 92	$5 \times 16^1 = 80$
80	
16^0 1) 12	$C \times 16^0 = 12$
12	92
0	

Exhibit B.8
More Examples of Conversion Between Base 10 and Other Number Systems

Base 10 to Base 2		Base 2 to Base 10
	101001101	
2^8	256) 333	$1 \times 2^8 = 256$
	256	
2^7	128) 77	$0 \times 2^7 = 0$
	0	
2^6	64) 77	$1 \times 2^6 = 64$
	64	
2^5	32) 13	$0 \times 2^5 = 0$
	0	
2^4	16) 13	$0 \times 2^4 = 0$
	0	
2^3	8) 13	$1 \times 2^3 = 8$
	8	
2^2	4) 5	$1 \times 2^2 = 4$
	4	
2^1	2) 1	$0 \times 2^1 = 0$
	0	
2^0	1) 1	$1 \times 2^0 = 1$
	1	333
	0	

Base 10 to Base 8		Base 8 to Base 10
	515	
8^2	64) 333	$5 \times 8^2 = 320$
	320	
8^1	8) 13	$1 \times 8^1 = 8$
	8	
8^0	1) 5	$5 \times 8^0 = 5$
	5	333
	0	

Base 10 to Base 16		Base 16 to Base 10
	14B	
16^2	256) 333	$1 \times 16^2 = 256$
	256	
16^1	16) 77	$4 \times 16^1 = 64$
	64	
16^0	1) 13	$B \times 16^0 = 13$
	13	333
	0	

These same techniques can be used for converting a base 10 number to base 16. For example 92_{10} is 5C in base 16. In Exhibit B.8, more examples are given for converting the base 10 number 333 to base 2, base 8, and base 16.

We have covered how to convert base 10 to base 2 and base 10 to base 8 or base 16. What about the reverse—going from base 8 to base 2 or base 16 to base 2? These latter operations are quite simple (Exhibit B.9).

Take each digit of the base 8 number and replace it with its three-bit equivalent. For example, 515_8 would be 101 001 101 in base 2. To convert from base 16 to base 2, you replace each digit with its four-bit equivalent. Thus $14B_{16}$ would be 0001 0100 1011 in base 2.

Conversely, to go from base 2 to base 8 take the binary number and convert each three-bit grouping to its base 8 digit (Exhibit B.10). To go from base 2 to base 16, convert each four-bit grouping into a base 16 digit. The binary number 1111110 is grouped into three-bit groups starting from the right side. This would give 001 111 110. Each three-bit group is converted to a base 8 digit, giving 176_8. To convert that same number 1111110_2 to hexadecimal, place it into four-bit groups, which give 0111 1110. Converting each group to a hexadecimal digit gives $7E_{16}$.

In a previous example, we started with the number 333_{10} and converted it directly to the binary number 101001101_2. We should get this same binary result if we go from base 10 to base 8 and then from base 8 to base 2, or from base 10 to base 16 and then from base 16 to base 2. Check the results in Exhibit B.8 to see if this is true.

How are these different number systems used in computer operations? Data are represented in one of two basic ways: either as **numerics,** numbers which can be manipulated arithmetically, or as **alphanumerics,** characters such as digits, letters, and special symbols. Generally, numeric data are represented using the binary number system, and binary arithmetic can be performed on it. In contrast, alphanumeric data such as ZIP code or phone numbers cannot be manipulated arithmetically, because they are represented by character codes such as EBCDIC or ASCII.

Hexadecimal or octal notation can be used for listing the contents of various memory locations in a form convenient for programmers to read. This is important when a program ends abnormally because of some error and the programmer needs to see the status of critical memory locations to understand

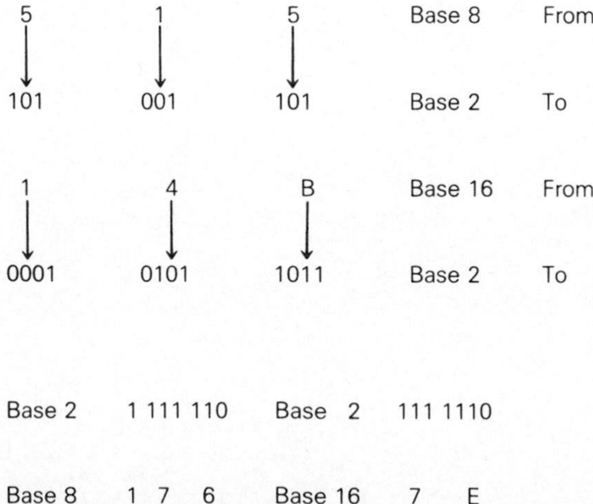

Exhibit B.9
Number Conversion from Base 8 or Base 16 to Base 2

Exhibit B.10
Number Conversion from Base 2 to Base 8 or Base 16

Exhibit B.11

A typical dump display listing the contents of primary memory with both hexadecimal and English

"Dump" display from "Program Patchwork" by Alan Hoenig. Reprinted by permission of *PC World,* (April 1985) published at 555 De Haro Street, San Francisco, CA 94107.

```
A>debug test.com
-d
108F:0100  E9 4D 0B BA AD 09 3D 02-00 74 18 3D 05 00 74 13   iM.:-.=..t.=..t.
108F:0110  BA 11 09 3D 08 00 74 0B-BA FD 08 3D 0B 00 74 03   :..=..t.:}.=..t.
108F:0120  BA EE 08 0E 1F E8 25 05-EB 0C CD 21 72 D5 B4 4D   :n...h%.k.M!rU4M
108F:0130  CD 21 2E A3 5E 0A E9 EE-00 FB 2E F6 06 BF 0A 03   M!.#^.in.{.v.?..
108F:0140  74 0C 2E F6 06 BF 0A 04-74 03 E9 14 0F CF 0E 1F   t..v.?..t.i..O..
108F:0150  B4 0D CD 21 F7 06 0D 0A-FF FF 74 03 E9 ED 02 33   4.M!w.....t.im.3
108F:0160  C0 8B E8 A2 6A 0A A2 6B-0A A2 C0 0A 39 06 66 0A   @.h"j."k."@.9.f.
108F:0170  74 06 C7 06 66 0A FF FF-38 06 5D 0A 75 03 E9 EB   t.G.f...8.].u.ik
-
-
```

what went wrong. Exhibit B.11 illustrates a **dump,** which is a printout of selected primary memory locations displayed in hexadecimal or octal format, depending on the computer used.

Generally, computers that have dataword lengths in multiples of 8 bits use hexadecimal printouts, such as IBM's 4341 series with its 32-bit dataword and the 3083 series with its 64-bit dataword. These computer datawords cannot be divided into the three-bit groups of the octal number system, but the four-bit groupings of hexadecimal fit nicely. On the other hand, Control Data Corporation's Cyber 170 series computers with their 60-bit dataword can use octal representation. It is important to stress again that the computer does not process or store data in octal or hexadecimal. Rather, binary data are converted to these forms for display purposes.

REVIEW QUESTIONS

1. What similarities exist between *binary* and *decimal* mathematical operations?
2. What are the basic rules of binary addition?
3. How is binary subtraction accomplished? Subtract 4 from 7 and give the binary result.
4. How are subtractions that produce a negative number handled in binary? Subtract 7 from 6.
5. What are the basic rules of binary multiplication? How is binary multiplication performed?
6. Briefly describe the octal and hexadecimal number systems. Use Exhibit B.5 to find the octal and hexadecimal equivalents of decimal 10.
7. Briefly describe the procedure followed to convert numbers from one base system to another.
8. What is the process for converting from base 8 or base 16 to base 2? Convert 20 (base 10) to its base 2 equivalent.
9. Convert 14_{10} to its octal and hexadecimal equivalents.
10. How are data represented in the computer? Why can't alphanumeric data be mathematically manipulated?
11. How are octal and hexadecimal notation used by programmers?
12. The Zenon Corporation's new micros feature a 32-bit processor. What number system is likely to be used in its memory dumps? Why?

APPENDIX C
The BASIC Programming Language

INTRODUCTION
BASIC'S FUNDAMENTAL DATA PROCESSING ELEMENTS
AN OVERVIEW OF THE BASIC PROGRAMMING LANGUAGE
SOME "DEFINITIONAL" STATEMENTS
ASSIGNMENT STATEMENTS
INPUT AND OUTPUT STATEMENTS
CONTROL STATEMENTS
WORKING WITH ARRAYS
FILE HANDLING
FUNCTIONS AND SUBROUTINES

INTRODUCTION

BASIC, which stands for **Beginner's All-purpose Symbolic Instruction Code,** was developed by John Kemeny and Thomas Kurtz of Dartmouth College. The program was first made available for general use in 1964. The professors' objective in developing BASIC was to create an **interactive** programming language that students could learn and use quickly and easily.

With an interactive programming language, you "converse" directly with the computer system to build, test, and run a program. Such interaction speeds up the learning process in two ways:

1. You rapidly discover your errors and successes in programming.
2. In a short period of time, you can change and rerun a program many times.

The BASIC programming language has only a few commands, which are fairly self-evident and handle many programming details for the programmer. As a result, many people are able to write relatively complex programs in BASIC after only a short period of instruction.

The purpose of this appendix is to introduce you to the BASIC programming language. Learning how to *program in BASIC* is covered in Appendix D. Before we start to explore BASIC, however, you need to understand two key aspects of this programming language.

As discussed in Chapter 14, programming languages should be **standardized** whenever possible for two main reasons. First, a program written in a standard version of a programming language can be run on many different computer systems. Second, a programmer can move easily from one computer system to another without having to learn a new version of the programming language. While a standard version for BASIC does exist, this standard is usually just a small subset of the versions used on most computer systems. Different versions of BASIC are provided with different computer systems. In fact, it is rare to find a BASIC program written for one computer system that can run on another system without some changes.

A reduced set of BASIC is covered in this appendix. As a result, programs written following the guidelines provided here should run under the versions of BASIC available on most computer systems. Any changes required should be minor. When, in this appendix, we must move from this reduced set of BASIC commands to a more complex set, we will use the Microsoft version of BASIC. This version has become the *current* de facto industry standard, since it is available with the IBM PC. Microsoft BASIC is also used with many other microcomputers.

As mentioned earlier in this appendix, BASIC is oriented toward **interactive** programming. Generally, input data are entered from a keyboard and output information displayed on a CRT screen. We follow such an approach in this appendix. Little standarization exists regarding other input or output activities, such as sending output to a printer or reading data from a disk file. As a result, we will not cover printed output and will discuss data file processing only briefly.

Summary

BASIC, which stands for *Beginner's All-purpose Symbolic Instruction Code,* was developed by John Kemeny and Thomas Kurtz of Dartmouth College. Their objective was to have an *interactive* programming language that people could learn and use easily.

BASIC has only a few commands, which are fairly self-evident and which handle many programming details for the programmer.

Programming languages should be *standardized* for two reasons. First, a standard version of a programming language can be run on many computer systems. Second, a programmer can move easily from one computer system to another without having to learn a new version of the programming language. While a standard version for BASIC does exist, this standard is usually a small subset of the versions existing on most computer systems. For this reason, a reduced set of BASIC is covered in this appendix.

Since BASIC is primarily an interactive programming language, input data are usually entered from a keyboard and output information displayed on a CRT screen. These forms of input and output are emphasized in this appendix.

BASIC'S FUNDAMENTAL DATA PROCESSING ELEMENTS

A programming language, essentially, allows you to specify a sequence of data operations. The capabilities of a language are largely determined by how the language organizes data items and by the nature of its operations on these data items. Thus, an important first step in learning a programming language is to understand the **types** of data that can be processed, the data **structures** that are allowed, and the data **operations** that can be performed.

Data Types

BASIC allows the use of both **numeric** and **alphanumeric** data items. Numeric data can be **integers** or **decimals:**

Integers	Decimals
2	2.38
−14	−14.929
13569	13569.1

One of the nice features of BASIC is that integers and decimals are handled in the same way. You do not have to distinguish between them. Here are two important rules to follow when keying in real numbers:

1. Always *precede* a negative number with a minus sign.
2. *Never* use commas to indicate "thousands," "millions," and so on.

All versions of BASIC also use another means to represent real numbers—**scientific,** or **engineering, notation.** These numbers are broken into two parts; the first part indicates the number's **actual digits** and the second part notes the **power of 10 to which these digits are being taken.** The following examples illustrate this method of representing numbers:

Regular Notation	Scientific Notation
20.334	2.0334E+01
0.00567	5.67E−03
−62939.6	−6.29396E+04

While you may not enter data using this notation, you may find it appearing as output!

Alphanumeric data can include any set of characters desired: digits, alphabetic letters, punctuation marks, and other special characters. In BASIC, an alphanumeric data item is referred to as a **string.** Strings are enclosed within quotation marks to identify them in a BASIC program:

"Sales Volume"
"Samuel Clemens"
"1600 Pennsylvania Avenue, Washington, D.C."

Data Structures

All versions of BASIC enable programmers to make use of the following four data structures: **constants, variables, arrays,** and **files.** These four data structures can handle almost any business data processing task.

Constants. A constant refers to a data item that cannot change its value when a program is run. Any real number or string can be used as a constant:

Real Numbers	Strings
2.0	"4567283"
−8	"(MILLIONS)"
−3745.66	"ENTER: YES OR NO"
35.567	"*********"

Variables. A variable refers to a data item that can change its value when the program is run. As described in Chapter 3: "The Central Processing Unit," the data items being processed in a program are stored in the computer system's primary memory. A variable, then, refers to a data item located in one specific storage location.

It is important to distinguish between a variable's **name,** or **address,** and its **contents.** A variable's name is the string constant used to refer to the data item. The different versions of BASIC have distinctly different rules for naming variables. The following rules, however, apply for all versions of BASIC:

1. **Numeric variable names** are denoted by:

   a single alphabetic character (A)

   a single alphabetic character followed by a single digit (A1)

2. **String variable names** are denoted by:

   a single alphabetic character followed by a dollar sign (A$)

The rather limited set of variable names that can be composed from these rules presents a major problem with this "reduced" set of BASIC capabilities—the names are not very meaningful. As a result, it can be difficult to understand exactly what a program is doing. If your version of BASIC has more liberal rules for naming variables, take advantage of them.

Exhibit C.1 illustrates a portion of a computer system's primary memory. When a variable is first used, its name is assigned a specific primary memory location. Any value then assigned to this variable name (i.e., that variable's contents) is physically stored in this primary memory location. As different values are assigned to the variable name, the contents of this storage location automatically change.

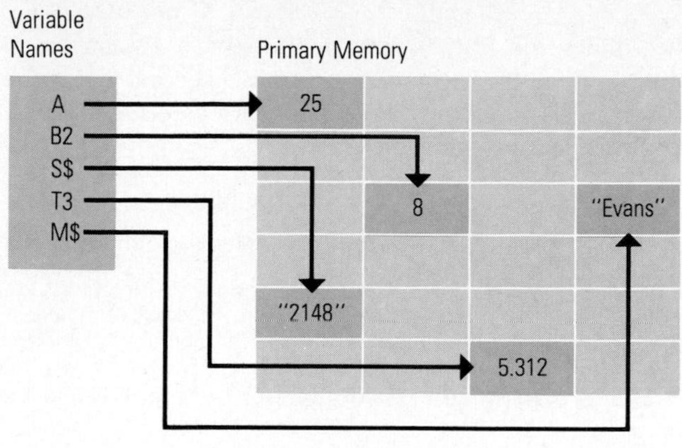

Exhibit C.1

Variable names indicate which primary memory storage locations are to be used in a program. The contents of these storage locations are the data values to be processed.

Primary Memory

28
42
23
37
36
49
26

Exhibit C.2

A one-dimensional array containing employees' ages

Arrays. An array refers to a set of data stored in a number of primary memory locations that are treated as a unit. By using a single array name, a programmer can refer to the entire set of storage locations.

All versions of BASIC enable a programmer to use one and two-dimensional numeric arrays, and most allow one-dimensional string arrays. A one-dimensional array can be thought of as a single column of data values. A two-dimensional array can be thought of as a table, consisting of multiple rows and columns of data values. Exhibits C.2, C.3, and C.4 illustrate a useful way of picturing how arrays are stored in primary memory. The exhibits may not represent the process exactly, but they do provide a way to think about how arrays are organized in primary memory when you program.

Arrays are named using the same rules that apply for variables. Numeric and string data items, however, **cannot** be placed within the same array.

123	521	.35
124	129	1.24
131	14	14.50
135	53	.08
138	426	1.56

Exhibit C.3

A two-dimensional array holding inventory information. Column "1" holds the part number, column "2" holds the quantity on hand for the part, and column "3" holds the cost of the part.

"Smith"
"Hankins"
"Thomas"
"Byrd"
"Nevins"
"Alvarez"
"Boykin"

Exhibit C.4

A one-dimensional array holding employees' names

Files. Files, like two-dimensional arrays, can be thought of as tables with multiple rows and multiple columns. Each row represents a **record** within the file, and each column represents a **field** within a record. However, files differ from two-dimensional arrays in the following ways:

1. Each column, or field, is a separate variable in a file but not in an array.
2. Both numeric and string variables, or fields, can be included within a file but not within an array.
3. Files are stored on secondary storage devices (e.g., diskettes) whereas arrays are stored within primary memory.

Exhibit C.5 illustrates a file that holds information about the employees of a firm.

Data Operations

Data values are transformed or created in BASIC by using three types of data operations: **arithmetical operations, relational operations,** and **logical operations.** Specific **operators** within each type of data operation actually indicate the nature of the operation to be performed. These operations are normally represented in **expressions,** which can be regarded as specific combinations of constants, variables, and operators. This system should become clear to you through the examples used to explain the different types of operations.

Arithmetical Operations. There are five arithmetical operators:

Operator	Operation
+	addition
−	subtraction
*	multiplication
/	division
^,**	exponentiation

EXHIBIT C.5

A data file holding information about a firm's employees

← FIELDS →

RECORDS ↕	Employee Number	Employee Name	Job Classification	Salary	Department	Employee Date
	42761	"JOSEPH BUTTONS"	05	32500	A	"05-23-71"
	42762	"SALLY WITHERS"	08	28000	F	"08-13-75"
	42763	"BENJAMIN JONES"	05	23000	G	"02-28-81"
	42767	"ANN MARTINEZ"	13	17500	B	"03-07-73"
	42768	"RICHARD VANTEL"	15	42500	A	"07-17-60"
	.	.	.	.	.	.
	.	.	.	.	.	.
	.	.	.	.	.	.
	61934	"MICHAEL ADAMS"	16	11500	C	"11-29-78"
	61935	"HARRIET TOMBS"	03	18000	C	"01-05-82"
	61936	"SARAH STONE"	05	22500	F	"08-15-83"

These operators, along with constants and variables, form **arithmetical expressions.** Arithmetical expressions are evaluated by following these rules:

1. All expressions within parentheses are evaluated first.
2. "Higher-order" operations are performed before "lower-order" operations. Exponentiation is the highest arithmetical operator. Multiplication and division comprise a middle level. Addition and subtraction are the lowest arithmetical operators.
3. Operations of the same order are performed by moving left to right across an expression.

These rules are illustrated in Example C.1.

Relational Operations. There are six relational operators:

Operator	Operation
>	greater than
>=,≥	greater than or equal to
<	less than
<=,≤	less than or equal to
=	equal to
<>,≠	not equal to

Example C.1
Evaluating Arithmetical Expressions

USE THESE VARIABLE VALUES IN EVALUATING THE EXPRESSIONS
A = 3   B = 4   C = 2

EXPRESSION	CALCULATION
A + 5 * C	A + (5*C) 3 + (5*2) 3 + 10 13
(A + 5) * C	(A+5)*C (3+5)*2 8 *2 16
B − A^2/2	B − ((A^2)/2) 4 − ((3^2)/2) 4 − (9 /2) 4 − 4.5 −.5
(B − A)^2/2	(B−A)^2/2 (4−3)^2/2 1^2 /2 1 /2 .5
C * B/(A*B-4)	C*B/((A*B)−4) 2*4/((3*4)−4) 2*4/(12 −4) 2*4/ 8 8 / 8 1

The relational operators are used to form **simple relational expressions.** The example below shows the form of a relational expression, whose value can be either *true* or *false:*

A-1	>	A-2
arithmetical expression	relational operator	arithmetical expression

Whether the value of the expression is "true" or "false" depends on the nature of the relationship between the two arithmetical expressions. There can be only one relational operator in a simple relational expression.

Example C.2 describes the relationships between the two arithmetical expressions that result in "true" and "false" values. Example C.3 illustrates how the values of relational expressions are evaluated.

Logical Operations. There are three logical operators:

Operator	Operation
NOT	Changes the value of a relational expression (i.e., a "true" expression is evaluated as being "false" or a "false" expression is evaluated as being "true").
AND	Evaluated as "true" only when both relational expressions are true.
OR	Evaluated as "true" when one or both relational expressions are true.

Example C.2

Definitions of the Relational Operators

AE1—first arithmetic expression
AE2—second arithmetic expression

OPERATION	EVALUATION
AE1 > AE2	TRUE: AE1 is greater than AE2 FALSE: AE1 is less than or equal to AE2
AE1 >= AE2	TRUE: AE2 is greater than or equal to AE2 FALSE: AE1 is less than AE2
AE1 < AE2	TRUE: AE1 is less than AE2 FALSE: AE1 is greater than or equal to AE2
AE1 <= AE2	TRUE: AE1 is less than or equal to AE2 FALSE: AE1 is greater than AE2
AE1 = AE2	TRUE: AE1 is equal to AE2 FALSE: AE1 is not equal to AE2
AE1 <> AE2	TRUE: AE1 is not equal to AE2 FALSE: AE1 is equal to AE2

Example C.3

Evaluating Relational Expressions

USE THESE VARIABLE VALUES IN EVALUATING THE EXPRESSIONS
A = 3 B = 4 C = 2

EXPRESSION	CALCULATION
A = 3	A = 3 3 = 3 [TRUE]
B+4 < 10	B+4 < 10 4+4 < 10 8 < 10 [TRUE]
2*A <= B	2*A <= B 2*3 <= 4 6 <= 4 [FALSE]
3+A <> 5*A	3+A <> 5*A 3+3 <> 5*3 6 <> 15 [TRUE]
A+C > 5*B	A+C > 5*B 3+2 > 5*4 5 > 5*4 5 > 20 [FALSE]

Example C.4
Evaluating Complex Relational Expressions

USE THESE VARIABLE VALUES IN EVALUATING THE EXPRESSIONS
A = 3   B = 4   C = 2

EXPRESSION	CALCULATION
A = 3 AND B = 4	A = 3 AND B = 4 3 = 3 AND 4 = 4 [TRUE] AND [TRUE] [TRUE]
B+2 < 4 AND 2*C > A	B+2 < 4 AND 2*C > A 4+2 < 4 AND 2*2 > 3 6 < 4 AND 4 > 3 [FALSE] AND [TRUE] [FALSE]
A+C = 5 OR B >= 3*A	A+C = 5 OR B >= 3*A 3+2 = 5 OR 4 >= 3*3 5 = 5 OR 4 >= 9 [TRUE] OR [FALSE] [TRUE]
B <> A+1 OR A > B*C	B <> A+1 OR A > B*C 4 <> 3+1 OR 3 > 4*2 4 <> 4 OR 3 > 8 [FALSE] OR [FALSE] [FALSE]
NOT B > A−C	NOT B > A−C NOT 4 > 3−2 NOT 4 > 1 NOT [TRUE] [FALSE]
NOT 2*C > B+A	NOT 2*C > B+A NOT 2*2 > 4+3 NOT 4 > 7 NOT [FALSE] [TRUE]

These logical operators are used to construct **complex relational expressions.** An example of a complex relational expression follows:

A = 3	AND	B = 4
simple relational expression	logical operator	simple relational expression

Example C.4 provides examples of how complex relational expressions are formed and evaluated.

A complex relational expression can contain more than one logical operator. With complex relational expressions, "NOT" operations are performed before "AND" operations, which are performed before "OR" operations. Exhibit C.6, which is referred to as the **hierarchy of operations,** should help you remember the relative order of all the different data operations.

Summary

The capabilities of a programming language are largely determined by the *types* of data that can be processed, the data *structures* that are allowed, and the data *operations* that can be performed.

Exhibit C.6

This list, known as the Hierarchy of Operations, gives the order in which data operations are performed in evaluating expressions. Higher-order operations are performed before lower-order operations.

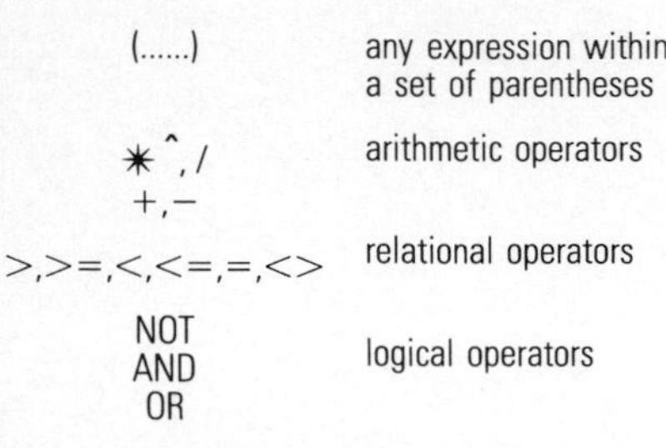

HIGHER-ORDER OPERATORS	
(......)	any expression within a set of parentheses
∗ ^, / +, −	arithmetic operators
>,>=,<,<=,=,<>	relational operators
NOT AND OR	logical operators
LOWER-ORDER OPERATORS	

BASIC allows the use of both *numeric* and *alphanumeric* data items. *Integer* and *decimal* numeric data items are handled in a similar fashion. *Scientific notation* can be used when entering or displaying numeric data items. Alphanumeric data items, which are termed *strings* in BASIC, must be enclosed within quotation marks.

All versions of BASIC provide four data structures: *constants, variables, arrays,* and *files.* Constants refer to data items that cannot change their value when a program is run. Variables refer to data items that can change their values. Variable *names,* or *addresses,* are used to direct a program to the particular location in primary memory where a data item is stored. The actual *contents* of a memory location is the variable's value. Variable *names* must follow a strict set of rules.

Arrays allow a programmer to refer to a set of data items stored in a number of primary memory locations. All versions of BASIC allow both one- and two-dimensional numeric arrays, and most provide for one-dimensional string arrays. A single array cannot contain both numeric and string data items. A one-dimensional array can be thought of as a single column of data values. A two-dimensional array can be regarded as a table of data values.

Files can be thought of as tables in which the columns represent different variables or *fields.* The table rows are referred to as *records.*

Data values are transformed or created in BASIC by using three types of data operations: *arithmetical, relational,* and *logical* operations. Data *operators* indicate the nature of the operation to be performed. These data operations are represented in *expressions,* or combinations of constants, variables, and operators.

The arithmetical operators form *arithmetical expressions* that perform the standard mathematical operations. Relational operators form *simple relational expressions* that compare the values of constants, variables, and *arithmetical expressions.* The logical operators form *complex relational expressions.* All relational expressions evaluate to a "true" or "false" value.

The order in which these data operations are performed follows a strict set of rules known as the *hierarchy of operations.* Exhibit C.6 summarizes these rules.

AN OVERVIEW OF THE BASIC PROGRAMMING LANGUAGE

Two types of **commands** are associated with the BASIC programming language:

1. Programming statements
2. System commands

Programming statements form the actual programs that direct the computer system's CPU in performing desired data processing tasks. **System commands,** on the other hand, direct the computer's operating system to work with a program currently being written or with a previously written program.

Programming Statements

As you can see from Program C.1, BASIC programming statements are built using three types of elements: **line numbers, programming commands,** and **expressions.** Notice that most of the programming statements in Program C.1 take a common form:

Line Number	Programming Command	Expression
10	REM	PROGRAM C.1
100	INPUT	P
120	LET	T = P*N
130	PRINT	T

We will discuss all of the programming statements in Program C.1 in this appendix. For now, try to follow exactly what happens in this program. The programming statements in line numbers 100 and 110 result in the program's user entering two values through the keyboard for variables P and N. Then, line number 120 multiplies these two variables together and places the answer in variable T. Line number 130 displays this answer on the CRT screen. Line number 170 displays a message asking the user if there are any more values to enter. Line number 180 takes in the user's answer, a "YES" or a "NO," and places it in a string variable named A$. Line number 190 tests A$ to see if the user's answer was "YES." If it was, the program repeats itself. If the answer was not "YES," the program flow moves down to line number 200, at which time the program stops.

```
OK
RUN
? 10
? 7
 70
ANY MORE? YES
? 3
? 5
 15
ANY MORE? NO
OK
```

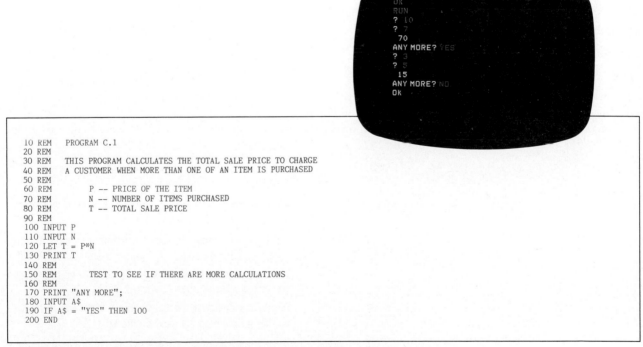

```
10 REM    PROGRAM C.1
20 REM
30 REM    THIS PROGRAM CALCULATES THE TOTAL SALE PRICE TO CHARGE
40 REM    A CUSTOMER WHEN MORE THAN ONE OF AN ITEM IS PURCHASED
50 REM
60 REM         P -- PRICE OF THE ITEM
70 REM         N -- NUMBER OF ITEMS PURCHASED
80 REM         T -- TOTAL SALE PRICE
90 REM
100 INPUT P
110 INPUT N
120 LET T = P*N
130 PRINT T
140 REM
150 REM        TEST TO SEE IF THERE ARE MORE CALCULATIONS
160 REM
170 PRINT "ANY MORE";
180 INPUT A$
190 IF A$ = "YES" THEN 100
200 END
```

Unless otherwise stated, all program listings in Appendix C have been written to accommodate both IBM Personal Computer BASIC for IBM microcomputers and APPLESOFT BASIC for Apple microcomputers.

Line numbers have two purposes. First, they indicate the **order** of the statements in a program. This is important because statements are executed sequentially unless the processing flow is directed to follow some other pattern. Second, they are used as **labels** to refer to particular statements in redirecting the processing flow.

Line numbers can take on any integer value between "1" and "99999." Most programmers do not specify their line numbers in increments of one in order to allow room for inserting additional statements into a program. Using increments of ten, as is done with Program C.1, is a good rule to follow.

Programming commands are **keywords** that indicate the type of data operation to be performed. These keywords, such as REM or LET, must be spelled correctly.

Expressions indicate the constants, variables, and/or different types of expressions that apply to the operation being performed. Usually, these expressions represent the specific values involved in a data processing operation.

System Commands

When a programmer begins a BASIC programming session, the computer system's primary memory is initially filled with zeroes. Programs are placed in memory in one of two ways.

First, programming statements can be entered one at a time from the keyboard to form a program. If the same line number is entered more than once, the last statement entered is the one kept in primary memory. For example, in entering Program C.1, the following two statements might be entered:

```
180 INPUT A
180 INPUT A$
```

Only the second of these two statements is contained in the program.

Second, an existing program, previously stored on a diskette, can be brought into primary memory by the operating system. These two alternatives are pictured in Exhibit C.7

The following six system commands are available with most versions of BASIC:

RUN	Directs the operating system to execute the program currently residing in primary memory.
LIST	Displays the entire program currently residing in primary memory on the CRT screen.
DELETE [line number]	Deletes from primary memory the program statement with the specified line number. A program statement can also be deleted by keying in its line number and then immediately keying the "return key."
NEW	Directs the operating system to zero out primary memory so that a new program can be entered.
SAVE "name"	Directs the operating system to write the program currently residing in primary memory on a secondary storage device. The rules for naming programs vary for different versions of BASIC. A relatively safe rule is to use names that begin

Directly from the keyboard:

Action:

① Statements entered into memory by keying in characters

② Statements displayed on CRT screen

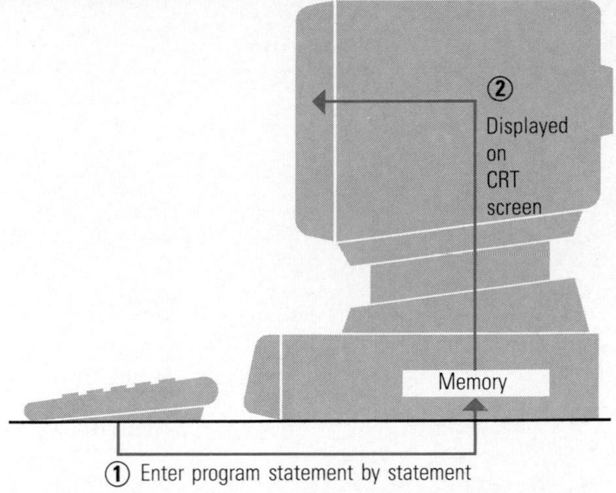

From a secondary storage device:

Action:

① Correct disk inserted into drive

② Instruction given to computer to read disk to retrieve program

③ Program read off drive

④ Instruction given to computer to list program

⑤ Program displayed on CRT screen

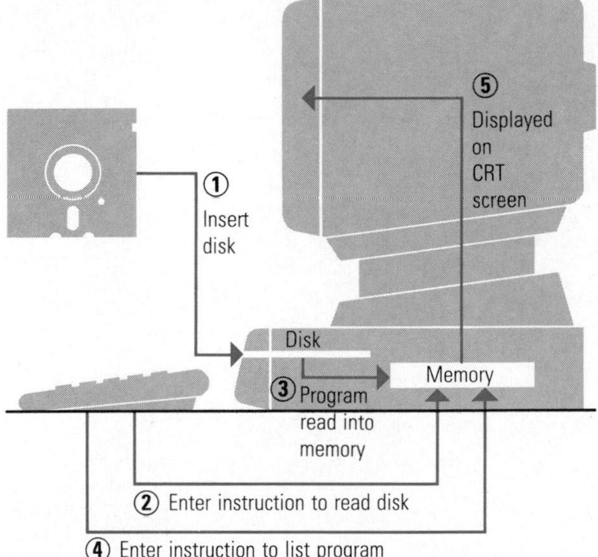

Exhibit C.7

Alternative ways of entering a BASIC program into a computer's memory

with an alphabetic character, that contain only letters and digits, and that use at most eight characters. This name may (Microsoft BASIC) or may not (Apple BASIC) have to be enclosed within quotation marks.

LOAD "name"	Directs the operating system to retrieve a previously written program from a secondary storage device. Again, the program's name may or may not have to be enclosed within quotation marks.

The LIST command can be used in a number of ways. In the descriptions that follow, "ln" is an abbreviation for "line number":

LIST	The complete program is displayed.
LIST ln	Only the specified line number with the program is displayed.
LIST ln1-ln2	Only the lines included within the specified range are displayed.

Example C.5 illustrates these uses of the LIST command.

Example C.5

Summary

The two types of BASIC *commands* include programming statements and system commands. *Programming statements* form the programs that direct the computer system's CPU to operate on data. *System commands* direct the computer's operating system to work with a program currently being written or with a previously written program.

Example C.5

Using the LIST System command. This example makes use of Program C.1.

```
SYSTEM COMMAND:   LIST

 10 REM      PROGRAM C.1
 20 REM
 30 REM      THIS PROGRAM CALCULATES THE TOTAL SALE PRICE TO CHARGE
 40 REM      A CUSTOMER WHEN MORE THAN ONE OF AN ITEM IS PURCHASED
 50 REM
 60 REM           P -- PRICE OF THE ITEM
 70 REM           N -- NUMBER OF ITEMS PURCHASED
 80 REM           T -- TOTAL SALE PRICE
 90 REM
100 INPUT P
110 INPUT N
120 LET T = P*N
130 PRINT T
140 REM
150 REM      TEST TO SEE IF THERE ARE MORE CALCULATIONS
160 REM
170 PRINT "ANY MORE";
180 INPUT A$
190 IF A$ = "YES" THEN 100
200 END
```

```
SYSTEM COMMAND: LIST 100

100 INPUT P
```

```
SYSTEM COMMAND: LIST 110-130

110 INPUT N
120 LET T = P*N
130 PRINT T
```

Programming statements are built using three basic elements: line numbers, programming commands, and expressions. *Line numbers* indicate the order of the statements in a program and serve as *labels* in redirecting the processing flow. *Programming commands* are *keywords* that indicate the type of data operation to be performed. *Expressions* usually represent the specific values involved in a data processing operation.

Programs are entered into a computer system's primary memory in one of two ways. First, programming statements can be entered one at a time from the keyboard. Second, a program previously stored on a diskette can be brought into primary memory by the operating system.

Most versions of BASIC include systems commands that execute a program (RUN), display a program on the CRT screen (LIST), remove programming statements from a program (DELETE), zero out primary memory so that a new program can be entered (NEW), write a program on to a diskette (SAVE), and retrieve a previously written program from a diskette (LOAD).

SOME "DEFINITIONAL" STATEMENTS

Some BASIC programming statements do not operate on data. Rather, they define specific features of a program. In this section we introduce a few of these "definitional" programming statements.

REM

The **Remark,** or **REM,** statement is used to **document** a BASIC program. Usually, these comments are used to define the overall purpose of a program, to define the variables in a program, and to identify important operations. By looking at Program C.1, you can see that the REM statement takes the following form:

60	REM	P—PRICE OF THE ITEM
line number	keyword	a text expression

Appropriately placed REM statements can make a BASIC program far more understandable for users. Notice in Program C.1 that having no text after the keyword REM results in a **blank line** appearing in the program listing.

REM statements are not read by the computer when a BASIC program executes. Their sole purpose is to make a program more understandable.

END

The **end,** or **END,** statement can be used in two related ways in BASIC. First, an END statement placed as the last programming statement in a program indicates there are no more statements in the program. Notice that all the programming examples in this appendix have an END statement as their final programming statement. Second, an executing program stops running whenever an END statement is reached. Many versions of BASIC, however, do allow a program to have more than one END statement. In this case, the END statement serves only the second purpose.

The END statement takes the following form:

```
200        END
line
number     keyword
```

DIM

The **dimension,** or **DIM,** statement is used to declare the existence and size of any arrays used in a program. Thus, a DIM statement must be placed in a program before the first use of an array.

An array is declared by listing a variable name and then indicating the number of rows and, if appropriate, columns the array possesses. With a one-dimensional array, only the number of rows is defined. With a two-dimensional array, the number of rows and columns must be defined. A one-dimensional array is declared in the following manner:

```
20         DIM        A(15)
line
number     keyword    variable name (number of rows)
```

And, a two-dimensional array is declared as follows:

```
50         DIM        C(5,2)
line                                  (number      number    )
number     keyword    variable name   (of rows,    of columns)
```

Integer constants must be used to indicate the number of rows and columns.

A single DIM statement can be used to declare a number of arrays. Consider the following DIM statement:

```
60 DIM A(15), B(25), C(5,4)
```

This would result in the following arrays being declared for use in a program:

A A one-dimensional array with 15 rows.

B A one-dimensional array with 25 rows.

C A two-dimensional array with 5 rows and 4 columns.

TRON and TROFF

The **trace,** or **TRON** and **TROFF,** statements are used to trace a program's processing flow. TRON "turns on" the tracing mechanism while TROFF "turns off" this mechanism. These statements take the following forms:

```
105        TRON
125        TROFF
line
number     keyword
```

By placing TRON and TROFF statements around a set of programming statements, the line numbers of these statements will be displayed on the CRT screen when the statements are executed. Program C.2 adds TRON and TROFF

```
10 REM    PROGRAM C.2
20 REM
21 REM    THIS PROGRAM ILLUSTRATES THE TRON AND TROFF STATEMENTS
22 REM
30 REM    THE PROGRAM CALCULATES THE TOTAL SALE PRICE TO CHARGE
40 REM    A CUSTOMER WHEN MORE THAN ONE OF AN ITEM IS PURCHASED
50 REM
60 REM         P -- PRICE OF THE ITEM
70 REM         N -- NUMBER OF ITEMS PURCHASED
80 REM         T -- TOTAL SALE PRICE
90 REM
91 REM    NOTICE THE TRON AND TROFF STATEMENTS ADDED AS
92 REM    LINE NUMBERS 105 AND 125
93 REM
100 INPUT P
105 TRON
110 INPUT N
120 LET T = P*N
125 TROFF
130 PRINT T
140 REM
150 REM          TEST TO SEE IF THERE ARE MORE CALCULATIONS
160 REM
170 PRINT "ANY MORE";
180 INPUT A$
190 IF A$ = "YES" THEN 100
200 END
```

```
OK
RUN
? 10
[110]? 7
[120][125] 70
ANY MORE? YES
? 3
[110]? 5
[120][125] 15
ANY MORE? NO
OK
```

Changes for APPLESOFT BASIC:

```
105 TRACE

125 NOTRACE
```

statements to Program C.1. Notice how the program's output displays each execution of the programming statements contained within the TRON/TROFF pair. As many TRON/TROFF pairs as needed can be placed within a single program. Be sure to delete these statements once a program has been debugged. Having these extra line numbers appear on a CRT screen can clutter up a program's output and make it virtually unreadable.

These very useful statements are not available with all versions of BASIC. Where they are available, the keywords may be different.

Summary

Some BASIC programming commands do not operate on data. Rather, they define specific features of a program. Some of these "definitional" programming commands are the *REM, END, DIM, TRON,* and *TROFF* statements.

The *remark,* or REM, statement is used to *document* a BASIC program. Usually, these comments define the overall purpose of a program, define its variables, and identify important operations.

The *end,* or END, statement can be used in two ways. It indicates the end of a program listing and, when reached, stops program execution.

The *dimension,* or *DIM,* statement is used to declare the existence and size of any arrays used in a program. A DIM statement must be placed in a program prior to the first use of the array.

The *trace,* or *TRON* and *TROFF,* statements are used to trace a program's processing flow. By placing TRON and TROFF statements around a set of programming statements, the line numbers of these statements will be displayed on the CRT screen when the statements are executed. TRON "turns on" the tracing mechanism while TROFF "turns off" this mechanism.

ASSIGNMENT STATEMENTS

Variables can be given data values in two ways without having to enter the data from the keyboard or from a diskette. Using the LET statement, data values can be directly assigned to variables. Using the READ and DATA statements, data values can be assigned to variables from a list of values kept with a program.

LET

The **assignment,** or **LET,** statement takes the following form:

120	LET	T = P✱N
line number	keyword	expression

This statement takes the value of the expression given on the righthand side of the "=" and places it into the storage location referred to by a variable name given to the left of the "=." Any prior values stored in the storage location are replaced by this new value.

Exhibit C.8 illustrates how this assignment process works using the LET statement given as line number 120 in Program C.1. The step-by-step actions are:

1. The value of variable *P* is brought into the CPU.
2. The value of variable *N* is brought into the CPU.
3. Variables *P* and *N* are multiplied; the result is temporarily kept in the CPU.
4. The value of variable *T* is brought into the CPU.
5. The product *P*✱*N* is assigned as the new value of *T*; the result is temporarily kept in the CPU.
6. The new value of *T* is placed in the storage location referred to as *T*.

The keyword LET is optional. Thus, the LET statement can appear as:

120	T = P✱N
line number	expression

However, beginning programmers are advised to use the LET keyword so that this statement is not confused with the "=" relational expression.

Exhibit C.8

Illustration of how values are assigned to variables with the LET statement

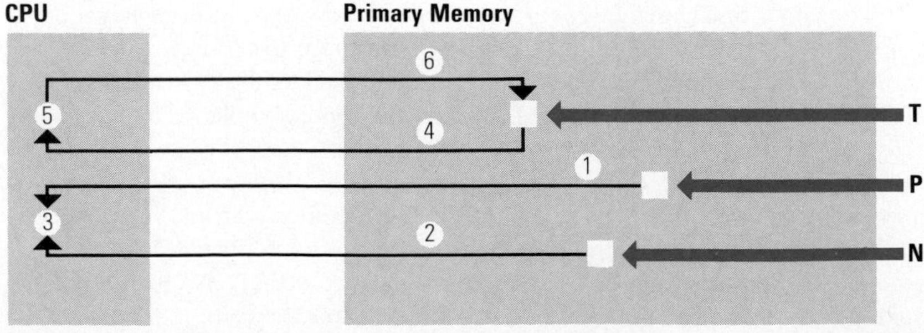

READ/DATA

The **READ** and **DATA** statements act together in the following way. The READ statement is located in a program where a variable is to be assigned a specific value. The data value to be assigned to this variable is placed in a DATA statement, which can be located anywhere in the program. Common strategies for placing DATA statements include the following:

1. Place the DATA statement containing the value immediately after the READ statement.
2. Place all DATA statements at the beginning of the program (usually just after the initial set of REM statements).
3. Place all DATA statements at the end of the program (just before the END statement). This is the strategy used in this appendix.

The standard form of the READ and DATA statements is:

100	READ	P	204	DATA	10
line number	keyword	variable name	line number	keyword	data value

When a program containing READ and DATA statements executes, the following occurs:

1. Just before the program's execution, all the data values contained in DATA statements are placed in a single data list in primary memory. The order in which the data values appear in this list follows the sequence, as denoted by line numbers, in which they are placed in the program.
2. A "data list pointer" is created and set so that it points to the first data value in the list. This pointer indicates which data value is the next one to be used from the list. As a data value is used, the pointer moves down to the next data value.
3. All DATA statements are ignored as the program runs.
4. Whenever a READ statement is executed, the data list value currently being pointed to is assigned to the variable given in the READ statement.

Program C.3 illustrates how READ and DATA statements could be added to Program C.1 so the user would not have to enter data values from the keyboard as the program executes. Program C.4 modifies Program C.3 to show that more than one data value can be placed on a single DATA statement. Notice that both programs give the exact same output.

If more data values are "requested" than actually exist in the data list, an error message is produced and the program will stop at the point where the additional data values were requested. No problems will arise if too many data values are provided in a data list. The most common error made with READ/DATA statements is to mix up the data values given in data lists so they fail to match the appropriate variables or variable types in the READ statements.

While READ and DATA statements are useful in learning how to program, they are not used very frequently in business programming. With business computing, data values usually come from data files or from users "conversing" with an information system.

RESTORE

Another programming command, the **RESTORE** statement, is often used with the READ/DATA pair of statements. The RESTORE statement serves a single

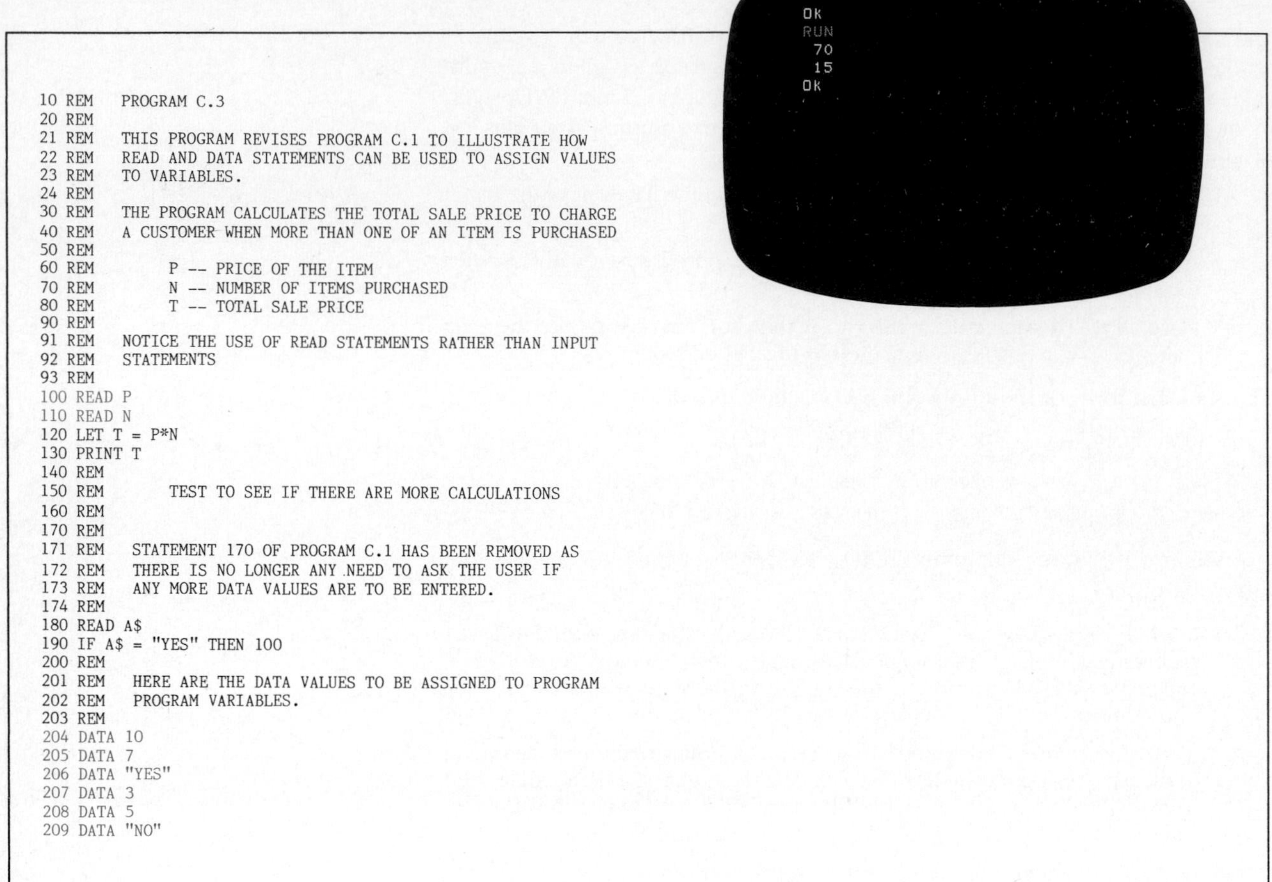

```
OK
RUN
 70
 15
OK
```

```
10 REM    PROGRAM C.3
20 REM
21 REM    THIS PROGRAM REVISES PROGRAM C.1 TO ILLUSTRATE HOW
22 REM    READ AND DATA STATEMENTS CAN BE USED TO ASSIGN VALUES
23 REM    TO VARIABLES.
24 REM
30 REM    THE PROGRAM CALCULATES THE TOTAL SALE PRICE TO CHARGE
40 REM    A CUSTOMER WHEN MORE THAN ONE OF AN ITEM IS PURCHASED
50 REM
60 REM         P -- PRICE OF THE ITEM
70 REM         N -- NUMBER OF ITEMS PURCHASED
80 REM         T -- TOTAL SALE PRICE
90 REM
91 REM    NOTICE THE USE OF READ STATEMENTS RATHER THAN INPUT
92 REM    STATEMENTS
93 REM
100 READ P
110 READ N
120 LET T = P*N
130 PRINT T
140 REM
150 REM        TEST TO SEE IF THERE ARE MORE CALCULATIONS
160 REM
170 REM
171 REM   STATEMENT 170 OF PROGRAM C.1 HAS BEEN REMOVED AS
172 REM   THERE IS NO LONGER ANY NEED TO ASK THE USER IF
173 REM   ANY MORE DATA VALUES ARE TO BE ENTERED.
174 REM
180 READ A$
190 IF A$ = "YES" THEN 100
200 REM
201 REM   HERE ARE THE DATA VALUES TO BE ASSIGNED TO PROGRAM
202 REM   PROGRAM VARIABLES.
203 REM
204 DATA 10
205 DATA 7
206 DATA "YES"
207 DATA 3
208 DATA 5
209 DATA "NO"
```

purpose. Whenever it is executed, the "data list pointer" moves back up to the top of the data list being kept in primary memory. In other words, the list of data values is "restored" to its initial state. This is useful when the same data values are to be assigned to a set of variables at multiple times during program execution. The RESTORE statement takes the following form:

450	RESTORE
line number	keyword

Summary

Variables can be given data values in two ways without having to enter the data from the keyboard or from a diskette.

Using the *LET* statement, data values can be assigned directly to variables. Here the value of an expression given on the righthand side of an "=" is placed into the storage location referred to by a variable name given to the left of the "=."

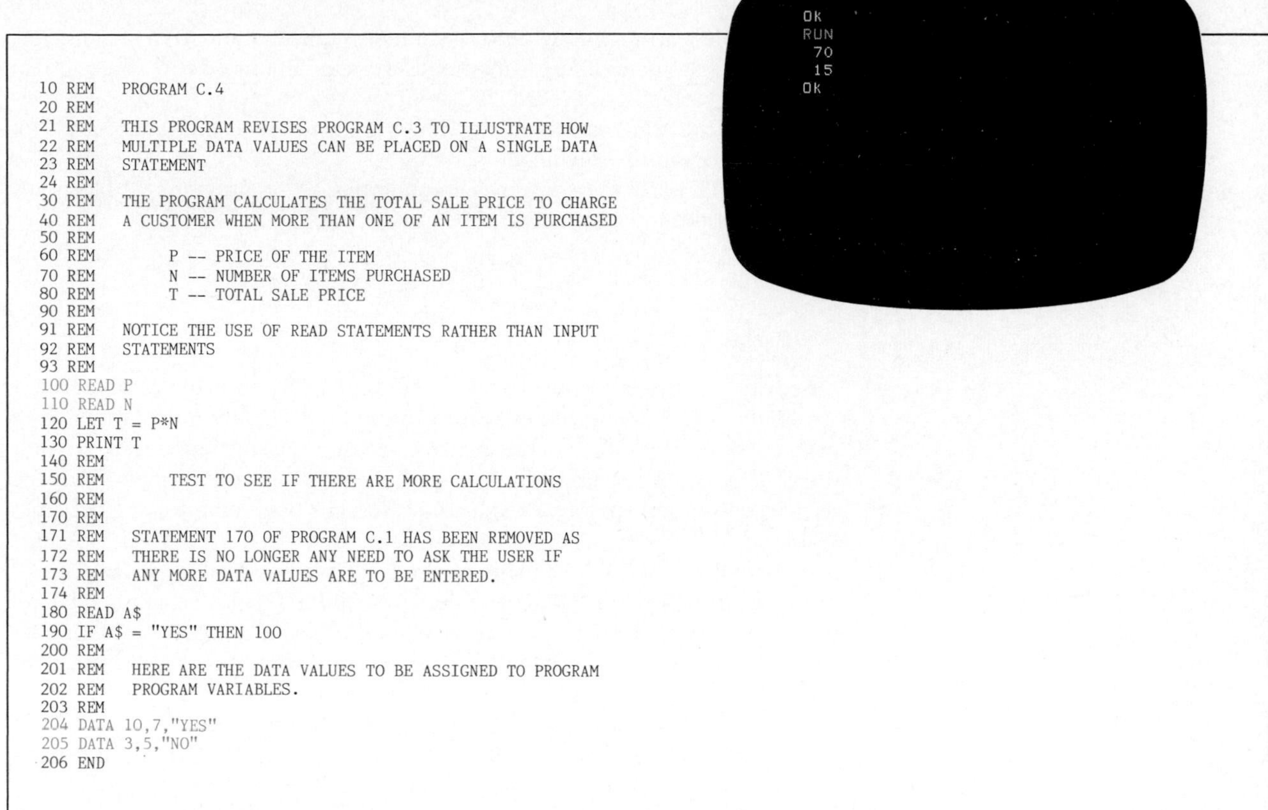


```
10 REM    PROGRAM C.4
20 REM
21 REM    THIS PROGRAM REVISES PROGRAM C.3 TO ILLUSTRATE HOW
22 REM    MULTIPLE DATA VALUES CAN BE PLACED ON A SINGLE DATA
23 REM    STATEMENT
24 REM
30 REM    THE PROGRAM CALCULATES THE TOTAL SALE PRICE TO CHARGE
40 REM    A CUSTOMER WHEN MORE THAN ONE OF AN ITEM IS PURCHASED
50 REM
60 REM         P -- PRICE OF THE ITEM
70 REM         N -- NUMBER OF ITEMS PURCHASED
80 REM         T -- TOTAL SALE PRICE
90 REM
91 REM    NOTICE THE USE OF READ STATEMENTS RATHER THAN INPUT
92 REM    STATEMENTS
93 REM
100 READ P
110 READ N
120 LET T = P*N
130 PRINT T
140 REM
150 REM        TEST TO SEE IF THERE ARE MORE CALCULATIONS
160 REM
170 REM
171 REM   STATEMENT 170 OF PROGRAM C.1 HAS BEEN REMOVED AS
172 REM   THERE IS NO LONGER ANY NEED TO ASK THE USER IF
173 REM   ANY MORE DATA VALUES ARE TO BE ENTERED.
174 REM
180 READ A$
190 IF A$ = "YES" THEN 100
200 REM
201 REM   HERE ARE THE DATA VALUES TO BE ASSIGNED TO PROGRAM
202 REM   PROGRAM VARIABLES.
203 REM
204 DATA 10,7,"YES"
205 DATA 3,5,"NO"
206 END
```

Using the *READ* and *DATA* statements, data values can be assigned to variables from a list of values kept with a program. The READ statement is located in a program where a variable is to be assigned a specific value. The data value to be assigned to this variable is placed in a DATA statement, which can be located anywhere in a program. Just prior to a program's execution, all the data values contained in DATA statements are placed in a single data list in primary memory. As READ statements are executed, values are taken one at a time from this data list.

The *RESTORE* statement is often used with the READ/DATA pair of statements. Whenever it is executed, the list of data values in primary memory is restored to its initial state.

INPUT AND OUTPUT STATEMENTS

Since BASIC is designed mainly as an interactive programming language, the **keyboard** is the primary device for entering data and the **CRT screen** is the primary device for displaying information. Correspondingly, the **INPUT** statement is used to enter data from the keyboard and the **PRINT** statement is used to display information on the CRT screen.

INPUT

Many people learning BASIC tend to confuse the INPUT and READ statements. The INPUT statement differs from the READ statement in that the values being assigned to variables in the INPUT statement are entered as a program is executed. With the READ statement, the values are entered via the DATA statement before a program is executed.

The INPUT statement given as line number 100 in Program C.1 illustrates the form of the input statement:

100	INPUT	P
line number	keyword	variable name

A **prompt character** is displayed on the user's CRT screen when an INPUT statement is executed to notify (prompt) the user to enter a data value. With most versions of BASIC, a question mark serves as this prompt character. After the prompt character has been displayed, the program stops and waits for the user to enter a data value. Once a data value has been entered, the program continues.

More than one variable name can be listed with one INPUT statement. For example, in Program C.5 line numbers 100 and 110 from Program C.1 have been combined to form a new line number 100. Notice that the values for both P and N, separated by a comma, are entered in response to the prompt character.

If fewer data values are entered than are given with an INPUT statement, the program will prompt the user for more variables. The nature of this prompt

```
10 REM   PROGRAM C.5
20 REM
21 REM   THIS PROGRAM ILLUSTRATES THAT TWO VARIABLES CAN BE
22 REM   LISTED ON A SINGLE INPUT STATEMENT
23 REM
30 REM   THIS PROGRAM CALCULATES THE TOTAL SALE PRICE TO CHARGE
40 REM   A CUSTOMER WHEN MORE THAN ONE OF AN ITEM IS PURCHASED
50 REM
60 REM        P -- PRICE OF THE ITEM
70 REM        N -- NUMBER OF ITEMS PURCHASED
80 REM        T -- TOTAL SALE PRICE
90 REM
91 REM   NOTICE HOW LINE NUMBERS 100 AND 110 FROM PROGRAM C.1
92 REM   HAVE BEEN COMBINED HERE.
93 REM
100 INPUT P,N
120 LET T = P*N
130 PRINT T
140 REM
150 REM        TEST TO SEE IF THERE ARE MORE CALCULATIONS
160 REM
170 PRINT "ANY MORE";
180 INPUT A$
190 IF A$ = "YES" THEN 100
200 END
```

```
Ok
RUN
? 10,7
 70
ANY MORE? YES
? 3,5
 15
ANY MORE? NO
Ok
```

varies for the different versions of BASIC. If more data values are entered than are given with the INPUT statement, the extra values are ignored.

When more than one variable is listed with an INPUT statement, data values must be entered in the same order that the variables were listed in the INPUT statement. Otherwise, the variables will be assigned the wrong values. For this reason, it is generally recommended that only one variable be listed with an INPUT statement. Another piece of good advice is to precede an INPUT statement with a PRINT statement that gives the name of the variable to be entered. This step will be illustrated after the PRINT statement has been introduced.

PRINT

The PRINT statement is used to display information on the CRT screen. The simplest forms of the PRINT statement are:

30	PRINT
line number	keyword

40	PRINT	"ANY MORE"
line number	keyword	string constant

50	PRINT	T
line number	keyword	variable name

60	PRINT	"ANSWER IS"	;	T
line number	keyword	string variable	semicolon	variable name

PRINT by itself, shown as line number 30 above, merely displays a **blank line** on the CRT screen. This simple indicator can help make program output more readable. PRINT with a string constant, shown as line number 40 above, displays a message to the user. PRINT with a variable name, shown as line number 50, displays the value of a variable. PRINT with a string constant and a variable name, shown as line number 60, displays the value of a variable preceded by a heading for the variable.

Program C.6 illustrates how even these elementary PRINT statements can make a program much easier to use. Notice that the PRINT statements given as line numbers 140 and 160 end with a semicolon. When this symbol ends a PRINT statement that immediately precedes an INPUT statement, the question mark is displayed *along with* the message. If the semicolon is left off, the question mark will appear just *under* the message. The semicolon in line number 190, however, serves a slightly different purpose. Here, the semicolon makes the heading and the variable's value appear next to each other on the CRT screen. How this works will be explained below.

The PRINT statement is highly flexible. Essentially, any list of constants, variables, or expressions—or any combinations of these—can be placed to the right of the PRINT keyword. Program C.7 illustrates some slightly more com-

```
OK
RUN

ENTER THE PRICE? 10
ENTER THE NUMBER PURCHASED? 7

THE TOTAL SALE PRICE IS $ 70
ANY MORE? YES

ENTER THE PRICE? 3
ENTER THE NUMBER PURCHASED? 5

THE TOTAL SALE PRICE IS $ 15
ANY MORE? NO
OK
```

```
10 REM   PROGRAM C.6
20 REM
30 REM   THIS PROGRAM ILLUSTRATES HOW A FEW SIMPLE PRINT
40 REM   STATEMENTS CAN MAKE A PROGRAM EASIER TO USE
50 REM
60 REM   THE PROGRAM CALCULATES THE TOTAL SALE PRICE TO CHARGE
70 REM   A CUSTOMER WHEN MORE THAN ONE OF AN ITEM IS PURCHASED
80 REM
90 REM         P -- PRICE OF THE ITEM
100 REM        N -- NUMBER OF ITEMS PURCHASED
110 REM        T -- TOTAL SALE PRICE
120 REM
130 PRINT
140 PRINT "ENTER THE PRICE";
150 INPUT P
160 PRINT "ENTER THE NUMBER PURCHASED";
170 INPUT N
180 LET T = P*N
185 PRINT
190 PRINT "THE TOTAL SALE PRICE IS $"; T
200 REM
210 REM       TEST TO SEE IF THERE ARE MORE CALCULATIONS
220 REM
230 PRINT "ANY MORE";
240 INPUT A$
250 IF A$ = "YES" THEN 130
260 END
```

```
OK
RUN
PRICE         NUMBER        TOTAL SALE

 10            7             70
 3             5             15
OK
```

```
10 REM   PROGRAM C.7
20 REM
30 REM   THIS PROGRAM ILLUSTRATES SOME SLIGHTLY MORE
40 REM   STATEMENTS CAN MAKE A PROGRAM EASIER TO USE
50 REM
60 REM   THE PROGRAM CALCULATES THE TOTAL SALE PRICE TO CHARGE
70 REM   A CUSTOMER WHEN MORE THAN ONE OF AN ITEM IS PURCHASED
80 REM
90 REM         P -- PRICE OF THE ITEM
100 REM        N -- NUMBER OF ITEMS PURCHASED
120 REM
130 REM   LINE NUMBER 150 SETS UP SOME COLUMN HEADINGS
140 REM
150 PRINT "PRICE", "NUMBER", "TOTAL SALE"
160 PRINT
170 READ P,N
180 PRINT P, N, P*N
190 REM
200 REM       TEST TO SEE IF THERE ARE MORE CALCULATIONS
210 REM
220 READ A$
230 IF A$ = "YES" THEN 170
240 DATA 10,7,"YES"
250 DATA 3,5,"NO"
260 END
```

plex PRINT statements. Specifically, line number 150 uses three string constants to display column headings, and line number 180 uses two variable names and an arithmetical expression to display three columns of values. Since the product *P*∗*N* was used in the PRINT statement, the program no longer requires the variable *T*. This was done for illustrative purposes only! It is not a good programming practice.

Program C.7 also demonstrates a number of other interesting features:

1. By entering data with READ/DATA statements, no INPUT prompts are displayed to distort the appearance of the output table. Using READ/DATA statements in this manner is similar to entering data values from data files.
2. Notice that the decimal points in the column headings are not centered over the data values. Most versions of BASIC provide a **PRINT USING** statement to produce neater columns of displayed values. Since the form of this statement varies greatly with different versions of BASIC, it is not discussed in this appendix.
3. Notice that the three columns all start in a specific column on the CRT screen. Each of these columns represents a **print zone.** All versions of BASIC divide the CRT screen into a number of print zones. The number of these zones and the length of each one vary from one BASIC version to another. Data values are indented one character within a print zone to leave space for a minus sign.

It is possible to "skip" across a print zone without displaying something in the zone. To do this, just place an extra comma in the PRINT statement's list of items to display. Program C.8 slightly revises Program C.6 to demonstrate the advantages of this step (see line number 145).

```
OK
RUN
                                TOTAL
PRICE          NUMBER           SALE
 10             7                70
 3              5                15
OK
```

```
10 REM    PROGRAM C.8
20 REM
30 REM    THIS PROGRAM ILLUSTRATES HOW TO SKIP OVER A
40 REM    PRINT ZONE
50 REM
60 REM    THE PROGRAM CALCULATES THE TOTAL SALE PRICE TO CHARGE
70 REM    A CUSTOMER WHEN MORE THAN ONE OF AN ITEM IS PURCHASED
80 REM
90 REM          P -- PRICE OF THE ITEM
100 REM         N -- NUMBER OF ITEMS PURCHASED
120 REM
130 REM   LINE NUMBERS 145 AND 150 SET UP SOME COLUMN HEADINGS
140 REM
145 PRINT ,,"TOTAL"
150 PRINT "PRICE", "NUMBER", "SALE"
160 PRINT
170 READ P,N
180 PRINT P, N, P*N
190 REM
200 REM         TEST TO SEE IF THERE ARE MORE CALCULATIONS
210 REM
220 READ A$
230 IF A$ = "YES" THEN 170
240 DATA 10,7,"YES"
250 DATA 3,5,"NO"
260 END
```

It is often desirable to "override" these print zones. One way to do so is to use the PRINT USING statement. Two other ways are to do the following:

1. Use semicolons rather than commas to separate the list of items to be displayed on the CRT screen.
2. Use the TAB function.

When a **semicolon** is used instead of a comma, the item to the right of the semicolon is displayed immediately after the item to the left of the semicolon. As was mentioned earlier, this is useful with prompts and with headings that precede a value being displayed.

The **TAB function** is used to "force" a value to be displayed starting in a particular column of the CRT screen. The basic form of the TAB function is as follows:

20	PRINT	TAB (20)	T
line number	keyword	function call	variable name

Functions will be described in more detail later in this appendix. Stated simply, a **function** is a predefined processing operation of general use. To use a function, you simply give its name. Most functions have arguments—or data values they use—that are enclosed in a set of parentheses right after the function name. Depending on the version of BASIC you are using, the TAB function's argument gives either the column in which the value is to be displayed or the number of columns to skip prior to displaying the value. In Microsoft BASIC, the argument represents the column in which printing of the value is to begin. Be sure you know which approach is followed by the BASIC version you are using. This argument can be a numeric constant, a numeric variable, or an arithmetical expression. Program C.9 uses the TAB function to make the columns displayed in our program more presentable.

Producing Printed Output

Much business programming requires **hard copy** output as well as CRT screen displays. Like many other BASIC programming commands, producing printed output is handled quite differently in various versions of BASIC. In most versions, however, the process is easy—you simply substitute the programming command that sends information to the printer for the PRINT command. With Microsoft BASIC, this is the **LPRINT** command.

Summary

Since BASIC is primarily an interactive programming language, the *keyboard* is the primary device for entering data and the *CRT screen* is the primary device for displaying information. Correspondingly, the *INPUT* statement is used to enter data from the keyboard and the *PRINT* statement is used to display information on the CRT screen.

With the INPUT statement, the values being assigned to variables are entered as a program executes. A *prompt character* is displayed on the CRT screen to "prompt" the user to enter a data value. The program stops until a data value has been entered, and then continues.

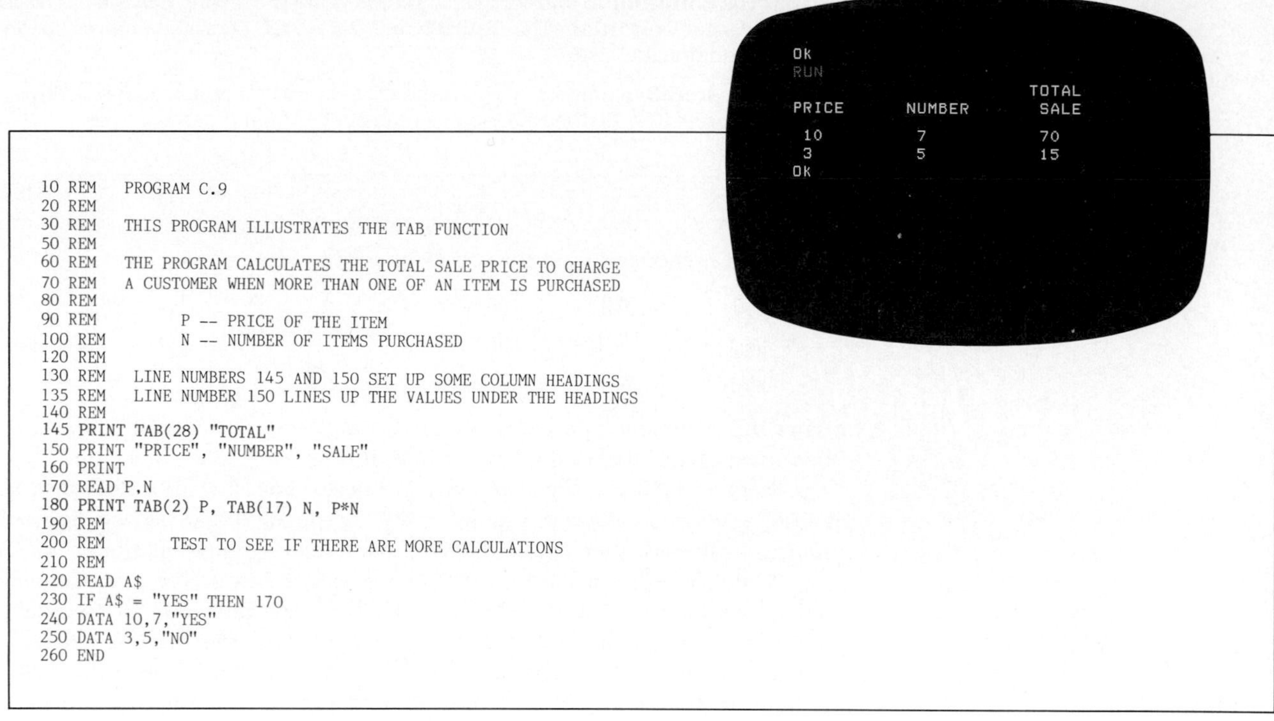

Ok
RUN
TOTAL
PRICE NUMBER SALE
10 7 70
3 5 15
Ok


```
10 REM    PROGRAM C.9
20 REM
30 REM    THIS PROGRAM ILLUSTRATES THE TAB FUNCTION
50 REM
60 REM    THE PROGRAM CALCULATES THE TOTAL SALE PRICE TO CHARGE
70 REM    A CUSTOMER WHEN MORE THAN ONE OF AN ITEM IS PURCHASED
80 REM
90 REM          P -- PRICE OF THE ITEM
100 REM         N -- NUMBER OF ITEMS PURCHASED
120 REM
130 REM    LINE NUMBERS 145 AND 150 SET UP SOME COLUMN HEADINGS
135 REM    LINE NUMBER 150 LINES UP THE VALUES UNDER THE HEADINGS
140 REM
145 PRINT TAB(28) "TOTAL"
150 PRINT "PRICE", "NUMBER", "SALE"
160 PRINT
170 READ P,N
180 PRINT TAB(2) P, TAB(17) N, P*N
190 REM
200 REM         TEST TO SEE IF THERE ARE MORE CALCULATIONS
210 REM
220 READ A$
230 IF A$ = "YES" THEN 170
240 DATA 10,7,"YES"
250 DATA 3,5,"NO"
260 END
```

The PRINT statement is a very flexible statement with which constants, variables, or expressions—or any combination of these—can be displayed on the CRT screen. A special form of the PRINT statement, the *PRINT USING* statement, can be used to tailor the appearance of information being displayed.

All versions of BASIC divide the CRT screen into a number of *print zones*. These print zones define where displayed information will be printed unless they are overridden. Three ways of overriding these print zones are to use the PRINT USING statement, to use *semicolons* rather than commas in separating the list of items to be displayed, and to use the *TAB function*.

Most business programming requires *hard copy* output as well as CRT screen displays. In most versions of BASIC, it is easy to produce printed output—simply substitute the programming command that sends information to the printer for the PRINT command. With Microsoft BASIC, this is the *LPRINT* command.

CONTROL STATEMENTS

BASIC programs normally follow a **sequential** processing flow. In other words, the next statement to be executed is the one with the next highest line number. **Control statements** change this sequential processing pattern by transferring the processing flow to another line number.

Three types of processing flow transfers can be executed via control statements:

1. The **unconditional** transfer, which immediately redirects the processing flow. The **GOTO** statement produces an unconditional transfer.

2. The **conditional** transfer, which redirects the processing flow on the basis of some **condition.** The **IF/THEN** and **ON . . . GOTO** statements produce a conditional transfer.

3. The **iterative** transfer, which redirects the processing flow in a repetitious manner. The **FOR/NEXT** statement produces an interative transfer.

GOTO

The GOTO statement takes the following form:

255	GOTO	130
line number	keyword	line number

When this statement is executed, the processing flow transfers to the line number given to the *right* of the keyword GOTO.

Program C.10 is a slight modification of Program C.6 that illustrates the GOTO statement. When line number 255 is executed, the processing flow returns to line number 130 so that two more values can be entered.

While the purpose of the GOTO statement is easy to grasp, a program written with too many GOTO statements can be extremely difficult to understand. If you find yourself "bouncing" all around a program because you have overused your GOTO statements, it might be best to stop programming and rethink your program design. You might find a more straightforward version. Program code that twists in many directions is termed **spaghetti code.**

```
10 REM    PROGRAM C.10
20 REM
30 REM    THIS PROGRAM MODIFIES PROGRAM C.6 TO ILLUSTRATE
40 REM    THE GO TO STATEMENT
50 REM
60 REM    THE PROGRAM CALCULATES THE TOTAL SALE PRICE TO CHARGE
70 REM    A CUSTOMER WHEN MORE THAN ONE OF AN ITEM IS PURCHASED
80 REM
90 REM          P -- PRICE OF THE ITEM
100 REM         N -- NUMBER OF ITEMS PURCHASED
110 REM         T -- TOTAL SALE PRICE
120 REM
130 PRINT
140 PRINT "ENTER THE PRICE";
150 INPUT P
160 PRINT "ENTER THE NUMBER PURCHASED";
170 INPUT N
180 LET T = P*N
185 PRINT
190 PRINT "THE TOTAL SALE PRICE IS $"; T
200 REM
210 REM        TEST TO SEE IF THERE ARE MORE CALCULATIONS
220 REM
230 PRINT "ANY MORE";
240 INPUT A$
250 IF A$ = "NO" THEN 260
255 GOTO 130
260 END
```

```
OK
RUN

ENTER THE PRICE? 10
ENTER THE NUMBER PURCHASED? 7

THE TOTAL SALE PRICE IS $ 70
ANY MORE? YES

ENTER THE PRICE? 3
ENTER THE NUMBER PURCHASED? 5

THE TOTAL SALE PRICE IS $ 15
ANY MORE? NO
OK
```

IF/THEN

The IF/THEN statement is the simplest of the two conditional transfer statements. With the IF/THEN statement, the pattern of the processing flow is determined by the value of a condition represented by a relational expression.

This statement takes the following form:

250	IF	A$ = "NO"	THEN	260
line number	keyword	condition	keyword	line number

Two rules govern the processing flow when this statement is executed:

1. If the value of the relational expression is "TRUE," the processing flow transfers to the line number given to the *right* of the keyword THEN.
2. If the value of the relational expression is "FALSE," the processing flow continues sequentially with the statement that immediately follows the IF/THEN statement.

The condition can be either a simple or a complex relational expression.

The example of the IF/THEN statement given above comes from Program C.10. Line number 250 evaluates the relational expression " A$ = "NO" " in determining if more data need to be processed. If A$ has a value of "YES," the condition is "FALSE" and the GOTO statement in line number 255 is executed, transferring the processing flow so that two more values can be entered. When A$ has a value of "NO," the condition is "TRUE," and the processing flow transfers to line number 260. The program then terminates.

ON . . . GOTO

The second conditional transfer statement is the ON . . . GOTO statement. Here, the value of an arithmetical expression serves as a condition that directs the processing flow to one of a series of possible program locations. The standard form of this programming statement is:

230	ON	D + 1	GOTO	260,	280,	300
line number	keyword	arithmetical expression	keyword	line number	line number	line number

If the value of "D + 1" equals "1," the processing flow transfers to the first line number in the list after the GOTO keyword. If the value of "D + 1" equals "2," the processing flow transfers to the second line number after the GOTO keyword. If the value of "D + 1" equals "3," the processing flow transfers to the third line number after the GOTO keyword, and so on.

The possible values of the arithmetical expression should match the number of line numbers contained in the list given to the *right* of the keyword GOTO. If the value is less than "1" or greater than the number of line numbers, the program may not work as you expect. Check the version of BASIC you are using to find out what will happen in these situations.

Program C.11 illustrates the ON . . . GOTO statement. This modification of Program C.9 allows an item's sale price to be discounted. This requires that a discount code be input along with an item's price and the number sold. The variable holding the entered discount code, *D,* is then used in the arithmetical expression directing the transfer of the processing flow (see line number 230).

```
OK
RUN
                                    TOTAL
PRICE           NUMBER              SALE

 10              7                   67.9
 3               5                   15
OK
```

```
10 REM   PROGRAM C.11
20 REM
30 REM   THIS PROGRAM ILLUSTRATES THE ON ... GOTO STATEMENT
40 REM
50 REM   THE PROGRAM CALCULATES THE TOTAL SALE PRICE TO CHARGE
60 REM   A CUSTOMER WHEN MORE THAN ONE OF AN ITEM IS PURCHASED
70 REM
80 REM   ALSO, A DISCOUNT CODE HAS BEEN ADDED THAT INDICATES
90 REM   WHETHER, AND HOW MUCH, THE SALE IS DISCOUNTED
100 REM
110 REM         P -- PRICE OF THE ITEM
120 REM         N -- NUMBER OF ITEMS PURCHASED
130 REM         D -- DISCOUNT CODE
140 REM
150 REM                 0 - NO DISCOUNT
160 REM                 1 - 3% DISCOUNT
170 REM                 2 - 5% DISCOUNT
180 REM
190 PRINT TAB(29) "TOTAL"
200 PRINT "PRICE", "NUMBER", "SALE"
210 PRINT
220 READ P,N,D
230 ON D+1 GOTO 260,280,300
240 PRINT "ERROR IN DISCOUNT FACTOR"
250 GOTO 390
260 LET T = P*N
270 GOTO 310
280 LET T = P*N - .03*P*N
290 GOTO 310
300 LET T = P*N - .03*P*N
310 PRINT TAB(2) P, TAB(17) N, T
320 REM
330 REM       TEST TO SEE IF THERE ARE MORE CALCULATIONS
340 REM
350 READ A$
360 IF A$ = "YES" THEN 220
370 DATA 10,7,1,"YES"
380 DATA 3,5,0,"NO"
390 END
```

After the discounted sale price has been calculated, the processing flow transfers to line number 310 to display the sale price. Notice that DATA statements 370 and 380 each contain a new value—the discount code.

FOR/NEXT

The FOR/NEXT statement provides an easy way to set up an iteration, or a **loop,** in a program's processing flow. Prior to illustrating this programming statement, this concept of a program loop will be described in more depth.

Program C.12 is a modification of program C.6, and demonstrates more clearly that a loop has been set up. This loop is located from line number 150 to line number 320. Each pass through this loop results in a new set of values being entered and processed. Program C.12 adds a **loop index,** given as variable *I,* which keeps track of how many sets of values have been processed.

Program C.13 modifies Program C.12 by using a FOR/NEXT pair of statements to define both the loop and the loop index. Here, line number 140 sets up the loop, initializes the loop index to a value of "1," and defines "2" to be the stopping value for the loop index. Line number 260 denotes the end of the loop. Notice that since the FOR/NEXT pair "controls" the processing flow through the loop, the program no longer asks the user if "ANY MORE" data values are to be entered.

```
OK
RUN

SET # 1

ENTER THE PRICE? 10
ENTER THE NUMBER PURCHASED? 7

THE TOTAL SALE PRICE IS $ 70
ANY MORE? YES

SET # 2

ENTER THE PRICE? 3
ENTER THE NUMBER PURCHASED? 5

THE TOTAL SALE PRICE IS $ 15
ANY MORE? NO
OK
```

```
10 REM    PROGRAM C.12
20 REM
30 REM    THIS PROGRAM MODIFIES PROGRAM C.6 TO ILLUSTRATE
40 REM    HOW A LOOP CAN BE SET UP IN A PROGRAM
50 REM
60 REM    THE PROGRAM CALCULATES THE TOTAL SALE PRICE TO CHARGE
70 REM    A CUSTOMER WHEN MORE THAN ONE OF AN ITEM IS PURCHASED
80 REM
90 REM          P -- PRICE OF THE ITEM
100 REM         N -- NUMBER OF ITEMS PURCHASED
110 REM         T -- TOTAL SALE PRICE
120 REM         I -- THE LOOP INDEX
130 REM
140 LET I = 0
150 LET I = I + 1
160 PRINT
170 PRINT
180 PRINT "SET #";I
190 PRINT
200 PRINT "ENTER THE PRICE";
210 INPUT P
220 PRINT "ENTER THE NUMBER PURCHASED";
230 INPUT N
240 LET T = P*N
250 PRINT
260 PRINT "THE TOTAL SALE PRICE IS $"; T
270 REM
280 REM        TEST TO SEE IF THERE ARE MORE CALCULATIONS
290 REM
300 PRINT "ANY MORE";
310 INPUT A$
320 IF A$ = "YES" THEN 150
330 END
```

```
OK
RUN

SET # 1

ENTER THE PRICE? 10
ENTER THE NUMBER PURCHASED? 7

THE TOTAL SALE PRICE IS $ 70

SET # 2

ENTER THE PRICE? 3
ENTER THE NUMBER PURCHASED? 5

THE TOTAL SALE PRICE IS $ 15
OK
```

```
10 REM    PROGRAM C.13
20 REM
30 REM    THIS PROGRAM MODIFIES PROGRAM C.12 TO ILLUSTRATE
40 REM    THE FOR/NEXT STATEMENT
50 REM
60 REM    THE PROGRAM CALCULATES THE TOTAL SALE PRICE TO CHARGE
70 REM    A CUSTOMER WHEN MORE THAN ONE OF AN ITEM IS PURCHASED
80 REM
90 REM          P -- PRICE OF THE ITEM
100 REM         N -- NUMBER OF ITEMS PURCHASED
110 REM         T -- TOTAL SALE PRICE
120 REM         I -- THE LOOP INDEX
130 REM
140 FOR I = 1 TO 2
160 PRINT
170 PRINT
180 PRINT "SET #";I
190 PRINT
200 PRINT "ENTER THE PRICE";
210 INPUT P
220 PRINT "ENTER THE NUMBER PURCHASED";
230 INPUT N
240 LET T = P*N
250 PRINT
260 PRINT "THE TOTAL SALE PRICE IS $"; T
300 NEXT I
330 END
```

The simplest form of these two statements is as follows:

140	FOR	I	=	1	TO	2
line number	keyword	loop index	equal sign	index starting value	keyword	index stopping value

300	NEXT	I
line number	keyword	loop index

A small set of rules govern the processing that occurs within this simple form of the FOR/NEXT loop:

1. The programming statements to be included within the loop must be "sandwiched" between FOR and NEXT statements having the same loop index.
2. While the loop index must be a numeric variable, the **starting** and **stopping** values for the loop index can be numeric constants, numeric variables, or arithmetical expressions.
3. The loop index is **incremented** by one with each pass through the loop. As soon as the loop index becomes greater than the stopping value for the index, the processing flow transfers to the programming statement that follows the NEXT statement.

The flexibility of the starting and stopping values of the loop index is very useful. For example, it is easy to give a user the capability to control the number of passes made though a loop. To do this, use a variable for the stopping value of the loop index and have the user enter the value for this variable.

```
OK
RUN
HOW MANY SETS OF VALUES DO YOU
WISH TO PROCESS? 2

SET # 1

ENTER THE PRICE? 10
ENTER THE NUMBER PURCHASED? 7

THE TOTAL SALE PRICE IS $ 70

SET # 2

ENTER THE PRICE? 3
ENTER THE NUMBER PURCHASED? 5

THE TOTAL SALE PRICE IS $ 15
OK
```

```
10 REM    PROGRAM C.14
20 REM
30 REM    THIS PROGRAM MODIFIES PROGRAM C.13 TO ILLUSTRATE
40 REM    HOW TO SET A STOPPING VALUE FOR THE LOOP INDEX
50 REM
60 REM    THE PROGRAM CALCULATES THE TOTAL SALE PRICE TO CHARGE
70 REM    A CUSTOMER WHEN MORE THAN ONE OF AN ITEM IS PURCHASED
80 REM
90 REM          P -- PRICE OF THE ITEM
100 REM         N -- NUMBER OF ITEMS PURCHASED
110 REM         T -- TOTAL SALE PRICE
120 REM         I -- THE LOOP INDEX
130 REM         S -- LOOP INDEX STOPPING VALUE
140 REM
150 PRINT "HOW MANY SETS OF VALUES TO YOU WISH TO PROCESS";
160 INPUT S
170 FOR I = 1 TO S
180 PRINT
190 PRINT
200 PRINT "SET #";I
210 PRINT
220 PRINT "ENTER THE PRICE";
230 INPUT P
240 PRINT "ENTER THE NUMBER PURCHASED";
250 INPUT N
260 LET T = P*N
270 PRINT
280 PRINT "THE TOTAL SALE PRICE IS $"; T
290 NEXT I
300 END
```

Note: The actual line length of some of your computer output may differ from the corresponding screen exhibits in this appendix.

FOR Statement	Successive Loop Index Values
FOR I = 1 TO 10:	I = 1,2,3,4,5,6,7,8,9,10
FOR I = 1 TO 10 STEP 3	I = 1,4,7,10
FOR I = 1 TO 10 STEP 4	I = 1,5,9
FOR I = 4 TO 15 STEP 2	I = 4,6,8,10,12,14
FOR I = 10 TO 2 STEP −1	I = 10,9,8,7,6,5,4,3,2

Example C.6

These FOR statements illustrate how different STEP increments change the values assigned to a loop index.

Program C.14 modifies Program C.13 to provide the user with this capability. Here, the variable S is used as the loop index stopping value, and the user is asked to enter the value for S in line number 150.

A more complex form of the FOR statement also exists:

```
220 FOR I = 1 TO 10          STEP          3
                                         index
                                       increment
[<--same as above--->]     keyword        value
```

Rather than having the loop index increment by one, it can be incremented by any value. As with index starting and stopping values, the increment value can be given as a constant, a variable, or as an arithmetical expression. Example C.6 illustrates how different loop index increments can cause the values assigned to the loop index to vary.

Finally, a FOR/NEXT loop can be **nested** inside another FOR/NEXT loop. When this occurs, the inside loop is fully processed with each iteration through the outside loop. Two nested loops are illustrated in Example C.7. The values assigned to these two sets of loop indexes indicate exactly how the processing flow moves through a set of nested loops. When FOR/NEXT loops are nested, the two loops cannot "straddle" one another. Rather, the inside loop must be fully within the outside loop. This is shown in Exhibit C.9.

Example C.7

Nested FOR/NEXT statements allow a programmer to put one loop inside another loop. These two examples illustrate how the loop indexes change their values as a program's processing flow goes through a nested loop.

Nested Loop #1	Nested Loop #2
10 FOR I = 1 TO 3	10 FOR M = 2 TO 4
20 FOR J = 1 TO 4	20 FOR K = 1 TO 2
.	.
.	.
.	.
100 NEXT J	100 NEXT K
110 NEXT I	110 NEXT M

Index Values (Nested Loop #1)

I	J
1	
	1
	2
	3
	4
2	
	1
	2
	3
	4
3	
	1
	2
	3
	4

Index Values (Nested Loop #2)

M	K
2	
	1
	2
3	
	1
	2
4	
	1
	2

Summary

BASIC programs normally follow a *sequential* processing flow. *Control statements* redirect this sequential processing pattern.

Three types of processing flow transfers are executed via control statements. The first is the *unconditional* transfer, which immediately redirects the processing flow. The *GOTO* statement produces an unconditional transfer. Second is the *conditional* transfer, which redirects the processing flow on the basis of some *condition*. The *IF/THEN* and *ON . . . GOTO* statements produce a conditional transfer. Third is the *iterative* transfer, which redirects the processing flow in a repetitious manner. The *FOR/NEXT* statement produces an iterative transfer.

With the GOTO statement, the processing flow transfers directly to the line number given to the *right* of the keyword GOTO. Programs with too many GOTO statements, which cause the processing flow to "bounce" around a program, are termed *spaghetti code*.

With the IF/THEN statement, a relational expression serves as a condition that determines the direction of the processing flow. If the value of the relational expression is "TRUE," the processing flow transfers to the line number

Exhibit C.9

Correct and incorrect vested FOR/NEXT loops

A correct FOR/NEXT loop:

```
10 FOR I = 1 TO 3          ┐
20 FOR J = 1 TO 4    ┐     │
   .                 │     │
   .                 ├ J-loop  ├ I-loop
   .                 │     │
100 NEXT J           ┘     │
110 NEXT I                 ┘
```

An incorrect FOR/NEXT loop:

```
10 FOR I = 1 TO 3                ┐
   .                             │
   .                             │
   .                             │
20 FOR J = 1 TO 4    ┐           ├ I-loop
   .                 │           │
   .                 │           │
100 NEXT I           ├ J-loop    ┘
   .                 │
   .                 │
   .                 │
140 NEXT J           ┘
```

given to the *right* of the keyword THEN. If the value of the relational expression is "FALSE," the processing flow continues sequentially.

With the ON . . . GOTO statement, an arithmetical expression serves as a condition that determines the direction of the processing flow. The possible values of the arithmetical expression should match the number of line numbers contained in a list given to the *right* of the keyword GOTO. The processing flow is redirected to the line number whose position in the list is equal to the value of the arithmetical expression.

With the FOR/NEXT statement, a *loop* is set up that causes the processing flow to cycle through a particular set of programming statements. The number of passes through this loop is determined by the starting, stopping, and increment values assigned to the *loop index.* These values can be defined through constants, variables, and arithmetical expressions. Also, one FOR/NEXT loop can be *nested* inside another FOR/NEXT loop.

WORKING WITH ARRAYS

Our earlier discussion of the DIM statement described how arrays are declared so they can be used in a BASIC program. In this section, we introduce the way in which array elements are referenced and used.

Arrays represent a set of primary memory storage locations named as a unit. Each of the storage locations referenced by an array name is an **element** of that array. It is these elements, and not the entire array, that are operated on with BASIC programming operations.

Program C.15 modifies the earlier program that allowed a discounted sale price. Rather than use the ON . . . GOTO statement to direct the processing flow to apply the correct discount amount, Program C.15 holds the discount amounts in an array named *A.* Line number 220 declares this array to be a one-dimensional array with three elements. Each of these array elements will hold a discount amount.

```
OK
RUN
ENTER DISCOUNT AMOUNT
FOR A CODE OF  1 ? 0
ENTER DISCOUNT AMOUNT
FOR A CODE OF  2 ? .03
ENTER DISCOUNT AMOUNT
FOR A CODE OF  3 ? .05
                               TOTAL
PRICE           NUMBER         SALE

  10               7            67.9
  3                5            15
OK
```

```
10 REM    PROGRAM C.15
20 REM
30 REM    THIS PROGRAM ILLUSTRATES THE USE OF A
40 REM    ONE-DIMENSIONAL ARRAY
50 REM
60 REM    THE PROGRAM CALCULATES THE TOTAL SALE PRICE TO CHARGE
70 REM    A CUSTOMER WHEN MORE THAN ONE OF AN ITEM IS PURCHASED
80 REM
90 REM    ALSO, A DISCOUNT CODE HAS BEEN ADDED THAT INDICATES
100 REM   HOW MUCH THE SALE IS DISCOUNTED.  THE DISCOUNT AMOUNT
110 REM   IS ENTERED INTO AN ARRAY NAMED A.  THE DISCOUNT CODE
120 REM   NOW INDICATES WHICH ELEMENT OF ARRAY A IS USED TO
130 REM   GET THE CORRECT DISCOUNT AMOUNT.
140 REM
150 REM           P -- PRICE OF THE ITEM
160 REM           N -- NUMBER OF ITEMS PURCHASED
170 REM           T -- TOTAL SALE PRICE
180 REM           A -- ARRAY HOLDING DISCOUNT AMOUNTS
190 REM           D -- DISCOUNT CODES (1,2,3) ASSIGNED
200 REM                BY THE USER
210 REM
220 DIM A(3)
230 FOR I = 1 TO 3
240 PRINT "ENTER DISCOUNT AMOUNT FOR A CODE OF ";I;
250 INPUT A(I)
260 NEXT I
270 PRINT
280 PRINT
290 PRINT TAB(29) "TOTAL"
300 PRINT "PRICE", "NUMBER", "SALE"
310 PRINT
320 READ P,N,D
330 LET T = P*N - A(D)*P*N
340 PRINT TAB(2) P, TAB(17) N, T
350 REM
360 REM        TEST TO SEE IF THERE ARE MORE CALCULATIONS
370 REM
380 READ A$
390 IF A$ = "YES" THEN 320
400 DATA 10,7,2,"YES"
410 DATA 3,5,1,"NO"
420 END
```

Array elements are referenced by the use of array **subscripts.** With a one-dimensional array, a single subscript is used. With a two-dimensional array, two subscripts are used; the first subscript indicates the array's row and the second subscript the array's column. Subscripts, which are enclosed within a set of parentheses immediately following the array name, can be given as constants, variables, or arithmetical expressions.

Exhibit C.10 pictures two arrays, *A* and *C,* that will be used to describe how array subscripting works. Array *A* is one-dimensional with 20 elements. Array *C* is two-dimensional with six rows and seven columns or 42 elements. The following examples indicâte how subscripts "point" to array elements (assume variable *I* has a value of 3):

A(4) — The fourth element in array *A*. Its value is 24.

A(12) — The twelfth element in array *A*. Its value is 13.5.

A(*I*+4) — The seventh element in array *A*. Its value is 18.

C(1,3) — The element in the first row, third column of array *C*. Its value is 15.

Exhibit C.10

Arrays used in describing how array subscripting works

Array A:

Array C:

		15				
					92	
			−25.3			
	75.3				−.03	

C(5,2) The element in the fifth row, second column of array *C*. Its value is 75.3.

C(4,4) The element in the fourth row, fourth column of array *C*. Its value is −25.3.

C(*I*,6) The element in the third row, sixth column of array *C*. Its value is 92.

Let's get back to Program C.15 to see how an array was used to hold the discount amounts. The FOR/NEXT loop in line numbers 230 to 260 prompts the user to enter the discount amount to be used with the three discount codes (1,2,3). The discount amount to be used with a discount code of "1" is put in the first element of array *A*, or *A*(1). The discount amount to be used with a discount code of "2" is put in the second element of array *A*, or *A*(2). The discount amount to be used with a discount code of "3" is put in the third element of array *A*, or *A*(3). The discount code, *D*, is entered as before (see line number 320). However, notice in line number 330 how variable *D* now serves as a subscript of array *A* in "pointing" to the appropriate element of the array. The calculations for the first set of data (see line number 400) are given in Example C.8.

Two-dimensional arrays are handled in a similar manner. Program C.16 is a simple program that makes use of a two-dimensional array. Here, the mileage between three cities is entered into array *D* from DATA statements. The DIM statement in line number 140 indicates that array *D* has three rows and three columns. The FOR/NEXT loop in line numbers 190 to 210 enters the mileage data into array *D* one row at a time. Exhibit C.11 pictures array *D* after the mileage data have been entered. When a user gives the codes for two cities, the program displays the mileage between these two cities. Notice how the mileage is "pulled" from primary memory in line number 300. Variable *J*, a code for one city, serves as a row subscript for array *D*. Variable *K*, a code for another city, serves as a column subscript for array *D*.

Example C.8

Calculating the discounted sales price for the first set of data processed in Program C.15

```
T = P∗N − A(D)∗P∗N
T = P∗N − A(2)∗P∗N
T = P∗N −  .03∗P∗N
T = 10∗7 −  .03∗10∗7
T =   70 −  2.1
T =   67.9
```

Summary

Arrays represent a set of primary memory storage locations named as a unit. Each of the storage locations referenced by an array name is an *element* of that array.

Array elements are referenced by the use of array *subscripts*. With a one-dimensional array, a single subscript is used. With a two-dimensional array, two subscripts are used; the first subscript indicates the array's row and the second subscript the array's column. Subscripts, which are enclosed within a set of parentheses immediately following the array name, can be given as constants, variables, or arithmetical expressions.

FILE HANDLING

In business programming, data items are regularly stored on secondary storage devices, such as disks, diskettes, and tapes, and then retrieved from these devices to be operated on in a program. Most often, data are **organized** into data files in secondary storage. Thus, the handling of data files is an important aspect of business programming.

```
10 REM   PROGRAM C.16
20 REM
30 REM   THIS PROGRAM ILLUSTRATES HOW TWO-DIMENSIONAL
40 REM   ARRAYS ARE USED.
50 REM
60 REM   THE PROGRAM LETS A PERSON FIND OUT THE DISTANCE
70 REM   BETWEEN THREE CITIES IN NORTH CAROLINA
70 REM
80 REM   USE THE FOLLOWING CODES FOR THE THREE CITIES:
90 REM
100 REM      1 - RALEIGH
110 REM      2 - CHAPEL HILL
120 REM      3 - DURHAM
130 REM
140 DIM D(3,3)
150 REM
160 REM  THIS FOR/NEXT LOOP OBTAINS THE MILEAGE AMOUNTS
170 REM  FROM THE DATA STATEMENTS
180 REM
190 FOR I = 1 TO 3
200 READ D(I,1), D(I,2), D(I,3)
210 NEXT I
220 PRINT "USE THE FOLLOWING CODES FOR CITIES:"
230 PRINT
240 PRINT "     1 - RALEIGH"
250 PRINT "     2 - CHAPEL HILL"
260 PRINT "     3 - DURHAM"
270 PRINT
280 PRINT "ENTER A CITY CODE ";
285 INPUT J
288 PRINT "ENTER A CITY CODE ";
289 INPUT K
290 PRINT
300 PRINT "THE DISTANCE IS "; D(J,K)
301 DATA 0,25,18
302 DATA 25,0,8
303 DATA 18,8,0
310 END
```

Ok
RUN
USE THE FOLLOWING CODES FOR CITIES:
1 - RALEIGH
2 - CHAPEL HILL
3 - DURHAM
ENTER A CITY CODE ? 3
ENTER A CITY CODE ? 2
THE DISTANCE IS 8
Ok

Exhibit C.11

The mileage array D for Program C.16

0	25	18
25	0	8
18	8	0

The manner in which different versions of BASIC handle data files is the least standardized aspect of BASIC. For this reason, this section will not be too detailed. The programming statements described are those for Microsoft BASIC. File handling programming statements for other versions of BASIC are likely to be quite different from these.

Several methods of organizing data files are described in Chapter 8: "File and Data Base Management." The discussion in this section, however, is limited to how **sequential** data files are processed in BASIC.

Five basic programming operations are involved in processing sequential data files:

open a file	Ready the file so it can be used in a program.
close a file	Release a file that had been opened earlier in a program.
read a record	Enter items from a data file into a program.
write a record	Store items onto a data file from a program.
end-of-file test	Determine if the end of the file has been reached when handling a data file from a program.

Open

Microsoft BASIC has three **OPEN** statements for opening a data file. The form of these statements is as follows:

230	OPEN	"B:INVENT.DAT"	FOR INPUT AS	#1
230	OPEN	"B:INVENT.DAT"	FOR OUTPUT AS	#1
230	OPEN	"B:INVENT.DAT"	FOR APPEND AS	#1
line number	keyword	file name	keyword phrase	device number

Notice that the keyword phrases are different: FOR INPUT AS #, FOR OUTPUT AS #, FOR APPEND AS #. The keyword phrase FOR INPUT AS # is used when opening an existing data file containing items to be entered into a program. The keyword phrase FOR OUTPUT AS # is used when opening a new data file on which items are to be stored. The keyword phrase FOR APPEND AS # is used when opening an existing data file to which items are to be added. A data file must be opened via an OPEN statement before the file is used in a program. This procedure is illustrated in Program C.17.

The **file name** with the OPEN statement serves as a **logical** link to data files stored, or to be stored, in secondary storage. Thus, these file names must follow the standard procedure for naming data files on the microcomputer being used.

The **device number** with the OPEN statement serves as a **physical** link to a particular secondary storage device. As Microsoft BASIC does not allow more than three data files to be used at one time, only device numbers "1," "2," and "3" can be used. The data file used with Program C.17, which is named "B:INVENT.DAT," is pictured as Exhibit C.12.

Exhibit C.12

This is a view of the inventory data file used in Program C.17.

Item ID Number	Item Price
100	3.50
101	15.00
102	6.95
103	.25
104	1.25
105	10.00
109	4.50
110	2.34
114	29.50
115	75.00
116	2.99
120	.75
121	1.25
125	6.50
126	13.80
127	1.43
128	8.35
129	9.25
130	.85

Close

The form of the **CLOSE** statement, used in closing a data file, is:

390	CLOSE	#1
line number	keyword	device number

More than one data file can be closed with a single CLOSE statement. Just list the device numbers, separated by commas, to the **right** of the keyword CLOSE. All data files should be closed before a program terminates.

In Program C.17, the OPEN and CLOSE statements are both inside the program's major processing loop (line number 230 to line number 440). This "repositions" the data file "B:INVENT.DAT" so that the INPUT # statement in line 290 will always begin by reading the first record in the data file. As a result, a user can enter item ID numbers in any order.

```
RUN
ENTER ITEM ID NUMBER ? 105
ENTER QUANTITY SOLD ? 20
TOTAL SALE PRICE IS $ 200
ANY MORE? YES
ENTER ITEM ID NUMBER ? 113
ENTER QUANTITY SOLD? 10
*** ERROR: NO MATCH FOR ITEM  113  **
ANY MORE? YES
ENTER ITEM ID NUMBER ? 114
ENTER QUANTITY SOLD ? 10
TOTAL SALE PRICE IS $ 295
ANY MORE? NO
Ok
```

```
10 REM   PROGRAM C.17
20 REM
30 REM   THIS PROGRAM ILLUSTRATES HOW DATA FILES STORED ON
40 REM   A DISKETTE ARE PROCESSED
50 REM
60 REM   THE PROGRAM ACCESSES AN "INVENTORY" DATA FILE WHOSE
70 REM   RECORDS HAVE TWO FIELDS:
80 REM
90 REM           I1 -- ITEM NUMBER
100 REM           P -- ITEM PRICE
110 REM
120 REM  A USER IS ASKED TO ENTER AN ITEM'S ID NUMBER AND
130 REM  THE QUANITITY SOLD.  THE PROGRAM READS THE CORRECT
140 REM  PRICE FOR THE ENTERED ITEM AND DISPLAYS THE TOTAL
150 REM  SALE PRICE.
160 REM
170 REM          I -- ENTERED ITEM ID NUMBER
180 REM          N -- NUMBER SOLD
190 REM          T -- TOTAL SALE PRICE
200 REM
210 REM  READY A DATA FILE FOR USE
220 REM
230 OPEN "B:INVENT.DAT" FOR INPUT AS #1
240 PRINT
250 PRINT "ENTER ITEM ID NUMBER ";
260 INPUT I
270 PRINT "ENTER QUANTITY SOLD ";
280 INPUT N
290 INPUT #1, I1, P
300 REM
310 REM  A TEST TO DETERMINE IF THE END OF THE DATA
320 REM  FILE WAS REACHED WITHOUT FINDING A MATCH
330 REM
340 IF EOF(1) THEN 480
350 IF I<>I1 THEN 290
360 LET T = P*N
370 PRINT
380 PRINT "TOTAL SALE PRICE IS $";T
390 CLOSE #1
400 PRINT
410 PRINT "ANY MORE";
420 INPUT A$
430 IF A$ = "YES" THEN 230
440 GOTO 510
450 REM
460 REM  ERROR MESSAGE IF NO MATCH IS FOUND
470 REM
480 PRINT
490 PRINT "*** ERROR: NO MATCH FOR ITEM ";I;" **"
500 GOTO 390
510 END
```

Changes for APPLESOFT BASIC:

```
230 REM CNT COUNTS THE DATA RECORDS IN THE INVENTORY FILE
231 CNT=1
232 PRINT "ENTER THE NUMBER OF DATA RECORDS IN THE INVENTORY FILE";
233 INPUT LIMIT
234 D$=CHR$(4)
235 PRINT D$,"OPEN INVENT.DAT,D2"
236 PRINT D$;"READ INVENT.DAT"

290 INPUT I1,P
291 CNT=CNT+1

340 IF LIMIT=CNT THEN 480

390 PRINT D$;"CLOSE INVENT.DAT"
```

Input # and Write

The programming statements for reading and writing data records are similar to the READ and PRINT statements:

line number	keyword	device number	list of variable names
290	INPUT	#1,	I1, P
690	WRITE	#2,	A,B,C

The **INPUT #** statement reads items from a data record into a program's variables. The **WRITE #** statement stores items in a data record from a program's variables.

EOF Function

When processing sequential files, it is possible to read through all the records in a file and reach the end of the file. Unless the process is handled in an appropriate manner, it will result in an **end-of-file error.** Thus, most versions of BASIC provide a means to detect and indicate when the end of a data file has been reached. In Microsoft BASIC, the following statement accomplishes this function:

340	IF	EOF	(1)	THEN	480
line number	keyword	end-of-file function	device number	keyword	line number

The **EOF** function has a value of "TRUE" only when the end of a data file has been reached. Otherwise, it has a value of "FALSE." When the end of a data file is reached, the processing flow moves to the line number given to the *right* of the keyword THEN. Often, as with Program C.17, an error message is displayed when an end-of-file error is detected. Line numbers 480 and 490 display this error message.

Summary

Business programming regularly requires the retrieval of stored data from secondary storage devices. Most often, such data are *organized* into data files.

Many of the data files used in business programming are organized *sequentially*. Five basic programming operations are used in processing sequential data files: *opening* a file, *closing* a file, *reading* a record, *writing* a record, and *end-of-file testing*.

The *OPEN* statement is used to ready a data file so that it can be used. A data file must be opened before the file is used in a program. Both a *file name,* which serves as a *logical* link to a particular data file, and a *device number,* which serves as a *physical* link to a particular secondary storage device, are given in the OPEN statement.

The *CLOSE* statement is used to release a file that had previously been opened. All data files should be closed before a program terminates.

The *INPUT #* statement is used to read items from a data record into a program's variables. The *WRITE #* statement is used to store items in a data record from a program's variables.

When processing sequential files, it is possible to read through all the records in a file and reach the end of the file. When this happens, an end-of-file error will occur unless the process is handled in an appropriate manner. The *EOF* function, which is used within an IF/THEN statement, provides a means of handling these end-of-file situations.

FUNCTIONS AND SUBROUTINES

Functions and *subroutines* serve two main purposes for programmers:

1. They provide a relatively easy way for programmers to use sets of programming statements that have already been written. This use can occur within one program or across many programs.
2. They make programs more understandable by clearly identifying programming statements that perform some particular task.

Programmers making good use of functions and subroutines can reduce the time and effort it takes to develop a program.

Functions

Functions assign a name to a specific data processing operation. Where the name is used in a program, the programming instructions required to perform the operation are physically inserted into the program at the time it is executed. Thus, functions can be thought of as a form of programming "shorthand."

Functions are used in the following way:

120	LET	R	=	SQR	(V)
line number	keyword	variable name	equal sign	function name	function argument

The programming statement from Program C.18 uses the SQR function in a LET statement to assign variable *R* the square root of variable *V*. Calculating a number's square root is a rather difficult programming task; however, many problems require the use of square roots. All versions of BASIC provide a function to calculate the square roots of numbers.

```
10 REM   PROGRAM C.18
20 REM
30 REM   THIS PROGRAM ILLUSTRATES THE USE OF A FUNCTION
40 REM
50 REM   THE PROGRAM SERVES AS A "CALCULATOR" TO
60 REM   CALCULATE SQUARE ROOTS FOR A USER
70 REM
80 PRINT
90 PRINT "ENTER THE VALUE FOR WHICH YOU WISH TO
100 PRINT "CALCULATE A SQUARE ROOT";
110 INPUT V
120 LET R = SQR(V)
130 PRINT
140 PRINT "THE SQUARE ROOT OF ";V;" IS ";R
150 PRINT
160 PRINT "ANY MORE";
170 INPUT A$
180 IF A$ = "YES" THEN 80
190 END
```

```
OK
RUN
ENTER THE VALUE FOR WHICH YOU WISH TO
CALCULATE A SQUARE ROOT? 457
THE SQUARE ROOT OF  457  IS  21.37756
ANY MORE? YES
ENTER THE VALUE FOR WHICH YOU WISH TO
CALCULATE A SQUARE ROOT? 45.7
THE SQUARE ROOT OF  45.7  IS  6.760178
ANY MORE? NO
OK
```

Exhibit C.13

Standard Predefined Functions

FUNCTION	DESCRIPTION		
TRIGONOMETRIC:	all require a single argument, which gives the desired angle in radians.		
SIN(x)	returns the sine of an angle		
COS(x)	returns the cosine of an angle		
TAN(x)	returns the tangent of an angle		
ATN(x)	returns the arc tangent of an angle		
EXPONENTIATION:			
LOG(x)	returns the natural logorithm of a number		
EXP(x)	raises the mathematical number 'e' to a power given by the argument x		
SQR(x)	returns the square root of a number		
MATHEMATICAL:			
INT(x)	returns the integer portion of a number		
	Examples:	expression	value
		INT (4.5)	4
		INT (23)	23
		INT (−3.6)	−4
SGN(x)	returns a '1' if the argument is positive, a '0' if the argument is zero, and a '−1' if the argument is negative		
ABS(x)	returns the absolute value of a number		
	Examples:	expression	value
		ABS (45.6)	45.6
RND	returns a random number between 0.0 and 1.0 (Note: While all versions of BASIC have a RND function, the form of the function varies.)		
STRING:	all these functions operate on strings rather than numbers		
LEN(s)	returns the length, i.e., the number of characters, of a string		
	Examples:	expression	value
		LEN("ABCDEF")	6
LEFT$(s,n)	returns the "n" leftmost characters in a string		
	Examples:	expression	value
		LEFT$("ABCDEF", 3)	"ABC"
RIGHT$(s,n)	returns the "n" rightmost characters in a string		
	Examples:	expression	value
		RIGHT$("ABCDEF", 3)	"DEF"
MID$(s,n,m)	starting with the "nth" character in a string, return the next "m" characters		
	Examples:	expression	value
		MID$("ABCDEF", 2, 3)	"BCD"
ASCII(s)	returns the ASCII code for the first character of a string		
	Examples:	expression	value
		ASCII ("T")	84
		ASCII ("$")	36
CHR$(e)	returns the string representation for the ASCII code given by the expression "e"		
	Examples:	expression	value
		CHR$(90)	"Z"
		CHR$(43)	"+"
VAL(s)	returns the numeric equivalent of a string		
	Examples:	expression	value
		VAL ("23.4")	23.4
STR$(e)	returns the string representation of the number given by the expression "e"		
	Examples:	expression	value
		STR$(5.78)	"5.78"

Notice that the function name is immediately followed by a set of parentheses. Enclosed in the parentheses is this function's argument. **Arguments** are values on which the programming statements represented by the function name operate. There can be zero, one, or many arguments to a function. These arguments can be constants, variables, or expressions. Also, notice that a function is used in a manner similar to any constant, variable, or arithmetical expression. A function can even be used as an argument for another function.

There are two categories of functions: **Predefined** functions and **user-defined** functions.

Predefined Functions.

Predefined functions, like the SQR function, are "built into" BASIC. This means they are available for use in any BASIC program being written. The number and type of *predefined* functions do vary across the different versions of BASIC. Most versions of BASIC, however, provide the functions given in Exhibit C.13.

User-defined Functions.

User-defined functions are defined by a programmer for use within a particular program. To use the function in a program, it must be defined with the **DEF** statement. As many user-defined functions as desired can be defined and employed within a program.

The programming statement used in defining a user-defined function takes the following form:

110	DEF	FNR	(X)	=	INT (X + .5)
line number	keyword	function name	function argument	equal sign	expression

The function name must begin with the letters "FN" and be followed by a single alphabetic character. With Microsoft BASIC only a single argument, which is used in the expression to the *right* of the equal sign, can be used. Some versions of BASIC, however, relax a few of these rules.

Program C.19 illustrates how user-defined functions are defined and employed. The program uses the following rule for "rounding" a number:

1. Round down if the fractional part of thc number is less than .5.
2. Round up if the fractional part of the number is at least .5.

This rule can be programmed quite easily by adding .5 to the number to be rounded and taking the integer portion of the result. Example C.9 illustrates this calculation. In Program C.19, line number 110 defines the function and line number 160 makes use of the function. Notice that the function defined in line number 110 makes use of the predefined INT function.

Example C.9

Example calculations for the rounding rule followed in Program C.19.

Value	Calculation	Integer Portion of Result
2.0	2.0 + .5 = 2.5	2
2.4	2.4 + .5 = 2.9	2
2.5	2.5 + .5 = 3.0	3
2.6	2.6 + .5 = 3.1	3
2.99	2.99 + .5 = 3.49	3

Subroutines

Subroutines are sets of programming statements that perform specific processing operations within a program. Often, a long or complex program can be made much more readable if its main processing parts are clearly distinguished by defining each as a separate subroutine. However, the programmer must document the processing flow carefully. An undocumented program with many subroutines can be extremely difficult to follow.

```
10 REM    PROGRAM C.19
20 REM
30 REM    THIS PROGRAM ILLUSTRATES A USER-DEFINED FUNCTION
40 REM
50 REM    THE PROGRAM ROUNDS-OFF A NUMBER FOR A USER
60 REM
70 REM
80 REM    THE FOLLOWING STATEMENT DEFINES THE
90 REM    USER-DEFINED FUNCTION
100 REM
110 DEF  FNR(X) = INT(X + .5)
120 PRINT
130 PRINT "ENTER A VALUE YOU WISH TO ROUND-OFF";
140 INPUT V
150 PRINT
160 LET R = FNR(V)
170 PRINT "THE ROUNDED-OFF VALUE OF ";V;" IS ";R
180 PRINT
190 PRINT "ANY MORE";
200 INPUT A$
210 IF A$ = "YES" THEN 120
220 END
```

Changes for APPLESOFT BASIC:

```
110 FN R(X) = INT(X + .5)

160 LET R = FN R(V)
```

```
Ok
RUN
ENTER A VALUE YOU WISH TO ROUND-OFF? 0.34
THE ROUNDED-OFF VALUE OF  .34  IS  0
ANY MORE? YES
ENTER A VALUE YOU WISH TO ROUND-OFF? 12.75
THE ROUNDED-OFF VALUE OF  12.75  IS  13
ANY MORE? YES
ENTER A VALUE YOU WISH TO ROUND-OFF? -5.79
THE ROUNDED-OFF VALUE OF -5.79  IS  -6
ANY MORE? NO
Ok
```

Two programming statements are used in defining and using subroutines: the *GOSUB* and *RETURN* statements.

GOSUB. The **GOSUB** statement directs a program's processing flow to the line number given to the *right* of the keyword GOSUB. It is at this line number that the subroutine's programming statements should begin. Thus, a GOSUB statement *calls* for the execution of a particular subroutine. The form of this statement is as follows:

390	GOSUB	590
line number	keyword	line number

For example, line number 390 in Program C.20 directs the processing flow to a subroutine used to enter a set of data. This subroutine begins at line number 590. Notice how REM statements are used to document both the GOSUB statement and the beginning of the subroutine.

RETURN. The role a **RETURN** statement plays for subroutines is similar to one an END statement plays for an entire program. First, it is used to signal the end of the set of programming statements making up a subroutine. However, more than one RETURN statement can exist in a given subroutine, as shown in Program C.20. Second, and more importantly, when a RETURN statement is executed, the program's processing flow is directed to the programming statement immediately following the GOSUB statement that first called for the subroutine's execution. The form of the RETURN statement is:

690	RETURN
line number	keyword

```
RUN
ENTER ITEM ID NUMBER? 105
ENTER QUANTITY SOLD? 20

ANY MORE? YES

ENTER ITEM ID NUMBER? 113
** ERROR: NO ITEM ID OF  113  **

ANY MORE? YES

ENTER ITEM ID NUMBER? 114
ENTER QUANTITY SOLD? 10
ANY MORE? NO
                TOTAL
        ITEM    PRICE

         105    $ 200
         114    $ 295
```

```
10 REM   PROGRAM C.20
20 REM
30 REM   THIS PROGRAM MODIFIES PROGRAM C.17 TO ILLUSTRATE
40 REM   HOW SUBROUTINES ARE USED
50 REM
60 REM   THE PROGRAM ACCESSES AN "INVENTORY" DATA FILE WHOSE
70 REM   RECORDS HAVE TWO FIELDS:
80 REM
90 REM           I1 -- ITEM NUMBER
100 REM           P -- ITEM PRICE
110 REM
120 REM  A USER IS ASKED TO ENTER AN ITEM'S ID NUMBER AND
130 REM  THE QUANITITY SOLD.  THESE ENTERED VALUES ARE PLACED
140 REM  IN ARRAYS SO THAT THEY ALL BE PROCESSED AT ONE
150 REM  TIME.  THE PROGRAM THEN RETRIEVES THE CORRECT
160 REM  PRICE FOR EACH ENTERED ITEM, CALCULATES THE TOTAL
170 REM  SALE PRICE, AND STORES THIS TOTAL IN AN ARRAY.
180 REM
190 REM          I -- ARRAY HOLDING ENTERED ITEM ID NUMBERS
200 REM          N -- ARRAY HOLDING NUMBER SOLD
210 REM          T -- ARRAY HOLDING TOTAL SALE PRICE
220 REM          K -- AN INDICATOR KEEPING TRACK OF THE
230 REM               NUMBER OF ITEMS THAT HAVE BEEN
240 REM               ENTERED
250 REM
260 REM
270 REM  AFTER THE ENTERED DATA HAVE BEEN PROCESSED, THE
280 REM  RESULTS ARE DISPLAYED IN A TABLE.
290 REM
300 REM  DECLARE ARRAYS I,N, AND T TO HOLD UP TO 20 ITEMS
310 REM
320 DIM I(20), N(20), T(20)
330 REM
340 REM
350 LET K = 0
360 REM
370 REM  ENTER A SET OF DATA
380 REM
390 GOSUB 590
395 PRINT
400 PRINT "ANY MORE";
410 INPUT A$
415 PRINT
420 IF A$ = "YES" THEN 390
430 REM
440 REM  PROCESS THE ENTERED DATA ITEMS
450 REM
460 GOSUB 770
470 REM
480 REM  DISPLAY PROCESSED DATA
490 REM
500 GOSUB 880
510 REM
520 REM TERMINATE PROGRAM
530 REM
540 GOTO 960
550 REM
560 REM
570 REM  THIS SUBROUTINE PROMPTS A USER IN ENTERING DATA
580 REM
590 LET K = K + 1
600 PRINT "ENTER ITEM ID NUMBER";
610 INPUT I(K)
620 OPEN "B:INVENT.DAT" FOR INPUT AS #1
630 INPUT #1, I1,P
640 IF EOF(1) THEN 700
650 IF I1 <> I(K) THEN 630
660 PRINT "ENTER QUANTITY SOLD";
670 INPUT N(K)
680 CLOSE #1
690 RETURN
```

Changes for APPLESOFT BASIC:

```
620 REM CNT COUNTS THE DATA RECORDS IN THE INVENTORY FILE
621 CNT=1
622 PRINT "ENTER THE NUMBER OF DATA RECORDS IN THE INVENTORY FILE";
623 INPUT LIMIT
624 D$=CHR$(4)
625 PRINT D$;"OPEN INVENT.DAT,D2"
626 PRINT D$;"READ INVENT.DAT"
```

(continuation of Program C.20)

```
700 PRINT "** ERROR: NO ITEM ID OF "; I(K); " ** "
710 LET K = K - 1
720 CLOSE #1
730 RETURN
740 REM
750 REM  SUBROUTINE TO PROCESS DATA
760 REM
770 FOR J = 1 TO K
780 OPEN "B:INVENT.DAT" FOR INPUT AS #1
790 INPUT #1, I1,P
800 IF I(J) <> I1 THEN 790
810 LET T(J) = N(J)*P
820 CLOSE #1
830 NEXT J
840 RETURN
850 REM
860 REM  THIS SUBROUTINE DISPLAYS RESULTS
870 REM
880 PRINT
890 PRINT TAB(14) "TOTAL"
900 PRINT TAB(7) "ITEM"; TAB(14) "PRICE"
910 PRINT
920 FOR J = 1 TO K
930 PRINT TAB(7) I(J); TAB(13) "$"; TAB(14) T(J)
940 NEXT J
950 RETURN
960 END
¶
```

```
630 INPUT I1,P
631 CNT=CNT+1

640 IF CNT=LIMIT THEN 700

680 PRINT D$;"CLOSE INVENT.DAT"

780 D$=CHR$(4)
781 PRINT D$;"OPEN INVENT.DAT,D2"
782 PRINT D$;"READ INVENT.DAT"

790 INPUT I1,P

820 PRINT D$;"CLOSE INVENT.DAT"
```

Program C.20 is a slightly longer and more complex version of Program C.17. Here, subroutines have been set up for prompting a user to enter data (line numbers 590 to 730); retrieve item prices from the data file "B:INVENT.DAT" and calculate the total price for an item (line numbers 770 to 840); and display the entered items and their total price (line numbers 890 to 950). Notice that the program's overall processing flow is given at the beginning of the program as line numbers 350 to 540. The GOTO statement given as line number 540 directs the processing flow to the END statement given as line number 960.

Summary

Subroutines are sets of programming statements that perform specific processing operations within a program. Often, a long or complex program can be made much more readable if its main processing parts are clearly distinguished by defining each one as a separate subroutine.

Two programming statements are used in defining and using subroutines: the *GOSUB* and *RETURN* statements.

The GOSUB statement directs a program's processing flow to a line number that begins a subroutine. Thus, a GOSUB statement *calls* for the execution of a particular subroutine.

The RETURN statement is used to signal the end of a subroutine and, more importantly, to direct the processing flow to the programming statement immediately following the GOSUB statement that "called" for the subroutine's execution.

REVIEW QUESTIONS

1. What is BASIC? Briefly discuss its major characteristics. What advantages are offered by a standardized language?
2. James Austin needs to place column headings in his BASIC program. What would the heading "Sales Volume" be called? How would it appear in a BASIC program?
3. What rules are used to evaluate arithmetical expressions in BASIC?
4. How are logical operations evaluated in BASIC?
5. Jan Harrison wishes to remove line 16 from her BASIC program. How can she accomplish this task?
6. Bill Yarnell wishes to place documentation in his BASIC program. What statements would he use for this purpose?
7. What is the purpose of the DIM statement in BASIC? What DIM statement would be used to define a one-dimensional array of 25 elements in your program?
8. Wendell Kirk desires to trace his program's programming flow from line 62 through line 97. How can this be accomplished?
9. What are the LET, READ, and DATA statements used for in BASIC?
10. What is the purpose of the BASIC GOTO statement? What problems can it cause?
11. What is the purpose of the BASIC FOR/NEXT statement? What rules does it follow?
12. What are the five BASIC programming operations involved with the processing of sequential data files?

APPENDIX D
Programming in BASIC

INTRODUCTION
A PROBLEM-SOLVING APPROACH TO PROGRAMMING
CALCULATING SKILLS
ANALYZING SKILLS
DEBUGGING SKILLS
SKILLS IN USING MENUS
SKILLS IN GROUPING DATA
EXERCISES

INTRODUCTION

The purpose of this appendix is to provide you with a fundamental set of programming skills, using the BASIC programming language. These programming skills, by themselves, will not make you an expert programmer. However, they should enable you to write some programs useful to you now in your college studies or later in your chosen career field.

The appendix begins by describing an approach to programming that is both **natural** and **problem oriented.** (A more thorough discussion of this approach to programming is given in Chapter 13, "Program Development.") Following the first section, a number of specific programming skills are developed. These include the following:

calculating	using the computer as an electronic calculator (Only data items entered into the computer are used in calculations.)
analyzing	creating new data items analyzing those entered into the computer
debugging	locating the errors that always crop up in writing a program
using menus	making it easier for the user to select a program's options and functions
grouping data	working with groups of data rather than individual data items

This introduction to programming in BASIC is intended to be used along with Appendix C, "The BASIC Programming Language." In this appendix, **programming** is stressed—not the details of the BASIC programming language.

A PROBLEM-SOLVING APPROACH TO PROGRAMMING

The most common mistake made by people learning to program is beginning to write, or **code,** a program before thinking through a complete solution to the problem being addressed. Here, problem solving occurs "on the fly" as coding progresses. Such an approach to programming usually produces many "false starts," "dead ends," and a seemingly constant need to rewrite and add program segments. Programs developed in this way tend to take much longer to write than the user expects and generally result in "patched-together" code that is difficult to understand.

Fortunately, there is an alternative solution. A programming problem should be approached in the same way many other problems are solved:

1. Define the problem to make sure the *right* one is being addressed.
2. Carefully assess the information available for use in solving the problem.
3. Consider alternative problem-solving approaches and then select the one that best fits the problem.
4. Check through the solution to make sure it is correct.

In the case of a programming problem, these problem-solving steps are expanded as follows:

1. **Define the problem.**
2. **Design the outputs** to be produced by a program that handles the problem.
3. **Identify the inputs** required to produce the program's outputs.
4. **Specify how these inputs are to be manipulated** in order to produce the program's outputs.
5. **Develop a logical design** of the program.
6. **Translate** this logical design into BASIC code.
7. **Test** the program.

Exhibit D.1 summarizes these steps.

Exhibit D.1
Steps in Developing a Program

1. Define the problem.
2. Design the outputs.
3. Identify the inputs.
4. Specify the data manipulations.
5. Develop a logical design.
6. Translate the design into BASIC code.
7. Test the program.

Define the Problem

Four key issues need to be raised in defining a programming problem:

1. What is the purpose of the program?
2. What are the desired outputs to be produced by the program?
3. What data items are available as inputs to the program?
4. Are any formulas or other data processing rules already known?

The more you learn about each of these issues, the better will be your initial program design. False starts, dead ends, program rewrites, and program additions most often occur because these issues are not fully explored until late in a programming project.

Design the Outputs

The objective of most business programs is to produce specific outputs. If a program's outputs are not clearly identified and described early in a programming project, it is unlikely that all required processing operations will be identified during the critical early stages of the project. All CRT displays, documents, and reports should be sketched out in detail as soon as possible.

Identify the Inputs

Given a complete set of outputs, it should be possible to identify all the data items that need to be entered into a program. If all needed input items are not defined early in a programming project, the rushed effort to "patch" the necessary code into a program often results in sloppy and awkward input procedures.

Specify the Data Manipulations

Given a complete set of both outputs and inputs, it should be possible to specify all the processing operations required to transform the program's inputs into program outputs. The aim is not to specify a detailed design, but rather to uncover all the major elements to include in a detailed design. When all required processing operations are known prior to developing the program's logical design, it is much more likely that a clear, easily understood processing flow will result.

Develop a Logical Design

We now have everything we need to solve the programming problem. The various solution parts are pieced together in a correct, straightforward manner. One of the best ways of doing this is to produce a logical design that is as close as possible to English. Most people can discover problems in program designs more quickly when the design is easy to follow and understand. The design language used here, **pseudocode,** was described in Chapter 13, "Program Development." Pseudocode uses everyday English, along with a few keywords and a style that clearly identifies logically related program segments, to express program designs.

Translate the Design into BASIC Code

Once this logical design has been completed and examined for errors, it is translated into the BASIC programming language. In this step, coding finally takes place! If your design is detailed enough, coding should be a mechanical task.

Test the Program

Both before and during program execution, the error-checking process known as **debugging** takes place. Here, errors are first detected and then corrected. It is rare that any program works correctly the first time it runs! A program should not be considered complete until correct outputs have been obtained using a broad range of values for the program's inputs.

Develop a Basic Set of Programming Skills

In this appendix, programming skills are introduced so they build on one another and, hence, can be used to solve increasingly sophisticated problems. When each new topic is presented, the programming "tools" being introduced are covered first. Business programming problems are then described and solved to illustrate how you can apply the tools.

Programming, to a large extent, is a craft. It is important to learn what tools exist and the way they work. Simply knowing the tools, however, is not the same as "learning how to program." It is how these programming tools are applied to solve particular problems that distinguishes *programming* from *coding.* Problems that at first glance seem complex may actually be quite simple when an appropriate set of tools is applied. Also, most programming problems can be solved in a variety of ways. There is *no one best way* to solve a programming problem.

Learning to program requires a lot of practice. While books on programming are helpful, perhaps the best way to become a skilled programmer is to work with skilled programmers. Observe the way they approach programming problems. Learn from the way they apply the various tools. Have them look at your programs while you are writing them and after they are completed. Ask their advice when you have problems.

Summary

This appendix first describes an approach to programming that is both *natural* and *problem oriented.* The programming skills developed include *programming tools* for *calculating, analyzing,* and *debugging* programs; *using menus* to handle program-user interactions; and *grouping data* to ease the processing of large collections of data items.

The most common mistake made by people learning to program is beginning to write, or *code,* a program before thinking through a complete solution to the problem being addressed. A programming problem should be addressed in the same way other problems are successfully solved. When approaching a programming problem, a seven-step process should be followed: *define the problem, design the outputs, identify the inputs, specify the data manipulations, develop a logical design, translate the design into BASIC code,* and *test the program.*

Programming is a craft. Simply knowing some programming tools is not the same as "learning how to program." It is how you apply programming tools to solve particular problems that distinguishes programming from coding. Problems that initially seem difficult may actually be quite simple when an appropriate set of tools is applied. Also, most programming problems can be solved in a variety of ways.

Learning how to program requires a lot of practice. Perhaps the best way to become a skilled programmer is to work with skilled programmers.

CALCULATING SKILLS

The simplest programs to write are those that perform processing tasks that could be done on a hand-held calculator. Program D.1 is a short calculating program that displays the square roots of values entered by a user. To perform this step, the program makes use of the square root function discussed in Appendix C, "The BASIC Programming Language." Most of the program's action takes place in line numbers 150 to 180. Line numbers 150 and 160 ask the user to enter a value, and line numbers 170 and 180 display the square root of the value.

Three programming tools are very useful when writing even simple calculating programs. These are:

1. A tool, usually termed a **counter,** to count the occurrences of some event.
2. A tool, usually termed an **accumulator,** to add a series of values.
3. A tool that lets a user **signal that no more calculations are to be performed.**

```
10 REM  PROGRAM D.1
20 REM
30 REM  THIS PROGRAM ACTS AS A "CALCULATOR"
40 REM
50 REM  THE PROGRAM ASKS THE USER TO ENTER A
60 REM  VALUE AND DISPLAYS THE SQUAREROOT OF
70 REM  THAT VALUE
80 REM
90 REM       V - THE ENTERED NUMBER
100 REM
110 PRINT "THIS PROGRAM DISPLAYS THE SQUAREROOT"
120 PRINT "OF THE VALUE ENTERED"
130 PRINT
140 PRINT
150 PRINT "ENTER A VALUE";
160 INPUT V
170 PRINT
180 PRINT "THE SQUAREROOT OF ";V;" IS "; SQR(V)
190 END
```

```
OK
RUN
THIS PROGRAM DISPLAYS THE SQUAREROOT
OF THE VALUE ENTERED

ENTER A VALUE? 20

THE SQUAREROOT OF  20  IS  4.472136
OK
```

Unless otherwise stated, all program listings in Appendix D have been written to accommodate both IBM Personal Computer BASIC for IBM microcomputers and APPLESOFT BASIC for Apple microcomputers.

Counter

Counters are the most common tool used in programming. Put simply, a counter is a variable that *counts* the number of times some event has occurred. That is, whenever the event occurs, a 1 is added to the counter. When the program terminates, the counter's value is the number of times the event has occurred.

Counters work in the following way:

Pseudocode	BASIC
set the counter to zero	180 LET I = 0
	.
	.
whenever the event occurs,	.
add 1 to the counter	240 LET I = I + 1

BASIC statement 180 **initializes** the counter to zero. This step is important because if the variable being used as the counter held a value other than zero, the count would be off by that amount. BASIC statement 240 adds 1 to the counter. Notice the expression to the right of the equal sign. First, a "1" is added to the current value of the variable. Then, the result of this addition is stored as the new value of the variable.

Program D.2 makes use of a counter that keeps track of the number of square root calculations that have been performed. The BASIC statements just described come from this program. Notice that line numbers 160 and 170 prompt the user to indicate how many square root calculations are to be performed. The user's response is placed in variable *N*. Variable *I*, the counter, keeps track of how many of these calculations have been performed. As long as the counter is less than *N*, more calculations need to be performed. Thus, the processing flow loops back to line number 190. When the counter equals *N*, the program terminates.

```
Ok
RUN
HOW MANY VALUES WILL BE ENTERED? 3

ENTER A VALUE? 10

THE SQUAREROOT OF  10  IS  3.162278

ENTER A VALUE? 20

THE SQUAREROOT OF  20  IS  4.472136

ENTER A VALUE? 30

THE SQUAREROOT OF  30  IS  5.477225
Ok
```

```
10 REM  PROGRAM D.2
20 REM
30 REM  THIS PROGRAM ILLUSTRATES A "COUNTER"
40 REM
50 REM  THE PROGRAM MODIFIES PROGRAM D.1 TO
60 REM  DISPLAY THE SQUAREROOTS FOR A NUMBER
70 REM  OF VALUES ENTERED BY A USER
80 REM
90 REM        V - A VALUE ENTERED BY A USER
100 REM       I - A COUNTER KEEPING TRACK OF
110 REM           THE NUMBER OF VALUES THAT
120 REM           HAVE BEEN PROCESSED
130 REM       N - THE NUMBER OF VALUES TO
140 REM           PROCESS
150 REM
160 PRINT "HOW MANY VALUES WILL BE ENTERED";
170 INPUT N
180 LET I = 0
190 PRINT
200 PRINT "ENTER A VALUE";
210 INPUT V
220 PRINT
230 PRINT "THE SQUAREROOT OF ";V;" IS "; SQR(V)
240 LET I = I + 1
250 IF I < N THEN 190
260 END
```

Accumulator

An accumulator is a more general version of a counter. Whereas counters always add a value of 1 to a variable, accumulators add any value to a variable. That is, they *accumulate* a series of values in a variable. Accumulators work in the following way:

Pseudocode	BASIC
set the accumulator to zero	220 LET A = 0
	.
	.
	.
	.
whenever another value becomes available, add the value to the accumulator	290 LET A = A + SQR(V)

As with counters, accumulators should always be initialized. BASIC statement 220 initializes variable *A*, which is to be used as an accumulator. BASIC statement 290 adds a value—in this case, the square root of variable *V*—to the current value of *A* and then stores the sum as the new value of *A*. The value being added to *A* in statement 290 could have been a constant, a variable, or any expression.

It is useful to recognize that accumulators, as well as counters, also can be used to perform a series of subtractions. In this case, the accumulator is initialized to a large starting value and the series of values are subtracted from, rather than added to, the accumulator.

Program D.3 modifies Program D.2 to illustrate an accumulator. Here, variable *A* accumulates the square roots being calculated and displayed. *A* is

```
10 REM  PROGRAM D.3
20 REM
30 REM  THIS PROGRAM ILLUSTRATES AN "ACCUMULATOR"
40 REM
50 REM  THE PROGRAM MODIFIES PROGRAM D.2 TO
60 REM  KEEP A RUNNING TOTAL OF THE SQUAREROOTS
70 REM  THAT ARE BEING DISPLAYED
80 REM
90 REM         V - A VALUE ENTERED BY A USER
100 REM        I - A COUNTER KEEPING TRACK OF
110 REM            THE NUMBER OF VALUES THAT
120 REM            HAVE BEEN PROCESSED
130 REM        N - THE NUMBER OF VALUES TO
140 REM            PROCESS
150 REM        A - AN ACCUMULATOR THAT KEEPS
160 REM            A RUNNING TOTAL OF THE
170 REM            SQUAREROOTS BEING DISPLAYED
180 REM
190 PRINT "HOW MANY VALUES WILL BE ENTERED";
200 INPUT N
210 LET I = 0
220 LET A = 0
230 PRINT
240 PRINT "ENTER A VALUE";
250 INPUT V
260 PRINT
270 PRINT "THE SQUAREROOT OF ";V;" IS "; SQR(V)
280 LET I = I + 1
290 LET A = A + SQR(V)
300 IF I < N THEN 230
310 PRINT
320 PRINT "THE SUM OF THESE SQUAREROOTS IS ";A
330 END
```

```
OK
RUN
HOW MANY VALUES WILL BE ENTERED? 2

ENTER A VALUE? 10

THE SQUAREROOT OF  10  IS  3.162278

ENTER A VALUE? 20

THE SQUAREROOT OF  20  IS  4.472136

THE SUM OF THESE SQUAREROOTS IS
7.634414
OK
```

Note: The actual line length of some of your computer output may differ from the corresponding screen exhibits in this appendix.

initialized in line number 220, and the square roots are added to *A* in line number 290. The sum of the displayed square roots is itself displayed in line number 320.

Signaling That No More Calculations Are to Be Performed

With most calculating tasks, operations on specific series of values are the major focus of the program. Thus, a user must be able to signal the program when no more values exist in a series of values. This signal is usually made in one of three ways:

1. Asking the user at the start of the program to indicate how many calculations are to be performed. Here, a counter is used to keep track of the number of calculations that have been performed. When the counter equals the value given by the user, no more calculations are to be performed.
2. Repeatedly asking the user, at the conclusion of each calculation, if another calculation is to be performed. Here, the user's **response** is used to signal the fact that no more calculations are to be performed.
3. Having the user enter a **trailer**—that is, a specific value that signals no more values will be entered; thus, no more calculations are to be performed.

Program D.2 made use of the first of these three strategies. The program prompts the user for the number of calculations to be performed in line numbers 160 and 170. This number is placed in variable *N*. Then, variable *I* is used

```
10 REM  PROGRAM D.4
20 REM
30 REM  THIS PROGRAM MODIFIES PROGRAM D.2 TO
40 REM  ILLUSTRATE HOW TO STOP A PROGRAM BY
50 REM  ASKING THE USER IF MORE PROCESSING IS
60 REM  REQUIRED
70 REM
80 REM  THE PROGRAM DISPLAYS THE SQUAREROOTS
90 REM  FOR A NUMBER OF ENTERED VALUES
100 REM
110 REM        V - A VALUE ENTERED BY A USER
120 REM       R$ - A VARIABLE HOLDING THE
130 REM            USER'S RESPONSE TO THE QUESTION
140 REM            ABOUT ANY MORE PROCESSING
150 REM
160 PRINT
170 PRINT "ENTER A VALUE";
180 INPUT V
190 PRINT
200 PRINT "THE SQUAREROOT OF ";V;" IS "; SQR(V)
210 PRINT
220 PRINT "ANY MORE VALUES";
230 INPUT R$
240 IF R$ = "YES" THEN 160
250 END
```

```
OK
RUN

ENTER A VALUE? 10

THE SQUAREROOT OF  10  IS  3.162278

ANY MORE VALUES? YES

ENTER A VALUE? 20

THE SQUAREROOT OF  20  IS  4.472136

ANY MORE VALUES? NO
OK
```

as the counter keeping track of the number of calculations that have been performed (see line number 240). Line number 250 then performs the check that determines whether or not another calculation is to be performed. As long as *I* is less than *N*, another calculation is performed.

Program D.4 modifies Program D.2 to illustrate the use of the second "stopping" strategy—repeatedly asking the user if another calculation is to be performed. Line numbers 220 and 230 ask the user to indicate if any more values are to be entered. The user's response is placed in variable *R$*. Line number 240 then determines whether or not another calculation is to be performed. If the value of *R$* is "YES," another calculation is done. If the value of *R$* is anything other than "YES," then no more calculations are performed.

Program D.5 modifies Program D.2 to illustrate the third "stopping" strategy—using a trailer. Line numbers 120 and 130 display a message to the user indicating how to stop the program. A trailer of "9999" is used as this value is unlikely to be involved in the calculation performed. Line number 170 then repetitively checks to see if this trailer value has been entered into variable *V*. When this step occurs, the processing flow is transferred to line number 210 and the program terminates.

Each of these three strategies has certain advantages and disadvantages. While repeatedly responding to a prompt asking if more calculations are to be performed is a "natural" way of controlling the program, the process can become tedious. On the other hand, this strategy does not require the user to know ahead of time how many calculations are to be performed or to remember a trailer value.

Summary

The simplest programs are those that perform processing tasks that could be done on a hand-held calculator.

```
OK
RUN
WHEN YOU WISH TO STOP, ENTER A
VALUE OF: 9999
ENTER A VALUE? 10
THE SQUAREROOT OF  10  IS  3.162278
ENTER A VALUE? 20
THE SQUAREROOT OF  20  IS  4.472136
ENTER A VALUE? 30
THE SQUAREROOT OF  30  IS  5.477225
ENTER A VALUE? 9999
OK
```

```
10 REM  PROGRAM D.5
20 REM
30 REM  THIS PROGRAM MODIFIES PROGRAM D.2 TO
40 REM  ILLUSTRATE HOW TO STOP A PROGRAM BY
50 REM  HAVING THE USER ENTER A "TRAILER"
60 REM
70 REM  THE PROGRAM DISPLAYS THE SQUAREROOTS
80 REM  FOR A NUMBER OF ENTERED VALUES
90 REM
100 REM         V - A VALUE ENTERED BY A USER
110 REM
120 PRINT "WHEN YOU WISH TO STOP, ENTER A
130 PRINT "VALUE OF: 9999"
140 PRINT
150 PRINT "ENTER A VALUE";
160 INPUT V
170 IF V = 9999 THEN 210
180 PRINT
190 PRINT "THE SQUAREROOT OF ";V;" IS "; SQR(V)
200 GOTO 140
210 END
```

Three programming tools are very useful when writing calculating programs: a *counter,* an *accumulator,* and a *means of signaling that no more calculations are to be performed.*

A counter is a variable that *counts* the number of times some event has occurred. That is, whenever the event occurs, a 1 is added to the counter.

An accumulator *accumulates* any series of values in a variable. These values can be represented as constants, variables, or expressions.

Counters and accumulators should both be *initialized,* or set to zero, before they are used.

Three strategies are commonly used to signal that no more calculations need to be performed. First, the user can be asked at the start of the program to enter the number of calculations to be performed. Second, the user can be asked repeatedly whether another calculation is to be performed. Third, the user can be required to enter a *trailer* to indicate that no more calculations are to be performed.

Sample Calculating Problems

The programming tools just introduced are extremely practical for business programming. The following two problems merely scratch the surface of the ways they can be used. Problem 1, which involves a simple calculation, illustrates the three strategies for stopping a series of calculations. Problem 2 makes heavy use of accumulators.

Problem 1: Calculating Mileage Expenses. A common business calculation is determining mileage expenses so employees can be reimbursed for offical business travel. Given a beginning mileage, an ending mileage, and a per-mile expense rate, the calculation should produce the amount of money to be returned to the employee.

As this appears to be a straightforward calculation, you might think that the problem is already clearly defined. The objective is to produce a total cost using the following formula:

total cost = rate ✱ (ending mileage − beginning mileage)

Exhibit D.2
Pseudocode Design for Problem 1

LEVEL 1:

enter data values

perform calculations

display results

LEVEL 2:

enter beginning mileage, ending mileage, and mileage rate

convert mileage rate
calculate mileage expense

display mileage expense

LEVEL 3:

enter beginning mileage, ending mileage, and mileage rate

rate = rate/100
expense = rate ✱ (ending mileage − beginning mileage)

display mileage expense

The program's output is the total cost, which is to be displayed as follows:

TOTAL MILEAGE EXPENSE IS $XXXXXXXXXX

The required input data are the two mileage figures and the mileage rate, as shown in the formula above.

Even this rather simple problem, however, needs more analysis. Does one mileage rate always apply? If not, how do you know which rate to use? Also, should the mileage rate be entered in dollars or cents? In this case, the same rate always applies and is to be entered in cents. The program then divides this rate by 100 to convert it to dollar terms.

Exhibit D.2 shows a pseudocode design for the program, which is given as Program D.6. Notice that the line numbers 100 to 130 are a one-for-one translation of Level 3 of the pseudocode design.

```
10 REM  PROGRAM D.6
20 REM
30 REM  THIS PROGRAM CALCULATES MILEAGE EXPENSES
40 REM  FOR A BUSINESS.
50 REM
60 REM       B -- BEGINING MILEAGE
70 REM       E -- ENDING MILEAGE
80 REM       R -- MILEAGE RATE (IN CENTS/MILE)
90 REM
100 INPUT B,E,R
110 LET R = R/100
120 LET C = R * (E - B)
130 PRINT "TOTAL MILEAGE EXPENSE IS $"; C
140 END
```

```
Ok
RUN
? 40234,40692,20
TOTAL MILEAGE EXPENSE IS $ 91.6
Ok
```

While Program D.6 does work, it could be improved:

1. No instructions were given to the user explaining the order in which data were to be entered. If these values were entered in any other order, the calculation would not be correct. Users should be reminded on the CRT screen of the order to input data items. And, as is discussed in Appendix C, it would be better to have the user enter one value at a time.
2. It may not be obvious to a user that an incorrect input has been entered. It is helpful to **echo** all entered items back to the user so that their values can be checked visually.
3. This program handles only one mileage calculation when it executes. The program would have to be executed multiple times if more than one calculation was to be performed. It might be better to design the program so that it could handle a number of mileage calculations.
4. Since the same mileage rate always applies, it needs only to be entered once when a series of mileage calculations are to be performed. Not only is this procedure easier for the user, it reduces the chance that an incorrect value will be entered for this rate.

The pseudocode design given in Exhibit D.3 makes use of these suggestions.

Program D.7 follows this logical design. Line numbers 110 and 120 prompt the user to enter the mileage rate. Line number 140 echos this value back to the user, and line numbers 150 to 170 are used in checking the correctness of this echoed value. Line numbers 200 to 250 and line numbers 260 to 310, respectively, prompt the user to enter a trip's beginning and ending mileage. Line numbers 360 to 390 ask the user if any more mileage calculations need to be performed. If the user responds with "YES," another set of mileage figures are processed. If the user responds with anything other than "YES," the program terminates.

While Program D.7 is more complicated than Program D.6, it is a more usable program. This does not mean that Program D.6 is inadequate. It

Exhibit D.3
Second Pseudocode Design for Problem 1

```
LEVEL 1:

  enter mileage rate
  convert mileage rate

  repeat
        enter beginning mileage
        enter ending mileage
        calculate mileage expense
        display mileage expense

        until (no more trips)

LEVEL 2:

  enter mileage rate
  check entered rate
  rate = rate/100

  repeat
        enter beginning mileage
        check beginning mileage
        enter ending mileage
        check ending mileage
        expense = rate * (ending mileage - beginning mileage)
        display mileage expense

        until (user response indicates no more trips)
```

```
OK
RUN
ENTER THE PER MILE EXPENSE IN CENTS? 20

THE CURRENT MILEAGE RATE IS  20  CENTS PER MILE
IS THIS CORRECT  (ENTER YES OR NO)? YES

ENTER BEGINNING MILEAGE? 40234
BEGINNING MILEAGE IS  40234
IS THIS CORRECT  (ENTER YES OR NO)? YES
ENTER ENDING MILEAGE? 40962
ENDING MILEAGE IS  40962
IS THIS CORRECT  (ENTER YES OR NO)? NO
ENTER ENDING MILEAGE? 40692
ENDING MILEAGE IS  40692
IS THIS CORRECT  (ENTER YES OR NO)? YES

TOTAL MILEAGE EXPENSE IS $ 91.6

DO YOU NEED TO CALCULATE MILEAGE EXPENSES
FOR ANOTHER TRIP  (ENTER YES OR NO)? NO
OK
```

```
10 REM  PROGRAM D.7
20 REM
30 REM  THIS PROGRAM MODIFIES PROGRAM D.6 TO
40 REM  MAKE IT EASIER TO USE.
50 REM
60 REM       B -- BEGINING MILEAGE
70 REM       E -- ENDING MILEAGE
80 REM       R -- MILEAGE RATE (IN CENTS/MILE)
90 REM      R$ -- USER RESPONSE
100 REM
110 PRINT "ENTER THE PER MILE EXPENSE IN CENTS";
120 INPUT R
130 PRINT
140 PRINT "THE CURRENT MILEAGE RATE IS ";R;" CENTS PER MILE"
150 PRINT "IS THIS CORRECT (ENTER YES OR NO)";
160 INPUT R$
170 IF R$ <> "YES" THEN 110
180 LET R = R/100
190 PRINT
200 PRINT "ENTER BEGINNING MILEAGE";
210 INPUT B
220 PRINT "BEGINNING MILEAGE IS "; B
230 PRINT "IS THIS CORRECT (ENTER YES OR NO)";
240 INPUT R$
250 IF R$ <> "YES" THEN 200
260 PRINT "ENTER ENDING MILEAGE";
270 INPUT E
280 PRINT "ENDING MILEAGE IS "; E
290 PRINT "IS THIS CORRECT (ENTER YES OR NO)";
300 INPUT R$
310 IF R$ <> "YES" THEN 260
320 LET C = R * (E-B)
330 PRINT
340 PRINT "TOTAL MILEAGE EXPENSE IS $";C
350 PRINT
360 PRINT "DO YOU NEED TO CALCULATE MILEAGE EXPENSES"
370 PRINT "FOR ANOTHER TRIP (ENTER YES OR NO)";
380 INPUT R$
390 IF R$ = "YES" THEN 190
400 END
```

produces correct answers when data are entered correctly. If this program is to be used only once and then discarded, the version represented by Program D.6 might be fine. However, if the program is to be used many times and, more importantly, by different people, then Program D.7 is the preferred version.

Program D.7 illustrates one of the three stopping strategies: repeatedly asking the user if another calculation is to be performed. Programs D.8 and D.9 are modifications of Program D.7 that make use of the other stopping strategies.

Program D.8 asks the user ahead of time for the number of trips for which travel expenses are to be calculated. This prompt occurs in line numbers 150 to 160. The total number of trips to be processed is stored in variable *N*. Notice that variable *I* serves as a counter keeping track of the number of trips that have been processed. Counter *I* is initialized in line number 240. A 1 is added to this counter in line number 400 after the data for each trip have been processed. Then, as long as *I* is less than *N*, line number 410 directs the program to begin processing data for another trip.

Program D.9 uses a trailer to indicate that no more calculations are to be processed. Line numbers 130 and 140 display a message that instructs the user in stopping the program: the user is to enter a "-1" (an improbable mileage

```
OK
RUN
HOW MANY TRIPS? 2
ENTER THE PER MILE EXPENSE IN CENTS? 20
THE CURRENT MILEAGE RATE IS 20 CENTS PER MILE
IS THIS CORRECT (ENTER YES OR NO)? YES

ENTER BEGINNING MILEAGE? 40234
BEGINNING MILEAGE IS 40234
IS THIS CORRECT (ENTER YES OR NO)? YES
ENTER ENDING MILEAGE? 40692
ENDING MILEAGE IS 40692
IS THIS CORRECT (ENTER YES OR NO)? YES
TOTAL MILEAGE EXPENSE IS $ 91.6

ENTER BEGINNING MILEAGE? 40792
BEGINNING MILEAGE IS 40792
IS THIS CORRECT (ENTER YES OR NO)? YES
ENTER ENDING MILEAGE? 41786
ENDING MILEAGE IS 41786
IS THIS CORRECT (ENTER YES OR NO)? YES
TOTAL MILEAGE EXPENSE IS $ 198.8
OK
```

```
10 REM  PROGRAM D.8
20 REM
30 REM  THIS PROGRAM MODIFIES PROGRAM D.7 TO
40 REM  HAVE THE USER BEGIN BY GIVING THE
50 REM  NUMBER OF TRIPS FOR WHICH CALCULATIONS
60 REM  ARE NEEDED
70 REM
80 REM       B -- BEGINING MILEAGE
90 REM       E -- ENDING MILEAGE
100 REM      R -- MILEAGE RATE (IN CENTS/MILE)
110 REM     R$ -- USER RESPONSE
120 REM      N -- NUMBER OF TRIPS
130 REM      I -- COUNTER FOR TRIPS PROCESSED
140 REM
150 PRINT "HOW MANY TRIPS";
160 INPUT N
170 PRINT "ENTER THE PER MILE EXPENSE IN CENTS";
180 INPUT R
190 PRINT "THE CURRENT MILEAGE RATE IS ";R;" CENTS PER MILE"
200 PRINT "IS THIS CORRECT (ENTER YES OR NO)";
210 INPUT R$
220 IF R$ <> "YES" THEN 170
230 LET R = R/100
240 LET I = 0
250 PRINT
260 PRINT "ENTER BEGINNING MILEAGE";
270 INPUT B
280 PRINT "BEGINNING MILEAGE IS "; B
290 PRINT "IS THIS CORRECT (ENTER YES OR NO)";
300 INPUT R$
310 IF R$ <> "YES" THEN 260
320 PRINT "ENTER ENDING MILEAGE";
330 INPUT E
340 PRINT "ENDING MILEAGE IS "; E
350 PRINT "IS THIS CORRECT (ENTER YES OR NO)";
360 INPUT R$
370 IF R$ <> "YES" THEN 320
380 LET C = R * (E-B)
390 PRINT "TOTAL MILEAGE EXPENSE IS $";C
400 LET I = I + 1
410 IF I < N THEN 250
420 END
```

figure) for the beginning mileage. Then, each time a new set of data are entered, line number 260 tests to see if this trailer value was entered into variable *B,* the beginning mileage. When *B* equals "-1," the processing flow is directed to line number 400 and the program terminates.

Given that the mileage rate never changes, the program might be made a bit easier to use by treating this rate as a constant rather than as a variable. The BASIC statement used to calculate total mileage expenses would then look as follows (using Program D.9):

```
370 LET C = .2 * (E - B)
```

Now the user does not have to bother entering a value for the mileage rate. While such a program would be simpler to use, line number 370 would have to be revised whenever the company's mileage rate was changed or the program would give the wrong result. Thus, this version actually becomes harder to use. A good rule to follow in designing programs is to use only constants for values that rarely, if ever, change.

```
OK
RUN
ENTER -1 FOR BEGINNING MILEAGE WHEN
YOU WISH TO STOP

ENTER THE PER MILE EXPENSE IN CENTS? 20
THE CURRENT MILEAGE RATE IS  20  CENTS PER MILE
IS THIS CORRECT  (ENTER YES OR NO)? YES

ENTER BEGINNING MILEAGE? 40234
BEGINNING MILEAGE IS  40234
IS THIS CORRECT  (ENTER YES OR NO)? YES
ENTER ENDING MILEAGE? 40692
ENDING MILEAGE IS  40692
IS THIS CORRECT  (ENTER YES OR NO)? YES
TOTAL MILEAGE EXPENSE IS $ 91.6

ENTER BEGINNING MILEAGE? -1
OK
```

```
10 REM  PROGRAM D.9
20 REM
30 REM  THIS PROGRAM MODIFIES PROGRAM D.7 TO
40 REM  HAVE THE USER ENTER A TRAILER OF "-1"
50 REM  FOR BEGINNING MILEAGE WHEN NO MORE
60 REM  CALCULATIONS ARE TO BE PERFORMED
70 REM
80 REM        B -- BEGINING MILEAGE
90 REM        E -- ENDING MILEAGE
100 REM       R -- MILEAGE RATE (IN CENTS/MILE)
110 REM      R$ -- USER RESPONSE
120 REM
130 PRINT "ENTER -1 FOR BEGINNING MILEAGE WHEN
140 PRINT "YOU WISH TO STOP"
150 PRINT
160 PRINT "ENTER THE PER MILE EXPENSE IN CENTS";
170 INPUT R
180 PRINT "THE CURRENT MILEAGE RATE IS ";R;" CENTS PER MILE"
190 PRINT "IS THIS CORRECT (ENTER YES OR NO)";
200 INPUT R$
210 IF R$ <> "YES" THEN 160
220 LET R = R/100
230 PRINT
240 PRINT "ENTER BEGINNING MILEAGE";
250 INPUT B
260 IF B = -1 THEN 400
270 PRINT "BEGINNING MILEAGE IS "; B
280 PRINT "IS THIS CORRECT (ENTER YES OR NO)";
290 INPUT R$
300 IF R$ <> "YES" THEN 240
310 PRINT "ENTER ENDING MILEAGE";
320 INPUT E
330 PRINT "ENDING MILEACE IS "; E
340 PRINT "IS THIS CORRECT (ENTER YES OR NO)";
350 INPUT R$
360 IF R$ <> "YES" THEN 310
370 LET C = R * (E-B)
380 PRINT "TOTAL MILEAGE EXPENSE IS $";C
390 GOTO 230
400 END
```

Problem 2: Calculating a Total Sales Price. A sales agent needs a program that will calculate the total sales price to be charged customers when they place orders. The total charge for an order depends on a number of factors including the retail price, the quantity sold, discounts, sales tax, and shipping charges. This problem is greatly simplified by the fact that the sales agent sells only one product.

The purpose of this program is clear: to produce a correct total sales price. The program will not be used to produce a sales invoice. If needed, the information will be taken from a CRT screen and entered manually onto a sales invoice. The output needs to display an itemized breakdown of the various price components: the total retail price, the discount, the sales tax, the shipping charge, and the total customer charge. The sales agent is expected to input the number of items sold, the applicable discount percentage, and the appropriate per-unit shipping charge (the sales agent has a booklet that provides these shipping costs). Sales tax is currently 5 percent. The current price of the product is $25.00.

The first design step is to specify how the output will appear. In this case, the following display is proposed and is agreeable to the sales agent:

```
CUSTOMER NAME:     XXXXXXXXXXXXXXXXXXXX
QUANTITY: XXXX     SHIPPING: XXXXX DISCOUNT: XX%

RETAIL PRICE       $ XXXXXXXXX
DISCOUNT           $ XXXXXXXXX
SALES TAX          $ XXXXXXXXX
SHIPPING           $ XXXXXXXXX

TOTAL CHARGE       $ XXXXXXXXX
```

To produce this CRT screen display, the following data items need to be entered: the sales tax rate, the product's price, the customer name, the quantity sold, the discount percentage, and the per-unit shipping charge. The calculations to be performed for each order are:

```
total retail price = price * quantity
total discount = total price * discount
adjusted price = total price − total discount
total tax = tax rate * adjusted price
total shipping = shipping charge * quantity
total charge = adjusted price + tax + shipping
```

The pseudocode for the program's logical design is shown in Exhibit D.4. The program itself is given as Program D.10. The variable *T* is the accumulator used to accumulate the total charge for an order. Notice in line number 370 that *T* is initialized to zero as each new order is processed. Otherwise, the charges associated with each new order would be accumulated "on top of" those of previous orders. Also notice that the program uses a READ statement to enter the tax rate and the product's price. Line number 270 is this READ statement, and line number 280 is its associated DATA statement. This was done because the tax rate and the product's price will not change often. Why require the user to enter values that *remain constant most of the time?* If and when these values change, the DATA statement will be modified to reflect the new values. Used in this way, the READ and DATA statements are effective programming tools.

ANALYZING SKILLS

The ability to analyze data in order to create "new" data that solve a programming problem is one mark of a good programmer. This process usually takes place in one of three ways:

summarizing A set of data are processed to produce new data describing some feature of the set.

classifying A set of data are processed so that items are assigned to one of a number of classifications based on certain features of the items.

filtering A set of data are processed so that many items are bypassed in order to handle certain of the items in some special way.

Exhibit D.4
Pseudocode for Problem 2

```
LEVEL 1:

   initialize program

   repeat

         initialize order processing
         enter data for an order
         perform price calculations
         display results

         until (there are no more orders to process)

LEVEL 2:

   set current sales tax rate and current price
   have the user enter the number of orders to process
   set order counter to zero

   repeat

         add one to order counter
         set total charge to zero

         enter order data
         check order data

         calculate total retail price
         accumulate into total charge
         calculate and display discount
         accumulate into total charge
         calculate and display sales tax
         accumulate into total charge
         calculate and display total shipping charge
         accumulate into total charge
         display total charge

         until (there are no more orders to process)

LEVEL 3:

   set current sales tax rate and current price
   have the user enter the number of orders to process
   set order counter to zero

   repeat
         add one to order counter
         set total charge to zero

         enter customer name
         enter quantity
         enter shipping charge
         enter discount %
         check enterred order data

         total retail price = price * quantity
         display total retail price
         add total retail price to total charge
         discount = total retail price * discount %
         display discount
         adjusted retail price = total retail price - discount
         subtract discount from total charge
         sales tax = adjusted retail price * sales tax rate
         display sales tax
         add sales tax to total charge
         shipping = shipping charge * quantity
         display shipping
         add shipping to total charge
         display total charge

         until (order counter is not less than the number of orders to process)
```

```
OK
RUN
ENTER THE NUMBER OF ORDERS
TO BE PROCESSED? 1
ENTER A CUSTOMER NAME? SMITH BROTHERS
ENTER QUANTITY ORDERED? 200
ENTER PER UNIT SHIPPING CHARGE? 2
ENTER DISCOUNT %? 3
CUSTOMER NAME:   SMITH BROTHERS
QUANTITY:  200    SHIPPING:  2    DISCOUNT: 3 %
IS THIS INFORMATION CORRECT (YES OR NO):? YES
RETAIL PRICE      $ 5000
DISCOUNT          $ 150
SALES TAX         $ 242.5
SHIPPING          $ 400
TOTAL CHARGE      $ 5492.5
OK
```

```
10 REM  PROGRAM D.10
20 REM
30 REM  THIS PROGRAM ILLUSTRATES THE USE OF ACCUMULATORS
40 REM
50 REM  THE PROGRAM CALULATES TOTAL SALES PRICE FOR A
60 REM  CUSTOMER ORDER TAKING INTO CONSIDERATION DISCOUNTS,
70 REM  SHIPPING CHARGES, AND SALES TAX
80 REM
90 REM          X - TAX RATE
100 REM         P - PRODUCT PRICE
110 REM         N - NUMBER OF ORDERS TO PROCESS
120 REM         I - A COUNTER KEEPING TRACK OF THE
130 REM             NUMBER OF ORDERS PROCESSED
140 REM         T - AN ACCUMULATOR THAT TOTALS THE
150 REM             SALES PRICE FOR AN ORDER
160 REM        C$ - CUSTOMER NAME
170 REM         Q - QUANTITY ORDERED
180 REM         S - SHIPPING CHARGE (PER UNIT)
190 REM         D - DISCOUNT %
200 REM        R$ - USER RESPONSE
210 REM        P1 - RETAIL SALES AMOUNT
220 REM        D1 - TOTAL DISCOUNT
230 REM        P2 - DISCOUNTED SALES AMOUNT
240 REM        X1 - TOTAL TAX
250 REM        S1 - TOTAL SHIPPING CHARGE
260 REM
270 READ X,P
280 DATA .05,25
290 PRINT "ENTER THE NUMBER OF ORDERS"
300 PRINT "TO BE PROCESSED";
310 INPUT N
320 LET I = 0
330 REM
340 REM    PROCESS AN ORDER
350 REM
360 LET I = I + 1
370 LET T = 0
380 PRINT
390 PRINT "ENTER A CUSTOMER NAME";
400 INPUT C$
410 PRINT "ENTER QUANTITY ORDERED";
420 INPUT Q
430 PRINT "ENTER PER UNIT SHIPPING CHARGE";
440 INPUT S
450 PRINT "ENTER DISCOUNT %";
460 INPUT D
470 PRINT
480 PRINT "CUSTOMER NAME:" TAB(18) C$
490 PRINT "QUANTITY:";Q TAB(18) "SHIPPING:";S TAB(35) "DISCOUNT:";D;"%"
510 PRINT "IS THIS INFORMATION CORRECT (YES OR NO):";
520 INPUT R$
530 IF R$ <> "YES" THEN 380
540 PRINT
550 LET P1 = P*Q
560 PRINT "RETAIL PRICE" TAB(18) "$";P1
570 LET T = T + P1
580 LET D1 = P1*(D/100)
590 PRINT "DISCOUNT" TAB(18) "$";D1
600 LET P2 = P1 - D1
610 LET T = T - D1
620 LET X1 = P2 * X
630 PRINT "SALES TAX" TAB(18) "$";X1
640 LET T = T + X1
650 LET S1 = Q * S
660 PRINT "SHIPPING" TAB(18) "$";S1
670 LET T = T + S1
680 PRINT
690 PRINT "TOTAL CHARGE" TAB(18) "$";T
700 IF I < N THEN 360
710 END
```

```
10 REM  PROGRAM D.11
20 REM
30 REM  THIS PROGRAM ILLUSTRATES DATA SUMMARIZATION
40 REM
50 REM  THE PROGRAM CALCULATES AND DISPLAYS THE
60 REM  AVERAGE VALUE FOR A SET OF DATA
70 REM
80 REM          N -- A COUNTER USED TO KNOW HOW MANY
90 REM               ITEMS ARE IN THE SET OF DATA
100 REM         A -- AVERAGE VALUE OF THE SET OF DATA
110 REM         V -- A VALUE FROM THE SET OF DATA
120 REM
130 PRINT "ENTER A VALUE OF 999 ONCE YOU HAVE"
140 PRINT "COMPLETED ENTERING THE SET OF DATA"
150 PRINT
160 LET N = 0
170 LET A = 0
180 PRINT "ENTER A VALUE";
190 INPUT V
200 IF V = 999 THEN 270
210 LET A = A + V
220 LET N = N + 1
230 GOTO 180
240 REM
250 REM    CALCULATE THE AVERAGE
260 REM
270 PRINT
280 PRINT "THE SUM OF THE ";N;" VALUES IS ";A
290 PRINT
300 LET A = A/N
310 PRINT "THE AVERAGE IS ";A
320 END
```

```
OK
RUN
ENTER A VALUE OF 999 ONCE YOU HAVE
COMPLETED ENTERING THE SET OF DATA
ENTER A VALUE? 5
ENTER A VALUE? 6
ENTER A VALUE? 11
ENTER A VALUE? 9
ENTER A VALUE? 5
ENTER A VALUE? 4
ENTER A VALUE? 3
ENTER A VALUE? 8
ENTER A VALUE? 3
ENTER A VALUE? 999
THE SUM OF THE  9  VALUES IS 54
THE AVERAGE IS  6
OK
```

Summarizing

Program D.11 is a summarizing program that calculates the average of a set of data. Thus, a new piece of data—the average value of the entire set of data—has been created. This new data item can now be used elsewhere in the program, stored in secondary storage, or simply displayed. In Program D.11, the average is displayed.

Program D.11 uses a counter and an accumulator, which are initialized in line numbers 160 and 170. Variable *N* counts the number of values that have been entered (see line number 220), while variable *A* accumulates the values as they are entered (see line number 210). The average of these values is then calculated in line number 300 by dividing *A* by *N*.

Classifying

Program D.12 makes use of the algorithm for calculating an average used in Program D.11 to analyze responses to a survey. Here, selected customers in a store were asked how many of a certain product they had purchased. Program D.12 calculates the average number of purchases by males and by females. To do so, the program needs to classify the purchase amounts by the sex of the customer surveyed.

In Program D.12, variables *N1* and *N2* represent counters that keep track of the number of males and females, respectively, that were surveyed. Similar-

```
RUN
ENTER A VALUE OF 999 ONCE YOU HAVE
COMPLETED ENTERING ALL THE DATA
ENTER NUMBER OF PURCHASES? 5
ENTER SEX CODE (M OR F)? M
ENTER NUMBER OF PURCHASES? 6
ENTER SEX CODE (M OR F)? F
ENTER NUMBER OF PURCHASES? 11
ENTER SEX CODE (M OR F)? F
ENTER NUMBER OF PURCHASES? 9
ENTER SEX CODE (M OR F)? F
ENTER NUMBER OF PURCHASES? 5
ENTER SEX CODE (M OR F)? M
ENTER NUMBER OF PURCHASES? 4
ENTER SEX CODE (M OR F)? M
ENTER NUMBER OF PURCHASES? 999

3  MALES AND  3  FEMALES WERE SURVEYED

AVERAGE PURCHASES FOR MALES:     4.666667
AVERAGE PURCHASES FOR FEMALES:   8.666667
OK
```

```
10 REM  PROGRAM D.12
20 REM
30 REM  THIS PROGRAM ILLUSTRATES DATA CLASSFICATION
40 REM
50 REM  THE PROGRAM MODIFIES PROGRAM D.11 TO CALCULATE THE
60 REM  AVERAGE PURCHASES BY MALES AND BY FEMALES IN A
70 REM  MARKET SURVEY.
80 REM
90 REM         A1 -- AVERAGE PURCHASES BY MALES
100 REM        A2 -- AVERAGE PURCHASES BY FEMALES
110 REM        N1 -- A COUNTER USED TO KNOW HOW MANY
120 REM              MALES WERE SURVEYED
130 REM        N2 -- A COUNTER USED TO KNOW HOW MANY
140 REM              FEMALES WERE SURVEYED
150 REM         P -- THE NUMBER OF PURCHASES THE PERSON
160 REM              INTERVIEWED MADE
170 REM        S$ -- A "M" IF THE PERSON INTERVIEWED WAS MALE
180 REM              OR A "F" IF THE PERSON WAS FEMALE
190 REM
200 PRINT "ENTER A VALUE OF 999 ONCE YOU HAVE"
210 PRINT "COMPLETED ENTERING ALL THE DATA"
220 PRINT
230 LET N1 = 0
240 LET N2 = 0
250 LET A1 = 0
260 LET A2 = 0
270 PRINT "ENTER NUMBER OF PURCHASES";
280 INPUT P
290 IF P = 999 THEN 450
300 PRINT "ENTER SEX CODE (M OR F)";
310 INPUT S$
320 IF S$ = "M" THEN 360
330 IF S$ = "F" THEN 390
340 PRINT "ERROR WITH SEX CODE:"; S$
350 GOTO 300
360 LET N1 = N1 + 1
370 LET A1 = A1 + P
380 GOTO 270
390 LET N2 = N2 + 1
400 LET A2 = A2 + P
410 GOTO 270
420 REM
430 REM    CALCULATE THE AVERAGE
440 REM
450 PRINT
460 PRINT N1;" MALES AND ";N2;" FEMALES WERE SURVEYED"
470 PRINT
480 LET A1 = A1/N1
490 LET A2 = A2/N2
500 PRINT "AVERAGE PURCHASES FOR MALES:   ";A1
510 PRINT "AVERAGE PURCHASES FOR FEMALES: ";A2
520 END
```

ly, variables *A1* and *A2* are used to accumulate the total purchases by males and females and to hold the averages calculated. Line numbers 230–260 initialize these variables.

Notice that the user enters two values for each customer surveyed: the person's number of purchases (see line numbers 270 and 280) and their sex code, an "M" or an "F" (see line numbers 300 and 310). The sex code, variable *S$*, is then used to classify the purchase amount as belonging to a male or a female. Line number 320 directs male purchases using *N1* and *A1* for the operation, and line number 330 directs female purchases using *N2* and *A2* for the operation.

Filtering

Program D.13 illustrates how to select certain data values from a set of data. Instead of determining averages for both males and females as was done in Program D.12, this program performs calculations only on responses by males. The IF statement in line number 330 serves as the filter. If the customer's sex code is "F," the processing flow is directed to line number 260 and another purchase amount is entered. Thus, all female responses are bypassed by the program.

More Programming Tools

Three programming tools useful in analyzing data include the concepts of a **flag,** an **anchor,** and a **control break.** Flags are used to control a program's

```
OK
RUN
ENTER A VALUE OF 999 ONCE YOU HAVE
COMPLETED ENTERING ALL THE DATA

ENTER NUMBER OF PURCHASES? 5
ENTER SEX CODE (M OR F)? M
ENTER NUMBER OF PURCHASES? 6
ENTER SEX CODE (M OR F)? F
ENTER NUMBER OF PURCHASES? 11
ENTER SEX CODE (M OR F)? F
ENTER NUMBER OF PURCHASES? 9
ENTER SEX CODE (M OR F)? F
ENTER NUMBER OF PURCHASES? 5
ENTER SEX CODE (M OR F)? M
ENTER NUMBER OF PURCHASES? 4
ENTER SEX CODE (M OR F)? M
ENTER NUMBER OF PURCHASES? 999

OF  6  PEOPLE SURVEYED  50 % WERE MALE

AVERAGE PURCHASES FOR MALES:      4.666667
OK
```

```
10 REM  PROGRAM D.13
20 REM
30 REM  THIS PROGRAM ILLUSTRATES THE USE OF DATA FILTERS
40 REM
50 REM  THE PROGRAM MODIFIES PROGRAM D.12 TO CALCULATE THE
60 REM  AVERAGE PURCHASES BY MALES AND THE PROPORTION OF
70 REM  INTERVIEWEES WHO WERE MALE.
80 REM
90 REM         A1 -- AVERAGE PURCHASES BY MALES
100 REM        P1 -- PROPORTION OF MALES IN THE SURVEY
110 REM        N1 -- A COUNTER USED TO KNOW HOW MANY
120 REM              MALES WERE SURVEYED
130 REM         N -- A COUNTER USED TO KNOW HOW MANY
140 REM              PEOPLE WERE SURVEYED
150 REM         P -- THE NUMBER OF PURCHASES THE PERSON
160 REM              INTERVIEWED MADE
170 REM        S$ -- A "M" IF THE PERSON INTERVIEWED WAS MALE
180 REM              OR A "F" IF THE PERSON WAS FEMALE
190 REM
200 PRINT "ENTER A VALUE OF 999 ONCE YOU HAVE"
210 PRINT "COMPLETED ENTERING ALL THE DATA"
220 PRINT
230 LET N1 = 0
240 LET N = 0
250 LET A1 = 0
260 PRINT "ENTER NUMBER OF PURCHASES";
270 INPUT P
280 IF P = 999 THEN 420
290 LET N = N + 1
300 PRINT "ENTER SEX CODE (M OR F)";
310 INPUT S$
320 IF S$ = "M" THEN 360
330 IF S$ = "F" THEN 260
340 PRINT "ERROR WITH SEX CODE:"; S$
350 GOTO 300
360 LET N1 = N1 + 1
370 LET A1 = A1 + P
380 GOTO 260
390 REM
400 REM    CALCULATE THE AVERAGE
410 REM
420 PRINT
430 LET P1 = 100*(N1/N)
440 PRINT "OF ";N;" PEOPLE SURVEYED ";P1;" % WERE MALE"
450 PRINT
460 LET A1 = A1/N1
470 PRINT "AVERAGE PURCHASES FOR MALES:   ";A1
480 END
```

processing flow. Anchors are used to assign a variable a specific value needed to carry out a particular algorithm. Control breaks are used to display sets of data in a readable manner.

Flag. Filtering, introduced above, made use of a program flag. In Program D.13, a sex code of "F" served as a flag to bypass all further processing of that customer. Program D.14 illustrates a common use of a flag: controlling whether a message is displayed to the user.

In Program D.14, variable *F$* is a flag indicating whether a user will be checking the values entered. Line numbers 220 and 230 ask the user if entered values are to be echoed back to let the values be checked visually. Line number 240 places the user's response, a "YES" or a "NO," into the flag *F$*. Then, line number 300 uses *F$* either to bypass or to process line numbers 310 to 330, which check values as they are entered. If *F$* equals "NO," the check is bypassed.

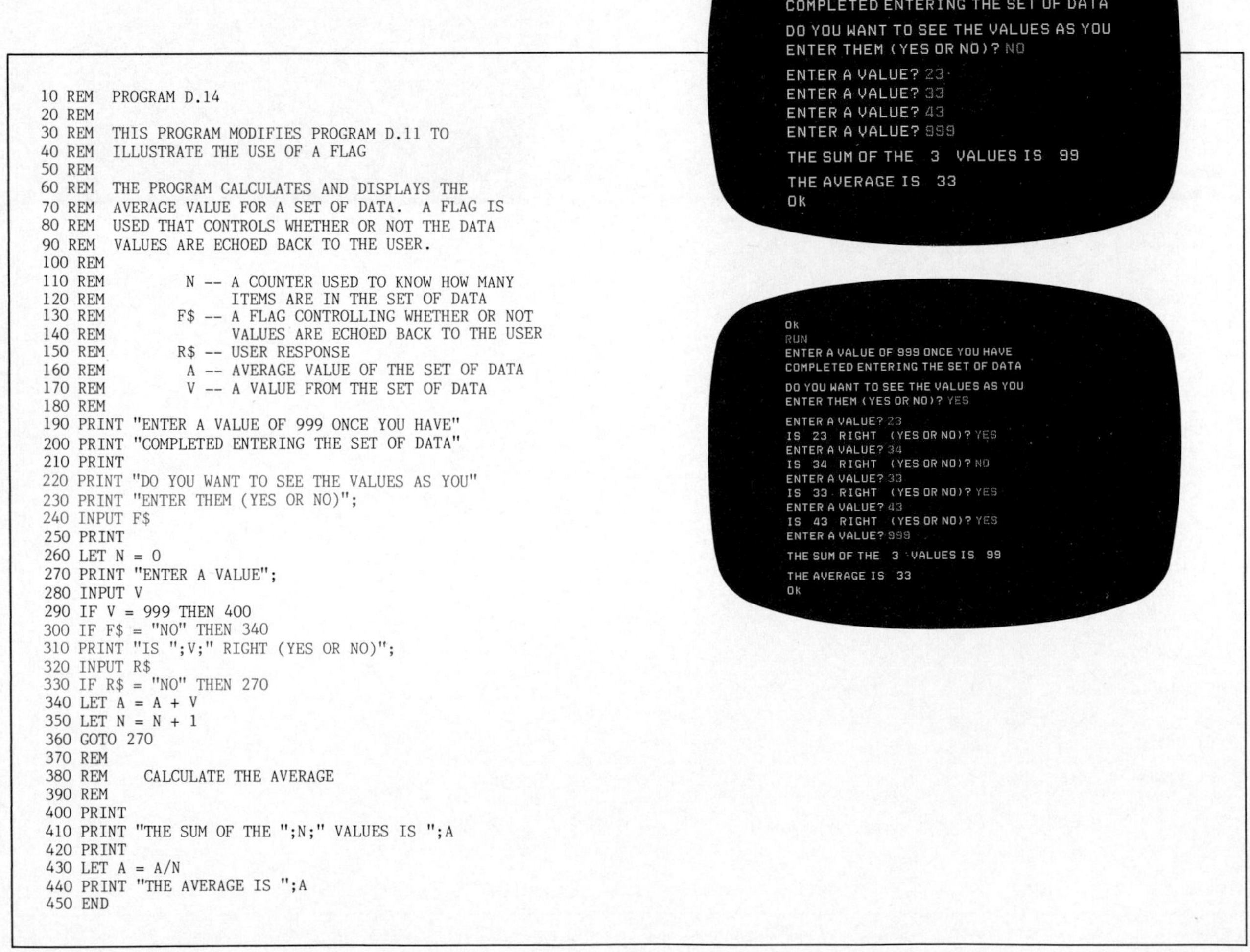

```
10 REM  PROGRAM D.14
20 REM
30 REM  THIS PROGRAM MODIFIES PROGRAM D.11 TO
40 REM  ILLUSTRATE THE USE OF A FLAG
50 REM
60 REM  THE PROGRAM CALCULATES AND DISPLAYS THE
70 REM  AVERAGE VALUE FOR A SET OF DATA.  A FLAG IS
80 REM  USED THAT CONTROLS WHETHER OR NOT THE DATA
90 REM  VALUES ARE ECHOED BACK TO THE USER.
100 REM
110 REM        N -- A COUNTER USED TO KNOW HOW MANY
120 REM             ITEMS ARE IN THE SET OF DATA
130 REM       F$ -- A FLAG CONTROLLING WHETHER OR NOT
140 REM             VALUES ARE ECHOED BACK TO THE USER
150 REM       R$ -- USER RESPONSE
160 REM        A -- AVERAGE VALUE OF THE SET OF DATA
170 REM        V -- A VALUE FROM THE SET OF DATA
180 REM
190 PRINT "ENTER A VALUE OF 999 ONCE YOU HAVE"
200 PRINT "COMPLETED ENTERING THE SET OF DATA"
210 PRINT
220 PRINT "DO YOU WANT TO SEE THE VALUES AS YOU"
230 PRINT "ENTER THEM (YES OR NO)";
240 INPUT F$
250 PRINT
260 LET N = 0
270 PRINT "ENTER A VALUE";
280 INPUT V
290 IF V = 999 THEN 400
300 IF F$ = "NO" THEN 340
310 PRINT "IS ";V;" RIGHT (YES OR NO)";
320 INPUT R$
330 IF R$ = "NO" THEN 270
340 LET A = A + V
350 LET N = N + 1
360 GOTO 270
370 REM
380 REM    CALCULATE THE AVERAGE
390 REM
400 PRINT
410 PRINT "THE SUM OF THE ";N;" VALUES IS ";A
420 PRINT
430 LET A = A/N
440 PRINT "THE AVERAGE IS ";A
450 END
```

Anchor. Often, an algorithm used in a programming problem requires that a variable be given an anchoring value. That is, the variable must be initialized a certain way or the algorithm will not work. Counters and accumulators, for example, must be anchored with a value of zero if they are to work correctly.

Program D.15 uses an anchor to find the maximum value in a set of data. The anchor is "set" in line number 200. Here, variable H is assigned a value of -9999, a number believed lower than the values in the set of data to be processed. With this algorithm, each value V is compared against H as it is entered (see line number 240). If V is greater than H, V is the "highest value entered so far." When this is the case, line number 250 assigns H the value of V. With this algorithm, variable H will contain the highest value in the set of data once the entire set of data has been entered. This algorithm only works if H starts off with a value lower than the actual maximum value in the set of data. Thus, H is anchored as a very low number.

Control Break. A control break links the sequence in which a set of data are entered with the manner in which the program's outputs are to be displayed. When this step is done correctly, the values entered direct the logic that displays program outputs.

```
OK
RUN
ENTER A VALUE OF 999 ONCE YOU HAVE
COMPLETED ENTERING THE SET OF DATA

ENTER A VALUE? 34
ENTER A VALUE? 43
ENTER A VALUE? 67
ENTER A VALUE? 2
ENTER A VALUE? -90
ENTER A VALUE? 32
ENTER A VALUE? 16
ENTER A VALUE? 36
ENTER A VALUE? 999

THE SUM OF THE  8  VALUES IS  140

THE AVERAGE IS  17.5

THE HIGHEST IS  67
OK
```

```
10 REM  PROGRAM D.15
20 REM
30 REM  THIS PROGRAM ILLUSTRATES THE USE OF AN ANCHOR
40 REM
50 REM  THE PROGRAM CALCULATES AND DISPLAYS THE
60 REM  AVERAGE AND HIGHEST VALUES FOR A SET OF DATA
70 REM
80 REM          N -- A COUNTER USED TO KNOW HOW MANY
90 REM               ITEMS ARE IN THE SET OF DATA
100 REM         H -- AN ANCHOR USED TO BOTH START OF THE
110 REM              ALGORITHM TO FIND THE HIGHEST VALUE
120 REM              AND HOLD THIS HIGHEST VALUE
130 REM         A -- AVERAGE VALUE OF THE SET OF DATA
140 REM         V -- A VALUE FROM THE SET OF DATA
150 REM
160 PRINT "ENTER A VALUE OF 999 ONCE YOU HAVE"
170 PRINT "COMPLETED ENTERING THE SET OF DATA"
180 PRINT
190 LET N = 0
200 LET H = -9999
210 PRINT "ENTER A VALUE";
220 INPUT V
230 IF V = 999 THEN 320
240 IF V <= H THEN 260
250 LET H = V
260 LET A = A + V
270 LET N = N + 1
280 GOTO 210
290 REM
300 REM    CALCULATE THE AVERAGE
310 REM
320 PRINT
330 PRINT "THE SUM OF THE ";N;" VALUES IS ";A
340 PRINT
350 LET A = A/N
360 PRINT "THE AVERAGE IS ";A
370 PRINT
380 PRINT "THE HIGHEST IS ";H
390 END
```

Program D.16 makes use of a control break to organize customer purchases by sex as they are displayed. Variable *B$* is the control break variable. When a sex code is entered, line number 380 compares the *B$* with *S$*, the variable holding the sex code. As long as *B$* equals *S$*, no special actions need to be taken. However, when the just-entered value for *S$* does not equal the current value of *B$*, a control break occurs. With Program D.16, the control break signifies that a new sex code is beginning. As a result, the display is adjusted accordingly: line numbers 400 and 410 print out a heading for the new sex code. Also, the control break variable is assigned this new sex code (see line number 390).

Summary

The ability to analyze data in order to create "new" data that solve a programming problem is one mark of a good programmer. Three common analysis techniques involve *summarizing, classifying,* and *filtering* data.

With summarizing, a set of data is processed to produce new data that describe some feature of the set of data. These new data can be used elsewhere in the program, stored in secondary storage, or simply displayed.

With classifying, a set of data is processed so that items are assigned to one of a number of classifications based on some feature of the items.

In filtering, a set of data is processed so that only certain items are selected for further processing.

Three programming tools useful in analyzing data include the concepts of a *flag,* an *anchor,* and a *control break.* Flags are used to control a program's processing flow. Variables are anchored by assigning them specific values required in making a particular algorithm work. A control break links the sequence in which a set of data is entered to the manner in which the program's outputs are to be displayed.

Sample Analyzing Problems

Much business programming, particularly that producing management reports, involves data analysis. The following three problems should indicate to you some of the ways management information can be created from business data. Problem 3 involves data summarizing and classifying. Problem 4 makes use of a flag, an anchor, and a filter. Problem 5 illustrates a control break.

Problem 3: Salary Analysis. The engineering manager of a small firm requests a program to analyze the salaries of the firm's fifty-two engineers and technicians. Specifically, this program is to calculate and display the following:

	Engineers	Technicians
Average salary for males		
Average salary for females		

The needed data—employee sex and salary—are readily available.

OK
RUN

 LISTING FOR SEX CODE: M

      PURCHASES: 5
      PURCHASES: 5
      PURCHASES: 4

 LISTING FOR SEX CODE: F

      PURCHASES: 6
      PURCHASES: 11
      PURCHASES: 9

 3 MALES AND 3 FEMALES WERE SURVEYED

AVERAGE PURCHASES FOR MALES: 4.666667
AVERAGE PURCHASES FOR FEMALES: 8.666667
OK

```
10 REM  PROGRAM D.16
20 REM
30 REM  THIS PROGRAM ILLUSTRATES THE USE OF A CONTROL BREAK
40 REM
50 REM  THE PROGRAM MODIFIES PROGRAM D.11 TO CALCULATE THE
60 REM  AVERAGE PURCHASES BY MALES AND BY FEMALES AND TO
70 REM  LIST THE SURVEY RESPONSES BY SEX CLASSFICATION.
80 REM
90 REM  THE VALUES MUST BE ENTERED BY SEX CLASSFICATION (ALL
100 REM MALES, THEN ALL FEMALES)
110 REM
120 REM        A1 -- AVERAGE PURCHASES BY MALES
130 REM        A2 -- AVERAGE PURCHASES BY FEMALES
140 REM        N1 -- A COUNTER USED TO KNOW HOW MANY
150 REM              MALES WERE SURVEYED
160 REM        N2 -- A COUNTER USED TO KNOW HOW MANY
170 REM              FEMALES WERE SURVEYED
180 REM         P -- THE NUMBER OF PURCHASES THE PERSON
190 REM              INTERVIEWED MADE
200 REM        S$ -- A "M" IF THE PERSON INTERVIEWED WAS MALE
210 REM              OR A "F" IF THE PERSON WAS FEMALE
220 REM        B$ -- CONTROL BREAK TEST VARIABLE
230 REM
240 REM  THIS PROGRAM USES READ AND DATA STATEMENTS FOR ENTERING
250 REM  DATA VALUES.  USE A VALUE OF 999 AS THE LAST VALUE IN
260 REM  THE DATA LIST TO INDICATE THAT ALL VALUES HAVE BEEN ENTERED.
270 REM  ENTER YOUR DATA VALUES IN PAIRS: FIRST THE NUMBER OF
280 REM  PURCHASES, THEN THE SEX CODE.
290 LET N1 = 0
300 LET N2 = 0
310 LET A1 = 0
320 LET A2 = 0
330 LET B$ = " "
340 READ P
350 IF P = 999 THEN 570
360 READ S$
370 IF S$ <> "M" AND S$ <> "F" THEN 460
380 IF S$ = B$ THEN 430
390 LET B$ = S$
400 PRINT
410 PRINT " LISTING FOR SEX CODE: ";S$
420 PRINT
430 PRINT "     PURCHASES: ";P
440 IF S$ = "M" THEN 480
450 IF S$ = "F" THEN 510
460 PRINT "ERROR WITH SEX CODE: "; S$
470 GOTO 710
480 LET N1 = N1 + 1
490 LET A1 = A1 + P
500 GOTO 340
510 LET N2 = N2 + 1
520 LET A2 = A2 + P
530 GOTO 340
540 REM
550 REM    CALCULATE THE AVERAGE
560 REM
570 PRINT
580 PRINT N1;" MALES AND ";N2;" FEMALES WERE SURVEYED"
590 PRINT
600 LET A1 = A1/N1
610 LET A2 = A2/N2
620 PRINT "AVERAGE PURCHASES FOR MALES:   ";A1
630 PRINT "AVERAGE PURCHASES FOR FEMALES: ";A2
640 DATA 5,"M"
650 DATA 5,"M"
660 DATA 4,"M"
670 DATA 6,"F"
680 DATA 11,"F"
690 DATA 9,"F"
700 DATA 999
710 END
```

The output of this program is the table just shown. The manager approves the following report format:

	Annual Salary Averages	
	Engineers	Technicians
Males	$ XXXXXXXX	$ XXXXXXXX
Females	$ XXXXXXXX	$ XXXXXXXX

To calculate these averages, the total dollar value of salaries and the total number of people must be aggregated for each of four personnel categories: male engineers, female engineers, male technicians, and female technicians. Given these sums, average salary is obtained by dividing the total salary figure by the number of employees. These sums are easily created by using counters and accumulators.

It would seem from the problem description that the only required input data items are the sex and salary for each employee. However, one additional data item is needed: a value indicating whether an employee is an engineer or a technician. As it turns out, the firm uses a job classification code in which "07" represents an engineer and "11" represents a technician. There are a total of 21 different job codes. Thus, the required data to be entered for each employee are: job code (07 or 11), sex code (*M* or *F*), and salary (in whole dollars).

Two major design decisions remain:

1. Should the employee data be entered with an INPUT statement or a READ statement?
2. How should the stream of input data be stopped?

Each of these questions will be answered in turn.

There are a total of 159 data items to enter into the program. If the INPUT statement is used and an error made on the 140th data item, the program would have to be started all over again. This would also mean reentering all 140 data items. It's unlikely the manager would find such a program very practical after even one such mistake had been made! By using READ and DATA statements, the complete set of data items could be entered and checked for accuracy prior to the execution of the program. This approach is preferred when a large number of data items are to be entered, and is the one we use in this program.

The question of how to tell the program that no more sets of data need to be read is a bit simpler. The program should be designed so that the following are true:

1. It will work even if the total number of engineers and technicians changes.
2. The manager does not need to count the sets of data to be entered.

The best choice here, then, is to use a trailer. As there are only 21 different job codes (01, 02, 03, . . . , 19, 20, 21), a value of 99 would be a good choice for this trailer.

The logical design for this program is given in Exhibit D.5. Program D.17 solves the problem. To save space, DATA statements for only 10 employees are given in the program. As a set of employee data is processed, different processing paths are taken depending on the following conditions:

1. whether the trailer value is read (line number 350);
2. whether the employee is an engineer or technician (line numbers 380 and 390); and
3. whether the employee is male or female (line numbers 450 and 550).

Exhibit D.5
Pseudocode for Problem 3

```
LEVEL 1:

   initialize program

   while (there are still employee data to read)

          read a set of data
          adjust the appropriate counter and accumulator

   calculate averages
   display averages

LEVEL 2:

   set counters and accumulators to zero
   display report headings

   while (there are still employee data to read)

          read job code, sex code, salary
          identify male and female engineers
          adjust the appropriate counter and accumulator
          identify male and female technicians
          adjust the appropriate counter and accumulator
          identify and handle incorrect job codes

   calculate average salary for each employee category
   display average salaries

LEVEL 3:

   set the four counters to zero
   set the four accumulators to zero
   display report headings

   read a job code
   while (job code does not equal 99)

          read sex code and salary
          if engineer
            then
                   if male then
                            adjust male engineers
                     else
                            adjust female engineers
            else
            if technician then
                   if male then
                            adjust male technicians
                     else
                            adjust female technicians
            else
                display job code error message
                stop program
          read a job code
   calculate salary averages for the four employee categories
   display salary averages
```

Notice how the headings for the report were displayed in line numbers 180 to 210 and how the TAB function was used in line numbers 690 and 710 to complete the report. Spending a little extra time working on output displays can greatly increase their readability.

Finally, notice that the job code was treated as a string variable rather than a numeric variable. This code could just as well have been a numeric value. If this had been the case, the variable name would have been *J* rather than *J$*. Treating the code as a string variable emphasizes that the "07" has no numeric meaning but is simply a code to classify data items.

```
OK
RUN
                    ANNUAL SALARY AVERAGES

                  ENGINEERS    TECHNICIANS

      MALES       $  26500     $  16000

    FEMALES       $  27000     $  16166.67
OK
```

```
10 REM PROGRAM D.17
20 REM
30 REM   THIS PROGRAM COMPARES THE SALARIES OF MALE AND
40 REM   FEMALE ENGINEERS AND TECHNICIANS.
50 REM
60 REM          J$ - JOB CODE
70 REM          S$ - SEX CODE
80 REM           S - SALARY
90 REM          N1 - NUMBER OF MALE ENGINEERS
100 REM         N2 - NUMBER OF FEMALE ENGINEERS
110 REM         N3 - NUMBER OF MALE TECHNICIANS
120 REM         N4 - NUMBER OF FEMALE TECHNICIANS
130 REM         A1 - AVERAGE SALARY OF MALE ENGINEERS
140 REM         A2 - AVERAGE SALARY OF FEMALE ENGINEERS
150 REM         A3 - AVERAGE SALARY OF MALE TECHNICIANS
160 REM         A4 - AVERAGE SALARY OF FEMALE TECHNICIANS
170 REM
180 PRINT TAB(25) "ANNUAL SALARY AVERAGES"
190 PRINT
200 PRINT TAB(22) "ENGINEERS     TECHNICIANS"
210 PRINT
220 LET A1 = 0
230 LET A2 = 0
240 LET A3 = 0
250 LET A4 = 0
260 LET N1 = 0
270 LET N2 = 0
280 LET N3 = 0
290 LET N4 = 0
300 REM
310 REM  JOB CODES - ENGINEER (7); TECHNICIAN (11)
320 REM  SEX CODES - MALE (M); FEMALE (F)
330 REM
340 READ J$
350 IF J$ = "99" THEN 650
360 READ S$
370 READ S
380 IF J$ = "07" THEN 550
390 IF J$ = "11" THEN 450
400 PRINT "  ERROR WITH JOB CODE: "J$
410 GOTO 830
420 REM
430 REM PROCESS SET OF TECHNICIAN DATA
440 REM
450 IF S$ = "F" THEN 490
460 LET N3 = N3 + 1
470 LET A3 = A3 + S
480 GOTO 340
490 LET N4 = N4 + 1
500 LET A4 = A4 + S
510 GOTO 340
520 REM
530 REM PROCESS SET OF ENGINEER DATA
540 REM
550 IF S$ = "F" THEN 590
560 LET N1 = N1 + 1
570 LET A1 = A1 + S
580 GOTO 340
590 LET N2 = N2 + 1
600 LET A2 = A2 + S
610 GOTO 340
620 REM
630 REM    FINISH UP PROCESSING
640 REM
650 LET A1 = A1/N1
660 LET A2 = A2/N2
670 LET A3 = A3/N3
680 LET A4 = A4/N4
690 PRINT TAB(11) "MALES" TAB(22) "$ ";A1 TAB(36) "$ ";A3
700 PRINT
710 PRINT TAB(9) "FEMALES" TAB(22) "$ ";A2 TAB(36) "$ ";A4
720 DATA "07","M",28500
730 DATA "11","F",16000
740 DATA "11","M",18500
750 DATA "07","F",23000
760 DATA "11","M",13500
770 DATA "07","M",22000
780 DATA "07","F",31000
790 DATA "11","F",18000
800 DATA "11","F",14500
810 DATA "07","M",29000
820 DATA "99"
830 END
```

Problem 4: A More Flexible Salary Analysis. After receiving the report produced by Program D.17, the engineering manager realized that her original problem description was not complete. In addition to the salary analysis for *all* engineers and technicians, she would also like the program to produce these statistics only for employees who had recently joined the firm. The manager asked that this feature be added to the program.

Program D.17 needs to be changed in the following ways to meet the manager's new request:

1. Enter the number of years of employment for each employee.
2. Add a flag that indicates whether the years-of-employment filter is to be used.
3. Add a prompt that asks the user to enter the number of years to use as the years-of-employment filter.
4. Add a filter that skips over any employee who has worked for the firm longer than the specified length of time.
5. Change the report heading so that it indicates that only certain employees, based on years of employment, are included within the salary analysis report.

This new report heading will be:

```
ANNUAL SALARY AVERAGES
    ( ALL PERSONNEL )
or,
 ANNUAL SALARY AVERAGES
( XX YEARS OR LESS SERVICE )
```

Program D.18 is the revised version of Program D.17. Note the changes:

1. Line number 260 anchors the years-of-employment filter *F* to a large number. It is unlikely that any employee would work for the firm more than 100 years!
2. Line numbers 270 to 290 ask the user if the analysis is to include a years-of-employment filter. If it is, the flag *F$* is set to "YES" and line numbers 310 to 330 prompt the user to enter the desired years of employment.
3. Line number 360 tests *F$* to determine which subheading needs to be printed (line number 370 or line number 390).
4. Line number 590 enters years of employment, variable *Y*, as an employee data item. Also notice that the DATA statements given in line numbers 1070 to 1160 now have a years-of-employment value.
5. Line number 600 tests to see if the employee data just entered should be skipped. If an employee's years-of-employment figure is greater than the value of *F*, then the employee is not included in the analysis and the processing flow immediately transfers to enter data for another employee.
6. Notice the extra tests done when calculating the average salaries (line numbers 880, 920, 960, and 1000). These prevent the program from attempting to "divide by zero" when there are no employees in a certain employee category.

Problem 5: Defective Parts Analysis. A purchasing manager in a small manufacturing firm wants to have a report produced that analyzes the percentage of defective parts obtained from each of five suppliers. With such a report, the quality of the suppliers' materials can be compared on a monthly basis.

```
10 REM PROGRAM D.18
20 REM
30 REM   THIS PROGRAM MODIFIES PROGRAM D.17 TO INCLUDE
40 REM   THE CAPABILITY TO PRODUCE THE SALARY ANALYSIS
50 REM   ONLY FOR EMPLOYEES WHO HAD BEEN WITH THE FIRM
60 REM   FEWER THAN A SPECIFIC NUMBER OF YEARS
70 REM
80 REM          F - YEARS OF EMPLOYMENT FILTER
90 REM         F$ - A FLAG THAT INDICATES WHICH TYPE
100 REM             OF ANALYSIS WILL BE PERFORMED (ALL
110 REM             PERSONNEL OR BASED ON YEARS OF
120 REM             EMPLOYMENT)
130 REM        J$ - JOB CODE
140 REM        S$ - SEX CODE
150 REM         S - SALARY
160 REM         Y - YEARS OF EMPLOYMENT
170 REM        N1 - NUMBER OF MALE ENGINEERS
180 REM        N2 - NUMBER OF FEMALE ENGINEERS
190 REM        N3 - NUMBER OF MALE TECHNICIANS
200 REM        N4 - NUMBER OF REMALE TECHNICIANS
210 REM        A1 - AVERAGE SALARY OF MALE ENGINEERS
220 REM        A2 - AVERAGE SALARY OF FEMALE ENGINEERS
230 REM        A3 - AVERAGE SALARY OF MALE TECHNICIANS
240 REM        A4 - AVERAGE SALARY OF FEMALE TECHNICIANS
250 REM
260 LET F = 100
270 PRINT "WILL THE ANALYSIS CHECK FOR YEARS OF"
280 PRINT "EMPLOYMENT (YES OR NO)";
290 INPUT F$
300 IF F$ = "NO" THEN 340
310 PRINT "ENTER THE MAXIMUM YEARS OF EMPLOYMENT"
320 PRINT "FOR THIS SALARY ANALYSIS";
330 INPUT F
340 PRINT
350 PRINT TAB(25) "ANNUAL SALARY AVERAGES"
360 IF F$ = "YES" THEN 390
370 PRINT TAB(28) "( ALL PERSONNEL )"
380 GOTO 400
390 PRINT TAB(22) "(";F;" YEARS OR LESS SERVICE )"
400 PRINT
410 PRINT TAB(22) "ENGINEERS     TECHNICIANS"
420 PRINT
430 LET A1 = 0
440 LET A2 = 0
450 LET A3 = 0
460 LET A4 = 0
470 LET N1 = 0
480 LET N2 = 0
490 LET N3 = 0
500 LET N4 = 0
510 REM
520 REM  JOB CODES - ENGINEER (7); TECHNICIAN (11)
530 REM  SEX CODES - MALE (M); FEMALE (F)
540 REM
550 READ J$
560 IF J$ = "99" THEN 910
570 READ S$
580 READ S
590 READ Y
600 IF Y > F THEN 550
610 IF J$ = "07" THEN 780
620 IF J$ = "11" THEN 630
630 PRINT "  ERROR WITH JOB CODE: "J$
640 GOTO 1180
650 REM
660 REM PROCESS SET OF TECHNICIAN DATA
670 REM
680 IF S$ = "F" THEN 720
690 LET N3 = N3 + 1
700 LET A3 = A3 + S
710 GOTO 550
720 LET N4 = N4 + 1
730 LET A4 = A4 + S
740 GOTO 550
750 REM
760 REM PROCESS SET OF ENGINEER DATA
770 REM
780 IF S$ = "F" THEN 820
790 LET N1 = N1 + 1
```

```
OK
RUN
WILL THE ANALYSIS CHECK FOR YEARS OF
EMPLOYMENT  (YES OR NO)? NO
                          ANNUAL SALARY AVERAGES
                            (  ALL PERSONNEL  )

                       ENGINEERS     TECHNICIANS

       MALES        $  26500        $  16000

     FEMALES        $  27000        $  16166.67
OK
```

```
OK
RUN
WILL THE ANALYSIS CHECK FOR YEARS OF
EMPLOYMENT  (YES OR NO)? YES
ENTER THE MAXIMUM YEARS OF EMPLOYMENT
FOR THIS SALARY ANALYSIS? 2
                         ANNUAL SALARY AVERAGES
                      ( 2  YEARS OR LESS SERVICE )

                       ENGINEERS     TECHNICIANS

       MALES        $  22000        $  16000

     FEMALES        $  0            $  0
OK
```

```
800 LET A1 = A1 + S
810 GOTO 550
820 LET N2 = N2 + 1
830 LET A2 = A2 + S
840 GOTO 550
850 REM
860 REM     FINISH UP PROCESSING
870 REM
880 IF N1 > 0 THEN 910
890 LET A1 = 0
900 GOTO 920
910 LET A1 = A1/N1
920 IF N2 > 0 THEN 950
930 LET A2 = 0
940 GOTO 960
950 LET A2 = A2/N2
960 IF N3 > 0 THEN 990
970 LET A3 = 0
980 GOTO 1000
990 LET A3 = A3/N3
1000 IF N4 > 0 THEN 1030
1010 LET A4 = 0
1020 GOTO 1040
1030 LET A4 = A4/N4
1040 PRINT TAB(11) "MALES" TAB(22) "$ ";A1 TAB(36) "$ ";A3
1050 PRINT
1060 PRINT TAB(9) "FEMALES" TAB(22) "$ ";A2 TAB(36) "$ ";A4
1070 DATA "07","M",28500,8
1080 DATA "11","F",16000,3
1090 DATA "11","M",18500,2
1100 DATA "07","F",23000,7
1110 DATA "11","M",13500,1
1120 DATA "07","M",22000,1
1130 DATA "07","F",31000,3
1140 DATA "11","F",18000,10
1150 DATA "11","F",14500,4
1160 DATA "07","M",29000,5
1170 DATA "99"
1180 END
```

This report should list the average percentage of defective parts for each supplier as well as the overall average for all five suppliers. The following data were available for each of the shipments the firm received from these five suppliers: supplier identification code (A,B,C,D,E); number of parts in the shipment; and number of defective parts in the shipment.

By accumulating the number of parts and the number of defective parts for each supplier, the *supplier's* percentage of defective parts can be calculated. By accumulating the same parts data across all suppliers, the *overall* percentage of defective parts can be calculated.

As with most programs, this problem can be solved in a number of ways. One approach is to set up separate accumulators for each supplier. If we use a control break, however, the program needs only two pairs of accumulators: one to use, in turn, with each of the suppliers and the second for the overall defective percentage. This second approach is used here. One benefit of this method is that additional suppliers can be added without changing the program.

The following report format was approved by the purchasing manager:

```
                    PERCENTAGE OF
                   DEFECTIVE PARTS

SUPPLIER A               XX
SUPPLIER B               XX
SUPPLIER C               XX
SUPPLIER D               XX
SUPPLIER E               XX

     OVERALL             XX
```

The input data items will be those listed earlier: supplier code, the number of parts in a shipment, and the number of defective parts in a shipment. Since the control break tool is being used, the data must be entered so that all shipments from a supplier are grouped together.

Exhibit D.6 shows the logical design for this problem and Program D.19 is a BASIC program that follows this logical design. As with Programs D.17 and D.18, only a small number of data values are used to illustrate the program's execution.

Exhibit D.6
Pseudocode for Problem 5

```
LEVEL 1:

  initialize program

  while (there are supplier data to process)

       enter a set of data
       adjust the overall accumulator
       adjust the supplier accumulator
       display supplier results

  display overall results

LEVEL 2:

  initialize variables
  display report heading

  while (there are supplier data to process)

       enter supplier code, parts, defective parts
       adjust overall accumulator
       if still on the "current" supplier
         then
             adjust supplier accumulator
         else
             calculate % defective for "prior" supplier
             display % defective for "prior" supplier
             set supplier accumulator to zero
             adjust supplier accumulator

  determine overall % defective
  display overall % defective

LEVEL 3:

  set accumulator to zero
  set control break variable to a blank
  display report heading

  enter a supplier code
  while (supplier code is not equal to "NO MORE")

       enter parts, defective parts
       adjust overall accumulator
       if control break variable is equal to supplier code
         then
             adjust supplier accumulator
         else
             calculate % defective for supplier
             display % defective for supplier
             set supplier accumulator to zero
             set control break variable to supplier code
             adjust supplier accumulator
       enter supplier code

  determine overall % defective
  display overall % defective
```

```
OK
RUN
                                   PERCENTAGE OF
                                  DEFECTIVE PARTS

                       SUPPLIER A      5
                       SUPPLIER B      6
                       SUPPLIER E      3

                       OVERALL         5
OK
```

```
10 REM  PROGRAM D.19
20 REM
30 REM  THIS PROGRAM ANALYZES THE DEFECTIVE
40 REM  PARTS A FIRM RECEIVES FROM ITS
50 REM  SUPPLIERS
60 REM
70 REM        P - OVERALL NUMBER OF PARTS
80 REM       P1 - NUMBER OF PARTS FOR A SUPPLIER
90 REM        D - OVERALL NUMBER OF DEFECTIVE PARTS
100 REM      D1 - NUMBER OF DEFECTIVE PARTS FOR A
110 REM           SUPPLIER
120 REM      S$ - SUPPLIER CODE
130 REM      N1 - NUMBER OF PARTS RECEIVED IN
140 REM           A SHIPMENT
150 REM      N2 - NUMBER OF DEFECTIVE PARTS RECEIVED
160 REM           IN A SHIPMENT
170 REM      C$ - CONTROL BREAK TEST VARIABLE
180 REM       A - PROPORTION OF DEFECTIVE PARTS
190 REM
200 LET P = 0
210 LET P1 = 0
220 LET D = 0
230 LET D1 = 0
240 LET C$ = " "
250 PRINT TAB(35) "PERCENTAGE OF"
260 PRINT TAB(34) "DEFECTIVE PARTS"
270 PRINT
280 READ S$
290 IF S$ = "NO MORE" THEN 390
300 READ N1,N2
310 LET P = P + N1
320 LET D = D + N2
330 IF C$ = " " THEN 350
340 IF S$ <> C$ THEN 390
350 LET C$ = S$
360 LET P1 = P1 + N1
370 LET D1 = D1 + N2
380 GOTO 280
390 LET A = INT( 100*(D1/P1) + .5 )
400 PRINT TAB(24) "SUPPLIER ";C$;TAB(40) A
410 IF S$ = "NO MORE" THEN 480
420 LET P1 = 0
430 LET D1 = 0
440 LET C$ = S$
450 LET P1 = P1 + N1
460 LET D1 = D1 + N2
470 GOTO 280
480 PRINT
490 LET A = INT ( 100*(D/P) + .5)
500 PRINT TAB(24) "OVERALL";TAB(40) A
510 GOTO 610
520 DATA "A",200,8
530 DATA "A",75,5
540 DATA "A",120,7
550 DATA "B",100,5
560 DATA "B",90,6
570 DATA "E",250,3
580 DATA "E",130,10
590 DATA "E",52,2
600 DATA "NO MORE"
610 END
```

Program D.19 has a number of interesting features:

1. The test using the control break variable *C$* in line number 330 is used to start the program. As the first supplier code will be different from the current value of *C$*, the program's normal logic would calculate and display the percentage of defective parts for the "prior" supplier. In this case, however, there is no prior supplier. The test in line number 330 jumps around the program's normal logic when *C$* holds a blank, which occurs only at the start of the program.

2. The trailer value, as seen in line numbers 290, 410, and 600, is the string "NO MORE." This string was chosen as it seems a natural way to indicate there are no more shipments to process.
3. The calculation of the percentage of defective parts may seem a bit unusual (see line number 490). This expression making use of the integer function does three things:
    1. Multiplying the result of the division by 100 converts the answer from a fraction to a percentage.
    2. Using this percentage as the argument of the integer function converts the percentage to an integer number.
    3. Adding .5 to the percentage rounds off this integer number.

The following example illustrates this procedure:

```
              let P = 198
              let D = 17
rate    =     INT ( 100*(D/P) + .5)
        =     INT ( 100*(17/198) + .5 )
        =     INT ( 100*(.08585859) + .5 )
        =     INT ( 8.585859 + .5 )
        =     INT ( 9.085859 )
        =     9
```

DEBUGGING SKILLS

No matter how much care is taken designing and coding a program, errors are bound to occur. Errors usually arise because the translation from the logical design to BASIC code is faulty or because of flaws in the logical design. In either case, these errors can be difficult to locate and correct. The process of locating and correcting programming errors is known as **debugging.**

Two programming tools valuable in debugging are a **trace flag** and a **debug print flag.** Each of these is described below.

Trace Flag

Most versions of BASIC provide a pair of programming statements, such as the TRON and TROFF statements in Microsoft BASIC, that "turn on" and "turn off" a flag. This operation results in the tracing of a program's processing flow. When the trace flag is on, the line number of every statement executed is displayed as the program runs. When the flag is off, the program executes normally.

Programs D.20A, D.20B, and D.20C present three versions of the same program to illustrate how tracing works. Program D.20A contains no trace flag, while Program D.20B makes use of it. The TRON statement in line number 225 turns the flag on, and the TROFF statements in line numbers 265 and 285 turn the flag off. Notice the numbers in brackets displayed when the program executes. These are the line numbers of the programming statements being executed while the trace flag is turned on. By following these line numbers, you can "trace" the program's processing flow. This feature can be valuable when you are trying to locate an elusive **bug** in your program.

Program D.20C provides an example of how *not* to use the trace flag. Notice that the GOTO statement in line number 280 branches to line number

```
OK
RUN
ENTER A PLUS ( + ) OR A MINUS ( - ) WHEN
PROMPTED TO INDICATE THE TYPE OF
OPERATION YOU WISH TO PERFORM? +

ENTER THE NUMBER OF OPERATIONS
YOU WISH TO PERFORM? 3

ENTER TWO VALUES: A,B? 3,4
 3  +  4  =  7

ENTER TWO VALUES: A,B? 65,37
 65  +  37  =  102

ENTER TWO VALUES: A,B? 359,932
 359  +  932  =  1291
OK
```

```
10 REM  PROGRAM D.20A
20 REM
30 REM  THIS PROGRAM DOES NOT USE A TRACE FLAG
40 REM
50 REM  THE PROGRAM SERVES AS A CALCULATOR THAT ADDS
60 REM  (A + B) OR SUBTRACTS (A-B) TWO VALUES
70 REM
80 REM              R$ - OPERATION CODE (+,-)
90 REM              N - NUMBER OF OPERATIONS TO PERFORM
100 REM             I - FOR/NEXT LOOP INDEX
110 REM             A - FIRST VALUE OF AN OPERATION
120 REM             B - SECOND VALUE OF AN OPERATION
130 REM
140 PRINT "ENTER A PLUS (+) OR A MINUS (-) WHEN"
150 PRINT "PROMPTED TO INDICATE THE TYPE OF"
160 PRINT "OPERATION YOU WISH TO PERFORM";
170 INPUT R$
180 PRINT
190 PRINT "ENTER THE NUMBER OF OPERATIONS YOU WISH TO PERFORM";
200 INPUT N
210 FOR I = 1 TO N
220 PRINT
230 PRINT "ENTER TWO VALUES: A,B";
240 INPUT A,B
250 IF R$ = "-" THEN 280
260 PRINT A;" + ";B;" = ";A+B
270 GOTO 290
280 PRINT A;" - ";B;" = "; A-B
290 NEXT I
300 END
```

```
OK
RUN
ENTER A PLUS ( + ) OR A MINUS ( - ) WHEN
PROMPTED TO INDICATE THE TYPE OF
OPERATION YOU WISH TO PERFORM? +

ENTER THE NUMBER OF OPERATIONS
YOU WISH TO PERFORM? 3

[230]ENTER TWO VALUES: A,B[240]? 3,4
[250][260] 3  +  4  =  7
[265]
[230]ENTER TWO VALUES: A,B[240]? 65,37
[250][260] 65  +  37  =  102
[265]
[230] ENTER TWO VALUES: A,B[240]? 359,932
[250][260] 359  +  932  =  1291
[265]
OK
```

```
10 REM  PROGRAM D.20B
20 REM
30 REM  THIS PROGRAM USES A TRACE FLAG
40 REM
50 REM  THE PROGRAM SERVES AS A CALCULATOR THAT ADDS
60 REM  (A+B) OR SUBTRACTS (A-B) TWO VALUES
70 REM
80 REM              R$ - OPERATION CODE (+,-)
90 REM              N - NUMBER OF OPERATIONS TO PERFORM
100 REM             I - FOR/NEXT LOOP INDEX
110 REM             A - FIRST VALUE OF AN OPERATION
120 REM             B - SECOND VALUE OF AN OPERATION
130 REM
140 PRINT "ENTER A PLUS (+) OR A MINUS (-) WHEN"
150 PRINT "PROMPTED TO INDICATE THE TYPE OF"
160 PRINT "OPERATION YOU WISH TO PERFORM";
170 INPUT R$
180 PRINT
190 PRINT "ENTER THE NUMBER OF OPERATIONS YOU WISH TO PERFORM";
200 INPUT N
210 FOR I = 1 TO N
220 PRINT
225 TRON
230 PRINT "ENTER TWO VALUES: A,B";
240 INPUT A,B
250 IF R$ = "-" THEN 280
260 PRINT A;" + ";B;" = ";A+B
265 TROFF
270 GOTO 290
280 PRINT A;" - ";B;" = "; A-B
285 TROFF
290 NEXT I
300 END
```

Changes for APPLESOFT BASIC:

```
225 TRACE

265 NOTRACE
```

```
OK
RUN
ENTER A PLUS (+) OR A MINUS (-) WHEN
PROMPTED TO INDICATE THE TYPE OF
OPERATION YOU WISH TO PERFORM? +
ENTER THE NUMBER OF OPERATIONS YOU WISH TO PERFORM? 3
[240]ENTER TWO VALUES: A,B[250]? 3,4
[260][270] 3 + 4 = 7
[280][300]
[240]ENTER TWO VALUES: A,B[250]? 65,37
[260][270] 65 + 37 = 102
[280][300]
[240]ENTER TWO VALUES: A,B[250]? 359,932
[260][270] 359 + 932 = 1291
[280][300]
OK
```

```
10 REM  PROGRAM D.20C
20 REM
30 REM  THIS PROGRAM USES A TRACE FLAG POORLY
40 REM
50 REM  THE PROGRAM SERVES AS A CALCULATOR THAT ADDS
60 REM  (A + B) OR SUBTRACTS (A-B) TWO VALUES
70 REM
80 REM            R$ - OPERATION CODE (+,-)
90 REM             N - NUMBER OF OPERATIONS TO PERFORM
100 REM            I - FOR/NEXT LOOP INDEX
110 REM            A - FIRST VALUE OF AN OPERATION
120 REM            B - SECOND VALUE OF AN OPERATION
130 REM
140 PRINT "ENTER A PLUS (+) OR A MINUS (-) WHEN"
150 PRINT "PROMPTED TO INDICATE THE TYPE OF"
160 PRINT "OPERATION YOU WISH TO PERFORM";
170 INPUT R$
180 PRINT
190 PRINT "ENTER THE NUMBER OF OPERATIONS YOU WISH TO PERFORM";
200 INPUT N
210 FOR I = 1 TO N
220 PRINT
230 TRON
240 PRINT "ENTER TWO VALUES: A,B";
250 INPUT A,B
260 IF R$ = "-" THEN 290
270 PRINT A;" + ";B;" = ";A+B
280 GOTO 300
290 PRINT A;" - ";B;" = "; A-B
300 TROFF
310 NEXT I
320 END
```

Changes for APPLESOFT BASIC:

```
230 TRACE
300 NOTRACE
```

300, a TROFF statement. Removing this debugging statement from the program would result in an error because there would now be no line number 300. (You would want to remove the TRON and TROFF statements once the program worked correctly. It is hard to read information being displayed with all the line numbers in brackets!) Do not tie debugging statements into the logic of your programs!

Debug Print Flag

While the trace flag does provide a step-by-step picture of how a program is executing, it does not display the values of a program's variables. Knowing how a program's variables change while a program executes is also helpful in debugging a program. The debug print flag provides this information.

Three operations are involved with using a debug print flag:

1. A flag is set to indicate whether the debug print statements are to be executed.
2. At critical points in a program's processing flow, the flag is tested with an IF statement to determine whether the flag is "on" or "off."
3. Print statements that display the values of some of the program's variables are linked to these IF statements.

When the debug print flag is on, the values of these variables are displayed. When the debug print flag is off, the program executes normally.

```
OK
RUN
 2
 3
 3
 4
 4
 5
OK
```

```
10 REM  PROGRAM D.21A
20 REM
30 REM  THIS PROGRAM DOES NOT USE A PRINT DEBUG FLAG
40 REM
50 REM  THE PROGRAM ILLUSTATES HOW A NESTED LOOP WORKS
60 REM  BY DISPLAYING THE SUM OF THE TWO LOOP INDICES,
70 REM  I AND J
80 REM
90 FOR I = 1 TO 3
100 FOR J = 1 TO 2
110 PRINT I+J
120 NEXT J
130 NEXT I
140 END
```

```
OK
RUN
I=  1  J=  1  --  2
I=  1  J=  2  --  3
I=  2  J=  1  --  3
I=  2  J=  2  --  4
I=  3  J=  1  --  4
I=  3  J=  2  --  5
OK
120 LET D$ = "OFF"
RUN
 2
 3
 3
 4
 4
 5
OK
```

```
10 REM  PROGRAM D.21B
20 REM
30 REM  THIS PROGRAM USES A PRINT DEBUG FLAG
40 REM
50 REM  THE PROGRAM ILLUSTATES HOW A NESTED LOOP WORKS
60 REM  BY DISPLAYING THE SUM OF THE TWO LOOP INDICES,
70 REM  I AND J
80 REM
90 REM  VARIABLE D$ IS A PRINT DEBUG FLAG.  SET IT TO "OFF"
100 REM IF YOU DO NOT WISH TO USE THIS DEBUGGING TOOL.
110 REM
120 LET D$ = "ON"
130 FOR I = 1 TO 3
140 FOR J = 1 TO 2
150 IF D$ = "OFF" THEN 170
160 PRINT "I= ";I;" J= ";J" -- ";
170 PRINT I+J
180 NEXT J
190 NEXT I
200 END
```

Programs D.21A and D.21B present two versions of the same program to illustrate the use of the debug print flag. Program D.21A does not use the debug print flag. Program D.21B, however, does make use of a **debug print flag,** given as variable *D$*. A string variable is being used for the flag so that the value assigned can be the words "ON" or "OFF." *D$* is set initially in line 120 and is tested in line number 150. Line number 160 displays the values of *I* and *J* only when *D$* is on.

The program must be modified to turn the print debug flag off. How this can be done is shown in the displayed output from Program D.21B. The information displayed with the flag turned off is the same as that obtained with the first version of the program.

Summary

No matter how much care is taken designing and coding a program, errors are bound to occur. The process of locating and correcting programming errors is known as *debugging*.

Two programming tools useful in locating and correcting program *bugs* are a *trace flag* and a *debug print flag*.

Most versions of BASIC provide a pair of programming statements that "turn on" and "turn off" a trace flag. When the trace flag is on, the line number of every statement that is executed is displayed. By following these line numbers, you can "trace" the program's processing flow.

The debug print flag is used to display the values of some of a program's variables at critical points in the program's processing flow. When the debug print flag is on, the values of these variables are displayed.

A Sample Debugging Problem

Problem 6: Calculating Employee Wage Increases. The personnel director of a hospital has requested a program to determine the new wage figures for the hospital's 325 hourly employees. The agreement worked out provides wage increases that depend on an employee's performance evaluation:

Performance Rating	Percentage Wage Increase
poor	0
satisfactory	4
good	5
outstanding	8

The input, processing, and output activities required for this problem are not difficult. Also, the personnel director has left all decisions about inputs and outputs to the programmer.

Two questions, however, remain:

1. How can error-free processing be guaranteed? The accuracy of this processing must be high.
2. How will the employee performance ratings be entered? They are not numeric values.

Each of these issues is resolved below.

Two types of business programming errors commonly occur in creating such programs. First, a program's logic can be faulty. That is, the program does not perform as specified or the program does not work correctly with some valid input data. Second, the program's logic is correct but invalid data are entered thereby producing incorrect output. The programmer can do several things to prevent both these errors from occurring:

1. Make use of debugging tools in developing the program. While you may not expect design errors, the output generated through the use of trace and debug print flags may enable you to discover errors that would otherwise be overlooked.
2. Test the program with well-chosen inputs. While you cannot make sure the program will work for all possible input values, carefully selected test data may help you discover errors that would otherwise be overlooked.
3. Have the program echo input values back to the user for visual verification. Thus, the user can check that the values just entered have been entered correctly.
4. Have the user enter data that are not actually used but that force the user to double-check the values that will be processed.

One way to handle the employee performance appraisals is to use alphabetic codes that are directly associated with the appraisal categories:

P–poor   S–satisfactory   G–good   O–outstanding

This approach is fine except for one drawback. The letter "O" for outstanding can be confused with a zero. It has been decided, therefore, to use the letter "E" (for "excellent").

Exhibit D.7 shows the logical design for this problem, given as Program D.22. A closer look at this program will indicate how the questions raised earlier were handled:

1. A likely place for a logic error to arise in this program is the code used to determine the percentage wage increase applied to an employee's current wage. Both a debug print flag, *D$*, and the trace flag are used to aid in debugging this segment of the program. *D$* is initialized in line number 190 and used in line number 550 to control line number 560. This flag triggers a display of the percentage wage increase to be applied to an employee's current wage. The trace flag is turned on in line number 410 and turned off in line number 580. By following the displayed line numbers, you can trace the exact path the program takes in determining this percentage increase for each set of entered employee data values.
2. A data entry echo and check are provided by line numbers 330 to 380.
3. The program design recognizes that a user might enter an incorrect performance rating. If this occurs, line number 530 displays an appropriate error message.

Exhibit D.7
Pseudocode for Problem 6

```
LEVEL 1:

  initialize program

  while (there are employee data to process)

        enter employee data
        determine correct wage increase %
        calculate new wage
        display output

LEVEL 2:

  set print debug flag on
  display message on how to stop the program

  enter an employee name
  while (employee name is not "NO MORE")

        enter employee number, wage, and rating
        echo back values just entered
        verify correctness of values just entered
        set % increase to zero
        if rating is "P" then
                increase is zero
          else if rating is "S" then
                increase is 4%
          else if rating is "G" then
                increase is 5%
          else if rating is "E" then
                increase is 8%
          else
                display error message
        wage change = wage * increase %
        new wage = wage + wage change
        display name, number, wage, wage change, new wage
        enter employee name
```

```
OK
RUN
ENTER 'NO MORE' WHEN PROMPTED FOR EMPLOYEE NAME
TO END THE PROGRAM

ENTER EMPLOYEE NAME? JAMES JONES
ENTER EMPLOYEE NUMBER? 23452
ENTER CURRENT WAGE? 6.85
ENTER PERFORMANCE APPRAISAL? G

NAME: JAMES JONES                       NUMBER: 23452
WAGE:  6.85    APPRAISAL: G
IS THIS CORRECT (ENTER YES OR NO)? YES

[420][430][440][490][500][550][560]% INCREASE = 5
[570][580]NAME: JAMES JONES     NUMBER 23452
OLD WAGE:  6.85
CHANGE:  .3425
NEW WAGE:  7.1925

ENTER EMPLOYEE NAME? NO MORE
OK
```

```
10 REM  PROGRAM D.22
20 REM
30 REM  THIS PROGRAM CALCULATES THE NEW HOURLY WAGE RATES
40 REM  FOR A HOSPITAL'S EMPLOYEES
50 REM
60 REM             D - PRINT DEBUG FLAG
70 REM            E$ - EMPLOYEE NAME
80 REM            N$ - EMPLOYEE'S JOB NUMBER
90 REM             W - EMPLOYEE'S CURRENT WAGE
100 REM           P$ - EMPLOYEE'S PERFORMANCE RATING
110 REM           R$ - USER RESPONSE
120 REM            R - % WAGE INCREASE
130 REM            C - WAGE CHANGE
140 REM           W1 - EMPLOYEE'S NEW WAGE
150 REM
160 REM  D$ IS A PRINT DEBUG FLAG.  SET D$ TO "OFF" IF YOU
170 REM  DO NOT WISH TO USE THE DEBUGGING TOOL.
180 REM
190 LET D$ = "ON"
200 PRINT "ENTER 'NO MORE' WHEN PROMPTED FOR EMPLOYEE NAME"
210 PRINT "TO END THE PROGRAM"
220 PRINT
230 PRINT
240 PRINT "ENTER EMPLOYEE NAME";
250 INPUT E$
260 IF E$ = "NO MORE" THEN 660
270 PRINT "ENTER EMPLOYEE NUMBER";
280 INPUT N$
290 PRINT "ENTER CURRENT WAGE";
300 INPUT W
310 PRINT "ENTER PERFORMANCE APPRAISAL";
320 INPUT P$
330 PRINT
340 PRINT "NAME: ";E$ TAB(30) "NUMBER: ";N$
350 PRINT "WAGE: ";W TAB(14) "APPRAISAL: ";P$
360 PRINT "IS THIS CORRECT (ENTER YES OR NO)";
370 INPUT R$
380 IF R$ = "NO" THEN 240
390 PRINT
400 LET R = 0
410 TRON
420 IF P$ = "P" THEN 570
430 IF P$ = "S" THEN 470
440 IF P$ = "G" THEN 490
450 IF P$ = "E" THEN 510
460 GOTO 530
470 LET R = 4
480 GOTO 550
490 LET R = 5
500 GOTO 550
510 LET R = 8
520 GOTO 550
530 PRINT "ERROR WITH PERFORMANCE APPRAISAL CODE -- ",P$
540 GOTO 240
550 IF D$ = "OFF" THEN 570
560 PRINT "% INCREASE = ";R
570 LET C = (R/100)*W
580 TROFF
590 LET W1 = W + C
600 PRINT "NAME: ";E$ TAB(30) "NUMBER ";N$
610 PRINT "OLD WAGE: ";W
620 PRINT "CHANGE: ";C
630 PRINT "NEW WAGE: ";W1
640 PRINT
650 GOTO 240
660 END
```

Changes for APPLESOFT BASIC:

```
410 TRACE

580 NOTRACE
```

SKILLS IN USING MENUS

Programs that are easy to use tend to be used more often. While this fact might seem obvious, you would be surprised how often programmers forget it. So far, we have discussed prompts as the primary means of easing program-user interactions. However, another technique, the menu, provides an alternative to prompts.

If the term *menu* makes you think of a restaurant, keep on thinking that way but "automate" your thoughts. A **menu** provides a user with a list of the alternative processing operations available in a certain segment of a program. When the user selects an item from the menu, that processing operation is performed.

Program D.23 uses a menu in order to improve the "calculator" program given earlier as Program D.20. The program lets a user choose one of four mathematical operations (addition, subtraction, division, and multiplication); prompts for two values; and then displays the results of the selected mathematical operation.

OK
RUN
MENU CHOICES: 1. ADDITION (A + B)
2. SUBTRACTION (A - B)
3. DIVISION (A / B)
4. MULTIPLICATION (A * B)
5. STOP THE PROGRAM
SELECT A MENU OPTION (1,2,3,4,5):? 3
A= ? 56
B= ? 245
56 / 245 = .2285714
SELECT A MENU OPTION (1,2,3,4,5):? 4
A= ? 45
B= ? .6
45 * .6 = 27
SELECT A MENU OPTION (1,2,3,4,5):? 6
MENU CHOICE ERROR: 6
SELECT A MENU OPTION (1,2,3,4,5):? 5
OK

```
10 REM  PROGRAM D.23
20 REM
30 REM  THIS PROGRAM ILLUSTRATES A MENU
40 REM
50 REM  THE PROGRAM SERVES AS A CALCULATOR PERFORMING
60 REM  SIMPLE ADDITION, SUBTRACTION, DIVISION, AND
70 REM  MULTIPLICATION
80 REM
90 REM         M - USER MENU CHOICE
100 REM        A - THE FIRST VALUE FOR A CALCULATION
110 REM        B - THE SECOND VALUE FOR A CALCULATION
120 REM
130 PRINT "MENU CHOICES:     1. ADDITION        (A + B)"
140 PRINT "                  2. SUBTRACTION     (A - B)"
150 PRINT "                  3. DIVISION        (A / B)"
160 PRINT "                  4. MULTIPLICATION  (A * B)"
170 PRINT "                  5. STOP THE PROGRAM"
180 PRINT
190 PRINT "SELECT A MENU OPTION (1,2,3,4,5):";
200 INPUT M
210 IF M = 5 THEN 390
220 IF M < 1 THEN 370
230 IF M > 5 THEN 370
240 PRINT "A= ";
250 INPUT A
260 PRINT "B= ";
270 INPUT B
280 ON M GOTO 290,310,330,350
290 PRINT ,A;" + ";B;" = ";A + B
300 GOTO 180
310 PRINT ,A;" - ";B;" = ";A - B
320 GOTO 180
330 PRINT ,A;" / ";B;" = ";A / B
340 GOTO 180
350 PRINT ,A;" * ";B;" = ";A * B
360 GOTO 180
370 PRINT "MENU CHOICE ERROR: ";M
380 GOTO 190
390 END
```

The program starts off by displaying the menu items available to the user. This is done with the PRINT statements in line numbers 130 to 170. Then line number 190 prompts the user for a menu choice. The program checks the validity of the menu choice in line numbers 220 and 230 and prints out an appropriate error message (line number 370) if an invalid choice was entered. Next, the user is prompted to enter the values to be used in the selected mathematical operation. Finally, the program uses an ON . . . GOTO statement to direct the processing flow to the correct operation (see line number 280).

Notice how the program terminates. The last menu item, Item 5 with Program D.23, will stop the program. This is a simple way for users to indicate that no more processing is to be performed.

As you can see with Program D.23, programs often use both prompts and menus for handling program-user interactions. One of the keys to good programming practice is knowing various ways to handle a particular data processing task, knowing the advantages and disadvantages of each, and then using the means most appropriate for that situation. The advantages and disadvantages of the different strategies for handling program-user interactions are discussed in Chapter 12, "Systems Development II."

Summary

Programs that are easy to use tend to be used more often. *Menus* can be used to make program-user interactions easier.

A menu provides a user with a list of the alternative processing operations available in a certain segment of a program. When the user selects an item from the menu, that processing operation is performed.

Including "stop the program" as one of the menu items provides a convenient way for a user to indicate that no more processing operations are to be performed.

A Sample Menuing Problem

Problem 7: Metric Conversions. An engineer who spends a lot of time working with a microcomputer has become frustrated with having to calculate metric conversions by hand. These irritating tasks not only take her away from the problem she is working on, she cannot remember the different conversion ratios. As a result, she has requested a program designed to perform these conversions on a microcomputer.

Specifically, the engineer has asked that the program handle the following types of conversions: feet and meters (1 meter = 3.28 feet); inches and centimeters (1 cm = .39 in); pounds and kilos (1 kilo = 2.2 lb); and grams and ounces (1 gram = .0353 oz). She wants the results to be displayed as:

```
8.5 FEET EQUALS 2.59 METERS
```

In total, eight conversions are to be performed: feet to meters, meters to feet, inches to centimeters, centimeters to inches, pounds to kilos, kilos to pounds, grams to ounces, and ounces to grams. These could be managed easily by using a menu with eight items. As with Program D.23, a ninth menu item can be added for stopping the program.

By employing a menu, the logical design for the program, shown as Program D.24, becomes very simple (see Exhibit D.8). As with Program D.23, an

```
CONVERSION OPTIONS: 1. FEET TO METERS
                    2. METERS TO FEET
                    3. INCHES TO CENTIMETERS
                    4. CENTIMETERS TO INCHES
                    5. POUNDS TO KILOS
                    6. KILOS TO POUNDS
                    7. OUNCES TO GRAMS
                    8. GRAMS TO OUNCES
                    9. STOP THE PROGRAM
SELECT CHOICE (1,2,3,4,5,6,7,8,9):?
CENTIMETERS= ?
                 45  CENTIMETERS EQUALS  17.55  INCHES
SELECT CHOICE (1,2,3,4,5,6,7,8,9):?
POUNDS= ?
                 165  POUNDS EQUALS  75  KILOS
SELECT CHOICE (1,2,3,4,5,6,7,8,9):?
OK
```

```
10 REM  PROGRAM D.24
20 REM
30 REM  THIS PROGRAM PERFORMS METRIC CONVERSIONS
40 REM
50 REM          M - MENU CHOICE
60 REM          A - MEASUREMENT TO CONVERT
70 REM          C - CONVERTED MEASUREMENT
80 REM
90 PRINT "CONVERSION OPTIONS:  1. FEET TO METERS"
100 PRINT "                    2. METERS TO FEET"
110 PRINT "                    3. INCHES TO CENTIMETERS"
120 PRINT "                    4. CENTIMETERS TO INCHES"
130 PRINT "                    5. POUNDS TO KILOS"
140 PRINT "                    6. KILOS TO POUNDS"
150 PRINT "                    7. OUNCES TO GRAMS"
160 PRINT "                    8. GRAMS TO OUNCES"
170 PRINT "                    9. STOP THE PROGRAM"
180 PRINT
190 PRINT "SELECT CHOICE (1,2,3,4,5,6,7,8,9):";
200 INPUT M
210 IF M = 9 THEN 760
220 IF M < 1 THEN 740
230 IF M > 9 THEN 740
240 PRINT
250 ON M GOTO 260,320,380,440,500,560,620,680
260 REM    FEET TO METERS
270 PRINT "FEET= ";
280 INPUT A
290 LET C = M/3.28
300 PRINT TAB(18) A;" FEET EQUALS ";C;" METERS"
310 GOTO 180
320 REM    METERS TO FEET
330 PRINT "METERS= ";
340 INPUT A
350 LET C = 3.28*A
360 PRINT TAB(18) A;" METERS EQUALS ";C;" FEET"
370 GOTO 180
380 REM        INCHES TO CENTIMETERS
390 PRINT "INCHES= ";
400 INPUT A
410 LET C = A/.39
420 PRINT TAB(18) A;" INCHES EQUALS ";C;" CENTIMETERS"
430 GOTO 180
440 REM        CENTIMETERS TO INCHES
450 PRINT "CENTIMETERS= ";
460 INPUT A
470 LET C = .39*A
480 PRINT TAB(18) A;" CENTIMETERS EQUALS ";C;" INCHES"
490 GOTO 180
500 REM        POUNDS TO KILOS
510 PRINT "POUNDS= ";
520 INPUT A
530 LET C = A/2.2
540 PRINT TAB(18) A;" POUNDS EQUALS ";C;" KILOS"
550 GOTO 180
560 REM        KILOS TO POUNDS
570 PRINT "KILOS= ";
580 INPUT A
590 LET C = 2.2*A
600 PRINT TAB(18) A;" KILOS EQUALS ";C;" POUNDS"
610 GOTO 180
620 REM        OUNCES TO GRAMS
630 PRINT "OUNCES= ";
640 INPUT A
650 LET C = A/.0353
660 PRINT TAB(18) A;" OUNCES EQUALS ";C;" GRAMS"
670 GOTO 180
680 REM        GRAMS TO OUNCES
690 PRINT "GRAMS= ";
700 INPUT A
710 LET C = .0353*A
720 PRINT TAB(18) A;" GRAMS EQUALS ";C;" OUNCES"
730 GOTO 180
740 PRINT "MENU SELECTION ERROR: ";M
750 GOTO 190
760 END
```

Exhibit D.8
Pseudocode for Problem 7

```
LEVEL 1:

  display metric conversion menu

  identify conversion to be performed

  perform conversion

  display results

LEVEL 2:

  display metric conversion menu

  enter menu choice
  while (conversion choice is not equal to 9)

       check validity of choice
       perform conversion
       display results
       enter menu choice

LEVEL 3:

  display metric conversion menu

  enter menu choice
  while (conversion choice is not equal to 9)
       if   menu choice is not 1 to 9 then
            display error message
            enter menu choice
       if   choice is feet to meters then
            enter feet
            meters = feet/3.28
            display result
       else if choice is meters to feet then
            enter meters
            feet = 3.28*meters
            display result
       else if choice is inches to centimeters then
            enter inches
            centimeters = inches/.39
            display result
       else if choice is centimeters to inches then
            enter centimeters
            inches = .39*centimeters
            display results
       else if choice is pounds to kilos then
            enter pounds
            kilos = pounds/2.2
            display result
       else if choice is kilos to pounds then
            enter kilos
            pounds = 2.2*kilos
            display result
       else if choice is ounces to grams then
            enter ounces
            grams = ounces/.0353
            display result
       else if choice is grams to ounces then
            enter grams
            ounces = .0353*grams
            display result
```

ON . . . GOTO statement (see line number 250) is used to direct the processing flow to the program segment performing the conversion requested by the user's choice of a menu item.

SKILLS IN GROUPING DATA

Up to now, the programs in this appendix have handled sets of data in a rather limited way:

1. The data are either maintained external to the computer system and entered via INPUT statements or maintained as part of a program in DATA statements and entered via READ statements.
2. Only a few items are stored in the computer's primary memory at any one time.
3. Values being entered into a program physically replace values previously entered.

While such an approach is relatively simple, it has a number of drawbacks:

1. Data tend to be tightly linked to a particular program. To use a set of data in another program, the data must be reentered through a keyboard by responding to INPUT prompts or by reproducing DATA statements.
2. One of two strategies must be taken to reuse a value that will be "lost" because a new value is to be entered into the variable holding this value:

   The value can simply be reentered when it is to be used again.

   The value can be stored in another variable.

   The first strategy is likely to mean extra work for the user. The second strategy will require defining extra variables, which may increase the complexity of the program.

3. The results of processing operations are not permanently captured. Again, one of two strategies must be taken to use these results in another program:

   The results can be printed onto paper and then entered into the program as data.

   The original data can be entered into the program, which also contains the processing operations that produce the needed results.

   Both of these strategies will require extra work by the program's user.

Programming tools that enable a programmer to **group** a set of data and treat the data as a single unit provide a means for overcoming these problems. Two such data grouping tools are **arrays** and **data files.**

With arrays, a set of data is manipulated as if it were a single variable. A major benefit of arrays is that the first items to be processed in a set of data will not be lost in order to process other items in the set. Also, the skilled use of arrays can often produce a rather simple solution to what initially appears as a complex programming problem. Arrays are perhaps the most powerful tool available to programmers.

With data files, a set of data to be processed is kept in secondary storage rather than being kept external to the computer system or as part of a program. These data files can hold raw data or the results of prior processing operations. In either case, the data can be accessed easily by many programs.

Arrays

Arrays enable a programmer to work conveniently with large sets of data in a program. Each value in the set of data is stored in an **element** of the array and is accessed through an array **subscript.** The first thing you need to learn about arrays is how subscripts work. Two helpful array operations will be covered as you are introduced to the use of subscripts: summing the values in an array and searching through an array for a certain value. Once you have become familiar with subscripts, two other common uses of arrays will be discussed: maintaining large sets of data in a program so that the values can be processed more than once and handling tables of data.

Summing Array Elements. Program D.25 sums the elements of a one-dimensional array. The DIM statement in line number 140 defines *A* as a one-dimensional array with five elements. Each of the two FOR-NEXT loops in Program D.25 serves a key role. The first loop, given in line numbers 180 to 200, fills the array with values from the DATA statement in line number 260. The loop index *I,* as it changes, inserts the values into successive elements of the array:

1. The "3" goes into the first element of *A,* or *A(1).*
2. The "5" goes into the second element of *A,* or *A(2).*
3. The "2" goes into the third element of *A,* or *A(3).*
4. The "7" goes into the fourth element of *A,* or *A(4).*
5. The "9" goes into the fifth element of *A,* or *A(5).*

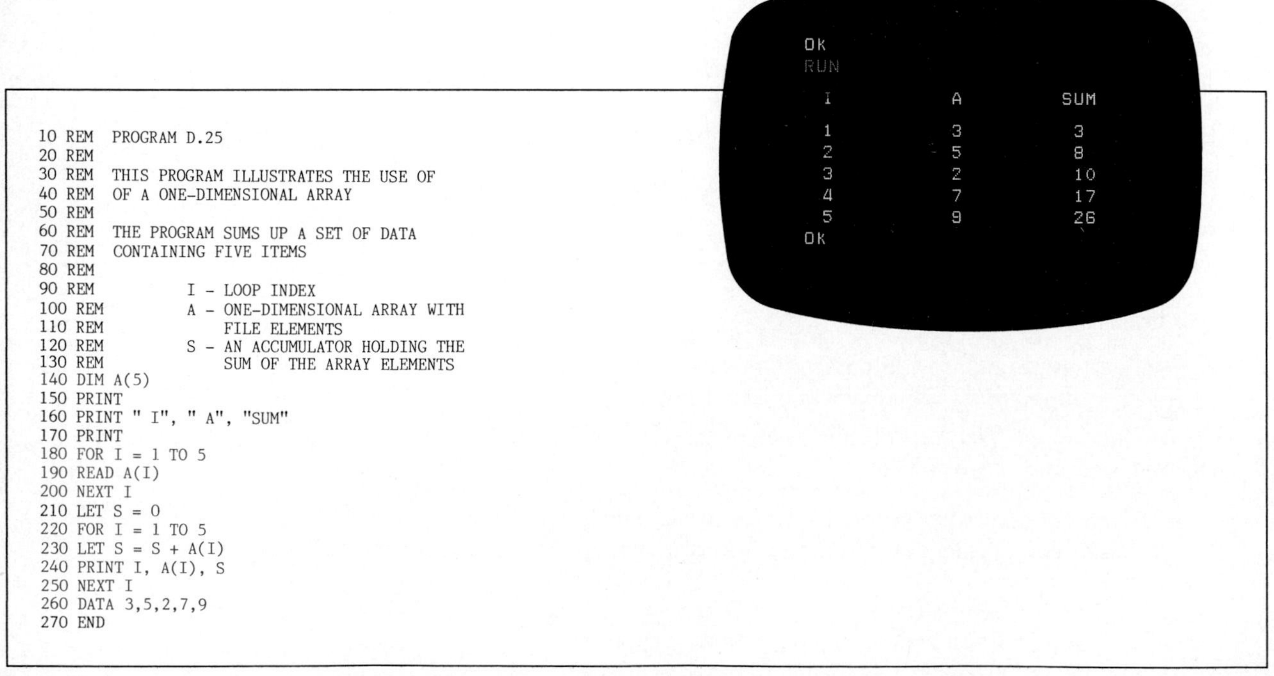

```
10 REM  PROGRAM D.25
20 REM
30 REM  THIS PROGRAM ILLUSTRATES THE USE OF
40 REM  OF A ONE-DIMENSIONAL ARRAY
50 REM
60 REM  THE PROGRAM SUMS UP A SET OF DATA
70 REM  CONTAINING FIVE ITEMS
80 REM
90 REM          I - LOOP INDEX
100 REM         A - ONE-DIMENSIONAL ARRAY WITH
110 REM             FILE ELEMENTS
120 REM         S - AN ACCUMULATOR HOLDING THE
130 REM             SUM OF THE ARRAY ELEMENTS
140 DIM A(5)
150 PRINT
160 PRINT " I", " A", "SUM"
170 PRINT
180 FOR I = 1 TO 5
190 READ A(I)
200 NEXT I
210 LET S = 0
220 FOR I = 1 TO 5
230 LET S = S + A(I)
240 PRINT I, A(I), S
250 NEXT I
260 DATA 3,5,2,7,9
270 END
```

OK
RUN
I A SUM
1 3 3
2 5 8
3 2 10
4 7 17
5 9 26
OK

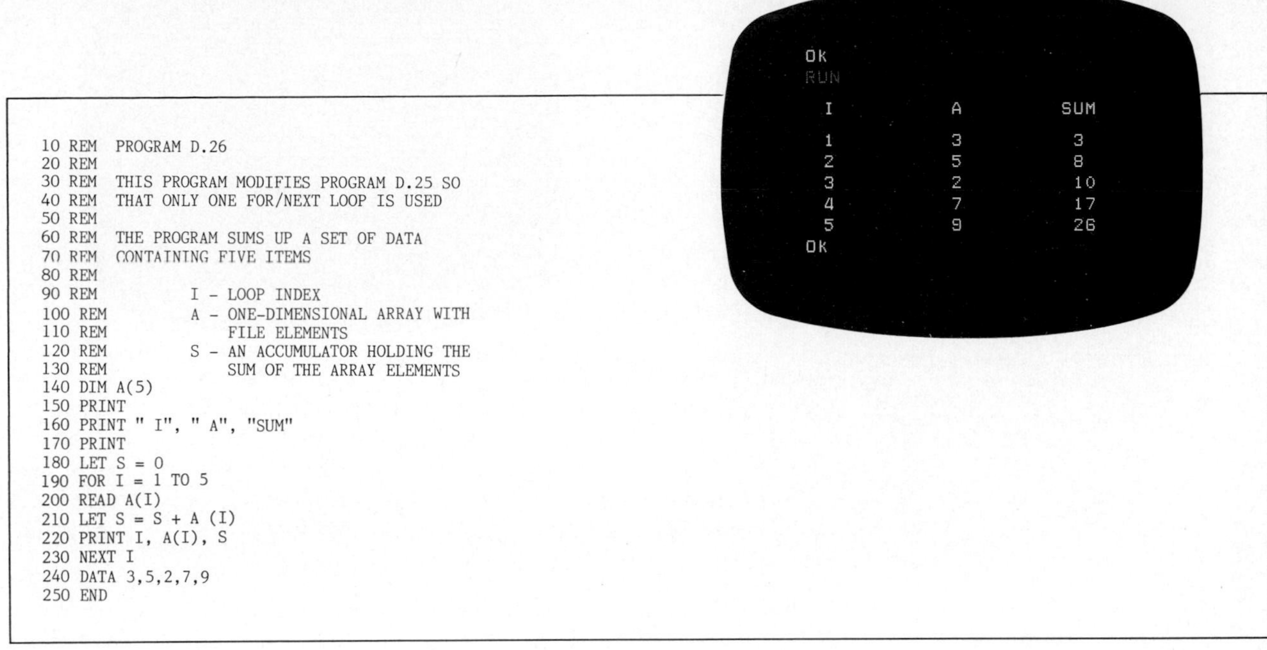

Ok
RUN
I A SUM
1 3 3
2 5 8
3 2 10
4 7 17
5 9 26
Ok

```
10 REM  PROGRAM D.26
20 REM
30 REM  THIS PROGRAM MODIFIES PROGRAM D.25 SO
40 REM  THAT ONLY ONE FOR/NEXT LOOP IS USED
50 REM
60 REM  THE PROGRAM SUMS UP A SET OF DATA
70 REM  CONTAINING FIVE ITEMS
80 REM
90 REM          I - LOOP INDEX
100 REM         A - ONE-DIMENSIONAL ARRAY WITH
110 REM             FILE ELEMENTS
120 REM         S - AN ACCUMULATOR HOLDING THE
130 REM             SUM OF THE ARRAY ELEMENTS
140 DIM A(5)
150 PRINT
160 PRINT " I", " A", "SUM"
170 PRINT
180 LET S = 0
190 FOR I = 1 TO 5
200 READ A(I)
210 LET S = S + A (I)
220 PRINT I, A(I), S
230 NEXT I
240 DATA 3,5,2,7,9
250 END
```

The second loop, given in line numbers 220 and 250, accumulates the values in array *A* into variable *S*. It then displays the loop index, the elements of *A*, and the accumulated sum.

Program D.26 is a shorter version of Program D.25. Notice that all the array operations have been placed within a single FOR-NEXT loop (see line numbers 190 to 230).

Program D.27 sums up each of the rows and columns in a two-dimensional array, *V*, which is defined as having two rows and three columns. Two one-dimensional arrays are also used: array *C* holds the three column sums, while array *R* holds the two row sums. Exhibit D.9 portrays this array as well as its row and column sums. Notice that nested FOR-NEXT loops were used in processing this two-dimensional array. The first loop, given in line numbers 190 to 230, fills array *V* with values from the program's two DATA statements. Here, the array is filled "row by row." That is, the first row is completely filled, and then the second row is completely filled. The second loop, given in line numbers 260 to 320, calculates row sums. The third loop, given in line numbers 350 to 410, calculates column sums. Notice how the loop indexes, which also serve as subscripts of array *V*, are switched in the second and third loops. In essence, the second loop works row by row (since the row subscript is the "outside" loop index), and the third loop works column by column (since the column subscript is the "outside" loop index).

Searching Array Elements. Arrays often hold tables of values critical to the data processing problem being solved. In order to obtain a particular value from such a table, the program must search through the array to locate the required value.

```
Ok
RUN
SUBSCRIPT:     1         2         3

ROW SUMS:      16        12
COLUMN SUMS:   5         8         15
Ok
```

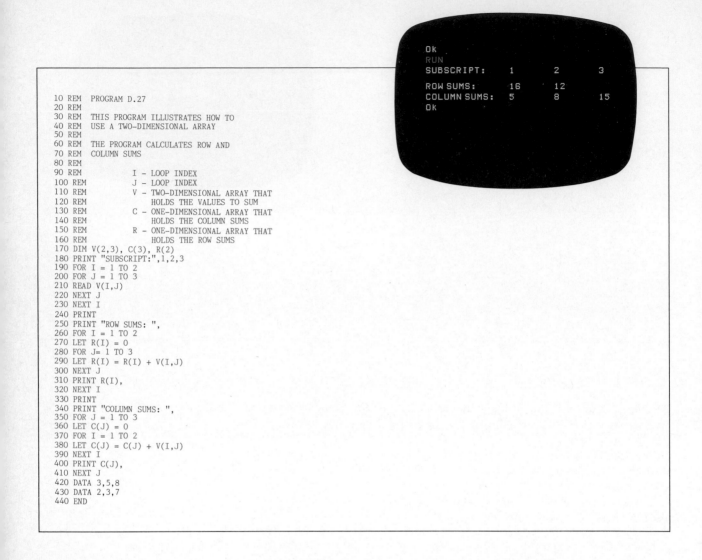

```
10 REM  PROGRAM D.27
20 REM
30 REM  THIS PROGRAM ILLUSTRATES HOW TO
40 REM  USE A TWO-DIMENSIONAL ARRAY
50 REM
60 REM  THE PROGRAM CALCULATES ROW AND
70 REM  COLUMN SUMS
80 REM
90 REM           I - LOOP INDEX
100 REM          J - LOOP INDEX
110 REM          V - TWO-DIMENSIONAL ARRAY THAT
120 REM              HOLDS THE VALUES TO SUM
130 REM          C - ONE-DIMENSIONAL ARRAY THAT
140 REM              HOLDS THE COLUMN SUMS
150 REM          R - ONE-DIMENSIONAL ARRAY THAT
160 REM              HOLDS THE ROW SUMS
170 DIM V(2,3), C(3), R(2)
180 PRINT "SUBSCRIPT:",1,2,3
190 FOR I = 1 TO 2
200 FOR J = 1 TO 3
210 READ V(I,J)
220 NEXT J
230 NEXT I
240 PRINT
250 PRINT "ROW SUMS: ",
260 FOR I = 1 TO 2
270 LET R(I) = 0
280 FOR J= 1 TO 3
290 LET R(I) = R(I) + V(I,J)
300 NEXT J
310 PRINT R(I),
320 NEXT I
330 PRINT
340 PRINT "COLUMN SUMS: ",
350 FOR J = 1 TO 3
360 LET C(J) = 0
370 FOR I = 1 TO 2
380 LET C(J) = C(J) + V(I,J)
390 NEXT I
400 PRINT C(J),
410 NEXT J
420 DATA 3,5,8
430 DATA 2,3,7
440 END
```

Exhibit D.9

Contents of Arrays V, R, and C in Program D.27

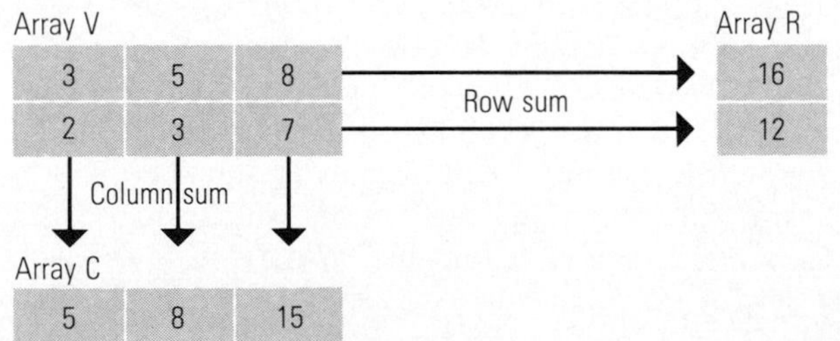

```
OK
RUN

ENTER PART NUMBER? 107

COST OF PART  107  IS $ 20.75
OK
RUN

ENTER PART NUMBER? 108
ERROR: NO MATCH FOUND FOR PART  108
OK
RUN

ENTER PART NUMBER? 113

COST OF PART  113  IS $ 30.5
OK
```

```
10 REM  PROGRAM D.28
20 REM
30 REM  THIS PROGRAM ILLUSTRATES HOW TO SEARCH
40 REM  THROUGH AN ARRAY
50 REM
60 REM  THE PROGRAM DISPLAYS THE COST OF A PART
70 REM  AFTER A USER HAS ENTERED A PART NUMBER
80 REM
90 REM          I - LOOP INDEX
100 REM         P - A TWO-DIMENSIONAL PARTS ARRAY
110 REM                 (COLUMN 1 - PART NUMBER)
120 REM                 (COLUMN 2 - PART COST)
130 REM         N - PART NUMBER
140 REM
150 DIM P(5,2)
160 FOR I = 1 TO 5
170 READ P(I,1), P(I,2)
180 NEXT I
190 PRINT
200 PRINT "ENTER PART NUMBER";
210 INPUT N
220 FOR I = 1 TO 5
230 IF N <> P(I,1) THEN 270
240 PRINT
250 PRINT "COST OF PART ";N;" IS $";P(I,2)
260 GOTO 340
270 NEXT I
280 PRINT "ERROR: NO MATCH FOUND FOR PART ";N
290 DATA 105,25.50
300 DATA 107,20.75
310 DATA 112,20.75
320 DATA 113,30.50
330 DATA 115,27.80
340 END
```

Program D.28 illustrates such an array operation. Array *P* contains the following table giving current costs for five parts that a firm uses in its manufactured products:

Part Number	Part Cost
105	25.50
107	20.75
112	20.75
113	30.50
115	27.80

Line number 150 defines *P* as a two-dimensional array having five rows and two columns. The part numbers are kept in the first column and the part costs are kept in the second column. Line numbers 160 to 180 fill this table from DATA statements. Line numbers 200 and 210 prompt the user for a part number, which is placed into variable *N*. The FOR-NEXT loop given in line numbers 220 to 270 actually performs the search. The key to this program is recognizing that each row of *P* holds the number and cost of a particular part. This FOR-NEXT loop searches down the first column of *P* looking for a match with the part number just entered into variable *N*. When a match occurs, the loop index *I* holds the row of the desired part. The value in the second column of this row, or *P*(*I*, 2), then contains the correct cost.

Maintaining Large Data Sets in a Program. Problems that require processing a large number of values at multiple locations within a program would be difficult to solve without using arrays. Arrays enable such problems to be handled with ease.

Program D.29 is a practical program for calculating the mean and standard deviation of a set of values. The formulas for these two calculations are:

$$\text{MEAN:} \quad M = \frac{\sum_{i=1}^{N} Vi}{N}$$

$$\text{STANDARD DEVIATION:} \quad S = \sqrt{\frac{\sum_{i=1}^{N} (Vi - M)^2}{N}}$$

Notice that the formula for the standard deviation uses the calculated value for the mean as well as each of the original values used in calculating the mean. Thus, the values in the set of data must be processed twice: once in calculating

```
OK

ENTER THE NUMBER OF DATA VALUES TO BE ANALYZED?
ENTER VALUES ONE AT A TIME AS A ? APPEARS
?
?
?
?
?
?
?
?
MEAN = 28
STD. DEV. = 4.1833
OK
```

```
10 REM  PROGRAM D.29
20 REM
30 REM  THIS PROGRAM ILLUSTRATES HOW ARRAYS LET YOU
40 REM  KEEP A SET OF DATA IN A PROGRAM SO THAT IT
50 REM  CAN BE OPERATED ON MORE THAN ONCE
60 REM
70 REM  THE PROGRAM CALCULATES THE MEAN AND STANDARD
80 REM  DEVIATION OF A SET OF DATA
90 REM
100 REM         I - LOOP INDEX
110 REM         V - ONE-DIMENSIONAL ARRAY HOLDING THE
120 REM             SET OF DATA TO BE ANALYZED
130 REM         N - NUMBER OF DATA VALUES TO BE ANALYZED
140 REM           - MEAN OF THE SET OF DATA
150 REM           - STANDARD DEVIATION OF THE SET OF DATA
160 DIM V(100)
170 PRINT
180 PRINT "ENTER THE NUMBER OF DATA VALUES TO BE ANALYZED";
190 INPUT N
200 PRINT "ENTER VALUES ONE AT A TIME AS A ? APPEARS"
210 PRINT
220 FOR I = 1 TO N
230 INPUT V(I)
240 NEXT I
250 REM         CALCULATE MEAN
260 LET M = 0
270 FOR I = 1 TO N
280 LET M = M + V(I)
290 NEXT I
300 LET M = M/N
310 REM          CALCULATE STANDARD DEVIATION
320 FOR I = 1 TO N
330 LET S = S + (V(I) - M)^2
340 NEXT I
350 LET S = SQR(S/N)
360 PRINT
370 PRINT "MEAN = ";M
380 PRINT "STD. DEV. = ";S
390 END
```

the mean (line numbers 260 to 300), and a second time in calculating the standard deviation (line numbers 320 to 350). By maintaining these values in an array, the problem is solved rather handily.

Program D.29 has one feature that deserves special attention. Array *V*, which holds the values to be analyzed, was defined as a one-dimensional array with 100 elements (see line number 160). This array size was selected as it was believed to be bigger than any set of data that might be analyzed. The user is prompted in line numbers 180 and 190 for the number of values to be analyzed. This value, variable *N*, is then used as the stopping value for the three FOR-NEXT loops in the program. In this way, only that portion of the array holding values is processed.

Handling Tables of Data. Many business programming problems require the use of tables of information such as shipping charges, shipping distances, and wage rates. These data tables usually are set up and accessed as either arrays or data files. Since arrays are maintained in primary memory and data files are maintained in secondary storage, maintaining data tables as arrays can result in faster and more convenient programs. As data tables become larger and their values change frequently, it is best to maintain the tables in secondary storage.

Program D.30 is a program used by a parts wholesaler that sums the total charge for a sales order, taking into consideration any discounts due the purchaser. This discount rate is obtained from the following table:

	PAYMENT CONDITIONS		
Total Purchase Amount ($)	With the Order	Upon Delivery	Within 30 Days
0 - 9,999	1%	0	0
10,000 - 24,999	2%	1%	0
25,000 +	3%	2%	0

The wholesaler carries 25 different products.

Program D.30 uses three arrays (see line number 250). Array *D*, which is defined as having three rows and three columns, holds the order discount data table just described. Array *P*, which is defined as having 25 rows and 2 columns, holds the part numbers and costs. Array *S*, which is also defined as having 25 rows and 2 columns, holds values to be displayed after the program has processed an entire order. Keeping the values to be displayed in array *S* prevents the program's data entry prompts from being intermixed with the program's outputs.

The program uses a menu to prompt the user for the payment condition of an order (see line numbers 370 to 420). The user's menu selection, variable *C*, then serves as the column subscript when a discount rate is "pulled" from array *D* in line number 600. Variable *R*, the row subscript for array *D* in line number 600, is obtained in another way. Line numbers 520 to 560 use variable *Q*, the order quantity for a part, and a series of IF tests to assign a value to *R* that corresponds with the rows of the discount table.

Finally, notice how the total charge for an order is determined. The FOR-NEXT loop in lines 700 to 730 displays each of the filled elements of array *S* and accumulates the discounted charge for each ordered part into variable *T*.

```
OK
RUN
PAYMENT CONDITIONS:     1 - WITH ORDER
                        2 - UPON DELIVERY
                        3 - OVER 30 DAYS
INDICATE PAYMENT CONDITION (1,2,3)?
HOW MANY DIFFERENT PARTS ARE BEING ORDERED?
ENTER PART NUMBER? 131
ENTER QUANTITY ORDERED? 40000
ENTER PART NUMBER? 152
ENTER QUANTITY ORDERED? 10000
                  PART NUMBER        CHARGE
                  131                509600
                  152                118800
                  TOTAL:             628400
OK
```

```
10 REM  PROGRAM D.30
20 REM
30 REM  THIS PROGRAM ILLUSTRATES ARRAYS CAN BE USED TO
40 REM  SET UP DATA TABLES
50 REM
60 REM  THE PROGRAM DETERMINES THE TOTAL COST FOR AN ORDER
70 REM  BASED ON PART COSTS AND AN ORDER DISCOUNT RATE
80 REM
90 REM              I - LOOP INDEX
100 REM             J - LOOP INDEX
110 REM             D - A TWO-DIMENSIONAL ARRAY HOLDING
120 REM                 THE DISCOUNT TABLE
130 REM             P - A TWO-DIMENSIONAL ARRAY HOLDING
140 REM                 PARTS DATA
150 REM             S - A TWO DIMENSIONAL ARRAY HOLDING
160 REM                 ORDER SUBTOTALS
170 REM             N - NUMBER OF DIFFERENT PARTS BEING
180 REM                 ORDERED
190 REM             C - PAYMENT CONDITION
200 REM            N1 - PART NUMBER
210 REM             Q - QUANTITY OF PARTS ORDERED
220 REM             R - ROW SUBSCRIPT FOR DISCOUNT TABLE
230 REM             T - TOTAL COSTS FOR A COMPLETE ORDER
240 REM
250 DIM D(3,3), P(25,2), S(25,2)
260 FOR I = 1 TO 3
270 FOR J = 1 TO 3
280 READ D(I,J)
290 NEXT J
300 NEXT I
310 FOR I = 1 TO 25
320 LET S(I,1) = 0
330 LET S(I,2) = 0
340 READ P(I,1),P(I,2)
350 NEXT I
360 PRINT
370 PRINT "PAYMENT CONDITIONS:  1 - WITH ORDER"
380 PRINT "                     2 - UPON DELIVERY"
390 PRINT "                     3 - OVER 30 DAYS"
400 PRINT
410 PRINT "INDICATE PAYMENT CONDITION (1,2,3)";
420 INPUT C
430 IF C < 1 THEN 770
440 IF C > 3 THEN 770
450 PRINT "HOW MANY DIFFERENT PARTS ARE BEING ORDERED";
460 INPUT N
470 FOR J = 1 TO N
480 PRINT "ENTER PART NUMBER";
490 INPUT N1
500 PRINT "ENTER QUANTITY ORDERED";
510 INPUT Q
520 LET R = 1
530 IF Q < 10000 THEN 570
540 LET R = 2
550 IF Q < 25000 THEN 570
560 LET R = 3
570 FOR I = 1 TO 25
580 IF N1 <> P(I,1) THEN 620
590 LET S(J,1) = P(I,1)
600 LET S(J,2) = Q*P(I,2) - D(R,C)*Q*P(I,2)
610 GOTO 650
620 NEXT I
630 PRINT "ERROR -- NO PART NUMBER: ";N1
640 GOTO 480
650 NEXT J
660 PRINT
670 PRINT ,"PART NUMBER", "  CHARGE"
680 PRINT
690 LET T = 0
700 FOR I = 1 TO N
710 PRINT , S(I,1), S(I,2)
720 LET T = T + S(I,2)
730 NEXT I
740 PRINT
```

```
750 PRINT ,"TOTAL:",T
760 GOTO 1050
770 PRINT "ERROR -- PAYMENT CONDITION: ";C
780 GOTO 410
790 DATA .01,0,0,.02,.01,0,.03,.02,0
800 DATA 114,40.00
810 DATA 122,75.00
820 DATA 125,35.00
830 DATA 126,33.00
840 DATA 128,32.00
850 DATA 129,12.00
860 DATA 131,13.00
870 DATA 132,14.00
880 DATA 133,15.00
890 DATA 134,13.00
900 DATA 135,14.00
910 DATA 136,12.00
920 DATA 137,10.00
930 DATA 138,9.00
940 DATA 139,8.00
950 DATA 140,9.00
960 DATA 141,13.00
970 DATA 142,14.00
980 DATA 151,11.00
990 DATA 152,12.00
1000 DATA 163,11.00
1010 DATA 164,17.00
1020 DATA 165,18.00
1030 DATA 166,19.00
1040 DATA 167,19.00
1050 END
```

Data Files

Three basic processing operations are performed in using data files:

file creating A data file is created and made available for use.

file updating Most business data files are established to keep track of some facet of a business's activities. As business events take place, the data describing these activities also change. As a result:

Some of the items in a data file will need to be *modified.*

Some new items may need to be *added* to a data file.

Some old items may need to be *deleted* from a data file.

file reporting Selected items are retrieved from a data file and displayed.

Developing programs for file creating and file reporting is generally not difficult. Thus, programs illustrating these operations will be described in this appendix. File updating, however, tends to be a more complex activity and will not be covered.

Programs D.31 and D.32 both involve a data file containing information on the current status of a firm's credit customers. Program D.31 creates such a data file. Program D.32 uses the file to produce a report listing customers who have reached or exceeded their authorized credit limits.

Line number 180 in Program D.31 informs the computer's operating system of the *external* file name, in this case NEWBALAN, that will be assigned to the data file being created. The "B:" preceding this file name indicates that the file is to be written on drive B, or the second disk drive on a two-disk drive microcomputer system. The "#1" assigns an *internal* file name to be used

```
OK
RUN

ENTER A VALUE OF 9999 FOR CUSTOMER ACCOUNT
NUMBER TO STOP THE PROGRAM

ENTER CUSTOMER ACCOUNT NUMBER: ? 2234
ENTER CURRENT ACCOUNT BALANCE: ? 200
ENTER CUSTOMER CREDIT LIMIT: ? 500

ACCOUNT: 2234  BALANCE:  200    LIMIT:  500
ARE THESE VALUES CORRECT? YES

ENTER CUSTOMER ACCOUNT NUMBER: ? 2235
ENTER CURRENT ACCOUNT BALANCE: ? 509
ENTER CUSTOMER CREDIT LIMIT: ? 800

ACCOUNT: 2235  BALANCE:  509    LIMIT: 800
ARE THESE VALUES CORRECT? NO

ENTER CUSTOMER ACCOUNT NUMBER: ? 9999
OK
```

```
10 REM  PROGRAM D.31
20 REM
30 REM  THIS PROGRAM ILLUSTRATES HOW TO CREATE A DATA
40 REM  FILE FROM DATA ENTERED FROM A KEYBOARD
50 REM
60 REM  THIS PROGRAM CREATES A DATA FILE "NEWBALAN"
70 REM  THAT CONTAINS THE FOLLOWING ITEMS FOR A
80 REM  FIRM'S CREDIT CUSTOMERS:
90 REM
100 REM      C$ - CUSTOMER ACCOUNT NUMBER
110 REM       B - CURRENT ACCOUNT BALANCE
120 REM       L - AUTHORIZED CREDIT LIMIT
130 REM
140 PRINT
150 PRINT "ENTER A VALUE OF 9999 FOR CUSTOMER ACCOUNT"
160 PRINT "NUMBER TO STOP THE PROGRAM"
170 PRINT
180 OPEN "B:NEWBALAN" FOR OUTPUT AS #1
200 PRINT "ENTER CUSTOMER ACCOUNT NUMBER: ";
210 INPUT C$
215 IF C$ = "9999" THEN 360
220 PRINT "ENTER CURRENT ACCOUNT BALANCE: ";
230 INPUT B
240 PRINT "ENTER CUSTOMER CREDIT LIMIT: ";
260 INPUT L
280 PRINT
290 PRINT "ACCOUNT: "; C$;"  BALANCE: ";B;"  LIMIT:";L
300 PRINT "ARE THESE VALUES CORRECT";
310 INPUT A$
320 PRINT
330 IF A$ <> "YES" THEN 200
340 WRITE #1,C$,B,L
350 GOTO 200
360 CLOSE #1
370 END
```

Changes for APPLESOFT BASIC:

```
180 C$=CHR$(4)
181 PRINT C$;"OPEN NEWBALAN,D2"
182 PRINT C$;"WRITE NEWBALAN"

340 WRITE C$,B,L

360 PRINT C$;"CLOSE NEWBALAN"
```

```
OK
RUN
                 CUSTOMERS AT OR OVER THEIR
                  AUTHORIZED CREDIT LIMITS

                ACCOUNT  BALANCE  LIMIT

                  2231     800      500
                  2234     500      500
                  2235     1050     1000
                  2237     800      500
                  2240     1200     1000
                  2242     1250     500
OK
```

```
10 REM  PROGRAM D.32
20 REM
30 REM  THIS PROGRAM ILLUSTRATES HOW TO GENERATE
40 REM  A REPORT FROM A DATA FILE
50 REM
60 REM  THE PROGRAM GENERATES A REPORT LISTING
70 REM  THOSE CUSTOMERS WHOSE CURRENT ACCOUNT
80 REM  BALANCES ARE EQUAL TO OR OVER THEIR
90 REM  AUTHORIZED CREDIT LIMIT
100 REM
110 REM         C$ - CUSTOMER ACCOUNT NUMBER
120 REM          B - CUSTOMER ACCOUNT BALANCE
130 REM          L - CUSTOMER CREDIT LIMIT
140 REM
150 PRINT TAB(19) "CUSTOMERS AT OR OVER THEIR"
160 PRINT TAB(20) "AUTHORIZED CREDIT LIMITS"
170 PRINT
180 PRINT TAB(18) "ACCOUNT" TAB(29) "BALANCE" TAB(42) "LIMIT"
190 PRINT
200 OPEN "B:OLDBALAN" FOR INPUT AS #1
210 IF EOF(1) THEN 260
220 INPUT #1,C$,B,L
230 IF B < L THEN 210
240 PRINT TAB(19) C$ TAB(29) B TAB(42) L
250 GOTO 210
260 CLOSE #1
270 END
```

Changes for APPLESOFT BASIC:

```
200 REM CNT COUNTS THE DATA RECORDS IN THE OLD BALANCE FILE
201 CNT=0
202 PRINT "ENTER THE NUMBER OF DATA RECORDS IN THE OLD BALANCE FILE";
203 INPUT LIMIT
204 D$=CHR$(4)
205 PRINT D$;"OPEN OLDBALAN,D2"
206 PRINT D$;"READ OLDBALAN"

210 IF CNT=LIMIT THEN 260
220 INPUT C$,B,L
221 CNT=CNT+1

260 PRINT D$;"CLOSE OLDBALAN"
```

within the program itself. When data values are written onto the data file in line number 340, the WRITE #1 statement places the values at the end of the data file earlier opened as File #1.

The CLOSE statement in line number 360 releases the data file NEWBALAN from this program. This step enables the internal name "#1" to be used for another data file in this program. It also enables the data file NEWBALAN to be used by another program. The data file NEWBALAN created via the execution of Program D.31 shown in the accompanying CRT screen display contains a single record with three fields:

```
"2234", 200, 500
```

Program D.32 produces the following report by retrieving values from a data file named OLDBALAN:

```
        Customers At or Over Their
         Authorized Credit Limits
  ACCOUNT       BALANCE        LIMIT
     .             .             .
     .             .             .
     .             .             .
```

Line number 200 identifies the data file to be accessed by the program. The data records contained in OLDBALAN are shown as Exhibit D.10.

The IF statement in line number 210 makes use of the **EOF function,** which tests to determine whether an **end-of-file mark** was reached on the data file being processed. This function provides an easy way to determine when there are no more values to be processed on the data file.

Exhibit D.10
The Data File OLDBALAN Used with Program D.32

```
"2230",100,500
"2231",800,500
"2232",600,1000
"2233",400,1000
"2234",500,500
"2235",1050,1000
"2236",700,1000
"2237",800,500
"2238",150,1000
"2239",0,500
"2240",1200,1000
"2241",350,500
"2242",1250,500
"2243",0,1000
"2244",750,1000
"2245",250,500
```

Summary

Programming tools that enable a programmer to *group* a set of data and treat them as a single unit can be helpful in solving business programming problems. Two data grouping tools are *arrays* and *data files.*

With arrays, a set of data is manipulated as if it were a single variable. A major benefit of arrays is that the first items to be processed in a set of data will not be lost in order to process other items in a set. Also, the skilled use of arrays can often simplify what initially appears to be a complex programming problem.

With data files, a set of data to be processed is kept in secondary storage rather than being kept external to the computer system or as part of a program. These data files can hold raw data or the results of prior processing operations. In either case, the data can be accessed easily by many programs.

When a set of data is created as an array, each value in the set is stored in an *element* of the array and is accessed through an array *subscript.*

Some of the useful operations that can be performed with arrays are summing the values in an array, searching through an array for a certain value, maintaining large sets of data in a program so that values can be processed more than once, and handling tables of data.

Three basic processing operations are performed using data files: file creating, file updating, and file reporting. With *file creating,* a data file is initially set up and made available for use. With *file updating,* some items in a data file are modified and others might be deleted from or added to the file. With *file reporting,* selected items are retrieved from a data file and displayed.

Data files are assigned *external* and *internal* names. External names distinguish one data file from the others in secondary storage. Internal names identify the data file within the program itself.

An *end-of-file mark* is placed at the end of a data file. An *EOF function,* which tests to see if the end-of-file mark has been reached, provides a simple way of determining when there are no more values to be processed on a data file.

Sample Data Grouping Problems

The data grouping skills just covered can greatly ease many business programming tasks. The three problems that follow are good examples of the usefulness of arrays and data files. Problem 8 makes use of a one-dimensional array. Problem 9 uses a one-dimensional array and a data file. Problem 10 retrieves data from two data files to produce a single report.

Problem 8: Present Value Analysis. A financial analyst wants a program to perform present value calculations. Present value analysis discounts future dollars as being less valuable than current dollars. Usually, the discount factor accounts for the expected inflation rate or a firm's cost of capital. The following is the formula used in this calculation:

$$\text{present value} = -C_0 + \sum_{i=1}^{n} \frac{C_i}{(1+d)^n}$$

where:

C_0 is the initial investment
C_i is the cash flow for year i
n is the number of years involved
d is the discount factor.

The financial analyst wants a program that will perform the analysis interactively. That is, prompts and menus should be used to define all aspects of the calculation: the number of years involved, the discount factor, the initial investment, and the yearly cash flows. Also, the analyst should be able to change any of the values involved with a calculation and then reanalyze the investment. Such a capability is termed **what-if** analysis. The results of the analysis should appear as shown:

```
  DISCOUNT FACTOR = XX%

INITIAL INVESTMENT = XXXXXXX

    YEAR        CASHFLOW
    ----        --------
     1          XXXXXXX
     2          XXXXXXX
     .             .
     .             .
     .             .
     N          XXXXXXX
PRESENT VALUE = XXXXXXXXXX
```

The key to solving this problem is to recognize that the stream of cash flows can be maintained in an array. This provides two main benefits:

1. The length of the cash flow stream can vary as needed.
2. The entire cash flow stream is kept in the program for subsequent "what-if" analyses.

No project is expected to span more than twenty-five years. Thus, the array holding the cash flows can be defined as a one-dimensional array with twenty-five elements.

The logical design for this problem is given in Exhibit D.11. Program D.33 solves the problem.

The "what-if" analysis is directed by the menu given in line numbers 500 to 580. A user can change any aspect of an investment except the number of years over which cash flows will occur. After the changes for a "what-if" analysis have been entered, menu option 4 directs the processing flow to line number 300 to display the new investment situation, perform the present value calculation, and display the results. Then, the user is again asked if another "what-if" analysis is to be performed.

Exhibit D.11
Pseudocode for Problem 8

```
LEVEL 1:

   specify an investment

   perform present value analysis

   display results

   while (the analyst wishes to do what-if analyses)

         change investment specification
         reanalyze the investment
         display results

LEVEL 2:

   enter years
   enter discount factor (%)
   enter initial investment
   enter initial yearly cash flows

   display investment situation
   convert discount % to a discount decimal
   assign negative initial investment to present value
   accumulate discounted cash flows into present value
   display present value

   enter response regarding what-if analysis
   while (response is "YES")

         display menu on investment changes
         enter menu choice
         repeat

               enter change value
               display menu on investment changes
               enter menu choice
               until (menu choice is "no more changes")

         display investment situation
         convert discount % to a discount decimal
         assign negative initial investment to present value
         accumulate discounted cash flows into present value
         display present value
         enter a response regarding what-if analysis
```

```
10 REM  PROGRAM D.33
20 REM
30 REM  THIS PROGRAM CALCULATES THE
40 REM  PRESENT VALUE OF AN INVESTMENT
50 REM
60 REM       Y - NUMBER OF YEARS
70 REM       D - DISCOUNT FACTOR (%)
80 REM      D1 - DISCOUNT FACTOR (DECIMAL)
90 REM       N - INITIAL INVESTMENT
100 REM      F - AN ARRAY OF CASH FLOWS FROM
110 REM          THE INVESTMENT
120 REM      P - PRESENT VALUE OF THE
130 REM          INVESTMENT
140 REM     R$ - USER RESPONSE
150 REM      C - USER MENU SELECTION FOR
160 REM          "WHAT-IF" ANALYSIS
170 REM
180 DIM F(25)
190 PRINT
200 PRINT "ENTER NUMBER OF YEARS";
210 INPUT Y
220 PRINT "ENTER DISCOUNT FACTOR (AS A %)";
230 INPUT D
240 PRINT "ENTER INITIAL INVESTMENT";
250 INPUT N
260 FOR I = 1 TO Y
270 PRINT "ENTER CASH FLOW FOR YEAR ";I;
280 INPUT F(I)
290 NEXT I
300 PRINT
310 PRINT TAB(12) "DISCOUNT FACTOR = ";D;"%"
320 PRINT
330 PRINT TAB(9) "INITIAL INVESTMENT = ";N
340 PRINT
350 PRINT TAB(15) "YEAR     CASH FLOW"
360 PRINT
370 LET D1 = D/100
380 LET P = -N
390 FOR I = 1 TO Y
400 LET P = P + F(I)/(1+D1)^I
410 PRINT TAB(17);I;TAB(23);F(I)
420 NEXT I
430 PRINT
440 PRINT TAB(7) "PRESENT VALUE = ";P
450 PRINT
460 PRINT "DO YOU WANT TO DO SOME WHAT-IF ANALYSIS";
470 INPUT A$
480 IF A$ = "NO" THEN 750
490 PRINT
500 PRINT "POSSIBLE PROBLEM CHANGES:"
510 PRINT
520 PRINT "    1. DISCOUNT FACTOR"
530 PRINT "    2. INITIAL INVESTMENT"
540 PRINT "    3. THE CASH FLOW FOR A YEAR"
550 PRINT "    4. NO MORE CHANGES"
560 PRINT
570 PRINT "SELECT ONE (1,2,3, OR 4)";
580 INPUT C
590 IF C < 1 THEN 620
600 IF C > 4 THEN 620
610 ON C GOTO 640,670,700,300
620 PRINT "MENU ERROR: ";C
630 GOTO 570
640 PRINT "ENTER DISCOUNT FACTOR";
650 INPUT D
660 GOTO 490
670 PRINT "ENTER INITIAL INVESTMENT";
680 INPUT N
690 GOTO 490
700 PRINT "ENTER YEAR";
710 INPUT Y1
720 PRINT "ENTER CASH FLOW"
730 INPUT F(Y1)
740 GOTO 490
750 END
```

```
RUN

ENTER NUMBER OF YEARS? 3
ENTER DISCOUNT FACTOR  (AS A %)? 12
ENTER INITIAL INVESTMENT? 10000
ENTER CASH FLOW FOR YEAR  1 ? 5000
ENTER CASH FLOW FOR YEAR  2 ? 10000
ENTER CASH FLOW FOR YEAR  3 ? 15000

            DISCOUNT FACTOR =  12 %

         INITIAL INVESTMENT =  10000

               YEAR    CASH FLOW

                 1     5000
                 2     10000
                 3     15000

PRESENT VALUE          = 13112.93

DO YOU WANT TO DO SOME WHAT-IF ANALYSIS? NO
OK
```

Problem 9: The Sales Contest. One of the major motivational devices used by a sales manager is a monthly sales contest for the sales staff. The salesperson who sells the most each month receives a free weekend vacation. Currently, the calculations to determine the monthly winners are performed by hand. The sales manager has requested a program that will perform this calculation.

A data file called ORDERS is available that contains the following information on each sales order processed during a month: order number, salesperson name, and amount of the sale. A small portion of this file is shown in Exhibit D.12. The winning salesperson is determined by totaling up the sale amounts for each person. Because of a high turnover rate among the sales force, the number of salespersons employed each month tends to vary. However, there have never been more than 100 salespersons working for the firm at any one time.

The solution to this problem involves a two-stage process:

1. Accumulate the total sales for each salesperson. As the composition of the sales force varies, this operation is not as simple as one might think.
2. Search through the sales totals to find the individual with the highest sales total and then display that person's name.

Salesperson names (a string variable) and salesperson sales totals (a numeric variable) must be maintained in memory. Thus, two one-dimensional arrays are used rather than a single two-dimensional array.

Exhibit D.13 presents a logical design for the sales context problem. Program D.34 solves the problem.

Knowing neither the number of salespersons on the firm's staff nor their names makes accumulating the sales totals the most difficult part of this program. Look closely at how this portion of Program D.34 works. Line number 290 reads the first set of order data from the ORDERS file. As *N* equals zero, the salesperson name and sales amount are placed in the first elements, respectively, of the name array, *T$*, and the sales totals array, *T*. Now that the name array *T$* and the totals array *T* have at least one entry, an iterative procedure can be used in processing the rest of the ORDERS file. This procedure is given in line numbers 310 to 390. When the name read is contained in array *T$*, the sales amount is added to that person's sales total in array *T*. When the name read is not contained in *T$*, the following occurs:

1. the number of salespersons, *N*, is increased by 1.
2. The new name is placed at the end of the name array, *T$*.
3. The new sales amount is placed at the end of the sales totals array, *T*.

Notice that variable *N* keeps a running total of the length of the two arrays, *T$* and *T*.

Exhibit D.12
Data File ORDERS Used with Problem 9

```
1012,"JONES",10000
1013,"SMITH",5000
1014,"BLACK",8800
1015,"SMITH",7700
1016,"LEE",6500
1017,"STEIN",5000
1018,"LEE",8500
1019,"STEIN",2500
1020,"JONES",12500
1021,"LEE",9000
1022,"SMITH",3500
1023,"TEMPLE",11000
1024,"BLACK",15000
1025,"LEE",6000
1026,"SMITH",1000
1027,"BLACK",7500
1028,"STEIN",4500
1029,"BLACK",9500
1030,"JONES",11000
1031,"TEMPLE",13000
1032,"STEIN",8000
```

Problem 10: The Parts Purchase Report. An inventory manager has requested that a report be produced from a firm's parts inventory file that will list the parts needing to be reordered, the necessary order amount, and the supplier's name. The parts inventory file, named PARTS, contains the following items for each part: part number (three digits), the amount on hand, the reorder point, the reorder quantity, an order flag (1 – an outstanding order exists; 0

Exhibit D.13
Pseudocode for Problem 9

```
LEVEL 1:
   accumulate total sales for all salespersons
   find highest total sales amount
   display results

LEVEL 2:
   while (there are sales orders to process)
          enter order data
          identify salesperson
          accumulate sales for that salesperson
   find highest sales amount
   identify salesperson with highest sales amount
   display sales totals for all salespersons
   display winning salesperson's name and total sales

LEVEL 3:
   set N, the number of salespersons identified, to zero
   enter order data from ORDERS file
   while (have not reached end-of-file)
          if N equals 0 then
                  add one to N
                  place salesperson's name in name array
                  place salesperson's sales in sales array
          if salesperson name not in name array then
                  add one to N
                  place salesperson's name in name array
                  place salesperson's sales in sales array
          if salesperson name already in name array then
                  find the person's location in sales array
                  add sales amount to that sales array location
   display report headings
   anchor highest sales amount, H, to zero
   set subscript I to zero
   repeat
          add one to I
          display salesperson's name and sales total
          if Ith value in sales array is greater than H then
                  set H to Ith value in sales array
                  assign Ith person's name to H$
          until (I equals N, the number of identified salespersons)
   display winning salespersons name
   display winning salespersons sales total
```

Exhibit D.14
Data File PARTS Used with Problem 10

```
206,110,90,40,0,10
207,110,125,30,0,12
210,110,130,40,0,11
211,200,190,50,1,13
222,300,200,100,0,12
223,80,100,50,0,10
228,50,200,100,1,12
230,300,200,150,0,10
231,180,200,150,0,11
232,600,500,300,0,12
235,400,500,200,0,13
236,50,75,50,0,10
237,150,100,100,0,11
238,200,200,100,0,13
```

– otherwise), and a supplier code (two digits). The reorder point indicates when it is time to prepare a parts order using the following rule:

> if the amount on hand is less than or equal to the reorder point,
> then prepare a parts order for the part

The reorder quantity gives the amount to order. The order flag indicates that a prior parts order has been issued but has not yet been received from the supplier. The supplier code identifies the part's supplier. Exhibit D.14 shows this data file.

Supplier names are available on another data file, named SUPPLIER. This file contains the following items for each supplier: supplier code (two digits), name, and address. Exhibit D.15 shows this data file. By cross-referencing the supplier codes in the two data files, PARTS and SUPPLIER, the correct supplier name can be located for each part being ordered.

```
OK
RUN

 SALES TOTALS
NAME        AMOUNT

JONES        33500
SMITH        17200
BLACK        40800
LEE          30000
STEIN        20000
TEMPLE       24000

 WINNING SALESPERSON:     BLACK
WINNING SALES AMOUNT:    $ 40800
OK
```

```
10 REM  PROGRAM D.34
20 REM
30 REM  THIS PROGRAM SOLVES THE SALES CONTEXT PROBLEM
40 REM
50 REM  THE PROGRAM READS A DATA FILE NAMED "ORDERS"
60 REM  THAT CONTAINS (FOR EACH SALES ORDER):
70 REM
80 REM          ORDER NUMBER
90 REM          SALESPERSON NAME
100 REM         AMOUNT OF SALE
110 REM
120 REM THE PROGRAM THEN ACCUMULATES TOTAL SALES AMOUNTS
130 REM FOR EACH SALESPERSONS AND DISPLAYS THE NAME OF
140 REM THE SALESPERSON WITH THE MOST SALES
150 REM
160 REM          O$ - ORDER NUMBER
170 REM          S$ - SALESPERSON NAME
180 REM           A - SALES AMOUNT
190 REM           N - NUMBER OF SALESPERSONS
200 REM          T$ - ARRAY OF SALESPERSON NAMES
210 REM           T - ARRAY OF SALESPERSON TOTAL SALES
220 REM          H$ - NAME OF SALESPERSON WITH MOST SALES
230 REM           H - HIGHEST AMOUNT OF SALES
240 REM
250 DIM N$(100), T(100)
260 OPEN "B:ORDERS" FOR INPUT AS #1
270 LET N = 0
280 IF EOF(1) THEN 400
290 INPUT #1,O$,S$,A
300 IF N = 0 THEN 360
310 FOR I = 1 TO N
320 IF S$ <> T$(I) THEN 350
330 LET T(I) = T(I) + A
340 GOTO 280
350 NEXT I
360 LET N = N + 1
370 LET T$(N) = S$
380 LET T(N) = A
390 GOTO 280
400 CLOSE #1
410 PRINT
420 PRINT "    SALES TOTALS"
430 PRINT "NAME","AMOUNT"
440 PRINT
450 LET H = 0
460 FOR I = 1 TO N
470 PRINT T$(I),T(I)
480 IF T(I) < H THEN 510
490 LET H = T(I)
500 LET H$ = T$(I)
510 NEXT I
520 PRINT
530 PRINT " WINNING SALESPERSON:   ";H$
540 PRINT "WINNING SALES AMOUNT: $";H
550 END
560 PRINT
```

Changes for APPLESOFT BASIC:

```
260 REM CNT COUNTS THE DATA RECORDS IN THE ORDERS FILE
261 CNT=0
262 PRINT "ENTER THE NUMBER OF DATA RECORDS IN THE ORDERS FILE";
263 INPUT LIMIT
264 B$=CHR$(4)
265 PRINT D$;"OPEN ORDERS,D2"
266 PRINT D$;"READ ORDERS"

280 IF CNT=LIMIT THEN 400
290 INPUT O$,S$,A
291 CNT=CNT+1

400 PRINT D$;"CLOSE ORDERS"
```

The report to be produced should appear as follows:

Parts Purchase Report

PART	AMOUNT	SUPPLIER
XXX	XXXXX	XXXXXXXXXXXXXX

A logical design for a program that produces the parts purchase report is shown in Exhibit D.16. Program D.35, which makes use of data from the PARTS and SUPPLIER data files in producing this report, is one of the shorter programs in this appendix.

Exhibit D.15
Data File SUPPLIER Used with Problem 10

```
10,"APEX CORP.", "222 WEST ST. CHICAGO ILL 60611"
11,"PARTS INC.","11 FIRST ST. ST. LOUIS MASS. 02301"
12,"TOOLS AND TOOLS", 22 LAST ST. AUGUSTA MAINE 02011"
13,"A & Z SUPPLIES", 44 9TH ST. WASHINGTON D.C. 04111"
```

Exhibit D.16
Pseudocode for Problem 10

```
LEVEL 1:
  display report headings

  while (there are parts to process)

       read data for a part
       evaluate order status
       display data on the part being ordered

LEVEL 2:
  display report headings

  open parts file
  read data for a part
  while (there are parts to process)

       if order flag is off then
         if amount on-hand <= reorder point then
           display data on part being ordered
       read data for a part

  close parts file

LEVEL 3:
  display report headings

  open parts file
  read data for a part
  while (have not reached end-of-file)

       if order flag is off then
         if amount on-hand <= reorder point then
           open supplier file
           read data for a supplier
           while (have not reached end-of-file)
                if match supplier codes then
                  display data on part being ordered
                read data for a supplier
           close supplier file

  close parts file
```

One question that you might have about this program is, why is the SUPPLIER file opened and closed *inside* the loop that processes parts data from the PARTS file? The supplier codes contained in the parts data are in no specific order. Consequently, the only way to locate a certain supplier is to move to the beginning of the supplier file and search through each set of data until a supplier code match occurs. Opening a file is one means of moving to the beginning of the file. Before a file can be reopened, however it must have been closed.

```
OK
RUN

        PARTS PURCHASE REPORT

      PART  AMOUNT  SUPPLIER

       207    30      TOOLS AND TOOLS
       210    40      PARTS INC.
       223    50      APEX CORP.
       231   150      PARTS INC.
       235   200      A & Z SUPPLIES
       236    50      APEX CORP.
       238   100      A & Z SUPPLIES
OK
```

```
10 REM PROGRAM D.35
20 REM
30 REM  THIS PROGRAM PRODUCES THE PARTS PURCHASE REPORT
40 REM
50 REM  THE PROGRAM READS TWO DATA FILES:
60 REM
70 REM      "PARTS":    P - PART NUMBER
80 REM                  A - AMOUNT ON HAND
90 REM                  R - REORDER POINT
100 REM                 Q - REORDER QUANTITY
110 REM                 F - AN "ON-ORDER" FLAG
120 REM                 S - SUPPLIER NUMBER
130 REM
140 REM "SUPPLIER":    S1 - SUPPLIER NUMBER
150 REM                N$ - SUPPLIER NAME
160 REM                A$ - SUPPLIER ADDRESS
170 REM
180 PRINT
190 PRINT TAB(20) "PARTS PURCHASE REPORT"
200 PRINT
210 PRINT TAB(13) "PART      AMOUNT      SUPPLIER"
220 PRINT
230 OPEN "B:PARTS" FOR INPUT AS #1
240 IF EOF(1) THEN 380
250 INPUT #1,P,A,R,Q,F,S
260 IF F = 1 THEN 240
270 IF A > R THEN 240
280 OPEN "B:SUPPLIER" FOR INPUT AS #2
290 IF EOF(2) THEN 350
300 INPUT #2,S1,N$,A$
310 IF S <> S1 THEN 290
320 PRINT TAB(13) P TAB(23) Q TAB(33) N$
330 CLOSE #2
340 GOTO 240
350 PRINT "NO MATCH -- PART: ";P;",   SUPPLIER:";S
360 GOTO 240
370 CLOSE #2
380 CLOSE #1
390 END
```

Changes for APPLESOFT BASIC:

```
230 REM  CNT1 COUNTS THE DATA RECORDS IN THE PARTS FILE
231 CNT1=0
232 PRINT "ENTER THE NUMBER OF DATA RECORDS IN THE PARTS FILE";
233 INPUT NO1
234 PRINT "ENTER THE NUMBER OF DATA RECORDS IN THE SUPPLIER FILE";
235 INPUT NO2
236 D$=CHR$(4)
237 PRINT D$;"OPEN PARTS,D2"
238 PRINT D$;"READ PARTS"

240 IF CNT1=NO1 THEN 380
250 INPUT P,A,R,Q,F,S
251 CNT1=CNT1 + 1

280 CNT2=0
281 REM CNT2 COUNTS THE DATA RECORDS IN THE SUPPLIER FILE
282 PRINT D$;"OPEN SUPPLIER,D2"
283 PRINT D$;"READ SUPPLIER"

290 IF CNT2=NO2 THEN 350
300 INPUT S1,N$,A$
301 CNT2=CNT2+1

330 PRINT D$;"CLOSE SUPPLIER"

370 PRINT D$;"CLOSE·SUPPLIER"
380 PRINT D$;"CLOSE PARTS"
```

Program D.35 follows the logical design given in Exhibit D.16 quite closely. However, one addition is made. If no match on supplier code occurs when searching the SUPPLIER data file, then the supplier code on the PARTS file must be incorrect. If an end-of-file is reached when reading the SUPPLIER file, the processing flow is immediately directed to line number 350 and an appropriate error message is displayed.

PROGRAMMING EXERCISES

Exercise 1 REM, READ, DATA, GOTO statements.
Write a program that reads and displays an employee's name, hours worked, and gross pay. The output should look as follows:

FRED SMITH	22	85.25
TOM JONES	40	212.85
MARY SMITH	10	95.25
JUDY JONES	6	25.36

Exercise 2 LET statement.
A program is needed to calculate the new balance for each credit customer. The old balance and payment amount are given as follows:

Customer	Old Balance	Payment
FRED SMITH	150.05	10.02
TOM JONES	1852.27	125.25
MARY SMITH	2700.25	356.31

The desired output is:

FRED SMITH	150.05	10.02	140.03
TOM JONES	1852.27	125.25	1727.02
MARY SMITH	2700.25	356.31	2343.94

Exercise 3 INPUT statement.
Write a program that will allow the user to enter an employee's name and wages. The program should calculate and display the income tax, which is 4.51% of the wages. Use the Break Key to end the program.

Data:		
	FRED SMITH	934.00
	TOM JONES	299.00
	MARY SMITH	100.00

Desired output:

ENTER THE EMPLOYEE NAME: FRED SMITH
ENTER THE WAGES: 934.00
THE TAX IS 42.1234
ENTER THE EMPLOYEE NAME: TOM JONES
ENTER THE WAGES: 299.00
THE TAX IS 13.4849
ENTER THE EMPLOYEE NAME: (hit the Break Key)

Exercise 4 IF statement.
The Jackson County Airport charges a fee for each aircraft that lands or takes off. The amount of the fee is based on the weight of the airplane. For aircraft weighing more than 5000 pounds the fee is $10.00. For aircraft 5000 pounds and under the fee is $5.00. Write a program to print a daily activity report for February 27, 1985, showing the aircraft number, fee, and weight. The data are as follows:

Aircraft	Weight
NZ9832	4312
ZC98732	3148
CL39872	5000
AC23137	2396
RX9873	15982

The report should be as follows:

AIRCRAFT	WEIGHT	FEE
NZ9832	4312	5
ZC98732	3148	5
CL39872	5000	10
AC23137	2396	5
RX9873	15982	10

Exercise 5 IF statement.
Write a program that will display a list of full-time students attending DP University. A full-time student is defined as one who takes 12 or more credits. A count of the number of full-time students should also be displayed. The data are as follows:

Student	Credits
MARY SMITH	14
TOM JONES	8
FRED JONES	18
LINDA SMITH	12

The report should be:

FULL-TIME STUDENTS

STUDENT NAME	CREDITS
MARY SMITH	14
FRED JONES	18
LINDA SMITH	12
THE NUMBER OF FULL-TIME STUDENTS IS	3

Exercise 6 IF statements.
Write a program that will calculate a payroll for a large company. The data consist of an employee name, number of hours worked, and rate of pay per hour. Pay is calculated by multiplying rate times pay, except that employees receive time-and-a-half for all hours worked over 40. The data are as follows:

Employee Name	Hours Worked	Rate per Hour
TOM JONES	36	4.97
MARY SMITH	42	4.25
BILL JONES	44	5.36
JILL SMITH	38	5.25

Output is as follows:

PAYROLL REPORT

NAME	HOURS	RATE	PAY
TOM JONES	36	4.97	178.92
MARY SMITH	42	4.25	182.75
BILL JONES	44	5.36	246.56
JILL SMITH	38	5.25	199.5

Exercise 7 Creating disk files.
Write a program that will allow the user to enter a student name and the number of credits that the student is working toward in a given term. The data are then to be stored in a disk file. Some data to be used are as follows:

TOM SMITH	13
RON REAGON	18
VAL JONES	12
BRIAN HILL	8

There is no displayed output.

Exercise 8 Reading a disk file.
Write a program that will read and display the file created in Exercise 7. The program should count the number of records in the file. Output is as follows:

STUDENT LISTING

NAME	CREDITS
TOM SMITH	13
RON REAGON	18
VAL JONES	12
BRIAN HILL	8
TOTAL STUDENTS	4

Exercise 9 Arrays and FOR/NEXT loops.
Your company needs a program to display a sales report. The company has 12 sales districts. The data to be read by the program consist of a product number, the amount of the sale, and the district in which the sale was made. Some sample data follow:

Product Number	Amount	District
1111	100.00	3
1115	9.80	6
1113	52.80	3
1121	8.60	3
1163	125.00	8
1171	92.88	6
1122	52.50	1
2233	111.00	10
2211	22.80	11

The report should consist of totals for each district, as shown below:

DISTRICT TOTALS

DISTRICT	TOTAL
1	52.5
2	0
3	161.4
4	0
5	0
6	102.68
7	0
8	125
9	0
10	111
11	22.8
12	0

Exercise 10 Functions, Subroutines.
Write a program that will list the square roots of a series of numbers. A subroutine should allow the user to enter a starting value and an ending value. The program should then list a series of numbers starting with the starting value and ending with the ending value. The square root of the numbers should be displayed also. Sample output follows:

ENTER A STARTING VALUE: 100
ENTER AN ENDING VALUE: 109

VALUE	SQUARE ROOT
100	10
101	10.0499
102	10.0995
103	10.1489
104	10.198
105	10.247
106	10.2956
107	10.3441
108	10.3923
109	10.4403

REFERENCES

LITERARY ACKNOWLEDGMENTS

Chapter 1

2 From "PCs Polish a PR Firm's Image" by Scott Kariya, *PC Magazine,* March 6, 1984, p. 166. Copyright © 1984 Ziff-Davis Publishing Company. Reprinted by permission. **5** Adapted from Figure 1 in "Could 1,000,000 IBM PC Users Be Wrong?" by Frank Gens and Chris Christiansen, *BYTE,* November 1983, p. 136. Copyright © 1983 McGraw-Hill, Inc., New York 10020. All rights reserved. Reprinted by permission. **11** From "Thumbs Up For Hands-On" by Ian Garvey, *PC Magazine,* August 1983, pp. 137, 142. Copyright © 1983 Ziff-Davis Publishing Company. Reprinted by permission. **25** From "The Automated Agent Helps Performers Get Gigs" by Hal Glatzer, *PC Magazine,* March 1983, pp. 286–291. Reprinted by permission of the author.

Chapter 2

30 From "Connecticut Mutual: Where PCs Sell Insurance" by Matt Kramer, *PC Week,* April 24, 1984, p. 54. Copyright © 1984 Ziff-Davis Publishing Company. Reprinted by permission. **33** From "Unmasking some myths about computer literacy," reprinted from the June issue of *Modern Office Technology,* and copyrighted 1984 by Penton/IPC subsidiary of Pittway Corporation. **38** From "Riding high on interactive computing," reprinted from the February issue of *Modern Office Technology,* and copyrighted 1984 by Penton/IPC subsidiary of Pittway Corporation. **44** Adapted from Figure 3 in "Personal Computers in the Eighties" by Greggory S. Blundell, *BYTE,* January 1983, P. 171. Copyright © 1983 McGraw-Hill, Inc., New York 10020. All rights reserved. Reprinted by permission. **47** From "Rides PC Wave," *PC Week,* May 8, 1984. Copyright © 1984 Ziff-Davis Publishing Company. Reprinted by permission. **53** From "For McKesson, Computers Are The Magic In Profit Margins" by Jui Cortino and Ellen C. Peck, *Management Technology,* July 1984, pp. 50–53. Reprinted by permission.

Chapter 3

80 "Minicomputer Revolution" from *Future Computing* by Portia Isaacson and Egil Juliussen. Copyright © 1979 by Portia Isaacson and Egil Juliussen. Reprinted by permission of the authors. **82** From "Grace Hopper: Conscience of the Industry" by Paul Gillin, *Computerworld,* September 10, 1984 and "Caltech microprocessors may rival supercomputers" by Tom Henkel, *Computerworld,* January 30, 1984. Copyright © 1984 by CW Communications/Inc., Framingham, MA 01701. Reprinted by permission.

Chapter 4

86 From "Hotel Chain Using Micros in Reservations Net," *Computerworld,* November 11, 1983. Copyright © 1983 by CW Communications/Inc., Framingham, MA 01701. Reprinted by permission. **101** Copyright © 1983 by Cahners Publishing Company, Division of Reed Holdings Inc. Reprinted with permission from *Mini-Micro Systems,* June 1983. **113** From "Hand-Held Computers Speed Service Reports," *Computerworld,* November 28, 1983. Copyright © 1983 by CW Communications, Inc., Framingham, MA 01701. Reprinted by permission.

Chapter 5

118 From "Stevie Wonder: Computers Make the Music in His Life" by Freff, *Enter,* April 1984. Copyright © 1984 Children's Television Workshop. Used by permission of Children's Television Workshop. **140** Copyright © 1982 by Cahners Publishing Company, Division of Reed Holdings Inc. Reprinted with permission of *Mini-Micro Systems,* December 1982.

Chapter 6

160 "Whence the Name Winchester" from *Business Computer Systems,* October 1982, p. 119. Copyright © 1982 by Cahners Publishing Company, Division of Reed Holdings Inc. Reprinted with permission.

Chapter 7

174 From "Microsoft's Drive to Dominate Software" by Stratford P. Sherman, *Fortune,* January 23, 1984, pp. 82–90. Copyright © 1984 Time Inc. All rights reserved. Reprinted by permission. **196** From "Why Software Won't Run on All PC Clones" by Donna Stein, *Business Computer Systems,* July 1983, pp. 95–100. Copyright © 1983 by Cahners Publishing Company, Division of Reed Holdings Inc. Reprinted with permission.

Chapter 8

200 From "Junkyards Polish Their Rusty Image," by Paul Hemp, *The New York Times,* August 30, 1984. Copyright © 1984 by The New York Times Company. Reprinted by permission. **217** Fernandez, Summers and Wood, *Database Security and Integrity.* Copyright © 1981, Addison-Wesley, Reading, Massachusetts. Adapted material. Reprinted with permission. **225** From "The PC Moves Into Real Estate" by Bil. Alvernaz, *PC Magazine,* November 1983. Reprinted by permission of the author.

Chapter 9

230 From "DDP 'Nets' Violaters in Ohio," *Data Management,* January 1981, pp. 24BB–24DD. Reprinted by permission of Data Processing Management Association. **251** "LAN Characteristics" from L. Jordon and B. Churchill, *Communication and Networking for the IBM PC,* p. 118 (Bowie, Maryland: Robert J. Brady Company, 1983). Reprinted by permission. **255** From "Federal Express Puts Dollars—$24 Million—Behind Demand for Unerring Communications," *Computerworld,* August 8, 1983. Copyright © 1983 by CW Communications/Inc., Framingham, MA 01701. Reprinted by permission.

Chapter 10

260 From "Selling Will Never Be the Same" by Greg Sanders, *Moonbeams,* November 1984. Reprinted courtesy of The Procter & Gamble Company. **266** From "How Chemical Bank Uses

Computers to Drive Hard Bargains" by John Herrmann, *Management Technology,* March 1984, pp. 42–46. Reprinted by permission. **275** From "Micros by the Millions: Future Computing Sizes Up the Desktop User Scene" by Susan J. Biagiotti with William F. Ablondi, *Management Technology,* December 1984, p. 62. Reprinted by permission. **276** From "PCs in Napa Valley" by Jonathan Littman, *PC Week,* November 13, 1984. Copyright © 1984 Ziff-Davis Publishing Company. Reprinted by permission. **278–79** From "On-Line Data Bases: The Facts You Want Are At Your Fingertips" by Stanley Stillman, *Management Technology,* November 1984, pp. 63–64. Reprinted by permission. **280** From "PCs Are Woven into Company Plan" by John Greitzer, *PC Week,* October 2, 1984. Copyright © 1984 by Ziff-Davis Publishing Company. Reprinted by permission.

Chapter 11

294 From "The Right Place at the Right Time" by J. Thomas Monk and Kenneth M. Landis, *Business Computer Systems,* October 1983. Copyright © 1983 by Cahners Publishing Company, Division of Reed Holdings Inc. Reprinted with permission. **302** From "Documenting An Infinite Number of Monkeys" by Corey Sandler, *PC Magazine,* August 1983. Copyright © 1983 Ziff-Davis Publishing Company. Reprinted by permission. **319** From "Gearing Up for Rapid Growth" by J. Thomas Monk and Kenneth M. Landis, *Business Computer Systems,* September 1983. Copyright © 1983 by Cahners Publishing Company, Division of Reed Holdings Inc. Reprinted with permission.

Chapter 12

324 From "Aetna Plans for 'No-Fault' OA" by Richard J. Telesca, *Datamation,* April 15, 1984. Reprinted with permission of *Datamation* ® magazine. Copyright © 1984 by Technical Publishing Company, A Dun & Bradstreet Company, all rights reserved. **328** From "How Color Communicates" by John Di Cocco, *Reference Magazine,* July/August 1983. Reprinted by permission of the author. **342** From "The Best-Laid Plans of Micros and Men" by Joel D. Krauss. Reprinted with permission from the March issue of *Modern Office Technology,* and copyrighted © 1984 by Penton/IPC subsidiary of Pittway Corporation. **349** From "Three-Person DP Staff Backs $21 Million Firm," *Computerworld,* March 14, 1983. Copyright © 1983 by CW Communications/Inc., Framingham, MA 01701. **350** From "Made-to Measure Software" by David Collopy. Reprinted with permission from *Personal Computing,* April 1983, pp. 80–85. Copyright © 1983, Hayden Publishing Company.

Chapter 13

372 From "Professionals Turn Progammers" by Kathy Chin, *Infoworld,* February 6, 1984, pp. 82–84. Copyright © 1984 by Popular Computing Inc. All rights reserved. Reprinted by permission. **381** From "Programming has wide DP application" by Debra Zahay, *Computerworld,* July 30, 1984. Reprinted by permission of the author. **394** From "The $2 Sure Thing" by Corey Sandler, *PC Magazine,* September 1983. Copyright © 1983 Ziff-Davis Publishing Company. Reprinted by permission.

Chapter 14

408 From "Modula-2: Pascal's powerful heir" by A. Winsor Brown and Richard E. Gleaves. Copyright © 1983 by Cahners Publishing Company, Division of Reed Holdings, Inc. Reprinted with permission from *Mini-Micro Systems* (September 1983). **410** From "Mature software tools speed development tasks" by Carl Warren. Copyright © 1984 by Cahners Publishing Company, Division of Reed Holdings Inc. Reprinted with permission from *Mini-Micro Systems* (August 1984). **419** From "Gimme That Old-Time Language" by Robert Glass. Reprinted from *Software News,* September, 1983. Copyright © 1983 Sentry Publishing Company, Inc., Westborough, MA 01581. **424** From "The Making of Modula-2" by Edward Joyce, *PC Magazine,* April 3, 1984. Copyright © 1984 Ziff-Davis Publishing Company. Reprinted by permission.

Chapter 15

432 From "IBM PCs Create a Winning Formula" by Lois Paul, *PC Week,* March 6, 1984. Copyright © 1984 Ziff-Davis Publishing Company. Reprinted by permission. **444** From "Modeling cash flow on your personal computer" by Bernard Denoyer and Bob Yeager, *Management Technology,* February 1984, pp. 27–28. Reprinted by permission. **446–47** From "Thinking and Writing with a PC" by Charles Spezzano, *Business Computing,* June 1984. Reprinted by permission of the author. **448** From "The New Look of Presentations" by Doran Howitt, *Infoworld,* December 24, 1984, pp. 28–31. Copyright © 1984 by Popular Computing Inc. All rights reserved. Reprinted by permission. **451** From " 'Mapper' Puts Trains On Right Track," *Management Information Systems Week,* September 7, 1983. Reprinted by permission of MIS Week. **456** From "Northrop: Resources for Mid-Sized Applications" in "A Concept Comes of Age" by Amy E. Smith, *Business Computer Systems,* November 1983. Copyright © 1983 by Cahners Publishing Company, Division of Reed Holdings Inc. Reprinted with permission. **459** From "How American Express Saves with PC XTs" by Arielle Emmett, *Business Computing,* December 1984. Reprinted by permission of PennWell Publishing Company.

Chapter 16

464 From "A Day at Xanadu: Family Life in Tomorrow's Computerized Home" by Roy Mason with Lane Jennings and Robert Evans, *The Futurist,* February 1984, pp. 17–18. Reprinted by permission of World Future Society. **481** From "External Data Sources: In Depth," *Computerworld,* April 1984, p. 7. Copyright © 1984 by CW Communications/Inc., Framingham, MA 01701. Reprinted by permission. **489** Reprinted with permission from "High-Tech Nomad" by Steven K. Roberts, published in the August 1984 issue of *Popular Computing* magazine. Copyright © 1984 by McGraw-Hill, Inc., New York. All rights reserved.

Chapter 17

494 "Biometrics Has A Touch for Spotting Phonies" by Eleanor Johnson Tracy, *Fortune,* April 15, 1985. Copyright © 1985 Time Inc. All rights reserved. Reprinted by permission. **496** From "The Path to Post-Industrial Growth" by Graham T. T. Molitor, *The Futurist,* April 1981, p. 85. Reprinted by permission of World Future Society. **502** From "Ergonomics" by Juanita Darling, *The Register,* August 19, 1984. Reprinted by permission of Freedom Newspapers, Inc., Santa Ana, California. **506** "Silent Watchers" from *Computerworld,* September 13, 1983, p. 90. Copyright © 1983 by CW Communications/Inc. Framingham, MA 01701. Reprinted by permission of Computerworld. **514** *DPMA Code of Ethics and Standards of Conduct.* © Data Processing Management Association. All rights reserved. Reprinted by permission. **516** "A Literate Man Called Boris" from "Teaching Computers the Art of Reason" by Tom Alexander, *Fortune,* May 17, 1982, p. 88. Copyright © 1982 Time Inc. All rights reserved. Reprinted by permission. **517** "Utah facility relies on Help" from *Computerworld,* July 9, 1984, p. 18. Copyright © 1984 CW Communications

/Inc., Framingham, MA 01701. Reprinted by permission of Computerworld. **519** "Recognition Dawns on the Computer" by Bill Silbert for *Fortune* in "Computers on the Road to Self-Improvement" by Tom Alexander, *Fortune,* June 14, 1982. Copyright © 1982 Time Inc. All rights reserved. Reprinted by permission. **522** "OA No Panacea for Economic Ills" by John B. Dykeman, *Modern Office Procedures,* July 1983. Copyright © 1983 Penton/IPC Publishing. Reprinted by permission.

Chapter 18

528 From "The Hard Sell Comes to Software" by Maggie McComas, *Fortune,* September 17, 1984. Copyright © 1984 Time Inc. All rights reserved. Reprinted by permission. **530, 531, and 532** From P. Archbold and J. Verity, "The Datamation 100," *Datamation,* June 1, 1985. Reprinted with permission of *Datamation* ® magazine. Copyright © Technical Publishing Company, A Dun & Bradstreet Company, 1985—all rights reserved. **533** From "Upstarts Outshine the Stars" by John W. Verity, *Datamation,* November 15, 1984, pp. 34–52. Reprinted with permission of *Datamation* ® magazine. Copyright © Technical Publishing Company, A Dun & Bradstreet Company, 1984—all rights reserved. **539** "Growth of Computer Specialty Stores" from *Computer Stores USA: Profiles and Directories* prepared by Future Computing, Inc. Reprinted by permission. **549** From "1985 Salary Survey and Career Planning Guide," *Source Personnel Services.* Reprinted by permission. **552** From "Pitching Computers to Small Business" by Bro Utal, *Fortune,* April 1, 1985. Copyright © 1985 Time Inc. All rights reserved. Reprinted by permission.

Appendix A

A-2 From *Breakthrough to the Computer Age* by Harry Wulforst. Copyright © 1982 by Harry Wulforst. Reprinted with the permission of Charles Scribner's Sons. **A-7** From "Ada, Countess of Lovelace, and Her Contribution to Computing" by Velma R. Huskey and Harry D. Huskey, *Abacus,* Vol. 1, No. 2, Winter 1984, pp. 22–29. Copyright © 1984 Springer-Verlag New York, Inc. Reprinted by permission. **A-9** From "A Brief History" by Don Sutherland, *Inc.,* October 1982, p. 64. Copyright © 1984 by Inc. Publishing Corporation. Reprinted by permission. **A-12** From *Stretching Man's Mind: A History of Data Processing* by Margaret Harmon (New York: Mason/Charter, 1975). Reprinted by permission of the author. **A-26** From *Fire in the Valley: The Making of the Personal Computer* by Paul Freiberger and Michael Swaine. Copyright © 1984 by McGraw-Hill, Inc. Reprinted by permission of Osborne/McGraw-Hill. **A-31** From *The New Alchemists* by Dirk Hanson. Copyright © 1982 by Dirk Hanson. Reprinted by permission of Little, Brown and Company.

PHOTO CREDITS

Positions of photographs are shown in abbreviated form as follows: top (t), bottom (b), center (c), left (l), right (r). All photos not credited are the property of Scott, Foresman and Company. Cover photo © Don Carroll, NY.

Chapter 1

2 Courtesy Ruder, Finn & Rotman **4** (l) Courtesy Fairchild Camera & Instrument Corporation, a Schlumberger Company **4** (r) Courtesy National Semiconductor Corporation **6** Reprinted from *Popular Science* with permission © 1984, Times Mirror Magazines, Inc. **7** (tl) Yoav Levy/Phototake **7** (tr) John McGrail/ Wheeler Pictures **7** (cl) Joe McNally/Wheeler Pictures **7** (cr) Paul Conklin **7** (bl) Tom Pantages photo/Courtesy MIT Experimental Music Lab **7** (br) Dan McCoy/Rainbow **11** Dan McCoy/Rainbow **13** Courtesy IBM **15** Courtesy Hayes Microcomputer Products, Inc. **16** (clockwise from top), Hank Morgan/Rainbow; Bohdan Hrynewych/Southern Light; Peter Angelo Simon/Phototake; Richard T. Nowitz/Phototake © Dawson Jones, Inc.; Dan McCoy/Rainbow

Chapter 2

30 © Michael Lennahan **32** Courtesy Lotus Development Corporation **36** (t) Courtesy IBM **36** (b) Steve Smith/Wheeler Pictures **38** Courtesy Wang Laboratories, Inc. **45** (t) Courtesy Quadram Corporation **45** (c&b) Courtesy Software Publishing Corporation **46** (l) Courtesy Software Publishing Corporation **46** (c) Courtesy Apple Computer, Inc. **46** (b) Phototake **48** (l) Courtesy TeleVideo Systems, Inc. **48** (r) Courtesy Software Publishing Corporation **49** Courtesy Lotus Development Corporation **53** Courtesy McKesson

Chapter 3

58 ©1984 Robert Hagedohm/LPI **71** Tom Pantages **73** (t) Berg & Assoc./Margaret C. Berg **73** (b) © Joel Gordon 1982 **74** Cameramann International, Ltd. **76** (l) Courtesy Radio Shack, a division of Tandy Corporation **76** (r) Steve Smith/Wheeler Pictures **77** (l) Dan McCoy/Rainbow **77** (c&r) Roger Ressmeyer/Wheeler Pictures **82** Official U.S. Navy Photograph

Chapter 4

86 Courtesy Ramada Inns, Inc. **93** Gary L. Kieffer, *U.S. News & World Report* **94** Cameramann International, Ltd. **95** (t) Reprinted by permission of Educational Testing Service **96** (t) Courtesy Recognition Equipment Inc. **96** (b) Cameramann International, Ltd. **98** Gary L. Kieffer, *U.S. News & World Report* **99** Courtesy Burroughs Corporation **100** Courtesy Interstate Voice Products **102** Chuck O'Rear/West Light **103** (t) Courtesy Diebold Inc. **103** (b) Courtesy Motorola Inc. **104** Courtesy Industrial Data Terminals Corp. **105** (t) Tom Pantages **105** (b) Michael Mauney **108** (tl) Art Pahlke **108** (tr) Courtesy Diebold Inc. **108** (bl) Peter Angelo Simon/Phototake **108** (br) © Dawson Jones, Inc. **109** (t) Courtesy Key Tronic Corporation **109** (b) Cameramann International, Ltd. **110** (t) Courtesy Hewlett-Packard **110** (b) Courtesy Apple Computer, Inc. **111** Courtesy Apple Computer, Inc. **112** Courtesy Apple Computer, Inc. **113** Courtesy Marquette Electronics, Inc.

Chapter 5

118 © Stan Fellerman **121** Cameramann International, Ltd. **122** Courtesy Polaroid **123** (l) Joe McNally/Wheeler Pictures **123** (r) Courtesy Zenith Data Systems **125** (br) Courtesy Apple Computer, Inc. **126** Courtesy Ashton-Tate **127** (t) Andy Levin/Black Star **127** (b) Courtesy Lawrence Livermore Laboratory **128** (l) Courtesy IBM **128** (r) Cameramann International, Ltd. **129** (t) Courtesy Osborne Computer Corporation **129** (c) Courtesy COMPAQ ® Computer Corporation **129** (b) Courtesy Data General Corporation **131** © Joel Gordon 1984 **132** John McGrail/Wheeler Pictures **134** Jeremy Elkin **135** Courtesy PrintaColor Corporation **136** Courtesy Hewlett-Packard **137** Courtesy Hewlett-Packard **138** Courtesy Eastman Kodak Company **139** Courtesy Digital Equipment Corporation **142** Courtesy Printronix **144** (l) Image produced by David Laidlaw, Huseyin Kocak & Thomas Banchoff of Brown University **144** (r) Courtesy MAGi Computer Slides

Chapter 6

148 (t) Richard Kalvar/Magnum Photos **148** (bl) Courtesy Drexler Technology **148** (br) Courtesy SmartCard International, Inc. (SCI) New York **152** (tl) Courtesy Apple Computer, Inc. **152** (tr) Bob Glaze/Artstreet **152** (bl) Courtesy Quadram Corporation and Communications Action Marketing, Inc. **152** (br) Eric Kamp/Phototake **154** Courtesy Hewlett-Packard **155** Harry N. Abrams, Inc. **159** (l) Courtesy Hitachi America, Ltd. **159** (r) Courtesy Drexler Technology Corporation **160** Courtesy IBM Archive **161** (t) Courtesy Industrial Data Terminals Corp. **161** (b) Courtesy Grid Systems Corporation **163** Bob Glaze/Artstreet **164** © Dawson Jones, Inc. **165** Courtesy IBM Archive **169** Courtesy Hitachi America, Ltd. **170** Courtesy Actronics Inc., Pittsburgh, PA

Chapter 7

174 Geoff Manasse **177** (l) © T. M. Wathen **177** (r) Brent Jones **178** Courtesy IBM Archive **179** (t) Courtesy Zenith Data Systems **179** (c) Courtesy Panasonic **179** (b) Courtesy Zenith Data Systems **181** Courtesy Chemical Bank **191** Courtesy McDonnell Douglas Information Systems Group **192** Photograph provided by Tandem Computers Incorporated **194** Courtesy Digital Research **196** Cameramann International, Ltd.

Chapter 8

200 Art Pahlke **225** Art Pahlke

Chapter 9

230 Courtesy State Highway Patrol of Ohio **232** Berg & Assoc./Gus Schonefeld **233** (l) Cameramann International, Ltd. **233** (r) Courtesy IBM **238** (tl) Courtesy Hayes Microcomputer Products, Inc. **238** (tr) Don & Pat Valenti/Hillstrom Stock Photo **238** (b) Courtesy Hayes Microcomputer Products, Inc. **242** (l) Robert P. Carr/BRUCE COLEMAN INC. **242** (r) Jon Brenneis/FPG **244** Cameramann International, Ltd. **245** AT&T Bell Labs **250** Cameramann International, Ltd. **255** Cameramann International, Ltd.

Chapter 10

260 Courtesy Procter & Gamble Co. **266** Courtesy Chemical Bank **276** Tom Myers **277** Tom Myers **287** Albert Hilton

Chapter 11

294 Scott Witte/Hillstrom Stock Photo **306** Cameramann International, Ltd. **319** © Dawson Jones, Inc.

Chapter 12

324 David A. Wagner/Phototake **328** Courtesy DICOMED Corporation **342** © Dawson Jones, Inc. **351** Robert G. Bryant

Chapter 13

372 Cameramann International, Ltd. **394** Focus On Sports

Chapter 14

400 Cameramann International, Ltd. **427** © Vincent J. Catania 1984

Chapter 15

432 Courtesy CIBA-GEIGY Corporation **441** Cameramann International, Ltd. **443** Courtesy Execucom **445** Cameramann International, Ltd. **448** Courtesy Ray Jacobson, LaSalle National Bank **451** Courtesy Sperry Corporation **452** (l) Cameramann International, Ltd. **452** (r) Courtesy Lotus Development Corporation **454** (t) Courtesy Digital Research **454** (b) Courtesy POLYTRON Corporation **456** Courtesy *Business Computer Systems* Magazine **457** Courtesy First National Bank of Boston **459** Albert Hilton

Chapter 16

464 Courtesy General Electric Company **467** Courtesy Apple Computer, Inc. **469** Courtesy NEC America, Inc. **470** Photo courtesy CPT Corporation **474** Dan McCoy/Rainbow **478** William Strode/Hillstrom Stock Photo **483** Courtesy Viewdata Corporation of America, Inc. **484** (t) Courtesy The Source Telecomputing Corp. **484** (b) Bo Rader **489** Steve Northup/*Time* Magazine

Chapter 17

494 Andrew Moore **497** Eugene Richards/Magnum Photos **501** Illustration Courtesy Steelcase Inc. **502** © Peter Aaron/ESTO **510** (l) Courtesy Anchor Pad International **510** (r) © Les Wollam **523** Chuck O'Rear/West Light

Chapter 18

528 Courtesy Cullinet Software **534** (t) Courtesy Apple Computer, Inc. **534** (b) Courtesy of Cray Research, Inc. **539** Cameramann International, Ltd. **540** Conroy-La Pointe Inc. **543** (l) Albert Hilton **543** (r) John McGrail/Wheeler Pictures **544** (t) Courtesy American Training International **544** (b) Lee McDonald **545** Courtesy Infomart **553** Terry Parke

Appendix A

A-2 Wide World Photos **A-3** (b) Norma Morrison/Hillstrom Stock Photo **A-4** Courtesy IBM Archive **A-5** (t) Culver Pictures **A-5** (br) British Crown Copyright. Science Museum, London **A-7** Culver Pictures **A-8** Brown Brothers **A-9** (l) Milwaukee Public Museum of Milwaukee County **A-9** (r) Photograph by Byron. The Byron Collection. The Museum of the City of New York **A-10** (t) Courtesy IBM Archive **A-10** (bl) Burroughs Adding Machine Co., Detroit, MI **A-10** (br) Library of Congress **A-11** (l) U.S. Department of the Interior, National Park Service, Edison National Historic Site **A-11** (r) Courtesy IBM Archive **A-12** Cover, Aug. 1926, *System: The Magazine of Business* **A-13** National Museum of History & Technology, Smithsonian Institution **A-14** (tl) Cruft Laboratory, Harvard University **A-14** (tr) Courtesy IBM Archive **A-14** (c) Wide World Photos **A-14** (b) Courtesy George Stibitz **A-15** (t&c) Iowa State University, Information Service **A-15** (b) Crown Copyright/PRO **A-16** UPI/Bettmann Newsphoto **A-17** (l) AT&T Bell Labs **A-17** (r) Chuck O'Rear/West Light **A-18** Courtesy National Semiconductor Corporation **A-19** (t) Courtesy Sperry Corporation **A-19** (b) Courtesy IBM Archive **A-21** Roger Tully © *Discover* Magazine 2/83, Time Inc. **A-22** Courtesy IBM Archive **A-23** (tl) NASA **A-23** (tr) AT&T Bell Labs **A-23** (c) Courtesy IBM Archive **A-24** Courtesy IBM Archive **A-25** Courtesy Intel Corporation **A-27** (t) Courtesy Intel Corporation **A-27** (c) Cameramann Intl., Ltd. **A-27** (bl) Courtesy Radio Shack, a division of Tandy Corporation **A-27** (br) Courtesy Chemical Bank **A-28** (tr) Courtesy Wang Laboratories, Inc. **A-28** (cl) William Strode **A-28** (bl) and (br) Courtesy Apple Computer, Inc. **A-31** Courtesy Apple Computer, Inc. **A-35** Courtesy IBM Archive

SELECTED BIBLIOGRAPHY

Adams, David R., Gerald E. Wagner, and Terrence J. Boyer. *Computer Information Systems: An Introduction.* Cincinnati, Ohio: South-Western Publishing Co., 1983.

Brooks, Frederick. *The Mythical Man-Month.* Reading, Mass.: Addison-Wesley, 1975.

Burch, John G., Jr., and Joseph L. Sardinas, Jr. *Computer Control and Audit.* New York: John Wiley & Sons, Inc., 1978.

Burkitt, Alan, and Elaine Williams. *The Silicon Civilization.* London: W. H. Allen, 1980.

Capron, H. L., and Brian K. Williams. *Computers and Data Processing.* Menlo Park, Calif.: Benjamin/Cummings Publishing Co., Inc., 1982.

Date, C. J. *Database: A Primer.* Reading, Mass.: Addison-Wesley, 1983.

Davis, William S. *Operating Systems: A Systematic View.* 2d ed. Reading, Mass.: Addison-Wesley, 1983.

De Voney, Chris. *IBM'S Personal Computer.* 2d ed. Indianapolis: Que Corporation, 1983.

Evans, Christopher. *The Making of the Micro.* New York: Van Nostrand Reinhold Co., 1981.

Feigenbaum, Edward A., and Pamela McCorduck. *The Fifth Generation.* Reading, Mass.: Addison-Wesley, 1983.

Fishman, Katherine Davis. *The Computer Establishment.* New York: Harper & Row, Publishers, Inc., 1981.

Fitzgerald, Jerry. *Business Data Communications.* New York: John Wiley & Sons, Inc., 1984.

Frank, Werner L. *Critical Issues in Software.* New York: Wiley-Interscience/John Wiley & Sons, Inc., 1983.

Freiberger, Paul, and Michael Swaine. *Fire in the Valley.* Berkeley, Calif.: Osborne/McGraw-Hill, 1984.

Glossbrenner, Alfred. *The Complete Handbook of Personal Computer Communications.* New York: St. Martin's Press, 1983.

Goldstine, Herman H. *The Computer from Pascal to Von Neumann.* Princeton, N.J.: Princeton University Press, 1972.

Hanson, Dirk. *The New Alchemists.* Boston: Little, Brown & Co., 1982.

Herman, Margaret. *Stretching Man's Mind.* New York: Mason/Charter Publishers, Inc., 1975.

Jordan, Larry E., and Bruce Churchill. *Communications and Networking for the IBM PC.* Bowie, Md.: Robert J. Brady Co., 1983.

Kernighan, Brian W., and P. J. Plauger. *The Elements of Programming Style.* New York: McGraw-Hill, 1974.

Kroenke, David M. *Business Computer Systems: An Introduction.* Santa Cruz, Calif.: Mitchell Publishing, 1984.

Kroenke, David M. *Database Processing.* 2d ed. Chicago: Science Research Associates, Inc., 1983.

Lancaster, Don. *Micro Cookbook: Volume II Machine Language Programming.* Indianapolis, Ind.: Howard W. Sams & Co., Inc., 1983.

Lechner, H. D. *The Computer Chronicles.* Belmont, Calif.: Wadsworth, Inc., 1984.

Ledin, George, Jr., and Victor Ledin. *The Programmer's Book of Rules.* Belmont, Calif.: Lifetime Learning Publications, 1979.

Mandell, Steven L. *Computers and Data Processing: Concepts and Applications with BASIC.* St. Paul, Minn.: West Publishing, 1982.

Mandell, Steven L. *Computers, Data Processing, and the Law.* St. Paul, Minn.: West Publishing, 1984.

Mandell, Steven L. *Introduction to BASIC Programming.* St. Paul, Minn.: West Publishing, 1982.

Martin, James. *An Information Systems Manifesto.* Englewood Cliffs, N.J.: Prentice-Hall, Inc., 1984.

Martin, James. *Application Development Without Programmers.* Englewood Cliffs, N.J.: Prentice-Hall, Inc., 1982.

Martin, James. *Principles of Data-Base Management.* Englewood Cliffs, N.J.: Prentice-Hall, Inc., 1976.

Martin, James, and Carma McClure. *Diagramming Techniques for Analysts and Programmers.* Englewood Cliffs, N.J.: Prentice-Hall, Inc., 1985.

McClellan, Stephan T. *The Coming Computer Industry Shakeout.* New York: John Wiley & Sons, Inc., 1984.

McCorduck, Pamela. *Machines Who Think.* San Francisco: W. H. Freeman & Co., 1979.

Metropolis, N., J. Howlett, and G. Tota, eds. *History of Computing in the Twentieth Century.* New York: Academic Press, Inc., 1980.

Peterson, James L., and Abraham Silberschatz. *Operating Systems Concepts.* Reading, Mass.: Addison-Wesley, 1983.

Randell, Brian, ed. *The Origins of Digital Computers.* New York: Springer-Verlag New York, Inc., 1982.

Reynolds, George W. *Introduction to Business Telecommunications.* Columbus, Ohio: Charles E. Merrill Publishing Co., 1984.

Rogers, Everett M., and Judith K. Larsen. *Silicon Valley Fever.* New York: Basic Books, 1984.

Rubinstein, Richard, and Harry Hersh. *The Human Factor.* Digital Press, 1984.

Sargent, Murray, III, and Richard L. Shoemaker. *The IBM Personal Computer from the Inside Out.* Reading, Mass.: Addison-Wesley, 1983.

Shelly, Gary B., and Thomas J. Cashman. *Introduction to BASIC Programming.* Brea, Calif.: Anaheim Publishing, 1982.

Shneiderman, Ben. *Software Psychology.* Cambridge, Mass.: Winthrop Publishers, Inc., 1980.

Stallings, Warren D., Jr., and Robert H. Blissmer. *Computer Annual.* New York: John Wiley & Sons, Inc., 1984.

Teague, Layette C., Jr., and Christopher W. Pidgeon. *Structured Analysis Methods for Computer Information Systems.* Chicago: Science Research Associates, Inc., 1985.

Weil, Ulric. *Information Systems in the Eighties.* Englewood Cliffs, N.J.: Prentice-Hall, Inc., 1982.

Wetherbe, James C. *Executive's Guide to Computer-Based Information Systems.* Englewood Cliffs, N.J.: Prentice-Hall, Inc., 1983.

Wexelblat, Richard L., ed. *History of Programming Languages.* New York: Academic Press, Inc., 1981.

Wulforst, Harry. *Breakthrough to the Computer Age.* New York: Charles Scribner's Sons, 1982.

Zaks, Rodnay. *Microprocessors: From Chips to Systems.* 3d ed., Berkeley, Calif.: Sybex, Inc., 1980.

Zmud, Robert W. *Information Systems in Organizations.* Glenview, Ill.: Scott, Foresman and Co., 1983.

GLOSSARY/INDEX

A

Abacus, invention of, A-3
ABC computer, A-15
ABI/Inform, 278
Ablative method: Method of recoridng data in which a hole is burned into the disk surface with a laser beam. 159
Abstraction, principle of, 297, 380–81
Acceptance tests: Tests that check on key performance factors. 339
Access: The way data are located in a file or data base system. 202, 221–22
Access arms: In multiple platter disk systems, the devices that move in and out to position the read/write heads over the appropriate tracks. 155
Access time: Amount of time it takes from the point of requesting data until the data are retrieved. 156, 165, 166
Accounting: Financial transactions involved with business activities. 37
Accounts payable: Business activity of paying suppliers. 36
Accounts receivable: Business activity of receiving and processing customer payments. 37
Accumulator: A specified register that is used to store the result of an arithmetic or logical operation. 67, D-5, D-7–D-8
Acoustic coupler: A portable modem that converts digital data into or from audible sounds that are "spoken" or "heard" through the normal telephone headset. 237
Actuator: device containing the read/write head, which swings in and out over the disk surface to locate the correct track. 155
Ada: Programming language designed to facilitate development of embedded computer systems. 423, A-7, A-29
Adaptor board: Interface board used to attach peripherals to a microcomputer. 233
Aetna Life & Casualty, 324, 325, 479
Aiken, Howard, A-13, A-16, A-17
Algorithms: Step-by-step instructions given to a computer that lead to the same result every time. 61
  development of, to read handwritten characters, 98
Allen, Barry, 261–62
Allen, Paul, A-26, A-29
Alphanumeric: Information presented in the form of letters, digits, and special characters. 121, 388, B-9, C-3
Alphanumeric printers, 130–31
  character formation, 131
  character transfer, 131–32
  printing speed, 132–34
Altair, A-26, A-29
ALU. *See* Arithmetic-logic unit (ALU)
Alvernaz, B., 225n
Amdahl Corp., 530, 531
American Airlines, and the development of SABRE reservation system, A-22, A-23
American Arithmometer Company, A-9
American Civil Liberties Union, 505
American Express, use of computers by, 459–60
American Heart Association, CPR learning system of, 170
American National Standards Institute (ANSI), 69, 409, 427
American Statistics Index (ASI), 481
American Training International (ATI), 544
Analog signals: Type of continuous wave pattern. 235
Analysis technique: Use of a speech synthesizer in which the digitized versions of individual words are stored in memory. 139
Analytical Engine, A-4, A-6, A-7
Analyzing skills, D-16–D-24
Anchor: Variable used in programming to initialize an algorithm. D-23
APL (A Programming Language): Programming language designed to facilitate development of programs involving matrix and mathematical computations. A-34
Apple Computer Corp., 529, 530, 532, 534, 552
  formation of, A-27, A-29, A-31
  Apple II, 532, A-27
  Apple IIe, 73–74
  Apple Lisa, 110, 111, 533, A-29
  Apple Macintosh, 74, 111, 125, 158, 533, 542, A-29
  and mail-order sales of software, 540
Apple v. *Franklin*, 512
Application generators: Prototyping tool that covers the full range of systems development activities. 348
Applications software: Programs that can perform specific user-oriented tasks. 13, 175, 535, 541
  and machine incompatibility, 178, 179–80
  and need for currency and accuracy of data, 204
Applied Data Research, 535
Arguments: Values on which the programming statements represented by the function name operate. C-43
Arithmetic-logic unit (ALU): Unit that contains the electronic circuits that actually perform the data processing operations. 11, 62, 67, 70
Arithmetic operations: Operations such as addition, subtraction, multiplication, and division. 20, 390, C-6–C-7
Array: Set of data stored in a number of primary memory locations. 389, C-5, C-34–C-36, D-45, D-46
  searching elements, D-47–D-49
  summing elements, D-46–D-47
Arrow keys: Keys used to facilitiate the movement of the cursor. 109
Artificial intelligence: Intelligence exhibited by a machine. 513
  heuristics and expert systems, 513–17
  Japan's fifth generation computing project, 517–21
Artificial test data: Data created just for testing. 336
ASCII: American Standard Code for Information Interchange. 69, 70, B-2, B-9
Ashton-Tate, 219, 528, 535
Assembler: Software that translates assembly programs into machine language instructions. 401, A-20
Assembly languages: Computer languages that replace the binary digits of machine language with abbreviations to indicate processing operations. 401, 403–4, A-20
Assignment statement: BASIC statement that assigns value to a variable. C-18–C-20
Association of Computer Machinery (ACM), 542
Asynchronous mode: Means of transmitting data one character at a time. 238–39

C

Communication industry, deregulation of, A-29
Communication network, use of, by Federal Express, 255
Communication satellite: Electronic device that receives, amplifies, and transmits signals between space and earth. 243
  use of, for telecommunications, 243–44
Computer Satellite Corporation (CSC), 245, 479
Communication software: Software that electronically links a personal computer to another computer system. 48
Communication support software (CSS): Software that provides terminal access, protocols, error detection and correction, and security. 253
  role of, 251, 253–54
COMPAQ, 129, 179
Compendex, 278
Compiler: Program that translates program language statement into object code. Each language has a different compiler. 401, A-20
Complement: That value which must be added to a number to get its number base, B-3
Complex calculator, A-14
Composite video monitor: Monitor that uses one electron gun to turn on the appropriate combination of red, green, and blue phosphor dots within each triad to display color. 123
Compuscan, 97
CompuServe, 481, 484, 485
Compustat, 278, 481
Computer: A set of electromechanical and electronic devices designed to process information signals. 10
  advances in, 79–81
  basic capabilities of, 23–24
  classification of, 75–76
  computing power of, 76–79
  history of, Appendix A
  use of, in law enforcement, 230, 231
Computer-aided design (CAD): The use of computer graphics terminals to aid designers in product design. 35, 126, 127, 149, 475
Computer-aided design/computer-aided manufacturing (CAD/CAM), 475
Computer-aided engineering (CAE): Use of a computer in testing engineering designs. 475–76
Computer-aided instruction (CAI): Training method in which a program is developed that instructs users through an interactive dialogue. 344, 497
Computer-aided manufacturing (CAM): The use of a computer to control the factory machines used in manufacturing products, 126, 127, 473–75
Computer applications, 15–16
Computer-assisted retrieval (CAR): System based on a minicomputer that uses an index to locate the specific cartridge of film that contains the desired data. 137
Computer-based learning (CBL): Instruction that simulates or models actual situations. 497
Computer bulletin boards, 486–87
Computer Center Corporation, A-26
Computer conferencing, 486–87
Computer consultant, choosing, 351–52
Computer crime: Generic term for the illegal acts that involve the computer. 505
  abuse of computer services, 507
  financial fraud, 507–8
  legislation dealing with, 512
  prevention and protection against loss, 509–13
  theft of data bases, 508
  theft of hardware, software, and trade secrets, 505–7
  vandalism, 508
Computer engineers: Individuals who design computer hardware. 551
Computer-generated images, 78
Computer generations: Eras in time representing particular stages in the development of computer technology. A-18
  fifth, 517–21
  first, A-18–A-21
  fourth, A-18, A-25–A-30
  second, A-18, A-21–A-23
  third, A-18, A-24–A-25
Computer industry, top fifty companies in, 529–30
Computer information systems education programs: College education programs located in the school of business that teach skills needed by application programmers and systems analysts. 550
Computerized scanners, 496
Computerland, 539
Computer literacy: An understanding of what computers are, how computers work, and what computers do. 8
Computer magazines, 360, 542
Computer output microform (COM): Technique in which a microphotographic copy of information is recorded on a microform such as a microfilm reel or a microfiche card. 136–38
Computer processor: The main component of a computer system, consisting of the central processing unit (CPU) and primary memory. 11
Computer-readable form, 19
Computer science education programs: College education programs located in the school of science that teach skills needed by systems support and data base programmers. 550
Computer Sciences Corp. (CSC), 530, 537, 538, 541, A-24, A-25
Computer security: Safeguards taken to protect a computer system and data from unauthorized access or damage. 509–11
Computer services industry, 536
  facilities management, 538
  network services, 537–38
  remote computing services (RCS), 536–37
Computer-specific: Operating system that is tailored to the specific hardware characteristics of a particular computer. 178
Computer storage, 149–50
  direct-access devices, 153–61
  fixed versus removable storage, 152–53
  mass devices, 164–69
  memory hierarchy, 165, 166–68
  sequential-access devices, 162–64
  sequential-access versus direct-access storage, 150–52
  trends in, 168–69
  volatile versus nonvolatile storage, 150
Computer system: Set of hardware and software used as a single unit. 10
Computer-Tabulating-Recording Company (CTR), A-11, A-12
Computer terminals
  general purpose, 105–7
  special function, 102–5
Computervision Corp., 530
Computing literacy: Ability to use the computer as a tool to enrich personal and professional life. 8
  levels of, 8–9
  progress in achieving, 33–35
Computing power: Measure of the number of instructions that can be processed in a given time period. 76
  volatile versus nonvolatile storage, 150
Concurrent operations: At a given point in time, the use of one computer resource by one program while another program uses a different resource. 189
Conditional controls: Control process that directs the processing flow on the basis of certain conditions. 390
Condition: Test of the values of one or more data items. 383
Connecticut Mutual, use of computer by, 30
Constants: Single memory locations whose contents do not change during program execution. 389, C-4
Constructive technique: Technique of speech synthesis that uses phonemes to construct a vocabulary. 139
Contention access method: Method used primarily with the bus network in which devices compete for access to transmit data on the cable. 249, 250–51

Contiguous memory: Memory location assigned as a block. 183
Continuous speech, 100
Contract programming, 339–40
Control break: Programming technique that links the sequence in which a set of data are entered with the manner in which the program's outputs are displayed. D-23–D-24
Control Data Corp. (CDC), 82, 520, 530, 531, 533, 537, B-10
Controllers: Processors that direct or coordinate other processors. 282
Control statement: BASIC statement that changes the sequential processing pattern by transferring the processing flow to another line number. C-27
Control unit (CU): Unit that contains the electronic circuits that direct and coordinate the processing activities. 11
Conversion: Manner in which a business converts from the old way of doing business to a new way. 344–45
Core memory, A-17
Correct program: Program that completely and accurately performs the information processing activities as specified in the systems design. 375
Cort, Donald, 230
Cosmic Cube, 82
Counter, D-5, D-6
Cox, Rodney, 508
CP/M (Control Program for Microcomputers), 194, 195, 362, A-29
CPU. *See* Central processing unit (CPU)
CPU utilization: Percentage of time that the CPU is actually working. 188
Crash conversion: Conversion process in which the old system is switched directly to the new system. 345
Cray, Seymour, 533
Cray Research, Inc., 82, 144, 533, 534
Cray–1, 82
Crosse, Andrew, A-7
CRT. *See* Cathode-ray tube
CRT radiation, problem of, 499
CRT screen: Primary device for displaying information. C-21
CRT screen generators: Software package available for prototyping. 348
CRT screen layout forms: Paper representations of a CRT screen. 316
Cullinet Software, 535
Cullinet's Integrated Data Management System (IDMS), 218
Cursor: Blinking symbol that shows where the next entered character will appear. 92
Custom software, 13
  development of, 339–40
  versus packaged software, 337–38
Cyber 205, 82
Cybernet, 537
Cyclic Redundancy Coding (CRC): Error check code often used in synchronous transmission. 239
Cylinder method: Method of organizing data on the disk that is based on a vertical plane. 155

D

Daisy wheel: Print mechanism used in computer printers in which each "petal" contains an embossed character. 131
Daisy wheel printer, 131, 132
Data: Symbols used to represent a fact, event, or thing. 10
  coding of, for computer use, 68–71
  input of, 18–19, 49
  output of, 23, 51
  processing of, 19–20, 50
  retrieval of, 21–23, 50–51
  skills in grouping, D-45–D-55
  storage of, 21–23, 50–51
Data base: Integrated collection of data items that can be retrieved in any combination necessary to produce needed information. 40, 201, 213
Data Base Administrator (DBA): Person that acts as the keeper of the data base. 216
Data Base Management System (DBMS): System that allows the programmer to be able to access data by specifying only the data items that are needed. 204, 212, 348
  accessing the data base, 221–22
  in action, 218–22
  data base administration, 216–18
  data base organization models, 214–16
  versus file systems, 222–24
  logical versus physical views, 213–14
  relational microDBMS, 219–21
Data capture: Conversion to computer-readable form. 94
Data communication: Movement of data from one location to another. 231
  external data paths, 231–33
  interface units, 233–34
Data currentness: The degree to which stored data represent a business's current activities. 330
Data dictionary: Complete description of the characteristics of a data base. 217, 332
Data encoding schemes, 68–70
Data encryption: Technique for converting data to be transmitted into a scrambled form. 253
Data entry design: Manner in which data are initially entered into an information system. 329–30
Data entry process, 87–88
  batch processing, 87, 88–91
  transaction processing, 87, 91–92
Data field: Collection of related characters. 21, 201
Data file: Organized set of related data items. 21, D-45, D-53–D-55
Data file activity: Proportion of records in a file that are retrieved and processed. 333
Data flow chart: A diagramming technique used to represent the flow of data through the processes that comprise an information system. 313
Data General Corp., 530, 532
Data General DG/One, 129
Data integrity: The degree to which stored data are accurate and secure. 330
Data item: Collection of related characters. 201
Data management routines, 176
Data management software: Support software used to provide an easier way for a programmer to create and maintain files and to retrieve data from them. 204, 361
  role of, 201–5
Data networks, 479–80
Data organization: The way in which data are arranged. 201
Data-oriented design: Design strategy that focuses on the data that are to be processed by the information system. 315
Data packet: The means of sending data in a telecommunication network. Start and stop information, origin and destination information, and error check bits are added to the encoded data. 238
Dataphone digital service (DDS): All-digital telecommunications network that can directly transmit the discrete digital signals of the computer. Can be used to integrate data, voice, and video transmission. 245
Datapoint Corp., 530
Datapro, 545
Data Processing Management Association (DPMA), 542
  code of ethics of, 513, 514–15
Data processing professionals, 546
Dataproducts Corporation, 141, 530
Dataquest, 545, 552
Data rate: Speed of telecommunication link. 237
Data record: Complete set of data describing each item, such as a part, an employee, a customer, etc., for which data is being stored within a data file. 21
Data redundancy: Abundance of files that contain many of the same data items. 211, 223
DATA statement: BASIC statement that assigns a specific value to a variable. C-19
Data structures: Alternative ways in which a set of data items can be organized. 389–90

Data transfer rate: Rate at which data can be transferred between peripherals and primary memory. 156
Data types: General classes of data that are processed by computer systems in particular ways. 388
Dataword length: Number of bits of data that can be retrieved from memory each machine cycle. 74, 78–79
Dayne Communication, 533
DBaseII, 219
Debugging: Testing of programs. 372, 378, D-4, D-34–D-37
Debug print flag: Programming tool used in debugging. D-34, D-36–D-37
Decentralized architecture: System in which data processing and data storage and retrieval are performed on multiple computer systems located throughout a firm. 271, 272
Decimals: Numeric data items comprised of whole and fractional parts. C-3
Decision-oriented design: Design strategy that focuses on the factors that are critical to the success of the business activity or task being handled by the information system. 315
Decision support system: System that allows management to produce management reports in an ad hoc fashion. 41, 149, 269–70
  example of, 266
  interaction of, in management information systems, 42–43
Decision support system generators: Software packages used to develop decision support systems. 269–70
Decision tables: A tool that can help in understanding the important factors behind specific business or user actions. 313
Dedicated computer systems: Computer systems that are designed to do one task very efficiently. 75
De facto standard: Standard informally accepted by vendors, generally because it has come to dominate a market segment of the business. 194
Default parameters: Policy parameters such as priority rules, I/O device assignments, and prespecified memory allocations. 181
Defective parts analysis, D-29–D-34
Defense, U.S. Department of, A-29
Definitional statements, C-15–C-17
Deltak, 543
Demand paging, 184–85
Demand reports: Reports that are distributed only when requested by a manager. 268
Demodulating process: Process in which the digital data are separated from the carrier signal. 236
Densmore, James, A-9
Desktop organizers: Integrated software that allows a business professional to juggle several small tasks simultaneously with a larger task. 454–55, 469
Detail diagrams: Diagrams that provide a more complete understanding of a software component's information processing activities. 334
Dewey, John, 11
Dialog, 481, 487
Dialogue design, 327, 329
DiCocco, J., 328n
Diebold Company, 103
Dietz, Larry, 553
DIF (data interchange format) files, 460
Difference Engine, A-4, A-5
Differential analyzer, A-13
Digital Equipment Corp. (DEC), 139, 530, 532, 535, 539, A-26
  DEC Rainbow, 195
  DECtalk, 139
  DEC VAX, 78
  PDP–1, A-21–A-22
  PDP–8, A-24, A-25
Digitally Aided Dispatch System, 255
Digital Productions, 144
Digital Research, 194, 535, A-29
Digital signals: Discrete pattern of impulses that is generated by on/off or high/low electrical signals to represent 1s and 0s. 235
Digital Telephone, 294, 295
Dimension, or DIM, statement: BASIC statement used to declare the existence and size of any arrays used in a program. C-16
Direct-access storage devices, 153
  bubble memory, 161
  magnetic disks, 153–58
  optical disks, 159–61
  versus sequential-access storage devices, 150–52
Direct or random access: Method in which data can be accessed directly. 150, 333
Disk cartridge: Single-platter removable disk. 157
Disk drive: An input device that reads data from or writes data to a disk or diskette. 12
Diskette: A small, flexible mylar plastic disk coated with magnetic oxide. Diskettes are available in a variety of physical sizes and all are designed to be removable. 153
Disk pack: Multiplatter hard disk, which can be loaded onto, and later removed from, a disk drive. 157
Displaced workers, 495–96
Distributed architecture: System in which multiple computer systems, connected in a computer network, are located throughout a firm. 271, 273–74
Distribution channels, 538
  manufacturer direct sales, 541–42
  retail outlets, 539–41
  systems houses, 541
Distribution technology, advances in, 53–54
Division/remainder method: Allocation method in which the key number identifier would be divided by the largest prime number less than the maximum number of records that will be needed. 209
Documentation: Permanent descriptions of the work performed during a systems development project. 300
  problems in writing, 302–3
  role of, in improving communication, 300
  in systems design, 336
  in systems implementation, 345
Dot-addressable display: Display in which each individual pixel is addressable. 124, 125
Dot-matrix printer, 131, 132, 134, 135, 142, 368
Double-density diskette: Diskette on which data are recorded at twice the normal density. 157
Double-sided diskette: Diskette on which data can be recorded on both the top and bottom surfaces. 157
Douthett, Roger, 39
Dowhile loop: Iteration pattern, 387, 393
Dow Jones News, 278, 481, 485
Dow Jones Quotes, 486
Downlink transmission: Sending of data from a communications satellite to an earth station on a certain carrier frequency. 243
Download: Transfer of data from a larger computer to a smaller computer. 48, 275
Drexler Technology, 148
Dreyfus, Hubert, 521
Drum plotter, 136
Drum printer, 142
Dumb terminal: Basic device used to enter data and display results. 106
Dumping: Means of moving all files, intact, from one location to another. 164
Dump: Printout of selected primary memory locations displayed in hexadecimal or octal format. B-10
Dunsprint, 481
Dvorak, August, 108
Dykeman, John B., 522–23

E

F

Fetch: Process of retrieving an instruction. 66
Fiber optics: Newest type of high bandwidth cable used for digital coding. Laser technology can be used to send an intense beam of highly focused light down these hair-thin strands. 244–45
Fifth generation computing project, 517–20
Fifth Generation, The (McCorduck), 521
File: Collection of similar type records. 201
File access methods (FAM): Support software that enables programmers to organize data into files and provides means for accessing data records. 204
File design, 331–33
File handling, with BASIC, C-36–C-40
File layout chart: Chart that shows how each record in a data file is organized. 332
File management: Software that transforms secondary storage into an electronic filing cabinet. 47
Filene's department store, use of computers by, 32
File system: Support software that provides the type of file organization and means for accessing the data for retrieval and updating. 205–6
 versus data base management systems, 222–24
 organization and access methods, 206–9
 sharing files, 209–12
Film industry, computer usage in, 144
Filtering, D-21
Final processing: The final stage of business programming in which summary outputs are produced and processing is terminated. 391–92
Financial analysis tools, 441–43
Financial modeling system: End-user tool that can perform financial analyses that are far too complicated for an electronic spreadsheet. 442
Financial planning, 485–86
Fingermatrix, 494
Firmware: Permanently coded instuctions within ROM. 72, 195
First-come-first-serve scheme: Scheduling scheme in which a list is kept of the order in which jobs arrive. Jobs are processed in that sequence. 182
First generation of computers, A-18–A-21
Fixed media: Media that cannot be touched or removed by the user. 152–53
Fixed partitions: Allocation method in which primary memory for use by user programs is divided into sections of a fixed memory size. 183
Flag: Programming tool used to control a program's processing flow. D-21–D-22
Flat-bed plotter, 136
Flat-panel displays, 128–30
Flexibility: Criterion used to judge printer effectiveness. 142
Flexible manufacturing system: System in which a set of machine tools are used to produce a variety of metal parts. 473
Floppy disk. *See* diskette
Flowcharts: Design tool that portrays a program's processing flow by showing the operations to be performed, the sequence in which they are to be performed, and the conditions that affect this sequence. 385
FLOW-MATIC, A-20
Fluegelman, Andrew, 427–29
Fonts: Type styles. 91
Foreground/background processing: Means of running both batch and interactive jobs to meet their very different response time requirements. 190
Format: Margins, spacing, page numbers, and headings of a document. 45
Forms design, 331
FOR/NEXT statement: BASIC statement used to set up an iteration or loop. C-30–C-33
FORTRAN (FORmula TRANslation): Program language often used for writing scientific and engineering programs. 70, 195, 412, 419, A-20, A-23
 example of, 412
 strengths of, 412
 weaknesses of, 412
FORTRAN IV, 419
FORTRAN 77, 419
Fourth generation of computers, A-25–A-30
Frames: Means of storing digitized patterns of images and sounds on an optical disk. 160
Framework, 452, 453, 528
Franciscan Vineyard, use of computers by, 276–77
Franklin Computer Corporation, 512
Fraud: Use of deceit to gain valuables. 507
Fredkin, Edward, 521
Freedman, David, 194
Freeman, Joseph P., 494
Freiberger, P., A-26n
Frequency division multiplexing, 240
Fridlund, Alan, 501
Friedl, Dr. Paul, A-34–A-35
Front-end processor: Micro- or minicomputer that functions as a specialized data communications handler. 254
Fujitsu, 529, 530, 531
Full-duplex channel: Communications path that allows data to be transmitted in different directions simultaneously. 240
Function: Predefined processing operation of general use. C-26, C-41–C-43
Function keys: Keys used to provide means of commanding common tasks in one step. 109, 368
Fylstra, Dan, A-29

G

Gantt chart: Project management tool that specifies the timing of a series of tasks so that it is easy to see whether the tasks are being completed on a schedule. 299
Garland, Steve, 429
Gates, William H. III, 174, 175, 424, A-26, A-29
Gateway: Interface device that provides the translations necessary to link two different types of networks. 251
General Electric, 497, 530, 537, A-20, A-21
General Motors, 497, 530
 use of computer-aided engineering by, 475–76
General-purpose computer, A-5, A-13–A-17
General-purpose computer systems: Flexible computer systems that can be programmed in different ways to perform significantly different tasks. 75
General-purpose programming language: Programming language that provides a set of processing capabilities that can be applied to most information processing problems. 406
George, Joe, A-35
Geosynchronization: Orbit for communications satellite in which the satellite is synchronized with the earth's rotation. 243
Gigabyte: One billion bytes or one thousand megabytes. 154
GigaHertz: GHz; billion cycles per second. 241
GIGO (garbage in, garbage out), 89–90
Glass, R., 419n
Gnostic Concepts, 545
Goldstine, Lieut. Herman H., A-2, A-3
Golf ball: One type of print mechanism used in computer printers. 131
GOSUB statement: BASIC statement that calls for the execution of a particular subroutine. C-44
GOTOs: Unconditional control in which the program flow jumps from one segment of a program to another. 390
GOTO statement: BASIC statement that directs the processing flow to a new line number. C-28
Grafix Partner, 448
Graphics: Pictures or graphs depicting information. 121
Graphics printers and plotters, 135–36
Greitzer, J., 280n
Grid chart: Tool that identifies the data files used with each major task. 313

J

Johnson, J. T., 457n
Joyce, E., 424n
Junior programmers: Newly hired programmers given mostly simple programming jobs. 340
Junkyards, use of computers in, 200, 201
Justification: Paragraph spacing that produces fixed paragraph borders, 444

K

K: Abbreviation for kilobyte, or 2 to the 10th, or 1024 bytes. 73
Kaiser Medical, 170
Kaufman, Felix, 2
Kemeny, John, 415, 427–29, A-22, A-23, C-2
Key: Field that can be used to identify a record. 201
Keyboard: Device for entering data. 368, C-21
  alternatives to, 109–12
  design of, 107–9
Key-to-disk device: Machine by which the operator can key data directly onto a disk. 94
Key-to-diskette data entry system: Machine, generally a microcomputer, by which the operator can key data directly onto a diskette. 94
Key-to-media equipment: Term for a number of keyboard devices that perform only the function of encoding data in a computer-readable form and placing them on media. 88, 93–94
Key-to-punched card devices: Machines that are used by an operator to key data onto punch cards. 93
Key-to-tape device: Machine with which an operator can key data directly onto magnetic tape. 93
Kilby, Jack, A-19, A 20
Kildall, Gary, A-29
Kilo: Prefix that means approximately 1000. Actually 2^{10} or 1024 in computer usage. 73
"Kitchen table computer," A-14
K mart, 541
Knight-Ridder newspaper chain, 482
Kob, Mary, 351
Kodak, 520
Krauss, J. D., 343n
Kurtz, Thomas, 415, 427–29, A-22, A-23, C-2
Kurzeil Reading Machine (KRM), 118

L

Laborlaw, 481
LAN. *See* Local area network (LAN)
Landis, K. M., 295n, 320n
Language translator: Program that translates the Englishlike program instructions of a high-level language, such as BASIC or COBOL, into the binary code language of machine. 176.
Large-scale integration: Microelectronic chips that each contain thousands of electronic components. A-25
Larson, Christopher, 196
LaSalle National Bank, 448
Laser printer, 134, 135
Laser technology, 159
Law enforcement, use of computers in, 230, 231
LEADS (Law Enforcement Automated Data System), 230
Leibnitz, Gottfried, A-4
Leibnitz wheel, A-4, A-30
LET statement: BASIC statement that assigns value to a variable. C-18
Letter quality printer, 368
Levi Strauss, 280
Levy, Joseph, 528
Lexitron, A-29
Lichack, Claire, 459–60
Light pen: Device, when used to touch the computer screen, causes changes in electrical potential, which in turn signals the computer to perform specific actions. 109
Linkage editor: System software module for linking or combining application program and other object modules. 187
Liquid crystal display (LCD) technology: Technology in which a thin layer of liquid crystal molecules are put between two sheets of glass. When voltage is applied to the liquid crystal in a specific cell, the material will turn opaque and block light, resulting in a black square. 129–30
LISP, 412, A-20
Little, Arthur D. Inc., 47
Littman, J., 277n
Live test data: Data taken from existing business records, which are used to assess how the software would handle day-to-day situations. 336
Load: the act of entering the appropriate instructions into the primary memory of a computer. 62
Load module: Software module that is in a form (object code) that can be processed. 187
Local area networks (LAN): Communication network for transferring data between microcomputers and shared peripherals within a building complex, such as an office or factory. 231, 246–47, 439
  characteristics of, 250–51
  common topologies, 247, 248
  connecting networks, 251
  and electronic mail, 467
  network access, 247, 249
  and office automation, 472
  transmission media, 249–50
Lockheed Missiles and Space Co., A-31
Logical design: Detailed description of the information system from the business, rather than the technical perspective. 307, 311, 357
  data-oriented, 315
  decision-oriented, 315
Logical operations: Complex relational operations. 390, C-8–C-9
Logical view: User's view of what data are needed to answer a variety of questions, in contrast to the physical view of how those data actually reside on the disk or are accessed. 213
Logic bombs, 508
Logic errors: Errors that indicate that the program design is incorrect. 378
Loop: interation. C-30
Loop index: Variable used to control interaction in a programming loop. C-30, C-32
Lotus Development Corp., 528, 529, 535
Lotus 1-2-3, 30, 32, 47, 49, 365, 448, 452, 453, 529, A-28
Lovelace, Ada Augusta, 412, A-7, A-29
LPRINT command: BASIC command that sends information to the printer for the PRINT command. C-26
Lyons, J. & Sons, A-20, A-21

M

Machine cycle: A combination of the I-cycle and the E-cycle. 67
Machine language: Lowest level of computer language. It consists of binary digits, 0 and 1. 401, A-19–A-20
Machines Who Think (McCorduck), 521
Magnetic disk: Rigid metal (hard disk) or flexible plastic ("floppy" diskettes) are coated with magnetic material. This material is used to store data in the form of magnetic bit patterns. 13, 153–56
  diskettes, 157–58
  hard disks, 156–57
Magnetic Ink Character Recognition (MICR): Means of character recognition frequently used by the banking industry as a standard method for processing checks. 98
Magnetic tape: A thin plastic tape that is coated with magnetic material. It is used in storing data as columns of magnetic spots. 12, 13, 150–51, 162–64, 166

N

O

Optical videodisc, 170
Optical wands, 102
ORBIT, 487
Orwell George, 505
Osborne, Adam, A-29
Osborne, I, 105, 118, 129, A-27, A-29
Output, 281
 classification of, 119–22
 of data, 23, 51
Output design, 326–27, 327, 328
Output devices: Devices used to move data and information out of the primary primary. 12
OUTPUT statements, C-21, C-23–C-26
Overlap processing: Processing in which the control unit can retrieve data from storage while the CPU is performing another task. 80
Overview diagrams: Diagrams describing the input, process, and output of the main software. 333

P

Pacific Bell, 245
Packaged software, 13–14
 evaluation of, 362, 363, 364–66
 versus customized, 337–38
 purchasing packaged, 338–39
Package evaluation matrix: Tool used to compare vendors' bids and to choose a software package. 338
Page: Means for dividing programs or memory into fixed-length blocks. 185
Page printers, 134, 142
Paging: Function that allows the user to, in one move, move up or down a document by the depth of an entire screen. 125
PALM microcomputer, A-34
Pansophic Systems, 535
Paper, invention of, A-3
Parallel: Method of sending data bits in which the eight bits representing a character are sent simultaneously. 232
Parallel conversion: Conversion process in which the old and the new information systems are run together for a period of time. 345
Parallel printing, 133
Parent: Higher-level data record. 214
Parity bit: Extra bit that makes the sum of bits representing a character either even or odd. It is a means of checking for errors that may have occurred during data transmission. 162, 239
Parts purchase report, D-59–D-63
Pascal: Programming language developed for teaching structured programming concepts. 412, 419, 421
 development of, A-24–A-25
 example of, 421–22
 and Modula-2, 423
 strengths of, 421
 weaknesses of, 421
Pascal, Blaise, A-4, A-25
Pascaline, A-4, A-30
Passwords: Confidential sequence of alphanumeric characters. 178–79
Patterson, John H., A-12
Paul, L., 432n
PCDOS (Personal Computer Disk-Based Operating System), 194
PC/Focus, 459–60
Penalty payments: Contract terms that cover instances where software is delivered late or fails to perform as expected. 339
Pen plotter, 135–36
Periodic reports: Reports that are distributed at regular intervals, such as daily, weekly, monthly, quarterly, or annually. 267
Peripheral devices: Devices that are added onto the computer processor. 11
Personal computer: Computer meant to be used by an individual. 4–5
 popularity of, 2, 3, 6
Personal computer support center: Facility with end-user tools that is directed toward microcomputer and users. 455 456, 457, 458
Personal computing: Use of personal computers to directly support business professionals in their work. 43
 business uses for, 43–49
PERT diagram: Project management tool showing the relationships among a project's tasks, as well as their timing. 299
Phased conversion: Conversion process in which the conversion is broken into smaller steps or phases. 345
Phelan, Mary, 319–20
Philips, N. V. Gloeilampenfabrieken, 530
Phonemes: Basic elements of speech. 139
Physical design: Description of the hardware, software, and operating procedures that should enable an information system to function. 325
Physical view: How the data actually reside on disk or are actually accessed. This is in contrast to the logical view which is the user's conceptual description of what data are needed. 213
Pilot study: Study in which the information system is used "live," but in a controlled manner. 341
Pixels: Picture elements on a visual display device that can be illuminated. 122, 123, 124, 125, 128, 144
PL/I (Programming language I): Programming language designed to provide extensive yet flexible support for all types of information processing tasks. 417, A-21
 development of, A-22, A-23
 example of, 417
 strengths of, 417
 weaknesses of, 417
Plotter: Output device that is specialized to produce graphics. 13, 135
Point-of-sale (POS) terminals: Electronic cash register terminals found in retail operations that can optically scan merchandise codes, record sales, and process transactions. 73, 96, 102, 107, 119
Polling: Access method used primarly with star network topology in which the central controller must go around the star network in sequential order asking each terminal if it wishes to transmit. 247, 250, 251
Portable computers, 105, 366, 489–90, A-27, A-34–A-35
Portable program: Program written in a programming language that is relatively easy to translate and execute on different computer systems. 409
Pournelle, Jerry, 35
Powers Accounting Machine Company, A-11, A-12
Powers, James, A-8, A-11
Precompilers, 222
Preliminary investigation. *See* Feasibility study
Presentation graphics: Tables, charts, and pictures used in reports. 445
Presentation graphics tools, 445, 448
Present value analysis, D-56–D-58
Prespecified reports: Carefully designed and programmed reports that can be produced very efficiently. 268
Previews and Premises (Toffler), 523
Primary key: Field that identifies a unique record. 201
Primary memory: Device that provides temporary storage for all the data and information being processed as well as the software directing the processing. 11, 78–79
Primary memory chips, 72–73
Prime Computer, Inc., 530, 532
Prime number: Number not divisible by any other number than itself and one. 209
Principle of abstraction: Structured design concept of capturing the essence of the object being designed. 297, 380–81
Principle of modularity: Structured design concept of representing a design as a collection of single-function modules. 297, 382
Principle of stepwise refinement: Structured design concept of building a design in

layers, where lower levels explain higher levels. 297, 382–83
Print and film devices, 130
alphanumeric printers, 130–34
computer output microform (COM), 136–38
graphics printers and plotters, 135–36
Printer: Device, similar to a typewriter, that uses paper as its output medium. 13
maintenance of, 143
selection criteria for, 140–43
types of, 368
Printing press, A-4
PRINT statement: BASIC statement used to display information on the CRT screen. C-21, C-23–C-26
Priority scheme: Scheduling scheme in which some programs are given a priority over other programs. 182
Privacy: The right to be left alone. 502–3
concerns on, 504–5
information, 503–4
Privacy Act of 1974, 504, 505, 506
Private line: Lines leased from the telephone company for the purpose of providing permanent connection between Point A and Point B. 242
Procedures design, testing of, 334–36
Process design, 331–34
Processing, of data, 19–20, 50, 62–66
Processing modes: Means by which transaction data can be either entered into a computer system and processed immediately or collected as batches and processed later. 87
Processing unit, memory capacity of, 74
Processors: System components that transform inputs into outputs. 281
Procter & Gamble, 260, 261
Program coding: Activity that translates the program design into a program using a programming language. 376
Program counter: Device used to keep track of where the next instruction is stored in primary memory. 66
Program data dependence: Situation in which subsequent changes in either the programs or data will have a significant effect on the other. 214
Program data independence: Situation in which changes in either programs or data can be made without significantly affecting the other. 214
Program design: Activity for producing a clear, logical flow for a program's information processing operations. 376
for business computing, 391–93
Program design tools, 383–85
flowcharts, 385
pseudocodes, 385–88
Program development, 375–76, 425
code program, 378
methods of designing, 380
process of, 376–78
program design, 377
program documentation, 378–79
programming teams, 379
test program coding, 378
test program design, 378
user participation, 379–80
Program Evaluation Review Technique (PERT). 299
Program maintenance, 425
Programmer: Individual who designs and develops computer programs. 15, 547
Programmers' manual: Descriptions of all the program development work that took place during a systems development program. 300, 336
Programming, 8, 373, 400
art of, 375
basic concepts in, 388–90
problem-solving approach to, D-2–D-5
skills needed for, 372, 373, 381
and the systems life cycle, 374
Programming languages. *See also specific language*
assembly, 401, 403–4
availability of, 425
comparison of levels, 409–10
control structure sophistication, 407
data structure sophistication, 407
ease of use, 408
evolution of, 401, 402
features of, 405–10
general-purpose, 406
and hardware control, 406
high-level, 401, 404–5, 410–29
interactive, 406–7
nonprocedural commands, 407
portability of, 425
standardization in, 408–9
very-high-level, 401, 405
Programs: Instructions to direct a computer in its information processing. 8
nature of, 425
performance objectives of, 425
Project definition: Overview of the information system. 307, 357
Project design, 357–59
Project management, role of, in improving communication, 297–99
Project manager: Manager responsible for planning and coordinating the tasks to be performed in a systems development project. 298–99
Project manual: Description of the work performed during a systems development project. 300
Project Match, 505
Project plan: Plan listing the main tasks to be accomplished, identifying who is to perform each task, and estimating the time and costs of each task. 311
review of, for systems design, 336
Project team: Team composed of managers, information system users, and computer specialists. 281
Prolok Magic diskette system, 510
Prompts: Simple instructions displayed on the computer screen that tell the user what to do next. 92, 329, C-22
Proprietary package, 541
PROSPECTOR, 517
Protection: Control of access to programs and data stored in the computer. 188
Protocol: Set of rules and procedures used for transmitting data between two hardware devices in a network. 253
Prototype homes, 464
Prototyping: Building a "quick-and-dirty" version of an information system. 348
advantages and disadvantages of, 348
guidelines for, 349
Pseudocodes: Design tool that produces a very readable program design. 385, 392, D-4
PTS PROMT, 279
Public-domain software, 365
Punched card: Card with 80 columns in which particular combinations of holes represent numbers, alphabetic letters, or special characters; sometimes called the IBM card. 88, 93, A-10
Punched-card equipment industry, A-11
Purchasing: Term for business function of buying and selling. 36

Q

Quad density diskette: Diskette in which data are recorded at four times the normal density. 157
Quasar Co., 113
Query language: Software that enables end-users to create data bases and then retrieve data to answer specific questions. 219
QWERTY keyboard, 107, 108

R

Radio Shack. *See* Tandy
RAM (Random Access Memory): Memory in which instructions or data can be written into or data read out of and transferred to the CPU for processing as needed. 72–73
volatile, 73
Ramada Inn, computer use by, 86, 87, 287–89

RAM disks: External add-on memory devices that can add up to one megabyte of storage. 168–69
Rand Corp., A-21, A-22
Range check: Process in which the computer can check to ascertain that certain data values fall within a specified range. 92
Rascomb, Inc., 342–43
Raster scan: Process of moving a beam of electrons across the screen to create brighter (on) or darker (off) points. 122–26, 134, 135
differences between vector technology and, 126–27
R:Base 4000, 219
RCA, 479
READ/DATA statements, C-19
READ statement: BASIC statement that assigns a specific value from a DATA statement to a variable. C-19
Read/write head: Mechanism used to directly locate the place where the data record is to be read or written. 151
Read/write memory: See RAM (Random Access Memory), 72
Ready-made software packages, 32
Real estate, use of computers in, 225
Real numbers: Numbers that can be given decimal values. 389
Real-time computing: Computing that allows events to be captured and processed as they occur. A-22–A-23
Real Trieve, 225
Recognition Equipment, Inc., 99
Record: A collection of all related data items. 201
Regis McKenna, Inc., A-31
Registers: Storage locations within the CPU that are used as temporary staging areas. 67
Relational data base structure: Data base structure that shows relationships among records by linking tables together as needed. 215, 216, 218
Relational Information Management (RIM), 219
Relational operations: Operations that can be applied to both numeric and alphanumeric data. 390, C-7–C-8
Relative file organization: File organization by which records are arranged by using the key value to directly calculate the relative location on disk. 208
Reliability: Percentage of time that the computer is up relative to the time it is scheduled to be up and running. 188
Remark, or REM, statement: Statement used to document a BASIC program. C-15
Remington, E. & Sons, A-6, A-9
Remington, Philo, A-9
Remington Rand, A-11, A-16, A-18, A-21, A-22
Remote computing services (RCS), 536–37
Remote job entry (RJE), 191
Removable media: Media such as magnetic tape and diskettes that allow the user to physically swap one set of data for another. 152
Repeatuntil loop: Iteration pattern, 387–88, 392
Report generation tools: Software that enables users to interactively define data files, enter and manipulate data, and produce reports. 348, 448–49
Report layout form: A paper representation of a management report. 316
Request for a Proposal (REP): Formal statement that describes selection criteria. 338
Requirements specification: Detailed statement of a business's information needs regarding an information system under development. 311 *See also* Logical design
Research firms, 545
Reservation systems, use of computers in, 86, 87, A-22, A-23
Resolution: Measure of the number of pixels that can be addressed on the screen. 124, 125
Resource management: The allocation and scheduling of computer resources. 182
Response time: The length of time between a user's request and the computer's response. 188
RESTORE statement: A BASIC statement that reinitializes the data values contained in a program's DATA statements. C-19–C-20
Retail Inventory Management System (RIMS), 280
Retail management, use of microcomputers in, 280
Retail market, 539–41
Retail sales, use of point-of-sale terminals in, 102
Retrieval, of data, 21–23, 50–51
Retrieval cue: Tag associated with a given fact or data item. 35
Retrieve: Accessing of data for use in producing desired information. 204
RETURN statement: BASIC statement used in a subroutine. C-44–C-46
Reuter Monitor, 279
Reverse video, 126
RGB monitors: Monitor that uses three electron guns to produce color. There is a gun for each of the red, green, and blue phosphor dots within a triad. 123
Riesenberg, J. H. & Associates, 350–52
Rifkin, Stanley, 508
Ring network topology: Pattern used to connect hardware devices in which each terminal is connected to two others. 247, 250
Ritty, James, A-8
Robertson's Auto Salvage, 200
Roberts, S. K., 490n
Robinson, Ken, 276
Robotics, 513
Robots: Mechanical devices that can be programmed to perform useful tasks. 474–75, 476. *See also* Industrial robots
and displaced workers, 495–96
Rollback strategy: A means of reconstructing a data base by undoing all the incomplete changes that were in process at the time of failure. 218
Rollforward strategy: A means of reconstructing a data base by using the last backup copy of the data base and applying all subsequently logged transactions to it. 218
ROM (Read Only Memory): Memory that can be used only to read data or written instructions that have been permanently loaded onto the chip. 72
advantages of, 73
electrically erasable programmable, 73
erasable programmable, 73
Rothchild, Edward, 161
Roth, Philip, 446
RPG (Report Program Generator): Programming language developed to duplicate punched card processing procedures. 417, A-24, A-25
strengths of, 418
weaknesses of, 418, 421
RS232-C input/output port, 232
Rubenstein, Seymour, A-29
Rufer, Finn & Rotman (RF&R), 2
Run: Processing of data. 89

S

SABRE reservation system, A-22, A-23
SAGE air defense system, A-19, A-20
Salary analysis, D-24–D-29
Sales: Business activity that covers the selling and delivering of goods. 37
Sales contest, D-59
Sales management, use of microcomputers in, 260
Sales price, calculation of total, D-15–D-16
Sanders, G., 260n
Sandler, C., 303n, 395n
SAS Institute, 535
Satellite Business Systems, 245
SBC (Satellite Business Corporation), 479
SCAMP (Special Computer APL Machine Portable), A-34–A-35

T

U

V

W

Weigand, Bob, 350–52
Wells, Larry J., 552
Westar satellites, 245
Western Electric, A-9
Western Union, 478, 479
What Computers Can't Do (Dreyfus), 521
Whirlwind Computer, A-13, A-17
Whitney, John, Jr., 144
Whittemore, John, 30, 31
Whitt, Walter, 459–60
Williams, Lance, 144
Williams, Samuel, A-13, A-14
Wilson, James, 280
Wilson, Robert, 349
Winchester technology: Technology that seals the hard disk inside a hermetic (airtight) container. 157, 160
Window(s): Function that allows the computer's display screen to be divided into separate areas or boxes. 125
Window manager: Software that allows the user to create a number of applications at the same time, to view each application in its own window, to change the size of windows, and to move data values among the windows. 453
Winery, use of microcomputers in, 276–79
Winery Information Management System, 276–77
Wirth, Niklaus, 421, 423, 424, A-24–A-25
Wonder, Stevie, 118, 119
Word processors: Software that transforms a terminal screen into sheets of paper to be electronically written on. 45, 104–5, 361, 444–45, 466, 496, A-24
advantages of using, 446–47
Wordstar, 365, A-29
Worker health, 499–502
Workshops: Training method that uses a classroom setting for training groups of users. 344
Workslate, A-27
Workstation: Enhanced microcomputer that can perform stand-alone data or word processing functions, function as a dumb terminal connected to a host computer, and do data communication tasks, such as electronic mail. 107
Works, The, 144
Wozniak, Steve, A-27, A-29, A-31
Write # statement, C-39–C-40
Wulforst, H., A-2n

X

Xanadu House, 464
XCON, 517
XENIX, 195
Xerox Corp., 249, 530, 539, A-29
X/Market, 481

Y

Yost, George Washington Newton, A-9

Z

Z80 microprocessor chip, 195
Zahay, D., 381n
Zilog Z-80A, 73, 74